Fundamental Perspectives on International Law

Third Edition

WILLIAM R. SLOMANSON
Thomas Jefferson School of Law
San Diego, California

West
Thomson Learning™

Australia • Canada • Denmark • Japan • Mexico • New Zealand • Philippines
Puerto Rico • Singapore • South Africa • Spain • United Kingdom • United States

Publisher: *Clark Baxter*
Developmental Editor: *Sharon Adams Poore*
Assistant Editor: *Cherie Hackelberg*
Editorial Assistant: *Melissa Gleason*
Marketing Manager: *Jay Hu*
Permissions Editor: *Joohee Lee*
Print Buyer: *April Reynolds*
Copy Editing, Production, Graphics, & Composition: *Summerlight Creative, Eugene, OR*
Cover Designer: *Lisa Merski Devenish*
Cover Images: *©1999 PhotoDisc, Inc.*
Printer: *R.R. Donnelley & Sons, Crawfordsville*

Printed in the United States of America

1 2 3 4 5 6 03 02 01 00 99

Library of Congress Cataloging-in-Publication Data
Slomanson, William R.
Fundamental perspectives on international law / William R. Slomanson. -- 3rd ed.
p. cm.
Includes bibliographical references and index.
ISBN 0-534-52984-4 (alk. paper)
1. International law. I. Title.
KZ3180.S59F86 1999
341--dc21 99-34802

Wadsworth/Thomson Learning
10 Davis Drive
Belmont, CA 94002-3098
USA
www.wadsworth.com

International Headquarters
Thomson Learning
290 Harbor Drive, 2nd Floor
Stamford, CT 06902-7477
USA

UK/Europe/Middle East
Thomson Learning
Berkshire House
168-173 High Holborn
London WC1V 7AA
United Kingdom

Asia
Thomson Learning
60 Albert Street #15-01
Albert Complex
Singapore 189969

Canada
Nelson/Thomson Learning
1120 Birchmount Road
Scarborough, Ontario M1K 5G4
Canada

This book is printed on acid-free recycled paper.

DEDICATION

Por la tercera vez para
LAMPC
Las luces de mi vida

Contents

Table of Cases

Principal case names are in ***bold italics***; names of cases cited or discussed in the text are in normal *italics*. Case names cited in principal cases and within other quoted materials are not included here.

Table of Treaties, Resolutions, and Miscellaneous Instruments

This index contains treaties, resolutions, and miscellaneous agreements. The various provisions of the UN Charter are not included here, but relevant provisions are indexed in the subject index (page 617).

Abbreviations

CSCE: Conference on Security and Cooperation in Europe
GATT: General Agreement on Tariffs and Trade
ICJ: International Court of Justice
IL: International Law
LON: League of Nations
NAFTA: North American Free Trade Agreement
NIEO: New International Economic Order
OAS: Organization of American States
PCIJ: Permanent Court of International Justice
UNGARES: United Nations General Assembly Resolution
UNSCRES: United Nations Security Council Resolution
WTO: World Trade Organization

Preface

This is a fascinating time to be studying International Law. The second edition was extensively reorganized to accommodate post–Cold War changes that had occurred between the first edition and 1995. This third edition required comprehensive updating to incorporate the whirlwind of developments over the last five years of the millennium. Using feedback from its adopters, *Fundamental Perspectives on International Law* has maintained the following ensemble of teaching materials: a narrative analysis of each theme; cases from many countries and international organizations to illustrate how International Law is applied; exercises for those teachers who use the problem-teaching method; bibliographies to supplement endnote resources for further research; and an Internet component to augment the teacher's ability to keep current and to offer a broader spectrum of materials for teaching International Law.

Daily headlines confirm that the lives of all humans are ever increasingly intertwined. Although the US has emerged as the lone superpower, it can neither dominate nor ignore its increasing dependence on a global community. Iraq cannot achieve regional dominance, while Iran's President has called for a dialogue between his nation and the US. NATO is expanding eastward, while the Organization for Security and Cooperation in Europe now embraces most of the continent. The UN has initiated international criminal tribunals to sustain the legacy of the Nuremberg Tribunal. Low-intensity conflict, just short of full-scale war, is expanding—while peace could ultimately prevail in Northern Ireland, the Middle East, and other historic hot spots. The "Euro" became the first truly international currency.

Learning more about International Law will prepare both its disciples and detractors for life in the twenty-first century. Evolving principles of self-determination, the expanding scope of organizational sovereignty, limitations imposed by maturing human rights and environmental regimes, and a growing cadre of non-State actors have all restrained the absolute control once wielded by the State over its inhabitants. Even the Internet presents a fresh challenge to State sovereignty, especially in relatively closed societies.

The China–Russia Joint Declaration on a Multipolar World and the Establishment of a New International Order thus proclaimed in 1997 that humankind "is on the threshold of a new era. The peoples of all countries are faced with the increasingly urgent question of the kind of international order they will live under in the next century. The Parties call on all countries to engage in an active dialogue on the establishment of a peaceful, stable, just and rational new international order, and they are prepared to take part in a joint discussion of any constructive proposals to this end."

◆ THIRD EDITION CHANGES

COURSE WEB SITE

http://home.att.net/~slomansonb/txtcsesite.html

This new Internet feature enables professors to incorporate the World Wide Web's rich vein of informational resources. Longer versions of key documents are maintained on this Web site, especially for those professors who prefer longer cases, treaties, and legislative materials than are normally appropriate for a snapshot of International Law "between two covers." The author can update prominent hypertext links that might otherwise become broken should the UN, an international tribunal, or some other decision maker decide to alter the Web address for its original material.

NEW MATERIALS AND SECTIONS

The third edition contains the following fresh materials:

- more original documents within the text or on the Course Web Site;
- new sections about the Internet and corrupt transactions;

- cases from the UN's new international criminal courts and the World Trade Organization;
- new decisions from existing tribunals such as the International Court of Justice and the European Court of Human Rights;
- section-by-section developments on the International Law Updates Web page (described below); and
- many new or revised problems for role playing and for probing student comprehension.

CHAPTER OPENING VIGNETTES

Major events and themes are displayed at the outset of each chapter and in selected sections to pique the reader's interest, place materials in context, and underscore the nexus between current events and International Law. These abstracts also illustrate contemporary applications of one or more principles that are covered in their respective sections.

INTERNET NOTES

A number of provocative excerpts, endnotes, and textbox inserts provide Web links to original documents on the Internet. This feature is especially useful for research papers and presentations.

REVISED APPENDIXES

The *Research Guide on International Resources* and the *Career Opportunities in International Law* appendixes (and UN Charter) of the second edition have been updated and moved to the Course Web Site.

◆ SUPPLEMENTAL MATERIALS

COURSE WEB SITE (CWS)

This novel resource contains or links to various documents, including the UN Charter, the PLO Charter, cases from international tribunals, key treaties, Helms-Burton legislation stating the US position on Cuba, and the Foreign Corrupt Practices Act. From the CWS, one may link directly to the:

- author's "A-to-Z" *International Website Appendix,* which offers links to Web sites about international legal matters around the world;
- *International Law Updates* Web page, which contains online information about developments after the publication of this edition; and
- CIA's extensive collection of world, regional, and country maps available on the Internet.

INSTRUCTOR'S MANUAL

This separate booklet highlights the major changes from the second edition for the convenience of professors who adopted the previous edition. It analyzes the end-of-chapter problems that will help students review and synthesize the materials. The manual also contains a test bank of actual International Law examinations.

◆ ACKNOWLEDGMENTS

The author thanks the following individuals for their support during his preparation of this edition: Sharon Adams Poore of Wadsworth Publishing for her sustained support of a project that integrates traditional pedagogy and a new Web component; Steven Summerlight for his dedicated work on the production process; Harvey Bass (TJSL '99) and Khurrum Wahid (TJSL '98) for their intuitive and trustworthy research support; and Tracy Carroll for her effervescent assistance in entering text for the new third edition excerpts.

Finally, the author thanks the following reviewers for their contributions to the third edition: Allan D. Cooper, Otterbein College; Robert F. Gorman, Southwest Texas State University; Dimitris Stevis, Colorado State University; Richard M.J. Thurston, Saint Peter's College; and Howard Tolley, University of Cincinnati.

William R. Slomanson
San Diego, California
June 1999

CHAPTER ONE

What Is International Law?

CHAPTER OUTLINE

SOUTH AFRICA, 1994—NELSON MANDELA (1918–), statesman and Nobel laureate, is elected first black president. He rose to national prominence as leader of the global protest against the white minority government's policy of racial segregation, known as *apartheid,* which officially ended in 1991.

During his twenty-six years in prison, Mandela became a symbol of worldwide resistance to South Africa's policy of apartheid—the subject of various UN General Assembly resolutions, opinions from the International Court of Justice, and a multilateral treaty.

—Adapted from Microsoft's Encarta Encyclopedia (CD-ROM, 1999)

INTRODUCTION

This edition begins with several recent scenarios where International Law has worked. These are followed by a practical but understated question: Why should one study International Law? As characterized by Columbia Law School Professor Louis Henkin, former President of the American Society of International Law, international lawyers often have had to defend the existence and relevance of International Law to world events. He is careful to add what critics do not seem to recognize: *"[A]lmost all nations observe almost all principles of international law and almost all of their obligations almost all of the time."*[1]

This chapter will help you appreciate what International Law is, the role of some related disciplines in its evolution, and the integral relationship between national and International Law. These materials will serve as the cornerstone for studying and digesting the ensuing chapters about the affiliated elements and corollaries of International Law. You will have launched your study of this fascinating and provocative subject, outfitted with a working knowledge of its fundamental building blocks.

◆ 1.1 INTERNATIONAL LAW AT WORK

The United Nations General Assembly declared the 1990s the UN Decade of International Law.[2] Former UN Secretary-General Boutros Boutros-Ghali underscored the developments that led to this ten-year program—in a way that indicates what this course will cover:

> The end of the cold war era and the developments which have occurred in the aftermath, have dramatically underlined the increasing importance of the rule of law in international relations. The need to reaffirm the link which exists between world peace and international law and to develop that law to meet the challenges of the present day situation was behind the proclamation. . . . Four main purposes were to be achieved by the Decade, namely: the promotion of the acceptance of and respect for the principles of international law; the promotion of means and methods for the peaceful settlement of disputes between States, including resort to and full respect for the International Court of Justice; the encouragement of the progressive development of international law and its codification; and the encouragement of the teaching, study, dissemination and wider appreciation of international law. The activities which are being carried out in the progressive development of international law and its codification in various fields remind us international law is a branch of law in constant evolution. Thus, there is a continuous need to increase awareness of the content of its rules, not only among government officials, but also among members of the public at large. The need for increasing such awareness is pressing particularly in certain areas, such as human rights, environment and development, drug-abuse control and peaceful settlement of disputes to mention a few.[3]

While the national responses to this UN program were not as effervescent as hoped for, International Law did work during the 1990s. The evidence includes: entry into force of one of the most widely ratified treaties of all time—the UN Convention on the Law of the Sea, and its new tribunal for maritime disputes (Chapter 6); establishment of the first truly international tribunals for prosecuting war crimes in Bosnia and Rwanda (Chapter 9); UN resolutions serving as a basis for the thirty-four-nation coalition that forced Iraq to withdraw from Kuwait (Chapter 10); abolition of apartheid in South Africa after years of intense international pressure and economic sanctions (Chapter 11); and creation of the World Trade Organization to replace the ailing GATT process for encouraging international trade and dispute resolution (Chapter 13).

One may begin the study of International Law by considering the alternative—being in a place where leaders decide to totally disregard International Law. This scenario was not limited to the Dark Ages—the comparatively uncivilized period between the thousand-year Pax Romana and the medieval Renaissance's rekindling of the need for international cooperation. A similar void materialized during the 1966–1976 Cultural Revolution in the People's Republic of China (PRC). All courses on International Law were canceled. The teachers were summarily dismissed and sent elsewhere for re-education. The Chinese government made no apologies about its distrust of International Law.[4] As one Chinese writer characterized the state of affairs, "in the Western capitalist world, suppression of the weak by the strong and the eating of small fish by big fish are not only tacitly condoned by bourgeois international law but also are cloaked with a mantle of legality."[5]

When the Cultural Revolution ended in 1976, the PRC's leaders chose to participate in the quest for world peace, notwithstanding competitive ideologies within the community of nations. In a 1982 review of the government's fresh perspective, the President of the Chinese Society of International Law in Beijing announced that the PRC had abandoned its parochial view of International Law. Any historical tendency to remain aloof and be sequestered from the society of nations had to be supplanted by the recognition that isolation was counterproductive to the country's national interests. Thus:

> China's international lawyers must begin to work diligently to rebuild her science of international law which serves to promote world peace and truly represents the interests of the people the world over. . . .
>
> We need to make an intensive study of not only the theory of international law, but the different realms and branches of international law as well to facilitate China's international activities and her legislative work. While doing scientific research in this field, we also have the responsibility to train a new generation of specialists and scholars in international law.[6]

This survey of International Law may be integrated with the study of other disciplines. Some individuals mistakenly perceive it as falling within the exclusive domain of the law schools. While there are many career opportunities for lawyers in this discipline,[7] the academic value of International Law is not limited to law students. Professor Chris Okeke advocates the following course objectives in Nigeria, where law is an undergraduate major (as in most countries):

> (i) To expose the students to a clear understanding of the fact of inter-dependence that . . . states and other subjects of International Law, do not live in isolation, but rather must necessarily be interdependent; (ii) To teach the students to appreciate the universal principles and rules designed to ensure normal relations . . . irrespective of the differences in their economic, political and social systems; (iii) To educate the students in the spirit of humanism, democracy and respect for the sovereignty of all nations and peoples; (iv) To make the students to be constantly aware of the need to fight for the extermination of the remnants (traces) of colonialism and all forms of racial and national oppression.[8]

Studying the doctrinal aspects of International Law exposes the tangible reality that national governments cannot operate their domestic institutions completely free of external constraint. As previously discussed, it took only one decade for the PRC to learn this lesson because of the isolation associated with the PRC's defunct Cultural Revolution. The materials in this text support the premise that conflict resolution is not limited to the actions of presidents or prime ministers and diplomats, international organizations such as the United Nations, or the judicial process. Non-governmental organizations such as the Red Cross or Amnesty International, journalists, and military decision makers play significant roles in the analysis and evolution of the events and reactions that affect international relations. How these participants respond to crises influences how nations behave. Therefore, they must understand the content of International Law and its varied applications.

Business interests are often directly affected by applications of International Law. Economic sanctions, for example, require a response in the corporate sphere of influence. In 1986, President Reagan ordered United States oil companies and civilians to leave Libya as a result of terrorist activity linked to the Libyan government. That decision denied Libya's access to US technical know-how and any export, shipping, and import infrastructure formerly operated by US enterprises. It also impacted the long-term operations of US interests in that region and limited access to Libyan oil. The subsequent decision of the Libyan government to ignore the United Nations Security Council has not improved Libya's posture in the global economy. Libya's refusal to release the terrorists allegedly responsible for the bombing of Pan Am Flight 103 over Lockerbie, Scotland, further isolated it from the world community and the modern wave of economic integration.

The demise of the medieval feudal systems demonstrated the need for a State system that could function as a community of nations, bound by commonly accepted norms of conduct—referred to as "International Law" for the last several hundred years. More than 150 years ago, when the world community was far less intertwined than today, Columbia University's prominent commentator James Kent commented on the importance of studying this branch of the law:

> A comprehensive and scientific knowledge of international law is highly necessary, not only to lawyers practicing in our commercial ports, but to every [person] who is animated by liberal views, and a generous ambition to assume stations of high public trust. It would be exceedingly to the discredit of any person who should be called to take a share in the councils of the nation, if [he/she] should be found deficient in the great leading principles of this law; and . . . the elementary learning of the law of nations, as not only an essential part of the education of an American Lawyer, but as proper to be academically taught.[9]

◆ 1.2 PUBLIC INTERNATIONAL LAW DEFINED

The terms *International Law, Law of Nations,* and *Public International Law* are used interchangeably unless otherwise distinguished. The related terms *nation, State,* and *country* are also used interchangeably throughout this text.

HISTORICAL STATE-DRIVEN DEFINITION

International Law is the body of rules by which nations are bound in their mutual relations. One may resort to several traditional sources for a more detailed explanation. One source is international jurists who sometimes employ useful definitions in their legal opinions. As articulated in a decision of the Permanent Court of International Justice (predecessor of the current world court):

> International law governs relations between independent States. The rules of law binding upon States therefore emanate from their own free will as expressed in conventions [treaties] or by usages [customary state practice] generally accepted as expressing principles of law and established in order to regulate the relations between these co-existing independent communities or with a view to the achievement of common aims.[10]

Opinio Juris Prior to the proliferation of treaties in the twentieth century, the primary source for determining the content of International Law was State practice—what States do in a particular situation. Professor Luigi Condorelli of the University of Geneva aptly characterizes this source of determining the applicable norm. His observation is that some States employ a common practice that ultimately becomes the expected result in the international relations between all States. This evolution of International Law is referred to in the academic literature as *opinio juris*—meaning juridically mandatory. Note that International Law does not necessarily consist of what States actually do. Rather, it is a blend of their respective expectations and actual practice.[11] The International Court of Justice (ICJ), which is the judicial branch of the UN, added the caveat that "[n]ot only must the acts concerned amount to a settled practice, but they must also be such, or carried out in such a way, as to be evidence of a belief that this practice is rendered obligatory by the existence of a rule of law requiring it. . . . The States concerned must therefore feel that they are conforming to what amounts to a legal obligation. The frequency or even habitual character of the acts is not in itself enough [to constitute *opinio juris*]."[12]

In addition to customary practice, the ICJ notes that requisite expectations might be derived from UN resolutions (§1.4). A 1986 ICJ case involving the alleged mining of Nicaraguan harbors by agents of the United States said that a UN General Assembly resolution may be evidence of *opinio juris*. The Court was referring to the Assembly's 1970 Resolution 2625(XXV), the Declaration on Principles of International Law Concerning Friendly Relations and Cooperation Among States in Accordance with the Charter of the United Nations. The Court explained that "the adoption by States of this text affords an indication of their *'opinio juris'* as to customary international law on the question."[13]

Consent-Based Governance This introductory section would be incomplete without a succinct reference to the governance model that distinguishes national from International Law (addressed in more detail in §1.7). Algeria's Mohammed Bedjaoui, a judge of the International Court of Justice, describes the consent-based structure of International Law in the following terms:

> Just as what is known as "municipal" law is the set of rules governing the relationships of individuals, juridical persons, groups and entities among themselves within a given State, the law known as "international" consists of a body of norms . . . intended to discipline the relationships of States among themselves. Thus, in principle, it regulates the conduct of States and not that of individuals. . . . The fundamental characteristic of this international law is thus that its function is to regulate the relations between States, in other words between entities known to be sovereign and which, in principle, assert their full independence of any legal order. This at once raises the problem . . . of how these States which affirm their sovereignty can be subject to international law. If one postulates at the outset that there is no higher authority than the State, how can the norm[s] of international law be produced for and applied by such a sovereign State? As might be expected, there is only [one] possible answer to this question, namely that, historically, it has not been possible for international law to be anything other than a law resting largely on *consent*, whether express or tacit, of States and that this situation is bound to continue for a long time to come. . . . It is more a law of *co-ordination* (between the sovereign jurisdictions of individual States) than a law of *subordination* such as municipal law, which regulates its subjects, where necessary through coercion exercised by the State['s internal] apparatus.[14]

MODERN DEFINITION AND OTHER ACTORS

While International Law governs the conduct of *States*, it is no longer limited to States only. It is also applicable to international organizations and, in limited circumstances, individuals.

The proliferation of international organizations since World War II expanded the scope of International Law, which can no longer be defined *solely* in terms of State practice. The increasing reliance of States on these organizations has thrust a degree of organizational vitality on these relatively new actors on the international scene (*see* §3.1). Their State members may delegate certain sovereign powers to the international organization which, in turn, requires its State members to observe the norms developed by the organization. For example, when the International Telecommunication Union allocates communication frequencies, its national members consent to be bound by its decisions.

Other non-State actors can no longer be diminished, as done in past discourses on International Law. There are actors—*other than* States (Chapter 2), international organizations (Chapter 3), and in certain cases individuals (Chapter 4)—who influence the evolution and application of International Law. An informative excerpt from a major symposium illustrates the increasing recognition of their role:

"New Players on the International Stage"

PETER SPIRO

International Legal Personality

2 *Hofstra [Law School] Law & Policy Symposium* 25-32 (1997)

III THE NEW ACTORS.

. . . What follows is a brief introduction to the most important non-state actors (NGOs, corporations, and subnational governments) and a concise description of the nature of their international presence and the legal status that is now accorded them.

1. Non-governmental organizations (NGOs).

NGOs are hardly new to the international scene. The Catholic Church is perhaps the original NGO, and the labor movement provides the other significant example of transnational non-governmental organizing from earlier eras. While both remain quintessential models today, they are now joined by a throng. An almost infinite variety of groupings has spawned institutional vehicles in the from of NGOs (defined as organizations of non-national definition and not-for-profit orientation). Among the more prominent NGO groupings are environmentalists, human rights advocates, women, children, gays, the elderly, consumers, and indigenous peoples, each of which has mobilized at the international level.

Many NGOs at least purport to represent memberships, and many act as advocates in and out of international institutional settings. Greenpeace and Amnesty International are perhaps the most prominent examples of the modern advocacy NGO. These advocacy NGOs are noteworthy in at least two important respects. First, they now act directly to influence international decisionmaking institutions and not only through the channel of "home states." Thus, a Greenpeace or Amnesty International [organization] will not stop at having members or national sections lobby their own governments. . . . Rather, they will move into the international stream as transnational entities seeking leverage wherever available. For example, a Greenpeace (with a largely North Atlantic membership) has had its positions voiced and advanced by delegations from small island states and lesser developed countries. In that fashion, advocacy NGOs become players outside the control of the states from which they nominally hale.

These NGOs have also been afforded a limited formal status in some international decisionmaking contexts. Pursuant to article 71 of the U.N. Charter, the Economic and Social Council (ECOSOC) has extended "consultative status" to international NGOs satisfying certain basic criteria. Recognition entitles an NGO access to ECOSOC proceedings and, for the more prominent organizations, rights to lodge oral and written interventions as well as to propose agenda items. NGOs have also been afforded limited rights of participation at UN-sponsored world conferences in recent years, including at Rio (on the environment), Cairo (population), and Beijing (women). Conferences on multilateral pacts on climate change and endangered species have afforded NGOs a place as observers to treaty monitoring proceedings. But in no institution save the International Labour Organisation have NGOs been formally extended a status even approaching parity with that of states. Nor have NGOs been afforded standing in international judicial forums, with prominent exceptions at the level of regional organizations.

In practice, NGO influence has far exceeded that indicated by their tentative formal standing in international institutions. NGOs have prompted states to undertake significant international legal initiatives, especially with respect to human rights and environmental protection. They have also been able to pursue global political agendas outside of institutions, either by shaming states (or other relevant actors, most notably corporations) through exposure and/or by mobilizing sympathetic consumer constituencies within the integrated global economy. The former is by now a well-honed tactic of the human rights movement through which objectives are secured by public relations mechanisms. The recent controversy surrounding Royal Dutch Shell's proposed scuttling of an oil rig [the Brent Spar] in the North Sea presents one recent example of the latter. Shell had received all appropriate domestic and international approvals to leave the Brent Spar rig on the ocean floor. Greenpeace objected and launched a campaign to boycott Shell gasoline. Within weeks, Shell's sales in Germany were down 30%, at which point the oil giant relented. Shell has since sought out Greenpeace for consultations in planning the decommission of other rigs. Similar tactics were deployed against France to protect its recent nuclear testing program in the South Pacific. Although the tests were completed as planned, the success of Greenpeace's consumer action campaign may have contributed to France's decision not to undertake more tests in the future.

Brent Spar–type tactics are effective in proportion to a corporation's or state's dependence on consumer trade. The potential for such activity will be enhanced by further integration of the global marketplace, which increases the exposure of target states and corporations. Granted, the mechanism may remain exceptional. Groups such as Greenpeace obviously cannot effectively attack every objective through outright confrontation. But the threat of membership mobilization will make repetitive deployment unnecessary in some cases. Potential targets may accede to NGO demands, or at least come to an informal negotiating table, out of an awareness that consumer campaigns have worked in the past. There will also be episodes in which the possible costs of boycott efforts will not outweigh the benefits of the activity that the NGO seeks to halt. This may help to explain Shell's continued presence in Nigeria notwithstanding objections to the human rights practices of the current regime there. While NGO power is not absolute, it is significant and growing.

2. Corporations.

As with the case of NGOs, corporations have long enjoyed a presence at the international level. The Hudson's Bay and British East India Companies were effectively sovereign over their far-flung trading realms, engaging in such characteristically governmental activity as coining currency, concluding treaties, and making war. During the 1960s and 1970s, the activities of multinational corporations were subjected to international scrutiny in the face of lesser developed countries' claims of capitalist exploitation.

In the interwar era of the 1920s and 1930s, the International Chamber of Commerce participated in a variety of League of Nations proceedings and even signed some League instruments as a party. Corporate alliances such as the ICC now participate in international contexts as NGOs, subject to the same requirements and enjoying the same rights as others under the consultative status system. Corporate interests have also organized themselves for the issues of the day, for example, by forming a highly effective Business Council on Sustainable Development to participate in multilateral forums relating to the international environment.

Corporations so grouped thus enjoy some formal status in international institutions. But, as with NGOs, the status is decidedly second class even as real-world corporate power grows. Except at the ILO [International Labor Organization], the corporate community does not enjoy a seat at the table, at least not in its own name. Corporations generally have no standing in public international judicial and dispute resolution bodies, even where they effectively may be the only real parties in interest. This may have been the case with the first decision handed down by the new World Trade Organization dispute resolution panel, which, though styled as a dispute between Brazil and the United States, was in fact more a dispute between two oil companies.

Excluding corporate actors from formal decision-making processes, as well as absolving them from ultimate accountability under international law, may have made sense in a world in which corporations had a clear national identity and could be adequately represented by and through particular states. Until recent years, this had held more and less true. Even during their vilification during the sixties and seventies, the so-called "multinationals" qualified as such by virtue of a mere presence in more than one country. The moniker "multinational" has not, as least until recently, implied true multinationality in the sense of being under the ultimate control of more than one nation, and thus in a sense being in the control of none. The United American Fruit Company, [at the turn of the Century] for example, was multinational insofar as it had operations in several Latin American counties, but it was exclusively a US enterprise at its core, clearly governed by the dictates of US law.

Today such national identity and control is no longer so apparent. Some large corporations are becoming truly multinational in the sense that it is now almost meaningless to describe them as, say, American or British or Dutch. Even a corporation so intertwined with US foreign relations as Coca-Cola is now moving to shed its national roots. The increasingly cosmopolitan nature of international corporate giants is reflected in corporate structures that make them difficult to regulate from any single state.

Indeed, it is becoming increasingly difficult for states to regulate even those corporations that maintain a strong national identification. As global capital becomes more mobile and the global economy more competitive, state efforts to constrain corporations may be doomed to fail in some contexts. The United States, for example, would find it very difficult, at best, to impose its domestic minimum wage laws on a US corporation's operations in Malaysia, for to do so would place the US corporation at a disadvantage against competitors from other nations not subject to the same regulation. In turn, a developing state like Malaysia could not itself impose a minimum wage so long as other countries did not do the same, for to do so would likely force the US corporation to relocate outside Malaysia. To the extent this description now reflects real-world conditions, the corporate community itself could become an ultimate repository of power.

No wonder that NGOs have moved on some issues to influence corporate behavior directly, rather than indirectly by winning state regulation to the same effect. Such has been the case with the Brent Spar incident and other boycott efforts. It has also characterized the shareholder responsibility movement, in which progressive interests enjoying large shareholding interests (most notably, US state and local pension funds as well as churches) pressure corporations through shareholder resolutions to adhere to environmental and human rights practices beyond those required by domestic or international law.

3. Subnational governments.

Subnational governments [like New York, Quebec, or Tijuana] are assuming an unprecedented role in global affairs. Subnational governments active at the international level include provinces, localities, and perhaps most notably the constitutive units of federative nation-states. The international profile of subnational governments has been most enhanced in recent years in the economic cultural spheres. Sister-city arrangements [in different countries] blossomed in the 1980s, and it is now routine for subnational officials to undertake international promotional campaigns (through trade delegations or permanent trade offices) to attract foreign investment into their jurisdictions. These activities have been facilitated by advances in global travel and communications, as well as by the global economic integration that makes transnational investment possible (and indeed necessary) to economic growth.

Subnational action has also had political implications at the global level. Conduct on the part of US states in the areas of tax policy and the treatment of aliens . . . has raised the ire of foreign governments. Even where subnational practice involves areas of core traditional authority (criminal or family law, for example), international norms may now elevate those practices to international significance. These cameo appearances by subnational authorities indicate that they may have interests at the international level distinct from the nation-states of which they are a part. . . .

There are, however, few direct links between subnational governments and international decisionmaking structures. A union of local elected officials enjoys consultative status at the UN, and municipal authorities were an important force in the UN-sponsored Habitat II world summit on housing and other problems common to urban governance that was convened in Istanbul in the summer of 1996. Such subnational geographic regions as Wales, the Basque land, and Catalonia have direct official links to the central organs of the European Union. The province of Quebec has a seat in the association of francophone states. But that appears to be the extent of formal subnational participation in international institutions.

Of course, this lack of status may be attributed to the fact that subnational authorities, by definition, remain under the control of national governments. Unlike corporations and NGOs, they are territorially fixed and cannot exploit mobility and transnational identities to defeat central government supervision. If the strength of central governments continues to flag, however, this control may emerge more formal than real, at least on some issues. In that case, the international significance of subnational governments is likely to be further enlarged, regardless of the legal status attributed to them under international law.

◆ *Notes*

The Swiss banking industry reached a settlement with lawyers representing Holocaust survivors in August 1998 after three years of negotiations. The Nazi regime had sent gold and other assets to Switzerland during World War II, a fact kept secret by the banks until a Swiss guard refused to shred some documentary proof in 1995. Some $1.3 billion dollars in reparations will be paid into an account, based on class-action litigation filed in three cases in the US (most notably, New York City). In 1995, the World Jewish Congress (WJC), with offices in more than eighty countries, pressured the Swiss banking industry and Swiss authorities to return these assets to their rightful owners. You can view various developments in the evolution of this embarrassing scenario (for Switzerland) on the World Wide Web at www.lib.uchicago.edu/~llou/nazigold.html.

The Swiss banks thereby averted economic sanctions —not by US federal authorities, but by "non-State" actors, including the cities of New York and Los Angeles. The latter entities, while governmental, are not "persons" under International Law (as opposed to the US and its government). The WJC likewise is not an international person that would otherwise be able to officially function in the international legal arena. However, both the cities and the WJC were able to forcefully influence the Swiss government (and, in turn, the Swiss banking industry) on a major issue in International Law with extremely sensitive political overtones. The influence of such non-State actors cannot be disregarded in the analysis of players on the international stage.

The current scope of International Law is routinely articulated in terms of States, international organizations, and in some cases, individuals or corporations. These entities will be the focus of this book. The American Law Institute—in a representative study by this prominent group of private lawyers, government officials, and law teachers dedicated to the clarification and improvement of national performance in the field of International Law—found that "International Law . . . consists of rules and principles of general application dealing with the conduct of states and international organizations and with their relations inter se [among or between themselves], as well as some of their relations with persons, whether natural or juridical [corporations]."[15]

SCOPE

As this course unfolds, you will begin to appreciate that International Law does not embrace a governmental structure like that of most nations. The UN Secretary-General is not a chief executive officer, nor is he or she the commander-in-chief of any armed forces. The UN General Assembly is not a legislative body which can *require* nations to act in accordance with a resolution. The International Court of Justice does not have the power to hear cases, absent the express consent of a State defendant. This comparatively primitive state of affairs— the hallmark of an international legal system in which the governed govern—necessitates that a State is not bound to act in a certain way unless customary State practice requires it or that State has expressly consented to the particular rule in a treaty.

The constant ebb and flow of national practice can make the task of ascertaining the precise content of International Law comparatively complex. There are continuous changes in State practice, clashing normative or cultural interpretations of the same legal dispute, and varying treaty reservations to the same treaty. One consequence is that the content of International Law sometimes evolves gradually, and briskly in other instances. A leading commentator, writing on behalf of the US Department of State, thus expressed that "International law is, more or less, in a continual state of change and development. In certain of its aspects the evolution is gradual; in others it is avulsive. [W]hereas certain customs are recognized as obligatory, others are in retrogression and are recognized as nonobligatory, depending upon the subject matter and its status at a particular time."[16]

Certain specialists in International Law perceive this evolutionary process as being so pervasive that one should not view International Law as a body of rules in the traditional normative sense. Instead, it is a *process*, invoking authoritative State decision making where rules are constantly made and remade. These commentators do not question the existence of International Law. They do question the utility of the common view that viable legal systems operate only when they are premised upon clearly defined systemwide rules that do not bend with the winds of political power. However, in the international legal system where States essentially govern themselves—and one often must look to State practice to determine the applicable substantive rule—the "distinction between law and politics is artificial, even preposterous."[17]

Universality? The definitional perspective in this section requires brief mention of two related questions: (1) Is universal acceptance required for a rule to become part of the content of International Law? (2) Can a powerful country, such as the United States, unilaterally change International Law—either theoretically or practically?

First, universal acceptance is *not* required for a norm to be incorporated into the body of International Law. If enough nations acknowledge a particular norm, by consistently using it in their international relations, their consensus will cause the norm to become a part of International Law.[18] However, the sovereign nature of each State authorizes the *express* rejection of what others might term a "universal" or "customary" rule. Acquiescence may bind the same sovereign nation, should it choose not to tender an objection through diplomatic processes or treaty reservations (§1.4).

Second, no single nation, regardless of its political or military strength, has the power to create or modify International Law. One nation's statute cannot create global obligations. A bilateral treaty between two nations creates obligations *inter se*, for which one incurs an admissible claim under International Law if the other breaches its treaty commitments. International Law is not created, developed, or abolished by the demand of one country or a small group of countries. Its contours are determined by the common consent of many nations. Even the United States, which enjoys a very unique and powerful position after the end of the Cold War, cannot either dominate or withdraw from the community of nations.

There are, of course, some wrinkles in the definitional fabric of International Law. Some commentators cautiously qualify the above consensus-based definition to require "democratic" and "civilized" components. Long before the demise of the Soviet Union, Moscow State University Professor Grigori Tunkin embraced the element of International Law consisting of democratic norms. He described it in his prominent 1974 treatise as the "aggregate of norms which are created by agreement between states of different social systems, [which] reflect the concordant wills of states and have a generally *democratic* character. . . ."[19] Other commentators add the qualification that International Law contains only those norms accepted by "civilized" nations. This limitation finds support in the Statute of the International Court of Justice. Article 38.1.c provides that the Court may rely on "the general principles of law recognized by *civilized* nations." Of course, what constitutes "civilized" often depends on the eye of the beholder.

◆ 1.3 HISTORY OF INTERNATIONAL LAW

Students of International Law must not fall victim to the modern penchant for ignoring the past. Looking back will help you to appreciate the remarkably accurate adage that "Those who ignore history are condemned to repeat it." One can value the historical evolution of International Law for several practical reasons. Most UN members (approaching 200, as opposed to the original 51) did not exist in 1945. Most members of the contemporary international community suddenly became subject to the existing rules of International Law developed over the course of many centuries. Past developments provided an immediate link with the present for these new States and international organizations with no comparable history to guide their international relations.

The following materials momentarily summarize the development of International Law and the schools of thought that shaped how we analyze and examine it in present contexts.

DEVELOPMENT

One could partition the history of Public International Law into three main periods: ancient, medieval, and modern.

Ancient International Law History records that people lived in parts of what is now the Middle East in roughly 25,000 B.C. Approximately 4000 B.C., the area spawned two communities that became the cradle of modern civilization—the Egyptians and the Babylonians.

The process by which International Law first developed was spawned by ancient Egyptian and Indian practices. Approximately 3100 B.C., two Mesopotamian city-states concluded a treaty that governed their international relations. Egyptian pharaohs also entered into treaties with neighboring kings beginning in 1400 B.C. These agreements recognized sovereign rights over certain geographical areas, the extradition of refugees, and the exchange of diplomatic envoys. In 1100 B.C., the Hindus advocated humaneness in the conduct of war. For example, poisoned weapons were prohibited. Around 800 B.C., the major Middle Eastern civilizations experienced a series of invasions—perhaps the most famous being that of Alexander the Great in approximately 300 B.C. His conquest introduced the Greek language into the area, followed by the 300-year Hellenic Age.

The Greek city-states and their philosophers believed that there was a legal hierarchy of authority, specifically local and "higher" laws. Local laws governed the conduct of individuals within each city-state. The laws of the city-state were subordinate to codes such as the Customs of the Hellenes. Accepted practice under this code included protection for aliens through a consular official to represent their interests, diplomatic immunity for foreign agents, and the right of asylum in certain cases.

Ancient Chinese tradition did not embrace law in the same way as it evolved in Western civilization. The need for a formalized legal order was perceived as the sign of a somewhat imperfect society. Nevertheless, the Confucian influence provided for minimum order, the essentials of which authorized the use of force. The Confucian philosophy of 600 B.C. perceived the Chinese ruler as Heaven's descendent. He was considered superior to the rulers of other nations, thereby providing a sense of legitimacy for China's early conquests and domination of its Asian neighbors. Extraterritorial applications of this descendence were conducted under the guise of self-defense, humanitarian intervention, and reprisals or punitive expeditions against barbaric rulers who dared engage in unauthorized invasions against China.

The Romans ultimately conquered most of the Middle East by approximately 30 B.C. The Pax Romana (beginning in 31 B.C.) was a period of relative peace among the Roman, Greek, and "barbaric" city-states of that era. Rome fought incessantly with those refusing to recognize its authority, while those subservient to it were free from war. Western civilization blossomed under Roman control. The ensuing thousand-year period effectively precluded attempts to reject internationally applicable norms. Roman law, for example, governed the rights of aliens—including development of the institution of the Praetor Pegreginus to settle legal disputes involving their interests. The Roman College of Fetiales negotiated treaties with non-Roman entities and decided legal matters associated with waging war against them. Upon conquering the Greeks, Rome was also exposed to their notion of universality. These distant subjects of Rome's control—and even Rome itself—were then perceived as integrated elements of a unified "international" system.[20]

Medieval International Law The medieval period in the evolution of International Law can be traced to several key developments in international relations. Charlemagne's coronation as Emperor of the West by Pope Leo III in A.D. 800 was a pivotal event. A new period in international relations followed—including expeditionary religious crusades, formation of codes such as the Law Merchant for medieval maritime dispute resolution, and the introduction of the "Just War" by Thomas Aquinas (who would later be canonized a saint by the Roman Catholic Church). Islam mounted its own crusades around A.D. 700. The Muslims conquered much of the Middle East. Like the ancient Chinese, their political tenets rejected any possible equality of nations with unacceptable religious and cultural systems.

The Roman system of colonial administration was ultimately replaced with a feudal system during the Dark Ages, eliminating the international personality of the State (or city-state) due to the ensuing merger of political authority and land tenure. Germanic and Viking influences impacted all of Europe where development of international norms had flourished. The fifteenth- and sixteenth-century intellectuals later coined the term *Dark Ages* for this period of cultural squalor between antiquity and the Renaissance—their own self-serving term, pregnant with metaphors ironically designed to inspire admiration for what would become a period of intense international conflict.

The Catholic Church sought to rekindle some form of unification after the feudal, or virtually tribal, existence of "civilization" in the Dark Ages. Church leaders believed in some unifying central authority, which led to the Pope's crowning of European monarchs in Rome. But the Protestant Reformation ultimately crushed the hopes of the Catholic Church to effectuate its version of international political stability. The feudal regions became sovereign in the sense now associated with statehood—but remained devoid of a community of nations in the modern sense (described below). War among what may be perceived today as "microstates" devolved into the Thirty-Years' War from 1618 to 1648. This hopeless anarchy was epitomized by the 350 German "States" of that era. Each exercised absolute sovereignty within its particular feudal region.

The Dutch writer Hugo Grotius (1583–1645) was a major contributor to the development of modern International Law. He is often referred to as the "Father of International Law," although the term *International Law* was later coined by the English philosopher Jeremy Bentham in 1789. Grotius's fundamental contribution to the theory of International Law was expressed in *The Law of War and Peace,* published in 1625. It postulated a voluntary law of nations based on consent. Since his native country (Holland) had just achieved independence after Europe's devastating Thirty-Years' War, Grotius developed support for the fundamental maxim that this newfound freedom from foreign domination necessitated an emphasis on the territorial sovereignty of each State. The transnational pretensions of the papacy and the Holy Roman Empire were ultimately supplanted by the postulate that States should be supreme in their respective spheres—subject to no external powers not expressly embraced by each's sovereign assent. The willingness to conform to transnational norms was then perceived as requiring express consent, in treaties, or implicit consent, drawn from customary State practice in international matters.

Modern International Law The modern era of international relations emerged from the 1648 Peace of Westphalia. It launched a series of treaties, rekindling the concept of a more broadly based sovereignty—unlike the more localized sovereignty of the preceding feudal period. Westphalia introduced the notion of collective self-defense found in contemporary treaties like the Charters of the League of Nations and Organization of American States. A representative passage from the 1648 agreement provided that "each of the contracting parties . . . shall be held to defend and maintain all and each of the dispositions of this peace, against whomsoever it may be [broken] without distinction of religion."[21] However, the Westphalian treaties proved unstable. There was no international organization to maintain the peace. Any prospects for collective security gave way to the formation of alliances serving nationalistic rather than collegial interests.

The next major development in the evolution of International Law was the Congress of Vienna in 1814–1815, initially designed to be an international organization for maintaining peace. Self-serving alliances later corrupted the possibility of world governance, however. One of the most infamous examples was the Conference of Europe, which divided Africa among European powers for colonial purposes. Ironically, US President Monroe would announce his famous "Monroe Doctrine" seven years later, designed partially to prevent any similar action in the New World.[22]

During the ensuing centuries, certain European powers became the most active and prominent members of this international community, joined by the US in the late 1700s and Latin American nations after the turn of the century. The period between the 1648 Peace of Westphalia and the outbreak of World War I in 1914 gradually solidified the contemporary perception of national sovereignty within the context of a community of nations. States in other parts of the world catered to this Western-driven paradigm, effectively acquiescing in the development of Eurocentric notions of International Law.[23]

The sovereignty pendulum began to swing in the other direction because of several events in the 1990s. One was with the collapse of the Soviet Union (USSR). Its demise was accompanied by a breakdown of statehood as contemplated in the 1648 Peace of Westphalia. The USSR evolved into some dozen States—almost overnight. Yugoslavia, once consisting of six provinces, later devolved into five new States. One of those States, Bosnia-Herzegovina, further decomposed into several State-like entities roughly approximating the indigenous Muslim, Croat, and Serbian populations. The evolution of non-State actors has had its impact as more of them have influenced State conduct and how people live (*see* Chapter 3 on international organizations and Chapter 4 on non-governmental organizations). Finally, the information revolution has somewhat diminished State sovereignty (§5.4 on State Jurisdiction and the Internet).

Chapter 2 presents the fundamental analysis of modern statehood. It will explain the concept of "State" and the contemporary influences affecting its historical role as the dominant feature of the international system.

SCHOOLS

Academic commentators developed several schools of thought for classifying the essence of Public International Law. The colleges within this theoretical university include the schools of Natural Law, Positivism, and Eclectics.

Natural Law This school, attributed to eighteenth-century European jurists, actually dates from the time of the ancient Greeks in approximately 500 B.C. Babylonia's (now Iraq) written Code of Hammurabi was based on Natural Law principles. The English Magna Carta also provided for certain natural rights linking morals and law.[24] Law must be in harmony with, or reflect the essential nature of, all peoples. Medieval disciples of this particular school of thought perceived legal order as being premised on the expectations that God or nature has injected into the essence of life. Such laws are immutable, existing even in the absence of a divine being. A properly functioning international legal order must thereby incorporate only those principles of justice rooted in the natural reasoning process.[25]

The Catholic Church's Thomas Aquinas contributed to this development by linking the philosophy of Aristotle and the theology of Catholicism. Harvard Divinity Professor Harvey Cox, in his essay regarding Islam's Koran, explains that "[t]o a Western reader, this important concept of 'the ethical common sense' . . . calls to mind the philosophical idea of natural law, or natural moral reason, which has played such an important part in the history of Western moral philosophy and predates the Christian era. The idea is also found in Christianity, as in St. Paul's Epistle to the Romans, in which he insists that all people are endowed with the capacity to know right from wrong."[26]

This was the prevalent theory in medieval times, when fewer international obligations were established by written treaties (or positive rules). Any contemporary academic or judicial momentum favoring Natural Law as the essence of International Law was likely spawned by the Nazi horrors perpetrated during the Holocaust.

> "Supposing these African negroes not to be slaves, but kidnapped . . . the treaty with Spain cannot be obligatory upon them; and the conflict of rights between the parties . . . must be decided upon the eternal principles of justice and international law."
>
> —US Supreme Court opinion in *US v. The Schooner Amistad,* 40 US 518, 595 (1841).

Jus cogens, a cornerstone of the Naturalist School, is Latin for compulsory law.[27] Article 53 of the Vienna Convention on State Treaties and the Vienna Convention on Treaties with International Organizations defines *jus cogens* as a peremptory norm of International Law "from which no derogation is permitted and which can be modified only by a subsequent norm of general international law having the same character."[28] Like a private individual being barred from enjoying the benefits of an illegal contract under national law, a State's violation of a *jus cogens* norm would likewise be barred from reaping the fruits of any such illegal agreement.

Although its existence is hotly debated, this theme has also appeared, at least nominally, in modern treaties and case law. The 1969 Vienna Convention on the Law of Treaties, the UN International Law Commission's 1976 Report of Its Draft Articles on State Responsibility, and the 1986 Vienna Convention on the Law of Treaties Between States and International Organizations all contain provisions concerning *jus cogens*. In 1969, the International Court of Justice, when referring to the UN Charter Article 2.4 prohibition against the aggressive use of force, chose not to embrace *jus cogens* in its legal analysis of a use-of-force issue. By 1986, however, the same Court thoroughly embraced it—as recommended by the UN's International Law Commission. The Court then characterized the prohibition on the aggressive use of force as a "conspicuous example of a rule in international law having the character of *jus cogens*."[29]

A certain polarity exists between *jus cogens* and State sovereignty. The former term is derived from the Natural Law concept that certain norms exist, from which no State may ever deviate. Such norms, assuming their existence, would not depend on the consent of States to nevertheless bind them. State sovereignty, on the other hand, may be characterized as authorizing States to do as they wish. Assume, for example, that all States were to agree that torture is an acceptable police tactic. No Natural Law or divinity-based norm could prevail over torture, assuming the latter's approval by the community of nations. The tension between *jus cogens* and State sovereignty has impaired any hope of widespread agreement about just what norms fall within this category.

Positivism School The Positivist School is a by-product of the Protestant Reformation. Its advocates perceive *consent* as the essential rationale for the current state of International Law. Thus, no international legal norm exists—no matter how staunchly ingrained in reason or morality—unless it is the product of consensual decision making among members of the international community. International Law process cannot exist independently of mutual consent, which is in turn based on customary practice, treaties, or other expressions of national consent. As the contemporary notion of "State" gradually developed its legal and political primacy, there was a predictable shift from Natural Law to Positivism as the underlying premise for defining the essence of International Law.

Some commentators have attacked the Positivist School because it lacks a yardstick for judging the morality of State conduct. If Hitler's Germany and Stalin's Russia could agree to divide Europe in 1939, then mere consent would produce an enforceable obligation to wage aggressive wars to achieve the treaty's objective. Others complain that it is too rigid, focusing upon the consent as the lynchpin for the international legal system. As stated by Professor T. W. Bennett of the University of Cape Town, regarding the imposition of English law on tropical Africa, "during the late nineteenth and early twentieth centuries, western legal thought was heavily influenced by positivism, a philosophy which has had a long-lasting and generally a malign[ing] effect on customary law. Positivism . . . provided a series of assumptions about the relationship of law and society which have been responsible for the distinctly 'legalistic' attitude that has characterized much subsequent work on the subject."[30]

Eclectic School This school occupies something of a middle ground, positioned somewhere between Natural Law and Positivism. Eclectic centrists ("Grotians") assert that International Law evolved through a periodic shifting of expedient emphases. Its progressive development was not significantly influenced by the more polarized alternatives premised on "nature" or "consent." Public International Law is, instead, a serviceable blend of both the naturalist's morality and the positivist's common assent of sovereign nations theories. Writers of the French and American Revolutions urged this approach as the basis for both national and international order.[31]

◆ 1.4 SOURCES OF INTERNATIONAL LAW

INTRODUCTION

The word *sources* is one of the most common but misunderstood terms in the jargon of International Law.[32] There is a confusing distinction between sources—referring to *what* the law is and *where* it may be found. In this section of the book, the term "source" means *where* a decision maker or researcher may look to ascertain the substantive content or applicable law. As used in this particular sense, "source" does *not* refer to the actual substance of International Law. Instead, it is a category of information which contains the applicable substantive rules.

The international community has agreed to the following list of sources for ascertaining the content of International Law, however. Under Article 38.1 of the Statute of the International Court of Justice (ICJ):

> The Court, whose function is to decide in accordance with international law such disputes as are submitted to it, shall apply:
>
> a. international conventions, whether general or particular, establishing rules expressly recognized by the contesting states;
> b. international custom, as evidence of a general practice accepted as law;
> c. the general principles of law recognized by civilized nations;
> d. . . . judicial decisions *and* the teachings of the most highly qualified publicists of the various nations, as subsidiary means for the determination of rules of law.

This portfolio of sources was extracted from Article 38 of the prior Statute, unanimously adopted by the First Assembly of the League of Nations in 1920 for the original world court—the Permanent Court of International Justice (PCIJ). This first world court used the same source list from 1920 until its judges fled from Holland during World War II. The PCIJ's version of Article 38 descended from the common practice of other tribunals that had used these same sources for finding evidence of the substantive content of International Law. While scholars have debated the completeness of this list of sources,[33] the UN Secretary-General commented (in 1949) that this major building block of International Law "has been repeatedly treated as authoritative by international arbitral tribunals."[34]

Not all nations use the identical list of sources of International Law. Their analysis is typically the same, however. The common statement of sources recommended for use in the United States, for example, is that of Washington, D.C.'s American Law Institute. It has published a number of restatements of various fields of law—a blend of what is, and what should be, the law in a particular field. Under §102 of the Foreign Relations Law of the United States, the *sources* of International Law are customary law, international agreement, and general principles "common to the major legal systems of the world." Under §103, the following are *evidence* of whether a rule has become International Law: decisions of international judicial and arbitral tribunals, decisions of national tribunals, the writings of scholars, and State pronouncements that are not seriously challenged by other States. General Assembly resolutions are "secondary" evidence, analogous to the ICJ Article 38 term "subsidiary" sources. Neither Article 38 nor the US Restatement rely on a General Assembly resolution as an indicator of the content of International Law. Comment *c.* to §103 thus provides that, unlike State practice or treaty commitments, international organizations "have no authority to make law, and their determinations of [what is] law ordinarily have no special weight." These general pronouncements are not legally binding on member nations. Yet such resolutions may be secondary evidence of International Law. Their declaratory pronouncements at least suggest some evidence of what the participating States consider the applicable norm.

Nations, international organizations, domestic or international courts, and arbitrators routinely examine the established sources of International Law to see whether the particular rule, which some participant is advocating, has been consented to by States. The London Court of Appeal articulated this forensic process with the following pronouncement: "Rules of international law, whether they be part of our law or a source of our law, must be in some sense 'proved,' and they are not proved in English courts by expert evidence like [testimony about] foreign law: they are 'proved' by taking judicial notice of international treaties and conventions, authoritative textbooks, practice and judicial decisions of other courts in other countries which show that they have attained the position of general acceptance by civilised nations."[35]

Article 38 Critics The 1944 Report of the Informal Inter-Allied Committee on the Future of the "Permanent" Court of International Justice stated that "although the wording of this provision is open to certain criticisms, it has worked well in practice and its retention is recommended."

Some critics question whether this aging articulation of the sources of International Law has continuing vitality. Some Western, Russian, and Chinese scholars have articulated forceful counter-arguments. Former University of Chicago Professor Morton Kaplan and former US Attorney General Nicholas Katzenbach argued in their book on the political foundations of International Law that this list of sources became "stereotyped." It failed to acknowledge their ever-changing nature. Literature from the former Soviet Union raised doubts concerning the "imperfect formulation" of Article 38 of the Statute of the International Court. Moscow State University Professor Grigori Tunkin comments that a "practice" might not be a *general* practice within the meaning of this Article, although it is recognized as a legally binding rule between two nations or within a particular region of the world. Chinese scholars perceive the Article 38 list of Western-derived sources as reflecting the external policy of the ruling classes, because these "sources of bourgeois international law are the external policy of the bourgeoisie which is also the will of the ruling class of those big capitalist powers."[36] "Third World" scholars embrace this latter perception regarding the Eurocentric roots of International Law. Their States were colonized long ago by the dominant States, which cultivated these rules prior to the independence movement of the 1960s.

Hierarchy Among Sources? The sequential arrangement of the sources within Article 38 of the ICJ Statute suggests an implicit hierarchy. The first layer of this ordering is that treaties, customs, and general principles are the primary sources for finding the content of International Law. Judicial decisions and scholarly writings are expressly designated as the "subsidiary" sources for determining the content of International Law.

A rule derived from one of those sources may somehow differ from the rule provided by another source. An example would be a rule drawn from a bilateral treaty between only two nations, as opposed to a contradictory rule implicit in a more universal customary practice. The local treaty may not relieve the contracting nations from compliance with a widely accepted custom. Hitler and Stalin agreed to divide Europe, but their treaty conflicted with the customary rule that aggression violates the prohibition against waging wars that violate territorial sovereignty.

The possibility of an explicit hierarchy of sources was nearly incorporated into the predecessor of Article 38, drafted for the Permanent Court of International Justice in 1920. The Committee of Jurists initially included a provision that the listed sources were to be considered *en ordre successif*—in successive order. These words were deleted, however, at the First Assembly of the League of Nations. The League's records do not indicate whether the deletion was meant to avoid a hierarchy, or, alternatively, was so unnecessary as to render these words *(en ordre successif)* surplusage. A treaty is the best evidence; a custom is easier than a general principle; and so on.[37]

Contemporary commentators rank the comparative importance of even the first part of the statutory list of sources. They consider custom to be not only at the top, but also the essential basis for other sources. University of Rome Professor Benedetto Conforti thereby insists that:

> Customary rules properly are placed at the top of the hierarchy of international norms. Included as a special category of customary rules, are general principles of law common to all domestic systems. Custom is both the highest source of international norms, and the only source of general rules. Treaties are second in ranking. Their obligatory character [itself] rests on a customary rule, *pacta sunt servanda* [good faith performance], and their entire existence is regulated by a series of customary rules known as the law of treaties. Third in the hierarchy are sources provided by agreements, including, most importantly, acts of international organizations.[38]

Other commentators characterize treaties as the most fundamental source. Frankfurt University's Professor Rudolf Bernhardt asserts that custom is often superseded by treaties. His informative perspective is that "normal customary law ... can as such be superseded by regional as well as universal treaties. States are in general free to conclude treaties which depart from customary law. This happens every day. Treaties on economic relations between certain States, double taxation agreements, defence alliances and human rights treaties all change the legal relations between the participating States, impose additional and different obligations, limit the existing freedom and sovereign rights of the States concerned, and [thereby] change the applicable norms. In this context, treaties have a 'higher' rank than customary law."[39]

This section of the book explores the meaning and effect of the listed (and other) sources of International Law: Custom, Treaties, General Principles, Judicial Decisions, Scholarly Writings, and UN Resolutions.

CUSTOM

Decision makers resolving international issues have historically looked to the customary practice of nations as the primary source for determining the content of International Law. An established State practice, accepted by many nations, qualifies as such a custom. This source has a rich and diverse history dating back to Roman times.[40] It has a persistent vitality because many international obligations are not expressed in treaties.

When is a custom "binding"? Moscow State University Professor Grigori Tunkin describes this question as one of the most important, and most complex, theoretical problems for diplomats, jurists, and researchers. It is therefore "natural that the question of customary norms of international law has been the object of constant attention of [the] specialists for a century."[41] This complexity has evolved from the dual process of having to determine both *where* to find evidence of the custom's existence and *when* it becomes obligatory.

There may be a continuum whereby a customary practice among a few nations ultimately ripens into an obligatory custom to be applied by all—on either a regional or a global basis. A common problem with proving the existence of a custom is thus determining whether a particular practice by some States is so recognized that it has matured into "Customary International Law" (CIL) that binds all nations. It then becomes necessary to research the actual practice of States to determine whether enough of them expect that practice to be applied by their respective decision makers. Oxford University's Professor Ian Brownlie conveniently assembles the four elements for resolving whether such a practice is CIL: (1) duration or passage of time; (2) substantial uniformity or consistency of usage by the affected nations; (3) generality of the practice, or degree of abstention; and (4) *opinio juris et necessitatis*—international consensus about, and recognition of, the particular custom as binding.[42]

The fourth element is arguably the most important, yet the most difficult to authenticate. The ICJ opinion in the 1969 *North Sea Continental Shelf* case authoritatively analyzed the requisite international consensus. It dealt with whether the UN's 1958 Convention on the Continental Shelf, containing an equidistance principle for allocating limited resources within the shelf, codified a customary rule that would bind nations *not* parties to that Convention. The Court stated that in order for *opinio juris* to render such a custom binding:

> Not only must the acts concerned amount to a settled practice, but they must also be such . . . as to be evidence of a belief that this practice is rendered obligatory by the existence of a rule of law requiring it. . . . The States concerned must therefore feel that they are conforming to what amounts to a legal obligation. . . . There are [otherwise] many international acts, e.g., in the field of ceremonial [behaviour] and protocol, which are performed almost invariably, but which are motivated only by considerations of courtesy, convenience, or tradition, and not by any sense of legal duty.[43]

Customs: Regional and Universal Regional customs used by a few nations may differ from international customs practiced by many other nations. Both categories of custom may be binding. For example, Colombia claimed in a 1950 ICJ opinion that "American International Law" required Peru to recognize Colombia's grant of asylum in the Latin American region. Diplomatic asylum was not recognized by customary practice elsewhere in the world. The Court rejected the existence of either a universal or regional custom, which would have recognized such asylum to be a binding practice (a decision for which it was harshly criticized, especially among African nations). Yet it tacitly approved the potential application of regional practices where they *could* be proven to exist.

The dispute emerged when Peru alleged that the Colombian embassy improperly granted asylum to a Peruvian national seeking to overthrow Peru's government. The ICJ explored the possibility that there might be a regional custom, as claimed by Colombia, that would bind Peru to honor this custom and allow the Peruvian to leave Peru without being prosecuted. A key passage illustrates what Columbia would have to prove in order to establish this source of International Law: "[t]he Party which relies on custom . . . must prove that this custom is established in such a manner that it has become binding on the other Party . . . [and] that the [claimed right of asylum] . . . is in accordance with a constant and uniform usage, practised by the States in question, and that this usage is the expression of a right appertaining to the State granting asylum [Colombia] and a duty incumbent on the territorial State [Peru]."[44]

Some commentators contend, however, that *universality* of practice is required for a custom to be binding under International Law.[45] This "requirement" has been advocated in socialist nations where International Law is not considered a part of the legal hierarchy of laws. The problem with this position is that universality is rarely achieved in an international system composed of many diverse nations. International custom gradually evolves through compromise and consistency of application. New York University Professor James Hsiung, writing on Chinese recognition practice, comments that the practice of States is not the ultimate basis of International Law. It is, instead, substantive evidence of a general consensus or acceptable expectation. Dissent or change of consensus is therefore an indicator that a certain norm is not supported by universal consensus. However, it is impossible to measure precisely how strong a dissent must be before an existing norm is changed, or precisely when a rejected norm ceases to exist. Dissent, or change of consensus, if supported by a growing number of States, may bring about a new norm or revision, or at least indicate a possible trend toward change.[46]

Custom Applied The following case illustrates how one group of decision makers determined whether a particular custom actually existed and whether it was sufficiently acknowledged by the international community to be binding International Law:

The Paquete Habana and The Lola

SUPREME COURT OF THE UNITED STATES, 1900

175 US 677, 20 S.Ct. 290, 44 *L. Ed.* 320

Author's Note: *The American press attributed the sinking of the USS Maine to a bomb planted aboard it by Spanish forces while at anchor in Havana Harbor. During the ensuing Spanish-American War of 1898, US vessels patrolled Cuban waters to prevent activities that might aid Spain. The US Navy seized two coastal fishing vessels near the coast of Cuba. One was* The Paquete Habana. *The other was* The Lola.

The "prize courts" of nations at war typically determine the lawfulness of military seizures of foreign vessels. A prize is a captured enemy or neutral vessel suspected of carrying materials to aid the enemy.[47] *The trial judge examined US domestic law to determine the validity of the seizure based on presidential executive decrees regarding the Law of Prize. He then addressed whether any exceptions authorized the return of the vessels and their fishing cargoes to their owners and to the crew members who were entitled to a percentage of the catch. The lower court's decision upheld the seizure of these coastal fishing vessels. The majority opinion surveyed how other nations answered such questions when the seizure allegedly violated the Law of Nations.*

COURT'S OPINION: Justice Gray delivered the majority opinion of the Court:

These are two appeals from decrees of the district court of the United States for the southern district of Florida condemning two fishing vessels and their cargoes as prize of war.

Each vessel was a fishing smack, running in and out of Havana, and regularly engaged in fishing on the coast of Cuba; sailed under the Spanish flag; was owned by a Spanish subject of Cuban birth, living in the city of Havana; was commanded by a subject of Spain, also residing in Havana; and her master and crew had no interest in the vessel, but were entitled to shares, amounting in all to two thirds, of her catch, the other third belonging to her owner. Her cargo consisted of fresh fish, caught by her crew from the sea, put on board as they were caught, and kept and sold alive. Until stopped by the blockading squadron she had no knowledge of the existence of the war or of any blockade. She had no arms or ammunition on board, and made no attempt to run the blockade after she knew of its existence, nor any resistance at the time of the capture.

Both the fishing vessels were brought by their captors into Key West. A libel [meaning the plaintiff's complaint asking] for the condemnation of each vessel and her cargo as prize of war [permitting the capture at sea of enemy property] was there filed on April 27, 1898; a claim was interposed by her master on behalf of himself and the other members of the crew, and of her owner; evidence was taken, showing the facts above stated; and on May 30, 1898, a final decree of condemnation and sale was entered, "the court not being satisfied that, as a matter of law, without any ordinance, treaty, or proclamation, fishing vessels of this class are exempt from seizure."

We are then brought to the consideration of the question whether, upon the facts appearing in these records, the fishing smacks were subject to capture by the armed vessels of the United States during the recent war with Spain.

By an ancient usage among civilized nations, beginning centuries ago, and gradually ripening into a rule of international law, coast fishing vessels, pursuing their vocation of catching and bringing in fresh fish, have been recognized as exempt, with their cargoes and crews, from capture as prize of war.

This doctrine, however, has been earnestly contested at the bar; and no complete collection of the instances illustrating it is to be found, so far as we are aware, in a single published work, although many are referred to and discussed by the writers on international law.

It is therefore worth the while to trace the history of the rule, from the earliest accessible sources, through the increasing recognition of it, with occasional setbacks, to what we may now justly consider as its final establishment in our own country and generally throughout the civilized world.

The Court next discussed the history of the custom allegedly exempting coastal fishers from capture in this scenario. This analysis commenced with King Henry IV's orders to his admirals in 1403 and then examined the relevant practices of France, Holland, Prussia, and the US.

Since the English orders in [the] council of 1806 and 1810 . . . in favor of fishing vessels employed in catching and bringing to market fresh fish, no instance has been found in which the exemption from capture of private coast fishing vessels honestly pursuing their peaceful industry has been denied by England or by any other nation. And the Empire of Japan (the last state admitted into the rank of civilized nations), by an ordinance promulgated at the beginning of its war with China in August, 1894, established prize courts, and ordained that "the following enemy's vessels are exempt from detention," including in the exemption "boats engaged in coast fisheries," as well as "ships engaged exclusively on a voyage of scientific discovery, philanthropy, or religious mission." Takahashi, *International Law,* 11, 178.

International law is part of our law, and must be ascertained and administered by the courts of justice of appropriate jurisdiction as often as questions of right depending upon it are duly presented for their determination. For this purpose, where there is no treaty and no controlling executive or legislative act or judicial decision, resort must be had to the customs and usages of civilized nations, and, as evidence of these, to the works of jurists and commentators who by years of labor, research, and experience have made themselves peculiarly well acquainted with the subjects of which they treat. Such works are resorted to by judicial tribunals, not for the speculations of their authors concerning what the law ought to be, but for trustworthy evidence of what the law really is.

This review of the precedents and authorities on the subject appears to us abundantly to demonstrate that at the present day, by the general consent of the civilized nations of the world, and independently of any express treaty or other public act, it is an established rule of international law, founded on considerations of humanity to a poor and industrious order of men, and of the mutual convenience of belligerent states, that coast fishing vessels, with their implements and supplies, cargoes and crews, unarmed and honestly pursuing their peaceful calling of catching and bringing in fresh fish, are exempt from capture as prize of war.

The exemption, of course, does not apply to coast fishermen or their vessels if employed for a warlike purpose, or in such a way as to give aid or information to the enemy; nor when military or naval operations create a necessity to which all private interests must give way.

On April 26, 1898, the [US] President issued another proclamation which, after reciting the existence of the war as declared by Congress, contained this further recital: "It being desirable that such war should be conducted upon principles in harmony with the present views of nations and sanctioned by their recent practice." This recital was followed by specific declarations of certain rules for the conduct of the war by sea, [although] making no mention of fishing vessels. 30 Stat. at L. 1770. But the proclamation clearly manifests the general policy of the government to conduct the war in accordance with the principles of international law sanctioned by the recent practice of nations.

The case then summarized the US admiral's argument in support of his seizure of The Paquete Habana *and* The Lola. *The sailors of the two seized vessels were members of the naval military reserves of Spain and were capable artillerymen. The majority of the Court concentrated, however, on the existence of a general custom against the capture of such vessels.*

The two vessels and their cargoes were condemned by the district court as prize of war; the vessels were sold under its decrees; and it does not appear what became of the fresh fish of which their cargoes consisted.

Upon the facts proved in either case [involving the vessels *Paquete Habana* and *Lola*], it is the duty of this court, sitting as the highest prize court of the United States, and administering the law of nations, to declare and adjudge that the capture was unlawful and without probable cause; and it is therefore, in each case—

Ordered, that the decree of the District Court be reversed, and the proceeds of the sale of the vessel, together with the proceeds of any sale of her cargo, be restored to the claimant [captain and crew], with damages and costs.

The relevant portion of the dissenting opinion of three Supreme Court justices who heard this case follows. They would have affirmed the seizure under the US Law of Prize because the custom relied on by the majority was not binding on the US: The President could decide not to use the international rules of war at any time. It also was not as clear to the dissenters that this custom of exempting coastal fishers had the degree of international recognition accorded it by the majority.

[We are] unable to conclude that there is any such established international rule, or that this court can properly revise action which must be treated as having been taken in the ordinary exercise of discretion in the conduct of war.

It cannot be maintained "that modern usage constitutes a rule which acts directly upon the thing itself by its own force, and not through the sovereign power" [quoting from *Brown* below]. That position was disallowed in *Brown v. United States,* and Chief Justice Marshall said:

> This usage is a guide which the sovereign follows or abandons at his will. The rule, like other precepts of morality, of humanity, and even of wisdom, is addressed to the judgment of the sovereign; and although it cannot be disregarded by him without obloquy, yet it may be disregarded. The rule is in its nature flexible. It is subject to infinite modification. It is not an immutable rule of law, but depends on political considerations which may continually vary.

Ruling!

◆ *Notes & Questions*

The *Paquete Habana* case analyzed the following issues relating to principles of customary International Law:

1. In what way was International Law deemed to be a part of the law of the United States?
2. Which international custom was applied to this dispute?
3. How did the judicial decision maker determine the existence of that custom?
4. The dissenting members of the Court minimized the impact of customary practice, based on what the US President may say in future executive orders about the applicability of International Law to the conduct of naval blockades. These judges would not have applied the exemption from capture under international custom, because the President had the power to order future admirals not to conduct a war in accordance with International Law. Which was more credible—the Court's majority or dissenting opinion?

TREATIES

There is a treaty on treaties. It provides that a treaty is "an international agreement concluded between States in written form and governed by international law, whether embodied in a single instrument or in two or more related instruments and whatever its particular designation."[48] International agreements may also be oral, as discussed below.

Treaties are the first source listed in the Article 38.1(a) (Statute of the International Court of Justice) restatement of the sources of International Law. Historically, they have been less prominent in international law making. As discussed in Chapter 8 on treaties, multilateral agreements are often achieved through compromise—thus providing only a generalized statement of principled values, easily stated in the abstract but hard to "pin down" to specific circumstances.

Treaties are the most convenient way, however, to quickly obtain reliable evidence of consensus on the issue before international decision makers. Ratified by many nations, a multilateral treaty is direct proof of rights and obligations accepted by parties to the treaty. When the participating countries intend to create a new or modify an existing rule, their treaty-based agreement adds to the substantive content of International Law. Therefore, it is a primary source for ascertaining the precise nature of just what participants have agreed to do or not do.

Regional or issue-specific treaties are not intended to have universal applicability. However, they are useful sources of International Law when they contain rules intended to bind certain nations. Examples include the Charter of the Organization of American States (OAS). It provides that all international disputes between American States shall be submitted to the peaceful procedures set forth in the OAS Charter, "*before* being referred to the Security Council of the United Nations."[49] Nations in the "American" region have thereby agreed to resolve their local disputes, conditioned upon first resort to regional OAS agencies—rather than commencing the resolution process with direct resort to the UN Security Council. While the UN Charter encourages such regionalism, this local treaty *requires* its members to seek an OAS solution first, before accessing a more universal forum. Conversely, a non-OAS nation is free to initiate its claim at the UN or in any other forum of its choosing.

Multilateral treaties may also provide evidence of international consensus, even when they are not universally adopted. One example is the UN Law of the Sea Treaty, which entered into force in November 1994. It is the best evidence of the respective rights and obligations of the parties who have accepted it. When enough nations have ratified such a treaty, it is the best source for resolving a maritime issue between the *ratifying* parties. Such a treaty may also bind *non*-parties as a matter of *Customary* International Law (CIL)—if it codifies the general practice of most or many nations. A rule stated in a treaty may pass into the body of CIL. This process was confirmed by the ICJ in its statement that a treaty may have "generated a rule which, while only conventional or contractual in its origin [between ratifying States], has since passed into the general *corpus* of international law, and is now accepted as such by the *opinio juris,* so as to have become binding even for countries which have never, and do not, become parties to the Convention. There is no doubt that this process is a perfectly possible one and does from time to time occur: it constitutes indeed one of the recognized methods by which new rules of customary international law may be formed."[50]

GENERAL PRINCIPLES

The statutory list of sources includes "general principles of law recognized by civilized nations." National and international decision makers thereby borrow principles from the internal law of various nations when an examination of customs or treaties does not yield an applicable rule. Examples include "equity" and "good faith."[51]

The evolution of International Law is thus supplemented by principles espoused in national legal systems. Some scholars, however, profess that only *International Law* principles may be drawn from decisions presented in national legal systems. Others perceive the general principles source as sufficiently broad to be reliable on any available principle to resolve the issue at hand. Russian scholars have interpreted "general principles" in this broader sense. Chinese scholars disagree. This source should be interpreted to refer only to the principles of *national* law that are generally applied by many nations.[52]

Why is this source of International Law necessary? Given the comparatively primitive development of the international legal system, in relation to the needs with which it is faced, international tribunals have decided fewer cases than those decreed by most (if not all) national legal systems. In any legal system, situations arise where the decision maker realizes that there *is* no law that applies to the issue under consideration. "General principles" serves as a stopgap. A judge can deduce an apropos rule, drawn from another legal system.

Both world courts have affirmed this source as an established and pragmatic source, for drawing certain principles from national jurisprudence, to answer questions arising under International Law. In an often-quoted statement from a 1937 PCIJ case, Judge Anzilotti commented on the commonly applied equitable principle that a nonperforming nation cannot take advantage of another's nonperformance. He was convinced that this general principle was "so just, so equitable, so universally recognized, that it must be applied in international relations" as one of those general principles of law recognized by civilized nations under Article 38 of the Court's Statute. The propriety of using national legal principles in international adjudication was reaffirmed in a 1970 ICJ case dealing with the general principle of judicial independence from other branches of the government. Notwithstanding differences in degree between various legal systems, it "may be considered as a universally recognized principle in most of the municipal [national] and international legal systems of the world."[53]

The induction of a general principle of national law into international decision making is classically illustrated by the following case opinion:

The AM&S Case
Austral[illegible]ng & Smelting Europe Ltd. v. E.C. Commission

[1982] *2 Common Market Law Reports 264*

Author's Note: *A commission of the European Community (EC) filed a proceeding questioning whether AM&S activities violated regional competition laws. The EC sought documents prepared by the company's lawyers. AM&S responded with this proceeding, seeking to avoid compliance, on the basis of an attorney–client privilege. There was no provision in the various EC treaties or regulations regarding this claimed privilege from discovery.*

The following excerpt is the Second Opinion of the Advocate General (Sir Gordon Slynn). Under applicable procedure, the attorney representing the EC files an opinion regarding issues in proceedings that are pending before the EC and judicial tribunals.

The following edited opinion assesses whether there is a general principle in the laws of the various EC member States to support the privilege claimed by AM&S. In certain sentences, italics were supplied by the author.

Court's Opinion: In February 1979, officials of the [European Community] Commission required the applicants to make available documents which they wished to see in connection with an investigation . . . of competitive conditions concerning the production and distribution of zinc metal and its alloys and zinc concentrates in order to verify that there is no infringement of Articles 85 and 86 of the EEC Treaty [the European Community's basic competition provisions]. The applicants produced copies of most of the documents. Some, however, were not produced . . . on the basis that they were covered by legal confidentiality, which entitled the applicants to withhold them.

The parties were invited to state at the re-opened oral hearing their views on the law as to, and legal opinions relating to, the existence and extent of the protection granted in investigative proceedings instituted by public authorities . . . to correspondence passing between . . . [lawyer and client].

The Commission's investigative powers for the purpose of carrying out the duties assigned to it . . . are so far as relevant conferred by Article 14 of Regulation 17. It may 'undertake all necessary investigations into undertakings and associations of undertakings' and, to that end, its authorised officials are empowered to examine books and business records, to take copies of them, and to ask for oral explanations. *There is no reference to any exemption or protection which may be claimed on the basis of legal confidence.* Is that silence conclusive that no such protection is capable of applying in any form and in any situation? In my view it is not. The essential enquiry is, first, whether there is a principle of Community law existing independently of the regulation, and, secondly, whether the regulation does on a proper construction restrict the application of that principle. The question is not whether a principle of Community law derogates from Article 14, but whether Article 14 excludes the application of principle of Community law. . . .

That general principles which have not been expressly stated in the Treaty or in subordinate legislation may exist as part of Community law, the observance of which the Court is required to ensure, needs no emphasis. . . . The Commission argue[s] that there has to be a consensus among the laws of all the member-States, and that the Court cannot establish a principle which goes beyond that accepted by any one of the member-States.

It cited no specific authority for that proposition, nor indicated what is the necessary level or degree of consensus required to establish the existence of a general principle.

That national law may be looked at on a comparative basis as an aid to consideration of what is Community law is shown in many cases. . . . Such a course is followed not to import national laws as such into Community law, but to use it as a means of discovering an *unwritten* principle of Community law. . . .

The Court has been provided with extracts from legislation, case decisions and the opinions of academic authors and a welter of case references. Rather than set those out in *extenso* I propose to summarise what seems to me to be the relevant features for present purposes, fully conscious of the risks that a summary may over-simplify and is incomplete. I deal first with the general position as to the protection of legal confidence and then consider the position in relation to competition law.

In Belgium, it seems that confidential communications between lawyer and client are protected and cannot be seized or used as evidence. . . . There exists also a more general principle which protects the privacy of correspondence—see Articles 10 and 22 of the [Belgian] Constitution.

In Denmark, the rules of the professional secret prevents lawyers from giving evidence of confidential information confided to them in their professional capacity, and a lawyer can refuse to produce documents covered by professional secrecy. Communications between an accused person and his lawyer are protected in the hands of the accused under section 786 of the Code of Procedure. This rule seems to apply also in civil proceedings [like the one now pending before the European Commission].

In Germany, confidential communications to a lawyer are protected in his hands, and breach of the professional confidentiality by a lawyer is a criminal offence. Thus such documents in the hands of the lawyer cannot be seized (section 97 of the Code of Criminal Procedure). . . .

In France, breach of the rule of professional secrecy is a criminal offence. . . .

In Greece, it seems that confidential communications in the hands of lawyers are protected in investigative proceedings instituted by judicial or administrative authorities. Documents in the hands of the client are covered by the general principle of privacy defined in Article 9 of the [Greek] Constitution. The power to search the client's premises is circumscribed by sections 253 *et seq.* of the Code of Criminal Procedure.

In Ireland and the United Kingdom, although there may be differences in detail, broadly the law of the two member-States is the same. . . . It should be repeated, however that it covers both (a) communications between a person and his lawyer for the purpose of obtaining or giving legal advice whether or not in connection with pending or contemplated legal proceedings and (b) communications between a person and his lawyer and other persons for the dominant purpose of preparing for pending or contemplated legal proceedings.

In Italy, as in most of the member-States, the law forbids lawyers from giving evidence of the information confided in them by their clients and entitles them to withhold documents covered by the doctrine of professional secrecy. On the other hand, it seems that, in the case of criminal investigations, documents held by a lawyer may be seized unless they have been entrusted to him for the preparation of his client's defence. Protection is wider in civil proceedings but it does not, in any case, appear to extend to documents in the hands of the client. It seems that . . . professional secrecy is a reflection of the right to a fair trial guaranteed by Article 24 of the [Italian] Constitution.

In Luxembourg, rules of professional secrecy and *'les droits de la défense,'* it would seem, protect legal confidences in the hands of the lawyer, and of the client after proceedings have begun, but little case law has been produced showing the application of these rules in practice.

Dutch law forbids the revelation of confidences by persons exercising a profession, such a lawyers. Coupled with this there is a right to refuse to give evidence on matters covered by professional secrecy. These matters include not only the information revealed by the client but also, in the case of lawyers, the legal advice they have given. Section 98 of the Code of Criminal Procedure provides that, when the premises of someone bound by professional secrecy are searched, the doctrine of professional secrecy must be observed and documents covered by it cannot be seized. There appears to be no authority holding or denying that legal correspondence found in the hands of the client is protected.

This summary is substantially, if not entirely, accepted by the Commission, the applicants and the body representing the Bars of all the member-States as being a fair and acceptable statement of the laws of member-States.

It seems to me significant that they were able to reach agreement as to the existence of the principles which are set out in the document which they prepared to read to the Court.

From this it is plain, as indeed seems inevitable, that the position in all the member-States is not identical. It is to my mind equally plain that *there exists in all the member-States a recognition that the public interest and the proper administration of justice demand as a general rule* that a client should be able to speak freely, frankly and fully to his lawyer. . . . Whether it is described as the right of the client or the duty of the lawyer, this principle has nothing to do with the protection or privilege of the lawyer. It springs essentially from the basic need of a man in a civilised society to be able to turn to his lawyer for advice and help, and if proceedings begin, for representation; it springs no less from the advantages to a society which involves complex law reaching into all the business affairs of persons, real and legal, that they should be able to know what they can do under the law, what is forbidden, where they must tread circumspectly, where they run risks. . . .

Judgment

By application lodged at the Court Registry on 4 October 1979, Australian Mining & Smelting Europe Limited (hereinafter referred to as "AM&S Europe') which is based in the United Kingdom, instituted proceedings . . . to have . . . Commission Decision 79/760/EEC of 6 July 1979 declared void. That provision required the applicant to produce for examination by officers of the Commission charged with carrying out an investigation all the documents for which legal privilege was claimed, as listed in the appendix to AM&S Europe's letter of 26 March 1979 to the Commission.

The application [by AM&S] is based on the submission that in all the member-States written communications between lawyer and client are protected by virtue of a principle common to all those States, although the scope of that protection and the means of securing it vary from one country to another. According to the applicant, it follows from that principle . . . that the protection is properly claimed on the ground that the documents in question are in fact covered by legal privilege. . . .

(a) *The interpretation of Article 14 of Regulation 17* [conferring investigatory powers on the EC] . . .

(b) *Applicability of the protection of confidentiality in Community Law* . . .

However, the above rules do not exclude the possibility of recognising, subject to certain conditions, that certain business records are of a confidential nature. *Community law,* which derives from not only the economic but also the legal interpenetration of the member-States, *must take into account the principles and concepts common to the laws of those States* concerning the observance of confidentiality, in particular, as regards certain communications between lawyer and client. That confidentiality serves the requirement, the importance of which is recognised in all of the member-States, that any person must be able, without constraint, to consult a lawyer whose profession entails the giving of independent legal advice to all those in need of it. . . .

(d) *The confidential nature of the documents at issue* . . .

In view of that relationship and in the light of the foregoing considerations, the written communications at issue must accordingly be considered, in so far as they emanate from an independent lawyer entitled to practice his profession in a member-State, as confidential and on that ground beyond the Commission's power of investigation under Article 14 of Regulation 17.

◆ *Notes & Questions*

1. Why did this opinion elaborate upon the laws of the EC member States?
2. There were some important differences between those laws. Did the opinion properly disregard them in reaching its decision?
3. What was the essential issue to be decided in the *AM&S* case, and what was the rationale for that decision?

Non-Judicial Application of General Principles

A definitive example of applying a general principle of law, outside of the judicial context, is found in the exchange of diplomatic correspondence between Mexico and the United States in 1938. While the United States claimed that international custom prohibited Mexico's expropriation of property owned by US citizens without compensation, both nations professed their own convenient applications of the general principles of "reason, equity, and justice." Mexico had expropriated farm land and oil properties without reimbursing the US owners.

The US government wanted Mexico to compensate them for these seizures. US Secretary of State Cordell Hull sent a communiqué to the Mexican Ambassador to the United States. Hull thereby generated an exchange of letters that would be a useful source for determining what these two countries considered to be the general principle governing expropriations. Hull wrote, on behalf of the United States government, that "we cannot admit that a foreign government may take the property of American nationals in disregard of the rule of [prompt, adequate, and effective] compensation under international law. Nor can we admit that any government unilaterally and through its municipal legislation can, as in this instant case, nullify this universally accepted principle of international law, based as it is on reason, equity and justice."

The Mexican ambassador denied the existence of a general principle of law requiring compensation under the circumstances. Under Mexico's view, "there is in international law no rule universally accepted in theory nor carried out in practice, which makes obligatory the payment of immediate compensation nor even of deferred compensation, for expropriations of a general and impersonal character like those which Mexico has carried out for the purpose of redistribution of the land. . . . As has been stated above, there does not exist in international law any principle [that is] universally accepted by countries, nor by the writers of treatises on this subject, that would render obligatory the giving of adequate compensation for expropriations of a general and impersonal character."

US Secretary Hull responded that "[t]he Government of the United States merely adverts to a self-evident fact when it notes that the applicable precedents and recognized authorities on international law support its declaration that, under every rule of law and equity, no government is entitled to expropriate private property, for whatever purpose, without provision for prompt, adequate, and effective payment therefor. In addition, clauses appearing in the constitutions of almost all nations today, and in particular in the constitutions of the American republics, embody the principle of just compensation."

Not wishing this statement to remain undeflected, Mexico responded that "[n]umerous nations, in reorganizing their economy, have been under the necessity of modifying their legislation in such manner that the expropriation of individual interests nevertheless does not call for immediate compensation and, in many cases, not even subsequent compensation; because such acts are inspired by legitimate causes and the aspirations of social justice, they have not been considered unusual or contrary to international law."[54]

Mexico and the US ultimately negotiated a settlement of this compensation dispute. The quoted diplomatic correspondence demonstrates one of the difficulties with ascertaining general principles of *national* law as a source for resolving a dispute having *International* Law implications (State responsibility for injury to aliens, as discussed in Chapter 2 of this book). Not all States necessarily agree about the general principle that a party may be advocating—in diplomatic correspondence, a judicial proceeding, or any occasion when an international decision maker is applying International Law to a given dispute. In this instance, Mexico and the US had posed mutually exclusive views regarding what each country perceived to be the applicable "general principle" governing compensation for the taking of foreign property.

◆ *Notes & Questions*

1. What was the "general principle" proposed by the US in the Mexican expropriation case?
2. What was Mexico's response to the US argument?
3. Which ambassador made the better argument?

JUDICIAL DECISIONS

Under Article 38 of the ICJ Statute, judicial decisions are a "subsidiary" source for determining the content of International Law. This source has historically drawn mostly upon *national* court decisions, which more frequently assess international issues than do international tribunals. The required State consent for resolving a case in an international tribunal has greatly limited the number of decisions available in such forums as a source for finding the content of International Law.

When a particular issue is decided the same way by the courts of various nations, a judicial tribunal will consider such consistent application as evidence of a State consensus about how to resolve that issue. Decision makers have also looked for uniformity in one State (usually their own). England's late Professor Hersch Lauterpacht commented that the "decisions within any particular State, when endowed with sufficient uniformity and authority, may be regarded as expressing the *opinio juris*," meaning an expression of what that State believes to be the accepted practice in international relations.[55]

This source is "subsidiary" because a judge's decision does not *make* law. The judge normally interprets the law and applies it to the pending case. This is particularly true in civil law countries, where judges have less discretion than that of their common law counterparts when they interpret the law. Many civil law commentators consider the common law judicial process to be one that produces an almost oxymoronic blend of judicial legislation because of the comparative latitude enjoyed by common law judges. In the United States, for example, Congress delegated the development of the federal law of admiralty to federal judges. Judicial pronouncements by the courts of one country cannot directly create or modify International Law, however. They provide incomplete evidence of a rule that the *judicial* branch of one member of the community of nations has adopted—not the executive branch, which normally determines national positions on international matters.

A national court may also rely upon foreign judicial decisions to resolve an internal matter with international implications. The US Supreme Court made an ambitious statement in 1815 about the utility of this practice. It was resolving a commercial dispute regarding a government seizure of sugar belonging to a citizen of another country during time of war. The Court therein stated that:

> The law of nations is the great source from which we derive those rules [regarding ownership of seized enemy property] which are recognized by all civilized and commercial states throughout Europe and America. This law is in part unwritten, and in part conventional [meaning the subject of a treaty]. To ascertain that which is unwritten, we resort to the . . . decisions of the Courts of every country, so far as they are founded upon a law common to every country, [which] will be received not as [binding] authority, but with respect. The decisions of the Courts of every country show how the law of nations, in the given case, is understood in that country, and will be considered in adopting the rule which is to prevail in this [case]. . . .[56]

Ironically, the "judicial decisions" source has evolved to the point where some commentators have characterized it as the most important factor in the progressive development of International Law. Some writers characterize judicial decisions as being entitled to greater significance than the "subsidiary" status accorded them by the ICJ Statute. As stated by the Court's President, decisions of international tribunals "exercise considerable influence as an impartial and well-considered statement of the law by jurists of authority made in light of actual problems which arise before them."[57]

Impact of ICJ Opinions The ICJ is fettered with a significant limitation not found in the national law of many UN members (particularly the common law countries such as Canada, England, and the United States). Under Article 38.1(d), judicial decisions are sources of the law "[s]ubject to the provisions of Article 59." Article 59 of the ICJ Statute provides that the "decision of the Court has no binding force except as between the parties and in respect of that particular case."

As stated by the PCIJ in 1926, the reason for this statutory limitation "is simply to prevent legal principles accepted by the Court in a particular case from being binding on other States or in other disputes."[58] Restated, national sovereignty was intended to limit the role of ICJ opinions in a manner not applied in national courts with common law backgrounds. The drafters of this provision, first applicable to the PCIJ and now to the ICJ, recognized that such a limit would encourage more States to submit their disputes to a distant tribunal in Holland. A bad result in one case would not haunt them in later disputes with other parties.

In practice, however, the ICJ has reapplied many principles relied on in its earlier cases. As its case precedent has expanded, a number of its prior opinions have been the basis for resolving the same issues resurfacing in subsequent cases. Perusing current ICJ opinions reveals that the current world court has not been satisfied with the limitation in Article 59 of deciding today, only to have its opinion disregarded tomorrow. Otherwise, there would be little consistency in its decision-making process and less respect for its ability to participate in the progressive development of International Law.

SCHOLARLY WRITINGS

Article 38.1(d) authorizes the use of "the teachings of the most highly qualified publicists of the various nations, as subsidiary means for the determination of rules of law." Analyses by influential "publicists," meaning prominent commentators in International Law, is the other statutory method for ascertaining evidence of the content of International Law.

As a practical matter, one who is deciding a question of International Law typically begins with academic writings for preliminary insight. Scholarly treatises have been helpful to international tribunals. The following passage in an opinion by the Permanent Court of International Justice illustrates the utility of this resource. The Court was considering the circumstances under which an individual could be prosecuted for a crime committed in international waters. The Court began its analysis by stating that "as regards teachings of publicists . . . it is no doubt true that all or nearly all writers teach that ships on the high seas are subject exclusively to the jurisdiction of the State whose flag they fly."[59] The judges in this case thereby incorporated the scholars' analyses of the jurisdictional issue to achieve a result which was consistent with International Law. This passage illustrates the impact which legal writers make on the progressive development of International Law.

Scholarly writers serve a related purpose. Their commentaries also record both historical and contemporary developments in State practice. Professor Karol Wolfke of Poland characterizes scholarly writings as an essential instrument for analyzing disputed issues, gathering information about prior resolutions of the same issue, and finding the latest trends in the ebb and flow of international legal norms. In addition to "attracting attention to international practice and appraising it, the writers indirectly influence its further evolution, that is, the development of custom."[60]

The use of scholarly writings for determining the content of International Law does have an inherent limitation, however. One reason is that scholarly writings often contain the author's perspective on what International Law *should* be, rather than what it *is*. This admonition was eloquently stated in an English appeals court opinion, declaring that "the views expressed by learned writers on international law have done in the past, and will do in the future, valuable service in helping to create the opinion by which the range of the consensus of civilized nations is enlarged. But in many instances their pronouncements must be regarded rather as the embodiments of their views as to what ought to be, from an ethical standpoint, the conduct of nations . . . [rather] than the enunciation of a rule or practice so universally approved or assented to as to be fairly termed . . . 'law.'"[61]

Given this admonition, one might characterize scholarly analysis as a behind-the-scenes "source" that applies in a peripheral sense. Yet scholarly writing is typically invoked by decision makers to obtain succinct and authoritative insights about the law's content—although not a law-making source for establishing the *opinio juris* (State expectations, based on the rules they observe in their relations with other States). Publicists thus write *about* the rules and may influence the rule-making process. But they can never make the rules, as accomplished by custom and treaties.

UN RESOLUTIONS

General Assembly Article 38 of the ICJ Statute is not necessarily the exclusive list of sources. Resolutions of international organizations may also assist in ascertaining the substantive content of International Law. There has been a vast proliferation of international organizations in the more than half-century since the initial version of Article 38 was prepared for use by the PCIJ. Although the UN General Assembly is not an international legislature, resolutions adopted by its State representatives reflect what States consider binding norms.

The strongest argument against characterizing General Assembly resolutions as either normative or rule-making may be drawn from the language of the UN Charter itself. The Assembly's given role is to make recommendations. Under Article 10, it "may discuss any questions or any matters within the scope of the present Charter, and . . . may make recommendations to the Members of the United Nations or to the Security Council. . . ." Under Article 11, the Assembly "may consider the general principles of cooperation in the maintenance of international peace and security . . . and may make recommendations with regard to such principles to the Members or the Security Council or both. . . ."

The former Legal Counsel of the United Nations characterized General Assembly resolutions as *non*-binding. Under his perspective, the "General Assembly's authority is limited to the adoption of resolutions. These are mere recommendations having no legally binding force for member states. Solemn declarations adopted either unanimously or by consensus have no different status, although their moral and political impact will be an important factor in guiding national policies. . . . The General Assembly, through its solemn declarations, can therefore give an important impetus to the emergence of new rules, despite the fact that the adoption of declarations per se does not give them the quality of binding norms."[62]

Some commentators nevertheless assert that the UN General Assembly's resolutions *are* sources of International Law that can bind member nations through their normative effect. While such resolutions are recommendations, they are also evidence of the customary practice of many States. The Polish Academy's Professor Krzysztof Skubiszewski notes that "[o]n various occasions, the developing States read into some recommendations the legal duty to conform to them. There is a whole gamut of arguments to justify this attitude. Some writers treat the nonbinding resolutions as a modern source (e.g., [ICJ] Judge [Mohammed] Bedjaoui). Others give an extensive interpretation of the powers of the resolution-making body ([ICJ] Judge T. O. Elias), so extensive that it obviously contravenes its constitutional position [as a body which only makes recommendations]."[63] Northwestern University Professor Anthony D'Amato notes that, although books have been written about this subject, "there has been no consensus. Therefore, International law would surely be a much easier subject to study and master if UN resolutions could be treated as definitive statements of rules of International Law."[64]

To more fully appreciate the importance of what follows—in the ensuing chapters of this course in International Law—one should acknowledge the distinction between "hard" and "soft" International Law. Recognizing the rationale for *why* UN resolutions do not appear on the Article 38 shopping list of International Law's sources aids in making the valuable connection between *hard* law (e.g., treaty obligations) and *soft* law (e.g., resolutions). Paul Szasz, Legal Advisor of the International Conference on the Former Yugoslavia, uses this distinction to explain how soft law, such as UN resolutions, often leads to hard law, like UN treaties, in the following terms:

> Hard international law is, by definition, binding, at least on some international entities (states or IGOs [inter-governmental organizations]), although not necessarily on all. By contrast, soft international law is not binding, though perhaps superficially it may appear to be so; nevertheless, international entities habitually comply with it, and it is this feature that makes possible reference to it as "law."...
>
> Soft law is usually generated as a compromise between those who wish a certain matter to be regulated definitely and those who, while not denying the merits of the substantive issue, do not wish (at least for a time) to be bound by rigid and obligatory rules—perhaps because they fear they cannot obtain whatever domestic legislative approval is necessary [say, to achieve ratification of a treaty through the ensuing internal processes required for State acceptance of an obligatory treaty].
>
> There are several reasons why soft law deserves to be included in a study of international law, especially one concerning the international legislative process. In the first place, soft law has much of the predictive value of hard law in regard to how states are expected to act. Indeed, in an international community where even hard and fast obligations are not always observed, there is at best a continuum ... between the predictive value of hard and soft law. Second, soft law does not often remain "soft." Frequently it becomes the precursor of hard law, either because states in complying with it eventually create customary law or because soft law may be part of the raw material taken into account when codifying or developing norms into treaty law; indeed, soft law in the form of solemn declarations is used often by the UN General Assembly as a stepping stone to treaty law.[65]

Language from several opinions by the International Court of Justice (ICJ) lends credence to the claim that at least *some* General Assembly resolutions may be binding. In the "Certain Expenses" case, involving the obligation of member nations to contribute to UN expenses, the Court commented that "Article 18 deals with the *'decisions'* of the General Assembly 'on important questions.' These 'decisions' ... have dispositive force and effect ... includ[ing] suspension of rights and privileges of membership, expulsion of Members and 'budgetary questions.'" In the *Namibia* case, dealing with South Africa's failure to comply with its trust obligations regarding the former South-West Africa, the ICJ stated that it would not be correct to assume that, because the General Assembly is in principle vested with only the power to recommend, "it is debarred from adopting ... resolutions which make determinations or have operative design." In the separate opinion of the prominent British ICJ judge, Sir Hersch Lauterpacht, in the *South-*

West Africa Voting Procedure case: "[a] Resolution recommending . . . a specific course of action creates *some* legal obligation which . . . is nevertheless a legal obligation and constitutes a measure of supervision."[66]

General Assembly resolutions, purporting to create legal norms without recourse to the treaty process, have created much confusion. One example is the 1946 "Nuremberg Principles," whereby the Assembly affirmed the Nuremberg trial process and judgments in a unanimous resolution. The same session unanimously adopted the "Genocide Convention," characterizing genocide as an international crime. Although the UN Charter does not provide the General Assembly with express authority to *declare* such matters, the Assembly has continued to do so without significant scrutiny. Columbia University's Professor Oscar Schachter questions the apparent assumption that such resolutions are entitled to legal validity. A vote for a resolution may not be intended to signify agreement on the legal validity of the asserted norm. In his words, governments do not always have that intent when they either vote for a resolution or fail to object to it. They may fairly assume that since Assembly resolutions are recommendations, "their vote should mean no more than that. They may cast their vote solely on political grounds in the belief that a resolution of the General Assembly is entirely a political matter without legal effect."[67]

Regardless of the varied positions on General Assembly resolutions as an extra-statutory source, they are a useful resource for seeking evidence of international norms—when professed by a sufficient number of countries. Examples include the unanimous affirmation of the principles contained in the Charter of the Nuremberg Tribunal punishing Nazi war criminals, and the unanimous resolution producing the ensuing Genocide Convention. These particular General Assembly resolutions expressed the opinions of *all* UN members that they would henceforth recognize global prohibitions against such State conduct.[68]

Although General Assembly resolutions are generally intended to reflect only a political view of the situation at hand, the ICJ recognizes some may provide the missing element of *opinio juris* (binding expectations recognized and practiced by State members) for resolving the pending case. The Court is then willing to rely on sources not found in the Court's Article 38 list of sources. In the 1986 *Nicaragua* case, for example, the Court considered the Declaration on Principles of International Law concerning Friendly Relations and Cooperation Among States in Accordance with the Charter of the United Nations as binding. It expressed the *opinio juris* of all UN members—although it was not the product of any debate. In this limited sense, then, the General Assembly's Declaration on Principles of International Law was effectively characterized as a source of International Law.[69]

Security Council Security Council resolutions are not normative or rule-making. They are reactions to violations of existing International Law principles. They typically address an aggressive use of force in violation of the UN Charter. The Council deals with such breaches on a case-by-case basis. (*See* §3.3 regarding the Council's authority.)

◆ 1.5 PRIVATE INTERNATIONAL LAW

While the line between "public" and "private" International Law may be blurred, there is a convenient functional distinction. *Public* International Law refers to the practices of States that they consider binding in their mutual relations. *Private* International Law refers to one of two legal regimes: (1) resolution mechanisms used by a State for disputes involving non-State entities, such as individuals or corporations; and/or (2) treaties that apply to the private conduct of individuals or entities in different legal systems.

Why is there a system of "Private" International Law—referred to in many countries as "conflict of laws?" As succinctly stated by Oxford University's P. M. North:

> The *raison d'être* of private international law is the existence in the world of a number of separate municipal systems of law—a number of separate legal units—that differ greatly from each other in the rules by which they regulate the various legal relations arising in daily life. The occasions are frequent when the courts in one country must take account of some rule of law that exists in another. A sovereign is supreme within his [its] own territory and, according to the universal maxim of jurisprudence, he [it] has exclusive jurisdiction over everybody and everything within that territory and over

every transaction that is there effected. He can, if he chooses, refuse to consider any law but his [its] own. The adoption, however, of this policy of indifference, though common enough in other ages, is impracticable in the modern civilised world, and nations have long found that they cannot, by sheltering behind the principle of territorial sovereignty, afford to disregard foreign rules of law merely because they happen to be at variance with their own territorial or internal system of law.[70]

HISTORICAL DERIVATION

The evolution of these two categories of International Law was closely enmeshed. Since the seventeenth century, the term *jus gentium,* or law of nations, has been used to refer to the public sector of International Law. The Romans used the same Latin phrase, however, to describe the body of law governing disputes between Roman citizens and foreigners. It was then used to describe what we would now call Private International Law. French and Italian scholars of the twelfth century developed principles, now referred to as "conflict of laws" principles, for resolving private transnational disputes.[71]

The public–private gap has narrowed over time, particularly since the end of World War II. Today, much of Public International Law applies to individuals and corporations—as illustrated in Chapters 3 and 4 of this book. And much of Private International Law applies to public entities such as State corporations engaged in international trade—as addressed in various chapters, including Chapter 13 on International Economic Relations.

A number of model international treaties have been drafted for disputes involving individuals from nations with different laws on the same subject. Some examples are the 1971 Hague Convention on the Law Applicable to Road Traffic Accidents, the 1973 Hague Convention on the Law Applicable to Product Liability, the 1980 UN Convention on Contracts for the International Sale of Goods (CISG), the 1988 Hague Convention on the Law Applicable to Succession to the Estates of Deceased Persons, and the 1988 UN Convention on International Bills of Exchange and International Promissory Notes. Two concrete examples follow, which will show the nature of the problems faced by individuals or corporations operating in an international context—where they are subject to different results depending on where they are sued.

Illustration 1: In July 1998, France's Cour de Cassation (a top-level court of review) resolved a dispute arising under Private International Law. French citizens sued a New York corporation in Paris, claiming that the gift of a museum in Venice, Italy, should be totally or partially revoked—because of the alleged failure of the museum's administration to carry out the conditions accompanying the donation. Because the defendant Guggenheim Foundation was registered with the tribunal in Venice, it responded in the French courts that this case could be heard in Italy, but not France. The New York Foundation thereby asserted that the French courts lacked jurisdiction over it, because it had effectively acquired a secondary Italian domicile for purposes of this litigation. *See* Introductory Note, "France: Court of Cassation Decision in *Foundation Solomon R. Guggenheim v. Helion & Rumney,*" 37 *Int'l Legal Mat'ls* 653 (1998).

Illustration 2: How do such treaties impact the private sphere, as opposed to the public sphere involving legal relations directly between States? An oral contract between private corporations, for example, may be legally enforceable under the law of Nation X but not the law of Nation Y. Under X law, an oral contract over $500 may be used to prove the existence of that contract, although it is based on an *oral* agreement. Under the law of Y, no contract for an amount over $500 can be enforced, unless it is made in *writing.* Assume that both nations have ratified the above UN Sale of Goods treaty—to facilitate international contracts between the exporters and importers of both nations, as well as to encourage dispute resolution. Article 11 of the CISG Convention provides that a "contract of sale need not be concluded in or evidenced by writing. . . . It may be proved by any means, including witnesses." The oral contract *is* enforceable by the testimony of witnesses, in the courts of both X *and* Y to prove the existence of, and to enforce, the contract. The CISG treaty commitments by nations X and Y therefore provide a predictable result for the enforceability of contracts by private traders in both nations. The result no longer depends on the particular nation wherein the plaintiff chooses to sue or arbitrate to enforce the oral contract.

France's Cour de Cassation summarized the dilemma often faced by courts in different countries when the litigation touches and concerns more than one country—with the potential for different results, depending upon which national court is the forum. Under the French Civil Code, jurisdiction in such cases is authorized when the plaintiff or defendant is a French citizen. Under the Dutch Code of Civil Procedure, there is jurisdiction if the plaintiff is a Dutch citizen. The German Code provides that the presence of a defendant's assets in the forum gives the courts jurisdiction, while the British courts can hear such a case if the defendant is served with process within the forum. The French court then analyzed two applicable treaties created to avoid such dilemmas; however, the defendant Foundation did not fit within their terms because the US was not a party to them. Thus, the New York defendant would have had to litigate the case involving the Italian museum in Paris, having been sued by French plaintiffs.

FEMINIST PERSPECTIVE

A *State* actor incurs international liability for gender discrimination only in the rare instance where the perpetrator's objectives include official crimes against women as such. An arguable example of State responsibility in the context of discrimination against women would be the Bosnian Serb tactic of encouraging the rape of Muslim (and other) women as a method for driving Muslims out of a particular area of Bosnia. If one were to assume that the self-styled head of state of the Bosnian Serbs were in fact the political leader of a de facto State *(within* Bosnia), then this tactic was a useful military strategy for facilitating "ethnic cleansing" to gain more territory in Bosnia-Herzegovina. The Bosnian Serbs have allegedly engaged in this heinous tactic, knowing that these women would not likely verify the fact of such atrocities because of their religious and cultural convictions.

The "public-private" International Law dichotomy has been characterized by certain legal theorists as perpetuating a disengagement of the State from certain historical, economic, and political realities. While the "State" is the primary actor in International Law, human rights law is designed to guarantee freedom and equality of the individual on the *international* level—in the same manner that liberal theory is designed to guarantee the rights of liberty and equality of the individual on the *national* level. Neither of these legal paradigms sufficiently distinguishes between individuals based on gender, nor do they fully accommodate the needs of women as a group. This inattention is perpetuated by traditional International Law theory. It supposedly protects the rights of the "individual," without accommodating the need to incorporate the disparate treatment of women into the dialogue. As asserted by the University of Sydney's Shelley Wright in a 1993 study by the American Society of International Law, "international law depends on an ambiguous definition of the state which includes [the elements of] territory, population, and government. The indeterminate nature of this definition means that women's unequal participation in the habitation, ownership, and use of territory and other material sources; women's primary role in the reproduction of population; and their absence from government is left unrecognized in international law. This [indifference] in turn ensures that male control of these processes at a national and global level remains undisturbed by international regulation."[72]

The 1979 Convention on the Elimination of All Forms of Discrimination Against Women—a product of the UN Decade of the Woman in the 1980s—entered into force in 1981. It specifically notes that, despite earlier instruments such as the UN Charter and the Universal Declaration of Human Rights (discussed in Chapter 11), "extensive discrimination against women continues to exist. Recalling that discrimination against women violates the principles of equality of rights and respect for human dignity, [it] is an obstacle to the participation of women, on equal terms with men, in the political, social, economic and cultural life of their countries [which] hampers the growth and prosperity of society and the family and makes more difficult the full development of the potentialities of women in the service of their countries and humanity." In 1988, the UN General Assembly called upon all States to ratify this treaty.[73] Nevertheless, ratifying nations have not necessarily incorporated the spirit of this treaty into their internal social discourse. The following excerpt presents a paradigm for pragmatically incorporating feminist perspectives into International Law discourse:

"Accountability in International Law for Violations of Women's Rights by Non-State Actors"

REBECCA J. COOK

Receiving Reality: Women and International Law, pp. 93–106 (Washington, D.C.: American Society of International Law, 1993)

Introduction

It can be shown that many states fail to discharge obligations under customary international law to protect women's human rights, and that they fail to protect such rights to which they have expressly committed themselves through voluntary membership of international human rights conventions, including the Convention of the Elimination of All Forms of Discrimination Against Women. Failures can be directly attributed to the executive, judicial and legislative organs of states. It may therefore be asked what is added to states' obligations by attempting to demonstrate and enforce their accountability in international law for violations of women's rights by *non*-state actors, including private persons. . . .

Women's human rights warrant defense when their violation originates in *state* action and also in *private* action. It is not a reason to disregard privately originating violations because violations also occur in the public sector of national life, or because they remain unremedied when they are directly attributable to organs of the state, or because they are more difficult to tackle when they arise through non-state actors. It will advance women's rights to address violations that occur both through direct state action and through state responsibility for the conduct of non-state actors. The pursuit of remedies for violations of rights originating through organs of state and through the conduct of non-state actors can be undertaken in tandem, and if such pursuit is frustrated in one area it nevertheless may be advanced in the other. The identification of violations of women's rights both by organs of state *and* by conduct of *non-state* actors for which the state can be shown accountable are complementary goals, and not alternatives to or in competition with each other. . . .

Customary international law and treaty law provide a number of approaches to engaging the responsibility of states. These approaches are addressed to consider how they might be applied to some of the more pervasive causes of violations of women's human rights by non-state actors.

Background Law

The law of state responsibility has evolved over the centuries as a principal area of concern within public international law, and has become subject to official codification under the League of Nations and the United Nations. The modern phase of codification, endorsed by the U.N. General Assembly in 1963, has produced the International Law Commission's Draft Articles on State Responsibility, Part I of which was adopted by the Commission between 1973 and 1980.

Article 11 (1) of the ILC Draft contains the classical proposition that the conduct of a person or a group of persons not acting on behalf of the state shall not be considered as an act of the state under international law. Detailed provisions govern when states may delegate powers to private persons, and when private persons may become empowered to act on behalf of a state, but the Article reflects the general propositions that private persons are not subjects of international law and that "[t]he acts of private persons or of persons acting . . . in a private capacity are in no circumstances attributable to the State."

It does not follow, however, that a state cannot incur international responsibility of its own because of the acts of private persons. When a state owes an obligation, for instance to protect a foreign diplomat or visitor, an act of a private citizen that harms such a protected person engages the responsibility of the state. It must provide adequate protection against repetition, police inquiries to identify and prosecute a criminal suspect, and access to due process in its justice system to compensate the victim.

State responsibility for failure to take proper measures to protect nationals of other countries, and to offer means of redress for their grievances, has been extended by international human rights law to require states to protect and provide justice for their own nationals. Where nationals are injured by acts of private persons, the state will have no greater accountability than under international customary law regarding the protection of nationals of other countries, unless the state has accepted a treaty obligation to assure that injury to its own national will not occur, or to afford a national victim justice through its own institutions and reasonable safeguards against the predictable repetition of private persons' injurious misconduct. . . .

State Responsibility for Non-State Actors Under Treaty Law

The evolution of post-1945 international human rights law has been to amplify and reinforce the legal protection that individuals enjoy against state power exercised by governments of their own nations. Accordingly, human rights treaties bind states in their treatment particularly of their own nationals. States are not obliged in principle to ensure compliance with treaty provisions in private law relations conducted between individuals or among non-state actors. In specific regards, states parties to treaties may commit themselves to a higher level of obligation, but the thrust of international human rights treaties is to hold states accountable only for violations of individual rights committed by state actors.

I. The Scope of State Responsibility

While it is obvious that states parties are responsible for their interference with human rights protected by treaties, a critical question concerns responsibility for failure of state action against private conduct that so denies individual rights protected by treaties as to impoverish a victim's enjoyment of life and citizenship. A state may be responsible for its failure to make its legal protection available to individuals against private action. Criminal law provides for the punishment and deterrence of private persons whose actions against victims endanger the well-being of the community. Civil courts enable individuals to employ the authority of the state to achieve justice for themselves in private relations. If the state refuses or fails to employ the state's protective power of individuals through its police and criminal justice system, or denies individuals reasonable access to self-protection through resort to the civil courts, the state may be considered in breach of its treaty obligation to protect human rights.

State responsibility for failure of its criminal law system was recognized by the European Court of Human Rights in *X and Y v. The Netherlands,* where the state had not enacted adequate criminal legislation to vindicate the rights of a mentally handicapped rape victim, and to deter such future assaults as required by the European Convention on Human Rights. Responsibility for failure to make civil justice accessible to individuals pursuing similarly protected rights was recognized by the Court in *Airey v. Ireland,* where the state offered no legal assistance to an applicant to a civil court whose processes were too complex for a lay person to undertake without legal aid. State responsibility is not for the conduct of private individuals that created the need for resort to the courts, but of the state's denial of justice to victims of crime and potential civil litigants when treaty rights have been violated. . . .

V. The Guarantee of the Elimination of All Forms of Discrimination Against Women

. . . By becoming states parties to the Women's Convention, states agree to "condemn discrimination in all its forms." The Preamble to the Women's Convention notes that the UN Charter, the Universal Declaration of Human Rights, the Women's Declaration, the two international human rights Covenants and UN and specialized agencies' resolutions, declarations and recommendations promote equality of rights of men and women. However, the drafters expressed concern in the Preamble "that despite these various instruments extensive discrimination against women continues to exist." The Preamble concludes with an expression of determination "to adopt the measures required for the elimination of such discrimination in all its forms and manifestation.". . .

The importance of eliminating all forms of discrimination against women is underscored by Recommendation 19 on Violence against Women of the Committee on the Elimination of Discrimination Against Women (CEDAW), established to monitor states parties' compliance with the Women's Convention, the draft UN Declaration on the Elimination of Violence against Women and the draft Inter-American Convention on Violence against Women. . . .

VI. Specific Guarantees

The Women's Convention commences with the agreement of states parties "to pursue by all appropriate means and without delay" a policy of eliminating discrimination against women, and to observe specific undertakings. Included are the significant commitments: "To take all appropriate measures to eliminate discrimination against women by any person, organization or enterprise" and "To take all appropriate measures, including legislation, to modify or abolish existing laws, regulations, customs and practices which constitute discrimination against women." The Convention follows with a number of specific duties by which states accept obligations, a number of which are "to ensure" outcomes such as the full development and advancement of women in such fields as politics, economics and culture, retention of nationality despite marriage, equal rights to education, and employment equity.

◆ *Notes & Questions*

1. Exhibit 1.1 (page 34) lists scenarios in which there may or may not be *State* responsibility for a violation of various treaties regarding women's rights, including those mentioned in this section of the book. Which of the circumstances listed in the exhibit—all occurring in the 1990s—would be likely to spawn State responsibility for a treaty violation under *International Law,* as opposed to criminal liability of an individual perpetrator under the *internal* law of the nation where the incident happened? Would there be State responsibility if a national government did not espouse the following as official policy, yet acquiesced in such actions by doing nothing to prevent them?

2. In §2.4 of this text, you will study State recognition of other States and governments. Afghanistan's fundamentalist Taliban government could be accused of conducting gender apartheid (*see* Exhibit 1.1 for the essentials). In summer 1998, religious police forces began to enforce the laws requiring destruction of televisions and other "harmful" influences on society. Assuming Afghanistan would incur State responsibility for violating the human rights of its female population, one might question what the international community could do to effectuate a change from external pressure.

   There are some options: (1) Withholding or withdrawing recognition (neither of which would affect Afghanistan's status as a State)—US President George Bush withheld recognition of six former Soviet republics until it was clear that they would adopt democratic principles of governing their peoples; Russia's President Boris Yeltsin called upon the three States that first recognized the Taliban government to withdraw their recognition. (2) The former Yugoslavia (Serbia and Montenegro, less several other provinces, now independent States) was relegated to an unclear status at the UN—not authorized to occupy the seat for "Yugoslavia," but not being expelled from the UN as a sanction for aggression in Bosnia, and other activities described in later chapters. (In April 1998, the UN Security Council imposed an arms embargo on "Yugoslavia," because of its violence against ethnic Albanians in the Kosovo region, near Yugoslavia's border with Albania.) The UN closed its offices in Afghanistan, and could do the same as done with the former Yugoslavia; or alternatively, vote to officially *expel* Afghanistan from the UN. (3) NATO or the UN could threaten or use economic or military measures against the Taliban government.

   Which, if any, of these options would be a viable strategy for exerting international pressure on Afghanistan to reverse its gender apartheid policies?

3. A number of commentators have expressed concern about the role of Islam, regarding the rights of women who have been subjected to centuries of disparate treatment based on their gender. In December 1997, the eighth annual Islamic Summit Conference in Iran proclaimed the following objective intended to respond to these negative perspectives: "20. *Emphasize* their full respect for the dignity and rights of Muslim women and enhancement of their role in all aspect[s] of social life in accordance with Islamic principles, and *call on* the [Islamic] General Secretariat to encourage and coordinate participation of women in the relevant activities of the OIC [Organisation of the Islamic Conference]." "Islamic Summit Conference: Tehran Declration," 37 *Int'l Legal Mat'ls* 938 (1997).

EXHIBIT 1.1 STATE RESPONSIBILITY VERSUS INDIVIDUAL PERPETRATOR'S RESPONSIBILITY

State	Event	"Treaty" Violation? (Notes)
Afghanistan	Taliban Islamic government forces women to quit jobs and not appear in public without burqa (covering almost entire body), travel with an unrelated male, or attend school. Only one-third of the female refugees are in camps—those on the outside are being subjected to harassment, because they are without their (deceased) husbands or any other proper male.	(only example of an *official* State policy)
India	Dowry killing of bride for inadequate dowry	
Israel	"Honor" killing of Druse women (ten *known* incidents since 1991) by male relative for leaving home twenty-two years earlier without parental permission.	
Pakistan	Only parents can determine who woman can marry (not currently limited to just Pakistan).	
Somalia	Female genital mutilation of young girls (100% in Somalia and practiced in thirty other countries—*see* Problem 11.C)	
Thailand	Forced prostitution of young girls	
US	Nationwide domestic violence against women in homes	

Is the above phrase—"in accordance with Islamic principles"—mere surplusage, or was it inserted as an institutional limitation on the rights of Islamic women in Muslim countries?

There is another important treaty that purports to protect women, without placing the requisite degree of responsibility on the responsible actor. This is the UN Declaration on the Elimination of Violence Against Women.[74] The treaty governs the conduct of ratifying States. However, it is *non-State* actors who typically batter or harass women. The responsible individuals normally incur no liability under International Law. Their liability is limited to national law, to the degree it protects women from abuse. It is "domestic" law, rather than International Law, that governs the liability of such non-State actors. A State would be responsible only if it had an express policy or implicit practice condoning violence against women. The extent to which international society must play some greater role is not yet perceived by traditional theorists as falling within the province of Public International Law.

The UNICEF (UN's International Children's Emergency Fund) 1997 Progress of Nations Report announced that violence against women is the world's most pervasive form of human rights abuse. As stated by its Executive Director, "[i]n today's world, to be born female is to be born high risk."

◆ 1.6 RELATED DISCIPLINES

This section of the text briefly summarizes other disciplines that have influenced the development of International Law. They are typically overlooked in legal studies. Each is a lens through which members of the diverse spectrum of nations view the precise nature of the generally worded norms that bind the community of nations.

INTERNATIONAL RELATIONS

The disciplines of International Law and International Relations share the common feature of examining how States behave. There are distinctions. One is that professors of International Relations do not have to defend the tangibility of their academic endeavor. Given the obvious fact that nations engage in mutual relations, the study of International *Relations* assesses the variables affecting good and bad relations. Those who profess International *Law* theory, on the other hand, must begin with a preliminary defense of its comparatively elusive existence. The need for this justification is dictated by differences between national and international enforcement mechanisms—discussed further in §1.7 on the national law versus International Law relationship, and §1.8 on whether International Law is really law.

Skeptics often invoke the mistaken assumption that States act only in their own best interests—without any earnest regard for the external legal controls imposed by International Law. They rely on the excesses of certain national members of the League of Nations, and the United Nations, as prominent examples of an ineffective legal system. This criticism is premised on the lack of effective executive, legislative, and judicial branches of government when compared to most national legal systems. Yet most nations nevertheless follow the rules of International Law. As illustrated by Columbia University's Professor Louis Henkin, the realist or pragmatic critics do not seem to recognize that *"almost all nations observe almost all principles of international law and almost all of their obligations almost all of the time."*[75]

Having previously defined International Law and its sources, this section of your coursebook now examines the parallel discipline of International Relations. The first step is to trace the development of the contemporary field of International Relations. It is routinely taught as one or more courses in the political science departments of many universities—and in the history or philosophy departments at others. An increasing number of universities offer a graduate degree in this field. Representative components of an International Relations course or major include International Relations Theory, American or English Comparative Foreign Policy Analysis, Arms Control (or Disarmament), International Law (or a related title), Comparative Politics, Regional Studies, International Development, and Peace Studies (or Conflict Resolution).

International Relations, as a distinct field of study, emerged early in the twentieth century. Post–World War I teachers, scholars, and diplomats recognized the need for the study of International Relations, premised on the platitude that history should not repeat itself. This field soon underwent a great transformation because of the harsh reality of the events leading to World War II. Political science "realists" perceived International Law as only a peripheral variable in the actual State practice of international relations. While both disciplines analyzed State behavior, law was characterized as being too abstract and inflexible to adjust to the political reality of international relations as actually practiced "in the trenches." As summarized by Professor Anne-Marie Burley of the University of Chicago (and now Harvard)

> the discipline of international relations was born after World War I in a haze of aspirations for the future of world government. These were quickly dimmed by World War II. The fledgling discipline was thus weaned on Political Realism . . . [by] seasoned observers of the interwar period [who] reacted against Wilsonian liberal internationalism, which presumed that the combination of democracy and international organization [the League of Nations] could vanquish war and power politics. They believed instead in the polarity of law and power . . . [because] states in the international realm were champions only of their own national interest. . . . The only relevant laws were the "laws of politics," and politics was a "struggle for power."[76]

Commencing in the late 1970s, International Relations theory shifted. Its analysts then began to acknowledge the contributions made by International Law and international organizations. These institutions were both perceived as encouraging positive State behavior in collaborative ways. International legal norms were recognized as actually assisting governments in their pursuit of desirable interests—not as divisions of a doctrinal paradigm referred to when convenient for governmental purposes.[77]

Events in the former Yugoslavia in the 1990s also exposed the previously suppressed ethnic dimension of international relations. The end of the Cold War did not end international rivalry. The demise of the Soviet Union unmasked repressed ethnic conflicts—never resolved under the Soviet Union's dominance over the international affairs of certain regions of the world.

The respective anti-Soviet and anti-American dimensions of First World and Second World global relations masked other hostilities that eventually surfaced with a vengeance in the form of "ethnic cleansing" (the 1990s euphemism for genocide). Many "Third World" regimes had been neither democratic nor communistic. The negative features of nationalism, based on ethnicity, "surfaced" with unexpected fury in nations like the now unified Germany and post–Cold War Yugoslavia. International communism may now be viewed in International Relations theory as an artificial interlude in the complex geopolitics that froze the normal growth of nationalist aspirations during the Cold War era. Editor of the *Journal of Political Science,* Clemson University Professor Martin Slann, succinctly articulated that

> Soviet disintegration . . . is not only a question of fifteen or possibly more republics [including five *additional* nations subsequently spawned by the breakup of Yugoslavia] establishing themselves as sovereign or of some of them combining in some sort of federated system [such as the Community of Independent States]; within many of the republics themselves there are ethnic and religious minorities who see no reason why they should be prevented from pursuing their own national destinies. Some of them will almost certainly do so. And many of them [have] do[ne] so at the expense of their neighbors.[78]

A number of the resulting human rights abuses are addressed in Chapter 11 of this book. Ethnic conflict was effectively "placed on the back burner" until the end of the Cold War, and the ensuing breakdown in national sovereignty is addressed in Chapter 2 on States in International Law.

RELIGION

The influence of religion was briefly addressed in §1.3 on the History of International Law. Christianity was the filter used to retain those portions of Roman law imported into modern legal systems. This section of the book addresses the impact of religion on the evolution of International Law.

Historical Affiliation There has long been an affiliation between religion and International Law—spawning both positive and negative results. They have, at times, drawn guidance from one other. Each has also contributed to a mutual and progressive development over the centuries. Exhibit 1.2 illustrates the ostensible tether between these two institutions.

The Vatican City-State Vatican City is the site of the Apostolic (or Holy) See—the central government of the Roman Catholic Church. The Pope, as Head of State, exercises a unique spiritual reign over the world's Catholics. The premises of this tiny State are located near Rome, based on a 1929 treaty with Italy.

The Vatican city-state is the only religious entity that has achieved governmental recognition with a status resembling a sovereign State. It has also maintained the longest tradition of diplomatic initiatives of any sovereign. Since the time of the Emperor Constantine in the fourth century A.D., the Pope has officially received numerous foreign emissaries. The Vatican currently maintains diplomatic relations with more than 120 nations. It finally established diplomatic ties with Israel in 1993, nearly a half-century after Israel achieved statehood.

Some of the prominent developments in Vatican history include its role in encouraging the medieval crusades; dividing the Atlantic between Spain and Portugal in 1493; the 1867 US congressional withdrawal of funding for a US delegation to the "Papal States"; President Franklin Roosevelt's sending a personal representative to the Pope on the eve of the outbreak of World War II; criticism for effectively acquiescing in the Nazi takeover of Europe; President Reagan's rekindling of the Vatican–US relationship in 1984 resulting in the opening of the Vatican embassy in Washington, D.C.; and occasional US Department of State briefings for the Pope when in Washington, D.C.

The Vatican's contemporary international presence has been the mediation of international crises to facilitate the maintenance of peace and global order. In 1965, for example, the Vatican embassy negotiated a cease-fire in the Dominican Republic conflict involving the departure of US troops from the Republic. In 1990, Panama's leader, Manuel Noriega, sought refuge in Panama's Vatican embassy. The Vatican's role prompted Noriega's surrender to troops who had surrounded the embassy shortly after the US invasion of Panama. The Holy See (Vatican) achieved worldwide attention in 1994, during the UN Conference on Population in Cairo, Egypt. The Pope consolidated forces with States such as Iran and Libya to avert a multilateral approach that might include abortion as a means for limiting the world's population. In 1997, the Pope made a much heralded visit to host Fidel Castro in Cuba.

Willamette University (Oregon) Professor James Nafziger penned the following excerpt, succinctly depicting the intriguing parallels between religion and International Law:

> Religion and international law often appear to be congruent. They share elements of ritual, authority

EXHIBIT 1.2 INFLUENCE OF RELIGION ON INTERNATIONAL LAW

485 B.C.: BABYLONIA Biblical Book of Esther: "And in every province, and in every city, whithersoever the king's commandment and his decree came, . . . many of the people of the land became Jews; for fear of the Jews fell upon them." (In December 1993, the Vatican finally recognized the State of Israel—forty-four years after Israel was admitted to the UN as a member State.)

OCTOBER 27, 1553: CITY-STATE OF GENEVA Civil authorities during the Inquisition execute Spanish physician for unorthodox beliefs about immortality of Jesus. Dr. Michael Servetus characterized Jesus as "Son of Eternal God," contrary to Church's teaching that Jesus is "Eternal Son of God."

1625: PARIS, FRANCE Hugo Grotius's *Prologue* to *The Law of War and Peace* (seminal work earning him title of Father of modern International Law): "Throughout the Christian world I observed a lack of restraint in relation to war . . . and that when arms have once been taken up there is no longer any respect for law, divine or human. . . ."

1849: LONDON, ENGLAND Henry David Thoreau publishes *On the Duty of Civil Disobedience*—cornerstone of Quaker philosophy: "If a thousand men were not to pay their tax-bills this year, that would not be [as] violent and bloody [a] measure, as it would be to pay them, and enable the State to commit violence and shed innocent blood."

JANUARY 1, 1961: MOSCOW, RUSSIA Article 227 of the Criminal Code amended: "Organizing or directing a group, whose activity . . . carried on with the appearance of preaching religious beliefs and performing religious ceremonies, is related to causing harm to the health of the citizens . . . shall be punished by deprivation of freedom for . . . up to five years or by exile. . . ."

SUMMER 1986: EGYPT Fundamentalist Muslim leader Umar al Talmasani: The predominant US attitude exports both Christianity, the traditional rival of Islam, and secularism, the modern rival of Islam. US foreign policy is "motivated by several factors, but the most important . . . [is] religious fanaticism . . . a continuation of the crusader invasion of a thousand years ago."

FEBRUARY 14, 1989: TEHRAN, IRAN Government leader Ayatollah Khomeini decrees that British author Salman Rushdie must be killed because *The Satanic Verses* blasphemes Islam. On fifth anniversary of decree, Iran announces it will not rescind decree because "repentance in such a case is a matter solely concerning divine mercy in afterlife." The West's continued support for Rushdie constitutes an insult to both Islam and Iran.

JANUARY 13, 1993: BAGHDAD, IRAQ Saddam Hussein: "Another battle has started. Another holy war ordained so that we can attain another great victory for . . . the Iraqi people." President Bush tells US soldiers: "You are doing the Lord's work."

DECEMBER 8, 1993: LONDON, ENGLAND Prince Charles proclaims intent to become king, leaving Britain to ponder the prospect of a divorced king becoming head of the Church of England. (The British monarch automatically becomes the supreme governor of the Church and must pledge during the coronation ceremony to uphold the Anglican faith.)

JANUARY 13, 1994: ROME, ITALY The Pope calls for ending the war in Bosnia via humanitarian intervention, declaring that per moral teachings of the church: "All military aggression is judged to be morally wrong. Legitimate defense, by contrast, is viewed as admissible and sometimes obligatory. The history of our century has confirmed this teaching numerous times."

JUNE 17, 1994: DHAKA, BANGLADESH Two thousand Muslim fundamentalists march through the streets of Dhaka to demand the execution of author Taslima Nasreen. A local court ordered her arrest based on charges disclosing her writings, which call for changes in Islamic laws to provide equal rights to women.

APRIL, 1995: BUENOS AIRES, ARGENTINA Upon urging by the Pope to examine their consciences, Argentina's Catholic bishops begged forgiveness for complicity in crimes committed by the Church during the "Dirty War" of the 1970s, wherein some 9,000 people disappeared and are presumed dead. Church leaders maintained relations with the military leaders responsible for this massive human rights abuse.

OCTOBER, 1996: KABUL, AFGHANISTAN Taliban government's religious army (established in 1994) begins to strictly enforce its version of Islamic rule, whereunder other religions cannot be tolerated.

and universality that "connect the legal order of any given legal society with that society's beliefs in an ultimate transcendent reality." There is, too, a certain sanctity to any body of law, just as there is an authoritative and often constitutive structure in religion. Judaism is based on a Covenant. In Martin Buber's terminology of I and Thou, both religion and international law are essentially dialogue; both seek to prove orientation of knowledge and a greater realization of life. In a sense, the whole concept and practice of global order presupposes a moral and teleological viewpoint that is essentially religious. United Nations Secretary General Javier Perez de Cuellar has referred to the UN Charter as "my religion.". . . As ethical systems, both law and religion address the global order in a profound manner; both are concerned with the manner in which we accept and organize the world and universe around us. . . .

Of course, conflict between religion and international law may sometimes be more apparent than real. Political and institutional factors, rather than genuine religious differences, may best explain theocratic defiance of international law that is expressed in religious terms. . . . Experts note that much of the tension between militant religiosity in the Third World and liberal, modernizing authority manifests not so much any real doctrinal differences as political claims by religious institutions (for example, by Shiite Muslims in Iran and the Afghan Mujahedeen) for recognition, full dignity, and equality—three values that many modern political and legal systems do not readily concede to religious forces.

In view of the discrepancies between religion and international law, it may be well to conclude that they are dimensions of each other; they are not so much congruent or united as they are related in a dialectical interdependence; they "stand or fall together. . . ."[79]

Integration of law and religion can, of course, result by definition whenever religious institutions or ideas are deliberately made the subject of international prescription. Examples include the Lateran Treaty between Italy and the Vatican . . . and the recognition of the Vatican as a state. "Right to life" provisions in human rights instruments that are intended or interpreted to prohibit abortion have religious foundations. An extraordinarily inflammatory issue was the [1975] "Zionism is racism" resolution of the United Nations General Assembly. . . .

Several global instruments articulate a fundamental freedom of thought, conscience and religion . . . [including the Universal Declaration of Human Rights, the International Covenant on Civil and Political Rights] and the Declaration on the Elimination of All Forms of Intolerance and Discrimination Based on Religion or Belief. . . . These provisions highlight the topic of religion's role in the international legal system, but do not reflect the positive functions of religion [even] when it is not deliberately made the subject of international prescription. . . .

Islamic Fundamentalist Movement The collapse of the Soviet Union effectively unleashed what the Cold War seemed to repress for the four decades since World War II–vintage religious rivalries. Post-war political order was essentially maintained by the NATO–Warsaw Pact paradigm. Then came the subsequent breakdown in statehood in terms of larger States, and entities such as the Soviet Union splitting into smaller sovereign powers.

Another form of association is evolving. A number of Western commentators have replaced the former Evil Empire (US President Reagan's term for the Soviet Union) with a new demon, often characterized or mischaracterized in their writings as "religious fundamentalism." The US post–Gulf War policy of respecting Iraq's borders, for example, is perceived by a number of Muslims as effectively neglecting ethnic Kurdish and religious Shiite claims to autonomy in and around Iraq. Freezing its borders, via no-fly zones and the like, arguably maintained the old world order rather than establishing a new one. As stated in a comprehensive study of what Western writers have called the fundamentalist post–Cold War insurgence,

> [f]undamentalists are boundary-setters: they excel in marking themselves off from others by distinctive dress, customs, and conduct. But they are also, in most cases, eager to expand their borders by attracting outsiders who will honor fundamentalist norms, or by requiring that nonfundamentalists observe fundamentalist codes. The state is the final arbiter of disputes within its borders. In cases in which the state is "fundamentalist" (e.g., Iran, Sudan) or has been influenced by fundamentalist socio-political agendas (Pakistan, India, Egypt, Israel), the fundamentalism of the enclave is encouraged or even

empowered to spill over its natural boundaries and permeate the larger society.[80]

A novel feature of the contemporary "fundamentalist struggle" involves what the West would describe as terrorist reactions to modern threats to fundamentalist doctrine. In March 1994, for example, suspected Muslim fundamentalists murdered two young schoolgirls in Algiers because they were unveiled. This action marked the bloody enforcement of a February 1994 vow undertaken in the name of religion. Muslim women who do not cover their heads in public have joined a growing list of targets, including the Algerian army, police, secularist intellectuals, artists, journalists, and certain unsympathetic foreigners. In 1996, the Taliban government in Afghanistan began to enforce its perception of an ordered society, wherein women are virtually under house arrest. They cannot leave their homes unless accompanied by a related male, attend school, work, or travel without a full-body garment (burqa).

There has been a historic tendency of religious leaders to participate in cross-border power struggles since the time of the medieval crusades. A number of Muslim nations supported the Afghan Mujahedeen for fourteen years during its struggle to disengage occupying Soviet troops. The rival factions within Afghanistan are tearing it apart, however, with political power struggles conducted in the name of Islam. If this scenario remains unchecked, religious violence could far surpass that done by the Inquisition and the crusades of the Roman Catholic Church in the medieval era. The destruction of religious icons could cost Afghanistan its predominant Islamic architectural heritage. Mosques have been special targets of violence because people use them as safe havens from battles fought by rival factions of the Mujahedeen. The famous Blue Mosque in Kabul was filled with women and children when it was bombed in March 1994 by air. The traditional acquiescence in the use of mosques as sanctuaries has apparently been forsaken by rival religious groups. Even the Soviet regime never dared to break that tradition while occupying Afghanistan (for a ten-year period beginning in 1979).

CULTURAL STUDIES

Overlooking *cultural* differences sows seeds of mistrust in both private and international relations. At least two layers of cultural difference adversely affect international communication. The first is the comparatively minor irritant associated with failing to appreciate a cultural contrast in a way that tends to undermine relationships. This recurring problem often surfaces when two nations possess unequal bargaining power. The conduct of the stronger nation's representative may indicate unawareness or ignorance. Protocol missteps are thus spawned by communication gaps. For example, during President Clinton's first official dinner function in a foreign nation in July 1993, he unexpectedly invited a translator to stand between himself and South Korea's President Kim, who was seated near the lectern. This event would have no cultural significance in the US. In Korea, however, it is an insult for anyone to stand between two heads of state. Strictly observed rules of etiquette apply in Korea, even between family members in *private* dinner settings. To add insult to injury, there had been an agreement that each president would deliver post-dinner remarks in their native tongues *without* the aid of an interpreter. The invitation to the translator to stand between them spawned another cultural faux pas, although there were no perceptible consequences.

The more significant form of cultural difference surfaces when an agreement is reached but applied differently by the parties to the agreement. What often appears perfectly clear to both sides, when formulated in abstract principles, may be interpreted quite differently. Diplomacy, the subject of Chapter 7 of this book, includes a cultural dimension worth considering at this point. Intelligent diplomacy requires the representatives to take account of cultural differences because they should be seeking a lasting result that will be satisfying to all participants. It is no secret that one should attempt to negotiate from a position of strength. Yet raw power politics, although a fact of international life, does not ultimately succeed as well as attempting to accommodate the cultural values of the "other side" in international relations. As articulated by St. John's University (New York) Professor Frank Ninkovich,

> [a]lthough diplomacy functions within cultural and intercultural contexts, historians of diplomacy have traditionally slighted cultural explanations of foreign policy in favor of tried and true concepts of power and interest . . . [but] insightful statesmen have always recognized that diplomacy also requires reckoning with cultural values which, because of their crucial role in shaping perceptions, are more significant than either ideological beliefs or abstract ideals. In one

> way or another, nearly all the major US statesmen of the twentieth century took cultural factors into account as part of their approach to diplomacy; indeed, culture played a prominent and often decisive role in their decision-making.[81]

The cultural aspects of international relations have not been sufficiently considered in published studies. Anthropologists have admittedly failed to explore, in any depth, the relationship between culture and many facets of what is governed by international norms. For example, Europe has been repeatedly ravaged by the scourges of war, more so than in any other region of the world. To what extent was the European concept of "State" the product of cultural biases favoring the waging of war on a grander scale than in any previous tribal era? Is warfare a cultural universal or, alternatively, is it a less prominent feature of certain societies?[82]

Culture and the modern "law" of human rights are also at odds. There is a serious issue regarding the universality of human rights norms, particularly those expressed in documents before the global decolonization movement of the 1960s. The 1948 Universal Declaration of Human Rights contains sweeping, all-inclusive language providing "universal" guarantees that have not been recognized in all cultures. The Universal Declaration has been attacked by Muslim fundamentalists as culture-bound, however, because of its Western-derived values. Female circumcision, for example, is abhorred by Western culture as a gross violation of women's basic human rights (Chapter 11). Yet it is an accepted practice in a number of African nations. The entire Western-derived International Bill of Rights, promulgated through the auspices of the UN, has been interpreted to apply in a more limited way in these cultures. A Muslim scholar would seriously question the universality of overly broad, culturally insensitive "rights" that other nations have sought to impose through international political and legal processes.

COMPARATIVE LAW

International Law is typically analyzed in terms of universal applicability. However, mutual expectations of members of the international community cannot be isolated from their distinct legal systems. Earlier in this text, you studied the theme that general principles of law drawn from various national legal systems may be used by an international decision maker as a stopgap measure to determine what norms are considered mutually binding in international relations. There are different national legal systems from which these international norms are extracted.

What, then, is "Comparative Law?" In the leading American casebook, it is succinctly described in the following terms: "As a practical subject, Comparative Law is a study of the legal borrowings or transplants that can and should be made; Comparative Law as an academic discipline . . . is . . . an investigation into the legal transplants that have occurred: how, when, why and from which systems they have been made; the circumstances in which they have succeeded or failed; and the impact on them of their new environment."[83]

The formal study of this comparative process began in Paris in 1900, when French scholars founded the International Congress for Comparative Law. This particular field of law still occupies a rather modest place in law school curricula, however.[84]

Just as well-rounded students should consider the impact of religion and culture on International Law, they should also acknowledge the influence of Comparative Law. There are many diverse legal traditions throughout the globe. National representatives in any international context—be they diplomats at the UN and multilateral conferences, or judges and arbitrators deciding international disputes—are far more likely to reach a workable result if they recognize that each representative's home-State law provides the lens through which one will perceive the international legal process. Differing legal traditions affect international problem-solving strategies. For example, two of the more prominent legal cultures are civil law (based on French law) and common law (based on English law). The former is derived from Napoleon's Civil Code of 1804. The latter has its roots in earlier medieval judicial practice.[85]

Assume that a civil law lawyer and a common law lawyer are contemplating a private business agreement, or are negotiating on behalf of their respective governments at an international conference. Each should come to the bargaining table prepared to address the question of how disputes will be resolved, and under what terms. They must be aware of the different legal cultures potentially affecting their negotiations. If they are negotiating a business contract with a dispute resolution clause, for example, they should be aware of the following differences: There will be no jury to resolve disputes, if the civil law tradition is applied; a common law judge will not be able to ask questions of trial witnesses; if there is a question of contractual interpretation, the common law judge will be less constrained by applicable legislation than will the civil law judge. Further, there are different standards for satisfying the burden of proof at trial. One of the most difficult phases in the development of the 1994 Rules of Procedure and Evidence for the UN's Bosnian War Crimes Tribunal was determining the extent to which the respective common law or civil law traditions would be utilized.[86]

◆ 1.7 NATIONAL–INTERNATIONAL LAW NEXUS

The internal law of each nation governs the relations among individuals, corporate entities, institutions, and the government within that nation's borders. This section of the text addresses the relationship between a nation's internal law and International Law.

Scholars have traditionally used the term *municipal law* to distinguish between the internal law of a nation and International Law. But the term "municipal" is ambiguous. Under US law, for example, a number of states of the United States have "Municipal Courts." Further, that term is not very descriptive of its international context. The term *national* will therefore be used synonymously with the terms employed by various commentators—domestic, internal, local, and municipal law. The commonly used term "domestic law" is avoided because of sexist connotations associated with that term by certain feminist writers.[87]

MONIST–DUALIST DEBATE

Scholars have debated the theoretical relationship between national and International Law for many decades. This controversy is typically described in terms of the "monist" versus "dualist" controversy.

Monist Approach The monist perspective is that the Law of Nations and the law of each nation form an integrated, universal legal order. International Law is inherently woven into the legal system of every nation, while International Law is part of the fabric of all national legal systems. Nations cannot reject International Law in principle. They may have reservations about certain components. Because so many national leaders have acknowledged the existence of International Law, it may be characterized as a part of human existence that is unrestrained by national borders.

National courts routinely apply International Law when they are directed to do so by their national legislatures or constitutions. International Law therein manifests its Natural Law roots (*see* §1.3). Otherwise, there would be legal anarchy in the absence of the foundational norms of State behavior. International Law is thus an integral part of all local legal systems.

The position of the UN's International Court of Justice is unmistakably clear—national law can never prevail in the event of a conflict with International Law. As stated by the Court in the 1988 case in which the US attempted to close the PLO Mission at the UN under antiterrorist legislation, it "would be sufficient to recall the fundamental principle of international law that international law prevails over domestic law. This principle was endorsed by judicial decision[s] as long ago as the arbitral award of 14 September 1872 in the *Alabama* case between Great Britain and the United States, and has frequently been recalled since, for example in the case concerning the *Greco-Bulgarian "Communities"* in which the Permanent Court of International Justice laid it down that it is a generally accepted principle of international law that in the relations between Powers who are contracting Parties to a treaty, the provisions of municipal law cannot prevail over those of the treaty."[88]

What are some contemporary examples of circumstances where a nation has expressly incorporated some feature of International Law into its national law? In 1973, Canada merged the 1951 UN Convention Relating to the Status of Refugees definition of refugees (persecution based on "race, religion, nationality, etc.") into its national laws. Canada has since produced a rich vein of judicial literature interpreting the rights of refugees under this international definition. In 1993, a California state court overruled a State Board of Prisons policy that barred foreign-born inmates from serving indeterminate sentences in their home countries. This incarceration policy conflicted with the Strasbourg Convention on Transfers of Sentenced Prisoners. The California policy violated the US Constitution's Supremacy Clause, which bars individual states of the US from undertaking policies that violate the federal government's treaty commitments. The French Constitution provides that treaties are "laws" that must be applied within the French legal system. Article 25 of the former West German Constitution provided that the "generally accepted rules of international law are binding upon the state power [to act] and upon every citizen." International Law thereby governs because there is no conflict with internal law.

The foremost proponent of the monist approach was probably the Austrian Professor Hans Kelsen. His articulation was that national law, and International Law, have always been a part of the same legal system of universal norms. In an earlier era, these norms provided the basis for a system that came to be known as International Law. The same behavioral norms also propelled national legal orders. States, through individuals who served as their agents, were expected to behave as people behave. International Law did not need to establish its primacy in relation to national law, given the interdependent—rather than hierarchical—relationship between these integrated legal systems.[89]

Dualist Approach Dualists reject the monist perception of International Law because it articulates an unrealistic assessment of two autonomous legal systems. International Law and national law are thus perceived as being distinct legal orders. Each nation retains the sovereign power to integrate, or isolate, the norms of International Law. National and International Law are not necessarily parts of a unified whole.

Why is International Law *not* an integrated legal system, since national and International Law both include standards of behavior affecting individuals and States? The quintessential feature of State sovereignty is consent. The modern state model, created by the 1648 Peace of Westphalia, evangelized an immutable dogma: No State may be bound without giving its consent. When a nation actively decides to incorporate International Law into its national law, only then is International Law the law of that land. As discussed earlier in this chapter, decision makers typically examine international customs or treaties to ascertain whether the requisite expression of consent exists. Just as general principles of national law may be incorporated into International Law, International Law *may* be similarly integrated into a State's national law. Until this occurs, International Law is more of a common goal or standard of achievement for that State in its capacity as an independent sovereign within the global legal community.

A judge must therefore apply his or her national law, such as executive and legislative directives, even if to do so would violate International Law. As illustrated in an opinion of the English Court of Appeals, International Law has no validity except insofar as its principles are accepted and adopted by England's internal law. Its courts must therefore acknowledge the existence of the rules that other nations may accept as binding among themselves. When determining issues arising under International Law, decision makers "seek to ascertain what the relevant rule is, and having found it they will treat it as incorporated into the domestic law, so far as it is not inconsistent with rules enacted by statutes or finally declared by their tribunals."[90] In a similar instance, a US court declared that international practice is law only insofar as the legislature allows the courts to apply it. International Law bends to the will of Congress because courts can annul legislation only when it is unconstitutional under national law. Judges therefore have the duty to enforce national legislation. An "act [congressional legislation] may contravene recognized principles of international comity, but that affords no more basis for judicial disregard of it than it does for executive disregard of it."[91]

Another example of the dualist perspective involves US prosecution of individual Nazi war criminals. Special legislation in Australia, Canada, and Great Britain authorizes the trial of former Nazi suspects for their war crimes. US law does not provide for prosecuting crimes against humanity, however. The violation of International Law, via the waging of "war crimes against humanity," was a pivotal segment of the Allied post-war Nuremberg (and Tokyo) Charter. The Nuremberg principles were expressly approved by a UN General Assembly resolution. Yet this component of International Law has not been incorporated into US law. As a result, the US has been prosecuting these individuals on the basis that they lied on their passport applications regarding their whereabouts and working circumstances during World War II. This scenario provides some practical proof for the dualist view regarding the derivative nature of International Law—which can only be utilized in national courts on the bases expressly recognized by national law.

Internal Law No Defense to Breach Even in dualist legal systems, however, a nation may not assert its internal law in defense of a breach of International Law. As stated in the UN International Law Commission's 1949 Draft Declaration on the Rights and Duties of States, every nation must carry out its obligations arising from treaties and other sources of International Law in good faith. A nation "may not invoke provisions in its constitution or its [other internal] laws as an excuse for failure to perform this duty." The Permanent Court of International Justice stated in 1931 that "a State cannot adduce as against another State its own Constitution with a view to evading obligations incumbent upon it under international law or treaties in force."[92]

INTERNATIONAL LAW "APPLIED"

Who actually *applies* International Law? One may conjure the notion of fifteen robed judges ceremoniously sitting in the ICJ's Peace Palace in the Netherlands, determining the great international legal issues of the day. That Court's docket, just barely into double figures in recent years, illustrates that the bulk of judicial decision making about international legal issues is done primarily elsewhere. Diplomats, presidents, treaty drafters, and other public servants have occasion to determine the "what, how, and when" of applying International Law. But it is the judges and arbitrators of the world's national legal systems who decide International Law decisions on a day-to-day basis. This "legal" aspect of International Law is routinely determined by what the University of Rome's Professor Benedetto Conforti calls "Domestic Legal Operators":

> Only through what we could term "domestic legal operators" can we describe the binding character of international law or, better still, its ability to be implemented in a concrete and stable fashion. "Domestic legal operators" are those charged by the State community to apply and enforce law and [thus] include judges, first and foremost. In every State system we find more or less similar provisions holding that actions must comply with international law as well as [with] municipal law. This being so, compliance with international law relies not so much on enforcement mechanisms available at the international level, but rather on the resolve of domestic legal operators such as public servants and judges to use to their limits the mechanisms provided by municipal law to ensure compliance with international norms [which are] . . . lacking in judicial and coercive enforcement procedures at the international level. . . .[93]

Can a national judge ignore the command of an applicable judgment of the judges of the International Court of Justice? This issue was considered in the following national court decision:

Committee of US Citizens Living in Nicaragua v. Reagan

UNITED STATES COURT OF APPEALS DISTRICT OF COLUMBIA CIRCUIT, 1988

859 *Fed. Rptr.* 2d 929

Author's Note: *In 1984, Nicaragua obtained a judgment against the US in the International Court of Justice (ICJ), based on US activities in Nicaragua designed to overthrow the "Sandinista" government (the political party so named in honor of Augusto Sandino, who led a peasant-guerilla army against US Marines in 1927–1933). The US attempted to withdraw from this case. The judges nevertheless proceeded (after the US purportedly withdrew) because the US had previously submitted to the ICJ's jurisdiction. The Court rendered a judgment against the US because of its activities directed against the Sandinista government of Nicaragua.*

In 1988, various organizations, and certain US citizens living in Nicaragua, subsequently sued President Reagan in his capacity as the President of the US. This suit sought relief in a US court for continuing US violations of the ICJ judgment which had prohibited the US from future acts against the government of Nicaragua. The plaintiffs pleaded with the judicial branch of the federal government to issue an injunction that would bar the continued US funding of the Nicaraguan "Contras." Plaintiffs argued that the congressional funding legislation, signed by the President, ignored the prior ICJ judgment. They alleged that the "Contra" funding violated the federal Administrative Procedure Act, the US Constitution, the United Nations Charter, and Customary International Law. The case was dismissed by the federal trial judge. Plaintiffs appealed.

The Court of Appeals held that the UN Charter requirement, whereby member nations must honor ICJ judgments, does not confer rights on these private individuals attempting to force their own country to comply with the ICJ judgment. The appellate court decided that only an aggrieved nation may seek such relief—in an international forum—to force the US to comply with the previous judgment of the international court.

Court's Opinion: Appellants Have No Basis in Domestic Law for Enforcing the ICJ Judgment

1. The Status of International Law in the United States' Domestic Legal Order

Appellants argue that the United States' decision to disregard the ICJ judgment and to continue funding the Contras violates three types of international law. First, contravention of the ICJ judgment is said to violate part of a United States treaty, namely Article 94 of the UN Charter. That article provides that "[e]ach Member of the United Nations undertakes to comply with the decision of the International Court of Justice in any case to which it is a party." Second, disregard of the ICJ judgment allegedly violates principles of customary international law. One such principle holds that treaties in force shall be observed. Appellants contend that another such principle requires parties to ICJ decisions to adhere to those decisions. Third, the United States may have violated peremptory norms of international law. Such norms, often referred to as *jus cogens* (or "compelling law"), enjoy the highest status in international law and prevail over both customary international law and treaties. Appellants . . . contend that the obligation of parties to an ICJ judgment to obey that judgment is not merely a customary rule but actually a peremptory norm of international law.

For purposes of the present lawsuit, the key question is not simply whether the United States has violated any of these three legal norms but whether such violations can be remedied by an American court or whether they can only be redressed on an international level. In short, do violations of international law have domestic legal consequences? The answer largely depends on what form the "violation" takes. Here, the alleged violation is the law that Congress enacted and that the President signed, appropriating funds for the Contras. When our government's two political branches, acting together, contravene an international legal norm, does this court have any authority to remedy the violation? The answer is "no" if the type of international obligation that Congress and the President violate is either a treaty or a rule of customary international law. If, on the other hand, Congress and the President violate a peremptory norm (or *jus cogens*), the domestic legal consequences are unclear. We need not resolve this uncertainty, however, for we find that the principles appellants characterize as peremptory norms of international law are not recognized as such by the community of nations. Thus, as we explain below in greater detail, none of the claims that appellants derive from violations of international law can succeed in this court.

2. The Effect of Subsequent Statutes Upon Prior Inconsistent Treaties

Although appellants' complaint alleges that Congress's funding of the Contras violates Article 94 of the UN Charter appellants seem to concede here that such a claim is unavailing. They acknowledge, as they must, that "[o]rdinarily, treaty obligations may be overridden by subsequent inconsistent statutes." Brief for Appellants at 32. . . .

At this stage of the present case, however, the key question is not whether Congress intended to abrogate Article 94. Since appellants allege that Congress has breached Article 94, we must determine whether such a claim could ever prevail. The claim could succeed only if appellants could prove that a prior treaty—the UN Charter—preempts a subsequent statute, namely the legislation that funds the Contras. It is precisely that argument that the precedents of the Supreme Court and of this court foreclose. We therefore hold that appellants' claims based on treaty violations must fail.

Our conclusion, of course, speaks not at all to whether the United States has upheld its treaty obligations under international law. As the Supreme Court said in the *Head Money* cases, a treaty "depends for the enforcement of its provisions on the interest and honor of the governments which are parties to it. If these fail, its infraction becomes the subject of international negotiations and reclamations . . . [but] with all this the judicial courts [within a nation that is a treaty party] have nothing to do and can give no redress." 112 US at 598, 5 S.Ct. at 253. This conclusion reflects the United States' adoption of a partly "dualist"—rather than strictly "monist"—view of international and domestic law. "[D]ualists view international law as a discrete legal system [which] . . . operates wholly on an inter-nation plane." Henkin, "The Constitution and United States

Sovereignty: A Century of Chinese Exclusion and Its Progeny," 100 *Harv. L. Rev.* 853, 864 (1987). . . .

Given that dualist jurisprudence, we cannot find—as a matter of domestic law—that congressional enactments violate prior treaties [i.e., the US has not generally adopted the monist approach]. . . .

The second paragraph of Article 94 provides that, "[i]f any party to a case fails to perform the obligations incumbent upon it under a judgment rendered by the [ICJ], the other party may have recourse to the Security Council, which may, if it deems necessary, make recommendations or decide upon measures to be taken to give effect to the judgment." U.N. Charter art. 94, para. 2. Because only nations can be parties before the ICJ, appellants are not "parties" within the meaning of this paragraph. Clearly, this clause does not contemplate that individuals having no relationship to the ICJ case should enjoy a private right to enforce the ICJ's decision. Our interpretation of Article 94 is buttressed by a related provision in the Statute of the ICJ, which is incorporated by reference in the U.N. Charter. See U.N. Charter art. 92. The Statute provides that "[t]he decision of the Court has no binding force except between the parties and in respect of th[e] particular case." Statute of the International Court of Justice, June 26, 1945, art. 59 (hereinafter "ICJ Statute"). Taken together, these Charter clauses make clear that the purpose of establishing the ICJ was to resolve disputes between national governments. We find in these clauses no intent to vest citizens who reside in a U.N. member nation with authority to enforce an ICJ decision against their own government. The words of Article 94 "do not by their terms confer rights upon individual citizens; they call upon governments to take certain action." *Diggs v. Richardson,* 555 F.2d at 851. We conclude that appellants' attempt to enjoin funding of the Contras based on a violation of Article 94 would fail even if Congress' abrogation of treaties were cognizable in domestic courts.

3. Customary International Law and Subsequent Inconsistent Statutes

. . . The question is whether such a violation is cognizable by domestic courts. Once again, the United States' rejection of a purely "monist" view of the international and domestic legal orders shapes our analysis. Statutes inconsistent with principles of customary international law may well lead to international law violations. But within the domestic legal realm, that inconsistent statute simply modifies or supersedes customary international law to the extent of the inconsistency. . . .

As with their refusal to take notice of statutory abrogation of treaties, the courts' disregard of statutory breaches of customary international law is not necessarily required by the Constitution. In Professor Henkin's view, "[t]he framers of the Constitution respected the law of nations, and it is plausible that they expected the political branches as well as the courts to give effect to that law. Other countries [applying the monist approach] . . . give effect to international law over domestic legislation." Henkin, "United States Sovereignty," 100 *Harv. L. Rev.* at 877 (footnotes omitted) (citing constitutions of West Germany, Italy, and Greece). Nonetheless, the law in this court remains clear: no enactment of Congress can be challenged on the ground that it violates customary international law. Those of appellants' claims that are predicated on this theory of illegality cannot succeed.

4. Peremptory Norms of International Law (*Jus Cogens*)

Appellants argue that the rule requiring parties who have submitted to an international court to abide by its judgment is not only a principle of customary international law but has become a form of *jus cogens.* Because such peremptory norms are nonderogable and enjoy the highest status within international law, appellants conclude that these norms are absolutely binding upon our government as a matter of domestic law as well. . . .

We need not decide whether an ICJ judgment would restrict Congress's foreign affairs power if that judgment were in fact a peremptory norm of international law. ICJ judgments simply do not meet the Vienna Convention's—or any other authority's—definition of *jus cogens.* . . .

Our conclusion is strengthened when we consider those few norms that arguably do meet the stringent criteria for *jus cogens.* The recently revised Restatement [of Foreign Relations Law of the US] acknowledges two categories of such norms: "the principles of the United Nations Charter prohibiting the use of force," and fundamental human rights law that prohibits genocide, slavery, murder, torture, prolonged arbitrary detention, and racial discrimination. But see Restatement §331, comment e (doctrine of *jus cogens* is of such "uncertain scope" that a "domestic court should not on its own authority refuse to give effect to an agreement on the ground that it violates a peremptory norm"). . . .

We think it clear, however, that the harm that results when a government disregards or contravenes an ICJ judgment does not generate the level of universal disapprobation aroused by torture, slavery, summary execution, or genocide. . . . In sum, appellants' attempt to enjoin funding of the Contras on the ground that it violates a peremptory norm of international law by contravening an ICJ judgment is unavailing. The ICJ judgment does not represent such a peremptory norm.

◆ *Notes & Questions*

1. The materials in other chapters in this book, especially Chapter 8 on treaties, will demonstrate that the UN Charter is not "self-executing." It does not create immediately binding obligations for UN member States. The Charter is, instead, a standard of achievement—a goal toward which nations are expected to aspire. If the *US Citizens* court had recognized this status, the court would likely have relied on it to avoid an extensive discussion of Charter Article 94 (regarding compliance with ICJ decisions). Yet the court accurately raises the issue, without deciding it, that such noncompliance might one day be characterizable as *jus cogens*. Would a US court's recognition of a member State's obligation to comply with ICJ judgments indicate adoption of the monist or dualist view of International Law?
2. The UN Convention for the Suppression of Terrorist Bombings requires each State to "adopt such measures as may be necessary, including domestic legislation, to ensure that criminal acts within the scope of this Convention . . . are punished by penalties consistent with their grave nature." Art. 5, reprinted in 37 *Int'l Legal Mat'ls* 249 (1998). Assume that State X adopts such legislation, pursuant to its ratification of this treaty. Does State X adhere to the monist or dualist model?
3. International Law is also applied by legislatures when they incorporate its principles into national law. In 1992, for example, while a Canadian criminal proceeding resulted in dismissal of the case, its judges were interpreting a criminal statute making war crimes and crimes against humanity occurring elsewhere a violation of Canadian law. The defendant had allegedly committed those crimes in Hungary in 1944. Section 7(3.71) of the Canadian criminal statute illustrates this incorporation of International Law into local law: "Every person who . . . commits an act or omission outside Canada that constitutes a war crime or a crime against humanity and that, if committed in Canada, would constitute an offense against the laws of Canada . . . shall be deemed to commit that act or omission in Canada at that time if . . . Canada could, in conformity with international law, exercise jurisdiction over the person. . . ." *See* "*Regina v. Finta,*" 104 *Int'l Law Rep.* 520, 526 (Ontario Ct. App., 1992).

◆ 1.8 IS INTERNATIONAL LAW REALLY LAW?

The following conversation has likely occurred on a number of occasions after the news of a serious breach of International Law saturates front-page headlines. The following words may have been uttered during either of the twentieth century's World Wars; after the facts of the Holocaust were exposed to world view; while Iran was holding American and Canadian diplomats hostage for 444 days; or when Saddam Hussein's forces torched more than 600 oil wells upon Iraq's flight from Kuwait:

> Of course, International Law isn't really law. Those who purport to be international lawyers, and the ivory-tower professors who teach and write on the subject, have a vested interest in trying to convince their clients and students that International Law is something more than a myopic fantasy. The evidence is all around us: if International Law were *really* law, Hitler, Khomeini, and Hussein would have been stopped in their tracks! International Law, if it is "law" at all, is quite primitive—because it lacks the essential powers of enforcement. Like God, one may

refer to International Law with great reverence while harboring doubts about its very existence!

A 1990 editorial appearing in a national magazine echoed these sentiments by describing the term *International Law* as self-canceling. In a prominent reporter's words, the term *International Law* "is virtually an oxymoron. Law without a sword is mere words: lacking an enforcement mechanism . . . [it is] merely admonition or aspiration . . . [and to be effective it] must be backed by coercion legitimized by a political process. The 'international community' has no such process."[94]

The superficial appeal of such arguments must be dissected before one can seriously proceed to study the field of International Law. There would be little sense in taking this course, or specializing in International Law or a related discipline, if the tangibility of this branch of law could not be authoritatively illustrated—and its reality ably defended.

International Law *is* primitive when compared to national legal systems. It lacks the same legislative, executive, and judicial enforcement mechanisms. Under the terms of the UN Charter itself, the General Assembly makes *recommendations,* not laws. The customary practice of States, and norm-creating treaties, are the essential lawmakers in the international legal system (*see* §1.4 on Sources of International Law). As will be seen later in this text, the UN Secretary-General does not have the power to intervene in any conflict beyond that which is expressly provided by the disputing parties or the veto-ridden Security Council. Thus, he or she cannot launch a military strike, has no standing forces, and can only refer matters affecting international peace to the Security Council. Finally, international dispute resolution mechanisms cannot be thrust upon any State without its consent. Unlike domestic lawbreakers, States are co-equal sovereigns who cannot be forced to appear in a courtroom to defend a claimed breach of International Law. As Chapter 9 will illustrate, the International Court of Justice cannot exercise jurisdiction in a case, absent a defendant State's express consent to the proceedings.

Critics of the international legal system therefore claim that International Law is not "law." This salvo is premised on the assumption that anything less than full and immediate enforcement power renders a legal system inherently impotent. "Realists" chastise the international legal system as being crude, in relation to the available enforcement powers in *national* legal systems. Their perspective does not adequately embrace a critical distinction, however. National law governs the relationship between the State and the individual—as opposed to International Law, which governs relations between States. The limitations of the international legal system, imposed by State sovereignty, render it comparatively "weak" in the judgment of these critics.

The response to this critique is that these systemic limitations were instituted by the State members of the international legal community—the governors, *and* the governed, in a system *designed* to temper the efficacy of enforcement measures with respect for national sovereignty. As articulated by one of the most prominent US Supreme Court chief justices, effectively drawing from the Westphalian model of the modern nation-State: "The jurisdiction of the nation within its own territory is necessarily exclusive and absolute. It is susceptible of no limitation not imposed by itself. Any restriction upon it, deriving vitality from an *external* source, would imply a diminution in sovereignty. . . ."[95]

Some analysts nevertheless perceive this state of affairs as rendering International Law either nonexistent, ineffectual, or both. One should distinguish between law and its enforcement mechanisms, however. While six months elapsed after Iraq's invasion of Kuwait, a thirty-four-nation coalition pitted Arab against Arab when Iraq violated the territorial sovereignty of Kuwait. Prior to the Iranian hostage crisis of 1979–1980, for example, States had observed the institution of diplomatic immunity for two millennia. It made little sense, even for nations at war, to "shoot the messenger." Iran admittedly ignored UN Security Council resolutions and a judgment of the ICJ, each calling for the release of the hostages. Yet it would be a mistake to say that, lacking an efficient enforcement mechanism in that instance, International Law does not exist. Iran was totally isolated in terms of the international response to its egregious breach of diplomatic immunity. No nation adversely reacted when the US froze billions of dollars of Iranian assets in the US as a means of pressuring Iran to comply with International Law. In the previous generation, a number of Hitler's henchmen paid with their lives for their roles in waging Germany's aggressive war—as a result of the work of the Allied Nuremberg War Crimes Tribunal.

The following scenario presents some refreshing perspectives on why International Law *is* "law," notwithstanding the intrinsic problems of enforcement and the actions of a few national leaders who believe that "might makes right."

OF TRAFFIC LIGHTS AND INTERNATIONAL LAW

One cannot appreciate why International Law works without first comprehending "law" as generating behavior that the particular community deems acceptable in spite of the indifference of certain scofflaws. Drawing upon a familiar scenario will help make this point.[96] Imagine that you are driving through a busy intersection with the usual array of traffic signals. Most motorists conform to the associated legal regulations by proceeding only when the light is green and stopping when the light is red. The routine observance of this regime prompts the following question: *Why* do most motorists observe the commands emitted from the directional commands when there is no policeman present to enforce the applicable rules?

Conforming behavior does not necessarily result from the fear of punishment. The motorists at the intersection observe the law due to their common desire to proceed safely. Otherwise, there would be chaos as each driver attempts to reach his or her respective destination. If most of them did not observe the traffic laws, there would be numerous collisions. These incidents would defeat the common goal of safely proceeding, although compliance may delay the immediate progress of some hurried drivers. Conformity with expectations enables all concerned to arrive at their destinations—even if they do not arrive on time. The few scofflaws are unlikely to ignore the traffic lights without at least minor (and in some cases major) consequences.

The international system similarly spawns an astonishing level of order between nations (motorists), because of the common interest they share in observing the fundamental expectations of global harmony (limiting serious collisions). While some States may occasionally ignore the norms of accepted behavior, the community has nevertheless imposed a legal framework for establishing mutual expectations. Most of these "drivers" in the international legal system engage in consistent and predictable behavior that does not offend the shared sense of global order.

The national decision to voluntarily observe International Law is premised on self-interest and the same cognitive survival instinct observable at traffic and international intersections. Self-interested States recognize that it is in their best interest to comply with the mutual expectations of International Law. Like most motorists, who observe almost all traffic laws almost all of the time, national interests are served best by a prevailing international order.

While the above traffic light analogy is not flawless, it does exemplify the analogous operation of International Law as an important cog in the wheel of international relations. One may avoid the all-too-common misperception that the legitimacy of governance depends primarily on coercive enforcement rather than commonly shared values. Hence, observance of the "law" does not have to be equated to the available degree of military or economic enforcement. States have observed International Law, in most instances, without a UN standing army, and without the comparable governmental institutions that are the benchmarks of national law.

◆ SUMMARY

1. International Law consists of rules governing the conduct of States. International organizations, individuals, and corporations are also subject to International Law in certain instances.
2. A customary practice of States may be incorporated into the body of International Law if States perceive it as being obligatory in their international relations.
3. The scope of International Law is sometimes unclear because it is not static. State practices vary vis-à-vis each other. What one State does in its own international relations varies from time to time.
4. Universality of acceptance is not required for a norm to be incorporated into International Law. Conversely, no single nation or small group of nations can independently alter global expectations.
5. The theoretical schools of thought for classifying International Law focus on Natural Law—based on immutable norms inherent in any ordered system of law; Positive Law—based solely on the expressed consent of nations; and Eclectics—a blend of maxims drawn from various schools of thought including Natural and Positive Law.
6. A State's legislation, executive decrees, and judicial opinions are sources for ascertaining the content of the law of that State. One must use a different paradigm when seeking sources as evidence of the content of *International Law,* because of the absence of

the same authoritative system of enforcement to limit State sovereignty.

7. International decision makers typically draw from five commonly recognized sources appearing in the Statute of the International Court of Justice: (a) treaties; (b) international customs; (c) general principles of law used by nations in resolving internal disputes; (d) the "subsidiary" source of judicial and arbitral decisions by national and international tribunals; and (e) the scholarly writings of experts in International Law. Another source might be a unanimous resolution of the UN General Assembly intended to create or modify the practice of its State members.
8. The ebb and flow of international consensus often makes it difficult to establish unchallenged evidence of the content of International Law, even when using these recognized sources.
9. Private International Law refers to resolution mechanisms for disputes involving non-State entities, such as individuals or corporations.
10. One feminist perspective is that the public–private International Law distinction is harmful, because it is imperfect and unrealistic. It has failed to properly govern the conduct of non-State abusers, who have historically been governed only by national laws.
11. International Relations study emerged as a distinct discipline after World War I. Liberal democratic theory embraced the hope that the League of Nations would put an end to war. The harsh reality of the events leading to World War II convinced political science "realists" that the companion discipline of International Law had only a peripheral value in International Relations theory.
12. More recently, International Relations theory acknowledges the contributions made by International Law and international organizations that facilitate positive State behavior in collaborative ways.
13. Religion and International Law share elements of ritual, authority, and universality. Sometimes these disciplines conflict, in part, because of cultural relativism. International protection of the rights of women, for example, are rejected by certain Islamic traditions.
14. Diplomacy requires the recognition of cultural values that, because of their crucial role in shaping perceptions, are sometimes more pivotal than ideological beliefs and abstract ideals.
15. The mutual expectations of members of the international community cannot be divorced from their respective legal systems. Each may contain different norms extracted for use in international legal transactions and when negotiating international rules.
16. Monists and dualists debate the theoretical relationship between national and International Law. Monists assert that International Law and the law of each nation form a unified, universal legal system. Dualists argue that International Law and national law are distinct legal systems. The State retains the essential sovereign power to integrate or ignore the norms of International Law.
17. Some States expressly integrate International Law into their national legal systems. In most, however, International Law has no validity unless its principles are expressly incorporated into national law.
18. A State may not assert its internal (national) law as a defense to its breach of International Law. It is liable for a breach of this "external" source of law, even when national law would compel the violation.
19. Some observers perceive International Law as weak and incapable of enforcement, asserting that the viability, or very existence of law, requires enforcement mechanisms like those available under national law.
20. International Law is primitive when compared with the enforcement mechanisms found in national legal systems. However, national sovereignty restricts the ways in which International Law is effectively enforced.
21. Most nations routinely observe International Law because it is in their best interests to do so, much like most motorists who observe traffic signals at busy intersections. One supporting rationale is that nations mutually recognize rights and duties regarding their sovereignty.

◆ PROBLEMS

Problem 1.A (end of §1.2) A member of the class will serve as the blackboard recorder. Another class member will begin this exercise by articulating his or her version of the definition of "International Law." Others may then suggest any modifications that would more fully or more accurately complete the definition.

Problem 1.B (end of §1.4) This hypothetical scenario examines whether certain of the Article 38 sources of International Law are entitled to more weight than others in resolving an international dispute. Assume that India becomes a party to a treaty with several other countries within its region of the world. Customary International Law (CIL) does not prevent a country from nationalizing the property of either its own citizens or foreign citizens. However, standard practice does require the nationalizing country to compensate foreign corporations for their expropriated assets. The government that takes the property must pay the foreign corporation the fair market value of the nationalized property at the time of the taking.

Under the regional treaty just ratified by India, the national parties have agreed that such compensation is no longer necessary. Under that treaty, the "Western-derived rule of International Law requiring prompt, adequate, and effective compensation is henceforth abrogated. Host State law determines the amount—and *whether*—payment is necessary under the circumstances." This international treaty agreement therefore contains a new rule that is contrary to the traditional practice of many countries throughout the world.

India then decides to nationalize a chemical plant belonging to a multinational corporation based in the US, a country that is *not* a party to the regional treaty that may limit or deny reimbursement. The US claims that its corporation is entitled to prompt, adequate, and effective compensation—asserting that CIL governs in this dispute. India responds that the US is nevertheless bound by the local treaty, because other countries in the region have adopted the new "no-compensation" rule by way of a treaty.

Assume that this dispute is submitted to the International Court of Justice (ICJ) for resolution. One student from India, one from the US, and another from a neutral country are ICJ judges. The three of you will now deliberate about which conflicting source—CIL vs. the treaty—governs the dispute between India and the US; and which source of International Law—the custom or the treaty—is entitled to more weight in the resolution of the compensation issue. The three of you must examine Article 38.1 of the ICJ Statute to find out whether it provides guidance for your ruling on the questions of which source should govern, whether one is entitled to more weight than the other, and why.

Problem 1.C (end of §1.4) D-Squad is a special unit within the State X police force. X is a Latin American nation whose typical, although unofficial, policy is to torture any citizen who is suspected of "civil disobedience." A treaty known as the Convention Against Torture and Other Cruel, Inhuman, or Degrading Treatment or Punishment was adopted by the UN General Assembly as Resolution No. 39/46 (1984). It entered into force when twenty nations ratified it (1987). The UN consisted of approximately 175 nations, including State X, at the time of the D-Squad acts and the effective date of the Torture Convention. Ratifying States may not employ torture as an official or unofficial policy.

State X is not a party to this treaty. There are *other* treaties prohibiting torture—including the American Convention on Human Rights and the Inter-American Convention to Prevent and Punish Torture—that have not yet been accepted by a number of nations in the Western Hemisphere.

The "Committee Against Torture" is an administrative agency established by the above Torture Convention to monitor State compliance with the treaty. In 1998, some D-Squad members acted in a way that clearly fit within the Convention's definition of torture. The Committee is conducting a hearing in which one of its representatives is presenting evidence to the treaty's Torture Committee about whether or not X's *de facto* torture policy (not official, but a "fact of life" in State X) violates International Law. A New York press conference has widely disseminated the events occurring in State X to both the foreign and domestic media. State X decides to participate in the resulting investigatory proceedings at the UN. The Committee's representative will now present the first phase of the potential case against State X—specifically identifying what sources of International Law are applicable to State X in this investigation.

A student who represents the government of State X (which denies the existence of an official torture policy) will respond to the Torture Committee representative's presentation of the case against State X.

Problem 1.D (§1.7, after n. 90) Assume that Israel and the PLO enter into a "Gaza Autonomy Taxation" treaty in 1998. Under its terms, Israel will retain the right to exact an income tax from all Gaza workers until the year 2005—when a new State called Palestine will have the exclusive right to tax Gaza's workers. The agreed-upon use of the revenue derived from this taxation treaty will be to create funds for enforcing Gaza's security. The income taxes are earmarked to pay for the police force that will keep the peace in Gaza. Until the

1998–2005 transition period is over, Israel has the exclusive fiscal responsibility to pay for the Gaza police force. After that, Palestine will assume the obligation to pay for the police force, as well as the right to tax Gaza residents who will benefit from the security provided by that force.

In the year 2000, a right-wing group within the PLO decides to conduct a terrorist campaign in Gaza, with the objective of driving Israel out of Gaza before the end of the transition period in 2005. The Israeli Knesset (parliament) responds to the terrorist campaign by enacting emergency legislation *extending* Israel's ability to collect and retain tax revenues derived from Gaza—for an indefinite period. The Knesset will determine when Gaza will be at least as secure as it was during the period leading up to the joint ratification of the 1998 sovereign tax treaty.

A Knesset representative advises her Palestinian counterpart that "Palestine" may never be able to collect Gaza's income taxes, even after the 2005 turnover date (under the 1998 treaty). It appears that Gaza will not be secure enough, until sometime well into the twenty-first century, for Israel to actually surrender this taxing power to the Palestinian Authority. Under International Law, Israel has a duty to perform its treaty obligations in good faith (as discussed in this textbook's treaty chapter). Assume that Israel has never addressed the question of whether its internal law or International Law would govern this potential "tax" treaty dispute with Palestinian authorities.

Two students will assume the role of the Israeli and Palestinian representatives. What arguments would each make regarding whether Israel's emergency legislation or the treaty governs whether the taxing authority will be shifted in timely fashion from Israel to the Palestinian Authority in 2005?

Problem 1.E (end of §1.7) A panel of students will present their perspectives on the following questions:

1. Does the US follow the monist view on the incorporation of International Law into national law?
2. The UN Charter is not a binding treaty creating immediate obligations (discussed further in Chapter 8). Could a US court nevertheless be bound to follow ICJ judgments under some source in International Law other than a treaty? Note that the *US Citizens* case suggests a basis for requiring the US to comply with the ICJ judgment prohibiting it from further supporting the Contra rebels in Nicaragua. Put another way, what would it take for the ICJ judgment to rise to a level of observance whereby post-Charter treaties and national legislation could *not* override the UN Charter Article 94 provision requiring national compliance with ICJ judgments? Is that basis for binding a nation to follow ICJ judgments currently in force?
3. Why would the plaintiffs in *US Citizens* not be able to obtain a remedy, even if they were able to establish that the US *must* observe all ICJ judgments?

Problem 1.F (end of §1.8) The Serbian post–Cold War advances in Bosnia-Herzegovina triggered a great deal of international frustration. Various rules of International Law, particularly the prohibition on violating territorial sovereignty, were ignored by the Serbs (primarily). The UN, NATO, and the US seemed powerless to act. The US and other NATO members wanted to carefully weigh the timing and degree of responsive action during a period when democracy and capitalism had not been staunchly incorporated into the various Yugoslavian territories involved in the Bosnian conflict. (England similarly appeased Hitler at the outset of World War II by its cautious response to German territorial advances taken in violation of the territorial sovereignty of various States in Europe.) With the possible exception of Moscow, there was no international outcry when an embargo was launched against the former Yugoslavia by the international community—nor when NATO aircraft proceeded to bomb a few Serbian positions in Bosnia.

Many skeptics claimed that this inaction proved that International Law is not "law." They viewed the international response to clear Serbian aggression as being strangled by political concerns—including the potential Russian reaction to any US–European measures against its traditional Serbian ally. Did they correctly equate cautious enforcement measures with the absence of any law to govern this war? Did the Bosnian crisis expose the political reality that expressions of caution by the international community are no more than a disguise for the fact that there is no applicable law to govern the relations between States?

Two students (or groups) will thus debate whether International Law is really law—and whether swift and effective enforcement measures against scofflaws, such as the former Yugoslavia (the "Serbs"), is the only genuine benchmark of an effective legal system.

◆ BIBLIOGRAPHY

§1.1 International Law at Work

W. Bishop, "Foreword to the Student: Why Study International Law?" in *International Law: Cases and Materials* xiii (3rd ed.). Boston: Little, Brown & Co., 1971.

R. Falk, "A New Paradigm for International Legal Studies: Prospects and Proposals," in R. Falk et al., *International Law: A Contemporary Perspective* 651. Dobbs Ferry, NY: Transnat'l, 1985.

M. Janis, *Careers in International Law.* Chicago: Amer. Bar Ass'n, 1993.

§1.2 Public International Law Defined

R. Bledsoe & B. Boczek, *The International Law Dictionary* (Santa Barbara, CA: ABC-Clio, 1987).

J. Grant et al. (eds.), *Parry and Grant Encyclopedic Dictionary of International Law* (2nd print. New York: Oceana, 1988).

L. Henkin et al., "The Nature of International Law," ch. 1 in *International Law, Cases and Materials* 1 (3rd ed. St. Paul: West, 1993).

M. Janis, "The Nature of International Law," ch. 1 in *An Introduction to International Law* 1 (2d ed. Boston: Little, Brown & Co., 1993).

M. Kaplan & N. Katzenbach, "The Theoretical Framework of International Law," ch. 3 in *The Political Foundations of International Law* 56 (New York: John Wiley & Sons, 1961).

O. Schachter, "The Nature and Reality of International Law," ch. 1 in *International Law in Theory and Practice* 1 (Dordrecht, Neth.: Martinus Nijhoff, 1991).

B. Weston et al., "The International Legal Process," ch. 1 in *International Law and World Order* 1 (2d ed. St. Paul: West, 1990).

§1.3 History of International Law

B. Chimni, *International Law and World Order: A Critique of Contemporary Approaches* (New Delhi: Sage Pub., 1993).

D. Kennedy, "A New Stream of International Law Scholarship," 7 *Wisconsin International Law Journal* 1 (1988).

"Historical Evolution of the International Community," ch. 2 (1868–1918) and ch. 3 (1918–present) in A. Cassese, *International Law in a Divided World* 34 & 55 (New York: Oxford Univ. Press, 1988).

§1.4 Sources of International Law

M. Akehurst, "The Hierarchy of Sources of International Law," 47 *British Yearbook International Law* 273 (1975).

D. Harris, "The Sources of International Law," ch. 2 in *Cases and Materials on International Law* 23 (4th ed. London: Street & Maxwell, 1991).

E. McWhinney, *United Nations Law Making: Cultural and Ideological Relativism and International Law Making for an Era of Transition* (New York: Holmes & Meier, 1984).

C. Parry, *The Sources and Evidences of International Law* (Manchester, Eng.: Manchester Univ. Press, 1965).

S. Rosenne, *Practice and Methods of International Law* (New York: Oceana, 1984).

"Sources of International Law," 19 *Thesaurus Acroasium*—Summer 1991 (Thessaloniki, Greece: Inst. Int'l Pub. L., 1992).

M. Villiger, *Customary International Law and Treaties: A Manual on the Theory and Practice of the Interrelation of Sources* (2nd ed. The Hague, Neth.: Kluwer, 1997).

§1.5 Private International Law

H. Charlesworth, C. Chinkin, & S. Wright, "Feminist Approaches to International Law," 85 *Amer. J. Internat'l Law* 613 (1991).

P. North & J. Fawcett, *Chesire and North's Private International Law* (12th ed. London: Butterworths, 1992).

§1.6 Related Disciplines

INTERNATIONAL RELATIONS

S. Burnett, "Implications for the Foreign Policy Community," ch. 13 in D. Johnson & C. Sampson (eds.), *Religion, The Missing Dimension of Statecraft* 285 (Oxford, Eng.: Oxford Univ. Press, 1994).

G. Maris, "The Relevance of International Law within International Politics," ch. 12 in *International Law: An Introduction* 363 (Lanham, MD: Univ. Press of America, 1984).

W. McWilliams & H. Piotrowski, *The World Since 1945: A History of International Relations* (3rd ed. Boulder, CO: Lynne Reinner, 1993).

J. Plano & R. Olton, *The International Relations Dictionary* (4th ed. Oxford, Eng.: ABC-CLIO, 1988).

N. Purvis, "Critical Legal Studies in Public International Law," 32 *Harvard International Law Journal* 81 (1991).

R. Powell, "Absolute and Relative Gains in International Relations Theory," 85 *American Political Science Review* 1303 (1991).

C. Sjolander & W. Cox, *Beyond Positivism: Critical Reflections on International Relations* (Boulder, CO: Lynne Reinner, 1994).

RELIGION

B. Grossfeld, "Religion and Law," ch. 14 in *The Strength and Weaknesses of Comparative Law* 107 (Oxford, Eng.: Oxford Univ. Press, 1990) (Weir translation).

CULTURAL STUDIES

R. Cohen, *Negotiating Across Cultures: Communication Obstacles in International Diplomacy* (Wash., DC: US Inst. of Peace Press, 1991).

COMPARATIVE LAW

M. Glendon, M. Gordon, & C. Osakwe, *Comparative Legal Traditions: Text, Materials and Cases on the Civil and Common Law Traditions* (2nd ed. St. Paul: West, 1994).

"Symposium: New Directions in Comparative Law," 46 *Amer. J. Comp. Law* 597–783 (1999).

C. Varga (ed.), *Comparative Legal Cultures* (New York: NYU Press, 1992).

§1.7 National–International Law Nexus

I. Brownlie, "The Relation of Municipal and International Law," ch. II in *Principles of Public International Law* 32 (4th ed. Oxford, Eng.: Oxford Univ. Press, 1990).

T. Frank & G. Fox (eds.), *International Law Decisions in National Courts* (Irvington, NY: Transnat'l, 1996).

L. Erades, *Interactions Between International and Municipal Law: A Comparative Case Law Study* (The Hague, Neth.: T.M.C. Asser Inst., 1993).

F. Kratochwil, "The Role of Domestic Courts as Agencies of the International Legal Order," in R. Falk et al., *International Law: A Contemporary Perspective* 236 (Dobbs Ferry, NY: Transnat'l, 1985).

K. Sik, "International Law in the Municipal Legal Order of Asian States: Virgin Land," in R. MacDonald (ed.), *Essays in Honour of Wang Tieya* 737 (Dordrecht, Neth.: Martinus Nijhoff, 1994).

§1.8 Is International Law Really Law?

R. Bierzanek, "Some Remarks on 'Soft' International Law," 17 *Polish Yearbook International Law* 21 (1988).

R. Falk, "International Jurisdiction: Horizontal and Vertical Conceptions of Legal Order," 32 *Temple Law Quarterly* 295 (1959).

D. Georgiev, "Politics or Rule of Law: Deconstruction and Legitimacy in International Law," 4 *European Journal of International Law* 1 (1993).

E. Niou & P. Ordeshook, "Stability in Anarchic International Systems," 84 *American Political Science Review* 1207 (1990).

◆ ENDNOTES

1. L. Henkin, "Preface," in *How Nations Behave: Law and Foreign Policy* (1st ed. New York: Columbia Univ. Press, 1968); *quote:* 2d ed. (1979), p. 47 (hereinafter *How Nations Behave*).
2. U.N.G.A. Res. 45/40, reprinted in Schaff, "United Nations Decade of International Law," 19 *Int'l J. Legal Info.* 130, 133–134 (1991).
3. Statement of the Secretary-General for the Newsletter of the American Society of International Law on the United Nations Decade of International Law; *see* www.law.cornell.edu/library/asil/issue1.htm#C.
4. *See* Wang T., "Teaching and Research of International Law in Present Day China," 22 *Colum. J. Transnat'l L.* 77 (1983).
5. H. Chiu, "Communist China's Attitude toward International Law," 60 *Amer. J. Int'l L.* 245, 250 (1966) (quoting Chinese-language source).
6. Huan, "Foreword" to first edition, *Chinese Yearbook of International Law* 4 (Taipei: Inst. Int'l Relations, 1983).
7. *See* "Postscript, International Law as a Career," 233 in A. D'Amato, *International Law: Process and Prospect* 233 (Dobbs Ferry, NY: Transnat'l, 1987).
8. C. Okeke, *The Theory and Practice of International Law in Nigeria* 277–278 (Enugu, Nigeria: Fourth Dimension Pub., 1986).
9. J. Kent, 1 *Commentaries on American Law* 20 (2d ed. New York: O. Halsted, 1832).
10. *The SS Lotus (France v. Turkey),* 1927 *PCIJ,* Series A, No. 10, 18. A panel of US jurists, referring to Nazi Germany's wrongful confiscation of a Swiss citizen's property in 1938, classically characterized International Law as "the relationship among nations rather than among individuals. It is termed the Law of Nations or International Law because it is relative to States or Political Societies and not necessarily to individuals, although citizens or subjects of the earth are greatly affected by it.'" *Dreyfus v. Von Finck,* 534 F.2d 24, 30 (2d Cir. 1976), *cert. den'd,* 429 US 825 (1976), *disavowed on other grounds, Filartiga v. Pena-Irala,* 630 F.2d 876 (2d Cir. 1980).
11. The concept, development, and usage is analyzed by Professor Condorelli in "Custom," ch. 7 in M. Bedjaoui (ed.), *International Law: Achievements and Prospects* 179, 187–192 (Paris: UNESCO, 1991).
12. "North Sea Continental Shelf Cases *(Fed. Rep. Germany v. Denmark/Netherlands),*" 1969 *ICJ Rep.* 4, 44.
13. "Case Concerning Military and Paramilitary Activities *(Nicaragua v. US),*" 1986 *ICJ Rep.* 101 (hereinafter *Nicaragua* case).
14. "General Introduction" in M. Bedjaoui (ed.), *International Law: Achievements and Prospects* 2 (Paris: UNESCO, 1991).
15. 1 *Restatement of the Foreign Relations Law of the United States* §101, 22 (3rd ed. St. Paul: Amer. Law Inst., 1987).
16. M. Whiteman, *Digest of International Law* 1 (Wash., DC: US Dep't State, 1963).
17. *See, e.g.,* M. McDougal & W. Reisman, "International Law as a Process of Authoritative Decision," ch. 1, §1 in *International Law in Contemporary Perspective* 4 (Mineola, NY: Foundation Press, 1981).
18. J. Charney, "Universal International Law," 87 *Amer. J. Int'l L.* 529 (Oct. 1993).
19. G. Tunkin, *Theory of International Law* 251 (Cambridge, MA: Harv. Univ. Press, 1974) (italics added).
20. Available electronic resources for additional historical detail include the University of Kansas World Wide Web Virtual Library, http://history.cc.ukans.edu/history/WWW_history_main.html; and the Index of Resources for Historians, http://history.cc.ukans.edu/history/index.html.
21. Text at www.yale.edu/lawweb/avalon/westphal.htm.
22. Text at www.law.ou.edu/monrodoc.html.
23. On the historical development of International Law, see A. Nussbaum, *A Concise History of the Law of Nations* (rev. ed. New York: MacMillan, 1953) (Mesopotamian treaty); Nanda, "International Law in Ancient Hindu India," ch. 3 in M. Janis (ed.), *The Influence of Religion on the Development of International Law* 51, 54 (Dordrecht, Neth.: Martinus Nijhoff, 1991) (Hindu disapproval of war); "A Brief History of Public International Law," ch. 15 in E. Paras, *International Law and World Organizations* 389 (4th rev. ed. Manila: Rex Book Store, 1985) (Greek city-state legal hierarchy); L. Chen, "The Confucian View of World Order," ch. 2 in M. Janis (ed.), *The Influence of Religion on the Development of International Law* 31, 37 (Dordrecht, Neth.: Martinus Nijhoff, 1991) (divinity basis for Chinese reprisals); "The Fetiales," ch. 1 in C. Watson, *International Law in Archaic Rome* 1 (Baltimore: Johns Hopkins Univ.

Press, 1993) (Roman college on legality of war); "The Historical Background of International Law," ch. 1 in C. Fenwick, *International Law* 9 (4th ed. New York: Appleton-Century-Crofts, 1965) (Greek universality introduced to Romans); Baskin & Feldman, "The Role of Hugo Grotius in the Formation and Development of the International Law Science," 1982 *Soviet Yearbk. Int'l L.* 275 (1983) (English trans.) ("father of International Law"); H. Lauterpacht, "The Grotian Tradition in International Law," 23 *Brit. Yearbk. Int'l Law* 1 (1946) (derivation of term *International Law*); "Historical Evolution of the International Community: The Former Setting (1648–1918)," ch. 2 in A. Cassese, *International Law in a Divided World* 34 (Oxford, Eng.: Clarendon Press, 1986) (European ascendancy).

24. Y. Danesh-Khoshboo, *The Civilization of Law: The Laws of Hammurabi and Magna Carta—Documents with Commentary* (Berrien Spring, MI: Vande Vere Pub., 1991).
25. *See, e.g.,* Kunz, "Natural-Law Thinking in the Modern Science of International Law," 55 *Amer. J. Int'l L.* 951 (1961); "Natural Law vs. Positivism," in G. Danilenko, *Law-Making in the International Community* 214–219 (Dordrecht, Neth.: Martinus Nijhoff, 1992).
26. H. Cox, "World Religions and Conflict Resolution," ch. 12 in D. Johnson & C. Sampson (eds.), *Religion, the Missing Dimension of Statecraft* 276 (Oxford, Eng.: Oxford Univ. Press, 1994).
27. A comprehensive analysis, commencing with the Peace of Westphalia, is provided in L. Hannikainen, *Peremptory Norms (Jus Cogens) in International Law* (Helsinki: Finnish Lawyers' Pub. Co., 1988).
28. *See* 1969 Convention, 155 UN Treaty Series 331; 1986 Convention, UN Doc. A/Conf. 129/15; *see also* Draft Article 18(2) in S. Rosenne, *The International Law Commission's Draft Articles on State Responsibility* (Dordrecht, Neth.: Martinus Nijhoff, 1991). *See also* Art. 18(2), 1996 Draft Articles on State Responsibility, 37 ILM 440 (1998).
29. **1969 case:** "North Sea Continental Shelf," 1969 *ICJ Rep.* 3, 42; **1986 case:** *"Nicaragua v. US,"* 1986 *ICJ Rep.* 14, 100.
30. T. Bennett, *A Sourcebook of African Customary Law for Southern Africa* 2 (Cape Town: Juta & Co., 1991).
31. *See* G. Schwarzenberger, "The Grotius Factor in International Law and Relations: A Functional Approach," ch. 12 in H. Bull, B. Kingsbury, & A. Roberts (eds.), *Hugo Grotius and International Relations* 301 (Oxford, Eng.: Oxford Univ. Press, 1992).
32. *See* §1, "Different Meanings of the Term 'Sources of Law,'" in V. D. Degan, *Sources of International Law* 1 (The Hague, Neth.: Martinus Nijhoff:, 1995).
33. *See, e.g.,* I. Brownlie, *Principles of Public International Law* 3 (4th ed. Oxford, Eng.: Oxford Univ. Press, 1990) (hereinafter Brownlie treatise); M. Akehurst, *A Modern Introduction to International Law* 23 (6th ed. London: Allen & Unwin, 1987); J. Brierly, *The Law of Nations* 56 (Waldock 6th ed. Oxford, Eng.: Clarendon Press, 1976). *But see* G. Maris, *International Law: An Introduction* 44 (New York: Univ. Press of Amer., 1984) (amidst chaos, there is no set rule of sources).
34. *Survey of International Law in Relation to the Work of Codification of the International Law Commission,* Sec.-Gen. Memo. A/CN.4/Rev.1, p. 22 (1949).
35. *"Trendtex Trading Corp. v. Central Bank of Nigeria,"* 1 *All English Rep.* 881, 902–03 (1977).
36. **Allied Report:** Cmd. Doc. 6531 (1944, p. 36); **Western criticism:** M. Kaplan & N. Katzenbach, *The Political Foundations of International Law* 231–236 (New York: John Wiley & Sons, 1961); **Soviet criticism:** G. Tunkin, *Theory of International Law* 118 (Cambridge, MA: Harv. Univ. Press, 1974) (hereinafter Tunkin treatise); **Chinese criticism:** H. Chiu, "Communist China's Attitude Toward International Law," 60 *Amer. J. Int'l L.* 245, 257 (1966), quoting Ying T'ao, "Recognize the True Face of Bourgeois International Law from a Few Basic Concepts," in *Studies in International Problems* 46–47 (1960) (Chinese-language periodical criticism).
37. *See* M. Akehurst, "The Hierarchy of the Sources of International Law," 47 *British Yearbk. Int'l L.* 273, 274 (1974).
38. "The Hierarchy of International Norms," in B. Conforti, *International Law and the Role of Domestic Legal Systems* 115–116 (Dordrecht, Neth.: Martinus Nijhoff, 1993) (Provost translation).
39. R. Bernhardt, "Hierarchy Among the Sources of International Law?" in D. Constantopoulos (ed.), *Sources of International Law,* XIX *Thesaurus Acroasium* 209 (Thessaloniki, Greece: Inst. Pub. Int'l Law, 1992).
40. *See* "The Elements of International Custom," ch. 1 in K. Wolfke, *Custom in Present International Law* 1 (2d rev. ed. Dordrecht, Neth.: Martinus Nijhoff, 1993).
41. Tunkin treatise, 113–114 (cited in note 36).
42. Brownlie treatise, 5–7 (cited in note 33).
43. 1969 *ICJ Rep.* 3, 44.
44. "Asylum Case *(Colombia v. Peru),*" 1950 *ICJ Rep.* 266, 276.
45. *See, e.g.,* G. Danilenko, "Customary Rule Formation in Contemporary International Law, 1982" *Soviet Yearbk. Int'l L.* 169, 170 (1983) (English translation).
46. J. Hsiung, "China's Recognition Practice and International Law," in J. Cohen (ed.), *China's Practice of International Law: Some Case Studies* 14, 17 (Cambridge, MA: Harv. Univ. Press, 1972).
47. The classic restatement of the law of prize issue under International Law is presented by Holland's Professor Verzijl. The latest compilation of his work is contained in W. Heere & J. Offerhaus, IX-C *The Law of Maritime Prize* (Dordrecht, Neth.: Martinus Nijhoff, 1991).
48. Vienna Convention on the Law of Treaties, art. 1(a) (1969). Further detail is provided in Chapter 8.
49. Article 20, 2 *US Treaties* 2394, 119 *U.N.T.S.* 3 (italics added).
50. "North Sea Continental Shelf Case," 1969 *ICJ Rep.* 3, 41–42.
51. **Equity:** C. Rossi, *Equity and International Law* 87 (Irvington, NY: Transnat'l, 1993). **Good faith:** J. F. O'Connor, *Good Faith in International Law* 17 (Aldershot, Eng.: Dartmouth, 1991).
52. Compare the Russian position in Tunkin treatise, 190–203 (cited in note 36) with H. Chiu, "Chinese Attitudes Toward

International Law in the Post-Mao Era, 1978–1987," 21 *Int'l Lawyer* 1127, 1140–41 (1987). Scholarly disagreement is further discussed in §12, "General Principles of Law," in R. Jennings & A. Watts, I *Oppenheim's International Law* (Part 1) 37, n.2 (9th ed. Essex, Eng.: Longman, 1992) (hereinafter Jennings treatise).
53. **PCIJ case:** "Diversion of Water from the Meuse," *PCIJ* Series A/B, No. 70, p. 25 (1937). **ICJ case:** "Barcelona Traction Case," 1970 *ICJ Rep.* 3, 33.
54. G. Hackworth, *Digest of International Law* 655–661 (Wash., DC: US Gov't Print. Off., 1942).
55. H. Lauterpacht, *The Development of International Law by the International Court* 20 (rev. ed. London: Stevens & Sons, 1958).
56. *Thirty Hogsheds of Sugar v. Boyle,* 13 US (9 Cranch) 191, 3 L.Ed. 701, 703 (1815).
57. Jennings treatise, 41 (cited in note 52 above).
58. "Case Concerning the Factory at Chorzow *(Germany v. Poland),*" 1926–1929 *PCIJ,* ser. A, No. 7, 19 (Judgment of May 25, 1926).
59. *"The SS Lotus (France v. Turkey),"* 1927 *PCIJ,* ser. A, No. 10, p. 26.
60. K. Wolfke, *Custom in Present International Law* 77 (2nd rev. ed. Dordrecht, Neth.: Martinus Nijhoff, 1993).
61. *West Rand Central Gold Mining Co. v. The King,* 2 King's Bench 391 (1905).
62. Suy, "Innovations in International Law-Making Processes," in R. McDonald et al. (eds.), *The International Law and Policy of Human Welfare* (Alphen aan den Rijn, Neth.: Sitjhoff & Noordhoff, 1978).
63. K. Skubiszewski, "Law-Making by International Organizations," in 19 *Thesaurus Acroasium: Sources of International Law* 364 (Thessaloniki, Greece: Inst. Public Int'l Law, 1992).
64. A. D'Amato, *International Law: Process and Prospect* 75–76 (Dobbs Ferry, NY: Transnat'l, 1987).
65. P. Szasz, "General Law-Making Processes" (from "Part I: The UN Sysytem as a Source of Law"), in O. Schachter & C. Joyner (eds.), 1 *United Nations Legal Order,* at 45–46 (Cambridge, Eng.: Cambridge Univ. Press, 1995).
66. "Certain Expenses of the United Nations: 1962," *ICJ Rep.* 151, p. 163; "Legal Consequences for States of the Continued Presence of South Africa in Namibia (South-West Africa) Notwithstanding Security Council Resolution" 276 (1970): 1971 *ICJ Rep.* 16, p. 50; "South-West Africa Voting Procedure: 1955" *ICJ Rep.* 67, p. 118.
67. O. Schachter, "Resolutions and Political Texts," ch. VI in *International Law in Theory and Practice* 88 (Dordrecht, Neth.: Martinus Nijhoff, 1991).
68. *See* M. Bergman, "The Norm-Creating Effect of a General Assembly Resolution on Transnational Corporations," in F. Snyder & S. Sathirathai (eds.), *Third World Attitudes toward International Law: An Introduction* 231 (Dordrecht, Neth.: Martinus Nijhoff, 1987) (some resolutions are "norm-creating" sources); and O. Asamoah, *The Legal Significance of the Declarations of the General Assembly of the United Nations* (The Hague: Martinus Nijhoff, 1966) (resolutions as sources when restating customary practice).
69. *See Nicaragua* case, pp. 99–100, 188 (cited in note 29 above).
70. P. M. North & J. J. Fawcett, *Private International Law* 3-4 (12th ed. London: Butterworths, 1992).
71. M. McDougal, "'Private' International Law: *Jus Gentium* Versus Choice of Law Rules or Approaches," 38 *Amer. J. Comp. L.* 521 (1990).
72. S. Wright, "Economic Rights, Social Justice and the State: A Feminist Reappraisal," in D. Dallmeyer (ed.), *Reconceiving Reality: Woman and International Law* 117, 135–136 (Wash., DC: Amer. Soc. Int'l L., 1993).
73. UN Gen. Ass. Res. 34/180, 34 U.N. GAOR Supp. (No. 46) at 193, U.N. Doc. A/34/46, entered into force Sept. 3, 1981. UN Gen. Ass. Res. 43/100 of Dec. 8, 1988, calls upon all nations that have not yet ratified or acceded to this treaty to do so as soon as possible.
74. UN Gen. Ass. Res. 48/104, 48 U.N. GAOR Supp. (No. 49) at 217, U.N. Doc. A/48/49 (1993).
75. *How Nations Behave, supra* note 1, at 47.
76. A. M. Burley, "International Law and International Relations Theory: A Dual Agenda," 87 *Amer. J. Int'l L.* 205, 207 (1993).
77. *See, e.g.,* R. Keohane, *After Hegemony: Cooperation and Discord in the World Political Economy* 246 (Princeton: Princeton Univ. Press, 1984); and Arthur Stein, *Why Nations Cooperate: Circumstance and Choice in International Relations* 113 (Ithaca, NY: Cornell Univ. Press, 1990).
78. M. Slann, "Introduction: Ethnonationalism and the New World Order of International Relations," ch. 1 in B. Schechterman & M. Slann (eds.), *The Ethnic Dimension in International Relations* 3 (Westport, CT: Praeger, 1993).
79. J. Nafziger, "The Functions of Religion in the International Legal System," in M. Janis (ed.), *The Influence of Religion on the Development of International Law* 147, 151–153 (Dordrecht, Neth.; Martinus Nijhoff, 1991) (footnotes omitted).
80. M. Marty & R. Appleby (eds.), *Introduction to Fundamentalisms and the State* 4 (Chicago: Univ. of Chicago Press, 1993).
81. F. Ninkovich, "Culture in US Foreign Policy Since 1900," ch. 8 in J. Chay (ed.), *Culture and International Relations* 103 (New York: Preager, 1990) (hereinafter *Chay treatise*).
82. *See, e.g.,* Wallace, "Is War a Cultural Universal? Anthropological Perspectives on the Causes of Warfare in Human Societies," ch. 2 in *Chay treatise,* p. 21 (cited in note 81).
83. R. Schlesinger et al., *Comparative Law: Cases—Text—Materials* 309 (5th ed. Mineola, NY: Foundation Press, 1988) (hereinafter *Schlesinger treatise*).
84. See "The Concept of Comparative Law," ch. 1 in K. Zweigert & H. Kotz, *An Introduction to Comparative Law* (2d rev. ed. Oxford, Eng.: Oxford Univ. Press, 1992).
85. *See generally* "Common Law and Civil Law—Comparison of Methods and Sources," in *Schlesinger treatise,* p. 229 (cited in note 83).
86. *See* "International Tribunal for the Prosecution of Persons Responsible for Serious Violations of International Humanitarian Law Committed in the Territory of the Former Yugoslavia Since 1991: Rules of Procedure and Evidence," 33 *Int'l Legal Mat'ls* 484 (1994).
87. *See* §1.5 of this book, "Feminist Perspective."

88. "Applicability of the Obligation to Arbitrate Under Section 21 of the United Nations Headquarters Agreement of 26 June 1947," 1988 *ICJ Rep.* 12, para. 57.
89. H. Kelsen, *General Theory of Law and the State* 363–380 (Cambridge, MA: Harv. Univ. Press, 1945).
90. *Chung Chi Cheung v. Regina,* 1939 *Court of Appeals* 160 (1939).
91. *Schroeder v. Bissell,* 5 Fed.2d 838 (D.C. Conn. 1925).
92. **ILC quote:** 1949 *Yearbook of the International Law Commission* 286, 289 (1949); **PCIJ quote:** "Polish Nationals in Danzig," 1931 *PCIJ Rep.,* ser. A/B, no. 44, p. 24.
93. B. Conforti, *International Law and the Role of Domestic Legal Systems* 8–9 (Dordrecht, Neth.: Martinus Nijhoff, 1993) (Provost translation).
94. G. Will, "The Perils of 'Legality,'" in *Newsweek,* 66 (Sept. 10, 1990).
95. *The Schooner Exchange v. McFadden,* 136 US (7 Cranch) 116, 136 (1812) (Marshall, C. J.) (italics added).
96. Saint Peter's College (New Jersey) political science Professor Richard Thurston inspired the development of this useful analogy.

CHAPTER TWO

States in International Law

CHAPTER OUTLINE

THIS UPRISING HAS COME TO FURTHER AFFIRM OUR people's unbreakable commitment to its national aspirations. These aspirations include people's firm national rights of self-determination and of the establishment of an independent state on our national soil under the leadership of the PLO, as our sole legitimate representative. The uprising also comes as further proof of our indefatigable spirit and our rejection of the sense of despair which has begun to creep into the minds of some Arab leaders who claim that the uprising is the result of despair.

—Concerning the Outbreak of the Intifada (1988), on the PLO's official Web site. See www.pna.net/facts/pal_14points_intifada.htm.

INTRODUCTION

There are various categories of international actors who either govern or are governed by International Law. These actors possess international legal personality—the legal capacity that carries with it certain entitlements and obligations arising under International Law.

The "persons" with this legal personality include States, international organizations, and, to some extent, private individuals within a State. This chapter focuses on the primary actor—*States*—an often misunderstood term.

After establishing the building blocks of the legal capacity of a State, this chapter surveys the unprecedented alteration in the infrastructure of International Law caused by the vast increase in the number of State actors since the end of World War II. This phenomenon was caused by events that included the 1960s decolonization movement and the 1990s splintering of larger States into smaller ones.

The important corollaries to statehood, once established, are:

- recognition by other States and organizations (the spark that ignited the "Bosnian War");
- State responsibility under International Law (substantive rules governing State conduct); and
- entitlement to sovereign immunity from suit in another country when a State is acting like a State (as opposed to a commercial trader).

◆ 2.1 LEGAL PERSONALITY OF THE STATE

A State's legal "personality," or "capacity," is the central feature of its status under International Law. Individuals and corporate entities within a nation have rights and duties arising under its internal laws. For example, they may petition for relief when their rights have been adversely impacted by the conduct of another individual, entity, or the government itself. They do not enjoy that status under International Law because they lack the legal capacity to engage in international relations or to act like a State within the community of nations.

If I steal your corporate assets, your company might sue me to recover the value of the lost assets. Your company has the legal capacity to sue me for that theft. If I were a government agent in another country, and I nationalized your corporate assets, your State would possess the legal capacity to sue my State in the International Court of Justice—because my conduct (on behalf of my government) harmed you by taking your property without proper compensation. You would not have the legal power to sue my State under general principles of International Law. Commentators often refer to your State's entitlement to react to such a theft as one that arises "on the *international* plane" or "at the *international* level."

There are contemporary pressures to break away from the historical perception of "State," as established by European powers in the 1648 Peace of Westphalia (Chapter 1). For example, large multinational corporations—with an annual budget much greater than most of the countries wherein they operate—enjoy a degree of autonomy that makes it difficult for States to exercise effective sovereign control. However, the fundamental player in international relations is still the State. UN Secretary-General Boutros-Ghali confirmed this primacy in his 1992 *Agenda for Peace* Report to the General Assembly whereby "[t]his wider mission [of making the UN stronger and more efficient] . . . will demand the concerted attention and effort of individual States, or regional and non-governmental organizations and of all of the United Nations system . . . [and the] foundation stone of this work is and must remain the State. Respect for its fundamental sovereignty and integrity are crucial to any common international progress." This principle was reaffirmed at the outset of his ensuing 1995 edition: "For almost three centuries, a set of principles of international cooperation has been in the making. . . . In almost every area, . . . nations working together, through the United Nations, are setting the global agenda."[1]

This view of the State as the primary international actor is not new. More than a generation ago, one of the most prominent International Law scholars described the continuing dominance of the State as the central feature of the international system. Columbia University Professor Wolfgang Friedmann acknowledged this primacy because it "is by virtue of their law-making power and monopoly that states enter into bilateral and multilateral compacts, that wars can be started or terminated, that individuals can be punished or extradited . . . and [the notion of "State" would be] eventually superseded only if national entities were absorbed in[to] a world state. . . ."[2]

The following materials now address several preliminary questions: What does the term "State" mean? Under what conditions does an entity become a "State" (the elements of statehood)? What is the relationship between a "State" (e.g., Bavaria) within a group of associated "States" (Germany) under International Law?

"STATE"

Like many other legal terms, the word *State* means different things to different people. A State is typically defined as a group of societies within a readily defined geographical area, united to ensure their mutual welfare and security. Commentators have debated the appropriate nomenclature for describing this entity, such as "nation" or "State," which is the cornerstone of International Law. The terms *State, nation, nation-state, community, country, people, government,* and *sovereign* have all been used interchangeably. They have distinct meanings, however. The following words in the Preamble to the UN Charter (emphasis supplied by the author) provide a convenient example of such usages: "We the *peoples* of the United *Nations* . . . [h]ave resolved to combine our efforts . . . [through] our respective *Governments*. . . ." There are also subtle differences among such terms that heads of State, diplomats, speakers, and writers do not always clarify for their respective audiences.

Reading the following definitions will generate a healthy degree of caution when one is attempting to digest the discourses on International Law found in various speeches, news reports, and texts (including this one):

- **State**—"a person of international law [that] should possess the following qualifications: (a) a permanent population; (b) a defined territory; (c) government; and (d) capacity to enter into relations with other States."
- **Nation**—"a practical association of human individuals who consider themselves to be a nation (on the basis of a shared religion, history, language or any other common feature)."
- **Nation-State**—the joinder of two terms, typically referring to a specific geographic area constituting a sovereign entity and possibly containing more than one group of nationals (individual citizens) based on shared religion, history, or language.
- **Community**—"a group of persons living in a given country or locality, having race, religion, language and traditions of their own, and united by the identity of such . . . in a sentiment of solidarity. . . ."
- **Country**—the territorial element of the term *State,* with attendant borders that define its land mass.
- **People**—"the permanently residing population of a territory with an internationally legal status (state, mandate territory, etc.)."
- **Government**—in International Law, the political group or entity responsible for engaging in foreign relations, which is the "true and lawful government of the state . . . which ought to exercise sovereignty, but which may be deprived of this right by a government *de facto.*"
- **Sovereign**—occasional synonym for State or nation, although it actually describes "the evolving relationship between state and civil society, between political authority and the community . . . [being] as both an idea and an institution integral to the structure of Western thought . . . and to a geopolitical discourse in which territory is sharply demarcated and exclusively controlled."[3]

STATEHOOD

Not all entities that are called a "State," and not all entities desiring recognition as a "State," may lay claim to that status under International Law. When *is* an entity entitled to statehood in the international sense of the word?

Four elements normally vest an entity with "international legal personality," meaning rights and duties identified with statehood arising under International Law. Under the 1933 Montevideo Inter-American Convention on the Rights and Duties of States, a "State as a person of international law should possess the following qualifications: (a) a permanent population; (b) a defined territory; (c) government; and (d) capacity to enter into relations with other States."[4] The simultaneous presence of these elements identifies a sovereign entity that possesses such international personality.

These legal criteria for statehood have been widely adopted. The extent of their acceptance, however, has not been matched by simplicity of application. One reason is that the absence of one or more of these statehood elements, even over a period of time, does not necessarily deprive a State of its international personality. Analytical problems most often arise when larger States break up into smaller ones—as in the former Yugoslavia after the demise of the Soviet Union; or one part of a nation attempts to secede—as in the American Civil War of the 1860s and Quebec's possible secession from Canada; or a foreign power exercises *de facto* control over another State—for example, Nazi Germany's expansion in Europe, or South Africa's long and illegal dominion of the South-West Africa Trust Territory, now Namibia.

Population Component The "permanent population" element is probably the least important of these elements of statehood. Neither a minimum population nor an express grant of nationality to the inhabitants is required for qualification as a state.[5] Nor does the absence of part of the population over a period of time necessarily vitiate state status. The nomadic tribes on the Kenya–Ethiopia border, for example, have been an ambulatory element of each nation's population for centuries. The transient nature of this significant component of each State's population has not diminished the permanence of either bordering State.

Deficiencies with the other elements of statehood—defined territory and a government engaging in foreign relations—have posed more serious problems.

Territorial Component The territorial element of Statehood has been occasionally blurred by mutually exclusive claims to the same territory. A classic example is the former Arab–Israeli territorial conflict, which had its roots in the United Nations plan to partition Palestine. This plan, devised in 1947 to divide Palestine into an Arab state and a Jewish state, was not implemented due to the Middle East War that erupted in 1948. Israel was able to expand its territory beyond that provided for by the UN plan, displacing millions of Arabs.

Columbia University's Professor Philip Jessup (who represented the United States in the UN Security Council in 1948 and later became a judge of the International Court of Justice) used the following illustration to demonstrate why Israel nevertheless satisfied the doctrinal elements of statehood as early as 1948:

On the Condition of Statehood

3 UN Security Council Official Records

383rd Meeting, at 9–12 (1948)

Over a year ago the United States gave its support to the principles of the majority plan proposed by the United Nations Special Committee on Palestine. That plan envisaged the creation of both a Jewish State and an Arab State in Palestine. We gave our support to the resolution of 29 November 1947 by which the General Assembly recommended a plan for the future government of Palestine involving, as one of its elements, the establishment of a Jewish State in part of Palestine. . . .

The Security Council now has before it the application of the Provisional Government of Israel for membership [in the UN].

The consideration of the application requires an examination of . . . the question of whether Israel is a State duly qualified for membership. Article 4 of the Charter of the United Nations specifies the following:

"Membership in the United Nations is open to peace-loving States which accept the obligations contained in the present Charter and, in the judgment of the Organization, are able and willing to carry out these obligations. . . ."

The first question which may be raised in analyzing Article 4 of the Charter and its applicability to the membership of the State of Israel, is the question of whether Israel is a State, as that term is used in Article 4 of the Charter. It is common knowledge that, while there are traditional definitions of a State in international law, the term has been used in many different ways. We are all aware that, under the traditional definition of a State in international law, all the great writers have pointed to four qualifications: first, there must be a people; second, there must be a territory; third, there must be a government; and, fourth, there must be capacity to enter into relations with other States of the world.

In so far as the question of capacity to enter into relations with other States of the world is concerned, learned academic arguments can be and have been made to the effect that we already have, among the Members of the United Nations, some political entities which do not possess full sovereign freedom to form their own international policy, which traditionally has been considered characteristic of a State. We know, however, that neither at San Francisco nor subsequently has the United Nations considered that complete freedom to frame and manage one's own foreign policy was an essential requisite of United Nations membership.

I do not dwell upon this point because . . . Israel is free and unhampered. On this point, I believe that there would be unanimity that Israel exercises complete independence of judgment and of will in forming and in executing its foreign policy. The reason for which I mention the qualification of this aspect of the traditional definition of a State is to underline the point that the term "State," as used and applied in Article 4 of the Charter of the United Nations, may not be wholly identical with the term "State" as it is used and defined in classic textbooks of international law.

When we look at the other classic attributes of a State, we find insistence that it must also have a Government. No one doubts that Israel has a Government. I think the world has been particularly impressed with the way in which the people of Israel have organized their government and have established a firm system of administration and of law-making under the most difficult conditions. Although, pending their scheduled elections, they still modestly and appropriately call themselves the Provisional Government of Israel, they have a legislative body which makes laws, they have a judiciary which interprets and applies those laws, and they have an executive which carries out the laws and which has at its disposal a considerable force responsive to its will.

According to the same classic definition, we are told that a State must have a people and a territory. Nobody questions the fact that the State of Israel has a people. It is an extremely homogeneous people, a people full of loyalty and of enthusiastic devotion to the State of Israel.

The argument seems chiefly to arise in connection with territory. One does not find in the general classic treatment of this subject any insistence that the territory of a State must be exactly fixed by definite frontiers. We all know that, historically, many States have begun their existence with their frontiers unsettled. Let me take as one example my own country, the United States of America. Like the State of Israel in its origin, it had certain territory along the seacoast. It had various indeterminate claims to an extended territory westward. But, in the case of the United States, that land had not even been explored, and no one knew just where the American claims ended and where French and British and Spanish claims began. To the North, the exact delimitation of the frontier with the territories of Great Britain was not settled until many years later. And yet, I maintain that, in the light of history and in the light of the practice and acceptance by other States, the existence of the United States of America was not in question before its final boundaries were determined.

The formulae in the classic treatises somewhat vary, one from the other, but both reason and history demonstrate that the concept of territory does not necessarily include precise delimitation of the boundaries of that territory. The reason for the rule that one of the necessary attributes of a State is that it shall possess territory is that one cannot contemplate a State as a kind of disembodied spirit. Historically, the concept is one of insistence that there must be some portion of the earth's surface which its people inhabit and over which its Government exercises authority.

◆ *Notes*

1. Prior to the 1995 Dayton peace agreement establishing various geopolitical entities within Bosnia, the Serbs in Bosnia sought to maintain control of an area now referred to as "Republica Srpska." Their objective was to drive out Muslims and Croats. They used unspeakable means to achieve this objective. In human rights litigation filed in a New York federal court, victims' attorneys served the self-proclaimed Bosnian Serb "President" Radovan Karadzic while he was there to attend a UN conference on peace in Bosnia. (This case is discussed in Chapters 9 and 11.)

   In the appellate decision reversing the trial court's dismissal of the case against Karadzic, the court addressed the issue regarding whether he was "acting under color of state law" for purposes of establishing his responsibility for numerous atrocities occurring in the Srpska area of Bosnia. On the question of whether this area was a "State," the court noted as follows:

   > The definition of a state is well established in international law: Under international law, a state is an entity that has a defined territory and a permanent population, under the control of its own government, and that engages in, or has the capacity to engage in, formal relations with other such entities. "[A]ny government, however violent and wrongful in its origin, must be considered a *de facto* government if it was in the full and actual exercise of sovereignty over a territory and people large enough for a nation. . . ."
   >
   > The customary international law of human rights, such as the proscription of official torture, applies to states without distinction between recognized and unrecognized states. It would be anomalous indeed if non-recognition by the United States, which typically reflects disfavor with a foreign regime—sometimes due to human rights abuses—had the perverse effect of shielding officials of the unrecognized regime from liability for those violations of international law norms that apply only to state actors. . . .
   >
   > Appellants' allegations entitle them to prove that Karadzic's regime satisfies the criteria for a state, for purposes of those international law violations requiring state action. Srpska is alleged to control defined territory, control populations within its power, and to have entered into agreements with other governments.It has a president, a legislature, and its own currency. These circumstances readily

appear to satisfy the criteria for a state in all aspects of international law. Moreover, it is likely that the state action concept, where applicable for some violations like "official" torture, requires merely the semblance of official authority. The inquiry, after all, is whether a person purporting to wield official power has exceeded internationally recognized standards of civilized conduct, not whether statehood in all its formal aspects exists.

—*Kadic v. Karadzic,* 70 Fed.3d 232 (2nd Cir., 1995), *rehearing den'd,* 74 Fed.3d 377 (2nd Cir., 1996), *cert. den'd* 518 US 1005 (1997).

2. Recognition thus plays no role in whether or not an entity is a "State" for the purpose of incurring international responsibility. The "President" of Republica Srpska, which was not a State in the traditional sense—and was initially contained within the boundaries of Bosnia-Herzegovina—could not avoid the characterization that he and his forces were operating as if they were a State. This decision thus supported the plaintiffs' claim that "President" Karadzic was acting under color of State law, a necessary element of their claim arising under the Alien Tort Statute, 28 US Code §1350. That legislation permits a foreign citizen to sue a foreign citizen in the US for acts occurring abroad that violate International Law. There is usually service of process on the defendant in the US when he is temporarily present. The plaintiff must assert that the defendant actor is conducting himself as if he were acting on behalf of a foreign State or political subdivision.

Government Component The "government" element of statehood is problematic when separate entities, operating in different regions within a State, claim that each is the legitimate government of the entire territory. Modern examples include Nationalist and Communist China, North and South Korea, and the two Vietnamese governments of the 1960s and 1970s. In each of these cases, separate entities possessing administrative and legislative authority claimed the exclusive right to govern. External interference by other States contributed to the rigidity that caused each government to adopt and maintain inflexible postures.

Another example of this overlapping governance arises in the awkward situation where a State's established government *should* be maintaining political order, yet a civil war or external threat has tempered its ability to actually "lead the way." The "Finland" of 1917 is a classic example. Shortly after achieving independence from what was destined to become a strong centralized Soviet Union, the Finnish government was engaged in a territorial dispute with Russia regarding some islands off Finland's coast. The League of Nations appointed some jurists who considered the issue of *when* Finland attained statehood after the territory's independence. They examined the fundamental requirement of an effective government (for statehood). Under their succinct description of this element:

> [T]he conditions required for the formation of a sovereign State did not exist. In the midst of revolution and anarchy, certain elements essential to the existence of a State . . . were lacking for a fairly considerable period. Political and social life was disorganized; the [civil] authorities were not strong enough to assert themselves; civil war was rife; further, . . . the Government had been chased from the capital and forcibly prevented from carrying out its duties; the armed camps and the police were divided into two opposing forces, and Russian troops, and after a time Germans also, took part in the civil war. . . . It is therefore difficult to say at what exact date the Finnish Republic, in the legal sense of the term, actually became a definitely constituted sovereign State. This certainly did not take place until a stable political organization had been created, and until the public authorities [of Finland] had become strong enough to assert themselves throughout the territories of the State without the assistance of foreign troops.[6]

Foreign Relations Component The attribute requiring the "capacity to enter into relations with other States" (Montevideo Convention) is arguably the most decisive criterion for statehood. Under International Law, a State must function independently of any external authority—other than that imposed by International Law. Not all entities referred to as a "State" possess this capacity.

A State may appear to possess the characteristics of a sovereign entity without actually being in control of its populace and territory. Foreign relations responsibilities may be entrusted to another State. Certain dependent

States may be monitored by other more established States. The governmental functions of such "mandated" (League of Nations) or "trust" territories (United Nations) have been exercised under the auspices of the League and the UN—discussed in Chapter 3 on the UN Trusteeship Council.

There is also the question of *which* government within a State is "the" government for purposes of International Law. A *national* government has the capacity to engage in international relations, not one of its component states or provinces. This rule applies in two contexts. First, a national entity may be controlled by an outside power and yet remain in charge of its international relations. Belorussia and the Ukraine were components of the dominant Soviet Union. Yet each retained the capacity to engage in international relations and were original members of the United Nations. Second, states within a federated State (a national entity) are not States in the international sense. The State of California is not a "State" under International Law. It does not engage in the type of relations that fall within the realm of International Law. This limitation may seem surprising, given the following facts. Until the 1990s, when its defense industry was adversely affected by military cutbacks, California had the world's seventh-largest economy. Its legislature declared in State Senate Bill 1909 that the expansion of international trade was vital to the overall growth of California's economy. California thereby established the California Trade and Commerce Agency in 1993, because current state efforts to develop relations with foreign countries are insufficient for effective coordination and mobilization of the resources necessary to promote economic growth and trade. The state's population (more than 30 million) and geographic size dwarf many nations of the world.

Only the national government of the US engages in the kind of foreign relations that are of concern to International Law. No state of the United States may enter into a treaty—a limitation expressly recognized under national law. Nor may the states located on the world's second-longest international border (some 2,000 miles with Mexico) impose either import or export duties on goods from Mexico or other nations (unless absolutely necessary for inspection purposes), without the consent of the US Congress.[7]

Under the internal law of some countries, the national government may even dismiss the state governments of lesser political entities within the country. In December 1992, for example, India's federal government dealt with Hindu militants by disbanding the state governments of three of India's northern states. The New Delhi national government then instituted its own rule in those states. A week before, a fourth state government was similarly ousted from power after rampaging mobs of Hindu militants razed a sixteenth-century mosque in the town of Ayodhya. This incident falls within the province of national rather than International Law. It would be quite a different matter, however, if the national government of South Africa ousted the government of the country of Lesotho, which is totally contained within South Africa's borders. Lesotho gained its independence (from Great Britain) in 1966, the year it also gained admission into the UN as a member nation. South Africa would thereby violate the territorial sovereignty of Lesotho if the government in Johannesburg suddenly decided to oust the government of Lesotho, thereby breaching the latter's sovereign status as an independent State.

◆ 2.2 CHANGING INFRASTRUCTURE

Earlier sections of this book introduced the fundamentals regarding the development, change, and application of International Law. This section offers a significant variable. A dramatic change has occurred in the makeup of the community of nations in a comparatively short period of time. The contemporary rules of modern International Law were developed over a span of approximately three centuries by a comparatively homogenous group of nations. Any symmetry among the principal actors—States that were initially the only infrastructure for International Law in the period immediately after World War II—has dissipated.

The genealogy of modern International Law is essentially European (*see* §1.3 on the History of International Law). Holland's Professor J. H. Verzijl emphatically noted in 1955 that "there is one truth that is not open to denial or even to doubt, namely, that the actual body of international law, as it stands today, is not only the product of the conscious activity of the European mind, but has also drawn its vital essence from a common source of European beliefs, and in both of these aspects it is mainly of Western European origin."[8]

This European essence of International Law is exemplified by the meetings of European nations in the nineteenth century. The 1815 Congress of Vienna established the Concert of Europe. That group of nations exercised what its members believed to be their manifest right to deny the *de jure* existence of certain nations without regard to their obvious *de facto* existence. The Berlin Congress of 1885, referred to as the West Africa Conference, decided that the African continent was sufficiently uncivilized—warranting its colonization in the best interests of all nations. In a valiant gesture, this conference of European powers deemed slavery abolished because of its origins, which violated the laws of nature. Their real reason for the abolition, however, was "prompted by [a] shortage of workforce[s] on the Western Coast of Africa, depopulated by the three-centuries-long export trade of slave labor to North and South America."[9]

Predictably, this Western-derived basis for International Law has been criticized by modern scholars from both Western and non-Western nations. Queen's University (Ireland) Professor George Alexandrowicz characterized this European essence of International Law as being unacceptably ethnocentric. In his view, "Asian States, who for centuries had been considered members of the family of nations, found themselves in an *ad hoc* created legal vacuum which reduced them from the status of international personality [statehood] to the status of candidates competing for such personality."[10]

In 1945, the sovereign nations of the world gathered at San Francisco to develop an agreement to set the basic parameters for future international relations. Those fifty nations incorporated what they deemed to be the appropriate political, social, economic, and humanitarian purposes into their agreement called the United Nations Charter. Since then, this community has nearly quadrupled in size to approximately 190 States, most of whom are UN members. The "charter" members no longer exercise the degree of control they enjoyed at inception, when five of them were able to "call the shots" as the permanent, nonrotating members of the Security Council—China (now the mainland People's Republic), the Soviet Union (now Russia), Great Britain, France, and the United States.

To better understand the nature of contemporary international legal process, one must acknowledge the drastic change wrought by the increase in this growing State infrastructure of the International Law system. The most influential participants in the conduct of world affairs at the close of World War II were nations with comparatively homogenous economic, political, and cultural outlooks. Most were in the Western Hemisphere or directly aligned with Western nations. A number of them had one or more colonies throughout the world at that time. Then came additions to the so-called global village, which were not mere changes in numbers. Major changes emerged with the decolonization movement of the 1960s and the demise of the Soviet Union in the 1990s.

Today, most of those colonies are independent nations. They became members of the United Nations. Admission to that body, which was flooded with applications in the 1960s after independence from the original colonizing members of the UN, provided a significant validation for these new admittees. The hoisting of their national flags at the UN, and in nations where they could afford to maintain embassies or consulates, signaled their participation in the community of nations.

Significant differences exist within that community today. Departure from the colonial status of an earlier era did not necessarily improve their economic, military, and political vitality. The UN membership now consists of radically different cultures, ideologies, and economic perspectives. This is one of the underlying reasons why, during the Reagan years, the US began to withdraw from various UN organs—including the International Court of Justice and UNESCO—UN Educational and Cultural Organization—because of the declining clout exercisable by the US, as host country, over UN affairs. The progressive development of International Law is of course affected by these differences. A comparison of Western European and Asian–African attitudes, for example, readily illustrates that the State structure of the international community is not as homogenous as it was during the centuries when its norms were being cultivated by a much smaller group of more similarly oriented nations.

One result of the induction of former colonies into the community of nations was their irrepressible consensus that colonial rule is a form of aggression to be challenged with force, if necessary, as an act of self-defense. However, the language of the UN Charter, drafted by the former colonial powers, permitted the use of force in self-defense—and only if an "armed" attack occurred against a UN member.[11] Some perceive this Charter provision as another ethnocentric limitation of International Law, imposed by the colonial pow-

New States receive one form of international recognition through admission to the UN. Here, the flags of Bangladesh, Grenada, and Guinea-Bisseau are raised for the first time at the UN Headquarters in New York City on September 18, 1974—one day after their admission as UN member States.

ers as a new means of maintaining the status quo after the decolonization of Africa in the 1960s.

The economic perspectives of these comparatively new States (former colonies) have affected the underlying structure of International Law. These lesser developed States want to redistribute the global resources, improve the living conditions of their peoples, and obtain greater equality. During the 1974–1982 UN Law of the Sea Treaty negotiations, for example, the less powerful nations of the world established, in principle, a primary economic goal. This treaty calls for "the equitable sharing of financial and other economic benefits" derived from an area encompassing about ninety percent of the natural resources of the oceans (Chapter 6, Range of Sovereignty). The economically dominant nations disagree with the principle of an equitable distribution of ocean resources. The more powerful seagoing nations refused to ratify the treaty, although it was acceptable in principle to most nations of the world. The US Reagan administration, for example, then feared that this redistribution motif would unfairly deprive the US of technical know-how and the traditional freedom to exploit global oceanic resources in the name of freedom of the seas. The more established members of the world community have spent a great deal of money on ocean fishing and mining development since World War II. Under the traditional application of International Law, wealthier nations are not required to share their economic gains from such activities with lesser developed nations.

This underlying difference in the economic perspectives of the more developed and lesser developed States is expressed in the so-called New International Economic Order (NIEO). International Law has traditionally prohibited a governmental taking of the property of a foreign citizen or business entity without compensation. The developed nations have historically claimed a

EXHIBIT 2.1 RENOVATED STATE INFRASTRUCTURE SINCE 1945

UN MEMBERS	AMERICAS		EUROPE		ASIA & OCEANIA		AFRICA	
1945 ORIGINAL MEMBERS	Argentina	Guatemala	Belgium	Turkey	Australia	Iraq	Egypt	South Africa
	Bolivia	Haiti	Belorussia	Ukraine	China • Taiwan until '71 • PRC now seated	Lebanon	Ethiopia	
	Brazil	Honduras	Czechoslovakia • split '93	USSR • until '91 • now the Russian Federation	India	New Zealand	Liberia	
	Canada	Mexico	Denmark	United Kingdom	Iran	Philippines		
	Chile	Nicaragua	France	Yugoslavia • split '92 • Serbia & Montenegro		Saudi Arabia		
	Colombia	Panama	Greece			Syria		
	Costa Rica	Paraguay	Luxembourg					
	Cuba	Peru	Netherlands					
	Dominican Republic	United States	Norway					
	Ecuador	Uruguay	Poland					
	El Salvador	Venezuela						
1945–1965	Jamaica	Trinidad & Tobago	Albania	Italy	Afghanistan	Kuwait		
			Austria	Malta	Burma • now Myanmar	Laos		
			Bulgaria	Portugal	Cambodia • now Kampuchea	Malaysia		
			Finland	Romania	Cyprus	Maldives		
			Hungary	Spain	Indonesia	Mongolia		
			Iceland	Sweden	Israel	Nepal		
			Ireland		Japan	Pakistan		
					Jordan	Singapore		
						Sri Lanka		
						Thailand		
						Yemen		

EXHIBIT 2.1 RENOVATED STATE INFRASTRUCTURE SINCE 1945 (CONTINUED)

UN MEMBERS	AMERICAS	EUROPE	ASIA & OCEANIA	AFRICA
1965–1985	Antigua & Barbuda; The Bahamas; Barbados; Belize (formerly British Honduras); Dominica; Grenada; Guyana; Saint Kitts and Nevis; Saint Lucia; Saint Vincent and the Grenadines; Suriname	Federal Republic of Germany • until '90 • now Germany; German Democratic Republic • until '90 • now Germany	Bahrain; Bangladesh; Bhutan; Brunei; Fiji; Oman; Papua New Guinea; Qatar; Solomon Islands; United Arab Emirates; Vanuatu; Vietnam; Western Samoa; Yemen	
1985–1999		Andorra; Armenia; Azerbaijan; Bosnia and Herzegovina; Croatia; Czech Republic; Estonia; Germany • including East Berlin and West Berlin; Georgia; Latvia; Liechtenstein; Lithuania; Macedonia; Moldova; Monaco; San Marino; Slovakia; Slovenia	Kazakhstan; Kyrgyzstan; Marshall Islands; Micronesia; North Korea; Palau; South Korea; Tajikistan; Turkmenistan; Uzbekistan	

NON–UN MEMBERS

Kiribati (formerly Gilbert Islands), Nauru, Niue[a], Serbia and Montenegro[b], Switzerland[c], Taiwan, Tonga, Holy See (Vatican City), Western Sahara (sovereignty unresolved), Gaza/West Bank (PLO[d])

[a]free association with New Zealand
[b]remainder of former Yugoslavia—status unresolved
[c]UN Observer Status
[d]UN Observer status, nonvoting GA seat. Table does not include territorial possessions of above-listed States.

Country Studies (C.I.A.) on the World Wide Web: www.odci.gov/cia/publications/factbook/country-frame.html

UN Membership Web site: www.un.org/Overview/unmember.html

right to "prompt, adequate, and effective" compensation when host State nations have taken the property of foreign corporations. But in 1974, the Group of 77 (G-77) nations thus declared their goal of injecting an NIEO into contemporary nationalization practice. The UN General Assembly announced the Declaration on the Establishment of a New International Economic Order and the Charter of Economic Rights and Duties of States.[12]

"G-77" (which quickly grew to 120) thereby professed two essential propositions in these 1974 declarations. First, the "greatest and most significant achievement during the last decades has been the independence from colonial and alien domination of a large number of peoples and nations which has enabled them [G-77] to become members of the community. . . ." Second, the essential orders contained in the NIEO's "new order" include (1) the regulation and supervision of the activities of transnational corporations to ensure the national sovereignty of the countries wherein they operate; and (2) the "active assistance to developing countries by the whole international community, free of any political or military conditions." The colonial requirement of "prompt, adequate, and effective" compensation is no longer consistent with what the international standard should be. Third World States seek the freedom to use their own national laws as the yardstick for resolving *whether* compensation is required under the circumstances of each case. And, *if* compensation is required under the nationalizing State's internal law (rather than International Law), that nation should be free to determine the extent of compensation without external pressures from wealthy nations who cling to historical formulas—like the requirement of paying fair market value for the nationalized property of foreign corporations. The lesser developed members of the UN maintain that this legal domination should cease so that internal law can provide the compensation yardstick, rather than the International Law devised in an era long before they became members of the international community of nations.

These Third World nations now constitute the majority of nations in the UN. They do not, however, control global resources in a way that has netted them the equitable redistribution of wealth sought under the 1974 NIEO. Such nations need to obtain credit and investment from the more powerful nations to expand their lesser developed export markets (discussed further in Chapter 13 on International Economic Relations).

◆ 2.3 CHANGES IN STATE STATUS

Upon achieving international personality within the community of nations, a State's condition may change in a number of ways:

- Two States may join together—East and West Germany joined to become Germany in 1990.
- A State may cease to exist—Kuwait would have been absorbed into Iraq, absent the international response to Iraq's 1990 invasion of Kuwait.
- Groups within a State may secede to create their own State—Bosnia-Herzegovina, Croatia, Macedonia, and Slovenia seceded from the former Yugoslavia during a two-year period beginning in 1992.
- One State may peacefully separate into two States—in 1993, Czechoslovakia divided into the new States of the Czech Republic and Slovakia.
- A former colony may become a part of a State, and then achieve independence—Eritrea became a State in 1993, having previously been part of Ethiopia.

This section addresses the effect of those changes in status that are particularly important in current world affairs: *succession, secession,* and *self-determination.* Each of these paradigms associated with the acquisition of international personality will now be summarized.

SUCCESSION

"Succession" refers to the circumstance where one or more States takes the place of another State. When two States merge, or when one State splits into two or more States, such entities acquire international personality or statehood.

Succession occurs in a variety of circumstances, including breakups and mergers. Contemporary examples include the 1993 split of Czechoslovakia into two States—the Czech Republic and Slovakia. These republics, in their respective territories, succeeded to the territory formerly occupied by the State of Czechoslovakia. This split was referred to as the "velvet divorce" due to the bloodless nature of this particular State's separation into two distinct States. Atypically, this particular breakup was not spawned by civil war or external pressure.

The converse situation is a merger, exemplified by the 1990 merger of the three territories of the Federal Republic of (West) Germany, the (East) German Demo-

> The Constitution of Bosnia and Herzegovina (BH) establishes a federal State . . . while also defining the two Entities (the Republika Srpska and the Federation of BH) and recognizing the citizenship of the two Entities. . . .
>
> The Constitution of the Republika Srpska establishes the Republic of Srpska as the sovereign State of the Bosnian Serb people.
>
> —Partial description of the European Commission for Democracy Through Law Opinion on the Compatibility of the Constitutions of the Federation of Bosnia and Herzegovina and the Republika Srpska, 35 *Int'l Legal Materials* 1567 (1996).

cratic Republic, and the City of Berlin. The legal status of Berlin was never fully resolved, although all issues were laid to rest by the multiparty treaty merging Berlin into the new integrated State of "Germany." This merger was fully agreed to by all the nations having a territorial interest—East Germany, West Germany, France, the (former) Soviet Union, the United Kingdom, and the United States.[13] These entities thereby succeeded to the territory that was once two sovereign States and a special zone, each losing its formerly distinct international legal personality in the process.

Succession may also occur when a State, or a portion of it, is first occupied and then administered by another State. Nazi Germany's puppet State, referred to as Vichy State, ruled in the southern part of France from 1940 to 1942. It subsequently functioned during a shadowy existence for two more years before dissolving in 1944. In 1992, French intellectuals called upon French President Mitterand to break a historical taboo by formally acknowledging that the Vichy regime persecuted French Jews—after a French court dropped charges of crimes against humanity involving a former Vichy police official. Mitterand responded that "the French state was Vichy and not the [French] republic." He sidestepped France's alleged complicity in war crimes by characterizing the Vichy government as an entity separate from the French Republic to the north.

Succession can also result from independence and partition. Contemporary India is an example of both. In 1947, the territory of India achieved full independence. The new State of India replaced the former territory of the same name, which had long been under British control. The Indian territory was split into two distinct States—India and Pakistan. This partition of the former territory of India established two new international States, each with its own international legal personality.

While there are many other succession scenarios,[14] a pervasive legal question lingers about the *effect* of succession under International Law. Under Article 2 of both the 1978 Vienna Convention on Succession of States in Respect of Treaties, and the 1983 Vienna Convention on Succession of States in Respect of State Property, Archives, and Debts, the term *succession* of States "means the replacement of one State by another in the responsibility for the international relations of the territory."[15] However, neither of these treaties ever entered into force. Specifically, what effect does succession have on (1) preexisting treaties, (2) its property or debts, and (3) the nationality of its citizens?

(1) Does the successor State take over the treaty obligations of the succeeded State? The historical view is that a new State commences its career with a clean slate. But global (and even interregional) perspectives are by no means uniform. When the original thirteen colonies obtained their independence from Great Britain in 1776, the newly formed "United States" began its existence with a clean slate—free from the obligations incurred by any prior treaties regarding the territory occupied by these colonies. The former Spanish colonies of South America likewise began statehood with a clean slate. When Colombia separated from Spain in 1823, however, the US position was that Colombia remained bound by Spain's prior treaty commitments, which had been incurred on behalf of its territory of Colombia. Then, in 1840, when the Texas territory gained independence from Mexico, the US likewise declared that all US treaty commitments with Mexico regarding Texas remained in effect.[16]

Today, there is no general rule of State succession to prior *bilateral* treaty obligations that are purely "political," as opposed to those that are less political in nature. Political treaties include the international alliances and neutrality arrangements of the predecessor State. Such treaties cease to exist when the State that concluded them ceases to exist. They specifically depend upon and assume the existence of the contracting State, and no longer function when that State dissolves. Although there is some disagreement, *non*-political treaties concluded by an extinct predecessor State, such as those involving commerce and extradition, generally fail to survive extinction. Yet the same treaties are likely to survive the succession, where two or more States agree to *unify*. When Nazi Germany absorbed Austria into Germany, the commerce treaties of the former State of Austria would not bind the successor German State. Yet commerce treaties of the former East and West Germanies would bind today's successor State of unified Germany.

Multilateral treaties ratified by the predecessor State, containing norms that have been adopted by many nations, survive succession. The successor State cannot claim a "clean slate" to avoid humanitarian treatment of the citizens of the predecessor State, when such treatment is the subject of a multilateral treaty to which only the predecessor is a party. This liability of the new or succeeding State is already rooted in norms of Customary International Law existing independently of the treaty, even where the succeeding State has not become a treaty party to that multilateral treaty.[17]

(2) Does the successor State take over the property and debts of the succeeded State? The property *and* the debts of an extinct State normally become the property of the successor State. The public international debts of an extinct State are the common illustration. The successor State is expected to absorb both the benefits and the burdens sustained by the former State.

An exception is often claimed when the debts of the succeeded State are contrary to the basic political interests of the successor State. International arbitrators have adopted the view that a successor State cannot be expected to succeed to such debts when they are repugnant to the fundamental interests of the succeeding State. When Yugoslavia reclaimed the territory of the "Independent Croatian State," an unrecognized puppet regime established on Yugoslavian territory during World War II, the successor State of Yugoslavia did not have to assume the debts of the former unrecognized fascist administration.[18]

The 1983 Vienna Convention on Succession of States in Respect of State Property, Archives, and Debts addressed this question, although it has not yet received sufficient ratifications to enter into force. The successor State is entitled to the property of the former State. Succession does not extinguish obligations, however, that are owed by the former State to public or private creditors. The Succession treaty provides that succession "does not as such affect the rights . . . of creditors."[19]

(3) Must the successor State provide its citizenship to the citizens of the succeeded State? When a State ceases to exist, so does the citizenship that it has previously conferred on its inhabitants. The former citizens of the extinct State must then look to the internal law of the successor State for new citizenship. This is generally a matter of internal rather than International Law. Yet international practice does suggest that the new State confer its citizenship on those who were citizens of the succeeded State, based on their habitual residence. On the other hand, the new State may not *force* its citizenship on individuals within what has become a subjugated State. This would preclude Israel, for example, from imposing its citizenship on people within the occupied territories it has acquired as a result of various wars.[20]

Succession of Governments Unlike the possible avoidance of obligations when a new State comes into existence, a new *government* may not claim a "clean slate." Otherwise, the stability of international relations would be significantly undermined if questions of succession to obligations arose every time a new government assumed power. International Law theory provides further support for the view that new governments cannot avoid international obligations because a "government" is not an international person.

SECESSION

While *succession* involves the takeover of another State's territory, *secession* is the severing of one portion of a State for the typical purpose of achieving independent statehood. Modern examples of secession arose in India and Yugoslavia. When Great Britain's rule over India ended in 1947 (during a general British withdrawal from Asia), Pakistan was created by partitioning part of India's northeastern territory. This partitioned State was intended to be a Muslim enclave, as orchestrated by the All-India Muslim League. Then in 1971, Bangladesh separated from Pakistan. This secession was rooted in Pakistan's attempt to base its national identity on religious grounds. In Yugoslavia, conflicts previously suppressed by the Cold War erupted in the 1990s. After the Soviet Union dissolved, ethnic conflict and resurging nationalism spawned the breakup of the former Yugoslavia into five separate States.

Some observers have characterized the contemporary rash of secessionist movements as a rather dangerous phenomenon. As aptly characterized by the University of Arizona's Philosophy Professor Allen Buchanan, "[if] each ethnic group, each 'people,' is entitled to its own state, then it [secession movements] is a recipe for virtually limitless upheaval, an exhortation to break apart the vast majority of existing states, given that most [States] if not all began as empires and include a plurality of ethnic groups or peoples within their present boundaries. . . . Secession can shatter old alliances . . . tip balances of power, create refugee populations, and disrupt international commerce. It can also result in a great loss of human life. And regardless of whether it acts or refrains from acting, each state takes a stand on each secessionist movement—if only by recognizing or not recognizing the independence of the seceding group."[21]

As with the prior *succession* (takeover) analysis, questions of continuing obligations may also arise after a *secession*. For example, had the Confederacy won the American Civil War of the 1860s, it is not clear whether the South would have retained the international obligations for its portion of the US. Prior to the end of World War II, international practice clearly supported the rule that a new State (seceding from another) could begin its existence without any restraints imposed by the treaty commitments of the State from which it seceded. After secession, the State from which another has seceded continues to be bound by its own existing treaty commitments that do not depend on the continued existence of the State that has seceded.

Since World War II, the unequivocal rule—authorizing a fresh start for seceding States—became somewhat equivocal. New States that have seceded from others still enjoy a "clean slate," but not as to those treaties creating law intended to bind all States. Humanitarian treaties are the prime example. These normally codify the existing customary practice of States. When Pakistan separated from India in 1947, it acknowledged a continuing obligation to remain a party to the 1921 Convention for the Suppression of Traffic in Women and Children. Pakistan's recognition of this obligation was specifically premised on India's acceptance of the 1921 treaty, when the Pakistani territory was still a part of India.[22]

SELF-DETERMINATION

> A fortnight ago, the FRY [Federal Republic of Yugoslavia], . . . Serb delegation, and the Kosovar delegation, summoned by the [NATO] Contact Group to meet, agreed to come to Rambouillet. The aim of these negotiations was to reach an interim agreement on substantial autonomy for Kosovo while respecting the FRY's national sovereignty and territorial integrity. The purpose was to allow the inhabitants of Kosovo to live again in peace. . . .
>
> Ministers recalled that they had [spelled] out in London on 29 January and [in] Paris on 14 February that those responsible for the failure of the talks would be held accountable.
>
> —Conclusions of The Contact Group, Rambouillet, France (February 20, 1999). *See* www.france.diplomatie.fr/actual/evenements/ramb30.gb.html.

Of the various modes of altering a territory's status, self-determination may be the least understood and most important. *Self-determination* is a people's right to choose how they will organize and be governed. They might not prefer self-governance; or, alternatively, they may opt for some form of autonomy that may or may not be statehood. Puerto Rico has been a part of the US for 100 years. Its people have not chosen to become an independent sovereign, nor have they chosen to become a state within the federated system of states within the US. If a majority of the people were to prefer complete independence from the US—much like the people of Canada's Quebec province have almost voted to do—then they would not be enjoying their right of self-determination.

Contemporary examples of claims that self-determination has been denied include those of the Palestinians and Russia's Chechens. The Palestinians living in several nations of the Middle East have claimed the right of self-determination over "Palestine" since the UN partition plan of 1947—which would have created a Palestinian State (in addition to Israel). The struggle of the inhabitants of Russia's predominantly Muslim region of Chechnya for full autonomy dates back to A.D. 965. During World War II, Stalin deported thousands of this area's inhabitants to Central Asia. In December 1994, a remarkable 40-mile human chain of 100,000 people protested Russia's continuing military assault on Chechnya.

The original *raison d'être* of self-determination dialogue was the decolonization of States, particularly on the African continent. One of the classic examples was the situation in Namibia—formerly called South-West Africa. It was controlled by South Africa, originating with a League of Nations mandate. South Africa refused to comply with various UN resolutions demanding that South Africa relinquish its control of South-West Africa. Ultimately, after seventy-four years of domination and a blistering decision from the International Court of Justice (ICJ),[23] South-West Africa finally achieved its own sovereign identity and was admitted to the UN as the nation of Namibia in 1990. The regional achievement of self-determination, through the decolonization movement of the 1960s, is graphically illustrated in Exhibit 2.1 (§2.2). It features the large number of States that were former colonies prior to the 1960s, which surpassed the number of States who were original members of the UN.

Another contemporary example of self-determination arose in the context of the Baltic States, which were overtaken by the Soviet Union in the 1940s. In February 1991, Estonians, Latvians, and Lithuanians voted to set themselves free from this domination by the Soviet Union. The takeover of the Baltic States remained unrecognized by many other States in spite of *de facto* Soviet control of the Baltics. Soviet President Gorbachev declared these votes "illegal" and dispatched orders to Soviet troops to increase army patrols in order to "maintain the civil order." After twenty deaths—and the European Union's withholding of $1 billion in food aid to the Soviet Union to protest the Soviet handling of the Baltics—the Kremlin withdrew its special troops in an effort to diffuse the confrontation over the Baltic right of self-determination. The European Union soon recognized the Baltics as independent States. In an official statement, the EU noted that it "warmly welcome[d] the restoration of sovereignty and independence of the Baltic states which they lost in 1940 [when Stalin annexed them into the Soviet Union]."

In 1992, the Canadian government signed an accord with Eskimo leaders to create a native-run territory in Canada's Northwest Territories to be called Nunavut. The agreement called for the establishment of Nunavut, with the Nunavut government gradually assuming greater power in that portion of Canada. The Arctic Eskimos ratified a land claim agreement via a referendum, which in turn resulted in the Canadian government's passing legislation establishing Nunavut in 1999.

The UN Charter serves as an explicit rallying point for the modern evolution of the law of self-determination. Article 1.2 of the Charter provides that one of the UN's essential purposes is "respect for the principle of equal rights and self-determination of peoples. . . ." The cornerstone, however, is the Article 73 Declaration Regarding Non-Self-Governing Territories: "Members of the United Nations [that] have or [will] assume responsibilities for the administration of territories whose peoples have not yet attained a full measure of self-government recognize the principle that the interests of the inhabitants of these territories are paramount, and accept as a sacred trust the obligation to promote to the utmost . . . the well-being of the inhabitants of these territories. . . ."

A key UN development surfaced in 1960, in the midst of the movement to decolonize the many territories controlled by the original members. In Resolution 1514(XV), the General Assembly proclaimed—over objections by Western nations—that the "subjection of peoples to alien subjugation . . . constitutes a denial of fundamental human rights, is contrary to the Charter of the United Nations . . . [because all] peoples have the right to self-determination . . . [and any inadequacy] of political, economic, social or educational preparedness should never serve as a pretext for delaying independence." That resolution also provides that:

> 2. All peoples have the right to self-determination; by virtue of that right they freely determine their political status and freely pursue their economic, social and cultural development. . . .
> 5. Immediate steps shall be taken, in Trust and Non-Self-Governing Territories or all other territories which have not yet attained independence, to transfer all powers to the peoples of those territories, without any conditions or reservations, in accordance with their freely expressed will and desire, without any distinction as to race, creed or colour, in order to enable them to enjoy complete independence and freedom.

Another General Assembly Resolution, 1541, further contemplated that non-self-governing territories might enjoy several possible outcomes in the quest for self-determination: (a) emergence as a sovereign independent State; or (b) free association with an independent State; or (c) integration with an independent State. Principle IX of that resolution declared that any "integration should be the result of the freely expressed wishes of the territory's peoples acting with full knowledge of the change in their status, their wishes having been expressed through informed and democratic processes, impartially conducted and based on universal adult suffrage. The United Nations could, when it deems it necessary, supervise these processes." The subsequent Declaration on Principles of International Law Concerning Friendly Relations and Cooperation Among States in Accordance with the Charter of the United Nations (Resolution 2625 [XXV]) added that:

> The establishment of a sovereign and independent State, the free association or integration with an independent State or the emergence into any other political status freely determined by a people constitute modes of implementing the right of self-determination by that people. . . . Every State has the duty to promote, through joint and separate action, realization of the principle of equal rights and self-determination of peoples in accordance with the provisions of the Charter, and to render assistance to the United Nations in carrying out the responsibilities entrusted to it by the Charter regarding the implementation of the principle.

As the decolonization movement of the 1960s shifted from rhetoric to reality, the rather general right of self-determination was further refined. Article 1.1 of both the 1966 International Covenant on Civil and Political Rights and the 1966 International Covenant on Economic, Social, and Cultural Rights was the next building block. It provides that "[a]ll peoples have the right of self-determination. By virtue of that right they freely determine their political status and freely pursue their economic, social and cultural development." While the General Assembly approved these covenants with near unanimity, certain Western powers maintained their reservations about the so-called right of self-determination. This document exemplified the shift in self-determination focus from "States" to "peoples."[24]

Now that UN diplomatic endeavors pointed in the direction of a State practice favoring the right of self-determination, the International Court of Justice (ICJ) was ready to assess the parameters of this right. In 1975, a legal controversy about the Western Sahara arose in the General Assembly, where it had lingered from 1966 to 1974. Due to the inertia of failing to implement prior resolutions on *Western Sahara,* the UN General Assembly requested an advisory opinion from the ICJ. Members of the Assembly thereby hoped to advance the right of the disputed area's peoples to self-determination. The General Assembly had previously resolved that the inhabitants possessed a right to self-determination, specifically finding that there should be a referendum conducted so that they could vote to determine the status of Western Sahara. The general right to self-determination was being politically foiled by the maintenance of the colonial status of Western Sahara—also referred to as Spanish Sahara under Spain's claim via colonization of the territory (in 1884), long before this particular dispute arose between Mauritania and Morocco. The Western Sahara was a Spanish protectorate from 1912 to 1976. After Morocco became a member of the UN in 1960, it claimed Western Sahara as a part of its national territory. The neighboring claimant Mauritania was prepared to acquiesce to the will of the peoples of Western Sahara. It did not wish to confront Spain with a direct legal claim—unlike Morocco, which was far more possessive.

The possibility of submitting this case to the Court was then pressed in the General Assembly by Morocco ". . . in order to guide the United Nations towards a final solution of the problem of Western Sahara. . . ." The disclosed purpose of a judicial analysis was to provide an authoritative analysis to the General Assembly. The Court's task was to determine the presence of any legal claims to this territory by the various nations involved—which might interfere or compete with the inhabitants' right to exercise their right to self-determination. Morocco argued that it had established ties of sovereignty over Western Sahara, under Islamic legal concepts of sovereignty, in effect at the time of its Spanish colonization. Morocco attempted to persuade the ICJ that the people of Western Sahara owed religious allegiance to the Sultan of Morocco—effectively resulting in a religious allegiance that amounted to territorial sovereignty.[25] In its advisory opinion, the ICJ concluded that "the Court has not found legal ties of such a nature as might affect the application of resolution 1514 (XV) in the decolonization of Western Sahara and, in particular, of the principle of self-determination through the free and genuine expression of the will of the peoples of the Territory."[26]

After this case was considered by the Court in 1975, Western Sahara was partitioned between Mauritania and Morocco. The Spanish army departed in 1976, based on an agreement reached the year before. Morocco and Mauritania took over this territory. An indigenous liberation movement protested the 1975 partition agreement, however. In 1979, Mauritania ceded its portion of Western Sahara, and Moroccan troops took over. There has been no referendum of the inhabitants. Control over the territory remains politically unsettled, due to hostilities between the Moroccan government and the indigenous liberation front. A UN-administered cease-fire between independence-oriented guerrillas and territorial authorities has been in effect since September 1991. In summer 1998, a UN mediator secretly met with Indonesian authorities, separatist guerillas, and other members of the local population; however, a promised referendum has not yet occurred.

The self-determination case arising in both a contentious and more clearly defined context (rather than being an advisory opinion with no State parties ro sharpen the issues in such a case) was the *East Timor* case:

◆

Case Concerning East Timor

(Portugal v. Australia)

International Court of Justice

June 30, 1995

General List No. 84

1995 *ICJ* 90 (1995)

Go to course Web page at

http://home.att.net/~slomansonb/txtcsesite.html

Click on Case Concerning East Timor

◆ *Notes & Questions*

1. What is the source of the right of self-determination of the people of East Timor, as claimed by Portugal?
2. What was the reason(s) for Portugal not joining Indonesia as a party to this suit?
3. Did the ICJ effectively ignore the eight UN Security Council and General Assembly resolutions regarding East Timor's right to self-determination?
4. Did the ICJ properly dismiss this case, even if it appeared to pay only lip service to the principle of "self-determination"?
5. How should the Court have ruled—or, was it correct in dismissing this case? Did the Court really do no more than dodge the issues, because Indonesia would not honor any judicial affirmation of the right of self-determination? Was this the real reason for Judge Oda's lengthy concurring opinion?
6. In June 1998, Indonesia's president offered residents of this territory a special status, whereby East Timor's culture and religion would be recognized, although Indonesia would retain political control. While it was not considered a serious gesture, it did signal willingness by Indonesia to improve the situation in its "27th province." In August 1998, Indonesia and Portugal announced an agreement on broad outlines of an autonomy plan for East Timor. The inhabitants would have local self-government and control of educational and cultural affairs. Indonesia would keep control over foreign, military, and monetary affairs. Indonesia did not answer the question, however, whether it thus intended to alter its position on absolute sovereignty over East Timor. Further analysis is available in G. Gunn, *East Timor and the United Nations: The Case for Intervention* (Patchogue, NY: Red Sea Press, 1997). Australia is the only Western nation to recognize Indonesian sovereignty over East Timor.

   In 1999, Indonesia and Portugal agreed that the residents of East Timor should choose between greater autonomy and independence. Shortly thereafter, anti-independence militiamen massacred twenty-five people in a Catholic churchyard after they had sought refuge from Indonesian forces.
7. On August 20, 1998, the Canadian Supreme Court articulated the following limitation on self-determination, summarized in paragraphs 123 and 138 of its opinion (italics added):

   > **123** International law grants the right to self-determination to "peoples." Accordingly, access to the right requires the threshold step of characterizing as a people the group seeking self-determination. However, as the right to self-determination has developed by virtue of a combination of international agreements and conventions, coupled with state practice, with little formal elaboration of the definition of "peoples," the

result has been that the precise meaning of the term "peoples" remains somewhat uncertain.

138 In summary, the international law right to self-determination only generates, at best, a right to *external* self-determination in situations of former colonies; where a *people* is oppressed, as for example under foreign military occupation; or where a *definable group* is denied meaningful access to government to pursue their political, economic, social and cultural development. In all three situations, the people in question are entitled to a right to external self-determination because they have been denied the ability to exert internally their right to self-determination. Such exceptional circumstances are manifestly inapplicable to Quebec under existing conditions. Accordingly, neither the population of the province of Quebec, even if characterized in terms of "people" or "peoples," nor its representative institutions, the National Assembly, the legislature or government of Quebec, possess a right, under international law, to secede unilaterally from Canada.

IN THE MATTER OF a Reference by the Governor in Council concerning certain questions relating to the secession of Quebec from Canada, available on the World Wide Web at:

www.droit.umontreal.ca/doc/csc-scc/en/pub/1998/vol2/html/1998scr2_0217.html

Has the Canadian Supreme Court inserted a limit not recognized by the ICJ in its *East Timor* case? Does the *East Timor* decision *exclude* this possible limitation in International Law? Further reading is available in "The Holders of the Right to Self-Determination and the Means of Ensuring Observance of the Right," ch. 6 in A. Cassese, *Self-Determination of Peoples: A Legal Reappraisal* 141 (Cambridge, Eng.: Cambridge Univ. Press, 1995).

◆ 2.4 RECOGNITION

There are several categories of recognition. The materials in this section deal with recognition by individual States and collective recognition by groups of States or international organizations.

RECOGNITION BY STATES

Introduction The first of the three common State recognition decisions involves the potential recognition of another State. There has been a vast increase in the number of States, particularly during the decolonization movement of the 1960s and the end of the Cold War (*see* Exhibit 2.1 in §2.2). This is the level where most recognition decisions occur.

A second category of recognition decision emerges when State A decides whether or not to continue relations with the new *government* of another State. A change of governments may trigger a host of political concerns in the recognizing State. A prominent example has been the continued US refusal to recognize the Castro regime since its overthrow of the prior government of Cuba in 1959.

A third form of recognition arises when one State decides to recognize a condition of *belligerency* in another State. Belligerents typically seek to overthrow the government of their home State. Other nations may wish to officially recognize a belligerent force or to covertly provide support to the military forces engaged in a civil war within a State. Recognition, whether *de facto* or *de jure,* may then give rise to a neutrality obligation on the part of the recognizing State. It is not supposed to act in a way that will adversely affect the territorial sovereignty of the State encountering the hostilities. In 1981, for example, France and Mexico officially recognized a leftist guerilla movement that had fought for several years against the Colombian Government. By recognizing this national liberation front as a "representative political force in Colombia," those nations also recognized the rebels' right to participate in negotiations to end the Colombian civil war. Then in 1992, the Colombian rebels were invited to Mexico City, where they signed a cease-fire agreement with Colombian leaders.

Writers and jurists have described recognition as one of the most chaotic and theoretically confusing topics in International Law. It is certainly one of the most sensitive and controversial.[27] These descriptions are unfortunately quite accurate: Recognition of another State, or an entity within it, typically involves the mixture of political, military, and international considerations described below. The following materials provide further detail on the conditions for recognition decisions.

Recognition of States Argentina's former Judge of the International Court of Justice aptly describes recognition of a new State as "a unilateral act whereby one or more States admit, whether expressly or tacitly, that they regard the . . . political entity as a State; consequently, they also admit that the . . . entity is an international legal personality, and as such is capable of acquiring international rights and contracting international obligations."[28]

Receiving recognition is a significant political goal for new States. Their leaders desire equality of status with the other members of the international community. Statehood, and the resulting recognition decision by other States, enables new States to engage in international relations. Recognition is a minimum requirement that, much like needing "two jacks or better to open" in a poker hand, elevates a new player to an enhanced stake in the game. Russia, for example, was keenly interested in the international recognition of its new republic—formed as a new commonwealth after a forty-year Cold War that stagnated its economy and embroiled it in adverse relations with democratic systems. The US recognized Russia (and a number of other members of the former Soviet Union) almost immediately after creation of the Commonwealth of Independent States in 1991. The US delayed recognition of Ukraine, on the other hand, until it was clear to the US that Ukraine could function in harmony with the same Russia that had dominated Ukraine for nearly 600 years.

A new State may be recognized almost immediately, or in some cases, years after it is formed. The very existence of the German Democratic Republic (formerly East Germany) was considered a breach of the Soviet Union's duties under its post–World War II treaties with the Allied powers regarding the administration of German territory. It was obviously a "State," in terms of its *de facto* status (*see* §2.1 on Legal Personality of the State). Many Western nations did not recognize East Germany's *de jure* existence, however, until 1973. A series of unilateral recognitions cured what they had initially perceived as an illegal State regime.

There may also be delayed *de jure* recognition of a *de jure* State recognized by many other States. The Vatican did not recognize the State of Israel until 1994, forty-five years after Israel was admitted to the UN as a member State. The Vatican's recognition, not undertaken until after the Israel–PLO accords of 1993, was premised on many centuries of distrust between Catholics and Jews. The week before this recognition occurred, Israel's largest-selling newspaper *(Yedioth Ahronoth)* stated: "The Catholic Church is one of the most conservative, oppressive, corrupt organizations in all human history. . . . The reconciliation can be done only if the Catholic Church and the one who heads it fall on their knees and ask forgiveness from the souls of the millions of tortured who went to heaven in black smoke, under the blessing of the Holy See." This news account was referring to the Catholic Church's Inquisition of the Middle Ages and the World War II Holocaust—whereby many Israelis believe that the Catholic Church did nothing to halt, or even clandestinely supported, Nazi Germany's appalling treatment of Europe's Jews.

De jure recognition may be prematurely granted. The European Community (now European Union, or "EU") recognized Slovenia and Croatia approximately six months after their vote of independence from the former Yugoslavia—an arguably premature decision that many consider to be the spark that fueled the fires between ethnic rivals in the former Yugoslavia. Recognition of Bosnia-Herzegovina was arguably premature. The Russian newspaper *Pravda* reported in its February 27, 1993, issue that the "international carnage has been largely caused by the hasty recognition [by countries including Russia] of the independence of the unstable state of Bosnia and Herzegovina." This perspective is based on the fact that Bosnia-Herzegovina was not in control of its territory during the flurry of international recognitions descending on it shortly after its secession from the former Yugoslavia.

The Yugoslavian government in Belgrade immediately protested that the EU's allegedly premature recognition of former territories of Yugoslavia violated International Law. Belgrade claimed that the virtually immediate international recognition by other countries violated Yugoslavia's territorial sovereignty over its secessionist regions. One can readily argue that there was no *de facto* basis for recognition by other countries (of Bosnia-Herzegovina), given the lack of control exercised over the territory and populace by the new Bosnian government. However, the political nature of recognition decisions suggests that Yugoslavia's claim of premature recognition did *not* trigger any State responsibility for harm to Yugoslavia.

Recognition decisions are granted or denied for a variety of reasons. Since the recognizing State is usually satisfied that the *legal* elements of statehood are present, the essential decision of whether to recognize another State has been traditionally quite *political* in nature. Examples include: (1) whether the new State has been recognized by other members of the international community; (2) ethnocentric motives stemming from the perceived inferiority of certain nations—effectively limiting the recognition of new States from outside the European community for a number of centuries; (3) a need to appease certain regimes—as when England recognized the nineteenth-century Barbary Coast, whose pirates were stealing British ships and cargoes; (4) humanitarian motives—many states refused to recognize Southern Rhodesia (now Zimbabwe) because of its internal racial policies; and (5) commercial and military motives.[29] For example, Cuba achieved its independence as a result of the Spanish-American War. The US then conditioned its 1903 recognition of Cuba on the demand that Cuba lease the Guantanamo Naval Base to the US. This base has been quite important to the political, military, and security interests of the US ever since (e.g., the 1962 Cuban Missile Crisis and the 1994 Haitian "invasion" staging area for US troops).

There are two theories of recognition discourse: the *constitutive* theory and the *declaratory* theory. Under the constitutive perception, members of the community of nations *must* recognize a new State in order to constitute or establish its *de jure* international legal personality. The declaratory view, on the other hand, is that recognition is *not* required for the new State to be considered legitimate. Recognition merely declares or acknowledges the existing fact of statehood.

Although the constitutive theory is still advocated by some States and scholars (requiring sufficient recognition for *de jure* statehood),[30] recognition is not generally required as a condition for statehood under International Law. Recognition is a matter of political decision making at the international level. Other States have no duty to recognize a new State merely because it possesses all the *legal* attributes of statehood. Recognition is, instead, a matter of discretion involving a *political* act with some legal consequences as discussed below. The former Yugoslavia is as much a State as its former region of Bosnia-Herzegovina, now recognized by many countries. That they decided *not* to recognize the Yugoslavian "rump" State did not breach any international obligation to the remaining Yugoslavian State.

The prevailing declaratory theory is manifested in regional treaties that specifically negate recognition as an element of the definition of statehood. Less powerful States do not want recognition decisions to influence their political goals. They do not want larger States to use recognition as a ploy to exact political concessions. Under Article 12 of the Charter of the Organization of American States, for example, the "political existence of the State is independent of recognition by other States. Even before being recognized, the State has the right to defend its integrity and independence, to provide for its prosperity, and consequently to organize itself as it sees fit. . . . The exercise of these rights is limited only by the exercise of rights of other States in accordance with international law."

Recognition of Governments The recognition of a new State may effectively include recognition of the government. Other States often reconsider prior recognition decisions when the government of an existing State changes, especially when there has been an unconstitutional change in government such as a coup d'etat in a former republic. When comparing the recognition of a State versus its government, one might make the analogy with a tree and the leaves that it drops from time to time. The tree is the State. The leaves are various governments. While governments (or forms of government) may come and go, the tree remains. Sometimes, another State may choose not to recognize either the tree or the leaf it bears; other times, that same State may decide only to withdraw recognition of the particular government.[31]

Recognition of new governments may be lawfully withheld or withdrawn. Recognizing States are often concerned about whether the populace under a new government has actually acquiesced in the change. In addition, a sudden change in the form of government can present significant economic, political, and military concern to other States. Many states did not recognize the Hanoi-installed Kampuchea government (Cambodia, 1975) because it took power while Prince Sihanouk's UN-recognized government was in exile. The US did not recognize the government imposed by the 1991 military coup in Haiti, occurring after the democratic election of a Haitian leader who was acceptable to the US. After eighteen months, only the Vatican recognized the new Haitian government, arguably premised on the Catholic Church's distaste for the ousted President Aristide—a former Catholic priest.

A number of new governments have reacted adversely to the renewed inquiry associated with recognition of governments. Large and economically dominant States reconsider recognition as a method for exacting new concessions from less powerful States.

While the recognizing State may be merely seeking assurances that prior international obligations will continue to be performed, they may also exact other less desirable concessions. When the new government is openly hostile to the recognizing State, the latter might break diplomatic relations, impose economic sanctions, or build up its military presence in or near the territory of the unrecognized government.

The "Estrada Doctrine" responded to this alleged abuse. This doctrine was named after Genaro Estrada, Mexico's Secretary of Foreign Relations, who introduced it in 1930. Estrada complained that a revolutionary change in government should not permit other countries to reconsider whether a new revolutionary government should be recognized.[32] By adopting the Estrada Doctrine, a number of Latin American nations argued that larger developed nations have misused their power of recognition to undermine new governments—with significant costs to the peoples of the affected countries. New governments perceive this renewed occasion for recognition as a device for treading on their sovereign right to conduct internal and foreign affairs as they deem appropriate. *How* the new government came into existence is not a matter for external recognition decisions by other States.

On the other hand, governments pondering a recognition decision profess a rather principled question about a new government that has usurped democratic processes via its violent overthrow of a democratic regime. In Haiti, the democratically elected leader was overthrown by a military coup in 1991. The rebel leaders in Rwanda massacred hundreds of thousands of people in 1994 when they seized power from the former government. There was a mass exodus of refugees fleeing for their lives due to the indiscriminate machete attacks by rebel forces in Rwanda. States with more democratic and less violent traditions thus tend to avoid international relations with "cutthroat" regimes.

There is an emerging international right to a democratic form of government. The 1991 EU Guidelines on Recognition refer to democracy as a factor in recognition decisions; a 1992 Organization of American States resolution demanded Haiti's return to democracy; and scholarly studies all support this developing attitude.[33] When there has been a bloody violation of that perceived right, a *failure* to reconsider recognition involves a moral dilemma. To what degree does the international community of nations, by turning its head the other way, acquiesce in the continued operation of a new government that is carrying out mass executions of innocent civilians?

If recognition is a matter for political decision makers, then what is the *legal* impact of recognition? A new government can face difficult legal barriers when it is not recognized by a particular country or the community of nations. An unrecognized government may not be able to effectively represent its interests elsewhere. For example, the unrecognized government and its citizens usually do not have access to the courts of the non-recognizing State. Such governments must endure the fiscal or political consequences of non-recognition.[34] A classic illustration of these consequences appears in the following case:

Bank of China v. Wells Fargo Bank & Union Trust Co.

UNITED STATES FEDERAL DISTRICT COURT
NORTHERN DISTRICT OF CALIFORNIA, 1952
104 Fed. Supp. 59

Author's Note: *The government-directed Bank of China at Shanghai deposited money into a US bank in San Francisco (Wells Fargo). Mao Tse-Tung subsequently overthrew the government of China in 1949. Wells Fargo then received conflicting demands to the ownership of the deposited money—from what were then the two "Banks of China." One demand was made by the Chinese mainland's new People's Republic of China—as the alleged successor to the government of all of China. The other claimant was the ousted Nationalist Chinese government seated in Formosa (now called Taiwan).*

President Truman announced that the US recognized the Nationalist government in Formosa as the de jure *or legiti-*

mate government for all of China, referring to both Taiwan and mainland China. Judge Goodman of the federal court in San Francisco then had to resolve which Bank of China would receive the nearly $800,000 deposited with the Wells Fargo Bank (prior to Mao's revolutionary takeover of China). The judge explored the rationales for making this decision on several grounds including: statehood, which entity more clearly represented the Chinese people, equitable division of the deposit, and whether recognition by the US executive branch would legally foreclose his ability to decide in favor of what was then the non-recognized mainland government.

Judge Goodman's decision was reversed for reasons unrelated to this portion of the case. His footnotes are omitted.

COURT'S OPINION . . .

The issue before the Court has therefore been reduced to a comparatively narrow one. . . . Which Bank of China is legally entitled to the funds deposited with the defendant Bank?

The controlling corporate authority of the Bank of China is effectively vested in the Government of China by virtue of its majority stock ownership, its dominant voice in the managing directorate, and the supervisory powers accorded by the Articles of Association to the Minister of Finance. A determination of what government, if any, should be recognized by this Court as now entitled to exercise this corporate authority over the deposit in suit, will govern the disposition of these causes.

The issue thus posed focuses attention at the outset on the fact that of the two governments asserting corporate authority, one is recognized by the United States [Nationalist China] while the other is not [the mainland PRC]. If this fact, per se, is determinative, the issue is resolved. If whenever this Court is called upon to determine whether there is a government justly entitled to act on behalf of a foreign state in respect to a particular matter, the Court is bound to say, without regard to the facts before it, that the government recognized by our executive is that government, then nothing more need be said here. To permit this expression of executive policy to usurp entirely the judicial judgment would relieve the Court of a burdensome duty, but it is doubtful that the ends of justice would thus be met. It has been argued that such is the accepted practice. But the authorities do not support this view.

There is, of course, the long line of New York decisions arising out of the nationalization of Russian corporations by the Soviet Government at a time when it was unrecognized by the United States. In those decisions, the New York courts stated time and again that no effect would be given to the acts of the unrecognized Soviet Government, in so far as property situated in this country was concerned. . . . Such decisions do not bar the way to giving effect to acts of non-recognized governments [however], even in respect to property within our borders, if justice so requires.

Some more recent decisions of the federal courts, involving Soviet nationalization of corporations of the Baltic states, give great weight to the executive policy of non-recognition. But it cannot be said that these decisions establish an all-embracing rule that no extra-territorial effect may ever be given the acts of an unrecognized government.

The [New York] decisions just set forth, as well as others in this field, reveal no rule of law obliging the courts to give conclusive effect to the acts of a recognized government to the exclusion of all consideration of the acts of an opposing unrecognized government. Nor does it appear that such a sweeping rule would be a sound one. . . .

This is not to suggest that the courts should regard executive policy in respect to recognition and non-recognition of foreign governments as meaningless or of little consequence. In any particular situation, executive policy may be crucial, as indeed it appears to be in the present case. But, it is a fact which properly should be considered and weighed along with the other facts before the Court.

Turning to the record in this case, it appears that two governments are governments in fact of portions of the territory of the State of China. The "Peoples" Government has supplanted the "Nationalist" Government in dominion over the entire Chinese Mainland with an area of more than 3,700,000 square miles, and a population of more than 460,000,000. The "Nationalist" Government controls one of the 35 provinces of China, the Island of Formosa, which has an area of 13,885 square miles and a population in excess of 6,000,000. It is obvious that the "Peoples" Government is now the government in fact of by far the greater part of the territory of the Chinese State. Nevertheless the "Nationalist" Government controls substantial territory, exceeding in area that of either Belgium or the Netherlands, and in population that of Denmark or Switzerland.

Each government, in its respective sphere, functions effectively. Each is recognized by a significant number of the nations of the world. Each maintains normal diplomatic intercourse with those nations which extend recognition. This has been the status quo for more than two years.

Each government is in a position to exercise corporate authority on behalf of the Bank of China. That is, each government is capable of utilizing the corporate structure and certain corporate assets to promote the corporate purposes. The Bank of China was chartered primarily to facilitate Chinese international commercial activities. . . . Each government is in a position to act through the corporate structure of the Bank of China to carry on these international functions in the areas abroad where such Government is recognized and these domestic functions within the territory such Government controls. Each government is in fact doing so. The Bank of China, as controlled by the Nationalist Government, continues to function on the Island of Formosa and through its foreign branches in the United States, Cuba, Australia, Japan, Indochina, and elsewhere where the Nationalist Government is recognized.

The Peoples Government as successor in fact to the Nationalist Government on the Chinese Mainland is exercising the prerogatives of the Government in respect to the Bank of China there. The Peoples Government has not nationalized the Bank of China, nor confiscated its assets, nor denied the rights of private stockholders. It exercises the authority vested in the Government of China as majority stockholder. The Bank of China continues to function in accordance with its Articles of Association under the guidance of the appointees of the Peoples Government and the majority of the directors previously elected by private stockholders on the Chinese Mainland and through branches in London, Hong Kong, Singapore, Penang, Kuala Lumpur, Batavia, Calcutta, Bombay, Karachi, Chittagong, and Rangoon.

The Nationalist and Peoples Governments have [each] maintained and strengthened their positions. Our national policy toward these governments is now definite. We have taken a stand adverse to the aims and ambitions of the [mainland] Peoples Government. The armed forces of that Government are now engaged in conflict with our forces in Korea. We recognize only the Nationalist Government [located on Formosa] as the representative of the State of China, and are actively assisting in developing its military forces in Formosa. The Bank of China now operates as two corporate entities, each performing within the area of its operations the functions bestowed upon the Bank of China by its Articles of Association. Each Bank of China is in a position to employ the deposit in suit for corporate purposes.

From a practical standpoint, neither of the rival Banks of China is a true embodiment of the corporate entity which made the deposit in the Wells Fargo Bank. The present Nationalist Bank of China is more nearly equivalent in the sense of continuity of management. The Peoples Bank is more representative in ability to deal with the greater number of private stockholders and established depositors and creditors. Were the Court to adopt a strictly pragmatic approach, it might attempt a division of the deposit between these two banks in the degree that each now exercises the functions of the Bank of China. Or the Court might award the entire deposit to the bank it deems to be the closest counterpart of the corporation contemplated by the Articles of Association.

. . . Such a course would ultimately entail determining which bank best serves the corporate interests of the State of China. That determination could not be made, while the State, itself, remains divided, except by an excursion into the realm of political philosophy. . . . Here, there co-exist two governments, in fact, each attempting to further, in its own way, the interests of the State of China, in the Bank of China. It is not a proper function of a domestic court of the United States to attempt to judge which government best represents the interests of the Chinese State in the Bank of China. In this situation, the Court should justly accept, as the representative of the Chinese State, that government which our executive deems best able to further the mutual interests of China and the United States.

Since the Court is of the opinion that it should recognize the Nationalist Government of China as legally entitled to exercise the controlling corporate authority of the Bank of China in respect to the deposit in suit, the motion for [the bank deposit] in favor of the Bank of China, as controlled by the Nationalist Government, is granted.

◆ *Notes & Questions*

1. Assume you are an appellate judge reviewing Judge Goodman's decision in the *Bank of China* case. On the basis of statehood, could you decide which government—the Nationalist Chinese or the Communist Chinese—should receive the deposited money?
2. What were the practical effects of the US President's decision to recognize Formosa's Nationalist government rather than the mainland PRC government?

Recognition of Belligerency That ill-defined situation referred to as a "belligerency" within a State may yield yet another basis for a recognition decision not involving statehood. The belligerent group, while not a State, may nevertheless achieve a degree of legal personality under International Law. Revolutionary groups attempting to seize power in their own country—or a portion of it—may thus be recognized. The recognition may come initially from the existing government in the State of the belligerency or externally from a foreign State.

The recognition of belligerency normally confers certain rights upon the belligerent entity, as well as on the government that opposes the belligerents. As stated by the US Supreme Court, these rights include the "rights of blockade, visitation, search and seizure of contraband articles on the high seas, and abandonment of claims for reparation on account of damages suffered by our citizens from the prevalence of warfare."[35] By blockading the South's Confederate ports, the Union government in the northern states, in effect, recognized that a state of belligerency existed between itself and the Confederacy.

When *another* country is not a party to a dispute between the belligerent forces and the forces of the regular government, it is expected to remain neutral until the belligerency is resolved. England recognized the Confederate States of the United States as "belligerents" when the Civil War between the Northern and the Southern states of the US began in 1861. England did not, however, observe its State duty to remain neutral as required under International Law. Ships for the Confederate South were built in British ports and prepared for war with the Union forces in the US. As a result, the Treaty of Washington of 1871 inaugurated the *Alabama Claims* international arbitration proceedings. Two years later, England paid over $15 million to the US as a consequence of the damages done by five vessels made in England for the belligerent Confederate forces. Ironically, Russian vessels paid port calls to New York and San Francisco in 1863, perceived by many observers as a tacit message that Russia then supported the Union in its quest to defeat the Confederacy. Czarist Russia observed its duty of neutrality because it took no active role in aiding the Union during the Civil War.

The essential elements of this duty to remain neutral are that the neutral State: (1) not take sides to assist either the belligerent or the regular government; (2) not allow its territory to be used as a base for hostilities by the belligerent forces; (3) acquiesce in restrictions imposed by the parties to the dispute if it wishes to remain entitled to respect of neutral State rights; (4) declare any change in status, as when it decides to side with the belligerency or the regular government; and (5) must accept State responsibility under International Law (§2.5) for any violation of its duty of neutrality.[36] Switzerland breached this duty during World War II by providing banking assistance to Germany and sending war materials to Japan. Angola, Rwanda, Uganda, and Zambia failed to remain neutral by providing military aid to rebels who took over some cities in the Congo in 1997.

A good example of a State's attempt to intervene while appearing to preserve its neutrality occurred in 1994 when France announced its intent to conduct a military intervention in Rwanda (a former Belgian colony). There had been a low-intensity conflict between the Rwandan government and the rebel Rwandan Patriotic Front since 1990. The intensity increased in 1994, when the outbreak of civil war caused civilian casualties

> That nevertheless, neither the Emperor, nor any of the States of the Empire, shall meddle with the Wars which are now on foot between them. That if for the future any Dispute arises between these two Kingdoms, the abovesaid reciprocal Obligation of not aiding each others Enemys, shall always continue firm. . . .
>
> —Treaty of Westphalia, Part IV, October 24, 1648, between the Holy Roman Emperor and the King of France and their respective Peace TreatyAllies. *See* course Web site at http://home.att.net/~slomansonb/txtcsesite.html. Click on Westphalia.

in the hundreds of thousands. This conflict also produced a mass exodus, driven by indiscriminate machete attacks on the populace. France advised the rebels that it would intervene for the exclusive humanitarian purpose of ending these massacres. The French Foreign Minister stated in early June 1994: "I want to underline the fact that we are making great efforts to convince the RPF [rebel forces] that this operation is not aimed against them." The rebels feared that France's intervention would thwart their interim successes in trying to overthrow the Rwandan government and its army. The French Foreign Minister thus assured all concerned that France would not proceed with its intervention, absent authority to do so by the UN Security Council (which was ultimately provided in late June). France's caution also served the neutrality interests of Zaire—the "jumping off" point for the departure of French troops to Rwanda. The UN ultimately established a Rwanda peacekeeping force to protect the populace from tribal warfare.

COLLECTIVE RECOGNITION

While State practice is normally emphasized in recognition analyses, an international organization or group of States may decide to extend (or withhold) collective recognition. Article 1(2) of the League of Nations Covenant provided for a form of collective recognition—permitting admission to this world body only if applicants expressed a commitment to observing international obligations. A State or other territory could attain membership "if its admission is agreed to by two-thirds of the Assembly, provided it shall give effective guarantees of its sincere intention to observe international obligations, and shall accept . . . regulations . . . in regard to its military, naval, and air forces and armaments." This article provided League members with a convenient basis for refusing to officially recognize or approve of the creation of new States by succession or unacceptable breaches of territorial sovereignty by aggressor States. As noted by the prominent Finnish statesman Erich in 1926, if the League of Nations did not succeed "in repelling an aggression or in preventing an occupation . . . of the territory of a Member, the other Members must not recognize that *de facto* change as final and valid *de jure*. If one of the direct consequences of that unlawful aggression has been the establishment of a new State, the Members of the League of Nations should . . . refuse to recognize that new State the existence of which is conflicting with the supreme values [of the League]. . . .[37]

The United Nations does not collectively recognize States. The UN Charter contains prohibitions against force, as did the League Charter. Unlike the League, mere admission into the UN is not regarded as an act of collective recognition. Many thought it unwise to imply recognition just from admission into this second-generation world body. The Cold War quickly revealed that the brass ring of universality was more difficult to grasp than contemplated by League of Nations members. In 1950, the Secretary-General expressly stated that the UN "does not possess any authority to recognize either a new State or a new government of an existing State. To establish the rule of collective recognition by the United Nations would require either an amendment to the Charter or a treaty to which all members would adhere."[38]

No such treaty ever materialized. There was a remarkable post-war influx of States onto the international scene (illustrated in Exhibit 2.1 in §2.2). The variousness of their backgrounds suggests that any attempt to qualify admission with the acceptance of conditions of recognition would again result in another form of Cold War—thereby defeating the underlying UN purpose of bringing the world community together in one place so as to diffuse conflicts and cultivate the essentials identified in the Charter's mandate.

The European Union or EU (formerly European Economic Community, EEC, and EC) has taken the leading role in developing recognition criteria. Its recognition requirements are comparatively objective, because State practice has never been very lucid about pinpointing the subjective criteria for recognizing other States. In 1991, the EU promulgated its Guidelines on the Recognition of New States in Eastern Europe and in the Former Soviet Union. This announcement was expressly linked to its commitment to the law of self-determination of States (*see* §2.3 on Changes in State Status). The EU and its member States adopted the following five criteria that States seeking recognition must satisfy:

1. respect for UN Charter provisions and its European counterpart (Conference on Security and Co-operation in Europe);
2. guarantees for ethnic and national minorities;
3. respect for the inviolability of all frontiers, which can be changed only by peaceful means and common agreement;

4. acceptance of international commitments regarding disarmament and nuclear nonproliferation; and
5. arbitration or like resolution of all disputes regarding succession and regional disputes.[39]

The EU will thereby withhold recognition from States, territories, or colonies resulting from international aggression. Recognition will not be given to States that violate territorial sovereignty or fail to observe international human rights guarantees. A number of nations including the US heartily supported this new objective approach in the development of the international law of recognition.[40]

◆ 2.5 STATE RESPONSIBILITY

INTRODUCTION

Prior sections of this text defined International Law, the various influences that shape it, the State as the principal actor in its evolution, and the changing infrastructure attributable to the momentous increase in States since 1945. This section briefly addresses another introductory theme: State responsibility under International Law. Once statehood is acquired, a State incurs obligations associated with its international status. It is required to make reparations for any international wrongdoing when it has achieved *de facto* statehood. This requirement is, of course, immutable once status as a *de jure* State entity has been confirmed via recognition. Otherwise, States would not be equal sovereigns under International Law, entitled to appropriate treatment because of their international personality.

Before delving into the specific content of International Law in this section and subsequent chapters, it will be useful to contemplate the general consequences of a State's wrongful conduct. When a State commits a wrongful act against another State, its breach of International Law activates the requirement that it make reparations for that harm. Law students study the law of torts, contracts, and criminal law in their first year of law school. They learn to appreciate the specific acts or omissions that breach the law, and how the resulting harm should be remedied. Assuming that a State has committed some wrong through its active or passive conduct, International Law is similarly concerned with defining the general contours of State responsibility.

Three fundamental elements trigger State responsibility under International Law: (1) the existence of a legal obligation recognized by International Law; (2) an act or omission that violates that obligation; and (3) some loss or articulable damage caused by the breach of the obligation.[41] These elements are drawn from a variety of sources, including various judicial and arbitral awards. In 1928, the quintessential articulation by the Permanent Court of International Justice was that "it is a principle of international law, and even a greater conception of [all] law, that any breach of an engagement [responsibility to another State] involves an obligation to make reparation."[42] In this particular instance, Germany was suing Poland in the former world court. While there is generally a sovereign right of expropriation, Germany sought reparations for Poland's breach of its *treaty* obligation not to expropriate a German factory once built in Poland.

Support for this principle can also be found in many arbitral decisions. In 1985, French agents destroyed the Greenpeace vessel *Rainbow Warrior* in a New Zealand harbor, after its crew protested French nuclear testing in the South Pacific, killing one crew member. In 1986, the UN Secretary-General ruled that France had thus incurred State responsibility for the acts of its agents. France was then supposed to transfer the responsible French agents to its base in the Pacific, where they would remain for at least three years. They were clandestinely repatriated to France, however, without New Zealand's consent. The *Rainbow Warrior* arbitration affirmed that "the legal consequences of a breach of a treaty, including the determination of the circumstances that may exclude wrongfulness . . . and the appropriate remedies for breach, are subjects that belong to the customary law of state responsibility."[43]

The above elements of State responsibility apply without regard to how one might characterize the obligation or the nature of the breach. The obligation may have been established by treaty or by customary International Law. The breach may be classified as either civil or criminal in nature. There is a persistent question, however, about whether the mere fact of some resulting harm is enough to trigger State responsibility; put another way, is some finding of fault or intent on the part of a State's agents required for State responsibility?

The ICJ's 1949 *Corfu Channel* opinion suggests that fault is required. Great Britain sued Albania when British naval vessels hit mines recently laid in an international strait off Albania's coast. Albania denied any knowledge of the presence of those mines—notwithstanding rather suspicious circumstances. The Court decided that "it cannot be concluded . . . that that state [Albania] necessarily knew, or ought to have known, of any unlawful act perpetrated therein, nor yet that it necessarily knew, or should have known, the authors [of the act of mine laying in the strait]."[44] Professor Malcolm Shaw of the University of Leicester in England points out, however, that this lone passage from the Court is *not* tantamount to its general adoption of a "fault" requirement that would limit State responsibility. While judicial and academic opinions are divided on this matter, most tend to agree that there is a strict liability standard—meaning that the State's fault, intent, or knowledge are *not* conditions for State responsibility. The State would thus be liable for harm, even in the absence of intent to harm another State or its citizens. It is not just heinous criminal activity that triggers State responsibility in International Law. A State can be liable if it fails to act, or is unaware of floating mines in its territorial waters through which foreign vessels routinely navigate.[45]

Draft Articles The study of International Law would, of course, be far simpler if it were only contained in a multilateral treaty to which all nations could agree. Yet this important area of the law is by no means easy to codify in a model treaty.

Three international drafting commissions have attempted to restate one major facet—the law of State responsibility under International Law. From 1924 to 1930, a Committee of Experts, working with the League of Nations, presented the first phase in this lengthy endeavor. Its draft articles were limited to the responsibility of States for injuries *within* their respective territories to foreign citizens or their property. The next phase, from 1949 to 1961, was undertaken by the UN's International Law Commission—a group of prominent international legal scholars nominated by the governments of UN member States.[46] From 1963 to date, the next wave of attempted codification of the law of State responsibility has crested at the UN Charter. The drafters for this phase broadened their efforts to cover State responsibility for all topics within the Charter's reach. The comparative length of this renewed endeavor is partially attributable to the remarkable increase in UN membership (illustrated in Exhibit 2.1 in §2.2).

A complete set of draft articles was finally adopted by the ILC's members in 1996. States were asked to provide responses by the beginning of 1998. Some did, resulting in more drafting.[47] The "Second Reading" of the draft, after incorporating State responses, is scheduled for 2001. The rules contained in this most recent draft focus on procedural ("secondary") rules, as opposed to substantive ("primary") rules that could have directly addressed what acts or omissions give rise to State responsibility for a breach of International Law.

This model law of State responsibility is thus couched in only the most general of terms—despite more than seventy years of laborious efforts to produce an acceptable draft for an international conference. Article 1 (of the sixty-article draft) almost bashfully provides as follows: "Every internationally wrongful act of a State entails the international responsibility of that State." Article 2 adds that every "State is subject to the possibility of being held to have committed an internationally wrongful act entailing its international responsibility." Article 51 professes that an "international crime entails all the legal consequences of any other internationally wrongful act. . . ."

Article 19 is the most controversial draft article and probably the one that most closely defines specifically prohibited State conduct. It deals with State responsibility for "international crimes and delicts." Subsection 3's examples include "aggression," "safeguarding self-determination of peoples," "slavery, genocide, and apartheid," and "massive pollution of the atmosphere or of the seas." These terms are not defined in any detail. Given the difficulty with securing State ratification of any multilateral treaty (as discussed in Chapter 8 of this text), it is not surprising that this work product appears in such general terms. Much remains to be done.

◆ 2.6 SOVEREIGN IMMUNITY

You have now studied the elements of statehood, rights and obligations incurred when there is a change in State status, and the general nature of responsibilities acquired when an entity achieves international legal personality by becoming a State. This section introduces an important adjunct to State status: Although a State may be clearly responsible for certain conduct, its status as a sovereign entity may shield it from having to respond to suits in the courts of another country. In this context, *when* sovereign immunity applies, one State's judge(s) cannot assert jurisdiction over another State in its courts.

This attribute of sovereignty is premised on one of the fundamental building blocks of International Law:

> The worst was yet to come: in the spring of 1944, Wolf and his family were captured and sent to Auschwitz-Birkenau. There his mother, father, and sister were murdered. Wolf was assigned to Birkenau, and then was sent to the slave labor camp Shventocholovitz. His treatment at both Auschwitz-Birkenau and Shventocholovitz was brutal, and he continues to suffer from the effects of the beatings he received. Finally, the Nazis sent him to Mauthausen in early April 1945, where he again was forced to work as a slave. . . .
>
> Wolf has no other suggestions for overcoming Germany's immunity under Section 1604 of the FSIA [US Foreign Sovereign Immunities Act], nor can we find any. We therefore agree with the district court that it lacked jurisdiction over the suit against Germany, *see* §1330(a), and that the claims had to be dismissed.
>
> —*Wolf v. Fed. Rep. Germany,* 95 F.3d 536 (7th Cir., 1996), *cert. den'd,* 117 S.Ct. 1112 (1997)

All States are entitled to equality. State B, being a coequal sovereign entity in the community of nations, should not be subjected to a lawsuit in the courts in State A. Assuming that the State A plaintiff is entitled to a remedy from the government or an agency of State B, it may be preferable to resolve the dispute through diplomatic negotiations—rather than in the courts of State A.

The expression of this equality is often found in the constitutive documents of international organizations. Article 2.1 of the UN Charter provides that the "Organization is based on the principle of the sovereign equality of all its Members." Article 9 of the Charter of the Organization of American States provides that "States are juridically [legally] equal, enjoy equal rights and equal capacity to exercise these rights, and have equal duties. The rights of each State depend not upon its power to ensure the exercise thereof, but upon the mere fact of its existence as a person under international law."[48]

The scope of the sovereign's immunity includes States, heads of State, and (since World War II) State government agencies that are conducting State business (as opposed to private enterprises). State practice has historically employed the *absolute* theory of sovereign immunity. The Kenya Court of Appeal provided a useful restatement of this theory. A resident of Kenya sued a British soldier for allegedly causing a motor accident in Kenya. The Claims Commission within Britain's Ministry of Defence, a government agency of Great Britain, was sued because it would normally be vicariously liable for the soldier's conduct undertaken in the course of his employment. This governmental defendant sought an order from the court, which did not result in the Ministry's dismissal until reversed on appeal. The immunity upheld by Kenya's appellate decision illustrates the rationale for dismissing the governmental defendant:

> [It was] . . . submitted before the learned [trial] judge that a foreign state could not be made party to a suit unless it consented. Mr. Waweru for the plaintiff does not appear to have seriously explained away that contention nor does the learned judge appear to have seriously considered the position of a foreign sovereign in our courts. . . . Nevertheless, it is a matter of international law that our courts will not entertain an action against certain privileged persons and institutions unless the privilege is waived. The class . . . includes foreign sovereigns or heads of state and governments, foreign diplomats and their staff, consular officers and representatives of international organisations like UNO [UN] and OAU [Organization of African Unity]. Mr. Frazer for the appellant [British governmental agency] cited the English case [citation omitted]. . . .
>
> [In that case, the] sovereign immunity was upheld . . . [and the] appeal was dismissed and the court said . . .
>
> The general principle is undoubtedly that, except by consent, the courts of this country will not issue their process so as to entertain a claim against a foreign sovereign for debt or damages. The reason is that, if the courts here once entertained the claim, and in consequence [thereby] gave judgment against the foreign sovereign, they [the courts rendering the judgment] could be called on to enforce it by execution against its property here. Such execution might imperil our relations with that country and lead to repercussions impossible to foresee. . . .
>
> As was held in *Mighell v. Sultan of Johore* [1894] 1 QB 149, the courts in one country have no jurisdic-

tion over an independent foreign sovereign of another country, unless he submits to the jurisdiction. There has been no [such] submission here.[49]

The scope of absolute sovereign immunity also depends on what entities are embraced within the term *State*. There is a distinction between heads of State and agencies of a State. Absolute immunity is almost universally recognized for heads of State regarding their public and private acts while they are in a foreign State. In the famous case cited in the above Kenya court decision, *Mighell v. Sultan of Johore*, England extended sovereign immunity to a foreign head of State who was sued in England for breach of his promise to marry. The case against the sultan was thus dismissed.[50]

One aberration in contemporary practice is the case of Manuel Noriega, Panama's former head of State. In 1989, the US invaded Panama, waited for him outside of the Vatican embassy there, seized him when he exited, and then returned him to the US for trial on drug-trafficking charges. This was perhaps the first time, since Roman leaders brought back captured foreign leaders in chains two thousand years ago, that a foreign ruler was captured abroad and returned for trial in the territory of the captors. The US relied on various legalities, including a state of war (commenced by the US invasion) and self-defense—premised on the danger that Noriega's dictatorship posed for US security interests in Panama. It was labeled as a "gross violation" of International Law by the former president of the American Society of International Law, while a US court rejected Noriega's claim of head of State immunity in 1997.[51] This is likely the lone incident marring the almost universal application of the absolute theory of sovereign immunity for foreign Heads of State.

Examples of the continued application of sovereign immunity for heads of State include the Bosnian Serb leader Radovan Karadzic. In 1993, he was granted a visa by the US to travel to the UN. Although he stands accused of war crimes in Bosnia, he was assured immunity from arrest for those crimes while in the US to attend UN peace talks. Sovereign immunity does not continue, however, for *former* rulers. While they normally are not sued just because they are no longer heads of State, a suit in foreign courts is nevertheless possible. The former Shah of Iran was served with a multibillion-dollar lawsuit in 1979 when he entered a New York hospital. This suit was dismissed on other grounds (*see* Chapter 9, Act of State). Deposed Philippine President Marcos was sued in the US on numerous occasions after his 1986 departure from the Philippines to Hawaii. He could not properly claim this immunity, however, because he was no longer a head of State (and the US government strongly supported Marco's successor in the Philippines). The successor government of the Philippines agreed that the suits against Marcos could proceed in the courts of the US—effectively waiving whatever sovereign immunity Marcos might have enjoyed in the absence of this waiver.

Today, there is another model for assessing sovereign immunity. Under the *restrictive* theory of sovereign immunity, most States no longer automatically extend "absolute" immunity to government-owned or -operated entities. *Military* units still enjoy absolute immunity from suits in foreign countries. But civilian entities, operated by a State in its capacity as a trader competing with other private merchants, are *not* necessarily given immunity from suit under the "restrictive" theory of sovereign immunity. This newer approach to sovereign immunity restricts the scope of available immunity—when the State stands in the shoes of a private trader—doing what any trader could do, rather than doing only what a sovereign can do.

Some States still apply the absolute theory of sovereign immunity, however, when the particular activity is closely associated with the political objectives of the foreign State within the host State. The following case from Poland is a useful illustration. A woman named Aldona was a typist employed by the weekly magazine *Voice of England*. This magazine was published in Kraków, Poland, by the British Foreign Office of the British government. Aldona was dismissed from her job. She was not paid the remainder of the salary due to her under the contract with the magazine. She sued Great Britain in a Polish court for the breach of her contract by the English agency publishing the magazine. The Polish courts dismissed her case because the defendant was a foreign sovereign. Aldona asserted that this dispute involved a mere contract of employment between a private person and a commercial magazine that was a profit-making enterprise—which was coincidentally published by an agency of the British government for diplomatic and other political purposes.

Aldona's unsuccessful argument was that publishing a magazine should be characterized as economic rather than diplomatic or some other State-related activity. Her lawyer argued that if Great Britain's magazine could thereby avoid paying her, on the basis of a dismissal on grounds of sovereign immunity, the contractual obligations of the British government in Poland would be meaningless. The Polish court first assessed the reciprocity concerns (suggested in the above case from Kenya). Absent a dismissal in this case, any subsequent suit against a Polish governmental entity in Great Britain would likely invite a British judge to allow a suit to proceed against Polish government agencies operating in Great Britain. The Polish court noted that, while the English magazine was a commercial entity—in the sense of selling magazines for a profit—its underlying *purpose* was unoffensive political activity on the part of England. The Polish Supreme Court also tied up an important loose end—the plaintiff's remedy was not in the courts, but rather through diplomatic negotiations on her behalf. Under the Polish Supreme Court's analysis:

> Polish Courts were unable, given the principle of reciprocity, to accept for deliberation the claim submitted by Aldona S., even if it concerned a commercial enterprise on behalf of the British authorities. However, such is really not the case, for the [lower Polish] Court of Appeal held that the publishing house of "Voice of England" is not a commercial enterprise. The objection of the plaintiff that this does not concern diplomatic but [rather] economic activity cannot be admitted as valid, for although the activity may not be diplomatic, it is political by its content, and economic only by its form. . . .
>
> Finally, the last objection of the plaintiff, that refusal of legal protection would render the obligations of the British Foreign Office as a publisher of a magazine in the territory of our State incomplete and unreal, is also unfounded, for, if the plaintiff does not wish to seek justice before English courts, she may take advantage of general international usage in connection with immunity from jurisdiction, and approach the [Polish] Ministry of Foreign Affairs, which is obliged to take up the matter with the [English] Ministry of Foreign Affairs of a foreign country with a view to obtain satisfaction for a just claim. This approach frequently produces speedier results than court procedure.[52]

Most States currently apply some form of the restrictive standard for resolving sovereign immunity questions. Certain States, such as the People's Republic of China, still adhere to the absolute immunity theory in *all* cases.[53] Western nations typically restrict a foreign sovereign's immunity from suit depending on whether the State is acting in a way that only States may act. Major distinctions are fabricated on distinctions like whether the State's conduct is: (1) sovereign versus private; (2) public versus private; (3) commercial versus noncommercial; or (4) political versus trade-related. These enumerated distinctions are easily stated but difficult to apply. Consider the following Austrian Supreme Court case.

> The plaintiff was an Austrian citizen whose automobile was damaged in a collision with a car owned by the US government in Austria. The driver of the US car was delivering mail to the US embassy. The lawyer for the US claimed sovereign immunity from suit in the Austrian courts, premised on the underlying purpose of the trip. The lower court, and the Austrian Supreme Court, allowed the case to proceed, however. It was the *act* of driving itself, rather than its underlying *purpose,* that would shape the scope of sovereign immunity in Austrian foreign sovereign immunity analysis. Any qualified driver can drive a car on an Austrian highway. Negligence on the highway, not the underlying purpose of delivering US government mail, therefore vitiated sovereign immunity for the US in the Austrian courts. As stated by the Austrian Supreme Court: "We must always look at the act itself which is performed by State organs, and not at its motive or purpose. We must always investigate the act of the State from which the claim is derived. Whether an act is of a private or sovereign nature must always be deduced from the nature of the legal transaction . . . the action taken or the legal relationship arising [as from the collision on an Austrian highway]. . . .
>
> [T]he act from which the plaintiff derives his claim for damages against the defendant is not the collection of mail but the operation of a motor car . . . and action as a road user. By operating a motor car and using the public roads the defendant moves in spheres in which private individuals also move.[54]

◆ *Notes & Questions*

1. Reciprocity among States was described by the *Aldona S.* court as the "most essential" principle in international

relations. Does that statement mean that the court would apply absolute immunity to even a relatively innocuous commercial contract, regardless of the circumstances, when the defendant is a foreign sovereign?

2. Aldona could not use the courts of Poland to recover her wages. Was she without a remedy? If she had another remedy, would it be better than a judgment for money damages payable to Aldona?
3. In the Austrian collision case, the court referred to the distinction between "private and sovereign acts." Was the delivery of mail to the US embassy in Austria a *private* or a *sovereign* act of the US government?
4. Does the emphasis on "the nature of the act" refer to the collection and delivery of embassy mail—or to the driving of a car on an Austrian highway?

Sometimes, a court must pursue a two-step appraisal: First, is the entity claiming the defense of sovereign immunity a "State" for the purpose of an immunity analysis? Second, is the entity's conduct that gives rise to the suit really sovereign or commercial in nature? If "sovereign," then the case is normally dismissed. If commercial, then the State is acting in a way that a private citizen may act, thus requiring the State to litigate the underlying claim on the merits. Also, the method by which such issues are managed by the executive branch of government, in judicial proceedings, exposes how immunity issues materialize in national courts—where private parties are litigating against a State, as opposed to two States resolving their conflict before an international tribunal. The following case illustrates this latter process in several countries:

The Holy See v. Starbright Sales Enterprises, Inc.

PHILIPPINES SUPREME COURT (EN BANC), 1994

102 *Int'l Law Rep.* 163 (1995)

Author's Note: *In 1990, Starbright brought this suit in the Philippine courts against The Holy See (HS—Vatican City). The HS had sold the land in dispute to Starbright, who sought an annulment of the sale, and damages, because the seller had failed to evict some squatters. The HS claimed that it was entitled to sovereign immunity from suit in the Philippine courts. The HS claimed that it had acquired the property as the site for its official mission in the Philippines, and then sold it. The reason was that the presence of the squatters—who may have had some right to be there—made development of this land for a diplomatic mission impossible.*

The trial court determined that the HS had waived its sovereign immunity by entering into this commercial contract to sell the land. The Supreme Court reversed the trial court's finding, however, resulting in dismissal of this suit.

COURT'S OPINION. The following is the text of the judgment of the Court, delivered by Quiason J [court's footnotes and citations omitted]: ...

Petitioner is The Holy See who exercises sovereignty over the Vatican City in Rome, Italy, and is represented in the Philippines by the Papal Nuncio.

Private respondent, Starbright Sales Enterprises, Inc., is a domestic corporation engaged in the real estate business.

This petition arose from a controversy over a parcel of land ... located in the Municipality of Paranaque, Metro Manila, and registered in the name of petitioner....

In view of the refusal of the squatters to vacate the lots sold to private respondent, a dispute arose as to who of the parties has the responsibility of evicting and clearing the land of squatters....

I

On 23 January 1990, private respondent filed a complaint ... [in] Manila for annulment of the sale of the three parcels of land, and specific performance and damages against petitioner, represented by the Papal Nuncio, and three other defendants: namely, Msgr

Domingo A. Cirilos, Jr., the PRC and Tropicana (Civil Case No. 90-183).

The complaint alleged that: (1) On 17 April 1988, Msgr Cirilos, Jr., on behalf of petitioner and the PRC, agreed to sell to Ramon Licup Lots 5-A, 5-B and 5-D at the price of P1,240.00 per square meter; . . . (5) thereafter, private respondent demanded from Msgr Cirilos that the sellers fulfill their undertaking and clear the property of squatters; however, Msgr Cirilos informed private respondent of the squatters' refusal to vacate the lots, proposing instead either that the private respondent undertake the eviction or that the earnest money be returned to the latter; (6) private respondent counterproposed that if it would undertake the eviction of the squatters, the purchase price of the lots should be reduced . . . (11) private respondent is willing and able to comply with the terms of the contract to sell and has actually made plans to develop the lots into a townhouse project, but in view of the sellers' breach, it lost profits of not less than P30,000,000.00. . . .

On 8 June 1990, petitioner and Msgr Cirilos separately moved to dismiss the complaint—[against] petitioner for lack of jurisdiction based on sovereign immunity from suit, and Msgr Cirilos for being an improper party. An opposition to the motion was filed by private respondent.

On 20 June 1991, the trial court issued an order denying, among others, petitioner's motion to dismiss after finding that petitioner "discarded [its] sovereign immunity by entering into the business contract in question. . . ."

Petitioner forthwith elevated [appealed] the matter to us. In its petition, petitioner invokes the privilege of sovereign immunity on its own behalf and on behalf of its official representative, the Papal Nuncio.

On 9 December 1991, a Motion for Intervention was filed before us by the Department of Foreign Affairs, claiming that it has a legal interest in the outcome of the case as regards the diplomatic immunity of petitioner [Holy See] and that it "adopts by reference, the allegations contained in the petition of the Holy See insofar as they refer to arguments relative to its claim of sovereign immunity from suit."

Private respondent [Starbright] opposed the intervention of the Department of Foreign Affairs. In compliance with the resolution of this Court, both parties and the Department of Foreign Affairs submitted their respective memoranda. . . .

II

The other procedural question raised by private respondent is the personality or legal interest of the Department of Foreign Affairs to intervene in the case on behalf of The Holy See.

In public international law, when a State or international agency wishes to plead sovereign or diplomatic immunity in a foreign court, it requests the Foreign Office of the State where it is sued to convey to the court that said defendant is entitled to immunity.

In the United States, the procedure followed is the process of "suggestion," where the foreign State or the international organization sued in an American court requests the Secretary of State to make a determination as to whether it is entitled to immunity. If the Secretary of State finds that the defendant is immune from suit, he, in turn, asks the Attorney General to submit to the court a "suggestion" that the defendant is entitled to immunity. In England, a similar procedure is followed, only the Foreign Office issues a certification to that effect instead of submitting a "suggestion."

In the Philippines, the practice is for the foreign government or the international organization to first secure an executive endorsement of its claim of sovereign or diplomatic immunity. But how the Philippine Foreign Office conveys its endorsement to the courts varies. . . .

In the case of bench, the Department of Foreign Affairs, through the Office of Legal Affairs moved with this Court to be allowed to intervene on the side of petitioner. The Court allowed the said Department to file its memorandum in support of petitioner's claim of sovereign immunity.

In some cases, the defense of sovereign immunity was submitted directly to the local courts by the respondents through their private counsels. In cases where the foreign States bypass the Foreign Office, the courts can inquire into the facts and make their own determination as to the nature of the acts and transactions involved.

III

The burden of the petition is [to prove] that respondent trial court has no jurisdiction over petitioner, being a foreign State enjoying sovereign immunity. On the other hand, private respondent insists that the doctrine of non-suability is not anymore absolute and that petitioner had divested itself of such a cloak when, of its own free will, it entered into a commercial transaction for the sale of a parcel of land located in the Philippines.

A. The Holy See

Before we determine the issue of petitioner's non-suability, a brief look into its status as a sovereign State is in order.

Before the annexation of the Papal States by Italy in 1870, the Pope was the monarch and, as The Holy See, was considered a subject of international law. With the loss of the Papal States and the limitation of the territory under The Holy See to an area of 108.7 acres, the position of The Holy See in international law became controversial.

In 1929, Italy and The Holy See entered into the Lateran Treaty, where Italy recognized the exclusive dominion and sovereign jurisdiction of The Holy See over the Vatican City. It also recognized the right of The Holy See to receive foreign diplomats, to send its own diplomats to foreign countries, and to enter into treaties according to international law.

The Lateran Treaty established the statehood of the Vatican City "for the purpose of assuring to The Holy See absolute and visible independence and of guaranteeing to it indisputable sovereignty also in the field of international relations. . . ."

The Vatican City fits into none of the established categories of States, and the attribution to it of "sovereignty" must be made in a sense different from that in which it is applied to other States. In a community of national States, the Vatican City represents an entity organized not for political but for ecclesiastical purposes and international objects. Despite its size and object, the Vatican City has an independent government of its own, with the Pope, who is also head of the Roman Catholic Church, as The Holy See or Head of State, in conformity with its traditions and the demands of its mission in the world. Indeed, the world-wide interests and activities of the Vatican City are such as to make it in a sense an "International State."

One authority wrote that the recognition of the Vatican City as a State has significant implication—that it is possible for any entity pursuing objects essentially different from those pursued by States to be invested with international personality.

Inasmuch as the Pope prefers to conduct foreign relations and enter into transactions as The Holy See and not in the name of the Vatican City, one can conclude that in the Pope's own view, it is The Holy See that is the international person.

The Republic of the Philippines has accorded The Holy See the status of a foreign sovereign. The Holy See, through its Ambassador, the Papal Nuncio, has had diplomatic representations with the Philippine Government since 1957. This appears to be the universal practice in international relations.

B. Sovereign Immunity

As expressed in Section 2 of Article II of the 1987 [Philippine] Constitution, we have adopted the generally accepted principles of international law. Even without this affirmation, such principles of international law are deemed incorporated as part of the law of the land as a condition and consequence of our admission in the society of nations.

There are two conflicting concepts of sovereign immunity, each widely held and firmly established. According to the classical or absolute theory, a sovereign cannot, without its consent, be made a respondent in the courts of another sovereign. According to the newer or restrictive theory, the immunity of the sovereign is recognized only with regard to public acts or acts *jure imperii* of a State, but not with regard to private acts or acts *jure gestionis.*

Some States passed legislation to serve as guidelines for the executive or judicial determination when an act may be considered as *jure gestionis.* The United States passed the Foreign Sovereign Immunities Act of 1976, which defines a commercial activity as "either a regular course of commercial conduct or a particular commercial transaction or act." Furthermore, the law declared that the "commercial character of the activity shall be determined by reference to the nature of the course of conduct or particular transaction or act, rather than by reference to its purpose." The Canadian Parliament enacted in 1982 an Act to Provide for State Immunity in Canadian courts. The Act defines a "commercial activity" as any particular transaction, act or conduct or any regular course of conduct that by reason of its nature is of a "commercial character."

The restrictive theory, which is intended to be a solution to the host of problems involving the issue of sovereign immunity, has created problems of its own. Legal treatises and the decisions in countries which follow the restrictive theory have difficulty in characterizing whether a contract of a sovereign State with a private party is an act *jure gestionis* or an act *jure imperii.*

The restrictive theory came about because of the entry of sovereign States into purely commercial activities only remotely connected with the discharge of governmental functions. This is particularly true with respect to the Communist States which took control of nationalized business activities and international trading.

This Court has considered the following transactions by a foreign State with private parties as acts *jure imperii:* (1) the lease by a foreign government of apartment buildings for use of its military officers; (2) the conduct of public bidding for the repair of a wharf at a United States naval station; and (3) the change of employment status of base employees.

On the other hand, this Court has considered the following transactions by a foreign State with private parties as acts *jure gestionis:* (1) the hiring of a cook in the recreation center, consisting of three restaurants, a cafeteria, a bakery, a store, and a coffee and pastry shop at the John Hay Air Station in Baguio City, to cater to United States servicemen and the general public; and (2) the bidding for the operation of barbers' shops in Clark Air Base in Angeles City. The operation of the restaurants and other facilities open to the general public is undoubtedly for profit as a commercial and not a governmental activity. By entering into the employment contract with the cook in the discharge of its proprietary function, the United States Government impliedly divested itself of its sovereign immunity from suit.

In the absence of legislation defining what activities and transactions shall be considered "commercial" and as constituting acts *jure gestionis,* we have to come out with our own guidelines, tentative [as] they may be.

Certainly, the mere entering into a contract by a foreign State with a private party cannot be the ultimate test. Such an act can only be the start of the inquiry. The logical question is whether the foreign State is engaged in the activity in the regular course of business. If the foreign State is not engaged regularly in a business or trade, the particular act or transaction must then be tested by its nature. If the act is in pursuit of a sovereign activity, or an incident thereof, then it is an act *jure imperii,* especially when it is not undertaken for gain or profit. . . .

In the case at bench, if petitioner [Holy See] has bought and sold lands in the ordinary course of a real estate business, surely the said transaction can be categorized as an act *jure gestionis.* However, petitioner has denied that the acquisition and subsequent disposal of Lot 5-A were made for profit but claimed that it acquired said property for the site of its mission or the Apostolic Nunciature in the Philippines. Private respondent failed to dispute said claim.

Lot 5-A was acquired by petitioner as a donation to the Archdiocese of Manila. The donation was made not for commercial purpose, but for the use of petitioner to construct thereon the official place of residence of the Papal Nuncio. The right of a foreign sovereign to acquire property, real or personal, in a receiving State, necessary for the creation and maintenance of its diplomatic mission, is recognized in the 1961 Vienna Convention on Diplomatic Relations (Articles 20–22). This treaty was concurred in by the Philippine Senate and entered into force in the Philippines on 15 November 1965.

In Article 31(a) of the Convention, a diplomatic envoy is granted immunity from the civil and administrative jurisdiction of the receiving State over any real action relating to private immovable property situated in the territory of the receiving State which the envoy holds on behalf of the sending State for the purposes of the mission. If this immunity is provided for a diplomatic envoy, with all the more reason should immunity be recognized as regards the sovereign itself, which in this case is The Holy See.

The decision to transfer the property and the subsequent disposal thereof are likewise clothed with a governmental character. Petitioner did not sell Lot 5-A for profit or gain. It merely wanted to dispose of the same because the squatters living thereon made it almost impossible for petitioner to use it for the purpose of the donation. The fact that squatters have occupied and are still occupying the lot, and that they stubbornly refuse to leave the premises, has been admitted by private respondent in its complaint.

The issue of petitioner's non-suability can be determined by the trial court without going to trial in the light of the pleadings, particularly the admission of private respondent. Besides, the privilege of sovereign immunity in this case was sufficiently established by the Memorandum and Certification of the Department of Foreign Affairs. As the department tasked with the conduct of the Philippines' foreign relations, the Department of Foreign Affairs has formally intervened in this case and officially certified that the Embassy of The

Holy See is a duly accredited diplomatic mission to the Republic of the Philippines exempt from local jurisdiction and entitled to all the rights, privileges and immunities of a diplomatic mission or embassy in this country. The determination of the executive arm of government that a State or instrumentality is entitled to sovereign or diplomatic immunity is a potential question that is conclusive upon the courts. Where the plea of immunity is recognized and affirmed by the Executive branch, it is the duty of the courts to accept this claim so as not to embarrass the Executive arm of the government in conducting the country's foreign relations. . . .

IV

Private respondent [Starbright] is not left without any legal remedy for the redress of its grievances. Under both public international law and transnational law, a person who feels aggrieved by the acts of a foreign sovereign can ask his own government to espouse his case through diplomatic channels.

Private respondent can ask the Philippine Government, through the Foreign Office, to espouse its claims against The Holy See. Its first task is to persuade the Philippine Government to take up with The Holy See the validity of its claims. Of course, the Foreign Office shall first make a determination of the impact of its espousal on the relations between the Philippine Government and The Holy See. Once the Philippine Government decides to espouse the claim, the latter ceases to be a private cause.

According to the Permanent Court of International Justice, the forerunner of the International Court of Justice:

> By taking up the case of one of its subjects and by resorting to diplomatic action or international judicial proceedings on his behalf, a State is in reality asserting its own rights—its right to ensure, in the person of its subjects, respect for the rules of international law.

Wherefore, the petition for certiorari is granted and the compliant in Civil Case No 90-183 against petitioner is dismissed.

SO ORDERED.

Most sovereign immunity questions involve acts of a recognized State, or one of its agencies, undertaking some activity that leads to a suit against it in a foreign country. The most dramatic case in the US is presented in the following proceeding. When reading it, consider whether sovereign immunity should be discarded as a vintage anachronism—held over from an era when States did not do business to the extent that they do today—or, alternatively, whether it still serves a utilitarian purpose in international relations. Reparations for the plaintiff's injuries may instead be the subject of diplomatic negotiations.

The law of sovereign immunity is not uniformly perceived by the various legal systems of the world, nor necessarily even by American judges. In this case alone, the trial, intermediate appellate, and Supreme Courts all differed on whether Saudi Arabia's sovereign immunity was waived by its recruiting and training of employees in the US. At the Supreme Court level, the justices were intensely divided on the question of whether this claim should be dismissed on the "technical" basis that the FSIA required the requisite degree of "commercial activity" for the Nelsons to be able to sue Saudi Arabia in the courts of the US. Only five of the nine justices agreed with the entire opinion of the majority (written by Justice Souter). One of those nine justices agreed with most, but not all, of the opinion. Two of them concurred with the result, but disagreed with some of the reasoning. Four justices concurred in part and dissented in part:

Saudi Arabia v. Nelson

SUPREME COURT OF THE UNITED STATES, 1993

507 US 349, 113 S.Ct. 1471, 123 *L. Ed.* 47

Author's Note: *The Nelsons, a married couple, filed this action against the Kingdom of Saudi Arabia, a Saudi hospital, and the hospital's purchasing agent in the United States. They alleged that the husband suffered personal injuries as a result of the Saudi government's unlawful detention, torture, and failure to warn him of the possibility of severe retaliatory action if he attempted to do his job by reporting on-the-job hazards. The Nelsons asserted jurisdiction under the US Foreign Sovereign Immunities Act of 1976, 28 United States Code §1605(a)(2)—or the FSIA. That legislation authorizes a US court to hear a case "based upon a commercial activity carried on in the United States by the foreign state."*

The federal trial court dismissed the Nelsons' claim for lack of subject-matter jurisdiction—ruling that the US courts did not have the power to hear this case against Saudi Arabia and its agents because the torture and detention were not "commercial" activities within the meaning of the FSIA. The intermediate appellate court reversed, concluding that Mr. Nelson's recruitment and hiring were "commercial activities" of Saudi Arabia, thereby authorizing the prosecution of the Nelsons' court action because Saudi Arabia and its agents were conducting "commercial" activity as envisioned by Congress under its FSIA.

The US Supreme Court reversed the intermediate Court of Appeals, reinstating the trial court's dismissal of this case. None of these courts was ruling on the merits of the Nelson case—they were merely determining whether such a case could even be presented in US courts (for a subsequent trial regarding liability and damages). The dismissal of such cases does not absolve the defendant of liability for State responsibility (see §2.5). Rather, its effect is that a trial judge is just not the appropriate decision maker.

The term "petitioner" refers to Saudi Arabia—the defendant in the courts below but the petitioner seeking reversal in the Supreme Court. The term "respondents" refers to the Nelsons—the plaintiffs below, and now responding to the Saudi attempt to reverse the Court of Appeals directive that the trial judge should proceed with this case. Citations have been deleted.

COURT'S OPINION. Justice SOUTER delivered the [majority] opinion of the Court.

The Foreign Sovereign Immunities Act of 1976 [generally] entitles foreign states to immunity from the jurisdiction of courts in the United States, subject to certain enumerated exceptions. One [exception] is that a foreign state shall not be immune in any case "in which the action is based upon a commercial activity carried on in the United States by the foreign state." We hold that respondents' action alleging personal injury resulting from unlawful detention and torture by the Saudi Government is not "based upon a commercial activity" within the meaning of the Act, which consequently confers no jurisdiction over respondents' suit.

I

. . . Petitioner Kingdom of Saudi Arabia owns and operates petitioner King Faisal Specialist Hospital in Riyadh [Saudi Arabia], as well as petitioner Royspec Purchasing Services, the Hospital's corporate purchasing agent in the United States. The Hospital Corporation of America, Ltd. (HCA), an independent corporation existing under the laws of the Cayman Islands, recruits Americans for employment at the [Saudi] Hospital. . . .

In its recruitment effort, HCA placed an advertisement in a trade periodical seeking applications for a position as a monitoring systems engineer at the Hospital. The advertisement drew the attention of respondent Scott Nelson . . . while Nelson was in the United States. After interviewing for the position in Saudi Arabia, Nelson returned to the United States, where he signed an employment contract with the Hospital, satisfied personnel processing requirements, and attended an orientation session that HCA conducted for Hospital employees. In the course of that program, HCA identified Royspec [hospital's agent in the US] as the point of contact in the United States for family members who might wish to reach Nelson in an emergency.

In December 1983, Nelson went to Saudi Arabia and began work at the Hospital, monitoring all "facilities, equipment, utilities and maintenance systems to insure the safety of patients, hospital staff, and others."

He . . . discovered safety defects in the Hospital's oxygen and nitrous oxide lines that posed fire hazards and otherwise endangered patients' lives. Over a period of several months, Nelson repeatedly advised Hospital officials of the safety defects and reported the defects to a Saudi Government commission as well. Hospital officials instructed Nelson to ignore the problems.

The Hospital's response to Nelson's reports changed, however, on September 27, 1984, when certain Hospital employees summoned him to the Hospital's security office where agents of the Saudi Government arrested him. The agents transported Nelson to a jail cell, in which they "shackled, tortured and bea[t]" him, and kept him four days without food. Although Nelson did not understand Arabic, Government agents forced him to sign a statement written in that language, the content of which he did not know; a Hospital employee who was supposed to act as Nelson's interpreter advised him to sign "anything" the agents gave him to avoid further beatings. Two days later, Government agents transferred Nelson to the Al Sijan Prison "to await trial on unknown charges."

At the Prison, Nelson was confined in an overcrowded cell area infested with rats, where he had to fight other prisoners for food and from which he was taken only once a week for fresh air and exercise. Although police interrogators repeatedly questioned him in Arabic, Nelson did not learn the nature of the charges, if any, against him. For several days, the Saudi Government failed to advise Nelson's family of his whereabouts, though a Saudi official eventually told Nelson's wife, respondent Vivian Nelson, that he could arrange for her husband's release if she provided sexual favors.

Although officials from the United States Embassy visited Nelson twice during his detention, they concluded that his allegations of Saudi mistreatment were "not credible" and made no protest to Saudi authorities. It was only at the personal request of a United States Senator that the Saudi Government released Nelson, 39 days after his arrest, on November 5, 1984. Seven days later, after failing to convince him to return to work at the Hospital, the Saudi Government allowed Nelson to leave the country. . . .

II

The Foreign Sovereign Immunities Act "provides the sole basis for obtaining jurisdiction over a foreign state in the courts of this country." Under the Act, a foreign state is presumptively immune from the jurisdiction of United States courts; unless a specified exception applies, a federal court lacks subject-matter jurisdiction over a claim against a foreign state.

Only one such exception is said to apply here. The first clause of §1605(a)(2) of the Act provides that a foreign state shall not be immune from the jurisdiction of United States courts in any case "in which the action is based upon a commercial activity carried on in the United States by the foreign state." The Act defines such activity as "commercial activity carried on by such state and having substantial contact with the United States," and provides that a commercial activity may be "either a regular course of commercial conduct or a particular commercial transaction or act," the "commercial character of [which] shall be determined by reference to" its "nature," rather than its "purpose."

There is no dispute here that Saudi Arabia, the Hospital, and Royspec all qualify as "foreign state[s]" within the meaning of the Act. 28 USC §§1603(a), (b) (term "foreign state" includes "an agency or instrumentality of a foreign state"). For there to be jurisdiction in this case, therefore, the Nelsons' action must be "based upon" some "commercial activity" by petitioners that had "substantial contact" with the United States within the meaning of the Act. Because we conclude that the suit is not based upon any commercial activity by petitioners, we need not reach the issue of substantial contact with the United States. . . .

[The Court's footnote here concludes that "where a claim rests entirely upon activities sovereign in character, as here, jurisdiction will not exist . . . regardless of any connection the sovereign acts may have with commercial activity."]

. . . Petitioners' tortious conduct itself fails to qualify as "commercial activity" within the meaning of the Act, although the [FSI] Act is too "'obtuse'" to be of much help in reaching that conclusion. We have seen already that the Act defines "commercial activity" as "either a regular course of commercial conduct or a particular commercial transaction or act," and provides that "[t]he commercial character of an activity shall be determined by reference to the nature of the course of conduct or particular transaction or act, rather than by reference to its purpose." If this is a definition, . . . it "leaves the critical term 'commercial' largely undefined." We do not, however, have the option to throw up our hands. The term has to be given some interpretation, and congressional diffidence necessarily results in judicial responsibility to determine what a "commercial activity" is for purposes of the Act.

Under the restrictive [codified in the FSIA], as opposed to the "absolute," theory of foreign sovereign immunity, a state is immune from the jurisdiction of foreign courts as to its sovereign or public acts *(jure imperii)*, but not as to those that are private or commercial in character *(jure gestionis)*. We explained [in an earlier case] . . . that a state engages in commercial activity under the restrictive theory where it exercises "'only those powers that can also be exercised by private citizens,'" as distinct from those "'powers peculiar to sovereigns.'" Put differently, a foreign state engages in commercial activity for purposes of the restrictive theory only where it acts "in the manner of a private player within" the market. We emphasized . . . that whether a state acts "in the manner of" a private party is a question of behavior, not motivation "[b]ecause the Act provides that the commercial character of an act is to be determined by reference to its 'nature' rather than its 'purpose,' [and] the question is not whether the foreign government is acting with a profit motive or instead with the aim of fulfilling uniquely sovereign objectives. Rather, the issue is whether the particular actions that the foreign state performs (whatever the motive behind them) are the type of actions by which a private party engages in 'trade and traffic or commerce.' . . ."

[T]he intentional conduct alleged here (the Saudi Government's wrongful arrest, imprisonment, and torture of Nelson) could not qualify as commercial under the restrictive theory. The conduct boils down to abuse of the power of its police by the Saudi Government, and however monstrous such abuse undoubtedly may be, a foreign state's exercise of the power of its police has long been understood for purposes of the restrictive theory as peculiarly sovereign in nature. Exercise of the powers of police and penal officers is not the sort of action by which private parties can engage in commerce. "[S]uch acts as legislation, or the expulsion of an alien, or a denial of justice, cannot be performed by an individual acting in his own name. They can be performed only by the state acting as such. . . ."

III

The Nelsons' action is not "based upon a commercial activity" within the meaning of the first clause of §1605(a)(2) of the Act, and the judgment of the Court of Appeals is accordingly reversed [thereby reinstating the trial court dismissal of this case without hearing the merits of the claim].

It is so ordered.

Justice WHITE, with whom Justice BLACKMUN joins, concurring in the judgment. . . .

The majority [opinion above] concludes that petitioners enjoy sovereign immunity because respondents' action is not "based upon a commercial activity." I disagree. I nonetheless concur in the judgment because in my view the commercial conduct upon which respondents base their complaint was not "carried on in the United States. . . ."

Justice KENNEDY, with whom Justice BLACKMUN and Justice STEVENS join . . . concurring in part and dissenting in part.

I join all of the Court's opinion except . . . where, with almost no explanation, the Court rules that, like the intentional tort claim, the claims based on negligent failure to warn are outside the subject-matter jurisdiction of the federal courts. . . .

Omission of important information during employee recruiting is commercial activity as we have described it. It seems plain that recruiting employees is an activity undertaken by private hospitals in the normal course of business. Locating and hiring employees implicates no power unique to the sovereign. In explaining the terms and conditions of employment, including the risks and rewards of a particular job, a governmental entity acts in "the manner of a private player within" the commercial marketplace. . . .

Justice STEVENS, dissenting [from dismissal of this case].

. . . In this case, as Justice WHITE has demonstrated [concurring in the result but arguing that the Saudi conduct was a commercial activity under the FSIA], petitioner's operation of the hospital and its employment practices and disciplinary procedures are "commercial activities" within the meaning of the statute, and respondent's claim that he was punished for acts performed in the course of his employment was unquestionably "based upon" those activities. The first statutory condition is satisfied; petitioner is not entitled to immunity from the claims asserted by respondent.

Unlike Justice WHITE, however, I am . . . convinced that petitioner's commercial activities . . . have sufficient contact with the United States to justify the exercise of federal jurisdiction. Petitioner Royspec maintains an office in Maryland and purchases hospital supplies and equipment in this country. For nearly two decades the Hospital's American agent has maintained an office in the United States and regularly engaged in the recruitment of personnel in this country. Respondent himself was recruited in the United States and entered into his employment contract with the hospital in the United States. Before traveling to Saudi Arabia to assume his position at the hospital, respondent attended an orientation program in Tennessee. The position for which respondent was recruited and ultimately hired was that of a monitoring systems manager, a troubleshooter, and, taking respondent's allegations as true, it was precisely respondent's performance of those responsibilities that led to the hospital's retaliatory actions against him. . . .

If the same activities had been performed by a private business, I have no doubt jurisdiction would be upheld [and that this case would thus be able to proceed]. And that, of course, should be a touchstone of our inquiry; for as Justice WHITE explains, when a foreign nation sheds its uniquely sovereign status and seeks out the benefits of the private marketplace, it must, like any private party, bear the burdens and responsibilities imposed by that marketplace. I would therefore affirm the judgment of the Court of Appeals [which, in reversing the trial court, would have allowed this case to proceed].

◆ *Notes & Questions*

1. Some US courts have considered the following argument for piercing the shield of sovereign immunity: A head of government or an agency of the State acts in a way that is "outside" or "beyond the scope of" duties associated with the exemplary features of conducting a government. The protective shield of sovereign immunity is no longer available. The alleged conduct is beyond the scope of allowable governmental conduct—as with torture, which violates International Law. The courts tend to distinguish between heads of government, versus a State or State agency, when addressing whether sovereign immunity remains available to such defendants in US courts. Compare *Hilao v. Estate of Marcos,* 25 F.3d 1467 (9th Cir. 1994)—no sovereign immunity because *head of State's* acts of torture, execution, and disappearances are obviously beyond scope of presidential authority—with *Seiderman de Blake v. Argentina,* 965 F.2d 699, 718 (9th Cir. 1992), *cert. den'd,* 507 US 1017 (1993)—alleged acts of torture perpetrated by *State* as responsible defendant for actions of military agent cannot be considered in US courts due to State's sovereign immunity.
2. *Should* the courts distinguish between a *State* defendant (shielded by sovereign immunity) and an *individual* defendant who was the head of State (no sovereign immunity) for the same conduct of torture and murder?
3. In 1996, the US Congress added an exception to §1605 of the Foreign Sovereign Immunities Act (FSIA). US citizens may now bring federal suits against seven designated terrorist countries, seeking damages resulting from torture, extrajudicial killing, aircraft sabotage, or hostage taking occurring in another country. State responsibility arises when an agent is carrying out his or her official duties, as delegated by the State. 28 USC §1605(a)(7). The specifically designated terrorist nations are Cuba, Iraq, Iran, Libya, North Korea, Sudan, and Syria.

   In March 1998, a US court rendered one of the first judgments under this revision to the FSIA. Iran was ordered to pay $247.5 million to the parents of an American woman killed in a 1995 suicide bombing in Gaza, for which Iran's Islamic Jihad claimed responsibility. *Flatow v. Iran,* 999 Fed. Supp. 1 (D.C. Dist., 1998). The money to pay this judgment could come from frozen Iranian assets in the US or from like Iranian assets in other nations willing to recognize such judgments. If collection efforts are unsuccessful, this case nevertheless signals a shift away from the previously ironclad immunity when a State was acting like a State—although not in a way that most States condone. For similar litigation against Cuba, in the notorious "Brothers to the Rescue" incident, *see Alejandre v. Republic of Cuba,* 996 Fed. Supp. 1239 (S.D. Fla., 1997). There are cases pending against Libya, previously dismissed but now refiled under the amendments to the FSIA, for Libya's role in the Pan Am Flight 103 bombing over Scotland in 1988.

◆ SUMMARY

1. The global community of nations has nearly quadrupled in size since the 1945 formation of the UN. The current majority is composed of many new States, with distinctly different cultures and values. International Law, developed mostly by State practice, has been altered by this influx of new States with diverse perspectives. This change in the infrastructure of the international legal system was triggered by the decolonization movement of the 1960s. Most existing States were once colonial territories of the original UN members.
2. States have rights and duties arising under International Law, referred to as arising "on the international plane." While States are the primary actors within the global community, their capacity as an *international* person is comparable to individual persons who have rights and obligations existing under national law.
3. A State possesses this international personality, or capacity, when it possesses (a) a permanent population, (b) a defined territory, (c) a government, and (d) the capacity to enter into relations with other States.
4. As a result of statehood, a State is responsible for its acts or omissions causing damage to another State. While attempts to codify this facet of International Law have not been completed, a State must make reparations to another State harmed by its wrongful conduct. It is unsettled whether fault or negligence is required to trigger State responsibility. Unlike States, new *governments* may not claim a "clean slate" regarding preexisting treaties and international obligations.
5. Succession results from one State taking over another State's territory. Secession refers to the separation of a State into two or more States. Self-determination is, essentially, the right of peoples within a State to choose self-governance or some related form of autonomy.
6. Recognition may be granted individually by one State or collectively by a group of States. Entities that may be recognized are new States, new governments, and belligerencies.
7. Recognition is not *required* under International Law. States are generally free to exercise their discretion about whether or not to grant recognition. While the decision to recognize is a political one, it has certain legal consequences—including access to the courts and assets located in the recognizing State.
8. Recognition is considered an element of statehood under the *constitutive* theory of recognition. Under the *declarative* theory, applied by most States, recognition merely declares the recognizing State's statement of *de jure* status of the recognized State (which has already attained statehood on a *de facto* basis).
9. States, heads of State, and State agencies are generally immune from being sued in the courts of another State. This defense to a lawsuit is referred to as sovereign immunity.
10. There are two theories of sovereign immunity: *absolute* and *restrictive.* The absolute theory provides total immunity from suit in other States regardless of the nature or purpose of the sovereign's acts. The restrictive theory withholds immunity for conduct that effectively places the foreign sovereign on equal footing with private actors in the State where the suit is filed.
11. Under the US Foreign Sovereign Immunities Act (FSIA), Congress intended that the courts examine the nature of the specific act—rather than the foreign sovereign's underlying purpose for doing the act. If the act can be done by a private individual, there is no immunity. If the act is sovereign in nature, immunity is granted to preclude suit when the foreign sovereign's acts are of a sufficiently political or sovereign character.

◆ PROBLEMS

Problem 2.A (§2.1, after Excerpt on Condition of Statehood) The Jessup excerpt presents the argument in favor of Israel's condition of statehood. Problem 2.a builds upon that paradigm with the related question of *Palestinian* statehood. The Palestine Liberation Organization (PLO) was created in 1964 to "liberate" Palestine from Israeli control. Its members include people who are citizens of various Arab States. They have lived together since ancient times, long before the Western nation-state model was incorporated into International Law. Materials regarding the PLO on the Internet are available at http://home.att.net/~slomansonb/txtcsesite.html; click on PLO.

In 1919, the Palestinian people were provisionally recognized as an independent State by the League of Nations, as well as in the 1922 Mandate for Palestine addressed to Great Britain. The UN's 1947 partition plan would have created a Palestinian State, but for the outbreak of war between Arab States and the new State of Israel. The drive for a Palestinian State gained momentum in the 1970s. The creation of the State of Palestine has international support only insofar as it would occupy the *additional* territories conquered by Israel in various Middle East wars in the 1960s and 1970s—but not that portion of "Palestine" that became the independent State of Israel in 1948. The PLO historically denied Israel's right to exist in what it considered as "Palestine," dating from biblical times. Palestinians routinely characterize the UN partition plan of 1947 as a criminal act that denied them rights they believed were guaranteed to them by the 1919 recognition of Palestine and 1922 League Mandate to Britain.

Led by Yasir Arafat, the PLO initially insisted that a Palestinian State should *replace* Israel because the Jewish state had no right to exist in its current location. The PLO later softened its position by supposedly recognizing Israel's right to exist (although some of its more militant members—Hamas—still disagree) and that the PLO should be given territory taken by Israel during various Middle East conflicts after the 1947 UN partition plan (UN Gen. Ass. Res. 181[II]). The 1998 peace negotiations included Israel's demand that the PLO revoke the provision in the 1964 Covenant that calls for Israel's destruction. Israel's borders have not been fixed by international agreement with its neighbors. The PLO argues that Palestine's borders are not yet established.

In 1974, the PLO was invited to participate in the UN General Assembly's debate on the Palestine question, and in an effort to secure peace in the Middle East. (*See* G.A. Res. 3210, 29 UN GAOR Supp. [No. 108] at 3, UN Doc. A/RES/3210[XXIX] [1974], and G.A. Res. 3375, 30 UN GAOR Supp. [No. 27] at 3, UN Doc. A/RES/3375[XXX] [1975].) The PLO was then officially recognized by Austria, India, and the Soviet Union. In July 1998, the PLO was also accorded a unique, non-voting "observer" status in the UN General Assembly. The PLO can now raise issues, co-sponsor draft resolutions, and make speeches in the General Assembly. Participation in the UN was previously limited to traditional States and less controversial nongovernmental organizations (such as the International Red Cross).

In 1987, the US Congress enacted legislation entitled the Anti-Terrorism Act. It was designed to close the PLO's UN observer mission in New York City. The basis for the desired closure was that the PLO's alleged terrorist activities could flow into the US through the PLO's observer mission at the UN. The US government subsequently filed a lawsuit in a US court under the antiterrorist law, seeking to close the mission.

The PLO responded from Algiers by proclaiming the existence of the new and independent "State of Palestine." This 1988 declaration includes the assertions that "the people of Palestine fashioned its national identity" and "the Palestinian people has not ceased its valiant defence of its homeland . . . [of Palestine, which] was subjected to a new kind of foreign occupation" when Israel took over. (*See* "Palestine National Council Political Communiqué and Declaration of Independence," reprinted in 27 *Int'l Legal Mat'ls* 1660, 1668 [1988]. It contains much of the history surrounding this conflict.) This Palestinian declaration of statehood was immediately recognized by the Soviet Union. As of 1988, then, the PLO claimed that the State of Palestine finally achieved *de facto*—if not *de jure*—existence as a State.

In 1989, the International Court of Justice ruled against the US on its unilateral attempt to close the PLO mission at the UN headquarters in New York City. The Reagan administration unsuccessfully argued that the antiterrorist legislation required closure "irrespective of any international legal obligations that the United States may have. . . ." The US noted that since the PLO was *not* a State, the space for its observer mission had been provided only as a mere courtesy—because the US was the host government for the UN's New York facilities. One basis for countering the US position materialized in mid-1988. Jordan's King Hussein severed all forms of legal and administrative ties between Jordan and the West Bank—where Jewish settlers were introduced by Israel, and which the PLO claims to be its territory.

The UN General Assembly adopted Resolution 43/177 in December 1988, whereby *it* recognized the new State of Palestine by according it observer-*State* status, augmenting the mere "observer" status the PLO achieved years before. As of 1990, 114 States had recognized the newly proclaimed State of Palestine, some twenty States more than the ninety-three that recognized Israel. In 1993, the PLO Chairman and the Prime Minister of Israel met on an historical occasion (with President Clinton and the worldwide press in Washington, DC) whereby they undertook to negotiate an end to the Middle East crisis. They established a program resulting in a partial turnover of autonomy over Gaza and the West Bank to the Palestinian National Authority—although the "land for peace" process was subsequently bogged down. In 1998, PLO Chairman Arafat announced that he would thus proclaim the *de jure* statehood of Palestine within two years, regardless of Israel's negotiating posture.

In March 1999, the European Union began to consider its potential recognition of a "Palestinian State." The EU reaffirmed the Palestinians' "right to self-determination" but did not actually recognize "Palestine."

Assume that the PLO is applying to the UN for full State membership. Did the PLO already satisfy any or all of the four traditional elements of statehood *before* the 1993–1994 Palestinian autonomy agreements? *After* the autonomy agreements?

Problem 2.B (end of §2.3) Members of the Palestine Liberation Organization (PLO) inhabit various countries in the Middle East. Although Israel and the PLO began to implement an autonomy agreement as to Gaza and the City of Jericho in 1994, the UN partition plan of 1947 "created" a Palestinian State—much of which devolved to other States as a result of ensuing wars between Arab States and Israel.

Are Palestinians within the States of Israel, Jordan, Lebanon, and Syria entitled to (1) secession, (2) succession, (3) self-determination, or (4) all of the above?

Problem 2.C (after §2.3 *East Timor* Case) In July 1998, the US began to give military aid to two Colombian Army units. The disclosed purpose was to protect human rights in Colombia. The US Department of State then commented that the aid includes night vision goggles, communications equipment, river boats, and aircraft—for the ostensible purpose of counter-narcotics operations.

Critics warned, however, that the real purpose for this "aid" is to augment the US role in Colombia's anti-guerilla war against indigenous forces desiring to overthrow the Colombian government. Colombian authorities noted that they have been given approval to use this materiel in a huge area of southern and eastern Colombia, which are the strongholds of the Revolutionary Armed Forces (RAF) of Colombia—one of Latin America's largest rebel forces.

Assume that the RAF has access to the UN general assembly or a media broadcast regarding this development in Colombia. The leader of the RAF claims that the US assistance to the Colombian Army has violated the indigenous population's right to self-determination. Three students (or groups) represent, respectively, the RAF, Colombia, and the US. They will now debate whether the various UN resolutions and ICJ cases (East Timor and Western Sahara) support the RAF's claim that Colombia and the US are thereby violating the Colombian people's right to self-determination.

Problem 2.D (end of §2.3) Europe's gypsies apparently began their westward exodus from India in the tenth century. They have been a migratory people with no territory, political influence, or formal organization. Their itinerant wandering is both the hallmark of their culture and their greatest conflict with structured societies. It is difficult to educate, tax, and count them in any nation's population census. The Nazis slaughtered numerous gypsies during World War II in a genocidal campaign to achieve racial purity. They have been driven from their homes by Bosnian Serbs and Croat military forces. Thousands fled to Italy and Germany in the 1990s, only to face attack by neo-Nazis and expulsion under strict immigration laws.

In 1997, the Czech Republic's President Havel admonished Czechs to end their intolerance of gypsies after a wave of them departed for Canada in the pursuit of a safe harbor. In 1991, a Sub-Commission of the UN Commission on Human Rights invited States with "Roma" communities to take all necessary steps to ensure equality and guarantee their protection and security within their various host States. UN Doc. E/CN.4/1992/2. Further details on this general dilemma for host States, and international humanitarian law, are provided in the "Gypsy Law Symposium," XLV *Amer. Journal Comparative Law* 225–442 (1997).

Perhaps one million Spanish gypsies now roam throughout Spain and camp in makeshift villages, literally on the edge of civilization, outside of towns and on the fringes of Spain's larger cities. Gypsies gathered in

Seville, Spain, in May 1994 for the first Gypsy Congress. This Congress was conducted under the auspices of the European Commission, the executive agency of the European Union. The Commission is trying to help gypsies help themselves in the current violence, surfacing with a fury in Europe's waves of ethnic violence that materialized after the Cold War.

Are Spain's gypsies entitled to self-determination? If so, how would that right be implemented?

Problem 2.E (end of §2.4) Under UN Security Council Resolution 777, the State of "Yugoslavia" ceased to exist, at least at the UN. In 1992, the former Yugoslavia split into what are currently five States—Bosnia-Herzegovina, Croatia, Macedonia, Slovenia, and the so-called rump State of Yugoslavia (consisting of Serbia and Montenegro).

Selection of the name "Republic of Macedonia" created a problem for one former Yugoslav territory and the fifteen States of the European Union (EU), including Greece. Greece was furious about the name chosen for this new country because of Greece's concern about its own province named Macedonia. The name "Macedonia" deeply resonates among the Greeks. Alexander the Great resided in this particular Greek province during his famous conquests of the Roman era. Now, Greece's northern province of Macedonia and the new Republic of Macedonia share a common international border of approximately 300 kilometers. Greece fears that the Republic of Macedonia—by selecting *that* particular name—has territorial aspirations for one day assimilating the Greek province of Macedonia. Greece refers to this area in the new Republic as "Skopje," the name of its capital city. The UN Secretary-General suggested that Macedonia at least change its name to "New" Macedonia, if that term were going to appear in its official country name.

The EU did not immediately recognize Macedonia, a territory desperately seeking recognition from other States. The EU had recognized Slovenia and Croatia approximately six months after their votes of independence from the former Yugoslavia. Regarding Macedonia, however, the EU leadership expressed that "there are still important matters to be addressed before a similar step by the Community and its member States will be taken." This was a smokescreen designed to temporarily delay recognition due to Greece's continuing objections to the recognition of Macedonia by member States of the EU. The EU then promulgated its Recognition Guidelines (§2.4) as the device for structuring mutually agreed upon succession, secession, and self-determination of the territories of the former Yugoslavia. All applicants for recognition by the EU must now comply with its requirements, including approval of the involvement of the UN Secretary-General, the Security Council, and the EU Conference on Yugoslavia for resolving conflicts.

The EU did not expressly recognize Macedonia. Instead, it determined that its member States "were willing to recognize that State as a sovereign and independent State . . . and under a name that can be accepted by all parties concerned [that is, Greece] . . . [while] member States look forward to establishing with the authorities in Skopje [Macedonia's capital] a fruitful cooperative relationship."

The US did not announce its intent to recognize Macedonia until February 1994, after six members of the European Union first recognized (the former Yugoslavian province) Macedonia as a State. The US had previously sent troops to "Macedonia" to help control the spread of the Yugoslavian conflict into other States, including Greece.

Questions: (1) Is Macedonia a "recognized" State? (2) What would Macedonia have to do in order to satisfy EU Guidelines for Recognition? (3) Did the EU member States essentially recognize Macedonia without recognizing its name? (4) *Should* Macedonia be recognized by other States outside of the EU?

Problem 2.F (§2.6, after *Nelson* Case) Assume that after the Supreme Court's *Nelson* opinion, the US senator who went to the aid of the Nelsons while the husband was confined in Saudi Arabia decides to help future litigants in another way. Senator Hawk proposes the following legislation to Congress as an amendment to the 1976 Foreign Sovereign Immunities Act:

> Be it hereby enacted that, from this day forward, all courts in the United States will—in doubtful cases involving the "commercial nature of the act" or conduct complained of—grant sovereign immunity to democratic sovereigns, and deny it by proceeding with cases against authoritarian sovereigns.

Two students will debate the propriety of this proposed legislation, specifically addressing whether Congress should thereby give democratic regimes greater sovereign immunity than authoritarian regimes.

◆ BIBLIOGRAPHY

§2.1 Legal Personality of the State

J. Hickey, Jr. (ed.), "International Legal Personality," 2 *Hofstra Law & Policy Symposium* 1–170 (articles on various topics).

R. Lapidoth & M. Hirsch (eds.), *The Arab–Israeli Conflict and Its Resolution: Selected Documents* (Dordrecht, Neth.; Boston: Martinus Nijhoff, 1992).

D. Murswiek, "The Issue of a Right of Secession—Reconsidered," in C. Tomuschat (ed.), *Modern Law of Self-Determination* 21 (Dordrecht, Neth.; Boston: Martinus Nijhoff, 1993).

A. Osiander, *The States System of Europe, 1640–1990: Peacemaking and the Conditions of International Stability* (Oxford, Eng.: Oxford Univ. Press, 1994).

N. Wallace-Bruce, *Claims to Statehood in International Law* (New York: Carlton Press, 1994).

W. Zartman (ed.), *Collapsed States: The Disintegration and Restoration of Legitimate Authority* (Boulder, CO: Rienner, 1995).

§2.2 Changing Infrastructure:

G. Abi-Saab, "The Newly Independent States and the Rules of International Law," 8 *Howard Law Journal* 95 (1962).

R. Anand, *Confrontation or Cooperation? International Law and the Developing Countries* (New Delhi: Banyan, 1986).

A. Bozeman, *The Future of Law in a Multicultural World* (Princeton: Princeton Univ. Press, 1971).

A. Carty, *The Decay of International Law? A Reappraisal of the Limits of Legal Imagination in International Affairs* (Dover, NH: Manchester Univ. Press, 1986).

W. Friedmann, *The Changing Structure of International Law* (New York: Columbia Univ. Press, 1964).

K. Ginther & W. Benedek (eds.), *New Perspectives and Conceptions of International Law: An Afro–European Dialogue* (Vienna: Springer-Verlag, 1983).

E. McWhinney, "The 'New' Countries and the 'New' International Law: The United Nations' Special Conference on Friendly Relations and Cooperation Among States," 60 *American Journal of International Law* 1 (1966).

S. Sinha, "Treatment of Asian and African Peoples under International Law during the Past Four Centuries," ch. 1 in *New Nations and the Law of Nations* 11 (Leiden, Neth.: A.W. Sijthoff, 1967).

W. Zartman (ed.), *Collapsed States: The Disintegration and Restoration of Legitimate Authority* (Boulder, CO: Reinner, 1995).

§2.3 Changes in State Status

SUCCESSION

S. Anaya, *Indigenous Peoples in International Law* (Oxford, Eng.: Oxford Univ. Press, 1996).

S. Bernanzez, "Succession of States," ch. 18 in M. Bedjaoui (ed.), *International Law: Achievements and Prospects* 381 (Dordrecht, Neth.: Martinus Nijhoff, 1991).

A. Cassese, *Self-Determination of Peoples: A Legal Reprisal* (Cambridge, Eng.: Cambridge Univ. Press, 1995).

V. D. Degan, "Equity in Matters of State Succession," ch. 14 in R. Macdonald, *Essays in Honour of Wang Tieya* 201 (Dordrecht, Neth.: Martinus Nijhoff, 1994).

Israel–Palestine Liberation Organization, "Agreement on the Gaza Strip and the Jericho Area," 33 *Int'l Legal Mat'ls* 622 (1994).

R. Lapidoth & M. Hirsch (eds.), *The Arab–Israeli Conflict and Its Resolution: Selected Documents* (Dordrecht, Neth.: Martinus Nijhoff, 1992).

SELF-DETERMINATION

A. Eide, "In Search of Constructive Alternatives to Secession," in C. Tomuschat (ed.), *Modern Law of Self-Determination* 139 (Dordrecht, Neth.: Martinus Nijhoff, 1993).

GENERAL

G. Ginsburgs, *From Soviet to Russian International Law: Studies in Continuity and Change* (The Hague, Neth.: Martinus Nijhoff, 1998).

§2.4 Recognition

C. Antonowicz, "On the Nature of Recognition of States in International Law," 8 *Polish Yearbook of International Law* 217 (1976).

C. Chinkin, "The Law and Ethics of Recognition: Cambodia and Timor," ch. 10 in P. Keal (ed.), *Ethics and Foreign Policy* 190 (St. Leonards, Australia: Allen & Unwin, 1992).

Kato, "Recognition in International Law: Some Thoughts on Traditional Theory, Attitudes of and Practice by African States," 19 *Indian J. of Int'l Law* 299 (1970).

G. Knight & H. Chiu, "The Law of the War and Neutrality in Warfare at Sea," ch. XV in *The International Law of the Sea: Cases, Documents, and Readings* (London: Elsevier, 1991).

J. Ruda, "Recognition of States and Governments," ch. 21 in M. Bedjaoui (ed.), *International Law: Achievements and Prospects* 449 (Dordrecht, Neth.: Martinus Nijhoff, 1991).

§2.5 State Responsibility

W. Butler, *Control over Compliance with International Law* (Dordrecht, Neth.: Martinus Nijhoff, 1991).

"State Responsibility," ch. 8 in R. Wallace, *International Law: A Student Introduction* 166 (2nd ed. London: Street & Maxwell, 1992).

Thesaurus Acroasium: Responsibility of States (Thessaloniki, Greece: Inst. Int'l Public Law & Int'l Relations, 1993).

J. Weiler, A. Cassese, & M. Spinedi (eds.), *International Crimes of State: A Critical Analysis of the ILC's Draft Article 19 on State Responsibility* (Berlin: De Gruyter, 1989).

§2.6 Sovereign Immunity

J. Dellapenna, *Suing Foreign Governments and Their Corporations* (Wash., DC: Bureau Nat'l Aff., 1988).

J. Donoghue, "Taking the 'Sovereign' Out of the Foreign Sovereign Immunities Act: A Functional Approach to the Commercial Activity Exception," 17 *Yale J. Int'l Law* 489 (1992).

"OAS Inter-American Draft Convention on Jurisdictional Immunity of States," 22 *Int'l Legal Mat'ls* 292 (1983).

S. Sucharitkul, "Immunity of States," ch. 16 in M. Bedjaoui (ed.), *International Law: Achievements and Prospects* 327 (Dordrecht, Neth.: Martinus Nijhoff, 1991).

"US Foreign Sovereign Immunities Act of 1976," 15 *Int'l Legal Mat'ls* 1388 (1976).

◆ ENDNOTES

1. **1992:** B. Boutros-Ghali, *An Agenda for Peace: Preventative Diplomacy, Peacemaking and Peace-keeping* 9 (New York: UN, 1992). **1995:** B. Boutros-Ghali, *An Agenda for Peace: Supplement to an Agenda for Peace* 1 (New York: UN, 1995).
2. W. Friedmann, *The Changing Structure of International Law* 214 (New York: Columbia Univ. Press, 1964).
3. *See generally* W. Rice, "Nation v. State—Judgment for Nation," 44 *Amer. J. Int'l L.* 162 (1950); M. Brandon, "State v. Nation: Fresh Evidence Admitted," 44 *Amer. J. Int'l L.* 577 (1950). **State:** Article 1, 165 *LON Treaty Series* 19, 49 US Stat. 3097. **Nation:** B. Driessen, *A Concept of Nation in International Law* 13 (The Hague, Neth.: T.M.C. Asser Inst., 1992) [hereinafter Driessen]. **Community:** "Greco–Bulgarian Communities Case," 1930 *PCIJ Rep.*, ser. B, No. 17, p. 33. **People:** Driessen, p. 17. **Government:** J. Fox, *Dictionary of International & Comparative Law* 75 (2d ed. New York: Oceana, 1997). **Sovereign:** J. Falk & J. Camilleri, *The End of Sovereignty? The Politics of a Shrinking and Fragmenting World* 11 (Hants, Eng.: Edward Elgar Pub., 1992).
4. 165 *LON Treaty Series* 19, 49 US Stat. 3097.
5. M. Gunter, "What Happened to the United Nations Ministate Problem?" 71 *Amer. J. Int'l L.* 110 (1977) (no minimum population); "Case Concerning Acquisition of Polish Nationality *(Germany v. Poland),*" 1923 *PCIJ,* ser. B, No. 7, p. 18 (Judgment of Sept. 15, 1923) (express grant not required).
6. League of Nations, Commission of Jurists on Aaland Islands Dispute, *Official Journal, Special Supp.* 4, at 8–9 (1920).
7. **Treaties:** US Const., Art. I, §10(1). **Duties:** Art. 1, §10(2).
8. J. H. Verzijl, "Western European Influence on the Foundations of International Law," 1 *Int'l Relations* 137 (1955).
9. E. Osmanczyk, *Encyclopedia of the United Nations and International Agreements* 95 (2nd ed. London: Taylor & Francis, 1990).
10. **Non-Western writer:** K. Sastri, "International Law and Relations in Ancient India," 1 *Indian Yearbk. Int'l Affairs* 97 (1952). **Western writer:** C. Alexandrowicz, "Mogul Sovereignty and the Law of Nations," 4 *Indian Yearbk. Int'l Affairs* 317, 318 (1955).
11. **Colonial aggression basis for self-defense:** R. Anand, "Attitude of the Asian–African States Toward Certain Problems of International Law," 15 *Int'l & Comp. Law Q.* 55, 63–66 (1966). **"Armed" attack requirement:** UN Charter, Art. 51. For UN Charter articles on the Web, *see* http://home.att.net/~slomansonb/txtcsesite.html.
12. The declaration is reprinted in 13 *Int'l Legal Mat'ls* 715 (1974). The G-77 charter is reprinted in 14 *Int'l Legal Mat'ls* 251 (1975).
13. *See* "Treaty on the Final Settlement with Respect to Germany," 29 *Int'l Legal Mat'ls* 1186, 1188 (1990) ("united Germany shall comprise the territory of the [FRG, GDR,] . . . and the whole of Berlin").
14. *See* R. Jennings & A. Watts, 1 *Oppenheim's International Law* (Part I) §§60–70 (9th ed. Essex, Eng.: Longman, 1993) [hereinafter *Oppenheim treatise*]. Regarding succession between *organizations,* the subject matter of Chapter 3, *see* P. Meyers, *Succession Between International Organizations* (London: Kegan Paul Int'l, 1993).
15. **1978 treaty:** UN Doc. A/Conf. 80/31. **1983 treaty:** UN Doc. A/Conf. 117/14 (neither yet in force).
16. **Colombia:** J. Moore, 5 *Digest of International Law* 341 (Wash., DC: US Gov't Printing Off., 1906). **Texas:** J. Moore, 3 *History and Digest of the International Arbitrations to Which the United States Has Been a Party* 3223 (Wash., DC: US Gov't Print. Off., 1898).
17. *Oppenheim treatise* (Part I), §62, 211–213 (cited in note 14).
18. "Regarding Dues for Reply Coupons Issued in Croatia," 23 *Int'l L. Rep.* 591 (1956).
19. *See* **1983 treaty,** Article 9 on property & Article 36 on debts (cited in note 15).
20. *Oppenheim treatise* (Part I), §62, 218–219 (cited in note 14).
21. A. Buchanan, *Secession: The Morality of Political Divorce from Fort Sumter to Lithuania and Quebec* 2 (Boulder, CO: Westview Press, 1991).
22. O. Schachter, "The Development of International Law Through the Legal Opinions of the United Nations Secretariat," XXV *British Yearbk. Int'l L.* 91, 107 (1948).
23. "Namibia (South-West Africa) Case," 1971 *ICJ Rep.* 55.
24. **Res. 1514:** Declaration on the Granting of Independence to Colonial Countries and Peoples, UN GAOR 15th Sess., Supp. No. 16 (A/4884), p. 66. **Res. 1541:** UN GAOR 15th Sess., Supp. No. 16 (A/4684), p. 29. **Res. 2625:** UN GAOR 25th Sess., Supp. No. 8 (A/8028), p. 121. **CPR Covenant:** 999 U.N.T.S. 171. **ESC Covenant:** 999 U.N.T.S. 3. **1970 Declaration:** UN GAOR 25th Sess., Supp. No. 8, (A/8028) p. 121. **Reservations:** *See, e.g.,* United Kingdom, UN GAOR 21st Sess., Third Comm., 1496th Mtg., 16 Dec. 1966, pp. 10–11.
25. This argument is explored in W. Cravens, "The Future of Islamic Legal Arguments in International Boundary Disputes Between Islamic States," 55 *Wash. & Lee Law Rev.* 529 (1998).
26. "Western Sahara (Advisory Opinion)," 1975 *ICJ Rep.* 12, para 162; reprinted in 14 *Int'l Legal Mat'ls* 1355 (1975).
27. P. Chandra, *International Law* 28 (New Delhi: Vikas, 1985) (chaotic); D. O'Connell, *International Law* 127 (2nd ed. New York: Oceana, 1970) (confusing); J. Dugard, *Recognition and the United Nations* 28 (Cambridge, Eng.: Grotius, 1987) (controversial) [hereinafter *Recognition*].

28. J. Ruda, *Recognition of States and Governments,* ch. 21 in M. Bedjaoui (ed.), *International Law: Achievements and Prospects* 450 (Dordrecht, Neth.: Martinus Nijhoff, 1991). On the historical evolution of recognition practice, *see* G. Abi-Saab, "International Law and the International Community: The Long Road to Universality" 36–39 (The Role of "Recognition"), ch. 1 in R. MacDonald (ed.), *Essays in Honour of Wang Tieya* (Dordrecht, Neth.: Martinus Nijhoff, 1994).
29. E. McDowell, "Contemporary Practice of the United States Relating to International Law," 71 *Amer. J. Int'l L.* 337 (1977) (recognition by other States); C. Fenwick, *International Law* 157–159 (4th ed. New York: Appleton-Century-Crofts, 1965) (ethnocentric motives); *see* "The Helena," 4 *Ch. Rob.* 3 (1801) (English case on pirate treaties), reprinted in W. Bishop, *International Law, Cases and Materials* 301 (3rd ed. Boston: Little, Brown & Co., 1971); G. Von Glahn, *Law Among Nations* 87–88 (6th ed. New York: Macmillan, 1992) (commercial and military motives).
30. Two major treatises sparked this post-war debate about the nature of recognition and are still the classics. Compare H. Lauterpacht, *Recognition in International Law* 63 (Cambridge, Eng.: Cambridge Univ. Press, 1947) (recognition is not primarily a manifestation of national policy, but the fulfillment of an international duty) with T. Chen, *The International Law of Recognition* 61 (Green ed. London: Stevens, 1951) (recognition is merely declarative of the existing fact of statehood).
31. The author thanks Mary Durfee, Associate Professor of the Social Sciences Department at Michigan Technological University, for this useful analogy.
32. Genaro Estrada's statement is reprinted in 25 *Amer. J. Int'l L. Supp.* 203 (1931). A provocative response was published in P. Jessup, "The Estrada Doctrine," 25 *Amer. J. Int'l Law* 719 (1930).
33. **EU Guidelines:** Reprinted in 31 *Int'l Legal Mat'ls* 1485 (1992) [hereinafter *Guidelines*]. **OAS Haiti resolution:** 86 *Amer. J. Int'l L.* 667 (1992). **Scholars:** R. Pinkney, *Democracy in the Third World* (Boulder, CO: Rienner, 1994); J. Dunn (ed.), *Democracy, The Unfinished Journey: 508 BC to AD 1993* (Oxford, Eng.: Oxford Univ. Press, 1992); T. Franck, "The Emerging Right to Democratic Governance," 86 *Amer. J. Int'l L.* 46 (1992).
34. *See* P. Brown, "The Legal Effects of Recognition," 44 *Amer. J. Int'l L.* 617 (1950); "Comment, Effects in Private Litigation of Failure to Recognize New Foreign Governments," 19 *Univ. Chicago L. Rev.* 73 (1951).
35. *The Three Friends,* 166 US 1, 63, 17 S.Ct. 495, 502, 41 L.Ed. 897 (1897).
36. "Unilateral and Third Party Claims: Neutrality," Section 13.4 in C. Chinkin, *Third Parties in International Law* 299 (Oxford, Eng.: Clarendon Press, 1993).
37. *See* English translation in "Collective Recognition and Non-Recognition Under the League of Nations," ch. 3 in *Recognition* 28 (cited in note 27). Arguments for and against are examined in "Recognition," ch. 4 in *Collective Recognition by the United Nations* 41 (note 27 above).
38. *Memorandum on the Legal Aspects of the Problem of Representation in the United Nations,* UN Doc. S/1466, Mar. 9, 1950.
39. *See Guidelines,* note 33 above.
40. *See, e.g.,* 2 *Foreign Pol. Bulletin* 39, 42 (Nov./Dec. 1991) (testimony of US Deputy Ass't of Dep't of State).
41. Whether damage is actually required is the subject of an intense debate. *See* A. Tanzi, "Is Damage a Distinct Condition for the Existence of an Internationally Wrongful Act?" in M. Spinedi & B. Simma (eds.), *United Nations Codification of State Responsibility* (New York: Oceana, 1987).
42. "Case Concerning the Factory at Chorzow," *PCIJ* ser. A, No. 17, p. 29 (1928).
43. "*Rainbow Warrior* Arbitration," 82 *Int'l L. Rep.* 499, 551 (1991). *See* UN Secretary-General's opinion contained in 81 *Amer. J. Int'l L.* 325 (1987).
44. 1949 *ICJ Rep.* 4, 18.
45. "State Responsibility," ch. 14 in M. Shaw, *International Law* 545–549 (4th ed. Cambridge, Eng.: Grotius, 1997).
46. *See* UN, *The Work of the International Law Commission* 121 (New York: UN, 1996). On the various phases of the ILC's work, *see* I. Sinclair, *The International Law Commission,* ch. II, at 45 (Cambridge, Eng.: Grotius, 1987). Various provisions, their genesis, and their development are discussed in S. Rosenne, *The International Law Commission's Draft Articles on State Responsibility* (Dordrecht, Neth.: Martinus Nijhoff, 1991).
47. **ILC draft:** reprinted in 37 *Int'l Legal Mat'ls* 440 (1998). **State responses:** *See* www.law.cam.ac.uk/rcil/ILCSR/Statresp.htm.
48. **OAS Web address:** *See* http://home.att.net/~slomansonb/txtcsesite.html; click on OAS Charter.
49. *"Ministry of Defence v. Ndegwa,"* 103 *Int'l Law Rep.* 235 (Kenya Court App., 1983).
50. "1 Queen's Bench 149" (1893), reported in *All Eng. Rep.* 1019 (1963).
51. **Violation of International Law:** L. Henkin, "The Invasion of Panama Under International Law: A Gross Violation," 29 *Columbia J. Transnat'l L.* 293 (1991). **Rejection of head of State immunity:** *US v. Noriega,* 117 F.3rd 1206 (11th Cir., 1997), *cert. den'd,* 118 US 1389 (1998).
52. *Aldona S. v. United Kingdom,* Supreme Court of Poland (1948), reported in 90 *Journal du Droit International* 191 (1963).
53. D. Fienerman, "Sovereign Immunity in the Chinese Case and Its Implications for the Future of International Law," in R. MacDonald (ed.), *Essays in Honour of Wang Tieya* 251 (Dordrecht, Neth.: Martinus Nijhoff, 1994).
54. *Collision with Foreign Government Owned Motor Car,* Supreme Court of Austria, reported in 40 *Int'l L. Rep.* 73 (1961).

CHAPTER THREE

International Organizations

NEW YORK, OCT. 24, 1998—ON UNITED NATIONS DAY, the UN Security Council voted 13–0 to endorse an October 12 NATO agreement that will allow 2,000 monitors to patrol the Yugoslavian region of Kosovo. Serb forces have driven many ethnic Albanians from their homes and into surrounding hills, spawning yet another round of ethnic cleansing in Yugoslavia since the end of the Cold War. NATO has threatened air strikes if Yugoslavia persists in using this method to control the Kosovo separatist movement.

This resolution is believed to be the first express UN endorsement of a NATO military operation. China and Russia abstained, asserting that the "unanimous" resolution, which was renegotiated in a rare Saturday session, does *not* authorize the use of force. It unquestionably targets the Yugoslavian government, which has allegedly killed thousands of Yugoslav Albanians and driven 300,000 from their homes, from February through October 1998.

The monitors will be provided by countries from the Organization for Security and Cooperation in Europe. Their task will be to verify Yugoslavia's commitment to cease its attack on ethnic Albanians.

This will be the first time that several international organizations have cultivated an arrangement governing a nation's conduct against its own citizens on its own soil.

—Adapted from a report by the Associated Press on October 25, 1998.

CHAPTER OUTLINE

INTRODUCTION

Chapter 2 addressed the legal identity and characteristics of the State, the primary actor in international affairs. This chapter continues with a related building block—the attributes of the international organization, an actor with increasing influence in global affairs.

There are important contrasts between the legal capacity of States and international organizations. Each State is an independent sovereign entity, enjoying equal status with other States—regardless of size or power—under International Law. Each one is endowed with the fundamental characteristic of statehood: power over persons and things within its borders. An international organization, on the other hand, owes its existence to the discretion of the States that created it (unlike the *non*-governmental organization, which is not beholden to a State or group of States for its existence).

After first outlining the legal essence of international organizations and then classification paradigms, this chapter will focus on the key *global* organization—the United Nations—and the most comprehensive *regional* organization—the European Union. The salient features of other regional organizations are succinctly described in this chapter, while *economic* international organizations are addressed in Chapter 13's analysis of International Economic Relations.

Like Chapter 2's analysis of *State* immunity, this chapter closes with fascinating details about *organizational* immunity of the UN and regional organizations operating within the boundaries of their member States. On completion of this third chapter, you will be prepared to undertake the final preliminary building block of International Law: the status of the *individual*.

◆ 3.1 LEGAL PERSONALITY OF ORGANIZATIONS

INTRODUCTION TO INTERNATIONAL ORGANIZATIONS

This chapter addresses "international organization" in terms of a formal institution providing the structure for accomplishing treaty-based objectives. These associations serve the diverse needs of member States, and also non-governmental citizens within those States, all of whom benefit by the existence of an international organization established to work toward defined objectives.[1]

What *is* an international organization? It is a formal and continuously operating institution established by agreement of the affiliated members that created it. This section of the book deals mostly with public international organizations established by three or more States. (Section 3.2 will address some private, *non*-governmental international organizations.) The typical intergovernmental organization is established by a treaty among States that desire the fulfillment of common objectives that they set forth in the constitutive instrument. For example, Canada, Mexico, and the United States established the North American Free Trade Agreement (NAFTA) in 1994. It was created to facilitate the trade objectives of its regional member States.

We begin this study by drawing a parallel between States and international organizations. The history of the modern *State* began 350 years ago with the 1648 Peace of Westphalia (§1.3). The idea of an international *organization* pursuing the common objectives of its member States is not a twentieth-century development.

Peace and religion were early motivators. The Egyptian Pharaoh Ikhnaton envisioned an international theological order some 3,400 years ago. The Amphictyon League of the ancient Greek city-states organized themselves with a view toward lessening the brutality of war. The medieval poet Dante proposed a global super-State operating under control of a central court of justice. Yet these were not organizations in the contemporary sense described below, and there were no permanent organizational institutions.

The following excerpt succinctly traces the evolution of international organization:

"Principles of the Institutional Law of International Organizations" (1996)

DR. CHITTHARANJAN AMERASINGHE

History of International Organizations (Pages 1–6)

Bilateral and even multilateral relations between States have a long history, but the establishment of public international organizations functioning as institutions is essentially a development of the late nineteenth century. Consular relations designed to protect interests in commerce, and diplomatic relations concerned with representation of States, go far back in history: the former to the times of the ancient Greeks and Romans; the latter to a somewhat later period, taking its modern shape in the fifteenth century. It is in these institutions that the origins of the more complex institutions which started evolving in the early nineteenth century can be found.

When bilateral relationships based on the existence of diplomatic embassies or missions were found to be inadequate to meet more complex situations arising from problems concerning not just two but many States, a means had to be found for representation in the same forum of the interests of all the States concerned. This was the international conference. It was the *ad hoc* temporary conference convened for a specific purpose and terminating once agreement was reached on the subject matter and a treaty was adopted that evolved ultimately into permanent international organizations with organs that function on a permanent basis and meet periodically.

The Peace of Westphalia of 1648 was the result of such a conference, as was the settlement in 1815 through the Congress of Vienna and the Treaty of Versailles in 1919. There were other conferences such as the Congress of Berlin of 1871 and the Hague Conferences of 1899 and 1907 which concerned other matters than peace. Conferences were convened to solve problems on a multilateral basis. The result of the conference would generally be a formal treaty or convention or, where such an agreement was not desirable or obtainable, a memorandum or minutes of the conference. . . .

These conferences proved inadequate for the solution of [specific, long-term] political problems. They were even more inadequate for the regulation of relations between the peoples of the different countries which were the result of their common interests. Thus, in the nineteenth century, there developed associations, international in character, among groups other than governments. There followed similar developments among governments which were, however, at that time rather in the administrative than in the political field.

In the western hemisphere, there were somewhat different but significant developments. The pan-American system resorted to conferences at a regional level, beginning in 1826, though they did not yield tangible results till the Washington Conference of 1885. These conferences had a periodic character after that and culminated in the formation of the OAS [Organization of American States]. They contributed to the techniques of international organizations in several ways: (i) the conferences were not convened at the initiative of any one State, but the time and place of each were decided by the previous one; (ii) the agenda of each conference was prepared by the governing body of the standing administrative organ, the Pan-American Union (established in 1912); (iii) a greater possibility existed to undertake preparatory work before each conference than in the case of *ad hoc* conferences; and (iv) the periodic character of the conferences made possible the development of more elaborate and formal procedural arrangements.

By contrast, the non-governmental unions or associations sprang from the realization by non-governmental bodies, consisting of both private individuals and corporate associations, that their interests had an international character which required that those interests be promoted in cooperation with similar bodies in other countries through permanent international associations. Perhaps the first conference of a private nature which led to the establishment of an association was the one which formulated the World Anti-Slavery Convention of 1840. Since then there have been a plethora of private associations or unions established, including the International Committee of the Red Cross (1863), the International Law Association (1873), the Inter-Parliamentary Union (1889) and the International Chamber of Commerce (1919), to mention only a few. Because of the proliferation of these private unions, in 1910 the Union of International Associations was formed to coordinate their activities, among other things. These private unions . . . anticipated and antedated the development of the public unions. Their appearance suggests that the growth of the international organization was the result of a universal human need.

The public international union which appeared also in the nineteenth century, especially in its second half, is more important for the development of the modern international organization. The public unions which sprang up at that time were international administrative unions—agencies which had a certain permanency and dealt with non-political technical activities. These were also associations of governments or administrations as contrasted with private bodies. The Congress of Vienna had proclaimed the principle of freedom of navigation which led to the appearance of many river commissions. A good example of these was the Rhine Commission which was invested with considerable powers, including both legislative and political powers. There were commissions for other rivers, such as the Danube, Elbe and Po. Numerous other administrative unions in many fields appeared pursuant to needs as they arose. The Universal Telegraphic Union was established in 1865 with an administration as its central organ. The

Universal Postal Union was established in 1874. There were other unions which sprang up such as the International Union of Railway Freight Transportation (1890), the International Bureau of Industrial Property (1883), the International Bureau of Literary Property (1886) and the International Office of Public Health (1907).

Such unions generally had periodical conferences or meetings of the representatives of member States, decisions being taken usually by unanimous vote, and a permanent secretariat (bureau) which performed the administrative tasks. One of the principal contributions of the unions to the concept of the international organization was the institutional element which was secured through a standing organ, the bureau, and provided the stepping stone from the technique of the conference to that of the organization. In some cases there were permanent deliberative or legislative organs as well (e.g., the UPU and the International Telegraphic Union). The trend toward the permanence of association was very marked. . . .

It was in 1919 after the Treaty of Versailles, when the League of Nations was created, that an attempt was made to create a political organization of an open and universal character. Since then the public inter-governmental or inter-State organization has become firmly established in international relations, a development which culminated in the establishment of the United Nations and its specialized agencies.

The nineteenth century has been described as 'the era of *preparation for* international organization,' this chronological period being between 1815 and 1914, while the years which have passed since the momentous event of 1914 must in a sense be regarded as 'the era of *establishment* of international organization, which, in these terms comes to be regarded as a phenomenon of the twentieth century.' The institutionalization today in inter-State relations has led to international organizations influencing far more than in the past the shaping of international relations and the development of the international law intended for their regulation. In an important sense great power diplomacy conducted at summit meetings has now given way increasingly to a new form of multilateralism achieved through international organizations like the UN as negotiating arenas available to all States. . . .

The post–Napoleonic Congress of Vienna of 1814–1815 temporarily set the stage for developing rules of international diplomacy. This Congress brought the nations of Europe together in *peacetime* to try to create rules for preventing another decades-long war in Europe. Unfortunately, this goal was not realized because of a variety of factors including the following: friction created by a waning British Empire attempting to control its historical leadership position in Europe; the expansionist leanings of the "Holy Alliance" of Austria, Prussia, and Russia as well as the Islamic Ottoman Empire; and a number of regional wars that deflected the Vienna Conference idea of meetings at regular intervals to *prevent* war rather than merely dealing directly with its consequences.

Prior to the close of World War I, public international organizations were not as ubiquitous as they are today. Some non-governmental organizations, such as the Hague Conferences of 1899 and 1907 and the International Red Cross, were created to control the negative aspects of State war potential. There were no public or intergovernmental organizations consisting of States and operating through permanent administrative organs. There had been a century of relative peace since the defeat of Napoleon. It then became evident that avoiding another global war would be of paramount interest to all States.

Governmental leaders recognized the role of the uncontrolled State in causing World War I. This was the greatest malfunction in State relations since the beginning of the Peace of Westphalia in 1648. The Westphalian model was also responsible for the modern conception of the State as being the *only* actor in International Law. This preoccupation had to change if a process of international organization were to materialize.

There had to be a period of relative global peace before international organizations could effectively function as international actors. The 1919 postwar meeting of the victorious nations at Versailles, France (like the 1814 meeting of Napoleon's victors), was the real cornerstone of modern international organization and regular intergovernmental collaboration. This body brought the notion of a "League of Nations" to fruition. Economic and social questions were not totally ignored. Such matters took a back seat, however, until the 1945

UN drafting conference at San Francisco. The League and the UN became the primary examples of intergovernmental organization. If swords were to be beaten into plowshares, then these twentieth-century international organizations would have to address economic and social matters as well. They would also have to consider individual rights, which were long excluded from direct protection on the international plane (a major contribution of the European Union, discussed in §3.4).

The Ford Foundation, a US-based research and policy-making institution, has traditionally advocated increased reliance on international organization as the vehicle for effecting positive changes in international relations. Its studies embrace the concept of international cooperation in an era when the State is the primary international player. In a 1990 study on international organizations and law, the Ford Foundation articulated a shifting paradigm whereby international organizations and non-governmental organizations would both assume a greater role in the progressive development of international order. As asserted in the foundation's serviceable position paper regarding the resulting need of more effective international organizations:

> [I]t is abundantly clear that no single nation now dominates our age. The United States, the architect of the postwar order, is no longer able to control events singlehandedly, if it ever could. Japan, the European Community, the newly industrializing countries . . . and the dominant nations in some regions have become influential international actors. . . . Partly as a consequence of this diffusion of power, international organizations face far different challenges now than they did forty years ago. The United Nations, Breton Woods institutions [establishing the International Monetary Fund], and the international trade system are all under strain. . . .
>
> Linking the fields of international organizations and international law to multilateral cooperation . . . suggests an underlying conviction that institutionalized global cooperation is a necessity . . . [that] should be based in law and should include enforceable rights and obligations.[2]

GROWTH IN INTERNATIONAL ORGANIZATIONS

There is a striking parallel in the growth of States and international organizations (IOs) since the close of World War II. The number of States increased dramatically, from fifty-one to nearly two hundred (*see* Exhibit 2.1 in §2.2). There has been an equally spectacular growth in the number of *international organizations,* from several hundred to nearly five thousand. Exhibit 3.1 (page 110) shows the dramatic growth in these organizations.

LEGAL CAPACITY UNDER INTERNATIONAL LAW

An international organization of States has legal capacity under International Law if it satisfies three essential elements. *First,* it must be a *permanent* association of State members with established objectives and administrative organs. The League of Nations, the predecessor of the United Nations, satisfied this prerequisite because its member States intended for it to function indefinitely. The League's peace objectives, and its organs geared toward achieving them, qualified it as an international organization. *Second,* an international organization must possess some power that is *distinct* from the sovereign power of its State members. Organs of the European Union can order a member State to act, over that State's objection, in matters defined by the Union's constitutive international treaties (discussed further in the Irish abortion case in §3.4). *Third,* the association's powers must be exercisable on an *international* level, rather than solely under the national legal systems of its member States. Public international organizations possess a legal personality or capacity to exercise certain "governmental" powers in a manner similar to those of their individual State members. When those States yield the requisite degree of sovereignty to the organization, it has truly international power—the capacity to engage in conduct otherwise reserved for States. Examples include the ability to conclude treaties with other organizations or individual States, and to require member States to act, or refrain from acting, in a particular way.

Not all international organizations are "public" entities in this sense. It is a popular myth, for example, that the International Criminal Police Organization (Interpol) operates on an international level that allows its agents to track and arrest international fugitives. In fact, Interpol's agents cannot act without the express consent of the national police of any State wherein it maintains a presence. It does not possess any international police power to apprehend criminals.[3]

The International Court of Justice provided a useful analysis of this capacity in the following case. In November 1947, UN General Assembly Resolution 181(II) par-

EXHIBIT 3.1 INTERNATIONAL ORGANIZATIONS BY YEAR AND TYPE (1909–1997)*

Year	Non-Governmental	Inter-Governmental	Total All Types
1909	176	37	213
1951	832	123	955
1960	1,268	154	1,422
1968	3,318	229	3,547
1976	6,222	252	6,474
1978	9,521	289	9,810
1983	17,030	2,549	19,579
1985	20,634	3,546	24,180
1987	23,248	3,897	27,145
1989	20,063	4,068	24,131
1991	23,635	4,565	28,200
1993	28,901	5,103	34,004
1995	36,054	5,668	41,722
1996	38,243	5,885	44,128
1997	40,306	6,115	46,421

*Adapted from Union of International Associations, Vol. 3, *Yearbook of International Organizations 1997–1998,* Table 2, Appendix 3, p. 1749 (34th ed. Munich: K.G. Saur Munchen Publishers, 1998).

titioned the former British Mandate, referred to as "Palestine," to create new Jewish and Arab States. This resolution was accepted by the Jewish community, but rejected by Arab States in the Middle East. Shortly after Israel declared its statehood in May 1948, hostilities began in and around what is now the State of Israel. Two weeks later, UN Security Council Resolution 50 called for a cessation of hostilities. A Norwegian, Count Bernadotte, was appointed the UN Mediator in Palestine for the purpose of negotiating a settlement. He was killed while pursuing this objective within the Palestinian territory. General Assembly Resolution 194(III) of December 1948 expressed a "deep appreciation of the progress achieved through the good offices of the late United Nations Mediator in promoting a peaceful adjustment of the future situation of Palestine, for which cause he sacrificed his life."[4] The issue for the International Court of Justice was whether the UN Charter gave the UN the legal capacity, as an international organization, to seek reparations from the responsible State or States whose agents killed UN employees:

Reparation for Injuries Suffered in the Service of the United Nations

ADVISORY OPINION, INTERNATIONAL COURT OF JUSTICE (1949)

1949 *International Court of Justice Reports* 174

Author's Note: *This is an International Court of Justice (ICJ) "Advisory Opinion." There is no State defendant—a process described further in Chapter 9 on the ICJ's caseload. The UN had requested that the Court render its opinion on the issue of whether the UN had the legal right to sue for damages to the UN, in its capacity as an organization* *employing international civil servants. In addition to the death of the UN's Mediator in Palestine, UN agents from various countries were being injured or killed while performing duties on behalf of the organization. Prior to the Court's decision in this case, only the victim's State of citizenship had the undisputed right to seek reparations for harm to that State—because of the death of its citizen, as explained in Chapter 4).*

In 1947, the UN thus asserted that there should be State responsibility to an international organization for injury to aliens (UN employees) caused by Israel, Jordan, and Egypt, where these individuals were working for the UN, in three separate incidents. The UN claimed that the responsible States failed to protect these individuals from private criminal acts. In the case of Israel, for example, two UN employees in Palestine were shot while driving through the Jewish portion of Jeru-salem. The UN sought compensation from Israel for the loss of their lives. Its claim was brought for Israel's "failure to exercise due diligence and to take all reasonable measures for the prevention of the assassination; liability of the government for actions committed by irregular forces in territory under the control of the Israel[i] authorities; and failure to take all measures required by international law and by the Security Council . . . to bring the culprits to justice." Israel refused to pay any compensation, claiming that only the State of the victim's nationality had the legal capacity to assert the State liability of Israel. (An account is available in 8 M. Whiteman, Digest of International Law *742 (Wash., DC: US Gov't Print. Off., 1967.)*

The Court analyzed whether the alleged harm to the UN, in its legal capacity as an international organization, could be reconciled with or supplant the right to seek reparations by the State of the victim's nationality. Put another way, if a Norwegian citizen is killed while abroad, only Norway could seek reparations from the responsible State prior to the creation of the UN. Could the UN Charter be construed, however, as furnishing the UN with the legal personality to sue in an international court for wrongs done to the UN in its capacity as the employer of the deceased?

Court's Opinion. The questions asked of the Court relate to the "capacity to bring an international claim"; accordingly, we must begin by defining what is meant by that capacity, and consider the characteristics of the Organization, so as to determine whether, in general, these characteristics do, or do not, include for the Organization a right to present an international claim [for injury to a UN agent].

Competence to bring an international claim is, for those possessing it, the capacity to resort to the customary methods recognized by international law for the establishment, the presentation and the settlement of claims. Among these methods may be mentioned protest, request for an enquiry, negotiation, and request for submission to an arbitral tribunal or to the Court in so far as this may be authorized by the Statute [of the ICJ].

This capacity certainly belongs to the State; a State can bring an international claim against another State. Such a claim takes the form of a claim between two political entities [i.e., States], equal in law, similar in form, and both the direct subjects of international law. It is dealt with by means of negotiation, and cannot, in the present state of the law as to international jurisdiction, be submitted to a tribunal, except with the consent of the States concerned. . . .

But, in the international sphere, has the Organization such a nature as involves the capacity to bring an international claim? In order to answer this question, the Court must first enquire whether the Charter has given the Organization such a position that it possesses, in regard to its Members, rights which it is entitled to ask them to respect. In other words, does the Organization possess international personality? . . .

The Charter has not been content to make the Organization created by it merely a centre "for harmonizing the actions of nations in the attainment of these common ends" (Article I, para. 4). It has equipped that centre with organs and has given it special tasks. It has defined the position of the Members in relation to the Organization by requiring them to give it every assistance in any action undertaken by it (Article 2, para. 5) and to accept and carry out the decisions of the Security Council; by authorizing the General Assembly to make recommendations to the Members; by giving the Organization legal capacity and privileges and immunities in the territory of each of its Members; and by providing for the conclusion of agreements between the Organization and its Members. Practice—in particular the conclusion of conventions to which the Organization is a party—has confirmed this character of the Organization, which occupies a position in certain respects in detachment from its Members, and which is under a duty to remind them, if need be, of certain obligations. . . . The "Convention on the Privileges and Immunities of the United Nations" of 1946 creates rights and duties between each of the signatories and the Organization (*see,* in particular, Section 35). It is difficult to see how such a convention could operate except upon the international plane and as between parties possessing international personality.

In the opinion of the Court, the Organization was intended to exercise and enjoy, and is in fact exercising and enjoying, functions and rights which can only be explained on the basis of the possession of a large measure of international personality and the capacity to operate upon an international plane. It is at present the supreme type of international organization, and it could not carry out the intentions of its founders if it was devoid of international personality. It must be acknowledged that its Members, by entrusting certain functions to it, with the attendant duties and responsibilities, have clothed it with the competence required to enable those functions to be effectively discharged.

Accordingly, the Court has come to the conclusion that the Organization is an international person. That is not the same thing as saying that it is a State, which it certainly is not, or that its legal personality and rights and duties are the same as those of a State. Still less is it the same thing as saying that it is a "super-State," whatever that expression may mean. It does not even imply that all its rights and duties must be upon the international plane, any more than all the rights and duties of a State must be upon that plane. What it does mean is that it is a subject of international law and capable of possessing international rights and duties, and that it has capacity to maintain its rights by bringing international claims.

The next question is whether the sum of the international rights of the Organization comprises the right to bring the kind of international claim described in the Request for this Opinion. That is a[n international organization's] claim against a State to obtain reparation in respect of the damage caused by the injury of an agent of the Organization in the course of the performance of his duties. Whereas a State possesses the totality of international rights and duties recognized by international law, the rights and duties of an entity such as the Organization must depend upon its purposes and functions as specified or implied in its constituent documents and developed in practice. The functions of the Organization are of such a character that they could not be effectively discharged if they involved the concurrent action, on the international plane, of fifty-eight or more Foreign Offices, and the Court concludes that the Members have endowed the Organization with capacity to bring international claims when necessitated by the discharge of its functions.

Having regard to its purposes and functions already referred to, the Organization may find it necessary, and has in fact found it necessary, to entrust its agents with important missions to be performed in disturbed parts of the world. Many missions, from their very nature, involve the agents in unusual dangers to which ordinary persons are not exposed. For the same reason, the injuries suffered by its agents in these circumstances will sometimes have occurred in such a manner that their national State would not be justified in bringing a claim for reparation on the ground of diplomatic protection, or, at any rate, would not feel disposed to do so. Both to ensure the efficient and independent performance of these missions and to afford effective support to its agents, the Organization must provide them with adequate protection.

The obligations entered into by States to enable the agents of the Organization to perform their duties are undertaken not in the interest of the agents, but in that of the Organization. When it claims redress for a breach of these obligations, the Organization is invoking its own right, the right that the obligations due to it should be respected. . . . In claiming reparation based on the injury suffered by its agent, the Organization does not represent the agent, but is asserting its own right, the right to secure respect for undertakings entered into towards the Organization. . . .

The question of reconciling action [this right to sue that is claimed] by the Organization with the rights of a national State may arise in another way; that is to say, when the agent bears the nationality of the defendant State. . . .

The action of the Organization is in fact based not upon the nationality of the victim but upon his status as agent of the Organization. Therefore it does not matter whether or not the State to which the claim is addressed regards him as its own national, because the question of nationality is not pertinent to the admissibility of the claim. . . .

◆ *Notes & Questions*

1. Article 104 of the UN Charter (*see* http://home.att.net/~slomansonb/txtcsesite.html; click on UN Charter) provides the UN with the "capacity as may be necessary" to exercise its functions and fulfill its purposes within the territory of each member State. What Charter gap was filled by the *Reparations* case?
2. Under Article 100 of the Charter, UN employees performing UN duties cannot "seek or receive instructions from any government or from any other authority external to the Organization." Assume that a UN agent—a citizen of Norway—is carrying out a mission on behalf of the UN in Norway. The *Reparations* case suggests reasons for conferring the protection of the UN on the injured individual, even though the UN employee is presumably still entitled to similar protection by his or her home State. Why?
3. There have been a number of incidents whereby the UN—or other international organizations such as the European Union—might sue to establish State responsibility, under the theory spawned by the ICJ's *Reparations* case:

   - In December 1991, the body of UN Colonel John Higgins was returned to the UN from Lebanon. While on a UN peacekeeping operation in 1989, he was kidnapped and later brutally murdered.
   - In January 1991, five European Community (now EU) truce observers were shot down in their helicopter by Serbian Yugoslavian military forces in Croatia. Of course, neither Lebanon nor what was then Yugoslavia claimed responsibility for the deaths of these agents while on peacekeeping missions for, respectively, the UN and the EU. It is precisely in this situation that these international organizations would hold the right, under the *Reparations* rationale, to seek redress from the responsible States.
   - In December 1992, Cambodia's Khmer Rouge freed eleven UN peacekeepers who had been kidnapped and threatened with execution. As a belligerent entity (*see* §2.4), the Khmer Rouge would bear responsibility under International Law for any harm that might have come to these UN peacekeepers.
   - In November 1997, gunmen stormed aboard a boat moored off Somalia to kidnap five aid workers from the UN and the EU.
   - In February 1998, four UN observers from the Czech Republic, Sweden, and Uruguay (two of the UN employees) were kidnapped by a heavily armed gang in Tbilisi, Georgia. The gang then presented the government of Georgia with the following demand: If seven prisoners accused of plotting to kill the President of Georgia were not released, these UN employees would be killed. Georgian police surrounded the house where the kidnapped UN personnel were being held and eventually captured the surviving gang members.

Question: In July 1998, four UN employees from Poland, Uruguay, Japan, and Tajikistan were shot in the former Soviet republic of Tajikistan. UN Secretary-General Kofi Annan said that they had been "ambushed and ruthlessly executed." You are the UN's lawyer: Who would be able to sue what country, or countries, and why?

Can the UN sue a member State in that State's courts? In the following case, the UN sued the US and a private shipping company—a non-State entity lacking the legal capacity to sue or be sued on the international plane. The US had specially designated the UN as an international organization, some years before this dispute arose, enabling the UN to enjoy the legal capacity in the host country to operate under US national law.[5]

The earlier *Reparations* case established the UN's right to sue a responsible State for wrongful conduct, harming the UN in its capacity as an international organization. This affirmatively answers the fundamental question about whether the UN has the capacity to sue a member State and a private non-governmental corporation in a commercial context:

Balfour, Guthrie & Co. v. United States

United States District Court, Northern District of California, 1950

90 Fed. Supp. 831

Author's Note: *In 1947, the United Nations International Children's Emergency Fund arranged for the shipment of powdered milk from ports on the US West Coast to Mediterranean ports. The ship that transported the milk was owned by the US government and operated by a US steamship company. The shipping contract between the UN agency and the US provided for the milk to be delivered to, and distributed in, Italy and Greece. One portion of the shipment never arrived. The other part arrived in damaged condition. The UN (and various shippers, including Balfour) sued the United States and a private US steamship company to recover for the loss of and damage to the milk.*

The UN's complaint is referred to as a "libel," which is the plaintiff's statement of the case against a defendant in a maritime suit.

Court's Opinion. Whether the United Nations may maintain these proceedings against respondent American Pacific Steamship Company can be first and more easily answered.

The International Court of Justice has held [*Reparations* case] that the United Nations is a legal entity separate and distinct from the member States. While it is not a state nor a super-State, it is an international person, clothed by its Members with the competence necessary to discharge its functions. Article 104 of the Charter of the United Nations provides that "the Organization shall enjoy in the territory of each of its Members such legal capacity as may be necessary for the exercise of its functions and the fulfillment of its purposes." As a treaty ratified by the United States, the Charter is part of the supreme law of the land. No implemental legislation would appear to be necessary to endow the United Nations with legal capacity in the United States. But the President has removed any possible doubt by designating the United Nations as one of the organizations entitled to enjoy the privileges conferred by the International Organizations Immunities Act, [which] states that "international organizations shall, to the extent consistent with the instrument creating them, possess the capacity (i) to contract; (ii) to acquire and dispose of real and personal property; and (iii) to institute legal proceedings."

The capacity of the United Nations to maintain the libel [suit] against the American Pacific Steamship Company is completely consistent with its charter. The libel asserts rights flowing from a contract made by a specialized agency of the United Nations in the performance of its duties. The agency, the International Children's Emergency Fund, was created by resolution of the General Assembly of the United Nations on December 11, 1946. Its function is to promote child health generally and in particular to assist the governments of countries that were the victims of aggression, to rehabilitate their children. The solution of international health problems is one of the responsibilities assumed by the United Nations in Article 55 of its Charter.

Whether the United Nations may sue the United States is a more difficult question. It is apparent that Article 104 of the Charter of the United Nations was never intended to provide a method for settling differences between the United Nations and its members. It is equally clear that the International Organizations Immunities Act does not amount to a waiver of the United States' sovereign immunity from suit. The precise question posed is whether the capacity to institute legal proceedings conferred on the United Nations by that Act includes the competence to sue the United States in cases in which the United States has consented to suits by other litigants.

The broad purpose of the International Organizations Immunities Act was to vitalize the status of international organizations of which the United States is a member and to facilitate their activities. A liberal interpretation of the Act is in harmony with this purpose.

The considerations which might prompt a restrictive interpretation are not persuasive. It is true that history has recorded few, if any, instances in which international entities have submitted their disputes to the courts of one of the disputing parties. But international organizations on a grand scale are a modern phenomenon. The wide variety of activities in which they engage is likely to give rise to claims against their members that can most readily be disposed of in national courts. The present claim is such a claim. No political overtones surround it. No possible embarrassment to the United States in the conduct of its international affairs could result from such a decree as this court might enter. A claim for cargo loss and damage is clearly susceptible of judicial settlement. Particularly is this so in this litigation inasmuch as the United Nations' claim is one of several of the same nature arising out of the same transaction or occurrence.

International organizations, such as the United Nations and its agencies, of which the United States is a member, are not alien bodies. The interests of the United States are served when the United Nations' interests are protected. A prompt and equitable settlement of any claim it may have against the United States will be the settlement most advantageous to both parties. The courts of the United States afford a most appropriate forum for accomplishing such a settlement.

Finally, it cannot be denied that when the Congress conferred the privileges specified in the International Organizations Immunities Act, it neither explicitly nor implicitly limited the kind or type of legal proceedings that might be instituted by the United Nations. There appears to be no good reason for the judicial imposition of such limitations [which would deny the UN the capacity to sue the US and the private shipping company in a US court].

◆ 3.2 CLASSIFICATION OF ORGANIZATIONS

International organizations can be classified in a variety of ways. This section illustrates what an organization is designed to do, based on who created it and why it was created.

TRADITIONAL MODEL

Cambridge University's Professor D. W. Bowett advocates the traditional paradigm of organizational classification by using a "functional" approach. International organizations thereby (1) are public or private, (2) are administrative or political, (3) are global or regional, and (4) possess or do not possess supranational power.[6]

This traditional model is a convenient, but aging, starting point for characterizing the power and purpose of the myriad of contemporary international organizations. The initial public versus private distinction refers to the establishment of "public" organizations by a group of States.[7] States often enter into written treaties to inaugurate international trade or communications associations which then implement the joint decisions of the State representatives.

Private international organizations are typically established by non-State entities (individuals or corporations) relying on non-governmental representatives to execute the mission of the particular organization—hence, the term "*Non*-Governmental Organization" or "NGO." This latter type of international organization is not created by a treaty between sovereign States. Examples include the International Chamber of Commerce (Paris) and the International Committee of the Red Cross (Geneva).

The administrative-versus-political distinction is somewhat blurred by modern practice. Administrative international organizations tend to have goals that are far more limited than those of their political analogues. The UN's International Telecommunications Union, for example, serves an administrative purpose that is *un*associated with maintaining or directing political order. Its delegates allocate radio frequencies including those used for communication in outer space. Many political associations, on the other hand, are inter-governmental entities designed to maintain military or political order. The UN was conceived to implement a system of collective security to discourage the unilateral use of military force. The UN Charter also contains provisions for improving social and economic matters that are administrative and political.

The global-versus-regional distinction is arguably less useful than the other traditional distinctions. The UN is the prime example of a "global" organization. Its impact, however, is not necessarily global. It is *not* a world government. It often serves as a forum for debating regional problems. Not all regional organizations are, in fact, regional. NATO is often referred to in the press as a Western European association. Yet the geographical position of certain long-term members such as the United States, Canada, and Iceland makes it difficult to analyze its work as limited to Western Europe—especially now that NATO is welcoming certain former Warsaw Pact members from the now dissolved Soviet Union (discussed further in §3.5).

The final traditional distinction involves organizations possessing—or not possessing—power over member States that requires them to act or not act in otherwise unacceptable ways. One definitional problem is that many international organizations are "supranational" ("supra" meaning "above"). They are associations of States with independent organs for implementing the goals of the participants. It would be incorrect, however, to characterize the UN as having supranational power. It cannot dispatch a peacekeeping force independently of the approval of the five permanent members of the Security Council. Nor does the Security Council traditionally dispatch troops without the consent of the State or States where they are to be stationed. In the European Union, on the other hand, members have ceded some of their sovereign powers to community organs that may, *and do,* require member States to act in ways that would not occur unilaterally (*see Open Door* case in §3.4).

EXPANDED CLASSIFICATION MODEL

A new, descriptive paradigm emerged after the dramatic numerical increase of States in the 1970s and 1980s (*see* Exhibit 3.1 in §3.1). The first cog in the more recent method for classifying IOs draws upon the "IGO–INGO" distinction—presented by University of Aberdeen's (Scotland) Professor Clive Archer.[8] This distinction builds upon UN Economic and Social Council Resolution 288(x) of 1950. It provided that every "international organization that is not created by means of international governmental agreements [treaties] shall be considered as a non-governmental international organization." IGO thus refers to international governmental organization, while INGO refers to an international *non*-governmental organization.

The UN is a global IGO. Its membership consists of States throughout the world. The European Union is an IGO that operates on a primarily regional international level.

Examples of INGOs include Amnesty International (London), the International Olympic Committee (Lausanne, Switzerland), the American Society of International Law (Washington, DC), the International Campaign to Ban Land Mines, and the comparatively amorphous group of terrorists allegedly training under Saudi multimillionaire Osama bin Laden.

Amnesty's members are individuals, from all over the globe, who are concerned about State observance of international human rights norms—often promoted through their respective Web sites.[9] Amnesty was not founded by a conference of governmental leaders. No State sends official representatives to its meetings. The Olympic Committee is a worldwide international organization, promoting sports competition to enhance State friendships. In 1998, its work under UN auspices promoted an agreement by 179 nations that there would be no hostilities during the Winter Olympics in Japan. The International Campaign to Ban Land Mines consists of about 1,000 groups worldwide. This organization received the Nobel Peace Prize for its work, which influenced 122 nations to sign the global treaty banning land mines in 1996. The American Society of International Law is composed of lawyers, judges, and professors from all over the world. It conducts seminars in and outside of the US. It is a professional association devoted to the study of International Law to promote State observance of International Law. The so-called Bin Laden group is allegedly responsible for various terrorists acts, including the August 1998 bombing of US embassies in Kenya and Tanzania. The work of this group is designed not only to target US citizens throughout the world, but also to influence governments to shun relations with the US. The renewed US interest in Africa, personified by US President Clinton's 1998 continental tour, is one basis for the supposition that Bin Laden desires to send a message to African nations who continue to pursue international relations with the US.

Some IOs consist of both IGOs *and* INGOs. Governments and private corporations have jointly formed an IO to deal with a particular problem. The Communication Satellite Corporation (COMSAT) is a mix of both States *(with* international legal capacity) and non-governmental corporations *(without* legal personality under International Law). They have combined to achieve various objectives involving the delivery of better worldwide communications.

The relationship between IGOs and INGOs may be symbiotic, whereby dissimilar organs exist in close association, or in a union, with each other to serve mutually beneficial interests. Certain INGOs, for example, possess a special status at the UN. The Palestine Liberation Organization (PLO), the International Committee for the

Red Cross, and the American Society of International Law have been accorded special "observer status" by different organs within the global international organization. When the General Assembly meets at the UN headquarters in New York City, for example, the PLO sends representatives to monitor the proceedings. As of July 1998, its representative may raise issues, co-sponsor draft resolutions, and make speeches in the General Assembly. The PLO, and the other INGOs enjoying observer status at the UN, may effectively participate in the work of the UN. While such INGOs are neither States nor IGOs, they do enjoy some degree of legal personality on the international level through their involvement with the most prominent IGO (the UN).

The International Red Cross, a private international union, enjoys yet another symbiotic relationship with IGOs. It was the Red Cross that promoted the intergovernmental Geneva Conventions of 1864, 1906, 1929, and 1949 (*see* Chapter 10 on the Laws of War). The Red Cross sometimes acts in ways that do not always draw the support of an individual State at war. The North Vietnamese were not particularly interested in Red Cross commentary on the degree of protection afforded US and South Vietnamese prisoners in the North during the Vietnam war. The Geneva Convention was characterized by the North Vietnamese as being inapplicable to this undeclared war. The Red Cross pressed all States to reconvene another Geneva Convention in 1977, however, which established added protections for prisoners in undeclared wars.[10] On the other hand, the Bosnian Serbs applauded the Red Cross assistance with the 1994 evacuation of thousands of Muslims and Croatians from the town of Prijefor in Bosnia. Although the objective was to save them from the Bosnian Serbs, this atypical Red Cross evacuation indirectly helped the Serbs in promoting their goal of ethnic cleansing.

In addition to the IGO–INGO distinction above, the remaining cogs in the contemporary analysis of organizational classification are: regional and universal organizations, purpose, and structure.

Regarding "purpose," one might contrast the UN Charter with the North American Free Trade Agreement (NAFTA). The Charter's first Article contains statements of purpose that are rather broadly worded. Member States therein "agreed" that:

> The Purposes of the United Nations are:
>
> 1. To maintain international peace and security . . . ;
> 2. To develop friendly relations among nations based on respect for the principle of equal rights and self-determination of peoples . . . ;
> 3. To achieve international cooperation in solving international problems of an economic, social, cultural, or humanitarian character . . . ;
> 4. To be a centre for harmonizing the actions of nations in the attainment of these common ends.

Courts and commentators have spent many years analyzing the scope of this very broad statement of purpose. It literally appears to "cover the universe," given its attention to peace, economic, social, and cultural objectives. NAFTA, on the other hand, is more limited, more specific, and less ambiguous. The liberal democracies within its membership are unlikely to go to war against each other. While equality or social improvements and cultural exchanges may be facilitated by NAFTA, its essential objective is to reduce trade barriers for the economic benefit of its trading partners. NAFTA Article 102.1 illustrates this contrast in purpose from the broader, egalitarian goals of the UN:

> The objectives of this Agreement . . . are to: (a) eliminate barriers to trade in, and facilitate the cross-border movement of, goods and services between the territories of the Parties; (b) promote conditions of fair competition in the free trade area; (c) increase substantially investment opportunities in the territories of the Parties; (d) provide adequate and effective protection and enforcement of intellectual property rights [copyright, trademark, and patent protection] in each Party's territory; (e) create effective procedures for the implementation and application of this Agreement, for its joint administration and for the resolution of disputes; and (f) establish a framework for further trilateral, regional and multilateral cooperation to expand and enhance the benefits of this Agreement.[11]

FUNCTIONAL SHIFT

Global and regional alliances are shifting from political to economic orientations. The Warsaw Pact, a prominent figure in international affairs until 1991, is military history. These former Soviet Union member States seek admission into NATO by way of its Partnership for Peace Program.

The Arab League is splintered. First, Egypt was expelled due to President Sadat's decision to enter into friendly treaty relations with Israel. The League virtually fell apart during the Persian Gulf War. Members who formerly advocated Israel's demise fought their Arab League ally Iraq in order to, among other things, protect Israel from Iraqi attack. The contemporary PLO autonomy further confirms the lack of unity about conquering Israel—the traditional military and political foe of League members.

The Organization of African Unity (OAU) is likewise devoid of its traditional political purpose: South Africa's unwinding of apartheid and the presidency of Nelson Mandela have inadvertently deprived the OAU of the one issue that united its otherwise fractious membership. The OAU is pursuing economic objectives to a much greater degree than in the past, now that these vestiges of colonialism have dissipated.

Numerous international common markets and free trade areas are working to advance the economic objectives of member States throughout the globe, especially now that the Cold War no longer drives international relations. (The major groupings will be covered in Chapter 13 on International Economic Relations.)

> 4. The Parties are of the view that the role of the United Nations and the Security Council must be strengthened, and that they highly appreciate United Nations efforts to maintain world peace and security. They believe that the United Nations, as the most universal and authoritative organization of sovereign States, has a place and role in the world that cannot be supplanted by any other international organization. The Parties are confident that the United Nations will play an important role in the establishment of the new international order.
>
> —Russian–Chinese Joint Declaration on a Multipolar World and the Establishment of a New International Order, adopted in Moscow on April 23, 1997.

◆ 3.3 UNITED NATIONS

This section of the text covers five central themes: events preceding creation of the UN (Historical Backdrop); the impact of politics in the UN process (Law and Politics); the UN's major institutions (UN Structure); successes and failures (UN Assessment); and proposed modifications (UN Reform).

HISTORICAL BACKDROP

League of Nations This was the first global international organization and the direct predecessor of the United Nations. The League of Peace, a private organization in the US, proposed a League of Nations in a 1914 newspaper editorial at the outset of World War I. Great Britain's League of Nations Society began to promote this ideal in 1916. The South African statesman who coauthored the Covenant of the League of Nations (and the UN Charter) proposed that the peoples in the territories formerly belonging to Russia, Austria-Hungary, and Turkey create an international organization to resolve their territorial disputes. All States would thereby abide by the fundamental principle that resolutions by "the league of nations should be substituted for any policy of national annexation."[12]

US President Woodrow Wilson was a key proponent of the League's creation. Drawing on the 1917 "Recommendations of Havana" prepared by the American Institute of International Law meeting in Cuba, Wilson's famous 1918 "Fourteen Points" speech to the US Congress advocated a "general association of nations [that] must be formed under specific covenants for the purpose of affording mutual guarantees of political independence and territorial integrity to great and small states alike." His essential purpose was to avoid a second world war, so that the first one would be the "war to end all wars." World leaders reacted by expressing their hope that the League would be the ultimate mechanism for avoiding a repetition of the secret military alliances and mutual suspicions that permeated the international atmosphere. The fear of another war thus generated the creation of this organization to encourage open diplomacy and cooling-off periods whenever international tensions threatened peace. Wilson witnessed the realization of his First Point—the creation of an international organization dedicated to open "covenants of peace, openly arrived at, after which there shall be no private international understandings of any kind but diplomacy shall proceed always frankly and in public view."[13]

The 1919 League of Nations Covenant, part of the Treaty of Versailles, was ultimately signed by seventy-three States. Its twenty-six articles dealt with a variety of problems, although the central theme was how to control military aggression. It was a progressive development in international relations because it established a two-organ permanent diplomatic conference (a General Assembly and a Security Council). The League was a central location for conference diplomacy. Unfortunately, it never achieved universality in terms of State participation.[14]

The dream that the League of Nations would maintain international peace and security failed the test of reality. The US Senate failed to ratify the League of Nations Covenant. The senators feared a diminution of US sovereignty should the nation participate. They believed that membership would instead draw the US into further wars. The US then opted for isolationism, which was a significant blow to the organization's potential effectiveness. League membership consisted essentially of the war-torn European countries.

While the League enjoyed some successes during its twenty-year existence, its failures eroded global confidence in the ability of an organization to maintain harmonious international relations. The League was unable to control the offensive military objectives of its member States. By the time the Soviet Union (USSR) finally joined the League in 1934, Brazil, Germany, and Japan had already withdrawn. The USSR later invaded Finland, Japan expanded into Manchuria, Germany annexed Austria into the Third Reich, and Italy invaded Ethiopia. A few League members reacted by an almost submissive form of economic sanctions—a brief boycott of Italian-made shoes. The global economic depression of the 1930s, coupled with US isolationism, the expulsion of the USSR (after it invaded Finland), and a somewhat xenophobic atmosphere, all contributed to the effective collapse of the League of Nations.

United Nations In 1942, a number of League members met to assess whether the League should continue. They decided that it should be replaced by another global international organization to pursue the ideal of collective security. The name "United Nations" was devised by US President Roosevelt.[15] It was first used in the "Declaration by United Nations" of January 1, 1942. Representatives of the twenty-six Allied nations therein pledged that their governments would continue their fight against the Axis powers.

The United Nations Charter was drawn up by the representatives of fifty allied countries during the UN Conference on International Organization, held in San Francisco from April through June 1945.[16] (Poland was not represented at the conference, although it later signed the Charter to become one of the original fifty-one member States.) Delegates deliberated the various proposals previously tendered by China, the USSR, the United Kingdom, and the US during meetings held in 1944. The summer 1945 drafting conference in San Francisco barely preceded the atomic bombing of Japan in August—which effectively ended the war. The new "United Nations" was officially established on October 24, 1945. That day is now celebrated globally as United Nations Day.

The UN's membership has dramatically changed since its inception in 1945—growing from 51 to almost 190 States. Exhibit 2.1 illustrates this progression (§2.2). Exhibit 3.2 provides a brief review of some of the other major UN developments since 1945, while Exhibit 3.3 furnishes a structural diagram of the United Nations system.

LAW AND POLITICS

Section 1.8 of this text drew on the analogy that most drivers (States) obey the traffic signals (international norms), even in the absence of a police presence on each corner to enforce the law (i.e., no standing UN army). Those who traverse the various intersections in international relations pursue their mutual, but distinct, interests by observing most of the norms most of the time.

Professor Oscar Schachter of Columbia University uses a comparable metaphor to describe the "patterns and politics" of the United Nations legal order. He succinctly describes the various entities discussed in this section of the text as a series of metropolitan and smaller areas linked by various roads, highways, and paths—the infrastructure consisting of the concepts, principles, and processes of the UN legal order. This excerpt provides a useful insight into the complex political processes of the UN and the ways in which they have affected the international legal order since its inception in 1945. When you read it, note how non-State actors, including other international organizations and individuals, are playing an increasingly greater role in the progressive development of International Law:

EXHIBIT 3.2 SELECTED CHRONOLOGY OF MAJOR UN EVENTS*

1945 UN Charter created and enters into force.

1946 First General Assembly (GA) London; reconvenes in New York.

1947 GA adopts plan to partition "Palestine" to create Arab and Jewish States.

1948 GA adopts Universal Declaration on Human Rights (Chapter 11).

1949 GA establishes office of High Commissioner for Refugees (Chapter 12).

1950 Soviet Union (SU) boycotts Security Council (SC) for failing to oust Nationalist (Formosa) government as representative for "China" seat. SC establishes Korean action under control of US (UN signed truce with North Korea in 1953).

1952 Over South Africa's objections, GA begins study of apartheid (SC arms embargo against South Africa: voluntary 1963; mandatory 1977).

1956 Hungary obtains SC resolution regarding SU invasion (unenforced). GA establishes first independent UN force to handle Suez Canal crisis.

1960 GA adopts Declaration on Granting Independence to colonies and peoples. GA: SU's Nikita Khrushchev accuses Secretary-General of abusing position.

1962 SC attempts to negotiate solution to Cuban Missile Crisis.

1963 World Food Program established by UN Food and Agricultural Organization.

1967 SC adopts Resolution 242 calling for Israeli withdrawal from occupied territories after Six-Day War with Middle East Arab States.

1968 GA approves Treaty on Non-Proliferation of Nuclear Weapons, calling for ratification (1993: North Korea announces intent not to renew).

1969 UN Convention on Elimination of All Forms of Discrimination becomes effective.

1971 GA expels Chinese Nationalist representative and seats PRC delegation.

1972 Kurt Waldheim begins service as Secretary-General 1972–1986 (later accused of Nazi-era war crimes).

1974 GA bars South African delegation from participating in GA operations despite Western objections; GA calls for New International Economic Order.

1975 GA passes resolution equating Zionism with racism (revoked in 1991).

1984 Office for Emergency Operations in Africa created for famine relief.

1989 GA announces the UN Decade of International Law (Chapter 1).

1990 Numerous SC and GA resolutions regarding Persian Gulf War (Chapter 10).

1991 End of Cold War signals improved atmosphere for SC peace efforts.

1992 UN concludes most expensive peace operation in history (Cambodia $2 billion).* SC bans former Yugoslavia from SC seat; status unresolved.

1993 US President's GA speech chides UN inability to fulfill agenda; promises US will pay past-due assessments *if* new funding formula developed. Secretary-General flees from attack by Somali residents. UN not key participant in Bosnia conflict. Russia's Yeltsin requests UN support for Russia to be guarantor of stability in former USSR. UN evacuates 700 refugees from Rwanda.

1994 GA establishes post of High Commissioner for Human Rights. US requests UN ban on worldwide arms sales to North Korea. SC authorizes French request for humanitarian intervention in Rwanda. UN establishes Rwanda peacekeeping operation. Bosnian Serbs isolate UN peacekeepers, making them virtual hostages.

1995 UN (Berlin) Greenhouse Conference negotiates new limits to control global warming.

1996 UN Conference on Human Settlements issues Habitat Agenda for urban living in 21st century; because of dues arrearage, US removed from panel regarding UN funding.

1997 In its first emergency session in 15 years, the GA demands that Israel stop building Jewish settlements in East Jerusalem. UN's International Criminal Tribunal for Former Yugoslavia conducts first international criminal trial since Nuremberg. New Secretary-General Kofi Annan installed to reform UN.

1998 Rome Conference establishes preliminary structure for first permanent International Criminal Court. Secretary-General advises US it must consult with UN before attacking Iraq.

*Further UN peacekeeping operations are addressed in Chapter 10.

"United Nations Law"

PROFESSOR OSCAR SCHACHTER

88 *American Journal of International Law* 1, 16–23 (1994)

As the United Nations system approaches its fiftieth anniversary, there is good reason to take a fresh view of its contribution to legal order in the contemporary world. . . . A half century of law creation and application by the United Nations and its specialized agencies has produced a *corpus juris* [body of law] of impressive breadth and diversity. Not surprisingly, the greater part of this law is known only to those specially concerned with a particular area or subject. Indeed, no one can be expected to be knowledgeable in all, or even most, of the fields covered. Still, along with the diversity, common elements can be found to enable us to characterize the total product as a distinctive, multilayered legal order. This essay is an overview of its essential and interesting features. It aims particularly at informing the many nonspecialists in and outside the international law community who have reason to be interested in the process and substance of the legal contribution of the UN system. . . .

An overview of the UN legal order reveals complex patterns. We see a multitude of specialized bodies of law, each with its distinctive features, many intricate and dense. They are fully accessible only to specialists, versed in doctrine and procedure that often seem arcane to outsiders. We might envisage them as separate communities, on a terrain that includes cities, towns, villages, hamlets. Extending this metaphor, we note that they are connected to each other by roads, highways and paths, that is, by concepts, principles and processes. The communities differ, of course, in size, influence and their linkages to each other.

Two areas of UN law that stand out in public interest are human rights and the law relating to peace and security (i.e., force, arms, etc.). They would be metropolises on our imaginary map. Human rights, in fact, could be likened to a metropolitan area, since it embraces a large core city and many connected towns and villages. . . .

A second "metropolis" on our map is the law of peace and security. In contrast to human rights, the goal of peace and security has been the *raison d'être* of the UN Charter. Under this head, we find the leading cases, the great dramas of the United Nations, the intense disputes about the interpretation and application of principles. This is the field of law in which the stakes are highest and the authority of the United Nations always on trial. Even though politics and national interests are rightly recognized as predominant, law has a role in almost every aspect of UN activity in this area. . . .

The metropolis of peace and security law, like human rights, has its suburbs. One of the most important is the regulation and prohibition of armaments, especially weapons of mass destruction. The legal pattern in this area is predominantly made up of negotiated agreements, on a global or regional basis. It also embraces inspection to ascertain compliance with legal obligations such as those contained in the Treaty on the Non-Proliferation of Nuclear Weapons or Security Council decisions under chapter VII as, for example, applied to Iraq. Efforts to outlaw mass weapons or their use on the basis of existing principles of customary law or the Charter itself persist in UN bodies but lack support by the major powers concerned.

Still another suburb in the peace and security area comprises the law developed by the Security Council and, to some degree, the General Assembly in respect of peace keeping, peace enforcement, inspection and control. However, as 1993 drew to a close, the lack of resolve on the part of major powers, along with weaknesses within the UN operations, augured a retreat from peace enforcement and perhaps from consensual peace keeping. While the main legal principles are not likely to be abandoned, we can expect changes in legal arrangements bearing on rules of engagement, command and control, and perhaps criteria for UN interventions. . . .

Not all the fields of law in the UN system are as large as those mentioned. Some would be only villages or hamlets on our metaphorical terrain. For example, the United Nations has generated and furthered an international treaty on enforcing maintenance obligations across national lines, a barely noticed legal instrument of great value to those entitled to support payments (in the main, mothers and children). Another "village" is concerned with aid to victims of crimes and abuses of power, a continuing project that seeks to prevent and curtail such victimization through legal and practical means. . . .

All of these subjects are part of the "terrain" of UN law since they were generated by UN organs or applied by them. Our metaphorical map reminds us that these various legal communities are not entirely separate, that highways and byways provide linkages in the form of common principles and processes. Without pressing the metaphor, we find interconnecting doctrine in the basic postulates of international law to which participants in the UN system, whatever the subject, profess adherence. States are regarded as the principal actors in creating and applying law. Their independence and formal equality are taken as axiomatic. The principles of territorial integrity and *pacta sunt servanda* [good faith performance of obligations], as well as the customary rules of diplomatic intercourse, are accepted in the UN system, as they are in general international law. Also accepted is the basic divide between the international and domestic domains, though, as indicated earlier, the line between them may change or blur in particular cases. All of these propositions are recognized as applicable to the legally relevant activities in the UN system. They are the connecting highways that run across the landscape and impart a degree of unity to the various activities.

These connecting highways—the concepts and principles of international law—are a conspicuous feature of UN debates. As the Secretary-General recently observed, "political discourse and the vocabulary of law mix cheerfully with one another . . . the dialectic between law and diplomacy is constantly at work." Perhaps it is not always "cheerful." The Secretary-General went on to say that "the United Nations shows, better than any other organization, the competition States engage in to try and impose a dominant language and control the juridical ideology it expresses." We are reminded that legal discourse is not divorced from political conflict. On the one hand, the concepts of international law provide a necessary code of communication, and therefore greatly facilitate the institutionalization of international society. On the other hand, international law is often relied upon by states to resist the transfer of their power to international authority. We have to look beyond international law itself to evaluate the likely consequences.

An overview of UN law reveals several other interesting characteristics of the UN system. I would begin with the characteristic modes of decision making in the UN system. These are essentially political processes, but they are shaped by the conditions of quasi-parliamentary procedures and the mandates of constituent instruments. What is perhaps most important in this respect is the central role of blocs and alliances in law creation and law application. State autonomy and equality are profoundly affected—that is, reduced—by the requirements of group cohesion. To be sure, these are not ironclad requirements. A member of the "77" (i.e., about 150 developing states) or of the European group may cast an independent vote, but this is exceptional. Many groups coexist, some based on particular interests (for example, petroleum producers), others on regional or historical ties. . . .

Still another characteristic of the UN system is its relative transparency and linkages to nonstate actors. This may surprise outsiders who feel excluded by its arcane language and somewhat elitist character. However, on a closer look at activities of legal significance, it becomes evident that member states are not the only participants, even if in a formal sense they are the designated players. In actuality most efforts directed to achieving new law or giving effect to existing law involve substantial participation by nonstate actors. Many enter as "experts" through governments or nongovernmental bodies. They are usually part of the "epistemic communities" that share and produce knowledge of particular subjects. They are necessary to informed decisions on seemingly technical questions. Although many are formally under governmental authority, their specialized expertise gives them a degree of independence and also raises the level of international cooperation.

A somewhat different role is played by groups and individuals outside governments who are dedicated to "causes" and take part indirectly in UN deliberations as "lobbyists" or "activists." Their influence varies with cause and case, but it would be a mistake to regard them in general as outsiders. I would guess that their actual role in the political and technical aspects of UN lawmaking is increasing. The communications revolution, the spread of democracy and the growth of transnational interest groups are factors that favor a larger role for nongovernmental bodies. . . .

As a final comment, I suggest an architectural metaphor. It views the UN legal order as a three-level structure:

On its ground floor, I place the actions of states—including the demands and goals of the governments and other organized groups in furtherance of their needs, wishes and expectations.

On the second level are the activities of a legal character—the formation and invoking of legal norms, and their application to particular situations.

On the third level, I would place the broad policy goals, aspirations and ideals that influence governments and the other actors.

Each of these levels exhibits its own values and processes. But there is continuous movement from level to level. The sphere of law in the middle level is influenced by the interests expressed below and the ideals and policy manifested above. The connections run both ways. Legal norms have an impact on the perceptions of interest and needs in the lower level and on the policies of the top level. This image helps us to see that the UN Legal Order is influenced by the multitude of demands and interests from below and by the ideals and principles on the higher level. It also reminds us that law exercises its influence in both directions, up and down.

Our metaphors may help to avoid a reductive conception of law in the UN system. To appreciate its achievement, we need to comprehend UN law in its full complexity and diversity. We may also envisage, as our metaphors suggest, the promise of continued legal developments responsive to practical needs and shared ideals.

UN STRUCTURE

The six principal organs of the UN are the: (1) General Assembly, (2) Security Council, (3) Economic and Social Council, (4) Trusteeship Council, (5) Secretariat, and (6) International Court of Justice (ICJ). Numerous other UN organs and specialized agencies also exist within the system in Exhibit 3.3.

General Assembly The General Assembly (GA) is composed of the UN's 185 member States. Various committees and commissions serve a variety of functions for the GA, including the making and consideration of reports on world events, discussion of principles of international cooperation, supervision of the UN's Trusteeship Council (discussed below), participation in selection of the judges of the ICJ, approval of budgets and applications for membership, and the appointment of the UN Secretary-General.

Six major committees drive the work of the General Assembly—referred to as the "First Committee," and so on. The following list suggests the structural arrangement of the day-to-day work of the Assembly: *First* Committee—Disarmament and International Security; *Second* Committee—Economic and Financial; *Third* Committee—Social, Humanitarian, and Cultural; *Fourth* Committee—Special Political and Decolonization; *Fifth* Committee—Administrative and Budgetary; *Sixth* Committee—Legal.[17]

World leaders have often addressed the General Assembly on very sensitive problems in international relations. In 1960, Nikita Khrushchev spoke to the GA, accusing UN Secretary-General Dag Hammarskjold of abusing his position as head of this global organ. Khrushchev proposed that Hammarskjold be replaced by a three-person directorate, so as to diffuse the power of the Secretary-General. It is unlikely that this criticism would have surfaced if the UN headquarters were located in Moscow rather than New York. Yasir Arafat, the leader of the PLO who negotiated the Gaza–Jericho autonomy agreement of 1993, spoke to the GA in 1974. His objective was to seek UN assistance in consummating the statehood of the dormant State of Palestine. In 1993, US President Clinton spoke in an effort to convince this body to reduce what he characterized as its overextended commitment to worldwide peacekeeping engagements. He also indicated that the US would pay its dues arrearage, if the UN would develop a new funding formula for its national assessments.

EXHIBIT 3.3 UNITED NATIONS STRUCTURE

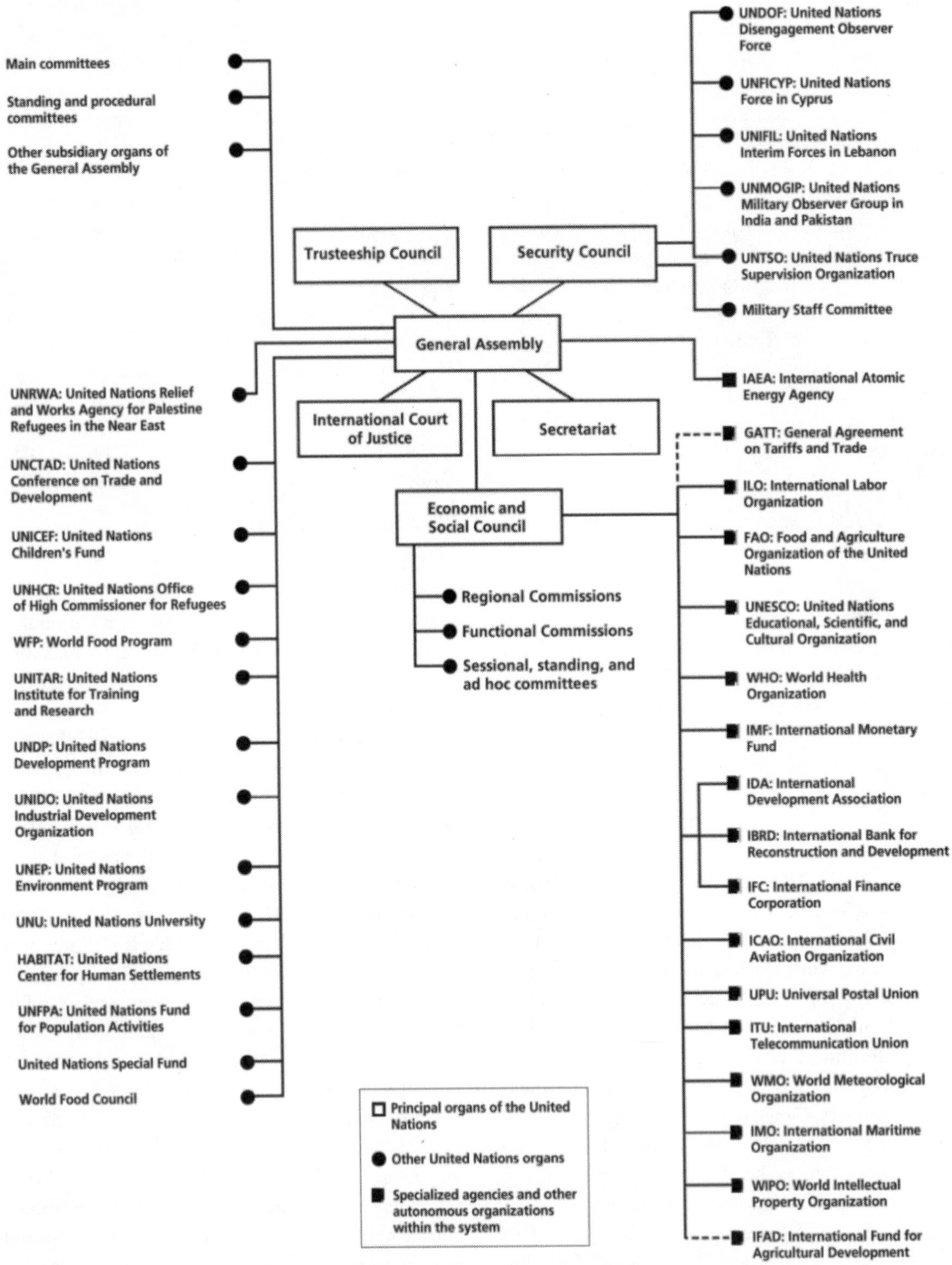

The GA is a global forum for resolving issues which fall within the scope of the UN Charter. Articles 10–17 of the Charter enable the GA to "discuss," to "consider," to "initiate studies and make recommendations," and to "receive and consider annual and special reports." England's University of Leicester Professor Malcolm Shaw thus characterizes the General Assembly as "essentially a *debating chamber,* a forum for the exchange of ideas and the discussion of a wide-ranging category of problems."[18]

The General Assembly became more than a mere debate chamber in 1950. Its members recognized that the Security Council's power to act in sensitive cases would be vitiated by the veto power of any of the five permanent members of the Council. The Assembly then adopted the "Uniting for Peace Resolution." Its purpose was to ensure a prompt UN response to threats to international peace—when the Security Council would not, or could not, take action to "put out the fire." The effect of this resolution, permitting the General Assembly to act in the absence of an express Charter authority to do so, is described in Chapter 10 of this text on the Security Council's authority to maintain peace.

The Assembly's Charter prerogatives are expressly limited to the initiation of studies and the recommendation of peaceful courses of action when confronted with pending hostilities. Its fundamental purpose is to promote international cooperation, in a political rather than military context, by encouraging the progressive development of International Law and its codification. Members of the Assembly therefore cooperate in the economic, social, cultural, educational, human rights, and health fields. They sometimes recommend measures for the peaceful adjustment of any situation deemed likely to impair friendly relations among nations.

The General Assembly is *not* a world legislature. It may pass resolutions, some of which ultimately become treaties. Other resolutions *may* indicate the degree of *opinio juris*—practices that States consider binding in their international relations (*see* §1.4). The Assembly does not, however, have the power to enact legislation like a national legislature such as the US Congress, Mexican Parliament, or Japanese Diet. The underlying reason is that State members are unwilling to yield the requisite degree of sovereignty to an international organization to authorize passage of laws that would bind all nations. As succinctly stated by the University of Pozman's Professor Krzysztof Skubiszewski (Poland), "[w]e know both from the reading of the UN Charter and the history of its drafting (the defeat of the Philippine proposal on this right presented at the [1945] Conference in San Francisco) that no power to make law for states has been conferred on the General Assembly or any other organ of the United Nations. For such power, whether comprising legislation by virtue of unanimous vote, or by majority decision with the guarantees of the system of contracting out, or by majority decision binding for all, must always be based on an EXPLICIT AND UNEQUIVOCAL TREATY AUTHORIZATION."[19]

General Assembly special "observer status" is extended to selected international organizations such as national liberation movements. These organizations may attend meetings of the GA. Their representatives may be seated in a special chamber just off the main hall of the GA. Non-State actors may thereby participate in, and serve as resources for, the Assembly's State members. Non-governmental observers, such as the Palestine Liberation Organization, often deal with governments on a *de facto* basis. This mechanism provides greater access to all elements of the international community that can contribute to the UN's overall peace process. Private research institutions are also designated as non-governmental observers of various UN organs operating under the GA. These include the Academic Council of the United Nations System (Rhode Island's Brown University) and the American Society of International Law (Tillar House, Washington, DC). These entities serve as think tanks for the pursuit of common objectives within the entire sphere of General Assembly activities.

The General Assembly was effectively controlled by the US throughout the 1950s. After a paradigm shift associated with the induction of new independent States that were former colonies, the so-called Third World began to control the overall direction of the Assembly by the mid-1960s. The Assembly provides an unparalleled form of recognition for these less powerful States. As aptly stated by Political Science Professor M.J. Peterson of Amherst University, the "egalitarian nature of the Assembly . . . makes it the favorite political organ of weak states . . . because it gives them an influence over decisions that they lack elsewhere in the international system. . . . The Third World Coalition . . . uses the Assembly more intensely than did the US-led coalition, but its relative lack of power has exposed more clearly the limits on Assembly control over outcomes in world politics."[20]

One of the resulting agenda shifts was the seventy-seven nation announcement of a New International Economic Order (Chapter 13). This platform advocated an equitable redistribution of the world's wealth. The Assembly-driven Law of the Sea Treaty, referred to as LOST by the more powerful nations who initially rejected it, became effective in November 1994. Its contemporary applicability illustrates some of the ways in which this redistribution is to be accomplished. While economically powerful nations have objected, the treaty text requires seagoing nations to contribute a portion of revenues they draw from mining and fishing the seas into an agency that, in turn, is supposed to repatriate a portion of these revenues to the less powerful non-seagoing States. However, all countries did accept the creation of a new Exclusive Economic Zone allowing coastal States—with no technology to exploit resources up to 200 nautical miles from their shores—to charge licensing fees to all who enter and use that zone (*see* Chapter 6).

Security Council: ***(a) Purpose and Structure.*** The Security Council (SC) is the UN organ with the primary responsibility for the maintenance of world peace. Under Article 39 of the Charter, the SC determines what constitutes a threat to peace and what measures shall be taken to maintain global peace and security. Under Article 47 of the Charter, the Council is responsible for submitting plans to UN members for establishing and maintaining a system to regulate armaments. Under Articles 41 and 42 of the Charter, the SC may decide what measures are employed to implement its decisions. The Council may order the complete or partial interruption of economic relations with States that violate International Law. If the Council considers such sanctions inadequate, it may use air, sea, or land forces as necessary to maintain or restore international peace and security. (The operations of multinational forces under the control of the Council are described in Chapter 10 of this book.)

The Security Council consists of fifteen countries. The Council's size was purposely limited to ensure prompt and effective action by the UN in contrast to the debating atmosphere of the *all*-member General Assembly. Nations can refer their disputes to the SC for resolution (as well as to the GA when it is in session). Unlike the Assembly, the Council functions continuously. A representative of each of the fifteen member States must be present at all times at UN Headquarters in New York City.

The Security Council includes five "permanent" members and ten "rotating" members periodically elected by the General Assembly. The five permanent members are China, France, Russia, the United Kingdom, and the United States. The "Russian" seat on the Council was formerly occupied by the Soviet Union until 1991. It is now occupied by Russia. The "China" seat has been occupied by the People's Republic of China since the Republic of China (Nationalist Chinese government) was ousted by UN action in 1971.

The makeup of the Security Council has always generated debates about its failure to reflect the General Assembly's composition. The latter is a richly diverse body, consisting of States from every corner of the world, innumerable cultures, all political systems, and every form of economic development. Under the original Charter, however, five of the (then only) eleven SC members occupied permanent seats on the Council. Any one of these five could block Council action by exercising its individual right to veto any proposed action. No *rotating* member can do so. Action by the SC therefore requires a unanimous vote of the five permanent members and a majority of the fifteen total members.

There have been two significant movements that changed the SC's composition. Since 1945, the permanent membership on the Security Council had not reflected the diverse nature of the community of nations. General Assembly member States believed that the Council should not ignore the less powerful but more populated States of Africa, Asia, and Latin America. In 1965, the UN therefore altered its structure to magnify the presence of such nations—many of which were former colonies of the charter UN members. The number of Council seats was then increased from eleven to fifteen. The four fresh seats were designated as additional "rotating" seats as opposed to "permanent" seats. A number of commentators viewed this as a minor concession, however, in the struggle to ameliorate the powerful-nation ("Permanent 5") dominance of the Council. After the demise of the Soviet Union and its attendant Cold War with the US, Germany and Japan have consistently sought an "upgrade" of their status from occasional rotating members to make seven permanent SC members rather than the current five.

Unlike the US, the British and French governments are opposed to such a change, as evinced by British Foreign Secretary Douglas Hurd's widely reported 1993 use of the old adage: "If it ain't broke, don't fix it." US Secretary of State Warren Christopher responded that the SC may not be broke; however, "[i]t's time for some reorganizing." Ironically, the Japanese and German Constitutions contain limitations on their ability to participate in SC military actions.[21]

(b) The Veto Dilemma. The League of Nations was plagued from the outset with its *unanimity* requirement for Security Council action. The UN strategy was initially perceived as an improvement. Nine of fifteen votes, rather than unanimity, is one of two conditions for Security Council action. The other condition has bedeviled the Security Council almost from the outset: The UN cannot act if one of the five permanent members casts a veto.

Ironically, the word *veto* is not contained in the UN Charter. Article 48 merely states that action "shall be taken by all the Members of the United Nations or by some of them, as the Security Council may determine." The Security Council Provisional Rules of Procedure contain the somewhat infamous veto provision adopted at the 1945 UN drafting conference in San Francisco. Mindful of the US decision not to join the League of Nations, and the Soviet Union's expulsion from the League for invading Finland, none of the five permanent Council members could be drawn into an armed conflict that it did not wish to enter.

National sovereignty was the real culprit in what would soon become apparent with the advent of the "Cold War": that powerful States did not want to cede the requisite power to enable the UN to effectively control threats to peace. There might be instances when a permanent SC member would want to clandestinely support the threatening State's action; or, alternatively, remain too indifferent to risk involvement in a particular threat to peace in another part of the world. The concern about sovereignty also thwarted materialization of the Article 43 standing army, which would have functioned as an international police force.

What triggered the post-war veto dilemma, pitting the two most powerful World War II allies against one another, in a way that would severely limit the UN's overall ability to respond to threats to peace? The USSR temporarily boycotted SC meetings in 1950. The USSR had insisted that the People's Republic of China (communist mainland China) was the appropriate entity to occupy the "China" seat on the Council, rather than the then-seated Republic of China (Nationalist government on Formosa—supported by the UN—now Taiwan). This historic absence allowed the SC to vote in favor of UN involvement in the Korean Conflict under the direction of a US military command. This would not have happened if the Soviet representative had been present for the vote, and possibly if the "China" seat had been occupied by mainland China, which came to the aid of North Korea during this 1950–1953 conflict. This event led to the infamous Cold War "veto" that continually paralyzed the SC's subsequent potential for fulfilling its mandate of maintaining international peace.

This negative impact of superpower politics has been most evident when the holders of the veto power have blocked an international response to their *own* threats to international peace. Recent examples by each Council member—armed with the knowledge that it could conveniently deflect Security Council action—arguably include the 1989 US invasion of Panama; France's involvement in the escape of the French agents responsible for the death of crew members on the Greenpeace vessel *Rainbow Warrior* in New Zealand in 1986; Great Britain's 1982 war with Argentina over the distant Falkland Islands just off Argentina's coast; the Soviet Union's takeover of Afghanistan in 1979; and any UN action that might have responded to the reported deaths of some 3,000 civilians in Beijing's Tiananmen Square during a demonstration for democracy in 1989.

Effective SC control of international conflict is arguably unlikely in the long run without significant change in Security Council voting procedure. All members of the permanent five thereby can have their cake and eat it too. The permanent five have all benefitted from the veto, which has unfairly been attributed solely to the obstructionism of the former Soviet Union.

(c) Peacekeeping Operations. The lack of effective UN involvement in various peacekeeping operations such as Bosnia and Somalia signal the lack of international commitment to reliance on the Security Council as a tool for facilitating an original ideal of the UN: "to save succeeding generations from the scourge of war." Although the frequency of the veto declined after the Cold War, the circumstances giving rise to the underlying conflict have not really changed. There will be no effective international control of such conflicts until there is a genuine interest by member States to integrate word and deed. In the words of UN Political Affairs Officer Anjali Patil, in her book on the Security Council veto: "It really doesn't matter who enjoys the veto power in the Security Council; international peace and security cannot be maintained until all States accept the need to identify with the whole of humanity. We have struggled over the centuries for absolute peace but have not yet achieved it. While creating the United Nations has enabled us to avoid a [third] world war, we have yet to create a genuine international society."[22]

In January 1992, world leaders conducted a summit-level meeting of the UN Security Council members in New York. This was the 3,046th meeting of the Council, but the *first* meeting of its heads of State. As proclaimed by Britain's SC President, on behalf of the Council to the heads of State at the close of this special meeting:

> This meeting takes place at a time of momentous change. The ending of the Cold War has raised hopes for a safer, more equitable and more humane world. . . .
>
> Last year, under authority of the United Nations, the international community succeeded in enabling Kuwait to regain its sovereignty and territorial integrity, which it had lost as a result of Iraqi aggression.
>
> The members of the Council also recognize that change, however welcome, has brought new risks for stability and security. Some of the most acute problems result from changes to State structures [*see* this book's Exhibit 2.1 in §2.3]. . . .
>
> The international community therefore faces new challenges in the search for peace. All Member States expect the United Nations to play a central role at this crucial stage. The members of the Council stress the importance of strengthening and improving the United Nations to increase its effectiveness.

Rather than themselves initiating just how this "strengthening and improvement" would happen, the Council's heads of State instead requested that the UN Secretary-General assume this task. In his responsive work product entitled *Agenda for Peace,*[23] Boutros Boutros-Ghali therein made specific recommendations in three areas: (1) *preventative diplomacy*—formal fact-finding mandated by the SC; meeting "away" from the Council's New York headquarters, notwithstanding this Charter requirement, so as to directly diffuse any underlying disputes based on the Council's presence in a major city of the major superpower; (2) *peacemaking*—mediation or negotiation by an individual to be designated by the SC; that the Council devise means for using financial institutions and other components of the UN system to insulate certain States from the economic consequences of economic sanctions under Article 41; that States undertake to make armed forces available to the Council, on a permanent basis, when it decides to initiate military action under Article 42; that the Council utilize peace-enforcement measures only in "clearly defined circumstances and with their terms of reference specified in advance"; (3) *peacekeeping*—that regional arrangements be undertaken in a manner that would effectively contribute to a deeper sense of participation, consensus, and democratization in international affairs.

The 1994 US reaction was interesting, to say the least. President Clinton signed a classified US Presidential Directive that one could characterize as defusing the UN Secretary-General's 1992 *Agenda for Peace* recommendations on peacekeeping operations. The Directive also modified the Bush administration's expansive UN policy and the unparalleled increase in UN peacekeeping operations associated with the SC's renaissance during the Persian Gulf War. The following analysis could not be directly based on the President's classified document, although the US Department of State provided a separate analysis summarizing the key elements of the fresh US–UN policy. The first paragraph addresses the general US voting posture in future SC matters. The second paragraph provides some specifics about the conditions for committing US troops to such actions:

> We have determined that the United States should support international action when a threat exists to international or regional peace and security, such as international aggression, an urgent humanitarian disaster or interruption of established democracy or gross violation of human rights that is coupled with violence. In determining whether to support international action, the US will consider whether operations have clear objectives, a defined scope, and an integrated politico-military strategy to achieve our objectives. An international "community of interests" should exist to support multilateral operations. For Chapter VI [presumably referring to Chapter VII] operations, a ceasefire should be in place. The availability of financial and human resources to carry out the strategy will be a critical

factor in US deliberations, as will the linkage of expected duration to clear objectives and realistic exit criteria for the operation.

The standards will be even more stringent when the US considers deploying American forces to participate in UN peacekeeping operations. The US will only participate in a peace operation when:

- It advances US interests and the level of risk is acceptable;
- US participation is necessary for the success of the operation;
- An integrated politico-military strategy exists to achieve our objectives;
- The personnel, funds, and resources are available to support the strategy;
- Command and control arrangements are satisfactory;
- Likely duration and exit conditions have been identified; and
- Domestic and Congressional support exists or can be marshaled.

We believe these factors are critical to the successful conduct of peace operations and to building public and Congressional support for US involvement in those operations. As for command and control arrangements, the President will never relinquish command over US forces. However, the President will, on a case-by-case basis, consider placing appropriate US forces under the operational control of a competent UN commander for specific UN operations authorized by the Security Council.[24]

◆ *Notes & Questions*

Assume you represent another member of the UN Security Council. How will you advise your country about the potential for US involvement in a SC action that your country is about to advocate to the rest of the Council?

There is a "mixed-bag" perception about UN performance. One illustration is the comparative results in Kuwait and Yugoslavia.

Kuwait and Iraq Security Council Resolution 687 was a milestone in UN history. This cease-fire resolution, among the many issued by the Council during and after the cessation of hostilities,[25] is a major break from prior resolutions—partially due to its breadth, but mostly due to its purported control over future State behavior. The Security Council ordered unprecedented and unparalleled controls on Iraq's future behavior in terms of observing international border delimitations, non-use of chemical and nuclear weapons, sanctions, and required war reparations. The relevant paragraphs of the SC's Resolution are reprinted below:

United Nations Security Council Resolution 687

2981st Meeting, April 3, 1991

The Security Council, . . .

Welcoming the restoration to Kuwait of its national sovereignty, independence, and territorial integrity and the return of its legitimate government, . . .

2. *Demands* that Iraq and Kuwait respect the inviolability of the international boundary . . .

4. *Decides* to guarantee the inviolability of the above-mentioned international boundary and to take as appropriate all necessary measures to that end in accordance with the Charter; . . .

8. *Decides* that Iraq shall unconditionally accept the destruction, removal, or rendering harmless, under international supervision, of:

(a) all chemical and biological weapons and all stocks of agents . . . ;

(b) all ballistic missiles with a range of greater than 150 kilometres and related major parts, and repair and production facilities; . . .

14. *Takes note* that the actions to be taken by Iraq . . . represent steps towards the goal of establishing in the Middle East a zone free from weapons of mass destruc-

tion and all missiles for their delivery and the objective of a global ban on chemical weapons; . . .

24. *Decides* that, in accordance with Resolution 661 (1990) and subsequent related resolutions and until a further decision is taken by the Council, all States shall continue to prevent the sale or supply . . . to Iraq by their nationals . . . of:

(a) arms and related materiel of all types. . . .

25. *Calls upon* all States and international organizations to act strictly in accordance with paragraph 24 above, notwithstanding the existence of any [prior] contracts, agreements, licenses, or any other arrangements; . . .

30. *Decides that,* in furtherance of its commitment to facilitate the repatriation of all Kuwaiti and third party nationals, Iraq shall extend all necessary cooperation to the International Committee of the Red Cross . . .

32. *Requires* Iraq to inform the Council that it will not commit or support any act of international terrorism . . .

34. *Decides* to remain seized of the matter and to take such further steps as may be required for the implementation of this resolution and to secure peace and security in the area.

The quoted portions of Resolution 687 provide the foremost statement of conditions ever made by the Security Council—because of their comprehensive nature and their purported control of future action by Iraq and all members of the international community. But for the Cold War veto described above, a similar resolution might have been issued in prior conflicts. This resolution signaled a zenith in the willingness of the Council to undertake its task of attempting to maintain global peace and security.

Adherence to this resolution was not as forthcoming as expected. Iraq chose to limit UN agents from conducting inspections of its war potential. Iraq even *seized* certain agents during their UN-sanctioned visits. In spite of such problems with implementation, this resolution heralded what would appear to be the effective return of the Security Council from its Cold War hiatus.

Security Council Activism The Security Council's Gulf War activism triggered the twin perceptions of the UN casting off the fetters of the Cold War, while simultaneously generating suspicion by nations that could be the future objects of the hegemony of its more powerful members. Many "Third World" countries—as they were typically characterized during the Cold War—perceived the Gulf War and the Council's activism as providing the potential for a new form of control by the States that remained dominant after the Cold War. This concern is aptly articulated by Kyoto University's Professor Yoshiro Matsui as follows:

> The Gulf War symbolizes the United Nations activism after the end of the Cold War. The Security Council adopted many resolutions under Chapter VII of the Charter [Action with Respect to Threats to the Peace] during and after the Gulf War, without being disturbed by the veto of its permanent Members, and this fact is highly appreciated . . . as illustrating a "rebirth" of the United Nations' collective security. . . .
>
> But . . . there spreads a wide suspicion, especially among the nonaligned and developing countries, that this United Nations activism may be a Great Power hegemony in disguise, since they are the only possible targets of this activism. This suspicion seems to be reinforced by the fact that almost all the resolutions . . . have not specified the concrete article of the Charter as their basis [for Council actions against Iraq]. This ambiguous constitutionality . . . is not a happy one for the United Nations activism, and Member States have legitimate interests to see that the Security Council acts within the framework of the Charter which they have accepted.[26]

Professor Matsui attributes this suspicion to the inherently limited scope of available UN controls—the Charter, the Security Council, and precedent do not give the Secretary-General authority to act in a military operation. The superpowers ensured their control of their own destiny in 1945, when the Charter emerged just short of providing such authority to the head of the

UN. No State later chose to provide the *standing* military forces called for in Article 43 of the Charter—as opposed to the resulting *ad hoc,* case-by-case approach, whereby each nation must consent to provide supporting military forces.

Another facet of this concern about the constitutionality of the Security Council's activism is spawned by Article 2.7 of the UN Charter. It provides that "[n]othing contained in the present Charter shall authorize the United Nations to intervene in matters which are essentially within the domestic jurisdiction of any state or shall require the Members to submit such matters to settlement under the present Charter; but this principle shall not prejudice the application of enforcement measures under Chapter VII [Action with Respect to Threats to Peace]."

Prior to the Gulf War, the Cold War period bred a restrictive application of Chapter VII. It was historically difficult for the Security Council to take an "activist" role in maintaining international peace. With world opposition to Iraq's invasion of Kuwait, it appeared that the Council was no longer employing a restrictive view of Article 2.7. This atmosphere set the stage for potential Security Council intervention in Yugoslavia (humanitarian aid), Somalia (where force was used *first* by UN troops), and Rwanda (humanitarian relief).

Subsequent Unilateral Action? For a number of years after the Persian Gulf War (PGW), Iraq played the "cat and mouse" game of frequently testing the UN resolve to ensure that any weapons of mass destruction would be found and dismantled. The US finally mounted a massive military presence in the Persian Gulf in 1998. The US relied on the language of the UN's PGW resolutions from 1991, including one that called on States to take all necessary measures to ensure the preservation of peace and Iraq's restoration of sovereignty to Kuwait. On the other hand, UN Charter Article 2.4 prohibits the use of force—the exceptions being self-defense (Article 51) and Security Council authorization (Article 42). The stalemate was broken, for the time being, by a Memorandum of Understanding between the United Nations and the Republic of Iraq, brokered by UN Secretary-General Kofi Annan.[27] This agreement thus put off the question of whether the US could legally attack Iraq, without the benefit of a fresh UN Security Council resolution authorizing this particular use of force seven years later.

Yugoslavia The Security Council's activism was reshelved during events unfolding in the former Yugoslavia beginning in 1992. Various regions of the former Yugoslavia voted for independence and were recognized by the international community. At the beginning of the "Gulf War" period, the first Security Council Resolution demanding Iraqi retraction from its invasion of strategically located and oil-rich Kuwait came ten hours after the invasion. The Council never "took charge," however, in the less strategically located and resource-poor arena of Bosnia-Herzegovina. The Bosnian Serbs perpetrated a full-scale war, marked by the brutal infliction of extreme violations of humanitarian norms on Bosnia's Muslim and Croatian civilian population. There was clear evidence of the indiscriminate bombing of civilians, including a widely reported attack on a marketplace in Sarajevo killing sixty-six people. The Serbs mistreated those in detention, ignored the basic international safeguards intended to protect civilians and medical facilities, and perpetrated a policy of "ethnic cleansing" resulting in the disappearance or uprooting of hundreds of thousands of refugees on the basis of their ethnicity and religion.

Unlike the Council's activism during the Persian Gulf War (PGW), there was a waning optimism about its continued role in actively maintaining peace—without the level of commitment available during the PGW. The Council engaged in a form of political "hot potato" regarding who should take charge of the international response to the Bosnia crisis. The Council authorized the use of force in three resolutions: (1) Resolution 770—"all necessary measures" *can* be "taken nationally or through regional agencies or arrangements" to deliver humanitarian assistance when needed in Bosnia-Herzegovina; (2) Resolution 816—States and regional groups *may* use necessary means that *they* may determine for enforcing no-fly zones established by the Council to contain this conflict; and (3) Resolution 836—UN member States "acting nationally or through regional organizations or arrangements" *may* use air power to protect UN peacekeepers on the ground in Bosnia (e.g., NATO bombing of Serb positions near Sarejevo in 1994). It appeared that the UN was now in search of a role.

The US feared ground-troop involvement in Bosnia, due to the fragile nature of its newly found relationship with Russia just after the Cold War. The Russian ties with the Serbs were too close for the US to risk extensive involvement. The NATO-based ultimatum, that Serb guns withdraw from UN-designated "safe havens," was the most effective tool for shifting political and military responsibility. NATO was simultaneously courting Russian membership, a convenient "regional arrangement" for finding peace, while serving as a face-saving device to "confront" the Serb defiance of various UN directives. The UN would thereby exercise some degree of control via its plan to give NATO authority to order air strikes as needed to achieve political objectives.

Economic and Social Council Unlike the League of Nations, which was concerned primarily about military and political problems, the UN system has been more attentive to economic and social matters. UN priorities include the observance of human rights and the general welfare of the individual.

ECOSOC, an agency of the UN headquartered in Paris, conducts studies and issues reports on international economic, social, cultural, educational, and health matters. The results of these studies are forwarded to the General Assembly, to the State members of the United Nations, and to other UN specialized agencies concerned with the promotion of human rights and fundamental freedoms for all people. ECOSOC also prepares draft conventions for submission to the General Assembly and arranges international conferences on matters within its competence. It is the lead international agency, for example, for addressing the impact of illegal drug trafficking.[28]

When the US Reagan Administration began to shun participation in various UN agencies in the 1980s, an ECOSOC specialized agency was the first UN entity from which the US withdrew (1984). This was the UN Educational, Scientific, and Cultural Organization (UNESCO). The US maintains that the vast UN bureaucracy has produced much paperwork without tangible benefits, as discussed below under "UN Assessment." In 1990, the US reaffirmed its opposition to rejoining UNESCO. US Secretary of State James Baker's remarks provided telling insight into the US position about the UN in general: "Bluntly stated, UNESCO needs the United States as a member far more than the United States needs UNESCO."

Trusteeship Council The Trusteeship Council (TC) is a distinct UN organ consisting of selected UN members and is responsible for the administration of territories that are incapable of self-government. Under Article 77 of the Charter, certain member States have supervised territories detached from enemy States, typically as a result of war. Under Article 73 of the Charter, supervising States accepting a "trust" territory must observe the principle that the interests of the inhabitants of these territories are paramount to any interests of the supervising State. The supervising State must therefore accept the obligation to promote the well-being of the inhabitants (*see* §2.3 on Self-Determination).

This "big brother" plan was devised to promote the political, economic, social, and educational advancement of the supervised territories that were not yet capable of self-governance. This posture made sense when the Charter was drafted in 1945, long before the decolonization movement of the 1960s. Another trusteeship objective was to help these territories achieve self-government through the progressive development of independent political institutions. The US, for example, administered the Trust Territory of the Pacific Islands beginning in 1947. Portions of the population later developed their own forms of government and constitutions. In 1986, the UN's Trusteeship Council determined that the United States had satisfied its obligation to administer most of this territory. The United States then declared its obligations to be discharged. The Micronesia and Marshall Islands portion of this US trust territory later joined the UN as independent States. Palau later became an independent nation. The speed of this internationally supervised development has depended on the particular circumstances of each territory, its people, and their stage of political advancement. Most of the TC's work has been completed, due to the success of the decolonization movement of the 1960s.

The leading example of a *breach* of this trust relationship is Namibia. This area was originally a League of Nations "Mandate," analogous to the League-generated British Mandate over Palestine. South Africa refused to yield to decades of UN pressure to release its trust territory of Namibia (formerly South-West Africa). South Africa finally agreed to permit Namibia to govern itself in 1990, the year that Namibia joined the UN as an independent State member.

There have been other alleged breaches of trust, or attempts by the governed territory to break free from the established State entrusted with the territory. Nauru, a tiny republic in the central Pacific Ocean, sued

Australia in the International Court of Justice (ICJ) in 1989—alleging neglect because of Australia's exploitation and removal of phosphates earlier in the twentieth century. Natives claimed that they were barred from seeking outside legal help to avoid such depletions during the Australian administration. In 1967, the UN General Assembly terminated the Trusteeship. In 1992, the ICJ rejected Australia's contention that the UN's termination of the trusteeship barred the Court from hearing this breach of trust case. Eventually, the parties agreed to discontinue the case, which has been dismissed.[29]

One trust territory sued its administrative host to terminate the trust relationship. The size of the Trust Territory of the Pacific Islands was reduced by the departure of Micronesia, the Marshall Islands, and the Commonwealth of the Northern Marianas—after the 1986 UN declaration that the US administration had been fulfilled as to these areas. The government of Palau then signed a "Compact of Free Association" with the US. This agreement was initially rejected by the people of Palau, however, in a series of UN-observed plebiscites. In 1990, this remaining Trust Territory of the Pacific Islands sued the US in a New York court in its bid for self-rule. The plaintiffs argued that continued UN trusteeship reneged on the lost promise of self-government. But any alteration of this trust relationship requires approval by the UN's Security Council under Charter Article 83. The US court dismissed this case, partially on the basis that US courts do not have the jurisdiction or power to hear cases to dissolve trust territory relationships—a power that is expressly reserved by the UN Charter to the Security Council in association with the Trusteeship Council.[30]

Although the TC may appear to be a relic of another era, it may nevertheless have some contemporary utility. A number of States are "failing," in the sense that they are experiencing difficulties in continued self-government. Famine, civil war, and economic deprivation are some of the contemporary causes. Liberia dissolved into chaos in 1990 when rival factions began to assert tribal rivalries—slaughtering tens of thousands in the crossfire. Similar events occurred in Rwanda in 1994. "Older" States from other regions of the world such as Afghanistan, Haiti, Mozambique, Somalia, and Zaire are bordering on the same fate. "Newer" States like Bosnia-Herzegovina and Azerbaijan are just one step further away from such failed status. As noted by the UN Secretary-General in 1995:

> Another feature of such conflicts [within States after the Cold War] is the collapse of State institutions, especially the police and judiciary, with resulting paralysis of governance, a breakdown of law and order, and general banditry and chaos. Not only are the functions of government suspended, its assets are destroyed or looted and experienced officials are killed or flee the country. . . .
>
> The United Nations is, for good reasons, reluctant to assume responsibility for maintaining law and order, nor can it impose a new political structure or State institutions. It can only help the hostile factions to help themselves and begin to live together again.[31]

The daunting question is this: When should such States be declared temporary wards of the UN? One of many problems would be the predictable reprisals of various local warlords, if under the auspices of the UN, a State or group of States attempted to intervene—no matter how humanitarian the motive. Another practical limitation would be UN's financial problems, caused by an increasing number of States that are in arrears on their imposed dues. Bosnia mediator Britain's Lord Owen and his US counterpart Cyrus Vance rejected this possibility for Bosnia. In 1992, the UN Secretary-General stated that the UN was "considering" this option. The alternative, however, is to idly observe such tragedy if it were to drag on indefinitely (should the NATO intervention fail).

Secretariat The Secretariat administers all of the programs of the UN. At its zenith, a staff numbering 26,500 persons (Geneva, New York, Vienna, and some other sites) was headed by the UN Secretary-General. This officer, appointed by the General Assembly on recommendation of the Security Council, is the chief administrative officer of the UN. He or she acts in that capacity when attending meetings of the various organs of the UN.

Employees of the Secretariat, including the Secretary-General, are expected to execute their duties independently of any national allegiances. Article 100 of the UN Charter provides that in the "performance of their duties the Secretary-General and the staff shall not seek or receive instructions from any other authority external to the Organization. They shall refrain from any action which might reflect on their position as international officials responsible only to the Organization." State members of the UN must therefore respect the exclusively international character and responsibilities of their citizens while serving on the UN staff.

A very important, but obscure, function of the office of the Secretary-General (SG) is preventative diplomacy. While the public has traditionally perceived the role of this office as rather titular, the SG has often undertaken quite perilous—and even monumental—negotiations to resolve international crises. Under Article 99 of the UN Charter, the SG "may bring to the attention of the Security Council any matter which in his opinion may threaten the maintenance of international peace and security." In Boutros Boutros-Ghali's *Agenda for Peace,* requested by the heads of State at the first meeting of the Security Council in 1992, he aptly notes the increasing importance of this role. In his words: "There is a long history of the utilization by the United Nations of distinguished statesmen to facilitate the processes of peace. . . . Frequently it is the Secretary-General himself who undertakes the task. While the mediator's effectiveness is enhanced by strong and evident support from the [Security] Council, the General Assembly and the relevant Member States acting in their national capacity, the good offices of the Secretary-General may at times be employed most effectively when conducted independently of the deliberative bodies."[32]

There is no clear theoretical framework, however, for a clear and consistent link between the SG's Article 99 obligation to bring peace-threatening matters before the Security Council, and the SG's ability to gather and evaluate conflict-prevention information. This is a critical gap in need of reform. The problem is succinctly stated by Professor of Peace Studies Thomas Boudreau of St. John's University in Collegeville, Minnesota: "Without a theoretical framework that justifies and clarifies a specific reform, each effort to improve the Secretary-General's ability to prevent conflict threatens to become a piecemeal 'band-aid' solution. In short, there is a need to . . . define and develop a clear and consistent link between the Secretary-General's obligation under Article 99 and his ability to gather, ascertain, and evaluate information concerning conflict prevention. There seems to be a bankruptcy of ideas in the realm of information gathering by the United Nations."[33]

International Court of Justice The ICJ is the UN's judicial organ. Unlike its predecessor, the Permanent Court of International Justice (which was *not* an organ of the League of Nations), the drafters of the UN Charter conceived this institution as being a forum wherein international disputes could be resolved in the courtroom rather than on the battlefield.

It is headquartered at The Hague, in the Netherlands, and is generally viewed as not having fully lived up to the dream envisioned by its creators who drafted the relevant UN Charter provisions (Articles 92–96) and the operational rules set forth in the companion Statute of the International Court of Justice. Here, too, national sovereignty has been the culprit in tarnishing the 1945 vision of beating swords into plowshares. This dilemma, related problems, and proposals for the Court's refurbishment are addressed in Chapter 9 of this text.

UN ASSESSMENT

Conflicting views abound regarding the UN's progress toward fulfilling its 1945 Charter objectives. This portion of the text summarizes the perspectives on whether the UN has played a significant role in discharging its Charter functions. Some commentators have asserted that it is only a place to let off steam, operating merely as a masquerade concealing the hegemony of its more powerful national members. The most accurate perception is one that carefully assesses both sides of the UN balance sheet. Although there have been pluses, many minuses can be attributed to the often-forgotten limitations imposed by State sovereignty.

Traditional Perceptions The UN has achieved about as much success as can be expected from an international organization composed of totally autonomous States—which have not ceded it the requisite degree of sovereignty so that it can act independently to preserve the peace and attain human rights for all peoples. It was never intended to be a supreme legislative body. Nor did its State creators endow it with supranational powers to force members to comply with the decisions of UN organs—as evidenced by the lack of Charter language vesting the Secretary-General with effective control over military operations. Despite that, successes have been achieved in advancing human rights, resolving territorial disputes, promoting economic and social welfare programs, and developing draft treaties for State adoption. The eight-year-long process, which produced the global constitution governing all oceans (Chapter 6, UN Conference on the Law of the Sea), is solid evidence of a monumental treaty undertaking that could not have materialized without this global forum to promote it.

While critics tend to focus on the limitations of the UN's politically sensitive bodies, such as the Security Council and the General Assembly, the UN has nevertheless commissioned more than forty existing agencies that pursue programs for improving the living conditions for millions of people (*see* Exhibit 3.3 on UN Structure). UN economic and social welfare programs have eliminated diseases and generated hundreds of treaties dealing with narcotics, trade, slavery, atomic energy, road transportation, and famine-relief efforts in Africa, among many others.[34] The UN can similarly be credited with the global proliferation of human rights treaties in the last several decades, discussed further in Chapter 11 of this text.

Various UN agencies have also resolved a number of territorial disputes. The International Court of Justice has decided many boundary disputes. The UN Committee on the Peaceful Uses of Outer Space undertook the foundational work necessary to conclude the 1967 Treaty on Principles Governing the Activities of States in the Exploration and Use of Outer Space Including the Moon and Other Celestial Bodies. The space treaties produced at the UN have provided a widely accepted paradigm for avoiding future territorial disputes and any militarization of space (*see* Chapter 6).[35]

One perception is that the UN has lost none of its relevance. A contemporary International Law specialist, Arpad Prandler of Hungary, asserts as follows:

> The Hungarian People's Republic, which in 1955 assumed the obligation to have respect for the Charter and implement its provisions, has taken a consistent stand . . . against concepts and suggestions which, though well-intentioned, have laid the blame on the Charter for both the failures of the World Organization and the negative tendencies for the international situation and which seek the cure for ills external to the Organization. . . . The aims and purposes of the Charter, namely the maintenance of international peace and security, the preservation and removal of threats to peace, the development of friendly relations among nations based on respect for the principle of equal rights and self-determination of peoples, and international cooperation in the economic, social and cultural fields are of unchanged significance and call for a fuller measure of implementation. . . . On the whole, the Organization . . . has stood the test of time.[36]

This perspective supports the view that the UN has managed at least to assist in repressing the military excesses and xenophobia that led to two World Wars in the twentieth century.

Another persistent view is that the UN has not accomplished its myopic goal of maintaining world peace. It is no stronger than the sum of its national parts.[37] Those who ascribe to this assessment of the UN's performance are most willing to predict that only the resurrection of *US* interest can save a floundering UN. The US reliance on the UN to support the Bush administration's interests in Kuwait triggered an about-face. The Reagan administration had previously adopted the attitude that the UN needed the US more than the US needed the UN—signaling the US withdrawal from various UN agencies in the 1980s. Suddenly, however, the Bush administration could not cite International Law enough when the US was seeking Arab support for the rescue of Kuwait from the Iraqi annexation of 1990.

A third perspective is that the UN has enjoyed both successes and failures, but now faces a major crisis. In the 1986 opening statement to the Forty-First Annual General Assembly, UN Secretary-General Javier Perez de Cuellar (Peru) stated that some nations had begun to jeopardize the future of the UN. There was a crisis of confidence in the UN, he claimed, because some of its member States were refusing to pay their assessed contributions to the UN's annual administrative budget. The US, for example, did not pay all of its assessed dues during the 1980s. Although this refusal violates an international obligation to pay such dues,[38] who can possibly force any UN member State to make such payments? If such members continue to renege on this commitment in their pursuit of political goals, the UN's ability to function will be in extreme peril unlike never before.

Supposed Failures Three general failures are typically attributed to the UN: (1) It is unable to control the use of force among states; (2) it is no more than a debate chamber; and (3) it is an expensive paper mill without tangible benefits.

Has the UN in fact failed to control the use of force? The most fundamental norm in the UN Charter is found in Article 2.4. It codifies the members' agreement to "refrain in their international relations from the threat or use of force against the territorial integrity or political independence of any state. . . ." But the UN does not control the military actions of its members. It *cannot* exercise greater power than that which is ceded to it by its member States. If the UN has failed in this instance, then it is the *States* that have caused the failure. One overlooked reason is that the UN's original member States failed to provide a standing military force for immediate deployment in crisis, as depicted in the Article 43.1 language that "All Members of the United Nations, in order to contribute to the maintenance of international peace and security, undertake to make available to the Security Council . . . armed forces, assistance, and facilities . . . necessary for the purpose of maintaining international peace and security."

Critics also routinely forget to incorporate Article 33 of the UN Charter into their appraisals. This provision directs that the "parties to any dispute, the continuance of which is likely to endanger the maintenance of international peace and security, shall, first of all, seek a solution by negotiation, . . . judicial settlement, resort to regional agencies or arrangements, or other peaceful means of their choice." Each nation is responsible for pursuing its Article 33 alternatives for maintaining good international relations. Contrary to popular belief, then, the UN *cannot* immediately step in to dissipate hostilities.

War and related hostilities are properly attributable to the UN's *members* for failing to control themselves, rather than to the UN itself for its supposed failure to control them. The UN has established some useful peacekeeping operations, as will be discussed in Chapter 10 on control of force by international organizations. But the UN members have failed to vest it with sufficient power and finances to control violations of the Charter's prohibition against the use or threat of force. Such operations cannot be conducted without the consent of the nations involved in the conflict. One cannot ignore that States never intended for the UN to be a supranational power, able to act without case-by-case consent. Otherwise, the State members would have contributed the standing military forces envisioned in Article 43 of the Charter.

Other important reasons may explain the so-called UN failure. A single veto of any one of the five permanent members of the Security Council vitiates the possible use of an international military force to control threats to peace. Further, the General Assembly did not exercise its Charter-based power to expel violators of International Law from the UN. The status of the former Yugoslavia is unclear, but the Assembly's State members did not expressly expel Yugoslavia for Serbia's role in the never-ending Bosnia conflict. As a result of such inaction by member States, the dream that the UN would enforce Charter norms has not been fully achieved. These limitations in the two major organs of the UN suggest that the original members did not create (nor do the major players actually want) a powerful international organization. These UN members want to retain the freedom to unilaterally preserve their sovereign powers to act, although they often pay lip service to general principles of peace, with which no member would publicly disagree.

UN paralysis can also be deadly, as demonstrated in Iraq, Cambodia, Africa, and Bosnia. Iraq has virtually mocked the UN with repeated violations of armistice agreements, long after the UN's US-led restoration of Kuwait's sovereignty. UN inspectors in Iraq were held captive while the UN negotiated their release. There was also a massive US military buildup in the Persian Gulf in 1998. The UN Secretary-General then secured Iraq's agreement to allow weapons inspections on a level *previously* negotiated—only to be thwarted by the subsequent Iraqi decision not to allow those inspections. UN humanitarian relief was barred from entering Iraq, as were UN inspection teams supposedly having unfettered access for the purpose of destroying Iraq's poison gas and nuclear weapons facilities. Khmer Rouge rebels in Cambodia seized six UN peacekeepers in 1992, claiming that they were agents of the Cambodian government sent to spy on rebel activities. In Africa, the Secretary-General was jeered and had to flee from rocks and garbage during his 1993 visits to Ethiopia and Somalia. UN rules of engagement permit gunfire to be returned only when a peacekeeper's life is in danger. The lone exception was briefly implemented after eighteen US soldiers were killed in Somalia in 1993 after irregular Somalian forces attacked a peacekeeping operation located in Mogadishu. In Bosnia, UN troops have stood idly by while Serbs bombed several of the UN-declared safe havens—prior to a relative period of peace enforced only by the threat of NATO air strikes on Serb artillery positions. Bosnia's Deputy Prime Minister Turajlic was murdered while under UN protection when he was riding with French troops.

The "Turkish bath" criticism is that the UN has failed because it serves only as a place to let off steam. This characterization is arguably accurate, while at the same time misleading. Jeanne Kirkpatrick, former US chief delegate to the UN Security Council, publicly analogized this body with a Turkish bath—unable to achieve its task of resolving international conflict. In 1986, UN General Assembly President Choudhury similarly proclaimed that the Assembly needs to be strengthened because it "has been reduced to a mere debating body."[39]

The UN's inability to act, or to achieve uniform compliance with international norms, cannot be characterized as a complete failure. One desirable UN function is that it provides adversaries with an opportunity for global access to information about regional problems. UN members meet both regularly and when there is a crisis. Without this forum, there would be no comparable opportunity for discussions that bring the force of public opinion to bear on the conduct of certain nations. Distant events would receive little attention outside of a particular country or region before they might erupt into war. Access to the UN's political organs such as the General Assembly and the Security Council serves the national political agenda of establishing and maintaining dialogues on the issues that nations consider important to the preservation of international peace.

The major powers structured this organization in a way that would not compromise their respective national interests. The permanent Security Council members' right of individual veto negated the possible impact that the UN might have had if given the requisite degree of power to actually beat swords into plowshares. Some commentators have asserted that the use, or threatened use, of the veto power has effectively resulted in a dictatorship within a democracy. The five permanent members thus "call all the shots," whether they will be fired, and at whom.

The third failure commonly attributed to the UN is the characterization that it is no more than a vast paper mill, existing to serve itself rather than its members. The UN is, of course, a very large business. At its zenith near the end of the Cold War, it employed some 26,500 people throughout the world, while generating more than one billion pages of documents each year. Its *six* official languages system of administration requires multiple translations and republication of the same information at virtually all levels. Under Article 111 of the Charter, the five original languages included those of the permanent members of the Security Council—Chinese, French, Russian, and English (US and Great Britain). Spanish was initially included as an official language due to the large percentage of the world's population that speaks Spanish. Arabic was added for the same reason in 1977.

Financial Crisis In the mid-1980s, certain countries began to withdraw from various organs of the UN and refuse to pay their full annual UN-assessed dues. The US's 1986 assessment, for example, was approximately $200 million, or 25 percent, of the UN's total $800 million annual budget. By 1993, the US dues assessment was $374 million in arrears—which the president promised to pay only if the UN alters its funding formula to reflect growth in other national economies (such as Germany and Japan, which pay far less in annual dues). The distinct US assessment for UN peacekeeping costs has been 31.7 percent of the total figure, often larger in absolute dollars than the regular annual budget. In 1994, the combined US share of the UN's annual general budget and special peacekeeping costs was $1.334 billion. This amount is now in the vicinity of $1.5 billion. The UN is owed much more because of delayed payments from other countries who have not received the attention spawned by the US arrearage. The UN will obviously reach the breaking point if members remain delinquent about paying these assessments. Its annual operating budget is approximately $2.5 billion—the same amount as the arrearage for the countries that have not timely paid their annual dues and peacekeeping assessments.

The UN finally created an independent Inspector General in 1994. The creation of this new watchdog post helped to clear the way for the US to repay the money it owes. The US Congress was unwilling to pay the arrearage in UN-assessed dues until this position was finalized, resulting in the naming of a German diplomat to probe bureaucratic mismanagement and waste. This international civil servant is also expected to placate national concerns about the inability to prosecute UN employees for their misconduct in office. The Inspector General is charged with the responsibility of ensuring strict financial oversight at the UN, as well as strengthening its accountability in ways that should generate greater confidence. There is the daunting question, however, of whether this measure is "too little, too late."

About 80 percent of the UN's budget is paid by only fifteen nations at a time when various UN agencies support a large number of staff in expensive cities such as Paris (UNESCO). It is understandable why traditional supporters like the US, which pays 25 percent of the fixed annual budget, should demand more for its involvement—just as any private corporate structure would have to reorganize to meet the demands of its stockholders who perceive their stock as dwindling in value because of mismanagement. The US Congress hopes to reduce this percentage assessment to 20 by the year 2000.

It is ironic that, in 1978, the US Department of State Legal Advisor concluded that the US—and all member States—must pay their assessed obligations. In his words, "the General Assembly's adoption and apportionment of the Organization's expenses create a binding legal obligation on the part of State members to pay their assessed shares." This analysis was based on Article 17 of the UN Charter and the 1962 International Court of Justice case interpreting the Charter as requiring members to pay the organization's expenses as a matter of International Law. Certain UN members had then objected to the UN peacekeeping commitments in the former Belgian Congo and the Middle East, unsuccessfully claiming that the related expenditures were not "expenses of the Organization" within the meaning of the Charter.[40]

One UN response was an offer to reduce the US portion of the organization's annual dues assessment—from 25 to 15 percent, which would have begun in the mid-1980s. The US Reagan administration refused. In her confirmation testimony before the US Congress, in January 1997, former US Ambassador to the UN Madeline Albright testified regarding the reason for the US refusal. Its denial was not because the proposed cut was insufficient; instead, the US was concerned that US influence in the UN would thereby be reduced.

By 1995, the US Congress was adamant about the perceived situation at the UN, where Republican Party leaders espoused the position that the US was not getting a sufficient political return on its investment. In the United Nations Withdrawal Act of 1995, the House of Representatives proposed that the US Mission to the UN be closed by 1999 and that the UN Headquarters Agreement Act be repealed so that the UN would cease to function in New York City. By 1999, had this Act been adopted into law, the US Congress would not have authorized any annual dues or peacekeeping funds. This Bill was referred to the House Committee on International Relations, and then to the Subcommittee on International Operations and Human Rights.[41]

The UN then began to exert more pressure on the US. A 1996 Secretary-General Report proposed administrative and budgetary reform, with a view toward appeasing US complaints about UN waste.[42] In November 1997, the UN removed the US from the key financial committee for failing to pay its dues (UN Advisory Committee on Administrative and Budgetary Questions). A 1998 US Senate Bill would have paid the UN accrued arrearage—$819 million in annual dues, and the $107 million peacekeeping assessment. However, an otherwise supportive President Clinton was essentially forced to veto this legislation because it contained a distinct and irrelevant abortion rider. UN Secretary-General Kofi Annan and the European Union denounced the resulting dues rejection, partially because it came in the same week that the US sought UN support for a military campaign against Iraq.

> Polls show that Americans overwhelmingly prefer collective security, [and] shared peacekeeping responsibilities in the post-Cold War world....
>
> "The public is very resistant to using force unilaterally. When the option of intervention is presented as a U.N. operation, it usually gets majority support, while . . . a US action is generally opposed."
>
> —J. Goldsborough, "The GOP's Phony War Against the UN," *San Diego Union Tribune,* Aug. 26, 1996 (op-ed column quoting Steven Kull of the University of Maryland)

The pressure for paying past dues materialized in an effective manner in 1997–1998. The Secretary-General notified the US that it would lose voting rights if the arrearage remained unattended. In 1997, the US lost the first of two annual bids for a seat on the powerful Advisory Committee on Administrative and Budgetary Questions—a committee on which the US served for fifty years, or since the inception of the UN. In 1998, the US paid only $197 million of its regular 1998 dues, the minimum necessary to avoid losing its GA vote.

The UN is not the only international organization suffering from the spread of national delinquency in paying assessed shares of organizational budgets. A number of African nations have fallen behind in their payments to the Organization of African Unity (OAU). Given the concerns about the impact of this development on operational integrity, the OAU resolved that its member States must no longer threaten its continued operation in this manner. In 1990, the organization resolved to limit its annual budget ceiling to 10 percent above the amount expended in the previous year. Another remedial measure was to remind delinquent member States that they could not participate in organizational decision making or present candidates for OAU posts.[43]

Under the United Nations dues system, 8 of 185 nations pay 75% of its $2.5 billion budget:

USA	25.0%
Japan	18.0
Germany	9.0
France	6.5
Italy	5.3
Russia, England, Canada	11.0
Others	<1.0 each

—Adapted from *USA Today* news report; *see* www.usatoday.com/snapshot/news/nsnap067.htm.

UN REFORM STUDIES

There have been a number of major proposals published on UN reform in addition to the Secretary-General's 1992 and 1995 *Agenda for Peace* suggestions described above.[44] One might begin this assessment by first reviewing a chronicle of the reform process—as opposed to prescriptions regarding what should be done.[45] There are at least five major studies addressing contemporary UN reform proposals, generated from different points on the political spectrum:

1. The 1980s reports of the Group of Intergovernmental Experts (UN);
2. The 1993 Ford Foundation report on more effective UN financing (private research corporation);
3. The 1993 report of the United States Commission on UN effectiveness (statutory entity created by the US Congress);
4. A 1994 Ford Foundation report written by former senior UN officials; and
5. The UN's 1997 collection of fifty key reform proposals.[46]

(1) During the 1980s, the UN General Assembly authorized a study of the UN for the purpose of exploring methods for improving its effectiveness. The 1986 report of the UN Group of Intergovernmental Experts from eighteen countries contained seventy-one recommendations—serving as their starting point for UN reform. These recommendations fall into several subdivisions. Recommendation 1(e) suggests streamlining the UN's "intergovernmental" machinery through greater coordination of the organization's numerous "conferences and meetings, in particular by staggering them throughout the year; this would ensure better utilization of conference facilities and established resources, limit the use of temporary personnel and reduce overtime." Another suggestion is to rearrange the structure of the Secretariat. Recommendation 15 would thus make a "substantial reduction in the number of staff members at all levels, but particularly in the higher echelons. . . ." In the overall area of personnel, Recommendation 50 is that the "Secretary-General should include in his annual reports to the General Assembly on personnel questions a [new and separate] section related to the ratings of the performance of staff and their promotion. The system of performance evaluation should be improved by introducing an element of comparison in the rating of staff."

This UN expert self-study made a number of recommendations for improving the UN's planning and budget procedures. Recommendation 68 proposes a clear agreement among the UN's member States on the content of the UN's budget. The precise concern expressed by the experts' report is the following: "[T]here is no clear linkage between priority setting and resource requirements either in the [periodic] medium term plan or in the [annual] programme budget. This has led to the fact that activities that are considered obsolete, of marginal usefulness or ineffective have not always been excluded from the programme budget."

(2) The 1993 Ford Foundation report *Financing an Effective United Nations* focused on two areas for improvement: the regular UN budget and peacekeeping. Regarding the annual UN budget, this group suggested that all members—particularly the larger contributors—pay their assessed dues *in full* and *on time.* Unlike the US presidential administrations of the 1980s and 1990s, this respected and independent US research institution did *not* favor the UN's scaling back of the US dues assessment. It said the US has much to gain from

continued participation in a strong UN. Members should pay their dues in quarterly installments, rather than in an annual lump sum. Delays would be penalized with interest assessments. This budgetary change would greatly assist in operating the UN's Working Capital Fund and help it anticipate such delays and facilitate responses on a more timely basis.

In the area of peacekeeping, the Ford Foundation assessment is that the international community should be prepared to accept increased peacekeeping costs in future years. The alternative of war and economic decline hold far greater disadvantages than allowing the world to slip into a chaotic series of uncontrolled conflicts. Finally, all member States with an above-average per capita gross national product should pay the same rate of peacekeeping assessments as their annual dues assessments.

(3) The third of the five major studies on improving UN effectiveness is a report of the US Commission on the Effectiveness of the UN. In September 1993, this congressionally mandated study released its recommendations on the eve of the opening of the UN's 48th Session in New York—after a two-year study that included public hearings from across the US. This Commission, viewing the UN from a perspective that would benefit the US, made several novel recommendations.

Probably the most controversial is the suggested creation of a 5,000- to 10,000-member UN Rapid Deployment Force of volunteers who are in turn volunteered by individual governments. This force would help to fill the vacuum left by the UN members' failure to provide a standing military force at the disposal of the UN under Article 43 of the Charter. UN headquarters would be equipped with state-of-the-art communications gear appropriate for such a modern and rapidly deployable force to "put out fires." The UN should earmark special UN forces to provide whatever logistical or tactical support is necessary to deal quickly with new conflicts.

This US Commission on the UN also recommended creation of an International Criminal Court to try international war criminals, terrorists, drug traffickers, and airline hijackers. The existence of such a Court would, of course, serve US interests. Such defendants might be triable in a way that would ameliorate public pressure on the US to do something when fundamental human rights are jeopardized in a theater that has little tactical significance for the US. Future "Noriegas" might not have to be captured during a US invasion of dubious legality. The UN actually later implemented this suggestion by creating two *ad hoc* International Criminal Courts for crimes in the former Yugoslavia and Rwanda (Chapter 9). This US Commission on UN reform also recommended the creation of another international court—one dealing specifically with human rights. This would be a specialty court under the UN umbrella—in addition to any International Criminal Court.

The US Department of State should train more professionals for handling UN affairs of interest to the US. This recommendation finally admits, although indirectly, the extent to which the US attitude has typically been that "the UN needs the US more than the US needs the UN."

The US Commission's final recommendation urges that the US should take the lead in advancing reforms at the UN. The US could thereby actively engage in constructive multilateral diplomacy. As stated in the Commission's report of its findings, the American people do not want to be the "world's police force." They *would* accept a collective responsibility, however, to be part of an international "highway patrol."

Some of the US Commission members believe that the UN has done so poorly that it should not be given any added responsibilities in the twenty-first century. There is no question that the UN could be better managed. Yet the majority of Commission members believe that abandonment would not improve global relations. Unlike an earlier era, when the US Senate shunned the League of Nations, this contemporary report of US attitudes affirms that this is no time for isolationism.

(4) The 1994 Ford Foundation's independent report (the second on the same subject in two years) urged the UN to create a common headquarters for the General Assembly, the Secretariat, and the specialized agencies—as was originally contemplated by the UN drafters in 1945. All such agencies would be grouped in a common seat, rather than the current practice of spreading them all over the world. Geneva and Bonn were suggested as possible sites, although such a move might further diminish US support.

(5) The most recent and extensive set of reform proposals is published in the UN-sponsored, three-volume work *Reforming the United Nations: New Initiatives and Past Efforts.*[47] This publication collates fifty of the major proposals for reform originating both from within and outside of the UN and spanning four decades.

One might begin an overview of this last collection of proposals with the following question: What would happen if the UN shut down today? Not unlike China's Cultural Revolution, where International Law was abandoned for a ten-year period (1966–1976),[48] suppose the *UN* were discarded! In an iconoclastic passage, challenging UN-driven programs seeking the redistribution of the world's wealth and resources, one proposal questions the continued vitality of the UN as follows:

> This [approach] raises the question, understandably, of whether the United Nations serves any positive purpose. If its influence is of no consequence or, indeed, negative, then the world may be better off without the U.N.... Today, however, the debate is not between competing theories, but is based on fact and history. The United Nations ... no longer is simply a well-intentioned glimmer in an idealist's eye or an embryonic body whose missteps and failures understandably should be overlooked. It is a full-grown organization with a real record and history. A discussion of the U.N. and of whether the world would be better without it, therefore now moves beyond theories and good intentions to a record of comprised facts and data, successes and failures.
>
> Only those situations improved by the U.N. argue for the continued existence of the organization. Even here, however, it is possible that other multinational organizations may be able to do as well or better than the UN.[49]

The essential question for the new millennium—after the Cold War era which dominated its initial evolution—is this: What kind of UN does the world community want? Rather than just being scrapped, as the above excerpt envisions, should the UN be reformed or basically redesigned? Also, are current attacks on the UN fresh examples of the old adage about "the pot calling the kettle black"? While observers are obsessed with fraud and waste at the UN, widespread dishonesty and mismanagement likewise plague the governments of the world. Regarding claims of UN impotence to realistically control threats to international peace, the major UN organs were always marginalized by the failure of States to cede the requisite degree of sovereignty to this organization so that it could function with true supranational powers—which could have required rogue States to observe international norms. One of the classic examples is the veto power of the five major powers who controlled the UN drafting process in 1945. That institution alone undermined the UN Charter's egalitarian concepts of equality among States and "one nation, one vote" from the outset of the organization's existence.

On the other hand, the balance sheet should not ignore some major breakthroughs, even if the resulting institutions have not operated as smoothly as envisioned. Relevant events just in the 1990s include the various international criminal tribunals now trying individuals for war crimes for the first time since Nuremberg (Chapter 9); the effectiveness of the UN Conference on the Law of the Sea, which drafted the widely accepted constitution for the oceans of the world that became effective in 1994 (Chapter 6); UN resolutions serving as a basis for the thirty-four nation coalition—pitting Arabs against Arabs—and forcing Iraq to withdraw from Kuwait (Chapter 10); the abolition of apartheid in South Africa after years of intense international pressure and economic sanctions (Chapter 11); and the 1998 creation of the new post of Deputy Secretary-General, who will oversee the administration of the UN bureaucracy.

Having considered the various UN assessments and reforms in this section of the book, it is now appropriate to probe another alternative. Regional associations of States have the potential to effectively achieve the goals enshrined in the UN Charter. Would these international organizations, focusing on *regional* problems, do the job better than a global organization—which often requires disinterested parties to take a position on matters that do not directly concern them?

◆ 3.4 EUROPEAN UNION

INTRODUCTION

The UN Charter recognizes the utility of autonomous international organizations in the various geographical regions of the world. Article 52(1) specifies that a State's membership in the UN does not preclude the simultaneous "existence of regional arrangements or agencies for dealing with such matters relating to the maintenance of international peace and security as are appropriate for regional action provided that such arrangements or agencies and their activities are consistent with the Purposes and Principles of the United Nations." Under Article 52(3), the UN Security Council encourages the settlement of local disputes through regional organizations. These provisions complement Article

33(1), whereby the State parties to any dispute "shall, first of all, seek a solution by negotiation . . . [or] resort to regional agencies or arrangements, or other peaceful means of their own choice." States have developed a number of regional defense, economic, and political organizations. These entities sometimes operate in harmony with the UN, at the global level, and with individual States at the regional level.

This textbook is not designed for a separate course in international organization. After reviewing the exponential growth in international organizations illustrated in Exhibit 3.1, it is quite evident that many organizations cannot be covered here if one is to learn the essentials of International Law. While several military and political organizations will be profiled in the next section, this section of the book will focus on the European Union. It is probably the best example of how a group of States has managed to integrate goals and results at the regional organizational level. Should this particular association of States continue to flourish since its 1957 inception, then there is hope that Europe might overcome its reputation as being the most belligerent region in history.

HISTORICAL BACKDROP

Long before the much-heralded European Union's Maastricht Treaty of 1992, the concept of an association of European States found political expression in both negative and positive ways. There were attempts to *impose* unity by Napoleon and Hitler. Napoleon sought to unite the Continent under French hegemony until his military demise at the beginning of the nineteenth century. Hitler aspired to the subjugation of Europe under the dictatorship of Germany's Third Reich.

Peaceful attempts to unite Europe followed World War I. In 1923, Austria led the Pan-European Movement. It beckoned creation of a United States of Europe modeled on the success of the Swiss struggle for unity with the 1648 Peace of Westphalia (§1.3), as well as the interim solidarity evinced by the German Empire of 1871. In 1929, in speeches before the League of Nations Assembly in Geneva, French and German leaders proposed the creation of a European Community within the framework of the League of Nations.

These positive bids for peaceful unification were overcome by a dominant tide of nationalism and imperialism. The Twentieth Century's two "great wars" demonstrated the futility of the constant rivalry between European nations over many centuries. Europe's collapse, its political and economic exhaustion, and its outdated national structures signaled the need for a fresh start and a more radical approach to the reordering of Europe.

The contemporary European Union is rooted in the creation of three communities. The first was the European Coal and Steel Community formed by the 1951 Treaty of Paris. The 1957 Treaty of Rome established the European Economic Community and the European Atomic Energy Community. The initial goal was to create a common market (no internal tariff barriers) in coal and steel for the six member States of Belgium, France, West Germany, Italy, Luxembourg, and the Netherlands. This union would, it was hoped, secure peace by loosely integrating both the victorious and the vanquished European nations of prior world wars. Although France rejected the added aspiration of an international *defense* organization, the original members built an economic community premised on the free movement of workers, goods, and services. Mutually agreeable agricultural and commercial policies were adopted by the end of the 1970s.

In 1972, Denmark, Ireland, and Great Britain applied for membership. The admission of these States was accompanied by new agreements regarding social, regional, and environmental concerns. Plans for a unified European monetary system were launched in 1979 as part of the grand design to enable the Community's member States to pursue common economic policies.

Greece, Spain, and Portugal joined in the 1980s, bringing the member-State total to twelve—while also bringing some disparity to the Community in terms of its members' respective stages of economic development. It was in this period that the Community began to grow in international stature, however. The Community, as an international organization, possessed the legal capacity to conclude treaties on behalf of its member States. One example is the loose form of association with a number of southern Mediterranean, African, and Caribbean–Pacific States under the four "Lome Conventions" concluded during the 1970s and 1980s.[50]

The Community's 1986 "Single Act" legislation was designed to formally establish a single market (similar to that enjoyed by the states of the United States) by 1992. One feature, yet to be actually realized, would have been a single currency—a key feature in promoting a true United States of Europe. The "1992" program prompted the applications of Austria, Finland, Norway (voter-rejected in 1994), and Sweden (admitted in 1995), plus Cyprus, Malta, Switzerland, and Turkey (not yet admitted)—all between 1987 and 1992. The current members have also resolved to further strengthen their economic and political ties. Under the "1992" legislation, the European Community is now referred to as the European Union.[51]

The end of the Cold War's East–West struggle, the demolition of the Berlin Wall, and the unification of Germany have all signaled potential movement toward forging a greater European Union (EU) while integrating its eastern neighbors. Yet ethnic rivalries in Europe, the breakdown of sovereignty (§§2.2–2.3), and the increasing influence of smaller commercial entities in the world market all suggest the possibility of an opposite result. Unless the EU is able to strengthen its internal structure and decision-making processes, it will never develop into the genuine union its members have now feverishly pursued over four decades. At this point in time, however, it is arguably the most advanced form of regional integration. The EU is the potential catalyst for uniting Europe in a way that could eliminate a number of barriers not limited to just trade. A summary of the essential institutions follows.

COMMUNITY LAW

The Treaty on European Union, or the "Maastricht Treaty," was signed in Maastricht, the Netherlands, in 1992. One objective was to amend all earlier treaties on varying Community subjects in a way that would bring all of them under one umbrella treaty and eliminate any inconsistencies.

The objectives stated in the Maastricht Treaty include some key features that define the anticipated future of this organization (Title I, Article B):

- "Creation of an area without [any] internal frontiers" (much like states of other federated unions such as the US);
- Social cohesion through an economic and monetary union, which will ultimately create a single currency (historically printed by each individual country);
- The further assertion of "its identity on the international scene, in particular through the implementation of a common foreign and security policy including the eventual framing of a common defence policy, which might in time lead to a common defense" (leaning toward the League of Nations and OAS Charter provisions providing that an attack upon one member of the international organization is an attack against all—a provision *not* employed in the UN Charter); and
- Strengthening the "protection of the rights and interests of the nationals of its Member States through the introduction of a citizenship of the Union" (facilitating even smoother international travel than currently permitted within the EU).

The latest "Community Law" involves the evolution of a single currency within the EU known as the European Monetary Union. The currency is referred to as the "Euro." A common currency will mean that nations with different economic needs will be bound by one common economic policy. The countries will effectively be yielding a degree of their sovereignty to a central bank located in Frankfurt. Members can qualify only if they achieve low inflation, low government budget deficits, and leaner social programs—at a time when unemployment in most member nations is relatively high (approximately 10 percent). This is essentially why England has opted out of participation in the Euro plan.

Trading in the Euro began on the first day of 1999, although the hard currency will not be in circulation for several years. After a transition period, and beginning on July 1, 2002, the Euro is scheduled to transition into full use with participating member nations. The other nonparticipants among the EU's members are Denmark, Sweden, and Greece (which will not qualify because of the budget deficit standard for participating). Nevertheless, eleven sovereign nations within the EU will cede national control over interest rates to an international body. This has *never* been done before in any international organization or in any other treaty arrangement.

What makes the EU different from the UN? Unlike the UN, the EU has a relatively homogeneous social, economic, and legal environment. The European Union was initially designed to integrate the European nations just economically. Europe was crushed by World War II; its Western nations had lost many of their colonies; and this community of nations needed to unite to compete with large powers—like the United States to the west and the Soviet Union to the east. The economic unification of Europe began with the reduction of trade barriers within the Community and the establishment of a common economic policy in relation to nonmember nations.

Europe's economic integration has occurred in two key phases. The first was the *reduction* of trade barriers. The second phase, commonly referred to as "1992," was designed to *eliminate* trade barriers by 1992. Like the 1994 North American Free Trade Agreement (NAFTA), the new arrangement would create a trading environment with initially reduced and ultimately eliminated tariffs and bring about a single economic market in which all participating countries could compete. This would enable member States to access each other's markets more freely while making it more difficult for nonmember countries. In such a market, the obstacles that would impede the movement of people, goods, services, or capital within the boundaries of the trading bloc would be first reduced and then eliminated. The EU's strategy was thus designed for the creation of one central bank, followed by one European currency for all member States. By contrast, there will never be a central bank for all UN members.

Another essential objective of this single market is the economic and political stability of Western (and maybe one day Eastern) Europe. Competitors within this Union will benefit because they will have larger markets, unimpeded by the usual customs inspections, tariffs, and other limitations on international business (Chapter 13). The comprehensive Maastricht Treaty, containing all of the "1992" laws, will be the basic source of Community developments for decades to come. The "1992" rules have a significant impact on foreign business operations in Europe. The rules govern even minutiae such as the brands of ketchup to be used in US-owned fast-food restaurants in Paris, the angle of Ford headlights made in London, and the airing of "I Love Lucy" reruns in Amsterdam.

The Maastricht Treaty on European Union affirms a rich history of Community case law to protect the social and other fundamental human rights of the citizens of member States. The UN balance sheet, by comparison, has been rather poor. Its financial crisis may even be its demise. As discussed in Chapter 11 on "Human Rights," the relevant provisions of the UN Charter contain only hortatory language setting a standard for common achievement. UN resolutions are often just that—resolutions, without necessarily binding effect (§1.4). The EU treaty, on the other hand, confirms a degree of solidarity in "relations between the member States and between their peoples." This phrase (treaty Title I, Article A) echoes the degree to which the rights of the individual are directly incorporated into the future of this international organization. It also indicates that member States must occasionally do that which they would never do if not for the advantages of membership in the EU.

> Many Britons—not only lawyers like myself—find it an insult to national pride that . . . the two 15-year-old Liverpool boys convicted five years ago by an English court of murdering 2-year-old James Bulger in a crime that shocked the world, will be allowed by the European Court of Human Rights in Strasbourg, France, to argue that the English legal system breached their human rights. . . .
>
> For many, myself included, the court is unpopular, despite the good work it has done.
>
> It is generally perceived as arrogant, unwieldy and the source of much chaos and delay. It is absolutely typical that when I telephoned recently to check the name of the chief judge, they were all at lunch. A recorded voice told me in French and English that someone would get back to me but, of course, no one did.
>
> —Fenton Bresler, "Can Foreign Court Pronounce on British Justice?" *National Law Journal,* June 8, 1998, at www.jlx.com/practice/internat/0608britjus.html

An essential difference between members of the UN and members of Europe's various international organizations is that the latter's institutions *are* generally endowed with the requisite degree of sovereignty to enable them to require member States to treat their citizens in ways that they would not otherwise consider under their own national laws.

The following case offers a dramatic illustration. The year 1992 was a stormy one in Ireland in terms of the very sensitive issue of abortion. Ireland's Constitution prohibits abortion, the result of a referendum of its voters in 1983. It is also a crime punishable by life imprisonment. A 1979 law had previously been enacted, making it unlawful to advocate or assist in the obtaining of an abortion in any manner. In one case litigated in 1992, a lower Irish court prohibited a raped fourteen-year-old girl from going abroad for the purpose of obtaining an abortion. After it became clear that she would commit suicide, the Irish Supreme Court overruled that opinion in a rather succinct one-sentence opinion. The European Court of Justice, seated in Luxembourg, had previously determined that it had no jurisdiction with regard to Ireland's national abortion law. Any issues related to that law were characterized as "lying outside the scope of [European] Community Law." This case was resolved by an institution not part of the EU, but nevertheless part of "Community Law." The European Court of Human Rights dates back to 1951, six years before the EU's predecessor—the European Community—was inaugurated by the Treaty of Rome. It nevertheless illustrates the internationalization of Community values in a way that transcends the national law of any one country within the "Community."

The following decision did not address whether family planning counselors in Ireland could advise women about the option of traveling to England, where abortion is legal. The defendants' lawyers attempted to resolve what they characterized as a "Community Law" issue. The defendants claimed that Ireland's judicial action, prohibiting abortion counseling, violated the European Human Rights Convention. In a companion case, some student newspapers were charged with publishing information about pregnancy alternatives in violation of Irish laws. The resulting opinion of the European Court of Human Rights, seated in France, effectively reversed the Irish Supreme Court injunction against the various defendants. It is also a classic illustration of how an international organization can require a State to act in a way that is contrary to its national law:

Case of Open Door and Dublin Well Woman v. Ireland

EUROPEAN COURT OF HUMAN RIGHTS, 1992

No. 64/1991/316/387–388

Author's Note: *The Irish Supreme Court affirmed a lower Irish court order requiring defendants—Open Door Counselling, Ltd., Dublin Well Woman, Ltd., and certain individual defendants—to cease counseling on the availability of abortions outside of Ireland. The court order had already resulted in the closure of defendant Open Door. The defendants applied to the European Court of Human Rights (ECHR) for relief under the European Convention on Human Rights (European Convention) provisions—which protect freedom of expression and prevent disclosure of information received in confidence.*

The ECHR did not rule directly on Ireland's constitutional ban on abortions. The majority of the Court's judges did rule, however, that preventing women from getting information on how to get abortions outside of Ireland violates the European Convention. Ireland could no longer use its own anti-abortion laws to deprive its citizens of human rights guaranteed by the European Convention. This was nevertheless an exceptionally divided court, the majority opinion carrying by a vote of fifteen to eight. Seven of twenty-three judges wrote their own separate opinions. The Court's numbering of paragraphs is omitted.

COURT'S OPINION. The case was referred to the Court by the European Commission on Human Rights [and] . . . by the Government of Ireland. . . . It originated in two applications against Ireland lodged with the Commission . . . by Open Door Counselling Ltd, a company incorporated in Ireland; the second by another Irish company, Dublin Well Woman Centre Ltd., and one citizen of the United States of America, . . . and three Irish citizens, Ms Ann Downes, Mrs X and Ms Maeve Geraghty [two employed as trained counsellors for one of these companies and two in their capacity as women of child-bearing age residing in Ireland]. . . .

The applicants complained of an injunction imposed by the Irish courts on Open Door and Dublin Well Woman to restrain them from providing certain information to pregnant women concerning abortion facilities outside the jurisdiction of Ireland. . . .

On 19 December 1986 Mr Justice Hamilton, President of the High Court [lower Irish court], found that the activities of Open Door and Dublin Well Woman in counselling pregnant women . . . to travel abroad to obtain an abortion or to obtain further advice on abortion within a foreign jurisdiction were unlawful [under] . . . the Constitution of Ireland.

He confirmed that the Irish criminal law [thus] made it an offence to procure or attempt to procure an abortion. . . . Furthermore, Irish constitutional law also protected the right to life of the unborn from the moment of conception onwards.

An injunction was accordingly granted " . . . that the Defendants [Open Door and Dublin Well Woman] and each of them, their servants or agents, be perpetually restrained from counselling or assisting pregnant women within the jurisdiction of this court [Ireland] to obtain further advice on abortion or to obtain an abortion."

Open Door and Dublin Well Woman appealed against this decision to the [Irish] Supreme Court which in a unanimous judgment . . . rejected the appeal [affirming the lower court's injunction requiring the defendants to cease giving information about the availability of abortions in Great Britain].

On the question of whether the above activity should be restrained as being contrary to the [Irish] Constitution, Mr Justice Finlay C. J. stated:

> . . . the issue and the question of fact to be determined is: were they thus assisting in the destruction of life of the unborn?
>
> I am satisfied beyond doubt that . . . the Defendants were assisting in the ultimate destruction of the life of the unborn by abortion.

In a companion case, an Irish anti-abortion society applied to the lower Irish court to restrain the publication of information in student newspapers regarding abortion information. That court referred this, and the Open Door and Well Woman matter, to the European Court of Justice in Luxembourg for a determination of whether this issue fell within the ambit of Community Law. But on appeal of that case referral, the Irish Supreme Court instead restrained the student publication from further publishing abortion counseling information. The dispositive statement from the Irish Supreme Court in the related newspaper case is provided by the ECHR in its Open Door and Dublin Well Woman decision at this point in the opinion.

> . . . I reject as unsound the contention that the activity involved in this case of publishing in the students' manuals the [Great Britain abortion clinic information] . . . can be distinguished from the activity condemned by this Court in [the Open Door Counselling case]. . . . It is clearly the fact that such information is conveyed to pregnant women, and not the method of communication, which creates the unconstitutional illegality. . . .

The ECHR next returned to its analysis of the Open Door and Dublin Well Woman defendants.

Section 16 of the Censorship of Publications Act 1929 . . . provides that:

> It shall not be lawful for any person, otherwise than under and in accordance with a permit in writing granted to him under this section . . . to print or publish . . . any book or periodical publication (whether appearing on the register of prohibited publications or not) which advocates . . . the procurement of an abortion. . . .

. . . In their applications lodged with the Commission . . . the applicants complained that the injunction[s] in question constituted an unjustified interference with their right to impart or receive information contrary to Article 10 of the [European Human Rights] Convention. . . .

The Commission had then ruled that the Irish Supreme Court injunctions did violate the European Convention, triggering the ECHR's jurisdiction to hear this case. Its analysis continues with the Open Door and Dublin Well Woman defendants.

> The applicants . . . invoked [Convention] Article 10 which provides:
>
> 1. Everyone has the right to freedom of expression. This right shall include freedom to hold opinions and to receive and impart information and ideas without interference by public authority and regardless of frontiers [within the Community].
>
> 2. The exercise of these freedoms . . . may be subject to such formalities, conditions, [and] restrictions . . . necessary in a democratic society . . . for preventing the disclosure of information received in confidence. . . .

In their submissions to the Court the [Irish] Government contested these claims and also contended that Article 10 should be interpreted against the background of Articles 2 . . . and 60 of the Convention the relevant parts of which state:

> [2.] 1. Everyone's right to life shall be protected by law. . . .
> 60. Nothing in [the] Convention shall be construed as limiting or derogating from any of the human rights and fundamental freedoms which may be ensured under the laws of any High Contracting Party. . . .

The Court cannot accept that the restrictions at issue pursued the aim of the prevention of crime since . . . neither the provision of the information in question nor the obtaining of an abortion outside the jurisdiction [i.e., in Great Britain] involved any criminal offence. However, it is evident that the protection afforded under Irish law to the right to life of the unborn is based on profound moral values concerning the nature of life . . . [which was] reflected in the stance of the majority of the Irish people against abortion as expressed in the 1983 referendum. . . .

The Court [however] is not called upon to examine whether a right to abortion is guaranteed under the Convention or whether the foetus is encompassed by the right to life as contained in Article 2. . . .

The only issue to be addressed is whether the [Irish] restrictions on the freedom to impart and receive information contained in the relevant part of the [Irish court's] injunction are necessary in a democratic society for the legislative aim of protection of morals. . . .

[T]he national authorities enjoy a wide margin of appreciation in matters of morals, particularly [when they] . . . touch on matters of belief concerning the nature of human life. . . .

However this power of appreciation is not unlimited. It is for the Court . . . to supervise whether a restriction [like this one] is compatible with the Convention. . . .

In this context, it is appropriate to recall that freedom of expression is also applicable to "information" or "ideas" that offend, shock or disturb the State or any sector of the population. Such are the demands of that pluralism, tolerance and broadmindedness without which there is no "democratic society." . . .

The [Irish] Government . . . [has] submitted that Article 10 should not be interpreted in such a manner as to limit, destroy or derogate from the right to life of the unborn which enjoys special protection under Irish law. . . . [T]he Court recalls [however] that the injunction . . . [and] the information that it sought to restrain was available from other sources. Accordingly, it is not the interpretation of Article 10 but the position of Ireland as regards the implementation of the [anti-abortion] law that makes possible the continuance of the current level of abortions obtained by Irish women abroad.

In light of the above, the Court concludes that the restraint imposed on the applicants from receiving or imparting information was disproportionate to the [governmental] aims pursued. Accordingly there has been a breach of Article 10.

◆ *Notes & Questions*

1. The Court held that Ireland violated Article 10 of the Convention and that it must pay damages to the defendant entities Open Door and Dublin Well Woman. These private corporations, and the individuals who were parties to this suit, were capable of personally enforcing their treaty rights provoked by Ireland's violations of the European Human Rights Convention. In the UN's International Court of Justice, however, only *States* may be parties to such enforcement proceedings (discussed further in Chapter 9). *Open Door* effectively means that an international organization may vary the traditional rules of International Law—which otherwise require a *State* to bring an action on behalf of its injured citizens against another State that is responsible for some alleged harm. Ireland would not, of course, be willing to advocate such treaty rights on behalf of its natural or corporate citizens. For Irish perspectives, *see* J. Kingston & A. Whelan, *Abortion and the Law: An Irish Perspective* (Dublin: Street & Maxwell, 1997).

2. *Should* the European Community provide this protection to individuals? Put another way, what *is* the special protection afforded to individuals and corporations under "Community Law" that is not available to them at the UN under traditional principles of International Law?

EUROPEAN COMMUNITY INSTITUTIONS

This international organization of States is managed by a number of common institutions. Unlike the UN, there are not nearly as many individual agencies (*see* Exhibit 3.3 in §3.3 showing major UN agencies). Yet one may characterize the European Community experience as not being as bogged down by a burdensome administrative superstructure. Exhibit 3.4 summarizes the major EC institutions and their respective functions.

All institutions of the European Union have been affected by the dramatic events occurring between the third round of European elections of 1989 and the fourth round of elections in 1994. Members of those institutions face a different Europe than that of 1989, when communists were in power from Berlin to Vladivostok. Few people outside of the Netherlands had heard of Maastricht, and political union was not considered a real priority.

The interim five years introduced the following astonishing events: the unification of Germany; the collapse of the Soviet Union; the potential for adding more State members to the EU, which had just completed the processes of democratic elections and the movement toward market economies; the breakdown of sovereignty into smaller units—particularly in Europe; renewed conflict in the Balkans—an area with a significant role in the two great wars of the twentieth century; and the flareup of ethnic rivalries. These events suggest some of the reasons why so many member parliaments did not share the same degree of urgency about ratifying the various "European" treaties, including the great Maastricht Treaty (envisioning a single currency within the EU).

The most recent event in the evolution of the EU process is the October 1997 signing (not ratification) of the Treaty of Amsterdam.[52] The 1992 Maastricht Treaty focuses on encouraging an economic and monetary union among EU member States. The 1997 Amsterdam Treaty, by contrast, contains new policies regarding social policies. This treaty is a reaction to the criticism that the EU has focused exclusively on economic interests to the detriment of issues such as social security, employment rights in the event of layoffs possibly associated with controls mandated by Maastricht's economic guidelines, and social welfare. Thus, the 1997 treaty is designed to reassure the public that basic social needs will not be sacrificed to market forces.

One critical feature for maintaining lasting peace in Europe may be the degree to which the EU and its eastern neighbors complete the process of integration. The EU is expected to lower, and then eradicate, its various trade barriers. Its central and eastern "associates" are expected to open their national markets to the EU products in a somewhat more gradual fashion in terms of movement of persons, capital, and services. As Exhibit 3.4 demonstrates, virtually all of these major EU institutions will have a significant role to play in this particular segment of the planned integration of the greater part of Europe.[53]

Expanding the EU to incorporate all States, including the eastern "associates," into other international organizations such as NATO has been proposed but would be no easy undertaking. Obvious problems have blocked NATO's being able to decisively handle the Bosnia situation, which continually threatens the area's peace. But the EU (and even the UN) did not do much better. It was not until July 1994 that the EU was able to demonstrate any significant peacekeeping progress in Bosnia's then two-year-old civil war. The EU took over the administration of Bosnia's city of Mostar in an effort to demilitarize a city typically divided by Muslim–Croat rivalry. This event came only after a US-brokered agreement whereby a portion of the city was taken over by EU forces.

Full political integration would mean that members of a very diverse political spectrum would be willing to effectively become a super-State or federated Europe—not unlike the federation of the states within the United States of America or the United States of Mexico. Further, Russia's path to democracy and a market economy is by no means clear or complete. Vladimir Zhirinovsky is the leader of the Liberal Democratic Party of Russia and a member of the Russian Parliament with a more significant following than reported by the Western media. He is described as a "dangerous radical" in western terms but is rather popular with many Russians. He has threatened EU member Germany with nuclear

EXHIBIT 3.4 EUROPEAN COMMUNITY'S MAJOR INSTITUTIONS (NOT LIMITED TO EU ENTITIES)

EUROPEAN PARLIAMENT (STRASBOURG, FRANCE): Committee meetings and limited sessions held in Brussels. ◆ 567 members directly elected by voters in EU countries. ◆ Political driving force for initiatives and legislation. ◆ Monitors day-to-day management via questions to Commission and Council (3,500 in 1992). ◆ Establishes periodic commissions of inquiry and examines petitions from Community citizens.

SECRETARIAT (LUXEMBOURG): 3,500 staff members plus political group staffs.

EUROPEAN COUNCIL: Heads of government and President of Commission. ◆ Acts as guiding force via two meetings per year.

COUNCIL OF THE EUROPEAN UNION (BRUSSELS): Certain meetings held in Luxembourg. ◆ 76 ministers from member States (agricultural, employment, foreign, etc.). ◆ Adopts major Community decisions based on Commission proposals. ◆ Responsible for intergovernmental cooperation.

EUROPEAN COMMISSION (HEADQUARTERS IN BRUSSELS, PLUS STAFF IN LUXEMBOURG): 17 State representative members who propose Community legislation. ◆ Primary guardian of Community treaties. ◆ Executive body that ensures correct application of treaties. ◆ May initiate infringement proceedings against States. ◆ Fines individuals and companies. ◆ Refers matters to Court of Justice. ◆ Administers budget and appropriations. ◆ 17,000 officials divided among 30 Directorates General.

ECONOMIC AND SOCIAL COMMITTEE (BRUSSELS): 189 members representing employees, employers, farmers, consumers, etc. ◆ Coal and steel matters referred to ECSC Consultative Committee ◆ 96 other representatives of producers, workers, consumers, traders.

COMMITTEE OF THE REGIONS (BRUSSELS): 189 members representing local and regional interests. ◆ Must be consulted prior to the adoption of decisions involving a region.

EUROPEAN INVESTMENT BANK (LUXEMBOURG): Raises funds to finance investments contributing to Community development. ◆ Makes loans to less developed countries (especially Central and Eastern Europe).

EUROPEAN COURT OF JUSTICE (LUXEMBOURG): 13 judges and 6 advocates-general ensure that European treaties are interpreted and implemented per Community Law. ◆ Judgments may be requested by member State, its courts, individual, company, or other Community institutions. ◆ Ensures compatibility of any legal instrument with Community Law.

EUROPEAN COURT OF HUMAN RIGHTS (STRASBOURG, FRANCE): 40 judges—one for each member State—adjudicate issues arising under the European Convention on Human Rights *(see, e.g., Open Door and Well Woman* case).

COURT OF FIRST INSTANCE (LUXEMBOURG): 12 judges ◆ Created in 1989 to deal mostly with actions brought by individuals (appeals may be lodged in Court of Justice).

COURT OF AUDITORS (LUXEMBOURG): 12 members appointed by Council to ensure sound financial management, all Community revenue collected, lawful expenditures made.

EUROPEAN MONETARY INSTITUTION AND CENTRAL BANK: Plan to administer single currency (ECU), which failed to become part of "1992" legislation but scheduled to be fully operational in mid-2002.

Note: Additional details about the various institutions are available on the European Union's Web site at www.europa.eu.int/index-en.htm.

attack if it "interferes" with Russian affairs. In his words, as reported in the Moscow newspaper *Izvestia*'s foreign affairs section, if elected, "I will not hesitate to use nuclear weapons."[54] He has also threatened the US over its ownership of Alaska. He declares that this takeover improperly deprived Russia of a valuable piece of what again must ultimately become Russian property.

◆ 3.5 OTHER INTERNATIONAL ORGANIZATIONS

While the European Union has received much global attention in recent decades, a number of other international organizations are also influential actors in international affairs. Some major *economic*

The European Parliament in session at Strasbourg, France.

organizations, including the World Trade Organization, the North American Free Trade Agreement, and the "Group of 77" will be covered in Chapter 13 of this text (International Economic Relations). The principal military and political international organizations are summarized in this section of the text:

- North Atlantic Treaty Organization (NATO)
- Organization for Security and Cooperation in Europe (OSCE)
- Commonwealth of Independent States (CIS)
- Organization of American States (OAS)
- League of Arab States (Arab League)
- Organization of African Unity (OAU).

NORTH ATLANTIC TREATY ORGANIZATION

The North Atlantic Treaty Organization (NATO) is the world's major military defense organization. Its solidarity has occasionally waned, particularly when France withdrew in 1966.[55] France then expressed its concern about NATO being the subject of US domination, largely because of its dependence on US military support. In 1997, France abandoned an interim two-year plan to reintegrate into NATO's military structure. France's strategy was premised on regaining control of one of the two regional command posts—the Southern Region in Naples, Italy, controlled by a US admiral. When the US refused, France's European allies did not provide the needed backing to wrestle command from the US. France's allies thus prefer that NATO's most powerful nation manage its military command structure, although that paradigm concentrates control in a non-European power.

In 1994, the US proposed an eastward extension of NATO to incorporate former members of the Soviet Union. Prior to Russia's 1994 decision to join NATO's

Partnership for Peace Program, the Clinton Administration took a cautious approach so that Moscow would not unnecessarily fear encirclement. NATO is a European intersection for Western powers, which formerly represented the Cold War interests of the United States in Europe and the Eastern States from the now defunct Warsaw Pact, which represented the interests of the former Soviet Union. At the height of the Cold War, NATO members had more than two million military personnel deployed in Western Europe. The Warsaw Pact nations deployed about four million troops in Eastern Europe. In 1989, prior to the fall of the Soviet Union, US President George Bush pledged a reduction of US forces equivalent to a 10 percent cut in all NATO forces. This pledge was designed to encourage a like Soviet reduction in the Warsaw Pact forces in the States of Eastern Europe.

The demise of the Soviet Union and the Warsaw Pact in the early 1990s ultimately resulted in an association between former Warsaw Pact nations and NATO. In the NATO Secretary General's 1990 speech to the Supreme Soviet in Moscow, just before the Warsaw Pact was dissolved, Germany's Manfred Worner proposed an association as follows:

> This visit in itself symbolizes the dramatic changes of the past year. The Cold War now belongs to the past. A new Europe is emerging . . . [yet] age-old fears and suspicions cannot be banished overnight; but they can be overcome. Never before has Europe had such a tangible opportunity to overcome the cycle of war and peace that has so bedeviled its history. . . .
>
> I have come to Moscow today with a very simple message: we extend our hand of friendship to you. And I have come with a very direct offer: to cooperate with you. The time of confrontation is over. The hostility and mistrust of the past must be buried. We see your country, and all the other countries of the Warsaw Treaty Organization, no longer as adversaries but as partners in a common endeavor to build what you [might] call a Common European Home, erected on the values of democracy, human freedoms, and partnership. . . .
>
> [The NATO Secretary General then proposed that out of the historical upheaval, because of the demise of communist control in Eastern Europe,] the Soviet Union gains partners that will help in its great domestic task[s] of reform and renewal. Partners who will cooperate to ensure that the Soviet Union is an active and constructive part of the dynamic Europe of advanced industrial economies and technological interdependence of the 21st century. . . . Beyond confrontation we can address the immense global challenges of today and tomorrow: environmental degradation, drugs, terrorism, hunger, population, the proliferation of immensely destructive military technologies in the Third World. . . . The Alliance I have the honour to represent wants partners in the building of a new Europe. . . . Let us look to a common future, and work for it with trust and imagination.[56]

In June 1994, Russia became the twenty-first State to sign the Partnership for Peace Program involving cooperation with NATO in joint military exercises, peacekeeping, and the exchange of military doctrine and weaponry. One week later, Russia's leader, Boris Yeltsin, signed an agreement with the European Union (EU) Commission President on economic matters—including the removal of quotas on Russian exports into EU countries. NATO invited former Warsaw Pact members to join, including the Czech Republic, Estonia, Hungary, Poland, and Slovenia. It has proposed a slower membership track for Bulgaria, Latvia, Lithuania, Romania, and Slovakia. (NATO expanded three times before: adding Greece and Turkey in 1952, West Germany in 1955, and Spain in 1982.) In 1999, Poland, Hungary, and the Czech Republic also became NATO members.

One must, of course, distinguish between merely signing a Partnership for Peace agreement and full NATO membership. The "Partnership" is only a step in what is a more complex process. Germany and the US are split on the issue of whether Russia should ultimately become a full-fledged member of NATO. Several months after Russia signed the NATO Partnership agreement—and one day after US troops finally withdrew from Berlin—Germany's defense minister proclaimed that allowing Russia to become a member would "blow NATO apart." Vintage rivalries are still generating concern about European security—in a way that may preclude the full integration of all "European" States into this regional organization. Further, the NATO collective security device has been quite a successful deterrent. An attack on one NATO member is considered an attack on all. Thus, one must question whether all NATO members are ready to view a military strike against any of these potential NATO members as if it were an attack on London, Paris, or Washington.

The NATO expansion is nevertheless quite the opposite of the post–World War I Western approach—which isolated Germany's Weimar Republic, deepened suspicions in the entire region, bankrupted Germany, and created an atmosphere that helped promote Hitler's ascension to power. While Russia is not a full-fledged NATO member, its loose association with NATO arguably vouches for Russia's protection from attack—economically from EU countries, and militarily from NATO countries. These events provide no guarantees, but are at least symbolic of the newfound penchant for East–West cooperation. In May 1997, NATO thus gave Russia a "voice," although not yet a vote, in NATO matters.

The West's position is that Russia should be less concerned about the entry of its Eastern European neighbors into NATO's military structure. Yet some commentators have argued that Russia is not being alarmist in perceiving this development as increasing worldwide US hegemony. Russia and China later proclaimed their joint declaration, emphasizing the need for a multipolar world. They articulated a new vision that would involve the UN in a "new international order" within a multipolar world. This strategy is designed to ensure that the US will not act unilaterally, as it has done in other matters (e.g., the 1998 military buildup in anticipation of an attack on Iraq discussed in §3.3).[57] While it is premature to speak in terms of a full-fledged strategic partnership between Russia and China, one could readily perceive the genesis as being the eastward expansion of NATO toward Russia's borders.

NATO could also be perceived as a relic of the Cold War. It has been arguably ineffective in dealing with local problems, such as containing the excessive military force used in the former Yugoslavia (Bosnia and Kosovo). However, NATO did authorize the use of air strikes in 1993, under extensive international pressure to react to the Bosnian Serb attacks on civilian targets, when the UN did not adequately respond. NATO awaited UN authorization for air strikes before it made the unquestioned threat that it would bomb Serbian positions if the Serbs failed to retreat from UN-designated safe havens in Bosnia. NATO vessels also carried out the UN embargo of the former Yugoslavia in the Adriatic commencing in 1993, although only a restricted amount of strategic material can reach that area by sea. In 1998, NATO troops from fourteen nations including Russia and Albania undertook joint military exercises as a reaction to Serbian attacks on Yugoslavia's Kosovo area—designed to uproot ethnic Albanians and check the successes of the Kosovo Liberation Army.

◆

NATO, the UN, and the Use of Force: Legal Aspects

"Kosovo, The Thin Red Line"

PROFESSOR BRUNO SIMMA,
UNIVERSITY OF MUNICH

9 *European Journal of International Law* (1999)

Go to course Web page at
http://home.att.net/~slomansonb/txtcsesite.html.

Click on Thin Red Line (see "NATO" under Miscellaneous Web Resources).

ORGANIZATION FOR SECURITY AND COOPERATION IN EUROPE

The Organization for Security and Cooperation in Europe (OSCE) is the other major regional international organization of Europe. It consists of fifty-four States, mostly European. Its members also include Canada and the US, while official "observer" status is extended to Japan—comparable to the UN extending observer status to entities like the PLO. The former Yugoslavia's attempt to assume the "Yugoslavian" seat in the OSCE was rejected—the same result as at the United Nations.

The OSCE's roots date back to the mid-1950s when the Soviet Union initiated "European Security Conferences" attended by representatives of Eastern European States. These meetings resulted in creation of the Warsaw Treaty Organization, which would become NATO's regional competitor. In the 1960s, the Warsaw Pact initiated additional conferences seeking greater peace and security in Europe. Thanks to the artful diplomacy by the Federal Republic of Germany in the field of East–West relations, the CSCE (Conference on Security and Cooperation in Europe—original name until 1995) was inaugurated in 1972, just after the conclusion of the first Strategic Arms Limitations Treaty between the US and the Soviet Union. The 1991 CSCE Madrid Conference produced the framework of the CSCE Parliament. The 1992 meeting of the CSCE Council of Ministers produced the Prague Document on the non-proliferation of nuclear weapons and limitations on arms transfers within Europe.[58]

There have been several defining moments in the CSCE–OSCE process. The first major achievement was the Helsinki Final Act of 1975 emphasizing concerns of regional security, economic matters, and humanitarian treatment. To ensure the equality of States—despite vast differences in economic, military, and political power—CSCE members resolved that its proceedings "shall take place outside military alliances." This has avoided a narrow NATO-versus-Warsaw-Pact–styled strategy for regional problem solving. The CSCE functions somewhat like a remodeled UN, whereby diverse players on the European stage continually meet for purposes including the provision of "confidence-building measures" regarding security and disarmament.

Other major achievements in the CSCE process include the 1989 Concluding Document of Vienna. It contains a mandate for the Negotiation on Conventional Armed Forces in Europe talks. This was followed by the 1990 Conventional Forces in Europe (CFE) Treaty of Paris.[59] A number of participating States—such as France, which has not rejoined the military wing of NATO—perceive the CSCE process as the *genuine* European alternative to resolving regional problems. The OSCE has thus played a role in monitoring events in Bosnia and Chechnya with a view toward maintaining the commitments tendered by the respective parties in those conflicts. It was the OSCE that undertook responsibility for the conduct of national and municipal elections, arms control negtiations, and human rights monitoring in Bosnia under the 1995 Dayton Peace Accords. When Serbian authorities would not recognize the 1996 election results, the OSCE called upon them to abide by the results.

Yet another facet of the lasting importance of this organization is its emphasis on human rights issues. The Conference on the Human Dimension meets annually to exchange information about questionable State practices and unresolved human rights problems. Prior to the destruction of the Berlin Wall, the US tapped the CSCE process as a vehicle for expressing concern that Eastern European members had failed to live up to professed objectives including the right to travel, freedom of religion, and freedom from psychiatric abuse while in detention. In March 1995, Russia's president, Boris Yeltsin, agreed to receive a permanent human rights mission from the CSCE to monitor events in Chechnya, the rebellious region consisting of mostly Muslims who seek independence.

Some limitations still hamper the CSCE process. Like the UN Charter, the CSCE 1975 Final Act is a political rather than a legally binding document. It is not a treaty in the sense of creating immediate obligations, although some participants have argued that the 1975 Act resulted in some binding commitments by member States to at least continued participation in a Pan-European process.[60] This should not be surprising, given the historical diversity of its member States.

Another institutional weakness is that the OSCE has exhibited a rather "light" institutional structure. The follow-up conferences have generally been *ad hoc,* although the number of these specialized conferences has increased. It would be difficult, of course, to obtain any degree of progress without the continued willingness of delegates from Europe's participating OSCE States to meet at least periodically.

The OSCE (formerly the CSCE) finally developed some permanent administrative and political organs in the early 1990s. One of the foremost analysts of the CSCE process, Professor Arie Bloed of the University of Utrecht in Holland, characterizes the "new" and revitalized CSCE process as shifting to a cooperational mode from its earlier confrontational mode during the Cold War. As he describes it:

> [N]owadays one could speak of an "old" CSCE which existed until the end of the 1980s and a "new" CSCE since the beginning of the 1990s. To a great extent the "old" CSCE is characterized by a "confrontational" approach by the participating States (in particular between the Western and East European States), whereas the emphasis in the "new" CSCE is on "cooperation" between all CSCE States. This fundamental change is also clearly reflected in the institutionalization of the CSCE. The "old" CSCE consisted of only periodic follow-up meetings and *ad hoc* conferences on specific subjects; the "new" CSCE is characterized by the establishment of regularly convening political organs and a number of small permanent administrative bodies. . . .
>
> In spite of all the changes, however, at present the "Cold War origins" of the CSCE are still clearly visible in many respects and it may be expected that this will be the case in the foreseeable future as well.[61]

One by-product of this cooperation was the March 1995 Pact of Stability. It requires former East bloc States, wishing to join either the EU or NATO, to first settle any border disputes and ethnic conflicts. The Pact requires that these former Soviet bloc countries agree to permit the OSCE to be the watchdog agency for ensuring compliance. If this bargain eventually performs as designed, new Yugoslavia-like conflicts will be resolved before they can erupt—also advancing the objectives of democracy and peaceful international relations on the European continent.

The OSCE is gradually assembling solid organizational infrastructure. In 1996, the OSCE heads of State announced the "Lisbon Summit Declaration." Its objective is to create a comprehensive security framework for Europe in the twenty-first century premised upon improved conflict-prevention measures, arms control, and meaningful assessment of security-related economic, social, and environmental problems. In 1997, the OSCE followed up by announcement of its Guidelines for a Charter on European Security.[62]

In 1998, the OSCE entered into its most prominent undertaking to date. NATO was on the eve of staging air strikes against the Federal Republic of Yugoslavia (FRY) because of its Serbian mistreatment of the ethnic Albanian majority in the troubled province of Kosovo. The agreement between the FRY and the OSCE sets forth rules for the OSCE Kosovo Verification Mission, established pursuant to a UN Security Council resolution. The FRY government endorsed the establishment of the Mission, and guaranteed the safety and security of the Mission and its participants—both of which enjoy the privileges and immunities set forth in the Vienna Convention on Diplomatic Relations. The Mission will be in operation for one year, subject to extensions. Its task is to verify compliance with Security Council Resolution 1199 and supervise elections in Kosovo. The Verification Mission is to travel freely throughout Kosovo, verify compliance with the cease-fire by all parties, and investigate roadblocks and other impediments to communication. The Mission will receive weekly reports from relevant FRY–Serbian military–police headquarters in Kosovo regarding movements of forces in or out of Kosovo. The OSCE Mission may accompany Serbian border control units and police in the performance of their normal activities. The Mission will assist international organizations, NGOs, and authorities from FRY, Serbia, and Kosovo in facilitating humanitarian assistance.

COMMONWEALTH OF INDEPENDENT STATES

The Commonwealth of Independent States (CIS) is roughly analogous to the former Soviet Union (SU). In 1991, seven of the fifteen States that would ultimately become new UN members signed the Agreement Establishing the Commonwealth of Independent States. The accompanying document announced by the heads of State of Belarus, Russia, and Ukraine acknowledged the deadlocks plaguing the CIS from its inception, including a profound economical and political crisis and a catastrophic drop in living standards. They nevertheless inaugurated the CIS with the following organizational objectives: "[pursuing] a policy of strengthening international peace and security. They undertake to discharge the international obligations incumbent on them under treaties and agreements entered into by the former Union of Soviet Socialist Republics, and are making provision for joint control over nuclear weapons and for their non-proliferation." These constitutive CIS documents contain guarantees of many of the same fundamental freedoms and human rights for individuals set forth in the UN Charter and the various OSCE statements on individual rights.

The companion Protocol contains the right of the other former States of the Soviet Union to accede to the CIS. This document, signed two weeks after the original CIS Declaration, contains the Alma Ata Declaration whereby former States of the SU commit to maintaining the inviolability of existing territorial borders and setting up lawfully constituted democratic States. This document expressed the regional solidarity favoring Russia as the entity to occupy the former seat held by the "SU" in the Security Council's permanent seat.[63]

Some progress has been achieved in fostering CIS unity since its 1991 inception. Six members facing bankruptcy pledged to achieve a new economic union in 1993—a "ruble zone" that could lead to restoration of a common currency in a region where the many new States would otherwise have to print and maintain their own money.

There have also been political setbacks within the CIS. Ukraine, the third largest nuclear power in the world, balked at yielding its nuclear weapons to Russia—the CIS partner that has threatened Ukrainian self-determination for some six hundred years. On the other hand, Ukraine elected a pro-Russian president in 1994. This result underscores the affection that many citizens still feel for the comparative predictability and security of the former Soviet Union. Russia's President Boris Yeltsin delayed the scheduled elections of the Russian president for the disclosed reason of controlling any potential right-wing return to communism. Ruling by such decrees, however, was a prominent feature of Czarist Russia. Until new political infrastructure is solidly in place, CIS regional solidarity remains threatened by the lack of international organization necessary to keep totalitarian controls from resurfacing.

One might characterize Russia as being in roughly the same dominant position as the US in the latter's relations with other members of the Organization of American States. During the February 1995 summit meeting of CIS leaders, there was no mention of Russia's attack on Chechnya—although many Russians and Russian military leaders openly disagreed with Russia's handling of this province seeking to exercise its claimed right to self-determination. Russia subsequently withdrew its troops and entered into an autonomy agreement with Chechnya, which ameliorated this threat to regional stability.

ORGANIZATION OF AMERICAN STATES

The Organization of American States (OAS), headquartered in Washington, DC, is composed of all States of the Western Hemisphere except Cuba. As a result of the 1962 Cuban Missile Crisis (Chapter 10), OAS members voted to suspend Cuba's participation because Cuba had "voluntarily placed itself outside of the inter-American system."[64]

The OAS is the world's oldest regional international association (discounting the less formal entities discussed in §3.3 on the history of international organizations). In 1890, several nations created a bureau later known as the Pan American Union. It was subsequently incorporated into another entity called the Organization of American States in 1948.[65]

Under Article 1 of its Charter, the OAS is a "regional agency" of the UN. These two international organizations are, however, quite distinct. The OAS is neither controlled by nor directly responsible to the UN. The loose association between these two organizations is an example of regionalism within a universal system. Arrangements like this were the preferred post–World War II apparatus for ensuring the coexistence of a new global organization and any regional groupings that might develop for the pursuit of local concerns. The earlier League of Nations Covenant similarly provided that the League's creation would not affect the vitality of "regional undertakings like the Monroe Doctrine [US control of the Western Hemisphere to exclude external powers] for securing the maintenance of peace."[66]

Article 4 of the 1948 OAS Charter establishes the organization's essential purposes: "(a) To strengthen the peace and security of the continent; (b) To prevent possible causes of difficulties and to ensure the pacific settlement of disputes that may arise among the Member States; (c) To provide for common action on the part of those States in the event of aggression; (d) To seek the solution of political, juridical and economic problems that may arise among them; and (e) To promote, by cooperative action, their economic, social and cultural development."

The OAS has changed its functional orientation several times. It was a commercial international organization when its predecessor was formed in 1890, but its members adopted a nonintervention theme after World War I to discourage unilateral action by any OAS member in hemispheric affairs. To promote joint military responses to external threats, the OAS's 1947 Rio Treaty proclaimed that "an armed attack by any State against an American State shall be considered as an attack against all the American States."[67] Each member thereby promised to assist the others in repelling such attacks. While OAS members are still concerned with defense matters, its current emphasis is on the development of economic and political solidarity in the hemisphere. In 1987, for example, member nations (other than the US) began to pursue the possible economic reintegration of Cuba into the OAS.

The OAS promotes regional trade and economic improvement pursuant to the Alliance for Progress program it announced in the 1960s. The OAS Charter addresses nearly all facets of economic and political life in the region, drawing on the parallel provisions and organization found in the UN Charter. For example, it has both an organ of consultation similar to the UN Security Council and an international court similar to the UN's International Court of Justice (Chapter 9).

The US dominance of this international organization has been a traditional feature of the OAS's lack of cohesiveness. In 1992, for example, the US provided $38 million of the annual $62 million OAS organizational budget. In 1994, Colombia's president was elected to the prestigious position of head of the OAS. Unfortunately for regional relations, this election was the first bid by Caribbean and Central American States to wrestle this position away from the South American States that have occupied it since its 1948 inception. US Secretary of State Warren Christopher spent a number of days prior to that election consulting with other conference representatives. Costa Rica's president, the heir apparent to the OAU post, blamed the US for its meddling, which allegedly cost Costa Rica the election.

The UN was not the only international organization seeking the restoration of Haiti's democratically elected president to power after the 1991 military coup. The OAS imposed an embargo on Haiti. In 1992, the US thereby seized an oil tanker bound for Haiti in violation of the embargo. This was the first time that an OAS embargo actually resulted in such action. Then, in 1997, an earlier amendment to the Charter entered into force, authorizing suspension of any State whose democratic government is forceably overthrown.

ARAB LEAGUE

The League of Arab States is an international organization composed of twenty-one Middle Eastern states and the Palestine Liberation Organization (PLO). The League was established in 1945 to promote comprehensive cooperation among countries of Arabic language and culture.[68] It then established the Council of Arab Economic Unity in 1964 to promote an Arab Common Market and various other economic programs. The resulting institutions include the Arab Fund for Economic and Social Development for projects in Arab countries (1968), the Arab Bank for Economic Development in Africa (1973), and the Arab Monetary Fund (1976).

> The Secretariat of the League of Arab States learned with resentment of the bombing by the United States [in Sudan on August 20, 1998]. . . .
>
> The Secretariat considers this unjustified act a blatant violation of the sovereignty of a State member of the League of Arab States, and of its territorial integrity, as well as against all international laws and tradition, above all the Charter of the United Nations.
>
> —Arab League Statement to UN Security Council, condemning US bombing in Sudan. UN Doc. S/1998/789, dated August 21, 1998

The historic League goal has been political collaboration for preserving the independence and the State sovereignty of its members. The Council of the League deployed inter-League peacekeeping forces in Kuwait in 1961 and Lebanon in 1976. The latter effort eventually failed in 1989, however, when Syria refused League demands to withdraw its troops from Lebanon and Iraq (Syria's archenemy).

One of the League's long-term goals is to operate as a collective self-defense organization like NATO. Some States within the League question why the US unilaterally engaged in a missile strike against Iraq in 1993 (in response to a threat on the life of former President Bush), while it would not readily engage in such tactics against the Bosnian Serbs.

The political solidarity of the League was adversely affected by a number of events occurring in the latter part of the twentieth century. Under the Camp David Agreements of 1978, US President Jimmy Carter facilitated a series of meetings between Egypt's President Anwar Sadat and Israel's Prime Minister Menachem Begin at Camp David near Washington, DC, leading to Egypt's establishing independent ties with Israel. Since this was contrary to League policy, Egypt was suspended from the League in 1979. Sadat was later assassinated. The 1991 Persian Gulf War further deteriorated Arab unity. Certain Arab members even went so far as to assist the US in protecting Israel from League member Iraq's missile attacks.

In 1993, the Israeli deportation of Muslim fundamentalists to Lebanon also helped rekindle the League's anti-Israel focus. The League sought worldwide support at the UN for the responsive Security Council resolution. Yet the evident lack of fervor in the private commentaries of Arab League representatives reflected a deep antipathy toward militant Arab fundamentalists. Many of them do not support the PLO's control of relations with Israel. Now that the PLO has negotiated an autonomy agreement with Israel in the Gaza Strip and the City of Jericho, the League has less of an anti-Israeli flavor. Yet the League's political cohesion remains in a state of flux because of worldwide claims that certain States within its membership have engaged in a systematic program of State terrorism to accomplish nationalistic goals.

ORGANIZATION OF AFRICAN UNITY

The Organization of African Unity (OAU), more than any other international organization, is rooted in the

Western-derived institutions of colonial rule and perceived inferiority of nations on the African continent. The OAU's traditional goal has been African political unity in terms of self-determination. As succinctly described by the University of East Anglia (England) Professor Gino Naldi:

> Pan-Africanism has its origins in nineteenth-century America where the American Colonization Society for the Establishment of Free Men of Color of the United States was formed in 1816 in response to the alienation and exploitation of the Negroes with the purpose of repatriating freed slaves. This led to the founding of Liberia in West Africa [by freed slaves from the US] as a free and sovereign State in 1847. Nevertheless, the Pan-African movement, which gathered momentum at the turn of the century, continued to struggle for the end of the colonial system in Africa and called for the dismantling of the colonial boundaries agreed upon at the Congress of Berlin in 1885 [due to Africa's perceived inability to govern itself without European influence]. . . . But it was the post–Second World War era that provided the impetus for self-determination in Africa. The demand for political, economic and cultural self-determination became a flood that the colonial powers could not dam. The independence of Ghana on 6 March 1957 marked the beginning of a new dawn in Africa.[69]

The OAU was initially a political organization, formally established in 1963 and headquartered in Ethiopia. It consists of all of the independent nations in Africa. Morocco withdrew and Zaire (now Democratic Republic of Congo) suspended its membership when the Western Sahara became an independent member in 1984—based on unresolved territorial claims (*see* §2.3, Changes in State Status).

The OAU's current orientation is increasingly economic, premised on the 1991 treaty establishing the OAU's economic community.[70] It has played virtually no role in the events in the member States of Somalia, Liberia, and Mozambique—all of which were the objects of UN peacekeeping operations in the 1990s. In 1998, however, an OAU delegation went to Ethiopia to mediate a territorial dispute involving invading Eritrean forces. The fundamental purpose has been the promotion of self-government and social progress throughout the African continent. Toward this end, the OAU has established a commission to mediate all disputes between African nations.[71]

The OAU's distinctive political feature was its support for the black nationalist movements in southern Africa. The six "Frontline Countries" are the bloc within the OAU that assisted the remaining colonial territories. The goal of the Frontline Countries was to assist specifically black South Africans who were subject to white minority rule under apartheid. These OAU internal institutions were dismantled just prior to Nelson Mandela's assumption of the presidency of South Africa in 1994. South Africa then joined the OAU. Another major goal, freeing South-West Africa from South African rule—held in violation of numerous UN resolutions—was accomplished with the independence, renaming, and entry into the UN of the new renamed State of Namibia in 1990.

Global and regional international organizations with a primarily economic focus are covered in Chapter 13 of this book.

◆ 3.6 ORGANIZATIONAL IMMUNITY

The concept of *State* immunity from being sued in the courts of another State was addressed in §2.6 of this book. This section raises a similar question: Are international *organizations* also entitled to immunity from suit in the national courts of its member States?

Chapter 2 describes State sovereign immunity from suit in the courts of another State. Such immunity depends on whether the forum where the suit is filed follows the absolute or the restrictive approach to *sovereign* immunity. The answer to the question of *organizational* immunity is more complex, although the same rationale generally exists for shielding organizations from suits in their member States. One reason for the dearth of available cases for analyzing this issue is that international organizations appear in national courts far less frequently than States.

UNITED NATIONS

The UN's physical facilities in the United States are inviolable. UN property and assets are immune from expropriation or from any other form of seizure. Its agents and their personal baggage are immune from arrest or detention. Most States guarantee these same protections by their participation in the Convention on the Privileges and Immunities of the United Nations.

This immunity was adopted by the General Assembly in 1946 and by the United States in 1970. The UN enjoys the same immunity in the US that is enjoyed by foreign governments.[72]

The degree of protection afforded UN civil servants in other countries is not as broad. In August 1998, the UN's Economic and Social Council requested an advisory opinion from the International Court of Justice (ICJ) pursuant to Section 30 of the Convention. The United Nations and the Government of Malaysia differ regarding the immunity from legal process of Mr. Dato' Param Cumaraswamy, the Special Rapporteur of the Commission on Human Rights on the Independence of Judges and Lawyers. He was named as a defendant in four civil defamation suits in Malaysia, resulting from statements he made in 1995 in an article in *International Commercial Litigation,* a magazine published in the United Kingdom and circulated in Malaysia. The UN Secretary-General issued notes confirming that, based on a determination by the UN Legal Counsel, Mr. Cumaraswamy's remarks were made in his official capacity as a Special Rapporteur—and that he should thus be immune from such litigation under the Convention. The Malaysian Ministry of Foreign Affairs asked the Malaysian courts to determine the immunity question. The High Court for Kuala Lumpur declined to find that Mr. Cumaraswamy was protected by the claimed immunity. The Malaysian government considered the Secretary-General's notes merely to be "opinions" with no binding legal effect. After further attempts to stay the court proceedings or reach some settlement, the UN and Malaysia agreed to refer the matter to the ICJ. The President of the ICJ issued an order, based on the submission of written statements and responses from the parties. It called on the Government of Malaysia to stay all court proceedings in this matter and to accept the advisory opinion as decisive.[73]

OTHER ORGANIZATIONS

The scope of immunity for *other* international organizations is not as clear. In some nations, international organizational immunity is likened to *diplomatic* immunity (Chapter 7). Other nations draw upon the analogy to State immunity (Chapter 2).

In a 1990 arbitration, the Federal Republic of Germany (the "FRG" before German unification) sought to tax certain activities of the European Molecular Biology Laboratory, or EMBL, an international organization that had negotiated a Headquarters Agreement with the FRG (similar to the agreement between the UN and US regarding the immunities of the organization's New York City facilities). The FRG imposed taxes and customs duties on income and goods related to the organization's canteen and guest house used by visiting staff and scientists, as well as maintenance of the residence of the Director-General of the EMBL. The organization believed that these taxes violated the Headquarters Agreement between Germany and the EMBL.

When ruling in favor of the EMBL, the arbitrators noted the special status, and immunity from such taxes and duties, of the international organization in the following terms:

> Therefore it was inadmissible [for the FRG] to tend to limit the privileges and immunities of the EMBL, and to interpret them restrictively. For the privileges and immunities were not intended to provide international organizations with individual legal entitlements, but to contribute to an effective discharge of the responsibilities by the organization and make the latter independent from internal jurisdiction [of the FRG courts over EMBL]. . . .
>
> Besides the general principle of the respect of the effective discharge of the responsibilities and of the independence of the organizations, the largely undisputed principle had to be respected that a host State must not draw financial advantages from the official activities of an international organization. Otherwise it would adversely affect the financial resources of the organizatuion at the expense of the financial contribution of the other member States.[74]

The following case more fully illustrates some of the reasons for insulating international organizations from such suits, including the reference to the analogous theme of State immunity:

Broadbent v. Organization of American States

UNITED STATES COURT OF APPEALS,
DISTRICT OF COLUMBIA CIRCUIT, 1980
628 *Fed. Rptr.* 2d 27

Author's Note: *Plaintiff Broadbent and some co-workers lost their jobs at the General Secretariat of the Organization of American States (OAS). The plaintiffs included US citizens and foreign nationals residing in the US who were employed at the OAS's permanent headquarters in Washington, DC. They believed that they were wrongfully terminated.*

They first filed a complaint with an OAS administrative tribunal set up to resolve personnel disputes. That OAS tribunal decided that these employees should be reinstated, awarding a small amount of money damages in the event that the OAS Secretary-General ultimately denied the reinstatement recommendation of the administrative panel. Plaintiffs then sued for $3 million in a federal court of the US—a completely separate tribunal also located in Washington, D.C. They alleged that the OAS had improperly breached their employment contracts.

The defendant OAS responded by seeking dismissal of their suit. The federal trial court did just that, holding that the OAS was "absolutely" immune—under any circumstances—from such suits. The federal appellate court agreed that the OAS was entitled to organizational immunity. This higher court's view, however, was that "restrictive" immunity was the applicable standard to apply to an international organization rather than the lower court's reliance on an absolute standard for gauging whether the organization was immune from suit.

Both the trial and appellate courts achieved the same result, because both courts dismissed the case against the OAS. But their respective legal yardsticks differed in terms of which standard was applicable—absolute or restrictive immunity.

The latter immunity standard would thereby authorize the prosecution of future suits against an international organization in US courts if, like State immunity, the organization's activities were sufficiently "commercial." The appellate court applied the Foreign Sovereign Immunities Act (FSIA) to the OAS, just as if it were a "State" within the meaning of the FSIA. If a foreign State would be entitled to immunity under the Act, so would an international organization like the OAS. The OAS was immune from suit if it was not conducting a "business" as a private trader when hiring and firing employees at the organization's Washington, DC, headquarters.

COURT'S OPINION. Section 1605 of the FSIA provides that foreign states shall not be immune from the jurisdiction of American courts in any case based upon their commercial activity in the United States, with the commercial character of an activity determined by reference to its "nature" rather than to its "purpose." The conceptual difficulties involved in differentiating *jure gestionis* [acts by a private trader] from *jure imperii* [acts by a State] have led some commentators to declare the distinction unworkable. The restrictive immunity doctrine is designed to accommodate the legal interests of citizens doing business with foreign governments on the one hand, with the interests of foreign states in avoiding the embarrassment of defending the propriety of political acts before a foreign court.

In our view [the appellate court], the employment by a foreign state or international organization of internal administrative personnel—civil servants—is not properly characterized as "doing business." That view is supported by the legislative history of the FSIA, and the definition of "commercial activity" in §1603. The House [of Representatives] Report commented:

> Commercial activity.—Paragraph (c) of section 1603 defines the term "commercial activity" as including a broad spectrum of endeavor, from an individual commercial transaction or act to a regular course of commercial conduct. A "regular course of commercial conduct" includes the carrying on of a commercial enterprise such as a mineral extraction company, an airline or a state trading corporation. Certainly, if an activity is customarily carried on for profit, its commercial nature could readily be assumed. At the other end of the spectrum, a single contract, if of the same character as a contract which might be made by a private person, could constitute a "particular transaction or act." . . . By contrast, . . . an activity whose essential nature is public or governmental . . . would not itself constitute a commercial activity. . . . *Also public or governmental and not commercial in nature would be the em-*

> *ployment of diplomatic, civil service,* or military personnel, but not the employment of American citizens or third country nationals by the foreign state in the United States.

This report clearly marks employment of civil servants as noncommercial for purposes of restrictive immunity. The Committee Reports establish an exception from the general rule in the case of employment of American citizens or third country nationals by foreign states. The exception leaves foreign states free to conduct "governmental" matters through their own citizens. A comparable exception is not applicable to international organizations, because their civil servants are inevitably drawn from either American citizens or "third" country nations. In the case of international organizations, such an exception would swallow up the rule of immunity for civil service employment disputes.

The United States has accepted without qualification the principles that international organizations must be free to perform their functions and that no member state may take action to hinder the organization. The unique nature of the *international* civil service is relevant. International officials should be as free as possible, within the mandate granted by the member states, to perform their duties free from the peculiarities of national politics. The OAS charter, for example, imposes constraints on the organization's employment practices. Such constraints may not coincide with the employment policies pursued by its various member states. . . . An attempt by the courts of one nation to adjudicate the personnel claims of international civil servants would entangle those courts in the internal administration of those organizations. Denial of immunity opens the door to divided decisions of the courts of different member states passing judgment on the rules, regulations, and decisions of the international bodies. Undercutting uniformity in the application of staff rules or regulations would undermine the ability of the organization to function effectively.

We hold that the relationship of an international organization with its internal administrative staff is noncommercial, and, absent waiver, activities defining or arising out of that relationship may not be the basis of an action against [the organization] regardless of whether international organizations enjoy absolute or restrictive immunity.

The appellants were staff members of the General Secretariat of the OAS. Their appointments, terms of employment, salaries and allowances, and the termination of employment were governed by detailed "Staff Rules of the General Secretariat" promulgated by the OAS. The Staff Rules further establish an elaborate grievance procedure within the OAS, with ultimate appeal to the Administrative Tribunal of the OAS.

The Tribunal is competent to determine the lawfulness of an employee's termination of employment. If an employee has been wrongfully discharged, the Tribunal may order reinstatement. If reinstatement is ordered, the Tribunal may also establish an indemnity to be paid to the employee in the event the Secretary General exercises his authority to indemnify the employee rather than effect the reinstatement.

The employment disputes between the appellants and OAS were disputes concerning the internal administrative staff of the Organization. The internal administration of the OAS is a non-commercial activity shielded by the doctrine of immunity. There was no waiver, and accordingly the appellants' action had to be dismissed.

◆ *Notes & Questions*

Section 2.6 of this book analyzes the distinction between the "absolute" and "restrictive" immunity of *States.*

1. How did the Broadbent trial and appellate courts apply that distinction in very different ways to an *international organization?*
2. There was no difference in the end result. Why?
3. Would it have made a difference if there had been *no* administrative tribunal at the OAS to handle such terminations?
4. In 1998, the same Court of Appeals stated that: (1) the scope of immunity accorded international organizations under the International Organizational Immunities Act (IOIA) of 1945 is probably broader

than that of States under the Foreign Sovereign Immunities Act (FSIA) of 1976; but (2) if the commercial activities exception to immunity were accorded to an international organization under the FSIA, garnishment of an employee's wages would not fall within that exception. This development suggests that US federal courts are moving in the direction of giving broader immunity to international organizations under the IOIA than to foreign States when they claim immunity from suit in the US under the FSIA. *Atkinson v. Inter-American Development Bank*, 156 Fed.3d 1335 (D.C. Cir., 1998) ("Even if we concluded that the IOIA's reference to the law of immunity of foreign sovereigns is an evolving one that incorporates the commercial activities exception to immunity, we think appellant's garnishment proceeding would not come within that exception."). The Court of Appeals did not clearly resolve whether Congress generally intended that greater immunity be accorded international organizations than States.

5. Sometimes, internal law requires action before an international organization can enjoy immunity from suit within that country. A treaty commitment by the executive branch of government may nevertheless supercede legislative inaction. In a 1983 case from the Philippines, a US shipping company sued the UN's World Health Organization (WHO) for failing to pay for goods delivered to the Philippines. WHO claimed organizational immunity on the basis that, in 1951, the Philippines became a party to the Convention on Privileges and Immunities of the Specialized Agencies of the United Nations. The plaintiff countered that the Host [country] Agreement negotiated between WHO and the executive branch of the government had not been ratified as required by the Philippine Constitution. The Court dismissed the shipper's complaint against the WHO. It was immune from suit because the ratified treaty was binding on the Philippines, although its Senate had not ratified the Host Agreement. *"United States Lines, Inc. v. WHO,"* 107 *Int'l Law Rep.* 182 (4th Div. Ct. App., Manila, 1983) (published 1984).

◆ SUMMARY

1. Most international organizations are established by treaty between three or more States to fulfill some common objective. They serve the varied needs of member States and citizens within those States who may benefit by the existence of an international organization established to work toward defined objectives.
2. An international organization has legal capacity under International Law if it satisfies three essential requirements: (1) It must be a permanent association of State members with established objectives and administrative organs; (2) it must possess some power that is distinct from the sovereign power of its member States; and (3) its powers must be exercisable on an international level, rather than solely within the national systems of its member States.
3. Certain organizations, such as the UN, have the legal capacity to bring a lawsuit in courts of its member States and to sue a member. Otherwise, the UN would not have the ability to carry out its Charter functions.
4. The numbers and functions of international organizations have increased dramatically since the end of World War II, making classification more complex than in past eras. Various classification schemes distinguish international organizations on the following bases: (1) public or private organizations, or, put another way, governmental (created by treaty) or non-governmental organizations; (2) administrative or political; (3) global or regional; (4) with or without the supranational power to require a member State to act in a certain way; (5) purpose for existence—such as political, humanitarian, military, economic, and so on.
5. International organizations not created by treaty are referred to as international *non*-governmental organizations, or NGOs. They fulfill an increasingly broad and complex scope of functions, sometimes in concert with *governmental* organizations (which consist only of States).
6. The UN structure consists of six principal organs: (1) General Assembly, (2) Security Council, (3) Economic and Social Council, (4) Trusteeship Council, (5) Secretariat, and (6) International Court of Justice. There are numerous other UN organs and specialized agencies within the system, as depicted in Exhibit 3.3.
7. The General Assembly consists of all member States. Its function is to make recommendations regarding

any matter falling within the broad purposes of the United Nations.

8. The Security Council, consisting of five "permanent" and ten "rotating" members, is a smaller body charged with maintaining international peace and security. The Cold War veto thwarted the Council's objectives. States will have to determine whether or not to cede the requisite degree of sovereignty to the UN and its Security Council if this international organization is to actually maintain international peace.
9. The Economic and Social Council oversees the numerous Charter-based programs involving economic, social, and cultural facets of this global international organization.
10. The Trusteeship Council was devised to assist territories not capable of self-governance at the close of World War II. This "big brother" program is not as viable as in 1945, when it was created, largely because of the colonial independence movement of the 1960s and the fulfillment of their right to self-determination.
11. The Secretariat, headed by the UN Secretary-General, is the large administrative staff that actually runs the UN and its various agencies at several locations throughout the world.
12. The International Court of Justice, located in the Netherlands, is the UN's judicial organ. Its role, although underutilized to date, is to provide a forum for resolving disputes in the courtroom rather than on the battlefield.
13. Several major studies of UN reform were conducted in the 1980s and 1990s. Some recommendations have already been implemented, including the UN creation of an International Criminal Court. Most suggestions, however, await further scrutiny by UN member States. If not implemented, there is a serious question about the degree to which the UN can carry out its Charter mandate of maintaining international peace.
14. The UN is a global organization attempting to deal with a multitude of problems in a variety of cultures. The European Union, by comparison, links a relatively homogeneous group of States whose interests are primarily economic.
15. The ultimate goal of the 1992 Maastricht Treaty is to bond the region's nations by economic ties, via a single currency, to help fulfill the vintage dream of a Europe united and at peace. The 1997 Treaty of Amsterdam is designed to implement social concerns associated with regional integration.
16. The institutions of the EU operate in a highly structured social, economic, and legal environment. Its achievements have provided a more successful model than the UN for integrating States in a way that is destined to maintain peace. It is far more difficult for the UN, because of its comparatively vast infrastructure of nations, in many different stages of economic and social development, to reach agreement on issues of global interest.
17. The North Atlantic Treaty Organization (NATO) is the primary regional military organization in the world. It consists of most European nations, the US, and Canada. Some question the need for its existence after the demise of the Warsaw Pact, made up of former members of the Soviet Union, and the emergence of the Organization for Security and Cooperation in Europe (OSCE).
18. The OSCE is becoming a major political organization in Europe. It consists of far more member States (fifty-four) than NATO—including France, which basically defected from NATO in 1966. As the OSCE's institutions mature—including the CSCE Parliament, which first met in 1992—it may obscure the need for other regional organizations dealing with the maintenance of peace and the regional security of Europe.
19. The Commonwealth of Independent States (CIS) is the contemporary international organization for States from the now defunct Soviet Union. The CIS was established to sustain Eastern Europe's desire for regional peace and security. This was the organization that facilitated the signing of the 1990 Conventional Forces in Europe arms reduction and Nuclear Non-Proliferation Treaty.
20. The Organization of American States (OAS) is the regional security agency of the States in the Western Hemisphere, except for Cuba. It is plagued with interregional rivalries and depends primarily for financial and military effectiveness on one member: the US.
21. The League of Arab States (Arab League) is similarly plagued with interregional differences in philosophy—many dealing with Israel. The Persian Gulf

War and the signing of the Israel–PLO autonomy agreements have deprived the League of the initial reason for its existence—eliminating the State of Israel.

22. The Organization of African Unity (OAU) existed primarily to break down regional barriers to African self-determination. The dismantling of apartheid, Nelson Mandela's presidency of South Africa, and the achievement of Namibia's statehood in the 1990s effectively deprived this organization of a rigorous political mission.
23. Many global and regional international organizations are retooling from a military and political perspective to one that is economic in scope.
24. There are various national approaches to the issue of organizational immunity. The UN and its agents are absolutely immune from suit in member States, including the US as host government. Other organizations derive their immunity from various analogies under the internal law of member States, including diplomatic immunity and State immunity.
25. In the US, it appears that the immunity analysis for international organizations is the same as for sovereign immunity, depending on whether the organization's conduct involves that of a governmental body or is comparable to that of a private trader.

PROBLEMS

Problem 3.A (after *Reparations* Case) In September 1991, in the aftermath of the Persian Gulf War, a UN nuclear inspection team entered Iraq for the purpose of ensuring that it was not producing weapons of mass destruction. This inspection was to be conducted under a Security Council resolution requiring Iraq to divest itself of such weapons. Iraq responded by seizing forty-four UN team members, including citizens of several nations. The Security Council then approved Iraqi demands, which included that the inspectors must make lists of Iraq's secret nuclear-weapons program papers that they intended to take with them for further analysis by the UN. This minor Security Council concession (allowing Iraq to make some demand of the UN) may have saved the lives of the UN's inspectors.

If they had been killed by Iraqi agents, to whom would Iraq have State responsibility for reparations under International Law? Are there two answers? Should there be an exclusive (that is, just one) remedy for this type of wrong?

Problem 3.B (end of §3.2) In 1991, military leaders overthrew the democratically elected government of Haiti. The US considered this coup to be quite adverse to the hemispheric interests of other democratic nations in the Caribbean, as well as to its own.

Assume that in January 2000 the US President announces that the US will undertake a "humanitarian intervention" in Haiti—as the President says—"to help the people of Haiti restore democracy." She or he refers to the French humanitarian intervention in Rwanda to assist inhabitants who were being massacred by rebel forces. Assume further that Haiti's military government responds to the US announcement with its own statement: "North American imperialism will never prevent the people of Haiti from achieving their rightful role in hemispheric affairs, which have been dominated by the US since establishment of various international organizations including the Organization of American States (1890) and the UN (1945)."

The UN previously imposed an embargo on oil bound for Haiti. Assume that the UN is unable to respond to *this* flare-up. The US has just vetoed a proposed UN Security Council resolution that would prohibit the US from acting unilaterally to invade Haiti. As covered in §3.3, the veto of one of the "permanent five" could preclude Council action on this matter (e.g., from dispatching peacekeeping forces to Haiti). Further, Haiti's military leaders are unlikely to agree to a UN intervention that might threaten their continued control of Haiti's government.

In February 2000, assume also that there was a local response to the events in Haiti. The Organization of Central American States (OCAS) has asked its members—consisting of States in Central America—to participate in a peace process. The organs of this international organization cannot act without the unanimous consent of all members of the OCAS. The dual goal of this conference will be to establish regional containment of this hypothetical Haitian scenario and to avoid a further confrontation between the US and Haiti. The OCAS is an independent international organization whose membership includes the US and Haiti. UN administrators have referred to this international organization as one of the UN's regional agencies. Under Article 33 of the UN Charter, regional agencies may attempt to resolve threats to international peace.

The Inter-American Economic and Social Council is part of the infrastructure of the Organization of Central American States. Its fundamental purpose is to promote the economic and social welfare of the member States of the OCAS through better utilization of all natural resources within the region. It has made many recommendations to OCAS member States dealing with economic and social matters. To accomplish its purpose, Council members voted to conduct a research study of the effect of both the US and the new Haitian regime on the worsening of the economic and social well-being of this Caribbean nation. Council members believe that the economic scenario in Haiti will undoubtedly worsen as a result of social and military problems resulting from the US–Haitian confrontation. The Council study, not yet completed, will address these interrelated matters for the US and other OCAS members to consider what collective action might be taken to avert the further escalation of hostilities in this region.

What is the nature of the OCAS, the international organization addressing this explosive situation? In other words, discuss the various ways in which one might classify this organization.

Problem 3.C (after Reading Security Council Materials in §3.3) The US has backed the addition of Germany and Japan as permanent members of the UN Security Council. Many other possible changes would arguably do a better job of making the Council "mirror" the Assembly by more accurately reflecting the factual composition of the community of nations.

1. Should Great Britain and France each continue to occupy a permanent seat?
2. Alternatively, should either nation cede its seat to Germany, or could all three somehow rotate that "permanent" slot on the Council—as the "European" delegate?
3. Would Japan be entitled to an Asian permanent seat, given its economic superiority in global affairs?
4. Should China share the permanent Asian seat with India, given the latter's immense population that surpasses that of all Council members except China?
5. Should Germany, Japan, or any other nation be added as a permanent SC member—but without the right of veto, thus providing for an interim status on the Council? This would be permanent status without the attendant right of automatic veto now exercisable by the original five permanent members.
6. Would any of these changes truly influence, in a positive way, the Security Council's ability to perform without diminishing its power to act?
7. Should there be some other change?
8. Should there be no change at all?

Class members will examine these various positions and resolve which would best suit the goals of (a) better representing the community of nations on the Security Council; and (b) better conducting the business of the Council under its Article 39 (or other) mandate(s).

Problem 3.D (within §3.3, to Expand on "Subsequent Unilateral Action?") A major legal question arose, as of the US 1998 military buildup in the Persian Gulf: Could the US unilaterally attack Iraq premised on aging 1991 UN resolutions—as opposed to soliciting a fresh UN Security Council resolution to authorize an attack on Iraq?

UN Charter Article 2.4 prohibits the use of force—the exceptions being self-defense (Article 51) and Security Council authorization (Article 42). As will be seen in Chapter 10 on the use of force, State practice has augmented the Article 51 requirement of an "armed attack" by relying on "anticipatory" self-defense—given advances in weapons technology since the Charter was drafted in 1945.

Resolution 678, passed before the PGW began, said that member States "can use all necessary force" to oust Iraq from Kuwait. However, seven years had passed by the time of the US saber rattling; Iraq had departed Kuwait; there had been a cease-fire; the US did not have the benefit of the same worldwide resolve to go to war in 1998 (not that of permanent SC members China, France, and Russia or any of the Arab nations that so staunchly supported the PGW in 1991); there was no provision in any SC resolution authorizing a UN member State to use force on its own initiative; and Article 2.4 of the UN Charter generally prohibits the use of force—which could be interpreted to require the express authorization of force by the Security Council rather than leaving a doubtful situation to the discretion of one member State.

The US position relied on several arguments, including the fact that Resolution 678 could be still be invoked, because peace and security had *not* been restored to the area; in 1994, Iraqi forces moved toward Kuwait, then pulled back when the US dispatched a naval carrier group to the Gulf; in 1996, Iraq sent forces into Northern Iraq to help a Kurdish group capture a key city inside a safe haven protected by US-led forces; and Article 51 of the UN Charter accorded the right of collective self-defense because of the potential use of the biological and chemical weapons thought to be hidden in Saddam Hussein's large presidential palaces. Thus, the continuing threat of biological warfare would mean that the war had never really ended—Iraqi compliance with the cease-fire agreements being construed as a condition precedent to an actual cease-fire (Resolution 686).

Two students (or groups) will debate whether the US possessed the authority to attack Iraq—as planned prior to the Secretary-General's successful intervention—without a fresh UN Security Council resolution. Only the basic arguments have been provided. There are others. This exercise presents some of the problems with potential UN solutions to threats to peace.

Problem 3.E (after Trusteeship Council Materials in §3.3) The aftermath of the Cold War included the breakdown, if not splintering, of State sovereignty. For example, the Soviet Union broke down into a number of smaller States. One State under its influence, Yugoslavia, further split into five additional States.

One consequence of the realization of Statehood, especially by former colonies in Africa, has been the increasing frequency of what many have referred to as "failed States." These are States that have achieved independence but not sufficient economic and political stature to thrive. Warring tribes and ethnic groups are responsible for mass terror, executions, fleeing refugees, and economic hardship for the citizens of such countries.

Somalia is just one example of the negative facets of post-colonial statehood: a State that has failed or will fail, thus producing anarchy. UN efforts to provide humanitarian relief have resulted in mass looting, anti-UN actions, and anti-UN sentiment expressed by various segments of the populace. The UN Secretary-General fled for his life during a 1993 visit to Somalia, during which he had hoped to bolster the spirit of the peacekeeping forces in Somalia.

Read Articles 75–85 of the UN Charter on the course Web site at http://home.att.net/~slomansonb/txtcsesite.html. Then reread the definition of statehood in §2.1 of this textbook. Should the UN attempt to reestablish the Trusteeship system in Somalia, because of its apparent failure as a State? Would the UN's current financial problems (discussed in §3.3) affect your decision?

Two students will now assume the roles of members of the UN's Trusteeship Council and Somalia. They will debate:

1. Whether or not the UN should bring Somalia "under its wings."
2. Which UN member State would administer such a Trust Territory (as proposed by the student advocating the creation of such a Trust).
3. Whether the Charter should be amended to delete the entire concept of trusteeship.

Problem 3.F (within UN Assessment Materials in §3.3) Reread Security Council Resolution 687, quoted in the text. Then see Chapter VII, Articles 39–49, of the UN Charter—set forth on the course Web site (http://home.att.net/~slomansonb/txtcsesite.html).

Consider the following 1974 statement in the General Assembly by Great Britain's representative (UN Gen. Ass. Records, 29th Sess., 2281st plenary meeting, 12 Nov. 1974, para. 55), speaking on the importance of continued adherence to Charter principles whenever State members fail to observe the rule of law in international affairs:

> [T]his Organization is governed by the Charter. It cannot, consistently with itself and with the role it is designed to play in international affairs, disregard that Charter. We are either a law-abiding, law-respecting body or we are nothing, a mere talking shop. If we put aside the Charter whenever its provisions may seem to a majority of us . . . to be inconvenient, then we lose all claim to authority and credence. In short, the Charter is and must be the constitutional foundation for all that we do. Respect for the Charter must permeate all our decisions.

1. Is Professor Matsui correct in his assertion (*see* §3.3, Security Council Activism) that the Charter does *not* give the Security Council express authority to act in and conduct a military operation?

2. Did the UN involvement in Kuwait violate the terms of UN Charter Article 2.7, because Iraq was only "reclaiming" its lost province of Kuwait?

Problem 3.G (within UN Assessment Materials, After "Financial Crisis," in §3.3) The UN Secretary-General threatened that the US would lose its General Assembly vote at the end of 1998 if it did not pay its arrearage of what was then more than $1.5 billion. (The US position in the Security Council would not be affected.) The US accounting system has generally created problems for the UN, because the UN expects dues to be paid at the beginning of the calendar year, but the US has normally paid its dues around October 1. As of the close of 1998, eighteen other nations had also fallen behind by failing to pay their dues for more than two years: Bosnia, Burundi, Cambodia, Comoros, Congo, Dominica, Equatorial Guinea, Georgia, Guinea-Bissau, Iraq, Liberia, Moldova, São Tomé, Somalia, Tajikistan, Togo, Vanuatu, and Yugoslavia.

Article 19 of the UN Charter provides as follows: "A member of the United Nations which is in arrears in the payment of its financial contributions to the Organization shall have no vote in the General Assembly if the amount of its arrears equals or exceeds the amount of the contributions due from it for the preceding two full years. The General Assembly may, nevertheless, permit such a Member to vote if it is satisfied that the failure to pay is due to conditions beyond the control of the Member."

Three students, or groups, will debate whether a nation in the position of the US should thus lose its vote. They will represent: (1) the US, (2) the UN, and (3) Japan (or other nations—such as US allies—that have timely paid their assessed dues). Japan shoulders the greatest financial burden, other than the US, notwithstanding Japan's economic recession.

BIBLIOGRAPHY

§3.1 Legal Personality of Organizations

P. Bekker, *The Legal Position of Intergovernmental Organizations: A Functional Necessity Analysis of Their Legal Status and Immunities* (Dordrecht, Neth.: Martinus Nijhoff, 1994).

W. Feld, R. Jordan, & L. Hurwitz, *International Organizations: A Comparative Approach* (3rd ed. Westport, CT: Praeger, 1994).

J. Hickey, Jr. (ed.), "International Legal Personality," 2 *Hofstra Law & Policy Symposium* 1–170 (articles on various topics).

F. Kirgis, *International Organizations in Their Legal Setting* (2nd ed. St. Paul: West, 1993).

P. Menon, *The Law of Treaties between States and International Organizations* (Lewiston, NY: Edwin Mellon Press, 1992).

§3.2 Classification of Organizations

V. Essien, "International Organizations: A Selected Bibliography," 10 *Fordham International Law Journal* 857 (Supplement, 1987).

"Persons Other than States as Subjects of International Law," in R. Jennings & A. Watts, 1 *Oppenheim's International Law* (Part I) §7, pp. 18–22 (9th ed. Essex, Eng.: Longman, 1993).

§3.3 United Nations

GENERALLY

S. Bailey & S. Daws, *The Procedure of the UN Security Council* (3rd ed. Oxford, Eng.: Clarendon Press, 1998).

B. Conforti, *The Law and Practice of the United Nations* (The Hague, Neth.: Kluwer, 1996).

G. Dirks et al., *State of the United Nations, 1993: North–South Perspectives* (Providence, RI: Acad. Council on UN System, 1993).

L. Finklestein (ed.), *Politics in the United Nations System* (Durham, NC: Duke Univ. Press, 1988).

J. Frowein & R. Wolfrum (eds.), *Max Plank Yearbook of United Nations Law: Volume 1–1997* (London: Kluwer, 1998).

A Global Agenda: Issues Before the 53rd General Assembly of the United Nations (New York: UN Ass'n of the US, 1998–1999 Annual Issue).

R. Gregg, *About Face? The United States and the United Nations* (Boulder, CO: Lynne Reiner, 1993).

C. Joyner (ed.), *The United Nations and International Law* (Cambridge, Eng.: Cambridge Univ. Press, 1997).

M. Marin-Bosch, *Votes in the UN General Assembly* (The Hague, Neth.: Kluwer, 1998).

M. Rajan, *The Expanding Jurisdiction of the United Nations* (Bombay: N.M. Tripathi Ltd., 1982).

B. Sloan, *United Nations General Assembly Resolutions in Our Changing World* (Ardsley Hudson, NY: Transnat'l, 1991).

K. Wellens (ed.), *Resolutions and Statements of the United Nations Security Council (1946–1992): A Thematic Guide* (2nd ed. Dordrecht, Neth.: Martinus Nijhoff, 1993).

R. Wells, *Peace by Pieces—United Nations Agencies and Their Roles: A Reader and Bibliography* (Metuchen, NJ: Scarecrow Press, 1991).

PEACEKEEPING

D. Daniel & B. Hayes (eds.), *Beyond Traditional Peacekeeping* (New York: St. Martin's Press, 1995).

W. Durch (ed.), *The Evolution of UN Peacekeeping: Case Studies and Comparative Analysis* (New York: St. Martin's Press, 1993).

R. Seikmann, *Basic Documents on United Nations and Related Peace-Keeping Forces: With an Appendix on UN Military Observer Missions* (2nd ed. The Hague, Neth.: T.M.C. Asser Inst., 1989).

UN, *The Blue Helmets: A Review of United Nations Peacekeeping* (2nd ed. New York: UN, 1993).

REFORM

Y. Blum, *Eroding the United Nations Charter* (Dordrecht, Neth.; Boston: Martinus Nijhoff, 1993).

B. Fassbender, *UN Security Council Reform and the Right of Veto: A Constitutional Perspective* (The Hague, Neth: Kluwer, 1998).

H. Kelsen, *The Law of the United Nations: A Critical Analysis of Its Fundamental Problems* (New York: Praeger Press, 1950).

J. Mueller, *The Reform of the United Nations* (New York: Oceana, 1992) (two-volume collection of UN resolutions, reports, and documents from the Annual Review of United Nations Affairs).

L. Sohn, "Important Improvements in the Functioning of the Principal Organs of the United Nations that Can Be Made Without Charter Revision," 91 *Amer. J. Int'l L.* 652 (1997).

LEAGUE OF NATIONS

B. Williams, *State Security and the League of Nations* (Baltimore: Johns Hopkins Press, 1927).

A. Zimmerman, *The League of Nations and the Rule of Law 1918–1935* (1936) (Holmes Beach, FL: Gaunt reprint, 1998).

§3.4 European Union

European Community (Luxembourg: Office for Official Pub. Euro. Comm., 1994).

R. Folsom, *European Community Law* (St. Paul: West, 1992).

R. Frid, *The Relations Between the EC and International Organizations: Legal Theory and Practice* (The Hague, Neth.: Kluwer, 1995).

R. Keohane & S. Hoffman, *The New European Community: Decisionmaking and Institutional Change* (Boulder, CO: Westview Press, 1991).

W. Nicoll & T. Salmon, *Understanding the New European Community* (New York: Harvester/Wheatsheaf, 1994).

J. Steiner, *Textbook on EEC Law* (3rd ed. London: Blackstone Press, 1992).

A. Toth, *The Oxford Encyclopaedia of European Community Law* (Oxford, Eng.: Clarendon Press, 1990).

Treaty on the European Union (Luxembourg: Office for Official Pub. Euro. Comm., 1992).

§3.5 Other International Organizations

S. Ali, *The International Organizations and World Order Dictionary* (Santa Barbara, CA: ABC CLIO, 1992).

A. Bloed (ed.), *The Conference on Security and Cooperation in Europe: Basic Documents, 1993–1995* (The Hague, Neth.: Martinus Nijhoff, 1997).

F. Kirgis, *International Organizations in Their Legal Setting* (2nd ed. St. Paul: West, 1993).

R. Lauwaars, "International Law: The Relationship between United Nations Law and the Law of Other International Organizations," 82 *Michigan Law Review* 1604 (1984).

G. Naldi (ed.), *Documents of the Organization of African Unity* (London: Mansell, 1992).

O. Stoetzer, *The Organization of American States* (2nd ed. Westport, CT: Praeger, 1993).

§3.6 Organizational Immunity

"Comment: United States Jurisdiction over Representatives to the United Nations," 63 *Columbia Law Review* 1066 (1963).

"Note: How Much Immunity for International Organizations?" 10 *North Carolina Journal of International Law & Commercial Regulation* 487 (1985).

ENDNOTES

1. A classic statement of the terms *international* and *organization* and distinctions between them is provided in "Definitions and History," ch. 1 in C. Archer, *International Organizations* (2nd ed. London: Routledge, 1992) [hereinafter Archer treatise].
2. *International Organizations and Law* 5–8 (New York: Ford Found., 1990).
3. **Capacity requirements:** *See* N. White, *The Law of International Organizations* 27 (Manchester, Eng.: Manchester Univ. Press, 1996). **Capacity on national but not international level:** *See* W. R. Slomanson, "Civil Actions Against Interpol: A Field Compass," 57 *Temple Law Quarterly* 553 (1984).
4. Further details on the resolutions and related events are provided in R. Lapidoth & M. Hirsch (eds.), *The Arab–Israeli Conflict and Its Resolution: Selected Documents* (Dordrecht, Neth.: Martinus Nijhoff, 1992).
5. International Organizations Immunities Act, 59 Stat. 669, 22 USCA §§288(a)–(f).
6. D. W. Bowett, *The Law of International Institutions,* 10–12 (4th ed. London: Stevens & Sons, 1982).
7. *See* H. Jacobson, W. Reisinger, & T. Mathers, "National Entanglements in International Governmental Organizations," 80 *Amer. Pol. Sci. Rev.* 141 (1986).
8. "Classification of International Organizations," ch. 2 in Archer treatise, 38 (cited in note 1 above).
9. **Web sites:** UN—www.un.org; EU—www.eurunion.org/websites/index.htm; International Olympic Committee—www.olympic.org/help/plugins.html; Amnesty International—www.amnesty.org; ASIL—www.asil.org.
10. *Protocols Additional to the Geneva Conventions of 12 August 1949* (Geneva: Int'l Comm. Red Cross, 1977).
11. **NAFTA text:** http://mgmt.tamu.edu/mgmt.www/nafta/index.htm.
12. A succinct but authoritative history is available in *League of Nations,* E. Osmanczyk, *Encyclopedia of the United Nations and International Agreements* 511–516 (2d ed. London: Taylor & Francis, 1990) [hereinafter *1990 UN Encyclopedia*]. For two more comprehensive studies, *see* F. Walters, *A History of the League of Nations* (London: Oxford Univ. Press, 1952); and A. Zimmern, *The League of Nations and the Rule of Law 1918–1935* (London: MacMillan, 1936).

13. *See* Vol. 2 of *Selected Literary and Political Papers and Addresses of Woodrow Wilson* (New York: Grosset & Dunlap, 1952) for Wilson's "Fourteen Points" speech.
14. **Text:** gopher://wiretap.spies.com:70/11/Gov/Treaties/League.
15. T. Hoopes & D. Brinkley, *FDR and the Creation of the U.N.* (New Haven, CT: Yale Univ. Press, 1997).
16. For a detailed analysis of the evolution of each article, *see* B. Simma (ed.), *The Charter of the United Nations: A Commentary* (Oxford, Eng.: Oxford Univ. Press, 1994).
17. **Historical committee structure:** B. Finley, *The Structure of the United Nations General Assembly: Its Committees, Commissions, and Other Organisms: 1974–1980s* (White Plains, NY: Kraus Int'l, 1988). **1993 committee reorganization:** Schaff, "More Organizational Changes at the UN," 22 *Int'l J. Legal Info.* 199 (1994).
18. M. Shaw, *International Law* 831 (4th ed. Cambridge, Eng.: Grotius, 1997) (italics added).
19. K. Skubiszewski, "The United Nations General Assembly and Its Power to Influence National Action," in *Proceedings and Committee Reports of the American Branch of the International Law Association 1964 Annual Meeting* 153–154 (1964).
20. M. J. Peterson, *The General Assembly in World Politics* 2–3 (Boston: Unwin Hyman, 1990).
21. Article 9 of the Japanese Constitution bars the maintenance of "war potential." *See generally* W. R. Slomanson, "Judicial Review of War Renunciation in the Naganuma Nike Case: Juggling the Constitutional Crisis in Japan," 9 *Cornell Int'l L.J.* 24 (1975). Articles 26 and 87(a) of the former "West" German Constitution banned the use of military forces for other than defensive purposes. Germany has sent troops to Somalia, while Japan has contributed financially to UN peacekeeping operations.
22. *The UN Veto in World Affairs 1946–1990: A Complete Record and Case Histories of the Security Council's Veto* (Sarasota, FL: UNIFO Pub., 1992).
23. UN Doc. DPI/1247, reprinted in 31 *Int'l Legal Mat'ls* 953 (1992) [hereinafter *Agenda for Peace*]. A supplement was published in January 1995. See UN Doc. A/50/60, S/1995/1.
24. Opening Statement of Dr. Edward Warner before the Senate Armed Services Subcommittee on Coalition Defense and Reinforcing Forces, in "US Department of Defense Statement on Peacekeeping," 33 *Int'l Legal Mat'ls* 814 (1994). *See also* D. Scheffer, "US Administration Policy on Reforming Multilateral Peace Operations," 33 *Int'l Legal Mat'ls* 795 (1994); and "US Department of State Statement on the Legal Authority for UN Peace Operations," 33 *Int'l Legal Mat'ls* 821 (1994).
25. A detailed account of the relevant "Kuwait" resolutions, plus supporting national materials, is available in M. Weller (ed.), *Iraq and Kuwait: The Hostilities and Their Aftermath* (Cambridge, Eng.: Grotius, 1993) (third volume in series).
26. Y. Matsui, "The Gulf War and the United Nations Security Council," ch. 36 in R. MacDonald (ed.), *Essays in Honour of Wang Tieya* 511 (Dordrecht, Neth.: Martinus Nijhoff, 1994).
27. *See* http://cnn.com/WORLD/9802/23/un.iraq.agreement/index.html.
28. *See, e.g.,* ECOSOC, *Commission on Narcotic Drugs Report of the Thirty-Sixth Session,* UN Doc. E/CN.7/1993/12/Rev.1, Supp. No. 9 (Vienna: UN, 1994). Further details are available from the UN Web site at www.un.org/esa.
29. **Termination does not bar subsequent proceedings:** "Certain Phosphate Lands in Nauru *(Nauru v. Australia),*" *ICJ Communiqué* No. 92/18 (Judgment on Preliminary Objections of June 26, 1992). **Dismissal as a result of settlement:** *ICJ Communiqué* No. 93/29 (Sept. 13, 1993) (whereby issues will never be publicly adjudicated). A book-length treatment of this subject is available in C. Weeramantry, *Nauru: Environmental Damage under International Trusteeship* (Melbourne: Oxford Univ. Press, 1992).
30. *"Morgan Guarantee Trust v. Republic of Palau,"* 924 *Fed. Rptr.* 2d 1237 (2nd Cir. 1991).
31. B. Boutros-Ghali, *Supplement to An Agenda for Peace: Position Paper of the Secretary-General on the Occasion of the Fiftieth Anniversary of the United Nations* 9 (2d ed. New York: UN, 1995).
32. B. Boutros-Ghali, *An Agenda for Peace: Preventative Diplomacy, Peacemaking, and Peacekeeping* 21–22 (New York: UN, 1992).
33. T. Boudreau, *Sheathing the Sword: The U.N. Secretary-General and the Prevention of International Conflict* 105–106 (New York: Greenwood Press, 1991).
34. An encyclopedic treatment of UN programs is available in *1990 UN Encyclopedia* (note 12 above).
35. See N. Jasentuliyana, "The Lawmaking Process in the United Nations," ch. 3 in N. Jasentuliyana (ed.), *Space Law: Development and Scope* 33 (Westport, CT: Praeger, 1992); C. Christol, "The Moon Treaty Enters into Force," 79 *Amer. J. Int'l L.* 163 (1985).
36. A. Prandler, "The Unchanging Significance of the United Nations Charter and Some International Legal Aspects of Its Application," in H. Bokor-Szego (ed.), *Questions of International Law* 191, 192 (Dordrecht, Neth.: Martinus Nijhoff, 1986).
37. *See* E. Van Den Haag & J. Conrad, *The U.N. In or Out? A Debate* (New York: Plenum Press, 1988); T. Franck, *Nation Against Nation: What Happened to the U.N. Dream and What the US Can Do About It* (New York: Oxford Univ. Press, 1985).
38. *See* R. Nelson, "International Law and US Withholding of Payments to International Organizations," 80 *Amer. J. Int'l L.* 973 (1986); and "Certain Expenses of the United Nations" (advisory opinion), 1962 *ICJ Rep.* 168, construing UN Charter Article 17.2 (requiring expenses to be borne by members as apportioned by the General Assembly).
39. *N.Y. Times,* Sept. 17, 1986, p.3 (Choudhury's opening statement to Assembly's 41st session in New York).
40. **Legal Advisor:** H. Hansell, Memo. of Aug. 7, 1978, reprinted in 1979 *Digest of United States Practice in International Law* 225, 226 (Wash., DC: US Gov't Print. Off., 1983). **Art. 17.2:** "The expenses of the Organization shall be borne by the Members as apportioned by the General Assembly." **ICJ case:** "Certain Expenses of the United Nations," 1962 *ICJ Rep.* 168. An illustrative analysis of these points is available in E. Zoller, "The 'Corporate Will' of the United Nations and the Rights of the Minority," 81 *Amer. J. Int'l L.* 610 (1987).

41. H.R. 2535, 104th Cong., Oct. 25, 1995, introduced by Rep. Scarborough. Web version at http://thomas.loc.gov/cgi-bin/query/z?c104:H.R.2535:.
42. *See, e.g.,* "Report of the Secretary-General: Administrative and Budgetary Aspects of the Financing of the United Nations Peacekeeping Operations," U.N. Doc. A/51/389 (1996), reprinted in 37 *Int'l Legal Mat'ls* 700 (1998).
43. *Resolution on Arrears of Contribution,* OAU Resolution 2 RADIC 660, reprinted in G. Naldi (ed.), *Documents of the Organization of African Unity* 45 (London: Mansell, 1992).
44. *See* text accompanying notes 31 and 32 above.
45. *See* the excellent two-volume text by J. Muller, *The Reform of the United Nations* (New York: Oceana, 1992).
46. (1) *Report of the Group of High-Level Intergovernmental Experts to Review the Efficiency of the Administrative and Financial Functioning of the United Nations,* Gen. Ass. Off. Records, 41st Sess., Supp. No. 49, Doc. No. A/41/49; (2) S. Ogata et al., *Financing an Effective United Nations: A Report of the Independent Advisory Group on U.N. Financing* (New York: Ford Found., 1993); (3) J. Leach et al., *Final Report of the United States Commission on Improving the Effectiveness of the United Nations* (Wash., DC: US Gov't Print. Off., 1993); (4) B. Urquhart & E. Childers, *Renewing the United Nations System* (New York: Ford Found., 1994); (5) J. Muller (ed.), *Reforming the United Nations: New Initiatives and Past Efforts* (New York & Dordrecht, Neth.: UN & Kluwer Law Int'l, 1997) (three volumes) [hereinafter *Reforming the United Nations*].
47. *Reforming the United Nations,* note 46 above.
48. *See* §1.1 of this text.
49. *Reforming the United Nations,* note 46 above, *Introduction to A World Without a United Nations: What Would Happen If the United Nations Were Shut Down,* at p. III.11/8 (presented by Wash., D.C.'s Heritage Foundation in 1984).
50. The 1975 "Lome I" Treaty and related documents are available in 14 *Int'l Legal Mat'ls* 595 (1975). The "Lome II" Treaties are available in 19 *Int'l Legal Mat'ls* 327 (1980). The 1984 modifications are available in 24 *Int'l Legal Mat'ls* 571 (1985) ("Lome III" Final Act). The Protocol relating to the Community's association with Cyprus is reported in "Notice of Other Recent Developments," 28 *Int'l Legal Mat'ls* 573, 574 (1989). The 1989 Lome IV Agreement, joining sixty-nine States in an association with the Community, is reprinted in 29 *Int'l Legal Mat'ls* 783 (1990).
51. Additional detail is available on the course Web site: http://home.att.net/~slomansonb/txtcsesite.html, click on European Union for text of various integrated treaties. Print resources include P. Fontaine, "A Brief History of European Integration," ch. 1 in *Europe in Ten Easy Lessons* 5–6 (Luxembourg: Office for Off. Pub. Euro. Comm., 1992). *See also* "The History of the European Community," ch. 1 in G. Berrmann et al., *Cases and Materials on European Community Law* (St. Paul: West, 1993).
52. *See* http://ue.eu.int/Amsterdam/en/treaty/treaty.htm.
53. For an elaborate analysis of the negative aspects of European integration, *see* G. Harris, *The Dark Side of Europe* (2nd ed. New York: Columbia Univ. Press, 1994) (written by this member of the European Parliament's Secretariat). The brighter side is available through EU press releases, on the World Wide Web at www.europa.eu.int/news/pr-en.htm.
54. Izvestia, "Personalities, Foreign Affairs," Dec. 12, 1993, p. 1.
55. An analysis of the French position is available in E. Stein & D. Carreau, "Law and Peaceful Change in a Subsystem: Withdrawal of France from NATO," 62 *Amer. J. Int'l L.* 577 (1968). Albania withdrew from the Warsaw Pact in 1968 after the Soviet invasion of Czechoslovakia.
56. *A Common Europe—Partners in Stability: Speeches by the Secretary General of NATO,* reprinted in *Change and Continuity in the North Atlantic Alliance* 191–195 (Brussels: NATO, 1990).
57. *See Russian–Chinese Joint Declaration on a Multipolar World and the Establishment of a New International Order,* adopted in Moscow on 23 April 1997, within insert at beginning of §3.3 of this text.
58. **Parliament:** "Final Resolution of the Madrid Conference Concerning the Establishment of the CSCE Parliamentary Assembly," 30 *Int'l Legal Mat'ls* 1344 (1991). **Arms:** "Prague Document on Further Development of CSCE Institutions and Structures and Declaration on Non-Proliferation and Arms Transfers," 31 *Int'l Legal Mat'ls* 978 (1992).
59. *See* S. Croft (ed.), *The Conventional Armed Forces in Europe Treaty: The Cold War Endgame* (Aldershot, Eng.: Dartmouth Pub., 1994).
60. *See, e.g.,* P. van Djik, "The Final Act of Helsinki—Basis for Pan-European System?" 1980 *Netherlands Yearbook International Law* 110.
61. A. Bloed, *The Conference on Security and Cooperation in Europe: Analysis and Basic Documents* 2–3 (Dordrecht, Neth.; Boston: Martinus Nijhoff, 1990).
62. **1996:** "Declaration on a Common and Comprehensive Security Model for Europe for the Twenty-First Century," 36 *Int'l Legal Mat'ls* 486 (1997). **1997:** "Guidelines on an OSCE Document-Charter on European Security," 37 *Int'l Legal Mat'ls* 693 (1998).
63. **Minsk Declaration on CIS:** *see* UN Doc. A/46/771 (1991), reprinted in 31 *Int'l Legal Mat'ls* 138 (1992). **Policy Declaration Protocol:** 31 *Int'l Legal Mat'ls* 142 (1992). The various documents are reprinted in W. Butler, *Basic Legal Documents of the Russian Federation* (New York: Oceana, 1992).
64. Meeting of Consultation of Ministers of Foreign Affairs of Jan. 31, 1962, reported in 46 *US Dep't State Bull.* 281, No. 1182 (1962).
65. The OAS Charter is available on the course Web site at http://home.att.net/~slomansonb/txtcsesite.html.
66. Article 21, League of Nations Covenant.
67. Article 3.1, Inter-American Treaty of Reciprocal Assistance, 21 *United Nations Treaty Series* 243, 62 US Stat. 1681.
68. The text of the constitutive agreement is reprinted in 39 *Amer. J. Int'l L.* 266 (1945). A commentary is available in Khadduri, "The Arab League as a Regional Arrangement," 40 *Amer. J. Int'l L.* 756 (1946).
69. *See* T. Elias, "The Commission of Mediation, Conciliation and Arbitration of the OAU," XL *Brit. Yearbk. Int'l L.* 336 (1964).

70. The treaty is reprinted in 30 *Int'l Legal Mat'ls* 1241 (1991).
71. G. Naldi, *The Organization of African Unity: An Analysis of Its Role* 3 (London: Mansell, 1989).
72. **Convention:** 1 *UN Treaty Series* 15 (1946). **Resolution:** Gen. Ass. Res. 22A, 1 Gen. Ass. Off. Records, Supp. p. 25, UN Doc. A/64 (1946). **US legislation:** International Organizations Immunities Act Section 2(b), 22 USCA §288 (1945) (1979 ed., 59 Stats. 669).
73. Request for an Advisory Opinion transmitted to the Court pursuant to Economic and Social Council decision 1998/297 of 5 August 1998, Difference Relating to Immunity from Legal Process of a Special Rapporteur of the Commission on Human Rights (Request and Order). *See* www.icj-cij.org/idocket/inuma/inumaframe.htm.
74. "European Molecular Biology Laboratory Arbitration," 29 June 1990, 105 *Int'l Law Rep.* 1, 19–20 (1990).

CHAPTER FOUR

Individuals and Corporations

CHAPTER OUTLINE

THE CITIZEN HIMSELF THEN IS ONLY DISTINGUISHED from the foreigner by the fact that the road to all public offices is open to him, that he may have to do military service, and that to make up for this he can . . . participate in elections. By and large this is all. For the protection of personal rights and of personal freedom is equally enjoyed by foreigners, [and] not seldom more so; in any case, this applies in our present German Republic.

—Adolf Hitler, *Mein Kampf*, p. 439 (Manheim trans. Boston: Houghton Mifflin Co., 1971); written in 1924 in his prison cell in Munich

INTRODUCTION

This is the final "preliminary" chapter. After surveying the meaning of the term International Law in the first chapter, the next two chapters identified the actors that have shaped its development—States since the 1648 Peace of Westphalia (§1.3), and international organizations, especially since the close of World War II. This chapter adds another dimension—the role of the "individual." While there are significant distinctions between natural persons and corporate persons under domestic and International Law, that level of detail is reserved for courses beyond the scope of this survey course.[1]

The historical perspective is that the individual plays no direct role in shaping the evolution of International Law—a system designed essentially to control the conduct of States in their mutual relations. The first section of Chapter 4 explores a comparatively recent development—the *international* legal personality of the individual. The recognition of the individual as another recognized actor on the international stage is most attributable to the abandonment of individual rights during the Nazi Third Reich.

The ensuing sections address nationality, statelessness, corporate nationality, and the special regime applicable to State conduct that targets aliens.

◆ 4.1 LEGAL PERSONALITY OF THE INDIVIDUAL

SOLDIER JONES HYPOTHETICAL

Assume that States X and Y share a common border. State X military intelligence indicates that State Y forces have been crossing into X from a small remote village in Y near the border. State Y villagers have been assisting State Y military forces by providing them with food and information about troop movements on the other side of the border in State X.

Jones is a soldier in the army of State X. His superior officer sends him into State Y on a secret mission called Operation Phoenix. The goal is to "neutralize" anyone who might help State Y forces cross into State X at the border village. Jones carries out his orders and kills most of the civilian men, women, and children in the village. Soldiers from State Y discover Jones in the act and pursue him to the Y coast near the village. Jones steals a yacht and escapes into international waters, as illustrated in Exhibit 4.1.

EXHIBIT 4.1 OPERATION PHOENIX

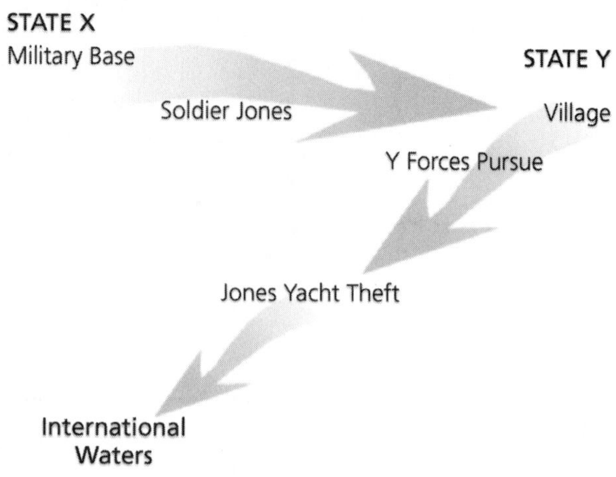

The remaining relatives of the slaughtered villagers want Soldier Jones and State X to pay for this brutal massacre. Operation Phoenix undoubtedly violated International Law. The military operation mounted by State X violated the territorial sovereignty of State Y. As argued by Afghanistan and Sudan, after the 1998 US bombing raids against a terrorist organization within their borders, another nation has conducted an extraterritorial military operation without first obtaining consent. It would be futile, of course, for the relatives of the deceased villagers from State Y to go personally to State X to see its leaders or to file suit in State X courts against Jones or the State X Army. It would be equally futile for them to file a lawsuit in their own State Y—whose courts would likely dismiss it because of State X's sovereign immunity in the courts of State Y (§2.6). A number of other limitations further preclude the *villagers* from a remedy against either Soldier Jones or State X, which are analyzed in this section:

- Can the State Y relatives *directly* negotiate with State X?
- Can they pursue Jones and State X in an *international* tribunal?
- Has Jones—an individual—violated International Law?

Historically, States have been the exclusive subjects of International Law. They created this body of rules, which they deem binding in their relations with each other. Individuals and business entities have historically been the subjects of the *national* or internal law of one or more States when their conduct arises in an international context. The laws of Morocco, for example, govern the conduct of a person living in Morocco or a corporation doing business there. If a private (non-governmental) Moroccan corporation wants to purchase metal from Germany, it will have to consult the internal law of Morocco for any local import restrictions on German metal. That corporation may not be able to import the same metal, however, for the purpose of making automatic machine guns. A violation would subject the corporation and its directors or owners to punishment under the national law of Morocco.

HISTORICAL LACK OF INDIVIDUAL CAPACITY ON THE INTERNATIONAL LEVEL

A vintage theoretical dispute dwells on whether the individual—clearly a subject of *national* law—is also a subject of *International* Law. The English philosopher Jeremy Bentham, who coined the term "International Law" in his famous treatise of 1789, articulated the historical perspective that only the State could be its subject: "Transactions which may take place between individuals who are subjects of different states . . . are regulated by the internal laws, and decided upon by the internal tribunals, of the one or the other of these states. . . . There remain then the mutual transactions between sovereigns as such, for the subject of that branch of jurisprudence which may be properly and exclusively termed *international*."[2]

Bentham embraced the perception that the individual was *not* a subject of International Law. In the Soldier Jones Hypothetical at the beginning of this section of the text, Jones would be incapable of violating International Law. He is an individual, not a State. Only State X could incur responsibility for the military slaughter of the Y villagers. Under Bentham's traditional view (and that of certain modern States), individuals lack the required "legal personality" or "capacity" to incur responsibility. Soldier Jones violated the national law of State Y. It was his home State, X, that violated International Law by ordering its agent to carry out Operation Phoenix. Jones was acting as an agent of State X. Only X possesses the capacity to incur State responsibility as a legal "person" subject to the rules of International Law.

This perspective still prevails in a number of countries. The existence of a direct relationship between the individual and International Law is denied by Chinese and former Soviet scholars. Chinese International Law texts published in the 1980s deny that individuals are the subjects of International Law.[3] A 1983 study by the East Asian Legal Studies Department of the University of Maryland corroborates the contemporary Chinese perspective that the sovereign quality of the State is inappropriately diminished by those who would subject State power to scrutiny by an individual under International Law. This study succinctly captures the attitude of the People's Republic of China: "Recognition of individual responsibility for personal acts under international law would . . . clash with Marxist principles regarding the class struggle in international relations. Moreover, the Chinese rejection of the concept of individuals as subject[s] of international law is an indisputable repudiation of the . . . conception of law which, by casting individuals in the role of international entities, attempted to circumvent the internal sovereign rule of the state. To the PRC, the only legitimate instrument to ensure the rights of individuals is the nation state."[4]

The Soviet perception presented another alternative. The status of the individual can be acknowledged by International Law only to the extent that it is expressly recognized by the national law. Otherwise, the United Nations Charter principles of State sovereignty and freedom from external intervention would be meaningless. The Soviet perspective was that even international organizations, heralding the human rights of the individual, could not circumvent the primacy of the State—for doing so would be tantamount to international interference in the internal affairs of the Soviet Union.

MODERN RECOGNITION OF INDIVIDUAL CAPACITY

The above historical model was challenged in the twentieth century by international jurists, as well as British and American scholars, who advocated that the individual *is* a subject of International Law in appropriate circumstances. They have asserted that individuals enjoy international rights—particularly human rights—and that those rights must be defended not only by the traditional protector (the State) but also directly by international organs possessing the legal power to interfere in the internal affairs of certain States. Professor Lung-chu Chen of New York University argues that authoritarian regimes deny individual status in International Law to conveniently serve the totalitarian purposes of those States that govern without legitimate authority. They "will not tolerate their nationals complaining to other state elites or the larger community of mankind [e.g., the UN] about the deprivations within their particular communities."[5]

In the last half of the twentieth century, Western commentators began to seek international recognition of the individual as possessing rights and liabilities arising directly under International Law. One basis for this argument was the eighteenth-century exception whereby individuals who committed certain types of crime were liable *as defendants* for violating the law of nations. Many jurists held that pirates were liable for their conduct directly under International Law—even when their conduct did not violate the law of the State where they could be found. Piracy was sufficiently heinous to be considered a crime against all nations. Individuals who committed this particular crime breached duties imposed upon them by International Law. (Section 5.2 addresses the related universal principle of international criminal jurisdiction.)

In the nineteenth century, however, the notion of individual liability under International Law faded. Most jurists and commentators then characterized the rights and duties of International Law as applicable exclusively to States. Individuals had obligations arising under national laws. Thus, they could breach *only* national laws.

The perspective recognizing that individuals could violate International Law (as well as national law) resurfaced as a result of the horrors perpetrated against individuals by Germany's Nazi regime. Western scholars and jurists revived the theory that an individual could breach International Law. This theory was memorialized in the 1946 Judgment of the Nuremberg Tribunal and companion war crimes trials in Tokyo. State practice then approved the trial of individuals for conduct deemed to violate *only* International Law. German law under Hitler's Third Reich not only authorized genocide and its related atrocities, but also demanded it in many instances. The resulting State denial of the dignity of the individual ultimately led France, England, the Soviet Union, and the United States to try the key Nazi war criminals as violators of *International Law* under the international agreements establishing the Nuremberg and Tokyo Military Tribunals.

The liability of the Nazi and Japanese defendants was based on the direct relationship between the individuals' conduct and International Law. The defendants claimed that they had no obligations under International Law. Their only duty was to the Nazi State, which, in turn, would bear any responsibility under International Law. The International Military Tribunal at Nuremberg disagreed in the following terms: "Individuals have international duties which transcend the national obligations of obedience imposed by the individual State [to which they owe allegiance]. He who violates the laws of war cannot obtain immunity while acting in pursuance of the authority of the State if the State in authorizing action moves outside its competence under international law" (discussed further in Chapter 5). This trial generated an intense global interest in acknowledging the individual's liability under *International* Law, premised largely on the genocidal conduct of the Nazi defendants.

PLAINTIFF VERSUS DEFENDANT DISTINCTION

Traditional International Law doctrine espouses the following remedy for individual plaintiffs harmed by the action of a State: Their home State may choose to pursue a claim, in an international context, for harm done to them by a foreign nation. In the Soldier Jones case, State Y—rather than the individual relatives of the deceased Y villagers—has the discretion to pursue a claim against State X for the acts of its military agents through diplomatic negotiations or by filing suit in an international tribunal. Under this theory, State Y was injured when its villagers were killed by State X agents like Soldier Jones when he executed Operation Phoenix. The harm to State Y is derived from the harm to its individual citizens living in the strategic village. The Permanent Court of International Justice characterized such claims in the following terms: "By taking up the case of one of its subjects and by resorting to diplomatic action or international judicial proceedings on his behalf, a state is in reality asserting its own rights—its right to ensure, in the person of its subjects, respect for the rules of international law."[6]

In the Soldier Jones Hypothetical, Jones, although an individual, could incur direct responsibility under International Law *if* his conduct amounted to genocide (Chapter 11) or piracy. Jones has then violated International Law and would be directly punishable as an individual *defendant* in an international tribunal. The UN's International Criminal Tribunals for the Former Yugoslavia and Rwanda were established to deal with such crimes in those particular theaters (Chapter 9). A relative of a deceased villager, however, would not have the capacity to be a *plaintiff* in an international tribunal. Only *States* or international organizations have the general capacity to pursue claims in international proceedings. State Y would, in its discretion, have the international legal capacity to pursue a remedy against Soldier Jones/State Y.

STATE AS PLAINTIFF ILLUSTRATION

What are the practical consequences of the State consensus that individuals cannot directly pursue their own claims as plaintiffs under International Law? The State enjoys the virtually exclusive discretion regarding whether or not to pursue a remedy on the international level—such as lodging a diplomatic claim or instituting proceedings in an international tribunal. The Permanent Court of International Justice recognized that "[r]ights or interests of an individual the violation of which rights causes damage are always in a different plane to rights belonging to a State, which rights may also be infringed by the same act. The damage suffered by an individual is never, therefore, identical in kind with that which will be suffered by a State; it can only afford a convenient scale for the calculation of the reparation due the State [whose citizen has been harmed]."[7]

National law, of course, embraces the discretionary nature of a State to espouse the claims of its citizens. In an unpublished opinion provided by the US Department of State, a federal trial court in Florida dismissed such a case on the basis that the judicial branch of government does not have the power to hear such a claim when it has already been denied by the executive branch. The plaintiff had alleged that her husband was the captain of a cargo ship, traveling from Miami to Montevideo, Uruguay. She claimed that a governor in

Brazil arranged for the deceased husband's ship to be hijacked—whereupon agents of the governor tortured her husband. She contended that her husband died from the resulting injuries. She filed this action because she wanted the court to require the US Secretary of State to submit her claim to the Brazilian government. The federal court in Miami dismissed this Petition for Mandamus on the basis that it could not require the Department of State to act in a situation where it had total discretion not to pursue this claim against Brazil. In the words of the federal court:

> Mandamus is available only when a government agency has a duty to act on the part of an individual. It is not available to review the discretionary acts of government officials. . . .
>
> The action is, in effect, a demand that the State Department "espouse" Petitioner's claim. Espousal is the assertion of the private claim of United States nationals by the government against another sovereign. The Secretary of State has the discretion to determine whether to espouse a claim.
>
> The Court finds that espousal being a discretionary function, it does not have jurisdiction to provide the mandamus relief sought by Petitioner.[8]

A major international tragedy that occurred in 1989 illustrates the application of this legal regime. Iran sued the US in the International Court of Justice for the 1988 destruction of an Iranian commercial airliner flying near a US naval vessel in the Persian Gulf. Under International Law, Iran's State status provided it with the legal capacity to present its claim in this international arena. The relatives of the Iranian citizens killed in the incident could not take such direct action against the US. The Iranian relatives, of course, expected Iran to act on their behalf. Iran was harmed when its citizens were harmed, triggering Iran's discretion to pursue a remedy against the offending nation. Iran claimed that the death of the Iranians on the ill-fated flight, and the destruction of the Iranian aircraft, constituted unprovoked violations of the right to fly over international waters. Further, any monetary compensation obtained by Iran for the destruction of the aircraft and the loss of life would belong to Iran. The victims' families would benefit only if Iran chose to give them that money. Many States do turn over such recoveries to the harmed individuals in these circumstances. Because of poor international relations, the US offered to provide compensation to the Iranian survivors conditioned on the special requirement that all payments would go directly to the victims' families—rather than pass through the hands of the Iranian government.[9]

CONCLUSIONS

The State was the exclusive actor on the international level since the dawn of modern statehood attributable to the European Peace of Westphalia in 1648. International organizations have blossomed as international actors in the twentieth century—beginning with global organization with the League of Nations and especially the United Nations. One legacy of the Nazi regime was the post-war proliferation of human rights. Such concerns revived the centuries-old notion of an individual incurring international responsibility for certain acts that harmed all inhabitants of the planet (described further in Chapter 9 on international tribunals and Chapter 11 on human rights). The individual's status in International Law is evolving toward recognition of the right to seek redress for grievances at the international level. University of Denver Professor Ved Nanda comments that "[h]istory will perhaps recall that the single most significant international law development in the second half of the twentieth century was the dramatic shift in the individual's status from a mere object to a subject of international law. Indeed, the human being as an individual is becoming a full-fledged claimant with standing to seek redress in the international arena. The protection of internationally recognized human rights is by all accounts a revolutionary change."[10]

There is no guarantee that individuals and organizations will continue to flourish in their contemporary capacity as actors on the international level. University of Florence's Professor Antonio Cassese warns that the State-centric nature of International Law could one day revert individuals and organizations to the station they once occupied (before the coming of the Nazi Third Reich). He encourages our acknowledgment that both remain dependent on the will of their State creators. One may therefore anticipate that:

> Like international organizations, individuals perform activities delegated to them by States. . . . On this score both organizations and individuals can be styled "ancillary" subjects of international law. This however also means that they are but instruments in the hands of States. They cease to exist internation-

ally the very day the groups of States by which they are begot decide to get rid of them.

It follows that, like international organizations, individuals are derivative subjects, in that they draw their existence from the formal decisions (normally a treaty) of other subjects [i.e., States].... Consequently one may distinguish between *primary* and *secondary* subjects, the former embracing States, the latter encompassing individuals, as well as all the other international subjects.[11]

◆ 4.2 NATIONALITY, STATELESSNESS, AND REFUGEES

> One of the first problems which presented itself in connection with the protection of minorities was that of preventing these States from refusing their nationality, on racial, religious or linguistic grounds, to certain categories of persons, in spite of the link which effectively attached them to the territory allocated to one or [the] other of these States.
>
> —*Acquisition of Polish Nationality* (Advisory Opinion), Permanent Court of International Justice, Ser. B, No.7, at 79 (1923 case interpreting nationality provision of WWI peace treaty between the Allied Powers and Poland)

An individual's nationality—often referred to as citizenship—is a bond between an individual and a State that establishes reciprocal rights and duties between them. This bond was once an automatic attribute of merely residing within the Roman Empire (except for certain "barbarians" who were not considered legal residents). In A.D. 212, the Edict of Caracalla conferred Roman citizenship on all individuals who lived within the area controlled by the Empire. There was no distinction between place of birth, parental citizenship, and whether one *wished* to become a Roman citizen or abandon that citizenship.[12]

This section analyzes general citizenship rules in the present day, State competence in such matters, and related consequences for affected individuals. The four major components are nationality, dual nationality, statelessness, and refugees. It is at this point that one may begin to appreciate the importance of nationality rules to the evolution of human rights (which are identified and analyzed in Chapter 11).

NATIONALITY

The bond known as "nationality" is a legal, political, and social link between an individual and a State. In 1955, the International Court of Justice defined nationality as "a legal bond having as its basis a social fact of attachment, a genuine connection of existence, interests and sentiments, together with the existence of reciprocal rights and duties. It may be said . . . that the individual upon whom it is conferred . . . is in fact more closely connected with the population of the State conferring nationality than with that of any other State. . . ."[13]

Nationality establishes mutual expectations for both the State that confers it and the individual who acquires it. The State has the right to require its citizens to serve in its military forces. The State may also tax an individual for earnings accrued anywhere in the world. The individual is correlatively entitled to certain expectations based on his or her nationality. One of the most important of these rights is the State protection of the individual. This right means, essentially, that the home State assists its nationals when they are abroad and are being mistreated by another State or its agents. A Canadian citizen who is mistreated by Saudi Arabia may seek Canada's assistance. The protection would likely materialize in the form of a Canadian diplomatic or consular officer's inquiry or protest on behalf of the Canadian citizen who was harmed by Saudi conduct that violated international expectations.

Nations have not always protected their citizens abroad. The concept of nationality was not introduced in mainland China, for example, until the mid-nineteenth century. The Chinese government historically showed little interest in protecting its citizens when they were abroad. Choosing to live abroad was *prima facie* evidence of disloyalty. Residing among "barbarians" rendered Chinese citizens unworthy of the State's protection.[14]

Is nationality a matter of national law or International Law? In 1923, the Permanent Court of International Justice responded that States were generally unlimited in making nationality decisions. Exceptions included those situations where there was a treaty obligation to *confer* or the *inability* to confer nationality under the particular circumstances. In one of the leading cases,

France conferred French nationality on residents of Tunis and Morocco over a British protest on behalf of British citizens living in those territories. The Court was asked to decide whether this was a matter falling exclusively within France's nationality laws. The Court decided that this matter involved an issue arising under *International* Law—although the conferring of nationality was normally a matter committed to the discretion of each State's national laws. In the Court's words: "[N]ationality is not, in principle, regulated by international law, [however] the right of a State to use its discretion is nevertheless restricted by obligations which it may have undertaken towards other States. In such a case, jurisdiction which, in principle, belongs solely to the State [e.g., conferring nationality on residents of its territories] is limited by rules of international law."[15]

Under this judicial formulation, a State would be free to *deprive* its citizens of citizenship against their wishes. In a prior 1915 case, the new Turkish government, fearing that Turkish Armenians were a dangerous "foreign element with cousins in the Russian army," deported them to Syria and other Middle Eastern areas. If the Turkish government had deprived them of their citizenship on the basis of their ethnic background, however, there would be no violation of International Law under the Court's (later) 1923 formulation. Subsequent refugee and genocide treaties now pose an impediment, as discussed below. In 1939, Stalin and Hitler signed a non-aggression treaty containing a secret protocol placing various nations, including Estonia, under Soviet influence. Stalin ordered the deportation of 60,000 Estonian nationalists to Siberia after taking away their Estonian citizenship. Under the PCIJ's 1923 approach, matters of nationality would fall exclusively within the jurisdiction of the Soviet Union because there was no nationality treaty between the Soviet Union and Estonia. Incidents like those involving the Armenians and Estonians stimulated international pressure to limit the total discretion exercisable by States in nationality matters. The results of such pressures are addressed below under "Statelessness."

Scholars are still divided on the degree to which International Law plays a role in State nationality decisions. Some believe that International Law does not impose significant limitations on the national right to grant or withdraw State citizenship. The International Law textbook used at Russia's Moscow State University provides that the status of citizenship "is above all a national institution." This statement is qualified, however, by the following acknowledgment that there may be limits on State control of that institution: In "modern international law, principles and norms relating to questions of nationality are contained primarily in the United Nations Charter [and related international Human Rights documents]. . . ."[16]

Some scholars take the position that State nationality decisions are governed by *both* national and International Law, although the role of the latter is secondary and uncertain. Western scholars disagree. They tend to argue that International Law plays a *significant* role in nationality matters. Members of the International Law Institute of the Netherlands, for example, undertook a major study, concluding that International Law limits the State in the application of its nationality laws. The head of the Department of International Law of the Institute writes that "international agreements . . . have been instrumental in shaping the Netherlands law on nationality. The relevant provisions have been incorporated into or implemented by municipal [national] statutory law, accounting for the amendments which the 1892 [Netherlands] Nationality Act has undergone in the course of time."[17]

How is nationality acquired? Individual nationality, also referred to as citizenship, may be acquired in three ways: (1) passively, by parentage; (2) passively, by being born in a State that considers a child born there its citizen; and (3) actively, by naturalization of an individual who voluntarily changes allegiance from one State to another:

(1) Citizenship derived from parentage is a rule drawn from the ancient Roman law. The child's citizenship is that of the parents. This rule is referred to as *jus sanguinis,* or "blood rule" for establishing citizenship. A child born of Roman parents in any region of the world not under Roman control was nevertheless a Roman citizen. The *jus sanguinis* basis for acquiring nationality is used in Europe, Latin America, and many English-speaking countries.

(2) Many countries apply a nationality-by-birth rule. This is the rule known as *jus soli,* or "soil rule" for granting citizenship. In the Middle Ages, birth within certain European territories automatically vested the newborn with that nation's citizenship. Under its contemporary application, a child born in England—whose parents are Italian citizens—is an English citizen under the immigration and nationality laws of England. (This child

would also be an Italian citizen because Italy follows the blood rule.)

Nationality determinations are often complicated by the simultaneous applicability of the laws of the country of parentage and the country of birth. Assume that a Japanese couple has a baby during a visit to the United States. Application of the parentage or *jus sanguinis* blood rule would make the baby a citizen of Japan. Application of the *jus soli* or soil rule would make the baby a citizen of the US. This child is a citizen of both countries and may have to choose one of the two citizenships on attaining adult status. To alleviate such problems in Europe, the Council of Europe's 1997 European Convention on Nationality provides that: Everyone has a right to nationality; States must automatically grant their nationality to persons having at least one parent who is a national of that State—although the relevant provision does not apply to persons born abroad. In that instance, the European Convention provides that there is an obligation to facilitate the acquisition of that State's nationality (although not automatically).[18]

There have been efforts to curtail the US application of the *jus soli* rule that automatically confers US nationality upon those born on US soil. The US Constitution provides that "All persons born or naturalized in the United States . . . are citizens of the United States. . . ."[19] In 1993, California's Governor Wilson made a proposal that, if adopted by Congress, would have amended the US Constitution. The change would have repealed the guarantee that children of foreign nationals (including those who are *undocumented)* born on US soil are automatically US citizens. Foreign citizens who are legally in the US would not have been affected.

(3) Individuals may actively—that is intentionally—change their nationality through a process called *naturalization*. The national law of the country from which nationality is sought establishes its naturalization requirements. States with adjacent borders may have very different views about naturalization matters.

In Western Europe, French and German leaders both sought to close and open the door to immigrants in the same month. In June 1993, France's National Assembly overwhelmingly approved a tougher immigration law that made it more difficult for foreign citizens to acquire French citizenship via marriage or residence with a family member in France. Immigration is one of France's most explosive social issues because of increasing crime, which the French press has attributed to "foreigners." Germany's Chancellor Helmut Kohl contemporaneously urged the German Parliament to make it easier to become a German citizen. Responding to pressure after fatal attacks on Turks in Solingen, Germany, Kohl attempted to initiate a process that would change Germany's eighty-year-old nationality law, barring many lifelong residents (including some who were *born* in Germany) from applying for German citizenship. Later that year, however, Germany introduced a tough immigration policy designed to halt the influx of immigrants spawned by the end of the Cold War. One year later (1994), illegal immigration had dropped by two-thirds, and the number of individuals seeking political asylum dropped 72 percent.

One major problem in immigration law involves naturalization undertaken for reasons not related to habitual residence in the naturalizing country. Granting citizenship under these circumstances does not necessarily entitle an individual to claim that he or she is a national of the naturalizing State. The relatively lax nationality laws of one State may be in conflict with the laws of another. In 1955, the International Court of Justice addressed this recurring problem in the following case:

Nottebohm Case (Liechtenstein v. Guatemala)

INTERNATIONAL COURT OF JUSTICE (1955)

1955 *International Court of Justice Reports* 4

Author's Note: *Nottebohm was a German citizen residing in Guatemala. He operated a successful business in both Guatemala and Germany before World War II. Guatemala's laws discriminated against foreign citizens and business entities that were nationals of countries with which it was at war. German citizens could not do business in Guatemala.*

Just before Guatemala declared war against Germany, Nottebohm went to Liechtenstein and applied for citizenship. His purpose was to avoid the discriminatory laws against foreign citizens so that he could continue his lucrative business in Guatemala. There was no state of war between Guatemala and Liechtenstein. Liechtenstein waived its usual three-year waiting period when it granted citizenship to Nottebohm. He immediately took an oath of allegiance, became a naturalized citizen of Liechtenstein, and was issued a passport prior to leaving for Guatemala. When Nottebohm attempted to return to Guatemala as a citizen of Liechtenstein, however, he was unable to reenter. His property in Guatemala was seized by the government. Guatemala still considered Nottebohm a German national and would not recognize Liechtenstein's grant of nationality. In 1946, Liechtenstein first asserted its right to protect Nottebohm, whom it considered to be its naturalized citizen. In 1951, after unsuccessful negotiations with Guatemala, Liechtenstein instituted this suit in the International Court of Justice. Liechtenstein wanted to recover for damages to Nottebohm caused by Guatemala's treatment of a person that Liechtenstein considered its citizen.

The Court's opinion addresses the requirements for the international recognition of citizenship conferred under national law. The legal question included whether Liechtenstein could present this claim on behalf of Nottebohm, and in turn, whether Guatemala had to recognize Nottebohm as a citizen of Liechtenstein.

COURT'S OPINION. [T]he Court must ascertain whether the nationality conferred on Nottebohm by Liechtenstein . . . bestows upon Liechtenstein a sufficient title to the exercise of protection in respect of Nottebohm as against Guatemala. In this connection, Counsel for Liechtenstein said: 'the essential question is whether Mr. Nottebohm, having acquired the nationality of Liechtenstein, that acquisition of nationality is one which must be recognized by other States.'

Guatemala expressly stated that it could not recognise that Mr. Nottebohm, a German subject habitually resident in Guatemala, has acquired the nationality of Liechtenstein without changing his 'habitual residence.' There is here an express denial by Guatemala of Nottebohm's Liechtenstein nationality.

The naturalization of Nottebohm was an act performed by Liechtenstein in the exercise of its domestic jurisdiction. The question to be decided is whether that act has the international effect here under consideration.

International arbitrators have given their preference to the real and effective nationality, that which accorded with the facts, that based on stronger factual ties between the person concerned and one of the States whose nationality is involved. Different factors are taken into consideration, and their importance will vary from one case to the next: the habitual residence of the individual concerned is an important factor, but there are other factors such as the centre of his interests, his family ties, his participation in public life, attachment shown by him for a given country and inculcated in his children, etc. [I]nternational law leaves it to each State to lay down the rules governing the grant of its own nationality. On the other hand, a State cannot claim that the rules it has laid down are entitled to recognition by another State unless it has acted in conformity with this general aim of making the legal bond of nationality accord with the individual's genuine connection with the State which assumes the defence of its citizens by means of protection as against other States.

According to the practice of States, to arbitral and judicial decisions and to the opinion of writers, nationality is a legal bond having as its basis a social fact of attachment, a genuine connection of existence, interests and sentiments, together with the existence of reciprocal rights and duties. It may be said to constitute the juridical connection of the fact that the individual upon whom it is conferred either directly by the law or as the result of an act of the authorities, is in fact more closely connected with the population of the State conferring nationality than with that of any other State. Conferred by a State, it only entitles that State to exercise protection vis-à-vis another State, if it constitutes a translation into juridical terms of the individual's connection with the State which has made him a national.

At the date when he applied for naturalization Nottebohm had been a German national from the time of his birth. His country had been at war for more than a month, and there is nothing to indicate that the application for naturalization then made by Nottebohm was motivated by any desire to dissociate himself from the Government of his country [Germany].

He had been settled in Guatemala for 34 years. He had carried on his activities there. It was the main seat of his interests. He returned there shortly after his naturalization, and it remained the centre of his interest and of his business activities. He stayed there until his removal as a result of war measures [passed by Guatemala] in 1943. He subsequently attempted to return there, and he now complains of Guatemala's refusal to admit him [now that he claims Liechtenstein rather than German nationality].

In contrast, his actual connections with Liechtenstein were extremely tenuous. No settled abode, no prolonged residence in the country at the time of his application for naturalization: the application indicates that he was paying a visit there and confirms the transient character of this visit by its request that the naturalization proceedings should be initiated and concluded without delay. If Nottebohm went to Liechtenstein in 1946, this was because of the refusal of Guatemala to admit him. No indication is given of the grounds warranting the waiver of the condition of residence. There is no allegation of any economic interests or of any activities exercised or to be exercised in Liechtenstein, and no manifestation of any intention whatsoever to transfer all or some of his interests and his business activities to Liechtenstein.

These facts clearly establish, on the one hand, the absence of any bond of attachment between Nottebohm and Liechtenstein and, on the other hand, the existence of a long-standing and close connection between him and Guatemala, a link which his naturalization in no way weakened. That naturalization was not based on any real prior connection with Liechtenstein, nor did it in any way alter the manner of life of the person upon whom it was conferred in exceptional circumstances of speed and accommodation. In both respects, it was lacking in the genuineness requisite to an act of such importance, if it is to be entitled to be respected by a State in the position of Guatemala. It was granted without regard to the concept of nationality adopted in international relations.

Naturalization was asked for not so much for the purpose of obtaining a legal recognition of Nottebohm's membership in fact in the population of Liechtenstein, as it was to enable him to substitute for his status as a national of a belligerent State [Germany] that of a national of a neutral State [Liechtenstein], with the sole aim of thus coming within the protection of Liechtenstein.

Guatemala is under no obligation to recognise a nationality granted in such circumstances. Liechtenstein consequently is not entitled to extend its protection to Nottebohm *vis-à-vis* Guatemala.

◆ *Notes*

1. The ICJ dismissed Liechtenstein's claim filed on behalf of Nottebohm. He was a citizen of Liechtenstein under that country's internal or national law. Under International Law, however, Liechtenstein could not confer its citizenship on Nottebohm for the purpose of requiring other countries to treat him as if he were a citizen of Liechtenstein. As a result, Guatemala could appropriately characterize Nottebohm as a German citizen—remaining free to apply its discriminatory laws against the citizen of a country with which Guatemala was at war.
2. The court never decided the merits of this claim regarding Guatemala's alleged mistreatment of Nottebohm—because he was not represented by a country with which he had the effective link of nationality. Liechtenstein therefore did not have the legal capacity to bring this claim. Only Germany possessed that right, which it did not invoke during or after the war.
3. The *Nottebohm* case validated the following factors for international recognition of naturalization by another State: residence, center of interests, family ties, participation in public life, and attachment shown for a particular State. Further details on the various national and international court decisions are available from the Finnish author Ruth Donner, "The Principle of the 'Link' in Nationality Law," ch. 2 in *The Regulation of Nationality in International Law* (2nd ed. Irvington-on-Hudson, NY: Transnational, 1994).

DUAL NATIONALITY

A person is a dual national when he or she possesses the citizenship of more than one nation. This status typically occurs when an individual: (1) is born in a nation that applies the *jus soli* rule of automatic nationality by birth, and (2) simultaneously acquires the parents' citizenship because their home nation applies the *jus sanguinis* rule of nationality by blood; that is, the nationality of the parents.

Dual nationality is also spawned by those nations that allow their nationals to emigrate, acquiring a new citizenship but keeping their original nationality status. In 1998, Mexico joined the growing number of countries recognizing dual nationality—in the sense that it no longer vitiates the original Mexican nationality, based solely on a Mexican becoming the citizen of another country. For example, while that individual is a citizen of just the US, he or she is also a dual national under Mexican law. A number of Mexicans who come to the US do not want to "betray" Mexico by opting for citizenship in the US. Mexico's objectives include building a larger following in the US, whereby affected individuals who are able to vote and hold office in the US, and own property in Mexico, can influence issues of interest to both nations. (The US does not favor dual citizenship, partially because of diplomatic problems regarding which country should represent a dual national who has been harmed in a third nation. Canada approved dual citizenship in 1977.)

An individual may encounter unusual burdens as a result of dual nationality. One is being subject to the jurisdiction of two countries, each of which considers that person its national. Each nation might then command that individual to return to it, such as when his or her testimony is required (§5.2 on the Nationality Principle of jurisdiction). Both nations may want to tax the income of such individuals or impress them into military service. Such individuals may not be able to predict which nation will protect them if they are harmed in a third nation. For example, a famous international arbitration decision denied Italy the right to espouse a claim on behalf of an Italian citizen born of Italian parents. He was an Italian national under the law of Italy. He was Peruvian, however, by birth. The tribunal refused to recognize Italy's attempt to bring a claim on his behalf against Peru. The international arbitrator was unwilling to allow Italy to represent a Peruvian national in a suit against Peru. As described earlier, various attributes flow from the bond of nationality between a nation and its citizens who happen to be abroad. One attribute is that an individual's home nation may be expected to provide diplomatic protection in a dispute involving mistreatment of the individual by another nation that considers that person an alien. Here Peru was in the awkward position of purporting to protect a Peruvian national against action taken by Italy—when he was also an Italian national because of his dual citizenship.[20]

Some multilateral treaties have attempted to ameliorate the adverse impact of dual citizenship, although they have accomplished little. The 1930 Hague Convention on Certain Questions Relating to the Conflict of Nationality Laws was the first multilateral treaty to address dual nationality. While it restates the basic nationality rules already discussed, none of its provisions resolves the dilemma posed for the individual dual national when two nations claim that person as their citizen. Under Article 3, for example, "a person having two or more nationalities may be regarded as its national by each of the States whose nationality he possesses." Under this early treaty on dual nationality, each nation may apply its own law to the same individual. Some relief was available in the wording of the 1930 Hague Protocol Relating to Military Obligations in Certain Cases of Double Nationality. This treaty provides a model for avoiding competing military service claims in the case of dual nationals. If it had been adopted by a sufficient number of countries, it would have eliminated double military service for individuals who were dual nationals. The 1964 Paris Convention Concerning the Exchange of Information with Respect to Acquisition of Nationality is another multilateral treaty designed to assist dual nationals. While useful for the purpose of acquiring information, none of its provisions addresses inconsistent obligations for dual nationals.[21]

The most effective devices for avoiding inconsistent burdens are the various *bilateral* treaties that specifically address dual nationality problems. The classic problem emerges when two States draft an individual into their respective armies. The Netherlands-Belgian Agreement of 1954, concerning the Military Service of Young Men Possessing Both Belgian and Netherlands Nationality, is a good illustration of international cooperation. It avoids the potential unfairness of having to serve in two armies just because an individual is a dual national. Military service for one nation automatically precludes military service obligations in another nation.[22]

The 1997 European Convention on Nationality is the most recent attempt to alleviate burdens associated with dual nationality. In contrast to the 1930 Hague Convention, this instrument does not decide the issue of diplomatic protection. Article 17 merely refers to the existing rules of Customary International Law—a reference that leaves much to the imagination. It does provide, in principle, that dual nationals are expected to fulfill any military obligation only once—although this standard does not apply in cases of an emergency mobilization of military forces.[23]

STATELESSNESS

The condition of statelessness is the lack of nationality in *any* State. Loss of one's original citizenship—typically conferred by birth or parentage—without obtaining a new citizenship renders the individual stateless. Such individuals cannot claim the bond of citizenship with any State that might otherwise protect them. There is no State to come to the aid of an individual in need of diplomatic representation.

During and after both world wars, numerous people became stateless. Many were refugees who lost their citizenship after fleeing from their native lands. They were not citizens of the State where they had found temporary refuge. Many fled certain Eastern European countries to avoid political persecution only to find that they had been deprived of their original citizenship for doing so. Under the 1948 Hungarian Nationality Act, for example, the government of Hungary could "deprive of his Hungarian nationality a person who . . . on going abroad contravenes or evades the statutory provisions relating to the departure from the country." The 1951 Polish Nationality Act provided that a Polish citizen who resided abroad would be deprived of Polish nationality if the government determined that such an individual "left the territory of the Polish State unlawfully" or "refused to return to Poland at the summons of the competent authority."

> 1. Everyone has the right to a nationality.
> 2. No one shall be arbitrarily deprived of his nationality nor denied the right to change his nationality.
>
> —Article 15, 1948 UN Declaration of Human Rights

The phenomenon of statelessness is not limited to the two world wars. Many refugees fled Cuba in the 1960s and Vietnam in the 1970s because of political persecution. They lost their citizenship as a result of their decision to flee. They were stateless before they underwent any naturalization proceedings in the countries where they found temporary or permanent refuge.

The significance of statelessness is that individuals who acquire this status encounter great difficulty in traveling and obtaining work. The absence of identity documents, like a birth certificate or a passport, typically precludes such aliens from entering or working in most countries. The following case is a classic illustration:

Re Immigration Act and Hanna

21 Western Weekly Reporter 400 (1957)

Author's Note: *In 1957, the Supreme Court of British Columbia reviewed a deportation order made by Canadian immigration authorities regarding an individual named Hanna. He had sought residence in Canada and a waiver of compliance with its Immigration Act due to his statelessness. Judge Sullivan's intriguing account of Hanna's dilemma follows.*

Court's Opinion. Hanna is a young man without a country—one of those unfortunate "stateless" persons of the world whose status is a matter of concern to humanitarians.

[He is] in the frustrating dilemma with which fate seems to have confronted him throughout his lifetime prior to his last arrival in Canada as ship-bound prisoner aboard a tramp motor-ship in her ceaseless meanderings from port to port throughout the world.

[The evidence was that] he was born at sea and that no known record of his birth is extant. The name of the vessel aboard which he was born, and particulars of her nationality or port of registry are unknown.

During his years of infancy and adolescence Hanna seems to have crossed and recrossed the international boundaries of Ethiopia, French Somaliland, British Somaliland and Eritrea without encountering difficulty with the immigration officials of those countries.

As he grew older Hanna seems to have encountered and had difficulty with the immigration officers of these adjacent countries, in none of which he could claim residence. He thereby learned that possession of a birth certificate is an indispensable requirement of modern society.

Almost three years ago, when he was in the port of Massaua, Eritrea, Hanna stowed away in an Italian tramp steamer in the hope of being carried in her to some country which would grant him asylum and right of residence. His plan met with frustration because upon arrival of such ship at any port he was immediately locked up and denied permission to land. After a year or more of such aimless wandering and imprisonment, Hanna escaped from the Italian vessel and concealed himself in the hold of the Norwegian motor-ship 'Gudvieg.' As a stowaway in such latter vessel he fared no better than before. He was [effectively] held prisoner aboard the 'Gudvieg' for more than 16 months and made three or more trips to Canada in her [prior to these proceedings].

From whatever angle one views it, so far as Hanna is concerned, this [Canadian] deportation order amounted to a sentence of imprisonment aboard the 'Gudvieg' for an indefinite term, and in my opinion and finding, no immigration officer has the legal right to exercise such drastic power.

◆ *Notes*

1. There is no record of what ultimately happened to Hanna. The judge in the *Hanna* case did *not* rule that Hanna could remain in Canada. Judge Sullivan merely ruled that Hanna could not be deported "as ordered" by immigration authorities. The immigration agency's order was, in effect, a decision that would have subjected Hanna to life imprisonment aboard the ship in which he arrived. The judge thus acknowledged that no country had allowed—or likely would allow—Hanna to leave that vessel.
2. In a similar deportation proceeding in the United States, a stateless seaman was detained at New York Harbor's Ellis Island for seven months. Like Hanna, he had been ordered deported without specifying a particular destination. The seaman instituted proceedings to modify this "pointless" deportation order. As in the Canadian *Hanna* case, the US judge acknowledged that a stateless seaman would be denied permission to land anywhere because there "is no other country that would take him without proper documents." *Staniszewski v. Watkins,* 80 Fed. Supp. 132, 134 (So. Dist. N.Y., 1948). This seaman was permitted to work in New York and periodically report to US immigration officials.
3. In 1994, a federal court in California ordered the release of a Cuban citizen confined in federal prisons since 1985. He was one of the Mariel Cubans, most likely released from a Cuban jail and sent to the US to reduce Cuba's prison population. He appeared on US shores in 1980. He was initially ordered returned to Cuba. That State, however, would not take him back, no longer considereding him a Cuban citizen. No other country was willing to accept him. For *fourteen* years he was subject to preventative detention. He was released from federal custody on grounds that his incarceration for such a long period was an excessive punishment. Then, in September 1994, the same federal appellate court decided that it would reconsider its prior decision to release him—resulting in his remaining in custody. This decision was approved in *Barrera-Echavarria v. Rison (Warden),* 44 F.3d 1441 (9th Cir. 1995), cert. den'd, 516 US 976 (1995). (Justice Pregerson dissented, quoting from another judge's observation in a related opinion that "[i]n our society no person may be imprisoned for many years without prospect of termination. The rights of the human person must be vindicated as part of the common good of our society." *Rison,* 44 F.3d, at 1452.)
4. Like Hanna, a *vessel* at sea may be deemed "stateless." In March 1995, a US Coast Guard airplane spotted a vessel on a routine patrol 600 miles south of the California–Mexico border. The vessel was not flying any flag, rendering identification from the air impossible. When the operator did not answer radio messages, a Coast Guard cutter crew boarded it—finding ninety-five undocumented Asian immigrants stowed aboard. It was not illegal for that vessel to be in international waters. But the failure to fly any flag or respond to attempts to communicate with a vessel in international waters rendered it "stateless" for the purpose of allowing this inspection. In 1994 alone, 1,168 Asian nationals were apprehended in their attempts to reach US shores.

5. The 1989 Convention on the Rights of the Child (Chapter 11) provides that a birth certificate is a child's first right, yielding an official identity and nationality. Only Somalia and the US have not ratified this Convention. In 1998, the UN Children's Emergency Fund (UNICEF) presented its annual Progress of Nations Report. UNICEF therein reported that *one-third* of the world's children do not have a birth certificate—approximately *forty million* children per year. This circumstance deprives the children of many developing countries health care, vaccinations, and access to education, and subjects them to premature military service. Many baby girls in China are not registered so families can avoid the PRC's policy of one child per family. Otherwise, the governmental rationale is the expense of individual registration and the parents' inability to pay any registration fee.

International organizations have attempted to alleviate the problems caused by statelessness. In 1921, the League of Nations established the Office of the High Commissioner of Refugees in response primarily to people made stateless by the Russian Revolution of 1917. Members of the United Nations later established the UN Relief and Rehabilitation Administration to deal with the statelessness resulting from World War II. The UN Conference on the Elimination or Reduction of Future Statelessness has conducted a number of meetings to address this problem—without much success. The UN High Commissioner for Refugees currently deals with such matters.

The right to change nationality means little if it is not accompanied by a corresponding right to acquire the nationality of another country. Several treaties therefore address (but have yet to resolve) the problem of statelessness. The goal of the above-mentioned 1930 Hague Protocol concerning Statelessness was to provide nationality to those deprived of it because of political dissension or military conflict. This draft treaty never became effective, because too few nations ratified its provisions. The Universal Declaration of Human Rights (Chapter 8), although not a binding treaty, nevertheless establishes a moral obligation that discourages UN member States from intentionally creating stateless persons. The UN Convention on the Reduction of Statelessness entered into force in 1975. It obliges its signatories to grant their citizenship to stateless people who are willing recipients and found within their borders. It also removes the State discretion to deprive inhabitants of citizenship except on grounds that are not associated with race, religion, and political beliefs. But there are only fifteen State members, hardly enough to signal a global commitment to the problem of statelessness. The 1997 European Convention on Nationality provides in its preambular wording that signatories should use their sovereign powers to avoid statelessness. Article 4 specifically provides that everyone has a "right" to nationality. Should this treaty become effective through a sufficient number of ratifications, then statelessness will have been significantly eliminated in the one area of the world that has produced millions of stateless persons because of two world wars. It would then become the first legally binding multilateral treaty containing a comprehensive set of rules to govern nationality problems.[24]

REFUGEES

State treatment of international refugees is a problem that sometimes overlaps with statelessness. This predicament received a great deal of attention because of the twentieth century's two world wars, culminating in the Refugee Convention discussed below. The plight of the refugee resurfaced with a fury after the Cold War—in Bosnia, Rwanda, and Kosovo, to name a few.

Refugee Conventions Shortly after World War II was over, it was evident that the refugee problems did not cease with that war. Rather than spontaneous *ad hoc* agreements, the UN initiated a process leading to the 1951 Geneva Convention on the Status of Refugees and its 1967 Protocol. The basic 1951 Convention applies to refugees spawned by events occurring prior to 1951. The 1967 Protocol applies to all refugees. This key convention is an important cog in the machinery of International Law, because the objective of refugee law is to establish fundamental rights of the individual. Former UN High Commissioner for Refugees Guy Goodwin-Hill captures this scenario in his articulation that "[a]s was the case with some of the inter-war arrangements [treaties replaced by the current Convention], the objective of the 1951 Convention and the 1967 Protocol is to both establish certain fundamental rights . . . and to prescribe certain standards of treatment. The refugee may be stateless and therefore, as a matter of law, unable to secure the benefits accorded to nationals of his or her country of origin. Alternatively, even if nationality is retained, the refugee's unprotected status can make obtaining such benefits a practical impossibility. The Convention consequently proposes, as a minimum standard, that refugees should receive at least that treatment which is accorded to aliens generally."[25]

These international refugee agreements do three things: They define *who* are refugees, determine their legal *status,* and provide the administrative and diplomatic *machinery* for implementing ameliorative treaty provisions.

Who are refugees under International Law? Article 1.A.(2) of the 1951 Refugee Convention defines a refugee as any person who "owing to [a] well-founded fear of being persecuted for reasons of race, religion, nationality, membership of a particular social group or political opinion, is outside the country of his nationality and is unable, or, owing to such fear, is unwilling to avail himself of the protection of that country; or who, not having a nationality and being outside the country of his former habitual residence as a result of such events, is unable, or . . . unwilling to return to it."

What is the refugee's legal status under International Law? One of the most important treaty protections is described in Article 33.1 of the Convention. A State may not *return* an individual to his or her homeland if "his life or freedom would be threatened on account of his race, religion, nationality, membership of a particular social group or political opinion."

US Interpretation The most famous case decided by any national court of a State party to the 1951 Refugee Convention has also been the most widely criticized. That is the following 1993 case, from the US Supreme Court, regarding Haitian refugees seeking asylum in the US. On September 30, 1991, a group of military leaders displaced the government of Jean-Bertrand Aristide, the first democratically elected president in Haitian history. All parties to the consequent litigation (below) agreed that since this military coup, "hundreds of Haitians have been killed, tortured, detained without a warrant, or subjected to violence and the destruction of their property because of their political beliefs. Thousands have been forced into hiding."

Following the coup, the US Coast Guard suspended repatriations for a period of several weeks, and the US imposed economic sanctions on Haiti. In the meantime the Haitian exodus expanded dramatically. During the next six months, the Coast Guard interdicted more than 34,000 Haitians. Because so many of them could not be safely processed on Coast Guard cutters, the Department of Defense established temporary facilities at the US Naval Base in Guantanamo, Cuba, to accommodate them during the screening process. In May 1992, the US Navy determined that no additional migrants could safely be accommodated at Guantanamo. This background set the stage for the US action that allegedly violated its commitments under the treaty.

President Clinton directed the Coast Guard to intercept vessels illegally transporting passengers from Haiti to the US and to return those passengers to Haiti *without first determining* whether they may qualify as "refugees" under the 1951 UN Convention Relating to the Status of Refugees. This reaction posed the question of whether such forced repatriation to Haiti violated the US Immigration and Nationality Act (INA) and Article 33 of the United Nations Protocol Relating to the Status of Refugees. The US Immigration Act was supposedly amended to codify the US treaty commitment under the 1951 Refugee Convention.

The treaty gap that triggered this litigation involved the term *returns* occurring on the high seas *before* entering US waters (or land)—rather than *after* arrival.[26] Put another way, does the French-language treaty term *refouler* broadly require a determination of refugee status for *all* returns or just those occurring *after* the asylum seeker has arrived *within* the territory (or territorial waters) of a State that is a party to the 1951 Refugee Convention?

The federal trial court decided against the Haitians, confirming the legality of President Clinton's directive requiring returns to Haiti without making the "Article 33 Refugee Convention" determination. The federal Court of Appeals disagreed. Its judges did not accept the US government's argument that the treaty did not bar returns made prior to the refugee's arrival in the US or its territorial waters. This interim Court of Appeal determined that the 1980 amendment to the INA had been intended expressly to conform US immigration law to the provisions of the Refugee Convention. This interim panel of judges read Article 33.1's "return" provision as "plainly" covering *all* refugees, regardless of their location when found and returned by the US Coast Guard. The US was engaged in the act of returning these refugees, even on the high seas, thereby triggering the Article 33.1 requirement of determining whether these "returns" would subject the Haitians to death or other heinous mistreatment on the basis of their political beliefs.

The text and the history of the US legislation, like that of Article 33 of the UN Convention, are completely silent on the applicability of returns undertaken *outside* territorial borders or waters. The "Respondents" (Haitians) argued that the 1967 Protocol's broad remedial goals prohibit a nation from repatriating refugees to their potential oppressors—whether or not the refugees are the objects of the US return *within* or *beyond* US territory. However, the US Supreme Court majority decided that in spite of the moral weight of this argument, Article 33 was not intended to have such *extraterritorial* effect. The treaty could not apply to a return ("refouler") occurring outside of US territorial waters, on the high seas, between Haiti and the US.

The drafters of the 1951 Convention, and the parties to the companion Protocol—like the drafters of the conforming 1980 US immigration law amendment—apparently did *not* contemplate that any nation would ever gather fleeing refugees and then return them to the very country from which they so desperately sought to escape. This action certainly violated the "spirit" of Article 33. But the Supreme Court majority found that no treaty can impose uncontemplated extraterritorial obligations on those who ratify it, regardless of the general humanitarian intent of the treaty. Simply put, because the text of Article 33 did not authorize a signatory's "returns" *outside* of its territory, it could not be interpreted to prohibit such actions.

Sale v. Haitian Centers Council, Inc.

SUPREME COURT OF THE UNITED STATES, 1993

509 US 155, 113 S.Ct. 2549, 125 *L. Ed.* 2d 128

Author's Note: *This is the dissent to the majority opinion paraphrased above. In the final paragraph of the Supreme Court majority's opinion, the judges presented their closing argument by quoting from the opinion of a lower court case with similar facts: "This case presents a painfully common situation in which desperate people, convinced that they can no longer remain in their homeland, take desperate measures to escape. Although the human crisis is compelling, there is no solution to be found in a judicial remedy" (implying the need for a diplomatic remedy or a treaty modification). In his dissent, Justice Blackmun agreed with the intermediate appellate court. According to Justice Blackmun, the lower court's judges correctly interpreted the "refouler" (return) provision of the Refugee Convention as prohibiting President Clinton's Executive Order to the Coast Guard in violation of the treaty.*

COURT'S OPINION. Justice BLACKMUN, dissenting.

When, in 1968, the United States acceded to the United Nations Protocol Relating to the Status of Refugees, Jan. 31, 1967, it pledged not to "return *(refouler)* a refugee in any manner whatsoever" to a place where he would face political persecution. In 1980, Congress amended our immigration law to reflect the Protocol's directives. Today's majority nevertheless decides that the forced repatriation of the Haitian refugees is perfectly legal, because the word "return" does not mean return, because the opposite of "within the United States" is not outside the United States, and because the official charged with controlling immigration has no role in enforcing an order to control immigration. . . .

Article 33.1 of the Convention states categorically and without geographical limitation: "No Contracting State shall expel or return *(refouler)* a refugee in any manner whatsoever to the frontiers of territories where his life or freedom would be threatened on account of his race, religion, nationality, membership of a particular social group or political opinion."

The terms are unambiguous. Vulnerable refugees shall not be returned. The language is clear, and the command is straightforward; that should be the end of the inquiry. Indeed, until litigation ensued, the Government consistently acknowledged that the Convention applied on the high seas.

The majority, however, has difficulty with the Treaty's use of the term "return ('refouler')." "Return," it claims, does not mean return, but instead has a distinctive legal meaning. For this proposition the Court relies almost entirely on the fact that *American* law makes a general distinction between *deportation* and *exclusion*. Without explanation, the majority asserts that in light of this distinction the word "return" as used in the Treaty somehow must refer only to "the exclusion of aliens who are . . . 'on the threshold of initial entry'" [citation omitted].

. . . The text of the Convention does not ban the "exclusion" of aliens who have reached some indeterminate "threshold"; it bans their "return." It is well settled that a treaty must first be construed according to its "ordinary meaning." Article 31.1 of the Vienna Convention on the Law of Treaties. The ordinary meaning of "return" is "to bring, send, or put (a person or thing) back to or in a former position." *Webster's Third New International Dictionary* 1941 (1986). That describes precisely what petitioners [US government agencies] are doing to the Haitians. By dispensing with ordinary meaning at the outset, and by taking instead as its starting point the assumption that "return," as used in the Treaty, "has a legal meaning narrower than its common meaning," the majority leads itself astray.

The straightforward interpretation of the duty of nonreturn is strongly reinforced by the Convention's use of the French term *refouler*. The ordinary meaning of "refouler," as the majority concedes, is "[t]o repulse . . . ; to drive back, to repel." [French] *Dictionnaire Larousse* 631 (1981). Thus construed, Article 33.1 of the Convention reads: "No contracting state shall expel or [repulse, drive back, or repel] a refugee in any manner whatsoever to the frontiers of territories where his life or freedom would be threatened. . . ." That, of course, is exactly what the Government is doing. It is no surprise that when the French press has described the very policy challenged here, the term it has used is *refouler*. See, e.g., Le bourbier haitien, *Le Monde,* May 31–June 1, 1992 ("[L]es Etats-Unis ont decide de refouler directement les refugies recueillis par la garde cotiere." (The United States has decided [de refouler] directly the refugees picked up by the Coast Guard). . . .

Article 33.1 is clear not only in what it says, but also in what it does not say: it does not include any geographical limitation. It limits only where a refugee may be sent "to," not where he may be sent from. This is not surprising, given that the aim of the provision is to protect refugees against persecution. . . .

The Convention that the [US] Refugee Act embodies was enacted largely in response to the experience of Jewish refugees in Europe during the period of World War II. The tragic consequences of the world's indifference at that time are well known. The resulting ban on *refoulement,* as broad as the humanitarian purpose that inspired it, is easily applicable here, the Court's protestations of impotence and regret notwithstanding.

The refugees attempting to escape from Haiti do not claim a right of admission to this country. They do not even argue that the Government has no right to intercept their boats. They demand only that the United States, land of refugees and guardian of freedom, cease forcibly driving them back to detention, abuse, and death. That is a modest plea, vindicated by the Treaty and the statute. We should not close our ears to it.

I dissent [therefore, from the majority's holding which affirms the legality of President Clinton's Executive Order authorizing returns to Haiti without the required determination of refugee status under the 1951 Refugee Convention].

◆ *Notes & Questions*

1. Unfortunately, as the above 1993 Haitian case illustrates, no UN program or treaty has fully accomplished the goal of eradicating the problems identified in *Sale v. Haitian Centers Council, Inc.* The primary barrier is national distrust. Many countries share the concern about potential UN or treaty interference with nationality decisions that they would like to make on a case-by-case basis. Their view, effectively, is that the State's treatment of individuals remains a matter that should be exclusively within national jurisdiction. *Sale* arguably provided another illustration of the disdain shown by certain national courts for broad interpretations of their treaty commitments.
2. Justice Blackmun was not the only "dissenter." The majority's decision was chastised by the President of the American Society of International Law in the Society's *Newsletter* of Sept.–Oct. 1993. Society President Louis Henkin therein reacted as follows:

[T]he Supreme Court has adopted an eccentric, highly implausible interpretation of a treaty. It has interpreted those treaties . . . not as other state parties would interpret them, not as an international tribunal would interpret them, [and] not as the US Supreme Court would have interpreted them earlier in our history when the justices took the law of nations seriously, when they appeared to recognize that in such cases US courts were sitting in effect as international tribunals [that is, prior to the establishment of the world courts by the League of Nations and the UN].

3. Consider this passage from possibly the most authoritative treatment of refugee law, penned by a former UN High Commissioner for Refugees, regarding the principle of "non-refoulement"—referring to the contemporary application of the 1951 Convention and its 1967 Protocol: "If each State remains absolutely free to determine the status of asylum seekers and either to abide by or ignore the principle of *non-refoulement,* then the refugee's status in international law is denied and the standing, authority, and effectiveness of the principles and institutions of protection are seriously undermined." *See* G. Goodwin-Hill, *The Refugee in International Law* 169 (2nd ed. Oxford, Eng.: Clarendon Press, 1996).

   Did the US Supreme Court's restrictive interpretation of the treaty's refoulement provision thereby violate US obligations under the Refugee Convention? Alternatively, should such situations be left to the discretion of each State to apply either a broad or narrow construction? Should the treaty be amended to clarify this point, or would there be a danger in reopening the treaty to national interpretation that might water down what rights are already expressed in the Convention and Protocol?
4. A primary objective of the Refugee Convention is to secure a hearing so that the country where the refugee is located will assess whether a "return" will subject him or her to unwarranted persecution or death. In a 1995 Canadian Supreme Court case, the Immigration and Refugee Board denied refugee status to a Chinese man whose wife was the target of a forced sterilization under the PRC's one-child-per-family government policy. He claimed persecution because of his pro-democratic activities in the PRC. The administrative denial was upheld by the Court of Appeals. The Supreme Court held that he had not presented adequate evidence of a well-founded fear of persecution. While he did not obtain the relief he sought, Canada observed its obligations under the Refugee Convention by affording him a hearing—unlike the facts in the *Sale* case. *Chan v. Minister of Employment and Immigration,* reprinted in 35 *Int'l Legal Mat'ls* 1 (1996).

◆ 4.3 CORPORATE NATIONALITY

INTRODUCTION

A corporation is considered a legal "person" under the national or internal law of most nations. While there are a variety of entities to which this section could apply, the most common form is that of the "corporation"—a business entity typically formed for the purpose of limiting liability beyond that which is available to a natural person. This section will use the term "corporation" to refer collectively to all such institutions. Studying corporations is important because a number of these "multinationals" generate annual earnings eclipsing the gross national product of the nations wherein they operate. Some have thus wielded a heavy hand in terms of influencing State behavior.

One of the more infamous examples is an antitrust case decided in 1909. Costa Rica nationalized the plaintiff US corporation's assets in Costa Rica. The apparent purpose of this property taking was another US corporation's conspiring with the government to monopolize the lucrative Central American banana trade. Given the traditional requirements for nationalization discussed later in this chapter, such conduct triggered Costa Rica's responsibility for a discriminatory taking of alien property in violation of customary international practice. After the decolonization of the 1960s, many lesser-developed nations of the world invoked the UN processes in 1974. The General Assembly then formulated a draft code of corporate conduct. This was to be a guideline for controlling foreign corporate activity designed to limit the profound influence of these major financial institutions on developing nations.[27]

Like a natural person, a business entity may possess nationality for the purpose of International Law. It, too, can be harmed in and by foreign countries. As discussed in §4.1 regarding the *individual's* traditional lack of international legal capacity, States have the right to present claims on behalf of their public and private corporations on the international level. This representation typically occurs through some diplomatic endeavor or through the pursuit of litigation in an international tribunal. But States are not *obligated* to present such claims on an international level.

The issue of *where* a corporation may properly claim citizenship can be a judicial quagmire in an age when so many corporations engage in business transactions throughout the globe. A number of European nations treat a multinational corporation as a national of the country where its headquarters or home office is located. In the United States, a corporation is a US national if it is incorporated in one of the fifty US states.

This chapter previously addressed the legal bond of nationality linking the individual and his or her native State. There are also occasions when a corporation may need protection on the international level. A corporation may be taxed by more than one country, each claiming that the corporation is its citizen. Alternatively, it may be nationalized by the host country without adequate (or any) compensation to the shareholders (Chapter 13).

The genuineness of an *individual's* nationality link with a particular State is comparatively easy to establish (§4.2 *Nottebohm* case). The genuineness of a *corporation's* link with a particular country is a more complex question. Today's multinational enterprises are often owned by parent corporations and, in turn, owned by numerous shareholders who reside in various countries. When the enterprise is harmed, it is the individual shareholder owners who are actually harmed. These investors sometimes seek the assistance of the States of their individual nationalities to help them obtain a remedy for the wrong done to the multinational enterprise.

PROPER STATE

Which country may present a claim on behalf of a corporation? Assume that Investco is a large multinational corporation located in Hong Kong. It is owned by shareholders from Brazil, France, Germany, South Africa, and the US. Assume further that the Chinese government nationalized Investco's assets after the 1998 takeover of Hong Kong without any compensation. Under International Law, not all of the "shareholder" nations have the capacity to present a claim for compensation against China. By analogy, the International Court of Justice (ICJ) determined that Mr. Nottebohm's receipt of a new nationality did not authorize Liechtenstein to present his property claim against Guatemala (§4.2). A similar analysis is appropriate in the case of corporations, when they have ties with more than one nation.

In the Investco nationalization hypothetical, a tribunal would have to decide which of the various nations best represents Investco's corporate personality. Under International Law, the appropriate State is normally the State where Investco is incorporated. There are exceptions, which will be discussed in the following case.

Barcelona Traction, Light, and Power Co.

INTERNATIONAL COURT OF JUSTICE

1970 *International Court of Justice Reports* (Second Phase) 3 (1970)

Author's Note: *Barcelona Traction was incorporated in Canada. It operated a power company in Spain. It was declared bankrupt by a Spanish court, which ordered the seizure of its assets. Belgium, England, Canada, and the US all tried to assist Barcelona Traction in resisting the seizure. Individual citizens in these countries owned the stock of the corporation. Its value would be decreased unfairly if the bankruptcy proceedings were inappropriately instituted. The shareholders believed that the Spanish authorities prematurely sought bankruptcy for some ulterior purpose. The corporation was a legal person separate from its stockholders—possessing its own Canadian nationality. Canada exercised its discretion, however, by choosing not to process this claim on behalf of the Canadian shareholders or the corporation. Belgian nationals owned eighty-eight percent of the Barcelona Traction stock at the time the bankruptcy was declared. Belgium thus decided to prosecute this action in the ICJ against Spain, because most of the harmed individual owners were Belgians.*

The ICJ dismissed this suit, ruling that Belgium could not represent Barcelona Traction. If the country of incorporation

(Canada) was unwilling to pursue the claim, the State of the majority of the individual shareholders (Belgium) could not do so. Selected portions of the ICJ's opinion portray the Court's rationale for vesting the country of incorporation with the exclusive right of representation on the international plane—in diplomatic or international judicial proceedings. The paragraph numbers are those of the Court.

Court's Opinion. 70. In allocating corporate entities to States for purposes of diplomatic protection, international law is based, but only to a limited extent, on an analogy with the rules governing the nationality of individuals. The traditional rule attributes the right of diplomatic protection of a corporate entity to the State under the laws of which it is incorporated and in whose territory it has its registered office.... However, in the particular field of the diplomatic protection of corporate entities, no absolute test of the 'genuine connection' has found general acceptance [as with *individuals* under the Court's *Nottebohm* case in §4.2]....

71. In the present case, it is not disputed that the company was incorporated in Canada and has its registered office in that country. The incorporation of the company under the law of Canada was an act of free choice. Not only did the founders of the company seek its incorporation under Canadian law but it has remained under that law for a period of over 50 years. It has maintained in Canada its registered office, its accounts and its share registers. Board meetings were held there for many years; it has been listed in the records of the Canadian tax authorities. A close and permanent connection has been established, fortified by the passage of over half a century. This connection is in no way weakened by the fact that the company engaged from the very outset in commercial activities outside Canada, for that was its declared object. Barcelona Traction's links with Canada are thus manifold.

72. Furthermore, the Canadian nationality of the company has received general recognition. Prior to the institution of proceedings before the Court, three other governments apart from that of Canada (those of the United Kingdom, the United States and Belgium) made representations concerning the treatment accorded to Barcelona Traction by the Spanish authorities. The United Kingdom Government intervened on behalf of bondholders and of shareholders. Several representations were also made by the United States Government, but not on behalf of the Barcelona Traction company as such....

75. The Canadian Government itself, which never appears to have doubted its right to intervene on the company's behalf, exercised the protection of Barcelona Traction by diplomatic representation for a number of years, in particular by its note of 27 March 1948, in which it alleged that a denial of justice had been committed in respect of the Barcelona Traction, Ebro and National Trust companies, and requested that the bankruptcy judgment be cancelled....

76. In sum, the record shows that from 1948 onwards the Canadian Government made to the Spanish Government numerous representations which cannot be viewed otherwise than as the exercise of diplomatic protection in respect of the Barcelona Traction company. Therefore this was not a case where diplomatic protection was [totally] refused or remained in the sphere of fiction. It is also clear that over the whole period of its diplomatic activity the Canadian Government proceeded in full knowledge of the Belgian attitude and activity....

78. The Court would here observe that, within the limits prescribed by international law, a State may exercise diplomatic protection by whatever means and to whatever extent it thinks fit, for it is its own right that the State is asserting. Should the natural [individuals] or legal [corporate] persons on whose behalf it is acting consider that their rights are not adequately protected, they have no remedy in international law. All they can do is to resort to municipal [internal] law, if means are available, with a view to furthering their cause or obtaining redress. . . . However, all these questions remain within the province of municipal law and do not affect the position internationally.

79. The State must be viewed as the sole judge to decide whether its protection will be granted, to what extent it is granted, and when it will cease. It retains in this respect a discretionary power the exercise of which may be determined by considerations of a political or other nature, unrelated to the particular case. Since the claim of the State is not identical with that of the individual or corporate person whose cause is espoused, the State enjoys complete freedom of action. Whatever the reasons for any change of attitude, the fact cannot in itself constitute a justification for the exercise of diplomatic protection by another government, unless there is some independent and otherwise valid ground for that....

88. It follows from what has already been stated above that, where it is a question of an unlawful act

committed against a company representing foreign capital, the general rule of international law authorizes the national State of the company alone to make a claim. . . .

96. The Court considers that the [unsuccessfully argued] adoption of the theory of diplomatic protection of shareholders as such, by opening the door to competing diplomatic claims, could create an atmosphere of confusion and insecurity in international economic relations. The danger would be all the greater inasmuch as the shares of companies whose activity is international are widely scattered and frequently change hands. It might perhaps be claimed that, if the right of protection belonging to the national States of the shareholders were considered as only secondary to that of the national State of the company, there would be less danger of difficulties of the kind contemplated. However, the Court must state that the essence of a secondary right is that it only comes into existence at the time when the original right ceases to exist [as when the State of incorporation ceases to exist—as discussed in this text's §2.3]. . . .

100. In the present case, it is clear from what has been said above that Barcelona Traction was never reduced to a position of impotence such that it could not have approached its national State, Canada, to ask for its diplomatic protection, and that, as far as appeared to the Court, there was nothing to prevent Canada from continuing to grant its diplomatic protection to Barcelona Traction if it had considered that it should do so.

◆ *Notes & Questions*

1. What general rule did the International Court of Justice apply for determining which State could represent a multinational corporation in international (judicial or diplomatic) proceedings?
2. Are there any exceptions that would allow *another* State to present an international claim on behalf of a corporation?
3. The Court's language in this 1970 opinion solidly vests the appropriate State with the sole discretion to determine whether it will process a claim for a corporation or an individual. As will be seen in later materials, including Chapter 11 on human rights developments, a State that harms its *own* citizen cannot hide behind this discretion in order to avoid State responsibility under international human rights law.
4. Should the rule for a corporation regarding who can represent it be the "genuine link" test for individuals from the *Nottebohm* case in §4.2? That might yield a less mechanical approach, because a court might decide that ownership of 88 percent of corporate stock is just as genuine a link as where the corporation was created—especially when many modern corporations do business around the world. Alternatively, would such a rule spawn abuses such as transferring stock in a way that provides shareholders with a wide latitude of discretion in selecting which country should present a corporate claim on the international level?

◆ 4.4 INJURY TO ALIENS

INTRODUCTION

There are various forms of State responsibility presented throughout this book. State responsibility is a vast component of International Law, necessarily handled by the somewhat scattered coverage of its diverse ingredients in various chapters. As discussed in §2.5, there have been numerous attempts to achieve consensus in articulating this facet of International Law—mostly without success. This section of the book covers State responsibility for *injury to aliens*—a matter well suited for treatment in the chapter on the individual and corporation in International Law. A State may be accountable for the acts of its agents harming aliens in a way that treats them differently from its own citizens.

Early commentators had practical reasons for focusing on this category of State responsibility. The nationals of one State—who have lived, traveled, or worked in another State—have endured abuse and discrimination throughout recorded history. As noted by a leading study: "Since ancient times foreigners have been regarded with suspicion, if not fear, either due to their nonconforming religious and social customs, their assumed inferiority, or because they were considered potential spies and agents of other nations. The Romans refused aliens the benefits of the *jus civile* [civil law], thirteenth-century England limited their recourse to the ordinary courts of justice [rather than all courts], and imperial Spain denied them trading rights in the New World."[28]

> It is an accepted maxim of international law that every sovereign nation has the power, as inherent in sovereignty, and essential to self-preservation, to forbid the entrance of foreigners within its dominions, or to admit them only in such cases and upon such conditions as it may see fit to prescribe.
>
> —*Nishimura Ekiu v. United States,* 142 US 651, 659 (1892)

The development of the law of State responsibility for injury to aliens began approximately two centuries ago. One of the foremost commentators of the eighteenth century, Emerich de Vattel, wrote in his book on the *Law of Nations:* "Whoever ill-treats a [foreign] citizen injures the State, which must protect the citizen."[29] His articulation was adopted by many international tribunals and commentators as the rationale for recognizing State responsibility for injury to aliens. Avoiding the escalation of this facet of discrimination became the linchpin of the law of State responsibility for injury to aliens.

This branch of State responsibility was essentially drawn from the internal tort law customarily applied by many States. Tort law governs civil wrongs by an *individual* for unreasonable conduct that harms another individual. If someone takes the property of another without justification, that person is liable under the internal tort law of many nations. Writers and jurists believed that a State should be similarly liable when its unreasonable acts or omissions harmed aliens. Such protection was necessary because national law typically insulated the State from the claims of its own citizens. When State X nationalized the property of a foreign citizen without compensation—that citizen's home—State Y could assert a case of State X's responsibility for the resulting harm to State Y, derived from the harm to its citizen.

CODIFICATION ATTEMPTS

As long as the law of State responsibility for injury to aliens is not codified in a multilateral treaty, the friction between "have" and "have-not" nations will continue to impair international business and governmental relations. An express agreement would incorporate diverse national perspectives about the appropriate contours of State responsibility for injury to aliens. The International Law textbook currently used at Moscow State University in Russia urges that "codification is now an urgent task. Members of the League of Nations sought to codify those norms of international law dealing with the responsibility of States for damage to the person or property of foreigners (which efforts served the interests of imperialist States)."[30]

Several attempts have been made to codify the law of State responsibility for injuries to foreign individuals and corporations. The first was the 1929 draft Convention on Responsibility of States for Damage Done on Their Territory to the Person or Property of Foreigners. It was compiled and produced under the auspices of the Harvard Law School Research in International Law Project during the period between the two world wars. Another campaign to codify this branch of State responsibility surfaced in 1953 when members of the UN General Assembly decided that "it is desirable for the maintenance of peaceful relations between States that the principles of international law governing State responsibility be codified." This UN resolution resulted in the drafting of several reports on various facets of State responsibility. Those reports did not, however, generate a written multilateral agreement.[31]

One of the most extensive presentations of the law of State responsibility toward aliens was published in 1961. It is the Draft Convention on the International Responsibility of States for Injury to Aliens. The authors of this draft treaty were Harvard University Professors Louis Sohn and Marvin Baxter. Their work exemplifies the Western view that underdeveloped nations have a significant interest in importing foreign investment and technological assistance and can profit by the just treatment of foreign corporations and employees. The Sohn–Baxter perspective is that both developed and lesser-developed nations should encourage the fair and non-discriminatory treatment of their citizens while abroad. The 1961 draft treaty does not incorporate the views of all commentators. It is an alternative, however, to the so-called Third World New International Economic Order (described below) under which a State *may* treat aliens differently than its own citizens in certain instances.[32]

Current UN efforts to codify State responsibility have not yet produced draft articles on this specific point. Even the 1998 draft is silent because "one should not find in the state responsibility draft articles a discussion of the law governing, for example, expropriation of the property of foreign nationals."[33] This project, as it continues to develop, will hopefully contain draft treaty articles that may serve as a basis for greater international cooperation in finding more widely accepted norms.

CATEGORIES OF INJURY

What specific State conduct triggers responsibility for injury to aliens? While classification is no simple task, the customary violations may be listed as follows: (1) non-wealth injuries; (2) denial of justice, including what some writers characterize as separate subcategories of wrongful arrest and detention, and lack of due diligence; (3) confiscation of property; and (4) deprivation of livelihood.

(1) Non-Wealth Injuries This form of State responsibility evolved from the unreasonable acts or omissions of State agents causing deaths or physical injuries of foreign citizens. A 1983 report by the Panel on the Law of State Responsibility of the American Society of International Law defined a "nonwealth injury" as "an injury inflicted by a State upon an alien either (1) directly through some act or omission causing physical or other personal injury to or the death of an alien, or (2) indirectly through some failure to act, including the failure under certain circumstances to prevent injury inflicted by another party, the failure to provide the injured alien with an effective remedy, or the failure to pursue, prosecute, and punish the responsible party."[34]

This category of harm is distinguished from the other types of State responsibility by its physical attributes. While a nonwealth injury can have economic consequences, the harm is not directed at the victim's pocketbook. In October 1965, for example, Indonesian army forces conducted a campaign directed at Chinese nationals in Indonesia. Chinese citizens were beaten, arrested without cause, and murdered. Further, Indonesia's army issued permits allowing civilians to demonstrate for the purpose of persecuting Chinese nationals. The Chinese government sought and received assurances from Indonesia's central government that this violence would end. Had the Indonesian government refused the Chinese demands, it would have incurred further responsibility for physical nonwealth injuries to the Chinese nationals.

(2) Denial of Justice: Discrimination Against Aliens A State's discriminatory application of its domestic laws to an alien is described as a "denial of justice." This is a somewhat "procedural" form of injury, rather than a physical harm. The standard procedures used (or not used) by the State are basically unfair because they do not affect local citizens in the same way.

There is no uniform definition of this form of injury. National and international tribunals have nevertheless found a denial of justice in countless cases. There are some limitations, however. In Latin American States, a "denial of justice" occurs only when the State has *completely* refused access to its courts or its courts will not take the necessary steps to render a decision. The regional perspective is that there can never be a denial of justice based on the quality or unsatisfactory nature of the procedures used by the tribunal when it is deciding an alien's claim. If there is *some* access to some tribunal, which at least decides the matter, a foreign citizen cannot complain about the quality of justice based on the use of different procedures than those in his or her own home state.[35]

Most nations adopt a broader interpretation of the term "denial of justice." A State can be responsible for injuring an alien when its tribunals do not provide adequate time or legal representation to prepare a defense. This must occur in a way that provides less protection than that afforded to the offending State's own citizens. If local citizens are allowed to seek legal assistance, it would be a denial of justice to withhold that right just because the prisoner is a foreign citizen.

Denial of Justice: "International Minimum Standard"? Another subcategory of denial of justice is the unreasonable arrest and detention of an alien. Incarceration is thereby unlawful when it discriminates against aliens and unreasonably departs from generally accepted procedures. An arresting State would be liable if it failed to give a reason for the arrest or detention of an alien defendant, or when trial is delayed for an unreasonable time after arrest.

Can a State incur liability for a denial of justice when it treats foreign citizens in the *same* way that it treats its own citizens? A variation on the denial of justice theme arises when a State treats a foreign citizen in a substandard way, and then defends on the basis of equal treatment of *all* individuals in the same circumstances. This problem triggers the daunting question of whether there is an "international minimum standard" (IMS) below which no State may fall in its treatment of the individual. The comparatively poor treatment of individuals is not discriminatory. Both foreign and local citizens are subjected to the same type of treatment. If an

IMS does exist, however, that State would not be able to use equality of treatment to justify its falling below the IMS regarding the treatment of both foreign and local citizens.

The historical maturation of such a standard has been retarded by economic and political differences between Western States and States in lesser-developed regions of the world. What is probably the most definitive (and equally broad) statement defining the international minimum standard was made by US Secretary of State Elihu Root in 1910:

> Each country is bound to give to the nationals of another country in its territory the benefit of the same laws, the same administration, the same protection, and the same redress for injury which it gives to its own citizens, and neither more nor less: provided the protection which the country gives to its own citizens conforms to the established standard of civilization.
>
> There is [however] a standard of justice very simple, very fundamental, and of such general acceptance by all civilized countries as to form a part of the international law of the world. The . . . system of law and administration shall conform to this general standard. If any country's system of law and administration does not conform to that standard, although the people of the country may be content to live under it, no other country can be compelled to accept it as furnishing a satisfactory measure of treatment of its citizens.[36]

The international minimum standard has been invoked in the following circumstances: The complaining State asserts that the responsible State departed from generally accepted standards of justice for the treatment of *any* individual—foreign or local. The responding State typically defends its action by reliance on the "national treatment" standard set forth in the 1933 Montevideo Convention on Rights and Duties of States (ratified mostly by Latin American nations). A foreign citizen is thereby entitled to no better treatment than the local citizens of the responding State. Equal treatment of local and foreign nationals precludes any international liability for injury to an alien. There is no clear consensus about the existence or scope of the IMS—partially due to the comparative economic positions of the nations usually involved in these controversies.

The respective positions are illustrated in the following case, one of the few but illustrative cases applying the IMS:

Roberts v. United Mexican States

UNITED STATES V. MEXICO GENERAL CLAIMS COMMISSION, 1926

4 *Rep. Int'l Arb. Awards* 77 (1974)

Author's Note: *Harry Roberts was a US citizen charged by Mexico with "assaulting a house." When he and several armed American companions gathered outside a house in Mexico, the owner summoned the Mexican police. After an exchange of small-weapons fire, the police arrested Roberts.*

The Mexican Constitution provided that prisoners had to be brought to trial within twelve months of their arrest. Roberts was in a Mexican jail for nineteen months with no hearing. His conditions of incarceration were typical for Mexican prisons but less tolerable than such conditions in other countries such as the US.

After his release, Roberts obtained US assistance for presenting this case against Mexico. The respective countries had established international arbitration machinery (General Claims Commission) to handle such disputes. The US therein argued that Mexico was responsible for a denial of justice to this US citizen, who was incarcerated in unenviable quarters in Mexico. The relevant portion of the Commission's decision appears below.

TRIBUNAL'S OPINION. This claim is presented by the United States of America in behalf of Harry Roberts, an American citizen who, it is alleged . . . was arbitrarily and illegally arrested by Mexican authorities, who held him prisoner for a long time in contravention of Mexican law and subjected him to cruel and inhumane treatment throughout the entire period of confinement. . . .

It is alleged that there were undue delays in the prosecution of the trial of the accused which was not instituted within one year from the time of his arrest, as required by the Constitution of Mexico. These delays were brought to the notice of the Government of Mexico, but no corrective measures were taken. During the entire period of imprisonment, he was subject to rude and cruel treatment from which he suffered great physical pain and mental anguish. . . .

The Commission is not called upon to reach a conclusion whether Roberts committed the crime with which he was charged. The determination of that question rested with the Mexican judiciary, and it is distinct from the question whether the Mexican authorities had just cause to arrest Roberts and to bring him to trial. Aliens of course are obliged to submit to proceedings properly instituted against them in conformity with local [national] laws. . . .

In order to pass upon the complaint [alleging abuse of the international minimum standard of treatment] with reference to an excessive period of imprisonment, it is necessary to consider whether the proceedings instituted against Roberts while he was incarcerated exceeded reasonable limits within which an alien charged with crime may be held in custody pending the investigation of the charge against him. Clearly there is no definite standard prescribed by international law by which such limits may be fixed. Doubtless an examination of local laws fixing a minimum length of time within which a person charged with crime may be held without being brought to trial may be useful in determining whether detention has been unreasonable in a given case. The Mexican Constitution provides . . . that . . . a person accused of crime "must be judged within four months if he is accused of a crime the maximum penalty for which may not exceed two years' imprisonment, and within one year if the maximum penalty is greater." From the judicial records presented by the Mexican Agent it clearly appears that there was a failure of compliance with this constitutional provision, since the proceedings were instituted on May 17, 1922, and that Roberts had not been brought to trial on December 16, 1923, the date when he was released. . . .

There is evidence in the record that Roberts constantly requested the American Consul at Tampico to take steps to expedite the trial. Several communications were addressed by American diplomatic and consular officers in Mexico to Mexican authorities with a view to hastening the trial. It was the duty of the Mexican judge under . . . the Mexican Constitution to appoint counsel to act for Roberts from the time of the institution of the proceedings against him. The Commission is of the opinion that preliminary proceedings could have been completed before the lapse of a year after the arrest of Roberts. . . .

With respect to this point of unreasonably long detention without trial, the Mexican Agency contended that Roberts was undoubtedly guilty of the crime for which he was arrested; that therefore had he been tried he would have been sentenced to serve a term of imprisonment of more than nineteen months; and that, since, under Mexican law, the period of nineteen months would have been taken into account in fixing his sentence of imprisonment, it cannot properly be considered that he was illegally detained for an unreasonable period of time. The Commission must reject this contention, since the Commission is not called upon to pass upon the guilt or innocence of Roberts but to determine whether the detention of the accused was of such an unreasonable duration as to warrant an award of indemnity under the principles of international law. Having in mind particularly that Roberts was held for . . . [nineteen] months without trial in contravention of Mexican law [allowing only a twelve-month period to elapse without trial], the Commission holds that an indemnity is due on the ground of unreasonably long detention.

With respect to the charge of ill-treatment of Roberts, it appears from evidence submitted by the American Agency that the jail in which he was kept was a room thirty-five feet long and twenty feet wide with stone walls, earthen floor, straw roof, a single window, a single door and no sanitary accommodations, all the prisoners depositing their excrement in a barrel kept in a corner of the room; that thirty or forty men were at times thrown together in this single room; that the prisoners were given no facilities to clean themselves; that the room contained no furniture except that which the prisoners were able to obtain by their own means; that they were afforded no opportunity to take physical exercise; and that the food given them was scarce, unclean and of the coarsest kind. The Mexican Agency did not present evidence disproving that such conditions existed in the jail. It was stated by the Agency that Roberts was accorded the same treatment as that given to all other persons, and with respect to the food Roberts received, it was observed in the answer that he was given "the food that was believed necessary, and within the [economic] means of the municipality." . . .

But such equality is not the ultimate test of the propriety of the acts of authorities in the light of international law. That test is, broadly speaking, whether aliens are treated in accordance with ordinary [minimum] standards of civilization. We do not hesitate to say that the treatment of Roberts was such as to warrant an indemnity on the ground of cruel and inhumane imprisonment. . . .

As has been stated, the Commission holds that damages may be assessed on two of the grounds asserted in the American memorial [stating the claim], namely, (1) excessively long imprisonment—with which the Mexican Government is clearly chargeable for a period of seven months, and (2) cruel and inhumane treatment suffered by Roberts in jail during nineteen months. After careful consideration of the facts of the case and of similar cases decided by international tribunals, the Commission is of the opinion that a total sum of $8,000.00 [in *1926* dollars] is a proper indemnity to be paid in satisfaction of this claim.

◆ *Notes & Questions*

1. On what basis did the United States allege that Mexico violated International Law? On what basis did Mexico respond that it did *not* violate International Law? Did the Commission actually impose US standards on Mexico, as opposed to "international" standards?
2. This was no "compromise" verdict—where a jury has otherwise decided for the plaintiff while awarding a rather nominal sum of damages. The $8,000 award was a significant sum of money in 1926—especially for the defendant nation at that time of its development.

Denial of Justice: Lack of Due Diligence A State may incur responsibility under International Law, although the principal actor is not an agent of the State. A State's failure to exercise due diligence to protect a foreign citizen is wrongful if the unpunished act of a private individual is a crime under the laws of that State (or generally recognized as criminal conduct elsewhere in the principal legal systems of the world). Responsibility then arises under International Law if that State fails to apprehend or control the individual who has committed the crime against the foreign citizen.

Examples include the 1979 storming of the US embassy in Iran by Iranian citizens. Iran's leader denied that his government had arranged for them to storm the embassy and take US citizens hostage because they were foreign citizens from a disfavored nation. Iran nevertheless incurred State responsibility for failing to take any action to stop the crowds from stampeding the persons and property of these foreign citizens (Chapter 7 "Hostage" case). A more common example of such State responsibility is the indifference of lower-echelon officials in circumstances where a *local* citizen would be given prompt assistance. States are expected to respond to such officials who act, or fail to act, in a way that unreasonably affects an alien.

(3) Confiscation of Property While a nation undoubtedly possesses the right to nationalize property belonging to foreigners (and local citizens), there are limitations. One prohibits the taking of property, referred to as confiscation or expropriation, in a way that discriminates against aliens. There is a significant conflict between traditional Western and contemporary non-Western models regarding whether International Law or host State law should apply.

Right to Nationalize Both national and International Law concede the State's sovereign right to expropriate ("nationalize," "take," or "appropriate") property. This is a recognized incident of the State's status as a sovereign entity. The State possesses such power over persons and things within its borders, absent some treaty commitment *not* to nationalize foreign property. As succinctly stated by a modern Chinese scholar:

> Public international law regards nationalization as [a] lawful exercise of state power. This is because each state, being possessed of sovereignty, naturally has the right within its own territory to prescribe whatever

> economic and social system it chooses to establish. Speaking more concretely, each state has the exclusive right to regulate . . . conditions of acquisition, loss, and contents of ownership. Consequently, when one approaches this question from the standpoint of the principle of state sovereignty, one must recognize that states enjoy the right to adopt nationalization measures. Nationalization belongs to matters of national jurisdiction and therefore . . . neither the United Nations nor other states have a right to intervene [when another country nationalizes the property of its citizens].[37]

One should first distinguish the following scenarios when analyzing State responsibility in expropriation cases. The analysis in this section of the book does not involve the first two of the four presented:

- State X takes property belonging to citizens of State X and to foreign citizens. All affected individuals may have claims under the law of State X for compensation. Such rights normally arise only under the *national* laws of State X.
- Alternatively, State X takes property belonging *only* to a foreign individual or corporation—but none belonging to its own citizens. As long as there is appropriate compensation for the taking, unrelated to the citizenship of the owner, State X does not incur any *international* responsibility. This is not considered an "injury to aliens" for the purpose of triggering State responsibility under International Law.
- State X takes only the property of a foreign citizen and either pays *no* compensation or *inadequate* compensation. This latter circumstance is one object of the law of State responsibility for injuring aliens via a confiscatory taking of property.
- State X specifically targets the property of either all foreigners, or a particular ethnic group. It does not take property belonging to its own citizens in like circumstances.

"Confiscation" Limitation If a State's taking of the property of a foreign citizen amounts to "confiscation," then there may be State responsibility in International Law. Under the traditional Western view, nationalizations must be undertaken for a "public" purpose. It must also be accompanied by "prompt, adequate, and effective" repayment for the property taken by the government.[38] There is no public purpose when the government takes property that merely adds to the personal holdings of a dictator. Further, the mere provision of *some* compensation does not mean that the compensation is adequate. A nationalization violates the Western-derived view of International Law if the terms of the compensation provided to its foreign owner are less favorable than those provided to citizens of the host State—or the amount is below the fair market value of the property taken by the State.

The standard for determining value is subject to a great deal of controversy. Some States do not feel compelled to use any of them. Concepts like "fair market value," "replacement cost," and "book value" are rather indefinite terms when applied by experienced accountants, let alone officials or mediators from different legal or social systems.

Nationalizations where compensation *is* paid may nevertheless give rise to a claim of State responsibility for injury to aliens. In a case with major political undertones, Fidel Castro orchestrated a revolutionary takeover of Cuba in 1959. The US subsequently imposed a quota on the amount of Cuban sugar importable into the US. Castro characterized this singular US sugar quota as an act of "aggression, [done] for political purposes." The Cuban government then nationalized the sugar interests of US individuals and corporations, but not Cuban-owned sugar interests. Cuba was willing to pay for the nationalized sugar interests in its own government bonds—payable *twenty* years later, at a rate of interest well below that of similar bonds. This type of compensation was legal under the laws of Cuba. The US Department of State viewed it as inadequate, however, referring to it as "manifestly in violation of those principles of international law which have long been accepted by the free countries of the West. It is in its essence discriminatory, arbitrary and confiscatory." Payment in long-term bonds, at a comparatively low rate of interest, was neither prompt nor adequate. The State Department claimed that Cuba's purpose was discriminatory because Cuba took the US property as a political response to the US import quota imposed on Cuban sugar.[39]

Non-Western Models A number of lesser-developed countries (LDCs) have adopted a different yardstick for measuring the appropriate degree of compensation. Their position is that the more-developed countries (MDCs), whose corporations operate within their borders, unfairly profited from these long-term economic relationships. Foreign multinational corporations have been characterized as extracting enormous profits with little return for the local citizens. The LDCs do *not* perceive uncompensated nationalizations of foreign property as necessarily being confiscatory takings in violation of International Law. One supporting argument is that the MDCs have effectively deprived the LDCs of their national sovereignty over natural resources through unacceptable business arrangements that have historically taken unfair advantage of the LDCs. Huge profits, they argue, have been expatriated to the private shareholders of the MDCs' multinational corporations. Instead, more of these profits should be injected into the sagging economies of the world's LDCs. An uncompensated nationalization returns only a *fraction* of what has been improperly taken from the LDC by one-sided business arrangements—which have diluted natural sovereignty over disappearing natural resources, with no tangible benefits for the LDCs.

Many LDCs decided to respond to the above Western-derived compensation requirements via their premise, as stated in the UN General Assembly Resolution of 1962 on Permanent Sovereignty over Natural Resources. Its objective was to machinate a paradigm in customary international practice, as it evolved while the LDCs were still colonial territories of the MDCs. A fresh standard for determining compensation for expropriations had to be determined under the *national* law of the host State where the taking occurs. This would be more representative than measuring compensation via the historical practice evolving from an era predating the existence of the vast majority of current members of the international community. The resulting Resolution therefore provides as follows: "[T]he owner shall be paid appropriate compensation, in accordance with the rules in force in the State taking such measures . . . [and] the national jurisdiction of the State taking such measures shall be exhausted. However, upon agreement by sovereign States . . . settlement of the dispute shall be made through arbitration or international adjudication. . . ."[40]

There is a tension between two competing policies in this East–West, or North–South, dialogue. One is the primacy of a State's territorial jurisdiction over persons and things within its territory. The opposing policy is the historical protection afforded to aliens by the external influence of International Law. The applicability of both policies often spawns a dilemma that pits them against one another. The University of Minnesota's Professor Gerhard von Glahn describes what is clearly the *Western* perception of the proper balance between these twin goals:

> Each state is the sole judge of the extent to which aliens enjoy civil privileges within its jurisdiction. But beyond those permissive grants, each alien, as a human being, may be said to be endowed with certain rights, both as to person and to property, that are his by virtue of his being. It is primarily in connection with those basic rights that a responsibility by the host state arises. It is in this sphere that claims originate and . . . may be advanced against the host state by the government to which the alien owes allegiance.[41]

The essential feature of this counter to the Western formulation is that national law rather than International Law would govern. Foreign shareholders, or the effected corporation, would be limited to the *local* remedies (if any) of the nationalizing State. That State would neither be accused of violating International Law nor would have to engage in international adjudication absent its consent. This is one of the basic tenets of the New International Economic Order (NIEO) promulgated in 1974 by many non-aligned nations (Chapter 13). Pace University (New York) Professor S. Prakash Sinha provides this summary:

> They challenge some of the rules of international law as not consistent with their view of the new order and they point to the need for international law to reflect a consensus of the entire world community, including theirs, and promote the widest sharing of values. They criticise the system of international law as being a product of relations among imperialist States and of relations of an imperial character between imperialist States and colonial peoples. . . . Moved by the desire to cut inherited burdens, to free themselves from foreign control of their economies, and to obtain capital needed for their programmes of economic reconstruction, the newly independent States have resorted to expropriation of foreign interests. In their opinion, the validity of such expropriation is not a matter of international law.[42]

On the other hand, this approach would foster economic suicide. Adoption would frustrate the free flow of capital to a State whose leader suddenly nationalized foreign property without paying compensation. Other corporate structures would fear similar treatment by State X. The resulting lack of investment would retard its economic growth.

Neither the Western position—which would apply the traditional International Law formulation requiring prompt, adequate, and effective compensation—nor the "Third World" NIEO—which would determine compensation, if any, exclusively under host State law—have been adopted in any multilateral treaty. This tension has retarded universal applicability of some major treaties. The UN Law of the Sea Treaty, for example, became effective in 1994. However, it contains a number of equitable redistribution provisions to which MDCs have either objected or have tendered reservations (§6.3).

The Latin American variation to the LDC perception of Western economic hegemony is the "Calvo Clause." It evolved from the tenet that no government should have to accept financial responsibility for civil insurrection resulting in mistreatment of foreign citizens at the hands of insurgents rather than the defending government. The relevant adaptation of this concept is that a State may impose conditions on foreign individuals and corporations who wish to do business within that State's borders. It may thus require, as a condition of doing business there, that foreigners be treated on equal footing with local citizens. A foreign company doing business in a "Calvo Clause" country must thereby relinquish its right, arising under International Law, to seek the diplomatic assistance of its home State when there has been a nationalization. As exemplified by Article 27.1 of the Mexican Constitution, foreigners must agree to "consider themselves as [Mexican] nationals in respect to such property, and bind themselves not to invoke the protection of their governments. . . ." This agreement thereby waives any right to claim the assistance of a foreign government when the Mexican government has decided to nationalize foreign property.

Iran–US Claims Tribunal One entity that could—but is unlikely to—develop a wider degree of consensus on international expropriation norms is the Iran–US Claims Tribunal. The Iranian revolution that led to the US Hostages Case *(see* §7.4) and the treaty that freed them in 1980 presented a rich environment for the progressive unification of the various models for evaluating applicable law and compensation rules. In this instance, host-State takings were outspokenly anti-American. They were done with utter disregard for any international norms. The Iranian government nationalized—or otherwise controlled—virtually all foreign property in all conceivable industries, with a view toward casting out the "US Demon." The US responded by freezing Iranian assets in the US. As part of the treaty agreement leading to release of the American hostages after 444 days in captivity, the US made these Iranian assets available to this tribunal for the purpose of satisfying claims against Iran.

This tribunal (Chapter 9) is unlikely to break new ground, however. Its mandate, agreed to by negotiators for the US and Iran, is to decide all cases "on the basis of respect for law, applying such . . . rules and principles of commercial and international law as the Tribunal determines to be applicable. . . ."[43] The Tribunal has had the unenviable task of interpreting this "governing law" term, but only in the several of the nearly five hundred cases it decided during its first ten years of existence. Most claimants avoided raising the issue of determining the precise international norms, perceiving the potential legal task as unproductively expensive due to the attendant ambiguity and complexity. As stated by a practicing lawyer who is one of the leading commentators on this issue: "In only a few cases has the issue been addressed, and in some of these, the awards suggest it was used more as a justification for achieving a result predetermined to be fair or equitable by the arbitrators than as a set of rules to be followed in reaching a reasoned decision based in law."[44]

Until a widely accepted treaty accomplishes a greater degree of international consensus, the debate about the appropriate compensation paradigm will continue to polarize the developed and developing States.

(4) Deprivation of Livelihood Another category of State responsibility for injury to aliens is the unreasonable deprivation of a foreign citizen's ability to enjoy a livelihood. The withdrawal of his or her ability to continue practicing a certain occupation is an unacceptable deprivation if done for a discriminatory purpose.

The US Supreme Court case of *Asakura v. City of Seattle* is a useful illustration (text in §8.1). Under a treaty between Japan and the US, the citizens of both countries were entitled to enjoy equal employment rights with the citizens of each country. The city of

Seattle subsequently passed a pawnbroker ordinance providing that "no such license shall be granted unless the applicant be a citizen of the United States." The Court determined that this ordinance "makes it impossible for aliens to carry on the business. It need not be considered whether the State, if it sees fit, may forbid and destroy business generally. Such a law would apply equally to aliens and citizens. . . ." The ordinance improperly discriminated against aliens in violation of the treaty specifically providing for equal treatment of Japanese citizens working in the US. If the court had ruled *against* the plaintiff Japanese pawnbroker who challenged the ordinance, the US would have incurred State responsibility for depriving foreign citizens of a livelihood during peacetime.[45]

◆ SUMMARY

1. The historical perspective was that the individual had no status (legal capacity) in International Law. Thus, an individual *claimant* could not pursue remedies for breaches of International Law at the international level. In certain cases such as piracy, however, an individual *defendant* could be punished under the law of nations for violating its rules.
2. The policies of the Nazi regime, whereby the State totally disregarded any dignity of the individual, led to a post–World War II revival of the status of the individual as a potential *defendant* who is legally capable of violating International Law.
3. The State has the discretion to pursue a remedy—through diplomacy or judicial action—on behalf of its citizens when another State violates their rights. This discretion does not *obligate* the home State to prosecute such claims, however, leaving the individual to pursue remedies available under national law.
4. Nationality may be acquired in three ways: (1) by birth in a country that applies the soil rule of *jus soli;* (2) by being born of parents, anywhere in the world, when the parents' home country applies the *jus sanguinis* blood rule; and (3) by naturalization, whereby the applicant attains a new nationality that differs from his or her previous nationality.
5. Nationality is normally a matter of national law. States do not have to recognize one another's decisions that confer nationality, however. Many international decision makers examine the extent of an individual's ties with the claimed country of nationality.
6. One who possesses nationality in two or more countries is a dual national and may thus be subjected to conflicting obligations including double taxation and military service.
7. Statelessness is the condition whereby an individual has no nationality in any country. Such individuals do not have a home country that could otherwise provide international protection. Post–World War II statelessness treaties have attempted to ameliorate the plight of those so affected by the lack of State protection because they have no nationality documents.
8. A refugee may or may not be stateless. The 1951 Refugee Convention (pre-1951 refugees) and its companion 1967 Protocol (*all* refugees) provide international protection for individuals who would be persecuted on being returned to their home State. There is some disagreement about the degree to which this treaty is applicable outside of the territory or territorial waters of States that have ratified this treaty.
9. Like individuals, corporations possess nationality that thereby entitles them to State protection. While most or all of the shareholders might be located in one State, only the State of incorporation generally has the international capacity to represent a corporation in international proceedings.
10. The State of incorporation has the discretion to represent its corporations in international proceedings. This right is not an obligation. The State's decision not to represent a corporation thus requires an injured corporation to seek remedies (if any) under national rather than International Law.
11. State responsibility for injuring aliens arose out of concerns for foreign citizens who have been treated differently than local citizens. The various methods of discrimination include: (1) nonwealth injuries; (2) denial of justice, including what some commentators characterize as the subcategories of wrongful arrest and detention and lack of due diligence; (3) confiscation of property; and (4) deprivation of livelihood.
12. The Western view emphasizes the primacy of customary international practice, which was developed to ensure that *international* norms govern State property takings. This traditional view requires prompt, adequate, and effective compensation for any expropriation. The perspective of lesser-developed States is that *national* law should govern. This perspective does not require compensation and depends on the circumstances of the particular case.

13. A regional application of the lesser-developed nations' response to the traditional compensation requirements is the Latin American "Calvo Clause." A foreign enterprise waives its right to diplomatic protection from its home State, even when its directors believe that there has been a discriminatory taking of property. Foreign corporations are effectively characterized as local citizens so as to avoid the potential application of any international norms regarding State responsibility for injuring aliens.

◆ PROBLEMS

Problem 4.A (end of §4.1) Two Libyan military intelligence officers were apparently responsible for blowing up Pan Am Flight 103 over Lockerbie, Scotland, in 1989. All 270 passengers, from various countries of the world including England and the US, died violent deaths. UN Security Council Resolution 731 of 1992 demanded the trial of these two suspects in the West. The Arab League negotiated with Libya's leader to turn over the suspects for trial outside of Libya. England and the US sought the extradition of these individuals from Libya for trial. Libya's leader (Colonel Gadhafi) refused all of these demands and requests. A 1998 arrangement for trial in the Netherlands nearly resolved this never-ending controversy. However, it failed to materialize when Libya demanded assurances that the two suspects would not be tried in England instead.

Under International Law, who may seek remedies for the death of the passengers on Pan Am Flight 103? Against whom?

Problem 4.B (after *Nottebohm* Case in §4.2) In June 1989, the best-known dissident in the People's Republic of China entered the US Embassy in Beijing to seek diplomatic asylum. Fang Lizhi, a prominent astrophysicist and human rights advocate, remained there until June 1990—refusing treatment for a heart ailment for fear of arrest. China's agreement to allow him to leave the US Embassy (without being arrested) for a new home in Great Britain signaled a thawing of Sino–US relations. The Chinese government acceded to US pressure to allow this dissident to leave China, possibly due to its desire to retain favorable trading status with the US.

Assume, instead, that Fang Lizhi is still residing in the US Embassy in Beijing. There has yet been no resolution of his request for asylum and no diplomatic arrangements made regarding his passage. He therein declares his intent to "defect" to either the US or Great Britain now that his immediate family is assembled with him in the US Embassy. They are ready to leave on short notice to any country that will take the family. The US ambassador initially says that "the granting of asylum at this critical time might jeopardize the US negotiations with China over human rights issues." After conferring with the US Secretary of State, and the British Foreign Minister, the parties decide that Fang Lizhi should apply for British citizenship. He has never been in Great Britain. The British government is apparently willing to waive all citizenship requirements, including a waiting period of three years (as in *Nottebohm).* After one week, Great Britain issues Fang Lizhi a British passport, which is delivered to him in the US Embassy in Beijing.

Assume further that (contrary to the actual facts in this case) the Chinese government protests, accusing the US and Great Britain of meddling in Chinese affairs. The PRC is *not* willing to allow safe passage so that Fang Lizhi can leave China. The Chinese government's Minister of Foreign Affairs advises all concerned that this dissident, engaging in anti-State conduct, will be arrested the moment that he departs from the embassy. In the eyes of the PRC, he remains a Chinese citizen.

What is Fang Lizhi's nationality? Must China recognize the British citizenship conferred on this individual under the *Nottebohm* case?

Problem 4.C (end of §4.2, after *Sale v. Haitian Centers Council* Case) As Justice Blackmun stated regarding Jewish refugees during the World War II era: "The tragic consequences of the world's indifference at that time are well known." One example might be the following incident. Even prior to US entry into World War II, the fate of the Jewish citizens and some other minorities of Nazi Germany was well known—*see* M. Gilbert, *Auschwitz and the Allies* (New York: Holt, Rinehart & Winston, 1981). US families were willing and qualified to sponsor a number of Nazi Germany's Jewish children. In 1939, however, the US Congress defeated proposed legislation that would have rescued about twenty thousand such children from Nazi Germany. The government's rationale was that this rescue would have exceeded the US immigration quota from Germany. *See A Brief History of Immigration to the United States* in T. Aleinkoff & D. Martin, *Immigration Process and*

Policy 52 (St. Paul: West, 1985), which described this event as "what may be the cruelest single action in US immigration history."

Beginning in 1994, daily newspaper accounts reported savage machete killings in Rwanda's civil war. Some one million Rwandans fled into Zaire (later renamed Democratic Republic of the Congo) and neighboring African nations. *Assume* that an organization like the Haitian Council is trying to save twenty thousand Rwandan orphans who are about to be expelled from Zaire. No one else is willing to take them. These children come from the "wrong" tribe. The successful rebel tribe leaders in Rwanda vow that such children will have no place in Rwanda's future if they return.

The US Embassy's ambassador to Zaire is approached by the Save the Rwanda Children Organization. Its representative presents a plan whereby willing and qualified US citizens will take the Rwandan refugees from Zaire to the US. A part of this plan is an application to the US for asylum for these children, who are being discriminated against on the basis of "membership in a particular social group" (the wrong tribe whose leaders fought the successful rebels) under Article 33.1 of the Refugee Convention. After consultation with the US Department of State, the US Embassy officer declines on the basis that the US "does not have the capacity to become the haven for the world's refugees." The US refusal in Zaire means that those children will be returned to Rwanda for likely extermination.

(1) Would the 1951 Refugee Convention affect the ability of the US to say no to this proposal, which will mean certain death for the children? (2) Blackmun's dissent in *Haitian Centers Council* scolds the Supreme Court majority for its refusal to apply the 1951 Convention on an "extraterritorial" basis; that is, in the international waters between Haiti and the US. Could Blackmun's argument be extended to this hypothetical, thus requiring the US to receive the Rwandan refugee children?

Problem 4.D (§4.4 after "Confiscation of Property" Subsection) Reynolds–Guyana (RG) was a foreign-owned mining corporation that mined bauxite in Guyana for a number of decades. The parent company was a US corporation. Guyana is a former British colony that achieved its independence and statehood in 1966. RG's profits were substantial, although there was an enormous start-up cost, including research and development.

In 1974, Guyana's government assessed an enormous "bauxite tax deficiency" against RG. The company immediately characterized this tax as being fabricated for confiscatory purposes. Guyana's Prime Minister responded that RG would be fully nationalized by the end of 1974. A US agency (the Overseas Private Investment Corporation) advised RG not to pay the bauxite tax deficiency. This agency then negotiated the sale of RG's mining operations to a third party on terms acceptable to the government of Guyana.

Assume the following: (1) A 1973 Guyana law, passed on the eve of this 1974 controversy, provides that a "Calvo Clause" is presumed to be a part of every contract involving any foreign business operation in Guyana; (2) this 1973 law contains a provision, similar to that contained in the Iran–US Claims Tribunal, stating that "any compensation dispute requires respect for the law, and the law to be applied to any nationalization is International Law."

The majority of RG shareholders are US citizens who have become quite wealthy as a result of their stock investment in RG. Negotiators are now deliberating about whether Guyana has incurred State responsibility to compensate RG's parent corporation (in the US) for injuries suffered by the enormous bauxite tax deficiency. (In this hypothetical, there has been no sale to a third party, as occurred in the actual 1974 case.) Two students (or groups) will now debate the effect of assumptions (1) and (2) above.

◆ BIBLIOGRAPHY

§4.1 Legal Personality of the Individual

C. Grossman & D. Bradlow, "Conference on Changing Notions of Sovereignty and the Role of Private Actors in International Law: Are We Being Propelled Towards a People-Centered Transnational Legal Order?" 9 *Amer. Univ. J. Int'l L. & Policy* 1 (1993).

R. Higgins, "Conceptual Thinking about the Individual in International Law," in R. Falk et al., *International Law: A Contemporary Perspective* 476 (Boulder, CO: Westview Press, 1985).

M. Janis, "Individuals and International Law," ch. 8 in *An Introduction to International Law* 227 (2nd ed. Boston: Little, Brown & Co., 1993).

§4.2 Nationality, Statelessness, and Refugees

G. Alfredsson & P. Macalister-Smith (eds.), *The Living Law of Nations: Essays on Refugees, Minorities, Indigenous Peoples and the Human Rights of Other Vulnerable Groups* (Kehl, Germany: N.P. Engel, 1996).

J. Hathaway, *The Law of Refugee Status* (Toronto: Butterworths, 1991).

H. Lambert, *Seeking Asylum: Comparative Law and Practice in Selected European Countries* (Dordrecht, Neth.: Martinus Nijhoff, 1995).

D. Miller, *On Nationality* (Oxford, Eng.: Clarendon Press, 1995).

G. Naldi, "Refugees," ch. 4 in *The Organization of African Unity: An Analysis of Its Role* 88 (London: Mansell, 1989).

§4.3 Corporate Nationality

J. Charney, "Transnational Corporations and Developing Public International Law," 1983 *Duke Law Journal* 748 (1983).

F. Rigaux, "Transnational Corporations," ch. 5 in M. Bedjaoui (ed.), *International Law: Achievements and Prospects* 121 (Dordrecht, Neth.; Boston: Martinus Nijhoff, 1991).

§4.4 Injury to Aliens

"Injury to the Persons and Property of Aliens on State Territory," ch. 23 in I. Brownlie, *Principles of Public International Law* (4th ed. Oxford, Eng.: Clarendon Press, 1990).

R. Jennings & A. Watts, "Property of Aliens: Expropriation," §407 in 1 *Oppenheim's International Law* (Part II) 911 (Essex, Eng.: Longman, 1992).

A. Mouri, *The International Law of Expropriation as Reflected in the Work of the Iran/US Claims Tribunal* (Dordrecht, Neth.: Martinus Nijhoff, 1994).

M. McDougal et al., "The Protection of Aliens from Discrimination and World Public Order: Responsibility of States Conjoined with Human Rights," 70 *American Journal of International Law* 432 (1976).

"Responsibility for Injuries to Aliens," in H. Kindred et al., *International Law: Chiefly as Interpreted and Applied in Canada* 540 (5th ed. Toronto: Edmond Montgomery Pub., 1993).

◆ ENDNOTES

1. I. Seidl-Hohenveldern, *Corporations in and Under International Law* (Cambridge, Eng.: Grotius, 1987).
2. J. Bentham, *An Introduction to the Principles of Morals and Legislation* 296 (Dover, NH: Longwood Press, 1970) (Burns & Hart edition).
3. *See* H. Chiu, "Book Reviews and Notes," 82 *Amer. J. Int'l L.* 892, 894–895 (1988).
4. D. Salem, *The People's Republic of China, International Law and Arms Control* 13 (Baltimore: Univ. of Maryland, 1983).
5. L. Chen, "The Individual," ch. 5 in *An Introduction to Contemporary International Law: A Policy Oriented Perspective* 76, 77 (New Haven, CT: Yale Univ. Press, 1989).
6. Mavrommatis Palestine Concessions case: *PCIJ*, ser. A, No. 2 (1924), reported in 2 *Int'l L. Rep.* 27. *See also* "rules creating individual rights and obligations . . . [are] enforceable by the national courts." "Danzig Railway Officials Case," *PCIJ*, ser. B, No. 15 (1928), reported in 4 *Int'l L. Rep.* 287.
7. *Case Concerning the Factory at Chorzow (Germany v. Poland),* 1928 *PCIJ*, ser. A, No. 17 (Judgment of Sept. 13, 1928).
8. *Brown v. Warren Christopher, Secretary of State,* No. 93-1375-CIV (S.D. Fla. Nov. 18, 1993) (unpublished opinion).
9. Iran and the US ultimately settled this suit for $61.8 million upon dismissal of the case from the ICJ's docket of cases. The order and surrounding facts are available in 35 *Int'l Legal Mat'ls* 550 (1996).
10. V. Nanda, "International Law in the Twenty-First Century," ch. 5 in N. Jasentuliyana (ed.), *Perspectives on International Law,* at 83 (London: Kluwer, 1995).
11. *See* A. Cassese, "Individuals," ch. 4 in M. Bedjaoui (ed.), *International Law: Process and Prospects* 114, 120 (Dordrecht, Neth.: Martinus Nijhoff, 1991).
12. E. Paras, "A Brief History of Conflict of Laws," ch. 15 in *Philippine Conflict of Laws* 438 (7th ed. Manila: Rex Book Store, 1990).
13. "Nottebohm Case *(Liechtenstein v. Guatemala),*" 1955 *ICJ Rep.* 4.
14. "Determination of Chinese Nationality," in 1 J. Cohen & H. Chiu, *People's China and International Law: A Documentary Study* 746 (Princeton, NJ: Princeton Univ. Press, 1974).
15. "Nationality Decrees in Tunis and Morocco (Advisory Opinion)," *PCIJ*, ser. B, No. 4 (1923), reported in 1 *World Court Rep.* 145.
16. G. Tunkin, *International Law* 338–339 (Moscow: Progress Publishers, 1982) (1986 English trans.) (hereinafter Tunkin treatise).
17. K. Sik, "The Netherlands and the Law Concerning Nationality," in 3 *International Law and the Netherlands* 3, 7 (Alphen aan den Rijn, Neth.: Sijthoff & Noordhoff, 1980).
18. *European Convention on Nationality, Done at Strasbourg, Nov. 6, 1997,* reprinted in 37 *Int'l Legal Mat'ls* 47 (1998) (hereinafter *1997 Nationality Convention*).
19. US Const., Amend. XIV (1868). An analysis is available in J. Guendelsberger, "Access to Citizenship for Children Born Within the State to Foreign Parents," 40 *Amer. J. Comp. L.* 379 (1992).
20. *"Canevaro Case (Italy v. Peru),"* 2 *Rep. Int'l Arb Awards* 397 (1949).
21. **Hague Convention:** "Convention of 12 April 1930," 179 *League of Nations Treaty Series* 89 (1938). **Protocol:** "Protocol of 12 April 1930," 178 *League of Nations Treaty Series* 227 (1937) (this series does not necessarily report treaties in chronological order). **Paris Convention:** *See* Sik article, p. 7 (cited in note 17 above).
22. "Exchange of Notes at The Hague of 9 June 1954," 216 *UN Treaty Series* 121 (1955).
23. *See 1997 Nationality Convention,* note 18 above.
24. *See 1997 Nationality Convention,* note 18 above (three ratifications are required for this treaty to enter into force).
25. G. Goodwin-Hill, *The Refugee in International Law* 298 (2nd ed. Oxford, Eng.: Clarendon Press, 1996).
26. *See generally,* H. Kahn, "Legal Problems Relating to Refugees and Displaced Persons," in *Hague Acad. Int'l Law,* 149 *Recueil des Cours* 287, 318 (1976).

27. **Case:** *American Banana v. United Fruit,* 213 US 347, 29 S.Ct. 511, 53 *L. Ed.* 826 (1909). **Code:** Gen. Ass. Reso. 3202 (S-VI) of 1 May 1974, Section 5. *See also* UNCTAD, *World Investment Report 1995: Transnational Corporations and Competitiveness* (Geneva: UN, 1995).
28. F. Dawson & I. Head, "National Tribunals and the Rights of Aliens," in 10 *International Law,* p. XI (Charlottesville, VA: Univ. Press of Va., 1971).
29. E. de Vattel, II *The Law of Nations* 136 (New York: Oceana, 1964) (translation of original 1758 edition).
30. Tunkin treatise, at 224 (cited in note 16 above).
31. **1929 draft:** "Responsibility of States," 23 *Amer. J. Int'l L.* Special Supp. 131 (1929). **1953 attempt:** Gen. Ass. Res. 799 (VIII), Dec. 7, 1953, contained in G.A.O.R. (8th Session) Supp. (No. 17) at 52, UN Doc. A/2630.
32. The draft convention is reprinted in L. Sohn & M. Baxter, "Responsibility of States for Injuries to the Economic Interests of Aliens," 55 *Amer. J. Int'l L.* 545, 548 (1961). The draft convention's principles were approved by the American Society of International Law's Panel on the Law of State Responsibility in 1980.
33. Quote from D. Kaye, "Introductory Note" to 1998 draft, contained in 37 *Int'l Legal Mat'ls* 440 (1998). *See* S. Rosenne, *The International Law Commission's Draft Articles on State Responsibility: Part 1, Articles 1–35* (Dordrecht, Neth.: Martinus Nijhoff, 1991); and M. Spinedi & B. Simma (eds.), *United Nations Codification of State Responsibility* (New York: Oceana, 1987).
34. G. Yates, "State Responsibility for Nonwealth Injuries to Aliens in the Postwar Era," in R. Lillich (Reporter), *International Law of State Responsibility for Injuries to Aliens* 213, 214 (Charlottesville, VA: Univ. Press of Va., 1983).
35. **Case examples:** The classic articulation is available in O. Lissitzyn, "The Meaning of the Term 'Denial of Justice' in International Law," 30 *Amer. J. Int'l L.* 632 (1936). **Latin American perspective:** I. Puente, "The Concept of 'Denial of Justice' in Latin America," 43 *Mich. L. Rev.* 383 (1944).
36. E. Root, "The Basis of Protection to Citizens Residing Abroad," 4 *Proceedings of the American Society of International Law* 20–21 (Wash., DC: Amer. Soc. Int'l Law, 1910).
37. Li Hao-p'ei, "Nationalization and International Law," in 1 *People's China and International Law: A Documentary Study* 719 (Princeton: Princeton Univ. Press, 1974).
38. This formulation appears in the diplomatic notes exchanged between Mexico and the US in 1938. *See* §1.4 of this text (General Principles), and 2 *Restatement (Third) of the Law of the Foreign Relations Law of the United States* §712 (St. Paul: ALI Publishers, 1987) (containing extensive commentary and examples).
39. These facts and quotes are taken from *Banco Nacional de Cuba v. Sabbatino,* 376 US 398, 84 S.Ct. 923, 11 *L. Ed.* 2d 804 (1964).
40. UN Gen. Ass. Res. 1803(XVII), reproduced in 2 *Int'l Legal Matl's* 223 (1963).
41. G. von Glahn, *Law Among Nations: An Introduction to Public International Law* 190 (7th ed. Boston: Allyn & Bacon, 1996).
42. S. Sinha, "Perspective of the Newly Independent States on the Binding Quality of International Law," in F. Snyder & S. Sathirathai, *Third World Attitudes Toward International Law: An Introduction* 23, 29 (Dordrecht, Neth.: Martinus Nijhoff, 1987).
43. *Undertakings of the Government of the United States of America and the Government of the Islamic Republic of Iran with Respect to the Declaration of the Government of the Democratic and Popular Republic of Algeria,* Art. V, reproduced in 20 *Int'l Legal Mat'ls* 229, 232 (1981).
44. J. Westberg, *International Transactions and Claims Involving Government Parties: Case Law of the Iran–United States Claims Tribunal* 66 (Wash., DC: Int'l L. Inst., 1991).
45. 265 US 332, 44 S.Ct. 515, 68 *L. Ed.* 1041 (1924).

CHAPTER FIVE

Extraterritorial Jurisdiction

CHAPTER OUTLINE

THE SECRETARIAT OF THE LEAGUE OF ARAB STATES learned with resentment of the bombing by the United States of the pharmaceutical factory near Khartoum, resulting in the loss of many civilian lives. . . .

The Secretariat considers this unjustified act a blatant violation of the sovereignty of a State member of the League of Arab States, and of its territorial integrity, as well as against all international laws and tradition, above all the Charter of the United Nations.

The Secretariat, deploring this attack, calls upon the United States . . . to respect international legality and to refrain from such acts which constitute violations of national sovereignty . . . thus endangering international peace and security.

—Statement by the Secretariat of the League of Arab States condemning the American bombing of Sudan [and Afghanistan] on August 20, 1998. UN Doc. S/1998/789

INTRODUCTION

Prior chapters have covered the essentials of International Law, including definitions and the actors who shape its contours. This chapter commences the analysis of substantive problems and solutions. The operational norms of International Law will be studied beginning with the acceptable parameters for exercising State power in an international or "extraterritorial" context.

This is the basic question: Under what circumstances can a State exercise its sovereign powers beyond its borders? This increasingly common feature of State practice may conflict with the norm that sovereignty is not permeable. Each State in the community of nations should render and receive equality and respect—regardless of its station within the community of nations.

Section 5.3 covers extradition. One State should not encroach on another's sovereign boundaries by arresting a wanted criminal within another State. No State sent agents into Libya, for example, to seize the Libyan terrorists apparently responsible for bombing Pan Am Flight 103 over Scotland in 1989—in spite of a UN resolution demanding their release for trial outside of Libya. The perceived benefits of invoking irregular alternatives to international extradition may yield exhilaration for the moment. Such benefits, however, are not worth the long-term burdens to State sovereignty.

◆ 5.1 DEFINITIONAL SETTING

State regulation of the activities of its inhabitants, or those whose conduct has an effect within its boundaries, is often described in terms of "jurisdiction" and "sovereignty." Each term means different things to different people, depending on the context. Although they are often used synonymously, there are some important distinctions between them.

SOVEREIGNTY

Sovereignty is the exclusive right of a State to govern the affairs of its inhabitants—and to be free from external control. A sovereign State has the international capacity to exchange diplomats with other States, to engage in treaty making, and to be immune from the jurisdiction of the courts of other States (when it is not acting like a private trader). A State possesses sovereignty when it is able to act independently of the consent or control of any other State.

Afghanistan emerged as a sovereign nation in 1709, for example, after centuries of feudal conflict. It became a sovereign member of the United Nations in 1946. The 1979 Soviet invasion of Afghanistan violated the latter's sovereignty over its own territory. Soviet troops were introduced without the consent of Afghanistan's president, who was executed. Rebels claimed that the government of Afghanistan was a "puppet regime," effectively controlled by the Soviet Union. Afghanistan no longer retained the sovereign power to control its own territory. The Soviet Union began to withdraw its troops in 1988. When the USSR collapsed in 1991, Afghanistan began to regain the supervision of its own affairs. Once again, it became a sovereign State. Neither the ensuing struggle for political power nor the 1998 US bombing of terrorist locations in Afghanistan vitiated its sovereignty.

International theorists describe State sovereignty in terms of a solid sphere—much like a billiard ball—whereby one nation cannot intrude into the internal affairs of another. When there is a clash between two or more such spheres of influence, the theoretical equality of every State rigidly repels the other "billiard ball" on the international playing surface. Examples of what one might call permeable sovereignty occurred in 1989 when the US invaded Panama in order to remove its leader (General Noriega) for trial in the US; and in 1990 when US DEA agents arranged for the abduction of a Mexican doctor from Guadalajara for trial in the US. One can readily appreciate that the US actions in these cases were not designed to assert US sovereignty over these countries. A more limited purpose was intended in each instance: to further some specific US policy interests in the Western Hemisphere. These actions were quickly ended—unlike the decade-long Soviet takeover of Afghanistan. The UN Charter prohibits the use of such force in international relations on the basis of the sovereign equality and dignity of all UN members.

Several historical events contributed to the emerging concept of State sovereignty. One was the regional consolidation of autonomous feudal fiefdoms, existing for thousands of years, in certain regions of the world. This development tainted the feudal power of numerous local rulers. A related development was the opposition to external intervention that surfaced in the Middle Ages. The leaders of the Holy Roman Empire had attempted to expand its influence into Western Europe and the Middle East during the medieval crusades. To repel these invaders, the people of the affected areas sought to consolidate local territorial power into statewide sovereignty. This centralization of sovereign power led these societies to adopt the concept of State sovereignty to help repel foreign intruders.

The following description of sovereignty is ironic because it was made by a prominent commentator from the former Yugoslavia before its breakup and apparent expulsion from the UN. Professor Branimir Jankovic of the Center for International Studies in Yugoslavia traces these roots of sovereignty. His perspective is as follows:

> [T]he idea of sovereignty originated when there appeared a growing opposition to feudal anarchy and to interference in the affairs of other states. The [emerging national] rulers of those times fought for their unlimited, sovereign authority, within their states as well as outside their borders. In this struggle to supersede the feudal retrogressive system and create a new social order, the idea of state sovereignty had a progressive significance. Although at first historically progressive, [sovereign] absolutism . . . was based upon an unlimited autocracy and brute force. It is in the ideology of absolutism that we find the roots of the theory of absolute sovereignty. . . . The sovereignty of a state means today its independence from external intervention. This is the supreme authority inherent in every independent state, limited only by the univer-

sally adopted and currently valid rules of international law. This supreme power extends within the borders of the national territory and is usually described as territorial sovereignty, or territorial jurisdiction of states.[1]

Spying is a form of extraterritorial jurisdiction in the sense that Nation X clandestinely sends an X citizen into Nation Y to spy, or uses a Nation Y citizen to spy on his or her own country.[2] While diplomats are not supposed to engage in this sort of activity, many have been expelled for precisely this reason (Chapter 7). Another format for this clandestine activity is using an international organization for the ulterior purpose of obtaining sensitive information about the targeted nation. The US has claimed that various UN representatives have thus been operatives for foreign nation information-gathering purposes. In January 1999, Iraq was finally able to credibly establish that US weapons inspectors, working for UNSCOM's international weapons inspection team, were executing an intelligence operation. It yielded information for the US military and political campaign against Iraq (apparently unknown to the chief weapons inspector Richard Butler, who denied that UNSCOM was being used for this purpose).

JURISDICTION

The term *jurisdiction* has several meanings. It includes the legal capacity or power of a State to (a) establish, (b) enforce, and (c) adjudicate rules of law within its boundaries. A State's legislature has the power to enact laws governing conduct within, and in some cases beyond, its borders. The executive branch of the State has the power to enforce its laws against those who would break the rules. The State's courts have the power to adjudicate cases against civil and criminal defendants under the laws of the State.

A preliminary but critically important limitation restricts these powers in International Law. An unauthorized exercise of sovereign power (jurisdiction), in the territory of another State, constitutes what is referred to as an "extraterritorial" jurisdiction—which violates International Law. The target State possesses the right, based on its status as a sovereign entity, to be recognized as sharing equal rights and dignity with all other members of the community of nations. The offending State has the correlative obligation not to interfere with another State's enjoyment of the exclusive right to control the activities within its borders.

By its consent, the Federal Republic of Germany ... has given permission for the United States of America ... to station a specific number of Pershing II and Cruise nuclear missiles on the territory of the [FRG, and] ... the authority to order the military operations of these weapons systems is vested in the President of the United States of America. ...

This legal effect of consent amounts to a transfer of sovereign rights. ... The Federal Republic has thereby given up an exclusive claim to sovereignty in this sphere ... which is under the control of a non-German sovereign authority. ...

The declaration of consent being challenged [by the parliamentary Green Party] grants to the United States of America the right to decide to release for military operation the weapons systems in question. ...

—Cruise Missiles Deployment (German Approval) Case, Federal Constitutional Court, 106 *Int'l Law Reports* 365, 375–376 (1997) (unsuccessful challenge decided in 1984)

The elemental jurisdictional questions analyzed in this chapter are then pursued in Chapter 6 on the "Range of Sovereignty." That closely related theme involves the degree to which one State may effectively exercise its sovereignty outside of its territorial confines, based on acceptable State practice. Some of the questions explored in these two chapters are as follows: Will a State X court have the jurisdiction to apply its internal criminal law to an event that occurs partially within and partially without the State's borders; occurs outside of State X, but produces an effect within State X; occurs on the high seas or in international airspace involving State X citizens or its vessels and aircraft? The real question is, to what extent does State X have "jurisdiction" to respond to such threats?

"EXTRATERRITORIAL" PROBLEM

Many States have, at one time or another, engaged in overt and covert activities within the territory of another State. What constitutes acceptable State practice is a matter of degree. The existence of an international diplomatic system, with its embassies and consulates, provides an acceptable level of engagement (Chapter 7). Arranging for the extraterritorial abduction of a foreign national for trial is quite another matter.

The US has been the object of much international attention, beginning essentially in the 1980s, because of legislation and presidential orders that have been unmistakably "extraterritorial" in nature. A few examples show the degree to which a State's jurisdiction can leap beyond its territory or territorial waters. A 1984 US law criminalized hostage taking outside of the US when the hostages are US citizens or the conduct is designed to influence a US governmental organization to act in a particular way. A 1986 law allowed the US Coast Guard to board vessels anywhere on the world's high seas when the object of the search is to prevent drugs from flowing into the US. In 1993, a federal court in Washington, D.C., approved the application of the National Environmental Protection Act to cover conduct in Antarctica (Chapter 12). In the same year, the US Supreme Court also approved the US Drug Enforcement Administration's participation in the abduction of a Mexican national from Mexico for trial in the US; the application of US antitrust law to London insurers engaged in a boycott affecting US insurers; and the US Coast Guard's return of potential refugees on the high seas near Haiti.[3]

One way the US has reacted to international objections to its "extraterritorial jurisdiction" has been to legislatively divest criminal defendants from raising this matter as a defense—specifically providing that a US court retains jurisdiction to proceed, even when to do so effectively condones an "extraterritorial" application of US law in violation of International Law. For example, an amendment to the US Maritime Drug Enforcement laws (Title 46, §1903) now provides that "[a] claim of failure to comply with international law in the enforcement of this chapter may be invoked *solely* by a foreign nation [and not by the criminal defendant], and a failure to comply with international law shall not divest a court of jurisdiction or otherwise constitute a defense to any proceeding under this chapter."

The exercise of "extraterritorial" jurisdiction is in some cases more acceptable—in terms of international relations—than in others. Prior to assessing some of the more questionable incidents, one should first examine the circumstances that empower a State to apply its laws to conduct occurring beyond its borders.

◆ 5.2 FIVE JURISDICTIONAL PRINCIPLES

Commentators use the term *international criminal law* (ICL) in two distinct contexts: (1) the penal features of International Law, and (2) the international application of a nation's criminal law. The first usage involves crimes that are in essence "internationalized" by the community of nations. The classic illustration is genocide. ICL, when used in this sense, means that if two nations were to enter into a treaty agreeing to eradicate a particular ethnic group, the treaty would be void from the outset. ICL clearly prohibits genocide under the rule of law adopted by the community of nations—through the 1946 Nuremberg and Tokyo Judgments in 1946, the ensuing General Assembly Resolution unanimously approving of those judgments, and the 1998 genocide decision of the International Criminal Tribunal for Rwanda (Chapter 9 on international tribunals and Chapter 11 on human rights).[4]

> Congress has the unquestioned authority to enforce its laws beyond the territorial boundaries of the United States. Whether Congress has exercised that authority in a particular case is a matter of statutory construction. In construing a statute to ascertain Congress' territorial intent, we begin with the presumption that "the legislation of Congress, unless a contrary intent appears, is meant to apply only within the territorial jurisdiction of the United States."
>
> —*Hong Kong and Shanghai Banking Corp. v. Simon,* 153 F.3d 991, 995 (9th Cir. 1998)

The other common usage of the term *international criminal law* involves applications of the national law of a particular nation. In this sense, a State is usually applying its internal criminal law to events occurring elsewhere but having an impact on that State. Uppsala University (Sweden) Professor Iain Cameron succinctly explains that "a state can criminalize conduct which occurs outside its territory, and provide for prosecution of the actors should they come within its territory. A state's assertion of [its jurisdictional] competence in this way can be referred to as 'extraterritorial criminal jurisdiction,' although the actual prosecution and punishment of

EXHIBIT 5.1 STATE X INTERNATIONAL JURISDICTIONAL GUIDE

Jurisdictional Principle	Conduct for Which State X May Prosecute
Territorial (Subjective)	Defendant's conduct violates State X law Conduct starts within State X Completed within State X or outside
Territorial (Objective)	Defendant's conduct violates State X law Conduct starts outside State X Completed or has "effect" within State X
Nationality	Defendant's conduct violates State X law Defendant is a citizen (national) of X Conduct may start and end anywhere
Passive Personality	Defendant's conduct violates State X law Victim is a citizen (national) of X Conduct may start and end anywhere
Protective	Defendant's conduct violates State X law Conduct may start and end outside State X (Territorial must either start or end in X) (Protective need not have "effect" in X)
Universality	Defendant's conduct sufficiently heinous to violate the laws of *all* States Conduct started and completed anywhere All States may prosecute (not just X)

the offender is intraterritorial. All states apply their criminal law to events and conduct occurring outwith [without] their territories to a greater and lesser extent, and so all states apply rules which lay down the spatial scope of their criminal law and grant competence to their courts to try and punish people who have committed abroad [the] acts defined in their criminal codes as offences."[5]

Other chapters (Chapters 9 and 11) will primarily focus on crimes that violate the Law of Nations such as genocide. This chapter deals primarily with ICL in the second sense: specifically, the limitations on a State's ability to proscribe and punish individuals who commit crimes beyond the borders of the prosecuting State.

In 1935, a major study at the Harvard Law School traced the continuing need for expanding criminal jurisdiction in this international context. The Introductory Comment of the study explained it as follows: "From its beginning, the international community of States has had to deal in a pragmatic way with more or less troublesome problems of penal jurisdiction. In exercising such jurisdiction . . . States became increasingly aware of the overlappings and the gaps which produced conflicts [between two States wanting to prosecute the same criminal] and required cooperation. . . . In the [nineteenth] century, with the increasing facility of travel, transport and communication . . . the problems of conflict between the different national systems became progressively more acute."[6] International practice ultimately acknowledged five customary bases for legitimate State regulation of an individual's conduct, occurring either partially or wholly beyond its borders. They are presented in Exhibit 5.1.

TERRITORIAL PRINCIPLE

Under this principle, the State's jurisdictional authority is derived from the location of the defendant's act. That conduct usually starts and ends within the State that is prosecuting the defendant. The State may thereby punish individuals who commit crimes within its borders. Of all jurisdictional principles, this application is the most widely accepted and the least disputed. This is only the starting point, however, because two other applications of the territorial principle have *international* applications; these are the "subjective" and "objective" categories.

Assume that the defendant is a foreign citizen. A State has the jurisdictional power to prosecute violators of its laws without regard to their nationality. Assume further that Italy wants to prosecute a Swiss citizen who plots the overthrow of the Italian government. That individual is captured by the Italian police in Rome. Italy possesses the territorial jurisdiction to prosecute and punish this defendant—although he or she is a foreign citizen. It does not matter whether the prohibited conduct began in Switzerland (ending in Italy) or began in Italy. As stated by Italy's Court of Cassation, in response to a Swiss defendant's claim that Italy would lack jurisdiction in such a case, there "is no rule of Italian public law or international law which exempts from punishment an alien who commits an act in Italy which constitutes a crime. . . . The crime of which the appellant [defendant] has been found guilty, is not less a crime because he is a Swiss national. . . . "[7]

Under International Law, Italy may also exercise its sovereign powers over those whose extraterritorial conduct violates its laws. The prior historical limitation—that a State could regulate *only* that conduct occurring within its geographical boundaries—no longer exists. Since the nineteenth century, improvements in travel and communication have greatly enhanced the criminal's ability to commit a crime (or parts of a crime) in more than one country. The unlawful conduct may occur partially inside and partially outside of Italy under the "territorial" principle.

The *subjective* form of territorial jurisdiction is used to justify legislation that punishes criminal conduct that commences within a State and is then completed abroad. A State has the power to punish the perpetrator of a crime finally consummated elsewhere when the intent to commit the crime and the initial act in furtherance of the crime occurred within that State. Nineteenth-century national legislation began to reflect this internationalization of criminal activity, which was made possible by the evolution of technology and communication.

The territorial principle has an alternative application when a State's jurisdiction is based on activities commencing outside of its borders. This is the "objective" variation of the territorial principle. It is applied to conduct that commences *outside* but is completed within the prosecuting State. It is also referred to as the "effects doctrine." This facet of territorial jurisdiction is more easily abused and thus subject to more limitations under International Law.

The leading international case on the "effects doctrine" was decided in 1927 by the Permanent Court of International Justice (PCIJ). Turkey arrested and prosecuted a French citizen for conduct that began and ended in international waters—as opposed to occurring within the territorial boundaries of a particular State's land or territorial sea. This is a significant case, because the finding that Turkish jurisdiction was authorized under International Law meant that international jurists condoned State practice that extended national criminal jurisdiction where the "effects" of the defendant's conduct somehow appeared in the prosecuting State:

The S.S. Lotus (France v. Turkey)

PERMANENT COURT OF INTERNATIONAL JUSTICE, 1927

Permanent Court of International Justice Reports, Series A, No. 10 (1927)

Author's Note: *In 1923, the French mail steamer* Lotus *was in international waters, headed for Constantinople. The* Lotus *collided with an outbound Turkish coal ship, the* Boz-Kourt. *Eight Turkish seamen were killed in the collision. When the* Lotus *arrived in Turkey, Turkish authorities arrested and prosecuted the French ship's watch officer, Lieutenant Demons (as well as the Turkish vessel's captain) for involuntary manslaughter. Defendant Demons' negligence allegedly cost the lives of Turkish citizens as well as substantial property damage to the Turkish vessel.*

France objected to Turkey's exercise of jurisdiction over its French citizen. The alleged criminal negligence did not occur on Turkish territory or in its territorial waters. After diplomatic protests, France and Turkey decided to submit the issue—France's objection to Turkey's exercise of its national jurisdiction—to the PCIJ for resolution. The following portion of the court's opinion addresses whether State practice acknowledged Turkey's jurisdiction over conduct far away on the high seas.

The PCIJ concluded that either France or Turkey could prosecute the French vessel's officer for involuntary manslaughter. (France could have done so under the Nationality Principle described later in this section.) Turkey was therefore authorized to prosecute Demons because the "effect" of his conduct was felt sufficiently within Turkey. The PCIJ herein confirmed the "objective" application of the territorial principle of State jurisdiction. Turkey did not violate International Law when it asserted its criminal jurisdiction in this high seas collision case outside of Turkish territory.

COURT'S OPINION. The violation, if any, of the principles of international law would have consisted in the taking of criminal proceedings against Lieutenant Demons. It is not therefore a question relating to any particular step in these proceedings [by Turkey] but of the very fact of the Turkish Courts exercising criminal jurisdiction. That is [because] the proceedings relate exclusively to the question whether Turkey has or has not, according to the principles of international law, jurisdiction to prosecute [France's citizen] in this case.

The prosecution was instituted in pursuance of [the following] Turkish legislation . . . : Any foreigner who . . . commits an offence abroad to the prejudice of Turkey or of a Turkish subject . . . shall be punished in accordance with the Turkish Penal Code provided that he is arrested in Turkey. . . .

Now the first and foremost restriction imposed by international law upon a State is that . . . it may not exercise its power in any form in the territory of another State. In this sense, jurisdiction is certainly territorial; it cannot be exercised by a State outside its territory except by virtue of a permissive rule derived from international custom or from a convention.

It does not, however, follow that international law prohibits a State from exercising jurisdiction . . . [over] acts which have taken place abroad. . . .

Such a view would only be tenable if international law contained a general prohibition to States to extend the application of their laws and the jurisdiction of their courts to persons, property and acts outside their territory. . . . But this is certainly not the case under international law as it stands at present. Far from laying down a general prohibition . . . it leaves them in this respect a wide measure of discretion. . . .

[I]t is certain that the courts of many countries, even of countries which have given their criminal legislation a strictly territorial character, interpret criminal law in the sense that offences, the authors of which at the moment of commission are in the territory of another State, are nevertheless to be regarded as having been committed in the national territory [of the prosecuting State] if one of the constituent elements of the offence, *and more especially its effects,* have taken place there [emphasis supplied by author].

The offence for which Lieutenant Demons was prosecuted was an act—of negligence or imprudence—having its origin on board the [French ship] *Lotus,* whilst its effects made themselves felt on board the [Turkish ship] *Boz-Kourt.*

◆ *Notes & Questions*

1. The PCIJ essentially held that Turkey could exercise its national criminal jurisdiction over a "foreigner" who violated the quoted Turkish penal code provision by committing an offense abroad. On these facts, "abroad" included international waters—which belonged to no one—as opposed to conduct *within* another State. The Court's articulation does not preclude the application of Turkish penal law to a *Turkish* citizen for his or her acts abroad that cause the same or similar effects within Turkey—such as the Turkish officer who was also responsible for damage to the Turkish vessel. The Court approved "wide discretion" for Turkey to apply its laws to foreigners on the high seas. As will be seen in the next chapter, this development is also referred to as the ability of a State to exercise its jurisdiction based on the "law of the flag." A Turkish vessel may be legally characterized as a floating extension of the Turkish territory. Which form of the territorial principle did the Court approve in *Lotus?*
2. The Court further recognized the applicability of the "passive personality" principle to the French officer's conduct. The victims of his negligence were Turkish citizens, as was the vessel. This application is further addressed later in this chapter.

NATIONALITY PRINCIPLE

A State may regulate the conduct of its own citizens, even when their acts occur entirely outside of that State. In 1992, US chess master Bobby Fischer defied a UN resolution imposing sanctions against the former Yugoslavia. No US citizen was permitted to travel to Yugoslavia as a part of US compliance with that resolution. When Fischer defied the travel ban, the US Treasury Department sent him a letter, warning him about the penalties for his refusal to comply. Although his conduct took place on foreign soil, the US could rely upon the nationality principle of jurisdiction to legitimize any ensuing prosecution for his acts.

Using the *Lotus* case as another example of the nationality principle, France could have prosecuted the French ship's officer for his negligence, because Lieutenant Demons was a French citizen who damaged a French public vessel. This potential exercise of State jurisdiction is premised on the legal bond between a State and its citizens. That link generates reciprocal rights and obligations. As previously analyzed in §4.2 (*Nottebohm* case), a State is expected to protect its citizens when they are abroad for as long as they owe it their allegiance. Conversely, a citizen's conduct may touch and concern the interests of his or her home State in a way that allows that State to request that the citizen return home. That State may also punish its citizen for certain conduct—for example, operating a public French vessel in a way that damages it in a collision at sea (based on the nationality link between France and its citizen in the *Lotus* case).

The nationality principle is invoked less frequently than the territorial principle. One practical reason is that the territorial and nationality principles often overlap. France would not *need* to invoke the nationality principle to exercise its jurisdiction if it wanted to prosecute Lieutenant Demons. The territorial principle would be conspicuously available, because his negligence harmed the French vessel in the *Lotus* collision—an extension of France's territory on the high seas. In the *Lotus* case, Turkey did not claim that its criminal jurisdiction was based in whole or in part on this principle, because the *Lotus*'s watch officer was not a Turkish citizen.

Under the nationality principle, States enjoy relatively unfettered legal control over their citizens. A State's treatment of its own citizens is usually of no concern to other states.[8] The following case explains why States possess wide discretion when exercising their jurisdiction based on the nationality of their citizens.

Blackmer v. United States

SUPREME COURT OF THE UNITED STATES, 1932

284 US 421, 52 S.Ct. 252, 76 *L. Ed.* 375

Author's Note: *This was a tax case arising out of the famous Teapot Dome Scandal during the administration of President Warren Harding in the 1920s. In litigation related to this scandal, the Supreme Court found that some high-ranking politicians had obtained oil leases through corrupt means. Blackmer, a US citizen, had some information needed by the US authorities to investigate them. He had moved to France but had not relinquished his US citizenship.*

A US consular officer in Paris served Blackmer with a notice to return to Washington to testify for the US government during criminal and civil investigations of the scandal. After Blackmer ignored this court order to return to the US, the trial judge found him in contempt of court for failing to appear. Blackmer then petitioned the US Supreme Court for relief from the lower court's contempt order and related fine. The following portion of the Supreme Court's opinion succinctly articulates the application of the nationality principle of jurisdiction requiring Blackmer's return.

COURT'S OPINION. Mr. Chief Justice HUGHES delivered the opinion of the Court.

The petitioner, Harry M. Blackmer, a citizen of the United States resident in Paris, France, was adjudged guilty of contempt of the Supreme Court of the District of Columbia for failure to respond to subpoenas served upon him in France and requiring him to appear as a witness on behalf of the United States at a criminal trial in that court. Two subpoenas were issued, for appearances at different times, and there was a separate proceeding with respect to each. The two cases were heard together, and a fine of $30,000 with costs was imposed in each case, to be satisfied out of the property of the petitioner which had been seizer by order of the court. The decrees were affirmed by the Court of Appeals of the District, and this Court granted writs of certiorari. . . .

The statute provided that whenever the attendance at the trial of a criminal action of a witness abroad, who is "a citizen of the United States or domiciled therein," is desired by the Attorney General, or any assistant or district attorney acting under him, the judge of the court in which the action is pending may order a subpoena to issue, to be addressed to a consul of the United States and to be served by him personally upon the witness with a tender of traveling expenses. Upon proof of such service and of the failure of the witness to appear, the court may make an order requiring the witness to show cause why he should not be punished for contempt, and, upon the issue of such an order, the court may direct that property belonging to the witness and within the United States may be seized and held to satisfy any judgment which may be rendered against him in the proceeding. . . .

While it appears that the petitioner removed his residence to France in the year 1924, it is undisputed that he was, and continued to be, a citizen of the United States. He continued to owe allegiance to the United States. By virtue of the obligations of citizenship, the United States retained its authority over him, and he was bound by its laws made applicable to him in a foreign country. Thus, although resident abroad, the petitioner remained subject to the taxing power of the United States. For disobedience to its laws through conduct abroad, he was subject to punishment in the courts of the United States. With respect to such an exercise of authority, there is no question of international law, but solely of the purport of the municipal law which establishes the duties of the citizen in relation to his own government. . . . Nor can it be doubted that the United States possesses the power inherent in sovereignty to require the return to this country of a citizen, resident elsewhere, whenever the public interest requires it, and to penalize him in case of refusal. . . . Compare Bartue and the Duchess of Suffolk's Case [citations omitted]. What in England was the prerogative of the sovereign in this respect pertains under our constitutional system to the national authority which may be exercised by the Congress by virtue of the legislative power to prescribe the duties of the citizens of the United States. It is also beyond controversy that one of the duties which the citizen owes to his government is to support the administration of justice by attending its courts and giving his testimony whenever he is properly summoned. And the Congress may provide for the performance of this duty and prescribe penalties for disobedience. . . .

PASSIVE PERSONALITY PRINCIPLE

This form of jurisdiction is based on the nationality of the *victim* when the crime occurs outside of the prosecuting State's territory. It is probably the least used jurisdictional basis, given its potential for abuse.

An unlimited application of the passive personality principle would result in the prosecution of people who harm citizens of the prosecuting State *anywhere* in the world. Although this principle is a recognized basis for exercising jurisdiction under International Law, it is generally not used unless another principle is also applicable. In the Permanent Court of International Justice's *Lotus* case, for example, Turkey relied on the passive personality principle to support its prosecution of the French ship's officer (in addition to territoriality). His conduct harmed Turkish citizens and property interests. Because the conduct took place outside of Turkey, the Court cautiously acknowledged the theoretical applicability of this principle. Some of the judges expressed their belief that International Law does not permit assertions of jurisdiction *exclusively* on this basis. Judge Moore warned that jurisdiction based *solely* on the victim's citizenship would mean "that the citizen [victim] of one country, when he visits another country, takes with him for his 'protection' the law of his own country and subjects those with whom he comes into contact to the operation of that law. In this way an inhabitant of a great commercial city, in which foreigners congregate, may in the course of an hour unconsciously fall under the operation of a number of foreign criminal codes. . . ."[9]

PROTECTIVE PRINCIPLE

Under this theory, the criminal act must threaten the security, territorial integrity, or political independence of the State. The protective principle allows a State to prosecute its own citizens, as well as citizens of other States, for such conduct outside of its territory. However, the perpetrator may choose not to enter the State whose laws have been violated. That State will then have to seek his or her extradition from a State where the offending individual is found.

The protective principle differs from the analogous territorial principle because the criminal's conduct does *not* have to be felt within the territory of the offended State. In a US case distinguishing these two principles, a Canadian citizen made false statements while trying to obtain a visa from the US Consulate in Montreal. The court noted that "the objective principle [requiring that the effects of the crime be directly felt within the territory] is quite distinct from the protective theory. Under the latter, all the elements of the crime occur in the foreign country and jurisdiction exists because these actions have a '*potentially* adverse effect' upon security or governmental functions . . . and there *need not be any actual effect* within the country as would be required under the objective territorial principle."[10]

Most states do not use this theory for exercising jurisdiction. In the leading treatise on International Law as applied by Canada, the authors explain that the focus on "security" underscores the potential for abuse:

> A state may exercise jurisdiction over acts committed abroad that are prejudicial to its security, territorial integrity and political independence. For example, the types of crime covered could include treason, espionage, and counterfeiting of currency, postage stamps, seals, passports, and other public documents.
>
> Canada and other countries such as the United Kingdom have not favored this principle when unaccompanied by other [jurisdictional] factors such as nationality or other forms of allegiance tying the accused to the forum.[11]

UNIVERSALITY PRINCIPLE

Certain crimes spawn "universal interest" because they are sufficiently heinous to be crimes against the entire community of nations. The perpetrators of these crimes are deemed to be enemies of all mankind. Any nation where the perpetrator is found is expected to arrest and try the perpetrator or extradite the criminal to a State that will prosecute. The universality principle has not been applied to civil (noncriminal) wrongs because they are not sufficiently outrageous. Nor has this principle been applied other than in the most shocking or morally degrading cases where it might be invoked as a matter of International Law.

There are several well-recognized universal crimes such as engaging in piracy (the earliest example), harming diplomats, hijacking aircraft, slave trading, engaging in certain wartime activities, and genocide. While some commentators may disagree with the length or completeness of this list, its moral accuracy cannot be contested.

This principle may be invoked when the other principles are not applicable. Piracy, for example, was (and is) usually committed on the high seas rather than within the territorial waters of any nation. The pirates often fled to distant lands or waters. Under the universal principle, all nations have the jurisdiction and the duty to apprehend pirates when they are present.[12]

The most prominent example of prosecution for a universal crime involved acts perpetrated during the Nazi Holocaust in World War II. In *Israel v. Eichmann,* Israel prosecuted Adolf Eichmann, Hitler's chief exterminator, under its Nazi Collaborators Punishment Law. That legislation and the ensuing prosecution were based on the application of universal jurisdiction. None of the other jurisdictional principles were available to Israel. The territorial principle could not apply, because Israel did not become a State until 1948. The nationality principle was inapplicable, because Germany would have to be the prosecuting State. The passive personality principle did not apply, because no victim could possibly be a citizen of the State of Israel during the time that the conduct occurred. If there was no Israel then, the protective principle could not be invoked to protect its interests.

Eichmann did commit crimes, however, constituting genocide against the citizens of various European States before Israel existed (Chapter 11). Eichmann was abducted from Argentina by Israeli commandos to stand trial in Israel. The resulting prosecution was undertaken in Israel's capacity as a member of the community of nations. The State asserted its universal jurisdiction to prosecute Eichmann. In the opinion of Israel's Supreme Court:

> The crimes defined in this [Israeli] law must be deemed to have always been international crimes, entailing individual criminal responsibility: customary international law is analogous to the Common

> Law and develops by analogy and by reference to general principles of law recognized by civilized nations; these crimes share the characteristics of crimes . . . which damage vital international interests, impair the foundations and security of the international community, violate universal moral values and humanitarian principles . . . and the principle of universal jurisdiction over "crimes against humanity" . . . similarly derives from a common vital interest in their suppression. The State prosecuting them acts as agent of the international community, administering international law.[13]

◆ 5.3 EXTRADITION

INTRODUCTION

Section 5.2 presented the five jurisdictional bases for prosecuting individuals engaged in international criminal activity. The theoretical availability of jurisdiction is pointless, however, if the alleged criminal is not present. Some States try criminals *in absentia* under their internal laws. This is not very satisfying, however, if the State cannot enforce its judgment on the convicted criminal. There is no global extradition treaty. Instead, there are hundreds of bilateral treaties listing the mutually agreeable conditions for the signatories to surrender accused or convicted criminals to one another.

Extradition is the customary State practice for securing the presence of the criminal. Under this process, State X requests that State Y turn over an individual located in State Y who has committed a crime that violated the laws of State X. State X thereby requests the extradition through diplomatic channels. If State Y agrees to X's request, then Y surrenders the accused to X authorities. This process has its origins in ancient civilization. The first recorded extradition treaty dates back to 1280 B.C., when an Egyptian Pharaoh foiled an attempted invasion by the bordering Hittite nation. The ensuing peace treaty provided for the exchange of the activists, who had returned to their respective nations, seeking shelter after the unsuccessful invasion attempt.[14]

UTILITY

Extradition treaties are necessary because extradition is not automatic. Under International Law, there is no duty to surrender a criminal to another nation. A citizen of Austria, for example, may commit a crime against his or her State and then flee to Germany. Germany may decide to honor—or ignore—Austria's request for the extradition of the Austrian criminal (absent a treaty). The US Supreme Court stated that "in the absence of a conventional or legislative provision, there is no authority vested in any department of the government to seize a fugitive criminal and surrender him to a foreign power. . . . There is no executive discretion to surrender him to a foreign government, unless that discretion is granted by law. It necessarily follows that as the legal authority does not exist save as it is given by act of Congress or by the terms of a treaty, it is not enough that statute or treaty does not deny the power to surrender. It must be found that [some] statute or treaty confers the power."[15]

On the other hand, there may be an internationally derived duty to surrender a fugitive for trial. Two Libyan intelligence officers were indicted by the UK and the US for their alleged role in the 1988 terrorist bombing of Pan Am Flight 103 over Lockerbie, Scotland, which claimed the lives of 270 people. Libya has refused to surrender them for trial. Several UN Security Council resolutions have demanded their release for trial. Although there was a new round of negotiations in 1998 calling for their trial in The Netherlands, they have yet to stand trial. Libya has countered that the UK and US violated a treaty to which all three (and most nations of the world) are parties. Libya claims that it *has* complied with this treaty. The UK and US are the alleged violators because a State in whose territory an offender is found has the obligation to try or extradite such individuals. Having submitted them to prosecution in Libya, there is supposedly no further Libyan obligation to extradite.[16] In the interim, severe economic sanctions have generated continued UN sanctions and Libyan interest in resolving this extradition matter.

Some countries even prohibit or greatly limit extradition. The Honduran Constitution, for example, prohibits the extradition of Honduran citizens to the United States. The constitutions of both Colombia (from 1991 to 1997) and Slovenia have barred extradition of their citizens to any foreign country. In 1993, a Pennsylvania judge claiming to be a Slovenian national fled from the US to Slovenia after being convicted of corruption—where he remains a fugitive and beyond the reach of US authorities. A related limitation is that—even when States X and Y have entered into such a treaty—the criminal may find a safe haven in State Z, which is not a party to the X–Y treaty.

When granted, extradition overcomes a major jurisdictional limitation closely linked to State sovereignty. Extradition allows States to accomplish indirectly what they cannot do directly. Austria's police agents cannot enter Germany to apprehend criminals. Austria's objective of prosecuting them for their crimes is met, however, when Germany grants Austria's extradition requests. Extradition circumvents the limitation that Austria's territorial jurisdiction cannot extend beyond its borders into Germany. Extradition also accomplishes the broader objective of facilitating international assistance for the apprehension of criminals. The British jurist Lord Russell classically stated in 1896 that "the law of extradition is . . . founded upon the broad principle that it is in the interest of civilised communities that crimes . . . should not go unpunished, and it is a part of the comity of nations that one State should afford to another every assistance towards bringing persons guilty of such crimes to justice."[17] The nation that honors a request for extradition today may want the requesting nation to return that favor tomorrow.

Extradition treaties typically list a mutually acceptable schedule of offenses subject to extradition. The crimes are usually major offenses against the law of both parties to the treaty. For example, Article II of the 1978 Treaty on Extradition Between the United States of America and Japan provides as follows:

> Extradition shall be granted in accordance with the provisions of this Treaty for any offense listed in the Schedule annexed to this Treaty . . . when such an offense is punishable by the laws of both Contracting Parties by death, by life imprisonment, or by deprivation of liberty for a period of more than one year; or for any other offense when such offense is punishable by the federal laws of the United States and by the laws of Japan by death, by life imprisonment, or by deprivation of liberty for a period of more than one year.[18]

The extraditable offenses in this treaty include murder, kidnapping, rape, bigamy, robbery, inciting riots, piracy, drug law violations, bribery, evasion of taxes, unfair business transactions, and violations of export–import laws.

"IRREGULAR" ALTERNATIVES

States do not always depend on extradition treaties when seeking to prosecute certain individuals. They may expel or deport "wanted" individuals without going through the process of extradition—even when there is no extradition treaty. States have also engaged in kidnapping.[19] The State whose sovereignty has been violated may protest. Under International Law, however, the resulting harm is to that State—rather than to the individual, who does not have the same legal capacity to use this violation of International Law for his or her criminal defense. In the *Eichmann* case (§5.2), Israel violated the territorial sovereignty of Argentina when its commandos went to Buenos Aires to capture him for trial in Tel Aviv. He was not able to invoke this violation as a defense to his prosecution.

In the case of some of the more notorious defendants such as Eichmann (the chief architect of the Holocaust's "Final Solution"), few nations are likely to protest such abductions. A national court may not be prone to seriously considering the defense that the *way* in which the criminal was brought to justice requires release. In 1994, Carlos "the Jackal" was finally brought to justice in France. He is the world-famous terrorist who allegedly trained many European and Middle East terrorist organizations during the 1970s and 1980s. As he was undergoing a medical operation in the Sudan, he was drugged and smuggled from the Sudan to Paris. While the Sudanese themselves may have arranged this kidnapping, his technical complaint about the method of capture and informal extradition were rejected by the French court. Alternatively, had French agents surreptitiously entered the Sudan without knowledge of the Sudanese, few nations would likely protest the violation of Sudan's territorial sovereignty.

In what is probably the most internationally criticized case ever decided by a national court, the US Supreme Court effectively took the position that the *absence* of an express provision barring international kidnapping did not deprive the US courts of their jurisdiction to try a kidnapped individual. In 1985, a US Drug Enforcement Administration (DEA) agent, Enrique Camerena, was brutally tortured for many hours in Mexico. A Mexican doctor reportedly kept him alive so that Mexican drug lords could torture him. This was one of the most sadistic murders in recorded history, and the first death of a US drug agent on Mexican soil. An individual convicted of conducting the torture was previously delivered by Mexican police, who pushed him through a fence onto the US side of the border in Texas.

Although there were earlier denials, President Bush conceded that a "system of rewards" was established to ensure the capture of the doctor who kept Camerena alive—specifically, a $50,000 bounty. A Mexican policeman was supposed to deliver this doctor to US authorities, but this arrangement fell through. Doctor Alvarez-Machain was then released from a Mexican jail. A private team of current and former US police officers assisted some Mexican nationals with kidnapping this doctor from his office in Guadalajara, Mexico; he then "appeared" in a Los Angeles federal court to face criminal charges related to the Camerena murder. The Mexican government protested, demanding that Alvarez-Machain be released, because of what it characterized as a violation of the general principles of International Law on territorial sovereignty and jurisdiction.

United States v. Humberto Alvarez-Machain

SUPREME COURT OF THE UNITED STATES, 1992

504 US 655, 112 S.Ct. 2188, 119 *L. Ed.*2d 441

Author's Note: *The defendant's lawyers defended him on several grounds, including the procedural argument that the way by which he appeared before the court was so outrageous that the US courts did not have jurisdiction to hold him for trial. Since the nineteenth century, the US courts had ruled that an individual criminal defendant may not obtain a dismissal based on how he or she was brought before the court—with the modern exception of conduct "shocking the conscience" of the court. In this instance, it was argued that the case against the doctor should be dismissed, because the manner of obtaining his presence for trial in the US violated the basic tenets of "due process of law."*

The US Government did not dispute the facts regarding the kidnapping. The federal trial judge in Los Angeles dismissed this case against the doctor, due to the "shocking" conduct of the US agents in violation of the laws of Mexico and the 1980 extradition treaty between the US and Mexico. In the words of the trial judge: "This court lacks jurisdiction to try this defendant." The intermediate Court of Appeals affirmed this dismissal—holding that the proper remedy was to release this Mexican national from US custody so that he could return to Mexico. The majority of the US Supreme Court's judges reversed, as follows:

COURT'S OPINION. THE CHIEF JUSTICE delivered the opinion of the Court.

The issue in this case is whether a criminal defendant, abducted to the United States from a nation with which it has an extradition treaty, thereby acquires a defense to the jurisdiction of this country's courts. We hold that he does not, and that he may be tried in federal district court for violations of the criminal law of the United States. . . .

Respondent moved to dismiss the indictment, claiming that his abduction constituted outrageous governmental conduct, and that the District Court lacked jurisdiction to try him because he was abducted in violation of the extradition treaty between the United States and Mexico. . . .

In the instant case, the Court of Appeals affirmed the district court's finding that the United States had authorized the abduction of respondent, and that letters from the Mexican government to the United States government served as an official protest of the Treaty violation. Therefore, the Court of Appeals ordered that the indictment against respondent be dismissed and that respondent be repatriated to Mexico. We granted certiorari, and now reverse [for purposes of authorizing further proceedings in the US]. . . .

In *Ker v. Illinois,* 119 US 436, 7 S.Ct. 225, 30 L.Ed. 421 (1886) . . . [this court held] in line with "the highest authorities" that "such forcible abduction is no sufficient reason why the party should not answer when brought within the jurisdiction of the court which has the right to try him for such an offence, and presents no valid objection to his trial in such court.". . .

The only differences between *Ker* and the present case are that *Ker* was decided on the premise that there was no governmental involvement in the abduction; and Peru, from which *Ker* was abducted, did not object to his prosecution. . . . Therefore, our first inquiry must be whether the abduction of respondent from Mexico violated the extradition treaty between the United States and Mexico. If we conclude that the Treaty does not prohibit respondent's abduction, the rule in *Ker* applies, and the court need not inquire as to how respondent came before it.

In construing a treaty, as in construing a statute, we first look to its terms to determine its meaning. The Treaty says nothing about the obligations of the United States and Mexico to refrain from forcible abductions of people from the territory of the other nation, or the consequences under the Treaty if such an abduction occurs.

More critical to respondent's argument is Article 9 of the Treaty which provides: "1. Neither Contracting Party shall be bound to deliver up its own nationals, but the executive authority of the requested Party shall, if not prevented by the laws of that Party, have the power to deliver them up if, in its discretion, it be deemed proper to do so." "2. If extradition is not granted pursuant to paragraph 1 of this Article, the requested Party shall submit the case to its competent authorities for the purpose of prosecution, provided that Party has jurisdiction over the offense."...

[But] Article 9 does not purport to specify the only way in which one country may gain custody of a national of the other country for the purposes of prosecution....

The history of negotiation and practice under the Treaty also fails to show that abductions outside of the Treaty constitute a violation of the Treaty. As the [US] Solicitor General notes, the Mexican government was made aware, as early as 1906, of the *Ker* doctrine, and the United States' position that it applied to forcible abductions made outside of the terms of the United States–Mexico extradition treaty. Nonetheless, the current version of the Treaty, signed in 1978, does not attempt to establish a rule that would in any way curtail the effect of *Ker.* Moreover, although language which would grant individuals exactly the right sought by respondent [Doctor Alvarez] had been considered and drafted as early as 1935 by a prominent group of legal scholars sponsored by the faculty of Harvard Law School [*see* note 4 to this chapter], no such clause appears in the current Treaty.

The language of the Treaty, in the context of its history, does not support the proposition that the Treaty prohibits abductions outside of its terms. The remaining question, therefore, is whether the Treaty should be interpreted so as to include an implied term prohibiting prosecution where the defendant's presence is obtained by means other than those established by the Treaty.

Respondent contends that the Treaty must be interpreted against the backdrop of customary international law, and that international abductions are "so clearly prohibited in international law" that there was no reason to include such a clause in the Treaty itself. The international censure of international abductions is further evidenced, according to respondent [doctor], by the United Nations Charter and the Charter of the Organization of American States. Respondent does not argue that these sources of international law provide an independent basis for the right respondent asserts not to be tried in the United States, but rather that they should inform the interpretation of the Treaty terms....

In sum, to infer from this Treaty and its terms that it prohibits all means of gaining the presence of an individual outside of its terms goes beyond established precedent and practice . . . [and] to imply from the terms of this Treaty that it prohibits obtaining the presence of an individual by means outside of the procedures the Treaty establishes requires a much larger inferential leap, with only the most general of international law principles to support it. The general principles cited by respondent simply fail to persuade us that we should imply in the United States–Mexico Extradition Treaty a term prohibiting international abductions.

Respondent [Alvarez] . . . may be correct that respondent's abduction was "shocking," and that it may be in violation of general international law principles. Mexico has protested the abduction of respondent through diplomatic notes, and the decision of whether respondent should be returned to Mexico, as a matter outside of the Treaty, is a matter for the Executive Branch. We conclude, however, that respondent's abduction was not in violation of the Extradition Treaty between the United States and Mexico, and therefore the rule of *Ker v. Illinois* is fully applicable to this case. The fact of respondent's forcible abduction does not therefore prohibit his trial in a court in the United States for violations of the criminal laws of the United States.

The judgment of the Court of Appeals is therefore reversed, and the case is remanded for further proceedings consistent with this opinion.

◆ *Notes*

1. Mexican (as well as some US and numerous Canadian) newspapers carried accounts of the extreme disappointment of the populace over this kidnapping of a Mexican citizen by agents of the US government for trial in the US. (Ironically, the North American Free Trade Agreement was enacted only two months after this decision.) Mexico and the US began to renegotiate the 1978 extradition treaty interpreted in this case, a process that remains unresolved. *See* Mexico–US Protocol to the Extradition Treaty, done at Washington, D.C., Nov. 13, 1997, reprinted in 37 *Int'l Legal Mat'ls* 154 (1998).

   Doctor Alvarez-Machain was later released for lack of evidence. His US lawyer then filed a $20 million lawsuit against the US, based on the circumstances described in this case and allegations of torture by US agents related to the abduction. In the following year, Costa Rica's Supreme Court effectively discarded the US–Costa Rican extradition treaty on grounds that the *Alvarez-Machain* decision made a mockery of such treaties that are concluded with the US.

2. Professor Louis Henkin, President of the American Society of International Law and Professor Emeritus of International Law at Colombia University School of Law, bashed the Supreme Court's reasoning with his statement that "the Court might have considered whether US courts should accept the fruits of such gross violations of international law by United States officials. The Supreme Court . . . failed international law: It failed to take international law seriously or to help assure that the United States take it seriously." Professor John Rogers of the University of Kentucky School of Law responded to Professor Henkin's Supreme Court bashing as "the kind of misreading that one might expect from a layperson. . . . There is a very respectable argument that permitting such a trial is perfectly consistent with United States obligations under customary international law, and that treaty has changed the customary rule." Professor Malvina Halberstam of Yeshiva University Law School in New York countered the outcry against the Supreme Court decision in *Alvarez-Machain* with her earlier assessment: "Commentators generally agree that the seizure of a person by agents of one state in the territory of another clearly violates international law. They also agree, however, that that does not deprive the court of jurisdiction over the person illegally seized." L. Henkin, "Professor Henkin Replies," *Amer. Soc. Int'l Law Newsletter,* p. 6 (Jan.–Feb. 1993). J. Rogers, "Response to President's Notes on Alvarez-Machain," *Amer. Soc. Int'l Law Newsletter,* p. 6 (Jan.–Feb. 1993). M. Halberstam, "In Defense of the Supreme Court Decision in *Alvarez-Machain,*" 86 *Amer. J. Int'l Law* 736, 737 (1992).

3. In a major 1975 federal case from New York, the defendant—an Italian citizen living in Uruguay—moved to dismiss the indictment against him on facts similar to *Alvarez-Machain*. He was abducted from his home by Uruguay's police, turned over to Brazilian police, tortured, sedated, and flown to the US—where he was immediately placed in the custody of the US Drug Enforcement Administration. He claimed that US officials participated in the abduction and torture. While the alleged conduct was not ultimately proven, the appellate court did rule on this potential defense as follows: "[W]e view due process as now requiring a court to divest itself of jurisdiction . . . where it has been acquired as the result of the government's *deliberate, unnecessary and unreasonable* invasion of the accused's constitutional rights. This conclusion represents but an extension of the well-recognized power of federal courts in the civil [case] context . . . to decline to exercise jurisdiction over a defendant whose presence has been secured by force or fraud." *US v. Toscanino,* 500 F.2d 267, 275 (2nd Cir. 1974) (emphasis supplied).

   This approach has not been adopted in other federal circuits. It has been raised by many defense attorneys, however, as a needed exception to the general rule that defendants cannot rely on the circumstances of their arrest in another country, resulting in their appearance before a US court, to avoid prosecution.

4. Under a little-known Mexican statute, Mexican authorities may act as an extension of the US prosecutor's office in order to try cases in Mexico on the basis of evidence provided by US authorities. In 1993, California prosecutors in Santa Clara County sent materials to Zacatecas, Mexico, resulting in a forty-five-year sentence imposed by the Mexican judge. A Mexican national had killed two people in California. This conviction was widely acclaimed in the US as providing a basis for "new" confidence in the Mexican legal system. From 1985 to 1992, San

Diego prosecutors (in a city on the international border) obtained sixty-three of sixty-four attempted convictions under this Mexican statute based on this alternative US arrangement with Mexico—one never mentioned in *Alvarez-Machain* or related cases.

Now read the following case from South Africa, dealing with precisely the same issue—but deciding that International Law clearly banned South African courts from exercising jurisdiction when agents of the State kidnapped a criminal defendant from another country (Swaziland).

State v. Ebrahim

Appellate Division for East/South-East Circuit, 1991

31 *Int'l Legal Mat'ls* 888 (1992)

Author's Note: *Ebrahim, a South African, previously completed a fifteen-year sentence in South Africa. In 1980, he left South Africa for Swaziland, because he was a leading member of the African National Congress (ANC), Nelson Mandela's political party. He was forcibly abducted from Swaziland in 1986 by unidentified persons. He was taken to the Republic of South Africa where he was formally arrested, tried, convicted of treason, and sentenced to twenty more years of imprisonment. Unlike the situation in* Alvarez-Machain, *in which Mexico protested the US assertion of jurisdiction, Swaziland did not object to the kidnapping in this case. This appeal (decided fifteen months before* Alvarez-Machain*) raises the same question of whether a person abducted by State agents is amenable to the criminal jurisdiction of the courts of the State to which he is abducted. Ebrahim lost his jurisdictional plea in the lower court.*

The appellate court first examined the historical antecedents, including the Roman and Dutch laws that are still applied in South Africa. Previous judicial decisions, in which criminal jurisdiction had been "properly" exercised over abducted persons, were discarded as a result of this case.

Court's Opinion. Appellant argues that the abduction was a violation of the applicable rules of international law, that these rules are part of our law, and that the violation of these rules deprived the trial court of competence to hear the matter. . . .

In *Nduli and Others v. Minister of Justice* [1978] this court decided that where the accused were abducted from Swaziland by members of the South African Police in breach of orders from their commanding officer, the South African state was not responsible and accordingly there was no violation of international law. Consequently the trial court was not deprived of its competence to try the accused. In that case, as in the present case, the accused were formally arrested in South Africa. In the present case, . . . the appellant was abducted from Swaziland to South Africa by persons who were not police but who acted under the authority of some state agency. . . .

According to [Roman Law] Digest 2.1.20:

"Paul Edict book 1: One who administers justice beyond the limits of his territory may be disobeyed with impunity." . . .

This limitation on the legal powers of Roman provincial governors and lawgivers is understandable and was unavoidable in the light of the great number of provinces comprising the Roman Empire in classical times, with their ethnic and cultural diversity, and their different legal systems which the politically pragmatic Romans allowed to remain largely in force in their conquered territories. Until late in the history of the Roman Empire certain provinces were controlled by the Senate and others by the Emperor. Intervention by one province in the domestic affairs of another was a source of potential conflict. . . .

It is inconceivable that the Roman authorities would recognize a conviction and sentence, and allow them to stand, when they were the result of an abduction of a criminal from one province on the order or with the cooperation of the authority of another province. This would not only have been an approval of illegal conduct, and therefore a subversion of authority, but would also have threatened the internal interprovincial peace of the Empire. . . .

One of the foremost Roman–Dutch jurists was Johannes Voet (1647–1713), a Professor of Law in the University of Leiden. According to Voet in his Commentarius and Pandectas 48.3.2:

> "So far however must the limits of jurisdiction be observed in seizing a person accused of crime that, if the judge or his representative pursues him when he has been caught in the judge's own area and has taken flight, he nevertheless cannot seize or pursue further than the point at which the accused has first crossed the boundaries of the pursuer. A judge is regarded as a private person in the area of another, and thus he would in making an arrest in that area be exercising an act of jurisdiction on another's ground, a thing which the laws do not allow.". . .

From the repeated exposition and acceptance of the above rule in its different forms it is clear that the unlawful removal of a person from one jurisdiction to another was regarded as an abduction and as a serious breach of the law in Roman–Dutch law. . . .

It is therefore clear that in Roman–Dutch law a court of one state had no jurisdiction to try a person abducted from another state by agents of the former state. The question must now be considered whether this principle is also part of our present law.

Our [English-based] common law is still substantially Roman–Dutch law as adjusted to local circumstances [in South Africa]. No South African statute grants or denies jurisdiction to our courts to try a person abducted from another state and brought into the Republic of South Africa. . . .

Several fundamental legal principles are contained in these rules, namely the protection and promotion of human rights, good inter-state relations and a healthy administration of justice. The individual must be protected against illegal detention and abduction, the bounds of jurisdiction must not be exceeded, sovereignty must be respected, the legal process must be fair to those affected and abuse of law must be avoided in order to protect and promote the integrity of the administration of justice. This applies equally to the state. When the state is a party to a dispute, as for example in criminal cases, it must come to court with "clean hands." When the state itself is involved in an abduction across international borders, as in the present case, its hands are not clean.

Principles of this kind testify to a healthy legal system of high standard. Signs of this development appear increasingly in the municipal law of other countries. A telling example is that of *United States v. Toscanino* 500 F. 2d 267, to which [defendant's counsel] Mr. Mahomed referred us. The key question for decision in that [1974 US] case was formulated as follows:

> "In an era marked by a sharp increase in kidnapping activities, both here and abroad . . . we face the question as we must in the state of the pleadings, of whether a Federal Court must assume jurisdiction over the person of a defendant who is illegally apprehended abroad and forcibly abducted by Government agents to the United States for the purpose of facing criminal charges here."

The Court refused to follow the decisions of *Ker v. Illinois,* 119 US 342 (1886), and *Frisbie v. Collins,* 342 US 519 (1952), for the following reasons:

> "Faced with a conflict between the two concepts of due process, the one being the restricted version found in *Ker-Frisbie* and the other the expanded and enlightened interpretation expressed in more recent decisions of the Supreme Court, we are persuaded that to the extent that the two are in conflict, the *Ker-Frisbie* version [whereby the offended State but not the abducted individual] must yield. Accordingly we view due process as now requiring a court to divest itself of jurisdiction over the person of a defendant where it has been acquired as the result of the Government's deliberate, unnecessary and unreasonable invasion of the accused's constitutional rights. This conclusion represents but an extension of the well-recognized power of federal courts in the civil context to decline to exercise jurisdiction over a defendant whose presence has been secured by force or fraud" (at 275). . . .

It follows that, according to our common law, the trial court had no jurisdiction to hear the case against the appellant. Consequently his conviction and sentence cannot stand.

AVOIDING EXTRADITION

States do not honor extradition requests for a variety of reasons. The laws of the requesting State may be perceived as violating fundamental human rights. For example, Canada does not apply the death penalty in criminal cases. The US does. Canada initially refused extradition of a US citizen accused of the sex-torture slaying of thirteen people in 1985 in California. In 1991, a Canadian jet flew this individual to the US after the Canadian Supreme Court restricted Canada's death-penalty limitation on extradition by interpreting the Canadian rule as inapplicable to non-Canadian citizens. In 1989, however, the European Court of Human Rights barred Great Britain from extraditing a West German citizen to the US—where he would face the death penalty.

Extradition treaties typically require that extraditable offenses be those that would violate the laws of *both* parties to the treaty. The conduct charged may violate the laws of both State X and State Y, but Y may prefer to try the accused. When Y's laws have *not* been violated, however, State practice varies on whether Y can refuse extradition and itself try the accused. Roorkee University (India) Professor Prakash Chandra comments on this contrast as follows: "Some jurists—Grotius, Vattel and Kent among them—hold that a state is bound to give up such fugitives but the majority . . . appear to deny such obligation. But mutual interests of states for the maintenance of law and order and the common desire to ensure that serious crimes do not go unpunished require that nations should cooperate with one another in surrendering fugitive criminals to the state in which the crime was committed."[20]

There is also a tendency to strictly interpret extradition treaties and their implementing statutes. For example, extradition may be granted only when a crime has been committed within the territorial jurisdiction of the offended State seeking extradition from the State where the fugitive is located. In 1997, the Nova Scotia Supreme Court denied extradition in a case in which Taiwanese crew members threw several Romanian stowaways overboard to their deaths. This was done in circumstances in which the stowaways could not reasonably survive. While both Romania and Taiwan desired the crew members' extradition for murder, the Canadian court determined that extradition was not warranted because the crime was not committed within Romanian or Taiwanese territory.[21]

Another reason for refusing extradition is the "political offense" exception to extradition. International treaties typically include some form of what might be characterized as an escape clause in order to provide the requested State an opportunity to deny extradition. An all-too-familiar reason for the refusal is that the requested State clandestinely supports the acts of the individual charged with a crime in the requesting State. Extradition can be denied when the requested State characterizes the crime as a "political offense." In an amendment to the 1986 US–UK extradition treaty, for example, "extradition shall not occur if . . . the request for extradition has in fact been made with a view to try to punish him on account of . . . political opinions."

The application of the political defense exception to extradition produced a useful breakthrough in the stormy political relationship between Taiwan and China. In 1994, China conceded that Taiwan could exclude certain hijackers from repatriation to China if a Taiwanese court found that the hijackers acted out of political motives. Between April 1993 and August 1994, there had been twelve such aircraft hijackings from China by dissidents seeking asylum in Taiwan. China ultimately decided to recognize this defense, avoiding the closing of this avenue of escape. As a result, China now recognizes the right of Taiwanese vessels to patrol the waters of the Taiwan Straits as well as the jurisdiction of Taiwanese courts over such matters.

What *is* a political offense? This question is subject to much debate. The 1935 Draft Extradition Treaty produced by the Harvard Research in International Law project used this perennial definition: "[T]he term 'political offense' includes treason, sedition and espionage, whether committed by one or more persons; it includes any offense connected with the activities of an organized group directed against the security or governmental system of the requesting State; and it does not exclude other offenses having a political objective." The commentary to this proposed article adds that no "satisfactory and generally acceptable definition of a political offense has been found yet, and such as have been given are of little practical value."[22] Sixty-five years later, there is still no consensus on what constitutes a political crime for the purpose of standardizing this basis for avoiding extradition.[23]

State practice vests the decision about the "political" nature of the defendant's crime with the *requested* State that has custody of the offender. Interpretations always depend on the circumstances of the particular case.

Under Article IV of the above US–Japan treaty, for example, extradition "shall not be granted . . . [w]hen the offense for which extradition is requested is a political offense or when it appears that the request for extradition is made with a view to prosecuting, trying or punishing the person sought for a political offense. If any question arises as to the application of this provision, the decision of the requested Party shall prevail." This typical "political offense" treaty exception is left purposefully vague. It therefore allows the requested party to determine unilaterally what constitutes a "political offense."

Because of dissatisfaction with the "political offense" exception to extradition, the 1998 UN Convention for the Suppression of Terrorist Bombings was the first multilateral treaty to specifically prohibit a party from allowing this defense to extradition.[24]

◆ 5.4 STATE JURISDICTION AND THE INTERNET

SHANGHAI, China—The Chinese government has extended it crackdown on dissidents to the Internet. Lin Hai, a Shanghai computer company owner, was prosecuted for giving the addresses of 30,000 Chinese computer users to *VIP Reference,* a pro-democracy journal published on the Internet by Chinese dissidents in the United States.

This was the first subversion prosecution of its kind. While the ruling Communist Party hopes to exploit the Internet commercially, the government does not want it to become an international forum for dissidents. Foreign reporters were not allowed to enter the courthouse, while police warned local residents not to talk to foreign reporters. The US Embassy in Beijing expressed concern that this was a closed trial.

Chinese efforts to control the Internet include its technology for blocking access to "subversive" web sites. Internet service providers must also register all users with the government.

—Adapted from Joe MacDonald, "China Prosecutes E-Mail 'Crime,'" Associated Press, Dec. 5, 1998

There is an attribute of the contemporary Information Revolution that States find increasingly unmanageable. Individuals are using the Internet to challenge the State's traditional ability to control activities occurring in and beyond its borders.

Some of the traditional jurisdictional theory—such as the "effects doctrine" and the protective principle of jurisdiction (§5.2)—provide the arguable bases for governmental control of individual and corporate activity on the Internet. Nevertheless, this is a new area of the law that has not been adequately addressed in the international dialogue about the emerging shift from a traditional domain toward an electronic environment. Both States and international organizations are therefore applying national law and entering into treaties to retain what power they can summon over offensive uses of the Internet—even when the conduct does not occur solely within their borders.

A NOT-SO-HYPOTHETICAL SCENARIO

An online travel service called OTS sells airline tickets to passengers in various markets. Much of OTS's business is done on the Internet. OTS asks Jane for her name, mailing address, telephone number, and e-mail address when she contacts its Web site. OTS then collects the following data to complete the transaction: Jane's name and mailing address so that OTS can deliver the ticket to her; her telephone number, should the airline have to contact Jane about a last-minute cancellation or change; and Jane's e-mail address, so that OTS can send confirmation that her ticket has been issued.

It is reasonable to conclude that by voluntarily engaging in this transaction Jane has consented to this use of her personal data. But OTS also wishes to use Jane's personal data for another purpose. OTS sends her e-mails containing announcements about its upcoming travel specials. OTS shares or sells data about Jane and other consumers to other companies. They use this information to market their own products. Jane has not consented to her personal data being used for these other purposes unrelated to her ticket purchase from OTS.

This recurring scenario raises important privacy questions. The use of computers, electronic data storage, and the Internet geometrically increased at the end of the twentieth century. It has now become even easier to collect, process, and disseminate personal information about individuals—with the click of a computer keyboard or mouse. At the same time, however, governments and the public have become aware of the lack of privacy illustrated by this routine transaction. One might envision a Fortune 500 company, whose data executive is bound for a country that does not afford the same degree of privacy as the country from which she has departed. The executive's laptop and various drives might be confiscated. Industry self-regulation alone is unlikely to protect Jane from the dissemination of her personal information by anonymous parties or foreign governments. National governments and international organizations are beginning to employ a regulatory approach to issues involving Jane's data privacy.

The European Privacy Directive (EPD) is a classic illustration of government control of Internet activities. This 1995 edict of the European Parliament and European Council stresses the privacy-oriented European Convention for the Protection of Human Rights and Fundamental Freedoms. The new rules became effective in October 1998. They prohibit, among other things, the transfer of data about individuals to non–EU nations that have not adopted sufficient privacy protection. Under the EPD, data collectors must disclose:

- the purpose for which the data is collected and used;
- who will receive, use, and process the data;
- the consequences of failing to provide the information; and
- the name and address of the entity collecting the data.

Individuals must also be informed of their right to obtain a copy of their personal data so they can correct any errors. Once obtained, the EPD requires that data be used and stored only for the purposes for which it was collected. Personal data must be stored in a secure manner that reasonably protects it from illegal use. It must be accurate, up-to-date, and kept only as long as is necessary to fulfill the purpose for which it was obtained. Greater protection applies to "sensitive" personal data on race or ethnic origin, political opinions, religious or philosophical beliefs, trade-union membership, health, and sexuality.

One who has not personally experienced the intrusive policies of the Nazi regime should acknowledge that Europeans are generally more concerned with privacy than are societies such as the United States, where having one's name in an electronic database might be more of an annoyance than a historical reminder of the Third Reich of the 1930s and 1940s. The EPD could result in the confiscation of laptops at airports if the data therein arguably contains offensive data. An executive such as Germany's former CompuServe Chief might violate the EPD if his computer contains a company's customer list of German citizens for use in the US. The European Directive thus expresses the European Parliament's concern about "data-processing systems [that] are designed to serve man; whereas they must, whatever the nationality or residence of natural persons, respect their fundamental rights and freedoms, notably the right to privacy, and contribute to economic and social progress, trade expansion and the well-being of individuals. . . ."[25]

The ultimate European Community objective is to ensure that its States establish criteria for data processing that falls within the terms of this policy directive, as well as ensuring that its citizens never again suffer the indignities of another era—when the rights of the individual were clearly compromised because of governmental excesses. As Article 7 of the Directive demonstrates:

> Member States shall provide that personal data may be processed only if:
>
> (a) the data subject [meaning the individual whose name is contained in any database] has unambiguously given his consent; or . . .
>
> (c) processing is necessary for compliance with a legal obligation to which the [information] controller is subject; or
>
> (d) processing is necessary in order to protect the vital interests of the data subject; or
>
> (e) processing is necessary for the performance of a task carried out in the public interest or in the exercise of official authority. . . .

One can readily discern that the government of any European member State can thereby access desired information *without* the data subject's consent whenever the government deems it necessary to investigate whether the individual is complying with local law (c), when "vital interests" not defined in the EPD are at stake (d), or as necessary in the "public interest" or "exercise of official authority" (e). Article 7, then, balances the sometimes competing needs to protect the individual's privacy and satiate governmental needs on a case-by-case basis.

The major barrier to the orderly transfer of data between the EU and other nations will likely be Article 25 of the EPD. The first paragraph requires member States to guarantee that "the transfer to a third country of personal data which are undergoing processing or are intended for processing after transfer may take place only if . . . the third country in question ensures an adequate level of protection." As a result, foreign companies doing business in the European Community may find their ability to engage in electronic commerce greatly restricted by the region's privacy concerns. Should litigation be initiated, a foreign company in other regions of the world may contend that the Directive is an extraterritorial law—in this case, generated by an international organization rather than a State—that effectively prohibits electronic commerce by business entities not located within Europe, not having any presence there, and not marketing there in any tangible manner. This issue will likely be one focus of the comprehensive World Trade Organization (§13.2) exploration of Internet issues pursuant to its Declaration on Global Electronic Commerce.[26]

A related problem is evolving in nations with comparatively expansive jurisdictional rules. For example, consider whether an Italian hotel with a Web site has to litigate claims filed by a guest who does the following: She views the hotel's Web site in the US, goes to Italy to stay in the hotel, gets hurt at the hotel, and sues when she returns to her own country rather than seek a remedy in Italy:

Weber v. Jolly Hotels

UNITED STATES DISTRICT COURT, EASTERN DISTRICT OF NEW JERSEY, 1997

977 F. Supp. 327

Author's Note: *This case arose out of Eileen Weber's accident while she was a guest at the defendant's hotel in Italy (Itajolly Compagnia Italiana Dei). When she sued the hotel in New Jersey, its lawyer asked the Court to dismiss this case because a US court should not have the "personal jurisdiction" over the person of the defendant Italian hotel in New Jersey (as opposed to an Italian court, where the incident giving rise to this suit occurred). The judge decided not to grant the motion to dismiss this case. Instead, the judge granted the plaintiff's request to transfer the case to the Southern District of New York—where a court might have the judicial power over the Italian hotel.*

Case and statutory citations have been omitted.

COURT'S OPINION. WOLIN, District Judge.

BACKGROUND

Defendant is an Italian corporation and its principal place of business is in Valdagno, Italy. Defendant owns and operates thirty-two hotels in Italy, and independent subsidiaries own and operate hotels in Holland, France, Belgium, and New York. Defendant does not conduct any business in New Jersey. However, it does provide "photographs of hotel rooms, descriptions of hotel facilities, information about numbers of rooms and telephone numbers" on the Internet.

In July 1993, defendant and Grand Circle Travel, a Massachusetts corporation, entered into an agreement whereby one of [the] defendant's hotels, the Jolly Diodoro Hotel in Taormina, Sicily, Italy, would allot a certain number of rooms per week at the hotel for Grand Circle Travel during the 1994 calendar year. . . .

Grand Circle Travel and plaintiff have a relationship [whereby] . . . plaintiff went on trips arranged by Grand Circle Travel. In late 1993 or early 1994, Grand Circle Travel sent plaintiff a brochure that described a tour of Italy. On February 25, 1994, plaintiff booked a trip to Italy through Grand Circle Travel. Included in the trip was a stay at the Jolly Diodoro Hotel.

On December 7, 1994, plaintiff sustained injuries when she fell at the Jolly Diodoro Hotel. At the time of the accident, plaintiff was a guest of the hotel. Plaintiff is a citizen of New Jersey. . . .

On June 26, 1995, plaintiff filed a Complaint and Jury Demand in the Superior Court of New Jersey, Law Division, Bergen County. She alleged that defendant knew or should have known of the dangerous condition on its premises. The case was removed to the United States District Court for the District of New Jersey on diversity grounds.

Defendant now moves the Court to dismiss the case for lack of personal jurisdiction.

DISCUSSION

1. Personal Jurisdiction: Standards . . .

The purpose of restricting personal jurisdiction is to protect the individual interests of non-resident defendants. A court may exercise personal jurisdiction over a non-resident defendant only where "minimum contacts" exist such that the exercise of jurisdiction "does not offend 'traditional notions of fair play and substantial justice.'" A defendant establishes minimum contacts with a forum state by committing some act by which he purposefully avails himself of the privilege of conducting activities within the forum state, thus invoking the benefits and protection of its laws. These contacts must be of the nature such that the individual non-resident defendant "should reasonably anticipate being haled into court there." What constitutes minimum contacts varies with the "quality and the nature of defendant's activity." . . .

2. Analysis

Plaintiff asserts that the Court has personal jurisdiction over defendant [because] . . . defendant's use of the Internet is equivalent to advertising in New Jersey. . . .

The [US] Supreme Court has long recognized that personal jurisdiction must adapt to progress in technology. Litigation involving the Internet has increased as the Internet has developed and expanded. Although the Internet is a new medium that raises new issues for the courts, district courts have successfully applied the principles established by . . . [the relevant case law] to cases involving the Internet. The cases that have addressed the relationship between the Internet and personal jurisdiction "reveal that the likelihood that personal jurisdiction can be constitutionally exercised is directly proportionate to the nature and quality of commercial activity that an entity conducts over the Internet."

The cases dealing with this issue can be divided into three categories. . . . The third category involves passive Web sites; i.e., sites that merely provide information or advertisements to users. Districts courts do not exercise jurisdiction in the latter cases because "a finding of jurisdiction . . . based on an Internet Web site would mean that there would be nationwide (indeed, worldwide) personal jurisdiction over anyone and everyone who establishes an Internet Web site. Such nationwide [or international] jurisdiction is not consistent with traditional personal jurisdiction case law. . . ."

Despite plaintiff's attempts to the contrary, this case clearly belongs in category three. Defendant placed information about its hotels on the Internet as an advertisement, not as a means of conducting business. In the past year, two district courts have refused to exercise jurisdiction over defendants who have a passive connection to the Internet. . . .

This Court agrees with the finding in *Hearst* that advertising on the Internet falls under the same rubric as advertising in a national magazine. This Circuit has consistently held that advertising in national publications "does not constitute 'continuous and substantial' contacts with the forum state." . . . ("In an age of modern advertising and national media publications and markets, plaintiffs' argument that such conduct would make a defendant amenable to suit wherever the advertisements were aired would substantially undermine the law of personal jurisdiction."). In addition, advertising on the Internet is not tantamount to directing activity at or to purposefully availing oneself of a particular forum.

Thus, the Court finds that exercising jurisdiction over a defendant who merely advertises its services or product on the Internet would violate the Due Process Clause of the Fourteenth Amendment. Exercising jurisdiction in such a case would be unjust and would disrespect the principles established by [case law]. . . .

3. Plaintiff's Request to Transfer

Plaintiff requests that the Court transfer the case to the Southern District of New York. . . .

In this instance, defendant has a subsidiary, Migdal Madison N.V., that owns a hotel in New York City. Migdal Madison is a Curacao corporation. Plaintiff claims that the New York hotel accepts reservations for all of defendant's hotels in Italy. Thus, plaintiff concludes that a New York court would have jurisdiction over defendant. . . .

Although the [New Jersey] Court is sensitive to the policies underlying section 1406(a) [case transfers] and to the dockets in other districts, the interests of justice dictate that this case be transferred to the Southern District of New York. The question of whether personal jurisdiction exists in New York should be decided after the transfer.

CONCLUSION

Thus, the Court finds that it does not have personal jurisdiction over defendant, but will order that the case be transferred to the Southern District of New York.

◆ *Notes & Questions*

1. Although the judge believed he lacked the power to require the Italian hotel to litigate this matter in New Jersey, he ruled that another court—within a dozen miles of his own—*might* have that power. Instead of this plaintiff, if you were hurt at the hotel, should you be able to return to the US and sue an Italian defendant in a New York court?
2. In Chapter 11 on Human Rights, we will discuss a US statute, 28 US Code §1350, and a case called *Filartiga*—whereby a New York court exercised such jurisdiction over a defendant from Paraguay, who killed the plaintiff's father in Paraguay. One could argue that this is an "extraterritorial" exercise of jurisdiction and well beyond the competence of a national court to adjudicate: a case between a plaintiff and defendant who are citizens of another country for recovery of damages for acts done outside the forum country. From an international perspective, the propriety of such jurisdiction might depend on factors yet to be discussed in this course (human rights perspectives regarding universal crimes, discussed in Chapter 9 on international adjudication).

◆ SUMMARY

1. Sovereignty is the right of a nation to govern the affairs of its inhabitants and to be free from external control. Jurisdiction refers to the power of a State to enact laws proscribing certain criminal conduct, to apprehend offenders, and to try them for violations.
2. The five internationally recognized bases for state jurisdiction are: (1) territorial principle, (2) nationality principle, (3) passive personality principle, (4) protective principle, and (5) universality principle.
3. Territorial jurisdiction is based on the location of the defendant's act. The two applications relevant to this course are the "subjective" principle (when the conduct commences within a State) and the "objective" principle (when the conduct commences outside but has the requisite "effects" within the prosecuting State).
4. Nationality jurisdiction is based on the nationality of the *defendant*. The passive personality principle, by comparison, is based on the nationality of the *victim*.
5. The protective principle authorizes a State to exercise jurisdiction over individuals for their criminal acts occurring outside its borders—when those acts threaten the security, territorial integrity, or political independence of the state. The protective principle differs from the territorial principle in that the effects of the defendant's conduct do *not* have to be felt within the territory of the nation that wishes to exercise its jurisdiction in the case.
6. The universality principle covers certain crimes that are considered to be against the entire community of nations. Any nation where the perpetrator of such a crime is found has the jurisdiction to arrest the criminal (who may be extradited). Such crimes include piracy, hijacking, and genocide.
7. Extradition is the process whereby one nation surrenders someone accused of a crime to another nation. It aids in the prosecution of criminals, because a nation cannot enter another's territory to apprehend them. To do so tarnishes the sovereign equality of all nations.
8. Nations need not extradite an accused in the absence of a treaty. Extradition treaties typically list a mutually acceptable schedule of offenses, subjecting those who commit them to extradition.
9. International Law prohibits one nation from abducting a criminal defendant from the territory of another nation. Authorities are divided as to whether the court of an abducting nation retains the jurisdiction to try kidnapped defendants.
10. Most extradition treaties contain an escape clause allowing the denial of extradition when a listed crime is a "political offense." The requested State has the dis-

cretion to deny extradition. There are no clearly adopted standards for the exercise of this discretion.

11. There is a growing concern about the extent to which a nation may civilly or criminally prosecute an individual or company for materials sent by e-mail or appearing on Web sites. As applied in many instances, this is arguably an extraterritorial exercise of State jurisdiction over events occurring in other States. Introducing materials into another country via such devices may subject the author to criminal prosecution or personal jurisdiction in civil damage cases.

◆ PROBLEMS

Problem 5.A (end of §5.2) In 1988, two Libyan citizens apparently planned and executed the bombing of Pan Am Flight 103 over Lockerbie, Scotland (within the United Kingdom). All 259 passengers aboard the flight met very violent deaths, and many more on the ground were killed by the falling plane. Pan Am is a US corporation. There were both UK and US citizens aboard this ill-fated flight.

The UK and the US indicted these individuals and demanded that Libya surrender them for trial—backed by a UN Security Council resolution demanding the same. (Libya said that it would cooperate, but only if former US President Ronald Reagan and former UK Prime Minister Margaret Thatcher be tried simultaneously for bombing Tripoli in 1986. That bombing was a reprisal for Libya's earlier bombing of a Berlin discotheque wherein a number of US soldiers died.)

On what bases may the UK and the US properly apply their criminal jurisdiction under the principles of "international criminal jurisdiction"?

Problem 5.B (end of §5.2) The Federal Kidnapping Act now provides as follows:

> (a) Whoever unlawfully seizes, confines, inveigles, decoys, kidnaps, abducts, or carries away and holds for ransom or reward or otherwise any person . . . when—
>
> (1) the person is willfully transported in interstate or foreign commerce;
>
> (2) any such act against the person is done within the special maritime and territorial jurisdiction of the United States;
>
> (3) any such act against the person is done within the special aircraft jurisdiction of the United States as defined in section 46501 of title 49;
>
> (4) the person is a foreign official, an internationally protected person [e.g., a diplomat] . . . ; or
>
> (5) the person is among those officers and employees designated in section 1114 of this title and any such act against the person is done while the person is engaged in, or on account of, the performance of official duties;
>
> shall be punished by imprisonment for any term of years or for life and, if the death of any person results, shall be punished by death or life imprisonment. . . .
>
> (e) If the victim of an offense under subsection (a) is an internationally protected person outside the United States, the United States may exercise jurisdiction over the offense if (1) the victim is a representative, officer, employee, or agent of the United States, (2) an offender is a national of the United States, or (3) an offender is afterwards found in the United States.

Assume that Student 1 is a defense lawyer, retained by a foreign national named Xena. She was brought to the US to stand trial. The charge is kidnapping a US citizen (under the quoted act). Xena was riding her horse in a faraway land known as Olympus when she noticed that "Citizen" was mistreating a local individual who was working on Citizen's property in Olympus. Citizen is the US diplomatic representative to the mythical country of Olympus. Xena plucks Citizen from the ground, straps him on her horse, and carries him with her throughout Olympus and a neighboring nation for several days. Her purpose is to show him that life is difficult enough without foreign officials coming to Olympus and mistreating local Olympians.

Student 2 is an attorney in the US Department of Justice prosecuting the criminal defendant Xena. She was extradited from Olympus, when the US requested her presence for trial on kidnapping charges.

Both lawyers are appearing before a specialized tribunal, whose obligation is to determine whether US and International Law would authorize her prosecution under this US legislation.

Problem 5.C (after *State v. Ebrahim* Case in §5.3) The US Supreme Court and the South African Supreme Court arrived at very different results on the issue of whether the abducting State's courts have the jurisdiction to proceed when the State is involved in the abduction of a defendant from foreign soil.

Assume that a South African citizen is abducted, through arrangements made by US agents, in order to stand trial in the US. South Africa protests, based on an extradition treaty between the two countries. South Africa and the US decide to resolve this matter in the International Court of Justice. The issue for the court is whether the US has the jurisdiction under International Law to proceed with the criminal case against the South African defendant.

Two students (or groups) will argue this matter before class members, who will serve as the ICJ judges deciding the case based on those presentations.

Problem 5.D (after *Jolly Hotels* Case in §5.4) In January 1998, a German prosecutor charged the former German Chief of Staff for CompuServe, a US-based Internet service provider (ISP), with transmitting child pornography over the Internet. In May 1998, a German trial court in Munich imposed a two-year term of probation and a DM 100,000 fine (US $57,000). An expert for the defense testified that the defendant could not have known about the child pornography being transmitted over the Internet by some CompuServe customers. The prosecutor dropped the charge, although the judge still found Felix Somm guilty. He was thus legally accountable for pornographic content transferred from private individuals to German citizens over the Internet, via CompuServe, although the Internet traffic may be as high as 100 gigabytes per day. Further details are available at www.freudenstadt.net/somm/english.html.

Assume that Joe, one of those child pornography providers, posted offensive materials on the Internet. Joe is a private CompuServe customer, living in New Jersey. He uses CompuServe as his ISP to send such information to other interested individuals. His materials are viewed in Germany. The German prosecutor issues an arrest warrant and thereafter seeks Joe's extradition to Germany for prosecution. This will be an important test case for the German government in its efforts to keep Internet pornography from coming into Germany. Joe is about to be extradited to Germany for sending an e-mail attachment to German citizens (and the rest of the cyberworld). It contained samples of the pornographic materials that are on his personal Web site. This site is provided by CompuServe, a US corporation. Joe's personal Web site (and its e-mail capacity) is one of the thousands of pages that CompuServe customers establish and insert desired content.

Two students—representing the respective German and US Departments of State—will debate whether extradition is a good idea in this case. Extradition in this case could mean future foreign prosecutions and extradition requests by other countries of the world. These governments would be interested in controlling the information made available to their citizens—because of e-mails sent by, and personal Web sites maintained by, millions of US citizens. The German government's interests include blocking the transmission of illegal materials via the Internet. The US interests include not wanting other governments to impose their views of what is illegal on US citizens.

◆ BIBLIOGRAPHY

§5.1 Definitional Setting

L. Henkin, "The Mythology of Sovereignty," ch. 24 in R. MacDonald (ed.), *Essays in Honour of Wang Tieya* 351 (Dordrecht, Neth.: Martinus Nijhoff, 1994).

"The Jurisdiction of States," ch. XII in O. Schachter, *International Law in Theory and Practice* 250 (Dordrecht, Neth.: Martinus Nijhoff, 1991).

R. Lapidoth, "Sovereignty in Transition," 45 *J. Int'l Affairs* 2 (1992).

K. Meessen (ed.), *Extraterritorial Jurisdiction in Theory and Practice* (London: Kluwer, 1996).

§5.2 Five Jurisdictional Principles

"International Conflict of Laws," ch. 10 in M. Janis, *An Introduction to International Law* 321 (2nd ed. Boston: Little, Brown & Co., 1993).

"Jurisdiction over Persons," ch. 9 in G. von Glahn, *Law Among Nations: An Introduction to Public International Law* 146 (7th ed. Boston: Allyn and Bacon, 1996).

C. Oliver, "The Jurisdiction (Competence) of States," ch. 15 in M. Bedjaoui (ed.), *International Law: Achievements and Prospects* 307 (Dordrecht, Neth.: Martinus Nijhoff, 1991).

§5.3 Extradition

M. Bassiouni, *International Criminal Law: Procedural and Enforcement Mechanisms* (Ardsley, NY: Transnational, 1998).

A Garcia-Mora, "Criminal Jurisdiction of a State over Fugitives Brought from a Foreign Country by Force or Fraud: A Comparative Study," 32 *Indiana Law J.* 427 (1957).

J. Gurule, "Terrorism, Territorial Sovereignty, and the Forcible Apprehension of International Criminals Abroad," 17 *Hastings Int'l & Comp. L. Rev.* 457 (1994).

E. Nadelmann, *Cops Across Borders: The Internationalization of US Criminal Law Enforcement* (University Park, PA: Penn. State Univ. Press, 1993).

§5.4 State Jurisdiction and the Internet

M. Rotenberg, *The Privacy Law Sourcebook: United States Law, International Law, and Recent Developments* (Wash., D.C.: Electronic Privacy Info. Center, 1998).

S. Salbu, "Who Should Govern the Internet? Monitoring and Supporting a New Frontier," 11 *Harv. J. Law & Tech.* 429 (1998).

"Symposium on Jurisdiction and the Internet," 32 *Int'l Lawyer* 959–1191 (1998).

◆ ENDNOTES

1. B. Jankovic, *Public International Law* 115–117 (Dobbs Ferry, NY: Transnational, 1983) (Pravo translation).
2. *See generally* "Territory and Espionage," ch. 3 in J. Kish, *International Law and Espionage* (The Hague. Neth.: Martinus Nijhoff, 1995).
3. **Hostage law:** 18 USC §1203. **Drug law:** 46 USC §1901 et. seq. **Environmental case:** *Environmental Defense Fund, Inc. v. Massey,* 986 Fed.2d 528 (D.C. Cir. 1993). **Abduction case:** *See* text of *US v. Alvarez-Machain* case in §5.3. **Antitrust case:** *Hartford Fire Insur. Co. v. Merrett Underwriting Agency Management. Ltd.,* 509 US 764, 113 S.Ct. 2891, 125 *L. Ed.* 2d 612 (1993). **Refugee case:** *See* text of *Sale v. Haitian Council* case in §4.2.
4. Further readings are available in J. Paust et al., *International Criminal Law: Cases and Materials* (Durham, NC: Carolina Academic Press, 1996); and L. Sunga, *The Emerging System of International Criminal Law* (The Hague, Neth.: Kluwer, 1997).
5. I. Cameron, *The Protective Principle of International Criminal Jurisdiction* 11–12 (Aldershot, Eng.: Dartmouth, 1994).
6. "The Research in International Law of the Harvard Law School, Jurisdiction with Respect to Crime," 29 *Amer. J. Int'l L. Supp.* 443 (1935) (hereinafter Harvard Research).
7. "Regarding *Penati,* Case No. 30," reported in 46 *Annual Digest and Reports of Public Int'l L. Cases* 74.
8. Human rights violations concern all States, however. Chapter 11 will explore the applicability of International Law to a State's treatment of its own citizens within its own borders.
9. *"The S.S. Lotus (France v. Turkey),"* *PCIJ,* ser. A, No. 10 (1927) (Judge Moore, dissenting).
10. *US v. Pizzarusso,* 388 Fed.2d 8 (2nd Cir. 1968), *cert. den'd,* 392 US 936, 88 S.Ct. 2306, 20 *L. Ed.* 2d 1395 (1968) (emphasis supplied).
11. H. Kindred et al., *International Law: Chiefly as Interpreted and Applied in Canada* 433 (5th ed. Toronto: Edmond Montgomery, 1993).
12. "Symposium on Piracy in Contemporary National and International Law," 21 *Calif. West. Int'l L.J.* 104 (1990).
13. *Attorney-General of Israel v. Adolf Eichmann,* Dist. Ct. of Jerusalem; reported in 36 *Int'l Law Rep.* 5, 15 (1968) (decided in 1961).
14. B. Yarnold, *International Fugitives: A New Role for the International Court of Justice* 11 (New York: Praeger, 1991).
15. *Valentine v. United States ex rel. Neidecker,* 299 *US Rep.* 5, 9, 57 S.Ct. 100, 102, 81 *L. Ed.* 5 (1936).
16. *See* "Questions of Interpretation and Application of the 1971 Montreal Convention Arising from the Aerial Incident at Lockerbie *(Libyan Arab Jamahiriya v. United Kingdom)*" at the ICJ's Web site: www.icj-cij.org/idocket/iluk/iluk2frame.htm.
17. *Re Arton,* 1 *Queen's Bench* 108, 111 (1896).
18. 31 *US Treaties* 892 (1979); *US Treaties and Other International Agreements Series,* No. 9625 (1980).
19. **Exclusion and deportation:** Evans, "Acquisition of Custody over the International Fugitive Offender—Alternatives to Extradition: A Survey of United States Practice," 40 *Brit. Yearbk. Int'l L.* 77 (1964). **Force:** Glennon, "State-Sponsored Abduction: A Comment on *United States v. Alvarez-Machain,*" 86 *Amer. J. Int'l L.* 746 (1992).
20. P. Chandra, *International Law* 80 (New Delhi: Vikas Pub.). *See also* "The Eisler Extradition Case," 43 *Amer. J. Int'l L.* 487 (1949), a British case in which the applicable laws of Great Britain differed from those of the US.
21. *Romania v. Cheng,* 114 C.C.C.3rd 289 (Nova Scotia S.Ct, 1997).
22. "Draft Convention on Extradition," Harvard Research, pp. 112–113 (cited in note 6 above).
23. G. Gilbert, "The Political Offence Exemption," ch. 6 in *Transnational Fugitive Offenders in International Law: Extradition and Other Mechanisms* 203 (The Hague, Neth.: Martinus Nijhoff, 1998).
24. Art. 5, reprinted in 37 *Int'l Legal Mat'ls* 249 (1998).
25. Directive 95/46/EC of the European Parliament and of the Council of Oct. 24, 1995, on the protection of individuals with regard to the processing of personal data and on the free movement of such data, *Official Journal of the European Communities,* No. L 281/31, preambular para. (1).
26. "The General Council shall, by its next meeting in special session, establish a comprehensive work programme to examine all trade-related issues relating to global electronic commerce, including those issues identified by Members." www.wto.org/wto/anniv/ecom.htm (adopted 20 May 1998).

CHAPTER SIX

Range of Sovereignty

CHAPTER OUTLINE

TRENTO, ITALY (AP)—AN ITALIAN JUDGE ON Monday dropped the case against the crew members of a Marine jet that severed a ski gondola cable in the Alps, leaving the decision to prosecute with U.S. courts. Twenty people were killed in the February 3 [1998] accident, which set off a crisis in U.S.–Italian relations and demands by some for a closing of U.S. bases in Italy.

Judge Carlo Ancona ruled that the Italian courts lacked jurisdiction in the case. Trento Prosecutor Francantonio Granero had pushed for manslaughter charges in Italy even though the Italian government has acquiesced in American prosecution of the four crewmen.

—http://cnn.com:80/WORLD/europe/9807/13/italy.cable.car.marines

INTRODUCTION

Chapter 2 introduced the fundamental concept of statehood. Chapter 5 added the related limitation that one State cannot unilaterally act within the territorial boundaries of another State. This chapter augments these themes by illustrating the scope of sovereign power exercisable in, over, and outside of a State actor. It answers this question: To what extent may a State exercise its sovereign powers without violating the sovereign rights of other States? This is obviously an issue of extreme importance to national interests.

As to land, the range of State sovereignty may be limited because some territories belong to no State, while others are incapable of ownership by any State. Regarding the oceans, a State may control the waters off its coast with the same completeness of control that it exercises over its land boundaries. Yet in other situations, that State may exercise varying degrees of control, depending on distance from the coast. Continuing questions are raised about the extent to which State sovereignty may be exercised in the airspace above the State, in the airspace over other States or international waters, and in outer space.

◆ 6.1 CATEGORIES OF TERRITORY

Four species of territory emerged under the modern system of States:

- Territory owned by a sovereign State (sovereign territory);

- Territory not owned by any State due to its special status (trust territory);
- Territory capable of ownership, although not yet under sovereign control *(terra nullius);* and
- Territory that cannot be owned by any nation *(res communis).*

SOVEREIGN TERRITORY

One attribute of a State's sovereignty is the right to the exclusive ownership and control of its territory. A State is entitled to exercise sovereignty over the land located within its territorial frontiers. The extent of that sovereignty is ordinarily limited by natural boundary lines. Oceans, mountains, and other natural frontiers usually provide geographical limits to a State's ability to control territory.

TRUST TERRITORY

A second category is land that is not subject to the sovereignty of any State because of a special status. Certain territories were the League of Nations' "mandates" and United Nations' "Trust Territories" (*see* §3.3) after World War II. No State, including the protecting State in whose care such a territory has been placed, may lay claim to ownership or sovereign title. Under the UN Charter, this category of territory does not have the ability to control its own area because it lacks political infrastructure. The League and the UN placed such areas under the protection of established States to promote the self-determination of the inhabitants.

TERRA NULLIUS

Certain territories were *capable* of being legally acquired. At one time, no State controlled them. These locations were referred to in the earlier colonial era as territories that were *terra nullius.* They were conveniently characterized as belonging to no one but capable of being legally acquired by the colonial European powers.

International Law, as shaped by European States, provided that they were competent to designate certain territories as *terra nullius.* In 1885, for example, the States attending the Conference of Berlin declared what was later deemed to be both immoral and illegal—that most of the African continent was *terra nullius* because the inhabitants of the continent were incapable of governing themselves. In a 1971 case before the International Court of Justice, South Africa argued that it was legally seized with the sovereign right to continue controlling Namibia (formerly South West Africa). The rationale was that the people of Namibia were incapable of governing themselves. The Court seized this opportunity to unreservedly declare that those European States "blundered" by characterizing Africa as *terra nullius* in the nineteenth century. As stated by the Court:

> African law illustrated . . . the monstrous blunder committed by the authors of the Act of Berlin, the results of which have not yet disappeared from the African political scene. It was a monstrous blunder and a flagrant injustice to consider Africa south of the Sahara as *terrae nullius,* to be shared out among the Powers for occupation and colonization, even when in the sixteenth century Victoria had written that Europeans could not obtain sovereignty over the Indies by occupation, for they were not *terrae nullius.*
>
> By one of fate's ironies, the declaration of the 1885 Berlin Congress which held the dark continent to be *terrae nullius* related to regions which had seen the rise and development of flourishing States and empires. One should be mindful of what Africa was before there fell upon it the two greatest plagues in the recorded history of mankind: the slave-trade, which ravaged Africa for centuries on an unprecedented scale, and colonialism, which exploited humanity and natural wealth to a relentless extreme. Before these terrible plagues overran their continent, the African peoples had founded states and even empires of a high level of civilization. . . .[1]

More than one State may attempt to control the activities of the people who inhabit areas that are *terra nullius.* This conflict generates the question of which State may legitimately claim territorial sovereignty when the area is not controlled exclusively by either. In the famous 1928 *Palmas Island* arbitration, the US and the Netherlands both claimed the exclusive right to an island located in the Philippine archipelago. The resulting arbitral opinion was a typical restatement of the imperialistic nature of the regime of *terra nullius* carried forward into twentieth-century legal thought:

> Territorial sovereignty belongs always to one [State] . . . to the exclusion of all others. The fact [is] that the functions of a State can be performed by any State within a given zone . . . in those parts of the globe which, like the high seas or lands without a master, cannot or do not yet form the territory of a State. . . .

> In the exercise of territorial sovereignty there are necessarily gaps, intermittence in time and discontinuity in space. This phenomenon will be particularly noticeable in the case of colonial territories, partly uninhabited or as yet partly unsubdued.[2]

As a condition for establishing its right to claim sovereignty, a State must normally establish that the particular zone was, in fact, *terra nullius* and thereby available for occupation and the ensuing claim to title. The International Court of Justice's 1974 *Western Sahara* case analyzed this prerequisite in a dispute between Spain and Morocco over control of a portion of the Western Sahara desert. The Court confirmed the international expectation that mere occupation is not enough to justify a claim of sovereignty over an occupied area. It also must have been a *terra nullius* if the claimant State seeks exclusive sovereign control. The Court therein traced the history of the term:

> [The] expression "terra nullius" was a legal term of art employed in connection with "occupation" as one of the accepted legal methods of acquiring sovereignty over a territory . . . [and it] was a cardinal contention of a valid "occupation" that the territory should be *terra nullius*—a territory belonging to no-one—at the time of the act alleged to constitute the "occupation.". . . A determination that the Western Sahara was a *terra nullius* at the time of colonization by Spain would be possible only if it were established that at that time the territory belonged to no-one in the sense that it was then open to acquisition through the legal process of "occupation."[3]

RES COMMUNIS

The fourth category of territory is incapable of ever being legally owned or controlled; it is typically referred to as *res communis.* It belongs to no one and must remain available for all to use. Under International Law, the entire community of nations must have unfettered access to such areas. These territories cannot be lawfully controlled by any State or group of States without the approval of the community of nations. The clearest examples of *res communis* are the high seas and outer space, as discussed later in this chapter.

It has been argued that Antarctica is a "land" area that is *res communis.* Article 4 of the 1959 Antarctic Treaty provides that States shall not recognize, dispute, or establish territorial claims there, and no new claims may be asserted by parties to this treaty. Some commentators have characterized Antarctica as *res communis* because of the harsh weather conditions making it difficult to occupy. Some scholars analogize Antarctica to the high seas, the deep seabed, outer space, and the Arctic (which has no land mass).[4] Chilean Professor Emilio Sahurie disputes the "occupation" analog, however. He notes that even the high seas have been appropriated (illustrated in §6.3). "Occupation" is becoming obsolete with advances in modern technology. Traditionalist scholars should acknowledge that only the moon and other celestial bodies are actually *res communis.* There is no territory on *earth* that is totally incapable of "exploitation"—which would be a more accurate measure of sovereignty than "occupation."[5]

◆ 6.2 DOMINION OVER LAND

A State ordinarily possesses the exclusive right to the use of its territory, the right to claim ownership or control, and the competence to exclude other nations from being present without consent. However, sovereignty disputes have existed for centuries.[6] Argentina's invasion of the Falkland Islands in 1982 was the contemporary phase of a dispute which began with England in 1833.

Resolution is complicated because judges, arbitrators, and diplomats often have to rely on documents that are centuries old. In a 1953 case in the International Court of Justice, England and France both claimed the exclusive right to two islets within the English Channel. The ICJ analyzed a number of medieval treaties in an effort to establish which State was entitled to this territory—including the Treaty of Lambeth of 1217, the Treaty of Paris of 1259, the Treaty of Calais of 1360, and the Treaty of Troy of 1420. The ICJ even considered a papal declaration in 1500 that transferred the Channel Islands from the French Diocese of Coutances to the English Diocese of Winchester. Since none of these documents specifically mentioned the disputed islets, the Court granted title to England based on its acts of possession.[7]

The materials in this section analyze the general modes for establishing sovereign title. The historical approach is presented first, followed by contemporary criticisms of these modes.

HISTORICAL APPROACH

The traditional methods for acquiring sovereignty over territory are as follows: occupation, conquest, cession, prescription, and accretion.

Occupation Exclusive *occupation* for an extended period of time is the routine basis for claiming sovereignty over a particular geographical area. This mode of acquisition is referred to as an "original" claim to territory as opposed to a "derived" basis for claiming sovereign title. In the latter instance, title may be expressly derived from a document, such as a treaty in which two or more States formally agree on exclusive or shared sovereignty over a particular territory.

During the previous colonization era, effective occupation required that the State occupy an area that was originally *terra nullius*—owned by no one but capable of ownership. The World Court has repeatedly stated that occupation is "legally an original means of peaceably acquiring sovereignty over territory . . . [however] it was a cardinal condition of a valid 'occupation' that the territory should be *terra nullius*—a territory belonging to no-one—at the time of the act alleged to constitute the 'occupation.' "[8]

Turkey's current occupation of Cyprus illustrates a violation of this principle. In 1974, Turkey began its occupation of a portion of the island of Cyprus over the objection of Greece. This was done for the expressed purpose of protecting the Turkish minority just after Greek Cypriots staged an unsuccessful coup that would have unified Cyprus and Greece. This was nevertheless an illegal occupation, because of the UN Charter prohibition on the use or threat of force in international relations. In 1997, the UN Secretary-General vowed an end to this occupation—a predicament that is still unresolved.

This method for authenticating sovereign title was typically proven initially by "discovery." The medieval perspective was that mere discovery, without actual possession, was sufficient to establish valid title. State practice in the later centuries of Europe's colonial expansion retreated from that view. After territory was discovered, there had to be at least some symbolic act signifying possession. State representatives thus planted a flag or created a more substantial tie, such as a settlement in the discovered territory. Discovery, coupled with such acts, established a colorable title—initiated but not necessarily perfected.

There is no general agreement about the effect of "discovery" on modern claims to State territory. Though some countries assert that discovery alone generates legal rights, others disagree. The US government claims that mere discovery yields *no* rights. When the US entered into a treaty with Russia in 1824 that established the boundaries of Alaska, the US declared that "dominion cannot be acquired but by a real occupation and possession, and an intention to establish it [by mere discovery] is by no means sufficient."[9] Under this view, some form of *occupation* was necessary to claim legitimate sovereignty over territory. Planting a US flag on the moon in 1969 did not establish any US sovereign rights or title to that territory.

The nineteenth-century European powers, relying on discovery as a basis for initiating claims of exclusive land title, carefully provided for protecting their respective claims to the territories of the African Continent. The 1885 Berlin Conference, whereby well-established African tribes were deemed incapable of self-governance, echoed the international practice that any form of occupation should be immediately communicated to the other colonial powers. Formal notification to all signatories was designed to prevent or ameliorate problems of successive discoveries of the same territory.

Discovery was supposed to be followed by effective occupation. States generally agreed that they did not have to *physically* occupy the territory in question. They did have to conduct some activity, however, to confirm actual governmental administration. The Europe-based Permanent Court of International Justice validated this requirement in the 1933 Danish–Norwegian dispute over eastern Greenland. The Court declared that sovereign claims to territory often depend "upon continued display of authority, involv[ing] two elements each of which must be shown to exist: the intention and will to act as sovereign, and some actual exercise or display of such authority."[10] In this case, Denmark did not physically occupy the contested portion of eastern Greenland. It did not establish settlements or send governmental officials to administer the area. Yet Denmark's title was successfully based on "the peaceful and continuous display of authority over the island." This was an "effective" occupation during the several centuries that Denmark engaged in diplomatic exchanges with other governments concerning eastern Greenland. These acts demonstrated a requisite degree of dominion to support Denmark's claim to sovereignty.

Conquest Another historical method for establishing title to territory is conquest. Nations often acquired territory by forcefully taking it. Israel conquered the West Bank of Jordan during its 1967 war with neighboring Arab nations. Germany annexed Austria in 1939. Japan annexed Korea in 1910. Belgium annexed the Congo in 1908.

The twentieth-century development of rules prohibiting the use of force outlawed this basis for *legitimately* claiming title to State territory (Chapter 10). In 1945, the UN Charter expressly prohibited the use of force in international relations. After two world wars, initiated by the expansionist territorial policies of a number of nations, the drafters effectively vitiated conquest as a basis for claiming title to property. Although there have been scofflaws, most States have observed this norm most of the time.

When Israel successfully concluded several wars allegedly initiated by Arab countries, it claimed added territory by conquest—both as a reprisal and as a defense to further attack. The affected territories included the West Bank of Jordan, the Gaza Strip formerly belonging to Egypt, and the Golan Heights of Syria. The UN responded in the cases of the West Bank and Gaza (and by implication the Golan Heights) with Resolution 242. This 1967 UN plea called for Israel to withdraw its forces "from territories occupied in the recent conflict." Israel withdrew from some of this territory in the mid-1970s and under the 1993–1994 Israeli peace accords with its neighbors—although it continues to establish living settlements in the area. Whether Israel will give up the strategic Golan Heights is another question.

This occupation received worldwide attention in 1997. On three occasions in four months, the UN General Assembly adopted resolutions condemning Israel for continuing to build housing in disputed territories. One of these was the first "emergency session" of the General Assembly in fifteen years. The vote was virtually unanimous: 131–3, with Israel, Micronesia, and the US voting against the last resolution. Israel has built approximately 200 settlements in the West Bank, Gaza Strip, and Golan Heights. One argument is that, under Article 49 of the post–World War II Geneva Conventions, occupying nations may not "transfer parts of its own civilian population into territory it occupies." In 1998, the US mediated the next step in the peace process, whereby the parties agreed as follows: Israel agreed to pull back its troops from an additional 13 percent of the West Bank, there would be a joint committee to discuss further withdrawals from occupied territory, and there would be safe passage for Palestinians moving between Gaza and other Palestinian areas in this part of the Middle East. The Wye River Memorandum, facilitated by US President Clinton, is designed to facilitate the implementation of the Interim Agreement on the West Bank and Gaza Strip (and subsequent agreements). A committee will be formed to discuss the Third Phase of the further redeployment of the respective forces. Both sides committed to resuming permanent status negotiations on an accelerated basis with the aim of reaching an agreement by May 4, 1999. They also pledged not to undertake unilateral actions affecting the status of the West Bank or Gaza.[11]

> The Security Council,
>
> Expressing its continuing concern with the grave situation in the Middle East.
>
> Emphasizing the inadmissibility of the acquisition of territory by war and the need to work for a just and lasting peace in which every state in the area can live in security.
>
> 1. Affirms that the fulfillment of Charter principles requires the establishment of a just and lasting peace in the Middle East which should include the application of both the following principles:
>
> 1. Withdrawal of Israeli armed forces from territories of recent conflict.
>
> 2. Termination of all claims or states of belligerency and respect for and acknowledgment of the sovereignty, territorial integrity and political independence of every state in the area and their right to live in peace within secure and recognized boundaries free from threats or acts of force.
>
> —UN Security Council Resolution 242 S/RES/242 (1967)

Another form of conquest is the establishment of a special "zone of peace" designed to provide a buffer between rival forces. The most prominent is the security zone that Israel set up in the southernmost portion of Lebanon in 1978. Because of many attacks from this area in the past, Israel has claimed the need for this zone—about 10 percent of Lebanon's landmass—in the name of self-defense.[12]

Cession An international agreement that deeds territory from one nation to another is called a *cession*. The grantee nation's right to claim title to the granted land is derived from such an agreement. In the 1928 *Island of Palmas Arbitration,* the Permanent Court of Arbitration (Netherlands) addressed the viability of transferring title by cession. The US unsuccessfully claimed sovereignty over an island in the Philippine archipelago founded on the 1898 Treaty of Paris between Spain and the US. Spain did not have proper title to the Island of Palmas at the time it ceded its treaty rights to the US. Spain could not, therefore, cede more rights to the US than Spain itself possessed. The opinion generally addressed the way in which title by cession is established:

> [Titles] of acquisition of territorial sovereignty in present-day international law are either based on . . . occupation or conquest, or, like cession, presuppose that the ceding [grantor] and the cessionary [grantee] Power, or at least one of them, have the faculty of effectively disposing of the ceded territory. . . . The title alleged by the United States of America . . . is that of cession, brought about by the Treaty of Paris, which cession transferred all rights of sovereignty which Spain may have possessed in the region indicated in Article III of the said Treaty and therefore also those concerning the Island of Palmas or Miangas.[13]

Cession has caused public resentment and smoldering hostility when it is forced on the granting State because it has lost a war. Germany was required to cede land to Poland after World War I. The ceded territory included more than one million ethnic Germans. For them, this change meant a drastic role reversal. The Polish government was suddenly confronted with a significant German minority in a region where power relationships had been quite different for more than a century. There may have been a legally sufficient transfer of title to this territory, but the German minority refused to consider itself subject to Polish rule. Germany, in turn, refused to formally renounce the region, although it had been forced to do so by the Treaty of Versailles. Poland was determined to create a homogeneous society in this region, and there were lingering socio-economic differences between the new "Polish" Germans and the other citizens of this new ceded territory—formerly in Germany and now in Poland.[14]

Prescription State A may derive title to territory—previously belonging to State B—by occupying State B, or some part of it, without objection from State B. After a period of time (not uniformly defined), the occupying State may validate its title by *prescription* if the original occupant does not effectively protest a prolonged presence.

Prescription is not universally accepted as a method for acquiring sovereign title. Some nineteenth-century jurists rejected the view that prescription is recognized under International Law. They asserted that one State could not legally claim title by merely usurping another's territory. Under this view, abandonment of disputed territory was an unacceptable legal fiction. The purported acquiescence in the prescriptive rights of the new occupant was merely a face-saving device. Most States, however, now recognize prescription as a valid basis for claiming sovereignty over territory.

One practical reason is that ineffective or excessively delayed opposition to hostile occupation conveniently removes defects in sovereign claims to disputed territory. Prescription is thus a common means for resolving long-term border disputes. The International Court of Justice addressed the underlying practicalities when it resolved a sixty-year-old boundary dispute between France (on behalf of Cambodia) and Thailand (formerly Siam). Each claimed sovereign rights to the area surrounding a sacred temple on the Siamese–Cambodian border. In the 1962 *Case Concerning the Temple of Preah Vihear,* Thailand claimed title based on a 1904 treaty. It did not, however, rebuff Cambodia's occupation of the disputed area until it seized the temple in 1954. The Court affirmed the utility of prescription as a device for acquiring title to property on the basis that

> it appears to have amounted to a tacit recognition by Siam of the sovereignty of Cambodia . . . over [the Temple] Preah Vihear, through a failure to react in any way, on an occasion that called for a reaction in order to affirm or preserve title in the face of an obvious rival claim. . . . In general, when two countries establish a frontier between them, one of the

> primary objects is to establish stability and finality. This is impossible if the line so established can, at any moment . . . be called in question . . . indefinitely [because] finality would never be reached. . . .[15]

Accretion The other historical method for establishing sovereign title is *accretion*. A State's territory may be augmented by new formations of land gradually deposited from bodies of water. Examples include additions to territory by the formation of islands within a State's territorial waters or a natural change in the flow of an international river.

In November 1998, China, Russia, and North Korea extended a World War II–era border agreement regarding the Tumen River. It flows from one of China's northern provinces into the Sea of Japan and separates the northern tip of North Korea from Russia. Its course has changed in the decades since the war. The three nations finally resolved resulting border issues, which had been on hold since a 1991 agreement between Russia and China. North Korea effectively delayed implementation because of political circumstances. However, such border disputes are sometimes even more complex, because of the passage of time and the circumstance where there has been *both* gradual *and* sudden changes in a river on an international border.

Sudden changes do not affect the boundary between two nations. The change must be gradual and imperceptible. The *Chamizal Arbitration* between the US and Mexico dealt with both types of change. One of the major boundaries between these two nations is the Rio Grande River. Treaties in 1848 and 1852 fixed this international boundary at a point farther north than that existing at arbitration in 1911. In the interim period, the gradual southward movement of the Rio Grande exposed a tract of land that was formerly *within* the river. This movement was exacerbated by a sudden flood in 1864. Both the gradual accretion and the flooding altered the course of the Rio Grande, producing a six-hundred-acre tract that became the subject of a territorial land dispute. The Mexican and US arbitrators thus described the legal impact of accretion in this instance as follows:

> [Because of] the progressive movement of the river to the south, the American city of El Paso has been extending on the accretions formed by the action of the river on its north bank, while the Mexican city of Juarez to the south has suffered a corresponding loss of territory. . . . The contention on behalf of the United States of Mexico is that this dividing line was fixed, under those treaties, in a permanent and invariable manner, and consequently that the changes which have taken place in the river have not affected the boundary line which was established and marked in 1852.
>
> On behalf of the United States of America it is contended that . . . if the channel of the river changes by gradual accretion, the boundary follows the channel, and that it is only in a case of a sudden change of bed that the river ceases to be the boundary, which then remains in the abandoned bed of the river.[16]

The arbitrators resolved this US–Mexican dispute by dividing the tract in accordance with the usual international rules applicable to accretion. They decided that the US was entitled to sovereignty over that portion of the Chamizal Tract resulting from the *gradual* southward accretion of land prior to the 1864 flood. Mexico was entitled to the remaining acres exposed by the flood. In 1967, the US put an end to the matter by formally transferring this portion of the Chamizal Tract to Mexico.

NEW MODES OF TERRITORIAL ACQUISITION

Title may now be acquired in ways other than those developed in previous centuries. These newer methods include renunciation, joint decision, and adjudication.

Renunciation By *renunciation,* a nation relinquishes title to its territory. There is no transfer of title, unlike the "treaty cession" that formally transfers or cedes territorial sovereignty to a grantee nation. In 1947, Italy renounced title (obtained by conquest) to its territories in northern Africa. These were involuntary renunciations orchestrated by the victorious Allied powers after Italy lost the war. A State may *voluntarily* relinquish its territorial sovereignty as well. This method of transferring sovereignty is sometimes referred to as *acquiescence, estoppel,* and even *prescription*.

The distinction between renunciation and prescription is sometimes rather blurred. One difference is the need for occupation in order to establish prescription. None of these terms has been clearly defined or distinguished in International Law. Although there is a lack of precision in their application, they share a common

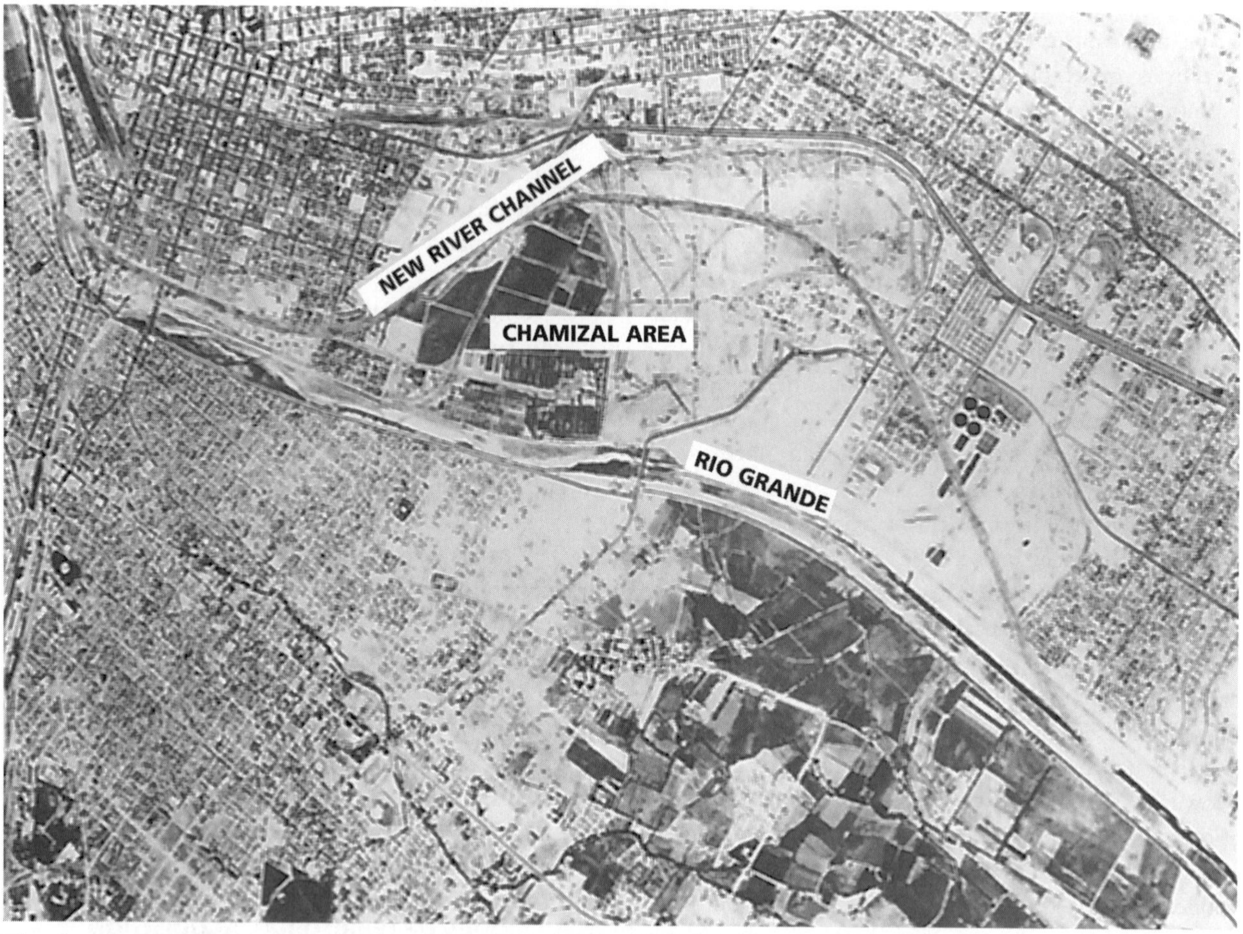

This photograph illustrates the disputed Chamizal Tract area of the Rio Grande River. The United States transferred the remaining acres exposed by the flood to Mexico and thus resolved this international dispute.

denominator. A State may not assert a territorial claim in a manner that is inconsistent with its conduct. In the 1968 *Rann of Kutch* arbitration, for example, Pakistan implicitly relinquished its title to an area on its common border with India. For more than one hundred years, Pakistan's predecessor did not react to obvious assertions of sovereignty (by England and then India) in the disputed border area. The arbitrators determined that Pakistan had acquiesced in India's exercise of sovereignty over the disputed area. Pakistan could not reclaim this land after another State had peacefully occupied it for so long a period of time.[17]

Joint Decision A joint decision by the victors of war is a twentieth-century device for transferring sovereignty over State territory. After each world war, victorious States claimed and exercised a right to dispose of certain property that the defeated States had obtained by forceful conquest. After World War I, certain victors decided to jointly dispose of the territory of the losers. The Permanent Court of International Justice recognized this method for transferring sovereign territory in 1923. After World War II, the victorious nations felt compelled to impose security measures on the losing nations. One such measure was the joint decision of the Allies to reduce certain German frontiers. As a result, Germany was forced to yield its sovereignty over that territory.[18]

Adjudication Another method for legitimizing the transfer of sovereignty is *adjudication*. Title disputes to State territory are often examined by judges and arbitrators. Although many of them have classified adjudication as an independent mode for "acquiring" title to State territory, this is a misnomer. International tribunals have no more power than that granted to them by the sovereign States that create them. Adjudication is the result of an international agreement that authorizes a mutually acceptable tribunal to resolve a dispute between the participating States.

Title by adjudication is similar to a treaty cession from a grantor to a grantee State. In both instances, the participating States enter into an agreement about how they will fix a boundary line. By adjudication, the parties agree to establish sovereign rights after the tribunal examines the facts and renders its decision. More decisions of the International Court of Justice have resolved territorial disputes than any other issue before the court.

CRITICISMS OF THE HISTORICAL APPROACH

Contemporary scholars have criticized the historical modes for acquiring sovereignty over State territory. According to Oxford University Professor Ian Brownlie, many "of the standard textbooks, and particularly those in English, classify the modes of acquisition in a stereotyped way which reflects the preoccupation of writers in the period before the First World War."[19] Some significant claims also arose (or resurfaced) after World War II. Professor Brownlie depicts some of the reasons why such claims will continue to adversely affect international relations in the following way:

> The pressures of national sentiment, new forms of exploitation of barren and inaccessible areas, the strategic significance of barren and inaccessible areas previously neglected, and the pressure of population on resources, give good cause for a belief that territorial disputes will increase in significance. This is especially so in Africa and Asia, where the removal of foreign political domination has left the successor states with a long agenda of unsettled [sovereignty] problems, legal and political.[20]

Other criticisms of the historical modes of acquiring title are found in the "Third World" attitudes about the development of International Law in the ethnocentric nations of the West. A number of States oppose the application of the long-established devices for validating sovereign title. These methods were developed long before many of today's nations became States. They seek a more significant role in the evolution of norms for determining contemporary territorial disputes. They oppose the conquest and cession bases for acquiring sovereign title. The legitimacy of conquest and treaties of cession as viable methods for legally establishing sovereignty over territory have been vitiated in this century by the development of League of Nations and UN norms prohibiting the use of force in international relations. Australian National University Professor D. W. Greig's comment on this conflict is that

> under *traditional* international law a cession [or treaty transferring sovereignty] imposed by force would be valid, the development of the twentieth century concept of the illegality of aggressive war would seem to cast doubts on the possibility that such a rule has survived. Indeed, prior to the Covenant of the League of Nations and to the Kellogg–Briand Pact [Renunciation of War] of 1928, a treaty of cession was not even necessary to validate a seizure of territory by force, for international law recognized annexation (or subjugation, or conquest, as it is variously termed) as a means of acquiring territory.[21]

Eastern scholars also criticize the traditional modes of acquiring sovereignty over territory—for a related reason. The thrust of their objection is that Western countries have perpetuated an ethnocentric view of what is acceptable State practice. They hold Western writers and jurists responsible for perpetuating the historical view that certain territories did not contain "civilized" people. Western colonial powers characterized the inhabitants of Asia, Africa, and Latin America (before the mid-twentieth century) as inferior and uncivilized—generating ethnocentric norms for acquiring title to territory. Any occupation based on the concept of *terra nullius* is completely rejected by most non-European States, especially new States once subjected to the expansionist colonialism of the more developed States. There is no moral or ethical basis in modern International Law for control based on the convenient analysis of *terra nullius.* This device was used by the colonizing powers only to rationalize what the lesser developed States now characterize as immoral or criminal acts by their former oppressors.

The following representative excerpt from the Chinese periodical *Studies in International Problems* provides the Chinese perspective on the Western development of the modes for acquiring State territory. It addresses why the historical modes are unacceptable by Chinese standards. A key theme in this excerpt is the criticism of the Western concepts of "original" and "derivative" acquisition of sovereignty. Original acquisition as a basis for title to territory conveniently surfaced when the particular territory did not have a sufficiently powerful entity controlling it. Derivative acquisition also perpetuated Western claims over territory even when it was previously owned by another social group of people or a "State," as analyzed immediately below:

"A Criticism of Bourgeois International Law on the Question of State Territory"

Hsin Wu

KCWTYC (newspaper) No. 7:44–51 (1960)
Reprinted and translated in J. Cohen & H. Chiu
Vol. 1 *People's China and International Law,*
323 Princeton University Press (1974)

Bourgeois international law sums up the various methods by which imperialist countries have historically seized territory by classifying them. Methods of acquiring territory are divided into *"original acquisition"* and *"derivative acquisition"* according to the different owners of the annexed territory.

Methods of acquiring territory are divided into *"acquisition by means of treaty"* or *"acquisition not by means of treaty"* according to the different methods adopted at the time of annexation. All these methods of acquiring territories are given legal status, and beautiful legal terms are used to conceal the reactionary essence of these actions. Let us now strip off the legal covers to see what is meant by . . . [these Western terms].

"Original Acquisition": According to the explanation of bourgeois international law, acquisition of land *"without an owner" [terra nullius]* is "original acquisition." What is land "without an owner"? Colonialists do not conceal the fact that this is not land which is entirely uninhabited, but merely land inhabited by what they do not regard as a "civilized people." They regard the vast lands in Asia, Africa, and Latin America as lands "without an owner," despite the fact that millions of owners live there and various nations exist there. They regard those people and nations as "barbarous" and "backward" and believe that they cannot be the owners of those lands. The lands should be occupied by "civilized" people and the acquisition of this territory by "civilized" countries is proper; it is a legitimate method of "original acquisition." In the words of the American scholar Hyde: "If the inhabitants of the territory concerned are an uncivilized or extremely backward people, deemed to be incapable of possessing a right of sovereignty, the conqueror may, in fact, choose to ignore their title, and proceed to occupy the land as though it were vacant." This statement shows how this authoritative American bourgeois scholar unabashedly defends aggressors. His reactionary theory is extremely absurd.

The inhabitants of lands "without an owner" are by no means the kind of people whom colonialists and bourgeois scholars have described as barbarous, ignorant, willing to be slaves, and unable to exercise sovereignty. These descriptions are a great insult and defamation to these inhabitants. The true situation is that, whether it was in Asia, Africa, or Latin America, the indigenous inhabitants all had their own excellent cultures. Bourgeois scholars may consider Africa, for example, as the most barbarous land. But, everyone knows that the African people once had excellent civilizations in the Nile River region, the Congo River region and in Carthage. Long before their contact with Europeans, the Africans were experts in various handicraft skills and technology and were able to refine iron and other mineral ores. They could make various instruments of production, weapons, and furniture. In certain areas of Africa, national art already had reached a comparatively high standard. African folk literature was rich, colorful, and full of attraction. The allegation that they were willing to become slaves and were unable to exercise sover-

Emphasis has been supplied by the author in certain passages.

eignty is a lie inconsistent with history.... It was not that they were unable to exercise sovereignty but rather that they were prevented from exercising their sovereignty by colonialists' use of massacre and suppression.

It should be pointed out that there has been a change in the view of bourgeois international law concerning the methods of "original acquisition." At first, bourgeois scholars argued that "occupation" was one method of "original acquisition," that is, a state which "first discovered a land 'without an owner'" should be the owner of that piece of land. It was through this method of acquisition that Portugal and Spain, two of the earliest colonial powers, occupied a large number of colonies. Later, bourgeois scholars proposed the view of "effective occupation." ... The theory of "occupation" did not meet the desire of the powerful imperialist countries that subsequently emerged, while "effective occupation" provides them with a legal basis for redistribution of the spoils.

"Derivative Acquisition": Bourgeois international law holds that the difference between "derivative acquisition" and "original acquisition" is that the former does not refer to the method of acquiring territory without an owner but refers to the method of acquiring territory originally belonging to another state. The imperialist powers' plundering of foreign territory naturally would not be limited to [only] lands "without an owner." After lands "without an owner" were carved up, they naturally would plunder lands "with an owner." Lenin said: "When the whole world had been divided up, there was inevitably ushered in an era of monopoly ownership of colonies, and, consequently, of particularly intense struggle for the division and redivision of the world." There is no limitation on imperialism's ambition with respect to plundering territory....

Sometimes, imperialism nakedly uses the method of aggressive war forcibly to seize another state's territory; sometimes it uses camouflaged measures or various pretexts to force another state in fact to place its territory under imperialism's occupation. In order to prove the legality of the above-stated methods of seizing territory, bourgeois international law further classifies "derivative acquisition" into acquisition by means of treaty and acquisition not by means of treaty.

What are the methods of "derivative acquisition" *by means of treaty?* Bourgeois international law considers cession one of these methods. Every country has the right to cede its territory, and it has the right to acquire ceded territory.... In a discussion on the form of cession [by treaty], "Oppenheim's International Law" described the annexation of Korea in 1910 by Japanese imperialism and the annexation of the Congo in 1908 by Belgian colonialists as a method of acquiring ceded territory through *peaceable* negotiation. But everyone knows that Korea was forcibly occupied by Japanese bandits and the Congo was a victim of the colonial system. From these instances, we may clearly discern that countries which ceded their territories were all under compulsion and that they were either weak, small, or defeated countries. Countries which acquired ceded territories were all imperialist countries engaging in territorial expansion. Bourgeois international law writings have never been able to cite a single case in which an imperialist power ceded its territory to a weak or small country. Therefore, it can be said that cession of territory is a method of plundering the territories of weak and small or defeated countries used by imperialist countries through the use of war and threat of force. . . . Most outspoken on this point is the American scholar Hyde, who writes in his book "International Law, Chiefly as Interpreted and Applied by the United States": "The validity of a transfer of rights of sovereignty as set forth in a treaty of cession does not appear to be affected by the motives which have impelled the grantor to surrender them." Obviously, according to such an interpretation, it was legitimate for Japan to force the Manchu government of China to cede Taiwan and Penghu through the unequal Treaty of Shimonoseki of 1895, after the Sino–Japanese War. This is tantamount to saying that if a robber steals property by brandishing a dagger before an owner and by threatening his life forces him to put his fingerprint on a document indicating his consent, then the act of robbery becomes legal. Is that not absurd? No wonder bourgeois international law has sometimes been described as the law of bandits. There is no exaggeration in such a description.

Besides cession, bourgeois international law also considers *lease* as a method of "derivative acquisition" of territory by means of treaty. . . . In 1898 Germany *leased* Kiaochow Bay, Britain *leased* Wei-hai-wei, and France *leased* Kuang-chou Wan from China. These leases were acquired by concluding unequal treaties. These unequal treaties absolutely were not concluded through "peaceable negotiations" as described by bourgeois international law. As a matter of fact, lease of the above-mentioned Kiaochow Bay and other places was executed under threat of force. In November 1897 Germany sent four men-of-war to Kiaochow Bay to occupy Tsingtao on the ground that its missionaries had been killed. It was under these circumstances of armed occupation that the "Treaty of the Lease of Kiaochow" was concluded. The leases of Wei-hai-wei and Kowloon were also obtained under similar conditions. . . .

Bourgeois international law considers "conquest" a method of *acquiring territory where no treaty exists.* So-called conquest means that a state uses its armed forces for long-term occupation of the territory or a part of the territory of another state. Undoubtedly, this is a savage and aggressive act. Bourgeois international law, however, considers such a method of acquiring territory lawful, even though it does not go through the process of concluding a treaty. In analyzing the causes of war, "Oppenheim's International Law" states: "If . . . territory cannot be acquired by peaceable means, acquisition by conquest alone remains if International Law fails to provide means of peaceful change in accordance with justice." Charles Rousseau, Professor of International Law at the University of Paris, in his book "Principles Generaux du Droit International Public," held that conquest is a means of acquiring sovereignty over a certain territory. The British jurist Schwarzenberger held: "In the international society law is subordinate to the rule of force. If the whole State machinery [of the defeated State] has collapsed, conquest would permit acquisition of title to the territory of this State." According to these theories, colonial wars or other aggressive wars started by imperialist countries in order to annex territories of other countries are lawful. The Japanese seizure of China's three northeastern provinces, Italy's annexation of Ethiopia, and Fascist Germany's occupation of Poland, Czechoslovakia, and so forth were all lawful.

"Prescription" is also considered a method of "derivative acquisition" of territory not by means of treaty. According to the explanation of bourgeois international law, "prescription" means the acquisition by a state of title to a territory through prolonged occupation. Obviously, this recognizes imperialism's acquisition of legal title to a territory through prolonged occupation by force. "Oppenheim's International Law" held that "a State is considered to be the lawful owner even of those parts of its territory of which originally it took possession wrongfully and unlawfully, provided that the possessor has been in undisturbed possession for such a length of time as is necessary to create the general conviction that the present condition of things is in conformity with international order." This means that any country, regardless of its motive or the means it used—whether by way of annexation or aggression—as long as it has the power to be in prolonged occupation by force of the territory of another state, may consider its aggressive act as "lawful." History shows that colonialists in fact frequently used the concept of "prescription" to plunder the territory of other countries. Even recently, in certain countries, certain persons in power and bourgeois scholars have attempted to resort to the concept of "prescription" as a legal basis for putting certain territory of China's Tibet under the jurisdiction of another country.

In view of the foregoing, the "derivative acquisition" either by means of treaty or not by means of treaty mentioned by bourgeois international law is a general term which describes the various methods used by imperialist countries to plunder the territory of colonized countries and weak and small countries.

◆ 6.3 LAW OF THE SEA

INTRODUCTION

The widely heralded norm "freedom of the seas" was a limitation that restricted national attempts to unreasonably extend the range of exclusive coastal sovereignty into international waters. Such claims conflicted with the rights of all States to fish and to navigate over international trade routes. The Dutch judge to whom the cannon-shot rule—fixing the outer limit of territorial sovereignty—is attributed refused to recognize greater sovereignty than that recognized under late medieval practice.[22] As characterized in a study by Yale Law School scholars,

> The concept of "freedom of the seas" entered the law of nations as a reaction against broad claims to territorial sovereignty over vast sea areas put forward by Spain, Portugal, England, and other states in the sixteenth and seventeenth centuries. The object of these claims was to monopolize fisheries, and trade with

areas thought particularly rich in resources. . . . No interference whatever with navigation was justified because effective occupation was impossible by the nature of the sea itself. The same principle was applicable to fisheries . . . for the additional reason that the resources of the sea were [then considered] inexhaustible. . . . The claim of the Dutch to free navigation . . . [evinces the] common interest in navigation and fishing [which] triumphed over monopoly, and that the great principle of "freedom of the seas" became in this sense universally accepted."[23]

Yet freedom of the seas served the interests of only the more powerful nations. It authorized their vessels to freely fish, mine, and navigate without limitation. A coastal State was precluded from interfering with a foreign vessel's activities, just three miles offshore, as well as the sovereignty of the nation whose flag it sailed under. By the dawn of the contemporary system of State sovereignty, introduced by the 1648 Peace of Westphalia, European powers had already assumed that the ocean's resources were unlimited. Thus the area beyond three nautical miles was an area—conveniently characterized as *res communis*—open to all comers. As succinctly described by University of Ottawa Professor Donat Pharand:

> Beginning in the seventeenth century, the Law of the Sea was developed and maintained to accommodate the interests of the major maritime powers. They developed a legal regime which protected their colonial, commercial and military interests. That legal regime was characterized by two basic principles: the freedom of the seas and the sovereignty of the flag State. The expression "freedom of the seas" designated mainly two types of freedom, fishing and navigation. It was thought that biological resources of the sea were inexhaustible and that any State, having the necessary fishing capability, could simply go out and help itself without any restriction whatever. As for the sovereignty of the flag State, it meant that the country under whose flag the ship was sailing had exclusive jurisdiction over all activities aboard the ship. Certainly this was the case when the ship was on the high seas, that is beyond the traditional three-mile territorial sea. Aside from two exceptions covering slave trade and piracy, this principle of sovereignty of the flag State remained untouched. In a nutshell this represented the state of the law of the sea until after World War II.[24]

The end of World War II signaled many beginnings. One was the coastal State tendency to extend sovereignty into marine areas well beyond the traditional three-mile limit of the "territorial" sea. Twentieth-century technology caused the free seas pendulum to swing in the opposite direction. Free accessibility to the High Seas resulted in a depletion of the world's marine resources and a reevaluation of the international penchant for a *laissez faire* ocean policy.

Various zones began to surface. Some States claimed full sovereignty over large areas, while other claims were comparatively limited. Indeed, all States had an important interest in guarding against illegal drug trafficking, immigration, and pollution—which know no boundaries. But a number of less-developed States watched in dismay while more-developed States entered their general maritime regions to fish and exploit the nearby oceans with technology not available to the coastal State. As more seagoing nations began to extract resources from the sea, pressure mounted to compress the notion of freedom of the seas. The colonial period was in decline (§2.2). The new resource-rich but technology-poor coastal States began to espouse the view that freedom of the seas continued to serve the ever-present colonial purposes of many large and economically powerful nations. The historical regime of freedom of the seas did not incorporate the interests of the *new* members of the international community—especially those coastal nations seeking to facilitate a more equitable distribution of the ocean's resources. These included former colonies that were not sovereign States until the 1960s. Previously, they were excluded from any role in the evolution of the Law of the Sea segment of International Law.

The UN thus sponsored various treaties with two objectives in mind: first, acknowledging limits on freedom of the seas; second, incorporating new coastal State perspectives about evolving sea zones that were unheard of before World War II. The most important and comprehensive of these treaties effectively codified a new constitution of the oceans, finally entering into force in 1994.

1982 LAW OF THE SEA TREATY

In November 1994, the most ambitious and comprehensive treaty of all times entered into force—the 1982

EXHIBIT 6.1 SEA ZONES

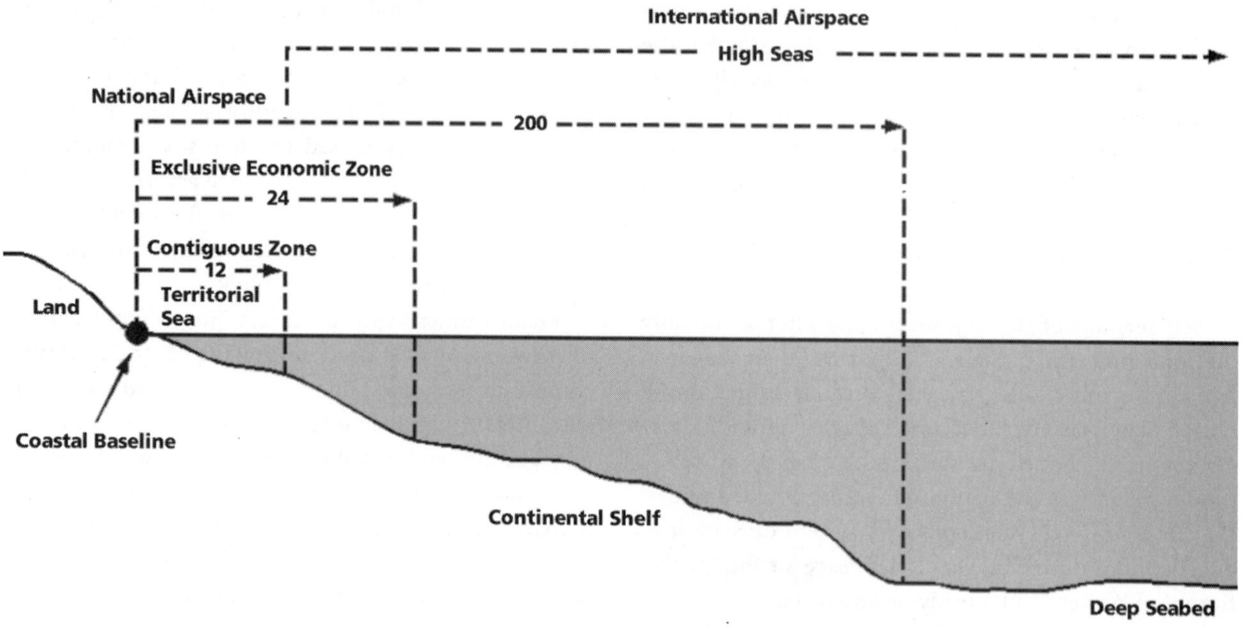

UN Convention on the Law of the Sea (UNCLOS).[25] It was the work product of the third multilateral treaty negotiation on the law of the sea, consisting of numerous meetings of the national delegates from 1974 to 1982. One-hundred and seventeen nations originally "signed" this treaty in 1982. One of the treaty provisions was that it would enter into force, codifying the International Law of maritime jurisdiction, one year after the sixtieth State (Guyana) so ratified the treaty (in 1993).

The UNCLOS has become *the* working document for all academics, practitioners, and decision makers concerned with ocean issues. This portion of the chapter addresses this comparatively new legal regime with its various sea zones. Much of the UNCLOS codifies prior State practice. A number of provisions were nurtured by progressive evolution during the negotiations. Some provisions were quite novel.

This section of the book explores the expanded range of State sovereignty in the now-established ocean-water areas: (1) Internal Waters, (2) Territorial Sea, (3) High Seas, (4) Contiguous Zone, (5) Exclusive Economic Zone, (6) the Continental Shelf, and (7) the Deep Seabed. Exhibit 6.1 depicts these zones at the outset to illustrate the first major theme of this section: The coastal State may undertake certain activities in ocean waters, including portions of the High Seas, thus limiting the activities of other States. This means that exercises of State sovereignty are not limited to the land territory of the coastal State. Its control of these various zones is itself limited, however. The farther away from the coast that it desires to so act, the less a State may impede the conduct of other States. Under this new constitution of the oceans, coastal States may preclude other nations from certain acts—up to 200 nautical miles from shore.

(1) INTERNAL WATERS

Article 8.1 of the UNCLOS defines internal waters as the "waters on the landward side of the baseline of the territorial sea." As with its land, a State has the sovereign right to control its bays, rivers, and other internal waters. Like repelling foreign invaders from its soil, a State has a strong interest in monitoring the military and commercial activities of foreign vessels within its internal waters. As depicted in Exhibit 6.1, the coastal baseline is the point where the sea intersects with the edge of the land on the sea coast. The baseline is a geographical yardstick for distinguishing internal waters from the sea and the starting point for measuring the various ocean water zones.

Two settings complicate the application of the *exclusive* jurisdiction of the coastal State over its internal waters. One is the problem of jurisdiction over events occurring on a foreign vessel while it is in port. The other situation involves conflicting rights in certain large coastal bays containing more open seas than the typical bay.

Ports For the purpose of separating a State's internal waters from the territorial waters off its coast, a port extends to the outermost permanent harbor facility forming an integral part of that harbor's system. A long entryway consisting of natural twists and turns is a part of the port. An artificial buoy area constructed *outside* of the mouth of that entryway, however, is not part of the port.

Under International Law, each State has the absolute right to control the internal waters contained within its ports. Customary practice has incorporated some limitations. When a foreign *warship* enters internal waters with permission, the port authorities do not board it—for mutual security reasons. Neither State wants to subject its military secrets to unnecessary scrutiny when its naval vessels enter a foreign port. Another limitation applies to *merchant* and other private vessels. They have the implied right to enter the internal waters of another State without express permission. They are routinely boarded, however, for customs or immigration purposes.

The UNCLOS does not cover the important jurisdictional problem associated with a member of a foreign crew who commits a crime while *in port* (as opposed to one committed on a ship passing through the Territorial Sea). When the vessel's sailors go ashore, they subject themselves to the laws or jurisdiction of the coastal State. When a crime is committed *on board* a foreign vessel in a port, however, *either* the laws of the coastal State *or* the laws of the State to which the vessel is registered might be applied.

The ancient rule was that any ship entering another nation's port became subject to the latter's complete control. Modern customary and treaty practice has altered that rule. In the case of crimes that do not affect the port's tranquility, the State of registry (the flag State)—rather than the port State—usually exercises primary jurisdiction to prosecute the criminal. That concession facilitates the smooth progress of international commerce and avoids undue interference in a ship's movements by the port State. But when the onboard crime causes a *significant* intrusion on the port's tranquility, the perpetrator becomes subject to prosecution by the port State.

Not all States automatically cede jurisdiction over on-board crimes to the flag State. In some regions, all crimes occurring within the internal or territorial waters trigger the coastal nation's competence to prosecute foreign sailors (absent the usual treaty exception for *military* personnel). Under customary practice, the flag State is competent to act if the port State chooses not to prosecute. For example, a court in Argentina had to determine the question of Argentina's jurisdiction over a theft that occurred aboard an Argentine merchant vessel at anchor in the port of Rio de Janeiro, Brazil. The ship left the Brazilian port and returned to Argentina with the thief still aboard. The thief was prosecuted in the Argentine court system. Although his lawyer argued that Argentina had no jurisdiction, because the crime occurred in Brazil, the court disagreed in the following terms:

> According to the rules of public international law . . . offences committed on board a private ship fall within the jurisdiction of the courts of the flag State if the ship is on the high seas, and fall within the jurisdiction of a foreign State only in the event that such offences have been committed while the ship is in the [internal or] territorial waters of that other State. . . . [The court then decided that Argentina nevertheless had jurisdiction because this] principle is not an absolute rule . . . for if the foreign State does not choose to exercise its right to institute proceedings because it considers that the act has not affected the community at large or the peace of the port (as maintained in French and Italian doctrine), the flag [State] may then assert full authority over the ship for the purpose of restoring order and discipline on board or protecting the rights of the passengers. . . .[26]

The rights of the port and flag States are not always left to judicial interpretation under customary International Law. The respective jurisdictional rights are often agreed to by treaty. Such treaties typically cede *primary* jurisdiction to the flag State. They frequently contain a "port tranquility" exception, permitting the port State to prosecute foreign sailors in specified situations.

What type of criminal conduct activates the "port tranquility" exception to the primary jurisdiction of the flag State? The US Supreme Court addressed this question in the following case—relied on by courts throughout the US on many subsequent occasions:

Mali v. Keeper of the Common Jail of Hudson County (Wildenhus Case)

SUPREME COURT OF THE UNITED STATES, 1887

120 US 1, 7 S.Ct. 385, 30 *L. Ed.* 565

Author's Note: *Wildenhus and Fijens were Belgian sailors aboard a Belgian steamship anchored in the port of Jersey City, New Jersey. In a fight below decks, Wildenhus stabbed and killed Fijens. The Jersey City police learned about this incident and arrested Wildenhus. Several Belgian crew members witnessed this incident. They also were placed in the port jail as witnesses for the proceedings against Wildenhus.*

The treaty between Belgium and the US ceded "primary" jurisdiction over onboard crimes to the respective flag States to which the vessels were registered. A Belgian consular official in New Jersey relied on this treaty and thus sought the release of the Belgian sailors to his custody. This foreign official was acting on behalf of Belgium, referring to himself as the "petitioner." The issue was whether the port tranquility doctrine should be applied to deprive the flag State (Belgium) of its primary jurisdiction under the treaty.

The first portion of the reported case is a factual account provided by the lawyers representing the US (on behalf of the prosecution by the state of New Jersey). In the latter portion of this opinion, the Chief Justice then delivered the Supreme Court's decision—agreeing with the lower courts that the treaty permitted New Jersey to prosecute the Belgian sailor under the circumstances. This particular homicide provided cause for invoking the port tranquility exception to Belgian jurisdiction over events occurring aboard its vessel.

COURT'S OPINION This appeal brought up an application made to the Circuit Court of the United States for the District of New Jersey, by Charles Mali, the "Consul of His Majesty the King of the Belgians, for the States of New York and New Jersey, in the United States," for himself as such consul, "and in behalf of one Joseph Wildenhus, one Gionviennie Gobnbosich, and one John J. Ostenmeyer," for the release, upon a writ of habeas corpus, of Wildenhus, Gobnbosich, and Ostenmeyer from the custody of the keeper of the common jail of Hudson County, New Jersey, and their delivery to the consul, "to be dealt with according to the law of Belgium." The facts on which the application rested were thus stated in the petition [requested by Belgium]: . . .

Second. That on or about the sixth day of October, 1886, on board the Belgian steamship Noordland, there occurred an affray between the said Joseph Wildenhus and one Fijens, wherein and whereby it is charged that the said Wildenhus stabbed with a knife and inflicted upon the said Fijens a mortal wound, of which he afterwards died. . . .

Fifth. That at the time said affray occurred the said steamship Noordland was lying moored at the dock of the port of Jersey City, in said state of New Jersey. . . .

Seventh. That said affray occurred in the presence of several witnesses all of whom were and still are of the crew of the said vessel, and that no other person or persons except those of the crew of said vessel were present or nearby. . . .

Article XI of a Convention between the United States and Belgium "concerning the rights, privileges, and immunities of consular officers" . . . is as follows:

> The respective consuls-general, consuls, vice-consuls, and consular agents shall have exclusive charge of the internal order of the merchant vessels of their nation, and shall alone take cognizance of all differences which may arise, either at sea or in port, between the captains, officers, and crews, without exception, particularly with reference to the adjustment of wages and the execution of contracts. The local authorities shall not interfere, except when the disorder that has arisen is of such a nature as to disturb tranquility and public order on shore, or in the port, or when a person of the country or not belonging to the crew, shall be concerned therein.

In all other cases, the aforesaid authorities shall confine themselves to lending aid to the consuls and vice-consuls or consular agents, if they are requested by them to do so, in causing the arrest and imprisonment of any person whose name is inscribed on the crew list, whenever, for any cause, the said officers shall think proper.

The claim of the consul was that, by the law of nations and the provisions of this treaty, the offence with which Wildenhus was charged is "solely cognizable by the authority of the laws of the Kingdom of Belgium," and that the State of New Jersey was without jurisdiction in the premises. The Circuit Court refused to deliver the prisoners to the consul and remanded them to the custody of the jailer. To reverse that decision this appeal was taken.

Chief Justice Waite orally restated these facts and then delivered the basic opinion of the Court as follows:

... [T]he courts of the United States have power to issue writs of habeas corpus which shall extend to prisoners in jail when they are in "custody in violation of the Constitution or a law or treaty of the United States," and the question we have to consider is, whether these prisoners are held in violation of the provisions of the existing treaty between the United States and Belgium.

It is part of the law of civilized nations that when a merchant vessel of one country enters the ports of another for the purposes of trade, it subjects itself to the law of the place to which it goes, unless by treaty or otherwise the two countries have come to some different understanding or agreement; for, as was said by Chief Justice Marshall in *The Exchange* [case], "it would be obviously inconvenient and dangerous to society, and would subject the laws to continual infraction, and the government to degradation, if such . . . merchants did not owe temporary and local allegiance, and were not amenable to the jurisdiction of the country." And the English judges have uniformly recognized the rights of the courts of the country of which the port is part to punish crimes committed by one foreigner on another in a foreign merchant ship. As the owner has voluntarily taken his vessel for his own private purposes to a place within the dominion of a government other than his own, and from which he seeks protection during his stay, he owes that government such allegiance for the time being as is due for the protection to which he becomes entitled.

From experience, however, it was found long ago that it would be beneficial to commerce if the local government would abstain from interfering with the internal discipline of the ship, and the general regulation of the rights and duties of the officers and crew towards the vessel or among themselves. And so by comity it came to be generally understood among civilized nations that all matters of discipline and all things done on board which affected only the vessel or those belonging to her, and did not involve the peace or dignity of the country, or the tranquility of the port, should be left by the local government to be dealt with by the authorities of the nation to which the vessel belonged as the laws of that nation or the interests of its commerce should require. But if crimes are committed on board of a character to disturb the peace and tranquility of the country to which the vessel has been brought, the offenders have never by comity or usage been entitled to any exemption from the operation of the local laws for their punishment, if the local tribunals see fit to assert their authority. Such being the general public law on this subject, treaties and conventions have been entered into by nations having commercial intercourse, the purpose of which was to settle and define the rights and duties of the contracting parties with respect to each other in these particulars, and thus prevent the inconvenience that might arise from attempts to exercise conflicting jurisdictions.

Next came a form of convention which in terms gave the consuls authority to cause proper order to be maintained on board and to decide disputes between the officers and crew, but allowed the local authorities to interfere if the disorders taking place on board were of such a nature as to disturb the public tranquility, and that is substantially all there is in the convention with Belgium which we have now to consider. This treaty is the law which now governs the conduct of the United States and Belgium towards each other in this particular. Each nation has granted to the other such local jurisdiction within its own dominion as may be necessary to maintain order on board a merchant vessel, but has reserved to itself the right to interfere if the disorder on board is of a nature to disturb the public tranquility.

The treaty is part of the supreme law of the United States, and has the same force and effect in New Jersey that it is entitled to elsewhere. If it gives the consul of Belgium exclusive jurisdiction over the offence which it is alleged has been committed within the territory of New Jersey, we see no reason why he may not enforce his rights under the treaty by writ of habeas corpus in any proper court of the United States. This being the case, the only important question left for our determination is whether the thing which has been done—the disorder that has arisen—on board this vessel is of a nature to disturb the public peace, or, as some writers term it, the "public repose" of the people who look to the state of New Jersey for their protection. If the thing done—"the disorder," as it is called in the treaty—is of a character to affect those on shore or in the port when it becomes known, the fact that only those on the ship saw it when it was done is a matter of no moment. Those who are not on the vessel pay no special attention to the mere disputes or quarrels of the seamen while on board, whether they occur under deck or above. Neither do they as a rule care for anything done on board which relates only to the discipline of the ship, or to the preservation of order and authority. Not so, however, with crimes which from their gravity awaken a public interest as soon as they become known, and especially those of a character which every civilized nation considers itself bound to provide a severe punishment for when committed within its own jurisdiction. In such cases inquiry is certain to be instituted at once to ascertain how or why the thing was done, and the popular excitement rises or falls as the news spreads and the facts become known. It is not alone the publicity of the act, or the noise and clamor which attends it, that fixes the nature of the crime, but the act itself. If that is of a character to awaken public interest when it becomes known, it is a "disorder" the nature of which is to affect the community at large, and consequently to invoke the power of the local government whose people have been disturbed by what was done. The very nature of such an act is to disturb the quiet of a peaceful community, and to create, in the language of the treaty, a "disorder" which will "disturb tranquility and public order on shore or in the port." The principle which governs the whole matter is this: Disorders which disturb only the peace of the ship or those on board are to be dealt with exclusively by the sovereignty of the home of the ship, but those which disturb the public peace may be suppressed, and, if need be, the offenders punished by the proper authorities of the local jurisdiction. It may not be easy at all times to determine to which of the two jurisdictions a particular act of disorder belongs. Much will undoubtedly depend on the attending circumstances of the particular case, but all must concede that felonious homicide is a subject for the local jurisdiction, and that if the proper authorities are proceeding with the case in a regular way, the consul has no right to interfere to prevent it.

The judgment of the Circuit Court is affirmed.

◆ *Notes & Questions*

1. What is the test for determining whether the port State or the flag State has jurisdiction when a crime has been committed aboard a vessel in port? Is the rule in *Wildenhus* likely the following: If the port authorities find out about a crime, they may characterize it as offending the port's tranquility?
2. The elasticity of the term *port tranquility* raises questions about the degree of discretion the port authorities may exercise in deciding whether to prosecute. You are the Jersey City District Attorney. There is a nonlethal fistfight between two Belgian citizens below decks on a Belgian merchant vessel. Would it offend the civility or tranquility of New Jersey? Would a fistfight *on* the decks offend its port tranquility?
3. Would it be more appropriate to vest *exclusive* jurisdiction in the coastal State only (the old customary rule) *or* in the flag State *only* (no port tranquility doctrine)?

Bays Most bays consist of only internal waters. Large bays with wide mouths present the question of whether they contain *only* internal waters or whether they also contain territorial *and* international waters. This type of bay illustrates the natural tension between freedom of the seas in international waters and the coastal State's need to control activities in a strategic bay that penetrates deep into its coastline. A classic illustration of this tension drew worldwide attention in 1986 when US warplanes were attacked over the Gulf of Sidra, in the large southern indentation of the Mediterranean Sea on Libya's coastline. Libya's leader, Mu'ammar Gadhafi, had proclaimed a "Line of Death" across the mouth of this gulf, approximately three hundred miles across. At its deepest indentation on Libya's coastline, this gulf extends well over one hundred miles into Libya's coastline on the Mediterranean Sea. Libya considers the entire gulf to be internal waters subject to its exclusive control. The US warplanes were operating over the gulf on the premise that it contains international waters, because of its immense width.

Article 10 of the UNCLOS defines a bay as "a well-marked indentation whose penetration . . . constitute[s] more than a mere curvature of the coast. An indentation . . . [must be] as large as, or larger than, that of a semicircle whose diameter is a line drawn across the mouth of that indentation." The mouth of a bay consists of its natural entrance points.

A coastal State may normally exercise complete sovereignty up to twelve nautical miles from its coast (*see* "Territorial Sea" below). In the case of a bay, if the Article 10 semicircle's diameter of the bay is *less* than twenty-four miles between each side of the mouth of the bay, its waters consist solely of internal waters. If the diameter is *greater* than twenty-four miles, the bay also contains High Seas (international waters) in the center of the mouth *and* territorial waters up to twelve miles from the entire coastline that forms the land boundary of the bay.

Bays are quite important to the national interests of coastal States.[27] The 1910 *North Atlantic Coast Fisheries* arbitration between England and the US addressed this significance in the following terms: "[A]dmittedly the geographical character of a bay contains conditions [that] concern the interests of the territorial sovereign to a more intimate and important extent than do those [interests] connected with an open coast. Thus conditions of national security and integrity, of defense, of commerce and of industry are all vitally concerned with the control of the bays penetrating the national coastline. This interest varies, speaking generally, in proportion to the penetration inland of the bay. . . ."[28]

Another type of bay is particularly important—the *historic* bay. Such bays contain only *internal* waters (as opposed to the "territorial" waters discussed below). The distinguishing feature is that their mouths are wider than the above twenty-four-mile limitation of the UNCLOS. Over a long period of time, a State may claim exclusive sovereignty over a large bay that would normally contain one or more of the other categories of ocean waters (Exhibit 6.1)—because of a distance between its natural entrance points that is *more than* twenty-four miles across. If other States do not dispute such a claim, then they acquiesce in the coastal State's treatment of the large historic bay as consisting of only internal waters.

One of the classic disputes is the aging US objection to Canada's claim that Hudson Bay is a "historic" bay consisting solely of internal waters. It is fifty miles wide at its mouth. As stated by the Canadian Minister of Northern Affairs and Natural Resources in 1957, "the waters of Hudson Bay are Canadian by historic title. . . . Canada regards as inland waters all the waters west of a line drawn across the entrance to Hudson Strait. . . ."[29] The US characterizes most of the Hudson Bay as *international* waters, however, on the basis that the US has consistently disputed Canada's internal waters claim. The international status of this bay has not been resolved, since neither nation has a strong enough interest to resolve this dispute.

(2) TERRITORIAL SEA

States have historically disagreed about the dividing line between the High Seas and the Territorial Sea. Bold, unilateral expansions of exclusive sovereignty crested during the fifteenth and sixteenth centuries. The range of these national claims extended deep into what is now considered the High Seas. Denmark and Sweden claimed large portions of the globe's northern seas. Each claimed complete sovereignty over the entire Baltic Sea. England claimed the entire English Channel and much of the North Sea. The Pope, as Head of the Holy See (Vatican State), ceded most of the Atlantic and Pacific oceans to Spain and Portugal in 1492. He viewed this concession as a natural adjunct of their rights in the trade routes to the New World.

These extravagant claims were opposed by other nations, and abandoned by the beginning of the eighteenth century. International practice never confirmed the Pope's authority to cede the right to entire oceans. The sheer inability to control such vast maritime areas afforded credibility to the "cannon-shot" theory of coastal jurisdiction: A nation could claim only that adjacent sea belt that it could actually control with its shore-based military power.

Under the UNCLOS, the Territorial Sea extends outward, twelve nautical miles from the national coastline. A coastal State exercises sovereignty over this portion of its territory, essentially to the same extent that it does so over its landmass. Its range of sovereignty includes the air over the Territorial Sea belt adjacent to the coast, the seabed below, and the subsoil within this zone.

A State *must* exercise its sovereign power in this adjacent strip of water. The minimum expectation is that the coastal State will chart the waters this close to its coast to provide warning of navigational hazards. As stated by England's Judge McNair, in a 1951 decision by the International Court of Justice: "To every State whose land territory is at any place washed by the sea, international law attaches a corresponding portion of maritime territory consisting of what the law calls territorial waters. . . . No maritime States can refuse them. International law imposes upon a maritime State certain obligations and confers upon it certain rights arising out of the sovereignty which it exercises over its maritime territory. The possession of this territory is not optional, not dependent upon the will of the State, but compulsory."[30]

Numerous definitional undercurrents muddied the scope of the Territorial Sea before the UNCLOS was negotiated. These included the location of the "baseline," the "breadth" of the Territorial Sea, what constitutes "innocent" passage, and the extent to which there exists a right to pass through straits that formerly contained international waters before the recent expansion of the Territorial Sea.

Baseline The Territorial Sea (TS) begins at the baseline (depicted in Exhibit 6.1). Each begins where the ocean's edge meets the coastline. Under Article 5 of the UNCLOS, the "normal baseline for measuring the breadth of the territorial sea is the low-water line along the coast as marked on large-scale charts officially recognized by the coastal State." The baseline is the yardstick for marking the inner boundary of the various coastal sea zones described in this chapter (*see* Exhibit 6.1).

The demarcations on the coastal State's official baseline charts do not mandate international recognition of its placement of the baseline. There are limitations. Under International Law, coastal baselines must follow the general direction of the coast. Unnatural land contours make it difficult, however, to establish indisputable baselines. Article 7.3 of the UNCLOS espouses the general principle that "the sea areas lying within the [base]lines must be sufficiently closely linked to the land domain to be subject to the regime of internal waters." This language, of course, begs the question of proper baseline placement for the inner edge of the TS on erratic coastlines.

The International Court of Justice at least set forth the guidelines for the international recognition of such baselines in the 1951 *Anglo–Norwegian Fisheries* case. When Norway announced the location of its baselines after World War II, it included a substantial portion of what were previously international fishing areas within its internal and territorial waters. Norway has many ramparts of rocks and small islets that interrupt the natural course of its coastline. Norway drew straight baselines, conveniently encompassing the rocks and islets off its coast, rather than using the traditional method of tracking the contour of its irregular coastline. By placing its baselines at the outer edge of these rock and islet configurations, Norway thus claimed a greater share of the common fishing area than Great Britain was willing to recognize. British fishermen had operated off Norway's coast *(within* the straight baseline area set by Norway) since the early 1900s. The parties to this dispute had exchanged diplomatic correspondence about their mutual rights to these fishing grounds over a period of years.

The ICJ delineated the general rules applicable to baseline placement for cases involving such unusual coastlines in the following passage:

> The delimitation of sea areas has always an international aspect; it cannot be dependent merely upon the will of the coastal State as expressed in its municipal [internal] law. . . .
>
> It is the land which confers upon the coastal State a right to the waters off its coasts. It follows that while such a State must be allowed the latitude necessary in order to be able to adapt its delimitation to practical needs and local requirements, the drawing of baselines must not depart to any appreciable extent from the general direction of the coast.
>
> Another fundamental consideration . . . is the more or less close relationship existing between certain sea areas and the land formations which divide or surround them. The real question raised in the choice of baselines is in effect whether certain sea areas lying within these lines are sufficiently closely linked to the land domain to be subject to the regime of internal waters. This idea, which is at the basis for

EXHIBIT 6.2 STRAIGHT BASELINE METHOD

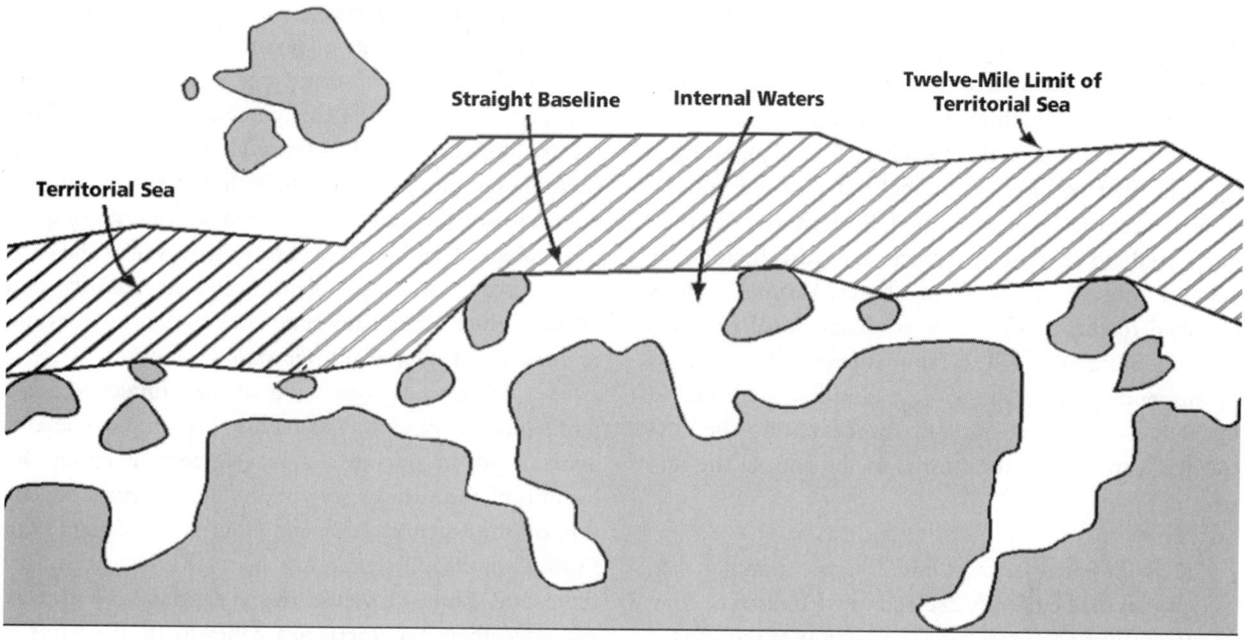

the determination of the rules relating to bays, should be liberally applied in the case of a coast, the geographical configuration of which is as irregular as that of Norway.

Finally, there is one consideration not to be overlooked, the scope of which extends beyond purely geographical factors: that of certain economic interest peculiar to a region, the reality and importance of which are clearly evidenced by a long usage.[31]

The majority of the ICJ's judges thereby approved Norway's straight baseline method in these unusual circumstances—because the resulting straight lines were sufficiently aligned with the general direction of the Norwegian coast. Although this method did not produce the usual replica of the coastal nation's coastline, it was acceptable in international practice. Exhibit 6.2 illustrates the Court's description of the method that Norway used to establish its baselines.

Territorial Sea Breadth The breadth of the Territorial Sea has long been the subject of major international controversies. In 1492, for example, Spain claimed exclusive territorial sovereignty over the entire Pacific Ocean. Portugal similarly claimed the Indian Ocean and most of the Atlantic Ocean.[32] Claims to entire oceans, however, were never recognized under International Law. States recognized the existence of a much narrower belt of water subject to the coastal State's exclusive control. In 1702, the writings of an often-quoted Dutch judge articulated the existing State practice about how to measure the breadth of this particular coastal zone: "Wherefore on the whole it seems a better rule that the control of the land [of its adjacent Territorial Sea] extends as far as a cannon will carry; for that is as far as we seem to have both command and possession. I am speaking, however, of our own times, in which we have those engines of war; otherwise, I should have to say in general terms that the control of the land ends where the power of men's weapons ends; for it is this, as we have said, that guarantees possession."[33]

This often-cited passage reveals that the three-mile shooting range of the eighteenth-century cannon established the width of the Territorial Sea. The coastal State could claim no more than it could control. Under this view, the maximum range of existing weapons was the yardstick for measuring the breadth of the Territorial Sea. Had this view persisted until the 1960s, the range of intercontinental missiles would make entire oceans the territorial waters of the launching nation.

After the American War for Independence, the United States claimed a Territorial Sea extending from the outer tips of various capes on its eastern coast. It used a straight baseline method that did *not* conform to its coastline. The resulting baselines were not a *natural* extension of the coastline (unlike Norway's straight baselines that connected the rocks and islets immediately adjacent to its coasts). The US Territorial Sea thus purported to extend its exclusive jurisdiction far beyond three miles from its shores. Various nations objected to this departure from international practice. In 1793, Secretary of State Thomas Jefferson responded by suspending this cape-to-cape baseline method. He formally advised England and France, noting the customary "cannonball" measure of the breadth of the Territorial Sea:

> [The] President of the United States, thinking that, before it shall be finally decided to what distance from our seashores the territorial protection of the United States shall be exercised . . . finds it necessary in the meantime to fix provisionally on some distance for the present government of these questions. You are sensible that very different opinions and claims have been heretofore advanced on this subject. The greatest distance to which any respectable assent among nations has been at any time given, has been the extent of human sight, estimated at upwards of twenty miles, and the smallest distance . . . is the utmost range of a cannonball, usually stated at one sea league [three nautical miles]. Some intermediate distances have also been insisted on, and that of three sea leagues has some authority in its favor. The . . . President gives instructions to the officers acting under his authority to consider those heretofore given are restrained for the present to the distance of one sea league or three geographical miles from the seashores.[34]

Certain coastal States claimed Territorial Sea boundaries much wider than the customary limit. Most of these claims were made by lesser developed nations with significant fishing or seabed resources adjacent to their coasts—while lacking the superior technology possessed by developed nations to take advantage of these resources. In 1952, for example, Chile, Ecuador, and Peru claimed a Territorial Sea of 200 nautical miles from their coasts. In 1956, a number of other nations in the same region of the world attended the Meeting of the Inter-American Council of Jurists in Mexico City, which adopted the following principle: "The distance of three miles as the limit of territorial waters is insufficient, and does not constitute a general rule of international law. Therefore, the enlargement of the zone of the sea traditionally called 'territorial waters' is justified. Each State is competent to establish its territorial waters within reasonable limits, taking into account geographical, geological, and biological factors, as well as the economic needs of its population, and its security and defense." Such statements generated worldwide pressure to expand the historical three-mile limit.[35]

In 1958, under sponsorship of the United Nations, representatives of eighty-six nations gathered in Geneva, Switzerland, to pursue a global agreement about the breadth of the various sea zones. The Geneva Convention on the Territorial Sea and Contiguous Zone (1958 LOS Convention) expressly adopted the customary three-mile limit. However, many nations subsequently extended their Territorial Sea zones to twelve nautical miles (*see* Exhibit 6.3). The 1982 Conference on the Law of the Sea (attended by 148 States) adopted this development in State practice. Under Article 3 of the UNCLOS, every "State has the right to establish the breadth of its territorial sea up to a limit not exceeding 12 nautical miles. . . ."

Shortly after its independence, the US announced its adherence to the customary three-mile limit and retained that limit for two centuries. Although some 140 nations adopted a twelve-mile limit at the UN's 1982 Conference, the US rejected the entire convention (as discussed below under deep seabed mining analysis). In 1988, however, President Reagan unilaterally extended the US Territorial Sea from three to twelve miles in "accordance with international law, as reflected in the applicable provisions of the 1982 United Nations Convention on the Law of the Sea."[36]

This quadrupling of the territorial waters zone had two major effects upon the Law of the Sea. First, it limited freedom of the seas because coastal States could regulate more activities because of the nine-mile expansion from three to twelve nautical miles. That development simultaneously extended the existing rules of "innocent passage." Second, many straits, through which ships pass from one part of the High Seas to another, no longer contained international waters (High Seas). Ships

EXHIBIT 6.3 BAY, BASELINE, HARBOR, ISLAND, AND TERRITORIAL SEA

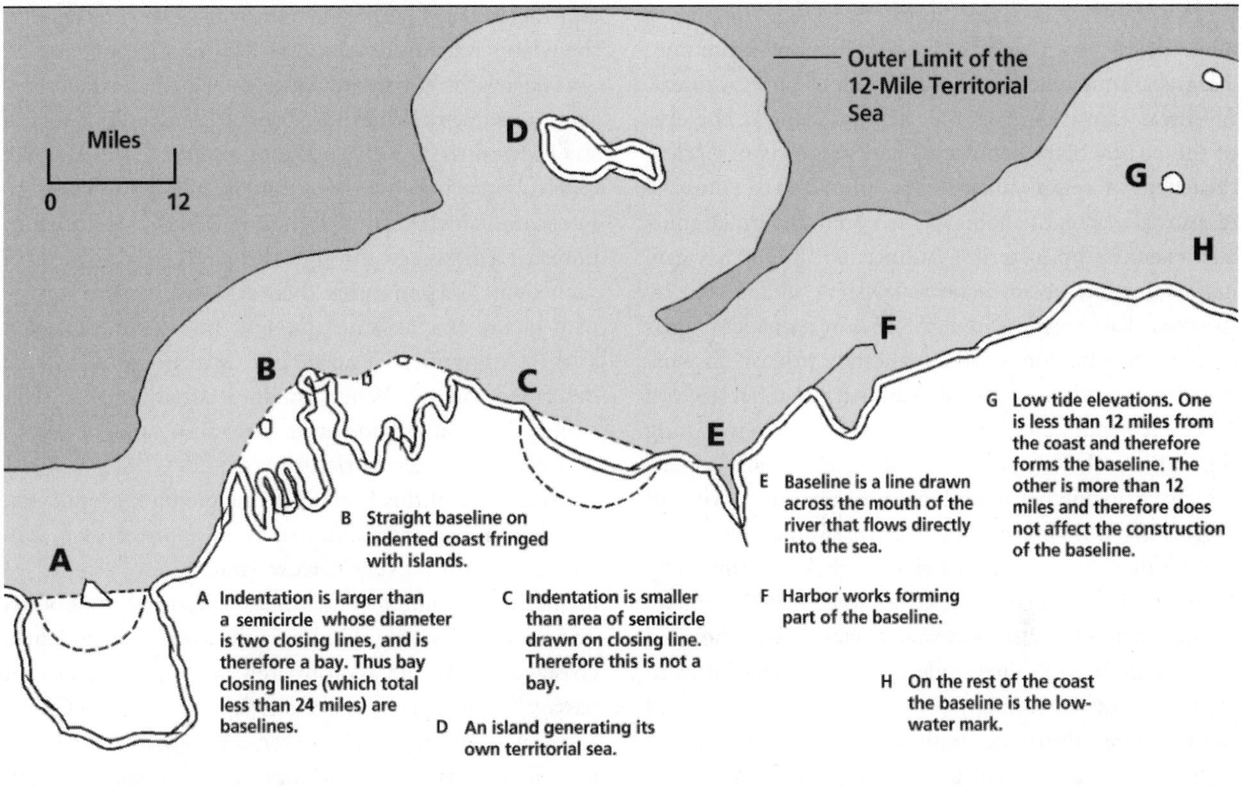
Outer Limit of the 12-Mile Territorial Sea
Miles
0
12
A
B
C
D
E
F
G
H
A Indentation is larger than a semicircle whose diameter is two closing lines, and is therefore a bay. Thus bay closing lines (which total less than 24 miles) are baselines.
B Straight baseline on indented coast fringed with islands.
C Indentation is smaller than area of semicircle drawn on closing line. Therefore this is not a bay.
D An island generating its own territorial sea.
E Baseline is a line drawn across the mouth of the river that flows directly into the sea.
F Harbor works forming part of the baseline.
G Low tide elevations. One is less than 12 miles from the coast and therefore forms the baseline. The other is more than 12 miles and therefore does not affect the construction of the baseline.
H On the rest of the coast the baseline is the low-water mark.

Source: Modified from R. Churchill & A. Lowe, *The Law of the Sea* 39 (Manchester, Eng.: Manchester University Press, 1988)

passing through such waters suddenly became subject to regulation by the coastal State on either side of the strait. Both of these developments were addressed in the UNCLOS as follows.

Innocent Passage One of the most tangible impacts of the change to a twelve-mile Territorial Sea was the extension of coastal State rules of "innocent passage." Article 18.1 of the UNCLOS Convention defines *passage* as "navigation through the territorial sea for the purpose of: (a) traversing that sea without entering internal waters . . . or (b) proceeding to or from internal waters. . . ."

But when is passage "innocent"? In 1986, two US naval vessels entered the Black Sea via the Turkish Straits. They were equipped with electronic sensors and sophisticated listening devices. Their disclosed purpose was to exercise what the US naval authorities characterized as their "right of innocent passage" through the territorial waters of the Soviet Union (SU). The SU placed all of its Black Fleet military vessels on combat alert. The SU protested this entry as unnecessarily provocative—and a clear violation of its territorial sovereignty.[37]

Under Article 19 of the UNCLOS, "innocent" passage means passage that is "not prejudicial to the peace, good order, or security of the coastal State." Further, the passing vessel may not stop or anchor, unless incidental to ordinary navigation or undertaken for the purpose of the authorized entry into a foreign port. A vessel may thus proceed to or from port, and render assistance to persons, ships, or aircraft needing emergency assistance.

Article 19 further requires foreign vessels to ascertain and comply with the innocent passage regulations promulgated by coastal States. Regulations relating to customs, immigration, and sanitation protect the coastal nation's interests in its territorial waters. An ocean liner carrying passengers into another country's territorial waters must comply with local tax laws affecting its cargo, passport regulations affecting its passengers, and waste-offloading requirements. Military vessels, when expressly permitted to enter a foreign port, normally give notice of their intended arrival at least several days in advance.

The application of the "innocent passage" regime is nevertheless elastic and ill-defined. Nations sometimes disagree about whether certain conduct poses a threat. A "threat" can take many forms, often being in the eyes of the coastal State beholder. There are, of course, clear breaches. A foreign military ship authorized to enter the territorial waters of another State could undertake military exercises upon arrival. Submarines might navigate below the surface in territorial waters, undetected by the coastal authorities. Foreign vessels can collect hydrographic information, conduct research, fish, or disseminate propaganda via radio signals. In September 1996, a North Korean submarine went aground when passing through South Korean territorial waters, clearly violating the principles that prohibit military entry without permission and entering such waters submerged.

Less threatening activities can be labeled as threats by a coastal State. During the Cold War, Soviet "fishing" trawlers with elaborate electronic devices aboard hovered just outside the US three-mile territorial water limits to gather information. Suppose that a private vessel called the *Greenpeace* distributes leaflets or displays signs against nuclear weapons to ships passing through the territorial waters of a major nuclear power. That State's coast guard vessel may stop the dissemination of such information because the activities of the *Greenpeace* would not be considered innocent. The UNCLOS provisions are ambiguous, but a better option than no definition at all.

The coastal State's discretion to arbitrarily apply locally defined rules of innocent passage are limited by the UNCLOS. Article 24 imposes a duty not to "impair" the innocent passage of foreign ships. The coastal State cannot impose navigational requirements that effectively deny the right of innocent passage. Failure to publicize dangers to navigation in the State's official navigational charts, for example, would make Territorial Sea passage impractical and dangerous. Article 24 also prohibits coastal States from promulgating regulations that discriminate against the ships or cargo of a particular nation—or ships carrying cargo to or from certain nations. The Arab embargo of Israeli shipping and goods would breach this provision of the treaty (*see* §8.4).

Strait Passage The second major effect of the UNCLOS expanded Territorial Sea from three to twelve nautical miles impacted a number of strategic straits, or natural sea passages that connect two large maritime areas. The Strait of Hormuz connects the Persian Gulf and the Indian Ocean. The Strait of Gibraltar connects the Mediterranean Sea and the Atlantic Ocean.

The relatively narrow width of the these straits presents a problem. When the navigable channel of such a strait is *more* than twelve miles from each of the national coasts bordering on the strait, it still contains some international waters or "High Seas." Ships are entitled to unrestricted passage through the High Seas portion of such straits, assuming that their activities are not repugnant to the coastal State's interests in other zones, such as the Contiguous Zone or Exclusive Economic Zone described below. When such a strait is *less* than twenty-four miles wide at its narrowest point, however, it contains only territorial waters.

As a result of this UNCLOS augmentation of coastal jurisdiction by nine additional miles, approximately 116 of these comparatively narrow "international straits"—formerly containing High Seas—suddenly embodied Territorial Seas *only*. Under customary State practice, coastal States would appropriately apply their "innocent passage" rules to such waters. Under the UNCLOS "strait passage" articles, however, the coastal State's innocent passage rules do *not* apply to these special straits (absent a treaty reservation submitted in opposition to this regime). Military and commercial vessels are entitled to *free* transit in them, just as if those special straits still contained slices of High Seas within them.

The Bering Strait between Russia (Siberia) and the United States (Alaska) provides a useful illustration. That strait is nineteen miles wide at its narrowest point. Ships pass through it when going between the Arctic and the northern Pacific oceans. The former Soviet Union claimed a twelve-mile Territorial Sea. Prior to 1988, the US three-mile Territorial Sea claim left a four-mile slice of High Seas at the narrowest point of passage. Military and commercial vessels could freely navigate in that strip of international waters in the middle of the Bering Strait. Now that the US has adopted a twelve-mile Territorial Sea, there are no High Seas left in that strait. All States would otherwise be subject to the potentially subjective "innocent passage" rules promulgated by Russia (on the eastern border of the strait) and the US (on its western border). At the narrowest point, the Bering Strait now contains only the *Territorial* Sea of both the US and Russia—normally delimited by an equidistance principle in the middle of the navigable channel.

Under the regime of "transit passage" proposed by the US to govern straits traditionally used for such international navigation, all States could navigate the Bering Strait as if it still contained a slice of High Seas in the middle. A number of States rejected this provision of the UNCLOS by tendering a reservation to its application when they ratified the treaty. The UNCLOS's "transit passage" provisions are designed to balance two competing national interests: the pre-1982 right to transit through straits containing some international waters—through the High Seas, when the norm was a three-mile Territorial Sea limit—and the post-1982 UNCLOS extension of the coastal State jurisdiction in this zone from three to twelve miles. Under Article 38.2, ships and aircraft *may* undertake "transit passage" through such straits now containing only territorial waters that formerly contained international waters "solely for the purpose of continuous and expeditious transit of the strait between one part of the high seas . . . and another part of the high seas. . . ." The coastal State or States may not impede such transit on the arguable basis that the otherwise amorphous rules of innocent passage apply to these waters that otherwise contain only territorial waters because of the narrowness of such a key navigational strait.

Under UNCLOS Article 42, the coastal State may, of course, promulgate rules ensuring transit passage that establish sea-lanes and traffic-separation schemes for safe navigation, as well as the prevention of pollution, fishing, and offloading of persons and commodities. None of these reasonable limitations may be applied, however, in a way that impedes the right of transit through such territorial waters when they bridge two portions of the High Seas.

Assume that the US and Russia were to agree upon applying this Article 38 transit passage provision. A Chinese ship, passing through the Bering Strait between the Arctic and northern Pacific oceans, would not be subject to either US or Russian innocent passage rules—although that strait would otherwise be just territorial waters at its narrowest point. Neither coastal State could prohibit the foreign commercial vessel from traversing their overlapping territorial waters, although the Chinese vessel would pass within twelve miles of the coasts of both the US and Russia. As long as the Chinese vessel was merely passing through this strait, the US–Russia adoption of the transit passage provisions under Article 38 of the UNCLOS would entitle that ship to pass freely through the strait, just as if it still contained High Seas.

(3) HIGH SEAS

The High Seas—often referred to as "international waters"—consist of that part of the ocean not subject to the complete territorial sovereignty of any State. States have "exclusive" jurisdiction only over their twelve-mile Territorial Seas. They have *some* powers in the zones seaward of their territorial waters. The degree of jurisdiction is more limited, however, as described later in this section of the book.

The most fundamental division among the various zones is the distinction between the coastal State's twelve-mile *Territorial Sea* and the *High Seas*—which is twelve nautical miles from the coastal State's baseline at shore's edge. (Two additional ocean water zones, the Contiguous Zone and the Exclusive Economic Zone, also begin at the coastal State's baseline.) As depicted in Exhibit 6.1, the outer edge of the Territorial Sea zone marks the inner edge of the High Seas.

Freedom of the High Seas has long been a universal tenet of International Law. In 1927, the Permanent Court of International Justice reaffirmed the ancient principle that this freedom was virtually absolute. The Court, noting that this liberty was subject to only those special limitations expressly recognized by State practice, stated the rule that it "is certainly true that . . . vessels on the high seas are subject to no authority except that of the State whose flag they fly. In virtue of the principle of the freedom of the seas, that is to say, the absence of any territorial sovereignty upon the high seas, no State may exercise any kind of jurisdiction over foreign vessels upon them. If a war vessel, happening to be at the spot where a collision occurs between a vessel [from its own country] . . . and a foreign vessel, were to send on board the latter an officer to make investigations or to take evidence, such an act would undoubtedly be contrary to international law."[38] The 1958 UN Law of the Sea Conference delegates captured the historical rule of complete freedom of the High Seas in Article 1 of the 1958 Convention on the High Seas.[39] It defined the High Seas as "all parts of the sea that are not included in the Territorial Sea or in the internal waters of a State." Article 2 added that the "high seas being open to all nations, no State may validly purport to subject any part of them to its sovereignty."

Freedom of the seas is no longer absolute. After the 1958 treaty, drafted before the decolonization period of the 1960s, the UN Law of the Sea Conference pendulum began to swing in the other direction. During the

1974–1982 UNCLOS process: The Territorial Sea was quadrupled, the size of the Contiguous Zone was doubled, and a *200*-mile Exclusive Economic Zone was created. The impact has been a "territorialization" of the oceans, once thought to belong to all. One result of these expansions and the related zone creation was the effective extension of the range of coastal sovereignty into what is now nearly 40 percent of the oceans. Further, the remainder of the High Seas are expected to come under control of an International Seabed Authority that will regulate *all* resource-extraction activities in the far reaches of the oceans under the UNCLOS regime described below. The High Seas could hardly continue to be characterized as *res communis* (belonging to all). As aptly stated by Professor Francis Ngantcha, in his book published by the Geneva Institute of International Studies:

> The Law of the Sea has traditionally been aimed at protecting the international community's interests over the inexhaustible uses of ocean space. To this end, the main pillar of the law has been freedom of the sea—with the implication that seagoing vehicles may freely roam the oceans. When much of the ocean space was considered *res communis,* this tenet was considered unquestionable.
>
> The 'territorialization' of the ocean space, i.e., its division into zones of coastal State sovereignty and/or jurisdiction, has put a stop to the 'old' system of 'free' global maritime communication and transportation. Consequently, the international networks of trade and commerce, naval mobility, overflight, etc., have come to depend upon the national maritime spaces of third States for purposes of passage.[40]

One major problem with coastal State jurisdiction in the High Seas is the degree to which it can protect itself against criminal activities that it perceives as threatening its national interests. Chapter 5 of this book addressed such exercises of sovereignty in terms of "extraterritorial jurisdiction" in its analysis of the various principles of international criminal jurisdiction (*see* §5.2). The increased drug trafficking problem of the last decade threatens coastal State interests long before the drugs reach any of the UNCLOS treaty zones. Consider the following scenario, wherein US customs inspectors seized drugs and arrested the leader of an international drug-smuggling ring just off the coast of Singapore:

United States of America v. Larsen

UNITED STATES COURT OF APPEALS, NINTH CIRCUIT, 1991

952 *Fed. Rptr.* 2d 1099

Author's Note: *The defendant was convicted of "aiding and abetting the knowing and intentional possession with intent to distribute marijuana" under federal controlled substances laws. The appellate court held that Congress intended that the following statute should be applied outside the US if necessary. US customs agents were thus authorized to seize a private vessel and arrest its crew in the High Seas near Singapore—thousands of miles from the California forum where the defendant was brought to trial for his violation of this statute.*

COURT'S OPINION. Before BROWNING, ALARCON, AND T.G. NELSON, Circuit Judges.

Charles Edward Larsen was convicted for his involvement in an international marijuana smuggling operation. . . . Larsen challenges the legality of his conviction on numerous grounds, including the court's extraterritorial application of 21 USC §841(a)(1) [the controlled substances law serving as the basis for his arrest near Singapore]. We affirm.

Larsen's conviction was based on evidence which established that he, along with codefendants and numerous other individuals, conspired to import shipments of Southeast Asian marijuana into the United States from 1985 to 1987, and to distribute the marijuana in the United States. The profits from these ventures were concealed by a fictitious partnership created by the defendant and others. This partnership was used to purchase the shipping vessel intended to transport the marijuana. During some of the smuggling operations, Larsen served as captain of the vessel.

Under Count Eight, Larsen was convicted of aiding and abetting codefendant Walter Ulrich in the crime of knowing and intentional possession with intent to distribute marijuana in violation of 21 USC §841(a)(1). The marijuana was seized by [US] customs inspectors from a ship on the high seas outside of Singapore. Larsen claims that the district court erred when it denied his motion to dismiss Count Eight because 21 USC §841(a)(1) does not have extraterritorial jurisdiction. . . .

Congress is empowered to attach extraterritorial effect to its penal statutes so long as the statute does not violate the due process clause of the Fifth Amendment. There is a presumption against extraterritorial application when a statute is silent on the matter. However, this court has given extraterritorial effect to penal statutes when congressional intent to do so is clear. Since 21 USC §841(a)(1) is silent about its extraterritorial application, we are "faced with finding the construction that Congress intended."

The [US] Supreme Court has explained that to limit the locus of some offenses "to the strictly territorial jurisdiction would greatly curtail the scope and usefulness of the statute and leave open a large immunity for frauds as easily committed by citizens on the high seas and in foreign countries as at home." Congressional intent to attach extraterritorial application "may be inferred from the nature of the offenses and Congress' other legislative efforts to eliminate the type of crime involved."

Until now, the Ninth Circuit [where appeals from California federal trial courts are heard] has not applied this "intent of congress/nature of the offense test" to 21 USC §841(a)(1); however, four other circuits have. They all held that Congress did intend the statute to have extraterritorial effect.

The Fifth Circuit held that Congress intended that 841(a)(1) have extraterritorial effect because it was a part of the Comprehensive Drug Abuse Prevention and Control Act of 1970, and the power to control illegal drug trafficking on the high seas was an essential incident to Congress' intent to halt drug abuse in the United States.

The Third Circuit held that Congressional intent to apply 841(a)(1) extraterritorially could be implied because "Congress undoubtedly intended to prohibit conspiracies to [distribute] controlled substances into the United States . . . as part of its continuing effort to contain the evils caused on American soil by foreign as well as domestic suppliers of illegal narcotics. . . . To deny such use of the criminal provisions 'would be greatly to curtail the scope and usefulness of the statute.' "

The First Circuit concluded that the district court had jurisdiction over a crime committed on the high seas in violation of 841(a)(1) because "[a] sovereign may exercise jurisdiction over acts done outside its geographical jurisdiction which are intended to produce detrimental effects within it."

The Second Circuit similarly held that "because section 841(a)(1) properly applies to schemes to distribute controlled substances within the United States," its extraterritorial application was proper.

Extraterritorial application of a drug possession/distribution statute comports with the reasoning behind the Supreme Court's *Bowman* decision, since such a statute is "not logically dependent on locality for the Government's jurisdiction, but [is] enacted because of the right of the government to defend itself against obstruction, or fraud wherever perpetrated" and "[i]t would be going too far to say that because Congress does not fix any locus it intended to exclude the high seas in respect of this crime" [citation omitted]. . . .

Larsen cites to a passing reference in *Hayes* which stated that Congress accepted the views of representatives from the Department of Justice and the DEA who testified that the Comprehensive Drug Abuse Prevention and Control Act of 1970 did not apply to American ships on the high seas. While the *Hayes* court acknowledged that some might conclude that §841(a)(1) does not apply extraterritorially because of this Congressional testimony, the court nevertheless held that §841(a)(1) did have extraterritorial application.

In affirming Larsen's conviction, we now join the First, Second, Third, and Fifth Circuit Courts in finding that 21 USC §841(a)(1) has extraterritorial jurisdiction. We hold that Congress' intent [to apply this drug law to the High Seas] can be implied because illegal drug trafficking, which the statute is designed to prevent, regularly involves importation of drugs from international sources.

[CONVICTION] AFFIRMED.

◆ *Notes & Questions*

1. *Larsen* deals with something different than extracting resources from the High Seas. The US was prosecuting a US citizen for criminal conduct occurring on the High Seas. *Should* the US have such jurisdiction to apply its laws *anywhere* on the High Seas under International Law?
2. Assume that the drug seizure and Larsen's arrest occurred in one of the following sea zones: (a) Singapore's Exclusive Economic Zone, (b) Singapore's Contiguous Zone, or (c) Singapore's Territorial Sea. Would the location of the arrest and seizure present greater concern to Singapore in any of these zones as opposed to another?
3. Would the US be violating any right of the nation of Singapore if the events in *Larsen* occurred in any of these zones (described in this section of Chapter 6—refer to Exhibit 6.1)?

---

(4) CONTIGUOUS ZONE

Coastal State sovereignty is *exclusive* in the Territorial Sea (TS) belt immediately adjacent to its landmass. A coastal State may also exercise *limited* jurisdiction in the Contiguous Zone (CZ), which extends from the baseline to twenty-four nautical miles from its coast. As depicted in Exhibit 6.1, the outer edge of the TS is the midpoint of the CZ.

Why *is* there a CZ? Sovereign rights in the CZ allow a coastal State to effectively monitor various national policies. Under Article 33.1 of the UNCLOS, the activities of foreign States or their vessels in the CZ are subject to the coastal State's jurisdiction for the express purposes of enforcing "customs, fiscal, immigration, or sanitary laws."

The CZ's proximity to the coastline requires a balance of international and coastal State rights to respectively use and control these waters. Enforcement of special maritime laws in this zone is not an unreasonable infringement of the international right to freely navigate through them. During the eighteenth and nineteenth centuries, State practice acknowledged the right to seize foreign and domestic vessels and arrest their occupants in international waters at some distance beyond the three-mile Territorial Sea. Coastal States were unwilling to ignore harmful or illegal activities occurring in this fringe area just beyond their Territorial Seas. The classic illustration was rumrunners during the US alcohol Prohibition era of the 1920s. They would hover there without dropping anchor. They sought opportunities to enter the Territorial Sea or to turn over their contraband to smaller boats that could then offload it at undisclosed locations ashore. This gave rise to the "hovering laws" extending coastal jurisdiction for the limited purpose of fending off anticipated violations of US liquor laws. The same concern exists today given the invasion by international drug traffickers.

A number of early twentieth-century developments impacted the creation and subsequent extensions of the CZ. The 1928 meeting of Stockholm's *Institut de Droit International* (Institute of International Law) was the first international attempt to react by assessing the proper scope of such hovering laws. The 1929 Harvard Law School study of the *Law of Territorial Waters* stated that "navigation of the high seas is free to all States. On the high seas adjacent to the marginal [territorial] sea, however, a State may take such measures as may be necessary for the enforcement within its territory or territorial waters of its customs, navigation, sanitary or police laws or regulations, or for its immediate protection."[41] The League of Nations' 1930 Conference on the Law of the Sea did not reach any express agreement about the precise scope or breadth of the CZ. The participants did agree on one important matter: Unlike territorial waters, where a coastal nation *must* exercise its sovereign control, a State had to expressly declare its claim to jurisdiction over a CZ. Under International Law, the CZ is *not* a necessary adjunct of the inherent scope of territorial sovereignty.

This consensus placed the burden on coastal States to justify any extension of sovereignty beyond their Territorial Seas. Other States did not have to recognize unusual jurisdictional claims in this area beyond the historic three-mile Territorial Sea. A major difference between the two zones was that a coastal State could not claim *exclusive* sovereignty over its CZ for all purposes. It could monitor and exclude hovering activities there. It could not limit passage that was otherwise unharmful to coastal State interests.

One problem with the 1958 UN Convention on the Law of the Sea was the specific twelve-mile breadth of the Contiguous Zone. Its establishment may have been a step backward. The drafters' intent was to place a single limit on the diverse national interests claimed by coastal States in this zone. States that wanted jurisdiction over a larger sea zone, however, did not ratify this provision of the 1958 Convention. They did not acquiesce in the prospect of their coast guard cutters idly standing by while contraband was being unloaded just outside the proposed twelve-mile Contiguous Zone. In a related extension, the 1958 UN Law of the Sea Convention provided for coastal jurisdiction over the Continental Shelf "to where the depth of the superjacent waters admits of the exploitation of the natural resources. . . ." This provision effectively permitted coastal States to monopolize the marine resources in and over their Continental Shelves—a portion of which extends into the Contiguous Zone.[42]

The third UN Law of the Sea Conference produced some answers to these problems through seaward extensions of sovereign control. As a result of negotiations from 1974 to 1982, the UNCLOS delegates expanded the Territorial Sea from the coastal baseline—to twelve miles—and the Contiguous Zone—to twenty-four miles. This treaty-based expansion, essentially codifying the existing State practice of the day, finally resolved the simmering dispute over the acceptable breadth of the CZ.

(5) EXCLUSIVE ECONOMIC ZONE

During the 1974–1982 negotiations, State representatives proposed a novel plan to accommodate the competing interests in the freedom of the High Seas and the interest in preventing the depletion of natural resources in those seas. Customary State practice had condoned the regulation of economic conduct in the waters off national shorelines involving fishing, mining, security, and certain other activities of interest to coastal States. These national interests were effectively codified by the 1982 UNCLOS provisions expressly establishing a two-hundred-mile Exclusive Economic Zone (EEZ), starting at the coastal baseline. This "economic" zone overlaps the twenty-four mile Contiguous Zone and the twelve-mile Territorial Sea. Although the general concept of an EEZ is now firmly established in International Law, the vagueness of the 1982 Convention—typical of any multilateral treaty where a wide degree of consensus is sought—masks the continued disagreement about the respective rights of different States in overlapping EEZs. The difficulty in reaching any agreement over the eight-year negotiating period was partially overcome by the use of vague language, enabling all participants to claim that their varied objectives had been achieved.

Under Article 56 of the UNCLOS, the coastal State enjoys sovereign rights in the EEZ for the purposes of "exploring and exploiting, conserving and managing the natural resources . . . of the waters superjacent to the sea-bed and its subsoil, and with regard to other activities for the economic exploitation and exploration of the zone, such as the production of energy from the water. . . ." This language provides no objective yardstick for measuring the *discretion* of the coastal State to exclude the activities of other states in its EEZ. For example, the coastal State may determine the "allowable catch" of fish to be taken by other States from its EEZ. This treaty language contains no concrete standard to define just what constitutes an allowable catch. Under Article 62, when a State fails to determine its allowable catch, or does not have the "capacity to harvest the entire allowable catch, it shall, through agreements . . . give other states access to the surplus of the allowable catch. . . ." This article requires the coastal State to provide for access to the surplus by other nations. Unfortunately, this provision means no more than an agreement to agree at a later time—without the benefit of guidelines to define specifically another State's right of access to the surplus resources of the EEZ.

Article 73 presents another example of the confusion spawned by treaty language which is very broad—and usually necessary to achieve consensus in a multilateral treaty setting—but forever in need of judicial interpretation to determine how to apply it. The following case illustrates this predicament. The UNCLOS International Tribunal for the Law of the Sea, seated in Hamburg, Germany, is the entity for resolving disputes arising under the Law of the Sea treaty. In its first judgment in 1997, the Tribunal was acutely divided over several issues including the type of activity which would result in a violation of coastal State fishing regulations in its Exclusive Economic Zone:

The M/V Saiga (Saint Vincent and the Grenadines v. Guinea-Bissau)

INTERNATIONAL TRIBUNAL FOR THE LAW OF THE SEA, 1997
www.un.org/Depts/los/judg_1.htm
Reprinted in 37 *Int'l Legal Mat'ls* 360 (1998)

Author's Note: *Rather than cover the various technical issues in this case, the edited version below acknowledges one of the many unanswered questions about what conduct constitutes an EEZ violation. A refueling vessel, flying the flag of Saint Vincent and the Grenadines, was captured by Guinea-Bissau. The alleged basis for seizure was that this tanker assisted three other unauthorized fishing vessels within 200 nautical miles of Guinea's coast. If Guinea could premise its seizure on an UNCLOS 200-mile EEZ violation rather than mere smuggling, the treaty would provide much greater coastal State jurisdiction than a seizure in international waters under Guinea's local smuggling laws.*

Also, under the UNCLOS treaty, a seized vessel must be promptly released when a bond has been posted—as done by Saint Vincent and the Grenadines. Guinea does not allow for such releases, however, for violations of its criminal smuggling laws. Initially, Guinea failed to release the tanker when Saint Vincent and the Grenadine posted a bond. Under the UNCLOS, Guinea could thus have a fund from which to recover any losses occasioned by the tanker's presence in its EEZ, and it would be obliged to immediately release the vessel under the treaty.

The majority opinion did not actually answer any substantive law question about what constitutes a violation of a coastal State's EEZ regulations. One reason was that this preliminary opinion had to focus first on whether the UNCLOS was applicable. If so, that treaty would thus furnish the Tribunal's power to decide this case. Both parties to this dispute subsequently agreed that the Tribunal should decide the merits of this dispute. Just before the Tribunal was about to decide whether Guinea had breached the UNCLOS treaty, however, Guinea decided to release the tanker and its crew.

The selected passages indicate the problems that future decision makers will encounter when attempting to use the UNCLOS to resolve issues arising under the Law of the Sea Treaty's EEZ provisions. The paragraph numbers are those of the Tribunal.

OPINION OF THE MAJORITY OF THE JUDGES

55. . . . It remains therefore to consider the question of the applicability of article 73. Article 73 reads as follows:

> *Article 73*
> *Enforcement of laws and regulations of the coastal State*
> *1. The coastal State may, in the exercise of its sovereign rights to explore, exploit, conserve and manage the living resources in the exclusive economic zone, take such measures, including boarding, inspection, arrest and judicial proceedings, as may be necessary to ensure compliance with the laws and regulations adopted by it in conformity with this Convention.*
> *2. Arrested vessels and their crews shall be promptly released upon the posting of reasonable bond or other security.*
> *3. Coastal State penalties for violations of fisheries laws and regulations in the exclusive economic zone may not include imprisonment, in the absence of agreements to the contrary by the States concerned, or any other form of corporal punishment.*
> *4. In cases of arrest or detention of foreign vessels the coastal State shall promptly notify the flag State, through appropriate channels, of the action taken and of any penalties subsequently imposed.*

56. In light of article 73 of the Convention and the contentions of Saint Vincent and the Grenadines, the question to be considered can be stated as follows: Is "bunkering" (refueling) of a fishing vessel within the exclusive economic zone of a State to be considered as an activity the regulation of which falls within the scope of the exercise by the coastal State of its "sovereign rights to explore, exploit, conserve and manage the living resources in the exclusive economic zone"? If this were the case, violation of a coastal State's rules

Made available by the Division for Ocean Affairs and the Law of the Sea, Office of Legal Affairs, United Nations, New York.

concerning such bunkering would amount to a violation of the laws and regulations adopted for the regulation of fisheries and other activities concerning living resources in the exclusive economic zone. The arrest of a vessel and crew allegedly violating such rule would fall within the scope of article 73, paragraph 1, of the Convention, and the prompt release of the vessel and crew upon the posting of a reasonable bond or other security would be an obligation of the coastal State under article 73, paragraph 2. . . .

57. Arguments can be advanced to support the qualification of "bunkering of fishing vessels" as an activity the regulation of which can be assimilated to the regulation of the exercise by the coastal State of its sovereign rights to explore, exploit, conserve and manage the living resources in the exclusive economic zone. It can be argued that refueling is by nature an activity ancillary to that of the refueled ship. Some examples of State practice can be noted. Article 1 of the Convention for the Prohibition of Fishing with Long Driftnets in the South Pacific of 23 November 1989 defines "driftnet fishing activities" as inter alia "transporting, transshipping and processing any driftnet catch, and cooperation in the provision of food, fuel and other supplies for vessels equipped for or engaged in driftnet fishing." As documented by Saint Vincent and the Grenadines, Guinea-Bissau, in its decree-law No. 4/94 of 2 August 1994, requires authorization of the Ministry of Fishing for operations "connected" with fishing, and Sierra Leone and Morocco routinely authorize fishing vessels to be refueled offshore.

58. Arguments can also be advanced, even though Guinea did not address this issue, in support of the opposite view that bunkering at sea should be classified as an independent activity whose legal regime should be that of the freedom of navigation (or perhaps—when conducted in the exclusive economic zone—that mentioned in article 59 of the Convention). The position of States with exclusive economic zones which have not adopted rules concerning bunkering of fishing vessels might be construed as indicating that such States do not regard bunkering of fishing vessels as connected to fishing activities. In support of this view it could also be argued that bunkering is not included in the list of the matters to which laws and regulations of the coastal State may, inter alia, relate according to article 62, paragraph 4, of the Convention.

59. It is not necessary for the Tribunal to come to a conclusion as to which of these two approaches is better founded in law. . . .

60. However, Guinea holds the view that the arrest of the M/V Saiga was in conformity with international law and that its release cannot be claimed on the basis of . . . the Convention. According to Guinea: (a) the bunkering must be qualified as an infringement of its customs legislation; (b) the bunkering took place in its contiguous zone (less than 24 nautical miles from the island of Alcatraz); and (c) the arrest was justified because it was effected following the exercise of the right of hot pursuit according to article 111 of the Convention. . . .

63. It has already been indicated that laws or regulations on bunkering of fishing vessels may arguably be classified as laws or regulations on activities within the scope of the exercise by the coastal State of its sovereign rights to explore, exploit, conserve and manage the living resources in the exclusive economic zone. The question now to be addressed is the following: Are there such laws and regulations in Guinea and, if so, is it relevant that Guinea qualifies them as "customs" or "smuggling" regulations? The main provisions that are relevant in this connection are those upon which the authorities of the detaining State relied at the time of arrest. It emerges . . . that the captain of the M/V Saiga is accused of a violation of article 40 of the [Guinea-Bissau] Maritime Code and Law 94/007/CTRM of 25 March 1994 which prohibits unauthorized import, transport and distribution of fuel in the Republic of Guinea (article 1).

64. The notion that bunkering is seen as an activity ancillary to fishing and connected thereto is not unknown in the law of Guinea. Article 4 of Law 94/007/CTRM specifically makes it an offence for the owners of fishing boats holding a fishing licence issued by the Guinean Government to refuel or attempt to refuel by means other than those legally authorized. . . .

65. From the pleadings and documents submitted by Guinea there also emerge indications that the violation of which the M/V Saiga was accused was seen as a violation concerning its rights in the exclusive economic zone.

66. Repeatedly, Guinea relies in its pleadings on article 40 of its Maritime Code, which defines Guinea's rights in the exclusive economic zone along the lines of article 56 of the Convention. Article 73 is part of a

group of provisions of the Convention (articles 61 to 73) which develop in detail the rule in article 56 as far as sovereign rights for the purpose of exploring and exploiting, conserving and managing the living resources of the exclusive economic zone are concerned. In the context of a violation concerning the bunkering of fishing vessels, a reference to article 40 of the Guinean Maritime Code, in view of its textual correspondence with article 56 of the Convention, must be read as dealing with the matters covered by article 73 of the Convention. . . .

68. . . . [The law of Guinea-Bissau] includes article 40 of the Maritime Code among the provisions which the captain of the M/V Saiga is accused of violating. How could this indication be relevant unless it meant that the violations of the substantive provisions listed afterwards are violations that are such when committed in the exclusive economic zone, and, consequently, relate to matters concerning the rights and jurisdiction of the coastal State in such zone? Moreover, GPV29 [Guinea's law] begins by referring to information received by the Guinean patrol boat on the "illicit presence of a tanker in the exclusive economic zone of [Guinean] waters." How could the presence of a tanker in the exclusive economic zone be seen as illicit were it not for suspected violation of the sovereign rights and jurisdiction of Guinea in the exclusive economic zone?

69. Of the several matters encompassed in the sovereign rights and jurisdiction of Guinea in the exclusive economic zone to which article 40 of the Maritime Code refers through its connection with article 56 of the Convention, "sovereign rights to explore, exploit, conserve and manage the living resources" as mentioned in article 73 are the only ones that can be relevant in the present case in light of the Guinean legislation referred to in paragraph 64 above and of the fact that it was fishing vessels that the M/V Saiga refueled.

70. The allegation that the infringement by the M/V Saiga took place in the contiguous zone and that the vessel was captured legitimately after hot pursuit in accordance with article 111, paragraph 1, of the Convention was advanced by Guinea only at the final stage of oral proceedings. This makes the classification of the laws allegedly violated as relating to "customs" or "smuggling" rather doubtful. From the point of view of facts, the only indication that the bunkering of the fishing vessels took place in the contiguous zone is the position given in the M/V Saiga's log book that became known to the Guinean authorities after, and not before, the arrest of the vessel. As late as in its Statement in response, Guinea indicated that the alleged infringement took place in its exclusive economic zone. As the position of the bunkering is close to the 24-nautical-mile limit measured from the low-water line of the island of Alcatraz, only a very accurate observation could have established that the bunkering took place in the contiguous zone. There is no evidence of such observation [therefore suggesting that violations, if any, occurred in Guinea's EEZ]. . . .

72. . . . [T]he classification as "customs" of the prohibition of bunkering of fishing vessels makes it very arguable that . . . the Guinean authorities acted from the beginning in violation of international law, while the classification under article 73 permits the assumption that Guinea was convinced that in arresting the M/V Saiga it was acting within its rights under the Convention. It is the opinion of the Tribunal that given the choice between a legal classification that implies a violation of international law and one that avoids such implication it must opt for the latter. . . .

Dissenting Opinion of President Mensah

11. As previously stated, the Judgment attaches considerable significance to the fact that [Guinea's law] PV 29 includes article 40 of the Maritime Code among the provisions which the Master of the M/V Saiga is "accused of violating." I am unable to see the justification of this assertion. Article 40 of the Marine Code reads as follows (informal translation):

> The Republic of Guinea exercises, within the exclusive economic zone which extends from the limit of the territorial sea to 188 nautical miles beyond that limit, sovereign rights concerning the exploration and exploitation, conservation and management of the natural resources, biological or non-biological, of the seabeds and their subsoils, of the waters lying underneath, as well as the rights concerning other activities bearing on the exploration and exploitation of the zone for economic purposes.

12. This article merely incorporates into Guinean law the provisions of article 56 of the Convention on the Law of the Sea. It contains nothing more than a

statement of the limits of the exclusive economic zone of Guinea, and the nature and extent of the "sovereign rights" which Guinea exercises in the zone. *It does not contain any rules or regulations which can be infringed nor does it create any offenses.* [Italics added.] It is, therefore, difficult to see in what sense the Captain of the Saiga, or indeed any other person, can be said to have "violated" article 40 of the Marine Code. [Thus, Guinea-Bissau arrested the tanker and its crew based on smuggling-related offenses—under circumstances which were beyond its jurisdictional competence under International Law—because the tanker's operations were conducted in the High Seas, beyond the Territorial Sea and Contiguous Zone.] . . .

Dissenting Opinion of Judges Park, Nelson, Chandrasekhara Rao Vukas and Ndiaye

. . . 13. The Applicant [Saint Vincent and the Grenadines] has not produced any evidence that the authorities of Guinea proceeded against the vessel as part of an anti-bunkering operation to protect fishing stocks in the EEZ of Guinea; nor is there any evidence for such a proposition in any of the documents placed before the Tribunal. Indeed, the Applicant's own submission reinforced this contention when it stated:

> In fact, so far as we are aware, despite extensive researches and the Guineans now having presented their case in an outline of their case before the Tribunal today, it would appear that the Guinean Government have not yet themselves enacted any specific legislation concerning the rights of bunkering vessels within [their] exclusive economic zone and consequently there is no legislation to which it could be said M/V Saiga was infringing or in breach of, and consequently it is not within the potential but as yet unexercised rights of the Government of Guinea to exercise powers over bunkering vessels in their exclusive economic zone to actually impose any penalty on M/V Saiga.

◆ *Notes & Questions*

1. A thoughtful analysis of the UNCLOS's dispute resolution mechanisms is available in J. Noyes, "Compulsory Third-Party Adjudication and the 1982 United Nations Convention on the Law of the Sea," 4 *Connecticut J. Int'l L.* 675 (1989).
2. For a book-length treatment of various issues arising under the EEZ regime, *see* D. Attard, *The Exclusive Economic Zone in International Law* (Oxford, Eng.: Clarendon Press, 1987). At pages 308–309, Professor Attard notes that "the division of the oceans today on the basis of sovereignty . . . is a solution as dangerous and as obsolete as the maintenance of an unrestricted concept of the freedom of the seas. Clearly, therefore, neither sovereignty nor freedom today provide an acceptable basis for a viable regime to regulate uses of the sea beyond the territorial sea." Would the work of international decision makers, such as the judges in this case, be more readily explained if the EEZ were expressly classified in the treaty as being either: (a) an extension of the coastal State's Territorial Sea, or (b) High Seas—as depicted in Exhibit 6.1—the current treaty regime?
3. To avoid jurisdictional overlaps, the UN generated an agreement regarding the respective jurisdictions of the International Court of Justice and the International Seabed Authority under UNCLOS. *See* "Agreement Concerning the Relationship Between the United Nations and the International Seabed Authority," 36 *Int'l Legal Mat'ls* 1492 (1997).

This newest sea zone is a product of the tension between historical expectations associated with freedom of the seas and modern pressures to decentralize the exploitation of ocean resources. After World War II, the more developed nations used their superior technology to extract the rich fishing and mineral resources contained in the sea and under the ocean's floor. Many of these natural resources were located just beyond the Territorial Seas of the lesser developed nations. They witnessed the resulting depletion of these natural resources—virtually within sight but beyond their grasp. Even some developed nations were concerned about protecting the resources off their own coasts from unlimited exploitation by other economic powerhouses. The sovereignty equation struck in the EEZ does not preclude *all* activity in this portion of the High Seas that could be characterized "economic." Although the coastal State enjoys some primary rights in this area, UNCLOS Article 58 provides that *all* States retain the right therein to navigate, overfly, and lay submarine cables and pipelines "compatible with . . . this Convention."

Such provisions authorize the *less* powerful coastal States to share in the wealth of natural resources near their shorelines. They have thus established licensing regimes for recapturing a percentage of the revenues derived when other States extract natural resources from the sea or the subsoil under the sea—up to 200 nautical miles from their coasts.

Some of the most powerful States have effectively *extended* this zone by augmenting it to accommodate what they characterize as special circumstances. In 1994, Canada enacted "emergency" legislation authorizing the arrest of violators of its new ban on catching the endangered "turbot" fish in the Grand Banks area 220 miles off Newfoundland. In March 1995, Spanish and Portuguese fishing trawlers were either seized or threatened with capture. The European Union then engaged in unsuccessful diplomatic attempts to convince Canada to cease this interference with the recognized right to fish in international waters beyond the 200-mile EEZ. Spain's resulting case against Canada was dismissed by the International Court of Justice on the basis of Canada's not having consented to the Court's jurisdiction.[43]

Now that the UNCLOS has entered into force (November 1994), coastal States expect to enjoy greater profits from their EEZs. They may—and do—charge licensing fees for taking fish or minerals from those zones. They may erect artificial islands or structures to harvest fish in the waters and minerals in the seabed of the EEZs. They may also conduct marine research and legitimately exclude other States from engaging in such activity.

Two further problems have limited the expansion of jurisdiction into the EEZ. First, the underlying purpose of equitably distributing global wealth will not be served by expanding coastal State rights in an EEZ without some correlative increase in the rights of *landlocked* States. They have no EEZ and no similar basis for developing their share of ocean resources. Under Article 70 of the UNCLOS, their rights were implicitly resolved. Landlocked or "geographically disadvantaged States shall have the right to participate, on an equitable basis, in the exploitation of an appropriate part of the surplus of the living resources of the exclusive economic zones of coastal States of the same subregion or region, taking into account the relevant economic and geographical circumstances of all the States concerned." But this language does not require that landlocked states receive any greater rights than any other group of States. If Paraguay, a landlocked state, fishes in Argentina's EEZ, it must pay the same license fees as any other nation. How, then, would Paraguay obtain the Article 70 benefit of equitable participation in Argentina's surplus fish available for such geographically disadvantaged states?

The second problem with creation of the EEZ, and its attendant expansion of the range of coastal sovereignty, is that many States cannot claim an *exclusive* 200-mile EEZ. Their respective shorelines are less than 400 nautical miles apart. Under Article 74 of the UNCLOS, States with opposing or adjacent coastlines are expected to resolve any inconsistent claims to their respective EEZs "by agreement on the basis of international law . . . in order to achieve an equitable solution." A similar problem arises with delimitation in facing or adjacent Continental Shelves (a regime that is addressed below). Between 1969 and 1993, the International Court of Justice heard *six* cases wherein it was called upon to establish respective rights in such EEZs or Continental Shelves in various regions of the world. The Court has not been able to produce a uniform principle other than the rather vague notion of "equidistance"—a term meaning different things to different nations.[44]

In practice, some nations have established their respective rights to overlapping coastal zones by using an equidistance principle. Italy and what was the former Yugoslavia, for example, face one another across the Adriatic Sea—which is only 100 miles across at many points. UNCLOS Article 74 mandates an agreement to "achieve an equitable solution" to the geographic inability of both nations to claim an entire 200-mile width across the Adriatic as their Exclusive Economic Zones. Under customary State practice, the Italian and (former) Yugoslavian EEZs would extend to a median line that is equidistant from both coasts. Italy and Yugoslavia would be entitled to comparable EEZs of some fifty nautical miles at certain points from their respective shores.

Article 59 of the 1982 LOS Convention says that conflicts over the control and the breadth of the EEZ are supposed to be resolved "on the basis of equity and in light of all the relevant circumstances, taking into account the respective importance of the interests involved to the parties as well as to the international community as a whole." This article is obviously vague. It does not define "equity," "relevant," or "interests." This vagueness is yet another illustration that consensus was achieved only through the use of broad terminology without clarity of application.

The international adoption of the EEZ regime has had the following impact upon the International Law of the Sea. Over one-third of all ocean space, containing 90 percent of global fishing resources, is now subject to the sovereignty of the coastal nations of the world. Now that the 1982 UNCLOS has been ratified by enough countries for it to enter into force, the lesser-developed nations have achieved one objective in their proposed redistribution of world wealth: an increase in the national sovereignty of such nations over global economic resources in the ocean waters near their shores but beyond both the older Territorial Sea and the Contiguous Zones.

On the other hand, there is no evidence that international approval of the 1982 Convention's EEZ articles have helped or will actually help the poorer or underdeveloped States, as envisioned by its proponents. As stated by Professor Arvid Pardo, Malta's former ambassador to the United Nations and an UNCLOS participant:

> [T]he Convention is grossly inequitable not only as between coastal States and landlocked and geographically disadvantaged States, but also as between coastal States themselves: only ten of these in fact obtain more than half of the area which the Convention places under national control [since so many nations separated by international waters are less than four hundred miles apart]. . . . It should be noted that adequate scientific capability, appropriate technology and substantial financial resources are required to effectively develop offshore resources, particularly mineral resources; thus, only wealthy countries and a few large developing countries such as China, Brazil, India and a few others have the means themselves to engage in significant offshore development. This could mean that marine areas under the jurisdiction of many small developing countries . . . could be exploited in practice predominantly for the benefit of technologically advanced countries with far-reaching political consequences.[45]

This perspective illustrates that comparatively wealthy and developed States are likely to continue extracting the usual benefits from their international ventures in the EEZs of other nations.

(6) CONTINENTAL SHELF

Historical Development The US devised a novel approach for protecting its natural resources: It was the first nation to claim a right to control the resources over its Continental Shelf (CS). In 1946, President Truman unilaterally announced a "fishing conservation zone" beyond the Territorial Sea. The US claimed limited jurisdiction over the Continental Shelf adjacent to its coasts—a distance of approximately 200 nautical miles on both coasts.

President Truman did not thereby claim *exclusive* sovereignty in this area of the High Seas. He expanded coastal sovereignty for the limited purpose of controlling *economic* activity in the waters over the Continental Shelf. Other nations retained the right to pass freely through the High Seas over the shelf. They could not fish there, however, without observing new US coastal fishing regulations. This "Continental Shelf Doctrine" was later adopted by some other nations and was the central theme of the 1958 United Nations Convention on the Continental Shelf.[46]

Many States have a continental shelf that differs drastically from that of the US. Chile, Ecuador, and Peru, for example, have shelves extending out to only a few miles from their coastlines before dropping off to great depths, unlike the much wider US shelf. They took a more direct approach to preserving their economic resources in the High Seas. In 1952, those three States simultaneously became the first nations to claim 200-mile-wide *Territorial* Seas. Unlike the US, they claimed *exclusive* territorial sovereignty in this large area adjacent to their coasts. They perceived little difference between their claim of exclusivity and the US-originated limited sovereignty Continental Shelf Doctrine.

UNCLOS Treatment Article 76 of the 1982 Law of the Sea treaty defines the CS as the coastal State's "seabed and subsoil of the submarine areas that extend beyond its territorial sea throughout the natural extension of its land territory. . . ." The range of the CS may vary from 200 nautical miles from the coastal baseline to 350 nautical miles, depending on the natural extension of the coastal State's underwater landmass—which often drops off to great depths relatively close to their coasts. The CS depicted in Exhibit 6.1 naturally slopes off without a sudden drop—as is the case with countries like the US. There is no CS, to speak of, off coastal States such as Chile, Ecuador, and Peru.

What happens when two or more coastal States *share* the same CS? What are their respective rights regarding use of their shared CS? The International Court of Justice addressed this matter in its 1969 *North Sea Continental Shelf* case decision. Germany, Denmark, and the Netherlands disputed the respective CS delimitations in the North Sea on each of their coasts. The Court stated that there was no obligatory method of delimitation. However, the delimitation was to be arranged "by agreement in accordance with equitable principles . . . in such a way as to leave as much as possible to each party all those parts of the continental shelf that constitute a natural prolongation of its land territory into and under the sea, without encroachment on the natural prolongation of the land territory of the other[s]. . . ."[47]

The 1982 UNCLOS essentially codified the *North Sea Continental Shelf Cases* decision in Article 83.1. States with opposite or adjacent coasts must thereunder enter into an "agreement on the basis of international law." Unfortunately, this is merely an agreement to agree—but typical of multilateral conventions where consensus is achieved by the use of question-begging language with which no State could disagree.

(7) DEEP SEABED

Historical Development Exploitation of marine life was the first of two major reasons for international interest in extending national sovereignty into the High Seas. The second reason was control of mineral exploitation in the seabed just beyond the Territorial Sea and Contiguous Zone. After World War II, the technology for deep seabed mining advanced quickly. Valuable ore deposits beyond the Territorial Sea became increasingly accessible and were extracted on a first-come, first-served basis. The coastal State could exercise exclusive sovereignty in the Territorial Sea, limited sovereignty in the Contiguous Zone, but no further control in the High Seas. Under International Law, the High Seas beyond these zones were *res communis*—belonging to no one and thus accessible by all. Many coastal States could not obtain, nor could they prevent other States from extracting, the mineral resources under these waters just beyond their sovereign control.

In 1970, the UN General Assembly proposed another ocean regime, designated the "Common Heritage of Mankind" (CHM). In Resolution 2749, the Assembly attempted to institutionalize the CHM in areas beyond national jurisdiction. Management, exploitation, and distribution of the resources of the ocean area beyond the national control of the coastal States should be governed by the international community rather than by the predilections of the more technologically advanced States and their multinational corporations. To this end, the UN General Assembly called for the convening of a new law of the sea conference that would reflect this change in attitude and draft articles to be negotiated by the international community.[48]

UNCLOS Provisions The work of the ensuing conference produced the most drastic revision of the historical conception of free seas. The 1982 Law of the Sea Treaty provisions on resources in the deep seabed, Part XI (Articles 136–153), address what is called the "Area." These provisions delayed the treaty's entry into force for more a decade. Developed nations had been profitably mining the oceans under the High Seas for decades before promulgation of the UNCLOS in 1982.

Article 1 of the UNCLOS defines the Area as the ocean floor and its subsoil "beyond the limits of national jurisdiction." Article 136 provides that the "Area and its resources are the common heritage of all mankind." This is the area under the oceans that does not otherwise fall within any of the zones described earlier in this section of the book. There are valuable minerals located in the High Seas, or the area beyond the Territorial Seas and the Contiguous and Exclusive Economic Zones.

While no *State* may exercise its exclusive or limited jurisdiction within the Area, a treaty-based organization called the International Seabed Authority (ISBA, or "the Authority") is supposed to control virtually all aspects of deep seabed mining in the Area. Article 137.2 of the UNCLOS contained an essential feature that drew objections from the major maritime powers: "All rights in the resources of the Area are vested in mankind as a whole, on whose behalf the [International Seabed] Authority shall act. These rights are not subject to alienation [sale or licensing by a national authority]. The minerals recovered from the Area, however, may only be alienated in accordance with this Part [XI] and the rules, regulations and procedures of the Authority."

Under the 1982 Convention, the ISBA consists of all national participants in the UNCLOS. It is to be based in Jamaica and funded by assessed contributions from

UN members. The ISBA is expected to organize and control all economic activities in the Area. Mineral resources within it are beyond national jurisdiction (outside of the exclusive economic zone of 200 miles), and fall within the Authority's control.

The 1982 Convention confers several fundamental tasks upon the Authority:

- to ensure that mining activities within the Area are "carried out for the benefit of mankind as a whole . . . taking into particular consideration the interests and needs of developing States and of peoples who have not attained full independence. . . . [The] Authority shall provide for the equitable sharing of financial and other economic benefits derived from activities in the Area through any appropriate mechanism. . . ." (Article 140);
- to establish regulations and procedures that will accomplish the required equitable sharing of the profits derived from the mineral resources in the Area (Article 160);
- to take measures to acquire technology for itself and to encourage the "transfer to developing States of such technology and scientific knowledge so that all States Parties [to the Convention] benefit therefrom" (Article 144.1); and
- to promote the "effective participation of developing States in activities in the Area. . . ." (Article 148).

These tasks will be accomplished by the Authority's operation of the "Enterprise," its mineral exploration and exploitation organ. Under the treaty, the Enterprise will monitor the commercial production of all mineral resources in the Area. It will be funded by "revenues [derived] by the Authority and the transfer of technology to the Enterprise" (Article 150d). The revenues derived from the Enterprise will be the royalty payments or profit shares of national or individual miners who extract minerals from seabeds in the area. The collection of these revenues and potential transfer of mining technology to the Authority's Enterprise are designed to circumvent what some 1982 Law of the Sea Conference delegates characterized as the monopolistic behavior of the larger developed nations. A small group within the community of nations possesses the requisite technology for mining these deep seabed resources. Under UNCLOS Article 150g, however, the Enterprise will ensure the "enhancement of opportunities for all . . . irrespective of their social and economic systems or geographical location, to participate in the development of the resources of the Area and the prevention of monopolization of activities in the Area."

Agreement on Implementation of Part XI In 1994, then–US Secretary of State Warren Christopher announced the US intent to sign the 1982 UNCLOS. The US realized that the UNCLOS would soon enter into force in November 1994, because the minimum number of ratifications (sixty) had already been deposited with the UN. This realization was a motivating factor for the July 1994 US "signing" (agreeing in principle, but not accepting it as obligatory—*see* §8.2 on treaty formation). The US Senate has not voted on the UNCLOS because the Chairman of the Senate Foreign Relations Committee has not conducted hearings on this issue.

While treaty ratification has stalled in the US Senate, executive-branch support is rooted in the successful negotiation of a separate agreement entitled the "Agreement Relating to Implementation of Part XI of the United Nations Convention on the Law of the Sea." Former Secretary of State Christopher lamented that the original UNCLOS Part XI provisions are "seriously flawed." Yet "it is imperative from the standpoint of our security and economic interests that the United States become a [ratifying] party to this Convention. . . . Its strategic importance cannot be overstated. . . . The result is a regime that is consistent with our free market principles and provides the United States with influence over decisions on deep seabed mining commensurate with our interests." He thus expressed the US intent to become a party to the UNCLOS if it can simultaneously ratify the two agreements (i.e., the 1982 Treaty and the special 1994 Agreement adopted by the UN General Assembly in 1994) as if they were a single instrument.[49]

The July 1994 special Agreement, approved by the General Assembly, restructured Part XI of the 1982 Treaty as a compromise designed to achieve more universal participation in a global law of the sea. The major maritime powers were reluctant to ratify Part XI as written. As stated in the August 1994 Report of the Section of International Law and Practice of the American Bar Association, recommending that the US sign (and ratify) the 1982 UNCLOS, "new threats to United States security posed by the end of the Cold War and by the rise of new nations and regional powers [make] . . .

it important to seek long-term stability of rules related to the oceans."[50]

The original treaty text suggests the creation of a new form of cartel—the Enterprise. This entity would be responsible for the mandated sharing of technology, the degree of production control and pricing, and an infrastructure not unlike that of the Organization of Petroleum Exporting Countries, which is responsible for worldwide price increases and production quotas—hardly a free market enterprise. As stated in the *Congressional Record,* the objections of industrialized States to Part XI of the 1982 treaty included that "it established a structure for administering the seabed mining regime that did not accord industrialized States influence in the regime commensurate with their interests; [and] it incorporated economic principles inconsistent with free market philosophy. . . ."[51]

The special 1994 Agreement removes a number of such objections to the deep seabed mining provisions of the original treaty previously articulated by the major industrialized powers. It removes objections to deep seabed mining resource allocation, which excluded the input of the major powers within the International Seabed Authority. It negates mandatory technology transfer, production limitations, more onerous financial obligations for the private enterprises of the mining nations, and a subsidized international entity (the Enterprise) that could compete unfairly with existing commercial enterprises. The essential objective of the fresh agreement was to retain a free market–oriented regime under which the major powers have flourished since World War II.

The 1994 Agreement specifically permits an industrialized nation to block decisions on a basis that reflects its comparative economic interests in the Law of the Sea. It may block the financial or budgetary decisions of the International Seabed Authority. This agency could otherwise decide to use revenues derived from the Enterprise to fund a liberation movement not in line with that nation's political interests. Under the 1994 special Agreement, the mandatory technology transfer provisions are supplanted by more cooperative arrangements, such as joint ventures involving procurement on the open market. The Enterprise will not have to be financed by the developed States only. There is also a form of "grandfathering" provision that allows mining, already licensed under national law, to operate on the same favorable terms as those previously granted by the Authority to French, Japanese, Indian, and Chinese companies whose mine site claims have already been registered. To meet yet another objection to the wording of the Part XI provisions of the UNCLOS, certain financial obligations otherwise imposed on mining nations at the exploration stage are eliminated under the special 1994 Agreement.

For those nations that are already parties to the 1982 LOS Convention, there is no specific time frame for either the Enterprise's commencement of mineral production or the Authority's equitable distribution of the revenues generated by the Enterprise. The UNCLOS contains two related timetables. Upon ratification by a sufficient number of nations (that is, in 1994), the Authority will review the progress made toward these production and distribution goals every five years. There will be another international review conference fifteen years after the Authority begins its commercial production of minerals in the Area. That conference will monitor the Authority's progress toward exploration, exploitation, conservation, and distribution of the resources from the ocean areas beyond national control.

PROGNOSIS

Individual conference participants in the drafting of the 1982 Treaty have provided mixed reviews about its achievements. Tommy Koh, Singapore's ambassador to the United Nations and President of the Conference, described the Area and Authority provisions as a success. In his view, the delegates reconciled the competing interests of many diverse groups of nations. His positive assessment is articulated as follows:

> [T]he international community as a whole wished to promote the development of the seabed's resources as did those members of the international community which consume the metals extracted from the . . . nodules [in the ocean's floor]. The developing countries, as co-owners of the resource, wanted to share in the benefits of the exploitation of the resources and to participate in the exploitation. . . . A seabed miner will have to pay to the International Seabed Authority either a royalty payment or a combination of a royalty payment and a share of his profits. . . . Under the Convention, a seabed miner may be required . . . to sell his technology to the Authority. This obligation has caused great concern to the industrialised

countries. It should be borne in mind, however, that the obligation [to transfer technology] cannot be invoked by the Authority unless the same or equivalent technology is unavailable in the open market. A contract study by the US Department of the Interior indicates that there is a relatively large number of suppliers of ocean mining system components and design construction services. If this is true, then the precondition [requiring technology transfer to the Authority] cannot be met and the obligation can never be invoked.[52]

The perspective of Arvid Pardo, Malta's Ambassador to the UN Conference on the Law of the Sea, is not as rosy as that of Ambassador Koh's. Ambassador Pardo's contrasting perspective is as follows:

> [T]he Convention reflects primarily the highly acquisitive aspirations of many coastal States, particularly of those developed and developing States with long coastlines fronting on the open ocean and of mid-ocean archipelagic States. Perhaps as much as forty percent of ocean space, by far the most valuable in terms of economic uses and accessible resources, is placed under some form of national control [by adoption of the exclusive economic zone]. . . . Additionally, elaborate provision is made for [the Authority's] international management of the mineral resources of the seabed beyond national jurisdiction. Nevertheless, the approach of the Convention to problems of marine resource management appears seriously deficient in several respects. . . . [T]he common heritage regime established for the international seabed is a little short of disaster. The . . . competence of the Authority is limited strictly to the exploration and exploitation of mineral resources; the decision-making procedures . . . ranging, according to the nature of the question, from a two-thirds majority to a consensus, are such as to render unlikely appropriate and timely decisions on important questions. . . . Thus, there arises the unpleasant prospect of the establishment of new and expensive international organizations incapable of effectively performing the functions for which they were created. . . . It is a pity that this side of the Convention has not been developed in a practical way. Instead a truly historic opportunity to mold the legal framework governing human activities in the marine environment in such a way as to contribute effectively to the realization of a just and equitable international order in the seas . . . has been lost.[53]

All of the ambitious provisions of the UNCLOS have not yet been implemented. But the signing by approximately 160 nations, ratification by some 110 nations, UNCLOS's 1994 entry into force, General Assembly acceptance of a renegotiated Part XI on deep seabed mining, establishment and functioning of a Law of the Sea Tribunal, and its regime for compulsory dispute resolution are all obviously rather positive developments.[47]

◆ 6.4 AIRSPACE ZONES

This section of the chapter identifies the various air zones, and the degree to which State authority may be exercised in each. The essential questions for analysis are: What are the State's rights and obligations: (1) in the airspace above its own territory? (2) in that of other States? (3) in air zones over international waters belonging to no one? (4) in outer space?

DOMESTIC AIRSPACE

Introduction A State has the sovereign right to control persons and things within its territory. Control of the *land* portion of State territory is addressed in §6.2. This section addresses the analogous national power over airspace.

Few branches of International Law developed as rapidly as International Air Law. Prior to World War I, there were no norms to govern international flight. The military use of aircraft quickly filled the vacuum. Hostile aircraft could approach more swiftly than approaching armies or warships. Rapid advancements in the technology of air travel profoundly accelerated the need to establish norms to control national airspace. Almost immediately, States claimed the right to include airspace within the definition of their "territory."

State practice quickly reflected the impact of air travel on international trade. A 1942 commentary in the *American Journal of International Law* addressed the significance of commercial air travel for internal security and foreign competition:

> The unprecedentedly accelerated speed of change in the last thirty years has been such that, politically, air navigation has already passed through many of the phases which it took sea navigation centuries to span.

> As to air navigation, it may be observed that in 1910 the states were preoccupied only with guaranteeing the safety of their territory; the necessity of permitting other states to navigate freely to and over their territory was recognized to the fullest extent where this freedom did not affect the security of the state. The period 1910–1919 can thus be compared with that period in the history of shipping in which the adjacent seas were appropriated primarily to secure the land from invasion.
>
> In 1919 the first consideration was still the security of the states, but . . . some small clouds were already appearing on the horizon of the free sky. In the minds of some . . . the idea took shape to use the power of the state over the air to protect its own air navigation against foreign competition. As in shipping, the pretensions to the appropriation of the sea and the power to restrict foreign sea commerce grew in proportion to the increase in the direct profits to be expected from them, so in aviation the pretensions to unrestricted sovereignty—not in doctrine but in practice—grew in proportion to the development of aviation during the period from 1919 to 1929.[54]

National legislation imposed various limitations on international air travel. It prohibited the unauthorized entry of aircraft. These laws restricted freedom of navigation, types of importable cargo, and conditions of passenger travel. States soon recognized the need to enter into international treaties for the purposes of establishing mutual expectations and facilitating international trade.

The vertical extension of State sovereignty first appeared in the 1919 Paris Convention Relating to the Regulation of Aerial Navigation. Article 1 provided for the mutual recognition "that every Power [State] has complete and exclusive sovereignty over the airspace above its territory." Under Article 15, each State party to this treaty could "make conditional on its prior authorisation the establishment of international airways and the creation and operation of regular international air navigation lines, with or without landing, on its territory."[55] As international commerce grew, the international community needed to solidify its expectations so that there could be a comprehensive air treaty regime.

1944 Chicago Convention The next air treaty and cornerstone of International Air Law is the 1944 Chicago Convention on International Civil Aviation. Most nations of the world are parties to this treaty. Its fundamental provisions are:

> *Article 1* The contracting States recognize that every State has complete and exclusive sovereignty over the airspace above its territory.
>
> *Article 2* For the purposes of this Convention the territory of a State shall be deemed to be the land areas and territorial waters adjacent thereto under the sovereignty . . . of such State.
>
> *Article 5* Each contracting State agrees that all aircraft of the other contracting States, being aircraft not engaged in scheduled international air services, shall have the right . . . to make flights into or in transit non-stop across its territory and to make stops for non-traffic purposes without the necessity of obtaining prior permission, and subject to the right of the State flown over to require landing.
>
> *Article 6* No scheduled [commercial] international air service may be operated over or into the territory of a contracting State, except with the special permission or other authorization of that State. . . .

These provisions codify the sovereign right to completely exclude air travel through the airspace above the State's landmass *and* above the territorial waters adjacent to its coastlines. France, for example, legally denied US President Ronald Reagan's request that US aircraft fly over France and its territorial waters during a 1986 retaliatory bombing mission into Libya. US warplanes were required to fly a circuitous route around France's territorial airspace and through the Straits of Gibraltar to gain access to Libya via the western entrance to the Mediterranean Sea.

In most instances, States encourage *commercial* flights through their airspace in order to maintain economic ties with other States. The Chicago Convention governs both the nonscheduled flights of private aircraft and the scheduled flights of commercial passenger and cargo air services. The key articles, their intended applications, and the essential provisions on military and other state aircraft are abstracted below.

Private Aircraft Noncommercial private aircraft enjoy the general right to fly into or over state territory (Article 5 above). They may land for refueling and other purposes without prior permission. An English citizen may land to refuel his plane at a French airport while en route to Ger-

> The government of Cuba, on February 24, 1996, in outrageous contempt for international law and basic human rights, murdered four human beings in international airspace over the Florida Straits. The victims were Brothers to the Rescue pilots, flying two civilian, unarmed planes on a routine humanitarian mission, searching for rafters in the waters between Cuba and the Florida Keys.
>
> As the civilian planes flew over international waters, a Russian-built MIG 29 of the Cuban Air Force, without warning, reason, or provocation, blasted the defenseless planes out of the sky with sophisticated air-to-air missiles in two separate attacks. The pilots and their aircraft disintegrated in the mid-air explosions following the impact of the missiles. The destruction was so complete that the four bodies were never recovered.
>
> —*Alejandre v. Republic of Cuba,* 996 *Fed. Supp.* 1239 (US Dist. Ct., Florida, 1997).

many. That pilot must, however, file a flight plan at the flight's point of origin. France may require an alteration of that flight plan if it interferes with any French regulation or security concerns. State practice is more restrictive in the case of *commercial* aircraft (Article 6 above). They may not fly over or land in the territory of another country without advance routing or landing arrangements.

The International Civil Aviation Organization (ICAO) regulates international commercial aviation. Established by the State parties to the Chicago Convention, this international organization schedules air routes, cargo delivery, and passenger service. Under Article 44 of the Chicago Treaty, the ICAO promotes "the safe and orderly growth of international civil aviation throughout the world . . . [by] development of airways, airports, and air navigation facilities . . . [and avoidance of] economic waste caused by unreasonable competition."

The organization's member States are encouraged to use a neutral tribunal to resolve disputes involving the ICAO's administrative decisions. Article 84 provides that States may appeal such decisions "to an *ad hoc* arbitral tribunal agreed upon with the other parties to the dispute or to the Permanent Court of International Justice." In 1972, the PCIJ's successor tribunal—the International Court of Justice—decided that it could also review ICAO decisions.[56] The ICJ accepted another such case in 1989. That case involved a judicial review of an ICAO decision that the US was not legally responsible when one of its naval vessels shot down an Iranian commercial aircraft over the Persian Gulf. Iran filed a suit, asking the court to declare the ICAO's decision erroneous. The parties ultimately dismissed this suit in 1994 after a number of delays in its pleading phase.

The 1944 Chicago Convention did not resolve many of the problems associated with the *scheduling* of air services. The commercial airlines of the world formed a private organization called the International Air Transport Association (IATA), which has focused its work on achieving the Chicago Convention goal of avoiding "unreasonable competition." The IATA is essentially a cartel of private airlines attempting to avoid destructive or excessive competition among international airlines—an unusually competitive business. The IATA, for example, ensures that flights by competing airlines do not leave the same airport at the same time. Such competition would ultimately destroy one or more of the competitors.

Some airlines have claimed that there is, in fact, a great deal of *anti*-competitive activity in international aviation. In 1983, Laker Airways of England filed lawsuits in England and the US, claiming that various Belgian, British, and Dutch airlines (IATA members) conspired to bankrupt Laker Airways because it offered very competitive airfares to the public. Members of the IATA allegedly perceived Laker's operations as a threat to the price structure established by their association. Plaintiff Laker claimed that during meetings of the IATA in 1977 the IATA airlines "agreed to set rates at a predatory level to drive Laker out of business." Laker also alleged that these international air carriers conspired to stop Laker from expanding its international air routes.[57]

Restrictive business practices in the international airlines industry are not limited to just private airline carriers. Many governments subsidize their government-owned or certain private international airlines, a practice facilitating continuing operation and increasing their share of the international market. These subsidies permit the favored airlines to charge lower fares or operate at a better profit margin, even when they charge the same or lower fares than their competitors. Subsidizing countries thereby create artificial economic barriers to normal market competition. They impose limitations on certain categories of importable cargo and on frequency of passenger aircraft entry into their airspaces. (Similar barriers to international competition are addressed in Chapter 13.) In 1998, the European Union's Court of First Instance thus annulled France's 1994 plan to provide 20 billion francs—about US $3.3 billion—to Air France.

State Aircraft Public (as opposed to private) aircraft are operated by the military, customs, and police authorities. These flights are not generally governed by the 1944 Chicago Convention, although it does make certain limited provisions for such aircraft. Under Article 3:

> (a) This convention shall be applicable only to civil aircraft, and shall not be applicable to state aircraft.
> (b) Aircraft used in military, customs and police services shall be deemed to be state aircraft. [However,]
> (c) No state aircraft . . . shall fly over the territory of another State or land thereon without authorization by special agreement.

Unlike *non*-scheduled private aircraft, government aircraft cannot enter another State's national airspace without its express prior consent. These agreements are often made on a case-by-case basis and otherwise by treaty arrangements between friendly countries. Before making an emergency landing in another State, a military pilot must seek permission to enter that State's airspace (and to land). This requirement prevents one State from sending its planes on a hostile mission under the pretext of a feigned emergency. Military flight agreements, such as those governing a State aircraft's entry into foreign airspace during joint military exercises, are normally made by formal agreements between affected States.

The following case is a classic illustration of national and international concerns about the presence of foreign State aircraft over a State's territory—even when the plane has no weapons systems. This case further illustrates that more than one State can violate International Law when a single plane makes an unauthorized entry into another nation's airspace:

Powers Case

UNION OF SOVIET SOCIALIST REPUBLICS

Military Collegium of the Soviet Supreme Court, 1960

30 *International Law Reports* 69 (1966)

Author's Note: *In 1960, the US authorized the flight of a U-2 military flight aircraft over the former Soviet Union. The U-2 is a reconnaissance aircraft without weapons capability. The U-2 was shot down, and the Soviet Union prosecuted its pilot for espionage. The following excerpts are from the military panel of the Soviet Supreme Court.*

In addition to noting any territorial sovereignty concerns, assess whether the Soviet Union was being unnecessarily technical about the threat posed by this unarmed aircraft in the upper periphery of its airspace where combat aircraft were unable to fly—and, alternatively, whether the Soviets had every right to be concerned about the presence of this aircraft in Russian airspace.

COURT'S OPINION. On May 1, 1960, at 5 hours 36 minutes, Moscow time, a military unit of the Soviet anti-aircraft defence in the area of the city of Kirovabad, the Tajik S.S.R., at an altitude of 20,000 metres, unattainable for planes of the civil air fleet, spotted an unknown aircraft violating the State frontier of the USSR.

The military units of the Soviet anti-aircraft defence vigilantly followed the behaviour of the plane as it flew over major industrial centres and important objectives, and only when the intruder plane had penetrated 2,000 kilometres into Soviet territory and the evil purpose of the flight, fraught with disastrous consequences for world peace in an age of thermonuclear weapons, became absolutely obvious, a battery of ground-to-air missiles brought the aggressor plane down in the area of Sverdlovsk at 8 hours 53 minutes as ordered by the Soviet Government.

The pilot of the plane bailed out and was apprehended upon landing. On interrogation, he gave his name as Francis Gary Powers, citizen of the United States of America. Examination of the wreckage of the plane which had been brought down showed that it was of American make, specially designed for high-altitude flights and fitted with various equipment for espionage reconnaissance tasks.

In April 1956, Powers was recruited by the Central Intelligence Agency of the United States for special intelligence missions in high-altitude aircraft.

After he had concluded a secret contract with the United States Central Intelligence Agency for a term of two years, Powers was allotted a high salary of 2,500 dollars a month for espionage activity. He underwent special training and was assigned to the intelligence air detachment under the code name of "Ten-Ten," stationed at the American–Turkish war base of Incirlik, near the town of Adana, in Turkey.

The Court has established that the detachment "Ten-Ten" is a special combination of the United States military and civilian intelligence designed for espionage against the Soviet Union with the help of reconnaissance planes sent into Soviet airspace. . . .

Having taken off from Peshawar airport in Pakistan, Powers flew over the territory of Afghanistan and for more than 2,000 kilometers over the Soviet Union in accordance with the established course. Besides Powers' testimony, this is confirmed by the American flight map discovered in the debris of the U-2 plane and submitted to the Court, bearing the route plotted out by Major Dulak, navigator of the detachment "Ten-Ten," and also notes and signs made by Powers, who marked down on this map several important defence objectives of the Soviet Union he had spotted from the plane.

Throughout the flight, to the very moment the plane was shot down, Powers switched on his special intelligence equipment, photographed important defence objectives and recorded signals of the country's anti-aircraft radar installations. The development of the rescued aerial photography films established that defendant Powers photographed from the U-2 plane industrial and military objectives of the Soviet Union—plants, depots, oil storage facilities, communication routes, railway bridges and stations, electric transmission lines, aerodromes, the location of troops and military equipment.

The numerous photos of the Soviet Union's territory, taken by defendant Powers from an altitude of 20,000 metres, in possession of the Military Collegium of the USSR Supreme Court, make it possible to determine the nature of industrial establishments, the design of railway bridges, the number and type of aircraft on the airfields, the nature and purpose of military material.

Powers tape-recorded impulses of certain radar stations of the Soviet Union with a view of detecting the country's anti-aircraft defence system.

Powers himself admitted that he realized when intruding into the airspace of the Soviet Union that he was violating the national sovereignty of the USSR and flying over its territory on an espionage mission, whose main purpose consisted of detecting and marking down missile launching sites. . . .

In considering the Powers case, the Military Collegium of the USSR Supreme Court takes into account that the intrusion of the American military intelligence plane constitutes a criminal breach of a generally recognized principle of international law, which establishes the exclusive sovereignty of every State over the airspace above its territory. This principle, laid down by the Paris Convention of October 13, 1919, for the regulation of aerial navigation, and several other subsequent international agreements, is proclaimed in the national legislations of different States, including the Soviet Union and the United States of America.

Violation of this sacred and immutable principle of international relations creates in the present conditions a direct menace to universal peace and international security.

At the present level of military technology, when certain States possess atomic and hydrogen weapons, as well as the means of delivering them quickly to targets, the flight of a military intelligence plane over Soviet territory could have directly preceded a military attack. This danger is the more possible in conditions when the United States of America, as stated by American generals, constantly keeps bomber patrols in the air, always ready to drop bombs on earlier marked-out targets of the Soviet Union.

Under these conditions the aggressive act of the United States of America, carried out on May 1 of this year by defendant Powers, created a threat to universal peace. . . .

After that the American leaders—President Eisenhower, Vice-President Nixon and State Secretary Herter—admitted that spying flights over Soviet territory by American planes constitute part of the "calculated policy of the United States of America."

Thus, the leaders of the United States of America proclaimed the violation of the sovereignty of other States and espionage against them as the official State policy of America. . . .

The Military Collegium of the Supreme Court of the Soviet Union has established that Powers could not have carried out the spy missions assigned to him without the use of the United States of America, for aggressive purposes, of the war bases and aerodromes on the territories of the States neighboring on the Soviet Union, including the territories of Turkey, Iran, Pakistan and Norway.

Powers' flight has proved that the Government of the United States of America, having bound Turkey, Iran, Pakistan, Norway and other States by bilateral military agreements, has established war bases and aerodromes on their territories for dangerous provocative actions, making these States accomplices in the aggression against the Soviet Union.

◆ *Notes & Questions*

1. What State or States violated Soviet airspace? Was the Soviet Union being overly technical about the threat posed by the unarmed US plane?
2. In 1983, a Korean Air Lines passenger jet, KAL Flight 007, was shot down over the Sea of Japan after it strayed into Soviet airspace. All 269 passengers and crew were killed. This was not a military mission. The Soviet pilot knew that it was a passenger aircraft. The US did not institute litigation against the Soviet Union. In some 100 US civil suits against the airlines, KAL has settled 75 with families of the deceased victims. KAL was found liable for the willful misconduct of the crew, which had flown off-course for a number of hours. Suits involving this incident have reached the US Supreme Court on more than one occasion. The latest is *Dooley v. Korean Air Lines,* 118 S.Ct. 1890 (1998).

There are a number of unresolved problems in International Air Law. Two of them are particularly sensitive. States have agreed neither on the permissible degree of response to violations of national airspace nor on the altitude that constitutes the upper limits of territorial airspace. The upper limit is important, because it separates national airspace from outer space—the latter being *res communis,* and thus available to all nations.

Excessive Force How much force may a State use to repel intruders? A number of military planes have purposefully or accidentally entered foreign airspace. A number of commercial aircraft have also encroached on territorial airspace. In some parts of the world, these unexpected intrusions are routinely ignored. In some cases, however, the intruder has been ordered to change course, escorted out of the offended State's territorial airspace, fired on as a warning, forced to land, or actually shot down.

In the decade after World War II, deadly force was employed in a number of incidents involving *non*-military aerial intrusions into national airspace. In the major international incident of 1955, an Israeli commercial plane flew into Bulgarian airspace while en route from Austria to Israel. A Bulgarian military aircraft shot it down over Bulgaria, killing all fifty-eight passengers. Israel instituted proceedings in the International Court of Justice. The court decided, however, that it could not hear the case because Bulgaria had not consented to the court's jurisdiction to hear such cases.[58] Israel and Bulgaria ultimately negotiated a compensation agreement in 1963.

Unfortunately, some States still use deadly force to react to nonmilitary intrusions of their airspace. The 1983 KAL downing, for example, generated a number of diplomatic protests, ICAO deliberations, and several meetings of the United Nations Security Council.[59]

The incident demonstrates the importance that the former Soviet Union attributed to the presence of *any* non-scheduled aircraft in its national airspace.

Upper Limit The upper limit of territorial airspace has not been precisely established. While the 1944 Chicago Convention is the centerpiece of International Air Law, it does not define the extent or height of national airspace. Different States, with varying political agendas, therefore claim different legal limits between national airspace and outer space. As noted by Robert Goedhart, in his work at the University of Utrecht in the Netherlands: "In spite of extensive discussions, anything but agreement on the said boundary has been arrived at . . . neither at a political level nor at a legal level, for which the tensions and enmity between the main spacefaring nations, the former Soviet Union and the United States, as a consequence of the Cold War are partly to blame."[60]

As a practical matter, territorial airspace is limited to the *navigable* airspace over State territory and its adjacent Territorial Seas—twelve nautical miles from the coastline under the Law of the Sea Treaty. This is the limit used by most States when they characterize the extent of their territorial airspace. Navigable airspace is the highest altitude attainable by military aircraft not in orbit.

AIRSPACE ABROAD

Although the 1944 Chicago Convention on International Civil Aviation is a fundamental air treaty, other treaties were needed to address issues that evolved with air travel after World War II. Could a State exercise jurisdiction over criminal offenses aboard its own aircraft when it was flying over international waters or in the airspace of another State? The need to expand jurisdiction over crimes aboard civil (non-military) aircraft became apparent as States began to experience prosecutorial limitations because of voids in applicable jurisdictional principles.

A classic instance of this vacuum emerged in 1950 when a US passenger assaulted several US citizens aboard a plane registered under a US airline company while it was flying over international waters. The Chicago Convention vests jurisdiction in the State where an incident occurs. But this event took place *beyond* national airspace. The American prosecutor resorted to US internal law. Under US law, there had to be a statute that specifically made the passenger's conduct a criminal act. The only relevant statute made it a crime to assault passengers on "vessels" that were "on the high seas." The plane was neither a vessel within the meaning of the only applicable statute nor was it "on" the high seas.[61] The US was *unable* to prosecute this individual, because of the absence of an applicable national law. The case was dismissed. The defendant was thus released from custody. The US Congress reacted by expanding this statute to include such offenses. This incident suggested the need for an international approach to such incidents, which could also occur above the airspace of another country. State representatives negotiated and ratified a series of international treaties to fill such legal gaps.

Tokyo Convention After World War II, the wartime concern about hostile flights appeared to be eclipsed by another problem. Airlines with large fleets of commercial aircraft were understandably concerned about their aircraft being subjected to the exclusive control of foreign nations while operating within foreign airspace. Within two decades after the war ended, members of the airline industry convinced their respective governments to negotiate the first multilateral air treaty containing *several* jurisdictional alternatives—the 1963 Tokyo Convention on Offences and Certain Other Acts Committed on Board Aircraft. It became effective in 1969 and has been ratified by most nations of the world.[62]

The Tokyo Convention established a framework for punishing individuals who commit violent crimes during international flights. This treaty emphasizes the jurisdiction of the aircraft's State of registration (often called the flag State) rather than that of the airspace of the State where the offense is committed. This treaty facilitated prosecution under jurisdictional principles not contemplated by the 1944 Chicago Convention while effectively expanding the range of sovereignty now exercisable in the airspace above distant lands. Because States had the exclusive sovereign power over the airspace above them (Chicago Convention), they had the correlative right to yield this total control of their airspace for mutually acceptable purposes. Under Article 3 of the Tokyo Convention, the "State of registration of the aircraft is competent to exercise jurisdiction over offences and acts committed on board [and each participating State] shall take such measures as may be necessary to establish its jurisdiction as the State of registration over offences committed on board aircraft registered in such State."

Under Article 4 of the Tokyo Convention, a State that is *not* the State of registration cannot interfere on the basis that its *territorial* criminal jurisdiction also applies in its own airspace—*except* in the following specific cases (covered in Chapter 5 on extraterritorial jurisdiction):

(a) The offense has an effect on the territory of such State (territorial principle);
(b) the offense has been committed by or against a national or permanent resident of such State (nationality and passive personality principles); and
(c) The offense is against the security of such State (protective principle).

Assume that a Japanese airliner is flying in an easterly direction 25,000 feet over Hawaii en route to Canada. A German passenger assaults and kills a French citizen during the flight. All of these countries are parties to both the Chicago and the Tokyo conventions. Under the territorial principle of international criminal jurisdiction, the incident occurred "in" the US because the Japanese aircraft was flying within the navigable airspace of a state of the US. Under the 1944 Chicago Convention, the US has "complete and exclusive sovereignty over the airspace above its territory." Japan is the State of registration (i.e., the flag State). Under Article 3 of the 1963 Tokyo Convention, Japan would be "competent to exercise jurisdiction over offences and acts committed on board [its airliner and should] take such measures as may be necessary to establish its jurisdiction." Since the US is a party to the Tokyo Convention, it will yield its territorial right to Japan to prosecute the German passenger. Japan will be obliged to prosecute this German citizen for the offense aboard the Japanese aircraft (unless it accedes to a US request to have the perpetrator tried in the US).

Under Article 4 of the Tokyo Convention, States other than the State of registration should not interfere by exercising their criminal jurisdiction over the offender. While the US has territorial jurisdiction over the German passenger, it should assist Japan in the latter's efforts to prosecute him. If the plane lands in Hawaii, the US should grant Japan's extradition request.

There are significant exceptions to the treaty norm of ceding jurisdiction to the State of registration. Other States may prosecute the German citizen in four situations. First, another State may prosecute him if his crime has an effect on its territory. This exception draws from the "effects doctrine" established by the Permanent Court of International Justice in the *SS Lotus Case* in 1927 (set forth in the text of §5.2). The Tokyo Convention thus provides for applications of the territorial principle of international criminal jurisdiction. If the captain of the Japanese airliner has to alter course or altitude to respond to the incident, that action might violate navigational rules established for the safety of aircraft. The US could then request the plane to land and prosecute the German for various crimes against the United States—over Japan's objection. This is an example of the territorial principle of jurisdiction, which remains available under the terms of the Tokyo Convention.

The second and third bases for States other than Japan (the State of the aircraft's registration) to exercise jurisdiction over the German citizen employ the nationality and passive personality principles of criminal jurisdiction. Germany and France may prosecute the German passenger under Article 4b of the above Convention: The "offense has been committed *by* or *against* a national or permanent resident of such State [that is a treaty party]." Germany may prosecute its national under the nationality principle; and France may prosecute the German passenger for killing a French citizen, under the passive personality principle.

The fourth exception to Japan's primary jurisdiction as the flag State involves the protective principle of jurisdiction. The German passenger may be prosecuted outside of Japan if this "offense is against the security" of some other State. It is unlikely that the US would actually claim that its security was threatened by the killing of the French citizen or, alternatively, by the unusual maneuvers of the Japanese aircraft over Hawaii. Suppose, however, that the French citizen was working for the US Central Intelligence Agency and was carrying sensitive documents, which the German stole and was the reason for the murder aboard the aircraft. US security interests might support the exercise of US jurisdiction—under the "security exception" to Japan's primary jurisdiction over its aircraft.

These additional jurisdictional bases for extending the range of State sovereignty have invoked all the typical rationales for international criminal jurisdiction except for one—the universality principle, which is discussed immediately below. The following treaty (Hague Convention) was needed because the Tokyo Convention was not intended to cover such interferences with civil aviation. This is why the Tokyo Convention paid lip service to primary jurisdiction of the State of registration while at the same time retaining all of the criminal jurisdictional principles. These were employed as express exceptions to the "rule" that the flag State (Japan) would have the "first shot" at criminal conduct occurring aboard its aircraft operating over another State and international waters (US).[63]

Hague Convention The 1970 Hague Convention for the Suppression of Unlawful Seizure of Aircraft added another jurisdictional alternative for prosecuting crimes on international flights. The universality principle provides that certain crimes are sufficiently heinous to be considered crimes against *all* States. Every State then has the jurisdiction to capture and punish or to extradite the perpetrator of such crimes (*see* §5.2). The Hague Convention extends the universality principle of jurisdiction to aircraft hijackings.

The treaty's fundamental theme is that all States must take the necessary steps to prosecute or extradite those who unlawfully seize commercial aircraft. This treaty is a direct response to the rash of international hijackings that began in the late 1960s. Too many nations clandestinely supported the political goals underlying those hijackings, seeking to publicize the political problems of the Middle East. These nations characterized brutal crimes aboard hijacked aircraft as "political conduct" rather than extraditable common crimes (*see* §5.3 on this exception to extradition). They granted asylum to or did not otherwise prosecute the responsible hijackers. Consequently, there was a growing international desire to deny such asylum to those involved in what most States characterized as "universal" crimes.

Some governments have invoked the convenient ploy of characterizing certain aircraft hijackings as "political" rather than common crimes (*see* §5.3 on "political" crimes). The 1970 Hague Convention neither addresses nor precludes this practice. Under the 1976 European Convention on the Suppression of Terrorism, however, offenses governed by the 1970 Hague Convention *cannot* be characterized as "political" offenses. This European treaty applies to only a handful of nations, however, that are parties to the Hague Convention.[64]

The Hague Convention was nevertheless the first *multilateral* step toward establishing air hijacking as a universal crime. More than 140 nations are parties to this treaty, which permits the exercise of jurisdiction over international flights by States other than the State of registration. Under Article 4 of the Hague Convention, each "[c]ontracting State shall take such measures as may be necessary to establish its jurisdiction over the offense . . . [and] shall likewise take such measures as may be necessary to establish . . . jurisdiction over the offense in the case where the alleged offender is present in its territory and it does not extradite him. . . ." Article 8 provides that the "offense shall be treated, for the purposes of extradition between Contracting States, as if it had been committed *not only* in the place in which it occurred *but also* in the territories of the States required to establish their jurisdiction in accordance with Article 4" (emphasis supplied by author).

Assume that the hypothetical German terrorist mentioned in this section forcefully takes control of the Japanese airliner over Hawaii. The hijacker causes it to land in Canada to refuel. The plane is then diverted to Libya. That nation does not comply with its treaty obligation to capture and prosecute the hijacker, who has committed a universal crime under the Hague Convention. The terrorist then escapes to Lebanon. All of these nations are parties to the Hague Convention. What States may thereby exercise jurisdiction over the German terrorist under the 1970 Hague Convention? Under Article 4, *each* State party must take measures to ensure that jurisdiction is somehow established. In this case, Japan *could* exercise its jurisdiction over the terrorist—but only if Lebanon were convinced to surrender the terrorist to Japan. The latter is the State of registration of the aircraft with "territorial" jurisdiction over events occurring aboard it anywhere in the world.

Under Article 6, any State "in the territory of which the offender or the alleged offender is present *shall* take him into custody or take other measures to ensure his presence." Canada or Lebanon would have the obligation to exercise jurisdiction in the case of such a "universal" crime. The Hague treaty requires them to take the necessary steps to prosecute or extradite the terrorist—either when the plane landed for refueling in Canada, or when it arrived at the final destination of Libya.

Since neither Canada nor Libya actually captured the hijacker, Lebanon would incur the ultimate obligation of prosecution or extradition under the Hague Convention. Lebanon would be justified in treating the terrorist's act "as if it had been committed not only in the place in which it occurred but also in the territories of the States required to establish their jurisdiction" over this hijacking incident. Lebanon is thereby obligated to capture this terrorist upon arrival in its territory. Mere custody of the terrorist would give Lebanon the right (or obligation) to either try or extradite him to Japan, Canada, or the US. Parts of the crime occurred in their respective territories.

Unfortunately, certain States have clandestinely supported hijacking incidents while appearing to satisfy their Hague Convention prosecution obligations. Under Article 7, a State that does not extradite a hijacker is "obliged, without exception whatsoever . . . to submit the case to its competent authorities for the purpose of prosecution." States that are sympathetic to the political cause of a particular hijacker, however, have sometimes allowed the terrorist to "escape." Alternatively, they have conducted mock trials for the purpose of concluding that the terrorists were *not* guilty of hijacking charges in violation of the Hague Convention. In 1973, for example, an Italian court released the hijackers of an Israeli passenger plane and tried them *in absentia*. Cyprus released Arab terrorists who attacked an Israeli plane in Cyprus after they were sentenced to imprisonment. These States technically met their treaty obligation to "prosecute" terrorists who seize commercial aircraft.[65]

Montreal Sabotage Convention The related 1971 Montreal Sabotage Convention similarly establishes universal jurisdiction over those who bomb or sabotage (rather than merely seize) commercial aircraft.[66]

The terrorist bombing of Pan Am Flight 103 over Lockerbie, Scotland, in 1988 triggered the criminal liability of the Libyan individuals allegedly responsible for the deaths of 230 passengers. Libya had, and still has, the responsibility to prosecute these perpetrators or turn them over for trial in the UK or the US, where they have been indicted. UN Security Council Resolution 731 of 1992 determined that Libya must release them for trial. Libya responded with a suit in the International Court of Justice, claiming that the US and the UK had themselves breached the Montreal Convention. Libya presented the theory in this case that the US and the UK had rejected Libyan efforts to resolve this matter in good faith. Libya claims that the US and the UK allegedly threatened the use of force. It requested that the ICJ issue an order prohibiting those countries from acting in any way that would further threaten peaceful relations. Libya was presumably concerned that, like the 1986 US bombing of Tripoli in response to another terrorist incident, these nations might undertake a military mission to extract the Libyan agents allegedly responsible for the bombing of Pan Am Flight 103.

The Court decided *not* to grant Libya's request for these measures pending the resolution of this matter between Libya and the US and UK. The essential stumbling block was that another UN organ, the Security Council, under Resolution 731, had already demanded that Libya turn over the terrorists for trial elsewhere. The ICJ did not want to be in the awkward position of rendering an injunction against US–UK action under the existing norm of International Law that prohibits the use of force to resolve disputes. The Court avoided this dilemma by noting that Libya chose instead to base its request for relief on the Montreal Convention—which does *not* involve any issue involving reprisals or the responsive use of force by another State. This possibility was never contemplated under the terms or intended scope of the Montreal treaty. In the words of the ICJ's Judge Shahabuddeen (from Guyana),

> the decision [that] the Court is asked to give [in favor of Libya] is one [that] would directly conflict with a decision of the Security Council. . . . Yet, it is not the jurisdictional ground for today's Order [denying Libya's request that the US and UK not take any action involving the use of force until this case is resolved on its merits]. This [denial] results not from any collision between the competence of the Security Council and that of the Court, but from a collision between the obligations of Libya under the decision of the Security Council and any obligation it may have under the Montreal Convention. The [UN] Charter says that the former [must] prevail.

In 1998, almost six years after Libya instituted this suit, the ICJ finally ruled that it did have jurisdiction.[67] In so doing, the ICJ acknowledged the potential for conflict between the UN Charter and other international agreements. Libya's claim under the Montreal Convention was that it was competent to investigate its own agents who were in Libya. But the Security Council had ordered Libya to release them for trial elsewhere, given Libya's apparent responsibility for State terrorism. Under Article 25 of the UN Charter, UN members agree to comply with decisions of the Security Council. Under Article 103 of the Charter, the Charter prevails "[i]n the event of a conflict between the obligations of the Members of the United Nations under the present Charter and their obligations under any other international agreement. . . ." Thus, Libya's treaty-based right to investigate and try these individuals was superseded by the Security Council action and the conflict resolution mechanism expressed in Charter Article 103.

At present, there have been only unsuccessful negotiations that would lift sanctions against Libya if it allowed the two allegedly responsible terrorists to stand trial in The Netherlands. The judges would be Scottish, Scottish law would apply, and sentences would be served in The Netherlands. However, Libya has backed out, several times at the last moment, on grounds that the plan is really a US–UK scheme to obtain custody of the two Libyans they have indicted for this crime.

OUTER SPACE

> Outer space, including the moon and other celestial bodies, is not subject to national appropriation by claim of sovereignty, by means of use or occupation, or by any other means.
>
> A State Party to the Treaty on whose registry an object launched into outer space is carried shall retain jurisdiction and control over such object, and over any personnel thereof, while in outer space or on a celestial body. . . .
>
> —Articles II and VIII, UN Treaty on Principles Governing the Activities of States in the Exploration and Use of Outer Space, Including the Moon and Other Celestial Bodies (1967)

The actual exploration of outer space began in 1957 when the Soviets launched their Sputnik satellite. This was the first man-made object to orbit the Earth. In 1961, the UN General Assembly resolved that international "law, including the Charter of the United Nations, applies to outer space and celestial bodies."[68]

The current status of outer space is analogous to the historical maritime concept of *res communis.* The High Seas are *res communis,* meaning that they are incapable of ownership and open to the peaceful use of all States (*see* §6.3). Under International Law, space and the planets within it are governed by the same regime. In 1967, the UN Treaty on Principles Governing the Activities of States in the Exploration and Use of Outer Space, Including the Moon and Other Celestial Bodies, established mutual State expectations about international relations in outer space. Under Article I of the Outer Space Treaty, as it is known, the "exploration and use of outer space . . . shall be carried out for the benefit and in the interests of all countries, irrespective of their degree of economic or scientific development, and shall be the province of all mankind."[69]

In the twenty-first century, people likely will inhabit space stations and other planets for extended periods of time, if not permanently. In November 1998, Russia launched the initial module of the International Space Station. Sixteen nations are participating in this project, consisting of 100 elements and scheduled to be completed by 2004. It will be an orbital home for at least fifteen years, followed by potential habitation on other planets. Will those societies govern themselves in accordance with the peaceable norms of International Law developed on the Planet Earth? The critical questions that will have to be answered include the following:

1. Will interplanetary colonization result in "States" as we now know them?
2. Will the UN Charter's prohibition against the use of force actually be extended into space? Or be abandoned? Or be supplanted by some other regime?
3. Will the national entities on Earth—referred to as States—apply Earth-bound legal principles to the vast reaches of outer space?
4. Alternatively, will various social groupings in space apply different paradigms that each planet or solar system considers appropriate for their independent galaxies separated by light years of travel?
5. Will the existence and discovery of another species of life make these questions irrelevant?

One must presume that, notwithstanding well-intentioned statements from the UN, nationalism and international tension could nevertheless be exported into

EXHIBIT 6.4 OUTER SPACE "CHARTER"

1958 UNGA RESOLUTION	UN General Assembly Res. 1348(XIII): Peaceful use of outer space and avoidance of national rivalries in outer space.
1959 UNGA RESOLUTION	Res. 1472(XIV): Freedom of space exploration.
1961 UNGA RESOLUTION	Res. 1721(XIV): Space to be used for benefit of all humankind.
1962 UNGA DECLARATION	General Assembly Declaration of Legal Principles Governing the Activities of States in the Exploration and Use of Outer Space: Resolved to conclude a nuclear test ban treaty; did not specifically recognize military use of outer space (3 *ILM* 157).
1963 TREATY	Treaty Banning Nuclear Weapon Tests in Atmosphere, Outer Space and Under Water: No nuclear explosions are permitted in outer space (2 *ILM* 883).
1963 UNGA RESOLUTION	Res. 1884(XVIII) Regarding Weapons of Mass Destruction: US and USSR are not to station nuclear or other weapons of mass destruction in outer space (2 *ILM* 1192).
1967 UNGA TREATY REGIME	Principles Governing the Activities of States in the Exploration and Use of Outer Space, Including the Moon and Other Celestial Bodies Outer Space Treaty: The Magna Carta of outer space regime; no weapons of mass destruction allowed; no military bases or maneuvers in space, although use of military for science; implicit acceptance of conventional weapons (6 *ILM* 386).
1971 CONVENTION	International Liability for Damage Caused by Space Objects: Launching State liable for damage caused by falling space debris (Liability Convention) (10 *ILM* 965).
1979 UNGA RESOLUTION	Moon Treaty: Clarifies ambiguities in 1967 Outer Space Treaty; moon subject to same demilitarization regime as other bodies. "Peaceful purposes" remains undefined (18 *ILM* 1434).
VARIOUS BILATERAL TREATIES	Most prominent are the SALT I and II Agreements between the US and former USSR providing for strategic arms limitations (20 *ILM* 477; 26 *ILM* 232).

*UNGA = UN General Assembly; *ILM* = *International Legal Materials*

space. This presumption was most evident during the Cold War, as illustrated by the following assessment of two US space specialists in 1986. Their view employed the typical perspective about the irreconcilable conflict in East–West relations:

> Thus we see two distinct and dissonant sets of values at work in the modern social arena. . . . These paradoxical, competing values are important both within and among countries. Totalitarian states, of course, adhere to military techniques both for survival and as the firmest foundation for loyalty and respect. They adhere to the atavistic view that the only true respect is born of fear. . . . The modern scientific view says that human diversity and sovereignty demand liberty both within and among states and that world peace will never be achieved otherwise . . . [although] many states do not seem to have learned this lesson fully. And since military tactics are to take by force, fire is fought with fire. All sides risk the incendiary consequences, because the chosen countertactic is counterforce . . . [although] the countertactic is endless escalation, perhaps even conflagration.[70]

While the superpower struggle of the Cold War has ended, the need remains to define the principles for peaceably governing activities in the rest of the universe in the twenty-first century. The following principles restate the International Law of Outer Space. The principal documents are chronicled in Exhibit 6-4.

The essential features of the current international legal regime for outer space include Article III of the 1967 Outer Space Treaty—the Magna Carta of outer space. It provides that "activities in the exploration and use of outer space . . . [are governed by] international law, including the Charter of the United Nations, in the interest of maintaining international peace and security and promoting international cooperation and understanding." International Law decisively mandates free access to outer space, the moon, and other celestial bodies. Unlike exploration on the Planet Earth, national exploration of the other planets will *not* give rise to any sovereign rights. For example, the US landed on the moon in 1969. Under the 1967 Outer Space Treaty, it did not thereby acquire any sovereign rights. The US can neither own the moon nor preclude other nations from gaining access to it. The universe may be explored for *scientific* purposes disassociated from any expansion of national sovereignty.

The Outer Space Treaty also demilitarizes outer space. Its national signatories "undertake not to place in orbit around the Earth any objects carrying nuclear weapons or any other kinds of weapons of mass destruction, install such weapons on celestial bodies, or station such weapons in outer space in any other manner . . . [because the] moon and other celestial bodies shall be used by all State Parties to the Treaty exclusively for peaceful purposes." The treaty does permit, however, a limited military presence in space. Article IV concurrently provides that the "use of *military* personnel for scientific research or for any other peaceful purposes shall *not* be prohibited" (emphasis supplied by author). In 1998, the US Departments of State and Defense thus objected to President Clinton's approval of satellite technology to the Peoples Republic of China. This was a "dual technology" transfer, usable for both commercial communications functions but readily convertible to weapons guidance systems. Like the aborted Star Wars Defense initiative of the Reagan administration, this transfer was perceived as violating various treaties including the 1972 Anti-Ballistic Missile Treaty, which outlaws missiles in outer space.

The demilitarization language in the 1967 Outer Space Treaty was drawn in part from the 1963 Nuclear Test Ban Treaty, whose original members were the United Kingdom, the former Soviet Union, and the US. Most nations of the world are parties to the Nuclear Test Ban Treaty. The principal provision in Article I of the Outer Space Treaty contains a promise that each member "undertakes to prohibit, to prevent, and not to carry out any nuclear weapon test explosion, or any other nuclear explosion, at any place under its jurisdiction or control. . . ." India and Pakistan's 1998 nuclear testing generated a fresh resolve to broaden participation in this particular treaty. Suddenly, the world seemed poised to deal with another crisis, although now between long-term regional rivals rather than the US and the former USSR.

The above language, contained in both the Test Ban Treaty and the Outer Space Treaty, is nevertheless ambiguous. It is really a compromise to ensure the participation of the then-existing space powers in the Outer Space Treaty, which would not have approved a *total* ban on a military presence in space. This article was a basis for the former Soviet claim that the US would violate the Outer Space Treaty if it had implemented the proposed Strategic Defense Initiative announced by the Reagan administration in 1983. Under that proposal, the US once considered placing nuclear military installations in outer space to defensively neutralize Soviet weapons—and those of other countries—before they could reach the US. Then, in 1997, the US military announced its plans to aim a laser at a US satellite in space. The purpose was to test methods for protecting satellites from jamming and being otherwise disabled. This spawned concern in the US Congress that Russia might respond by resurrecting its own testing involving ballistic missile shots at its satellites.

The Outer Space Treaty incorporates *non-military* concerns of the international community. It requires participants to assume full civil liability for their activities in outer space that cause harm to any of Earth's inhabitants. Under Article VI, launching nations "bear international responsibility for national activities in outer space. . . ." This requirement inspired the creation of the 1971 Liability Convention, under which ratifying States have accepted automatic responsibility for damage caused by their spacecraft upon reentering Earth's atmosphere.

Under Article II of the 1971 Liability Convention, a "launching State shall be absolutely liable [even if its conduct is not negligent] to pay compensation for damage caused by its space object on the surface of the earth or to aircraft in flight." The launching State should provide advance notification of an anticipated breach of airspace caused by a falling object. This convention was applied in 1979 when Canada lodged a claim against the former Soviet Union, alleging that the latter nation did not comply with its treaty obligation to notify Canada of a nuclear-powered satellite's potential reentry into

Canadian airspace. Canada claimed that when "Cosmos 954" fell, it deposited harmful radioactive debris in various parts of Canada's Northwest Territories. Canada's claim was later resolved diplomatically.[71]

The research and exploration of outer space is "on hold" in the sense that there is no longer a space race between the two superpowers of the Cold War. Further, economic considerations make it difficult for the US and Russia to continue the massive planning that occurred immediately after the Soviet Sputnik went into orbit in 1957—culminating in the US landing the first man on the moon in 1969. Yet all States are interested in pursuing the age-old dream of space travel. With world financial markets on a virtual roller coaster in the 1990s, international cooperation may be the only way to tap the resources available in outer space.

"Where do we go from here?" This familiar question has special meaning in the context of outer space, especially as the population continues to outgrow food supply—and the environment is unable to meet demands being currently placed on it. There are over 500 satellites operating in space. Hundreds more are expected to be in orbit in the coming decade, especially as the information age evolves via space technology. The militarization of space has been outlawed by UN efforts. There is no guarantee that existing charters and organizations will be able to meet the evolving demands of life in the twenty-first century.

Because there has been an effective worldwide organization for the last half of the twentieth century—the UN—the time may be ripe for a World Space Organization. It would develop and possess the specialized expertise for achieving objectives like those contained in the UN Charter—although in a far more "universal" sense. The international political environment appears to be amenable now that the confrontations of the Cold War superpower era is gone. Yet the cost and complexity of space exploration is astronomical. Such an organization could act as a catalyst for managing resources, technology, and manpower in an independent way that would benefit all nations (not unlike the work of the UN's International Seabed Authority for the oceans of the globe).[72]

◆ SUMMARY

1. There are four general types of territory: (1) territory owned by a sovereign State, (2) territory not owned by any State, (3) territory capable of ownership but not yet under sovereign control, and (4) territory that is not capable of ownership by any State.
2. Certain territories are not subject to the sovereignty of any nation because of their special status. These were the League of Nations "mandates" and United Nations "trust" territories.
3. An area that is *terra nullius* belongs to no one. It is capable of acquisition. In the event of a sovereignty dispute, a State can usually establish a legitimate claim by showing that the disputed territory was initially *terra nullius.*
4. Territories that are *res communis* belong to no one and must remain available for all to use. They are incapable of ownership or control by any sovereign State. Antarctica is in this category, based primarily on the inability of States to effectively occupy it. The High Seas and outer space are the best examples of *res communis.*
5. Five historical methods were used to acquire title to land: (1) occupation, (2) conquest, (3) cession, (4) prescription, and (5) accretion. *Occupation* must be "effective." When two States claim title to the same territory, the successful State usually establishes its title by actual possession. Modern prohibitions on the use of force have outlawed *conquest* as a legitimate basis for claiming sovereignty over a conquered territory. In a cession treaty, the grantor State cedes its title to the grantee State. Title by *prescription* occurs when another State's territory is occupied without a clear legal basis, but the supposed State owner does not protest the occupation for some period of time. *Accretion* may alter international boundaries by the gradual accumulation of land deposits. Sudden changes do not affect the boundary between two nations. The change must be gradual and imperceptible.
6. Title may also be established by renunciation, joint decision, and adjudication.
7. The historical methods for acquiring sovereignty over State territory have been criticized for ignoring the rights of the prior inhabitants of territories that States conveniently characterized as "uncivilized."
8. Internal waters are the waters on the land side of the coastal baseline. The baseline is the point where the ocean meets the coast, separating internal waters from the Territorial Sea.

9. Some special problems with the regime of internal waters include crimes committed aboard a vessel in port—normally subject to the jurisdiction of the vessel's flag (home) State of registration. The port State may prosecute, however, when the crime sufficiently disturbs the port's tranquility. A bay is a well marked indentation with a penetration too deep to constitute a mere curvature of the coastline. Bays wider than twenty-four miles at their mouths normally contain international waters. They may be historic bays, instead, that contain most or only internal waters.
10. The Territorial Sea (TS) begins at the baseline, which marks the inner boundary of the various coastal sea zones. The TS extends out to twelve nautical miles from the coastal baseline. This portion of the ocean is subject to the *exclusive* sovereignty of the coastal State.
11. Two related problems with the Territorial Sea involve passage of oceangoing vessels. The coastal State administers its rules of innocent passage in the TS zone. Under International Law, passage is innocent as long as it does not "prejudice the peace, good order, or security of the coastal State." A number of straits formerly containing international waters may be subject to the rules of innocent passage, because of recent expansions of territorial jurisdiction under customary practice and the UN Convention on the Law of the Sea. Under the Law of the Sea Treaty, which entered into force in 1994, many of these straits will be subject to a more liberal form of coastal jurisdiction referred to as "strait" passage. Ships will be authorized to pass through them as if they still contain High Seas (absent a treaty reservation by the coastal State).
12. The High Seas is that part of the ocean not subject to the *exclusive* territorial sovereignty of any nation. These waters are beyond the national sovereignty exercisable in a coastal State's Territorial, Contiguous, or Exclusive Economic Zones.
13. The UNCLOS extended coastal State jurisdiction in the High Seas in several ways. It adopted a twenty-four-mile Contiguous Zone (formerly twelve miles). The coastal State may therein protect its interests in enforcing its laws governing matters such as immigration, customs, and drug control. The Continental Shelf (CS) regime of the UNCLOS further permits coastal State control of resources in the CS, in some cases from 200 to 350 nautical miles from the coast. There is also an Exclusive Economic Zone (EEZ), which authorizes State control over resources in the waters up to 200 nautical miles from shore. Other nations must pay fees for using the resources within the coastal State's EEZ. This provides some redistribution of the wealth within the EEZ to a coastal State that lacks the technology to take advantage of its nearby resources.
14. The deep seabed beyond the EEZ is not subject to coastal control. Provisions of the 1982 UNCLOS, objected to by the major maritime powers, provide that the oceans are otherwise subject to international control by the International Seabed Authority. The Authority is supposed to supervise the equitable distribution of the world's ocean resources. Under a 1994 special agreement, generated by the US and other major maritime powers, a number of the UNCLOS provisions will *not* apply to those nations. They may ratify the UNCLOS without subjecting themselves to the required technology transfer, sharing of revenues, and decision-making process that would otherwise disregard the pro rata interests of these major maritime powers.
15. The lesser-developed nations of the world want to participate effectively in the exploration and exploitation of the natural resources adjacent to their coastlines, as well as throughout all of the oceans. The coastal State EEZ and the International Seabed Authority are some of the treaty-based tools for accommodating the conflict between the historical rule of freedom of the seas and the modern penchant for an equitable distribution of ocean resources.
16. Airspace is included within the concept of "State territory." Under general principles of International Law, States enjoy exclusive sovereignty in the airspace above their territory. They may limit the entry of aircraft into their national airspace and may also restrict freedom of navigation—that is, the types of importable cargo and the scope of passenger airlines operations within their territories.
17. Various treaties have impacted the original notion of exclusivity of sovereignty over national airspace. The 1944 Chicago Convention on International Civil Aviation contains the fundamental principles of International Air Law. Also, two international organizations regulate international commercial aviation.

The *public* entity, whose membership consists of States, is the International Civil Aviation Organization. The International Air Transport Association is a *private* entity, a cartel of commercial airlines designed to control destructive competition.

18. *State* aircraft are operated by the military, customs, or police authorities of a State. They cannot enter another country's national airspace without express prior consent, often the subject of preexisting treaty arrangements.
19. As to private (nongovernment) aircraft, States have agreed to limit their absolute jurisdiction over their airspaces under various international treaties. Under the 1963 Tokyo Convention on Offences and Certain Other Acts Committed on Board Aircraft, the *State of registration* has primary jurisdiction or control over its own aircraft wherever they are operating. The 1970 Hague Convention for the Suppression of Unlawful Seizure of Aircraft provides for "universal" jurisdiction. Hijacking is thereby considered a crime against *all* nations, and each nation has the jurisdiction to capture and punish or to extradite aircraft hijackers. And certain treaties contain provisions that prohibit or limit the state practice of treating aircraft hijacking and other violent crimes as "political offenses" based on the motives of the offender. These treaties preclude excusing hijackers under the political offense exception to most extradition treaties.
20. Unexpected intrusions by a foreign commercial aircraft are often ignored. States may thus order course changes, escort offending planes out of their airspace, fire warning shots, or force landings. During the Cold War, some nations considered *any* intrusion to be of major significance, warranting the most extreme measures to repel such flights—including those of *commercial* aircraft.
21. The fundamental outer space treaties of the Outer Space Charter are the 1967 Outer Space Treaty and the 1963 Nuclear Test Ban Treaty. The Outer Space Treaty and the Nuclear Test Ban Treaty provide that outer space cannot be owned or claimed by any nation, is accessible to all nations, and shall be used for peaceful and scientific purposes. The language of these treaties extends existing principles of International Law into outer space. It is possible, however, that these norms will be ignored and replaced with a new regime—either constructive or destructive—as outer space activities develop in the twenty-first century.

◆ PROBLEMS

Problem 6.A (end of §6.2) Assume the following facts: Iran (or its predecessor Persia) has exercised sovereignty over the island of Qais in the Persian Gulf near Iran's coastline as a result of a military conquest 500 years ago. Iran and Iraq are now at war (sometime during their more contemporary 1980–1988 war). Iraq's military forces seize Qais and refuse to return it to Iranian control. Iraq does not physically occupy Qais, but its military vessels prohibit Iran from gaining any access to Qais. Iran takes no action until fifteen years later when it lodges a formal diplomatic protest with Iraq, disputing Iraq's current control of Qais. Iran insists that Qais remains under Iraq's historical territorial sovereignty.

Two students will act as representatives for Iran and Iraq. They will debate whether Qais is now legally owned by Iran or Iraq.

Problem 6.B (§6.3 at end of (2) Territorial Sea) The US and the hypothetical nation of Estado are on the verge of a military confrontation. A sizable US fleet is steaming toward Estado to engage in what some cantankerous senators have branded "gunboat diplomacy"—a show of force designed to illustrate the US decision to back up its political position with a show of military strength.

The US fleet crosses into what Estado has claimed to be its 200-nautical-mile "Territorial Sea" (announced in 1952). Estado has never announced a sovereign claim to any other sea zone. Estado claims exclusive sovereignty over all of Bahia Grande, the large bay adjacent to its northern coastal border. This would be the first time that foreign vessels have ever entered Bahia Grande without Estado's permission.

The fleet continues to head directly for Estado's Port El Centro on the southern edge of Bahia Grande. The bay's east–west mouth is forty nautical miles wide. The Port's outer harbor facilities are on the coastal baseline twenty miles south of the mouth (or entrance points of the bay). These facilities are on a point of the bay's coastline that is equidistant from the entrance points forming the mouth of the Bahia Grande.

The US military forces pass through the center of the bay's navigable channel in the middle of the mouth of the bay. The armada pauses at a point fifteen miles from the outer edge of Port El Centro on the coastline and equidistant from the sides of the semicircular coastline forming the edges of Bahia Grande. This resting point is also five miles south of a line that could be drawn across the bay between its entrance points. All US military forces are operating in Combat Readiness Alpha, the highest degree of preparation for actual combat. Various units in this task force have nuclear capabilities.

When the US forces come to rest in the bay, are they located in the *internal* waters of Estado or in *international* waters as defined by International Law?

Problem 6.C (§6.3 at end of (2) Territorial Sea) A US Navy vessel and a US passenger ship are about to pass through an international strait between two coastal nations. The strait's natural width varies from fifteen to twenty-five nautical miles between the bordering coastal States. Each State has ratified the 1982 Convention on the Law of the Sea. The navigational officer (NO) does not know whether the two coastal States have ratified Articles 37–44 of the UN Convention on the Law of the Sea authorizing "strait passage." (The NO's petty officer is researching the ships' records, which will be subsequently reported to the captain.)

NO 1 is the navigational officer aboard the Navy vessel. NO 2 is the navigational officer aboard the passenger ship. The NOs will advise their respective captains (that is, the class) of the rights of each ship and the coastal States. The NOs will review the various rules of passage outlined in the materials in this section of the book—(2) Territorial Sea.

Problem 6.D (end of §6.3) Refer to Problem 6.2 above, wherein the US fleet steams into Estado's Bahia Grande. Assume that Bahia Grande is *not* a historic bay that contains only internal waters.

Refer to the Exhibit 6.1 Sea Zones chart at the beginning of §6.3. Assume that Port El Centro's outer harbor facilities are located on that chart at the point marked "Coastal Baseline."

Apply the 1982 UNCLOS principles—and any applicable customary International Law principles—to answer the following questions:

1. Did the US violate Estado's territorial waters when it crossed into Estado's 200-mile Territorial Sea?
2. What coastal zone did the US fleet first enter when it was en route to Estado?
3. Did the US fleet ever enter Estado's contiguous zone? If so, where?
4. Did the US fleet ever enter Estado's territorial waters? Where?
5. Where do Estado's internal waters meet its Territorial Sea?

Problem 6.E (end of §6.3) Assume that the US and the hypothetical nation of Estado enter into a treaty giving US corporations the right to establish business operations in Estado. Assume that a large multinational enterprise called Mineco is the US-based corporate parent for many worldwide subsidiary corporations. Mineco has established a foreign corporate subsidiary in Estado. None of Mineco's key management personnel are citizens of Estado, although all of Mineco's blue-collar workers are Estado nationals.

Under the Estado–US licensing agreement, Mineco is solely responsible for all mining of Wondore, a valuable ore found mainly in and near Estado. Wondore is used to create energy. US scientists are now exploring whether it can also serve as the energy alternative to oil. Under the licensing agreement with Estado, Mineco has the exclusive right to do all of the drilling in and near this resource-rich nation. There are vast reserves of Wondore in the seabed adjacent to Estado's shores—up to 300 nautical miles from its coastline. Mineco is now examining the viability of drilling under the ocean floor in a corridor that stretches from Estado to 300 nautical miles seaward from its coast.

Assume that Estado is a party to and has ratified the 1982 Law of the Sea Treaty, which entered into force in 1994. The US position is not relevant, because any rights involving mining in or near Estado waters will depend on Estado's position regarding the UNCLOS. You should assume the following alternatives: (a) Estado *is* and (b) Estado *is not* a party to the special 1994 Agreement (prompted by the US to avoid the impact of the UNCLOS's Part XI provisions regarding the mining of deep seabed resources). How does the new UNCLOS affect Estado's and Mineco's right to extract these minerals from the 300-mile corridor?

Problem 6.F (§6.4 after Powers Case) The US and a Caribbean neighbor are engaged in what may turn out to be a hostile conflict. A US fleet containing US Marine and Naval forces is now steaming toward the hypothetical State of Estado. A US multinational corporation owns a satellite that is orbiting over Estado at an altitude of 22,500 miles. That corporation allows the US forces to use its satellite to monitor events occurring in Estado. This sophisticated satellite permits a monitor aboard the fleet command ship to count individual troops in Estado.

US fighter–bomber aircraft are launched in international waters and fly over Estado after the satellite confirms that all Estado military aircraft are on the ground. Does the *presence* of the US satellite "over" Estado violate its airspace under the 1944 Chicago Convention or customary State practice?

Problem 6.G (end of §6.4) This problem continues with the US–Estado potential military confrontation. Read Problem 6.F first.

Assume that Estado and the US are parties to all the treaties contained in §6.4 on outer space. Could the *use* of the US satellite violate any of those treaties? How?

Problem 6.H (§6.4 after n. 65) This problem builds on the US–Estado potential military confrontation described in prior problems. A group of Estado extremists seizes a US commercial airliner as it flies over Jamaica. There are eighty US citizens on board the aircraft. The hijackers divert the plane to Estado. En route, they broadcast that their reason for seizing the aircraft is to bring world attention to the plight of Estado. They proclaim that their only way of dealing with US imperialism is to capture one of its aircraft and bring the US hostages to Estado. They arrive in that State and are hidden from public view. It is not clear whether Estado's government played a role in planning this hijacking.

The Estado hijackers are tried in an Estado "People's Tribunal" and found *not* guilty. The tribunal decides that the defendants have committed a "political" crime rather than an ordinary crime under Estado law. Estado is a party to all of the multilateral treaties dealing with commercial air flights described in the air zones section of this chapter. Estado is not a party to any regional air treaty, such as the referenced European Convention.

Has Estado breached the air treaties to which it is a party? How?

◆ BIBLIOGRAPHY

§§6.1–6.2 Categories of Territory, Dominion Over Land

M. Dixon & R. McCorquodale, "Sovereignty over Territory," ch. 7 in *Cases and Materials on International Law* 225 (London: Blackstone Press, 1991).

D. Harris, "Territory," ch. 5 in *Cases and Materials on International Law* 173 (4th ed. London: Street & Maxwell, 1991).

A. Kacowicz, *Peaceful Territorial Change* (Columbia: Univ. So. Caro. Press, 1994).

S. Sharma, *Territorial Acquisition, Disputes and International Law* (The Hague, Neth.: Martinus Nijhoff, 1997).

§6.3 Law of the Sea

E. Brown, *International Law of the Sea* (Brookfield, VT: Ashgate Pub., 1994) (two volumes).

J. Charney & L. Alexander, *International Maritime Boundaries* (Dordrecht, Neth.: Martinus Nijhoff, 1991) (two volumes).

G. Galdorisi & K. Vienna, *Beyond the Law of the Sea: New Directions for US Oceans Policy* (Westport, CT: Praeger, 1997).

"Law of the Sea Forum: The 1994 Agreement on Implementation of the Seabed Provisions of the Convention on the Law of the Sea," 88 *Amer. J. Int'l Law* 687 (1994).

F. Vicuna, *Exclusive Economic Zone: A Latin American Perspective* (Boulder, CO: Westview Press, 1984).

P. Yuan, "The United Nations Convention on the Law of the Sea from a Chinese Perspective," 19 *Texas Int'l L.J.* 415 (1984).

§6.4 Airspace Zones

AIRSPACE

A. Ciampi, "*Public Prosecutor v. Ashby:* Italian Decision Under NATO Status of Forces Agreement to Try US Military Officers for Deaths Caused When Aircraft Severed Ski Lift Cable," 93 *Amer. J. Int'l Law*, 219 (1999).

P. Dempsey, *Law and Foreign Policy in International Aviation* (Dobbs Ferry, NY: Transnational Publishers, 1987).

I. Diederiks-Verschoor, *An Introduction to Air Law* (The Hague, Neth.: Kluwer, 1997).

C. Johnsson, *International Aviation and the Politics of Regime Changes* (New York: St. Martin's Press, 1987).

R. Jennings & A. Watts, "Jurisdiction at Sea and in the Air," 1 *Oppenheim's International Law* (Part I), §141, p. 479 (Essex, Eng.: Longman, 1993).

OUTER SPACE

K. Bockstiegel & M. Benko (eds.), *Space Law: Basic Legal Documents* (Dordrecht, Neth.: Martinus Nijhoff, 1990).

N. Jasentuliyana (ed.), *Space Law: Development and Scope* (Westport, CT: Praeger, 1992).

K. Li (ed.), *World Wide Space Law Bibliography* (Montreal: McGill Univ.—De Daro Pub., 1978) (two volumes with annual supplements).

N. Matte (ed.), *Space Activities and Emerging International Law* (Montreal: McGill Univ., 1994).

◆ ENDNOTES

1. *"Namibia (South-West Africa) Case,"* 1971 *ICJ Rep.* 55.
2. *US v. The Netherlands,* Permanent Court of Arbitration, No. XIX, 2 *Rep. Int'l Arb. Awards* 829 (1949).
3. 1975 *ICJ Rep.* 4 (and set forth in §2.3 of this text).

4. Regarding both regions, *see* "The Legal Regimes of the Polar Regions, Part II," in D. Rothwell, *The Polar Regions and the Development of International Law* 49 (Cambridge, Eng.: Cambridge Univ. Press, 1996).
5. **Antarctica is *res communis:*** Balch, "The Arctic and Antarctic Regions and the Law of Nations," 4 *Amer. J. Int'l L.* 265 (1910); **is not *res communis:*** E. Sahurie, *The International Law of Antarctica* 420 (Dordrecht, Neth.: Martinus Nijhoff, 1992). **Treaty text:** *See* 54 *Amer. J. Int'l L.* 476 (Supp. 1960) or 19 *Int'l Legal Mat'ls* 860 (1980).
6. *See generally* S. Sharma, *Territorial Acquisition Disputes and International Law* (The Hague, Neth.: Martinus Nijhoff, 1997); and G. Goetz & P. Diehl, *Territorial Changes and International Conflict* (London: Routledge, 1992).
7. "The Miniquiers and Ecrehos Case *(France v. United Kingdom),*" 1953 *ICJ Rep.* 47 (1953).
8. "Western Sahara Case *(Spain v. Morocco),*" 1975 *ICJ Rep.* 3, citing the Permanent Court of International Justice *Legal Status of Greenland* case, *PCIJ,* ser. A/B, No. 53 (1933).
9. *See* G. von Glahn, "Title to Territory, Air, and Space," ch. 14 in *Law Among Nations* 297 (7th ed. Boston: Allyn & Bacon, 1996).
10. *Legal Status of Greenland* case (cited in note 8 above).
11. **1995 Interim Agreement:** 36 *Int'l Legal Mat'ls* 551 (1997). **1997 Note for the Record:** 36 *Int'l Legal Mat'ls* 650 (1997). **1998 Wye River Agreement:** www.israel-mfa.gov.il/peace/wye.html.
12. *See generally* S. Subedi, *Land and Maritime Zones of Peace in International Law* (Oxford, Eng.: Clarendon Press, 1996).
13. 1928 Permanent Court of Arbitration No. XIX, 2 *Rep. Int'l Arb. Awards* 829 (1949).
14. *See* R. Blanke, *Orphans of Versailles: The West German Minority in Western Poland, 1918–1939* (Lexington: Univ. Press of Kentucky, 1993).
15. 1962 *ICJ Rep.* 6.
16. Award by the United States–Mexico International Boundary Commission Constituted by Treaty of June 24, 1911, 11 *Rep. Int'l Arb. Awards* 309 (1962).
17. *See* "Summary of the Indo-Pakistan Western Boundary *(Rann of Kutch)* Case *(India v. Pakistan),*" 1968 *Int'l L. Rep.* 2 (1976); excerpts reprinted in 7 *Int'l Legal Mat'ls* 635 (1968).
18. **PCIJ application:** "Jaworzina Boundary Case," *PCIJ,* ser. B, No. 8 (1923). **Post–World War II application:** I. Brownlie, *International Law and the Use of Force by States* 408 (Oxford, Eng.: Oxford Univ. Press, 1963).
19. I. Brownlie, *Principles of Public International Law* 131 (4th ed. Oxford, Eng.: Clarendon Press, 1990) (hereinafter Brownlie treatise).
20. Brownlie treatise, p. 127 (cited in note 19 above).
21. D. Greig, *International Law* 160 (2nd ed. London: Butterworths, 1976) (emphasis supplied).
22. C. van Bynkershoek, *De Dominio Dissertatio* (Possession of the Sea Dissertation), reprinted in ch. 2 *Classics of International Law* 44 (Wash., DC: Carnegie Endowment for Int'l Peace, Magoffin translation, 1923).
23. M. McDougal & N. Schlei, "The Hydrogen Bomb Tests in Perspective: Lawful Measures for Security," 64 *Yale Law Journal* 648, 661–662 (1964).
24. "The Law of the Sea: An Overview," ch. 1 in D. Pharand & U. Leanza, *The Continental Shelf and the Exclusive Economic Zone: Delimitation and Legal Regime* 5 (Dordrecht, Neth.: Martinus Nijhoff, 1993).
25. UN Doc. A/CONF. 62/122 (1982), reprinted in 21 *Int'l Legal Mat'ls* 1261 (1983). Click on Law of the Sea link on the course Web page at http://home.att.net/~slomansonb/txtcsesite.html.
26. "Re Bianchi, Camara Nacional Especial [special chamber of the national court of] Argentina," 24 *Int'l L. Rep.* 173 (1961) (decided in 1957).
27. *See* G. Westerman, *The Juridical Bay* (Oxford, Eng.: Clarendon Press, 1987).
28. *Tribunal of the Permanent Court of Arbitration,* reprinted in Sen. Doc. No. 870, Vol. I, 61st Congress, 3rd Sess., p. 64 (1912).
29. Excerpt from Canadian Parliamentary debate, reprinted in H. Kindred et al., *International Law Chiefly as Interpreted and Applied in Canada* 665–666 (5th ed. Toronto: Edmond Montgomery Pub., 1993).
30. "Anglo-Norwegian Fisheries Case *(England v. Norway),*" 1951 *ICJ Rep.* 116, 160 (Judgment of Dec. 18, 1951).
31. *Id.,* 18 *Int'l Law Reports* 86, at 95.
32. *See* 2 *Yearbk. Int'l L. Comm.* 36, UN Doc. A/CN.4/17 (1950) on the Vatican's proclamations granting these rights.
33. Bynkershoek, *De Dominio Dissertatio* (Possession of the Sea Dissertation), reprinted in ch. 2 *Classics of International Law* 44 (Wash., DC: Carnegie Endowment for Int'l Peace, Magoffin translation, 1923).
34. J. Moore, *Digest of International Law* 702–703 (Wash., DC: US Gov't Print. Off., 1906).
35. **1952 declaration:** *see* US Naval War College, 51 *Int'l Law Situation and Documents* 1956, p. 265 (1957). **1956 declaration:** *see* US Naval War College, 50 *Int'l Law Situation and Documents* 1955, p. 244 (1957).
36. "Presidential Proclamation on the Territorial Sea of the United States," 24 *Weekly Compilation of Presidential Documents* 1661 (1989), reprinted in 28 *Int'l Legal Mat'ls* 284 (1989).
37. Shortly after this incident, the US and the USSR decided that one another's commercial vessels could enter their respective ports and pass through territorial waters. A minimum of two days' notice was required. This 1990 agreement expressly excluded "war vessels." "Agreement Regarding Certain Maritime Matters between the Government of the United States of America and the Government of the Union of Soviet Socialist Republics," *US Treaties and Other International Agreements Series,* No. 11453 (1990).
38. *"The SS Lotus (France v. Turkey),"* *PCIJ,* ser. No. 10 (1927); case text in §5.2.
39. 450 *UN Treaty Series* 82 (1963).
40. F. Ngantcha, *The Right of Innocent Passage and the Evolution of the International Law of the Sea: The Current Regime of "Free" Navigation in Coastal Waters of Third States* 1 (London: Pinter, 1990).

41. "Harvard Research Draft, Art. 20," reprinted in 23 *Amer. J. Int'l L.* 250 (1929).
42. **Expanded CZ:** "Convention on the Territorial Sea and Contiguous Zone," Art. 24.2, 516 *UN Treaty Series* 205 (1964). **Shelf agreement:** "Convention on the Continental Shelf," Art. 1, 499 *UN Treaty Series* 311 (1964).
43. *Case Concerning Fisheries Jurisdiction (Spain v. Canada).* Various proceedings are available on the ICJ's Web site at www.icj-cij.org. Regarding the dismissal for lack of jurisdiction, *see* www.icj-cij.org/idocket/iec/iecframe.htm.
44. *See* L. Henkin, R. Pugh, O. Schachter & H. Smit, *International Law: Cases and Materials* 1283 n. 1 (3rd ed. St. Paul: West, 1993).
45. A. Pardo, "The Convention on the Law of the Sea: A Preliminary Appraisal," in F. Snyder & S. Sathirathai, *Third World Attitudes Toward International Law* 737, 741, and 747 n. 32 (Dordrecht, Neth.: Martinus Nijhoff, 1987) (hereinafter *Third World Attitudes*).
46. **Truman's CS declaration:** 10 *Fed. Register* 12304, 59 *Statutes at Large* 884 (1945)—Presidential Proclamations 2667 and 2668. **1958 CS Convention:** 400 *UN Treaty Series* 311 (1961). The evolution of Continental Shelf principles is presented in D. Pharand & U. Leanza (eds.), *The Continental Shelf and the Exclusive Economic Zone: Delimitation and Legal Regime* (Dordrecht, Neth.: Martinus Nijhoff, 1993).
47. 1969 *ICJ Rep.* 3, 53.
48. **CHM Resolution:** Gen. Ass. Reso. 2749 (XXV), UN Gen. Ass. Off. Rec. (GAOR), 25th Sess., Supp. No. 28, p. 24, reprinted in 10 *Int'l Legal Mat'ls* 220 (1971). **Analysis:** Joyner, "Legal Implications of the Concept of the Common Heritage of Mankind," 35 *Int'l & Comp. L.Q.* 190 (1986).
49. **1994 Agreement:** Annex I to *Consultations of the Secretary-General on Outstanding Issues Relating to the Deep Seabed Mining Provisions of the United Nations Convention on the Law of the Sea,* UN Doc. A/48/950 (1994) (revising UN Doc. SG/LOS/CRP.1/Rev.1), reprinted in 33 *Int'l Legal Mat'ls* 1309 (1994). **Christopher quote:** "United States to Move Ahead with the Law of the Sea Convention," 140 *Congressional Record–Senate,* 103 Cong., 2nd Sess. (June 30, 1994). An extensive review of Law of the Sea developments is available in J. Noyes, "International Legal Developments in Review: 1996 Public International Law of the Sea," 31 *Int'l Lawyer* 703 (1997).
50. The author thanks Prof. John Noyes of the ABA's International Section for providing a copy of this Recommendation.
51. *See* transmittal document to the Senate Foreign Relations Committee, Treaty Doc. 103-39, 103rd Cong., 2nd Sess., Oct. 7, 1994, regarding Part XI and Agreement on Implementation of Part XI, at 59.
52. T. Koh, "Negotiating a New World Order for the Sea," in *Third World Attitudes* 715, 725–726 (cited in note 45 above).
53. A. Pardo, *Third World Attitudes* 737, 741–744 (note 45 above).
54. D. Goedhuis, "Civil Aviation After the War," 36 *Amer. J. Int'l L.* 596, 605 (1942) (referring to World War I).
55. 11 *League of Nations Treaty Series* 173 (1922). The US was never a party to this first international air treaty.
56. "Jurisdiction of the ICAO Council *(India v. Pakistan),*" 1972 *ICJ Rep.* 46.
57. *Laker Airways v. Sabena,* 731 Fed.2d 909 (D.C. Cir. 1984). A history of the various English and American cases regarding *Laker* is available in 1 *Restatement of the Foreign Relations Law of the United States* 252–253 (3rd ed. Wash., DC: Amer. Law Inst., 1987).
58. "Case Concerning the Aerial Incident of July 27, 1955 *(Israel v. Bulgaria),*" 1957 *ICJ Rep.* 182.
59. A thoughtful analysis of this incident is provided in Fitzgerald, "The Use of Force Against Civil Aircraft: The Aftermath of the KAL Flight 007 Incident," 22 *Canadian Yearbook Int'l L.* 291 (1984).
60. R. Goedhart, *The Never-Ending Dispute: Delimitation of Air Space and Outer Space* 4 (Gif-sur-Yvette, France: Editions Frontieres, 1996).
61. *See US v. Cordova,* 89 Fed.Supp. 298 (E.D. N.Y. 1950).
62. 704 *UN Treaty Series* 219 (1969).
63. *See* M. Milde, "Law and Aviation Security," in T. Masson-Zwaan & P. Mendes de Leon, *Air and Space Law;* De Lege Ferenda, *Essays in Honor of Henri A. Wassenbergh* 93 (Dordrecht, Neth.: Martinus Nijhoff, 1992).
64. Reprinted in 15 *Int'l Legal Mat'ls* 1272 (1976).
65. These and similar examples are collected in W. Slomanson, "ICJ Damages: Tort Remedy for Failure to Punish or Extradite International Terrorists," 5 *Calif. West. Int'l L.J.* 121 (1974).
66. 610 *UN Treaty Series* 205 (1967).
67. **Preliminary jurisdictional ruling:** "Questions of Interpretation and Application of the 1971 Montreal Convention Arising from the Aerial Incident at Lockerbie *(Libyan Arab Jamahiriya v. United Kingdom),* Request for the Indication of Provisional Measures," reprinted in *Official Documents,* 86 *Amer. J. Int'l L.* 638 (1992). **Case quote:** *id.,* p. 651 (Shahabuddeen, J., Separate Opinion). **Final jurisdictional decision:** *see* ICJ Web site www.icj-cij.org.
68. Gen. Ass. Reso. 1721(XVI) of Dec. 20, 1961.
69. 610 *U.N. Treaty Series* 205 (1967).
70. G. Robinson & H. White, *Envoys of Mankind: A Declaration of First Principles for the Government of Space Societies* 30–31 (Wash., DC: Smithsonian Inst. Press, 1986), reprinted with the permission of the Smithsonian Institution.
71. The diplomatic exchanges between Canada and the former USSR are reproduced in 18 *Int'l Legal Mat'ls* 899 (1979).
72. *See* S. Courteix, "Towards a World Space Organization?" in G. Lafferranderie (ed.), *Outlook on Space Law over the Next 30 Years* 423 (The Hague, Neth.: Kluwer, 1997).

CHAPTER SEVEN

Diplomatic Relations

CHAPTER OUTLINE

A WOMAN IS BRUTALLY RAPED, YET HER ATTACKER goes free. A man is fatally hit by a car, and the driver is not charged with a crime. Drug smugglers are seized, kidnappers identified, thieves caught in the act—and all go free. What is responsible for this breakdown of justice?

DIPLOMATIC IMMUNITY. All of these outrageous crimes were committed by members of the diplomatic corps—people who live above the law. And here, for the first time, is a documented exposé of the frightening, secret crimes they don't have to answer for. . . . *Diplomatic Crime* is the shocking account of these tragedies—and the routine governmental cover-ups that followed them.

[W]e have officially labeled thirty-seven thousand visitors currently [1987] living in . . . [major] cities as above and beyond the law.

Most of these given this enormous exemption from civilized behavior are not diplomats. They are the wives, children, drivers, and valets of ambassadors and ministers sent to this country to represent their nations. . . .

This immunity is particularly bizarre since it is not limited to incidents occurring in the course of "official duties" but rather serves as an absolute security blanket.

—Cover & pp. 14–15, C. Ashman & P. Trescott, *Diplomatic Crime* (New York: Knightsbridge Publishing, 1988)

INTRODUCTION

Diplomacy plays a significant role in shaping international legal developments. Kings, queens, and presidents rely on their diplomats to address the day-to-day crises that are often resolved through quiet diplomacy. The UN Secretary-General does not merely preside over various UN meetings. Under Article 99 of the UN Charter, he or she "may bring to the attention of the Security Council any matter which in his opinion may threaten the maintenance of international peace and security."

This chapter depicts the working environment of and some significant legal ramifications for the institution of the "diplomat." The preliminary analysis shows how diplomatic relations are initiated and broken. Once established, what is the nature, respectively, of diplomatic and consular functions? What are the legal effects of acts undertaken within an embassy or consular premises when the laws of the host country differ? What are the relevant legal principles for the many famous cases involving diplomatic asylum? Do newspaper stories and books fairly characterize the supposedly deplorable situation when some diplomat has "once again" avoided civil or criminal prosecution?

◆ 7.1 FOREWORD TO INTERNATIONAL DIPLOMACY

HISTORICAL DEVELOPMENT

For centuries, special envoys have represented the interests of their rulers in other regions of the world. A treatise, supposedly written in the third century B.C., described Greek practice around 800 B.C. There were already three categories of what we now call diplomats, consuls, and couriers: those with ministerial rank, those with slightly lesser rank, and the mere conveyers of messages. The Greek city-states developed lasting rules of diplomatic exchanges, inaugurating an era that protected messengers who brought bad news from distant lands.[1]

Around A.D. 1500, permanent representatives called "ambassadors" were first established in Italy. This institution then flourished elsewhere in Western Europe, although other nations resisted it for several more centuries. As chronicled by London School of Economics Professor M. S. Anderson:

> [B]y the middle of the fifteenth century there were clearly taking root in Italy new diplomatic techniques and institutions. These formed the basis of a system of interstate relations recognizable as the direct ancestor of the one which exists today. . . . [M]ost of the Italian peninsula was divided between a fairly small number of relatively well-organized states. . . . These competed with one another intensely for power, for territory, [and] in the last analysis for survival. It was therefore essential for their rulers to watch closely each other's doings and to be as well informed as possible about each other's policies and ambitions. . . . In Italy it was therefore possible to raise day-to-day government to a high pitch of efficiency, to control the territory of these states effectively from a single centre, in a way which was still impracticable in France, Spain, or the growing Habsburg [dynasty in Hungary]. . . .
>
> Fifteenth-century Italy, then, was in miniature what in the following hundred years most of western Europe and later the rest of the continent [and modern diplomacy] was to become.[2]

The 1814–1815 Vienna Congress focused on the norms for engaging in international diplomacy. Most European States thereby established the mutually acceptable institutions that governed their international relations. Previously considered a somewhat discredited activity, diplomacy was finally perceived as a very positive institution. Preventative diplomacy was viewed as a vehicle that would not necessarily prevent war, but would serve the long-term interests of *both* the international community and individual States.

The drafters of the 1945 UN Charter included a provision implicitly recognizing the importance of maintaining diplomatic ties. Should a State fail to carry out its peaceful membership obligations, Article 41 authorizes the Security Council to call on its members to sever or limit diplomatic relations with the offending State. This sanction was conceived as a technique for disrupting conduct that constituted a threat to international peace. The target State would lose the benefit of trade and other ties with the remaining UN member States. In 1992, for example, the UN imposed sanctions against Libya for its failure to surrender the two Libyan terrorists allegedly responsible for the bombing of Pan Am Flight 103 over Lockerbie, Scotland, in 1988. Those sanctions prohibited arms sales to Libya and commercial flights into that country, and forced the scaling back of Libya's diplomatic missions throughout the world.

States are expected to employ diplomatic alternatives before resorting to international courts (Chapter 9) or the use of force (Chapter 10). In 1957, the International Court of Justice (ICJ) aptly articulated this practical condition precedent in a case in which India objected to Portugal's premature filing of a case against India in the ICJ. The Court's formulation of this principle was that "Portugal, before filing her application in the present case, did not comply with the rule of customary international law requiring her to undertake diplomatic negotiations and continue them to the point where it was no longer profitable to pursue them. . . ."[3] The existence of active negotiations is not an impediment to the ICJ's exercise of jurisdiction. Prior resort to diplomatic negotiations is significant evidence, however, of the existence of a legal dispute—in the event of a jurisdictional objection by one of the parties on grounds that there is no tangible dispute requiring ICJ involvement.

The respective 1961 and 1963 Vienna Conventions on Diplomatic and Consular Relations are the current encyclopedias of diplomatic practice. They form the core materials for this chapter.

PERCEPTIONS OF DIPLOMATIC ROLE

The role of the diplomat has not been characterized uniformly. Host governments have often considered them to be "spies." In Czarist Russia, leaders feared that the presence of foreign ambassadors would be an invitation to spy on Russia. Allegations of espionage continued to plague international diplomacy during the Cold War.[4] In 1985, the former Soviet Union (which now hosts a number of foreign diplomatic missions in Moscow) charged a group of US diplomatic personnel with spying. They were required to leave Russia. The US responded by ejecting a number of Soviet diplomats from the United Nations in New York City. Then, in 1987, the US refused to occupy a newly constructed diplomatic complex in Moscow because the walls contained hidden listening devices. In 1994, the US expelled a diplomat identified as Russia's senior intelligence agent. France expelled four American diplomats in 1995 for their alleged industrial and political espionage. The US Central Intelligence Agency's station in Paris supposedly obtained secrets about France's nuclear arsenal and its planned trade posture toward US industry.

The Chinese have characterized the diplomat as a "fighter." During the 1966–1976 Cultural Revolution, the Chinese press often referred to diplomats in this context, as illustrated in the following excerpt:

> The diplomatic personnel of great socialist China are proletarian diplomatic fighters. At any time and in any place, they . . . show a dauntless revolutionary spirit, a firm and correct political orientation, an unconquerable fighting will. They are capable of accomplishing all the missions of proletarian revolutionary diplomacy however complicated or perilous the situation. The proletarian fighters on the diplomatic front . . . can distinguish friends from enemies. They are most modest in their attitude toward [other] revolutionary people and countries; they respect them; they resolutely support their revolutionary struggles, displaying the proletarian internationalist spirit. They repudiate all manifestations of great-power chauvinism. They wage a firm, blow-for-blow struggle against the imperialists, modern revisionists and all reactionaries, and relentlessly rebuff their provocations.[5]

There are, of course, less dogmatic definitions of the role of the modern diplomat. The nineteenth-century European conception was that diplomacy was the art of negotiation or communication. Harold Nicolson, a twentieth-century British diplomat and prolific writer, defined international diplomacy as "the application of intelligence and tact to the conduct of official relations between the governments of independent states."[6] Most contemporary commentators perceive diplomats in the more familiar context of being foreign-based emissaries who promote friendly relations. Their role includes maintaining the vigilance necessary to ensure that State interaction is harmonious and that all applicable legal relationships conform to expectations.

Then there is the battle of ideologies involving "idealists" and "realists." The perspective of certain idealists is that State representatives have the moral and ethical obligation to solve problems in a way that benefits all immediate parties—and any other State or entity affected by international negotiations. The State, through its representatives, should not use international relations as a device for improving its destiny at a significant cost to another State or the community of nations. On the other hand, political realists do not perceive diplomats as carrying out just their titular functions and being guided by the norms of International Law. Indeed, the integrity of the international system is often called into question by the periodic diplomatic protests over State conduct that another State considers incompatible with existing law (discussed further in §7.2).

During the emergence of the so-called realist period of the 1960s, renowned US commentator Hans Morgenthau criticized any legalistic perception of modern diplomacy as myopic idealism. He characterized diplomats as, in reality, practical manipulators of power relationships—not facilitators of International Law. Under this view, diplomats merely negotiate on the basis of the respective strength of the States they represent. This role parallels the Chinese view that the diplomat is a fighter. Morgenthau thus contended that international "politics, like all politics, is the struggle for power [and that the] means at the disposal of diplomacy are three: persuasion, compromise and threat of force." US President Nixon and Secretary of State Kissinger restated this theme as their justification for unpopular tactics utilized during the Vietnam War, specifically echoing Morgenthau's sentiment that we "must negotiate from a position of strength." A closely related perspective is that, unlike the individual, the State itself is not endowed with any ethical responsibility in the conduct of its diplomatic corps. Under this view, there is no ultimate authority to which the State must answer. Wales University College of Swansea's Professor David Boucher thus comments: "The state itself is [often] implicitly and explicitly personified. It, like individuals, has interests, and is motivated by the same psychological factors. The state as the creator and sustainer of morals internal to itself is not itself constrained by a moral code in its relations with other states. The international sphere is *devoid* of the notions of justice and injustice because no ultimate authority exists to subordinate the individual states to it and create the conditions necessary for the emergence of morality."[7]

Former Canadian Prime Minister Lester Pearson advocated the realist theory—that the character of diplomacy depends on the particular issue at hand. In his assessment of nuclear diplomacy, he stressed that force must be recognized as the essential backdrop for successful control of the arms race. In his words: "Protection from these grim consequences of our own [nuclear] genius requires possession of overwhelming, destructive power" to avoid mutual destruction. Those States with nuclear powers must negotiate from a position of strength. This power theory is echoed by the leading Soviet publicist, Moscow State University's Professor Grigori Tunkin. He characterizes diplomacy as the most important means of accomplishing a State's foreign policy. He defines diplomacy as the activity of "heads of states, of governments, of departments of foreign affairs, of special delegations and missions, and of diplomatic representations appertaining to the effectuation by peaceful means of the purposes and tasks of the foreign policy of a state."[8]

In an informative exchange at the 1983 annual meeting of the American Society of International Law in Washington, D.C., two diplomats espoused their respective idealist and realist perspectives on the degree to which diplomats rely on International Law. The summary of that exchange includes Canada's ambassador to the United States, Ambassador Gottlieb, aptly describing the idealist perspective on the conduct of diplomacy. He states that there is a "need to anchor the conduct of diplomacy in international law, as well as the need to develop this body of law. . . . [One] hope[s] that international law would keep pace with the demands imposed by these trends and that, in some cases, international law might even exceed the requirements placed on it." In contrast, the Venezuelan ambassador to the United States expressed his view that international law was *not* important in the conduct of diplomacy—which is controlled primarily by the will of governments rather than rules of law. Ambassador Perez-Chiriboga's "realist" perspective was that "international law did play a[n effective] role in the practice of international diplomacy, but that not all steps taken in the conduct of diplomacy fell within the parameters of international law. . . . [D]iplomacy was conditioned by the will of governments and the role of international law in this field would increase [only] if governments respected international law."[9]

Any attempt to synthesize these varied definitions and perspectives on diplomacy produces at least two related conclusions: (1) Diplomats often deal with each other from diverse political perspectives about the fundamental nature of their respective roles, and (2) diplomatic practice has evolved and adapted to the needs of changing international environments. These starting points in a discourse on diplomacy provide some insight into why diplomatic negotiations often deteriorate: The participants often pursue varying purposes from different moral, political, and sociological perspectives.[10]

Diplomats must decide what particular methods are best suited to achieve their respective foreign policy objectives. To do this, they must first determine what those objectives are and what alternatives are available to accomplish them. Diplomats must be prepared, for example, to deal with different constitutional and social systems in the host State. A new ambassador cannot expect to achieve diplomatic goals without knowing what results can be realistically achieved. The ambassador must continue to assess the objectives of the host State and the degree to which he or she can reasonably negotiate in favor of the home State. Next, the diplomat must gauge the extent to which the objectives of the sending and receiving State are compatible. Finally, the diplomat must employ means that are suitable to the pursuit of desired objectives.[11]

ALTERED DIPLOMATIC STATUS

The technological innovations of the twentieth century changed diplomacy in two dramatic ways. First, they altered the *status* of the diplomat. Nineteenth-century diplomats, serving far from the seat of their governments, had much wider discretion when reacting to problems at their outposts. Travel and communications were difficult and slow. An ambassador had to react to local crises without the benefit (or detriment) of immediate directions from his government. Instantaneous communications and supersonic travel now limit the need to rely on such undirected judgment.

The scope of diplomacy itself was also changed. Summit diplomacy by heads of State has limited the role of ambassadors. Presidents, prime ministers, emperors, and sheikhs attend well-publicized conferences on major issues. In 1972, Richard Nixon, the first US president to visit the People's Republic of China, personally directed the establishment of more friendly international relations between these two powers. Leaders now negotiate directly with each other, reaching agreements on general principles. In 1992, the fifteen heads of State in the nations then serving on the UN Security Council met for the first time to discuss their respective interests in the operations of this UN body.

The role of the diplomat in international relations—once the sole province of ambassadors—has been minimized, in comparison to that of his or her nineteenth-century counterpart. In the US, for example, there has been an increasing tendency toward the centralization of foreign policy decisions at the White House.[12] Modern "shuttle diplomacy," typified by President Nixon's use of Secretary of State Henry Kissinger in Middle East and Vietnamese negotiations, further limited the degree of autonomy once enjoyed by US ambassadors.

Another twentieth-century development significantly influenced the role of the diplomat: international terrorism, which has been facilitated by increases in speed of travel and advanced weapons technology. Diplomats must sometimes conduct their affairs in the hostile shadow of intimidation from terrorist groups. A number of these obscure groups have been clandestinely supported by certain governments as a crude instrument for furthering their foreign policy interests. Diplomats at all levels of government have encountered the threat of assassination by those States or individual groups whose political philosophies differ from their own.

Examples are not limited to any particular region or target nation. Egypt's leader Anwar Sadat paid with his life for the 1978 Camp David Agreements, which he directly negotiated with Israel through President Carter's mediation. Egypt thereby became the first Arab State to directly negotiate with Israel. Sadat's murder was attributed to extremists within (and probably also outside) Egypt who feared that this would one day lead the way to friendly relations with Israel.[13] Israel's Prime Minister Yitzhak Rabin paid for the 1993 US-brokered Middle East peace accord with his life when he was shot by an Israeli law student who opposed the agreement.

The student of diplomacy must also recognize that modern diplomacy has been used as both a sword and a plowshare. The 1994 US–North Korea energy aid agreement is a *positive* example of economic diplomacy. In 1993, North Korea announced its intent to withdraw from the Nuclear Nonproliferation Treaty (Chapter 10), which had been signed by 153 nations. It denied access to its nuclear facilities to inspectors from the UN's International Atomic Energy Agency. The US, after a round of preliminary negotiations, threatened sanctions. The international community was concerned that North Korea's aging leader was unwilling to move beyond the Cold War era in order to cooperate in international controls on nuclear proliferation. Under the 1994 agreement, the US will provide $4 billion of energy aid to ameliorate North Korea's desperate economic situation and to dissuade the further development of its nuclear weapons capability. This program is designed to provide economic assistance, vitiate North Korea's isolationism, and promote diplomatic and other ties. North Korea then conducted a missile test in 1998, with a trajectory that overflew Japan. While this event has significant political and military implications for regional stability, one might at least recognize that the missile did not go *into* Japan. North Korea would not likely risk confrontation with the US and the loss of financial gains from the prior economic aid deal.

The Arab boycott of Israeli goods could be described as one of the *worst* examples of economic diplomacy. The Arab League's official policy was to influence other States not to buy from or sell to Israel—a scenario that was not expected to survive the diplomatic breakthrough associated with the 1993 Israeli–PLO Peace Accords signed in Washington. (This boycott is presented and analyzed in Chapter 8.)

SECRET DIPLOMACY

What diplomats do is sometimes less important than *how* they do it. For example, should diplomacy be conducted openly or in secret? President Woodrow Wilson's famous "Fourteen Points" speech to the US Congress in 1918 advocated "[o]pen covenants of peace, openly arrived at, after which there shall be no private international understandings of any kind but diplomacy shall proceed always frankly and in public view." Wilson was thereby admonishing certain governments who had engaged in secret arrangements that led to World War I. The skillful British diplomat and commentator Sir Harold Nicolson articulated the position that international policy-making should never be undertaken in secret. Consider his remarks, regarding World War II, which have unarguably retained their appeal to this day: "No system should ever again be tolerated [that] can commit men and women, without their knowledge or consent, to obligations which will entail upon them, either a breach of national good faith, or the sacrifice of their property and lives."[14]

The pendulum may now be swinging in the other direction. In March 1986, US Secretary of State George Shultz complained that diplomats and heads of State *cannot* effectively conduct their affairs in public. Shultz felt that the US's Cold War relations with the Soviet Union were becoming far less productive. Diplomatic exchanges about nuclear arms control were being conducted in public forums. He perceived the presence of the media as unduly influencing the effectiveness of these critical diplomatic efforts. He called on the leaders of both Cold War powers to engage in a more "quiet" diplomacy conducted via private discussions rather than open conversations effectively directed at the public and the media—as opposed to only the respective negotiators. In 1994, US Secretary of State Warren Christopher received a rather blunt lecture about secret diplomacy from the Chinese Communist Party's leader. After Christopher had met secretly with China's leading dissident, while on a trade mission to Beijing, the Chinese leader claimed that the result of this meeting was that "public opinion flared up, and US officials made accusations against China" that would not survive public scrutiny in any country. The Chinese reaction made it far more difficult for the US to exact human rights concessions in exchange for the US continuing to grant China favorable trade status.

The following materials address some other benchmarks of international diplomacy—the current operating functions of diplomats and consular officials; State practice regarding the regime applicable to an act undertaken within an embassy, which has different legal results under host country law; norms involving diplomatic asylum; and the ways of dealing with a diplomat who has abused his or her immunity.

◆ 7.2 DIPLOMATIC AND CONSULAR FUNCTIONS

SYSTEMIC OVERVIEW

When two States agree to establish diplomatic relations, they exchange representatives who usually work in the respective capitals of each State. The representative is often referred to as "ambassador," "minister," or "head of mission." The terms *embassy* and *mission* are popular descriptions of the building where foreign officials undertake many of their diplomatic tasks. However, the term *embassy* is a technical one that describes the function of the ambassador. The term *mission* is the actual process of maintaining permanent diplomatic offices in the host State. The term *premises* refers to the buildings and land used for the purposes of the foreign mission. A *chargé d'affaires* is normally the second-ranking official in the delegation. He or she takes charge of the mission and premises in the absence of the primary diplomat. (*See* Exhibit 7-1.)

No State has established diplomatic offices in every other State of the world. Financial limitations have even closed many consulates and embassies. The US maintains approximately 140 embassies abroad. It hosts about 130 foreign embassies in Washington, D.C. The US also maintains more than 100 "consular posts" to deal with commercial matters throughout the world. Certain States can afford embassies in only a few places, however. In 1993, the Philippines announced that it would close its consulates in a number of US cities. It also closed its embassies in Cuba, Jordan, Micronesia, Morocco, Peru, Poland, Romania, Senegal, and Sri Lanka.

The host State may close (or withhold occupancy of) an embassy—without necessarily breaking diplomatic relations. The US closed Rwanda's Washington embassy in July 1994. The Rwandan diplomats were ordered to leave the US with only five days' notice. (The US then sought to remove the Rwandan representative from the UN Security Council.) President Clinton explained that the US was not breaking formal ties with Rwanda but attenuating relations to a lower level of interaction. In President Clinton's words: "The US cannot allow representatives of a regime that supports genocidal massacres to remain on our soil." In 1990, the military government of Lebanon was no longer recognized by the US. Despite claims emanating from "leaders" in Lebanon, the US refused to allow Lebanon's former representative to occupy the Lebanese embassy in Washington. And in

EXHIBIT 7.1 REPRESENTATIVE US DIPLOMATIC MISSION

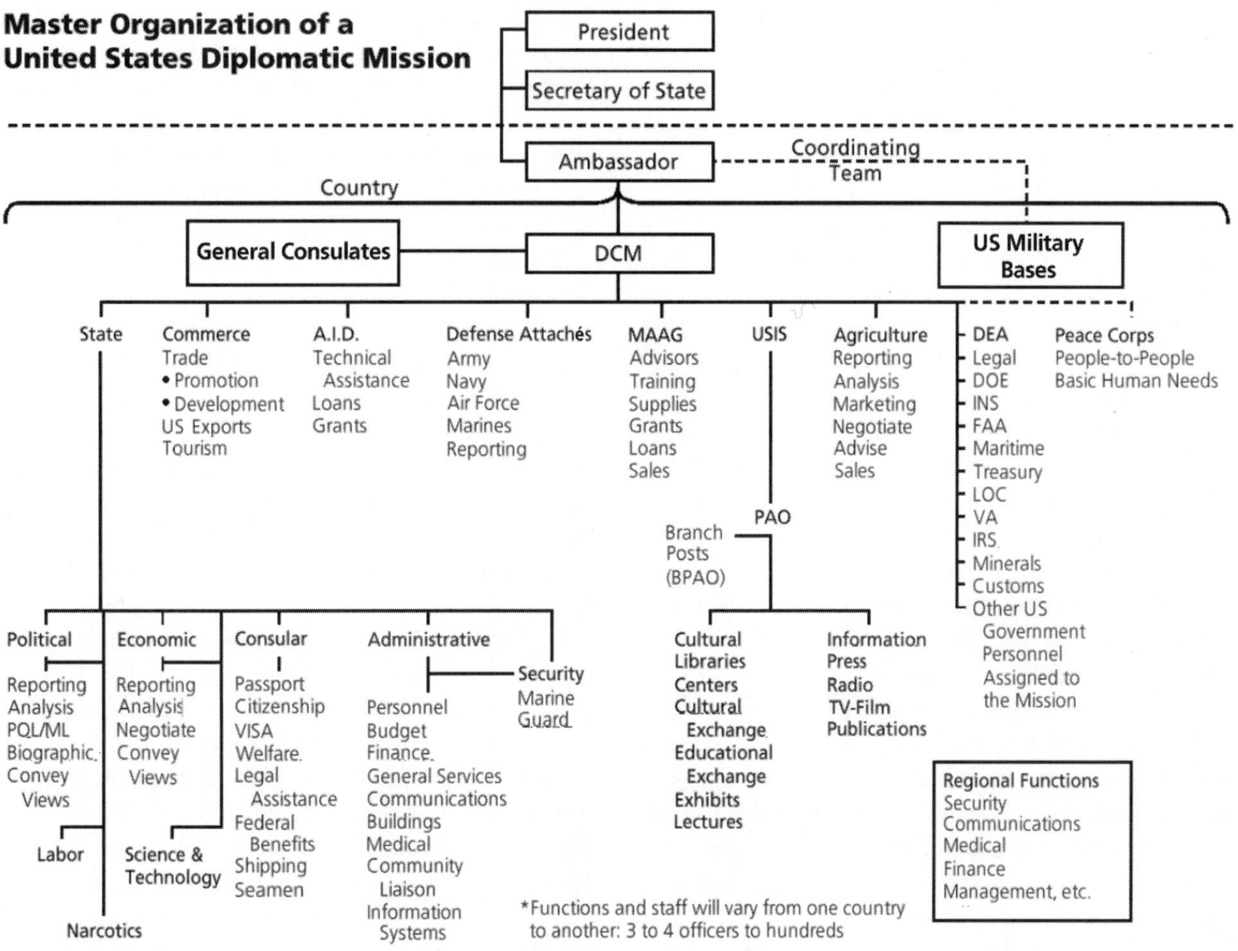

Source: D. Mak & C. Kennedy, Appendix C, *American Ambassadors in a Troubled World* (Westport, CT: Greenwood Press, 1992). Printed with permission.

1992 and 1981, China downgraded the Beijing missions of France and the Netherlands, respectively, because of their sales of fighter planes and submarines to Taiwan.

The process of exchanging diplomats begins with an "accreditation." The State A host government must consent to the particular diplomat dispatched from State B. State B's agent typically presents his or her "credentials" to a representative of the head of State A. The credential is a document that identifies the State B agent as State B's official representative. State A's consent is confirmed by an *agrément* that indicates its approval of State B's diplomat.[15] During the failed 1991 coup by certain Russian military leaders against Mikhail Gorbachev, the ranking US diplomat refused to present his credentials to the coup's leaders. He was forced to leave Russia but was hastily replaced by a new US ambassador who immediately presented his credentials to Gorbachev as a show of US support for maintaining the democratic reforms sought by Gorbachev.

Certain States have arranged for *multiple* accreditations, whereby the same diplomatic premises contain the embassies of more than one foreign government. Conversely, some States do not have any diplomatic presence, often relying on their United Nations mission in New York or Geneva to promote their diplomatic interests.

The *location* of the diplomatic premises occasionally signals a political aperture. Foreign missions are normally located in the capital city of the host State. Massachusetts Avenue in Washington, D.C., is commonly referred to as "Embassy Row," because of the large number of foreign missions located on that street. In Israel, most States have located their diplomatic premises in Tel Aviv. They do not recognize Jerusalem as the capital of Israel (which Israel has claimed since 1950). In 1993, the essentially Muslim State of Kyrgyzstan established its embassy in Jerusalem—a major holy center for Muslims. The president of that former Soviet republic announced this decision during his visit to Jerusalem. Only El Salvador and Costa Rica had previously maintained embassies in Jerusalem (rather than Tel Aviv). In 1998, US Speaker of the House Newt Gingrich acquiesced in a White House request that he *not* visit the proposed site of the new US embassy in Jerusalem. Both Israel and Palestine claim Jerusalem as their capital city. His visit would have triggered more bloodshed in Middle East peace negotiations

Diplomatic relations, once established, do not always proceed smoothly. An adverse development in the international relations between two States may occur. A diplomat may act in a manner considered unacceptable to the host State and may then be asked to leave—with or without specified reasons. The host State would thus declare the sending State's diplomat *persona non grata* (unwelcome), necessitating his or her departure. On the eve of the 1991 UN-imposed Iraqi departure date from Kuwait (and the ensuing Persian Gulf War), Iraq's ambassador was summoned to the US State Department in Washington and advised that he must reduce the size of his diplomatic staff to four people who could travel no farther than twenty-five miles from their embassy. The rest of the staff was ordered to leave the US—including the Iraqi ambassador himself. While the US did not then "break" diplomatic relations with Iraq, it did close the US embassy in Baghdad.

Not all States follow this customary practice of merely withdrawing a particular diplomat's acceptability. Contrary to International Law, diplomats are sometimes held captive and have even been prohibited from exiting the host State. During its Cultural Revolution, the People's Republic of China withdrew the diplomatic status of a representative in the Indian embassy and forbade his departure until he was punished for the "crimes" with which he had been charged. In a similar episode during the same period, a Dutch chargé d'affaires in China was declared *persona non grata*. Rather than facilitating his return to the Netherlands, China did not grant this officer an exit visa until after five months of confinement. In response to this episode, Chinese diplomats in the Netherlands remained secluded in their offices—to avoid having to testify about this affair to Dutch officials. China's actions violated both the customary practice of States and the fundamental diplomatic treaty discussed below. This incident illustrates how host States can readily interrupt and interfere with the normal conduct of diplomatic relations.[16]

Suspension or termination of diplomatic relations is completely *discretionary* under State practice. International Law does not require a legal basis for such disruptions. States may abruptly refuse to deal with each other. The sending and host States may opt to recall their respective diplomatic agents. During the student demonstrations in Beijing in 1989, the US did not break diplomatic relations with China. The US did prepare its diplomats to leave Beijing for their safety—an action designed to demonstrate the US protest of the massacre of students seeking democratic reform in China.

In 1979, the US recognized the government of the People's Republic of China as the political entity responsible for "China." The US nevertheless maintains relations with Taiwan, which is treated as a State and permitted access to US courts—unlike the People's Republic of China and the former Soviet Union when they were not recognized by the United States. Prior to 1993, when mainland China and Taiwan took the first steps to resolve forty years of political hostility, their proximity required unofficial communications on a regular basis—notwithstanding lack of diplomatic ties and their mutual nonrecognition. As succinctly described by the University of Leicester's G. R. Berridge: "Intermediaries are valued by hostile states seeking some kind of accommodation when at least one of the parties regards the political price of direct talks as unacceptably high, or believes that the participation of a third party in any negotiation with its enemy will bring it material gain and additional security from any settlement."[17]

Severing diplomatic ties does not necessarily cut off the continuing need to deal with each other—even when there are no "official" links. This unconventional diplomacy—when States and other entities without diplomatic relations must nevertheless talk to the "enemy"—is a worldwide phenomenon. This form of diplomatic exchange is the product of the need for communication between States or other entities publicly at war but privately seeking a reconciliation or some other mutually recognized objective.

One of the more common devices for this shadowy form of diplomacy is to employ the diplomatic corps of third parties who enjoy good relations with both hostile States. Cuba and the US have had indirect dealings with each other ever since Fidel Castro assumed political power in 1959. The US broke diplomatic relations with Cuba, but the Swiss and former Czechoslovakian embassies in Havana exchanged information on behalf of the US and Cuban government for many years. The Cuban Interest Section of the former Czechoslovakian embassy in Washington, D.C., also acted as a go-between in such matters. In March 1995, an Iraqi court sentenced two Americans to an eight-year prison term because they strayed into Iraqi territory during a visit with friends in the demilitarized zone between Kuwait and Iraq. The US and Iraq had no *official* diplomatic ties. Poland had such ties with both countries. Its diplomats served as go-betweens to negotiate the release of the US citizens.

States also undertake other forms of unconventional diplomacy when they do not recognize one another. Israel and the Palestine Liberation Organization secretly communicated for many years before their 1993 Washington peace accord. The United Kingdom and Sinn Fein (seeking independence for Northern Ireland) engaged in private negotiations before the 1994 announcement of their new working relationship. The clandestine methods for international communication include disguised embassies and ceremonial occasions such as the "working funeral" when a prominent dignitary has died.

1961 VIENNA CONVENTION ON DIPLOMATIC RELATIONS

Diplomatic functions are globally defined in the Vienna Convention on Diplomatic Relations. The diplomat thus:

(a) Represents the sending State in the receiving State;
(b) Protects the interests of the sending State and of its nationals, within the limits permitted by the receiving State's internal laws and International Law;
(c) Negotiates with the Government of the receiving State;
(d) Ascertains, by lawful means, conditions and developments in the receiving State, and reports them to the Government of the sending State; and
(e) Promotes friendly relations between the sending State and the receiving State by prodding the development of their economic, cultural, and scientific relations.[18]

The key members of State A's embassy staff are usually nationals of State A. They *may* be citizens of some other State but only with the consent of the host (receiving) State B. This special provision helps to ensure that State A's diplomatic mission represents *only* the interests of State A. If a diplomat representing State A were a citizen of State B, for example, this hypothetical "A" diplomat would face constant conflicts of interest while trying to represent the interests of State A—and simultaneously representing the potentially conflicting interests of his or her own State B.

Protecting the interests of State A includes providing diplomatic (or consular) assistance to a State A citizen who is present in and has allegedly been harmed by host State B or its agents (*see* §4.2 on nationality). The State A representative in State B may have to deal with a variety of problems confronting his or her fellow citizens. These include making arrangements for a criminal defense or the transfer of deceased individuals or their property between the host State and the home State.

1963 VIENNA CONVENTION ON CONSULAR RELATIONS

Consular officials are not usually "diplomatic" representatives. They are not generally accredited to the host State, although they are official agents of the sending State. Consular officers often conduct "diplomatic" negotiations in international trade matters, however. Such matters are sometimes handled through the institution of the *honorary consul*. This is an individual who assists in the promotion of trade policies. He or she is typically a national of the *host* State, possessing expertise in host State business matters.

One of the most sensitive consular functions is providing access to jailed nationals of the home State of local consular officials. Denial of access or delays often generate friction in international relations. In 1993, for example, the US protested to Israel about its treatment of three jailed Palestinian-Americans from Chicago. They were visiting relatives in the occupied West Bank—where they were arrested and confined without prompt access to either lawyers or US consular officials. The resulting US protest occurred during the period when the US was attempting to bring Israel and the PLO together for the long-awaited peace accords (ultimately achieved in Washington several months later).

Historical Evolution Consular institutions have had a longer and more varied history than the medieval Italian diplomatic mission described above. The forerunner of the modern consul appeared almost as early as people began to trade. The Preamble to the 1963 Vienna Convention acknowledges that "consular relations have been established between peoples since ancient times." As succinctly described by Professor Luke Lee of American University in Washington, D.C.:

> [T]he many political contributions of the Greek city-states . . . [include] the early development of the consular system; the *prostates* and the *proxenos* are considered forerunners of the modern consuls. The *prostates* were chosen by Greek colonists to live abroad to act as intermediaries in legal and political relations between the foreign (Greek) colony and the local government [of a distant land]. About the sixth century B.C. the Egyptians allowed Greek settlers . . . to select *prostates,* who administered Greek law to the Greeks. In the same period, similar institutions could be found in certain parts of India.
>
> During the first millennium B.C., *proxenoi* were appointed in the Greek city-states to look after the interests of the appointing [city-]State. The *proxenos,* though more a political than commercial agent, has been likened to the modern honorary consul, and was [thus] chosen from the nationals of the receiving State.[19]

Modern Treaty The 1963 Vienna Convention on Consular Relations contains the globally defined consular functions.[20] Consular officials thus:

(a) protect the interests of the sending State and its nationals, within the limits permitted by International Law;
(b) further the development of commercial, economic, cultural and scientific relations—and otherwise promote friendly relations;
(c) ascertain conditions and developments in the commercial, economic, cultural, and scientific life of the receiving State—and report thereon to the government of the sending State and other interested persons;
(d) issue passports and travel documents to nationals of the sending State, and visas or appropriate documents to persons wishing to travel to the sending State;
(e) safeguard the interests of nationals, including minors and other persons lacking full capacity of the sending State;
(f) represent or arrange appropriate representation for nationals of the sending State before the tribunals and other authorities of the receiving State—where such nationals are unable to assume the defense of their own rights and interests—including the transmission of judicial documents or the taking of evidence for the courts of the sending State;
(g) exercise rights of supervision and inspection provided for in the laws and regulations of the sending State for vessels having the nationality of the foreign State—as well as aircraft registered in that State; and
(h) assist vessels and aircraft and their crews, or take statements regarding the voyage of a vessel, examining and stamping the ship's papers, or conduct investigations into any incidents that occurred during the voyage (*see Wildenhus* "port tranquility" case in §6.3).

Consular officers thus prepare trade reports, gather information relevant to international trade, and investigate alleged infractions of commercial treaties in or by the host State. Consuls also supervise international shipping. Seagoing vessels must be registered to a particular country and fly that country's flag. Consuls authenticate the registration papers of their home State's ships in the host State. Consuls help their home State's nationals resolve host State customs and immigration problems. Consuls also provide needed services to fellow citizens who become ill or indigent while in the host State. They take charge of the estates of deceased home State nationals and arrange for property distribution under the host State's laws. Unlike diplomats, consuls often directly assist their fellow nationals with personal problems—such as obtaining legal representation in host State courts—that normally have no sensitive political repercussions. The following case was a major exception, drawing worldwide attention to one country's failure to provide rights guaranteed under the 1963 Vienna Convention:

Case Concerning the Vienna Convention on Consular Relations (Paraguay v. United States of America) Request for the Indication of Provisional Measures: Order

INTERNATIONAL COURT OF JUSTICE, 1998
37 *Int'l Legal Mat'ls* 810 (1998)

Author's Note: *Paraguay instituted proceedings against the US on April 3, 1998, for violations of the Vienna Convention on Consular Relations (VCCR). A Paraguayan national named Angel Breard was scheduled for execution by the State of Virginia on April 14. He admittedly committed the rape and murder for which he was sentenced to death. However, the state of Virginia failed to provide the right to assistance by the consular officers of Paraguay—as required by the VCCR—on the occasion of his arrest and detention under the US–Paraguay friendship treaty. Had this been done, the defendant might not have made a number of apparently unreasonable decisions during the criminal proceedings against him.*

Paraguay argued that the ICJ order was necessary, because Breard's scheduled execution would deprive it of an effective remedy—should the ICJ rule in Paraguay's favor on the merits at some point in the future. US Secretary of State Albright wrote to the Governor of Virginia, seeking a delay of this execution on grounds that the "execution of Mr. Breard in the present circumstances could lead some countries to contend incorrectly that the US does not take seriously its obligations under the [Vienna] Convention."

On April 9, the ICJ issued this order to the US—that the execution be delayed until the accused could be given his procedural rights under the treaty.

On April 14, the US Supreme Court declined to stay the execution. Its essential reason was that the US admittedly had an obligation to afford Mr. Breard his rights under the 1963 treaty. However, Congress passed the 1996 Antiterrorism and Effective Death Penalty Act. It provides that habeas corpus petitioners, claiming treaty violations, cannot seek federal relief unless they have previously raised this claim in the state proceedings leading to their conviction. Mr. Breard did not do so. (Under US law—discussed in Chapter 8—a subsequent statute, which is in conflict with a prior treaty, supercedes the earlier treaty.) Virginia thus executed Mr. Breard that evening.

ICJ ORDER. The International Court of Justice . . . [a]fter deliberation . . . makes the following Order *[the paragraph numbers are those of the Court]*: . . .

2. Whereas, in the Application, it is stated that in 1992 the authorities of the Commonwealth of Virginia arrested a Paraguayan national, Mr. Angel Francisco Breard; whereas it is maintained that he was charged, tried, convicted of culpable homicide and sentenced to death by a Virginia court (the Circuit Court of Arlington County) in 1993, without having been informed, as is required under Article 36, subparagraph 1 (b), of the Vienna Convention, of his rights under that provision; whereas it is specified that among these rights are the right to request that the relevant consular office of the State of which he is national be advised of his arrest and detention, and the right to communicate with that office; and whereas it is also alleged that the authorities of the Commonwealth of Virginia also did not advise the Paraguayan consular officers of Mr. Breard's detention, and that those officers were only able to render assistance to him from 1996, when the Paraguayan Government learnt by its own means that Mr. Breard was imprisoned in the United States; . . .

3. Whereas, in the Application, Paraguay states that Mr. Breard's subsequent petitions before federal courts in order to seek a writ of habeas corpus failed, the federal court of first instance having, on the basis of the doctrine of "procedural default," denied him the right to invoke the Vienna Convention for the first time before that court . . . [and] whereas Paraguay also filed a petition for a writ of certiorari in the Supreme Court, which is also still pending; and whereas Paraguay furthermore engaged in diplomatic efforts

with the Government of the United States and sought the good offices of the Department of State;

4. Whereas, in its Application, Paraguay maintains that by violating its obligations under Article 36, subparagraph 1 (b), of the Vienna Convention, the United States prevented Paraguay from exercising the consular functions provided for in Articles 5 and 36 of the Convention and specifically for ensuring the protection of its interests and of those of its nationals in the United States; whereas Paraguay states that it was not able to contact Mr. Breard nor to offer him the necessary assistance, and whereas accordingly Mr. Breard "made a number of objectively unreasonable decisions during the criminal proceedings against him, which were conducted without translation"; and "did not comprehend the fundamental differences between the criminal justice systems of the United States and Paraguay"; and whereas Paraguay concludes from this that it is entitled to . . . "the re-establishment of the situation that existed before the United States failed to provide the notifications . . . required by the Convention";

5. Whereas Paraguay requests the Court to adjudge and declare as follows: . . .

> "(3) that the United States is under an international legal obligation not to apply to the doctrine of 'procedural default,' or any other doctrine of its internal law, so as to preclude the exercise of the rights accorded under Article 36 of the Vienna Convention; and
>
> (4) that the United States is under an international legal obligation to carry out in conformity with the foregoing international legal obligations any future detention of or criminal proceedings against Angel Francisco Breard or any other Paraguayan national in its territory, whether by a constituent, legislative, executive, judicial or other power, whether that power holds a superior or a subordinate position in the organization of the United States, and whether that power's functions are of an international or internal character;
>
> and that, pursuant to the foregoing international legal obligations,
>
> (1) any criminal liability imposed on Angel Francisco Breard in violation of international legal obligations is void, and should be recognized as void by the legal authorities of the United States;
> (2) the United States should restore the status quo ante, that is, re-establish the situation that existed before the detention of, proceedings against, and conviction and sentencing of Paraguay's national in violation of the United States' international legal obligations took place; and
> (3) the United States should provide Paraguay a guarantee of the non-repetition of the illegal acts"; . . .

18. Whereas at the hearing [seeking a provisional order to stay the execution until trial of this case on its merits], the United States argued that Mr. Breard's guilt was well established, and pointed out that the accused had admitted his guilt, which Paraguay did not dispute; whereas it recognized that Mr. Breard had not been informed, at the time of his arrest and trial, of his rights under Article 36, subparagraph 1 (b), of the Vienna Convention, and indicated to the Court that this omission was not deliberate; whereas it nonetheless maintained that the person concerned had had all necessary legal assistance, that he understood English well and that the assistance of consular officers would not have changed the outcome of the proceedings brought against him in any way; whereas, referring to State practice in these matters, it stated that the notification provided for by Article 36, subparagraph 1 (b), of the Vienna Convention is unevenly made, and that when a claim is made for failure to notify, the only consequence is that apologies are presented by the government responsible; and whereas it submitted that the automatic invalidation of the proceedings initiated and the return to the status quo ante as penalties for the failure to notify not only find no support in State practice, but would be unworkable; . . .

20. Whereas the United States furthermore maintained that Paraguay's contention that the invalidation of the sentence of a person who had not been notified pursuant to Article 36, subparagraph 1 (b), of the Vienna Convention could be required under that instrument, has no foundation in the relevant provisions, their *travaux préparatoires* or the practice of States,

and that, in the event, Mr. Breard has not been prejudiced by the absence of notification; and whereas it pointed out that provisional measures should not be indicated where it appears that the Applicant's argument will not enable it to be successful on the merits; . . .

22. Whereas the United States finally alleged that the indication of the provisional measures requested by Paraguay would be contrary to the interests of the States parties to the Vienna Convention and to those of the international community as a whole as well as to those of the Court, and would in particular be such as seriously to disrupt the criminal justice systems of the States parties to the Convention, given the risk of proliferation of cases; and whereas it stated in that connection that States have an overriding interest in avoiding external judicial intervention which would interfere with the execution of a sentence passed at the end of an orderly process meeting the relevant human rights standards; . . .

28. Whereas at the hearing, the United States contended, for its part, that Paraguay had not established that the Court had jurisdiction in these proceedings, even prima facie; whereas it argued that there is no dispute between the Parties as to the interpretation of Article 36, subparagraph 1 (b), of the Vienna Convention and nor is there a dispute as to its application, since the United States recognizes that the notification provided for was not carried out; whereas the United States maintained that the objections raised by Paraguay to the proceedings brought against its national do not constitute a dispute concerning the interpretation or application of the Vienna Convention; . . .

29. Whereas the United States moreover indicated to the Court that it had expressed its regret to Paraguay for the failure to notify Mr. Breard of his right to consular access, engaged in consultations with Paraguay on the matter and taken steps to ensure future compliance with its obligations under the Vienna Convention at both the federal and state level; . . .

37. Whereas the execution of Mr. Breard is ordered for 14 April 1998; and whereas such an execution would render it impossible for the Court to order the relief that Paraguay seeks and thus cause irreparable harm to the rights it claims; . . .

40. Whereas measures indicated by the Court for a stay of execution would necessarily be provisional in nature and would not in any way prejudge findings the Court might make on the merits; and whereas the measures indicated would preserve the respective rights of Paraguay and of the United States; and whereas it is appropriate that the Court, with the cooperation of the Parties, ensure that any decision on the merits be reached with all possible expedition;

41. For these reasons, THE COURT unanimously,

I. Indicates the following provisional measures:
The United States should take all measures at its disposal to ensure that Angel Francisco Breard is not executed pending the final decision in these proceedings, and should inform the Court of all the measures which it has taken in implementation of this Order;

II. Decides, that, until the Court has given its final decision, it shall remain seized of the matters which form the subject-matter of this Order.

◆ *Notes & Questions*

1. This is one of the handful of cases where a foreign government has sought redress for a treaty violation in a US federal court. It is also the *first* case where an international tribunal has intervened in ongoing domestic proceedings. A useful analysis is available in W. Aceves, "International Decisions," 92 *Amer. J. Int'l L.* 517 (1998). Paraguay ultimately sought and obtained a dismissal of this proceeding.
2. If Breard admitted committing the rape and murder for which he was convicted, what would be gained by a delay of the execution until after a full hearing on the merits by the US courts—as argued by the

dissenters in the US Supreme Court case of *Breard v. Greene,* 118 S.Ct. 1352 (1998) and as ordered by the ICJ?

3. Although Breard was executed, the case is still pending in the ICJ, because of the significant issues it raises that are not limited to just Mr. Bread's case. As of April 1998, there were sixty-five other prisoners on death row in the US who had been convicted in violation of the rights supposedly accorded foreign nationals under the 1963 VCCR. A symposium is available on the issues raised by this case in "Agora: Breard," 92 *Amer. J. Int'l Law* 666–712 (1998).
4. On October 8, 1998, the wife of a television anchorman, Hugh Finn, obtained judicial approval to remove her husband's life support system (at his Virginia nursing home). He was comatose for three years and six months since his auto accident, brain dead, and had stated—several years before, in a case on which he was reporting—that he would not want to be kept alive under such circumstances. Virginia governor Gilmore, who did not wish to delay Angel Breard's execution on April 14, 1998, was instrumental in the court battle wherein the State of Virginia sought to delay Mrs. Finn's removal of the life support system.
4. Another case like *Breard* was filed by Germany against the US in the ICJ. The US Supreme Court again refused to stay the execution of a foreign citizen. The ICJ unsuccessfully ordered the US to "take all measures at its disposal to ensure that Walter LeGrand is not executed pending the final [ICJ] decision in these proceedings." *See* "Case Concerning the Vienna Convention on Consular Relations *(Germany v. USA),*" *ICJ Rep.,* paragraph 28 (1999).

◆ 7.3 EXTRATERRITORIALITY AND ASYLUM

Prior sections discussed diplomatic and consular functions. There are two important corollaries: First, what is the effect of an act undertaken in a foreign embassy or consulate when the consequences would be different in the host State where the building is located? Second, may a foreign State give diplomatic asylum within its embassy or consular premises when to do so would offend the wishes of the host State?

EXTRATERRITORIALITY FICTION

The special international status of embassies and consular premises long ago generated the question of whether they are legally a part of the host State or sending State. Historically, they were considered an extraterritorial extension of the sending State rather than the receiving State. This legal fiction meant that acts done within an embassy or consulate would be governed by the law of the *sending* State, even when contrary to host State law.

The historical basis for this view is derived from the practice of medieval "Christian" States. Their consuls exercised full civil and criminal jurisdiction over their fellow nationals located in *non*-Christian States. This exclusion from the jurisdiction of the local tribunals was rooted in the convenient legal fiction of "extraterritoriality." Foreign nationals could invoke the protection of the more favorable laws of their own home States—a subtle form of extraterritorial jurisdiction (*see* §5.1). The Sino–Russian Treaty of Nerchinsk of 1689 provided that criminals would be delivered to the consular officers of their own countries for prosecution. The Franco–US Consular Convention of 1788 similarly provided for consular jurisdiction of the respective nations over civil disputes between Frenchmen when both were in the US, and between Americans when both were in France. The Japanese–American Treaty of 1858 was a model for a number of similar pacts that provided for this extraterritorial regime, conferring jurisdiction to resolve such disputes on foreign consular officers located in the host State.[21]

An increasing number of contemporary courts apply a pragmatic analysis of such immunity, which has effectively rejected this historical fiction. Egypt's consulate in London, for example, would have been historically characterized as being located on Egyptian soil. The contemporary approach is that the Egyptian consulate in London is located in England for *all* purposes. The modern approach acknowledges the basic need for protecting diplomatic and consular premises. However, there is no need for the extraterritoriality fiction that provided an unnecessary degree of protection for foreign nationals located in the host State. The following case illustrates both the historical fiction and the modern status of the sending State's diplomatic and consular premises:

Radwan v. Radwan

FAMILY DIVISION—LONDON, ENGLAND, 1972

3 *All England Reports* 967 (1972)

Author's Note: *Mr. Radwan was an Egyptian national who entered into a polygamous marriage with an English woman at the Egyptian consulate in Paris.*

Mr. Radwan subsequently moved to England. He entered the Egyptian consulate in London to divorce his English (second) wife by employing the Middle Eastern "talaq" procedure: In her absence, he orally decreed three times that they were divorced. This talaq procedure constituted a valid divorce under the laws of Egypt but not under English law.

Several years later, the English wife filed her own divorce suit in the English courts, anticipating that she would be entitled to a better divorce settlement under English law than Egyptian law. Her English lawyer argued that the talaq divorce, while performed within the Egyptian consulate in London, was not entitled to recognition under English law. It could not be recognized as a divorce performed "outside of" England. Mr. Radwan, hoping to avoid an unfavorable English divorce decree, responded to his "wife's" suit in the English courts by claiming that he had already obtained a valid divorce—when he performed the talaq procedure in the Egyptian consulate. Thus, he argued, his talaq divorce was effective, because it was legally performed in "Egyptian territory" (that is, in Egypt's consulate in London). Judge Cummins's decision disagreed as follows. (The court's footnotes are omitted.)

COURT'S OPINION. I have read the relevant subparagraph of the petition whereby the talaq divorce is pleaded. The husband put in evidence the affidavit of Mustapha Kamil Abdul Fata, Deputy Consul General of the Consulate General of the United Arab Republic of Egypt in Kensington Palace Gardens in London. In it he swore [in his capacity as an expert on Egyptian law] as follows:

(1) The Egyptian Consulate in London is regarded as being Egyptian territory on Egyptian soil.

(2) The divorce . . . registered in Cairo . . . is valid and recognised by Egyptian law. . . .

I also received the affidavit of Jamil Nasir, a person qualified in Egyptian law. In that affidavit he says that . . . under Egyptian law the Consulate General of the United Arab Republic in London is regarded as Egyptian territory. He does not give any reasons for that opinion, but I note that it corresponds with the [above-quoted] statement of the deputy consul of the Consulate General in London. . . .

The facts are as follows. The husband was born in Cairo. He is and at all material times was a Mohammedan. He was and remains a subject of the United Arab Republic. . . . On 1st [of] April 1970 he entered the Egyptian Consulate in London; the procedure stated in the affidavit of the deputy consul of the Consulate General was followed. The husband three times declared the prescribed [talaq] form of divorce in the presence of two witnesses. All the steps were carried out in accordance with Egyptian law. After the prescribed 90 days the divorce was finalised in accordance with Egyptian law, and in accordance with that law it was no impediment to the efficacy of the proceedings that the wife knew nothing about it at all. . . .

The question for my decision is whether by *English* law the Consulate General of the United Arab Republic is part of a country outside the British Isles within the meaning of the Recognition of Divorces and Legal Separations Act of 1971. By that Act the relevant sections providing for recognition will have effect in respect of overseas divorces if they have been obtained by means of judicial or other proceedings *in any country outside the British Isles,* and it is necessary for the efficacy of the talaq divorce that it should have been obtained outside the British Isles by reason of the fact that at the material time the husband had acquired English domicile *[emphasis supplied by author].*

Curiously, the question has not arisen for decision in England before, that is, the question whether the premises of an embassy or consulate are part of the territory of the sending state as compared to the territory of the receiving state.

Issue!

I quote and adopt the observations of [legal commentator] Mr J E S Fawcett:

> There are two popular myths about diplomats and their immunities which we must clear away: one is that an embassy is foreign territory, and the other is that a diplomat can incur no legal liabilities in the country in which he is serving. The first is a confusion between territory or property and jurisdiction over it, and it is important to clarify it for it has sometimes arisen over ships and aircraft. The building occupied by a foreign embassy and the land on which it stands are part of the territory of what we call the receiving state: it is therefore under the jurisdiction of that state. But the members of the mission and their activities in the embassy are primarily under the control and jurisdiction of the sending state. International law avoids conflict between these jurisdictions by laying down rules to cover the whole field of diplomatic relations. These rules have been embodied in the Vienna Convention [on Diplomatic Relations of] 1961, which may be taken as reflecting existing law and practice. This Convention, and that on Consular Relations drawn up in 1963, are among the first steps . . . in the successful codification of international law. The premises of a mission are inviolable, and the local authorities may enter them only with the consent of the head of the mission. But this does not make the premises foreign territory or take them out of the reach of the local law for many purposes: for example, a commercial transaction in an embassy may be governed by the local law, particularly tax law; marriages may be celebrated there only if conditions laid down by the local law are met; and a child born in it [the diplomatic premises] will, unless his father has diplomatic status, acquire the local nationality.

Judge Cummins then considered similar cases involving this issue arising in other countries. This is a useful illustration of how a decision maker resorts to customary State practice as a basis for ascertaining the content of International Law.

FRANCE: *Nikitschenkoff* case: The court was dealing with murderous assaults on the first secretary of the Russian embassy in the Russian embassy in Paris, and an argument was submitted that the place of the crime being the premises of the Russian embassy was a place situated outside the territory of France and not governed by French law. The decision was a decision under art. 3 of the Code of Napoleon. The court said:

> [that] all those who live in the territory [France] are subject to [French] police and security laws; Whereas, admitting as exceptions to this rule of public law the immunity which, in certain cases, international law accords to the person of foreign diplomatic agents and the legal fiction in virtue of which the premises they occupy are deemed to be situated outside the territory of the sovereign to whom they are accredited; Whereas, nevertheless, this legal fiction cannot be extended but constitutes an exception to the rule of territorial jurisdiction . . . and is strictly limited to the ambassador or minister whose independence it is designed to protect and to those of his subordinates who are clothed with the same public character; Whereas the accused is not attached in any sense to the Russian Embassy but, as a foreigner residing for the time in France, was subject to French law; and Whereas the place where the crime which he is charged with committing cannot, in so far as he is concerned, be regarded as outside the limits of [French] territory . . . the jurisdiction of the French judiciary [is] clearly established.

> GERMANY: *Afghan Embassy* case.
> ITALY: *[citing several cases].*

In all these cases the court rejected the argument that diplomatic premises were not part of the territory of the receiving state. . . .

Although international conventions [treaties] do not have the force of law unless embodied in municipal legislation [of an individual state], they may in the field of international law be valuable as a guide to the rules of international law which this country as a signatory respects. . . .

If it was the view of the high contracting parties [to the Vienna Convention] that the premises of missions were part of the territory of the sending state, that would undoubtedly be formulated [within the language of those treaties].

◆ *Notes & Questions*

1. In the initial phase of this stormy divorce, Judge Cummins ruled that Mr. Radwan did not legally divorce his English wife in a place "outside of" England merely because he was in the Egyptian consulate. The talaq divorce procedure was performed *in* England, was ineffective under English law, and would not be recognized by England. Mr. Radwan was still married to his English wife under the laws of England. His purported divorce (in the London consulate) failed to bar his English wife from prosecuting her subsequent divorce action in the English courts. If the talaq procedure had *actually* occurred in Egypt, on the other hand, England would then have recognized the divorce.
2. The English wife did pursue her independent divorce proceedings in England. In that case, the same Judge Cummins decided the related question of whether the Radwan "marriage" was governed by Egyptian or French law. Their marriage (performed in the Egyptian consulate in Paris) and Mr. Radwan's talaq divorce (performed within the Egyptian consulate in London) would both be valid under *Egyptian* law. But neither event took place in Egypt. Judge Cummins consistently ruled in Radwan No. 2 that the marriage occurred in France rather than in Egypt. He noted that the extraterritoriality fiction regarding foreign consulates was not recognized under French law (nor under English law, as he had decided in Radwan No. 1). The marriage undertaken in the Egyptian consulate in Paris was *also* void under host State (French) law. *Radwan v. Radwan* (No. 2), 3 *All England Law Reports* 1026 (1972).
3. The popular misconception is that embassies and consulates are on "foreign" soil. The Vienna Conventions are mentioned in the *Radwan* opinion, because they effectively replaced the extraterritoriality fiction—with an express protection for diplomatic premises. Judge Cummins bases his opinion on what is *not* said in those treaties. How, then, does their silence on this matter support the proposition that "extraterritoriality" is a fiction no longer needed in International Law?

DIPLOMATIC ASYLUM

Asylum is the protection from arrest or extradition when given to a host-State political refugee by a foreign-State diplomat. During the 1989 Tienanmen Square demonstrations in the People's Republic of China, the US granted asylum to China's top dissident. He and his wife stayed in the US embassy in Beijing. Chinese authorities had ordered his arrest for treason, demanding that the US government surrender him to the local authorities waiting outside the US embassy in Beijing. At the same time, the Chinese sealed their international borders to prevent any clandestine escape attempts.

The Vatican and the US were involved in two other prominent asylum incidents. In the most recent of the two, the US invaded Panama in 1989. Its dictator, General Manuel Noriega, remained in hiding for five days. He then entered the Vatican embassy in Panama City after evading US military personnel seeking to take him to the US for trial on drug-trafficking charges. The Vatican diplomat initially refused to turn Noriega over to the invading US forces—which had surrounded the embassy with US troops, tanks, and helicopters to prevent any possible escape. After an agreement with US authorities, the Vatican decided to surrender Noriega to the US forces. He was brought to the US for trial. Whether the Vatican actually granted him asylum became a moot issue. Noriega was able to obtain temporary refuge in the embassy until he could arrange a satisfactory bargain with the US authorities. This was not the first time that the Vatican effectively granted asylum to someone wanted by US authorities. In 1866, Pope Pius XI granted diplomatic asylum to John Surratt, Jr., who had conspired with John Wilkes Booth to assassinate US President Lincoln. Ultimately, the Pope surrendered Surratt to the US for prosecution.

Other sensational asylum cases have generated the popular belief that individuals are *routinely* granted such refuge in foreign embassies. Political relations may be harmed, however, when asylum is granted. A classic case was that of Hungary's Cardinal Jozsef Mindszenty, who remained within the premises of the US embassy in Budapest, Hungary, for fifteen years. He had been arrested for anti-government activities in 1948, jailed in 1949, and freed for several days during a popular revolt in 1956. He then sought refuge in the US embassy. Although the US did not normally grant asylum, it considered this particular request a special case. Mindszenty remained in the embassy under a grant of diplomatic asylum from 1956 to 1971—when Hungary finally agreed to his safe passage to the Vatican.

In the leading international judicial opinion on diplomatic asylum, the International Court of Justice articulated the general principle that States do not *officially* recognize a right of asylum. Diplomatic asylum had been granted with some frequency, however, in Latin America. The following case presents a unique situation because the Court failed to acknowledge the *regional* custom of granting asylum—a decision for which it was much criticized:

Asylum Case: Colombia v. Peru

INTERNATIONAL COURT OF JUSTICE, 1950

1950 *ICJ Rep.* 266

***Author's Note:** Haya de la Torre was a Peruvian national who led an unsuccessful rebellion against Peru in 1948. When the Peruvian government issued a warrant for his arrest on criminal charges related to this political uprising, de la Torre went to the Colombian embassy in Lima, Peru. He requested and was granted diplomatic asylum by the Colombian ambassador on behalf of the government of Colombia. Colombia then requested permission from Peru for de la Torre's safe passage from the Colombian embassy, through Peru, and into Colombia. Peru refused.*

Colombia then brought this suit against Peru in the ICJ, asking the Court to declare that Colombia had properly granted asylum, pursuant to a recognized regional practice of granting asylum in such political cases. Peru's lawyers responded that Colombia could not unilaterally grant asylum over Peru's objection. De la Torre had committed a common crime, subjecting him to prosecution by Peru, just like any other criminal. Colombia had no right to employ asylum as a means of avoiding Peru's criminal laws.

OPINION. In the case of diplomatic asylum, the refugee is within the territory of the State where the offence was committed. A decision to grant diplomatic asylum involves a derogation from the sovereignty of that State. It withdraws the offender from the jurisdiction of the territorial State and constitutes an intervention in matters which are exclusively within the competence of that State [Peru]. Such a derogation from territorial sovereignty cannot be recognised unless its legal basis is established in each particular case. . . .

The Havana Convention on Asylum of 1928 . . . lays down certain rules relating to diplomatic asylum, but does not contain any provision conferring on the State granting asylum a unilateral competence to qualify the offence with definitive and binding force for the territorial State. . . .

A competence of this kind is of an exceptional character. It involves a derogation from the equal rights of qualification which, in the absence of any contrary rule, must be attributed to each of the States concerned; it aggravates the derogation from territorial sovereignty constituted by the exercise of asylum. Such a competence is not inherent in the institution of diplomatic asylum. This institution would perhaps be more effective if a rule of unilateral and definitive qualification were applied. But such a rule is not essential to the exercise of asylum. . . .

The Colombian Government has finally invoked "American international law in general" [to justify its grant of asylum]. In addition to the rules arising from agreements, . . . it has relied on an alleged regional or local custom peculiar to Latin-American States. The Party which relies on a custom of this kind must prove that this custom is established in such a manner that it has become binding on the other Party, . . . that it is in accordance with a constant and uniform usage practised by the States in question, and that this usage is the expression of a right appertaining to the State granting asylum and a duty incumbent on the territorial State. This follows from Article 38 of the Statute of the Court, which refers to international custom "as evidence of a general practice accepted as law." . . .

[T]he Colombian Government has referred to a large number of particular cases in which diplomatic asylum was in fact granted and respected. But it has not shown that the alleged rule of unilateral and definitive qualification was invoked or . . . that it was, apart from conventional stipulations, exercised by the States granting asylum as a right appertaining to them and respected by the territorial States as a duty incumbent on them and not merely for reasons of political expediency. The facts brought to the knowledge of the Court disclose so much uncertainty and contradiction, so much fluctuation and discrepancy in the exercise of diplomatic asylum and in the official views expressed on various occasions, there has been so much inconsistency in the rapid succession of conventions on asylum, ratified by some States and rejected by others, and the practice has been so much influenced by considerations of political expediency in the various cases, that it is not possible to discern in all this any constant and uniform usage, mutually accepted as law, with regard to the alleged rule of unilateral and definitive qualification of the offence.

The Court cannot therefore find that the Colombian Government has proved the existence of such a custom. But even if it could be supposed that such a custom existed between certain Latin-American States only, it could not be invoked against Peru which, far from having by its attitude adhered to it, has, on the contrary, repudiated it by refraining from ratifying the Montevideo Conventions of 1933 and 1939, which were the first to include a rule concerning the qualification of the offence [as "political" in nature] in matters of diplomatic asylum. . . .

Article 2 lays down in precise terms the conditions under which asylum shall be granted to [political] offenders by the territorial State . . . the essential justification for asylum being in the imminence or persistence of a danger for the person of the refugee. It was incumbent upon the Government of Colombia to submit proof of facts to show that [this] condition was fulfilled. . . .

Asylum may be granted on humanitarian grounds . . . to protect political offenders against the violent and disorderly action of irresponsible sections of the population. It has not been contended that Haya de la Torre was in such a situation at the time when he sought refuge in the Colombian Embassy at Lima. . . .

In principle, it is inconceivable that the Havana Convention could have intended the term "urgent cases" to include the danger of regular prosecution to which the citizens of any country lay themselves open by attacking the institutions of that country, nor can it be admitted that in referring to "the period of time strictly indispensable for the person who has sought asylum to ensure in some other way his safety," the Convention envisaged protection from the operation of regular legal proceedings. . . .

In principle, asylum cannot be opposed to the operation of justice. An exception to this rule can occur only if, in the guise of justice, arbitrary action is substituted for the rule of law. Such would be the case if the administration of justice were corrupted by measures clearly prompted by political aims. Asylum protects the political offender against any measures of a manifestly extra-legal character which a Government might take or attempt to take against its political opponents. The word "safety," which . . . determines the specific effect of asylum granted to political offenders, means that the refugee is protected against arbitrary action by the Government, and that he enjoys the benefits of the law. On the other hand, the safety which arises out of asylum cannot be construed as a protection against the regular application of the laws and against the jurisdiction of legally constituted tribunals. Protection thus understood would authorise the diplomatic agent to obstruct the application of the laws of the country whereas it is his duty to respect them; it would in fact become the equivalent of an immunity, which was evidently not within the intentions of the draftsmen of the Havana Convention.

It has not been shown that the existence of a state of siege [in Peru] implied the subordination of justice to the executive authority, or that the suspension of certain constitutional guarantees entailed the abolition of judicial guarantees. . . .

The Court cannot admit that the States signatory to the Havana Convention intended to substitute for the practice of the Latin-American republics, in which considerations of courtesy, good-neighbourliness and political expediency have always held a prominent place, a legal system which would guarantee to their own nationals accused of political offences the privilege of evading national jurisdiction. Such a conception, moreover, would come into conflict with one of the most firmly established traditions of Latin-America, namely, nonintervention [for example, by Colombia into the internal affairs of another State—Peru]. . . .

[The court must] reject the argument that the Havana Convention was intended to afford a quite general protection of asylum to any person prosecuted for political offences, either in the course of revolutionary events or in the more or less troubled times that follow, for the sole reason that it must be assumed that such events interfere with the administration of justice. It is clear that the adoption of such a criterion would lead to foreign interference of a particularly offensive nature in the domestic affairs of States; besides which no confirmation of this criterion can be found in Latin-American practice, as this practice has been explained to the Court.

In thus expressing itself, the Court does not lose sight of the numerous cases of asylum which have been cited....

If these remarks tend to reduce considerably the value as precedents of the cases of asylum cited ... they show none the less, that asylum as practised in Latin-America is an institution which, to a very great extent, owes its development to extra-legal factors. The good-neighbour relations between the republics, the different political interests of the Governments, have favoured the mutual recognition of asylum apart from any clearly defined juridical system. Even if the Havana Convention, in particular, represents an indisputable reaction against certain abuses in practice, it in no way tends to limit the practice of asylum as it may arise from agreements between interested Governments inspired by mutual feelings of toleration and goodwill....

The Court considers that there did not exist a danger constituting a case of urgency within the meaning of Article 2, paragraph 2, of the Havana Convention.

◆ *Notes*

1. The ICJ decided that Haya de la Torre's asylum should be terminated because Colombia could not properly grant it. Colombia's unilateral decision that de la Torre was engaged in "political activity," rather than a common crime against Peru, was not entitled to recognition by other countries (§5.3 addresses this distinction).
2. Although the ICJ ruled that this asylum was not *legally* valid, Peru's citizen was effectively sheltered anyway. Peru could not enter the Colombian embassy to force his surrender. Colombia, on the other hand, could not force Peru to grant de la Torre safe passage out of Peru. After this decision, Colombia and Peru ultimately negotiated an end to the stalemate by permitting de la Torre to leave Peru for Colombia.
3. Four years after this judgment, Peru ratified the Caracas Convention on Diplomatic Asylum. Article 2 therein provides that "every State has the right to grant asylum...." Article 4 adds that it "shall rest with the State granting asylum to determine the nature of the offense [common crime versus political act] or the motives for the persecution." These provisions require treaty signatories to recognize unilateral grants of asylum rather than depend on a distant court's interpretation or application of the *general* International Law that may differ from a *regional* State practice. *See* "Comment, Diplomatic Asylum in the United States and Latin America: A Comparative Analysis," 13 *Brooklyn J. Int'l L.* 111 (1987).
4. The ICJ's judgment in the *Asylum* case was criticized by many States—especially in Latin America, where diplomatic asylum was a common regional practice. Commentators characterized the Court as suffering from the continuing influence of *European* judicial perspectives. A representative criticism by a Brazilian author is as follows:

> [The various judicial pronouncements in the Asylum case] received wide publicity and were the object of various learned papers; those written in Spain and Latin America were, with rare exception, highly critical of the stand taken by the [ICJ]....
>
> From a Latin American point of view, [the judgment] contains certain affirmations which simply went to prove that the Court was not qualified to pass judgment since it had examined a typical Latin American juridical institution [diplomatic asylum] exclusively from a European and biased point of view.... Just as the [reasoning] ... of the International Court of Justice on the question of the international status of South-West Africa made most Afro-Asian States distrust the court, the Haya de la Torre case alienated most Latin American States, contributing to the atmosphere of ill-will which characterizes the relations of most States with the principal judicial organ of the United Nations [the ICJ].[22]

In the referenced *South-West Africa* case decided by the ICJ in the same year as the *Asylum* case, the Court ruled that South Africa had no obligation to place

South-West Africa (a former League "mandate") under the UN Trusteeship system. As a result, this territory remained subject to domination by the white minority government until independence forty years later (as the new State of Namibia). *See* "International Status of South-West Africa," 1950 *ICJ Rep.* 128.

5. In May 1999, João Vieira, the president of Guinea-Bissau, was driven from power by a segment of his nation's army. He successfully sought political asylum in the Portuguese embassy in the capital city of Bissau. Vieira's nineteen-year rule has been criticized on the basis of entrenched corruption. Portugal's prime minister offered Vieira asylum, although there was no guarantee that Vieira would be able to leave the embassy to go to Portugal.

◆ 7.4 IMMUNITIES AND ABUSE OF IMMUNITY

This section addresses two integral themes to the International Law of Diplomacy: the extent to which the sending State and its representatives may invoke immunity from prosecution in the host State; and the pressure to seek a waiver of immunities when a diplomat engages in conduct unbecoming his or her position.

DIPLOMATIC AND CONSULAR IMMUNITIES

Evolution Many centuries ago, it was customary practice to protect the representatives of other governments. Otherwise, they could not perform their economic and political functions without fear of injury or death. Protective measures—now referred to as immunities—were created to limit the absolute power or jurisdiction of the host States wherein they served. The mutual interests of the sending and receiving States required the creation of special privileges and immunities from local prosecution. Diplomats were thus protected from both host State authorities and private citizens in civil and criminal matters. The foreign envoy could then focus on diplomatic endeavors, without fear of arrest or time-consuming involvement in litigation unrelated to the diplomat's official functions.

Oxford University's Professor Ian Brownlie explains the rationale for diplomatic immunity as follows: The "essence of diplomatic relations is the exercise by the sending government of state functions on the territory of the receiving state by license [permission] of the latter. Having agreed to the establishment of diplomatic relations, the receiving [host] state must take steps to enable the sending state to benefit from the content of the license. The process of giving 'full faith and credit' to the license results in a body of 'privileges and immunities.'"[23]

This vintage practice, now known as *diplomatic immunity,* has additional roots in the medieval State practice that recognized the need for safe passage through third States. In the fifteenth and sixteenth centuries, a ruler who hoped to defeat an alliance between two other rulers would literally select their respective emissaries as targets. He needed only to kill or imprison any intermediary who was passing through his kingdom. For example, the French envoys Rinco and Fregoso were murdered by Emperor Charles V. Spain's Ambassador Mendoza was imprisoned in France for four months while on a mission to England. Incidents such as these ultimately led to State recognition of diplomatic immunities and privileges.[24] Unfortunately, many States failed to appreciate the practicality of "not shooting the messenger." Ultimately, certain States began to codify their expectations about diplomatic immunity in their internal laws. England's Diplomatic Privileges Act of 1708, for example, was a direct result of the arrest and detention of the Russian ambassador and his coach by English authorities. The Act was designed "to prevent like insolences for the future."[25]

Consular immunity is more limited than diplomatic immunity. The diplomat and his or her staff are granted *full* immunity from the jurisdiction of the host State. Consular officers enjoy less insulation from host State arrest or civil litigation. One reason for this distinction is that they usually represent less sensitive interests than ambassadors and diplomats. As restated by Stefan Sawicki in the *Polish Yearbook of International Law,* "members of the consulate enjoy the immunity *only* in relation to official acts considered as [an] expression of a sovereign State. . . ."[26]

Modern Treaty Paradigm The contemporary rules of diplomatic immunity are contained in the Vienna Convention on Diplomatic Relations of 1961.[27] Its essential provisions, observed by approximately 150 State parties, are:

> **Article 22.1.** The premises of the mission shall be inviolable. The agents of the receiving State may not

Rescuers carry a woman from the US Embassy over the rubble of a collapsed building next to the embassy in Nairobi, Kenya. Terrorist bombs exploded minutes apart outside the US embassies in the Kenyan and Tanzanian capitals on August 7, 1998. Twelve Americans were among the dead, and the US ambassador to Kenya was injured, according to the the US State Department. The bombings killed 224 people and wounded 5,000. AP photo by Khalil Senosi (reprinted with permission of AP/World Wide Photos).

enter them, except with the consent of the head of the mission. 2. The receiving State is under a special duty to take all appropriate steps to protect the premises of the mission against any intrusion or damage and to prevent any disturbance of the peace of the mission or impairment of its dignity. 3. The premises of the mission, their furnishings and other property thereon and the means of transport of the mission shall be immune from search, requisition, attachment [seizure resulting in custody and control by a court] or execution [sale of property to satisfy court judgment].

Article 24. The archives and documents of the mission shall be inviolable at any time and wherever they may be.

Article 27.1. The receiving State shall permit and protect free communication on the part of the mission for all official purposes. In communicating with the Government and the other missions and consulates of the sending State, wherever situated, the mission may employ all appropriate means, including diplomatic couriers and messages in code or cipher. However, the mission may install and use a wireless transmitter only with the consent of the receiving State. 2. The official correspondence of the mission shall be inviolable. Official correspondence means all correspondence relating to the mission and its functions. 3. The diplomatic bag shall not be opened or detained. . . . 5. The diplomatic courier, who shall be provided with an official document indicating his status and the number of packages constituting the diplomatic bag, shall be protected by the receiving State in the performance of his functions. He shall enjoy personal inviolability and shall not be liable to any form of arrest or detention.

Article 29. The person of a diplomatic agent shall be inviolable. He shall not be liable to any form of arrest or detention. The receiving State shall treat him with due respect and shall take all appropriate steps to prevent any attack on his person, freedom or dignity.

Article 30.1. The private residence of a diplomatic agent shall enjoy the same inviolability and protection as the premises of the mission. 2. His papers, correspondence and . . . his property shall likewise enjoy inviolability.

Article 31.1. A diplomatic agent shall enjoy immunity from the criminal jurisdiction of the receiving State. He shall also enjoy immunity from its civil and administrative jurisdiction [regarding torts, contracts, and other legal matters].

A number of these provisions—found also in the 1963 Vienna Convention on Consular Relations[28]—were the subject of worldwide attention during the Iranian Hostage Crisis of 1979–1980. Their continuing vitality, notwithstanding 444 days of diplomatic stalemate between Iran and the US, was illustrated by the fact that *no* State supported Iran's actions. The UN Security Council unanimously resolved that Iran should immediately release the diplomatic and consular personnel who were seized at the US embassy and various consular offices in Iran. The crisis, together with its international legal implications, is analyzed in the following case:

Case Concerning United States Diplomatic and Consular Staff in Tehran

INTERNATIONAL COURT OF JUSTICE, 1980

19 *Int'l Legal Mat'ls* 553 (1980)

Author's Note: *On November 4, 1979, the US embassy in Tehran, Iran, was overrun by several hundred of the 3,000 Iranians who had been demonstrating at the embassy gates. They seized diplomats, consuls, and Marines and began their occupation of the embassy premises. Two US consulates in other cities in Iran were also occupied and closed on the following day. The embassy personnel in Tehran were physically threatened and denied any communication with either US officials or relatives. Several hundred thousand demonstrators converged on the US embassy premises on November 22, 1979. The Iranian government made no effort to intervene or to assist the hostages inside the building. While a few hostages were released, most were removed to unknown locations beyond the embassy's premises.*

The US instituted this suit against the International Court of Justice, alleging that Iran breached the Vienna Conventions on Diplomatic and Consular Relations, the Vienna Convention on the Prevention of Crimes against Internationally Protected Persons, and the 1955 US–Iran Treaty of Amity.

The position of the Iranian government is contained in correspondence it submitted to the court. Iran refused to send lawyers to represent Iran, to file any official papers, or to directly participate in these proceedings. The ICJ nevertheless considered Iran's correspondence and made preliminary reference to it as follows.

COURT'S OPINION—IRANIAN CORRESPONDENCE. The Government of the Islamic Republic of Iran . . . draws the attention of the Court to the deep-rootedness and the essential character of the Islamic Revolution of Iran, a revolution of a whole oppressed nation against its oppressors and their masters, the examination of whose numerous repercussions is essentially and directly a matter within the national sovereignty of Iran. . . .

For this question [regarding detention of the diplomatic hostages] only represents a marginal and secondary aspect of an overall problem, one such that it cannot be studied separately, and which involves . . . more than 25 years of continual interference by the United States in the internal affairs of Iran, the shameless exploitation of our country, and numerous crimes perpetrated against the Iranian people, contrary to and in conflict with all international and humanitarian norms.

The problem involved in the conflict between Iran and the United States is not [merely] one of the interpretation and the application of the treaties upon which the American Application is based, but results from an overall situation containing much more fundamental and more complex elements. Consequently, the Court cannot examine the American Application divorced from its proper context, namely the whole political dossier of the relations between Iran and the United States over the last 25 years. This dossier includes . . . all the crimes perpetrated in Iran by the American Government, in particular the *coup d'etat* of 1953 stirred up and carried out by the CIA, the overthrow of the lawful national government of Dr. Mossadegh, the restoration [then] of the Shah and of his regime which was under the control of American interests, and all the social, economic, cultural and political consequences of the direct interventions in our internal affairs, as well as grave, flagrant and continuous violations of all international norms, committed by the United States in Iran.

OPINION OF THE COURT. *The paragraph numbers are those of the court.*

22. The persons still held hostage in Iran include, according to the information furnished to the Court by the United States, at least 28 persons having the status, duly recognized by the Government of Iran, of "member of the diplomatic staff" within the meaning of the Vienna Convention of Diplomatic Relations of 1961; at least 20 persons having the status, similarly recognized, of "member of the administrative and technical staff" within the meaning of that Convention; and two other persons of United States nationality not possessing either diplomatic or consular status. Of the persons with the status of member of the diplomatic staff, four are members of the Consular Section of the Mission.

23. Allegations have been made by the Government of the United States of inhumane treatment of hostages; the militants and Iranian authorities have asserted that the hostages have been well treated, and have allowed special visits to the hostages by religious personalities and by representatives of the International Committee of the Red Cross. The specific allegations of ill-treatment have not however been refuted. Examples of such allegations, which are mentioned in some of the sworn declarations of hostages released in November 1979, are as follows: At the outset of the occupation of the Embassy some were paraded bound and blindfolded before hostile and chanting crowds; at least during the initial period of their captivity, hostages were kept bound, and frequently blindfolded, denied mail or any communication with their government or with each other, subjected to interrogation, threatened with weapons.

24. Those archives and documents of the United States Embassy which were not destroyed by the staff during the attack on 4 November have been ransacked by the militants. Documents purporting to come from this source have been disseminated by the militants and by the Government-controlled media. . . .

36. . . . [T]he seizure of the United States Embassy and Consulates and the detention of internationally protected persons as hostages cannot [despite Iran's written communication to the ICJ] be considered as something "secondary" or "marginal," having regard to the importance of the legal principles involved. It also referred to a statement of the Secretary-General of the United Nations, and to Security Council resolution 457 (1979), as evidencing the importance attached by the international community as a whole to the observance of those principles in the present case as well as its concern at the dangerous level of tension between Iran and the United States. . . .

46. [The court *is* able to hear this case because the] United States' claims here in question concern alleged violations by Iran of its obligations under several articles of the Vienna Conventions of 1961 and 1963 with respect to the privileges and immunities of the personnel, the inviolability of the premises and archives, and the provision of facilities for the performance of the functions of the United States Embassy and Consulates in Iran. . . . By their very nature all these claims concern the interpretation or application of one or other of the two Vienna Conventions.

47. The occupation of the United States Embassy by militants on 4 November 1979 and the detention of its personnel as hostages was an event of a kind to provoke an immediate protest from any government, as it did from the United States Government, which despatched a special emissary to Iran to deliver a formal protest. . . .

It is clear that on that date there existed a dispute arising out of the interpretation or application of the Vienna Conventions and thus one falling within the scope of the Protocols [which are a part of the Vienna

Conventions on Diplomatic and Consular Relations *requiring* States to submit such disputes to the ICJ for resolution]. . . .

61. The conclusion just reached by the Court, that the initiation of the attack on the United States Embassy on 4 November 1979, and of the attacks on the Consulates at Tabriz and Shiraz the following day, cannot be considered as in itself imputable to the Iranian State does not mean that Iran is, in consequence, free of any responsibility in regard to those attacks; for its own conduct was in conflict with its international obligations. By a number of provisions of the Vienna Conventions of 1961 and 1963, Iran was placed under the most categorical obligations, as a receiving State, to take appropriate steps to ensure the protection of the United States Embassy and Consulates, their staffs, their archives, their means of communication and the freedom of movement of the members of their staffs.

62. Thus, after solemnly proclaiming the inviolability of the premises of a diplomatic mission, Article 22 of the 1961 Convention continues in paragraph 2:

> *"The receiving State is under a special duty to take all appropriate steps to protect the premises of the mission against any* intrusion or damage and to prevent any disturbance of the peace of the mission or impairment of its dignity." [Emphasis supplied by the Court.]

So, too, after proclaiming that the person of a diplomatic agent shall be inviolable, and that he shall not be liable to any form of arrest or detention, Article 29 provides:

> "The receiving State shall treat him with due respect and *shall take all appropriate steps to prevent any attack on his person, freedom or dignity."* [Emphasis supplied by the Court.]

The obligation of a receiving State to protect the inviolability of the archives and documents of a diplomatic mission is laid down in Article 24, which specifically provides that they are to be "inviolable at any time and wherever they may be." Under Article 25 it is required to "accord full facilities for the performance of the functions of the mission," under Article 26 to "ensure to all members of the mission freedom of movement and travel in its territory," and under Article 27 to "permit and protect free communication on the part of the mission for all official purposes." Analogous provisions are to be found in the 1963 [Consular] Convention regarding the privileges and immunities of consular missions and their staffs (Art. 31, para. 3, Arts. 40, 33, 28, 34 and 35). In the view of the Court, the obligations of the Iranian Government here in question are not merely contractual obligations established by the Vienna Conventions of 1961 and 1963, but also obligations under general international law.

63. The facts set out in paragraphs 14 to 27 above establish to the satisfaction of the Court that on 4 November 1979 the Iranian Government failed altogether to take any "appropriate steps" to protect the premises, staff and archives of the United States' mission against attack by the militants, and to take any steps either to prevent this attack or to stop it before it reached its completion. They also show that on 5 November 1979 the Iranian Government similarly failed to take appropriate steps for the protection of the United States Consulates at Tabriz and Shiraz. In addition they show, in the opinion of the Court, that the failure of the Iranian Government to take such steps was due to more than mere negligence or lack of appropriate means. . . .

77. . . . Paragraphs 1 and 3 of that Article [22] have also been infringed, and continue to be infringed, since they forbid agents of a receiving State to enter the premises of a mission without consent or to undertake any search, requisition, attachment or like measure on the premises. Secondly, they constitute continuing breaches of Article 29 of the same Convention which forbids any arrest or detention of a diplomatic agent and any attack on his person, freedom or dignity. Thirdly, the Iranian authorities are without doubt in continuing breach of the provisions of Articles 25, 26 and 27 of the 1961 Vienna Convention and of pertinent provisions of the 1963 Vienna Convention concerning facilities for the performance of functions, freedom of movement and communications for diplomatic and consular staff, as well as of Article 24 of the former Convention and Article 33 of the latter, which provide for the absolute inviolability of the archives and documents of diplomatic missions and consulates. This particular violation has been made manifest to the world by repeated statements by the militants occupying the Embassy, who claim to be in possession of documents from the archives, and by various government

authorities, purporting to specify the contents thereof. Finally, the continued detention as hostages of the two private individuals of United States nationality entails a renewed breach of the obligations of Iran under Article 11, paragraph 4, of the 1955 Treaty of Amity, Economic Relations, and Consular Rights. . . .

79. . . . [J]udicial authorities of the Islamic Republic of Iran and the Minister for Foreign Affairs have frequently voiced or associated themselves with a threat first announced by the militants of having some of the hostages submitted to trial before a court or some other body. These threats may at present merely be acts in contemplation. But the Court considers it necessary here and now to stress that, if the intention to submit the hostages to any form of criminal trial or investigation were to be put into effect, that would constitute a grave breach by Iran of its obligations under Article 31, paragraph 1, of the 1961 Vienna Convention. This paragraph states in the most express terms: "A diplomatic agent shall enjoy immunity from the criminal jurisdiction of the receiving State." Again, if there were an attempt to compel the hostages to bear witness, a suggestion renewed at the time of the visit to Iran of the Secretary-General's Commission, Iran would without question be violating paragraph 2 of that same Article of the 1961 Vienna Convention which provides that: "A diplomatic agent is not obliged to give evidence as a witness.". . .

83. In any case, *even if the alleged criminal activities of the United States in Iran could be considered as having been established,* the question would remain whether they could be regarded by the Court as constituting a justification of Iran's conduct and thus a defence to the United States' claims in the present case. The Court, however, is unable to accept that they can be so regarded. This is because diplomatic law itself provides the necessary means of defence against, and sanction for, illicit activities by members of diplomatic or consular missions. [Emphasis supplied by author.] . . .

85. Thus, it is for the very purpose of providing a remedy for such possible abuses of diplomatic functions that Article 9 of the 1961 Convention on Diplomatic Relations stipulates:

> "1. The receiving State may at any time and without having to explain its decision, notify the sending State that the head of the mission or any member of the diplomatic staff of the mission is *persona non grata* or that any other member of the staff of the mission is not acceptable. In any such case, the sending State shall, as appropriate, either recall the person concerned or terminate his functions with the mission. A person may be declared *non grata* or not acceptable before arriving in the territory of the receiving State.
>
> 2. If the sending State refuses or fails within a reasonable period to carry out its obligations under paragraph 1 of this Article, the receiving State may refuse to recognize the person concerned as a member of the mission."

87. . . . The Iranian Government did not, therefore, employ the remedies placed at its disposal by diplomatic law specifically for dealing with activities of the kind of which it now complains. Instead, it allowed a group of militants to attack and occupy the United States Embassy by force, and to seize the diplomatic and consular staff as hostages; instead, it has endorsed that action of those militants and has deliberately maintained their occupation of the Embassy and detention of its staff as a means of coercing the sending State. It has, at the same time, refused altogether to discuss this situation with representatives of the United States. The Court, therefore, can only conclude that Iran did not have recourse to the normal and efficacious means at its disposal, but [instead] resorted to coercive action against the United States Embassy and its staff.

◆ *Notes & Questions*

1. What rules of International Law were breached by Iran in the *Hostage* case?
2. Assume that the US *was* responsible for the violations of International Law—as asserted by Iran in the preliminary passage of this case (directly before the numbered paragraphs of the court's opinion). Do such violations justify Iran's kidnaping the hostages or taking over the embassy?

Staff members from the US embassy in Tehran, Iran, pose for a group picture after their release from being held hostage for 444 days. They were seized when militant Iranian students overran the embassy in 1979, seeking the return of the former Shah of Iran who was deposed and then living in the US.

3. Would the ICJ rule differently if Iran were *not* a party to the Vienna Conventions on Diplomatic and Consular Relations?

General (Mis)perception There are many contemporary criticisms of diplomatic immunity. Journalists have sensationalized abuses of diplomatic immunity with a view toward revisiting the protection afforded by the Vienna Convention on Diplomatic Relations (VCDR).[29] This perspective is not unique. Not all States observe the general international rule of diplomatic immunity from criminal prosecution. During the Cultural Revolution (1966–1976), representatives of the People's Republic of China "declared that diplomatic immunities were of bourgeois origin and . . . had no place in a socialist society."[30]

But the evolution of diplomatic privileges and immunities spans thousands of years. The 1961 VCDR finally codified State expectations, most of which were rooted in reciprocity. The University of Reading's J. Craig Barker illustrates that "[e]ven if it were considered desirable to amend the law to deal with the problem of abuse, the question must be asked as to whether such amendment is possible, given the reciprocal nature of diplomatic relations and the manifest desire of each State to ensure the fullest protection for its diplomatic personnel working abroad. On the other hand, does that mean that abuse of diplomatic privileges is simply a necessary evil which must be endured in order to ensure the greater good that is the maintenance of proper international relations?"[31]

This scenario, in which an accredited diplomat abuses his or her general protection from civil or criminal prosecution, should be distinguished from a State's attempt to secure a wider degree of diplomatic immunity than is available under the VCDR. (*See* Problem 7.C.)

Contemporary Alternatives The above examples of moral indignation with diplomatic immunity do not always acknowledge that there are alternatives available to deal with such abuses—as suggested in the *Hostage* case set forth above. The ICJ therein refers to the following remedies for abuse of immunity in its paragraph 86: *"Even in the case of armed conflict* or in the case of a breach in diplomatic relations those provisions require that both the inviolability of the members of a diplomatic mission and of the premises, property and archives of the mission must be respected by the receiving State. Naturally, the observance of this principle does not mean—and this the Applicant Government expressly acknowledges—that a diplomatic agent *caught in the act* of committing an assault or other offence may not, on occasion, be *briefly arrested* by the police of the receiving State *in order to prevent the commission* of the particular crime [italics supplied by author]."

The participation of more than 150 States in the Vienna Convention on Diplomatic Relations suggests that the benefits have not been vitiated by the occasional costs. Assume that a State A diplomat commits a crime in host State B. The interests of both States are better served if State B declares State A's offending ambassador *persona non grata* (*see* §7.2). If State B were to arrest the State A diplomat, State B would risk reciprocal treatment—the authorities in State A might one day respond by arresting a State B diplomat or consular officer who commits a crime or civil wrong while working in State A.

Insurance is another alternative. State B citizens can be protected against certain consequences of diplomatic conduct through this risk-shifting device. A portion of the risk of having A's diplomats in State B is borne by State A, which has sent them to B. This insurance benefits State B nationals. While the State A diplomat is not thereby subject to suit in State B's courts, a State B insurer can thereby assume a portion of the risks associated with the diplomat's negligence. B nationals would thus have a monetary remedy like that available to them when they insure themselves against the conduct of *private* (nondiplomatic) individuals in State B. This convenient compromise permits the A diplomat to continue his or her duties without the inconvenient disruption of having to defend lawsuits in B's courts. The insurer will do this instead, and the responsible diplomat does not fully "escape" liability. The US Department of State has promulgated standards regarding compulsory diplomatic insurance.[32]

"Waiver" of diplomatic immunity is an alternative in appropriate criminal cases. Assume that an individual is entitled to immunity under the Vienna Diplomatic or Consular Convention. She has allegedly committed a serious criminal offense. The host State might request that the sending State waive diplomatic immunity of this agent. There have been several attempts by the US to enact legislation whereby it could *automatically* initiate proceedings in cases involving serious crimes. US Senator Jesse Helms has proposed a "Diplomatic Immunity Abuse Prevention Act" on several occasions—and it may one day survive congressional opposition. Under its terms, a request for waiver would be initiated in all such cases by the US Secretary of State. In the interim, States are not precluded from requesting such waivers on an *ad hoc* basis when circumstances so warrant. The sending State could ensure the continuance of mutually beneficial relations if one of its diplomats committed a serious crime (which would violate the laws of both nations). Such waivers would not unjustly surprise any diplomatic representative who occupies that position, because of her awareness of host-State culture and general norms of conduct.

There is a blossoming culture of acquiescence in host-State requests for waivers of diplomatic immunity. In 1996, Zaire's president waived diplomatic immunity for the country's ambassador to France. This ambassador's speeding caused a car accident in Menton, France, that killed two 13-year-old French children and brought protests from 5,000 marchers. In 1997, the Republic of Georgia's second-ranking diplomat was drinking and speeding in Washington, D.C., where he caused four other cars to crash and the death of a 16-year old woman. The US Department of State immediately sought and obtained a waiver of his diplomatic immunity. The request in this case was arguably premised on the then-recent statement by Georgia's President Shevardnadze that the moral principle of just punishment outweighed what he considered to be the antiquated, Cold War–era practice of diplomatic immunity. The former Georgian diplomat is now serving a 21-year sentence.

Diplomatic Bag Complaints about diplomatic immunity include the occasional problem with the "diplomatic bag." Article 27.3 of the Vienna Convention on Diplomatic Relations provides that a "diplomatic bag shall not be opened or detained." The following excerpt from a French journal *(Review of Public International Law)* demonstrates the competing considerations that often arise when there has been an abuse:

"Seizure of Arms in Baggage of Diplomat in Transit"

78 *Revue Generale de Droit International Public* 247 (1974)

Five hand grenades, five revolvers, eight kilos of explosive devices, and 21 letter bombs not yet addressed, rifles and ammunition were discovered on the evening of October 23, 1972, by Dutch customs officers at the airport of Schiphol in the baggage of an Algerian diplomatic agent accredited to a South American nation which the Dutch Minister of Justice refused to identify. Aged 32, born in Jordan, but carrying an Algerian diplomatic passport, the diplomat, who was identified only by the initials II.R., came from Damascus via Frankfurt and was en route to Rio de Janeiro. He declared himself to be entirely ignorant of the contents of his baggage, explaining only he thought he was carrying documents delivered to him in Damascus and destined for an Algerian embassy in a South American republic, which he declined to identify further. He added nevertheless he had bought the rifles, which were found separately, for diplomatic colleagues. The Queen's prosecutor [of the Netherlands] did not institute judicial proceedings against the diplomat because in his judgment it had not at all been established that the diplomat was actually aware of the contents of his baggage. As a result the diplomat was authorized to continue his trip to South America, but his bags were retained for an investigation.

Following the discovery, the Israeli government—which was convinced the arms seized were to be used in organizing an attack upon its embassy in Brazil—requested an explanation from the Dutch government, because in its opinion the Algerian diplomat should have been held by the authorities at the airport "because diplomatic immunity applies only in the countries where diplomatic agents are accredited and not in the countries through which they are only in transit." One should have some reservations about this assertion which is contrary to established practice and is contradicted by Article 40 of the Vienna Convention of April 18, 1961, on Diplomatic Relations by whose terms a diplomatic agent in transit through the territory of a third state is given "inviolability and every other immunity necessary for his passage or return." But, inasmuch as the acts here were outside official functions, the immunity of agents in transit, already subject to strict limitations, obviously ceases in a case of flagrant offense.

The UN's International Law Commission has been working on draft provisions that would amend the status of the diplomatic courier and the diplomatic bag—through optional protocols to the Vienna Convention. The objective is to provide the State parties to the Vienna Convention on Diplomatic Relations an opportunity to place further restrictions on such immunity in a way that would better control potential abuse. The UN's Sixth Committee (Legal) is conducting informal consultations on the question whether the General Assembly should convene an international conference for the purpose of creating draft articles on this sensitive topic.[33]

◆ SUMMARY

1. International diplomacy is the conduct of relations between governments. Diplomatic relations are established through the mutual consent of the sending and host States. Ambassadors represent the head of State of the sending State. They normally reside in the national capital of the host State.

2. Modern modes of communication and transportation have altered the diplomatic role. Ambassadors no longer have the degree of autonomy exercised by their predecessors—who were often out of contact with their home States for lengthy periods of time. Further, heads of State now engage directly in international diplomacy.
3. The diplomat's duties include: (a) representing the sending State, (b) protecting the interests of the sending State, (c) negotiating with the host government, (d) reporting conditions in the host State to the sending State, and (e) promoting friendly relations.
4. Diplomacy is traditionally undertaken in private settings. Some world leaders have directed their diplomatic efforts toward a comparatively public audience during joint summit meetings. Foreign policy making is appropriately debated in a public arena, but negotiations to implement national policies are often best handled by career diplomats in a private setting.
5. Consular officers are not necessarily diplomatic representatives. They may occasionally undertake diplomatic tasks by conducting their affairs from within the embassy premises rather than in a separate office in the host State. Consuls typically implement the trade policy of the sending state. Their immunities are not as broad as those of the "diplomat" who enjoys complete immunity from the jurisdiction of the host State. Consular immunity is extended only for those official acts that directly represent the interests of the sending State.
6. The extraterritoriality fiction was that foreign embassies and consulates were considered to be on "foreign" soil—treated as if it were in the sending State rather than in the host State. This practice arose under customary State practice to validate certain activities occurring within those premises. The adoption of the Vienna Convention on Diplomatic Relations (and its companion Consular Convention) eliminated the need to rely on the historical fiction—by expressly providing for the comprehensive protection of institutions like the premises, occupants, and diplomatic bag.
7. There is no general right of diplomatic asylum under International Law. Such a right may exist under regional practice or treaties, however. The UN's International Court of Justice has been criticized for not applying such regional practices to cases involving States in the affected region. A conflict may arise when one State's embassy grants asylum to a host-State national accused of a crime. The lack of a *general* right of asylum can result in an impasse: The host State cannot legally enter the premises of the diplomatic mission to arrest the accused; the sending State cannot obtain a right of passage out of the host State territory surrounding the diplomatic premises.
8. A State may suspend or completely terminate international relations with another State. States may recall their diplomats from the respective capitals. They may also break formal diplomatic ties, even when there is a continuing need to deal with one another. Some States have facilitated this clandestine communication with the assistance of third States.
9. Immunity from the application of the host State's law permits diplomatic and consular representatives to carry out their functions without fear of arrest or involvement in litigation. The Vienna Conventions on Diplomatic and Consular Relations specifically provide for the inviolability of: (a) embassy and consulate premises; (b) the documents on these premises; (c) the diplomatic bag, wherever it is located; (d) the person of the diplomatic agent; and (e) his or her private residence.
10. When a diplomatic representative abuses the immunity conferred under International Law, the host State may declare that individual *persona non grata,* which results in his or her expulsion. Absent a waiver of the sending State, host State authorities may not arrest or try diplomatic representatives for their crimes or civil wrongs (for example, causing an automobile accident).

◆ PROBLEMS

Problem 7.A (end of §7.2) A sending State's diplomat, who is formally accredited under the VCDR procedure, is clearly entitled to such immunity in the host State. And while there is no formal treaty, heads of State are always accorded similar immunity under the umbrella of State immunity (§2.6).

It is up to the host State to determine whether to provide like immunity to *other* individuals. Chile's former dictator, Augusto Pinochet, is the individual most identified with human rights abuses in Chile from 1973 through 1990, including the death and disappearance of numerous political opponents of his regime. Prior to leaving office, he arranged for an amendment to the Chilean Constitution, making him a senator for life. In October 1998, he traveled to London on a Chilean diplomatic passport. Spain issued an arrest warrant, requesting that England extradite him to Spain to be tried for the murder of numerous Spaniards living in or visiting Chile. He was arrested in London.

Chile lodged a diplomatic protest with England. At this point, it was up to England to decide whether to honor or decline the Spanish arrest warrant on the basis of Chile's supposed "diplomatic immunity" from prosecution. (Assume that England awaits resolution of the debate initiated at the end of this problem.) Chile's president, Eduardo Frei, sought Pinochet's release on the basis that Pinochet had been accorded immunity from prosecution in Chile and was thus entitled to amnesty for any crime committed while in office. This amnesty is not unlike South Africa's post-Apartheid Truth Commission process, whereby its former president could be accorded immunity from prosecution—by cooperating and thus bringing out the whole truth about disappearances and torture during the era when the white government controlled South Africa's black population via its official apartheid regime.

One might argue that under the dictatorship of Franco, Spain did not progress toward democracy as quickly as Chile did after Pinochet stepped down as head of a military dictatorship. In the case of Spain, there was no truth commission, no national soul-searching like that of Chile and South Africa, and no convictions for crimes committed: just amnesty for Franco. One could further argue that such immunity is the price tag for obtaining truth, peace, and closure. In a perfect world, there would be perfect justice.

In October 1998, the first British court of appeal to rule in this case held that Pinochet must be released.[34] In its opinion, the intermediate appellate court found that, pursuant to the State Immunity Act of 1978 and the Diplomatic Privileges Act of 1964, "a former head of state is clearly entitled to immunity in relation to criminal acts performed in the course of exercising public functions." The Court distinguished the Nuremberg Charter and Statutes of the International Tribunals for Rwanda and Former Yugoslavia, which strip head-of-state immunity for criminal acts, on grounds that these international tribunals were established by international agreements regarding jurisdiction. The House of Lords overruled the Divisional Court the following month, finding that Gen. Pinochet did *not* have immunity. A second House of Lords decision reversed, after Pinochet's lawyers chastised the ruling for bias because one of the Lords is director and chairman of Amnesty International, a participant in the legal proceedings. (The judge's wife also worked for that organization.) For a valuable analysis of the dangers of denying immunity to this former head of State in this case, *see* a former US Legal Advisor's illustration of the disadvantages at www.lawnewsnetwork.com/opencourt/stories/dec/c121498a.html.

In March 1999, the House of Lords ultimately stripped Pinochet of his "diplomatic" immunity that derived from his status as a former head of State.

One might argue that if perpetual immunity were not granted, then all officials (former diplomats or heads of State) could find themselves enmeshed in a provoked traffic accident on the first day of assuming privileged duty—and have such liability hang over their heads forever—or, in the case of genocide or "crimes against humanity," find themselves at the discretion of either right-wing or humanitarian judges. The latter might well choose to indict people like Yasir Arafat or Ariel Sharon and thus jeopardize ongoing Middle East peace negotiations. Nobody with such potential liability hanging over their heads would accept any position of public authority anywhere. On the other hand, should there be an exception for crimes against humanity? In July 1998, delegates at the Rome Conference regarding an international criminal court hammered out the following provision in Article 27 of the proposed permanent court's statute: "2. Immunities or special procedural rules which may attach to the official capacity of a person, whether under national or international law, shall not bar the Court from exercising its jurisdiction over such a person."

Four students (or groups) will represent, respectively, Chile, England, Spain, and the UN—specifically, a UN civil servant whose task is to monitor State practice and compliance with both the Vienna Convention of Diplomatic Relations and human rights abuses. The issue for debate is whether England and Spain should recognize or ignore the diplomatic (or former head of State) immunity accorded Pinochet by Chile. If recognized, he will be released and allowed to return to Chile. If ignored, "ambassador" Pinochet will be extradited to Spain to be prosecuted for torturing and "disappearing" Spanish citizens during his admittedly barbaric tenure as Chile's head of State.

Problem 7.B (end of §7.3) In 1992, Peru's ex-President Alan Garcia sought refuge in the Colombian embassy in Peru. This Peruvian president (from 1985 to 1990) was an outspoken opponent of his successor. Garcia had been in hiding since the new president dissolved the Peruvian Congress and temporarily closed the Peruvian courts. Colombia decided to grant Garcia diplomatic asylum. Colombia then began steps to process Garcia's orderly departure from Peru. Did Colombia violate International Law by granting diplomatic asylum to former President Garcia in 1992? Would Peru be required to let Garcia leave the Columbian Embassy and exit from Peru?

Problem 7.C (end of §7.4) In 1994, a Berlin appellate court reinstated an arrest warrant issued for Syria's former Ambassador "S." It determined that neither the Vienna Convention on Diplomatic Relations (VCDR) nor general International Law prohibited his arrest and prosecution for assisting in the 1983 bombing of a French arts center in West Berlin. Explosives used in the attack had been temporarily stored in the Syrian embassy in East Berlin. Syria's Ambassador S. was instructed by his government to aid the terrorist organization led by "Carlos" in carrying out this attack, which claimed one life and severely injured twenty-three people. Although the Syrian embassy officer declined to transfer the explosives to West Berlin, storage there did help to conceal their whereabouts before the blast.

The German court determined that the diplomatic immunity accorded to a Syrian head of mission by the German Democratic Republic (East Germany) was not binding on *third* States—including the Federal Republic of Germany ("West Germany" before reunification in 1990). In the court's words: "Diplomatic immunity is only effective in the receiving state. Third states have not consented to the diplomat's activity. . . ." The court also reasoned that the incorporation of former East Germany into the new Germany did not require (reunified) Germany to respect the immunity accorded by a "third state" to this diplomat. *"S. v. Berlin Court of Appeal and District Court of Berlin-Tiergarten,"* 24 *Europaische Grundechte-Zeitschrift* 436 (1994). *See* B. Fassbender, "International Decisions," 92 *Amer. J. Int'l Law* 74 (1998).

Three students or groups will debate the soundness of this decision. One will act as the German prosecutor who successfully argued this case on appeal. The other will represent Syria. A third will represent the UN International Law Commission—having been summoned as a "friend to the court" to advise all parties about the proper application of the VCDR to this case.

Problem 7.D (end of §7.4) The following hypothetical is adapted from actual events. Many of the applicable rules of International Law are set forth in the 1961 Vienna Convention on Diplomatic Relations and the 1980 *Hostage* case. Students will engage in diplomatic negotiations to achieve what they believe to be the best resolution under International Law. This exercise is designed to illustrate the rules of immunity and some of their practical limitations.

The Problem. Rieferbaan's is a discotheque in Germany near a US military base. US soldiers often socialize at Rieferbaan's. Magenta is a State that has an embassy in Germany but no diplomatic relations with the US. Magenta's embassy is ten minutes from Rieferbaan's by car.

The first secretary of Magenta's diplomatic mission in Germany is Chargé d'Affaires Mann. The leader of Mann's home State (Magenta) has directed Mann to openly criticize the United States and take all steps necessary to publicize Magenta's belief that the US should pull its troops out of Western Europe. Magenta's leader directs Chargé d'Affaires Mann to set off a bomb at the discotheque when it is crowded with US soldiers. Mann and the Magenta head of State communicate secretly via coded radio signals.

Unknown to Mann, the Army Intelligence Office at the US military base (in conjunction with a government radio station in Germany) has broken Magenta's code for diplomatic transmissions. The US and German governments are fully aware of the terrorist plot. They want it to develop, however, to a point where Magenta cannot deny responsibility.

Chargé d'Affaires Mann has assembled a group of armed anti-US "freedom fighters" at Magenta's embassy premises and at various points between the embassy and Rieferbaan's. The Army Intelligence Office learns that there will be a very extraordinary but apparently innocuous message transported directly from Magenta's leader to Mann (into Magenta's embassy) via diplomatic pouch. It contains the signal to go ahead with the terrorist bombing at the Rieferbaan Disco. Magenta's diplomatic courier arrives at a German airport, is detained by US soldiers, and is then arrested by German police. The State of Magenta's official diplomatic pouch is seized and opened. The US soldiers and the German police intercept the message that would have resulted in the bombing of the discotheque and a massive loss of life.

German police later surround Magenta's embassy where the key "freedom fighters" are located. They advise Chargé d'Affaires Mann by telephone that the plot has been discovered and that the courier and pouch have been seized due to Magenta's "abuse of transit" via the diplomatic pouch brought into Germany. Everyone in the embassy is ordered to immediately come outside and cross the street onto "German soil."

Three students will act as diplomatic representatives. Student 1 will be Hans Smit, a German career diplomat assigned to negotiate a successful conclusion to this crisis. Student 2 will be Joanna Shultz, the US Ambassador to Germany. Student 3 will assume the role of Chargé d'Affaires Mann, Magenta's ambassador to Germany.

Part One. Hans Smit (student 1) and Joanna Shultz (student 2) confer at a government building in Germany near the Magenta embassy. They are trying to decide whether Chargé d'Affaires Mann should be invited to join them. Germany, the US, and Magenta are parties to the Vienna Convention on Diplomatic Relations. Smit and Shultz should assess whether Mann can be characterized as having waived the treaty's immunity provisions. If Mann decides to confer with them outside the Magenta embassy, they should further assess the possibility of revoking his diplomatic immunity to arrest him.

Part Two. Assume that Smit and Shultz decide to invite Mann to negotiate but not to arrest him. Can Mann reasonably claim that Germany and the US have nevertheless violated the Vienna Convention? What specific claims will Mann be able to assert?

Part Three. The three ambassadors are discussing whether the "freedom fighters" in the Magenta embassy should be permitted to go freely from Germany to France as they have requested. If Germany decides against this resolution, what can it do to the "freedom fighters"?

◆ BIBLIOGRAPHY

§7.1 Foreword to International Diplomacy

J. Chay (ed.), "Diplomatic History and International Relations," ch. 3 in *Culture and International Relations* 34 (New York: Praeger, 1990).

R. Cohen, *Negotiating Across Cultures: Communication Obstacles in International Diplomacy* (Wash., DC: US Inst. Peace, 1991).

J. Findling, *Dictionary of American Diplomatic History* (2nd ed. New York: Greenwood Press, 1989).

L. Chen, "The Diplomatic Instrument," ch. 15 in *An Introduction to Contemporary International Law: A Policy-Oriented Perspective* 253 (New Haven, CT: Yale Univ. Press, 1989).

D. Mak & C. Kennedy, *American Ambassadors in a Troubled World: Interviews with Senior Diplomats* (Westport, CT: Greenwood Press, 1992).

K. Tomasevski, *Development Aid and Human Rights Revisited* (London: Pinter Pub., 1993).

§7.2 Diplomatic and Consular Functions

L. Dembinski, *The Modern Law of Diplomacy: External Missions of States and International Organizations* (Dordrecht, Neth.: Martinus Nijhoff, 1988).

A. Kapur (ed.), *Diplomatic Ideas and Practices of Asian States* (Leiden, Neth.: E.J. Brill, 1990).

A. Kremenyuk (ed.), *International Negotiation, Analysis, Approaches, Issues* (San Francisco: Jossey-Bass Pub., 1991).

L. Lee, *Consular Law and Practice* (Oxford, Eng.: Clarendon Press, 1991).

B. Murty, *The International Law of Diplomacy: The Diplomatic Instrument and the World Public Order* (New Haven, CT: New Haven Press/Martinus Nijhoff, 1989).

B. Sen, *A Diplomat's Handbook of International Law and Practice* (3rd ed. Dordrecht, Neth.: Martinus Nijhoff, 1988).

§7.3 Extraterritoriality and Asylum

R. Jennings & A. Watts, "So-Called Diplomatic Asylum," §495 in 2 *Oppenheim's International Law* 1082 (9th ed. Essex, Eng.: Longman, 1993).

C. Ronning, *Diplomatic Asylum: Legal Norms and Political Reality in Latin American Relations* (The Hague, Neth.: Martinus Nijhoff, 1965).

§7.4 Immunities and Abuse of Immunity

L. Frey & M. Frey, *The History of Diplomatic Immunity* (Columbus: Ohio State Univ. Press, 1999).

C. Lewis, *State and Diplomatic Immunity* (London: Lloyd's of London Press, 1985).

L. Shapiro, "Foreign Relations Law: Modern Developments in Diplomatic Immunity," 1989 *Annual Survey American Law* 281 (New York: NYU, 1990).

J. Ure, *Diplomatic Bag: An Anthology of Diplomatic Incidents and Anecdotes from the Renaissance to the Gulf War* (London: John Murray Pub., 1994).

A. Zeidman, "Abuse of the Diplomatic Bag: A Proposed Solution," 11 *Cardozo Law Review* 427 (1989).

◆ ENDNOTES

1. *See* B. Murty, "Diplomacy in Historical Perspective," §1.2 in *The International Law of Diplomacy: The Diplomatic Instrument and the World Public Order* 3 (New Haven, CT: New Haven Press, 1989) (hereinafter *International Law of Diplomacy).*

2. M. Anderson, *The Rise of Modern Diplomacy 1450–1919,* pp. 2–3 (London: Longman, 1993).
3. "Right of Passage Case (Preliminary Objections)," 1957 *ICJ Rep.* 125, 130.
4. J. Kish, *International Law and Espionage* (The Hague, Neth.: Martinus Nijhoff, 1995).
5. Translation provided by P. Ardant, "Chinese Diplomatic Practice during the Cultural Revolution," ch. 3 in *China's Practice of International Law: Some Case Studies* 92–93 (Cambridge, MA: Harv. Univ. Press, 1974) (hereinafter "Chinese Diplomatic Practice").
6. **European perspective:** Garden, 1 *Traite Complet de Diplomatie ou Theorie Generale des Relations Exterieures des Puissances de L'Europe* 1 (Paris 1833) (diplomacy is the science or "art of negotiation"); C. Calvo, 1 *Dictionnaire de Droit International Public et Privie* 25 (Berlin, 1885) (science of state relations, or simply the "art of communication"). **Nicolson perspective:** H. Nicolson, "The 'Old' and the 'New' Diplomacy," in R. Pfaltzgraff (ed.), *Politics and the International System* 425 (2nd ed., Philadelphia: Lippincott, 1972).
7. **Morgenthau view:** H. Morgenthau, *Politics Among Nations* 541 (3d ed. New York: Knopf, 1960) (hereinafter Morgenthau treatise). **Boucher view:** D. Boucher, "Reconciling Ethics and Interests in the Person of the State: The International Dimension," ch. 3 in P. Keal (ed.), *Ethics and Foreign Policy* 44, 46 (St. Leonards, Aust.: Allen & Unwin, 1992) (italics added).
8. L. Pearson, *Diplomacy in the Nuclear Age* 64 (Cambridge, MA: Harv. Univ. Press, 1959); G. Tunkin, *Theory of International Law* 273 (Cambridge, MA: Harv. Univ. Press, 1974).
9. **Idealist (Canadian):** Panel, *International Law in International Diplomacy,* in *Proceedings of the 77th Annual Meeting* 99 (Wash., DC: Amer. Soc. Int'l Law, 1985). **Realist (Venezuelan):** *id.,* p. 103.
10. *See generally* K. Hamilton & R. Langhorne, *The Practice of Diplomacy: Its Evolution, Theory and Administration* (London: Routledge, 1995).
11. Morgenthau treatise, pp. 539–540 (cited in note 7 above).
12. *See* Bacuss, "Diplomacy for the 70's: An Afterview and Appraisal," 68 *Amer. Pol. Science Rev.* 736 (1974) (post–World War II tendency encouraged by all US presidents).
13. *See* N. Hevener (ed.), *Diplomacy in a Dangerous World: Protection for Diplomats under International Law* (Boulder, CO: Westview Press, 1986).
14. **Wilson quote:** 2 *Selected Literary and Political Papers and Addresses of Woodrow Wilson* (New York: Grosset & Dunlap, 1927). **Nicolson quote:** reprinted in T. Couloumbis & J. Wolfe, *Introduction to International Relations* 161 (3rd ed. Englewood Cliffs, NJ: Prentice-Hall, 1986).
15. *See* "Vienna Convention on Diplomatic Relations of 1961," Articles 1–5, 500 *UN Treaty Series* 95 (1964), reprinted in 18 *Int'l Legal Mat'ls* 149 (1979) [hereinafter Diplomatic Convention].
16. Accounts of these incidents are available in "Chinese Diplomatic Practice," pp. 100 (Raghunath Affair) and 103 (Jongejans Affair) (cited in note 5 above).
17. **Taiwan relations:** Taiwan Relations Act of 1979, 22 US Code §3303 (1986) (change of recognition status of Taiwan does not affect legal rights vested prior to recognition of the PRC). *See* §2.4 of this book on the specific legal effects of nonrecognition. **Unconventional diplomacy:** G. Berridge, *Talking to the Enemy: How States without "Diplomatic Relations" Communicate* 129 (New York: St. Martin's Press, 1994).
18. Diplomatic Convention, Art. 3 (cited in note 15 above).
19. L. Lee, *Historical Evolution,* ch. 1 in *Consular Law and Practice* 4 (Oxford, Eng.: Clarendon Press, 1991) [hereinafter *Consular* treatise].
20. 596 *UN Treaty Series* 261 (1967), Art. 5, reprinted in E. Osmanczyk, *Encyclopedia of the United Nations and International Agreements* 987 (2nd ed. New York: Taylor & Francis, 1990) [hereinafter Consular Relations Convention].
21. *See* "Extraterritoriality" in *Consular* treatise, pp. 6–7 (cited in note 19 above).
22. G. Do Nascimento e Silva, *Diplomacy in International Law* 104–106 (Leiden, Neth.: Sijthoff, 1972). "In the South-West Africa Cases *(Ethiopia and Liberia v. South Africa),*" 1966 *ICJ Rep.* 6, the ICJ held that the plaintiff States did *not* have a sufficient interest to represent the rights of persecuted natives in South Africa. The suit was dismissed, leaving those natives without an effective remedy.
23. I. Brownlie, *Principles of Public International Law* 348 (4th ed. Oxford, Eng.: Clarendon Press, 1990).
24. "Claims to Formal Bases of Capability," ch. 7 in *International Law of Diplomacy* 333, 424–425 (cited in note 1 above).
25. *See Empson v. Smith,* 2 *All England Rep.* 881, 883 (1965) (discussing the Russian ambassador's detention).
26. XV *Polish Yearbk. Int'l L.* 119, 120 (1986) (italics added).
27. Diplomatic Convention (cited in note 15 above).
28. Consular Relations Convention (cited in note 20 above).
29. *See, e.g.,* text box on first page of this chapter.
30. *See* "Chinese Diplomatic Practice," p. 94 (cited in note 5 above).
31. J. Barker, *The Abuse of Diplomatic Privileges and Immunities: A Necessary Evil?* 12 (Aldershot, Eng.: Dartmouth, 1996).
32. *See* Note, "Insuring Against Abuse of Diplomatic Immunity" 38 *Stanford L. Rev.* 1517 (1986). **US Department of State standards:** "Regulations on Compulsory Liability Insurance for Diplomatic Missions and Personnel," 22 *Code of Fed. Regs.* 151 (1980), reprinted in 18 *Int'l Legal Matl's* 871 (1979). **Federal statute:** 22 US Code §254e.
33. *Report of the Secretary-General on United Nations Decade of International Law,* UN Doc. A/47/384, para.153, p. 49 (Aug. 26, 1992).
34. The Web version of this case is available at: http://tap.ccta.gov.uk/courtser/judgments.nsf/cb15085535271b6a8025655900762c34/b415b144908598e2802566ad0062261b?OpenDocument.

CHAPTER EIGHT

Treaty System

CHAPTER OUTLINE

In the event of a conflict between the obligations of the Members of the United Nations under the present Charter and their obligations under any other international agreement, their obligations under the present Charter shall prevail.

—UN Charter, Art. 103

(1) All persons within the enacting country are forbidden to conclude any agreement . . . with any person or organization (i) situated in Israel; (ii) affiliated with Israel through nationality; or (iii) working for or on behalf of Israel, regardless of place of business or residence; and

(2) Importation . . . is forbidden of all Israeli goods, including goods manufactured elsewhere containing ingredients or components of Israeli origin or manufacture.

—Unified Law of 1954 (Arab League Boycott Law)

INTRODUCTION

States have established their respective rights and obligations through treaties for many centuries—first orally, then in writing. Today's primary method of determining mutual expectations is the written treaty, which is governed on a global basis by the 1969 Vienna Convention on the Law of Treaties (effective 1980).

This chapter begins with the question "What *is* a treaty?" This first level of analysis is then accompanied by a useful compass: a method for classifying the various categories of treaties.

The next section then summarizes the central themes in the international treaty process: formation, performance, termination, and suspension. Each facet of the treaty system has its own special standards, consisting of obligations that must be observed if international relations are to function smoothly. Studying each subtopic will greatly enhance your understanding of the international system.

Although this is a survey course in *International* Law, there is a global interest in the operation of the *US* treaty system and how it varies from the international norm. One section of this chapter is thus devoted to US treaty practice.

The final section is a brief but comprehensive problem based on a fascinating treaty regime, one that was actually designed to drive a State out of existence. It reviews the important elements of treaty practice, while providing a charged political context as a basis for studying this fundamental segment of International Law—as well as setting the stage for some of the trade measures covered in Chapter 13 on International Economic Relations.

◆ 8.1 DEFINITION AND CLASSIFICATION

DEFINITIONAL CONTOURS

The word *treaty* means different things to different people. As a starting point in this chapter on treaties, the UN International Law Commission (ILC—an organ of the General Assembly) undertook an exhaustive study of the term. The ILC characterized *treaty* as a "generic term covering all forms of international agreement in writing concluded between states."[1] (The ILC study did not address *oral* agreements.)

Some three dozen terms are used interchangeably with the word *treaty*. As a result, a major study of International Law at the Harvard Law School described treaty law as "confusing, often inconsistent, unscientific and in a perpetual state of flux." The legal distinctions among these various terms are minimal, however, in the sense that each synonym creates binding obligations under International Law. The above ILC study nevertheless concluded that "judicial differences, in so far as they exist at all . . . lie almost exclusively in the method of conclusion and entry into force." Article 2.1 of the 1969 Vienna Convention on the Law of Treaties defined a treaty as "an international agreement concluded between states in written form and governed by international law, whether embodied in a single instrument or in two or more related instruments and whatever its particular designation."[2]

Other definitional preliminaries include the important theme that a treaty may be made not only by a State, the centerpiece of the international system, but also by an international organization. In 1991, for example, the International Monetary Fund signed an accord with the Soviet Union (on the eve of its demise). That agreement established a special association, whereby this international organization could advise the Soviets on economic and fiscal policy. The underlying instrument was made at the insistence of the Group of Seven industrialized States. They wanted to avoid marginalizing what would soon be former Soviets by helping them with the regional transition to a market economy.

The 1969 Vienna Convention on the Law of Treaties (VCLT) deals only with *State* treaties. The drafters wanted to concentrate first on *State* treaty matters, saving the analysis of the treaties of international organizations, such as the European Community, for another day. The 1986 Vienna Convention on the Law of Treaties Between States and International Organizations or Between International Organizations provides the *organizational* counterpart of international treaty law.[3]

Like other disputes, treaty disputes have adversely affected international relations on many occasions and in a variety of contexts. There have been many interpretational problems with the formation, observation, and termination of treaties. The UN thus developed a code to govern international agreements—that is, a treaty on treaties. The ILC spent a number of years drafting a blueprint for resolving these problems. The result of that commission's work was the 1969 VCLT. It governs *written* treaties made *after* 1980—when the convention was ratified by the required minimum number of nations to become effective. It provides the best insight into the treaty practice of States, and it is the core of this chapter on the treaty system.

ANALOGY TO CONTRACT LAW?

There is a daunting question regarding treaties between nations and whether they are sufficiently analogous to contracts between private individuals. If not, there will always be inconsistencies with the VCLT's reliance on contractual analogies from the internal law of States.

The first major study of the International Law of Treaties was the Harvard Draft of 1935, which made the aforementioned characterization of treaty law as confusing, inconsistent, unscientific, and perpetually in flux. The drafters of the second twentieth-century attempt to produce a global yardstick—the 1969 VCLT—may have oversimplified treaty law, as described by Professor Andreas Gasis of the Hellenic Institute of International and Foreign Law (Greece):

> As is well known, man, when faced with a problem not previously encountered, frequently resorts to a familiar solution, derived from an analogous situation. . . . This practice is widespread in the realm of European Continental Law, where the more elaborated Civil Law of Roman origin has systematically been used as the root onto which new branches of law have been grafted. . . . This method, however,

reflects a kind of imposed and contingent solution, not always successful, in the face of real changes in society, and slowly the new areas of law thus defined begin to operate autonomously and evolve in their own way.

The . . . phenomenon has also appeared in the realm of international law, where there has been an attempt to codify a Law of Treaties in recent years. Thus, the relevant Vienna Convention on the Law of Treaties, 1969, takes a notoriously narrow "contract" view of Treaties. . . . Hence, when reading the text . . . , one cannot escape the impression of being at the forefront of . . . [some species of] a Continental Civil Code governing private law contract, or . . . the common law tradition [both of which govern contracts between *private* individuals rather than the *public* law embodied in international agreements involving States or international organizations].[4]

The essential objection, then, is that the VCLT is too doctrinal. It fails to incorporate the fact that an international treaty is something different than a contract governing private relationships between individuals (who often speak the same native language). It has been argued that a treaty should not be thought of as a "concluded" agreement that expresses the complete intent of the parties to the treaty. Instead, it is merely evidence of an underlying legislative purpose that, while ascertained by international consensus, is only *partially* expressed in the terms of the treaty. Even an agreed-upon meaning associated with a particular treaty word can undergo subsequent alteration—when there has been a lapse of time or a change in State practice regarding the application of that term. Nineteenth-century writer Robert Phillimore opined that "due construction of the instrument may require a [k]nowledge of the antiquated as well as the present use of the words. . . ."[5]

Professor Gasis (quoted above) adds that the "scientific" approach of the Vienna Convention, in its attempt to typecast treaty language for the nations of the world, nevertheless bridges *distinct* cultures and legal traditions. This may effectively produce a disconnect that quashes the intended meaning of a treaty term in the VCLT for one or more of the ratifying parties—the same consequence often discovered in other treaties between nations embracing different social or legal cultures. The VCLT, of course, induces objective standards. However, these may emasculate the subjective intent of one or more State parties. While this often happens in the case of private contracts *within* Country X and between its private traders, it is far more risky in the international context—where a written agreement may be only one part of a larger understanding (or misunderstanding) among Countries X, Y, and Z. States generally prefer less formal agreements so that they may retain flexibility in their mutual dealings. University of Helsinki Professor Jan Klabbers comments that "[a]ll too formal and visible agreements make it politically difficult for states to change their policies. The necessity of sending proposed agreements through cumbersome procedures of approval in their national legislatures reduces states' freedom of action. Further, agreements allowing for quick renegotiation or modification are by definition not as inflexible as agreements which do not make [such an] allowance. Finally, agreement can be reached more swiftly . . . the more informal the proposed instrument is considered to be."[6]

The issue is whether a treaty and a State's internal law, which it applies to private contracts, are sufficiently analogous for the parties to an agreement to realistically appreciate the full scope of what they have agreed upon. This question is implicitly answered in the affirmative, because of States' resort to the VCLT, which they have ratified, to resolve questions of treaty interpretation. One should nevertheless acknowledge that the twentieth-century treaty–contract analogy is not without its critics.

CLASSIFICATIONS

Many treaty classifications are possible. For example, one could distinguish between a "legislative" and an "executive" treaty.[7] Because §8.3 below addresses this comparative distinction in the context of US treaty practice, the materials in *this* section deal with the more fundamental benchmarks for assessing the nature of the various treaty regimes throughout the globe. There are four distinctions that conveniently illustrate the fundamental nature of such treaties: oral or written; bilateral or multilateral; lawmaking or contractual; and self-executing or a declaration of intent.

Oral Versus Written The VCLT was drafted in terms of "written" treaties. While most treaties are written, States routinely incur international obligations based on oral agreements. State representatives often enter into oral agreements that contain mutual obligations for their respective constituencies. Denmark and Norway established Denmark's sovereignty over Eastern Greenland in a manner far less formal than a written treaty. The right to this vast area had been disputed since the 1819 termination of their union. In a recorded conversation in 1919, the Norwegian Minister of Foreign Affairs and a Danish diplomat agreed that Norway would not object to Danish control over all of Greenland—including the disputed portion of its eastern coast. The Permanent Court of International Justice held that this oral understanding resulted "in the settlement of this [sovereignty] question."[8] The Court accorded great weight to the context in which this particular conversation occurred. Although not as formal as a written treaty, this agreement was nevertheless binding on Norway, because of the person saying it and the subject of the discussion. It was made between two diplomats on a question falling within the negotiating authority each possessed on behalf of his State.

Bilateral Versus Multilateral A *bilateral* treaty establishes mutual rights and obligations between two States. It normally affects only them and no others. Other States typically derive no benefits or duties from such a treaty. The States entering into this type of treaty do not intend to establish rules that contribute to the progressive development of International Law. For example, there are hundreds of bilateral extradition treaties, each listing the circumstances under which the two treaty parties agree to return criminals to the State requesting extradition. The respective States do not intend to make a change to international practice when they agree on which crimes are thereby subject to extradition.

A *multilateral* treaty, on the other hand, is an international agreement among three or more States. Most of the military, political, and economic organizations discussed in Chapter 3 were created by multilateral treaties—expressing the mutual rights and duties of the member States, and the competence of the particular organization created by their treaty.

There has been a significant proliferation of multilateral treaties in the twentieth century. Writing on the impact of the 1982 UN Convention on the Law of the Sea (§6.3), for example, George Washington University Professor Louis Sohn traces this phenomenal increase since the end of World War II:

> International lawyers have by now accepted the fact that rules for drafting and putting into force such [multilateral] agreements are flexible. . . .
>
> This flexibility is due primarily to the tremendous increase in the last fifty years in the role being played by international institutions and multipartite diplomacy. Originally, evidence of the existence of a rule of international law could be found only in books written by eminent professors or in briefs prepared by practitioners in disputes involving international law. . . . The Hague Peace Conferences of 1899 and 1907 inaugurated a new approach: the contracting parties, acting on behalf of 'the society of civilized nations,' agreed on a number of lawmaking conventions . . . [regarding] 'the principles of equity and right on which are based the security of States and the welfare of peoples . . . and the dictates of public conscience.'
>
> During the period of the League of Nations, while the 1930 Codification Conference [on treaty practice] did not prove successful, the number of multipartite treaties increased considerably. Professor Manley O. Hudson collected in the first eight volumes of *International Legislation,* covering the period 1918 to 1941, 610 international multipartite treaties of that period. Since the Second World War, the United Nations, acting not only through the International Law Commission, but also through its specialized agencies and special conferences . . . together with the increasing number of regional organizations and various groups of states dealing with specific topics of international law, has given birth to several thousands of multipartite agreements covering practically every conceivable subject [more than 33,000 when this article was written].[9]

Bilateral treaties do not confer benefits on or create obligations for third States—unless that is the express intent of the contracting parties. Multilateral treaties normally contain no third-party benefits or obligations. However, they are more likely to do so if the treaty is ratified by a large number of nations and it codifies customary State practice (§1.2).[10]

Lawmaking Versus Contractual Treaties may also be classified as either "lawmaking" or "contractual." A lawmaking treaty creates a *new* rule of International Law designed to modify existing State practice. The 1982 United Nations Law of the Sea Treaty contains a number of new rules governing jurisdiction over the oceans. Although it codifies (restates) some previously existing rules that States applied in their mutual relations, this multilateral treaty also contains some novel law*making* provisions. For example, an International Seabed Authority would control the ways in which the ocean's resources are globally (re)distributed. Free "transit passage" would replace the otherwise applicable regime of restricted "innocent passage" through the territorial waters of coastal States (§6.3). Ratification of these provisions would *change* State practice, which has not previously required either an equitable redistribution of global resources or transit passage.

On the other hand, some treaties are merely "contractual." A treaty regulating the imports and exports of States typically sets forth only those rights and obligations that are *already* available under common international practice. In one sense, the North American Free Trade Agreement (NAFTA) broke new ground by legally associating Canada, Mexico, and the US in a large free-trade area. Yet there was nothing novel or law*making* about their reduction of trade barriers or entry into a form of common economic market. Many States had already done so. NAFTA merely created an international contract that established the respective rights and duties of the State parties, just like a private contract would do so between merchants engaged in cross-border transactions. NAFTA did not attempt to establish new principles that should generally govern trade practices under International Law. NAFTA deals only with the rights of the contracting States, not the rights of the entire community of nations. In this sense, NAFTA was not a lawmaking treaty. One could distinguish the new 1995 World Trade Organization (WTO), however, which replaced the established General Agreement on Tariffs and Trade process (Chapter 13). The WTO process involves a law*making* treaty, because of novel provisions designed to change the way in which nations resolve their international trade disputes.

Some commentators challenge the continuing vitality of the lawmaking versus contractual distinction. The proliferation of lawmaking treaties, typified by the 1899 and 1907 Hague process, contained new norms of International Law. These were designed to govern international society as a whole. In modern times, however, the distinction between the lawmaking and the merely contractual treaty is somewhat blurred. Comparatively fewer masterpieces of legislation, in the lawmaking sense, are being created. International treaties now tend to address mostly "contractual" matters between States, rather than creating fresh norms of international conduct that are suddenly applicable to all (when ratified by the requisite number of States). French Professor Paul Reuter, in his distinguished treatise on treaty law, succinctly recounted that "[t]he development of treaties during the second half of the nineteenth century prompted several new doctrinal distinctions. . . . [T]he expressions 'law-making treaties' and 'contractual treaties' came into use, the former referring to the treaties [that] first laid down general conventional rules governing [all of] international society. . . . It is important to make clear, when speaking of treaties as either [normative] 'legislation' or [mere] 'contracts,' whether they are being viewed from a legal or sociological standpoint."[11]

Professor Reuter then proceeds to explain that the great collective instruments of modern society are no longer contracts or treaties in the sense originally elicited by either term. From a sociological point of view, the private contract is well suited for application to private individuals. They are the relatively equal subjects of the private contract law of the one or two States involved in their transaction. Equal bargaining power is hardly the case in the community of nations, however. On the other hand, modern multilateral treaties are rarely lawmaking treaties that create new norms of International Law. They are usually cast in the most general of terms so as to encourage greater participation with the use of very broad terms that do not purport to modify customary State practice.

Self-Executing Versus Declaration of Intent A treaty may be further classified as "self-executing" when it imposes immediate obligations within the treaty itself, or alternatively as merely a declaration of intent, when it contains general statements of principle setting a standard of achievement for all parties. A self-executing treaty requires *no further action* to impose binding obligations on its signatories. It is instantly incorporated into both International Law *and* the internal law of each treaty member by the express terms of the treaty. There is no need for additional executive or legislative action by the State parties to create immediately binding legal obligations. On the other hand, treaties declaring intent to achieve a certain goal *require subsequent State action* before the parties incur any obligation under the treaty.

Most multilateral treaties are *not* self-executing. The State drafters who sign them intend that they be *only* statements of principle that do not impose *immediate* legal obligations. Sometimes, a ratifying nation will tender reservations, including a statement that the particular treaty is not self-executing—as done by the US when it ratified the International Covenant on Civil and Political Rights. Such treaties are intended to articulate mutually agreeable goals or standards of achievement. Each participant must undertake some subsequent act under its internal law, however, to ripen the stated standards into a binding legal obligation requiring the nation to actually apply the treaty. If treaties *were* normally self-executing, few States would participate. There is a vast difference in economic, cultural, political, and military ability to perform all features of a major multilateral treaty. Therefore, participation by all—which is attainable on the basis of merely stating aspirational goals—accommodates these differences while expressing common objectives with which the signing (but not yet ratifying) States could at least agree in principle.

One might begin with the fundamental question: Is the United Nations Charter a treaty that merely contains statements of principles or does it impose immediately binding obligations on nations who join the UN?

Sei Fujii v. State of California

SUPREME COURT OF CALIFORNIA, 1952

38 Cal.2d 718, 242 P.2d 617

Author's Note: *A Japanese citizen named Sei Fujii lived in California. He held title to his land but was ineligible for US citizenship under then-applicable naturalization laws (which were subsequently repealed). California's alien land law at the time prohibited alien ownership of land in the State. This law was enacted before the US became a party to the United Nations Charter in 1945.*

Sei Fujii's land was taken by the state of California in 1948. He then sued the state, seeking a declaration that its prohibition against alien ownership of land conflicted with the UN Charter's provisions prohibiting racial discrimination. (The Court decided, on the basis of US law, that the state's Alien Land Law violated the Equal Protection Clause of the federal Constitution's 14th Amendment—which generally prohibits states from treating aliens differently solely because they are aliens.)

A portion of the Court's often-quoted opinion addressed the question of whether the UN Charter could be classified as "self-executing." If so, the Charter would be the type of treaty that imposes an immediate obligation on governmental entities within the US (including the California legislature) to extinguish any existing laws that permitted discrimination on the basis of race or alienage. If not self-executing, then California could legally continue to so discriminate—although the US would have the moral responsibility to achieve the UN Charter's nondiscrimination objective at some time in the future.

Justice Gibson delivered the opinion of the California Supreme Court as set forth below. The Court's footnotes and citations are omitted. The italics in the opinion have been supplied by the author.

COURT'S OPINION. It is first contended that the land law has been invalidated and superseded by the provisions of the United Nations Charter pledging the member nations to promote the observance of human rights and fundamental freedoms without distinction as to race. Plaintiff relies on statements in the preamble and in Articles 1, 55 and 56 of the charter [containing the pledge to achieve "human rights and fundamental freedoms for all without distinction as to race"].

It is not disputed that the charter is a treaty, and our federal Constitution provides that treaties made under the authority of the United States are part of the supreme law of the land and that the judges in every state are bound thereby (US Const., Art. VI). *A treaty, however, does not automatically supersede local laws which are inconsistent with it unless the treaty provisions are self-executing.* In the words of Chief Justice Marshall [in an earlier US Supreme Court decision]: A treaty is "to be regarded in courts of justice as equivalent to an act of the Legislature, whenever it operates of itself, without the aid of any legislative provision."

In determining whether a treaty is self-executing courts look to the intent of the signatory parties as manifested by the language of the instrument, and, if the instrument is uncertain, recourse may be had to the circumstances surrounding its execution. . . .

In order for a treaty provision to be operative without the aid of implementing legislation and to have the force and effect of a statute, *it must appear that the framers of the treaty intended to prescribe a rule that, standing alone, would be enforceable in the courts* [without further action by the parties to that treaty]. . . .

It is clear that the provisions of the preamble and of Article 1 of the charter which are claimed to be in conflict with the alien land law are *not* self-executing. They state general purposes and objectives of the United Nations Organization and *do not purport to impose legal obligations* on the individual member nations or to create rights in private persons. It is equally clear that none of the other provisions relied on by plaintiff is self-executing. Article 55 declares that the United Nations "shall promote . . . universal respect for, and observance of, human rights and fundamental freedoms for all without distinction as to race, sex, language, or religion," and in Article 56, the member nations *"pledge themselves to take joint and separate action* in cooperation with the Organization for the achievement of the purposes set forth in Article 55."

Although the member nations have obligated themselves to cooperate with the international organization in promoting respect for, and observance of, human rights, it is plain that *it was contemplated that future legislative action by the several nations would be required to accomplish the declared objectives,* and there is nothing to indicate that these provisions were intended to become rules of law for the courts of this country upon ratification of the charter.

The language used in Articles 55 and 56 is not the type customarily employed in *treaties which have been held to be self-executing* and to create rights and duties in individuals. . . .

It is significant to note that when the framers of the charter intended to make *certain* provisions effective without the aid of implementing legislation they employed language which is clear and definite and manifests that intention. For example, Article 104 provides: "The Organization shall enjoy in the territory of each of its Members such legal capacity as may be necessary for the exercise of its functions and the fulfillment of its purposes." Article 105 provides: "1. The Organization shall enjoy in the territory of each of its Members such privileges and immunities as are necessary for the fulfillment of its purposes. 2. Representatives of the Members of the United Nations and officials of the Organization shall similarly enjoy such privileges and immunities as are necessary for the independent exercise of their functions in connection with the Organization." In *Curran v. City of New York,* these Articles [in the UN Charter] were treated as being self-executory.

The provisions in the charter pledging cooperation in promoting observance of fundamental freedoms lack the mandatory quality and definiteness which would indicate an intent to create justiciable rights in private persons immediately upon ratification. Instead, they are framed as a promise of future action by the member nations. Secretary of State Stettinius, chairman of the United States delegation at the San Francisco Conference where the charter was drafted, stated in his report to President Truman that Article 56 "pledges the various countries to cooperate with the organization by joint and separate action in the achievement of the economic and social objectives of the organization without infringing upon their right to order their national affairs according to their own best ability, in their own way, and in accordance with their own political and economic institutions and processes." . . .

The humane and enlightened objectives of the United Nations Charter are, of course, entitled to respectful consideration by the courts and legislatures of every member nation, since that document expresses the universal desire of thinking men for peace and for equality of rights and opportunities. The charter represents a moral commitment of foremost importance, and we must not permit the spirit of our pledge to be compromised or disparaged in either our domestic or foreign affairs. We are satisfied, however, that the *charter provisions relied on by plaintiff were not intended to supersede existing domestic legislation,* and we cannot hold that they operate to invalidate the Alien Land Law.

The UN Charter was not generally intended to impose across-the-board obligations on the community of nations. With varying degrees of development and financial ability to achieve the Charter's objectives, many nations had not yet even begun to recover from the impact of World War II. The essential distinction is whether States that ratify a particular treaty mean it to simply suggest standards of achievement, as opposed to immediate legal obligations enforceable by the individuals who would benefit from the treaty's objectives.

The following excerpt from a US Supreme Court decision construes the effect of a bilateral treaty with Japan that conflicted with a law enacted by a state within the US. In this instance, Japan and the US intended that their respective citizens should benefit from their treaty agreement. If the treaty were self-executing, a governmental entity within the US could not properly enact conflicting legislation.

Asakura v. City of Seattle

SUPREME COURT OF THE UNITED STATES, 1924

265 US 332, 44 S.Ct. 515, 68 *L. Ed.* 1041

Author's Note: *The italics in certain passages have been supplied by the author.*

COURT'S OPINION. Plaintiff in error is a subject of the Emperor of Japan, and, since 1904, has resided in Seattle, Washington. Since July, 1915, he has been engaged in business there as a pawnbroker. The city passed an ordinance, which took effect July 2, 1921, regulating the business of pawnbroker and repealing former ordinances on the same subject. It makes it unlawful for any person to engage in the business unless he shall have a license, and the ordinance provides "that no such license shall be granted unless the applicant be a citizen of the United States." Violations of the ordinance are punishable by fine or imprisonment or both. Plaintiff in error brought this suit in the Superior Court of King County, Washington, against the city, its Comptroller and its Chief of Police to restrain them from enforcing the ordinance against him. He attacked the ordinance on the ground that it violates the treaty between the United States and the Empire of Japan, proclaimed April 5, 1911. . . . It was shown that he had about $5,000 invested in his business, which would be broken up and destroyed by the enforcement of the ordinance. The Superior Court granted the relief prayed. On appeal, the Supreme Court of the State held the ordinance valid and reversed the decree. . . .

Does the ordinance violate the treaty? Plaintiff in error invokes and relies upon the following provisions: "The citizens or subjects of each of the High Contracting Parties shall have liberty to enter, travel and reside in the territories of the other to carry on trade, wholesale and retail, to own or lease and occupy houses, manufactories, warehouses and shops, to employ agents of their choice, to lease land for residential and commercial purposes, and generally to do anything incident to or necessary for trade upon the same terms as native citizens or subjects, submitting themselves to the laws and regulations there established. . . . The citizens or subjects of each shall receive, in the territories of the other, the most constant protection, and security for their persons and property. . . ."

A treaty made under the authority of the United States "shall be the supreme Law of the Land; and the *Judges in every State shall be bound thereby,* any Thing in the Constitution or Laws of any State to the Contrary notwithstanding." Constitution, Art. VI, §2.

The treaty-making power of the United States . . . extend[s] to all proper subjects of negotiation between our government and other nations. . . . The treaty [in this instance] was made to strengthen friendly relations between the two nations. As to the things covered by it, the provision quoted establishes the rule of equality between Japanese subjects while in this country and native citizens. Treaties for the protection of citizens of one country residing in the territory of another are numerous, and make for good understanding between nations. . . . *The rule of equality established by it cannot be rendered nugatory in any part of the United States by municipal ordinances or state laws* [unlike the treaty analyzed in the *Sei Fujii* case above, which did *not* impose immediate obligations]. It stands on the same footing of supremacy as do the provisions of the Constitution and laws of the United States. It [the US–Japan friendship treaty] *operates of itself without the aid of any legislation,* state or national; and it will be applied and given authoritative effect by the courts. . . .

The purpose of the ordinance complained of is to regulate, not to prohibit, the business of pawnbroker. But it makes it impossible for aliens to carry on the business. It need not be considered whether the State, if it sees fit, may forbid and destroy the business generally [applying its laws equally to all, regardless of race or citizenship]. Such a law would apply equally to aliens and citizens, and no question of conflict with the treaty would arise. The grievance here alleged is that plaintiff in error, *in violation of the treaty, is denied equal opportunity* [under the Seattle ordinance]. . . .

Decree reversed [so that the plaintiff Japanese citizen may continue to practice his profession as pawnbroker; and the defendant city must repeal its city ordinance, which violated the treaty].

◆ *Notes & Questions*

The Seattle pawnbroker ordinance in *Asakura* violated an international treaty. The California land statute in *Sei Fujii* did not. Why was one of these treaties enforceable, but not the other?

◆ 8.2 FORMATION, PERFORMANCE, CESSATION

This section of the book deals with the overall treaty process—how a treaty is formed, expectations regarding its performance, and the circumstances whereby treaty obligations may be interrupted.

TREATY FORMATION

This analysis focuses on the multilateral treaty process. Formation and implementation involve several phases: negotiations, signature, ratification, reservations, entry into force, and registration. The final formation problem addressed in this section is treaty "invalidity"—a matter of particular concern to some less powerful treaty partners.

Negotiations The emergence of a multilateral treaty often begins when an international organ, such as the UN's International Law Commission or the General Assembly, decides to study some problem of global concern. The UN General Assembly might then resolve that this particular problem should be the subject of an international conference. State representatives often begin the treaty process with preliminary negotiations through an international conference. Maritime nations of the world first met in 1974, for example, to develop an International Law of the Sea. Their initial discussions expanded over the course of the next eight years, during which most nations of the world negotiated their respective positions on proper use of the oceans and their natural resources. These representatives drafted and redrafted a form of "constitution" that formed the final treaty text—satisfactory to the participants at least in principle (§6.3).

Conference representatives must possess the authority to negotiate on behalf of their respective States. Not unlike diplomats and their credentials, conference participants are normally vested with "full powers" by the State they represent. A document from each State's government is presented to a chair or conference committee at the inception of the conference, vesting that agent with various powers: to negotiate, provisionally accept, or perform any act necessary for completing this initial phase of the treaty process. The "full power" instrument facilitates assurances that conference developments will be acceptable to the governments that will one day have to decide whether to ratify the final draft of the treaty text negotiated by their representatives.

The lack of such authority adversely affected international relations when a former US minister to Romania signed two bilateral treaties, but without the President's authority to do so. In one instance, the US minister improperly advised the President that he was signing a different treaty than the one he actually signed with Romania. As to the other agreement, he had *no* authority whatsoever to actually bind the US. The US attempt to avoid its obligations under those treaties was resisted by Romania because the US had already officially entered into these two agreements.[12]

To help clarify treaty expectations in such instances, Article 8 of the VCLT provides that any "act relating to the conclusion of a treaty performed by a person who cannot be considered . . . as authorized to represent a State for that purpose is without legal effect unless afterwards confirmed by the competent authority of the State." This language theoretically creates the potential for abuse, whereby a State can enter into a treaty and subsequently disavow the authority of its representative. In practice, however, the representative's presentation of documentary powers at the inception of a conference notifies all participants of the extent of a particular delegate's powers—which in some cases may be limited by the dispatching government.

Signature The next significant step in the treaty process is the "opening for signature." States, and any participating international organizations, are invited to *sign* (not the same as subsequent *ratification*). A State that signs a treaty has agreed, in principle, to the general wording of the articles appearing in the text of its final draft. Drawing upon the example of the Vienna Convention on Diplomatic Relations (Chapter 7), negotiations were concluded in 1969. The representatives had thereby finished drafting this new "constitution" on diplomatic relations. In one sense, this was only the beginning. Under Article 81 of the VCLT, "[t]he present Convention shall be open for signature by all States Members of the United Nations . . . and by any other State invited by the General Assembly to become a party to the Convention . . ." (until a given date, at Austria's Federal Ministry for Foreign Affairs in Vienna, where negotiations took place, and subsequently at the UN in New York).

Similarly, a State may "accede" to a treaty. That State thereby consents to be bound, albeit in principle, like any States that may have signed the treaty at the conclusion of the drafting conference. Alternatively, accession may express a State's willingness to accept the treaty's obligations—*immediately* and without the necessity of ratification (discussed below). Accession is normally employed by States that did not participate in the initial process whereby the treaty was drafted.

Ratification In the next major stage of the treaty process, States must decide whether to accept or reject all the rights and obligations in the final draft of the treaty. Unanimous and immediate consent of all States is possible, but quite atypical, for reasons addressed in the "Reservations" portion of this section. Acceptance of the treaty and the obligations it contains normally evolves through two related stages. The first stage is *provisional* acceptance of the treaty by the conference delegates. This stage expresses consent to the general wording of the final conference draft. Unless otherwise specified, the signature of a representative on a multilateral treaty merely indicates that his or her State agrees in principle with the essence of the treaty. *Final* acceptance would follow when various States express their willingness to be legally bound by the treaty's terms.

Such consent may occur in a variety of ways, including adoption (unanimous consent when the conference ends), signature of the representatives at the conference (*if* the treaty's express terms so provide), and "ratification."[13] Post-conference ratification is the typical mode for each State's full acceptance of a treaty. The conference delegate has already submitted the provisionally accepted treaty text to the proper authority in his or her State for final approval—to be determined in accordance with that State's internal laws on treaty acceptance. Oxford University's Sir Humphrey Waldock provides a useful explanation for the necessity of post-conference ratification by each potential State party:

> Ordinarily there are two stages in the making of a treaty: . . . [first,] signature . . . of the contracting states, and [second] its ratification by or on behalf of the heads of those states. There are good reasons why this second stage should be necessary before a treaty . . . becomes actually binding. In some states, for example, constitutional law vests the treaty-making power in some organ which cannot delegate it to the plenipotentiaries [treaty conference delegates], and yet cannot itself carry on negotiations with other states; for example, in the United States the power is vested in the President, but subject to the advice and consent of the Senate. But apart from such cases, the interests with which a treaty deals are often so complicated and important that it is reasonable that an opportunity for considering the treaty as a whole should be reserved. A democratic state must consult public opinion, and this can hardly take shape while the negotiations, which must be largely confidential, are going on. These being the reasons that render ratification necessary, it is clearly impossible, as is done by some writers, to specify the circumstances in which a refusal to ratify is justified and those in which it is not.[14]

Reservations Acceptance of a treaty is not necessarily an "all-or-nothing" proposition. A reservation is a State's unilateral variation from a general term contained in the negotiated text. Notwithstanding ratification of the overall treaty, the State thereby excludes or modifies the legal effect of its obligations arising under that particular article—as applied to *that* State. The State is expressing its agreement with the text generally but does not wish to become obligated on *all* terms. A State's provisional acceptance at the drafting conference does not preclude it from tendering such subsequent reservations long after it has signed the treaty.

A reservation to a specific provision in a treaty is a conditional consent that limits the application of a specific treaty provision(s) to that State. If the reservation is acceptable to the other parties, it limits the scope of the reserving State's consent. Although *that* State is not then bound by what it considers an "objectionable" treaty provision, indicated via its reservation, it is bound by all *other* terms of the ratified treaty.

In the case of a *bilateral* treaty between just two nations, reservations are almost nonexistent. One of the two parties may still have a "reservation," but it is effectively a new proposal that materializes in the joint negotiations over which terms will ultimately be inserted into the final treaty text. Both States must agree on all terms of a bilateral treaty, although they may have different interpretations of a specific provision at some point in the future.

Hypothetical reservation illustration: Assume that the representatives of States A, B, C, and D provisionally accept the final text of a treaty at the conclusion of their drafting conference. They all express their agreement to be bound by the broadly worded principles stated in this hypothetical treaty. They now open this treaty for signature (and subsequent ratification). Because the terms of this treaty are *not* likely to be self-executing—the conference delegates did not have the power to ratify the treaty immediately upon conclusion of the drafting stage—no State is yet entitled to the rights or bound to perform the obligations specified in the treaty. Each State must subsequently accept the treaty through the respective State ratification processes. When State A's leaders subsequently review this treaty for possible ratification, they decide to object to the application of one of the treaty clauses. State A will tender a reservation to that particular provision of the treaty. Assuming that A's reservation is acceptable to B, C, and D, State A is excused from performing that provision of the treaty. Assume that B, C, and D do *not* tender the same reservation when *they* ratify this treaty. Unlike State A, they *are* bound by this treaty clause among themselves, although it does not apply to A. States B, C, and D must therefore perform the relevant obligation contained in that general treaty clause vis-à-vis one another. They do not have to do so, however, in their dealings with State A. That particular provision of the final draft treaty—the subject of A's reservation—is *not* effective between State A and any other party to this treaty.

Why are reservations permitted? They encourage wider participation in multilateral treaties through a very practical compromise. Broad participation is better than limited participation by only those few States that might be willing to accept *all* terms of a draft treaty. For example, few States would agree to be sued in the International Court of Justice (ICJ) if they were unable to make reservations to the final draft treaty provision regarding the ICJ's competence to hear and decide cases. Article 36.6 of the UN's Statute of the ICJ provides that any disputes over the Court's jurisdiction—the power to hear the particular case—are to be determined by the Court itself. Nearly all States of the world are parties to this Statute—which is itself a treaty. The original UN members provisionally agreed in principle with the Statute's directive that the *Court* is to decide whether it can hear a particular case. Many of those same States ultimately decided *not* to give their full consent to Article 36.6, however. Many of them tendered reservations to this treaty-based competence of the *ICJ* to decide its jurisdiction. Those States reserved the question of the Court's power to hear a case unto *themselves* when summoned as a defendant before the Court, rather than allowing the ICJ to decide its own jurisdiction under the ICJ's Statute. States also had the option regarding whether or not to *unconditionally* submit to the jurisdiction of the Court in all cases or, alternatively, to tender reservations that would limit the Court's competence to hear only certain types of cases. This somewhat complex feature of the Court's jurisprudence is analyzed in Chapter 9. Suffice it to say that at this juncture there was a practical need for compromise in this particular treaty context. Without the possibility of such a treaty reservation, a number of major powers would not have recognized a distant Court's power to hear all international controversies. Reservations like these accommodate the special interests of States that would not otherwise participate in the overall process of international adjudication by the ICJ.

Such conditional assent cannot be used in *all* treaties. The drafting conference negotiators may decide to insert a prohibition *against* reservations within the express language of the final treaty text. The 1995 Agreement for Implementation of the Provisions of the United Nations Convention on the Law of the Sea of 10 December 1982 Relating to the Conservation and Management of Straddling Fish Stocks and Highly Migratory Fish Stocks prohibits reservations. Predictably, such a provision can limit effective participation. While the US Senate gave its approval to this treaty in 1996, members of that body warned other nations that this should not be construed as US acquiescence in future treaties containing a like provision.[15]

There is a highly sensitive problem when a treaty says nothing about whether reservations are permitted. The classic example is the United Nations Genocide Convention.[16] The general principles of this 1948 instrument were unanimously adopted by all UN members in the aftermath of the Holocaust in Nazi Germany. Many States, however, did not ultimately ratify the Genocide Convention. They were reluctant to accept it without knowing what specific obligations might one day materialize—because the term *genocide* has meant different things to different people. States encountered the dilemma of knowing that they must be willing to accept the Convention's obligations in general, yet they feared that the absence of a reservation provision might one day subject them to scrutiny on grounds that they had never contemplated. The US, for example, did not become a party until nearly forty years later (1986) because of prior senatorial concern about the meaning and application of its various terms.

The International Court of Justice's *Genocide* case addresses this problem. In 1948, the UN General Assembly unanimously adopted the Convention on Genocide. As discussed in §1.4 of this text, this resolution would not be an immediate treaty source in International Law. It could not directly bind the State members of the General Assembly without further action via individual State ratifications. In 1950, the UN General Assembly requested an advisory opinion (noncontentious litigation and no defendant, as discussed in Chapter 9). The 1948 Convention had just entered into force, because of the deposit of the minimum number of ratifications by 1950. There was no provision on the extremely sensitive question of whether reservations were permitted. If reservations *were* to be authorized, then States could theoretically exclude certain forms of genocide from their consent to be bound by this treaty.

Some parties to the Genocide Convention were understandably concerned about the possibility that subsequent ratifications might include reservations purporting to retain the sovereign power to act in ways that could be interpreted as genocide. The General Assembly wanted the ICJ to interpret the Genocide Convention to determine whether a State might ratify the Convention while also tendering a limiting reservation to its broad terms.

Reservations to the Convention on Genocide

INTERNATIONAL COURT OF JUSTICE, 1951

1951 *ICJ Reports* 15

Author's Note: *The Court dispensed a very general and abstract analysis of this sensitive question. Noting the apparent divergence of State views on the possibility of any reservation, the ICJ decided that this treaty implicitly contained the right to become a party—while simultaneously presenting a reservation—as long as it was "compatible" with the language and purpose of the treaty. The relevant portion of the opinion follows—unsigned by any member of the Court. Italics in certain passages have been supplied by the author.*

COURT'S OPINION. [T]he precise determination of the conditions for participation in the [Genocide] Convention constitutes a permanent interest of direct concern to the United Nations which has not disappeared with the entry into force of the Convention....

It is well established that in its treaty relations a State cannot be bound without its consent, and that consequently no reservation [by one state] can be effective against any [other] State without its agreement thereto. It is also a generally recognized principle that a multilateral convention is the result of an agreement freely concluded upon its clauses and that consequently none of the contracting parties is entitled to frustrate or impair, by means of unilateral decisions or particular agreements, the purpose and *raison d'etre* of the convention. To this principle was linked the notion of the integrity of the convention as adopted, a notion which in its traditional concept involved the proposition that *no reservation was valid unless it was accepted by all* the contracting parties without exception, as would have been the case if it had been stated during the negotiations.

This concept, which is directly inspired by the notion of contract, is of undisputed value as a principle. However, as regards the Genocide Convention, it is *proper to refer to a variety of circumstances which would lead to a more flexible application of this principle.* Among these circumstances may be noted the clearly universal character of the United Nations under whose auspices the Convention was concluded, and the very wide degree of participation envisaged by Article XI of the [Genocide] Convention. Extensive participation in conventions of this type has already given rise to greater flexibility in the international practice concerning multilateral conventions. More general resort to reservations, very great allowance made for tacit assent to reservations, the existence of practices which go so far as to admit that the author of reservations which have been rejected by certain contracting parties is nevertheless to be regarded as a party to the convention in relation to those contracting parties that have accepted the reservations—all these factors are manifestations of a new need for flexibility in the operation of multilateral conventions.

It must also be pointed out that although the Genocide Convention was finally approved unanimously, it is nevertheless the result of a series of majority votes. The majority principle, while facilitating the conclusion of multilateral conventions, may also make it necessary for certain States to make reservations. This observation is confirmed by the great number of reservations which have been made in recent years to multilateral conventions.

In this state of international practice, it could certainly *not be inferred from the absence* of an article providing for reservations in a multilateral convention that the contracting States are *prohibited from making . . . reservations.* Account should also be taken of the fact that the absence of such an article or even the decision not to insert such an article can be explained by the desire not to invite a multiplicity of reservations. The character of a multilateral convention, its purpose, provisions, mode of preparation and adoption, are factors which must be considered in determining, in the absence of any express provision on the subject, the possibility of making reservations, as well as their validity and effect. . . .

The Court recognizes that an understanding was reached within the General Assembly on the faculty [ability] to make reservations to the Genocide Convention and that it is permitted to conclude therefrom that States becoming parties to the Convention gave their assent thereto. It must now determine *what kind of reservations may be made* and what kind of objections may be taken to them.

The solution of these problems must be found in the special characteristics of the Genocide Convention. The origins and character of that Convention, the objects pursued by the General Assembly and the contracting parties . . . furnish elements of interpretation of the will of the General Assembly and the parties. The origins of the Convention show that it was the intention of the United Nations to condemn and punish genocide as "a crime under international law" involving a denial of the right of existence of entire human groups, a denial which shocks the conscience of mankind and results in great losses to humanity, and which is contrary to moral law and to the spirit and aims of the United Nations (Resolution 96(I) of the General Assembly, December 11th, 1946). The first consequence arising from this conception is that the principles underlying the Convention are principles which are recognized by civilized nations as binding on States, even without conventional obligation. A second consequence is the universal character both of the condemnation of genocide and of the cooperation required "in order to liberate mankind from such an odious scourge" (Preamble to the Convention). The Genocide Convention was therefore intended by the General Assembly and by the contracting parties to be definitely universal in scope. It was in fact approved on December 9th, 1948, by a resolution which was unanimously adopted by fifty-six States.

The objects of such a convention must also be considered. The Convention was manifestly adopted for a purely humanitarian and civilizing purpose. It is indeed difficult to imagine a convention that might have this dual character to a greater degree, since its object on the one hand is to safeguard the very existence of certain human groups and on the other to confirm and endorse the most elementary principles of morality. In such a convention the contracting States do not have any interests of their own; they merely have, one and all, a common interest, namely, the accomplishment of those high purposes which are the *raison d'etre* of the convention. Consequently, in a convention of this type one cannot speak of individual advantages or disadvantages to States, or of the maintenance of a perfect contractual balance between rights and duties. The high ideals which inspired the Convention provide, by virtue of the common will of the parties, the foundation and measure of all its provisions.

The foregoing considerations, when applied to the question of reservations, and more particularly to the effects of objections to reservations, lead to the following conclusions.

The object and purpose of the Genocide Convention imply that it was the *intention of the General Assembly* and of the States which adopted it that *as many States as possible should participate*. The complete exclusion from the Convention of one or more States would not only restrict the scope of its application, but would detract from the authority of the moral and humanitarian principles which are its basis. It is inconceivable that the contracting parties readily contemplated that an objection to a minor reservation should produce such a result. But even less could the contracting parties have intended to sacrifice the very object of the Convention in favour of a vain desire to secure as many participants as possible. The object and purpose of the Convention thus limit both the freedom of making reservations and that of objecting to them. It follows that it is *the compatibility of a reservation with the object and purpose of the Convention* that must furnish the criterion for the attitude of a State in making the reservation on accession as well as for the appraisal by a State in objecting to the reservation. Such is the rule of conduct which must guide every State in the appraisal which it must make, individually and from its own standpoint, of the admissibility of any reservation.

Any other view would lead either to the acceptance of reservations which frustrate the purposes which the General Assembly and the contracting parties had in mind, or to recognition that the parties to the Convention have the power of excluding from it the author of a reservation, even a minor one, which may be quite compatible with those purposes.

It has nevertheless been argued [independently of these proceedings] that any State entitled to become a party to the Genocide Convention may do so while making any reservation it chooses by virtue of its sovereignty. The Court cannot share this view. It is obvious that so extreme an application of the idea of State sovereignty could lead to a complete disregard of the object and purpose of the Convention.

◆ *Notes & Questions*

1. What test did the International Court of Justice use to determine whether a reservation to a multilateral treaty is permissible?
2. The former Yugoslavia ratified the Genocide Convention in 1950. The current rump State of Yugoslavia does not currently enjoy the right to occupy the Yugoslavian seat at UN General Assembly sessions in New York (Chapter 2). Thus, it might claim that the prior Yugoslavian ratification of the Genocide Convention does not apply to this current Yugoslavian entity. The 1998 genocide involving ethnic Albanians in Serbia's Kosovo province would not be covered directly under this Convention (although certainly under customary International Law). How likely would the current Yugoslavia agree to become a full-fledged member of the UN on condition that it renounce Serbian ethnic-cleansing policies in Kosovo? in Bosnia? China in Tibet? This list does not end here.
3. The year 1998 was the 50th anniversary of the UN's promulgation of the Universal Declaration of Human Rights. Reservations to this document might likewise present a host of problems in the work of supervisory organs—whose task consists of reducing the potentially detrimental impact of reservations to the various human rights instruments that do not address the permissible scope of reservations. For a fascinating analysis, *see* L. Lijnzaad, *Reservations to UN-Human Rights Treaties: Ratify and Ruin?* (Dordrecht, Neth.: Martinus Nijhoff, 1995). *See also* J. Gardner (ed.), *Human Rights*

as General Norms and a State's Right to Opt Out: Reservations and Objections to Human Rights Conventions (London: Brit. Inst. Comp. Law, 1997).

Entry into Force The next phase of the treaty process is "entry into force." The participants may have provisionally accepted the treaty's final draft language at the drafting conference, followed by final acceptance of the treaty by their individual ratifications. Unlike bilateral treaties, where only two States have to agree for a treaty to legally materialize, multilateral treaties usually require greater indicia of international consensus before they are binding. An "entry into force" provision ensures that an agreed-upon minimum number of States ratify the treaty.

Nothing precludes certain parties or international organizations from claiming that a treaty not yet entered into force is nevertheless evidence of what States already consider binding in their mutual relations. For example, no State would claim that the Genocide Convention's ratification by the minimum number of States was a condition precedent to the illegality of an official State policy of genocide. But the objectives of the Convention were to codify this customary expectation, while further defining the specific acts that would qualify as genocide (Chapter 11).

The *manner* and *date* of entry into force is determined from the particular treaty's express provisions. Multilateral treaties normally enter into force when a minimum number of ratifications are deposited at some central location such as the UN. The Genocide Convention, for example, did not enter into force until twenty States had deposited their ratifications with the UN Secretary-General. The 1982 UN Law of the Sea Convention (Chapter 6) did not enter into force until 1994, one year after the sixtieth State ratified it, pursuant to an express provision so stating in that treaty.

States that have not ratified a treaty are not bound by its terms once it has entered into force. They may be bound by its underlying norms if the treaty codifies the existing practice of most States (Chapter 1). Those States may also subsequently consent to be bound by submitting their ratifications and any compatible reservations.

Registration Treaties must be registered, meaning that they must be sent to the UN Secretariat or other appropriate international institution for dissemination to interested parties. Both of the Vienna Conventions—governing the treaties of States and of international organizations—refer to this obligation to register treaties.[17] This requirement approximates the filing of an important document, such as a pleading filed with a court. Registration ensures that international agreements are public, as opposed to the secret treaties that led to World Wars I and II. Treaties are usually registered at the UN—or at the headquarters of the international organization most directly involved with the object of the particular treaty.

Publication is typical but not necessarily required. Both bilateral and multilateral treaties are published in the UN's publication entitled the *United Nations Treaty Series*.[18] Certain countries, especially those with the economic capacity to do so, publish all of their treaties. While some government representatives might prefer to engage in "quiet" diplomacy and treaty negotiations, the product of their efforts must be subjected to public scrutiny. The US Congress therefore requires publication in the comprehensive source *United States Statutes at Large*. Once published therein, US laws and treaties "shall be legal evidence of laws . . . treaties, and international agreements other than treaties [that is, executive agreements]."[19]

There is a peculiar difference between the League of Nations Covenant and the UN Charter regarding the registration requirement embraced by both documents. Article 18 of the Covenant contained an outright bar that voided the potential effects of any unregistered treaty. Secret treaties were characterized as void from the outset. UN Charter Article 102, on the other hand, provides that a party to an unregistered treaty may not "invoke that treaty or agreement before any organ of the United Nations." This does not "void" the treaty. It declares that the instrument cannot be used in any proceedings involving the UN, such as judicial proceedings in the International Court of Justice. In 1992, a London newspaper reported that presidential candidate Bill Clinton had struck a secret deal with the head of the European Community. A new world trade agreement (World Trade Organization—effective 1995—Chapter 13) would be delayed until after his election. This report was denied. Hypothetically, if such an agreement were made, it would be void under League practice and unusable should any dispute involving the 1992 compact arise in UN proceedings.

As a practical matter, many treaties are not registered (or published). Because of the time and money inherent in the registration–publication process, certain international organizations have narrowly construed the meaning of the word *treaty* to limit which treaties are subject to the UN Charter registration requirement. The UN, although subject to budgetary constraints (§3.5), has resolved to improve the availability of its documents on the Internet. General Assembly Resolution 211(C) of 1997 "[r]equests the Secretary-General to ensure that the texts of all new public documents . . . are made available through the United Nations Web site . . . and are accessible to Member States without delay. . . ."[20]

Invalidity International agreements should be the product of a mutually beneficial decision to create rights and honor obligations. Unfortunately, a number of treaties have been imposed by one State on another because of their inherently unequal bargaining positions. During the seventeenth and eighteenth centuries, writers first raised the question of whether treaties were valid in the absence of any real bargaining or negotiations. In 1646, the famous Dutch author Hugo Grotius distinguished between equal and unequal treaties. He described an unequal treaty as one that is forced on one nation by another, rather than being the product of a negotiated process. In 1758, Swiss author E. de Vattel examined the problem of unequal treaties—concluding that States, as well as persons, should deal fairly with one another. The principle that individuals did not have the right to impose their wishes on others should apply with equal force to sovereign States. De Vattel hypothesized that because States "are no less bound than individuals to respect justice, they should make their treaties equal, as far as possible." Neither of these influential writers, however, questioned the *legal validity* of such treaties. They presumed that "unequal" treaties were nevertheless legitimate. A bargained-for exchange was not considered a necessary prerequisite for a valid treaty between sovereign States. But as later stated by American author H. Halleck in 1861, "the inequality in the . . . engagements of a treaty does not, in general, render such engagements any the less binding upon the contracting parties."[21]

There are many examples of such unequal treaties. In 1807, Napoleon threatened to place the king of Spain on trial for treason unless the king surrendered his throne. Having no choice, King Ferdinand entered into an agreement with France that was devoid of any bargained-for advantages for Spain. In the 1856 Treaty of Paris, Russia was prohibited from maintaining a naval fleet on the Black Sea at its geographically sensitive southwestern border. In 1903, the US condition for recognizing Cuba's independence from Spain was the Guantanamo Naval Base Treaty. The US thereby "acquired" the lease for a military base that proved critical to US interests (for example, during the 1962 Cuban Missile Crisis and the 1994 Haitian operation). The 1903 Panama Canal Treaty validated US control over the Canal (until relinquished in 1977), a former province of Colombia. The Treaty of Versailles, which ended World War I, was signed by German delegates who had unsuccessfully objected to terms requiring that the responsible party (Germany) pay the other treaty parties (the victors) for their damages incurred during the war. And just prior to World War II, Hitler threatened to bomb Czechoslovakia, forcing the creation of a treaty placing the Czechs under German "protection."[22]

In the twentieth century, several events led legal commentators to review the historical presumption that unequal treaties are valid. National Chengchi University (Taipei) Professor Hungdah Chiu summarized them as follows:

> After the 1917 Bolshevik revolution in Russia, the Bolshevik government offered to abolish and later did abolish some former Tzarist treaties imposed upon China, Persia, and Turkey; and Soviet writers then began to discuss the question of the validity of those "coercive, predatory, and enslaving" treaties, although the term "unequal treaties" was not widely used after World War II. This early development in the Soviet Union, however, was generally ignored by Western scholars.
>
> In the 1920s, however, the problem of unequal treaties received world-wide attention when China demanded the abolition of some treaties that it termed unequal. Only then did some Western writers renew interest in the problem. In 1927, at the annual meeting of the American Society of International Law, a session was devoted to the discussion of China's unequal treaties. With the abolition of what were presumed to be the last of China's unequal treaties in the early 1940s, Western scholars again lost interest in the subject.
>
> With the emergence of many new states in Asia and Africa in the 1960s, the question of unequal treaties again began to attract worldwide attention.

When the Draft Articles on the Law of Treaties prepared by the United Nations International Law Commission was sent to UN member states for comment, many states expressed concern about the question of unequal treaties.[23]

In the 1960s, many of the "new" nations (former colonies) in Africa and Asia advocated the proposition that unequal treaties were no longer acceptable under International Law. Their forums for advocating this perspective were the conference negotiations resulting in the Vienna Convention on the Law of Treaties. One supporting argument was that Article 2.4 of the UN Charter requires all members to "refrain in their international relations from the threat or use of force . . . [which is] inconsistent with the purposes of the United Nations." If force is illegal, then coercion in the treaty process should invalidate the legality of a treaty.

The result of the VCLT negotiations was the incorporation of two articles applicable to treaties concluded after the effective date of the VCLT (January 27, 1980). Article 51 provides that the "expression of a State's consent to be bound by a treaty which has been *procured by the coercion of its representative* through acts or threats directed against him shall be without any legal effect" (italics added). Article 52 provides that a "treaty is void if its conclusion has been *procured by the threat or use of force in violation of the principles of international law* embodied in the Charter of the United Nations" (italics added). Although coerced treaties concluded prior to the VCLT were presumed valid by some writers, Articles 51 and 52 expressly negated that presumption for subsequent treaties. As stated by the International Court of Justice, there "can be little doubt, as is implied in the Charter of the United Nations and recognized in Article 52 of the Vienna Convention on the Law of Treaties, that under contemporary international law an agreement concluded under the threat or use of force is void."[24]

During the Vienna Conference negotiations, a number of Eastern communist bloc and African states advocated the view that Article 52's prohibition against force should expressly include "economic, military, and political" coercion. Their attempts to ban treaties procured through these categories of force were rebuffed by Western representatives. The Western position was that, given the difficulty of defining "force" in the treaty process, it would be too difficult to determine whether a treaty was invalid because it was allegedly signed as a result of such duress.

Article 52 of the VCLT therefore does not contain a specific definition of force. Instead, it generally prohibits the threat or use of force in violation of the principles of International Law embodied in the UN Charter. This language meant only that "the precise scope of the acts covered by this definition should be left to be determined in practice by interpretation of the relevant provisions of the [UN] Charter." Yet Article 2.4 of the Charter only vaguely prohibits the use of force "against the territorial integrity or political independence of any state. . . ." The Vienna Convention Article 52 definition of force in the treaty process was left purposefully vague, because it relies on the vague definition of force as expressed in the UN Charter.[25]

Some of the ambiguity about the scope of the term *force* was offset at the conclusion of the VCLT. The delegates adopted the *separate* Declaration on the Prohibition of Military, Political or Economic Coercion in the Conclusion of Treaties. They therein stated that the United Nations Conference on the Law of Treaties "*solemnly condemns* the threat or use of pressure in any form, whether military, political, or economic, by any State in order to coerce another State to perform any act relating to the conclusion of a treaty in violation of the principles of the sovereign equality of States and freedom of consent. . . ."[26] This Declaration was actually made independently of the VCLT rather than directly expressed within the text of the Article 52 prohibition of force in the conclusion of treaties. This exclusion—which more precisely defined force, but outside of the treaty text itself—was a compromise that illustrates Western opposition to nonmilitary duress as a basis for invalidating a treaty. Because the VCLT itself defines coercion only by the reference to the "principles of international law embodied in the Charter of the United Nations," it is difficult to determine when a treaty would be void on the basis of duress in its creation.

TREATY OBSERVANCE

There are several yardsticks for determining whether a State has performed or properly rebuked "its end of the deal": good faith performance of national treaty obligations; changed circumstances justifying nonperformance; express and implied consent to suspension or termination of a treaty; material breach by one party justifying another's nonperformance; impossibility of performance; and conflict with a peremptory norm of International Law.

Good Faith Performance Under Article 2.2 of the United Nations Charter, "Members . . . shall fulfill in good faith the obligations assumed by them in accordance with the present Charter." The universal character of this norm was aptly articulated by the former Dutch ambassador to the UN in 1967: "The principle of good faith itself . . . extends beyond the scope of this article and is generally recognized as expressing a fundamental concept underlying the entire structure of the international public order. It applies to the observance and interpretation of treaties and even to the obligation not to frustrate the object of a treaty prior to its entry into force, as well as to the fulfillment of obligations arising from other sources of international law. Particularly in the context of the law of treaties the principle of good faith . . . clearly emerges as having a fundamental and universal nature."[27]

This limitation on State conduct directs that a State not act in such a way as to frustrate the purpose of the treaty. It may not pass subsequent internal legislation that is inconsistent with its obligations under a treaty it has signed or ratified. In a US–UK treaty delineating the fishing rights of US citizens in Canadian waters, the UK's post-treaty regulations limited those rights in a way that was not contemplated by the wording of the treaty. The arbitrators in this important proceeding noted that such regulations had to be "drawn according to the principle of international law that treaty obligations are to be executed in perfect good faith, therefore excluding the right to legislate at will concerning the subject-matter of the treaty, and limiting the exercise of sovereignty of the States . . . to such acts as are consistent with the treaty. . . ."[28]

Various cases decided by the International Court of Justice nevertheless illustrate some of the problems with *applying* the good faith performance standard. In two significant cases, the ICJ dealt with what it perceived to be tardy claims that were not, under the circumstances, made apparently in good faith. In the 1960 *Case Concerning the Arbitral Award Made by the King of Spain,* a bilateral treaty required Honduras and Nicaragua to arbitrate their boundary dispute. Spain's king was the agreed-upon arbitrator after the treaty-designated arbitrator failed to act. When the king decided this boundary dispute in 1960, neither country objected to his decision. Years later, Nicaragua challenged the validity of his award because the king "was not designated arbitrator in conformity with the provisions of the . . . Treaty [which] had elapsed before he agreed to act as arbitrator." Honduras responded that Nicaragua was thereby acting in bad faith, waiting too long to assert this potential bar to enforcement of the king's award. The ICJ held that Nicaragua could not in good faith raise such procedural problems so many years after the arbitration was complete and the treaty purpose fulfilled. In the words of the ICJ:

> Having failed to challenge the competency of the King as sole arbitrator before or during the course of the arbitration but, on the contrary, having invited him to make an award on the merits, Nicaragua was thereafter precluded from contesting the regularity of the appointment.
>
> All the relevant facts relating to that appointment were known to it when it participated in the arbitration. Each State party to the arbitration proceedings was entitled to place faith upon the deliberate conduct of the other State in the course of such proceedings. Nicaragua cannot be permitted to be placed in the position where, had the Award been satisfactory from its point of view, it could have accepted it, if not be free to disregard it as a nullity.
>
> It would be contrary to the principle of good faith governing the relations between States were it [Nicaragua] permitted now to rely upon any irregularity in the appointment to invalidate the Award. Its conduct up to the moment of the Award operated in my opinion so as to preclude it thereafter from doing so. . . .[29]

In a similar case, Cambodia and Siam (now Thailand) agreed to a boundary delimitation made by a "Mixed Commission" of individuals from Thailand and Cambodia. The commission's work was completed in 1907. A subsequent dispute arose over an important religious site situated at the border but not mentioned in surveys conducted by the commission's officers. The commission's surveys apparently placed the temple area within the territory comprising French Indochina (included in what is now Cambodia). The commission members from Siam received copies of the surveys and did not object at the time of that body's findings. Years later, Thailand refused to cede authority over the area to Cambodia. In the 1960 proceedings before the ICJ, Thailand had two objections to the treaty-based boundary of 1907: First, the surveys were not actually the work of the treaty-designated commission; second, they contained material errors in the placement of the Thai–Cambodian boundary. The ICJ rejected Thailand's claim for two reasons: It was not made in good faith, because of the tardiness in asserting it. Also, Thailand had apparently acquiesced in the boundary line fixed by the commission decades before it presented an objection. Both forms of conduct led to the Court's useful articulation regarding the importance of good faith treaty performance:

> The primary foundation of this principle is the good faith that must prevail in international relations, inasmuch as inconsistency of conduct or opinion on the part of a State to the prejudice of another is incompatible with good faith. Again, I submit that such inconsistency is especially inadmissible when the dispute arises from bilateral treaty relations. A secondary basis of the principle is the necessity for security in contractual relationships. A State bound by a certain treaty to another State must rest in the security that a harmonious and undisturbed exercise of the rights of each party and a faithful discharge of reciprocal obligations denote a mutually satisfactory state of things which is permanent in character and is bound to last as long as the treaty is in force. A State cannot enjoy such a situation and at the same time live in fear that some day the other State may change its mind or its conduct and jeopardize or deny rights that for a long time it has never challenged. A continuous and uncontroverted fulfillment of a treaty is tantamount to a pledge, a security renewed day by day that the treaty rights, passiveness or any form of express or tacit acquiescence, and other disputes have been decided against litigant States on the general basis of inconsistency between the claims of States and their previous acts.[30]

The lack of a precise definition of good faith treaty performance raises the question of whether it is in fact a general principle of International Law. Professor Charles Fenwick, former director of the Department of Legal Affairs of the Pan American Union, asserted the doubtful applicability of this norm. He used treaties of peace—imposed by the victor on the vanquished—as his prime example that good faith was not really expected in treaty matters. When a vanquished State wanted to repudiate a treaty imposed on it by a victorious nation, the simple solution was another war. Given this fact of international life, he argued that "[a]ppearances could be saved, if [even] necessary, by finding other grounds of war, and then, if the outcome were successful, taking back what had been previously granted under duress. . . . Thus the faithful execution of treaties of peace was adjusted to shifts in the balance of power, and the principle of good faith was maintained while being indirectly undermined."[31]

Various organizations have attempted to articulate a standard for resolving questions about the precise content of the rather elastic "good faith" yardstick—often referred to as *pacta sunt servanda.* The UN's International Law Commission (ILC)—an organ of the UN General Assembly—commenced its study of the *pacta sunt servanda* "norm" shortly after the UN was created. The ILC's first work product on this subject was the Draft Declaration on the Rights and Duties of States. Article 13 provided that every "State has the duty to carry out in good faith its obligations arising from treaties . . . and it may not invoke provisions in its constitution or its [internal] laws as an excuse for failure to perform this duty."[32] This attempt to define good faith was *so* acceptable that it was virtually useless as a functional device for describing content. Some Vienna Conference delegates even argued in favor of *eliminating* the term from international treaty law due to the perennial inability to satisfactorily define it.[33]

The very general wording chosen for Article 26 of the VCLT achieved a consensus. It provides that every treaty "is binding upon the parties to it and must be performed by them in good faith." That language is no more specific than any earlier attempt to define good faith. Thus, good faith performance of treaty obligations does not mean literal compliance to the maximum extent possible. Performance should be assessed by reference to the circumstances of each particular case.

Change in Circumstances A treaty is no longer binding if there has been a fundamental change in circumstances. This concept is referred to in international literature as the doctrine of *rebus sic stantibus.* While a treaty is a solemn contract between States, a party may invoke changed circumstances as an excuse for suspending or terminating that contract.

This concept typically arises as a defense to good faith performance. Defining "changed circumstances" is as difficult as defining "good faith." Commentators, diplomats, and jurists are unable to agree on the precise circumstances for properly invoking this basis for avoiding treaty obligations. This obstacle has not impeded either the academic or judicial utility of the doctrine of *rebus sic stantibus.* The spectrum of views is that it is "clearly a reasonable doctrine [that] . . . international law should recognize," merely an "alleged principle of international law," and "an unsuitable method for altering treaty obligations to accommodate changed conditions." The prolific Chinese scholar Wang Yao-t'ien viewed changed circumstances as a contrivance fashioned by capitalist States to abrogate treaties at will. In his 1958 treatise on trade treaties, he wrote that two States should *renegotiate* their treaty rather than one of them unilaterally suspending or terminating its treaty obligations. In his words: "There is a doctrine of *'rebus sic stantibus'* in the works of bourgeois international law. . . . In international relations, sometimes it is necessary to revise or abrogate a treaty in the light of fundamental change of circumstances. However, capitalist states frequently use this principle as a pretext to justify their unilateral [abrogation] of treaties. Generally, the process should be: When a fundamental change of circumstances occurs, the contracting states should seek revision or reconclusion of the original treaty through diplomatic negotiation."[34]

Columbia University Professor Oliver Lissitzyn most accurately referred to the changed circumstances doctrine as a right with unsettled contours. In his words:

> After centuries of doctrinal discussion, the existence, scope and modalities of such a right remain controversial and perplexing. Its practical importance may at times be exaggerated; but nations dissatisfied with the *status quo* continue to regard it as a welcome device for escaping from burdensome treaties, while others fear it as a threat to stability and to their interests. Terminology has complicated the problem. . . . Governments, in asserting the right, have variously employed or refrained from employing such terms as *rebus sic stantibus.*[35]

Most theorists do not believe that changed circumstances permit a *unilateral* abrogation of treaty commitments. When circumstances beyond the control of the parties necessitate the alteration of a treaty commitment, the remedy is usually suspension or termination of the treaty—depending on the extent of the conditions that have changed. In practice, however, the State claiming changed circumstances may no longer want to fulfill commitments that have become inconvenient or not as beneficial as anticipated. During the 1960s, the drafters of the Vienna Convention on the Law of Treaties attempted to clarify the legal contours of the changed circumstances doctrine. The drafting committee's members articulated their concern as follows:

> Almost all modern jurists, however reluctantly, admit the existence in international law of the principle . . . commonly spoken of as the doctrine of *rebus sic stantibus.* . . . Most jurists, however, at the same time enter a strong *caveat* as to the need to confine the scope of the doctrine within narrow limits and to regulate strictly the conditions under which it may be invoked; for the risks to the security of treaties which this doctrine presents . . . [are] obvious. The circumstances of international life are always changing and it is easy to allege that the changes render the treaty inapplicable.[36]

The ultimate work product of the Vienna Convention on changed circumstances was Article 62. The essential provision (Art. 62.1) provides that a "fundamental change in circumstances which has occurred with regard to those existing at the time of the conclusion of a treaty, and which was not foreseen by the parties, may not be invoked as a ground for terminating or withdrawing from the treaty unless: (a) the existence of those circumstances constituted an essential basis of the consent of the parties to be bound by the treaty; and (b) the effect of the change is radically to transform the extent of obligations still to be performed under the treaty."

The existence of the changed circumstances doctrine has been reluctantly conceded in international litigation. In 1929, the Permanent Court of International Justice grudgingly recognized its vitality. The Court refused to assess its contours, however, ultimately choosing not to apply it.[37] In the early 1970s, the International Court of Justice ruled against a State's changed circumstances defense to its unilateral termination of a treaty. The segment of this case dealing with changed circumstances is presented below. It echoes the sentiment of the VCLT commentators that renegotiation, or judicial settlement, is the preferred alternative to unilateral termination based on "changed circumstances":

Fisheries Jurisdiction Cases

INTERNATIONAL COURT OF JUSTICE, 1973

[1973] *ICJ Reports* 49

Author's Note: *Various nations have fished in the waters surrounding Iceland for centuries. After World War II, Iceland became concerned that these nations, using advanced technology, were rapidly depleting valuable fishing resources—Iceland's primary livelihood. In 1959, the Althing, its parliament, declared that "Iceland has an indisputable right to fishery limits of 12 miles (rather than 3), that recognition should be obtained of Iceland's right to the entire continental shelf area (about 50 miles) and that fishery limits of less than 12 miles [when the international norm was a three-mile territorial sea] from the baselines around the country are out of the question."*

In 1961, Iceland and England were engaged in a diplomatic Exchange of Notes that ultimately became a treaty. Iceland agreed to give England six months' notice of any further extension of Icelandic fisheries jurisdiction and to submit future fisheries disputes to the ICJ. In 1971, Iceland advised England about Iceland's intent to extend its fisheries jurisdiction again—this time to the entire Continental Shelf surrounding Iceland's shores. (The US had similarly created a 200-mile Continental Shelf zone in 1945.) England objected, because a coastal state's ability to control fishing in international waters was well under the fifty-mile limit suddenly claimed by Iceland (at a time when there was no Exclusive Economic Zone).

In 1972, the Althing adopted a resolution that the twelve-mile agreement of 1961 had to be repealed because of changed circumstances. England (and Germany) sued Iceland in the ICJ to preserve their fishing rights under the 1961 treaty. Although Iceland chose not to appear in the proceedings, it did provide the Court with a written defense: The technological circumstances had changed so drastically that Iceland was compelled to unilaterally abrogate its 1961 treaty with England. The court ruled (in Iceland's absence) that Iceland could not properly invoke changed circumstances. English ships were not precluded from fishing within the fifty-mile area claimed by Iceland.

The portion of the opinion dealing with changed circumstances follows. The paragraph numbers are those of the Court. Italics have been added by the author at various points.

COURT'S OPINION. 35. In his letter of 27 June 1972 to the Registrar [of the Court] the Minister for Foreign Affairs of Iceland refers to 'the changed circumstances resulting from the ever-increasing exploitation of the fishery resources in the seas surrounding Iceland.' Judicial notice should also be taken of other statements made on the subject in documents which Iceland has brought to the Court's attention. Thus, the resolution adopted by the Althing on 15 February 1972 contains the statement that 'owing to changed circumstances the Notes concerning fishery limits exchanged in 1961 are no longer applicable.'

36. In these statements the Government of Iceland is basing itself on the principle of termination of a treaty by reason of change of circumstances. International law admits that a fundamental change in the circumstances . . . [that] resulted in a radical transformation of the extent of the obligations imposed by it [the treaty], may, under certain conditions, afford the party affected a ground for invoking the termination or suspension of the treaty. This principle, and the conditions and exceptions to which it is subject, have been embodied in Article 62 of the Vienna Convention on the Law of Treaties, which may in many respects be considered as a codification of existing customary law on the subject of the termination of a treaty relationship on account of change of circumstances.

37. One of the basic requirements embodied in that Article is that the change of circumstances must have been a fundamental one. In this respect the Government of Iceland has, with regard to developments in fishing techniques, referred . . . to the increased exploitation of the fishery resources in the seas surrounding Iceland and to the danger of still further exploitation because of an increase in the catching capacity of fishing fleets. The Icelandic statements recall the exceptional dependence of that country on its fishing for its existence and economic development. . . .

In this same connection, the resolution adopted by the Althing on 15 February 1972 had contained a paragraph in these terms:

> That the Governments of the United Kingdom and the Federal Republic of Germany be again informed that because of the vital interests of the

> nation and owing to changed circumstances the Notes concerning fishery limits exchanged in 1961 are no longer applicable and that their provisions do not constitute an obligation for Iceland.

38. The invocation by Iceland of its 'vital interests,' which were not made the subject of an express reservation to the acceptance of the jurisdictional obligation under the 1961 Exchange of Notes, must be interpreted, in the context of . . . the traditional view that the changes of circumstances which must be regarded as fundamental or vital are those which imperil the existence or vital development of one of the parties.

39. The Applicant [England], for its part, has expressed before the Court the view that 'the danger of overfishing has not yet materialized,' and made it clear, in its oral argument, that it was not to be understood as accepting the correctness of the claim by the Government of Iceland that the technical development of fishing equipment and modern fishing techniques had made it more pressing than before to take conservation measures in order to prevent overfishing in the waters around Iceland. . . .

41. It should be observed in this connection that the exceptional importance of coastal fisheries to the Icelandic economy is expressly recognized in the 1961 Exchange of Notes, and the . . . point is not disputed.

42. Account must also be taken of the fact that the Applicant, in its contentions before the Court, expressed the opinion that if Iceland, as a coastal State specially dependent on coastal fisheries for its livelihood or economic development, asserts a need to procure the establishment of a special fisheries conservation regime (including such a regime under which it enjoys preferential rights) in the waters adjacent to its coast but beyond the exclusive fisheries zone provided for by the 1961 Exchange of Notes, it can legitimately pursue that objective by collaboration and agreement with the other countries concerned, *but not by unilateral assumption of exclusive rights within those waters.* The exceptional dependence of Iceland on its fisheries and the principle of conservation of fish stocks having been recognized, the question remains as to whether Iceland is or is not competent unilaterally to assert an exclusive fisheries jurisdiction extending beyond the 12-mile limit. . . .

43. Moreover, in order that a change of circumstances may give rise to a ground for invoking the termination of a treaty, it is also necessary that it *should have resulted in a radical transformation of the extent of the obligations still to be performed. The change must have increased the burden of the obligations to be executed to the extent of rendering the performance something essentially different from that originally undertaken.* In respect of the obligation with which the Court is here concerned, this condition is wholly unsatisfied; the change of circumstances alleged by Iceland cannot be said to have transformed radically the extent of the jurisdictional obligation which is imposed in the 1961 Exchange of Notes. The compromissory clause enabled either of the parties to submit to the Court any dispute between them relating to an extension of Icelandic fisheries jurisdiction in the waters above its continental shelf beyond the 12-mile limit. The present dispute is exactly of the character anticipated in the compromissory clause of the Exchange of Notes. Not only has the jurisdictional obligation not been radically transformed in its extent; it has remained precisely what it was in 1961.

44. The Applicant, in the oral proceedings, advanced the contention that the assertion of changed circumstances does not . . . release the State invoking them from its treaty obligation *unless* it has been *established, either by consent* of the other party *or by judicial or other settlement* between the parties, that the changed circumstances are of a kind which justifies release from existing treaty obligations.

◆ *Notes & Questions*

In a 1992 decision, a French administrative body reviewed the government's unilateral suspension of a series of bilateral treaties. Each of them had exempted foreign nationals from visa requirements for visiting France. The new, post-treaty legislation was a response to a wave of terrorist attacks. A Moroccan national, unable to produce a visa, was being expelled because he was no longer legally present in France. Although France was not a party to the Vienna Convention on the Law of Treaties (VCLT), the opinion nevertheless seizes upon the VCLT, the International Court of Justice, scholars, and customary State practice, to support France's right to suspend its "no visa" treaties—on the basis of a fundamental change in circumstances. As stated in "*Prefect of La Gironde v. Mahmedi, France (Conseil d'Etat),*" 106 *Int'l L. Rep.* 204, 206–207 (1992):

> It is the last-mentioned eventuality, otherwise known as *rebus sic stantibus,* which the [French] Minister invoked in his letter to Morocco: 'As the Government of the Kingdom of Morocco is aware, terrorist attacks have increased and intensified . . . during the last several weeks. This development constitutes a fundamental change in circumstances. . . .'
>
> The 'doctrine of fundamental change in circumstances' was explicitly accepted by the International Court of Justice as a reason for suspension of treaties. . . . The doctrine is enshrined in Article 72 of the Vienna Convention. . . . The fact that France is not a party to that Convention does not alter the [government's] position because it merely codifies preexistent rules and principles of international law. . . .
>
> It should be added that legal writers unanimously recognize the existence of this doctrine and only disagree with regard to its basis.

A number of terrorists have been found in France for a variety of reasons, including a historically liberal environment for immigrants and visitors. The *Mahmedi* case involved France's 1986 legislative change to its 1983 "no visa" treaty with Morocco. A government that has had to deal with the many faces of terrorism in the past might arguably be expected to anticipate such problems when it enters into such a treaty commitment. Does the ICJ's *Fisheries Jurisdiction* case, and the other materials in this section, point toward—or away from—the validity of France's unilateral suspension of its "no visa" treaty with Morocco on the basis of the changed circumstances doctrine?

TREATY TERMINATION AND SUSPENSION

There are other, more viable methods of treaty suspension or termination. The stability of the treaty system is nourished by the State fulfillment of treaty commitments. International agreements normally remain in force until the contracting parties jointly decide to modify them. States may legitimately terminate or suspend their treaty obligations, however, by employing several other devices.

Express Consent States typically enter into treaties of indefinite duration. Yet a treaty can terminate by its own terms in conformity with provisions expressed by the parties. The expiration of a specified amount of time is a routine basis for termination. The People's Republic of China commonly makes treaties that remain in force only for a designated period. For example, the 1950 Sino–Soviet Treaty of Friendship, Alliance, and Mutual Assistance provided that the "present treaty will be valid for thirty years. If neither of the contracting parties . . . desire[s] to renounce the treaty, it shall remain in force for another five years and will be extended in compliance with this rule."[38]

Treaties more typically contain provisions for advance notification of termination. The 1955 Sino–Indonesian Treaty on Dual Nationality provided that if "after the expiration of twenty years, one party requests its termination, it must so notify the other party one year in advance and in written form; and the present treaty shall be terminated one year after the tendering of such notification." The 1954 Mutual Defense Treaty between the United States and the Republic of China (Taiwan) provided that it would remain in force "indefinitely [although] either Party may terminate it one year after notice has been given to the other Party." In 1978, President Carter gave notice that he intended to terminate the treaty with Taiwan. That treaty was terminated by the US one year later when he officially recognized the People's Republic of China (mainland China) as the *de jure* government of China.

A treaty may be terminated or suspended even when it does *not* contain revocation or notice provisions. The participants may simply repeal it in another treaty. Under Article 58 of the Vienna Convention on the Law of Treaties, two (or more) nations may suspend a treaty as it relates to their mutual obligations to one another.

Implied Consent The parties to an international agreement can effectively disapprove it by *implication.* If a subsequent treaty is silent about the continued validity of a prior treaty on that subject, termination or suspension can be implied from the circumstances. The State parties may enter into a subsequent agreement containing the same subject matter as an earlier treaty. If provisions in the second treaty conflict with the first, then the first is cancelled by the implied consent of the parties.

Two treaty agreements or the conflicting provisions within them must, of course, be incompatible in order to imply termination of the earlier treaty. In a 1939 case in the Permanent Court of International Justice (PCIJ), a majority of the Court ruled that the two related agreements were compatible. Justice Anzilotti's dissent in that case succinctly stated the general requirements for implicit treaty abrogation: There "was no express abrogation [of the 1931 treaty]. But it is generally agreed that, beside express abrogation, there is also tacit abrogation resulting from the fact that the new provisions are incompatible with the previous provisions, or that the whole matter which formed the subject of these latter [understandings] is henceforth governed by the new provisions."[39]

Under Article 59(b) of the 1969 Vienna Convention on the Law of Treaties (VCLT), the parties may consent by implication to treaty termination when a subsequent treaty is "so far incompatible with the earlier one that the two treaties are not capable of being applied at the same time."

The other basis for implied consent to treaty termination is a failure of compliance. A treaty can be negated by implication when all of the parties ignore it. The absence of objections constitutes an implied understanding that the treaty is no longer in force.

Material Breach One party's treaty breach may allow the other(s) to consider the treaty as either suspended or terminated.[40] The breach must be material rather than minor. Under Article 60 of the VCLT, material breach of a *bilateral* treaty by one party permits the other party "to invoke the breach as a ground for terminating the treaty or suspending its operation in whole or in part." Material breach of a *multilateral* treaty similarly entitles "the other parties . . . to suspend the operation of the treaty . . . in the relations between themselves and the defaulting State [but not one another]. . . ." The clearest example of a material breach under Article 60 would be an outright repudiation of a treaty. The other party would then be authorized to suspend or terminate its own obligations under that treaty.

In practice, it is often difficult to establish what constitutes a *material* breach and *which* party is actually responsible for the breach. In 1966, North Vietnam claimed that South Vietnam had materially breached the Geneva Accords. That international agreement—agreed to by representatives of both governments—called for a cessation of hostilities in Vietnam, the reduction of military forces, and reunification through free elections. The North Vietnamese claim of material breach by South Vietnam was based on the introduction of US military forces into the Southern portion of the country in rapidly increasing numbers. The US justified South Vietnam's departure from the Geneva agreement on the basis of a material breach by North Vietnam. The US claimed that the "substantial breach of an international agreement by one side [North Vietnamese aggression in South Vietnam] permits the other side to suspend performance of corresponding obligations under the agreement. South Vietnam was allegedly justified in refusing to implement the provisions of the Geneva Accords," which otherwise would have required it to limit expanded military involvements and to arrange unification elections. Specifically, the introduction of military personnel into the southern portion of the country "was justified by the international law principle that a material breach of an agreement by one party [North Vietnam] entitles the other [South Vietnam] at least to withhold compliance . . . until the defaulting party is prepared to honor its obligation."[41] North Vietnam and South Vietnam accused each other of materially breaching their respective commitments under the Geneva Accords.

In a 1972 case in the International Court of Justice, Pakistan complained that India materially breached several aviation treaties. An Indian aircraft had been hijacked and diverted to Pakistan. India then revoked Pakistan's right to fly over Indian territory. For reasons unrelated to the merits of this case, the ICJ did not resolve whether India breached the aviation treaties when it refused to allow Pakistani aircraft in Indian airspace. It did find, however, that the Indian suspension of Pakistan's treaty rights to pass over Indian territory and to land in India constituted material breaches of their aviation treaty.[42]

Impossibility of Performance A party to a treaty may invoke impossibility of performance as a basis for suspending or terminating its obligations under that treaty. Article 61 of the VCLT provides that impossibility "results from the permanent disappearance or destruction of an object indispensable for the execution of the treaty." The drafters of the VCLT used the following examples: submergence of an island that is the object of a treaty relationship, the drying up of a river, and the destruction of a dam or hydroelectric installation indispensable for the execution of a treaty. The extinction of these objects would terminate (or temporarily suspend) rights and obligations arising under a treaty governing their use.[43]

A fundamental change that *radically* alters the nature of treaty obligations has been characterized by some jurists as impossibility of performance—adducing a fine-line distinction from the above "changed circumstances" analysis. Although there are similarities, the criteria employed for applying "impossibility" differ. Every impossibility of performance involves a changed circumstance, but not every changed circumstance constitutes impossibility of performance. The changed circumstances doctrine may excuse *difficulty* of performance, while impossibility excuses only that performance that would be totally *impossible*. This excuse exonerates one or both parties from treaty performance when the relevant circumstance renders the treaty meaningless.[44]

Assume that Spain and Portugal establish their respective rights to fish in an area on either side of a boundary in the international waters near their coasts. They agree to regulate their respective fishing fleets on either side of the line separating Spain's area from Portugal's area. The purpose of the treaty is to maintain an equal distribution of the resources near their respective coasts. If the fish unexpectedly migrated into Portugal's area, then the treaty would be suspended. The changed circumstance is that fish are *temporarily* unavailable in equal numbers to both Spain and Portugal. Spain's fishermen would be permitted to fish in Portugal's area of the High Seas due to the treaty's mutually agreed purpose of equitable distribution. The same fishing treaty would be terminated under the impossibility doctrine if all of the fish were *permanently* driven away by contamination of the treaty area. The treaty would be meaningless because the object of that agreement would no longer exist.[45]

Conflict with Peremptory Norm A treaty is void if it conflicts with a peremptory norm of International Law. The common descriptive term for such a norm is *jus cogens,* referring to a supposedly universally acknowledged law from which no State could deviate (§1.4). Article 53 of the Vienna Convention on the Law of Treaties defines this term as a norm that is "accepted and recognized by the international community of States as a whole as a norm from which no derogation is permitted and which can be modified only by a subsequent norm of general international law having the same character." However, the VCLT does not define what constitutes such a norm.

Some jurists and commentators deny the functional existence of *jus cogens,* because even the most generally accepted rules have not achieved universality. Moscow State University's Professor Grigori Tunkin explains that the "arguments of opponents of *jus cogens* can be reduced to the fact that such principles are possible only in a well-organized and effective legal system, and since international law is not such a system, the existence of principles of general international law having the character of *jus cogens* is impossible."[46]

One can make a reasonable theoretical argument, however, that *jus cogens* would render certain treaties void. When two States have entered into a treaty in which they agree to invade another country, that agreement violates the most fundamental UN Charter article—Article 2.4's prohibition on the use of force in international relations. Such a treaty violates an undisputable Charter norm. Today, Stalin and Hitler's 1939 agreement to divide Europe could not legitimately circumvent the Article 2.4 prohibition of force.

VCLT Applied In 1997, the International Court of Justice adjudicated the following dispute between Hungary and Slovakia. Hungary relied on a number of Vienna Convention on the Law of Treaties provisions—all discussed in this section of the book—as its rationale for terminating its 1977 Budapest Treaty with Czechoslovakia.

Case Concerning the Gabcíkovo–Nagymaros Project (Hungary v. Slovakia)

INTERNATIONAL COURT OF JUSTICE, 1997

Go to course Web site at http://home.att.net/~slomansonb/txtcsesite.html; click on Hungary/Slovakia Treaty Breach Case.

◆ Notes

1. This particular ICJ opinion is enlightening, because it applies so many of the principles contained in the Vienna Convention on the Law of Treaties in a liti-

gious context based on arguments submitted by the respective parties. On the other hand, the Court's decision merely directed the parties to negotiate a final resolution in good faith to achieve the objectives of the 1977 treaty—rather than ordering the parties to take any *specific* action to build and complete this joint power project on the Danube.

2. The Court's "resolution" in this case found that both parties had breached the 1977 Budapest Treaty, while directing them to apply the principles announced in its opinion. They later initialed a draft Framework Agreement in March 1998. After the elections of March 1998, however, Hungary's new government disavowed the ICJ judgment's direction to fulfill Hungary's 1977 treaty obligations. Slovakia thus filed a request in September 1998, asking the court to render an additional judgment—because of Hungary's alleged unwillingness to actually implement the Court's "decision."

Limitations Suspension or termination is subject to some other limits. The severance of diplomatic or consular relations does not necessarily affect treaty rights and obligations. Article 2.3 of the Vienna Convention on Consular Relations (VCCR) provides that the "severance of *diplomatic* relations shall not *ipso facto* [automatically in and of itself] involve the severance of *consular* relations" (emphasis supplied). Article 45 of the VCCR expressly provides that a break in diplomatic relations does *not* alter the continuing obligation to honor treaty obligations that have nothing to do with diplomatic or consular matters. Therefore, war and other hostile relationships do not terminate all treaty obligations of parties to the conflict. States are expected to continue to perform their obligations under treaties like the Geneva Conventions of 1949 dealing with Red Cross assistance, the laws of war, and treatment of prisoners of war (Chapter 10).

Theory and practice, however, often diverge when nations are at war. The outbreak of war does not automatically terminate treaty obligations. The US war with Germany did not automatically terminate the 1923 US treaty obligation to transmit property of deceased individuals to German citizens.[47] A *prolonged* state of war often presents problems with the performance of treaty requirements, and continuing these obligations may make no sense.

◆ 8.3 UNITED STATES TREATY PRACTICE

Under *International Law,* there are two general rules regarding conflicting laws. One is that the UN Charter prevails when it conflicts with another international instrument.[48] The other is that a nation's internal law cannot be used as a defense to its breach of an international obligation.

This section deals with *US treaty practice.* It begins with two key components. The first is the significant distinction between the terms "treaty" and "executive agreement." Under International Law, all presidential executive agreements are treaties. Under US law, however, executive agreements are not necessarily treaties. The second major theme is the resolution of conflicts between treaties or executive agreements, the US Constitution, and federal statutes.

TREATY VERSUS EXECUTIVE AGREEMENT

As discussed in §8.2, *treaty* is a generic term that is often used synonymously with some three dozen words signifying an international agreement. Under *International* Law, the particular description of the international instrument does not affect its binding nature. Under US *internal* law, the word *treaty* has a narrower meaning. It has spawned scholarly debate and lawsuits between the legislative and executive branches of government. Certain US senators sued President Carter in 1977 over his use of executive agreement to relinquish US control of the Panama Canal rather than a treaty made with the consent of the Senate.

Under the US Constitution, the President makes all treaty commitments. But the term *treaty* technically refers only to those international agreements made by the President *with the consent of the Senate.* The President may also enter into "executive agreements" that do not require Senate approval. This *treaty* versus *executive agreement* distinction was spawned by early US practice under the Treaty Clause in Article II of the US Constitution. It provides that the President "shall have the Power, by and with the Advice and Consent of the Senate, to make Treaties, provided two-thirds of the Senators present concur. . . ." During the Constitutional

Convention of 1787, the House of Representatives was ultimately excluded from an express treaty-making role with the Senate as originally proposed. After debating the matter, the delegates acknowledged the widespread feeling that diplomatic negotiations required a degree of secrecy possible only in the smaller senatorial body (then twenty-six senators from thirteen colonies). The fervor of this debate effectively overshadowed the importance of what remained in the final draft of the Constitution—excluding the House and including the President.[49]

Almost immediately, US presidents—*without* seeking the consent of the Senate—began to enter into "executive agreements." This form of international treaty making was (and is) not a "treaty" under the US Constitution. This contrast evolved, in part, because the US Constitution does not define "treaties." When it was adopted in 1787, its drafters apparently saw no need to define a concept that was then well known in international practice.[50] The Treaty Clause has not been interpreted by the judicial branch of the US government to mean that the President *must* have the Senate's advice and consent for *all* international agreements. The President may thus enter into executive agreements, which do not require Senate approval.

During the early development of relations between the executive and congressional branches of government, two factors influenced the Senate to acquiesce in executive agreements, which were treaties made *without* its advice and consent. First, the relationship between the President and the Senate had evolved in favor of such action. Second, the Senate had to support the President's general management of foreign relations. It had no constitutional authority to negotiate directly with foreign governments—unlike the President, who is empowered to "make" treaties with other States (and now with international organizations).

Two types of executive agreement evolved. One is the *congressional*–executive agreement whereby the President can request approval of an executive agreement by a joint resolution of both houses of Congress. Columbia University Professor Louis Henkin presents the following vindication for this implied presidential power:

> Neither Congresses, nor Presidents, nor courts, have been seriously troubled by these conceptual difficulties and differences [between a *treaty* and an *executive* agreement]. Whatever their theoretical merits, it is now widely accepted that the Congressional–Executive agreement is available for wide use . . . and is a complete alternative to a treaty: The President can seek approval of any agreement by joint resolution of both houses of Congress rather than by two-thirds of the Senate. Like a treaty, such an agreement is the law of the land, superseding inconsistent state laws, as well as inconsistent provisions in earlier treaties, in other international agreements, or in acts of Congress.[51]

The other category of executive agreement is the *sole* executive agreement. While congressional approval for executive agreements is often sought, it has been completely avoided in some instances. The President has exercised the inherent power to incur an international obligation independently of the Senate (Article II treaty) or both houses of Congress (congressional–executive agreement). Columbia University Professor Oliver Lissitzyn succinctly describes the historical but troubled development of the President's executive agreement power:

> The making of executive agreements is a constitutional usage of long standing [that] apparently rests upon the President's vast but ill-defined powers in the fields of foreign relations and national defense. Neither the usage nor the decisions of courts, however, provide clear-cut guidance as to the *scope* of the treaty-making power and the scope of the executive agreement–making power [which] are not mutually exclusive. What may be properly accomplished by executive agreement may also be accomplished by treaty. . . .
>
> It is not believed that any attempt to delimit rigidly the scope of the executive agreement–making power is likely to be successful or to result in a correct portrayal or prediction of actual practice. Some writers, while refusing to regard the executive agreement–making power as co-extensive with the treaty-making power, wisely refrain from attempting to define the scope of the former. . . .
>
> It may be proper, therefore, to regard the executive agreement–making power as extending to all the occasions on which an international agreement is

believed by the Chief Executive to be necessary in the national interest, but on which resort to the treaty-making procedure is impracticable or likely to render ineffective an established national policy. The test here suggested is the only one that adequately accounts for the variety of situations in which the President, with or without the approval of Congress, has resorted to the executive-agreement procedure. It also accounts for the increasing frequency of resort to the executive-agreement method in recent years, with the growth of complexity in international affairs and of pressure of work in the Senate.[52]

The President has undertaken certain executive agreements both *before* and *after* seeking input from the legislative branch of the government. Some international agreements involved *prior* Senate or congressional approval, while others have been concluded with *subsequent* approval. This feature of the President's power in the field of foreign relations thus could be well defined as ill-defined. *Why* a particular agreement falls within one of these three categories is probably best explained by congressional acquiescence in presidential discretion when exercising control over foreign affairs.

Exhibit 8.1 illustrates the historical comparison between "treaties," in the constitutional sense of requiring the Senate's advice and consent, and "executive agreements," undertaken as either the congressional or sole variations of that term. It is readily evident that the executive agreement has far surpassed the treaty in terms of how the President exercises his or her power as the maker of international agreements.

EXHIBIT 8.1 EXECUTIVE AGREEMENT–TREATY COMPARISON

Era	"Executive Agreements"	Article II "Treaties"
1789–1799	0	8
1800–1899	115	312
1900–1932	388	411
1933–1979	8,405	550
Totals	8,908	1,281

Source: Adapted from L. Margolis, *Executive Agreement and Presidential Power in Foreign Policy* 108 (New York: Praeger, 1985).

The Senate has occasionally expressed concern about this spiraling use of executive agreements, which seem to be emasculating its constitutional role in the treaty-making process. The most heated debate occurred between 1952 and 1957. Senator John Bricker generated an intense challenge by his proposed amendment to the Constitution's Treaty Clause. He advocated that *all* international agreements by the US should become effective *only* when legislation passes in both the House of Representatives and the Senate. If he had been successful, the proposed constitutional amendment would have eliminated the President's ability to enter into *any* international agreement without express congressional approval. He or she would have been more of a negotiator than a maker of treaties.

Although the Bricker Amendment failed, Congress did pass the Case Act in 1972. It requires the President to advise Congress (in writing) of *all* international agreements made *without* the consent of the Senate *or* without a joint resolution of Congress. The President may believe that public disclosure would prejudice national security, however. In this instance, he or she may secretly enter into and later transmit a completed executive agreement to the Senate Committee on Foreign Relations and the House Committee on Foreign Affairs.[53]

The US Supreme Court has occasionally described but not really defined the scope of the President's executive agreement power. In a case growing out of President Carter's 1979 executive agreement with Iran—which ended the hostage crisis and provided a basis for resolving business claims against Iran—the Court characterized that general power as follows: "In addition to congressional acquiescence in the President's power to settle [such] claims, prior cases of this Court have also recognized that the President does have *some* measure of power to enter into executive agreements without obtaining the advice and consent of the Senate."[54]

The following case illustrates the difficulty in drawing a precise legal demarcation between the President's executive agreement power and the required Senate consent under the US Constitution.

Weinberger v. Rossi

SUPREME COURT OF THE UNITED STATES, 1982

456 US 25, 102 S.Ct. 1510, 71 *L. Ed.* 2d 715

Author's Note: *In 1968, President Johnson made an executive agreement with the Republic of the Philippines. It provided for the preferential employment of Filipino citizens at US military bases in the Philippines. Its purpose was to ensure the availability of suitable employees on those bases. The underlying rationale was that giving these jobs to local Filipino nationals would result in lower wage costs and less turnover in these positions. There was a comparatively limited pool of US citizens, typically military dependents, to work in these positions on foreign military bases. To accomplish this goal, the President decided to establish conditions favoring foreign nationals as employees on those bases.*

Three years later, Congress enacted a law prohibiting any employment discrimination against US citizens on US overseas military bases—unless a "treaty" expressly permitted such discrimination as necessary to the national interests of the US. Four more executive agreements followed, providing for preferential treatment of foreign citizens at various military bases overseas—after passage of the 1971 nondiscrimination legislation. However, none of them was submitted to the Senate for its advice and consent as required by the 1971 law.

In 1978, several US citizens working at one of the US naval bases in the Philippines were notified that their jobs had been converted into "local" positions (pursuant to the discrimination authorized by executive agreement with the Philippines). This meant that they would be discharged from their employment with the US Navy so that "local" Filipino citizens could obtain those "local" jobs. The Rossis and others who had lost their jobs sought reinstatement in their employment. They sued the US government (in the name of Secretary of Defense Weinberger) for violating the 1971 antidiscrimination statute.

The Supreme Court had to interpret the "treaty exception" in Section 106 of the statute. This legislation prohibited discrimination unless there was a "treaty" allowing such discrimination in favor of local nationals (as opposed to US military dependents). Did this exception mean that discrimination against US citizens would be permitted only under a "treaty"—in the constitutional sense of that term—that requires Senate consent to discriminate against US citizens abroad? Alternatively, did Congress intend to leave untouched the President's power to enter into an executive agreement permitting job discrimination? If the latter were the case, then an executive agreement would be a "treaty" for purposes of the federal nondiscrimination statute. In this sense, there would be no distinction between an "Article II treaty" and an executive agreement made only by the President without the Senate's consent.

The Supreme Court's task was to construe the federal statute, which provides as follows: "Unless prohibited by treaty, no person shall be discriminated against . . . in the employment of civilian personnel . . . in any foreign country because such person is a citizen of the United States or is a dependent of a member of the Armed Forces of the United States." Justice Rehnquist's opinion illustrates the difficulties with distinguishing between "treaties" and "executive agreements," in a very sensitive context with significant foreign policy ramifications.

COURT'S OPINION. Our task is to determine the meaning of the word "treaty" as Congress used it in this statute. Congress did not separately define the word, as it has done in other enactments. We must therefore ascertain as best we can whether Congress intended the word "treaty" to refer solely to [the Constitution's] Art. II, §2, cl. 2, "Treaties"—those international agreements concluded by the President with the advice and consent of the Senate—or whether Congress intended "treaty" to also include executive agreements such as the BLA [Base Labor Agreement permitting discrimination].

The word "treaty" has more than one meaning. Under principles of international law, the word ordinarily refers to an international agreement concluded between sovereigns, regardless of the manner in which the agreement is brought into force. Under the United States Constitution, of course, the word "treaty" has a far more restrictive meaning. Article II, §2, cl. 2, of that instrument provides that the President "shall have Power, by and with the Advice and Consent of the Senate, to make Treaties, provided two thirds of the Senators present concur."

Congress has not been consistent in distinguishing between Art. II treaties and other forms of international agreements. For example, in the Case Act, 1 U. S. C. §112b(a) [*see* analysis accompanying this text's note 48 above], Congress required the Secretary of State to "transmit to the Congress the text of any international agreement, other than a treaty, to which the United States is a party" no later than 60 days after "such agreement has entered into force." Similarly, Congress has explicitly referred to Art. II treaties in the Fishery Conservation and Management Act of 1976, 16 USC §1801, and the Arms Control and Disarmament Act, 22 USC §2551.

On the other hand, Congress has used "treaty" to refer only to international agreements *other than* Art. II treaties. In 39 USC §407(a), for example, Congress authorized the Postal Service, with the consent of the President, to "negotiate and conclude postal treaties or conventions." A "treaty" which requires *only* the consent of *the President* is not an Art. II treaty. It is not dispositive that Congress in §106 used the term "treaty" without specifically including international agreements that are not Art. II treaties [emphasis supplied]. . . .

Thus, if Congress intended to limit the "treaty exception" in §106 to Art. II treaties, it must have intended to repudiate these executive agreements that affect the hiring practices of the United States only at its military bases overseas. One would expect that Congress would be aware that executive agreements may represent a *quid pro quo* [bargained for exchange whereby] the host country grants the United States base rights in exchange for the preferential hiring of local nationals [of the host State]. . . .

At the time §106 was enacted, there were in force 12 agreements in addition to the BLA providing for preferential hiring of local nationals on United States military bases overseas. Since the time of the enactment of §106, four more such agreements have been concluded, and none of these were submitted to the Senate for its advice and consent. We think that some affirmative expression of congressional intent to abrogate the United States' international obligations is required in order to construe the word "treaty" in §106 as meaning only Art. II treaties. We therefore turn to what legislative history is available in order to ascertain whether such an intent may fairly be attributed to Congress.

The legislative history seems to us to indicate that Congress was principally concerned with the financial hardship to American servicemen which resulted from discrimination against American citizens at overseas bases. As the Conference Committee Report explains:

> "The purpose of [§106] is to correct a situation which exists at some foreign bases, primarily in Europe, where discrimination in favor of local nationals and against American dependents in employment has contributed to conditions of hardship for families of American enlisted men whose dependents are effectively prevented from obtaining employment."

The Conference Report, however, is entirely silent as to the scope of the "treaty" exception. Similarly, there is no mention of the 13 agreements that provided for preferential hiring of local nationals. Thus, the Conference Report provides no support whatsoever for the conclusion that Congress intended in some way to limit the President's use of international agreements that may discriminate against American citizens who seek employment at United States military bases overseas.

On the contrary, . . . Congress was not concerned with limiting the authority of the President to enter into executive agreements with the host country, but with the *ad hoc* decisionmaking of military commanders overseas. In early 1971 [just before Congress passed §106], Brig. Gen. Charles H. Phipps, Commanding General of the European Exchange System, issued a memorandum encouraging the recruitment and hiring of local nationals instead of United States citizens at the system's stores [on US military bases]. The hiring of local nationals, General Phipps reasoned, would result in lower wage costs and turnover rates. Senator Schweiker, a sponsor of §106, complained of General Phipps' policy [of discriminating against US nationals on US military bases in Europe]. . . .

While the question is not free from doubt, we conclude that the "treaty" exception contained in §106 extends to executive agreements as well as to Art. II treaties [characterizing these executive agreements as "treaties" for the purpose of authorizing discrimination against US nationals on foreign US military bases]. . . .

◆ *Notes & Questions*

1. The Supreme Court effectively "lent its hand" to the President's intentional discrimination against US citizens who hoped to work on US military bases abroad. This meant that military dependents, typically spouses of enlisted personnel with a generally lower

wage structure than that of military officers, would be unable to work—and in many cases thus unable to accompany their military spouses during overseas assignments. The intermediate appellate court decision, *Rossi v. Brown,* 206 US.App.D.C. 148 (1980), was overruled. If the Supreme Court's decision seemed unfair to US military dependents, then what was the countervailing rationale for promoting US interests?

2. The materials in this section suggest a two-part process for deciding whether the President's exercise of the executive agreement power transgresses any limits contained in the constitutional Treaty Clause or limiting congressional legislation (although *Rossi* did not interpret §106 of the antidiscrimination statute as posing a bar to the President's powers in this particular instance). First, the President (through the appropriate federal agency) must determine whether his or her proposed executive agreement falls within the parameters of the Treaty Clause—which may (or may not, per *Rossi)* require Senate consent. Second, the President must examine existing congressional legislation and attitudes to determine whether congressional approval should or must be obtained. As stated in the principal treatise on US constitutional law in the US—L. Tribe, "Treaties and Executive Agreements," in §§4–5 of *American Constitutional Law* 228–229 (2nd ed. Mineola, NY: Foundation Press, 1988):

> The precise scope of the President's power to conclude international agreements without the consent of the Senate is unresolved. At one extreme, the proposition that the treaty is the exclusive medium for affecting foreign policy goals and, consequently, that executive agreements are ultra vires [unconstitutional] seems adequately refuted. . . .
>
> At the other extreme, the notion that executive agreements know no constitutional bounds proves equally bankrupt. Executive agreements, no less than treaties, must probably be limited to appropriate subject matter. The more difficult question is whether there exist species of international accord that may take the form of a treaty, but not that of an executive agreement.

SUPREME LAW OF THE LAND

The treaty versus executive agreement distinction is just one of the major problems in US treaty practice. Another involves a conflict between the US Constitution or a federal statute on the one hand, and a clear international treaty commitment on the other hand. In parts of Europe, Mexico, and certain other regions, treaties *must* take precedence over internal law in the event of a conflict.[55] The constitutions of Burkina Faso, Congo, Mauritania, and Senegal expressly provide that a treaty is superior to internal law—although there is apparently no reported judicial decision that affirms this elevated status.

An internal law of the US may occasionally clash with and supersede a prior international agreement. This portion of the book addresses the resolution of such conflicts under *US* law—as opposed to *International* Law, where a State may not rely on its internal law to avoid international obligations.

The US Constitution does not provide a direct answer to the resolution of such conflicts. Article VI provides only that the "Constitution, and the Laws of the United States [federal statutes] which shall be made in Pursuance thereof and all Treaties made . . . shall be the supreme Law of the Land. . . ." This wording does not establish any relative hierarchy in the event of a conflict.

For this conflict to arise, the treaty in question must, of course, be a part of US national law. This can be accomplished in several ways: The US might consent to a self-executing treaty, the Congress might enact legislation that implements a treaty previously signed by the US, or the President might enter into an executive agreement with another country.

Treaty Versus Constitution The US Supreme Court has consistently held that the Constitution prevails when it conflicts with legislation or treaties. Both a federal statute *and* a treaty (executive agreement) were in conflict with the Constitution in the 1957 case of *Reid v. Covert.*[56] The Court held that civilian wives who had killed their military husbands on US bases in England and Japan could not be tried by a military court-martial. The Supreme Court examined several distinct sources of US law to arrive at this conclusion. The Uniform Code of Military Justice (UCMJ) is federal legislation that provided then for a court-martial in this situation. Presidential executive agreements governing crimes occurring on US bases abroad incorporated these provisions of the Uniform Code—making them expressly applicable to military dependents. The court found that neither the Military Justice Code nor the executive agreements could deny the spouses' constitutional rights to indictment by a civilian grand jury and to a jury trial by their peers. These rights, enshrined in the US Constitution, could not be vacated by either the federal statute (UCMJ) or an executive agreement (applying the UCMJ to military dependents abroad).

Treaty Versus Statute Treaties and federal statutes are on equal footing under Article VI of the Constitution. Each is therein referred to as the "supreme law of the land." Neither is superior to the other under the Constitution's express terms. The US Supreme Court applies the following rule: "The last in time prevails." As stated in the above *Reid* decision, the Court has "repeatedly taken the position that an Act of Congress . . . is on full parity with a treaty, and that when a statute which is subsequent in time is inconsistent with a treaty, the statute to the extent of conflict renders the treaty null."[57] This position was reaffirmed in 1998 when the Court construed the 1996 Antiterrorism and Effective Death Penalty Act as foreclosing a Paraguayan defendant from appealing the failure of the Virginia state court system to notify Paraguay of his arrest and detention. Such notification is required by the 1963 Vienna Convention on Consular Relations (*see* §7.2 for the full case).[58]

Thus, under the internal law of the US, Congress may *denounce* treaties. In its comprehensive Anti-Apartheid Act of 1986, Congress expressly repudiated a presidential executive agreement providing for air service with South Africa (prior to the improvement in international relations when the white minority government stepped down from power in 1993).[59]

Yet another related conflict may arise. The internal laws of the US may be incompatible with *customary* International Law not expressed in a treaty. The practice of States is a major source of this category of International Law (§1.4). However, US courts will not necessarily apply it. US courts must adhere to the will of the US Congress as expressed in federal legislation. If Congress intended that a US statute violate the customary practice of States, then a US judge must follow the will of Congress.

US courts do not *blindly* apply internal law, however, when to do so would unnecessarily conflict with International Law. Judges presume, where the legislation they are interpreting is not unrelenting, that Congress did not *intend* to violate International Law when enacting a federal statute. This presumption is often used to interpret US legislation in a way that avoids violations of the customary practice of States. This presumption cannot be invoked, however, if Congress unmistakably intended to disregard some principle of customary international law. (*Larsen* case, §6.3—where Congress implicitly intended the application of US drug laws on the High Seas.)

The applicability of this presumption was aptly articulated in a 1925 Prohibition-era rum-running case:

> If we assume for the present that the national legislation has, by its terms, made the acts complained of a crime against the United States . . . then there is no discretion vested in the federal court, once it obtains jurisdiction, to decline enforcement [on the basis of a violation of International Law]. International practice is law only in so far as we adopt it, and like all common or statute law it bends to the will of the Congress . . . [because] it . . . follow[s] that in construing the terms and provisions of a statute it [the court] may . . . assume that such principles were on the national conscience and that the congressional act did not deliberately intend to infringe them. In other words, unless it unmistakably appears that a congressional act was intended to be in disregard of a principle of international comity, the presumption is that it was intended to be in conformity with it.[60]

Likewise, legislation by the individual political subdivisions within the federated system of states may not override the will of Congress. In a US Supreme Court case directly on point, the state of Missouri could not properly pass legislation that effectively controlled matters that fell within the federal government's treaty power. Missouri could not purport to control the hunting laws regarding migratory birds while they were en route from Canada, through the US, to Mexico and other countries. This is a matter that squarely fell within the *national* treaty power, which had already taken priority over the right of Missouri to control the people and things (migratory animals) temporarily within its boundaries.[61]

◆ 8.4 ECONOMIC COERCION CASE STUDY

INTRODUCTION

Arab nations began their boycott of Israeli products shortly after World War II. The details are provided below. This scenario will be used to analyze and review materials contained in this chapter. This boycott serves as a useful basis for analyzing the nature and scope of international treaty commitments in a context adapted from this very real-world scenario. For nearly fifty years, it has been a vivid reminder of how the treaty system can be used for the most sensitive of political purposes: to drive a nation out of existence. In the late 1998 Washington-brokered peace effort, Israel and the PLO finally agreed about the removal of the clause from the 1964 Palestinian Charter, which called for the dismantling of Israel.

Several events have impacted the solidarity once enjoyed by the twenty-one member States of the Arab League (§3.5). Egypt broke ranks with the League by its decision to meet with Israel—incident to the 1979 "Camp David" agreements, which were facilitated by US President Carter near Washington, D.C. A dozen years later, Kuwait was no longer interested in the Arab boycott of Israeli goods in the aftermath of the Persian Gulf War when it was rescued from Iraqi conquest. That particular war pitted various Arab League members against its own League member Iraq. The 1993 Washington Peace Accords between PLO Chairman Yasir Arafat and Israeli Prime Minister Yitzhak Rabin presented an important breakthrough for ending the Arab boycott of Israel—which threatened international relations in the Middle East for more than four decades.

For the purpose of the following problem, assume that the Arab League boycott is still in existence and as tangible as it was before the 1993 Washington peace accords. This assumption is not totally hypothetical. In 1997, US Defense Secretary William Cohen learned that the Air Force was excluding Jews from working for a private contractor on a US military base in Saudi Arabia. That predicament was spawned by the Arab boycott of Israel. Given the US law that prohibits compliance with that discriminatory boycott, the Secretary ordered all US military installations to ensure strict compliance with the US anti-discrimination law designed to counter the effects of the Boycott.

ESSENTIAL FACTS

Members of the Council of the Arab League of Nations drafted and unanimously approved the 1954 Unified Law on the Boycott of Israel. The Council was composed of State representatives from each State in the League. The Council was established to promote cooperation through periodic meetings of the foreign ministers of each Arab State. The Arab States agreed to prohibit the purchase of Israeli exports when they approved the Unified Law as follows:

> (1) All persons within the enacting country [in the Arab League] are forbidden to conclude any agreement or transaction, directly or indirectly with any person or organization (i) situated in Israel; (ii) affiliated with Israel through nationality; or (iii) working for or on behalf of Israel, regardless of the place of business or residence; and
>
> (2) Importation into the enacting country [adopting this boycott] is forbidden of all Israeli goods, including goods manufactured elsewhere [outside of Israel] containing ingredients or components of Israeli origin or manufacture.

All League members implemented the Unified Law adopted by the Council in 1954. Their national legislation contains only minor variations from the above terms. Saudi Arabia's version, for example, provides as follows:

> **Code of Regulation for the Boycott of Israel**
> 1(a). All persons, whether natural or legal [meaning corporate entities], are prohibited from concluding, whether directly or through an intermediary, any covenant with any entities or persons resident in Israel, of Israeli nationality, or working for . . . Israel, wherever they may reside.
>
> 2(a). The introduction or importation of Israeli goods, merchandise, and products of all kinds, or of financial documents or other negotiable instruments into the [Saudi] Kingdom is prohibited. . . .

In 1972, the Arab League announced a revision of the boycott law called the General Principles for the Boycott of Israel. This version retained the broad language of the original agreement and supplemented it by imposing three specific categories of prohibitions. A *primary* boycott bars Arab nations from exporting goods to and importing goods from Israel. A *secondary* boycott generally bans trade between League members and countries that trade with Israel. Israel's trading partners are thus placed on a blacklist that limits their ability to trade with nations in the Arab League. A *tertiary* boycott further discourages trade with Israel. League members may not deal with companies that do any business with blacklisted countries, such as a company contracted to supply buses to Saudi Arabia. When the Saudis learned that the seats were made by another firm located in a blacklisted country, they threatened to cancel the bus order. The bus manufacturer then substituted seats with those made by a different firm *not* located in a blacklisted country. The Saudis decided that the contract was acceptable, and the buses were delivered to Saudi Arabia.[62]

The League's Unified Law further prohibits trade with persons "affiliated with Israel through nationality." Some commentators asserted that this language was a euphemism for persons of the Jewish faith. If so, the Arab boycott applies to all Jewish-owned businesses, wherever they are located throughout the world. Some States, including the US, passed legislation to *punish compliance* with this boycott. League members rejected this characterization of the boycott. The above-quoted Saudi version of the Unified Law, for example, prohibits trade with persons "of Israeli nationality." The Saudi statute differs from the text of the Arab League's Uniform Law. It is *not* susceptible to the argument that it conceals racism directed at *all* Jews, wherever they may reside. The Saudi law merely limits trade with Israeli citizens without regard to ethnic background or "affiliation with" Israel.[63]

The Arab boycott of Israel has been a comparatively hostile form of non-military pressure. Travelers in the Middle East were not surprised to see lists at airport customs booths listing Israeli-made goods or those from "offending" countries that dealt with Israel that travelers could not bring into the port of entry.

Boycotts are not, of course, unique to the Middle East. Economic boycotts and embargoes have been used by other countries as an alternative to military coercion. The US, for example, has participated in boycotts against Cuba, Iran, Nicaragua, North Korea, and Vietnam. The UN has established its own boycotts. The international boycott of South Africa was based in part on UN resolutions that condemned apartheid.

◆ *Problem*

Based upon the above facts and materials presented in this chapter, respond to the following questions. The section number(s) indicate which part of the chapter is most directly applicable to the particular question:

1. Is the Unified Law on the Boycott of Israel and related General Principles a treaty? *See* §8.1 for definitions.
2. There are several categories of treaties. How should this treaty be classified? *See* §8.1 on classification and §8.2 on formation and performance.
3. Assume that it is 1955, one year after passage of the Arab League's Unified Law. Saudi Arabia has just adopted the boycott agreement (the Unified Law), which prohibits trade with persons "affiliated with Israel through nationality." Saudi Arabia, however, submits a reservation to the League at the time it registers its consent to accept its obligations. The Saudi version of the Unified Law is a prohibition against trade with "persons of Israeli nationality who are residents of Israel." This language was carefully chosen to avoid any implication of *worldwide* discrimination against Jewish businesses. Assume that the League's Unified Law is a treaty. Does Saudi Arabia's reservation permit it to become a party to the Unified Law? What test would decide this question? *See* §8.2 on formation.
4. Assume that the League's boycott agreement was not self-executing. Assume further that one of the States in the Arab League, State X, has a constitutional system like that of the United States. State X's leader must obtain the consent of X's legislative body to enter into certain treaties—but not all treaties. Would that leader be more likely to use an executive agreement or an Article II treaty to implement the boycott? *See* §8.3 on United States Treaty Practice.
5. Egypt was a member of the Arab League and a party to the original boycott agreement of 1954. Egypt terminated its participation in the boycott in 1979, incident to the US-brokered Camp David agreement described in the background for this problem. Under International Law, did Egypt have a basis for terminating its boycott obligations? *See* §8.2 on termination, suspension, and invalidity.

◆ SUMMARY

1. Under International Law, the term *treaty* is a generic one, describing many forms of international agreement. Legal distinctions as to treaty names or designations relate primarily to the way in which the treaty is made. All such commitments are binding under International Law.
2. There are some political reasons for seeking flexibility in international agreements—a factor that mili-

tates against a rigid approach that advocates a formal treaty process for all international agreements. Nevertheless, the uniform State expectations about treaty formation and observance issues are contained in the Vienna Convention on the Law of Treaties. It defines the term *treaty* as a "written" agreement between states that is governed by International Law. A treaty need not be written, however, to be binding. No multilateral instrument yet governs oral agreements.

3. Treaties may be classified as (a) oral or written, (b) bilateral or multilateral, (c) lawmaking or contractual, or (d) self-executing or statements of principle. The difference between a bilateral and multilateral treaty is the number of participants. Unlike law*making* treaties, contractual treaties are not intended to *create* rules of International Law. Self-executing treaties create immediate legal obligations. Some treaties contain only declarations of principle that merely set goals or standards of achievement for the participating States.
4. The treaty process consists of several essential stages: negotiations, signature, ratifications, reservations, entry into force, and registration.
5. The negotiations stage will hopefully result in the production of a final treaty text that is acceptable in principle to all conference delegates. Subsequent State acceptance typically involves a two-stage process. The first stage is provisional acceptance. This means that the final draft is acceptable in principle to the treaty-drafting participants. The second stage is the post-conference ratification by each nation.
6. A reservation is a limitation on a State's acceptance of the obligations expressed in the final draft of a multilateral treaty. The reserving State expresses its general consent to be bound by the treaty. But its final acceptance is limited by the terms of its reservation. Other States that give their consent without any like reservation are bound by all of the terms of the final draft of the treaty in their relevant expectations regarding one another's conduct governed by treaty terms.
7. A reservation must be *compatible* with the object and purpose of the treaty. By permitting reservations, member States encourage the widest participation for attaining the objectives of a multilateral treaty.
8. Various conditions may invalidate a treaty, including the use of force. "Invalidity" may also arise in the context of the so-called equal and unequal treaties. Unequal treaties are *imposed* on one of the parties. There is no fair exchange of treaty rights and obligations. One State *must* accept what the other State or States demand. Under the Vienna Convention on the Law of Treaties, a treaty is invalid when the threat or use of force violates "principles of international law embodied in the Charter of the United Nations." At the close of the Vienna Conference, the participants declared (in a separate document) that economic, military, and political coercion was specifically unacceptable. Not all States adhere to the more specific definition of force in that post-conference Declaration.
9. US treaty practice distinguishes between treaties and executive agreements, both of which are equally binding under *International* Law. Under US law, the Constitution provides that the President cannot enter into a treaty without Senate approval. The President can nevertheless make an executive agreement without Senate consent. Presidents often obtain some form of congressional approval for treaty agreements, although none will be sought in matters that are not sensitive exercises of this inherent presidential power.
10. The US Constitution overrides conflicting federal statutes and international treaties. Statutes and treaties, on the other hand, are on equal footing. In the event of a conflict, the latest in time prevails. US courts presume that where the intent of Congress is unclear, its legislation is *not* designed to intentionally violate International Law. Where such intent *is* clear, however, US courts must apply subsequent federal legislation that violates either an earlier treaty or customary International Law.

◆ PROBLEMS

Problem 8.A (§8.1, after *Asakura* Case) Refer to the 1980 *Hostage Case* from the International Court of Justice and the 1961 Diplomatic Relations Convention provisions—both set forth in §7.4 of the text. Answer the following questions, based on the materials in §8.1:

1. Did the Diplomatic Convention's articles have to be "self-executing" for the US to claim that Iran breached that treaty?
2. *Are* those provisions self-executing? Can this be answered by reading the given articles? Based on the *Sei Fujii* and *Asakura* cases, how would you resolve

the question of whether the Diplomatic Relations treaty is self-executing?

Problem 8.B (§8.2, after *Reservations* Case) Article 17(2) of the 1969 Vienna Convention on the Law of Treaties states that when "it appears from the . . . object and purpose of the treaty that the application of the treaty *in its entirety* between all the parties is an *essential condition* of the consent of each one to be bound by the treaty, a reservation requires acceptance by *all* the parties" (italics added). VCLT Article 19(1)(a) provides that the legal effect of a reservation is that it "[m]odifies for the reserving state the provisions of the treaty to which the reservation relates to the extent of the reservation."

Assume the following facts: La Luce del Pueblo—meaning "Light of the People," or LLP—is an ultra-radical group of citizens within a hypothetical Caribbean State called Haven. Last September, Haven's military leader placed the LLP in charge of guarding some kidnapped US citizens. They were being held incommunicado during hostilities with the US. Without authority from the country's leader, some members of LLP decided to mistreat the US citizens. Several were beaten. One was brutally murdered. His body was then dumped on the steps of the US embassy in Haven, where journalists had gathered to learn about the latest developments in the ongoing hostilities.

A number of foreign newspapers printed a picture of the body of the dead US citizen on the US embassy steps. Their news story about the beatings and execution assigned responsibility to "LLP, the zealous group of Haven idealists who say that they resent the decades of the US dominance in hemispheric affairs." The newspaper account included LLP's statement to these journalists: "We plan, for the benefit of the People's Revolutionary Party (led by Haven's military leader), to eliminate all US citizens in Haven who hinder our progress." Subsequently, US citizens were randomly attacked and beaten in Haven's restaurants and bars. Nationals from other countries were not harmed in these incidents. Haven's leader denied any involvement with what he characterized as "an idealistic, but irresponsible splinter group of radicals to be dealt with *if found.*" Worldwide media attention now focused on Haven and its growing confrontation with the US.

Some US senators thus stated for the *Congressional Record* that "Haven had added genocide to the long list of international obligations breached by Haven in the last decade. Haven has failed to adhere to the bilateral treaties between the two nations, to the wishes of the Organization of American States, and to the unmistakable minimum standards of international behavior." Under the Genocide Convention, genocide is the killing of members of a particular ethnic group with the intent to destroy it.

Under US–Haven treaties, murder is an extraditable offense. Last October, the US Department of State demanded that Haven extradite those responsible for killing the US citizen so that they could be tried either in the US or in some international tribunal for the crime of genocide. Haven refused this extradition request because "those who have killed the US citizen may have committed murder, but they are not thereby responsible for genocide."

Assume that Haven, attempting to show its solidarity with the world community, chooses this point in time to become a party to the Genocide Convention. Haven tenders its consent to the appropriate international authority. It also submits the following reservation: "Haven hereby adopts the Genocide Convention as binding. Haven reserves the sovereign right, however, to use *any* means at its disposal to eliminate external threats to Haven's territorial integrity."

Is it possible for Haven to tender this reservation to the Genocide Convention? Specifically, is this reservation permissible under the ICJ's *Reservations Case* and the Vienna Convention on the Law of Treaties?

Problem 8.C (§8.2, after "Invalidity" Materials) In 1980, the Vienna Convention on the Law of Treaties became effective because the minimum number of national ratifications were deposited with the UN. During the negotiating process, US hostages initially remained captive in the American embassy and, for most of the time, at other locations in Iran. The US and Iran had no direct diplomatic relations. Algeria assisted US President Jimmy Carter in negotiating a treaty with Iran to secure the liberation of these hostages. They were released in exchange for the release of Iranian assets in the US, which had been frozen by Carter near the outset of the crisis. The US also agreed to return assets subject to its control that belonged to the family of the former Shah of Iran. Various documents about that treaty and related matters are reprinted in 20 *Int'l Legal Mat'ls* 223–240 (1981). A criticism of the US Department of State's decision *not* to raise the question of force in this particular treaty process is presented in *Iranian Hostage Agreements,* in Malawer book, p. 27 (cited in note 23 of this chapter).

A very sensitive provision of this treaty required arbitration of any subsequent disputes related to the "Hostage Crisis." This provision precluded the hostages, their families, or any governmental entity from suing Iran in the US, the International Court of Justice, or anywhere else. President Carter's economic sanctions were not working, and he did not want to undertake further military action to retrieve the hostages from Iran, after a failed rescue attempt in 1979. Instead, he entered into an executive agreement to resolve this crisis and obtain the guaranteed safety of the hostages. Subsequent suits by several hostages were dismissed by US courts on the basis of the President's agreement not to permit suits against Iran that were spawned by the Hostage Crisis.

Assume that the US Senate is debating the propriety of President Carter's negotiations that led to the executive agreement between the US and Iran. The topic of this hypothetical Senate debate is *not* whether the Senate's advice and consent were necessary for the hostage-release agreement with Iran. The Senate has decided that the US will not rely on any of its internal laws as a basis for avoiding this treaty's obligations to Iran. The Senate has instead chosen to debate whether it can avoid the US obligations under the treaty on the basis that the President had to enter into the hostage-release treaty under duress.

Senator Dove represents a number of colleagues who do not wish to alter or negate the effect of the President's arrangement with Iran. They do not want to risk renewed hostilities or create the impression that America goes back on its obligations. Dove contends that "there was no physical, military, or economic coercion that forced this powerful nation into President Carter's treaty. It was the *United States* that employed forceful tactics, rather than Iran, when Carter's military rescue mission failed."

Senator Hawk represents an opposing group of senators. She and her colleagues hope to refreeze Iranian money accounts and gold bullion still within the US or controlled by private US businesses in foreign countries. She wants to renew the *Hostage* case litigation in a separate phase in the International Court of Justice. (*See* §7.4 for excerpts from the ICJ case involving the Court's order that Iran free the US hostages.) Relying on Article 52 of the Vienna Convention on the Law of Treaties, Hawk believes that the ICJ should render an authoritative decision characterizing the hostage treaty as invalid on the basis of duress.

Senator Hawk thus contends that "the Iranian treaty would never have seen the light of day if we were not forced into it by the hostage situation. Senator Dove's litmus test for validating the treaty is an imaginary bright line that separates military and nonmilitary coercion in all circumstances. "The proper approach, in my opinion, is to invalidate the Iranian deal by distinguishing between *lawful* and *unlawful* coercion—rather than Senator Dove's approach, which isolates military duress [to invalidate the treaty] from nonmilitary duress [whereby the treaty would be unaffected]."

Make the following assumptions: (a) Iran is a party to the Vienna Convention on the Law of Treaties; (b) it did not make any reservations; (c) the hostages have been released, but the Iranian assets are still available for seizure; (d) the Carter hostage release agreement was made *after* the January 27, 1980, "start" date for the prospective applicability of the VCLT. Two students will present the arguments that Senators Dove and Hawk might use in their Senate debate on the applicability of the VCLT. Can the US void its treaty obligations to Iran under President Carter's executive agreement?

Problem 8.D (§8.2, after *Fisheries Jurisdiction* Case) The US and the hypothetical Latin American State of Estado entered into the 1953 Treaty of Friendship, Commerce, and Navigation (FCN). This general treaty initiated their international relationship and covered a number of details. In the relevant treaty clause, the US agreed that Estado could nationalize American business interests. In return, Estado was required to provide reasonable compensation, which was defined in the treaty as "the fair market value of all nationalized assets."

The US–Estado relationship turned sour in the 1990s. The government of Estado nationalized a major US corporation's property in Estado with no compensation. Estado resisted the US claim of entitlement to compensation under the 1953 friendship treaty. Estado's Minister of State issued the following statement:

> A fundamental change in circumstances has precluded the continued viability of the 1953 FCN Treaty. The 1974 United Nations Declaration on the Establishment of a New International Economic

Order obviously necessitates termination of the compensation requirements of the outmoded US–Estado FCN Treaty [*see* §4.4 of this text on the NIEO]. The changed circumstance is that our nation, so rich in natural resources, need no longer fall prey to another nation's multinational enterprises. The United States corporation has plundered untold billions of dollars in excessive profits from the very core of Estado, and all of the profits have been repatriated back into the United States rather than benefiting the Estado economy. The content of International Law was developed by powerful nations over the many centuries before Estado even existed. It is a self-perpetuating vehicle used by countries like the United States to justify its asserted right to compensation in the amount of the "fair market value" of nationalized property. Due to changed circumstances, Estado may reasonably justify its refusal to pay *any* compensation to a corporation that has already acquired much more than it could ever repay to Estado. As a showing of good faith on the part of my Government, Estado will not seek reimbursement in an international forum, settling instead for the fair market value of the nationalized assets, which is only a small fraction of what the United States enterprise has already taken from the people of Estado.

Can Estado properly invoke the doctrine of *rebus sic stantibus* to terminate its treaty obligation to repay fair market value for nationalizing the US corporation?

Problem 8.E (end of §8.2) Refer to Problem 8.D above. Assume that Estado later repealed *all* treaty commitments with the US after the US senators widely condemned its nationalization of the US corporate property. *Questions:* (1) Is the US now required to perform its obligations under any treaty with Estado? (2) Does the US have any remedies under the Vienna Convention on the Law of Treaties?

◆ BIBLIOGRAPHY

§8.1 Definition and Classification

D. Johnson, *Consent and Commitment in the World Community: The Classification and Analysis of International Instruments* (Irvington-on-Hudson, NY: Transnational, 1997).

M. McDougal et al., *The Interpretation of Agreements and World Public Order* (New Haven, CT: Yale Univ. Press, 1967).

§8.2 Formation, Performance, Cessation

F. Horn, *Reservations and Interpretive Declarations to Multilateral Treaties* (The Hague, Neth.: T.M.C. Asser Inst. 1988).

A. McNair, *The Law of Treaties* (Oxford, Eng.: Clarendon Press, 1961).

"Note: Effect of Duress on Iranian Hostage Settlement Agreement," 14 *Vanderbilt J. of Transnat'l Law* 847 (1981).

S. Rosenne, *Breach of Treaty* (Cambridge, Eng.: Grotius, 1985).

S. Rosenne, *The Law of Treaties—A Guide to the Legislative History of the Vienna Convention* (Dobbs Ferry, NY: Oceana, 1970).

A. Vamvoukos, *Termination of Treaties in International Law: The Doctrines of* Rebus Sic Stantibus *and* Desuetude [Acquiescence] (Oxford, Eng.: Clarendon Press, 1985).

Wehberg, "Pacta Sunt Servanda," 53 *American Journal of International Law* 775 (1975).

P. Wesley-Smith, *Unequal Treaty: 1898–1997* (rev. ed. Hong Kong: Oxford Univ. Press, 1984).

§8.3 United States Treaty Practice

M. Glennon, "The Senate Role in Treaty Ratification," 77 *Amer. J. Int'l Law* 257 (1983).

L. Henkin et al. (eds.), *Foreign Affairs and the US Constitution* (Ardsley-on-Hudson, NY: Transnat'l, 1990).

E. Surrency, "How the United States Perfects an International Agreement," 85 *Law Library Journal* 343 (1993).

§8.4 Economic Coercion Case Study

P. Areeda, "Remarks on the Arab Boycott," 54 *Texas Law Review* 1432 (1976).

◆ ENDNOTES

1. Comment (2) to Art. 2, "Int'l L. Comm'n Commentary on the Vienna Convention on the Law of Treaties," in "Official Documents-United Nations Reports of the International Law Commission," 61 *Amer. J. Int'l L.* 248, 287 (1967) (hereinafter "Commentaries").
2. **Harvard study:** "Draft Convention on the Law of Treaties," 29 *Amer. J. Int'l L.* 652, 712 (Supp., 1935). **Multiple terms:** A comprehensive table depicting these terms, with accompanying details, is available in D. Myers, "The Names and Scope of Treaties," 51 *Amer. J. Int'l L.* 574, 576 (1957). **ILC study:** "Commentaries," Comment (3) to Art. 2, p. 288 (cited in note 1 above). **VCLT definition:** The text of this convention is reprinted in 63 *Amer. J. Int'l L.* 875 (1969) and 8 *Int'l Legal Mat'ls* 679 (1969) (hereinafter VCLT).
3. **European Community:** M. Kaniel, *The Exclusive Treaty-Making Power of the European Community up to the Period of the Single European Act* (The Hague: Kluwer, 1996). **Vienna Convention:** UN Gen. Ass. Doc. A/CONF.129/15 of March 20, 1986, reprinted in P. Menon, *The Law of Treaties Between States and International Organizations* 159 (Lewiston, NY: Edwin Mellon Press, 1992) (hereinafter Organizational Treaty).

4. A. Gasis, "Preface" to E. Raftopoulos, *The Inadequacy of the Contractual Analogy in the Law of Treaties* XIII (Athens: Hellenic Inst. Int'l & Foreign Law, 1990) (hereinafter *Contractual Analogy).*
5. R. Phillimore, 2 *Commentaries Upon International Law* 99 (3rd ed. London: Butterworths, 1892).
6. **Scientific approach:** "The Public Law View of Treaties in the 19th and the Early 20th Century," ch. 5 in *Contractual Analogy* 151 (cited in note 4 above). **Informal approach:** "Treaty-Like Instruments: An Overview," ch. 1 in J. Klabbers, *The Concept of Treaty in International Law* 27 (The Hague: Kluwer, 1996).
7. *See* S. Reisenfeld & F. Abbott (eds.), *Parliamentary Participation in the Making and Operation of Treaties: A Comparative Study* (Dordrecht, Neth.: Martinus Nijhoff, 1994).
8. "Status of Eastern Greenland *(Denmark v. Norway),*" 1933 *PCIJ,* ser. A/B, No. 53.
9. L. Sohn, "International Law Implications of the 1994 Agreement," 88 *Amer. J. Int'l L.* 696, 701–702 (1994).
10. The general rule against creation of third-party obligations is exhaustively examined in C. Chinkin, "States as Third Parties to Treaties: Formal Prescriptions," ch. 2 in *Third Parties in International Law* 25 (Oxford, Eng.: Clarendon Press, 1993). Potential exceptions are also addressed in A. Verdross, *Volkerrecht* 143-144 (5th ed. Vienna: Springer Verlag, 1964). An English-language statement of the Verdross Position is provided in G. I. Tunkin, *Theory of International Law* 93 (Cambridge, MA: Harv. Univ. Press, 1974) (Butler translation from Russian language) (hereinafter Tunkin treatise).
11. P. Reuter, *Introduction to the Law of Treaties* 20 (2d ed. London: Pinter Pub., 1989) (Mico & Haggenmacher translation).
12. An account of this event is provided in 4 G. Hackworth, *Digest of International Law* 467 (Wash., DC: US Gov't Print. Off., 1942).
13. *See* "Commentaries," Articles 10–12, at 303–313 (VCLT, cited in note 2 above). These terms are defined in Articles 9–13 of the final text of the VCLT.
14. J. L. Brierly, *The Law of Nations* 319–320 (Waldock 6th ed. London: Oxford Univ. Press, 1963) (hereinafter Brierly treatise).
15. **Treaty:** UN Doc. A/Conf. 164/37 (1995), reprinted in 34 *Int'l Legal Mat'ls* 1542 (1995). **Senate reaction:** "[T]he Senate's approval of this treaty should not be construed as a precedent for acquiescence to future treaties containing such a provision." Dep't State Files L/T, discussed in 90 *Amer. J. Int'l L.* 270 (1996).
16. "Convention on the Prevention and Punishment of the Crime of Genocide of December 9, 1948," 78 *UN Treaty Series* 277 (1951).
17. **States:** VCLT, Art. 80.1 (cited in note 2 above). **Organizations:** Organizational Treaty, Art. 81.1 (cited in note 3).
18. This UN publication, approaching nearly 1,500 print volumes, is available in electronic form at www.un.org/Depts/Treaty. While there is currently no charge for accessing this Web site, the UN will be charging a fee after a trial period. Researchers can still obtain no-cost electronic versions of the major multilateral treaties from online university collections and the Web pages of individual professors. *See,* for example, this book's course Web page for links to the major treaties discussed in the course at http://home.att.net/~slomansonb/txtcsesite.html and http://home.att.net/~slomansonb/intlweb.html; scroll down to "Education-University Home Pages" and "Treaties."
19. 1 *US Code* §112.
20. UN Web site: www.un.org.
21. **Grotius:** 2 *De Jure Belli Ac Pacis* [The Law of War and Peace] 394 (Kelsey translation, Wash., DC: Carnegie Endowment for Int'l Peace, 1925). **E. de Vattel:** 3 *Le Droit de Gens ou Principes de la Loi Naturelle* [The Law of Nations or Principles of Natural Law] 165 (Wash., DC: Carnegie Endowment for Int'l Peace, 1916 reprint of 1758 treatise). **American author:** H. Halleck, *International Law* 196 (San Francisco: Bancroft, 1861).
22. **Treaty of Paris:** An account of this event and its related treaty validity problems is provided in the Brierly treatise at 332–333 (cited in note 14 above). **Treaty of Versailles:** This treaty and its consequences are described in C. Fenwick, *International Law* 531–532 (4th ed. New York: Appleton, 1965) (Fenwick translation from the French) (hereinafter Fenwick treatise). **Hitler treaty:** A detailed account of the events is provided in G. Von Glahn, *Law Among Nations* 479–480 (7th ed. Boston: Allyn and Bacon, 1996).
23. H. Chiu, "Comparison of the Nationalist and Communist Chinese Views of Unequal Treaties," in J. Cohen (ed.), *China's Practice of International Law: Some Case Studies* 241–242 (Cambridge, MA: Harv. Univ. Press, 1972) (footnotes omitted). A brief assessment and criticism of the Soviet writers on this subject is available in S. Malawer, "Soviets and Unequal Treaties," in *Essays on International Law,* at 101 (Buffalo, NY: Hein, 1986) (hereinafter Malawer book).
24. "Fisheries Jurisdiction *(U.K. v. Iceland),*" 1973 *ICJ Rep.* 1, 14 (decided after 1969 VCLT conference and before 1980 effective date).
25. **Communist, African position:** An account of the varied perspectives of the participants is available in R. Kearney & R. Dalton, "The Treaty on Treaties," 64 *Amer. J. Int'l L.* 495, 532–535 (1970) (hereinafter "Treaty on Treaties" article). **"Force" left undefined:** "Commentaries," Art. 49 [now Art. 52], Comment (3), p. 407 (VCLT cited in note 2 above).
26. UN Doc. A/CONF. 39/26, contained in *Documents of the Conference,* p. 285, May 22, 1969. The text is reprinted in 8 *Int'l Legal Mat'ls* 733 (1969).
27. P.-H. Houben, "Principles of International Law Concerning Friendly Relations and Cooperation among States," 61 *Amer. J. Int'l L.* 703, 725 (1967).
28. "North Atlantic Coast Fisheries Arbitration," Permanent Court of Arbitration No. VII (1910), 11 *Royal Inst. Foreign Affairs* 167 (1932).
29. *"Honduras v. Nicaragua,"* 1960 *ICJ Rep.* 192 (Judgment of Nov. 18, 1960).
30. "Case Concerning the Temple of Preah Vihear *(Cambodia v. Thailand),*" 1962 *ICJ Rep.* 6 (Judgment of June 15, 1962).

31. Fenwick treatise, p. 531 (footnote omitted) (cited in note 22).
32. *See Proposed Article 13, Report of the International Law Commission Covering Its First Session,* contained in UN GAOR, 4th Session, Supp. No. 10, Doc. A/925, p. 8 (1949).
33. *See* "Treaty on Treaties" article, pp. 516–517 (cited in note 25 above). The proposed exclusion is therein reported by members of US Department of State participants in the VCLT.
34. **Spectrum of views:** The quoted characterizations are contained in the Brierly treatise, p. 338 (cited in note 14 of this chapter) (clearly reasonable); Briggs, "The Attorney General Invokes *Rebus Sic Stantibus,*" 36 *Amer. J. Int'l L.* 89, 93 (1942) (alleged principle); M. Akehurst, *A Modern Introduction to International Law* 145 (7th ed. London: Routledge, 1997) (unsuitable). **Chinese view:** This excerpt is from *International Trade Treaties and Agreements* (Peking: 1958) and is reprinted in 2 J. Cohen & H. Chiu (eds.), *People's China and International Law,* p. 1257 (Princeton: Princeton Univ. Press, 1974) (hereinafter *People's China).*
35. O. Lissitzyn, "Treaties and Changed Circumstances *(Rebus Sic Stantibus),*" 61 *Amer. J. Int'l L.* 895 (1967) (hereinafter "Changed Circumstances" article).
36. "Commentaries," Art. 59 (now Art. 62), pp. 428–429 (cited in note 1 above).
37. *See* "The Free Zones of Upper Savoy and the District of Gex *(Switzerland v. France),*" 1929 *PCIJ,* ser. A, No. 22, and ser. A/B No. 46, 2 *World Court Rep.* 448 (1971).
38. Translation provided in 2 J. Cohen & H. Chiu, *People's China* 1166, 1167 (cited in note 34).
39. "Electricity Company of Sofia and Bulgaria *(Belgium v. Bulgaria),*" 1939 *PCIJ,* ser. A/B, No. 77, p. 64 (dissenting opinion of Judge Anzilotti).
40. *See generally* M. Gommaa, *Suspension or Termination of Treaties on Grounds of Breach* (The Hague: Martinus Nijhoff, 1996).
41. The US government's brief is reprinted in US Department of State, "The Legality of United States Participation in the Defense of Viet-Nam," 60 *Amer. J. Int'l L.* 565, 585 (first quote) and 577 (second quote) (1966). For additional detail, *see* American Society of International Law, *The Viet-Nam War and International Law* (Princeton: Princeton Univ. Press, 1968) (three volumes).
42. "Appeal Relating to the Jurisdiction of the ICAO Council *(India v. Pakistan),*" 1972 *ICJ Rep.* 46 (Judgment of Aug. 18, 1972).
43. "Commentaries," Art. 58 (now Art. 61), Comment (2), p. 427 (cited in note 1).
44. "Changed Circumstances" article (cited in note 35).
45. *See* American Law Institute, *Restatement Second of the Foreign Relations Law of the United States,* §153, Illustration 1 (St. Paul: West, 1965). (Unlike the prior *Restatement,* the new *Restatement Third* does not use illustrations in the replacement §336.)
46. **Judicial denial:** *See* "Commentaries," Comment (1) to Art. 50 (now Art. 53), p. 409 (cited in note 1). **Academic denial:** Tunkin treatise, p. 149 (cited in note 10).
47. *Clark v. Allen,* 331 US 503, 67 S.Ct. 1431, 91 *L. Ed.* 1633 (1947).
48. *See* ICJ's analysis regarding the Pan Am Flight 103 Libyan terrorist bombing case in §6.4 of this book under "Montreal Sabotage Convention." UN Charter Article 103 was thus characterized as controlling, notwithstanding the conflicting treaty that would otherwise accord Libya the exclusive right to resolve this matter within its judicial system.
49. The process is recounted in A. Bestor, "Advice from the Very Beginning, Consent When the End is Achieved," in L. Henkin, M. Glennon & W. Rogers, *Foreign Affairs and the US Constitution* 6 (Ardsley-on-Hudson, NY: Transnat'l Pub.: 1990).
50. An analysis of the drafters' intent is available in L. Henkin, "International Concern and the Treaty Power of the United States," 63 *Amer. J. Int'l L.* 272 (1969).
51. L. Henkin, *Foreign Affairs and the United States Constitution* 217 (2nd ed. Oxford, Eng.: Clarendon Press, 1996) (footnotes omitted).
52. O. Lissitzyn, "The Legal Status of Executive Agreement on Air Transportation," 17 *J. Air L. & Comm.* 436, 439–442 (1950) (footnotes omitted).
53. The relevant section of the Case Act is contained in 1 *US Code* §112b(a).
54. *Dames & Moore v. Regan,* 453 *US Rep.* 654, 682, 101 S.Ct. 2972, 2988, 69 *L. Ed.* 2d 918 (1981) (noting that the President's power to settle claims regarding international relations had been exercised for 200 years with congressional acquiescence) (italics added).
55. **Switzerland:** *"Librairie Hachette, S.A. v. Societe Cooperative,"* XXV *Annuaire Suisse de Droit International* 239 (1968). **Belgium:** *"Minister for Economic Affairs v. S.A. Fromagerie Franco-Suisse,"* 1972 *Common Market Law Rep.* 330. **Mexico:** Constitution, Art. 133.
56. *Reid v. Covert,* 354 US 1, 77 S.Ct. 1222, 1 *L. Ed.2d* 1148 (1957).
57. *Reid,* 354 US 18, 77 S.Ct. 1231.
58. *Breard v. Greene,* 118 S.Ct. 1352 (1998).
59. See *"South African Airways v. Dole,"* 817 *Fed. Rptr.* 2d 119 (D.C. Cir. 1987).
60. *Schroeder v. Bissell,* 5 Fed.2d 838 (D.C. Conn., 1925). Such cases build upon the 1804 statement by the US Supreme Court that "an act of congress ought never to be construed to violate the law of nations, if any other possible construction remains." 6 US (2 Cranch) 64 (1804).
61. *Missouri v. Holland,* 252 US 416, 40 S.Ct. 382, 64 *L. Ed.* 641 (1920).
62. *See* S. Doyle, "International Boycotts," in V. Nanda, *The Law of Transnational Business Transactions* 13–14 (New York: Clark Boardman, 1984).
63. **Laws punishing compliance:** *See* H. Fenton, "United States Antiboycott Laws: An Assessment of Their Impact Ten Years after Adoption," 10 *Hastings Int'l & Comp. L. Rev.* 211 (1987). **Arguable applicability to all persons of Jewish faith:** 3 A. Lowenfeld, *International Economic Law: Trade for Political Ends* 314 (New York: Clark Boardman, 1983).

CHAPTER NINE

Arbitration and Adjudication

CHAPTER OUTLINE

IRRELEVANCE OF OFFICIAL CAPACITY

1. This Statute shall apply equally to all persons without any distinction based on official capacity. In particular, official capacity as a Head of State or Government, a member of a Government or parliament, an elected representative or a government official shall in no case exempt a person from criminal responsibility under this Statute, nor shall it, in and of itself, constitute a ground for reduction of sentence.

2. Immunities or special procedural rules which may attach to the official capacity of a person, whether under national or international law, shall not bar the Court from exercising its jurisdiction over such a person.

—Rome Statute of the International Criminal Court, Article 27, adopted July 1998. For Statute, see www.un.org/icc/romestat.htm.

INTRODUCTION

Earlier chapters included materials about resolving conflicts between the parties to a dispute. The chapters introducing International Law and States depicted various political, economic, and military modes of dispute resolution. The chapter on international organizations covered certain bodies whose function is to promote peaceable dispute resolution, the UN Security Council being the classic illustration. Chapters 7 and 8 also dealt with dispute resolution through diplomacy and the treaty process.

This chapter examines the third-party dispute resolution mechanism: arbitration and adjudication of international conflict. Its essential objective will be to help you develop a sense of when, where, and why States are willing to rely on some third party or entity as an alternative to direct negotiations or hostilities.

After an overview of the international arbitration and litigation models, the materials in this chapter will proceed through the maze of global, regional, and national court alternatives for resolving a contemporary international controversy.

◆ 9.1 ARBITRATION AND ADJUDICATION BLUEPRINT

INTRODUCTION

- *Who* can pursue a remedy for a violation of International Law?
- *Where* can a violation of International Law be adjudicated?
- *Should* it be resolved by arbitration or a panel of judges?
- *What institutions* are available as alternatives to the more hostile forms of conflict?
- *How feasible* is litigation in cases involving international relations between States? Between individuals? Between a State and an international organization? In cases involving sensitive matters as opposed to those of lesser importance to national interests?

A State's pursuit of *litigious* remedies against another State is often complicated by developments in their international relations. The allegedly offending State will not readily admit its liability, even in the clearest of circumstances. In the case of a conspicuous breach, an apology or a promise that the offending act will not be repeated may be unattainable for political or security reasons. For example, the US never admitted international liability when an American U-2 reconnaissance aircraft violated Russian airspace in 1960. The plane was shot down two thousand kilometers inside the Soviet border, but the pilot claimed that he had merely strayed off course (*Powers* case, §6.4). In 1983, the Soviet Union did not admit liability when a Russian pilot shot down a Korean commercial aircraft that strayed off course over Russian territory. Nearly three hundred civilian passengers and crew were killed, although the aircraft posed no security threat to Russian sovereignty. The Soviets claimed that warnings were given and that this response to an intrusion of its airspace did not involve the use of "excessive force." This theme could be applied to contemporary atrocities in Bosnia, Kosovo, and the Middle East to name a few.

States are understandably reluctant to admit that they have breached International Law. National representatives must always assess the practicality of attempting to resolve a dispute with the help of a third-party arbitral or adjudicatory body. The litigation option has not been viable in situations involving *sensitive* disputes or open hostilities. The States involved must first consent to being sued in international tribunals. Unfortunately, the comparatively diminutive docket of the UN's International Court of Justice is the envy of most national judges, who are far busier in terms of their comparative volume of cases. Additionally, factors such as the financial crisis at the UN have impacted the International Court of Justice's ability to swiftly resolve such cases. Since the 1980s, the average length of a judicial proceeding, from filing to disposition, grew from 2.5 to 4 years.[1] Arbitration is often the preferable option for those disputes susceptible to resolution by the more formal adjudicatory modes.

The common questions regarding third-party dispute resolution by persons or entities *not* a party to the dispute form the core of this chapter. Arbitration will be addressed at the outset, because more international disputes have been resolved through arbitral tribunals than by international courts. Judicial remedies follow.

ARBITRATION: HISTORICAL DEVELOPMENT

The city-States of ancient Greece used arbitration as a method for resolving their disputes. A treaty in 445 B.C. grew out of the Peloponnesian War between Athens and Sparta. They agreed not to resort to war as long as the other was willing to resolve a dispute via arbitration. A violation of this treaty subsequently resulted in a ten-year war, whereafter the parties once again agreed not to engage in war—and to submit their future disputes to arbitration.[2]

Modern international *commercial* law is based on practices developed in medieval Europe by merchants engaged in international trade. These standard expectations were called the "Law Merchant." This body of law was created and developed by specialized tribunals in various Mediterranean ports—where private merchants resolved their domestic and international business disputes via arbitration. The Law Merchant flourished in the twelfth-century Italian city-States, later spreading to other commercial centers. The customary practices developed by these tribunals were ultimately incorporated into the commercial laws of many nations.

International arbitration had its own "Dark Ages," lasting until just before the nineteenth century. The famous Jay Treaty (Convention of Amity) of 1794 between Great Britain and the United States established a regime whereby an equal number of British and American nationals were selected to serve on an arbitral commission. Its mandate was to settle matters arising out of the Revolutionary War, which remained unsettled by British–American diplomacy.[3] The two countries further encouraged the use of international arbitration in their 1871 Treaty of Washington Arbitration. The US claimed that Great Britain had violated the neutrality rules arising under customary international practice. Great Britain had aided the South during the American Civil War by building ships for the Confederate Navy. The arbitral tribunal ordered Great Britain to compensate the US for its ensuing losses. When Great Britain complied, there was a renewed interest in using inter-State arbitration to settle international disputes. The national practice of inserting arbitration clauses into treaties increased dramatically. Arbitration began to flourish with the establishment of some two hundred arbitral tribunals that would decide hundreds of cases.

Russia's Czar Nicholas then decided to invite State members of the international community to meet at the Netherlands city of The Hague. National delegates attended the Hague Peace Conferences of 1899 and 1907. The resulting 1899 Hague Convention for the Pacific Settlement of International Disputes recognized arbitration as "the most effective and at the same time the most equitable means of settling disputes which diplomacy has failed to settle." The 1907 Convention for the Pacific Settlement of Disputes was the first multilateral treaty to provide that "International Arbitration has for its object the settlement of disputes between States by judges of their own choice and on the basis of respect for law." Before and ever since these Conventions, most of the arbitrators were not "judges." They were heads of State, academics, national agencies, and politicians.[4] The Hague Conference process thus produced the Permanent Court of Arbitration in 1907—which is still operable, but without a significant caseload for a half-century. This "Court" will be addressed later in this chapter.

Articles 12 and 13 of the Covenant of the League of Nations "mandated" that League members would not go to war if the subject of their dispute had already been submitted to arbitration. Three months were to elapse *after* an award before one State could resort to war against another. This Covenant also created the first "World Court"—the Permanent Court of International Justice (PCIJ) at The Hague. As a result, resort to international arbitration declined—from the PCIJ's inception in 1920 until after World War II. Treaties containing either an arbitration clause or requiring State parties to submit disputes to the PCIJ continued to climb.

With establishment of the second "World Court"—the International Court of Justice (ICJ) at The Hague in 1945—the State members of the international community once again envisioned the submission of legal disputes to a *permanently* constituted judicial body, but not necessarily to the *ad hoc* bodies typically invoked in State practice. The foremost collection of data regarding international arbitrations has been compiled by Nijmegan University (Netherlands) Professor A. M. Stuyt. His *Survey of International Arbitrations* lists nearly 180 inter-State arbitrations between 1900 and 1945. In the last half of this century, roughly the same period of years (1945–present) produced only 43 inter-State arbitrations.[5]

A growing class of international disputes has nevertheless been submitted to various permanent arbitral tribunals. While States generally moved away from *inter-State* arbitration, other forms of international arbitration involving private parties began to flourish, as described in §9.3 below.

ADJUDICATION: HISTORICAL DEVELOPMENT

Before the twentieth century, international disputes were usually resolved by diplomatic negotiation, occasionally by arbitration, and often by war. Negotiations did not always subdue the use of force—which unfortunately remained the ultimate instrument of diplomacy. Arbitration was not a good vehicle for preventing the escalation of international disputes. If States chose arbitrators on an *ad hoc* basis, it was to handle a specific problem *after* the dispute arose. This would effectively permit the stronger State to dictate terms that were not a fully bargained-for exchange. Furthermore, States rarely consented to arbitrating their more sensitive problems in the absence of a forced compromise.

Some national leaders wanted a more durable dispute-resolution alternative. The Latin American participants in the Hague Conferences proposed and then implemented a judicial response to the perennial problems with inter-State dispute resolution. They established the Central American Court of Justice in 1908, the first international court designed to address local problems. It ceased to function, however, in 1918. One reason was the forecast that the French-conceived League of Nations and the Permanent Court of International Justice (PCIJ) would supplant any need for *regional* international courts. A global court would, it was hoped, shift the resolution of inter-State disputes from the battlefield to the courtroom. The States creating the PCIJ wanted it to play a role in the achievement of world peace through law. Some believed that this court would function as a judicial buffer between adversaries who would otherwise resolve their disputes in a military arena. Others anticipated that such a world court would be, at the very least, a neutral forum for settling certain disputes. A number of national leaders, including US President Woodrow Wilson, believed that an international court could positively influence national adherence to International Law.

The concept of a *world* (as opposed to *regional*) international court evolved through two phases, each commonly associated with a particular international organization: the former Permanent Court of International Justice (PCIJ) and the current International Court of Justice (ICJ). The PCIJ was *not* an organ of the League, however. A State desiring to use it would enter into a treaty with another State. Several hundred bilateral treaties among the various nations of the world conferred jurisdiction on the PCIJ. On the other hand, States joining the UN are automatically parties to the Charter's companion treaty—the Statute of the International Court of Justice. While they are not *required* to use the ICJ, this involuntary nexus with the Court's Statute attested to the judicial existence of the latter world court.

The PCIJ was the first permanently constituted dispute-resolution mechanism available to all nations of the world. In the case of States unwilling to actually litigate their differences, organs of the League of Nations could (and did) request "advisory" opinions from the PCIJ, which had the power to theoretically apply International Law to situations where a potentially liable State was unwilling to appear in judicial proceedings as a defendant. From 1922 to 1940, the PCIJ heard twenty-nine cases between adversaries who litigated their cases in the court. It also rendered twenty-seven advisory opinions (a special form of "adjudication" analyzed in §9.4).[6]

Two paradoxes contributed to the demise of the PCIJ. First, while this court was sponsored by the League of Nations, it was not an official organ of the League. Second, while US President Wilson played a fundamental role in developing international support for the League, the US did not join the League and never appeared as a litigant in the PCIJ. The Senate blocked US participation in the League. Because of rampant post–World War I isolationist sentiment, US senators feared *any* international alliances because any one of them might one day draw the US into a second world war.

The outbreak of World War II in 1939 destroyed the potential effectiveness of the PCIJ. The court conducted its last public sitting in that year—when most of the judges fled to Geneva to take advantage of Switzerland's wartime neutrality.

The dream of a global judicial body was not totally shattered by the abrupt reality of war. In 1943, the "Four Powers" (China, the Soviet Union, Great Britain, and the US) determined that another global international organization should replace the League of Nations. The possibility of another world court was also rekindled by Great Britain's invitation to a group of International Law experts who met in London. These experts agreed that another global court was needed. It would have to be a completely new court in order to diffuse the criticism of the earlier PCIJ—perceived by many States as a European institution designed by European jurists to dominate the legal affairs of other nations.

◆ 9.2 ALTERNATIVE DISPUTE RESOLUTION

The emergence of modern International Law in the seventeenth century (*see* Peace of Westphalia in §1.3) was not accompanied by either a world government or the discontinued use of force by States. As the international community grew in size, there was less to share—and more pressure on peaceful cohabitation of the planet because of limited landmass, airspace, oceans, and natural resources. Disputes became a predictable element of international relations. The United Nations process responded by codifying several important guidelines in the search for viable alternatives to hostilities. They are presented in Exhibit 9.1.

The various alternative dispute resolution (ADR) mechanisms are typically less formal than either arbitration or court proceedings. They include the following means of settlement: negotiation, inquiry, mediation, conciliation, and minitrial.

NEGOTIATION

Negotiation differs from the other informal modes of ADR because its conduct is completely controlled by the immediate parties to the dispute. Negotiations between States are normally conducted through diplomatic channels. They may be performed by heads of State, ambassa-

EXHIBIT 9.1 UN DIRECTIVES ON NONMILITARY DISPUTE RESOLUTION

UN Charter Article 2.4	The Charter's most fundamental norm: "All Members shall refrain . . . from the threat or use of force. . . ."
UN Charter Article 2.3	States shall "settle their international disputes by peaceful means in such a manner that international peace and security . . . are not endangered."
UN Charter Article 33.1	"The parties to any dispute . . . shall, first of all, seek a solution by negotiation, enquiry, mediation, conciliation, arbitration, judicial settlement . . . or other peaceful means of their own choice."
General Assembly Res. 2625(XXV) of 1970	Regarding the application of Charter Article 2.3: States "shall accordingly seek early and just settlement of their international disputes by negotiation, enquiry, mediation, conciliation. . . ."

dors, draft treaty–conference participants, respective foreign ministers, or other designated representatives.

The parties may *consult* with one another in their attempt to resolve a dispute. Consultation facilitates problem solving before any adverse action has been taken by either party. The acting State might alter its proposed action in a way that accomplishes its objectives, but with a less significant impact on the consulted State. After the 1982 Falkland Islands War, Argentina and Great Britain hoped to avoid unnecessary confrontations because of the presence of their respective military forces in the same area. In 1990, they entered into an Interim Reciprocal Information and Consultation System. It provides that their consultation system will govern "movements of units of their Armed Forces in Areas of the South West Atlantic. The aims of this system are to increase confidence between Argentina and the United Kingdom and to contribute to achieving a more normal situation in the region [including a direct communication link]."[7]

INQUIRY

Unlike direct negotiations, the other ADR modes invoke the assistance of a third party. An inquiry is conducted by someone not a party to the dispute who attempts to provide adversaries with an objective assessment. A continuing stalemate typically leads to more confrontational modes for settling the contest. Thus, the presence of a third party facilitates the injection of a more balanced approach to resolving the dispute before it erupts into hostilities.

The term *inquiry* is commonly used in two senses. The broader connotation refers to the process itself: A court, arbitral body, international organization, or individual tries to resolve a dispute between other States or entities. The narrower connotation of this term as used in this section of the book refers to some specific arrangement other than arbitration or some other ADR mode that requires an independent investigation of the underlying facts of the disputed issue.[8] The 1899 Hague Convention for the Pacific Settlement of International Disputes (§9.1) contains six articles that call on States to establish commissions of inquiry to attain objective fact-finding in international disputes.

In the famous *Dogger Bank Inquiry,* a group of Russian war vessels were en route from the Baltic Sea to the Far East in 1904 to engage hostile forces in the war with Japan. The Russian ships steamed directly into a fleet of private English fishing vessels at the Dogger Bank in the North Sea. The Russian fleet assumed that it was under attack by English war vessels, which were reportedly in this area. The Russians fired on the fishing vessels, sinking one, damaging others, and killing and wounding a number of civilian fishermen. England then made plans to intercept the Russian fleet. France intervened, convincing Russia and England to establish a commission of inquiry under the Hague Convention paradigm. Five admirals from Austria-Hungary, England, France, Russia, and the United States spent two months hearing evidence from witnesses. This commission found that the Russian admiral had no justification for opening fire—although the report was worded so as to not discredit the Russian admiral. Russia received the commission's findings and decided to pay damages as a result of the conduct of this Russian squadron.[9]

MEDIATION

Mediation is another ADR device that invokes the assistance of an "outsider" who is not a party to the dispute. Unlike the commission of inquiry, which is basically a fact-finding tool, the mediator is typically authorized to advance his or her own proposal for resolving the dispute. Nothing is binding about the mediator's role, otherwise, he or she would really be an arbitrator or judicial officer, who is seized with the power to require a particular result. There is no prior commitment by the parties to accept the mediator's proposal.

The mediator can make his or her proposals informally, based on information supplied by the parties. The mediator does not undertake an independent investigation (as would a commission of inquiry). Where negotiations are deadlocked, the mediator can attempt to move the parties in the direction of at least considering his or her proposal. Such proceedings are normally informal and private, unlike an arbitration or judicial proceeding, with its formal procedures for taking evidence from witnesses in an open-hearing context. The Red Cross often acts as a mediator in those conflicts where the parties are unlikely to negotiate face-to-face. Algeria served in this capacity, mediating the Iran–US Hostage Crisis in 1979–1980.

"Good offices" is a variant of the mediation technique. A third party communicates the statements of the disputing parties to one another. This is a useful technique when the dispute involves States that do not maintain diplomatic communications. Good offices may also involve the "outsider" inviting the disputing parties to a settlement conference or undertaking other steps to facilitate their communications. This theme was the focal point of the 1936 Inter-American Good Services and Mediation Treaty, as well as the 1948 American Treaty on Peaceful Settlement of Disputes (the "Bogotá Treaty"). The UN Secretary-General has often used his position to facilitate inter-State settlement of disputes through the "good offices" of the UN.

In October 1998, four nations used various features of the mediation technique to resolve a border dispute between two other nations. From 1941 to 1995, Ecuador and Peru had fought three wars over a 48-mile strip of jungle on their 1,050-mile common border. Argentina, Brazil, Chile, and the United States mediated during three years of deadlocked negotiations. The disputing parties felt that they had not obtained all that they were entitled to receive under this mediation. However, their joint agreement ended this dispute on terms that were an acceptable alternative to another war.

CONCILIATION

The so-called textbook definition of conciliation was provided by late Professor Clive Parry of Cambridge, England. It is the "process of settling a dispute by referring it to a commission of persons whose task it is to elucidate the facts and (usually after hearing the parties and endeavoring to bring them to an agreement) to make a report containing proposals for a settlement, but not having the binding character of an [arbitral] award or [court] judgment."[10]

The conciliator is designated by the potential litigants to help them reconcile their differences. Because the parties often resort to formal litigation when one of them is unwilling to listen to what the other has to say, this "outsider" attempts to reconcile their differences by depicting the negative aspects of their respective positions so that all approaches to characterizing and resolving the problem will be articulated and perceived for what reasonableness they actually convey.

Conciliation places third-party dispute-resolution assistance in a more formalized setting than negotiation or mediation. Like the commission of inquiry, a conciliation commission *may* engage in a fact-finding role. Yet, a conciliation commission normally attempts to promote a resolution. This is a step beyond fact-finding inquiries, although less formal than an arbitration or judicial proceeding.

In 1922, the League of Nations General Assembly resolved that States should conclude treaties requiring the submission of disputes to conciliation commissions—unless the parties were already willing to resolve the dispute via arbitration or by litigation in the Permanent Court of International Justice. Some twenty treaties contained a conciliation requirement—including the famous Locarno agreements between Germany on the one hand, and Belgium, France, Czechoslovakia, and Poland on the other. The Locarno Treaty was then incorporated into the League's 1928 General Act for the Pacific Settlement of Disputes. League members established either *ad hoc* or permanent conciliation commissions to act, unless they submitted their disputes to the PCIJ or to binding arbitration. Nearly 200 such treaties were concluded between the two World Wars.

Conciliation is no longer a creature of bilateral treaties. Certain multilateral treaties provide for conciliation as an alternative for the adopting States and international organizations in various regions. These include the following:

- 1957 European Convention for the Peaceful Settlement of Disputes;
- 1965 Washington Convention for the Settlement of Disputes Concerning Investments Between States and Nationals of Other States;
- 1963 Charter of the Organization of African Unity;
- 1975 Convention on the Representation of States in Their Relations with International Organizations of a Universal Character;
- 1978 Vienna Convention on Succession of States in Respect of Treaties;
- 1981 Treaty Establishing the Organization of Caribbean States; and
- 1982 UN Convention on the Law of the Sea.[11]

Although these treaties provide for conciliation, not all are effective. The 1957 European Convention for the Peaceful Settlement of Disputes has not come into force. Too few States decided to ratify it. The Arbitral Tribunal of the Organization of African Unity (OAU) is another tribunal that never materialized. Instead, OAU members continue to rely on traditional diplomatic negotiations to settle disputes.

MINITRIAL

While quite similar to conciliation, the minitrial is the latest approach to international dispute resolution. It is not a real trial. The parties confront one another in a similar context, however, and must verify their positions before a neutral third party. The "judge" is typically an expert in the particular field, and not necessarily a sworn judicial officer or lawyer. These "trials" often take place before negotiators who are senior employees of the respective parties. Each negotiator, in turn, then proceeds to illustrate the weaknesses to his or her employer's position—long before a costly arbitration or judicial proceeding at some point in the future.

Italy's Mauro Rubino-Sammartano, who practices in French and Italian courts, illustrates the successes with this comparatively new device in his book on international arbitration:

> Xerox Corporation entered into a distribution agreement with a Latin American company. . . . [T]he distributor construed the contract as applying not to one line of computers only, but to all the computers sold by Rank Xerox throughout Latin America rather than in a more limited territory. One year after proceedings had been started before the California courts [in the US], an extremely quick mini-trial took place (Rank Xerox presenting its case in one hour and forty minutes), which produced a positive result ending in a promptly performed settlement.
>
> Another positive mini-trial is the Telecredit-TRW dispute concerning trademarks, conducted before the parties' negotiators and a neutral advisor; the dispute was settled 60 days after completion of the mini-trial.
>
> A third positive mini-trial is reported as having taken place between a German manufacturer and an American distributor. Settlement was reached after a presentation of [just] one hour by each party.[12]

One must, of course, recognize some inherent limitations with this new ADR device. Goodwill is an essential element in such a process. Its absence has frustrated ADR schemes in virtually every legal system to date. On the other hand, large corporate enterprises have little to lose by such devices as opposed to the time and expense associated with the more formal resolution mechanisms addressed in the remaining sections of this chapter.

◆ 9.3 ARBITRAL CLASSIFICATIONS AND TRIBUNALS

Arbitration is a comparatively formal mode of dispute resolution. Adversaries rely on a third party to hear the evidence and resolve the dispute by issuing a binding arbitral award. This section of the book covers the types of arbitration and selected arbitral tribunals.

CLASSIFICATION

Arbitration may be classified as follows: *ad hoc* versus permanent; by the nature of the parties; composition of the tribunal; and category of dispute.

***Ad Hoc* Versus Permanent** Arbitrations have been historically *ad hoc.* After a dispute arises, the parties determine *what* will be decided and *who* will do the deciding. They agree on the general terms and limitations that they will impose on the arbitrators called upon to help resolve a particular dispute. *Ad hoc* arbitration imparts the recurring problem of not having procedures already in place, with the resulting lack of predetermined procedures that are satisfactory to all concerned. On the other hand, the overwhelming number of parties to these arbitrations have fulfilled their international obligations established by binding arbitration.[13]

The terms of an international arbitration agreement may leave much to the discretion of the arbitrator and the participants. In 1988, for example, an international arbitration panel ruled in Egypt's favor in a border dispute with Israel, leaving the parties to work out the details of actually determining the precise boundary line. Such freedom of choice in fashioning the ultimate resolution is not available when a permanently established court decides such disputes. In contrast, mutually acceptable arbitration procedures may be tailored after the fact to match the circumstances of the particular case. This flexibility avoids the jurisdictional objections that have plagued courts such as the UN's International Court of Justice since its inception. The parties may also experience less flexibility when they submit their case to a standing arbitral tribunal with its own pre-established set of rules and procedures.

Permanently established "institutional" arbitration tribunals provide predictability and stability in resolving business disputes. As aptly depicted by McGill University (Canada) Professor Stephen Troope:

> Since the 1960s, the international business community has manifested an increasing interest in arbitration as a dispute resolution mechanism. Concurrent with this increased attraction to arbitration has been the emergence and growth of more and more arbitral institutions . . . providing facilities and organisational mechanisms for the arbitral resolution of commercial disputes . . . [and] with the increasing scale of international trade, arbitration has very much come into its own. . . .
>
> Because of the potential application of contemporary commercial arbitration in many economic contexts . . . one can understand the superficial attraction of institutional arbitration which provides a stable organisational base for an arbitration, a staff trained to administer arbitration and more importantly, a set of pre-established procedural rules which should prevent renegotiation during a heated dispute, thereby helping to ensure that the arbitration goes forward even in the face of a recalcitrant party. It is asserted, therefore, that institutional arbitration enhances the values of certainty and predictability.[14]

Nature of the Parties Arbitration historically involved inter-State disputes, achieving its heyday in the first half of the twentieth century. The prime example is the Permanent Court of Arbitration (PCOA), a product of the 1899 Hague Peace Conference. Various nations met in Holland to explore ways to achieve peace and disarmament. They adopted the Convention on the Pacific Settlement of International Disputes. Treaty participants viewed the PCOA as an egalitarian device that would implement their goal of peacefully resolving international disputes. It commenced operations in 1913 and still functions today at its seat in The Hague.

The PCOA is not a court. Its "judges" are mostly lawyers who have expertise in international business matters and are willing to travel. They serve on small arbitration panels. Each of the seventy-five participating countries appoints four individuals to provide arbitration services for a fixed number of years. The national parties to a dispute choose several of these experts to serve on a panel that will deliberate their particular problem.

The occurrence of inter-State arbitration has significantly declined since World War II, because the growing infrastructure of the increasingly diversified community of nations has not provided the type of stability necessary for States to arbitrate their disputes.[15] The postwar creation of the Permanent Court of International Justice in The Hague diverted national attention from the PCOA. Prior to 1931, the PCOA heard twenty-four cases. Since then, it has heard only several, including the Iran–US Claims Tribunal, which the PCOA's 1990 Annual Report claims as its third case since WWII. The sixty-five-year-old PCOA was immediately available to carry out the details of the US–Iran 1980 Hostage Treaty. The PCOA was a somewhat untapped resource that could immediately begin to consider the difficult compensation issues arising out of that dispute. The availability of panels (chambers) of less than all judges of the International Court of Justice further limits the need for this arbitral tribunal (§9.4).

Another "States-only" arbitral tribunal was established by the Charter of the Organization of African Unity (OAU): the OAU's Commission of Mediation, Conciliation and Arbitration, seated in Addis Ababa,

Ethiopia. Its twenty-one members have "jurisdiction" (noncompulsory) to resolve any inter-State dispute referred to it by the parties or by certain governmental entities of the OAU or its State members. The essential role of the OAU Commission is to facilitate alternative dispute-resolution mechanisms between the various African States.

Contemporary "international" arbitrations typically occur between a private individual or corporation and a State *and between* private persons, corporations, and international organizations. This flexibility encourages treaty provisions that provide for virtually all conceivable categories of arbitration. The 1987 France–United Kingdom Channel Tunnel Treaty expressly authorizes the reference of disputes to arbitral tribunals for disputes *between* (a) the State parties, (b) States and concessionaires, or (c) just concessionaires. All public and private entities have access to a convenient dispute-resolution mechanism without regard to the status of any particular tunnel-service provider. There are no sovereign immunity problems for concessionaires. A claimant does not have to surmount potential sovereignty objections between the States involved in the tunnel's operation. There is no need for a business entity to first enlist the assistance of its home State in order to present a claim against an international person (for example, France or the United Kingdom). A private non-governmental corporation may then arbitrate a dispute with its own home State without resorting to the traditional International Law requirement that it seek sovereign representation at the international level. This procedure avoids the awkward scenario when a contractor's dispute is with its own country. The major *multilateral* treaties that provide for this form of mixed State–private party arbitration are the New York Convention, the Inter-American Convention on International Commercial Arbitration, and the Washington Convention.[16]

Composition and Category A functional classification is (a) mixed international arbitration, (b) private disputes involving a public interest, and (c) administrative arbitration.

In a "mixed" arbitration, one party is a State and the other is either a private party or a business entity. A classic instance is the Algiers Accords—the agreement creating the Iran–United States Claims Tribunal in 1981. The US hostages being held in Iran were released, and Iran was able to regain control over some of its assets, which had been frozen at the inception of this major international dispute. US individuals and corporations were provided with a means of redress against Iran. The Tribunal then began its task of resolving claims against the Iranian funds, which would be disbursed as a result of its decisions. Due to the animosity between the parties and the high claims at stake, the Tribunal's lasting value was rather evident. It was unlikely that a negotiated settlement between the US and Iran could have been reached without this independent mechanism for "post-hostility" claims adjudication—typical of postwar tribunals formed to resolve private claims against State parties.[17]

In 1991, the UN Security Council established the UN Compensation Commission (UNCC), which is headquartered in Geneva. Its mandate is to process, determine, and pay any claims against Iraq arising from the 1991 Persian Gulf War. This tribunal was created under the Council's Chapter VII powers whereby the UN Charter was designed to control threats to peace. The UNCC's function is to decide the amount and validity of claims arising on or after August 2, 1990, the date of Iraq's invasion of Kuwait. It has issued approximately twenty decisions, *announcing* settlements in claims involving serious personal injury or death that resulted from Iraq's annexation of Kuwait.[18] In 1996, the UNCC began to issue checks based on money obtained from Iraqi sales of oil—30 percent of which is retained for the payment of UNCC claims.

Another form of international arbitration is "commercial" arbitration between business enterprises.[19] While there are a number of such tribunals, several bear special mention. The International Court of Arbitration of the International Chamber of Commerce (ICC Court) is a prominent arbitral organization based in Paris. It has resolved commercial disputes since 1923 and currently receives approximately 350 cases per year. Under Article 1.1 of the ICC's Rules of Conciliation and Arbitration, the "function of the Court is to *provide for* the arbitration of business disputes of an international character. . . ."[20] The parties submit their requests for dispute resolution assistance to the Secretariat of the ICC Court of Arbitration. The "court" then delegates the power to arbitrate matters referred to it. The Secretariat appoints either one or three individuals to consider the dispute, depending on its complexity. These individuals sit on the ICC National Committee located in each participating country.[21]

EXHIBIT 9.2 SELECTED INTERNATIONAL ARBITRAL TRIBUNALS

Tribunal	Headquarters	Dispute Category ◆ Function
Chambers of the International Court of Justice	The Hague, Netherlands	Inter-State ◆ Parties may request special three-judge chamber to arbitrate disputes
Court of Arbitration of the International Chamber of Commerce	Paris, France	International business between private persons or corporations ◆ ICC delegates requests for ICC arbitration to local experts on National Committees in participating States
International Centre for Settlement of Investment Disputes	Washington, D.C., USA	Mixed arbitration ◆ Individual or corporation may deal directly with State ◆ Builds confidence in private foreign investment
International Labor Organization Administrative Tribunal	Geneva, Switzerland	Inter-State and administrative ◆ Resolves disputes regarding international labor standards ◆ Jurisdiction extended to various UN agency labor practices
Iran-US Claims Tribunal	The Hague, Netherlands	Mixed arbitration ◆ Resolves claims from 1979–1980 Hostage Crisis ◆ Hears claims of US nationals v. Iran
London Court of International Arbitration	London, England	International business ◆ Between private persons or corporations ◆ Highly reputed center for commercial arbitration
NAFTA Free Trade Commission	NAFTA Secretariat at national office in each country	Cabinet-level entity supervises implementation of the NAFTA Agreement and resolves disputes that may arise. Any consulting country may initiate panel proceedings, which resemble those conducted under GATT and WTO procedures.
Permanent Court of Arbitration	The Hague, Netherlands	*Ad hoc* tribunals ◆ Designated arbitrators settle disputes between States (or organizations of States) and between States and private parties
Stockholm Chamber of Commerce Arbitration	Stockholm, Sweden	International business ◆ Between private persons or corporations ◆ Highly reputed center for commercial arbitration
UN Administrative Claims Tribunal	New York, NY, USA	Administrative arbitration ◆ Resolves claims between UN and its employees
UN Compensation Commission	Geneva, Switzerland	Mixed arbitration ◆ UN Security Council organ reresolves individual claims against Iraq due to invasion of Kuwait
World Trade Organization	Geneva, Switzerland	International business ◆ Inter-State panels determine whether a State's businesses are complying with GATT requirements

The International Centre for Settlement of Investment Disputes (ICSID) is another active commercial arbitral body. The 1966 Convention on the Settlement of Investment Disputes between States and Nationals of Other States established the ICSID,[22] which is sponsored by the UN's International Bank for Reconstruction and Development located in Washington, D.C. This tribunal was designed to develop confidence in private foreign investment through arbitration. It differs from other international arbitral bodies such as the Hague Permanent Court of Arbitration because use of ICSID facilities is not limited to governmental parties. An individual or corporation may arbitrate directly with a foreign State ("mixed" arbitration). An individual does not need to seek and obtain governmental or diplomatic assistance from his or her own country to arbitrate a claim. Like the ICC International Court of Arbitration, the ICSID does not directly arbitrate disputes at its headquarters. It maintains panels of legal and business experts who are willing to arbitrate claims submitted to it. They arbitrate many contract disputes between private corporations and the foreign States with which they deal.[23] In 1993, the ICSID rendered the first award ever given under the law of a bilateral investment treaty to which the US was a party.[24]

There are also "special purpose" commercial arbitral bodies that specialize in specific areas of law or trade. The World Intellectual Property Organization (WIPO) is a specialized agency of the UN with headquarters in Geneva. It maintains panels for resolving international problems involving alleged copyright, patent, and trademark-infringement claims. This body published revised ADR rules that became effective in 1994. It may become a particularly expeditious and suitable means for accommodating the special problems associated with intellectual-property disputes. A patent or trademark holder may have instant access to a body of intellectual-property experts. A claim that a foreign company is making or marketing the owner's product—without entering into a licensing arrangement with the patent or trademark owner—may be lodged with the WIPO. The owner does not have to pursue either diplomatic or judicial remedies, which would depend on the willingness of the owner's home State to one day pursue such claims.

"Administrative" arbitration typically involves the inner workings of international organizations. In the case of *Yakimetz v. The Secretary-General of the United Nations,* a UN staff member from the Russian delegation at the UN in New York applied for asylum in the US. He also requested a career appointment at the UN, based on his excellent service record. When his request was denied, he filed an administrative action in the United Nations Administrative Tribunal. The UN Tribunal decided that the Secretary-General's decision was "flawed," although it would not reverse the UN's employment denial.[25]

SELECTED ARBITRAL TRIBUNALS

Given the number and scope of contemporary arbitral tribunals, complete coverage is not possible in an introductory text on International Law. Exhibit 9.2 provides a snapshot, however, of existing arbitral tribunals and the roles they serve in international dispute resolution.

Two other regional (economic) courts are in various stages of development: the Court of Justice of the Economic Community of West African States, and the Economic Court of the Commonwealth of Independent States. Both were mentioned in related treaty processes in 1994. Neither has yet resolved a dispute.

◆ 9.4 INTERNATIONAL COURT OF JUSTICE

INTRODUCTION

The dream of world peace entwined with the adjudication of disputes is not new. The medieval Florentine poet Dante proposed a world State under a central court of justice in his *De Monarchia.* The twentieth century was the first millennium to produce a world organization dedicated to peace. The first of two courts known as the "World Court" was ironically designated the *Permanent* Court of International Justice—spawned by the first World War, but mooted by the second.

The dream of a global judicial body that might substitute the courtroom for the battlefield was not completely shattered by the abrupt reality of World War II. The possibility of a revived World Court began with the UK's invitation to a group of International Law experts to confer in London. They agreed that another global court should be created. This would be a completely new court, thereby diffusing the criticism of the previous World Court that it was a European institution designed by European jurists to dominate the legal affairs of the larger community of nations.

In 1943, the Four Powers (China, Soviet Union, United Kingdom, United States) determined that another global international organization should replace

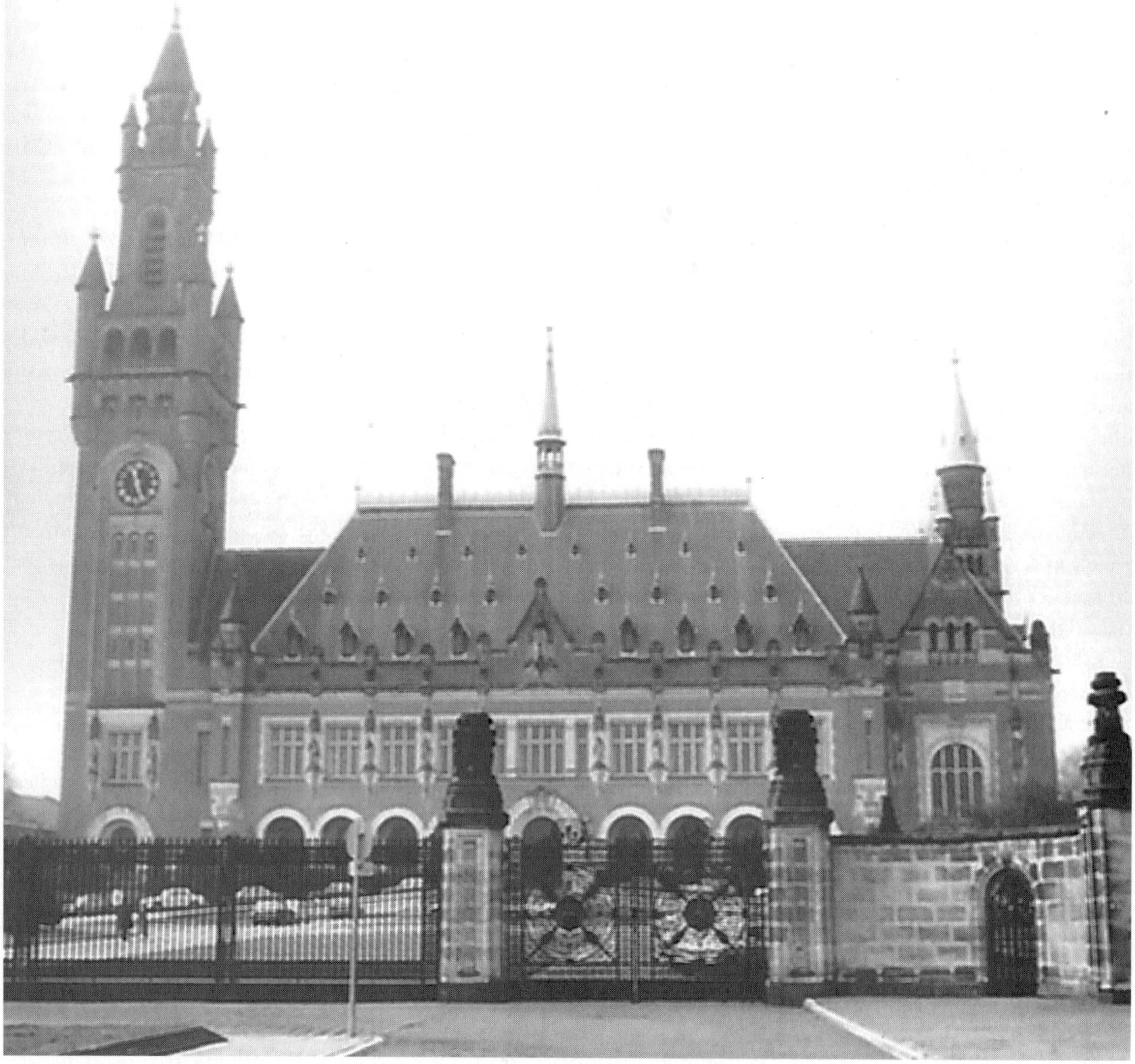

The International Court of Justice in the Peace Palace at The Hague, in the Netherlands.

the League of Nations. In 1944, they published their proposals about world peace. These were ultimately debated during the 1945 UN development conference in San Francisco. These meetings forged the principles now contained in the UN Charter and its annexed Statute of the International Court of Justice. Contrary to the approach taken by the League of Nations, UN participants decided that the powers of the new Court must be directly incorporated into the UN Charter. It would be the judicial branch of this new peace organization. The status of the International Court of Justice would thereby be on a par with the other major organs of the UN.

This section describes the contemporary operations of the International Court of Justice (ICJ)—what it is and is not designed to do.

CHARTER PROVISIONS

The UN's founding members decided to place the "constitutional" basis for the ICJ in the UN Charter. This dovetailed the international organization and its new World Court—unlike the loose "association" that existed

The judges of the International Court of Justice seated for proceedings in the Peace Palace.

between the League of Nations and the *distinct* Permanent Court of International Justice (PCIJ).[26] Contrary to popular belief, the PCIJ was *not* a part of the League of Nations. The ICJ, on the other hand, is the judicial arm of the UN. It shares responsibility with the other major UN organs for monitoring national observance of the principles set forth in the UN Charter.

Charter Article 95's description of the ICJ as the UN's "principal" judicial organ did not mean that other judicial organs would be developed or incorporated into a worldwide hierarchy with the ICJ at the apex. The Charter encouraged States to consider "entrusting the solution of their differences to other tribunals." Unlike the ICJ, however, any regional international tribunals were not to be formally linked to UN operations.

The *UN Charter* sets forth the general functions of the Court in Articles 92 through 96. The *Statute of the International Court of Justice* contains the procedures for submitting and resolving national disputes. The following materials survey the UN Charter provisions on the Court, summarize the Court's functions under its statute, and analyze how the Court's functions have been affected by State practice that developed after the Charter materialized in 1945.

The UN Charter provides that: (1) all member States are automatically parties to the Statute of the International Court of Justice, (2) members promise to comply with the decisions of the Court, and (3) the Security Council may undertake enforcement measures if this promise is breached. To encourage national use of the ICJ, Article 93.1 of the Charter requires all State members to become "*ipso facto* [by joining the UN] parties to the Statute of the International Court of Justice." This statute is often referred to as being "annexed" to the Charter. The drafters wanted the Charter and the ICJ's Statute to be jointly adopted by all States that would join the UN. This Statute, discussed below, became operative in 1951. Several States that were *not* UN members (for several decades after it came into existence) initially became parties to the ICJ Statute, but not to the UN Charter (Liechtenstein, San Marino, and Switzerland; only the last is not a current UN member).

Under Article 94.1 of the Charter, each UN member "undertakes to comply with the decision of the International Court of Justice in any case to which it is a party." This is a fundamental requirement of any organized judicial system. While the judgments of the ICJ have been honored by most State parties, some States have ignored its judgments. And, as usual, certain commentators have concentrated on this negative aspect of the UN's judicial process, construing the conduct of several scofflaws as a fatal blow to the continuing willingness of most States to abide by ICJ judgments.

The conspicuous examples of State defiance of ICJ decisions include the following. Libya disobeyed the Court's order to turn over the two Libyan terrorists allegedly responsible for blowing up Pan Am Flight 103 over Lockerbie, Scotland, in 1988 (§6.4). South Africa refused to honor the Court's "advisory" order in the 1971 *Namibia Presence* case to terminate control of the area of South-West Africa, which is now the independent State of Namibia. In the 1973 *Fisheries Jurisdiction* cases, the ICJ ordered Iceland and the United Kingdom to negotiate an equitable solution to foreign fishing rights in the international waters near Iceland's coast (§8.2). This matter was not seriously negotiated and has not been resolved. In the 1980 *Hostage Case,* Iran refused to release the US diplomats held hostage in Tehran. And from 1984 to 1988, the US refused to participate in or honor the ICJ's judgments in the *Nicaragua* case (discussed below).

Defiance does not go unnoticed under the UN Charter. Article 94.2 provides that if "any party to a case fails to perform the obligations incumbent upon it under a judgment rendered by the Court, the other party may have recourse to the Security Council, which may, if it deems necessary, make recommendations or decide upon measures to be taken to give effect to the judgment." A State may notify the Security Council when another State has failed to comply with any Charter obligations.

The Council has occasionally referred cases to the ICJ. But the Council has never undertaken *effective* enforcement action after an ICJ judgment. By the early 1950s, a handful of States had failed to perform their obligations as determined by the Court. Although the Charter does not specify *what* measures may be taken in this instance, the Security Council could have devised and announced post-judgment compliance measures.

The Security Council formulated what was probably its most significant (although unsuccessful) ICJ enforcement measure after the Court rendered its opinion in the 1971 *Namibia Presence* case (§2.3). The Court ordered South Africa to terminate its control of South-West Africa (Namibia). The Council then ordered South Africa to comply with the ICJ's judgment. It also ordered other States to abstain from dealing with South Africa in any way that was inconsistent with the ICJ's divestment opinion. South Africa ultimately agreed to cooperate with the UN. Two decades later, South-West Africa (Namibia) finally achieved its independence from South Africa.

The Security Council has had very limited experience with enforcing judgments—and little incentive to develop enforcement measures. Under UN Charter Article 36.3, "legal disputes should as a general rule be referred by the parties to the International Court of Justice in accordance with the provisions of the Statute of the Court." States do not, as a general rule, refer their more sensitive legal disputes to the ICJ. This is one reason why States litigating disputes in the ICJ have generally complied with its judgments. The result is usually not particularly adverse to the critical political or economic interests of the litigants.

UN TRUST FUND

One reason for limited use of the ICJ is the financial condition of the UN's smaller States. As noted in §7.2, many of them do not have the resources to maintain a diplomatic presence in other States. Many cannot operate any embassy *anywhere* due to quite limited financial resources. The same problem has historically limited their access to the ICJ as a dispute-resolution center. It is costly to maintain a local presence at The Hague (Netherlands), where the ICJ is located, even for the limited purpose of filing pleadings, conducting the research necessary to adequately participate in judicial proceedings on a distant continent, and paying the cost of scientific studies and expert testimony in the Court's proceedings. A partial remedy has been proposed at the UN.

In UN Secretary-General Boutros Boutros-Ghali's 1992 report on preventive diplomacy, he recognized that while the Court's docket has grown, it is an underutilized resource. He urged UN members to "support the Trust Fund established to assist countries unable to afford the cost involved in bringing a dispute to the Court. . . ."[27] This is an inducement to States to submit their disputes to the ICJ. This fund constitutes a form of international legal aid as envisioned by Secretary-General Javier Perez de Cuellar in 1989. It is financed by voluntary contributions from the comparatively prosperous States, international organizations, and non-governmental organizations. Thirty-four States had contributed over a half-million dollars to the fund as of the Secretary-General's 1992 annual report. Chad is one State that disclosed its ability to participate in ICJ proceedings only because of the availability of this fund (during a public hearing at the ICJ on July 14, 1993, in the ICJ *Territorial Dispute* case between Libya and Chad). While some commentators view this fund as a make-work device for the Court, the ICJ itself is not an intended beneficiary. A permanent fund is preferable to the common scenario whereby needy States must seek financial assistance from other States. The latter may, of course, exact a future concession for such grants or loans.

As reported by a staff member of the ICJ, the fund's resources were essentially depleted (after only two successful applications). Thus, "new incentives are needed to raise the level of contribution by wealthier states and enable a larger number of less fortunate states to settle their disputes peacefully in the World Court."[28] It is unfortunately evident that smaller States' access to the ICJ is not a priority of the larger States. The penchant for redistributing the world's wealth was discussed in Chapter 6 on the UN's two-decade drive to effectuate the Convention on the Law of the Sea in 1994. The UN still has a long way to go in currying support in favor of funding the UN Secretary-General's Trust Fund.

ICJ STATUTE

Earlier materials in this section identified the basic UN Charter provisions on the ICJ. The various provisions of the companion "Statute of the International Court of Justice" provide additional details regarding the ICJ's judges, its functions, the pivotal "optional" clause, and the Court's "advisory" jurisdiction (as opposed to its "contentious" jurisdiction).[29]

Judges The International Court of Justice is composed of fifteen judges, each from a different UN member State. Recurring suggestions that there be more judges have not been adopted, primarily because it would not be practical to conduct the Court's business with a larger number of jurists. Also, the cost of additional judges would not be supported by the Court's limited caseload to date. The UN Secretary-General invites State members who are parties to the Permanent Court of Arbitration to submit names of judicial candidates. They are then elected by the UN General Assembly and Security Council. There are triennial elections of five judges to the Court, each serving a nine-year term.

Article 2 of the Statute of the International Court of Justice establishes the eligibility requirements for its judges. They must be independent, "elected . . . from among persons of high moral character, who possess the qualifications required in their respective countries for appointment to the highest judicial offices, or are jurisconsults [learned in International Law] of recognized competence. . . ." About one-third of the judges actually have been judicial officers in their countries. Most have been law professors and practicing lawyers. Some judges have been senior government administrators, and two were heads of State.[30]

Unlike other branches of the UN or certain regional tribunals, ICJ judges do not represent their governments. They must act independently. Under Articles 16 and 17 of the Statute, judges cannot "exercise any political or administrative function, or engage in any other occupation of a professional nature." They cannot "act as agent, counsel, or advocate in any case." Since the judges are not national delegates, their respective governments cannot dismiss them from the ICJ for their judicial opinions. Only the Court itself can vote to dismiss a judge. It has never done so.

Functions The Court's basic function is to hear and determine all cases involving interpretations and applications of the principles set forth in the UN Charter. Under ICJ Statute Article 36.1, the Court's jurisdiction consists of "all cases [that] the parties refer to it and all matters specially provided for in the Charter of the United Nations or in treaties. . . ." Under Article 38, the Court relies on the following sources of International Law to disputes submitted for its consideration: (1) treaties; (2) customary State practice; (3) general principles of law applied by civilized nations; (4) national or other international court decisions; and (5) scholarly writings of the experts in International Law (*see* §1.4 of this book on sources of International Law).

The original UN members designed the ICJ to promote the peaceful settlement of international disputes. The Court soon began to execute this function in a fitting manner. The Court's first contentious case (between adverse litigants) was the 1948 *Corfu Channel* litigation. The United Kingdom sued Albania when UK warships hit mines laid in Albania's territorial waters. The Court decided that the UK had a right to navigate through these waters, holding Albania responsible for the damage to the UK war vessels. After the judgment, this problem did not resurface. In the 1950 *Protection of French Nationals and Protected Persons in Egypt* case, France sued Egypt for harming French citizens residing in Egypt. After the suit was filed, Egypt rescinded its objectionable measures. The ICJ discontinued the proceedings because Egypt's remedy satisfied France. The Court was apparently headed for a bright future.

The manner in which the Court was constituted by the UN Charter and its companion ICJ Statute created special jurisprudential problems, however. Nigeria's former Judge and President of the ICJ, T.O. Elias, observed that "[t]he ICJ or World Court is unique in a number of ways and, as such, generates no international legal system of its own." Unlike national tribunals, the ICJ has no bailiffs or prison system to ensure compliance with its interim orders and judgments.[31] There were no special forces dispatched to Libya, for example, when the Court ordered Libya to turn over its two citizens apparently responsible for the 1988 bombing of Pan Am Flight 103 over Lockerbie, Scotland. Even if Libya had turned over those individuals, there would be no UN jail at the disposal of the ICJ—necessitating reliance instead on the aid of some State member to carry out such an order.

There is another significant jurisprudential problem with the Court: It is a trial court, not an appellate court. Reviewing tribunals in national legal systems routinely rely on an extensive judicial record from a lower court, whose lawyers refine and advocate the respective view of the precise nature of the issue to be resolved. New York University Professor Thomas Franck notes the inherent limitation of not having a record from which to draw:

> [T]he Court, as both trial court and court of ultimate jurisprudential recourse, is in a far more difficult position than domestic [national] courts, where it is customary to make fact-determination the principal concern of the lower court while leaving it to a higher tribunal to devote itself almost exclusively to the jurisprudential issues applicable to predetermined facts. Moreover, to this burden of duality should be added the disadvantage of distance. That The Hague is very far . . . [from] the forests of El Salvador or the jungles of Thailand and the desert of Western Sahara, is self-evident. Less immediately apparent is the . . . Court's cultural diversity, [because] few members can draw upon personal experience to imagine the substantive realities as to which the pleadings establish contradictory assertions. . . . In the [ICJ's] Peace Palace, the judges . . . cannot . . . reach into their life experiences to weigh the comparative probabilities. Even where contradictory witnesses are concerned, how can they rely on socio-culturally conditioned instinct to feel who is likely to be lying . . . when the witnesses are from a culture that is wholly unfamiliar to most members of the Court?[32]

While the ICJ has always functioned as a trial court, it could arguably undertake a form of judicial review of UN agency actions. In the *Libya* (§10.7) and *Bosnia* cases (§11.1), these countries claimed that the ICJ must review and overrule Security Council sanction decisions that were allegedly beyond the Council's powers under the UN Charter. In a democratically constituted national court system, such a balance-of-power principle unquestionably authorizes judicial review of the constitutionality of executive action.[33] The ICJ has never reviewed a sanction decision by the Security Council, however, for the purpose of determining its "constitutionality" under the UN Charter.

There are related problems with procedures to be employed and evidentiary burden of proof. An international tribunal such as the ICJ consists of judges from different legal systems. The term "burden of proof" has different meanings in common law and civil law countries. And contrary to the national law model, there are no rules of evidence that are internationally accepted. As depicted by the UN Compensation Commission's Dr. Mojtaba Kazazi, "similar to other aspects of international law, party autonomy is a major factor in determining the rules of evidence, including those on the burden of proof. Generally speaking, States are free to agree as they wish with respect to the burden of proof, when establishing an international tribunal for the peaceful settlement of their disputes." He also notes, "[i]n practice, however, in most of the cases no specific rules regarding evidence can be found in the *compromise* [statement of the case], and the parties to an international litigation usually empower the concerned international tribunal to determine its rules of procedure and evidence itself."[34]

OPTIONAL CLAUSE

Compulsory Jurisdiction Member States do not *have* to submit their disputes to the ICJ. All State members of the UN are automatically parties to the ICJ Statute per Article 93.1 of the UN Charter. Its terms "dictate" as follows: "All Members of the United Nations are *ipso facto* parties to the Statute of the International Court of Justice." That rather commanding language does not mandate ICJ dispute resolution for all cases, however. This "requirement" is one of form, rather than of substance. Those who created the ICJ anticipated that sovereign States would not be willing to vest the ICJ with the full judicial power necessary to require them to appear in a lawsuit filed by another State. The prospect of a distant tribunal rendering judgments against the more powerful nations of the world was too myopic to compel compulsory jurisdiction in all cases. If such a mandate had been placed in the Charter or ICJ Statute, the UN would be a far smaller organization than it is today.

The drafters of the ICJ Statute provided for several methods of accepting the compulsory (mandatory) jurisdiction of the ICJ after a State joins the UN. Article 36 of the Statute provides that the Court will have jurisdiction to hear and decide cases against a consenting State:

- in "cases [that] the parties refer to it" [for example, by inserting a clause in a treaty specifically referring any potential dispute to the ICJ *or*]
- "States parties to the present Statute may . . . declare [*unilaterally* by an appropriate filing with the UN Secretary-General that the filing State] recognizes as compulsory . . . and without special agreement [that is, a mutually agreeable treaty] the jurisdiction of the Court in all legal disputes concerning:

  (a) the interpretation of a treaty;
  (b) any question of international law;
  (c) the existence of any fact which, if established, would constitute a breach of an international obligation;
  (d) the nature or extent of the reparation [such as damages] to be made for the breach of an international obligation."

The ICJ Statute's provisions for "compulsory jurisdiction" depend completely on the will of States to accept the Court's power over them—in the specific circumstances expressed in each Declaration of Acceptance. The specific methods for exercising these alternatives are succinctly summarized by Polish Academy of Sciences Professor Renata Szafarz in his book on the Court's compulsory jurisdiction:

> The consent may be expressed *ad hoc* once a dispute has arisen. It may also be expressed *post hoc* by a party to the dispute when the case has been brought before the court by another party. Finally, consent may be expressed *ante hoc,* in advance, with reference to all legal disputes to be submitted in the future or to certain categories of dispute. The latter form of jurisdiction is usually, though not very precisely, termed compulsory or obligatory jurisdiction. Since the compulsory jurisdiction of the ICJ results either from the acceptance by states of the so-called optional clause . . . or from the acceptance of judicial clauses contained in treaties a considerable majority of states have accepted the compulsory jurisdiction of the ICJ, at least to some extent . . . even though . . . there should be more than the present 54 declarations accepting the optional clause and that there should be fewer reservations to [such] judicial clauses.[35]

Optional Clause Application This new UN blueprint for a judicial dispute resolution mechanism was a practical compromise. The organization's judicial process could not mandate *compulsory* jurisdiction for all of the UN's sovereign members all of the time. States did not want to be locked into the submission of all future disputes for resolution by this new and untested tribunal. But the potential UN members could be given the *option* to do so with the prerogative of accepting the ICJ's jurisdiction. The compromise contained in the optional clause was a peculiar and unique application of the "compulsory" jurisdiction commonly exercised by national courts. States joining the UN would automatically "accept" the ICJ Statute, although it contained a "compulsory jurisdiction" clause. That clause would only be triggered, however, by the member State's *subsequent* decision to actually subject itself to the jurisdiction and judgments of the UN's Court. Acceptance also did not have to be an all-or-nothing proposition.

This unique limitation is found in Article 36.2 of the ICJ Statute: States party "to the present Statute *may at any time* declare that they recognize as compulsory . . . the jurisdiction of the Court in all legal disputes. . ." [italics added]. This limitation on the Court's statutory jurisdiction to hear cases is another application of the treaty reservation theme examined in §8.2 of this book. Expressly authorizing limiting reservations in the Statute avoided an all-or-nothing approach to the decision whether to join the UN. Lacking this option, the world's more powerful nations would otherwise be unlikely to swell the membership ranks of the new world organization. This is one reason why the UN Charter refers to other dispute-resolution mechanisms (Exhibit 9.1).

The "compulsory" jurisdiction to hear cases is the most controversial and misunderstood feature of the ICJ's jurisdiction. States have unilaterally tendered a variety of acceptances: very *narrow* acceptances of the ICJ's compulsory jurisdiction, very *broad* ones, and others in-between. Egypt's declaration of 1957 was probably the narrowest, accepting ICJ jurisdiction *only* in the event of an international dispute directly involving its operation of the Suez Canal. The broadest acceptance comes from countries like Nicaragua, which have submitted unconditional unilateral acceptances of the ICJ's jurisdiction to hear *any* case involving Nicaragua. That country has little to lose in a forum where it can theoretically "square off" with the major powers of the world. Somewhere in between lies the declaration accepting ICJ jurisdiction on specified terms, such as those that function for a limited period of years (subject to renewal). Under Article 36.3, national declarations opting to accept the compulsory jurisdiction of the ICJ may thus be made (1) unconditionally, (2) for a limited time, or (3) on the condition of reciprocity.

Jurisdiction to Determine Jurisdiction A non-statutory limitation on ICJ jurisdiction clashes with the express terms of the ICJ Statute. State practice that evolved after the promulgation of the Statute's final draft in 1951 created yet another obstacle to realization of the dream of substituting the courtroom for the battlefield. Article 36.6 provides that in "the event of a dispute as to whether the Court has jurisdiction, the matter shall be settled by the decision of the Court." This provision was interpreted by the ICJ in the Court's 1955 *Nottebohm* case (*see* text in §4.2). The relevant passage addresses the virtually global practice that a court has the jurisdiction to determine its own jurisdiction when one of the parties questions whether it has the power to hear the case:

> Paragraph 6 of Article 36 merely adopted . . . a rule consistently accepted by general international law . . . [whereby] an international tribunal has the right to decide to [resolve questions about] its own jurisdiction and has the power to interpret for this purpose the instruments which govern jurisdiction. This principle, which is accepted by general international law in the matter of arbitration, assumes particular force when the international tribunal . . . is an institution which has been pre-established by an international instrument defining its jurisdiction and regulating its operation, and is in the present case the principal judicial organ of the United Nations. . . . The judicial character of the Court and the rule of general international law referred to above are sufficient to establish that the Court is competent to adjudicate on its own jurisdiction in the present case.[36]

The ICJ does *not* possess the exclusive power to decide its own jurisdiction. The major powers began to limit their declarations when they filed so-called acceptances of the Court's compulsory jurisdiction. Their reservations to that statutory language, when tendered in advance of any dispute, specified that the defendant State—not the ICJ—would decide whether the Court could hear and decide international disputes wherein they were summoned to appear as a defendant. Try to imagine a national judge's reaction if a defendant told the judge that the court did not have the power to act, that the *defendant* had decided this question, and that the judge could do nothing about it. This is exactly what many States did by invoking the optional clause and thus limiting their "acceptances." The ICJ Statute does not *require* a State to accept the Court's jurisdiction. This is the reason why the Court has been powerless to act in some widely publicized instances.

France's acceptance (withdrawn in 1974) is a good example. Its acceptance "does not apply to differences relating to matters that are essentially within the national jurisdiction *as understood by the Government of France* [italics added]." In this instance, France extracted the language from Article 2.7 of the UN Charter: Nothing "contained in the present Charter shall authorize the United Nations to intervene in matters [that] are essentially within the domestic jurisdiction of any state. . . ." France (and a number of other nations) have thereby invoked the UN Charter's limitation on its general power to act as a basis for (a) appearing to submit to the jurisdiction of the Court, and (b) actually retaining the ability to avoid certain ICJ disputes by classifying a case as one that is essentially "domestic" rather than "international" in scope.

Canada's acceptance of the ICJ's compulsory jurisdiction was limited as follows: In a 1994 reservation to the UN Law of the Sea Treaty (Chapter 6), Canada's Declaration accepted jurisdiction "over all disputes . . . other than . . . disputes arising out of or concerning conservation and management measures taken by Canada with respect to vessels fishing in the NAFO Regulatory Area . . . and the enforcement of such measures." This area is the subject of conflicting fishing rights and an ICJ case wherein Spain sued Canada because of its assertion of fisheries jurisdiction *beyond* the economic zone established in the UN treaty.

Reciprocity This basis for limiting national acceptances of the ICJ's compulsory jurisdiction acknowledged that not all States would recognize the Court's jurisdiction on the identical basis. A potential defendant State might consider it unfair for a plaintiff State—which had previously tendered a *narrower* acceptance of the Court's jurisdiction before any dispute arose—to sue in circumstances whereby the plaintiff State would not be similarly amenable to the Court's jurisdiction.

Assume that France and Norway independently tendered their separate Declarations of Acceptance of ICJ jurisdiction years ago. Before any dispute arose between them, each thereby agreed to accept the ICJ's power over them and to be bound by its judgments. Neither country did so, however, on an *un*conditional basis. Each accepted the "compulsory" jurisdiction of the ICJ with a limitation. France's hypothetical declaration consents to jurisdiction in all matters with one exception not included in Norway's acceptance: "France will *not* appear as a defendant in cases involving armed conflicts between France and any another country." Assume that Norway's prior declaration also accepted the Court's jurisdiction, but with a different reservation: "Norway accepts the Court's compulsory jurisdiction on the condition of reciprocity."

In this hypothetical situation, Norway attacks France. France then sues Norway in the ICJ, possibly for the psychological value of media reports depicting France as the victim in this armed conflict. The more limited nature of France's acceptance of the Court's compulsory jurisdiction would be borrowed by Norway to avoid this litigation. Norway's previous acceptance was made "on the condition of reciprocity." France previously limited its jurisdictional submission by effectively repressing the Court's power to hear any case of armed conflict involving France. Norway may invoke the narrower acceptance of a State that is suing Norway. Norway may substitute France's narrower acceptance of the Court's jurisdiction. If France could avoid the same suit if it were a defendant, then so may Norway. The Court would have to dismiss France's case against Norway. Norway's "reciprocity"-based acceptance of the Court's jurisdiction would permit Norway to borrow France's "armed conflict" reservation to the Court's jurisdiction.

The following ICJ case illustrates the problems spawned by national declarations containing individual reservations arguably not contemplated by the drafters of the ICJ Statute. This case demonstrates how both the reciprocity and domestic jurisdiction limitations may deprive the ICJ of its fundamental judicial power to decide whether it can hear a case arising under International Law.

Case of Certain Norwegian Loans (France v. Norway)

INTERNATIONAL COURT OF JUSTICE, 1957
1957 *ICJ Reports* 9

Author's Note: *From 1885 to 1909, the Norwegian Government borrowed money from French sources. Norway's loans were secured by banknotes, wherein the government promised to repay the loans in gold. In 1914 (when World War I began in Europe), Norway wanted to retain its gold reserves. It therefore suspended the convertibility of its banknotes into gold for an indefinite period. Norwegian law provided that when creditors refused to accept payment in Bank of Norway notes (rather than the promised gold), Norwegian debtors could postpone payment of their loans in gold. French citizens were unable to obtain their repayment in gold as promised under the express terms of the loans to Norway.*

The French government suggested that this dispute be submitted to either an international commission of financial experts or any mutually acceptable arbitral body—or, alternatively, to the International Court of Justice. Norway consistently refused all of these alternatives on the basis that this matter should be heard only in Norwegian courts. Norway considered this problem to be a local matter involving no more than an alleged breach of contract that was governed by the local laws of Norway. France ultimately filed this case in the ICJ. In its application for relief, the French government sought a judgment that Norway's loans should be discharged only by payment in gold as promised.

The ICJ did not reach the merits of France's case. The Court could not exercise jurisdiction to hear this particular case. Its inherent power to proceed was vitiated by the combined effect of France's "domestic jurisdiction" reservation and Norway's "reciprocity" reservation. The opinion of the majority of the judges discusses why the ICJ did not have the power to act. Judge Lauterpacht's concurring opinion agreed with the result reached by the majority of the judges (that the court lacked jurisdiction). He based his conclusion, however, on different footing: France's purported submission to the compulsory jurisdiction of the court was illusory—a rather daunting theme that continues to plague the Court to this day.

Both opinions in this case reveal how national limitations on the power of the ICJ to hear international disputes have frustrated the goals of the Statute of the International Court of Justice as well as full utilization of the Court's resources. Emphasis in certain paragraphs has been added by the textbook author.

COURT'S OPINION.

MAJORITY OPINION OF THE COURT

The Application [by France for a judgment against Norway] expressly refers to Article 36, paragraph 2, of the Statute of the Court and to the acceptance of the compulsory jurisdiction of the Court by Norway on November 16th, 1946, and by France on March 1st, 1949. The Norwegian Declaration reads:

> I declare on behalf of the Norwegian Government that Norway recognizes as compulsory *ipso facto* and without special agreement . . . *on condition of reciprocity,* the jurisdiction of the International Court of Justice in conformity with Article 36, paragraph 2, of the Statute of the Court, for a period of ten years as from 3rd October 1946.

The French Declaration reads:

> On behalf of the Government of the French Republic, and subject to ratification [which was later given], I declare that I recognize as compulsory *ipso facto* and without special agreement . . . on condition of reciprocity, the jurisdiction of the International Court of Justice . . . for all disputes which may arise [unless] the parties may have agreed or may agree to have recourse to another method of peaceful settlement. This declaration does not apply to differences relating to matters which are essentially within the national jurisdiction [of France] as understood by the Government of the French Republic. . . .

The Norwegian Government maintained that the subject of the dispute was within the exclusive domain of the municipal [internal] law of Norway, and that the Norwegian Government relied upon the reservation in the French Declaration [excluding] matters which are essentially within the national jurisdiction [of France] as understood by the French Government. . . .

[Norway explained that] There can be no possible doubt on this point. If, however, there should still be some doubt, the *Norwegian Government would rely upon the reservations made by the French Government* in its Declaration of March 1st, 1949. By virtue of the principle of reciprocity, which is embodied in Article 36, paragraph 2, of the Statute of the Court and which has been clearly expressed in the Norwegian Declaration of November 16th, 1946, the Norwegian Government cannot be bound, vis-à-vis the French Government, by undertakings which are either broader or stricter than those given by the latter Government [of France]. . . .

[In a subsequent portion of the opinion, the Court responded as follows.] In the Preliminary Objections filed by the Norwegian Government it is stated:

> The Norwegian Government did not insert any such reservation in its own Declaration. But it has the right to rely upon the [narrower] restrictions placed by France upon her own undertakings.
>
> Convinced that the dispute, which has been brought before the Court by the Application of July 6th, 1955, is within the domestic jurisdiction, the Norwegian Government considers itself fully entitled to rely on this right [as France would do if a defendant in this Court]. Accordingly, it requests the Court to decline, on grounds that it lacks jurisdiction, the function which the French Government would have it assume.

In considering this ground of the Objection, the Court notes in the first place that the present case has been brought before it on the basis of Article 36, paragraph 2, of the Statute and of the corresponding Declarations of acceptance of compulsory jurisdiction; that in the present case the jurisdiction of the Court depends upon the Declarations made by the Parties in accordance with Article 36, paragraph 2, of the Statute on condition of reciprocity; and that, since two unilateral declarations are involved, such *jurisdiction is conferred upon the Court only to the extent to which the Declarations coincide* in conferring it. A comparison between the two Declarations shows that the French Declaration accepts the Court's jurisdiction within narrower limits than the Norwegian Declaration; consequently, the common will of the Parties, which is the basis of the Court's jurisdiction, exists within these narrower limits indicated by the French reservation. . . .

France has limited her acceptance of the compulsory jurisdiction of the Court by excluding beforehand disputes relating to matters which are essentially within the national jurisdiction as understood by the Government of the French Republic. In accordance with the condition of reciprocity to which acceptance of the compulsory jurisdiction is made subject in both Declarations and which is provided for in Article 36, paragraph 3, of the Statute, Norway, equally with France, is entitled to except from the compulsory jurisdiction of the Court disputes understood by Norway to be essentially within its national jurisdiction. . . .

The Court does not consider that it should examine whether the French reservation is consistent with the undertaking of a legal obligation and is compatible with Article 36, paragraph 6, of the Statute [the core of Justice Lauterpacht's concurring opinion] which provides:

> *In the event of a dispute as to whether the Court has jurisdiction, the matter shall be settled by the decision of the Court.*

The validity of the [French] reservation has not been questioned by the Parties. . . .

The Court considers that the *Norwegian Government is entitled, by virtue of the condition of reciprocity, to invoke the reservation contained in the French Declaration* of March 1st, 1949; that this reservation excludes from the jurisdiction of the Court the dispute which has been referred to it by the Application of the French Government; that consequently the Court is without jurisdiction to entertain the [French] Application. . . .

The ICJ then voted twelve to three that it lacked the necessary jurisdiction to hear and determine France's claim.

Separate Opinion of Judge Sir Hersch Lauterpacht

While I concur in the operative part of the Judgment inasmuch as the Court has declared itself incompetent to decide on the merits of the case submitted to it, I much regret that I do not find myself in agreement with the *grounds* of the Judgment. . . .

I consider it *legally impossible for the Court to act in disregard of its Statute* which imposes upon it the duty and confers upon it the right to determine its jurisdiction. That right cannot be exercised by a party to the dispute. The Court cannot, in any circumstances, treat as admissible the claim that the parties have accepted its jurisdiction subject to the condition that they, and not the Court, will decide on its jurisdiction. To do so is in my view contrary to Article 36 (6) of the Statute which, without any qualification, confers upon the

Court the right and imposes upon it the duty to determine its jurisdiction. Moreover, it is also contrary to Article 1 of the Statute of the Court and *Article 92 of the Charter of the United Nations which lay down that the Court shall function in accordance with the provisions of its Statute.* It is that question which I now propose to consider in connection with the examination of the validity of the French Acceptance [whereunder it decides jurisdiction rather than the ICJ]. . . .

Moreover, the particular [French] *reservation now at issue is not one that is contrary to some merely procedural aspect of the Statute. It is contrary to one of its basic features.* It is at variance with the principal safeguard of the system of the compulsory jurisdiction of the Court. Without it, the compulsory jurisdiction of the Court being dependent upon the will of the defendant party, expressed subsequent to the dispute having been brought before the Court, has no meaning. *Article 36 (6) is thus an essential condition of the system of obligatory judicial settlement as established in the Statute.* That provision was inserted in the Statute with the deliberate intention of providing an indispensable safeguard of the operation of the system. Article 36 (2) speaks of the recognition by the parties to the Statute of the 'compulsory' jurisdiction of the Court. But there is no question of compulsory jurisdiction if, after the dispute has arisen and after it has been brought before the Court, the defendant State is entitled to decide whether the Court has jurisdiction. . . .

Accordingly, in my view the entire *French Declaration* of Acceptance must be treated as *devoid of legal effect* and as incapable of providing a basis for the jurisdiction of the Court. It is for that reason that, in my view, the Court has no jurisdiction over the dispute.

◆ *Notes & Questions*

1. The *Norwegian Loans* case illustrates that there are fundamental problems with the "compulsory" jurisdiction of the ICJ. While the legal relationship existed between the parties before the Court came into existence, both litigants had expressly agreed to use the Court to decide such international disputes. Yet both litigants were able to reserve the "right" to avoid the Court's compulsory jurisdiction. France's narrow acceptance retained the ability to characterize a claim as one arising under France's internal law rather than International Law. Norway merely piggybacked onto France's narrower Declaration of Acceptance because Norway had accepted the ICJ's compulsory jurisdiction via its own "reciprocity" Declaration of Acceptance. Consider the following questions:
   (a) Under the Statute of the ICJ, who decides whether the Court has jurisdiction?
   (b) What is the "optional clause," and which State or States invoked it in *Norwegian Loans?*
   (c) When a State invokes the optional clause, what obligation does it thereby accept?
   (d) The text of the optional clause includes the word *compulsory.* What does this term mean? What limitations does the ICJ Statute contain?
   (e) States do not have to unconditionally accept the jurisdiction of the ICJ in *all* matters. How did Norway limit the declaration in which it previously submitted itself to the compulsory jurisdiction of the ICJ?
   (f) Why was Norway able to avoid litigating the *Norwegian Loans* case?
   (g) Why did Judge Lauterpacht characterize France's submission to the compulsory jurisdiction of the ICJ as invalid?

2. Spain (representing the interests of the European Union) sued Canada in the ICJ, claiming that Canada's special fisheries jurisdiction—some 220 nautical miles off Canada's coast, well beyond the 200-mile Exclusive Economic Zone—violates International Law (discussed in §6.3). In December 1998, the ICJ dismissed this suit on the basis that it lacked jurisdiction to hear the case. One year before enacting this special legislative fishing-conservation zone, Canada tendered a fresh acceptance to the compulsory jurisdiction of the ICJ. Canada thus limited its consent to suit in the ICJ by excepting any case against Canada regarding Canada's amended Coastal Fisheries Protection Act.

   The Court rejected Spain's assertion that the Canadian reservation should be considered inadmissible, which would have otherwise permitted the Court to proceed with the case if the new reservation were interpreted as being inconsistent with general International Law. Further details are available on the ICJ Web site at http://www.icj-cij.org/idocket/iec/iecframe.htm.

ADVISORY JURISDICTION

During the first forty years of its existence (1946–1986), the International Court of Justice had fifty-three "contentious" cases wherein the State litigants argued either jurisdictional objections or the merits of their cases. During the same period, the ICJ also rendered eighteen "advisory" opinions in cases where States were *not* parties to the proceedings. The Court therein invites States or international organizations to provide information to assist in its advisory deliberations. Unlike the ICJ's contentious litigation, there is no plaintiff or defendant.

The ICJ succinctly summarized the fundamental difference between its contentious and advisory jurisdiction as follows:

> The participation of interested States had conferred on the present proceedings a wholly unusual character tending to obscure the difference in principle between contentious and advisory proceedings. Whereas in contentious proceedings the Court has before it parties who plead their cause and must, where necessary, produce evidence in support of their contentions, in advisory proceedings it is assumed that the Court will itself obtain the information it needs, should the States not have supplied it. In contentious proceedings, if a party does not succeed in producing good grounds for a claim, the Court has only to dismiss it, whereas in advisory proceedings the Court's task is not confined to assessing the probative force of the information supplied by States, but consists in trying to arrive at an opinion with the help of all the elements of information available to it.[37]

The ICJ's advisory jurisdiction resolves sweeping questions of International Law in a non-adversarial context. An advisory resolution fills the gap created by the general lack of State commitment to resolving sensitive international disputes in contentious (adversarial) litigation. States are normally unwilling to submit their major disputes to the Court. Some States have even registered objections when a UN agency has sought an advisory opinion. An early ICJ opinion on point (1950) determined that State consent is *not* required for an advisory opinion: "It follows that no State, whether a Member of the United Nations or not, can prevent the giving of an Advisory Opinion which the United Nations considers to be desirable in order to obtain enlightenment as to the course of action it should take. The Court's [advisory] Opinion is given not to the States, but to the organ which is entitled to request it; the reply of the Court, itself an 'organ of the United Nations,' represents its participation in the activities of the Organization, and, in principle, should not be refused."[38]

Who initiates advisory proceedings and why? Under Article 65 of the Statute of the International Court of Justice, the "Court may give an advisory opinion on any [international] legal question at the request of whatever body may be authorized by or in accordance with the Charter of the United Nations to make such a request." An individual State may bring a problem to the attention of one of these bodies. Under UN Charter Article 96, however, only the General Assembly, the Security Council, and specialized agencies authorized by the General Assembly may "request advisory opinions of the Court on legal questions arising within the scope of their activities." The Court then interprets and applies International Law in the absence of State litigants. In 1993, for example, the General Assembly's World Health Organization sought an advisory opinion from the ICJ requesting guidance on the question of whether the threat or use of nuclear weapons is permitted in *any* circumstances.

The judicial arm of the overall organization may also resolve conflicting interpretations of the Charter by different UN organs. In the 1945 Statement on Charter Interpretation contained in UN Conference Document No. 933, the drafting committee provided as follows:

> Difficulties may conceivably arise in the event that there should be a difference of opinion among organs of the Organization concerning the correct interpretation of the Charter. Thus, two organs may conceivably hold and may express or even act upon different views. . . . [I]t would always be open to the General Assembly or to the Security Council . . . to ask the International Court of Justice for an advisory opinion concerning the meaning of a provision of the Charter.

Another reason for the ICJ's advisory jurisdiction is that only *States* may be parties in the Court's contentious cases. Unlike certain regional international courts (§9.6), other international organizations, their agencies, and individuals cannot be parties in ICJ litigation. They lack the international personality to directly participate in contentious litigation. Supplementing the ICJ's contentious jurisdiction with the power to hear cases, by or against international organizations, had been suggested but not implemented—mostly due to the uncertain contours of the relationship between States and international organizations when the UN Charter and ICJ Statute were created. Advisory opinions were designed to provide guidance about matters involving the UN's organs and specialized agencies. The Court could thereby settle potential disputes among the various organs of the UN.

Among the Court's more prominent advisory opinions are the 1950 *Competence of the Assembly* case, the 1951 *Genocide Reservations* case, and the 1988 *PLO UN Mission* case. In the first of these opinions, the ICJ resolved a dispute involving the respective powers of the UN's General Assembly and Security Council. The Court decided that the UN Charter could not be interpreted to permit the General Assembly to unilaterally admit members to the UN. It was *unwilling* to condone the suggestion—contrary to the Charter's language—that a recommendation of the Security Council was not required. In a second advisory opinion, the General Assembly sought guidance about the permissibility of potential reservations to the Genocide Treaty. While the court did not clearly answer this question (*see* case text in §8.2), it did decide that State treaty reservations must be generally compatible with the underlying purpose of a treaty. In the 1988 *PLO UN Mission* case, the Court decided that the US could not close the mission of the Palestine Liberation Organization in New York. The US obligations to the UN precluded closure of the PLO's UN Mission on the basis of antiterrorism.[39]

Given the political interest that States sometimes exhibit in proceedings related to an advisory opinion, the difference between advisory and contentious litigation can be obscured. Normally, the Court obtains what information it desires when exercising its advisory jurisdiction—particularly when one or more interested States are not forthcoming in providing factual details for the Court's legal analysis. But in some advisory cases, State interest generates a degree of participation virtually on a par with that manifested by the ICJ's contentious cases. In the 1975 *Western Sahara* advisory opinion (analyzed in §2.3), for example, the UN General Assembly requested an ICJ advisory opinion regarding the status of the referenced territory. The Court called upon Spain, Morocco, and Mauritania to submit information regarding their respective claims to this region. The proceedings resembled contentious litigation, because of the presentation of conflicting adversarial views to the Court—although the case technically involved only the advisory jurisdiction of the Court.

CHAMBERS OF THE COURT

Under Article 26 of the ICJ Statute, the "Court may form from time to time one or more chambers, composed of three or more judges . . . for dealing with particular categories of cases." Upon the request of a party to a dispute, the president of the ICJ determines whether the other party is agreeable to the formation of a chamber to hear the dispute. The original intent—to provide chambers to hear labor, transit, and communications cases—expanded in 1982. Various ICJ chambers began to consider border disputes between the US and Canada, Mali and Upper Volta, and El Salvador and Honduras.[40]

The chamber mode of dispute resolution offers two advantages. One is that the judges may decide matters on a summary basis. Article 29 of the ICJ Statute provides that with "a view to the speedy dispatch of business, the Court shall form annually a chamber composed of five judges which, at the request of the parties, may hear and determine cases by summary procedure." The judges can dispense with certain court rules and procedures when deemed appropriate. The other advantage is that States do not have to submit their cases for consideration by the *full* Court. The entire tribunal of fifteen jurists may include judges from States having poor relations with a party to a particular dispute.

In 1972, the ICJ amended its court rules to permit its president to ascertain the litigants' views on the judicial composition of their particular chambers. The legality and desirability of those consultations is still being debated. Article 26 of the Statute of the International Court of Justice provides for party approval of the *number* of judges. It does not defer to party approval about *which* judges will sit on a particular panel. The 1972 compromise is designed to encourage greater use of the Court. When this issue was being considered, the ICJ president stated that parties' input about which judges sat on their panel would breathe new life into the use of the Court. The receipt of their input does not change the fact that the Court itself still elects the members of its chambers. The president of the Court acknowledged that from "a practical point of view, it is difficult to conceive that in normal circumstances those [judicial] Members who have been suggested by the parties would not be elected."[41]

Others view this development as an indicator of the increased politicalization of the ICJ. The American Society of International Law's 1987 study on the ICJ indicates that the parties have a decisive impact on the composition of the chambers. They are able to comment on the makeup of the particular chamber, which relieves national apprehension about submitting cases to judges from unfriendly governments. Some States have recommended that the ICJ chambers device be supplemented by creating *regional* chambers. These devices for increasing the use of the ICJ would, in the view of some commentators, support the perspective that the Court has become a political institution.[42]

ICJ ASSESSMENT

Is the concept of global adjudication as an alternative to war too idealistic to be workable? In the UN Secretary-General's 1992 special report to the UN Security Council, Boutros Boutros-Ghali recommended the following steps to reinforce the role of the ICJ: "(a) All member States should accept the general jurisdiction [rather than the usual reliance on special treaty clauses] of the International Court . . . without *any* reservation, before the end of the United Nations Decade of International Law in the year 2000. (b) When submission of a dispute to the full Court is not practical, the Chambers jurisdiction should be used. (c) States should support the Trust Fund established to assist countries unable to afford the cost involved in bringing a dispute to the Court. . . ."[43]

It is unlikely that States will rekindle the interest in international adjudication that blossomed from 1944 through 1946. In 1944, even before World War II ended, some of the world's most powerful nations planned a global organization of states that would avert further wars. In 1945, they drafted unassailable principles calling for the peaceful settlement of disputes. These norms were then incorporated into both the UN Charter and the ICJ Statute. The language in these constituting documents expressed the hope that the Court would play a role in managing subsequent hostilities. UN Charter Article 36.3 states "that legal disputes should as a general rule be referred by the parties to the International Court of Justice in accordance with the provisions of the Statute of the Court." The Court was designed to serve as a buffer for adversaries who might thereby avoid the various forms of hostility (Chapter 10) to settle their disputes. If an offending State failed to comply with the Court's interim orders or final judgments, the Security Council was to devise measures to ensure compliance.

In practice, this paradigm did not close the gap between hope and reality. Many of the original UN members refused to yield sovereign control over their own disputes to an international organization headquartered in a distant land—or its judicial organ in Europe. Charter Article 33, for example, provides that adversaries are expected to resort first to local or regional mechanisms before invoking the aid of the UN. This rather amorphous prescription provided a convenient basis for avoiding direct resort to the ICJ.

A fundamental problem of mistrust remains. Many UN delegates at the 1945 UN drafting conference mistrusted the first World Court (PCIJ), which had been conceived by the French and staffed with mostly European judges. To these delegates, it may have been more palatable to entrust sensitive disputes to a local or regional judicial body as opposed to a global institution hundreds or thousands of miles away in the Netherlands. Socialist States have generally avoided the submission of their disputes to a distant international tribunal, perceiving such pressures as a bourgeois threat to their sovereign decision-making prerogatives. Many lesser developed States lack familiarity with formal adjudication and are thus rather cautious about formal mechanisms like "compulsory jurisdiction."[44]

On the other hand, the US and Russia tendered a joint proposal in 1993 at the UN that encouraged greater use of the ICJ via the "chambers" process described above. The objective is to encourage resort to a convenient dispute-resolution mechanism, at least in cases involving the terrorism and narcotics treaties signed by both States in the aftermath of the Cold War. The other UN Security Council members—France, Great Britain, and China—were asked to support and ultimately join the US–Russia chambers proposal. Disputes would be resolved by "panels" of fewer than all fifteen judges. But Great Britain and a number of commentators characterized this proposal as a step backward. It supposedly *discourages* use of full-court powers. France and China remain so suspicious of the ICJ that their endorsement of this plan remains unlikely.

Article 59 of the ICJ Statute is an arguable manifestation of the general sovereign mistrust of "outside" judicial resolutions of local disputes. The court's decisions "have no binding force except as between the parties and in respect of that particular case." Although the Court is expected to provide some direction in the progressive development of International Law, its Statute expressly limits the binding effect of the ICJ's judgments for use in subsequent cases. Decisions legally bind *only* the immediate parties in the immediate suit. The parties are not necessarily bound in the event of a similar issue arising between them in the future. *Stare decisis* is generally rejected in countries employing Civil Law jurisprudential principles (*e.g.*, France)—as opposed to Common Law countries (*e.g.*, England), where case precedent is a central feature of national jurisprudence. The Court has nevertheless relied on its prior decisions as evidence of the content of International Law. It would be a waste of judicial resources, however, not to consider earlier decisions when the same point of law is later presented in another case.[45]

Although numerous criticisms persist, the ICJ has been useful. It has decided a number of significant disputes. Most of its decisions have been implemented by the participating States. In 1992, for example, El Salvador and Honduras accepted an ICJ border-dispute judgment that ended a two-century dilemma in their international relations. As stated by Honduras's President Rafael Callejas, two Central American States illustrated "that any dispute, however complex, can be resolved in a civilized and conciliatory way." The Court has also been able to proceed to an important judgment even in the absence of the defendant State. Such cases have significantly aided in the progressive development of International Law (as in the *Nicaragua* judgment against the US after its withdrawal—described earlier in this section and set forth in Chapter 10).

The utility of the ICJ includes the plaintiff State's ability to file a case with a view toward encouraging settlement when diplomatic negotiations are deadlocked. Nicaragua filed a transborder armed-conflict claim against Honduras in 1988. Honduras responded by attacking the jurisdiction of the Court. The Court determined that it did have jurisdiction over this dispute. The parties then reached an out-of-court agreement, likely facilitated by Honduras's recognition that it could obtain more via settlement than by a possibly all-or-nothing court judgment. Nicaragua then requested that this case be discontinued after the two nations fully resolved their dispute diplomatically.

Success is, of course, tempered by the realization that States tend *not* to submit their most sensitive disputes to the Court. The Court has played a tangible role in facilitating the continuous development of International Law as it ebbs and flows with the complex developments of State practice. Through no fault of its own, however, it has *not* contributed significantly to the preservation of world peace. It cannot realistically control disputes when the participants who would be governed by its jurisprudence have failed to employ its resources. The ICJ cannot be fairly accused of "failing." It was never vested with the independent power to require the participation of potential defendant States or render enforceable legal solutions. In the last analysis, the "compulsory" jurisdiction of the Court is solely dependent on State consent for its very existence. Some States have even deprived the Court of the otherwise universally exercised judicial power to determine its own jurisdiction to proceed. England's Sir Hersch Lauterpacht, one of the most prominent members of the Court, explained that

> it would be an exaggeration to assert that the Court has proved to be a significant instrument for maintaining peace. The degree of achievement of this end by an international court, as indeed by any other court, is dependent upon the state of political integration of the society whose law it administers. But international society has in this respect, in the years following the two World Wars, fallen short of the expectation of those who in the Covenant of the League of Nations and in the Charter of the United Nations intended to create, through them, the basis of the future orderly development of the international community.[46]

Some individuals claim that the International Court of Justice is the classic ivory tower occupied by a group of theoreticians. Its jurists supposedly generate pointless discourses that are unrelated to how States actually behave in the real world. These criticisms are misdirected. The UN was not intended to be a world government. Its decisions were not really designed by its State membership to replace the primacy of national sovereignty. The UN's judicial arm was not intended to be a world court in the sense that it might become a principal tool for dispute resolution. The *optional* nature of sovereign submission to the ICJ's power to hear and determine cases arising under International Law is the built-in Achilles heel of the UN's judicial process.

A more useful perspective is that the UN has not replaced States as the core element in the structure of the international system. Its members never transferred the necessary jurisdictional powers to the ICJ or the necessary enforcement powers to the UN. States did not want to vest such organizational entities with the power to resolve international disputes absent the full consent of the participating States on an almost case-by-case basis. The original fifty-one members of the UN had various reasons for limiting the power of this judicial body. The older and more developed powers perceived the potential change in the postwar composition of the community of nations as an unwelcome shift in the balance of power. Nearly three-fourths of the UN's current members did not exist in 1945 when the other quarter created the organization. (Exhibit 2.1 in §2.2 graphically depicts this evolution.)

The newer States do not share the same political and economic perspectives of certain of the older, powerful, and more economically established members. In the 1970s, these "Third World" States expressed the common view that they should become members of the international community on equal terms with the original UN members. From the perspective of new States, many aspects of modern International Law (developed by Europeans incident to the 1648 Peace of Westphalia described in §1.3) discourage the Third World's military and economic development. One might argue that the ICJ, and the ability of the more powerful UN members to manipulate it, is just another facade for perpetuating the dominance of the older members of the international community. This perspective suggests that until international tribunals command a wider constituency, national courts provide a more realistic medium for *judicial* development of International Law. The ICJ cannot be a talismanic cure for international disputes absent a greater political integration of the community of nations.

Many observers of the International Court of Justice exude a religious reverence for the Court and a demonic disdain for States that have not used it. This perspective is also misleading. The ICJ is not like a national supreme court, typically exercising the powers to command the presence of adversaries and enforce national court judgments. The States that produced the ICJ cast it onto a stage directed by world politics. In the absence of world government, they did not want the ICJ to function like their own national courts. As classically depicted by the improper US withdrawal from ICJ jurisdiction in the *Nicaragua* case (without the minimum notice of withdrawal as promised in its acceptance of the Court's jurisdiction), the compulsory jurisdiction of the Court is not serving the role envisioned by the UN drafters.

US POSITION ON THE ICJ

The US has been rather reserved about the ICJ from the outset. In 1946, the US Senate debated whether the US should accept the jurisdiction of the UN's new court. Senator Connally, Chairman of the Senate Foreign Relations Committee, expressed his concern that the US would be effectively surrendering the fate of important national interests to the UN by generally accepting the Court's compulsory jurisdiction. In his words: "I am in favor of the United Nations, but I am also for the United States of America. I do not want to surrender the sovereignty or the prestige of the United States with respect to any question which may be merely domestic in character . . . [when the] best hope of the world lies in the survival of the United States with its concepts of democracy, liberty, freedom, and advancement under its [own] institutions."[47]

The US nevertheless "accepted" the ICJ's jurisdiction in 1946, but not without reservations. Key US limitations that would preclude the Court from hearing cases were: (a) entrusted to *other* tribunals by a distinct treaty provision; (b) essentially within the domestic jurisdiction of the US, *as determined by the US;* and (c) cases arising under a multilateral treaty—unless all parties to the dispute were also parties to the particular treaty and agreed on submitting a dispute to the ICJ.

After accepting the Court's jurisdiction, subject to the above limitations, the US became a major proponent of increased use of the ICJ. In 1974, the US Senate asked the US President to consider the feasibility of increasing the nation's participation in the ICJ. In 1977, the resulting US Department of State study concluded that the "underlying presumption of this Senate Resolution is that it is desirable to widen access to the International Court of Justice in order to increase its activity, use and contributions to the development of international law. As a general proposition, the Department of State strongly endorses that presumption."[48]

In the 1980s, the US "roller coaster" approach to ICJ adjudication began another descent. The US had begun to withdraw from various organs of the UN, as well as refusing to pay its assessed share of UN dues (§3.3). In 1984, the US refused to participate in Nicaragua's suit against the US, claiming that the US Central Intelligence Agency had arranged the mining of key Nicaraguan harbors. The US withdrew its acceptance of the Court's jurisdiction virtually on the eve of the filing of the case by Nicaragua. In its 1946 declaration accepting the jurisdiction of the ICJ, the US had promised a minimum of six months' notice for any withdrawal. US Secretary of State George Schultz nevertheless stated that the immediate withdrawal from any case involving any Central American State was necessary "to foster the continuing regional dispute settlement process which seeks a negotiated solution to the interrelated political, economic, and security problems of Central America." As the US could not legally withdraw without giving six months' notice, the Court proceeded with the case and entered a judgment against the US.[49]

A sharp debate nevertheless lingered about the legality and political propriety of the US withdrawal. George Mason University (Virginia) Professor Stuart Malawer made the following observation in opposition to the US withdrawal from this case:

> The World Court [judges] in absolutely astonishing majorities rejected the American arguments concerning the lack of jurisdiction and inadmissibility of Nicaragua's claim against it. Reading the recent court decision, one must wonder how anyone ever believed the [Court's] decision could have been otherwise.
>
> Why is it that the United States, the country which has championed international law in foreign affairs and the development of the World Court, has gotten itself into such an embarrassing position, and is now on the verge of being branded an outlaw state, when the transgressions of so many others are so great?
>
> My answer is simple. The legal advice given by the lawyers in the State Department must have been terrible.[50]

Although scholars may debate the legality of the US withdrawal, one conclusion is inescapable. The US did not comply with its reservation promising to give six months' notice of its intent to withdraw its acceptance of the Court's compulsory jurisdiction.

Then, in 1985, the US terminated its general acceptance (in 1946) of ICJ compulsory jurisdiction. The US position was that, of the five permanent members of the UN Security Council, only the US and the UK had previously accepted the Court's compulsory jurisdiction (in a rather limited form). Given the lack of universality hoped for by the US when it originally accepted the Court's jurisdiction, the US had never been able to bring a case against another State—while itself having been sued three times. Therefore, the US presidential administration publicly blamed Nicaragua, Cuba, and the former Soviet Union for using the Court's processes as a political weapon in the Cold War.

The last indication of the ultimate US position on the Court itself—other than what one may deduce from failing to pay UN dues—can be gleaned from the 1993 *Final Report of the United States Commission on Improving the Effectiveness of the United Nations.* This special government commission was established by the US Congress under the Foreign Relations Authorization Act of 1988. It studied the role of the UN and its place in US foreign policy. In the *Findings and Recommendations,* this Commission (consisting of House members and other special appointees) determined that the US should take the lead in advocating wider acceptance of the compulsory jurisdiction of the Court. The Commission recommended as follows: "that, to set a standard of leadership, the US consider reaccepting the compulsory jurisdiction of the Court. . . ."[51] As to the Court's *advisory* jurisdiction, the Commission also recommended a gradual expansion of this facet of the ICJ's competence. Specifically, States are thus encouraged to refer questions of International Law from their national courts to the ICJ.

◆ 9.5 INTERNATIONAL CRIMINAL COURTS

INTRODUCTION

Victorious States have often punished losing States. In earlier eras, the motivation was revenge. In the twentieth century's experiences with an International Criminal Court, the motivation has been to punish those guilty of outrageous human rights violations. This section opens with the text of the most famous international tribunal: the World War II "Nuremberg Trial" of Nazi Germany's notorious war criminals and the companion Tokyo Trial of Japanese war criminals. It then explores the currently functioning *ad hoc* tribunals for crimes occurring in Yugoslavia (Bosnia) and Rwanda. Finally, these materials present a succinct overview of a potential shift from dream to reality—given the opening for signature of the 1998 Rome Statute for a permanent International Criminal Court.

> The topic under discussion today is particularly important for the ICRC. Through its activities, the ICRC witnesses the commission of atrocities on a wide scale, including war crimes, which are all too often left unpunished. This situation simply cannot continue, and we firmly believe that the international community must ensure that those responsible are made accountable for their acts. Although States already have a duty to prosecute, and also to undertake all the necessary steps to adapt their national legislation and to provide effective penal sanctions, today's reality shows that this duty is not fulfilled. It is in this context that the establishment of an international criminal court is so important to change this pattern of impunity.
>
> —Statement of the International Committee of the Red Cross before the United Nations Preparatory Committee for the Establishment of an International Criminal Court, New York, February 14, 1997

The concept of a war crimes trial is not unique to the revered Nuremberg trial in post–World War II Germany. There are accounts of a war crimes trial in 405 B.C. near what is now Turkey; a trial of a European governor for his actions in 1427, when his troops raped and killed innocent individuals; and a post–World War I trial of a submarine commander who torpedoed a British hospital ship and then sank its lifeboats. The League of Nations produced an international penal code and related Convention on the Establishment of the International Criminal Court (within the PCIJ)—signed by Belgium, Bulgaria, Cuba, Czechoslovakia, France, Greece, Spain, Monaco, the Netherlands, Romania, Turkey, the USSR, and Yugoslavia. This treaty never entered into force, however, due to the lack of sufficient ratifications.[52]

In 1994, Ethiopia commenced war crimes trials against the leaders of its former Marxist dictatorship. After these leaders seized power in 1974, some 250,000 people were killed or died in forced relocation programs. In one six-hour period during 1988, 2,500 civilians were killed by helicopter gunships and fighter planes.

Between 1946 and 1993 (the dates of establishment of the Nuremberg and Bosnia-oriented tribunal for crimes in the former Yugoslavia), there were many calls for the creation of the second exclusively criminal international tribunal to try various types of "international" crimes. These would be the crimes that may serve as a basis for universal jurisdiction such as war crimes, terrorism, and hijacking (*see* §5.2). Building on the 1934 League of Nations draft Convention for the Creation of an International Criminal Court, an unofficial nongovernmental organization attempted to assert pressure on the community of nations to bring such a tribunal into existence. The organization, the Foundation for the Establishment of an International Criminal Court, conducted two drafting conferences in 1972. These gatherings were attended by experts from all over the world. And in 1986, the US Congress asked President Reagan to explore the possibility of international pressure being exerted to establish an ICC to deal with international terrorists.

This theme was ignited by problems with securing the extradition of terrorists from reluctant nations. An asylum State would be in a very awkward position if it refused to yield an offender to such a tribunal—improving the prospects for a truly *international* response to terrorism and the convenient "political offense" exception to extradition treaties (discussed in §5.3). In 1992, the UN Secretary-General appointed a Commission of Experts to document violations of humanitarian law in the former Yugoslavia, before the 1993 establishment of the Yugoslavian tribunal.[53]

In theory, the trial of "international" criminals would be best accomplished by an *international* court—as opposed to a *national* court. The 1921 Leipzig trials of German nationals in Germany for war crimes against the Allies, plus the 1961 Israeli trial of Hitler's chief exterminator, Adolf Eichmann, in Israel, are classic examples of the judicial dilemma associated with such *national* tribunals. It was arguably difficult for both of those judicial bodies to exercise the impartiality that is the hallmark of the judicial role. One could also claim that the impartiality of the 1990 US prosecution of Panama's former dictator was tainted by the prior relationship between Noriega and the US Central Intelligence Agency. As stated in a 1992 study of the future of international courts:

> The existence of international crimes and the recognition of individual responsibility for such crimes logically suggests that there should be an *international* tri-

bunal with power to try individuals for the commission of international crimes. It is just as important to have an international criminal court to administer international criminal law as it is to have national criminal courts to administer national criminal law. For however objective and impartial national courts in fact may be, because they are courts of particular states there will inevitably be a suspicion of bias when a national court tries an international criminal. . . .

[T]rying international criminals before municipal courts is haphazard, unjust and militates against the development of a *universal* criminal law. The administration of international criminal law will only become systematic, just and universal when the organ of its administration is a *permanent* international criminal court.[54]

Although there is now an ICC Statute awaiting ratification by the global community (*see* Permanent ICC below), it has been argued that altering the Statute of the *existing* International Court of Justice would be preferable. States did not have to create a new judicial tribunal to deal with matters that might have fallen within the province of the UN's existing International Court of Justice (ICJ), which has been in place since 1946. In other words, States would have to change the requirement that only States may be parties before the ICJ. This sentiment was aptly articulated by Florida International University's Professor Barbara Yarnold:

One issue that requires attention is whether it might be advisable to create a new international criminal tribunal, rather than utilizing the International Court of Justice. . . .

[T]he International Court of Justice is the best forum for the adjudication of state and international crimes, for several reasons. . . . Although the ICJ has fallen into disuse recently, its performance has commanded the respect of many states in the world community over the years, due to its presumed expertise and impartiality. Hence, the International Court of Justice already has a certain level of legitimacy and support among states [as opposed to any tribunal yet to be established].

Second, the concept of establishing a new international tribunal may be more difficult to sell than that of transferring new responsibilities to a preexisting international tribunal.

Third, much work has already been put into developing the International Court of Justice. . . . The Statute of the International Court of Justice would not have to be discarded. Instead, the [ICJ] Statute could be amended where necessary [to provide the requisite criminal jurisdiction].

Certainly, this recommendation that the International Court of Justice be given jurisdiction over international crimes [rather than leaving it to State jurisdiction] . . . will be opposed by those superpowers in the world community that historically have favored the use of force over the rule of law.[55]

The following materials will help you appreciate a relevant historical dilemma: Given the debate about whether national or international tribunals should be trying international criminals, there has always been the underlying question about whether there is actually an "international" criminal law—or just international crimes that fall within the jurisdiction of either national courts or the two *ad hoc,* limited-purpose tribunals (Yugoslavia and Rwanda). Until the 1998 Statute of the permanent ICC is ratified by a sufficient number of States, there will be no real international "point person" (entity) to ensure the progressive development of International Criminal Law.[56]

NUREMBERG AND TOKYO TRIBUNALS

The desire to establish the first modern and truly International Criminal Court surfaced in 1945 as a device for deterring future misuses of force. The victorious Allied powers established two major international tribunals to try war crimes. One, the eleven-nation International Military Tribunal of the Far East, tried twenty-five Japanese defendants for war crimes. All were found guilty. Seven were sentenced to death. The most famous tribunal, however, was the four-nation body established by the Nuremberg Charter. The United States, Great Britain, France, and the former Soviet Union created the Nuremberg Tribunal by international agreement. The fundamental objective was to try Nazi "war criminals whose offenses have no particular geographical location whether they be accused individually or in their capacity as members of [military] organizations" of the German government.[57]

The treaty, known as the Nuremberg Charter, contained what the Allied powers perceived as a novel method for deterring the national misuse of force. Germany's key planners were tried and imprisoned or executed for their war crimes. The essential basis for their liability was the violation of prewar international agreements that outlawed war. The following excerpt from the resulting Nuremberg Judgment analyzes the role of international law in outlawing the tactics planned and executed by German leaders during World War II:

Judgment of the International Military Tribunal (1946)

22 *International Military Tribunal, Trial of the Major War Criminals* 411 (1948)

Court's Opinion. The charges in the indictment that the defendants planned and waged aggressive wars are charges of the utmost gravity. War is essentially an evil thing. Its consequences are not confined to the belligerent states alone, but affect the whole world.

To initiate a war of aggression, therefore, is not only an international crime; it is the supreme international crime differing only from other war crimes in that it contains within itself the accumulated evil of the whole.

The first acts of aggression referred to in the indictment are the seizure of Austria and Czechoslovakia; and the first war of aggression charged in the indictment is the war against Poland begun on the 1st September 1939. Before examining that charge it is necessary to look more closely at some of the events which preceded these acts of aggression. The war against Poland did not come suddenly out of an otherwise clear sky; the evidence has made it plain that this war of aggression, as well as the seizure of Austria and Czechoslovakia, was premeditated and carefully prepared, and was not undertaken until the moment was thought opportune for it to be carried through as a definite part of the preordained scheme and plan.

For the aggressive designs of the Nazi Government were not accidents arising out of the immediate political situation in Europe and the world; they were a deliberate and essential part of Nazi foreign policy. From the beginning, the National Socialist movement claimed that its object was to unite the German people in the consciousness of their mission and destiny, based on inherent qualities of [an allegedly superior] race, and under the guidance of the Fuhrer.

For its achievement, two things were deemed to be essential: The disruption of the European order as it had existed since the Treaty of Versailles, and the creation of a Greater Germany beyond the frontiers of 1914. This necessarily involved the seizure of foreign territories.

War was seen to be inevitable, or at the very least, highly probable, if these purposes were to be accomplished. The German people, therefore, with all their resources, were to be organized as a great political-military army, schooled to obey without question any policy decreed by the State.

The Charter defines as a crime the planning or waging of war that is a war of aggression or a war in violation of international treaties. The Tribunal has decided that certain of the defendants planned and waged aggressive wars against 10 nations, and were therefore guilty of this series of crimes. This makes it unnecessary to discuss the subject in further detail, or even to consider at any length the extent to which these aggressive wars were also "wars in violation of international treaties, agreements, or assurances." These treaties are set out in . . . the indictment. Those of principal importance are the following [which are herein summarized by the Tribunal]:

(A) HAGUE CONVENTIONS

In the 1899 Convention the signatory powers agreed: "before an appeal to arms . . . to have recourse, as far as circumstances allow, to the good offices or mediation of one or more friendly powers." A similar clause was inserted in the Convention for Pacific Settlement of International Disputes of 1907. In the accompanying Convention Relative to Opening of Hostilities, article I contains this far more specific language:

> The Contracting Powers recognize that hostilities between them must not commence without a previous and explicit warning, in the form of either a declaration of war, giving reasons, or an ultimatum with a conditional declaration of war.

Germany was a party to [and thus bound by] these conventions.

(B) VERSAILLES TREATY

Breaches of certain provisions of the Versailles Treaty are also relied on by the prosecution . . . to "respect strictly the independence of Austria" (art. 80); renunciation of any rights in Memel (art. 99) and the Free City of Danzig (art. 100); the recognition of the independence of the Czecho-Slovak State; and the Military, Naval, and Air Clauses against German rearmament found in part V. There is no doubt that action was taken by the German Government contrary to all these provisions. . . .

The question is, what was the legal effect of this [Kellogg-Briand] pact? The nations who signed the pact or adhered to it unconditionally condemned recourse to war for the future as an instrument of policy, and expressly renounced it. After the signing of the pact, any nation resorting to war as an instrument of national policy breaks the pact. In the opinion of the Tribunal, the solemn renunciation of war as an instrument of national policy necessarily involves the proposition that such a war is illegal in international law; and that those who plan and wage such a war, with its inevitable and terrible consequences, are committing a crime in so doing. War for the solution of international controversies undertaken as an instrument of national policy certainly includes a war of aggression, and such a war is therefore outlawed by the pact.

◆ *Notes*

1. The Nuremberg result was not well received in all sectors of the political spectrum. US Senator Robert Taft, Republican Majority Leader after the war, referred to this case as a "miscarriage of justice [that] the American people would long regret." In his opinion, "the trial of the vanquished leaders could not be impartial no matter how it was hedged about with the forms [appearance] of justice." This perspective, and others, are analyzed in Migone, "After Nuremberg, Tokyo," 25 *Texas L. Rev.* 475 (1947).
2. Criticisms were not limited to just the Nuremberg proceedings. India's dissenting judge in the Tokyo trials complained that there was no body of law prior to World War II for the majority's decision that war was unlawful under International Law. In Justice Pal's words, national resort to war was a "recognized rule of international life." Although there were a number of noble statements made in treaties—most of which were honored in the breach—customary State practice necessitated the legal conclusion that "war was a legitimate instrument of self-help" when peaceful solutions failed. His views on this subject were published in R. Pal, *International Military Tribunal for the Far East: Dissident Judgment* 103 (Calcutta: Sanyal, 1953).

The principles enshrined in this Nuremberg Judgment were later approved by the UN General Assembly. In 1946, shortly after the Judgment was published, the Assembly adopted Resolution 95(1) to express its sentiment that the "Nuremberg principle" had been incorporated into International Law. Under this principle, a State and its agents who wage an aggressive war commit the supreme international crime, one punishable by any nation able to bring the planners to justice. The responsible leaders thereby incur criminal responsibility—arising directly under International Law—for the conduct that makes them liable for this supreme crime. The validity under the internal laws of Germany did not provide them with a defense. They were tried and punished for their participation as agents of the State in its unlawful use of force against other States. As articulated by the judges at Nuremberg, "[C]rimes against international law are committed by men, not by abstract entities, and only by punishing individuals who commit such crimes can the provisions of international law be enforced."

Neither the Nuremberg principles nor the ensuing UN resolution had a significant impact on subsequent decisions to use or refrain from using force. This was the last time that "victorious" nations ever established a tribunal to try agents of a defeated nation for waging war. (The 1993 UN "Yugoslavian" and subsequent Rwandan tribunals, discussed below, do not involve victors imposing such jurisprudence on the vanquished. They were the product of UN Security Council resolutions.) In 1974, the University of Michigan's late Professor William Bishop expressed his frustration with this predicament by posing the following question:

> What then, has . . . international law done for the welfare of humanity since its promulgation? The

The leading Nazi defendants are pictured during these proceedings in 1945 at Nuremberg, Germany. Hermann Goering, Rudolph Hess, and Joachim von Ribbentrop are seated in the dock's first row (left to right). All three were found guilty of war crimes, crimes against peace, and crimes against humanity. Goering and von Ribbentrop were sentenced to death. Hess was sentenced to life imprisonment.

answer is clear and simple: nothing. Since Nuremberg, there have been at least eighty or ninety wars (some calculators exclude armed invasions of neighbors too weak to attempt resistance), some of them on a very large scale. The list includes the Korean War, the Suez invasion [by France and Great Britain] of 1956, . . . the four Arab-Israeli wars, the Vietnam wars (including the accompanying fighting in Laos and Cambodia), and the invasion of Czechoslovakia by the Soviet Union and its myrmidons. In none of these cases, nor in any other, was an aggressor arrested and brought to the bar of international justice, and none is likely to be. For all the good it has done, the doctrine that aggressive war is a crime might as well be relegated to the divinity schools.[58]

For many years, the work of DePaul University (Chicago) Professor M.C. Bassiouni and Benjamin Ferencz of New York, did a great deal to keep the vision of a permanent ICC from fading into obscurity. Their exhaustive studies served as a model for the UN's creation of the current *ad hoc* tribunals for atrocities committed in Yugoslavia and Rwanda.[59]

AD HOC INTERNATIONAL CRIMINAL TRIBUNALS

Yugoslavia Unlike the Allied Powers' treaty arrangement that established the Nuremberg and Tokyo tribunals, the current Yugoslavian and Rwandan ICCs were established by UN Security Council Resolutions. In 1993, the first of the two specialized tribunals was the International Criminal Tribunal–Yugoslavia (ICTY). This modern version of an International Criminal Court has brought individuals to justice who committed major atrocities in Bosnia from 1991 to 1995 (from the breakup of the former Yugoslavia through the restoration of peace). Its seat is in The Hague, in the Netherlands, which is also the seat of the International Court of Justice.

The ICTY consists of two trial chambers and an appellate chamber. The executive organs include a registry for the court and a prosecutor's office. In September 1993, the UN General Assembly elected eleven judges to serve four-year terms from a slate of candidates nominated by the UN Security Council. The judges are professors and lawyers from all over the world. The first president of the International Tribunal (and its appellate chamber) was from Italy. The vice-president was from Costa Rica. A female judge from the US is president of one of the two trial chambers—of particular importance because of the alleged mass rapes of Muslim women by Serbian soldiers as part of an ethnic-cleansing plan. A Nigerian is president of the other trial chamber.

The ICTY applies the rules of international humanitarian law applicable to armed conflict. These are the 1949 Geneva Convention for the Protection of War Victims, the 1948 Genocide Convention, the crimes against humanity formulation contained in the 1946 Nuremberg Judgment, and the 1907 Hague Convention on the Laws and Customs of War on Land (further addressed in Chapter 10 on the use of force). Prosecution focuses on such crimes as murder, rape, torture, and ethnic cleansing, as well as similar human rights violations.[60]

The tribunal's first verdict in 1997 was possibly its most significant because of the legal precedents it established for subsequent prosecutions:

◆

Prosecutor v. Dusko Tadic aka "Dule"

International Tribunal for the Prosecution of Persons Responsible for Serious Violations of International Humanitarian Law Committed in the Territory of Former Yugoslavia since 1991 (ICTY)
Case No. IT-94-1-T, 7 May 1997

Go to course Web Page at http://home.att.net/~slomansonb/txtcsesite.html; click on Tadic Case.

◆ *Notes & Questions*

1. In the penalty phase of Tadic's trial, he was convicted of eleven of thirty-one counts and sentenced to twenty years in prison. He was not convicted of murder (insufficient evidence) or rape (a witnesss would not testify). He was characterized as not being the "butcher," but rather the "bully" who is a karate expert. Such sentences are being served in Finland and Italy, the two nations that house those convicted by the ICTY. Tadic was not given the possible life sentence. Neither the ICTY nor the Rwandan tribunal has the power to sentence a convicted war criminal to death. (*See* Problem 9.E.) For other opinions, and various orders from the ICTY, *see* the UN Web site at www.un.org/icty.
2. The ICTY (and Rwanda) tribunal was established differently than the UN's International Court of Justice. How so? Does the source from which the ICTY originates suggest that it will more likely be subject to the political will of its creator than the ICJ?
3. The result nevertheless has two arguable advantages over prior practice. First, the ICTY is a more broadly based institution in International Law, because prior tribunals were established by a group of victorious powers over those whom they conquered—specifically, the Allied Power post–World War II trials at Nuremberg and Tokyo. Second, the new ICTY and Rwandan tribunals are truly international. They do not involve trials of "international crimes" by national tribunals, whose judges might not be perceived as impartial. If you were an Israeli judge, analyzing the guilt or innocence of Adolf Eichmann (Hitler's chief exterminator) when he was tried in Israel years after the Nuremberg trial was completed, your impartiality might be questioned by the so-called world court of public opinion.
4. In December 1998, ICTY Judge Gabrielle McDonald reported that the Federal Republic of Yugoslavia (FRY) has obstructed Security Council resolutions. She stated that the FRY failed to comply with Resolution 1207, which sets forth the Security Council's demand to immediately and unconditionally execute arrest warrants against three individuals. The FRY has continued to deny visas to the Prosecutor's investigators in contravention of various Security Council Resolutions. Judge McDonald concluded with a plea to the Security Council "not to let one State stand in

the way of peace [and] . . . not to allow the FRY's obstructionism to go unchecked, for it sets a dangerous precedent. . . ." *See* her report at www.un.org/icty/pressreal/p371-e.htm.

Rwanda In the year after the UN Security Council's establishment of the ICTY (1993), the Council established the International Criminal Tribunal for Rwanda (ICTR) in Arusha, Tanzania. Rwanda did not support establishment of this tribunal, partly because it was outside Rwanda. The Security Council opted against a Rwandan location on a variety of grounds including security risks, lack of appropriate infrastructure, and perceptions of judicial partiality normally associated with conducting trials in the very nation where the atrocities occurred. In 1998, one of six judges at the Tribunal stepped down, claiming mismanagement and a lack of leadership. The UN Secretary-General had previously fired the administrative head of the tribunal. Nevertheless, this tribunal has tried and convicted various individuals, including a mayor and the former premier of Rwanda (life terms) for their roles in the genocidal massacre (including rape and other crimes) of some one-half million Tutsis by the ruling Hutu majority government in 1994.[61]

In the Rwandan premier's case, the ICTR drew upon the Appellate Tribunal's analysis contained in the ICTY's Tadic case (*see* above Web-page version for Tadic trial proceedings). The judges of the ICTR were ruling on an important defense motion, challenging the jurisdiction of the ICTR to hear and determine such cases.[62] This phase of this particular proceeding illustrates the basis not only for the Rwandan court's power to prosecute, but also for that of the permanent ICC spawned by the 1998 Rome Conference (discussed below). There were five principle objections, all of which were rejected by the ICTR.[63]

First, Rwanda's State sovereignty had been allegedly violated, because the ICTR was not created by a treaty ratified by Rwanda. One problem with this theory was that Rwanda had requested establishment of an *ad hoc* ICC to adjudicate cases regarding the 1994 genocide occurring within its borders. Its reasons for not approving the final draft statute did not depend on sovereign objections. Also, Article 25 of the UN Charter requires States to comply with Security Council decisions. Should the permanent ICC not materialize or not function as anticipated, it is arguable like defenses in any future *ad hoc* tribunal would likewise be denied. Should the State where the atrocities occur not request formation of an *ad hoc* tribunal (unlike Rwanda), one could expect a UN Charter Article 2.7 defense that the organization cannot interfere in matters which that State considers as falling exclusively within its domestic adjudicatory power.

Second, the defense asserted that the UN Security Council exceeded its authority when it relied on its Chapter VII powers to create this tribunal. This was supposedly not a threat to international peace, and the UN Charter never contemplated formation of such a judicial tribunal as a matter related to peace preservation. However, perpetrators of genocide and other violations of international human rights would inherently support the Council's authority to prevent such future threats to peace.

Third, the former Rwandan premier's defense team challenged the primacy of the international tribunal—vis-à-vis the national courts of Rwanda. The Trial Chamber of the ICTR noted the applicability of the general principle that persons accused of crimes should retain their right to be tried by the regular domestic courts, rather than by a politically founded *ad hoc* tribunal that might fail to provide impartial justice. The Appellate Chamber decision in the Yugoslavian *Tadic* case led to the assessment that the ICTR's proper establishment under the Security Council's Chapter VII powers enabled the ICTR to prosecute a Rwandan citizen even in the absence of Rwandan consent.[64] "Primacy" in ICTY proceedings is expressed in Article 9(2) of the ICTY Statute, whereby it "shall have primacy over national courts. . . . [ICTY] may formally request national courts to defer to the competence of the International Tribunal. . . ."

Fourth, the defense argued that the UN Charter did not encompass the possibility that a UN-based tribunal could confer jurisdiction over individuals, as opposed to States (*see* §9.4 on the ICJ Statute's limitation to States). Also, the Council had never done so in the past when clear violations of human rights laws had occurred. The Court responded that by establishing the ICTY and the ICTR the Security Council had effectively extended international criminal responsibility directly to individuals for violations of international humanitarian law.

Finally, the defense raised the other potentially recurring issue: The ICTR is not an impartial entity, because of its establishment by the Security Council—a political body. However, the Tribunal is not bound to apply Rwanda's rules of evidence, the judges explicitly are not accountable to the Council, and a fair trial was guaranteed by the Tribunal's Statute and Rules for the Court's operations. Ironically, the defense did not mention the advantage of being tried by the international tribunal rather than in the national courts of Rwanda—where the death penalty applies and has been applied to a number of defendants convicted of like crimes. In April 1998, for example, twenty-two men were tied to stakes and shot, with large crowds as witnesses, despite pleas for clemency by Pope John Paul II. In some instances, the convicts had no lawyers, and no witnesses were called in their defense in the national proceedings.

The Rwandan experience has received mixed reviews. As stated by two of the leading commentators on the proceedings of the ICTR (and ICTY):

> The establishment of the Rwanda Tribunal constitutes one of the most important milestones in the history of international criminal law. The significance of this event becomes clear only when it is viewed in its historical context, taking into account the difficulties encountered in previous efforts to create *ad hoc* international criminal tribunals and in the continuing efforts to create a permanent international criminal court. . . .
>
> Perhaps the greatest failing of the Rwanda Tribunal was the amount of time it took to bring those responsible . . . to justice [genocide in 1994, first judgment in 1997]. . . .
>
> While some of the causes of the delay were perhaps unavoidable, the major cause of the delay resulted from the need to build an entire international institution from the ground up. . . . Yet the delay could have been avoided if there had existed a permanent international criminal court. . . . Since the establishment of the Rwanda Tribunal, the members of the Security Council have experienced . . . 'tribunal fatigue.' . . . Notwithstanding a host of other atrocities . . . at least one permanent member of the Security Council [possessing the right of veto]—China—has openly expressed concern about using the Yugoslavia and Rwanda Tribunals as precedent for the creation of other *ad hoc* [by country or incident] criminal tribunals. Moreover, the expense of establishing *ad hoc* tribunals, each with its own staff and facilities, is simply seen as too much for an organization [UN] whose budget is already stretched too thin. Thus, the requests by Burundi and Cambodia to establish similar tribunals to address the atrocities committed in those countries have not received a favorable response by the Security Council to date.[65]

PERMANENT ICC

In July 1998, representatives of approximately 150 nations gathered in Rome to draft the first global International Criminal Court Statute. The ICC's seat will be in The Hague in the Netherlands. Trials will be permitted elsewhere. After the treaty enters into force on ratification by sixty countries, this ICC will try individuals accused of the following: *genocide,* as defined in the 1949 Genocide Convention; *international and internal war crimes,* "committed as a part of a plan or policy or as part of a large-scale commission of such crimes"; and *crimes against humanity,* which are a "widespread or systematic" part of a plan or policy directed against civilians. Unlike the Nuremberg and Tokyo tribunals, there is no death penalty. Rather than dealing with such crimes on an *ad hoc* basis like the Yugoslavian and Rwandan Tribunals established by UN Security Council vote, this ICC will be a permanent fixture of the international community of nations. Oddly, the use of poison gas and exploding bullets are punishable, but not the use of nuclear weapons, land mines, or chemical weapons (*see* §8.2 regarding the usual compromises necessary to achieve such a broad consensus).

One hundred twenty countries voted in favor of establishing this permanent International Criminal Court (ICC), twenty countries abstained, and seven opposed. The United States is among the several dissenters. This is ironic, because it was the US that shepherded creation of the Nuremberg, Tokyo, Rwanda, and Yugoslavia international tribunals. President Clinton frequently spoke in favor of the ICC and appointed a first-ever Ambassador at Large for War Crimes Issues to focus the administration's efforts. The US delegation participated extensively in all of the preparatory negotiations once they began in 1995. However, the US position is that the ICC should operate only with the approval of the UN Security Council. The US would thus be able to exercise its veto power. The world's Conference delegates wanted an ICC that was able to proceed without being thwarted by the Security Council's veto, which has plagued the Council almost since its inception (*see* §3.5).

Another US objection was that US peacekeeping forces might be subjected to ICC jurisdiction, although the Rome Treaty contains a number of procedural safeguards designed to prevent such action only in the most egregious of circumstances. For example, a case cannot be heard in the following circumstances: A State with jurisdiction is already investigating, unless that state "is unable or unwilling genuinely to carry out the investigation"; a State has made a good faith decision not to investigate; or the accused has already been tried for the conduct alleged. A case is also inadmissible if it is "not of sufficient gravity to justify further action by the Court." An ICC investigation may be commenced only by the Security Council, a State that is a party to the Rome Statute, or by the ICC Prosecutor. In investigations launched by a State or the ICC Prosecutor, the Court will need the consent of either the State on whose territory the crime occurred or the State of the nationality of the accused, otherwise the ICC cannot act (unless there is a UN Security Council referral).[66]

In January 1999, the French Constitutional Council ruled in a case brought by France's president and prime minister that the French constitution would have to be amended before France could ratify the Rome Statute of the International Criminal Court. The ICC Statute (see textbox on the first page of this chapter) waives immunity from any criminal responsibility of a head of state or government or members of a ratifying government and parliament. The Council held that this treaty provision would contradict the constitutional provisions regarding the special responsibility of State officials. The Rome Statute (Articles 17 and 20) authorize the ICC to ignore national rules providing for amnesty and other limitations on its jurisdiction. See story (in French) at www.conseil-constitutionnel.fr/decision/98/98408/index.htm.

That 120 nations voted in favor of this ICC Statute indicates the strongest commitment to date for a strong and independent international criminal court. The Treaty is fraught, of course, with the usual compromises that may ultimately allow States or the Security Council to hamper investigations and delay prosecutions; the Treaty is also opposed by the US Senate. Yet the creation of this permanent ICC after more than fifty years of discussion since Nuremberg represents a major step toward implementing the evasive Rule of Law. Whether the new ICC will effectively control despotic governments will depend on the will of the international community, which has the power to turn promise into reality.

◆ 9.6 REGIONAL COURT ADJUDICATION

INTERNATIONAL LAW IN REGIONAL COURTS

Article 33 of the UN Charter provides that the "parties to any dispute . . . shall, first of all, seek a solution by negotiation, . . . arbitration, . . . resort to regional agencies or arrangements, or other peaceful means of their own choice." This section of the book surveys regional litigation, theoretical advantages, and practical problems with this form of international dispute settlement.

For many centuries, international disputes were not resolved by international courts. Diplomatic negotiations and occasional *ad hoc* arbitrations served this purpose. Successful postwar diplomacy often established international "Claims Commissions." These temporary bodies heard evidence from representatives of the States involved in the particular dispute. The resolution of claims dissolved the commission.

The trend has been away from the use of temporary regional tribunals toward more permanent institutions. During the twentieth century, a number of regional courts (and two global courts) have been created by international agreement. Full-time judges and permanent staffs are available to the parties, thereby submitting disputes to these tribunals. Unlike the Yugoslavian and Rwandan criminal tribunals (§9.5), one does not have to await a several-year organizing process before filing an action and proceeding with a comparatively prompt resolution. There is no need for creating the tribunal and then selecting the arbitrators or judges.

In theory, regional courts should be more viable dispute-resolution mechanisms than global courts. But like the International Court of Justice, they are generally underutilized. Mistrust of the institution should be, of course, less of a problem in a regional court. Local judges are normally in a better position to resolve international problems originating within their own region, where they are likely to be familiar with regional norms of conduct. The two "World Courts," both seated in the heart of Europe, have been criticized for not fully comprehending the impact of regional practices.

The comparative enforceability of judgments is a related benefit of the regional court process. Unlike judgments from the UN's International Court of Justice, which have sometimes been ignored, judgments from the regional tribunals in Europe are unquestionably incorporated into the fabric of the European Union's member States. With the exception of this particular region, however, it is not clear that regional courts have been more effective than global courts. A number of regional courts have not survived. Those that have do not hear many cases. A Central American Court, the first regional international court, was established by treaty in 1907. The State participants soon decided that any need for regional courts would be supplanted by the Permanent Court of International Justice. The Central American Court was therefore disbanded in 1918.

The belief that regional courts would be viable dispute-resolution mechanisms resurfaced after the demise of the first "World Court." In 1945, the States that created the UN inserted Article 33 into the UN Charter, indicating that disputes might be considered first by "regional arrangements." This language therein incorporated the theme that regional courts could play an effective role in shifting international disputes from the battlefield to the courtroom.

The absence or presence of a major regional power has affected the viability of regional adjudication. The regional European legal process described below accommodates the major powers of France and Great Britain. Their influence has significantly advanced adjudication at the regional level. The comparative frailty of the Latin American regional court process could be attributed to the lack of US resolve to engage in regional adjudication with its OAS neighbors. The lack of a major regional power also has limited the effectiveness of regional tribunals. International courts in other regions of the world are unlikely to achieve the European brand of success without a significant economic or military power acting as a stimulant.

A related limitation of the regional court system is that its success depends on the solidarity of the member States. In most cases, the political and economic unity of the region has been minimal. This discourages national resort to these courts for the resolution of disputes. In the European Union, on the other hand, members have demonstrated the necessary cohesiveness to support a regional court system for an entire generation. The participating States possess similar economic and political interests—a fact that has contributed significantly to the success of the region's political organization and judicial dispute-resolution processes. In most regions, a lack of political solidarity has limited the potential for a more effective regional court process.

In a perfect world, the resolution of international disputes would not be affected by political considerations. The decision about whether to go to court, however, is itself a major political consideration. Many States avoid regional (and global) courts for reasons unrelated to the legal issues or merits of their disputes. National leaders may decide that the filing of a lawsuit in a public forum will only exacerbate national differences that can be otherwise managed more effectively through less sensitive avenues of diplomacy. A State may oppose judicial resolutions of international disputes, because a public airing of the problem may escalate (or create) a rift in international relations. In a different political environment, the same State may seek a judicial resolution. Amicable relations may be preserved by submission of the case to an impartial international tribunal.

Another problem limits the viability of regional adjudication. States have not given regional courts the compulsory jurisdiction to litigate. When States have created regional courts, they theoretically agree that the availability of a standing tribunal is a good idea. In practice, however, they do not require themselves to submit to the judicial processes of the regional courts they create. They fear the loss of sovereignty they typically associate with submitting sensitive cases to a public forum they do not control.

The lack of a defined relationship between the global and regional court systems further limits the potential for the judicial resolution of international disputes. Issues arising under International Law have been adjudicated both in the various regional courts and in the International Court of Justice. UN Charter Article 95 grants the ICJ the power to hear cases arising under International Law. No Charter provision, however, creates or even suggests a relationship between the ICJ and the various regional courts. Charter Article 33 merely provides for prior resort to "regional agencies or arrangements" for the resolution of international disputes. The same case could be lodged in both a regional court and the ICJ. Certain State violations of an individual's human rights, for example, could be heard in the European Court of Human Rights, the International Court of Justice, or the UN's International Criminal Court for the trial of war crimes in the former Yugoslavia.

The lack of a hierarchy among national, regional, and global courts is a related limitation on the viability of regional adjudication. While the litigants are expected to exhaust local remedies in national courts before coming to the ICJ (*see* §2.5 on State responsibility), the ICJ has never required its litigants to resort first to available regional courts. Neither the UN Charter nor the Statute of the ICJ give the ICJ power to suspend regional court proceedings so the ICJ might provide a global response to the problem at hand. In 1998, the US ignored the command of the ICJ to delay execution of a Paraguayan citizen who had not been accorded his treaty-based right to access to the local consular officer from Paraguay (*Breard* case in §7.2).

A lack of uniformity also limits the international system of adjudication. Regional courts operate independently of national courts, the ICJ, and each other. Regional international courts function as trial courts from which there is no right of appeal. States have never ceded appellate powers to regional (or global) courts over their national judiciaries. When creating the international courts discussed later in this section of the book, States generally avoid the common model existing within their own court systems. In many national court systems, cases normally proceed through a hierarchy of judicial levels. This progression creates a trial-court record resolving factual issues so that an appellate tribunal may then concentrate on the legal issues involved in the dispute. This promotes uniformity of decision within national legal systems. A higher appellate court may then provide guidance to the various national trial courts, thus promoting uniform application of the law within that national system.[67]

The general lack of a legal relationship among regional courts—and between regional courts and the ICJ—has generated other problems. The predicament of having entirely independent regional court systems was forecast by prominent English commentator Professor Jenks. In 1943, prior to creation of the regional courts that exist today, he cautioned against such a system because "[t]he coexistence of the Permanent Court of International Justice and of entirely independent regional international courts would involve at least two dangers. There would be a danger of conflicts regarding jurisdiction, and a danger that regional courts might be inspired by regional legal conceptions to such an extent that their decisions might prejudice the future unity of the law of nations in respect of matters regarding which uniform rules of worldwide validity are desirable."[68]

Jenks's concern about parochial definitions of International Law was well founded. The interpretation of what constitutes a local custom has jeopardized prospects for a smooth relationship among national, regional, and global courts. What one type of court perceives as falling within the general parameters of International Law may be a rather parochial perspective. The ICJ's 1950 *Asylum* case (set forth in §7.3) illustrates this problem. Colombia relied on a regional practice to establish its claim that Peru had failed to honor the right of asylum existing in the Latin American region of the world. There was, in fact, support for this being characterized as a customary regional practice. The ICJ did not affirm the right of asylum because it was not practiced on either a regional level in Europe or on a more global level. The ICJ ruled that Colombia "failed to meet its burden" of proving the existence of such a right under International Law. The ICJ was harshly criticized for its failure to recognize and apply this regional practice.

The next subsection surveys the operations and aspirations of the various regional courts.

OPERATIONAL REGIONAL COURTS

Several regional courts currently hear issues arising under International Law. They include the following courts, which are discussed below: (1) the European Court of Justice, (2) the European Court of Human Rights, (3) the Inter-American Court of Human Rights, and (4) the Andean Court of Justice. These courts essentially interpret the treaties that created the political or economic organizations they serve. (*See* Exhibit 9.3.)

There have been other dormant or defunct regional courts. The former Central American Court of Justice ceased to function in 1918. While it was supposedly reestablished in 1965, it has not yet issued a case. The Court of Justice of the European Coal and Steel Community was replaced by the current European Court of Justice in 1973. The League of Arab States has contemplated establishing an Arab Court of Justice since 1950. The proposed court is described in a draft statute. However, insufficient political solidarity in the region has prevented its activation.[69]

European Court of Justice The 1957 Treaty of Rome established the first European regional court: the

EXHIBIT 9.3 REGIONAL INTERNATIONAL COURTS

Court	Location (Date)[a]	Bench	Affiliation(s)	Cases Heard
Court of Justice of the European Communities[b]	Luxembourg (1973)	15 judges: 1 from each European Union member State; and president	Council of Europe, European Union	◆ Commission v. State ◆ Private v. EU institution ◆ Cases referred from national courts
European Court of Human Rights[b]	Strasbourg, France (1958)	3-judge Committees, 7-judge Chambers, 17-judge Grand Chamber (40 total from Council of Europe members)	Council of Europe, European Union	Determines State violations of European Convention on Human Rights
European Court of First Instance[b]	Luxembourg (1989)	15 judges: 1 from each European Union member State	Council of Europe, European Union	◆ Actions brought by individuals ◆ Appeals to Court of Justice
Inter-American Court of Human Rights	San Jose, Costa Rica (1979)	6 part-time judges, 1 full-time president (all from OAS member States)	Organization of American States	Determines State violations of American Convention on Human Rights
Andean Court of Justice	Quito, Ecuador (1979)	5 judges: 1 from each member State	Andean Pact, Latin American Free Trade Association	Reviews State compliance with Pact economics
Central American Court of Justice	(1907 & 1965)[c]	Presidents of member States' judiciaries	Organization of Central American States	Disputes between States and between individual and State[d]
Arab Court of Justice	Cairo, Egypt (1965)	[d]	League of Arab States	[d]
African Economic Community Court of Justice[e]	(1991)	[d]	Organization of African Unity	[d]

[a]Date established, reestablished

[b]Compulsory jurisdiction over member States

[c]Hiatus from 1918 until reconstituted in 1965; *see* D. Bowett, *The Law of International Institutions* 287 (4th ed. London: Stevens & Sons, 1982)

[d]Proposed but not yet operational

[e]*See* A. Yusuf (ed.), 1 *African Yearbook of International Law* 237 (Art. 7) & 241 (Art. 18) (Dordrecht, Neth.: Martinus Nijhoff, 1994)

Court of Justice of the European Coal and Steel Community. Article 3 of the 1973 Convention on Certain Institutions Common to the European Communities transferred the powers of this court to the current European Court of Justice (ECJ), which is located in Luxembourg. The ECJ's judges, from European Union (EU) member countries, decide about 200 cases per year.

The ECJ, sometimes called the "Supreme Court" of Europe, resolves disputes between the national laws of member States and European Community law. For example, EU nations are not supposed to create import duties or non-tariff barriers on most products imported from other EU members. This Court decided that Italy violated community transportation rules by prohibiting an Irish airline from picking up passengers in England and flying them to Milan.

The judicial power of this remarkably successful tribunal is succinctly described by the University of Exeter (England) Professor John Bridge, as follows:

> The ECJ is an "international court" in more than one sense of that term. It is international in the fundamental sense that it is a creation of international law through the joint exercise of the treaty-making powers of the Member States. In organizational terms it is international in that it is composed of judges of the different nationalities of the [EU] Member States. In jurisdictional terms it is international in the classic sense that it is competent to hear and determine cases alleging the failure of Member States to fulfill treaty obligations. Another aspect of its international character lies in its authority to review, with reference to the Treaties, the legality of acts and omissions by the institutions set up by the Treaties to serve the purposes of the Communities. The ECJ also has jurisdiction to rule on the compatibility with the EEC Treaty of proposed agreements between a Community and either third states or an international organization. It also serves as an international administrative tribunal through its jurisdiction in disputes between the Communities and its servants.[70]

The ECJ differs from the traditional international tribunals. Unlike the practice of the global International Court of Justice, where only States may be parties, individuals and corporations may participate in certain proceedings before the ECJ (especially through its Court of First Instance). The first two cases heard by the European Court were filed by private (non-governmental) corporations. Individuals who have been fined by an administrative body of the European Union may appeal to the ECJ. Individuals and corporations may also ask the ECJ to annul administrative decisions and regulations of EU agencies, which allegedly violate EU norms. In one case, a British citizen filed suit in the ECJ to recover damages incurred during an assault in Paris. The administrator of a French fund for French citizens had denied the British citizen's claim on the basis of his foreign nationality. In another case of great constitutional significance, a French political group was able to successfully attack the European Parliament's allocation of funds from its budget to certain political parties. This clarified the Court's position that the decisions of all EU institutions, including the European Parliament, were open to judicial review via suits brought by private individuals or non-governmental entities.[71]

National tribunals may also invoke the expertise of the ECJ. Under Article 177 of the EEC Treaty and Article 150 of the Euratom Treaty, courts and other tribunals from within the EU's member States have requested the ECJ to rule on a treaty matter arising within their particular national systems.

This Court's practice further differs from routine international litigation in the UN's International Court of Justice. Unlike the EU, the UN is composed of approximately 185 member States. The objectives of the UN members are quite diverse in comparison with those of the much smaller EU, whose member States are comparatively homogeneous. Also, the respective constitutional charters are quite different. The UN Charter is not a legally enforceable document. It did not create immediately enforceable obligations applicable to all member States. These were, instead, standards of achievement, or a form of global political aspiration (*see* §8.1). On the other hand, the various treaties applicable to the comparatively integrated European Union were intended to create legal obligations from the outset. EU member States are thus subject to the economic directives contained in its various self-executing treaties. The EU may enforce those provisions in the same manner that a national court may require compliance with its internal law.

This difference accounts for the comparative volume of cases heard by the ECJ. The range of the ECJ's jurisdiction has had an impact on States outside of the EU—including the US. There is an understandable global obsession with the "extraterritorial application" of the laws of the US.[72] The ECJ exercises similar power, however, under its own case law, which allows it to enforce Community legislation against even non-members. The ECJ has thus relied on US antitrust case law in support of its judicial authority over corporate anti-competitive conduct beyond the EU.

The following case depicts this novel ability of an international organization to enforce its economic solidarity through its integrated legislative, executive, and judicial policy. The ECJ thereby furthers the interest of the entire community of member States to govern the conduct of citizens in nonmember States (having an impact within the EU).

Ahlstrom Oy and Others v. EC Commission

COURT OF JUSTICE OF THE EUROPEAN COMMUNITIES, 1988 CASE NO. 89/85,
Euro. Court Rep. 5193, 4 *Common Mkt. L. Rep.* 901

Author's Note: *A cartel of US, Canadian, and other private wood pulp companies conspired to align their prices in a way that eliminated price competition among these companies for sales to various customers within the EU. Their conduct did not violate US law. US companies may conspire to fix prices, as long as their arrangement involves only exports. The EU's executive authority (the "Commission") fined these foreign wood pulp companies for their anti-competitive conduct, based on their activity outside of the EU having an effect within the EU. The defendants claimed that an international organization did not have the power to sanction the conduct of foreign companies that were not citizens of any State within the European Economic Community. The ECJ herein addressed the related issue of whether the Community could apply its antitrust law to foreign individuals and corporations—an action on par with State exercises of this so-called extraterritorial jurisdiction.*

After the preliminary statement of facts, the bulk of the reported ECJ case opinion contains the analysis by the Advocate-General assigned to this case. Six individuals, who are ECJ employees, serve in this special capacity. They do not represent any party. Unlike the US system, where there is no similar judicial officer, the ECJ judges rely heavily on the analysis prepared by the Advocate-General assigned to its cases. The "Commission" is the administrative body that developed the record in this case. It had fined the foreign companies, which was the basis for their appeal to the ECJ.

Emphasis and bolding have been supplied by the author at several points within this opinion. Citations to authority have been omitted.

COURT'S OPINION. These applications [for relief] are directed against the Commission Decision of 19 December 1984 establishing that 41 wood pulp producers, and two of their trade associations, all having their registered offices outside the Community, [illegally] engaged in concerted practices on prices....

[I.] *A. The product and the producers*

Wood pulp is used in the manufacture of paper and paperboard.

. . . The product in question in these cases is a chemical pulp known as 'bleached sulphate pulp.' Of all wood pulps it is the best in quality and its characteristics are such that it can be used in the manufacture of quality paper (writing paper or printing paper) and quality paperboard (milk cartons)....

The more than 800 paper manufacturers established in the Community are supplied by some fifty pulp producers from at least eighteen countries. The Community is the most important market for bleached sulphate pulp, relatively little of which is produced in the Community....

B. The contested decision

1. The operative part of the decision

In its decision, the Commission has established a number of infringements [of Community legislation and policies]....

In respect of all those practices, the Commission imposed fines on 36 of the 43 addressees of the decision.

. . . However, the Commission states that it also took into account the submission of the United States addressees that they were unaware that their behaviour infringed Community law. . . .

2. **Whether the Community has jurisdiction to apply its competition rules in this case**

In its decision the Commission states:

Article 85 of the EEC Treaty applies to restrictive practices which may affect trade between member-States even if the undertakings and associations which are parties to the restrictive practices are established or have their headquarters *outside* the Community, and even if the restrictive practices in question also affect markets outside the EEC.

In this case all the [defendant] addressees of this decision were during the period of the infringement exporting directly to or doing business within the Community. Some of them had branches, subsidiaries, agencies or other establishments within the Community. The concertation [illegal agreement] on [fixing] prices, the exchange of sensitive information relative to prices, and the clauses prohibiting export or resale all concerned shipments made directly to buyers in the EEC or sales made in the EEC to buyers there. The shipments affected by these agreements and practices amounted to about two-thirds of total shipments of bleached sulphate wood pulp to the EEC and some 60 percent of EEC consumption. . . . The effect of the agreements and practices on prices announced and/or charged to customers and on resale of pulp within the EEC was therefore not only substantial but intended, and was the primary and direct result of the agreements and practices. . . .

D. Procedure before the Court . . .

On 8 July 1987, the Court decided that the parties should first of all be heard on the question *whether the Community has jurisdiction to apply its competition rules* to undertakings whose registered office is situated outside the Community. . . .

Questions asked by the Court

The Court asked the Commission the following . . . :

Does the Commission maintain that it has jurisdiction in these cases by reason of *conduct* which has taken place *within* the Community and, if so, what is that conduct? *Or* does it [the Commission] base its jurisdiction on the *effects within* the Community of conduct which took place outside the Community and, if so, what is that conduct and what are its effects?

The Commission answered that question as follows:

On the basis of Article 3(f) of the Treaty, the Commission considers that the primary objective of the rules on competition in the EEC Treaty is to ensure that the conduct of economic activity in the Community should not be distorted [by anti-competitive price-fixing]. Therefore, in considering what constitutes the relevant conduct for the purposes of Article 85, the Commission must determine how the agreement, decision or concerted practice has been implemented. In the case of a concerted practice, this means identifying the practices that have been concerted. . . .

The Commission acknowledges that *it is not always easy to distinguish 'the effects' of 'conduct' from the conduct itself.* . . .

Thus the communication of announced prices was made *in* the Community. The transaction prices themselves were charged in the Community by the producers themselves, by their subsidiaries, branches or other establishments, or by their agents or employees. . . .

Finally, as regards . . . price recommendations, . . . that *conduct admittedly took place outside the Community. However, the substantial, foreseeable and direct effect of that conduct is a restriction of competition within the Common Market,* that is to say an effect which clearly took place within the Community.

Next, the Commission considers whether that kind of jurisdiction may be claimed under international law. . . .

In this case, the Commission considers that if the Community's jurisdiction in this case is considered to be based on conduct which occurred *within* the Community, it is not in breach of any prohibitive rule of international law. The same holds true in so far as its jurisdiction is based on the effects within the Community of conduct which occurred elsewhere. The Community has not acted in a manner which is contrary to the laws or national interests of non-member countries, nor has it substantially interfered with the economic policy of the countries concerned, as is clear from the lack of any reaction from those countries [that is, no diplomatic or other protest by non-Community countries to the Community's imposition of fines].

There is nothing in international law which obliges the Commission to interpret away the word 'effect' in

Article 85 of the Treaty as soon as that effect is produced [from some other location] across international boundaries. Although the 'effects doctrine' is still contested under international law, the Commission considers that the objections come primarily from the United Kingdom and not from . . . other countries. The Commission maintains that, in that respect, the Community should not be subject to a more restrictive jurisdictional criterion than that accepted for *States* [merely because the Community is an international organization]. . . .

[I]t is said that there is nothing in the wording of Article 85 of the Treaty to *allow* it to be extended to cover undertakings outside the Community solely by reason of anti-competitive effects produced within the territory of the Community. Secondly, it is suggested that the case law of the Court can be construed as rejecting the effects doctrine. Let me state at once that I will advise the Court to uphold neither of those objections. . . .

Principles laid down by the Court in its case law

Although the Court has not, in its decision to date, formally upheld the effects doctrine with regard to the application of competition law to undertakings outside the Community, that does not imply that it rejects the doctrine. . . .

II. The effects doctrine in the light of international law

. . . Is the location of effects doctrine, as a basis for jurisdiction, consistent with the rules of international law? In order to answer that question, it is necessary first of all to consider the very nature of international law. . . .

Academic writers are divided on that point. The discussion has revolved essentially around the significance and scope of the LOTUS judgment, delivered on 7 September 1927 by the Permanent Court of International Justice ((1927) PCIJ ser A, no 10). That judgment, adopted by the President's casting vote, states in particular that international law does not prohibit a *State* from exercising jurisdiction in its own territory, in respect of any case which relates to acts which have taken place abroad. . . .

And what is thus permissible for *States* must necessarily also be permissible for the *Community,* as a ["person" who is a] subject of international law, where the jurisdiction of the Community has been substituted for that of the member-States. . . .

That having been said, it is undoubtedly in United States law that are to be found the most far-reaching deliberations and efforts to determine the circumstances permitting a State to exercise its prescriptive jurisdiction in situations involving extraneous elements. That is not surprising. The [US] Sherman [Antitrust] Act dates back to 1890. It has given rise to a very considerable body of case law and academic writing, evidencing the concern to reconcile legitimate national interests with the imperative requirements of international law and international relations. That is why I propose to refer to the most noteworthy decisions of the United States courts [in the following passages of this opinion].

III. The principles of United States law

. . . In the context of this attempt to circumscribe the effects doctrine, reference should be made to the judgment of Judge Choy in the TIMBERLANE LUMBER case ((9th Cir 1977) 549 F 2d 597). . . .

Judge Choy came to the conclusion that, in certain circumstances, the interests of the United States were too weak and the incentive for restraint in order to preserve harmony in its international relations too strong to justify an assertion of extraterritorial jurisdiction. . . .

In that regard, United States law, as it now stands, rests [firmly] on two principles. The first is that the United States will assert jurisdiction [over conduct outside the US] where the effects on its trade are direct, substantial and foreseeable. According to the second [principle], the courts should assess the 'balance of interests' in order to ensure that the exercise of such jurisdiction is reasonable [given the respective national interests involved]. . . .

DECISION [OF THE ECJ]:

. . . The [wood pulp] producers in this case *implemented* their pricing agreement *within* the Common Market. . . .

Accordingly the Community's jurisdiction to apply its competition rules to such conduct is covered by the territoriality principle as universally recognised in public international law. . . .

It should further be pointed out that the United States authorities raised no objections regarding any conflict of jurisdiction when consulted by the Commission pursuant to the OECD [regional Organization for Economic Cooperation and Development] Council Recommendation of 25 October 1979 concerning Cooperation between member Countries on Restrictive Business Practices affecting International Trade (Acts of the Organisation, Vol 19, p 377)....

Accordingly it must be concluded that the Commission's decision is not contrary to Article 85 of the Treaty or to the rules of public international law relied on by the applicants.

◆ *Notes & Questions*

1. The case of the *SS Lotus,* referred to in the ECJ's opinion, is set forth in the text of §5.2, which analyzes jurisdictional principles under International Law. That case from the Permanent Court of International Justice differed in certain respects from the issue before the ECJ in *Ahlstrom* in terms of where the conduct occurred. How so?
2. The ECJ refers to the absence of a US protest to the Commission fine in the context of the ECJ's exercise of jurisdiction over the US wood pulp companies. Had there been such a protest, would it likely have changed the Court's decision?
3. In a case of first impression, a federal appellate court decided that the US Justice Department could apply US antitrust law to criminally prosecute price-fixing activities by a Japanese corporation—having a substantial and intended effect in the US. *See US v. Nippon Paper Industries,* 109 F.3d 1 (1st Cir., 1997), *cert. den'd,* 118 US 685 (1998), *reh'g den'd,* 118 US 1116 (1998).

European Court of Human Rights The European Court of Human Rights (ECHR) is the other major international court in Europe. Established by the 1950 European Convention for the Protection of Human Rights and Fundamental Freedoms, the ECHR became operational in 1958. In 1959, it began to hear cases arising under the European Convention in Strasbourg, France. There are forty European State signatories to this treaty. Its jurisdiction, while focusing on human rights issues, is effectively more extensive than that of the European Court of Justice—in terms of the number of State parties to the treaty that created the Court.

Article 45 of the Convention provides that the ECHR may hear "all cases concerning the interpretation and application of the present Convention." The Court's basic role is to provide judicial protection for the fundamental rights of the individual. It may thus hear cases that might not be heard under the laws of the aggrieved individual's home State. In Great Britain, for example, there is no written constitution that enumerates a list of individual rights. Neither the medieval Magna Carta nor any other document guarantees the right of British citizens against any capricious act of government agents. Great Britain's commitment to the preservation of human rights under the European treaty, however, does provide certain written guarantees to British citizens. They may file claims against their government in the ECHR at its seat in Strasbourg France.[73]

Member States may litigate suits in the ECHR. Individuals do not have the legal capacity to be parties, although they could petition the former European Commission on Human Rights to correct State action that allegedly failed to comply with the Human Rights Treaty (*see, e.g., Open Door* case set forth in text of §3.4).

Members of the European Community (and some nonmember States) have submitted disputes to the compulsory jurisdiction of the European Court of Human Rights. They have promised to participate in all cases alleging breaches of their treaty obligation to preserve fundamental human rights. State participation in this regional judicial process demonstrates a greater sense of commitment than many of those same nations have shown to any global judicial process. They have relinquished their sovereign immunity, which would otherwise shield them from being sued without their express consent. The resistance of the same States to the compulsory jurisdiction of the International Court of Justice illustrates their preference for *regional* enforcement of human rights under their regional treaty.

Another comparative advantage of the ECHR (versus the ICJ) is that ECHR judgments are directly enforceable in the national courts of the parties to the European Convention on Human Rights. This eliminates the major enforcement problem plaguing the ICJ. Even when States appear and litigate in the ICJ's proceedings, there is no supranational executive body to oversee national compliance with the ICJ judgments. Nor is there a comparable treaty provision making ICJ judgments directly enforceable by treating them as if they were made by a national court of the State parties to the dispute.

There are, of course, questions about the proper scope of the ECHR's decisional law and how its exercise has affected the willingness of member States to submit to its compulsory jurisdiction. The classic example of this conflict was spawned by the Court's decision in the 1979 *Sunday Times* case wherein the ECHR overturned a major decision by the British House of Lords. A succinct summary of the events in this ECHR case follows:

British proceedings: The drug Thalidomide was made in (former West) Germany and marketed in Great Britain. In 1961, large numbers of pregnant women who used this sedative began to give birth to children with severe deformities. The manufacturer withdrew the drug from the British market that year. During the 1971 settlement negotiations regarding the funding of a charitable trust established in 1968 for the children, the British newspaper *Sunday Times* criticized the small amounts to be placed in this trust, considering the severity of its effect on the children involved. The *Times* announced that a future article would detail how this tragedy occurred as a result of a lack of proper testing of the drug. The British Attorney-General (AG) obtained a court injunction barring the publication of this story—subjecting the *Times* to contempt of court if it published the article. Unlike the US, British law prohibits "trial by newspaper" so as to avoid pretrial publicity that will adversely affect pending litigation. In this case, however, the trial judge decided that the public's need to know outweighed the rationale for banning the intended newspaper story on pending litigation. The British AG appealed. The appellate court refused the AG the relief sought. The AG then further appealed to the House of Lords, effectively the "court of last resort" in Great Britain. The House directed that the trial court issue an injunction against publication, which again subjected the newspaper to contempt of court sanctions if it published the subject article.

ECHR proceedings: The newspaper then sought relief from the (former) European Commission on Human Rights, an administrative step prior to the court proceedings. The Commission found that the injunction violated Article 10 of the European Human Rights Convention. That article protects the right to freedom of expression, including the right "to hold opinions and to receive and impart information and ideas without interference by public authority and regardless of frontiers." The European of Court Human Rights in Strasbourg, France, then affirmed this administrative decision, thereby relieving the paper of liability for contempt of the court in London. The ECHR held that the House of Lords' injunction against publication was not necessary for the maintenance of public confidence in the British judicial system. (Other nations, including Canada, also generally prohibit pretrial publicity like that which hindered the objective conduct of the famous 1994 O. J. Simpson case in Los Angeles, California).

Criticism: A prominent British lawyer, F. A. Mann, wrote that the ECHR, sitting in France, effectively undermined confidence in its regional judging by this ruling, which uprooted the staunchly ingrained British legal tradition. In his incisive analysis:

> [C]ontempt of court is undoubtedly one of the great contributions the common law [of England] has made to the civilised behaviour of a large part of the world beyond the continent of Europe where [the ECHR sits but] the institution [of restraining pretrial newspaper publicity to preserve confidence in the courts] is unknown. . . . Yet it is that very branch of the law which the European Court of Human Rights has seriously undermined by, in effect, overturning the unanimous decision of the House of Lords . . . a unique event in the [extensive] history of English law. In fact, it is probably no exaggeration to say that the gravest blow to the fabric of English law has been dealt by the *majority of eleven judges* coming *from* Cyprus, Denmark, Eire, France, Germany, Italy, Portugal, Spain, Sweden and Turkey, who over the *dissent of nine judges from* Austria, Belgium, Holland, Iceland, Luxembourg, Malta, Norway, Switzerland and the United Kingdom, decided in favour of the *Sunday Times*. . . . The [real issue is] whether the Strasbourg Court arrogated unto itself powers . . . which it cannot possibly exercise convincingly . . . and whether the level of [sound] judicial reasoning is higher in London or Strasbourg?[74]

Inter-American Court of Human Rights The Organization of American States (OAS) is the regional political association of States in the Western hemisphere (*see* §3.5). OAS member State representatives drafted the American Convention on Human Rights, which became effective in 1978.[75] Approximately two-thirds of the OAS's more than thirty member States have adopted this treaty (but not the US).

In 1979, the OAS established the Inter-American Court of Human Rights (IAC) in San Jose, Costa Rica. It has since heard several contentious cases and has rendered about a dozen advisory opinions. The court's primary function is to interpret the American Convention. The IAC hear claims alleging that an individual's civil and political rights have been infringed by State action. Unlike the practice developed in Europe's regional courts, individuals can never appear either directly or indirectly in the IAC. Under Article 61(1) of the Convention, "only States Parties and the [Human Rights] Commission shall have the right to submit a case to the Court."

The IAC hears disputes between States when one accuses another of violating individual freedoms guaranteed under the American Convention. The participating States must consent, however, to the jurisdiction of this Court to resolve such disputes. Unlike the practice of the two European courts (discussed above), only a few OAS member States have accepted the compulsory jurisdiction of the IAC.

The IAC may also issue "advisory" opinions. These do not employ the presence of an offending nation. The purpose of this power, similar to that of the International Court of Justice's advisory jurisdiction, is to provide judicial guidance to member States about certain practices that violate the Human Rights Convention.[76] The Court is thereby able to develop the regional Latin American law regarding State compliance with the provisions of the American Convention.

One of the Convention's key provisions prohibits States from harming their citizens for political purposes. In a landmark trial in 1988, the IAC heard the first contentious trial against a Latin American State for the politically motivated murders of its own citizens. Honduras was tried for the disappearance and murders of 90,000 people since the 1950s.[77] The IAC is only the second regional court (after the European Court of Human Rights) to judge States for violations of internationally recognized human rights.

The IAC is something more than a temporary arbitral body and something less than a permanent judicial institution. Its seven jurists, from different OAS nations, do not conduct proceedings on a full-time basis. Funding has been withheld, pending development of the Court's jurisprudence to a point where full-time judges are necessary. This part-time status is, unfortunately, unique among the regional courts of the world. The Court's Chief Justice, George Washington University Professor Thomas Burgenthal, laments that ". . . a part-time tribunal might give that body an *ad hoc* image, likely to diminish the prestige and legitimacy it might need to obtain compliance with and respect for its decisions in the Americas. But the [OAS] General Assembly opted instead for a tribunal composed of part-time judges . . . [who are] free to practice law, to teach, and to engage in whatever other occupations they may have in their native countries."[78]

This tribunal oversees a rather ambitious set of goals set forth in the various regional human rights documents (Chapter 11). Its theoretical utility has not been matched, however, by State usage. The region does not enjoy the comparatively lengthy period of development and degree of solidarity that exists in the European Union's two regional tribunals. Absent the sense of liberal democracy enjoyed in other regions of the world, the work of this Court will likely remain rather limited in terms of actual accomplishments. As aptly described by University of Canterbury (New Zealand) Professor Scott Davidson:

> The malaise [that] the nonuse of the contentious procedure signifies lies deeper than the pure mechanics of making an instrument and its institutions work more efficiently: it lies more likely in the political and economic structures of the states of the region and in the perceptions which these structures engender. If certain states continue to see the inter-American human rights system as a threat to entrenched positions rather than an aid to furthering support for the forms of liberal democracy which the Court and the instruments upon which it relies clearly support, then such states are unlikely to encourage its [expanded] use.[79]

Andean Court of Justice The 1969 Treaty of Bogotá, often referred to as the "Andean Pact," was adopted by five South American nations. They hope to develop an economic union similar to that of the European Union. The national members are Bolivia, Colombia, Ecuador, Peru, and Venezuela. (Chile previously withdrew.)

In 1983, the Andean Pact countries created the Andean Court of Justice (ACJ), which sits in Quito,

Ecuador. It has five judges—one from each member State. Contrary to the more flexible practice in the Inter-American Court of Justice, the judges of the ACJ must live near Quito. They may not undertake any other professional activities.[80]

Under Article 32 of the ACJ agreement, judgments are directly enforceable in the national courts of member States. There is no need for any national incorporation of the regional court's judgments into internal law. Similar to the practice in the European Court of Justice, Article 33 provides that States cannot submit any controversy arising under the Andean Pact "to any [other] court, arbitration system or any other procedure not contemplated by this Treaty." This limitation is designed to promote uniformity of decision and application of the same judicial standards to economic disputes arising throughout the region. Judges of national courts within Andean Pact states may also request that the regional court interpret the Andean Pact's economic provisions when such issues are litigated in their national courts. This power encourages regional solidarity in matters of Latin American economic integration.

The court is able to overrule decisions by the Andean Pact's other major organs. A member State's alleged noncompliance with the Pact's economic integration plan is first considered by either the Commission—the Pact's major administrative organ—or the Junta—its chief executive organ. These bodies may submit a dispute with a member nation to the Court. The Court can nullify decisions of the Commission or the Junta and require the offending State to comply. In the ACJ's first case, decided in 1987, Colombia questioned a resolution of the Junta. The Court ruled that the Junta improperly limited Colombia's introduction of protective measures against imports from Venezuela.[81]

Under Article 25 of the treaty creating the ACJ, the offending nation's noncompliance permits the court to "restrict or suspend, totally or partially, the advantages deriving from the Cartagena [Andean Pact] Agreement which benefit the noncomplying member country." Suppose that a member State does not reduce its tariffs on exports of another member State—as required by the terms of the Andean Pact regulations. The ACJ Court has the power to render a judgment requiring the offending State to comply with the treaty or its related regulatory rules. The Court has never issued such an opinion, however. Like other international courts, the ACJ may also render advisory opinions.

The ACJ has not been utilized extensively for a variety of economic and political reasons. The underlying Cartagena Agreement (Andean Pact) was modified in 1989 by the Quito Protocol with a view toward bringing the Andean regional process in line with that of the European Union. In that year, the member States also issued a manifesto whereby they committed themselves to fully implementing the Andean Common Market.[82]

◆ 9.7 INTERNATIONAL LAW IN NATIONAL COURTS AND THE US

This section addresses the following themes:

- Is International Law applied in national courts?
- *Is* International Law a part of the law of the US?
- *When* does national law take precedence over International Law?
- In *what courts* can suits involving International Law be brought?
- *How* do US courts and litigants *avoid* the resolution of such issues?

INTERNATIONAL LAW IN NATIONAL COURTS

Most court decisions involving issues arising under International Law are those of national courts. There are nearly 190 nations in the world, with varying degrees of judicial independence, most of which routinely produce case law addressing such matters.[83] George Slyz, New York University Fellow for the Center for International Studies, explains: "International Law has a long history of influencing and forming the basis for decisions of national courts. In the seventeenth century, for example, English and French courts regularly applied international prize law in cases concerning the lawfulness of seizures of a belligerent's commercial vessels during military conflict. Today, national courts increasingly confront issues of international law as a result of the unprecedented increase in activity on the part of international organizations and states' newfound willingness to submit their disputes to international tribunals."[84]

The nexus between national and international systems was addressed in §1.7 of this text on the related interplay between national and International Law.

> The commonly recognized principles and norms of the international law and the international treaties of the Russian Federation shall be a component part of its legal system. If an international treaty of the Russian Federation stipulates other rules than those stipulated by the [Federation] law, the rules of the international treaty shall apply.
>
> —Russian Constitution, Article 15(4)

> This Constitution, and the Laws of the United States which shall be made in Pursuance thereof; and all Treaties made, or which shall be made, under the Authority of the United States, shall be the supreme Law of the Land. . . .
>
> —United States Constitution, Article VI(2)

> The rights and freedoms set forth in the European Convention for the Protection of Human Rights and Fundamental Freedoms and its Protocols shall apply directly in Bosnia and Herzegovina. These shall have priority over all other law. All competent authorities in Bosnia and Herzegovina shall cooperate with and provide unrestricted access to: any international human rights monitoring mechanisms established for Bosnia and Herzegovina; the supervisory bodies established by any of the international agreements listed in Annex I to this Constitution; the International Tribunal for the Former Yugoslavia . . . ; and any other organization authorized by the United Nations Security Council with a mandate concerning human rights or humanitarian law.
>
> —Bosnia & Herzegovina Constitution, Sections II(2) and (8)

Reviewing those materials will help you focus on the theme of this section: national judicial applications of International Law. Canadian applications are available in the classic text *International Law: Chiefly as Interpreted and Applied in Canada*. Mexican applications are available in the prominent *Derecho Internacional Publico*.[85] The US approach is the focus of the remaining portions of this section.

PRIMA FACIE INCORPORATION IN US COURTS

The question of whether US courts apply International Law is not explicitly answered by the US Constitution. Its legislative article proclaims that Congress has the power to "define and punish . . . Offenses against the Law of Nations." Another article provides that treaties "shall be the supreme Law of the Land." Yet neither of these constitutional provisions expressly incorporated *International Law* into the "laws" of the United States. The US Supreme Court professed to do so in its *Paquete Habana* case. In 1900, the Court announced that "International law is part of our law, and must be ascertained and administered by the courts . . . as often as questions of right depending upon it are duly presented for their determination."[86]

RESOLUTION OF CONFLICTS WITH NATIONAL LAW

May national law take precedence over International Law in the United States? In practice, the above Supreme Court statement—and the Constitutional language that treaties are "supreme"—are subject to a number of qualifications. The Constitution's drafters hoped that US law would develop in a way which would respond to the necessities of the era. Characterizing treaties with other nations as the "Law of the Land" would give the least offense to the established European powers that were in a position to threaten the existence of the new republic. So there is certainly no conflict between US and International Law that one can find in the express terms of the Constitution. Nevertheless, a conflict may exist due to a hierarchy that evolved among the Constitution, federal statutes, and treaties.

Constitutional Supremacy The US Constitution *always* takes precedence over treaties, US statutes, and customary (nontreaty) rules of International Law. The following case classically illustrates how an international treaty, a federal statute, and the US Constitution could clash. As you read this case, bear in mind that the importance and applicability of International Law were *presumed* by the drafters of the 1787 US Constitution during the formative years of the new republic. That is one reason why they did not address the possibility of an express conflict between national and International Law in the Constitution of 1787.

Reid v. Covert

SUPREME COURT OF THE UNITED STATES, 1957

354 US 1, 77 S.Ct. 1222, 1 *L. Ed*. 2d 1148

Author's Note: *In two cases considered simultaneously by the Court, civilian wives killed their husbands, who were members of the US armed forces assigned to bases overseas. Mrs. Covert killed her husband at a US base in Great Britain. Mrs. Smith killed her husband at a US base in Japan. Warden Reid was the nominal defendant, because he was the Superintendent of the Jails housing certain civilian dependents serving sentences imposed by military courts-martial overseas.*

Some years before the homicides in this case, the President had entered into executive agreements—"Status of Forces" (SOF) agreements—between the US and the countries where these homicides occurred. As a result of those agreements, any civilian dependents accompanying their spouses were tried on the US military base where a crime occurred. They were prosecuted under the Uniform Code of Military Justice (UCMJ), the federal statute that governs criminal trials of military personnel. The UCMJ and the SOF treaties with Great Britain and Japan assured these countries that crimes occurring at US military posts on their soil would be prosecuted and that those responsible would be swiftly tried and punished by American military authorities.

The year before this opinion was rendered, the US Supreme Court had decided that the military trials of Mrs. Covert and Mrs. Smith did not violate their rights under the US Constitution. The Court had determined that their Constitutional rights—including the right to a jury of one's peers (that is, a civilian jury rather than a military jury)—did not apply to American citizens for their conduct in foreign lands. The Supreme Court nevertheless granted a subsequent petition that resulted in the rehearing of the cases against Mrs. Covert and Mrs. Smith. On rehearing, the Court reversed its earlier decision approving the courts-martial of Covert and Smith. This time, the Supreme Court held that trial by courts-martial improperly deprived the civilian wives of their Constitutional rights. The UCMJ permissibly withheld the Constitutional rights associated with jury trial as applied to military personnel. The UCMJ could not be applied, however, to authorize military courts-martial of their civilian dependents. Unlike the UCMJ, the US Constitution provides for civilian juries and related safeguards expressed in the Constitution's Bill of Rights. The wives' lawyers argued that the presidential SOF agreements, which incorporated the UCMJ, could not override safeguards expressly guaranteed to civilians by the US Constitution.

The relevant portions of Justice Black's majority opinion follow, representing only four of the seven justices who participated in the case. Emphasis in certain passages of the Supreme Court's opinion has been supplied by the author.

COURT'S OPINION. These cases raise basic constitutional issues of the utmost concern. They call into question the role of the militia under our system of government. They involve the power of Congress to expose civilians to trial by military tribunals, under military regulations and procedures, for offenses against the United States thereby depriving them of trial in civilian courts, under civilian laws and procedures and with all the safeguards of the Bill of Rights. These cases are particularly significant because for the first time since the adoption of the Constitution wives of soldiers have been denied trial by jury in a court of law and forced to trial before courts-martial.

In No. 701 Mrs. Clarice Covert . . . was tried by a court-martial for murder under Article 118 of the Uniform Code of Military Justice (UCMJ). The trial was on charges [made] by Air Force personnel and the court-martial was composed of Air Force officers. The court-martial asserted jurisdiction over Mrs. Covert under Article 2 (11) of the UCMJ, which provides:

> "The following persons are subject to this code: . . . "(11) Subject to the provisions of any treaty or agreement to which the United States is or may be a party or to any accepted rule of international law, all persons serving with, employed by, or accompa-

nying the armed forces without the continental limits of the United States. . . ."

Counsel for Mrs. Covert . . . petitioned the District Court for a writ of habeas corpus to set her free on the ground that the Constitution forbade her trial by military authorities. . . .

In No. 713 Mrs. Dorothy Smith . . . charged that the court-martial was without jurisdiction because Article 2 (11) of the UCMJ was unconstitutional insofar as it authorized the trial of civilian dependents accompanying servicemen overseas. . . .

At the beginning we *reject* the idea that *when the United States acts against citizens abroad it can do so free of the [Constitution's] Bill of Rights.* The United States is entirely a creature of the Constitution. Its power and authority have no other source. It can only act in accordance with all the limitations imposed by the Constitution. When the Government reaches out to punish a citizen who is abroad, the shield which the Bill of Rights and other parts of the Constitution provide to protect his life and liberty should not be stripped away just because he happens to be in another land. This is not a novel concept. To the contrary, it is as old as government. It was recognized long before Paul successfully invoked his right as a Roman citizen to be tried in strict accordance with Roman law. . . .

The rights and liberties which citizens of our country enjoy are not protected by custom and tradition alone, they have been jealously preserved from the encroachments of Government by express provisions of our written Constitution.

Among those provisions, Art. III, §2 and the Fifth and Sixth Amendments are directly relevant to these cases. Article III, §2 lays down the rule that:

> "The Trial of all Crimes, except in Cases of Impeachment, shall be by Jury; and such Trial shall be held in the State where the said Crimes shall have been committed; but when not committed within any State, the Trial shall be at such Place or Places as the Congress may by Law have directed."
>
> The Fifth Amendment declares:
>
> No person shall be held to answer for a capital, or otherwise infamous crime, unless on a presentment or indictment of a Grand Jury, except in cases arising in the land or naval forces, or in the Militia, when in actual service in time of War or public danger;"
>
> And the Sixth Amendment provides:
>
> "In all criminal prosecutions, the accused shall enjoy the right to a speedy and public trial, by an impartial jury of the State and district wherein the crime shall have been committed."

The [above] language of Art. III, §2 manifests that constitutional protections for the individual were designed to restrict the United States Government when it acts outside of this country, as well as here at home. After declaring that all criminal trials must be by jury, the section states that when a *crime* is *"not committed within any State, the Trial shall be at such Place or Places as the Congress may by Law have directed."* If this language is permitted to have its obvious meaning, §2 is applicable to criminal trials outside of the States as a group without regard to where the offense is committed or the trial held. From the very first Congress, *federal statutes* have implemented the provisions of §2 by providing for trial of murder and other crimes committed outside the jurisdiction of any State *"in the district where the offender is apprehended, or into which he may first be brought."* The Fifth and Sixth Amendments, like Art. III, §2, are also all-inclusive with their sweeping references to "no person" and to "all criminal prosecutions."

This Court and other federal courts have held or asserted that various constitutional limitations apply to the Government when it acts outside the continental United States. While it has been suggested that only those constitutional rights which are "fundamental" protect Americans abroad, *we can find no warrant,* in logic or otherwise, *for picking and choosing among the remarkable collection of "Thou shalt nots" which were explicitly fastened on all departments and agencies of the Federal Government by the Constitution and its Amendments.* Moreover, in view of our heritage and the history of the adoption of the Constitution and the Bill of Rights, it seems peculiarly anomalous to say that trial before a civilian judge and by an independent jury picked from the common citizenry is not a fundamental right.

At the time of Mrs. Covert's alleged offense, an executive agreement was in effect between the United States and Great Britain which permitted United States' military courts to exercise exclusive jurisdiction over offenses committed in Great Britain by American servicemen or their dependents. For its part, the United States agreed that these military courts would be willing and able to try and to punish all offenses against the laws of Great Britain by such persons. In all material respects, the same situation existed in Japan when Mrs. Smith killed her husband. Even though a court-martial does not give an accused trial by jury and other Bill of Rights protections, the Government contends that Art. 2 (11) of the UCMJ, insofar as it provides for the military trial of dependents accompanying the armed forces in Great Britain and Japan, can be sustained as legislation which is necessary and proper to carry out the United States' obligations under the international agreements made with those countries. The obvious and decisive answer to this, of course, is that *no agreement with a foreign nation can confer power on the Congress, or on any other branch of Government, which is free from the restraints of the Constitution.*

Article VI, the Supremacy Clause of the Constitution, declares:

> "This Constitution, and the Laws of the United States which shall be made in Pursuance thereof; and all Treaties made, or which shall be made, under the Authority of the United States, shall be the supreme Law of the Land. . . ."

There is nothing in this language which intimates that treaties and laws enacted pursuant to them do not have to comply with the provisions of the Constitution. Nor is there anything in the debates which accompanied the drafting and ratification of the Constitution which even suggests such a result. These debates as well as the history that surrounds the adoption of the treaty provision in Article VI make it clear that the reason treaties were not limited to those made in "pursuance" of the Constitution was so that agreements made by the United States under the Articles of Confederation, including the important peace treaties which concluded the Revolutionary War, would remain in effect. It would be *manifestly contrary to the objectives of those who created the Constitution,* as well as those who were responsible for the Bill of Rights—let alone alien to our entire constitutional history and tradition—to construe Article VI as permitting the United States to exercise power under an international agreement without observing constitutional prohibitions. In effect, such construction would permit amendment of that document in a manner not sanctioned by Article V. The prohibitions of the Constitution were designed to apply to all branches of the National Government and they cannot be nullified by the Executive or by the Executive and the Senate combined. . . .

This Court has also repeatedly taken the position that *an Act of Congress,* which must comply with the Constitution, *is on a full parity with a treaty,* and that *when a statute which is subsequent in time is inconsistent with a treaty, the statute* to the extent of conflict *renders the treaty null.* It would be completely anomalous to say that a treaty need not comply with the Constitution when such an agreement can be overridden by a statute that must conform to that instrument.

In summary, we conclude that the Constitution in its entirety applied to the trials of Mrs. Smith and Mrs. Covert. *[The Court then ordered the release of Mrs. Smith and Mrs. Covert from custody, freeing them from any further prosecution.]*

◆ *Notes*

1. The presidential SOF treaty agreements incorporated the federal statute (UCMJ). The latter, in turn, then provided for trial and punishment of civilian dependents by military courts-martial. Those agreements accommodated Japanese, British, and US sovereign concerns. When military personnel were killed on US bases on their soil, those countries were willing to cede their sovereign power or control over the civilian perpetrators to the US so that they could be courts-martialed rather than be tried in the local courts where the US Constitution would not apply. In Japan, for example, there were no juries. The SOF agreements were based on the expectation that such crimes would be punished. The *Reid* case illustrates that when the US takes action affecting its citizens abroad, it can do so, but subject to the limitations imposed by the US Constitution. Under *US* law, the

Constitution had to prevail, although it conflicted with the international obligations spawned by crimes on US military bases in other countries. As a result of *Reid,* these two murders went unpunished.

2. The US released the convicted wives from custody. They were not extradited to Great Britain or Japan. These defendants could not be prosecuted (at that time), because the President's prior SOF arrangements presumed that such matters would be governed exclusively by the UCMJ. Because they could not be applied to civilian dependents, who were entitled to be tried by a jury of their peers, there was no other law under which to prosecute or hold the wives in custody.
3. In the dissenting opinion in *Reid,* certain members of the Court expressed their concern that the peacetime failure to apply the UCMJ to civilian dependents created a gap that would allow US citizens to be prosecuted by foreign authorities in such cases. The dissenters believed that it would be preferable to try Mrs. Smith by court-martial, rather than in the Japanese system, where there are no juries.
4. Under International Law, the US Constitution cannot be applied to events occurring in other countries. Only a foreign nation has the sovereign power to prosecute criminals for conduct occurring within its borders absent consent to some other arrangement. Like the prior SOF agreements, a treaty may still provide the US and another country with the *concurrent* jurisdiction, or mutual opportunity, to try and punish such defendants. The US usually obtains "primary jurisdiction" to try its own military and civilian defendants. If it declines to prosecute, then the foreign country may do so.

One such agreement is the subsequent US–Japanese Protocol Agreement. That agreement deals with *on-base* offenses against members of the American armed forces and their dependents. Under its terms, the US has the *primary* or first right to try the perpetrators of such offenses (court-martial for military personnel, and civilian jury trial in the US for dependents). Civilians may be turned over to Japanese authorities, however, if the US declines its option to try them in civilian courts of the US under federal law enacted after the *Reid* decision. This Protocol was then approved by the US Supreme Court (after *Reid*).[87]

Statute Versus Treaty US legislators do not normally propose laws that purport to violate International Law. For example, the object of the Anti-Terrorism Act of 1987—which required the closure of the Palestine Liberation Organization's New York (UN) and Washington, D.C., offices—was to suppress terrorism. A US court nevertheless held that this law violated US obligations to the UN. A clearer example of the US breach of an international obligation would be a statute that, under US law, withholds or extinguishes the US obligation to pay assessed UN dues.[88]

What happens when a statute does conflict, either expressly or implicitly, with a treaty? The US rule is that the *later in time* prevails. This rule is derived from a judicial interpretation of Article VI of the Constitution providing that "the laws of the United States [including federal statutes] . . . and all Treaties . . . shall be the supreme Law of the Land." This equality means, however, that an obligation arising under an international treaty may be negated by a subsequent statute. Under the US Supreme Court's time-honored "parity" rule, which merely treats the last in time as controlling, "an Act of Congress . . . is on full parity with a treaty, and . . . when a statute [that] is subsequent in time is inconsistent with a treaty, the statute to the extent of the conflict renders the treaty null."[89]

What happens when a federal statute conflicts with a norm of International Law that is *not* contained in a treaty? This problem is presented when a criminal defendant claims that the application of a US statute to his or her crime cannot survive scrutiny because of its "extraterritorial" effect. Under US law, a statute that *expressly* proscribes criminal conduct abroad must be applied by a US judge, regardless of whether there may be a breach of International Law. Such statutes normally address acts which are intended to have an effect within the US, such as drug-smuggling operations on the High Seas. A statute that is silent, however, is presumed *not* to apply to extraterritorial conduct. This presumption may be overcome, however, when the circumstances unmistakably lead to the implication that Congress intended to apply US law on an extraterritorial basis.

The US decision in the *Noriega* case contains a useful illustration of conflict between a federal criminal statute and the norm of International Law, which generally precludes the application of national law outside of the country enacting that law. Panama's former military leader had been indicted in the US for drug trafficking by misusing his position to direct the importation of thousands of pounds of cocaine into the US via Miami. After the US invasion of Panama and Noriega's extraction for prosecution in the US, Noriega claimed that the relevant drug trafficking statutes could not be properly applied to him. The court disagreed, quoting various authorities including the US Supreme Court:

> Section 959, prohibiting the distribution of narcotics intending that they be imported into the United States, is *clearly meant to* apply extraterritorially. The statute expressly states that it is "intended to reach acts of manufacture or distribution committed outside the territorial jurisdiction of the United States" 21 USC §959(c). The remaining statutes, by contrast, do *not on their face* indicate an express intention that they be given extraterritorial effect. Where a statute is silent as to its extraterritorial reach, a *presumption* against such application normally applies. However, "such statutes *may* be given extraterritorial effect if the nature of the law permits it and Congress intends it. Absent an express intention on the face of the statutes to do so, the exercise of that power *may be inferred* from the nature of the offenses and Congress' other legislative efforts to eliminate the type of crime involved."[90]

WHO CAN BE SUED AND WHERE?

When a claim arising under International Law is adjudicated in the US, who may be sued—and where? In US federal courts, each lawsuit must be based on a specific Constitutional grant of power to hear and determine the particular type of case. Article III of the Constitution furnishes the power whereby federal courts may resolve cases involving ambassadors, consular officers, and diplomats.[91] Congress may restrict the application of this Constitutional power to certain courts. The federal Judicial Code thus limits the resolution of cases against ambassadors and consuls to only the federal courts. The purpose of this restriction—giving *exclusive* jurisdiction to the federal but not state courts—is to seek harmony in the judicial application of International Law when foreign diplomats and consular officers are sued in a court in the United States. Then there is one federal system resolving such cases, rather than fifty-one state and federal systems resolving such matters. This limitation limits the potential for the judiciary in the US to render conflicting decisions on matters of interest to the international community.

Federal courts share certain *concurrent* powers with the states of the US. The respective court systems routinely resolve controversies *between* a state or its citizens *and* foreign countries or their citizens (§2.6 on Sovereign Immunity). Disputes involving issues of International Law, other than cases that fall within the *exclusive* province of the federal courts, may be adjudicated in the courts of all fifty states—as well as in the ninety-three federal districts of the US.

Federal courts have interpreted the Supremacy Clause of the Constitution to require states of the US to apply *federal law* when dealing with issues of International Law. Decisions by federal courts take precedence over any conflicting decisions by state courts when a question of International Law is presented in either system (state or federal). Put another way, state court judges cannot decide an issue concerning International Law in a manner that conflicts with a federal decision on that point of law. One reason is that the individual US states no longer exercised any *international* powers once the US was formed. The 1787 US Constitution established the US as a federal entity for this purpose and thus distinguishable from the thirteen colonies. The sovereignty of the federal government in international affairs is thus complete. The US Supreme Court established this federal–state hierarchy when it reasoned that as "a member of the family of nations, the right and power of the United States in that field [international law] are equal to the right and power of the other members of the international family. Otherwise, the United States is not completely sovereign."[92] When the federal government decides not to recognize a foreign government, for example, state court judges cannot allow that government to appear in their courts as either a plaintiff or a defendant.[93]

AVOIDING INTERNATIONAL LAW ISSUES

Can a US court completely avoid the resolution of an issue arising under International Law without abdicating its judicial responsibility to resolve cases and controversies? US courts have devised a number of judicially created doctrines to *avoid* the resolution of issues arising under International Law. The prominent ones are the Political Question Doctrine, the Act of State Doctrine, and Lack of Standing.

Political Questions The judicial branch of government was not designed to exercise political functions. Under the Political Question Doctrine, judges will not resolve controversies that should be resolved by the *political* branches of government: the executive or legislative branches. The conduct of foreign affairs is Constitutionally committed to the president, who is the chief of the executive branch of government. When it is claimed that the *US* has violated International Law, a "political question" is presented that often falls within the province of the President's foreign relations powers.

A number of these political questions were presented in various state and federal courts during the Vietnam War. President Nixon's decisions to mine North Vietnamese harbors and bomb Cambodia were challenged by individuals in the US Army and in the House of Representatives. Their lawsuits claimed that these US military actions violated the United Nations prohibition against the aggressive use of force in international relations. The courts dismissed such cases, however, on the grounds that they involved military decisions that were insulated from judicial review and thus *political* rather than judicial questions. The judiciary did not wish to second-guess the President's military strategy in foreign conflicts.[94]

In a more recent application, survivors and estate representatives brought a negligence suit against the United States on behalf of members of the crew of a Turkish destroyer. They sought money damages for injuries and deaths that occurred in 1992 when the Turkish destroyer was struck by live missiles fired from an American warship during a NATO training exercise. The trial and appellate courts did not consider this case on its merits, because this action presented a non-justiciable political question. As stated by the appellate court:

> Restrictions derived from the separation of powers doctrine prevent the judicial branch from deciding "political questions," controversies that revolve around policy choices and value determinations constitutionally committed for resolution to the legislative or executive branches. . . .
>
> Foreign policy and military affairs figure prominently among the areas in which the political question doctrine has been implicated. The Supreme Court has declared that "[m]atters intimately related to foreign policy and national security are rarely proper subjects for judicial intervention." The Constitution commits the conduct of foreign affairs to the executive and legislative branches of government. . . .
>
> In a related manner, the political branches of government are accorded a particularly high degree of deference in the area of military affairs. The Constitution emphatically confers authority over the military upon the executive and legislative branches of government. . . . The Supreme Court has generally declined to reach the merits of cases requiring review of military decisions, particularly when those cases challenged the institutional functioning of the military in areas such as personnel, discipline, and training. . . .
>
> As with many cases that directly implicate foreign relations and military affairs, the instant controversy raises a nonjusticiable political question.[95]

Act of State This doctrine (AOS) is another convenient device for avoiding the litigation of issues arising under International Law. It is used to avoid a judicial resolution of challenges to the conduct of *foreign* leaders or governments performed within their own territories, as opposed to political decisions of the US president.

Probably the major incident in which the AOS doctrine was applied to avoid such litigation occurred after the Cuban government nationalized property belonging to US citizens in 1959. (The US did not approve of Fidel Castro's coming to power. It imposed a quota on Cuban sugar imports, which resulted in Cuba's nationalizations of US business interests.) In the ensuing suits in various US courts, individuals and businesses alleged violations of International Law spawned by Cuba's inadequate compensation for these nationalizations. The US courts dismissed these claims because Cuba's conduct in Cuba could not be challenged in US courts, *assuming* that Cuba had violated International Law by its nationalization of alien property without the requisite compensation. In the famous *Sabbatino* case, the US Supreme Court authoritatively echoed the traditional position that every national government is "bound to respect the independence of every other sovereign State, and [that] *the courts of one country will not sit in judgment on the acts of the government of another [country] done within its own territory.* Redress of grievances by reason of such acts must be obtained through the means open to be availed of by sovereign powers as between themselves [through diplomatic negotiations or litigation in *international* tribunals]."[96]

The dismissal of such suits under the AOS doctrine does not mean that there is no redress for the underlying grievances. It does mean that aggrieved individuals should pursue *legislative* or *executive* remedies. An example of the latter would be individual pressure on the US Department of State to negotiate for monetary compensation from Cuba on behalf of the US sugar corporations adversely affected by the Cuban nationalizations.

The courts are reluctant to resolve issues that touch upon the Constitutional powers of the executive branch of government. The President is Constitutionally required to conduct foreign affairs, not the courts. Judges do not want to hinder the international diplomacy of the Department of State by making pronouncements on sensitive points of International Law. The State Department, acting on behalf of the President, may be engaged in negotiations with another government on behalf of *all* US citizens harmed by that foreign government's actions. A US court judgment for *one* US citizen in a particular case—heralding the foreign State's violation of International Law—could easily jeopardize those negotiations.

Congress disliked the US Supreme Court's well-intentioned AOS doctrine, because judges in the US were thereby encouraged to dismiss suits involving the acts of foreign governments against US citizens that violated International Law. Congress responded to the Court's *Sabbatino* case by amending a federal statute to *encourage* courts to resolve such issues, *unless* the President deems it appropriate to seek a dismissal. This is the famous "Hickenlooper Amendment" to the US Foreign Assistance Act. The alteration of this legislation provides that the judge should proceed to decide cases that allege foreign government violations of International Law harming US citizens. The exception is that the court should dismiss, however, if there is an executive suggestion that hearing and determining the case would adversely affect some sensitive diplomatic negotiations (or for any other political reason for not proceeding to judgment). The Hickenlooper Amendment provides as follows:

> Notwithstanding any other provision of law [that is, US Supreme Court authority], no court in the United States shall decline on the ground of the federal act of state doctrine to make a determination of the merits giving effect to the principles of international law in a case in which . . . [a] right to property is asserted by any party . . . based on the confiscation . . . by an act of that state in violation of the principles of international law including the principles of compensation . . . : *Provided,* That this subparagraph shall not be applicable (1) in any case [where a bank letter of credit secures the claimant's right to the value of the nationalized property] . . . , or (2) . . . the President determines that application of the act of state doctrine [i.e., dismissing the case] is required in that particular case by the foreign policy interests of the United States and a suggestion to this effect is filed on his behalf in that case with the court.[97]

If the President (through the Department of State) does *not* file a suggestion with the court requesting a dismissal, then the judge normally proceeds to decide the case, even if the court effectively passes judgment on the question of whether a foreign government or its agency has violated International Law. Congress therein reversed the impact of the US Supreme Court's AOS decision. *Sabbatino* had directed trial courts to *automatically* decline to hear and determine such issues. The ensuing congressional directive dovetails the interests of the executive branch with those of the judicial branch in a way that may accomplish the same result. The courts need not be concerned about embarrassing the President in the conduct of foreign relations. The State Department receives notice from the courts anytime such an issue is pending. The President has an opportunity to effectively intervene for the purpose of seeking a dismissal.[98]

Both the Act of State and Political Question doctrines were addressed in a fascinating case involving a self-styled head of State, "President" Radovan Karadzic. He was served with process in New York City while attending UN negotiations regarding Bosnia prior to the 1995 Dayton Peace Accords. There were numerous International Law issues in this case, including whether his "Republica Srpska" within Bosnia insulated him under either the Political Question Doctrine or the Act of State Doctrine.

Kadic v. Karadzic

UNITED STATES COURT OF APPEALS, SECOND CIRCUIT, 1995

70 Fed.3d 232, *rehearing den'd,* 74 Fed.3d 377, *cert. den'd* 518 US 1005

Author's Note: *Two groups of victims from Bosnia-Herzegovina brought actions against the self-proclaimed president of the unrecognized Bosnian-Serb entity called Republica Srpska under the Alien Tort Claims Act for violations of international law* (Filartiga *case, Chapter 11). The United States District Court for the Southern District of New York dismissed these actions for lack of subject matter jurisdiction.*

The Court of Appeals reversed, holding that the plaintiffs sufficiently alleged violations of Customary International Law and the laws of war for purposes of the Alien Tort Claims Act; that they had sufficiently alleged that the unrecognized Bosnian Serb entity of "Srpska" was a "state," thus resulting in the defendant acting under color of law for purposes of international law violations requiring official action; that the defendant was not immune from personal service of process while an invitee of the United Nations; and that these suits were not precluded by either the Political Question Doctrine or the Act of State Doctrine, which had been waived.

Most case citations have been omitted from this edited version of the case.

COURT'S OPINION. III. Justiciability

We recognize that cases of this nature might pose special questions concerning the judiciary's proper role when adjudication might have implications in the conduct of this nation's foreign relations. We do not read *Filartiga* [set forth in Chapter 11, holding that foreign citizens may sue foreign citizens in the US for certain violations of the Law of Nations] to mean that the federal judiciary must always act in ways that risk significant interference with United States foreign relations. To the contrary, we recognize that suits of this nature can present difficulties that implicate sensitive matters of diplomacy historically reserved to the jurisdiction of the political branches. *See First National Bank v. Banco Nacional de Cuba,* 406 US 759, 767, 92 S.Ct. 1808, 1813, 32 *L. Ed.*2d 466 (1972). We therefore proceed to consider whether, even though the jurisdictional threshold is satisfied in the pending cases, other considerations relevant to justiciability weigh against permitting the suits to proceed.

Two nonjurisdictional, prudential doctrines reflect the judiciary's concerns regarding separation of powers: the political question doctrine and the act of state doctrine. . . . Although we too recognize the potentially detrimental effects of judicial action in cases of this nature, we do not embrace the rather categorical views as to the inappropriateness of judicial action urged by [certain judges] . . . . Not every case "touching foreign relations" is nonjusticiable, and judges should not reflexively invoke these doctrines to avoid difficult and somewhat sensitive decisions in the context of human rights. We believe a preferable approach is to weigh carefully the relevant considerations on a case-by-case basis. This will permit the judiciary to act where appropriate in light of the express legislative mandate of the Congress in section 1350 [Alien Tort Statute], without compromising the primacy of the political branches in foreign affairs. Karadzic maintains that these suits were properly dismissed because they present nonjusticiable political questions. We disagree. Although these cases present issues that arise in a politically charged context, that does not transform them into cases involving nonjusticiable political questions. . . .

A nonjusticiable political question would ordinarily involve one or more of the following factors: [1] a textually demonstrable constitutional commitment of the issue to a coordinate political department; or [2] a lack of judicially discoverable and manageable standards for resolving it; or [3] the impossibility of deciding without an initial policy determination of a kind clearly for nonjudicial discretion; or [4] the impossibility of a court's undertaking independent resolution without expressing lack of the respect due coordinate branches of government; or [5] an unusual need for unquestioning adherence to a political decision already made; or [6] the potentiality of embarrassment from multifarious pronouncements by various departments on one question.

With respect to the first three factors, we have noted in a similar context involving a tort suit against the PLO that "[t]he department to whom this issue has been 'constitutionally committed' is none other than our own—the Judiciary." *Klinghoffer,* 937 F.2d at 49 [suit against the PLO for terrorist attack and death of a US citizen]. Although the present actions are not based on the common law of torts, as was *Klinghoffer,* our decision in *Filartiga* established that universally recognized norms of international law provide judicially discoverable and manageable standards for adjudicating suits brought under the Alien Tort Act, which obviates any need to make initial policy decisions of the kind normally reserved for nonjudicial discretion. Moreover, the existence of judicially discoverable and manageable standards further undermines the claim that such suits relate to matters that are constitutionally committed to another branch.

The fourth through sixth . . . factors appear to be relevant only if judicial resolution of a question would contradict prior decisions taken by a political branch in those limited contexts where such contradiction would seriously interfere with important governmental interests. Disputes implicating foreign policy concerns have the potential to raise political question issues, although, as the Supreme Court has wisely cautioned, "it is 'error to suppose that every case or controversy which touches foreign relations lies beyond judicial cognizance.' "

The act of state doctrine, under which courts generally refrain from judging the acts of a foreign state within its territory, might be implicated in some cases arising under section 1350. However, as in *Filartiga,* we doubt that the acts of even a state official, taken in violation of a nation's fundamental law and wholly unratified by that nation's government, could properly be characterized as an act of state.

In the pending appeal, we need have no concern that interference with important governmental interests warrants rejection of appellants' claims. After commencing their action against Karadzic, attorneys for the plaintiffs in *Doe* [trial court plaintiff] wrote to the Secretary of State to oppose reported attempts by Karadzic to be granted immunity from suit in the United States; a copy of plaintiffs' complaint was attached to the letter. Far from intervening in the case to urge rejection of the suit on the ground that it presented political questions, the Department responded with a letter indicating that Karadzic was not immune from suit as an invitee of the United Nations. After oral argument in the pending appeals, this Court wrote to the Attorney General to inquire whether the United States wished to offer any further views concerning any of the issues raised. In a "Statement of Interest," signed by the Solicitor General and the State Department's Legal Adviser, the United States has expressly disclaimed any concern that the political question doctrine should be invoked to prevent the litigation of these lawsuits: "Although there might be instances in which federal courts are asked to issue rulings under the Alien Tort Statute or the Torture Victim Protection Act that might raise a political question, this is not one of them." Though even an assertion of the political question doctrine by the Executive Branch, entitled to respectful consideration, would not necessarily preclude adjudication, the Government's reply to our inquiry reinforces our view that adjudication may properly proceed.

As to the act of state doctrine, the doctrine was not asserted in the District Court and is not before us on this appeal. Moreover, the appellee has not had the temerity to assert in this Court that the acts he allegedly committed are the officially approved policy of a state. Finally, as noted, we think it would be a rare case in which the act of state doctrine precluded suit under section 1350. *Banco Nacional* was careful to recognize the doctrine "in the absence of . . . unambiguous agreement regarding controlling legal principles," such as exist in the pending litigation, and applied the doctrine only in a context—expropriation of an alien's property—in which world opinion was sharply divided. Finally, we note that at this stage of the litigation no party has identified a more suitable forum, and we are aware of none. Though the Statement of the United States suggests the general importance of considering the doctrine of forum non conveniens [which might otherwise require a dismissal because of where the events took place], it seems evident that the courts of the former Yugoslavia, either in Serbia or war-torn Bosnia, are not now available to entertain plaintiffs' claims, even if circumstances concerning the location of witnesses and documents were presented that were sufficient to overcome the plaintiffs' preference for a United States forum.

Conclusion

The judgment of the District Court dismissing appellants' complaints for lack of subject-matter jurisdiction is reversed, and the cases are remanded for further proceedings in accordance with this opinion.

◆ *Notes & Questions*

1. What was defendant Karadzic's political question defense?
2. A head of State of a foreign country can usually claim that he or she undertook acts of State, which should not be second-guessed by courts of another country—as authoritatively announced in the *Sabbatino* case, which is referred to in the text of this case *(Karadzic)* and in the text of this book under "Act of State" above. *See, e.g., Credit Suisse v. Dist. Court,* 130 Fed.3d 1342 (9th Cir., 1997), wherein action by victims of human rights violations under the Marcos regime in the Philippines were barred from prosecuting their suit under the Act of State (AOS) doctrine. Did the US court in *Karadzic* violate the AOS principle?

Lack of Standing This doctrine precludes a criminal defendant from asserting the rights of a third party who is not present in the litigation. A related form of the "standing" motif was previously presented in §5.3 of the text. The *Alvarez-Machin* case involved the claim of a kidnapped Mexican doctor who was a defendant in a US court after his abduction from Guadalajara. *He* could not assert *Mexico's* potential claim that the US had violated its territorial sovereignty by arranging the abduction of a Mexican citizen for trial in the US.

General Manuel Noriega presented a similar claim after the US invasion of Panama. He was taken by US military forces to the US, for prosecution under US drug-trafficking laws. The US judge relied on this standing doctrine to avoid the issue of whether the US invasion violated International Law. The relevant passages of the court's standing analysis are set forth immediately below:

United States of America v. Manuel Antonio Noriega

UNITED STATES DISTRICT COURT OF SOUTHERN FLORIDA, 1990

746 Fed.Supp. 1506, *aff'd,* 117 F.3d 1206 (11th Cir., 1997), *cert. den'd,* 118 S.Ct. 1389 (1998)

Author's Note: *The Court's original footnotes 29–32 have been replaced by author's footnotes a–d in the text of this version of the opinion. Emphasis in certain passages has been supplied by the author.*

OPINION. B. Violations of International Law

In addition to his due process claim, Noriega asserts that the *invasion of Panama violated international treaties and principles of customary international law*—specifically, Article 2(4) of the United Nations Charter,[a] Article 20[17] of the Organization of American States Charter,[b] Articles 23(b) and 25 of the Hague Convention,[c] Article 3 of Geneva Convention I, and Article 6 of the Nuremberg Charter.[d]

Initially, it is important to note that individuals lack standing to assert violations of international treaties in the absence of a protest from the offended government. Moreover, the *Ker-Frisbie* doctrine establishes that violations of international law alone do not deprive a court of jurisdiction over a defendant in the absence of specific treaty language to that effect. To defeat the Court's personal jurisdiction [over the defendant], Noriega must therefore establish that the treaty in question is self-executing in the sense that it confers *individual* rights upon citizens of the signatory nations, and that it by its terms expresses "a self-imposed limitation on the jurisdiction of the United States and hence on its courts."

As a general principle of international law, *individuals have no standing to challenge violations of international treaties* in the absence of a protest by the sovereign involved. [Citing US case authorities:] "[R]ights under international common law must belong to the sovereigns, not to individuals"; "Under international law, it is [only] the contracting foreign government that has the right to complain about a violation." The rationale behind this rule is that treaties are "designed to protect the sovereign interests of nations, and it is up to the offended nations to determine whether a violation of sovereign interests occurred and requires redress." . . .

Consistent with that principle, a treaty will be construed as creating enforceable *private rights* [assertable by criminal defendants in US courts] only if it expressly or impliedly provides a *private* right of action [assertable by nationals of the contracting States].

No such rights are created in the sections of the U.N. Charter, O.A.S. Charter, and Hague Convention cited by Noriega. Rather, those provisions set forth broad general principles *governing the conduct of nations toward each other and do not by their terms speak to individual or private rights.* [Citing US case authorities:] (articles phrased in "broad generalities" constitute "declarations of principles, not a code of legal rights"); (Articles 1 and 2 of the United Nations Charter "contain general 'purposes and principles,' some of which state mere aspirations and none of which can be sensibly thought to have been intended to be judicially enforceable at the behest of individuals"). ([I]ndividual may not invoke Article 2(4) of the U.N. Charter or Article 20[17] of the O.A.S. Charter if the sovereign state involved does not protest); (Hague Convention confers no private right of action on individuals). . . . Thus, under the applicable international law, Noriega lacks standing to challenge violations of these treaties in the absence of a protest by the Panamanian government that the invasion of Panama and subsequent arrest of Noriega violated that country's territorial sovereignty.

It can perhaps be argued that reliance on the above body of law, under the unusual circumstances of this case, is a form of legal bootstrapping. Noriega, it can be asserted, is the government of Panama or at least its *de facto* head of state, and as such he is the appropriate person to protest alleged treaty violations; to permit removal of him and his associates from power and reject his complaint because a new and friendly government is installed, he can further urge, turns the doctrine of sovereign standing on its head. This argument is not without force, yet there are more persuasive answers in response. First, as stated earlier, *the United States has consistently refused to recognize* the Noriega regime as Panama's legitimate government, a fact which considerably undermines Noriega's position. Second, Noriega *nullified the results of the Panamanian presidential election held* shortly before the alleged treaty violations occurred. The suggestion that his removal from power somehow robs the true government of the opportunity to object under the applicable treaties is therefore weak indeed. Finally, there is no provision or suggestion in the treaties cited which would permit the Court to ignore the absence of complaint or demand from the present duly constituted government of Panama. The current government of the Republic of Panama led by Guillermo Endara is therefore the appropriate entity to object to treaty violations. In light of Noriega's lack of standing to object, this Court therefore does not reach the question of whether these treaties were violated by the United States military action in Panama.

Article 3 of Geneva Convention I, which provides for the humane treatment of civilians and other non-participants of war, applies to armed conflicts "not of an international character," i.e., internal or civil wars of a purely domestic nature. Accordingly, Article 3 does not apply to the United States' military invasion of Panama.

Finally, Defendant cites Article 6 of the Nuremberg Charter, which proscribes war crimes, crimes against peace, and crimes against humanity. The Nuremberg Charter sets forth the procedures by which the Nuremberg Tribunal, established by the Allied powers after the Second World War, conducted the trials and punishment of major war criminals of the European Axis. The Government maintains that the principles laid down at Nuremberg were developed solely for the prosecution of World War II war criminals, and have no application to the conduct of US military forces in Panama. The Court cannot agree. As Justice Robert H. Jackson, the United States Chief of Counsel at Nuremberg, stated: "If certain acts in violation of treaties are crimes, they are crimes whether the United States does them or whether Germany does them, and we are not prepared to lay down a rule of criminal conduct against others which we would not be willing to have invoked against us." Nonetheless, Defendant fails to establish how the Nuremberg Charter or its possible violation, assuming any, has any application to the instant prosecution. As stated above, the *Ker-Frisbie* doctrine makes clear that violations of treaties or customary international law alone do not deprive the court of jurisdiction over the defendant in the absence of limiting language to that effect. Defendant has not cited any language in the Nuremberg Charter, nor in any of the above treaties, which limits the authority of the United States to arrest foreign nationals or to assume jurisdiction over their crimes. The reason is apparent; the Nuremberg Charter, as is the case with the other treaties, is addressed to the conduct of war and international aggression. It has no effect on the ability of sovereign states to enforce their laws, and thus has no application to the prosecution of Defendant for alleged narcotics violations. "The violation of international law, if any, may be redressed by other remedies, and does not depend upon the granting of what amounts to an effective immunity from criminal prosecution to safeguard individuals against police or armed forces misconduct." *United States v. Cadena,* 585 F.2d at 1261. *The Court therefore refrains from reaching the merits of Defendant's claim under the Nuremberg Charter.*

◆ *Notes & Questions*

1. What is the court's rationale for deciding that the cited treaties did *not* yield any protection to Noriega?
2. The court makes two interesting statements about Noriega's claims: First, "the United States has consistently refused to recognize the Noriega regime as Panama's legitimate government, a fact which considerably undermines Noriega's position." Second, "Noriega nullified the results of the Panamanian presidential election held shortly before the alleged treaty violations occurred." Do these judicial counters mean that lack of recognition and how Noriega came to power are legal bases for the US invasion and the ensuing prosecution of Noriega?
3. Could Noriega have properly raised an Act of State defense to this prosecution?

◆ SUMMARY

1. Arbitration differs from diplomatic and judicial methods of international dispute resolution. In diplomacy, the national participants do not submit their disputes for resolution by a third party or "outside" entity. In litigation, the court's composition and power to act are established *before* the dispute arises. In arbitration, the parties often determine who will decide and what will be decided after the dispute arises.
2. The various *ad hoc* arbitration alternatives share a common problem: States must freshly design each arbitral body for every arbitration. Unlike a *permanent* arbitral entity, such as the Permanent "Court" of Arbitration, there are no preestablished rules and procedures predating the agreement to arbitrate. Permanent arbitral bodies are immediately available with objective rules and procedures for resolving international disputes.
3. The permanent arbitral entities include (1) the Permanent Court of Arbitration, (2) the International Chamber of Commerce Court of Arbitration, and (3) the International Centre for Settlement of Investment Disputes. The Permanent Court of Arbitration (Netherlands) is not a court. Its "judges" serve on small arbitration panels available for the arbitration of *inter*-State disputes. The Court of Arbitration of the International Chamber of Commerce (France) facilitates the arbitration of *private* business disputes. The International Centre for Settlement of Investment Disputes (US) refers mixed arbitration disputes (between a State and a private individual or corporation) to panels of legal and business experts who arbitrate claims submitted to it.
4. A global court for judicially resolving international disputes between States materialized after World War I: the Permanent Court of International Justice. The leaders of many nations believed that a universal judicial tribunal might one day supplant the use of military force to resolve conflicts. The 1939 outbreak of World War II signaled the demise of the first World Court.
5. In 1945, the UN created a new World Court—the International Court of Justice—via UN Charter provisions and a new Statute of the International Court of Justice. All States that join the UN become parties to the relevant treaty provisions that expressly established the judicial power of the ICJ. The Court may hear cases referred to it as follows: as specifically provided in the UN Charter; in the ICJ Statute; or under special international agreements between nations.

6. Under the "Optional Clause" of the ICJ Statute, States *have* the option of consenting to the jurisdiction of the ICJ. States may choose to submit themselves to the Court's jurisdiction without imposing any conditions or limitations on their consent. Most States, however, have incorporated reciprocity or some other limitation into their acceptance of the ICJ's jurisdiction. This compromise facilitated the number of acceptances, although the actual acceptances have often been rather limited.
7. The ICJ possesses both "contentious" and "advisory" jurisdiction. In a contentious case, the plaintiff State and the defendant State take part in the proceedings as adversaries. The Court may also issue advisory opinions (*noncontentious* cases). There is no plaintiff and no defendant participating in the Court's proceedings. UN agencies such as the General Assembly or the Security Council may request that the ICJ apply International Law to a given set of facts. The ICJ may then issue an advisory opinion to aid in the progressive development and interpretation of International Law.
8. The ICJ has been criticized for its ineffectiveness. It was formed within a political arena, however. The State participants did not really want it to decide all international disputes. In the absence of a true world government, they did not want this World Court to function like their national courts.
9. The first contemporary International *Criminal* Court (ICC) was the Nuremberg Tribunal, constituted by the victorious Allies after their defeat of the Axis Powers in 1945. German and Japanese defendants were prosecuted in an international forum for various crimes, including crimes against peace and humanity.
10. The UN Security Council established a contemporary ICC in 1993 to prosecute war crimes in the former Yugoslavia. In 1994, it established another *ad hoc* tribunal for like crimes in Rwanda. The Council has since resisted requests to establish more of these special tribunals. In 1998, the UN hosted a conference on a permanent ICC in Rome. Delegates from nearly 160 nations met there and established a draft ICC Statute, a treaty that is now in the process of being ratified.
11. A number of regional courts have been created by an international treaty. Their judges hear disputes arising under International Law within their regions as structured by the treaty creating the particular courts. There are several functioning regional courts, including the European Court of Justice, the European Court of Human Rights, and the Inter-American Court of Human Rights.
12. The future of regional courts will depend on the solidarity of the political organizations of the member States with which they are associated. In most instances, the limited political and economic integration of the member States discourages the use of regional courts for resolving international disputes. Some States avoid regional litigation for reasons that are unrelated to the legal issues or merits of a potential court case. They refuse to participate because of the fear of losing cases in a public forum consisting of third parties or judges that the defendant State does not control. The European courts have been the most successful, because members have ceded them the requisite degree of sovereignty to make their decisions binding within member nations.
13. There is no defined relationship between the global and regional court systems. The UN Charter does not address the relationship between the International Court of Justice and regional courts. The Charter merely provides for the option of prior resort to "regional agencies or arrangements" for resolving international disputes. Appeal from a regional court decision to the global court is not possible. Regional judges do not defer cases for resolution by the ICJ. The ICJ cannot order regional courts to delay their proceedings for a decision by the ICJ.
14. The European Court of Justice interprets the trade obligations contained in the treaties and regulations of the various segments of the European Union. The European Court of Human Rights, the other regional court in Europe, is one of the two major European regional courts. This court judicially monitors State protection of the fundamental rights of the individual under the European Convention on Human Rights.
15. The Organization of American States established the Inter-American Court of Human Rights. The primary function of that court is to hear disputes between States, when one accuses another of violating the fundamental freedoms guaranteed under the American Convention on Human Rights.
16. The Andean Pact is composed of five South American nations that created the Andean Court of Jus-

tice. Judges of national courts within Andean Pact States may request that the regional court interpret the Andean treaty's provisions when such issues are litigated in their national courts. This promotes uniformity of judicial decision making on matters of regional economic integration. Several members of the Organization of American States created a separate organization of states known as the Central American Organization of States. Its judicial organ, the Central American Court of Justice, has not been as effective as other regional courts.

17. The US Constitution provides that treaties are the "supreme Law of the Land." The US Supreme Court has added that "International law is part of our law." These provisions are subject to a number of qualifications, however. The US Constitution always takes precedence over treaties, statutes of the US, and customary (nontreaty) rules of International Law. When a treaty and a statute conflict, the later in time prevails. When the intent of Congress is clear, legislative violations of International Law do not excuse the courts from following the will of Congress. US courts do presume, however, that US legislation is intended to be in harmony with the rules of International Law.
18. US federal courts *exclusively* resolve cases involving ambassadors and consuls. State and federal courts in the US exercise *concurrent* jurisdiction over other cases containing issues arising under international law. The Supremacy Clause of the US Constitution requires that states of the US apply federal law to issues arising under International Law.
19. A number of doctrines are used by US courts to avoid a judicial resolution of issues arising under International Law:
    a. Under the Political Question Doctrine, a judge will not resolve a controversy that should be resolved by the political branches of the government.
    b. The Act of State Doctrine is used to avoid challenges to the conduct of foreign leaders occurring within their own territories. Judges do not want to impede any diplomatic efforts with distinct judicial pronouncements on sensitive questions of International Law. In 1964, the US Supreme Court directed judges to dismiss cases alleging a foreign sovereign's violation of International Law (*Sabbatino* case). The US Congress responded to that decision by its amendment to the US Foreign Assistance Act (Hickenlooper Amendment). Judges now proceed with such cases, and give notice to the Department of State that a relevant issue alleging a breach of International Law by a foreign sovereign is pending before the court. This notice provides the President with an opportunity to file a suggestion with the court that it would be in the best interests of the US for the judge to dismiss the case (due to ongoing political negotiations).
    c. A lack of "standing" prevents a criminal defendant from asserting the rights of his or her home State, when brought before US courts via a violation of the territorial sovereignty of that foreign State. Absent a protest by the defendant's home State, US courts routinely proceed to resolve such cases.

◆ PROBLEMS

Problem 9.A (§9.4 after *Norwegian Loans* Case) The ICJ opinion in *Reservations to the Convention on Genocide* is set forth in this book in §8.2. The Court held that to be an acceptable reservation to a multilateral treaty, a reservation must be "compatible" with the underlying purposes of the treaty. In the *Norwegian Loans* case, France's reservation provided that *France* would decide if the ICJ has jurisdiction in cases which it might characterize as falling within its dometic jurisdiction. Under the ICJ Statute, the *ICJ* decides whether it has the power to act. Is France's reservation therefore *incompatible* with the underlying purpose of the ICJ Statute (which is a treaty)?

Problem 9.B (end of §9.4) Two groups of students will meet separately to draft their versions of a new "World Court Statute." Each group must draft clauses defining the court's power to act. These clauses will address whether the UN membership should do the following:

1. Automatically be parties to this new World Court Statute;
2. Have the option to accept the court's compulsory jurisdiction—
    a. without any possible reservation, or
    b. with reservations;
3. If 2(b) is permitted, authorize any reservations (conditional acceptances) necessary to ensure wide participation in the new "World Court Statute."

Problem 9.C (§9.5, after ICTY *Tadic* Case) After his killings, sexual assaults, torture, and so on, defendant Tadic was sentenced to twenty years in prison. The sentences for his various crimes actually added up to ninety-seven years. The court opted to minimize his sentence by having the respective sentences served concurrently. He was not given the possible life sentence.

Neither the ICTY nor the Rwandan tribunal has the power to sentence a convicted war criminal to death. One reason is the sentiment expressed by some commentators that the death penalty violates International Law. *See, e.g.*, W. Schabas, *The Abolition of the Death Penalty in International Law* (2nd ed. Cambridge, Eng.: Cambridge Press, 1997). The tribunal remarked that Tadic was a lower level functionary, operating out of a deep hatred that was spawned by a party and governmental campaign of terror that many carried out, while only a few were captured and prosecuted. Should the tribunal have sentenced Tadic to life in prison? Would "life" be more than necessary to send the message that war criminals can no longer undertake such acts with the impunity that so many of them have savored since Nuremberg? Would the alternative, the harshest penalty possible (life in jail), suggest that the tribunal was unnecessarily flexing its muscles in an effort to make an example of this lower level criminal? Or was the tribunal not harsh enough, because it sentenced Tadic to only twenty years?

Two students will represent, respectively, the ICTY prosecutor's office and Tadic's defense counsel. They are conducting a "rehearing" in the mock penalty phase of this trial. They will debate these (and any related) questions that may arise.

Problem 9.D (§9.6 after European Court of Human Rights *Sunday Times* Case Materials) Unlike English law, the laws of many countries of continental Europe do *not* generally prevent pretrial publicity (via routine court injunctions against publishers of pretrial information). Similar to the famous O. J. Simpson murder case of 1994 in Los Angeles, California, there may be the same "news organization feeding frenzy" prior to criminal trials—complete with interviews and opinion editorials appearing in newspapers, tabloids, books, and on television and radio.

One advantage of the public dissemination of such information is that the public can thereby learn about dangers to its safety and what is being done to protect it. On the other hand, it is also difficult (as in the O. J. Simpson trial) to obtain an impartial finding of fact at trial because of the widespread effects of such publicity.

Assume that a contemporary "Jack the Ripper" has been arrested in London after an extraordinary murder investigation. A number of individuals have been murdered in the same way that Jack allegedly killed a famous London socialite, who was well known for her exhaustive charity work in the slums of London. Jack's sensational murder trial will soon begin in London. There have been no similar murders since Jack's capture. A German-owned broadcasting company beams satellite-based information about Jack's pending trial throughout the continent of Europe and over British airwaves.

After obtaining the usual London trial-court injunction banning this form of pretrial publicity, British authorities prosecute this German company for its continued dissemination of the satellite-based information—from Germany—about the pending trial in London. After exhausting all appeals under the British system, the German company seeks relief from the European Court of Human Rights—based on the London court's violation of the Convention Article 10 right to free expression.

Great Britain's judiciary has had a long and unbroken history of banning pretrial publicity. German courts have rarely ever made such "gag orders." Great Britain did not express its concern in a reservation to Article 10 of the ECHR treaty regarding "free expression." Both countries are parties to the European Human Rights Convention, which does not contain any specific guidance as to the application of the treaty's "free expression" clause.

Two students (or groups) will debate whether the European Court of Human Rights should rule as it did in the ECHR "Thalidomide" case set forth in §9.6. Specifically, should this regional *international* court overrule the British *national* court's injunction, which is designed to control the adverse effects of pretrial publicity on the English judicial system?

Problem 9.E (§9.8 after *Noriega* Case) A US citizen is traveling in the Middle East. He is riding on the crowded public bus that was the target of a terrorist "suicide bomb" in October 1994. He is killed when the bomb carrier leaves it on board the bus, killing twenty-one people and injuring many others during rush hour in Tel Aviv.

"Hamas" claims responsibility. The group consists of people of Palestinian origin who hope to use such terrorist events as political bargaining chips to defeat the Middle East peace process being negotiated by the PLO and various governments in the region. Hamas is seeking a greater Palestine than agreed to by Yasir Arafat, the PLO's representative.

The US Department of State is considering an Israeli plan that the US and Israel jointly undertake a secret mission to go into whatever State in which the Hamas perpetrators are ultimately found and extract the perpetrator who left the bomb on the Israeli bus. Any other captured Hamas members will be tried in Israel for their participation in the 1994 bombing.

You are the judge in a trial court in your state of the United States, where the deceased US citizen lived. The spouse of the murdered citizen has recently filed a suit against Hamas in your court. Needless to say, Hamas does not respond to this suit. The US Department of State, acting on behalf of the US President, files papers in this suit asking you to dismiss this case because of sensitive Department of State negotiations with Israel. The essential Department of State requests are as follows:

a. The Department of State lawyer says that the Political Question Doctrine requires dismissal of this case. How will you rule?
b. The Department of State lawyer says that the Act of State Doctrine is applicable and requires dismissal of this case. How will you rule?
c. The Department of State lawyer says that if you deny the US Government's request to dismiss this case, and the Hamas bomber is captured and returned to the US for trial, the perpetrator will have the standing to claim that your court cannot prosecute him. In other words, it is argued that you will have to dismiss this case anyway. How will you rule?

◆ BIBLIOGRAPHY

§9.1 Arbitration and Adjudication Blueprint

M. Butlerman & M. Kuijer (eds.), *Compliance with Judgments of International Courts* (The Hague, Neth.: Martinus Nijhoff, 1996).

A. Lowenfeld, *International Litigation and Arbitration* (St. Paul, MN: West, 1993).

S. Muller & W. Mijs (eds.), *The Flame Rekindled: New Hopes for International Arbitration* (Dordrecht, Neth.: Martinus Nijhoff, 1994).

J. Ralston, *International Arbitration from Athens to Locarno* (Stanford, CA: Stanford Univ. Press, 1929).

§9.2 Alternative Dispute Resolution

R. Ostrihansky, "The Future of Dispute Settlement within GATT: Conciliation v. Adjudication," in M. Brus, S. Muller, & S. Weimers (eds.), *The United Nations Decade of International Law: Reflections on International Dispute Resolution* 125 (Dordrecht, Neth.: Martinus Nijhoff, 1991).

Panel, "New Trends in International Dispute Settlement," in *Proceedings of the 87th Annual Meeting of the American Society of International Law* 2 (1993).

§9.3 Arbitral Classifications and Tribunals

S. Cromie & W. Park, *International Commercial Arbitration* (London; Boston: Butterworths, 1990).

A. Lowenfeld, *International Litigation and Arbitration* (St. Paul: West, 1993).

§9.4 International Court of Justice

W. Coplin & J. Rochester, "The Permanent Court of International Justice, the International Court of Justice, the League of Nations and the United Nations: A Comparative Empirical Survey," 66 *Amer. Pol. Sci. Rev.* 529 (1972).

R. Falk, *Reviving the World Court* (Charlottesville, VA.: Univ. Press of Va., 1986).

T. Franck, *Judging the World Court* (London: Allen & Unwin, 1986).

S. Gorove, "Formation of Internal Subdivisions of International Tribunals—Some Comparative Highlights and Assessment," 38 *American Journal of International Law* 353 (1990).

B. MacPherson, *World Court Enhancements to Advance the Rule of Law* (Livingston, NJ: Center for UN Reform Education, 1994).

S. Rosenne, *The World Court and How It Works* (5th rev. ed. Dordrecht, Neth.: Martinus Nijhoff, 1994).

H. Thirlway, "The Law and Procedure of the International Court of Justice 1960–1989," 63 *British Yearbook International Law* 1 (1992).

§9.5 International Criminal Court

M. Bassiouni, *The Statute of the International Criminal Court: A Documentary History* (Ardsley, NY: Transnat'l, 1998).

L. Beres, "Toward Prosecution of Iraqi Crimes Under International Law: Jurisprudential Foundations and Jurisdictional Choices," 22 *Calif. West. Int'l L.J.* 127 (1991).

F. Buscher, *The US War Crimes Trial Program in Germany, 1946–1955* (New York: Greenwood Press, 1989).

R. Clark & M. Sann (eds.), *The Prosecution of International Crimes* (New Brunswick, NJ: Transnat'l, 1996).

J. Jones, *The Practice of the International Criminal Tribunals for the Former Yugoslavia and Rwanda* (Ardsley, NY: Transnational, 1998).

V. Morris & M. Scharf, *An Insider's Guide to the International Criminal Tribunal for the Former Yugoslavia: A Documentary History and Analysis* (Irvington, NY: Transnat'l Pub., 1994) (two volumes).

P. Piccigallo, *The Japanese on Trial: Allied War Crimes Operations in the East, 1945–1951* (Austin: Univ. of Texas Press, 1979).

M. Scharf, "Trial and Error: An Assessment of the First Judgment of the Yugoslavia War Crimes Tribunal," 30 *New York Univ. J. Int'l Law and Politics* 167–201 (1998).

§9.6 Regional Court Adjudication

J. Bengoextea, *The Legal Reasoning of the European Court of Justice: Toward a European Jurisprudence* (Oxford, Eng.: Clarendon Press, 1993).

V. Berger, *Case Law of the European Court of Human Rights* (Dublin: Round Hall Press, 1991) (two volumes).

S. Davidson, *The Inter-American Court of Human Rights* (Aldershot, Eng.; Brookfield, VT, USA: Dartmouth Press, 1992).

M. Janis, *International Courts for the Twenty-First Century* 235 (Dordrecht, Neth.: Martinus Nijhoff, 1992).

P. Kempees, *A Systematic Guide to the Case-Law of the European Court of Human Rights 1960–1994* (The Hague, Neth.: Martinus Nijhoff, 1996) (two volumes).

§9.7 International Law in National Courts and the US

GENERALLY

L. Erades, *Interactions Between International and Municipal Law: A Comparative Case Law Study* (The Hague, Neth.: T.M.C. Asser Inst., 1993).

B. Conforti, *International Law and the Role of Domestic Legal Systems* (Dordrecht, Neth.: Martinus Nijhoff, 1993).

A. Oppenheimer (ed.), *The Relationship Between European Community Law and National Law: The Cases* (Cambridge, Eng.: Grotius, 1994).

US

J. Charney, "Judicial Deference in Foreign Relations," in L. Henkin, M. Glennon, & W. Rogers (eds.), *Foreign Affairs and the US Constitution* 98 (Ardsley-on-Hudson, NY: Transnat'l Pub., 1990).

M. Glennon, *Foreign Affairs and the Political Question Doctrine* in L. Henkin, M. Glennon, & W. Rogers (eds.), *Foreign Affairs and the US Constitution* 107 (Ardsley-on-Hudson, NY: Transnat'l Pub., 1990).

T. Franck & M. Glennon, "The Law of Nations as Incorporated into United States Law," ch. 2 in *Foreign Relations and National Security Law* 108 (2nd ed. St. Paul: West, 1993).

J. Paust, *International Law as Law of the United States* (Durham, NC: Carolina Academic Press, 1996).

◆ ENDNOTES

1. ICJ Communiqué No. 98/14, 6 Apr. 1998, at 1, para. 4.
2. *See* L. Sohn, "International Arbitration in Historical Perspective: Past and Present," in A. Soons (ed.), *International Arbitration: Past and Prospects* 9 (Dordrecht, Neth.: Martinus Nijhoff, 1990).
3. 8 *US Statutes at Large* 196 (1802), *US Treaty Series* No. 108.
4. *See* "Introduction," in A. Stuyt, *Survey of International Arbitrations: 1794–1989,* p. 3 (3rd ed. Dordrecht, Neth.: Martinus Nijhoff, 1990) (hereinafter *Survey of International Arbitrations*).
5. *See generally, Survey of International Arbitrations* (note 4 above).
6. Details about the PCIJ are available in S. Rosenne, *The Law and Practice of the International Court, 1920–1996* (The Hague, Neth.: Martinus Nijhoff, 1997) (four volumes) (hereinafter *The International Court*). *See also* A. Zimmern, *The League of Nations and the Rule of Law 1918–1935* (Gaunt [Holmes Beach, FL] reprint of London: MacMillan & Co., 1936).
7. Reprinted in Appendix A to J. Merrills, *International Dispute Settlement* 312 (3rd ed. Cambridge, Eng.: Grotius, 1998) (hereinafter *International Dispute Settlement*).
8. An excellent discussion of this distinction, and ADR modes in general, is available in *International Dispute Settlement,* p. 43 (note 7 above).
9. The facts are available in *International Dispute Settlement,* pp. 44–46 (note 7 above).
10. C. Parry et al., *Parry and Grant Encyclopaedic Dictionary of International Law* 71 (New York: Oceana, 1988) (citing authority).
11. *See International Dispute Settlement,* pp. 59–75 (note 7 above).
12. M. Rubino-Sammartano, "Abitration and Alternative Disputes Resolution," ch. 1 in *International Arbitration Law* 8–9 (Deventer, Neth.: Kluwer Law and Taxation Pub., 1990).
13. *See generally, Survey of International Arbitrations* (note 4 above). In the prior edition of that work, the author reported that a party failed to comply with only 3 of 443 reported decisions.
14. S. Troope, *Mixed International Arbitration* 200–201 (Cambridge, Eng.: Grotius, 1990).
15. *See* §2.2, Exhibit 2.1, on the transformation of the community of nations—especially since the 1960s.
16. **New York Convention:** "United Nations Convention on Recognition and Enforcement of Arbitral Awards," 330 *UN Treaty Series,* No. 4739 (1958) (more than 90 State parties). **Inter-American Convention:** *See* US implementing statutes in 9 *US Code* §§301–307 (1990) (approximately thirteen State parties and likely to increase with US ratification). **Washington Convention:** "Convention on the Settlement of Investment Disputes Between States and Nationals of Other States," 575 *UN Treaty Series* 159 (1965) (more than 100 State parties) (hereinafter Washington Convention).
17. See T. Von Mehron, "The Iran–US Arbitral Tribunal," 31 *Amer. J. Comp. L.* 713 (1983) and R. Lillich & D. Magraw (ed.), "The Iran–United States Claims Tribunal: Its Contribution to the Law of State Responsibility" (Irvington-on-Hudson, NY: Transnational, 1998).
18. R. Lillich (ed.), *The United Nations Compensation Commission* (Irvington-on-Hudson, NY: Transnational, 1995).
19. *See generally* W. Reisman et. al., *International Commercial Arbitration: Cases, Materials and Notes on the Resolution of International Business Disputes* (Westbury, NY: Foundation Press, 1997).

20. The ICC's arbitration rules are reprinted in 15 *Int'l Legal Mat'ls* 395 (1976) (italics added).
21. Further details about the work of the ICC are available in S. Jarvin, Y. Derains, & J. Arnaldez, *Collection of ICC Arbitral Awards: 1986–1990* (Deventer, Neth.: Kluwer Law and Taxation Pub., 1994).
22. *See* Washington Convention (note 16 above).
23. Further details about the work of the ICSID are available in R. Rayfuse (ed.), *ICSID Reports* (Cambridge, Eng.: Grotius, 1993).
24. *Amer. Manufacturing & Trading, Inc. v. Republic of Zaire,* ICSID Case Arb/93/1, reprinted in 36 *Int'l Legal Mat'ls* 1531 (1997).
25. Case No. 332, Judgment No. 333, reported in *Judgments of the United Nations Administrative Tribunal,* Nos. 301–370, p. 239 (1992). *See also Broadbent v. OAS,* featured in the text of §3.6 of this book (employee's termination of employment action against OAS dismissed as a matter internal to OAS).
26. *See* M. Hudson, *International Tribunals* 145 (Wash., DC: Carnegie Endowment for Int'l Peace, 1944).
27. B. Boutros-Ghali, *An Agenda for Peace* 23 (New York: UN, 1992), first printed in 28 *Int'l Legal Mat'ls* 1589 (1989). This proposal was repeated in his 1995 *Supplement to Agenda for Peace* 54 (New York: UN, 1995) (hereinafter *Supplement).*
28. **Commentators:** *See* O'Connell, "International Legal Aid: The Secretary General's Trust Fund to Assist States in the Settlement of Disputes through the International Court of Justice," ch. 12 in M. Janis, *International Courts for the Twenty-First Century* 235 (Dordrecht, Neth.: Martinus Nijhoff, 1992) (hereinafter *International Courts).* **Resources quote:** P. Bekker, "International Legal Aid in Practice: The ICJ Trust Fund," 87 *Amer. J. Int'l L.* 659, 668 (1993).
29. The full ICJ Statute is reprinted in E. Osmanczyk, *Encyclopedia of the United Nations and International Agreements* 454 (2nd ed. New York: Taylor & Francis, 1990) (hereinafter *UN Encyclopedia)* and in L. Henkin et al., *Basic Documents Supplement to International Law Cases and Materials* 123 (3rd ed. St. Paul: West, 1993).
30. A more detailed description is available in *The International Court* 23 (note 6 above).
31. "The World Court and the International Legal System," ch. 8 in T. O. Elias, *The United Nations Charter and the World Court* 111 (Lagos, Nigeria: Nigerian Inst. Advanced Legal Studies, 1989).
32. T. Franck, "Fact-Finding in the ICJ," in R. Lillich, *Fact-Finding Before International Tribunals* 21–22 (Ardsley-on-Hudson, NY: Transnat'l Pub., 1992).
33. This principle is enshrined in the jurisprudence of the US Supreme Court, building on the case wherein the Court asserted its power to review the Constitutional validity of actions taken by other branches of the government: "It is emphatically, the province of the judicial department, to say what the law is. . . . If two laws conflict with each other, the courts must decide the operation of each." *Marbury v. Madison,* 5 US (1 Cranch) 137, 177–178 (1803).
34. M. Kazazi, *Burden of Proof and Related Issues: A Study on Evidence Before International Tribunals* 3 (The Hague, Neth.: Kluwer Law Int'l, 1996).
35. R. Szafarz, *The Compulsory Jurisdiction of the International Court of Justice* X (Dordrecht, Neth.; Martinus Nijhoff, 1993) (explanatory clauses deleted).
36. "Nottebohm Case," 1953 *ICJ Rep.* 119–120 (preliminary order).
37. "Western Sahara Case (Advisory Opinion)," 1975 *ICJ Rep.* 3, 104 (Judge Petren's separate opinion).
38. "Interpretation of Peace Treaties with Bulgaria, Hungary and Romania (Advisory Opinion)" 1950 *ICJ Rep.* 71, para.71.
39. **Competence case:** "Competence of the General Assembly for the Admission of a State to the United Nations," 1950 *ICJ Rep.* 4. **Reservations case:** "Reservations to the Convention on Genocide," 1951 *ICJ Rep.* 15. **PLO case:** "Applicability of the Obligation to Arbitrate Under Section 21 of the United Nations Headquarters Agreement of 26 June 1947," 1988 *ICJ Rep.* 12.
40. Accounts of these cases are available in S. Schwebel, "Ad Hoc Chambers of the International Court of Justice," 81 *Amer. J. Int'l L.* 831, at 843 (1987).
41. E. De Archaga, "The Amendments to the Rules of Procedure of the International Court of Justice," 67 *Amer. J. Int'l L.* 1, 3 (1973).
42. M. Leigh & S. Ramsey, "Confidence in the Court: It Need Not Be a 'Hollow Chamber,'" in L. Damrosch, *The International Court of Justice at a Crossroads* 106, 112–117 (Dobbs Ferry, NY: Transnat'l Pub., 1987) (hereinafter *ICJ at a Crossroads).*
43. B. Boutros-Ghali, *An Agenda for Peace: Preventative Diplomacy, Peacemaking and Peace-Keeping* 22–23 (New York: UN, 1992) (original text reprinted in the 1995 *Supplement,* cited in note 27).
44. Analyses of this form of mistrust and caution are available in R. Anand, "Attitude of the 'New' Asian–African Countries Toward the International Court of Justice," in F. Snyder & S. Sathirathai, *Third World Attitudes Towards International Law* 163 (Dordrecht, Neth.: Martinus Nijhoff, 1987); E. Whinney, *The World Court and the Contemporary International Law-making Process* (Alphen aan den Rijn, Neth.: Sijthoff & Noordhoff, 1979).
45. *See generally* M. Shahabuddeen, *Precedent in the World Court* (Cambridge, Eng.: Grotius, 1996).
46. H. Lauterpacht, *The Development of International Law by the International Court* 4 (Cambridge, Eng.: Grotius Publications, 1982).
47. 92 *Congressional Record* 10,696 (1946).
48. The Senate study is reprinted in 16 *Int'l Legal Mat'ls* 187, 188 (1977).
49. "Case Concerning the Military and Paramilitary Activities in and Against Nicaragua *(Nicaragua v. USA),*" 1986 *ICJ Rep.* 98.
50. S. Malawer, *World Court and the US, in Essays on International Law* 95 (Buffalo, NY: Hein, 1986). The Department of State's

position is summarized in Stevenson, "Conclusion," in *ICJ at a Crossroads* 459–461 (note 42 above).

51. Copies are obtainable from the UN Sales Office in New York City. Quote drawn from *Final Report,* p. 28.
52. **Early trials:** *See* R. Hingorini, *Modern International Law* 353 (2nd ed. New York: Oceana, 1984). **League of Nations ICC:** This account is available in *UN Encyclopedia,* at 202 (cited in note 29 above).
53. **NGO:** *See* Gross, "International Terrorism and International Criminal Jurisdiction," 67 *Amer. J. Int'l L.* 508 (1973). **US Congress, political offense concern:** discussed in "The Political Offense Exemption," ch. 6 in G. Gilbert, *Aspects of Extradition Law* 113, 156–162 (Dordrecht, Neth.: Martinus Nijhoff, 1991).
54. J. Bridge, "The Case for an International Court of Criminal Justice and the Formulation of International Criminal Law," ch. 11 in *International Courts* 213, 223 (note 28 above) (italics added).
55. B. Yarnold, "The International Court of Justice as an Adjudicator of State Transnational and International Crimes," ch. 7 in *International Fugitives: A New Role for the International Court of Justice* 104–105 (New York: Praeger, 1991) (italics added).
56. *See generally* J. Paust et al., *International Criminal Law: Cases and Materials* (Durham, NC: No. Carolina Acad. Press, 1996); and L. Sunga, *The Emerging System of International Criminal Law: Developments in Codification and Implementation* (The Hague, Neth.: Kluwer Law Int'l, 1997); "Developments in International Criminal Law," 93 *Amer. J. Int'l Law,* 1–123 (1999).
57. **Tokyo Trial:** *See* J. Ginn, *Sugamo Prison, Tokyo: An Account of the Trial and Sentencing of Japanese War Criminals in 1948* (Jefferson, NC: McFarland & Co., 1992); J. Keenan & B. Brown, *Crimes Against International Law* (Wash., DC: Public Affairs Press, 1950). **Nuremberg Trial:** G. Ginsburgs & V. Kudriavtsev, *The Nuremberg Trial and International Law* (Dordrecht, Neth.: Martinus Nijhoff, 1990); J. Fried, "The Great Nuremberg Trial" 70 *Amer. Pol. Sci. Rev.* 192 (1976).
58. W. Bishop, *Justice Under Fire* 284 (New York: Prentice-Hall, 1974).
59. *See* M. Bassiouni, "The Time Has Come for an International Criminal Court," 1 *Indiana Int'l & Comp. L. Rev.* 1 (1991) (one of the author's many publications in this field); and B. Ferencz, *An International Criminal Court: A Step Toward World Peace—A Documentary History and Analysis* (New York: Oceana, 1980) (two volumes).
60. *See generally* V. Morris & M. Scharf, *An Insider's Guide to the International Criminal Tribunal for the Former Yugoslavia* (Irvington-on-Hudson, NY: Transnational, 1995) (two volumes).
61. **Mayor case:** *Prosecutor v. Jean-Paul Akayesu,* Case No. ICTR-96-4-T (Judgment), www.un.org/ictr/english/judgements/akayesu.html. **Premier case:** *Prosecutor v. Jean Kambanda,* Case No. ICTR 97-23-S (Judgment and Sentence), www.un.org/ictr/english/judgements/kambanda.html.
62. *Prosecutor v. Kanyabashi,* Case No. ICTR-96-15-T (Jurisdiction, 18 June 1997). The ICTY case relied on by the ICTR in ruling on jurisdictional objections is *Prosecutor v. Tadic, Decision on Jurisdiction,* No. IT-94-1-T (Aug. 10, 1995), *aff'd,* Appeal on Jurisdiction, No. IT-94-1-AR72 (Oct. 2, 1995).
63. An excellent summary is available in B. Oxman, "International Decisions," 92 *Amer. J. Int'l Law* 66 (1998).
64. *See* B. Brown, "Primacy or Complementarity: Reconciling the Jurisdiction of National Courts and International Criminal Tribunals," 23 *Yale J. Int'l Law* 383 (1998).
65. V. Morris & M. Scharf, *The International Criminal Tribunal for Rwanda* 1, 707–709 (Irvington-on-Hudson, NY: Transnational, 1998).
66. The resulting Rome Statute is available at www.un.org/icc/romestat.htm.
67. *See* authorities cited in note 32 above.
68. C. Jenks, "Regionalism in International Judicial Organization," 37 *Amer. J. Int'l L.* 314 (1943).
69. **Central American Court:** *See* D. Bowett, *The Law of International Institutions* 287 (4th ed. London: Stevens & Sons, 1982). **Arab Court:** *See* E. Foda, *The Projected Arab Court of Justice: A Study in Regional Adjudication with Specific Reference to the Muslim Law of Nations* (Westport, CT: Hyperion Press, 1981).
70. *International Courts* 87–88 (cited in note 28 above).
71. Case 294/83, *Partie Ecologiste "Les Verts" v. European Parliament,* 1986 *Euro. Ct. Rep.* 1339, analyzed in "Judicial Review of Community Acts," ch. 7 in L. Brown & T. Kennedy, *The Court of Justice of the European Communities* 123, 128 et seq. (4th ed. London: Street & Maxwell, 1994).
72. *See, e.g.,* the US Supreme Court's effective validation of the US Drug Enforcement Administration's role in kidnapping a Mexican national from Mexico for trial in the US; set forth in §5.3 (*Alvarez-Machain* case).
73. *See* F. Newman, "Legal Anomaly: Lacking Bill of Rights, Britons Seek Redress at a Court in France," *Wall Street Journal,* Oct. 21, 1985, at p.1.
74. F. Mann, "Contempt of Court in the House of Lords and the European Court of Human Rights," 95 *Law Quarterly Rev.* 348, 348–349 (1979) (italics added).
75. The text of this convention is reprinted in 9 *Int'l Legal Mat'ls* 673 (1970).
76. *See* T. Burgenthal, "The Advisory Practice of the Inter-American Human Rights Court," 79 *Amer. J. Int'l L.* 1 (1985).
77. A detailed account of this and two related cases is available in C. Cerna, "The Inter-American Court of Human Rights," in *International Courts,* 117, 131 (cited in note 28 above).
78. T. Burgenthal, "The Inter-American Court of Human Rights," 76 *Amer. J. Int'l L.* 231, 233 (1982).
79. S. Davidson, *The Inter-American Court of Human Rights* 207 (Aldershot, Eng.: Dartmouth Press, 1992).
80. The Andean Pact is reprinted in 8 *Int'l Legal Mat'ls* 910 (1969). The Andean Court agreement is reprinted in 18 *Int'l Legal Mat'ls* 1203 (1979).
81. Pierola, "The Andean Court of Justice," 2 *J. Int'l Dispute Reso.* 11, 35–36 (1987).
82. **Alignment with European process:** "Quito Protocol," 28 *Int'l Legal Mat'ls* 1165 (1989). **Implementation goal:** "Manifest of Cartagena de Indias," 28 *Int'l Legal Mat'ls* 1282 (1989).

83. The most comprehensive compilation of such cases is contained in the widely available *International Law Reports,* published by Grotius Publications. *See, e.g.,* J. Barker, *Consolidated Tables of Cases and Treaties: Volumes 1–80* (Cambridge, Eng.: 1991). One may therein select a particular treaty and quickly ascertain the identity of national cases that have interpreted that treaty.
84. G. Slyz, "International Law in National Courts," ch. 5 in T. Franck & G. Fox (eds.), *International Law Decisions in National Courts* 71 (Irvington-on-Hudson, NY: Transnational, 1996).
85. **Canada:** H. Kindred et al., *International Law: Chiefly as Interpreted and Applied in Canada* (5th ed.Toronto: Edmond Montgomery, 1993), and documentary supplement. **Mexico:** M. Vazquez, *Derecho Internactional Publico* (10th ed. Mexico City: Editorial Purrua, 1991) (Spanish language text).
86. "Punish Offenses": Art. I, Section 8, Clause 10. "Law of the Land": Article VI, clause 2. Supreme Court quote: 175 US 677 (1900)—set forth in §1.4 of this text.
87. The US–Japanese Protocol Agreement is discussed in *Wilson v. Girard,* 354 US 524, 77 S.Ct. 1409, 1 *L. Ed.* 1544 (1957).
88. **PLO case:** *US v. PLO,* 695 *Fed.Supp.* 1456 (So. Dist. N.Y., 1988). The Reagan administration decided not to appeal the court's decision. **UN dues:** *See* §3.3 of this text, regarding the president's potential breach (as opposed to the hypothetical statute—which was not enacted).
89. *Reid v. Covert,* 354 US 1, 77 S.Ct. 1222, 1 *L. Ed.* 2d 1148 (1957)—case text set forth earlier in this section of the book.
90. *US v. Noriega,* 746 *Fed.Supp.* 1506, 1515 (So. Dist. Fla., 1990), *aff'd,* 117 F.3d 1206 (11th Cir., 1997), *cert. den'd,* 118 S.Ct. 1389 (1998).
91. *See* 28 USCA §1351. The diplomatic immunity afforded by the 1961 Vienna Convention on Diplomatic Relations has essentially withdrawn the possibility of a §1351 suit against a diplomat.
92. **US Federal supremacy:** *United States v. Curtiss-Wright Export Corp.,* 299 US 304, 57 S.Ct. 216, 220, 81 *L. Ed.* 255 (1936). **European Union:** P. Dubinsky, "The Essential Function of Federal Courts: The European Union and the United States Compared," XLII *Amer. J. Comparative L.* 295 (1994).
93. Effect of federal nonrecognition: *See Russian Socialist Federated Soviet Republic v. Cibrario,* 235 N.Y. 255, 139 N.C. 259 (1923) (dismissing state court suit against Russia's unrecognized Bolshevik government); *Wulfsohn v. Russian Socialist Federated Soviet Republic,* 234 N.Y. 372, 138 N.C. 24 (1923) (dismissing state court suit by that unrecognized government).
94. *See, e.g., DaCosta v. Laird,* 471 F.2d 1146 (2d Cir. 1973) (Vietnam harbor mining), and *Holtzman v. Schlesinger,* 484 F.2d 1307 (2d Cir. 1973) (Cambodian bombing).
95. *Aktepe v. USA,* 105 F.3d 1400 (11th Cir., 1997), *cert. den'd,* 118 S.Ct. 685 (1998).
96. *"Banco Nacional de Cuba v. Sabbatino,"* 376 *US Rep.* 398, 416, 84 S.Ct. 923, 934, 11 *L. Ed.* 2d 804 (1964) (italics added).
97. 22 USC §2370(e)(2), as amended.
98. *See Senate Foreign Relations Committee Report on [the second] Hickenlooper Amendment,* S. Rep. No. 1188, pt. I, 88th Cong., 2d Sess. 24 (1964).

CHAPTER TEN

Use of Force by States and Organizations

CHAPTER OUTLINE

THE SECURITY COUNCIL, . . .
Noting with alarm the decision of Iraq on 31 October 1998 to cease cooperation with the United Nations Special Commission, and its continued restrictions on the work of the International Atomic Energy Agency (IAEA), . . .
Acting under Chapter VII of the Charter of the United Nations,
1. ***Condemns*** the decision by Iraq of 31 October 1998 to cease cooperation with the Special Commission as a flagrant violation of resolution 687 (1991) and other relevant resolutions;
2. ***Demands*** that Iraq rescind immediately and unconditionally the decision of 31 October 1998, as well as the decision of 5 August 1998, to suspend cooperation with the Special Commission and to maintain restrictions on the work of the IAEA, and that Iraq provide immediate, complete and unconditional cooperation with the Special Commission and the IAEA. . . ."

—UN Security Council Resolution 1205, Nov. 5, 1998

Over the past year we have deepened our engagement with the forces of change in Iraq, reconciling the two largest Kurdish opposition groups, beginning broadcasts of a Radio Free Iraq throughout the country.

We will intensify that effort, working with [the US] Congress to implement the Iraq Liberation Act, which was recently passed, strengthening our political support to make sure the opposition, or to do what we can to make the opposition a more effective voice for the aspirations of the Iraq[i] people.

Let me say again, what we want and what we will work for is a government in Iraq that represents and respects its people, not represses them."

—Excerpt from US President Clinton's Statement on Iraq, Nov. 15, 1998, after recalling a planned cruise missile strike on Baghdad

INTRODUCTION

The introductory chapters on States and international organizations depict the hostile environment often associated with issues arising under International Law. Later chapters on diplomacy, treaty relations, and dispute-resolution mechanisms similarly link International Law with the quest for controlling the ultimate instrument of diplomacy—the use of force.

This chapter focuses on when force is legitimately invoked, the many faces of the term *force,* and its capacity to disrupt international relations. After defining the term and classifying its uses, the remaining sections will depict some rather sensitive issues involving force: humanitarian intervention, rescue missions, the Laws of War, State terrorism, and arms sales. The chapter closes with a brief analysis of the struggle among the political branches of *US* government to control presidential force via congressional directives. This theme is of special interest now that the US is "the" remaining post–Cold War superpower and often called on to intervene in foreign conflicts.

◆ 10.1 DEFINING "FORCE" AND ITS ROLE

This section analyzes the historical evolution of force in the international community, what the term *force* includes, and the variables affecting its legitimate use.

HISTORICAL AND MODERN APPLICATIONS

War was not condemned in ancient Greece or Rome. On the other hand, Aristotle wrote that it was regarded as the antithesis of happiness and leisure: "We make war in order that we may live at peace. . . . Nobody chooses to make war or provokes it for the sake of making war; a man would be regarded as a bloodthirsty monster if he made . . . [friendly nations] into enemies in order to bring about battles and slaughter."[1]

The apparently insatiable obsession of the nation-State system that developed in the aftermath of the 1648 Peace of Westphalia might be explained by thinking of war as a systemic essential. A valuable perspective is provided by Yale University Professor Michael Reisman in his provocative essay on a global system that promotes war:

> The rhetoric of peace is more than neutralized by the symmetrical prominence of the military in competing governments. The manifest drive is for security, in a system which is structured for insecurity. . . . The allocation of power is, of course, an inescapable concern, but one of the functions of a system of nation-states . . . is to perpetuate insecurity through artifacts such as the "balance" or imbalance of power. . . . While a war system requires a culture of parochialism, self-sacrifice, and the paraphernalia of wars, it does not require wars. Rather it requires a pervasive *expectation* of impending violence in order to sustain and magnify personal insecurity. Small wars can be nourished as a neat means of keeping this expectation alive. . . .
>
> The viciousness of a war system is circular as well, for even those who concede its horror and absurdity [can readily] perceive . . . a situation in which the sense of insecurity can be quite accurate and rational. . . . In international politics there is, indeed, a very real enemy with very real operations-plans [prepared in anticipation of war].[2]

During the formation of modern International Law in the eighteenth and nineteenth centuries, the use of force was often characterized as a "necessity." The more powerful European States developed convenient justifications for their aggressive use of force. One such convenience was the common claim that force was the only effective device for enforcing International Law. An aggrieved State could not allow the violation of International Law to go unpunished for fear of anarchy. Force was characterized as an inherent right—one beyond question—when a State, in its discretion, deemed it necessary to use force in the name of God and country.

Great Britain's Sir Hersch Lauterpaucht was one of the most prolific legal historians, teachers, writers, and judges (International Court of Justice). His ubiquitous writings on war aptly described it as the ultimate instrument for enforcing national policy. It was also the self-acclaimed enforcement mechanism of International Law, needed in the absence of an international organization (prior to the twentieth century). Lauterpacht traced the development of the legal justification for the unilateral use of force as follows:

> [T]he institution of war fulfilled in International Law two contradictory functions. In the absence of an international organ for enforcing the law, war was a means of self-help for giving effect to claims based or

> alleged to be based on International Law. Such was the legal and moral authority of this notion of war as an arm of the law that in most cases in which war was in fact resorted to in order to increase the power and the possessions of a State at the expense of others, it was described . . . as undertaken for the defence of a legal right. This conception of war was intimately connected with the distinction, which was established in the formative period of International Law and which never became entirely extinct, between just and unjust wars. . . .
>
> In the absence of an international legislature it was a crude substitute for a deficiency in international organization. As [the English legal analyst] Hyde, writing in 1922, said 'It always lies within the power of a State to gain political or other advantages over another . . . by direct recourse to war.' International Law did not consider as illegal a war admittedly waged for such purposes. . . .
>
> War was in law a natural function of the State and a prerogative of its uncontrolled sovereignty.[3]

In the nineteenth century, the unbridled use of force became the centerpiece of national policy for certain leaders. They employed it to preserve the "national security."[4] However, the defensive implication of that term did not emasculate the very aggressive nature of their *realpolitik*. Napoleon used force to dominate Europe in the late eighteenth and early nineteenth centuries. Hitler's twentieth-century use of force expanded Germany's national frontiers and influence throughout Europe. His aggressive policies sparked World War II.

The use of force has also been perceived as a useful dimension of the political struggle for achieving national objectives. Under this view, the use of force is necessary to achieve political power, both internally and in International Relations. China's revolutionary leader from a recent generation in Chinese political thought, Mao Tse-Tung, viewed "politics as war without bloodshed and war as politics with bloodshed."[5] During and after his rise to power in 1949, Mao asserted that war would no longer be necessary after international communism eliminated the world's social and economic classes. Aggressive military means were justified by the end.

The former Soviet Union championed a distinct communist perspective that was designed to avoid the use of force. Prior to the Soviet demise in the 1990s, the use of force was characterized as becoming obsolete as other nations fully comprehended the principle of "peaceful coexistence" enshrined in the Soviet Constitution. The basic premise was that two nations with opposed political and economic ideologies can nevertheless coexist in peace—if each is able to pursue distinct social, political, and economic goals during the global transition from capitalism to communism. Commentators often referred to the Soviet Union's official foreign policy with the West as "détente." This policy necessitated tolerance of the Western capitalist system until it could be overcome. Moscow State University Professor Grigori Tunkin explains it as follows:

> The principle of peaceful coexistence of states with different social systems presupposes the existence of other major principles of international law, such as non-use of force or threat of force, respect for sovereignty and non-intervention in internal affairs. It reflects their substance in a general form even though it goes beyond these principles. The principle of peaceful coexistence prohibits policies that are directed at confrontation between states belonging to different social systems and requires that policies be directed at developing cooperation between them, in short, be policies of détente. . . .
>
> It follows that the principle of peaceful coexistence is directed against anti-communism in interstate relations. That is why it is so strongly disliked by reactionary circles of capitalist countries who assert that this principle does not exist in international law.[6]

Contemporary "realists" discount the accuracy of claims that history has ever produced binding limitations on the use of force. Their perspective is that international rules about force are meaningless in a crisis. There is no practical utility in the legal formulations that purport to legally justify or control the State use of force. Analyzing the legitimacy of aggressive conduct in reality is theoretical and unproductive. The role of law in international relations, in their view, is overstated. One example is that States retained the inherent right to use force, notwithstanding the contemporary prohibition in the UN Charter. It is thus unrealistic to expect States to justify their conduct to anyone. Australian National University Professor D. W. Greig describes this view as follows:

> The extent to which a state is entitled to use force in the conduct of its international relations raises a profusion and a confusion of politico-legal problems [that] are scarcely capable of analysis, let alone solution. . . .
>
> In no area is international law more vulnerable to the taunt that "it really doesn't work" than in the context of the rules which are claimed to exist [about] prohibiting or restricting the use of force. The reason why this type of assertion is made is partly due to the fact that widespread publicity is given to instances of the use of force by states, while peaceful inaction or cooperation, that is, the normal situation in the relations of states, merits scarcely a mention in the news media. However, *the making of such an assertion discloses a fundamental misunderstanding of the role of international law.* It has already been demonstrated that legal principles are only allowed to be the sole determinants within a limited area (i.e. mainly within the jurisdictional competence of the International Court). The more important the issue, the less traceable it is to anything other than political compromise in which the part played by the legal rules is correspondingly limited. And if one assumes that states will only have recourse to force as a last resort when they consider their vital interests most gravely threatened or affected, the role of legal principle may well vanish altogether, even though the states concerned will often advance reasons which purport to establish the legality of their actions within the existing or supposed legal order.[7]

The contemporary norm is a bright-line rule that legally tolerates *no* use of aggressive force—including threats. This is the UN Charter perspective, proclaimed in the 1945 constitutive document of the international organization possessing the "official" monopoly on the use of force. The contours of this apparently unwavering limitation—and the realities of its boundaries—are addressed in §10.2.

In practice, a number of States do not characterize force, or at least certain applications, as being inherently mischievous. Certain nations have employed combinations of military action, threats, and economic coercion to achieve political objectives—such as the 1998 US stance with Iraq described in the opening text box of this chapter. Most nations ostensibly characterize force as being "bad" in the abstract. It often becomes a "necessary evil," however, when a critical national interest is at stake.

The preceding summary of just *some* of the perspectives on force suggests that there are probably more shades of gray to describe this subject than in any other in International Law. Expressing the most correct articulation is, of course, not as important as recognizing the underlying concern: Will the international community effectively control national uses of aggressive force when sophisticated weaponry can consummate Armageddon?

WHAT IS "FORCE"?

Force is a broad term that applies to a variety of circumstances. It has been applied when States are at war, on the brink of war or exchanging political or economic potshots, or when one adversary is unaware of the clandestine acts of another. States have invoked measures short of war that have had rather devastating effects on the target nation.

War Many major "wars" have erupted since the end of World War II—mostly in the Third World. One may differentiate between declared and undeclared wars, large-scale military combat and low-intensity conflict, and civil and international wars.

What is the significance of the distinction between a declared and an undeclared war? Declared wars include the familiar circumstance in which one nation or group, such as the Allies or Axis powers of World War II, advises another that a formal state of war exists between them. Early twentieth-century agreements required formal advance notice in the event of one State's plans to declare war on another. An undeclared war involves the participation of two or more States in hostilities that have not been formally declared a "war." During the Vietnam War, successive US presidents committed US military forces to this unpopular military conflict. Combat troops sent abroad created at least two significant political conflicts. First, Congress never exercised its Constitutional power to declare war on North Vietnam, ultimately leading to the 1973 confrontation facilitated by the War Powers Resolution (§10.8). Second, the North Vietnamese viewed the lack of a declared war, in what it perceived as a *civil* war, as rendering the protections of the Geneva Conventions inapplicable for military prisoners of war. US POWs did not receive Red Cross visits, and conditions of incarceration were matters of local rather than International Law (§10.6).

Low-intensity conflict is another point on the force spectrum, somewhere between an all-out war of nations and mere political hostility. The word *war* typically generates visions of the two world wars of the twentieth century or the more contemporary Persian Gulf War in which two dozen States joined in the fight to liberate the oil-rich sheikhdom of Kuwait from Iraq. There have been hundreds—if not thousands—of smaller conflicts wherein death and destruction have been just as exacting for the affected individuals. Residents of Bosnia-Herzegovina experienced one of these low-intensity conflicts. Inhabitants would hardly consider their conflict as being anything less intense than a larger geopolitical conflict. Yet the hostile actions are designated by outsiders as "low intensity" in the sense that they are limited to one location and often ignited or fueled by external military or political sparks that fuel the flames of war.

The US military definition of this phenomenon provides some useful insight about this instrument for conducting foreign affairs:

> Low-intensity conflict is a politico-military confrontation between competing states or groups *below* conventional war and *above* the routine, peaceful competition among states. It frequently involves protracted struggles of competing principles and ideologies. Low-intensity conflict ranges from subversion, such as training and paying paramilitary rebels, to the use of armed force. It is waged by a combination of means, employing political, economic, informational, and military instruments. Low-intensity conflicts are often localized, generally in the Third World, but contain regional and global security implications.[8]

This category of "war" includes, but is not limited to, the following: large-nation interventions such as the 1994 US military operation in Haiti to restore democracy; border wars between Third World countries; the conflict between Israel and its Middle East neighbors; and wars involving national liberation fronts, such as US support of the Contras, which was designed to topple Nicaragua's Sandinista government (*see Nicaragua* case in §10.2). Such conflicts will continue to surface in the aftermath of the Cold War. The post-1945 Soviet objective of worldwide communism, and any US exaggeration of the Soviet threat to control US allies, are no longer factors in the suppression of such conflict.[9]

An analysis of this form of conflict is contained in a 1988 US Government Printing Office publication reporting the findings of the Commission on Integrated Long-Term Strategy. While it was prepared before the collapse of the Soviet Union, this analysis still suggests the continuing interest in low-intensity conflicts and their implications for US national security:

> To help protect US interests and allies in the Third World we still need more of a national consensus on both means and ends. Our means should include:
>
> - Security assistance at a higher level and with fewer legislative restrictions. . . .
> - Versatile mobile forces, minimally dependent on overseas bases, that can deliver precisely controlled strikes against military targets.
> - In special cases, US assistance to . . . insurgents who are resisting a hostile regime that threatens its neighbors. The free world will not remain free if its options are only to stand still and retreat.[10]

"Civil" war is another category of hostility, invoking special rules of International Law on the use of force. Uninvolved States may neither participate absent a declaration of war nor clandestinely support one of the belligerent parties. Great Britain violated this principle during the US Civil War when it outfitted a number of the Southern Confederacy's ships for use against the North. In the 1872 *Alabama Claims* arbitration, the British government was ordered to pay compensation to the US for this violation of the principle of neutrality (§2.4). The International Court of Justice rebuked the US on similar grounds in its 1986 *Nicaragua* case, holding that the US had not properly invoked a collective right of self-defense by not so clandestinely aiding the Contras in their fight against the Nicaraguan government (§10.2).

Brink of War Force has been used in a variety of contexts that might be characterized as brinkmanship: lighting the fuse without actually firing. Examples include reprisals, countermeasures, and "gunboat" diplomacy.

A *reprisal* is a coercive measure that typically involves the State-authorized seizure of property or persons. It retaliates for a prior wrong to the initiating State or its citizens. While not uncommon during war, it is not authorized during times of peace. The 1970 UN Declaration on Principles of International Law Concerning Friendly Relations and Cooperation Among States in Accordance with the Charter of the United Nations explicitly prohibits acts of reprisal using force.[11]

Reprisal was a more common strategy prior to the twentieth century. It took the forms of public and private reprisals. Public reprisals were once confined to injuries sustained by the State itself. In the eighteenth century, however, governments began to authorize reprisals for injuries to their citizens caused by foreign governments. When the ship of an English Quaker was seized in French waters, for example, England's Lord Cromwell demanded redress from the French government. When he was ignored, he sent orders to English warships to seize the French vessels and goods. Private reprisals were executed by individuals, as opposed to State military forces, who were harmed by the acts of a foreign government. The individual would petition his or her State for the issuance of "letters of marque and reprisal." In times of peace, the carrier of such a letter would be authorized, in his or her home State, to seize property or citizens of the offending State under authority of the issuing State's letter.[12]

Countermeasures are a form of sanctions that do not usually employ military force. Examples include a State's decision not to apply a treaty with the targeted State; the confiscation of goods or freezing of assets, such as when US President Carter froze Iranian bank accounts during the hostage crisis of 1979–1980 (§9.3); a boycott, such as the Arab boycott of Israel (§8.4); and an embargo. While a reprisal is a countermeasure, the peacetime use of this individualized remedy is rare.

Countermeasures are often premised on a theory of self-defense. While legitimate self-defense is a justification for the use of force, certain countermeasures undertaken for other purposes may not be justifiable uses of force. A State that clandestinely finances a terrorist group is, in effect, undertaking a countermeasure against the State where the terrorists strike (§10.7).

Gunboat diplomacy is another form of force. It is one State's somewhat hostile or threatening act that is designed to intimidate another State. In the International Court of Justice's 1949 *Corfu Channel* judgment, for example, Great Britain successfully established that Albania was responsible for safe passage of international shipping through the channel between Albania and the Greek Island of Corfu. A British warship hit a mine while navigating within those waters. Albania had previously contested the presence of foreign military vessels in these waters. One could argue that the presence of the warships in that strait was itself a hostile act provoking Albania to take countermeasures. In the famous Tonkin Gulf incident of 1964, US warships were continuously present off the coast of North Vietnam as US military advisors were being introduced into South Vietnam. Two Navy warships were supposedly attacked by North Vietnamese patrol boats, which provided the fodder for escalating the American involvement in the Vietnam conflict. US naval vessels began to patrol the Gulf's international waters off North Vietnam in growing numbers. The message to North Vietnam, sent by the mere presence of these vessels, was that the US was always on the horizon. The adjacent Tonkin Gulf was thus known throughout the world as "Yankee Station."

More recent examples of this form of force involve the post–Gulf War tension between Iraq and the US. Iraq engaged in such cat-and-mouse diplomacy with its 1994 military buildup in southern Iraq near Kuwait's northern border. The US responded to this show of force by conducting military exercises in the immediate area. US warplanes then dropped bombs on Iraqi tanks abandoned in the Kuwait desert during the Persian Gulf War. In March 1995, Iraq deployed some 6,000 troops and chemical weapons near the edge of the Persian Gulf. This buildup was apparently well beyond Iraq's reasonable defense requirements—and intended as a regional show of force. In 1998, two US military buildups in and around the Persian Gulf sent the message that the US was willing to engage in major military attacks against Iraq. The message, occasioned by the presence of troops, was that Iraq must rescind its decision to thwart UN weapons inspectors from doing their job of monitoring Iraq's potential for producing weapons of mass destruction.

VARIABLES AFFECTING LEGITIMACY

Economic and Political Force States compete with one another, employing various forms of economic and political force. There can be a fine line between mere competition and aggression. The Arab boycott of Israel classically illustrates economic intimidation designed to drive a State out of existence. Just after the establishment of the State of Israel, members of the Arab League unanimously planned the economic collapse of Israel as follows: a primary boycott of Israeli goods sold in the international marketplace; a secondary boycott, whereby Arab States discouraged other States from trading with Israel; and a tertiary boycott in which other States that did trade with Israel were blacklisted from obtaining international contracts of any kind with this boycott's overseers (*see* §8.4).

Other forms of economic coercion are quite hostile, although not designed to eradicate an opposing State. In 1979, US President Carter ordered a freeze on the transferability of billions of dollars worth of Iranian assets found in the US or controlled by US entities in response to Iran's seizure of US diplomats. Freezing Iran's vast financial assets ultimately played a related role. These funds helped establish the Iran–US Claims Tribunal for resolving post-hostility claims against Iran, which was premised on its State responsibility for the uncompensated taking of US property during this crisis (§9.3).

Multinationally imposed economic sanctions are another form of force. The breakdown of South African apartheid was, to a significant degree, facilitated by UN-imposed sanctions. These were leveled against South Africa because of its official policy of separating the races at all levels of society. The UN directed its member States to boycott South African goods and investments. The long-term effects of this economic deprivation were partially responsible for that government's decision to abandon apartheid in order to avoid the adverse long-term effects of this external economic pressure.

Aggressive and Defensive Force Another significant feature of any analysis or classification of force is the actor's posture as either an aggressor or a victim who has no choice but to defend its sovereign existence. As disclosed in §10.2 on self-defense, this distinction is often rather ambiguous. The underlying question is whether the particular use of force constitutes using a sword or a shield.

State and Organizational Actor Before further studying the complexities of whether a particular use of force violates International Law, one must consider whether the State actor is undertaking unilateral action or acting at the directive of an international organization that is attempting to restore peace.

A classic dispute arose in 1998 when the US engaged in two miliary buildups in the Persian Gulf. Iraq had consistently thwarted UN efforts to conduct inspections in search of weapons of mass destruction. In 1991, UN Security Council Resolution 678 authorized the use of all necessary force to eject Iraq from Kuwait. By 1998, however, it was not clear that the US could continue to rely on such authority to use force against Iraq. There had been no fresh Security Council resolution in the interim seven years. The UN Secretary-General advised the US that a new Security Council resolution would be necessary before the US could employ forceful measures in this instance. Three Council members (France, PRC, and Russia) objected to the US assertion of virtually carte blanche authority to invade Iraq. This was no longer the scenario in which the US would be defending Kuwait's sovereignty. There was no longer a widely accepted Arab coalition in favor of multilateral action against Iraq. The US nevertheless argued that it retained the authority to use force. Iraq had failed to comply with UN weapons-inspection mandates after the Persian Gulf War. If this were a breach, however, would fresh Council authority be necessary for the US to attack Iraq? Alternatively, would a US attack constitute an aggressive use of force in violation of UN Charter principles?

While widely debated, but never resolved, this is the type of problem that this chapter is designed to explore. The next section presents the essentials regarding contemporary perspectives on acceptable uses of force.

◆ 10.2 UNITED NATIONS CHARTER PRINCIPLES

The UN Charter contains some deceptively simple rules on the use of force: (1) States may not use force aggressively, although the Charter does not define the term *force;* (2) States may expressly use force defensively when there is an "armed" attack, although there is no mention of the implicit need to defend when the enemy has not quite pulled the trigger; and (3) the UN Security Council possesses the legal monopoly on the use of force, although the Charter Article 43 UN military force never materialized. The UN's drafters hoped to control the same aggressive behavior that led to World War II and the demise of the post–World War I League of Nations. The key Charter's provisions on the use of force were cast in the following terms:

> **Article 2.4** All Members shall refrain in their international relations from the threat or use of force against the territorial integrity or political independence of any state, or [behave] in any other manner inconsistent with the Purposes of the United Nations.

> **Article 51** Nothing in the present Charter shall impair the inherent right of individual or collective self-defence if an armed attack occurs against a

> Member of the United Nations, until the Security Council has taken measures necessary to maintain international peace and security....
>
> **Article 39** The Security Council shall determine the existence of any threat to the peace, breach of the peace, or act of aggression and shall ... decide what measures shall be taken in accordance with Articles 41 [countermeasures *not* involving armed force] and 42 [countermeasures involving armed force], to maintain or restore the peace.

HOW IS ARTICLE 2.4 APPLIED?

Scope of Article 2.4 This article is the most fundamental principle in International Law. Yet its proscription on force almost immediately generated a debate about whether this Charter prohibition is a *meaningful* norm. Unlike earlier multilateral treaties on the use of force—such as the 1928 Paris Peace Pact that expressly condemned war—the UN Charter neither mentions the terms *war* or *aggression* nor defines a number of key terms that became subject to varied interpretations. Some commentators have therefore argued that Article 2.4 is deficient as a legal norm because it is too broad to have any specific meaning. Others have argued that the drafters' use of such broad terms was intended to avoid any narrow interpretation of Article 2.4. Columbia University Professor Oscar Schachter, former Director of the UN Legal Division, provides a useful perspective on the position that Article 2.4 was intended to broadly outlaw all forms of aggressive force:

> Admittedly, the article does not provide clear and precise answers to all the questions raised. Concepts such as "force," "threat of force" or "political independence" embrace a wide range of possible meanings. Their application to diverse circumstances involves choices as to these meanings and assessments of the behavior and intentions of various actors. Differences of opinion are often likely even among "disinterested" observers; they are even more likely among those involved or interested. But such divergences are not significantly different from those that arise with respect to almost all general legal principles. . . . [A]rticle 2.4 has a reasonably clear core meaning. That core meaning has been spelled out in [subsequent] interpretive documents . . . adopted unanimously by the General Assembly. . . . The International Court and the writings of scholars reflect the wide area of agreement on its [intended] meaning. It is therefore unwarranted to suggest that article 2.4 lacks the determinate consent necessary to enable it to function as a legal rule of restraint.[13]

Some States and commentators interpret Article 2.4 more narrowly. They do not view economic coercion, for example, as falling within the meaning of the Charter's prohibition against force. Under this delimiting view, a trade embargo against a particular State's products is not "force" within the meaning of the Charter.

This legal debate began to take shape in 1952. The General Assembly established the Special Committee on the Definition of Aggression. Many States, particularly those in the Western hemisphere, urged that since International Law had already banned the use of force, further definitions of "aggression" were unnecessary. The Committee and the General Assembly ought to concentrate, it was argued, on defining the Charter terms "armed attack" and "self-defence." A more detailed definition of aggression would only serve to hamper the UN's organs in ways that might preclude the Security Council from exercising its control over breaches of the peace under its "Chapter VII" powers (Articles 39, 41, and 42). This blocking move was countered with the argument that the major powers, in reality, wanted only to retain their own discretion to act in ways that were not *expressly* prohibited in UN-related terms.

In its 1956 *Report to the United Nations Special Committee on the Definition of Aggression,* the US representative asserted the futility of attempting to derive *global* refinements. It had signed a number of more specific *regional* definitions, including the OAS 1947 Inter-American Treaty of Reciprocal Assistance. Such "instruments belonged to the same geographical area and were united by many bonds, including a feeling of solidarity, which were not present to the same degree among the Members of the United Nations."[14] Further expressions about the meaning of the term *force* were arguably more readily controlled by a *regional* process in which the US was the major regional force.

Given the evolution of this definitional debate, something needed to be done to clarify the scope of the Charter's terse statement prohibiting the use of force or threats. Under Article 13.1(a) of the UN Charter, the General Assembly is responsible for "promoting international cooperation in the political field and encouraging the progressive development of international law. . . ." The Assembly thus resolved to fill the Charter's use-of-force definitional gap by proclaiming three major resolutions in 1970, 1987, and 1998.

Post-Charter Declarations on Force In 1970, the UN General Assembly further defined the term *force* in its Declaration on Principles of International Law concerning Friendly Relations and Cooperation among States in Accordance with the Charter of the United Nations.[15] This comparatively lengthy Declaration contains provisions drawn from a variety of interim UN documents regarding the use of force. The basic purposes of the 1970 Declaration were to interpret these documents and to confirm that States should agree to a more *broadly* constructed norm than the Charter's mere prohibition against the use of force.

The 1970 Declaration "recalls" the duty of States to refrain from military, political, economic, or any other form of coercion directed at the political independence or territorial integrity of another State. It specifies that such "a threat or use of force constitutes a violation of international law and the Charter of the United Nations and shall never be employed as a means of settling international issues." This Declaration provides that a State may not use "propaganda," "terror," or "finance" to coerce another State into acting in a particular way.

The 1970 Declaration was a UN General Assembly resolution that was not debated. It was adopted without a vote. It was not the product of a negotiated process, whereby the national members of the UN exchanged concessions to achieve a workable agreement. It is another statement of laudatory principles containing commonsense provisions that belabor the obvious. The final paragraph, for example, provides that the "principles of the Charter [that] are embodied in this Declaration constitute basic principles of international law, and consequently [it] appeals to all States to be guided by these principles in their international conduct and to develop their mutual relations on the basis of the strict observance of these principles."

In 1987, the General Assembly approved another declaration that even further refined the Charter prohibition on force. This was the Declaration on the Enhancement of the Effectiveness of the Principle of Refraining from the Threat or Use of Force in International Relations. This second attempt to more clearly define aggression was the product of ten years of committee work. Like the UN's 1970 Declaration on Friendly Relations, the General Assembly ultimately adopted the 1987 UN Declaration without a vote.[16]

The 1987 Declaration contains significant clarifications. States must:

- refrain from "organizing, instigating, or assisting or participating in paramilitary, terrorist or subversive acts, including acts of mercenaries, in other States";
- abstain from threats against the economic elements of another State; and
- avoid "economic, political *or any other type of measures* to coerce another State" for the purpose of securing advantages of any kind.

In 1998, the UN passed General Assembly Resolution 53/10 on the Elimination of Coercive Economic Measures as a Means of Political and Economic Compulsion. It thus urged States not to unilaterally impose coercive economic measures. The underlying concern is the severe impact such measures have on the economy and free trade of the State against whom they are applied (such as the US embargo against Cuba). The Assembly called for the repeal of unilateral, extraterritorial laws that impose such "sanctions on corporations and nationals of other States." It also called on States to cease applying or recognizing such unilateral measures. Finally, the Assembly requested the UN Secretary-General to report on the implementation of this resolution. In the first week of January 1999, the Clinton administration announced a new policy that allowed any US resident to send limited amounts of money to Cuban families and organizations—a privilege formerly limited to those with family in Cuba. Cultural exchanges of academics, athletes, scientists, and others will also become easier.

There are two significant similarities in these UN Declarations. First, they broadened the Charter rule prohibiting force by expressly prohibiting particular uses not specifically mentioned in the 1945 Charter. Second, these Declarations share the same infirmity. In each of them, the national members of the General Assembly did not include concrete measures to *enforce* the principles they purported to add to the UN's trilogy of basic articles on force (2.4, 51, and 39). These declarations are arguably just that—declarations. On the other hand, they do serve as clarifications or expanded indications of what conduct arguably falls within the Charter's prohibition on the use of force.

ICJ Position The International Court of Justice's 1986 *Nicaragua* case takes the position that the Article 2.4 "armed attack" provision of the UN Charter is no longer the *exclusive* blueprint for employing force in International Law. While Nicaragua and the US agreed that Article 2.4 is the fundamental norm, the Charter's language is only one module of the legal foundation for the use of force.

Military and Paramilitary Activities in and Against Nicaragua (Nicaragua v. United States)

INTERNATIONAL COURT OF JUSTICE, 1986

1986 *ICJ Reports* 14

Author's Note: *Nicaragua alleged that the US had mined its harbors, trained counterinsurgents, and promoted civil dissent against a government that was unpopular with the US. The excerpted paragraphs—which are those of the Court—address the interplay of Article 2.4 and customary State practice:*

COURT'S OPINION. . . .

183. . . . [T]he Court has next to consider what are the rules of customary international law applicable to the present dispute. For . . . the Court recently observed,

> It is of course axiomatic that the material of customary international law is to be looked for primarily in the actual practice and *opinio juris* [commonly accepted practice] of States, even though multilateral conventions [such as the UN Charter] may have an important role to play in recording and defining rules deriving from custom, or indeed in developing them. . . .

188. The Court thus finds that the Parties thus both take the view that the fundamental principle in this area is expressed in the terms employed in Article 2, paragraph 4, of the United Nations Charter. . . . The Court has however to be satisfied that there exists in customary international law an [commonly accepted State practice] as to the binding character of such abstention. This may . . . be deduced from . . . the attitude of the Parties and the attitude of States towards certain General Assembly resolutions, and particularly . . . [the 1970 Declaration concerning Friendly Relations]. The effect of [unanimous] consent to the text . . . may be understood as an acceptance of the validity of the rule or set of rules declared by the resolution themselves. The principle of non-use of force, for example, may thus be regarded as a principle of customary international law. . . .

191. As regards . . . the principle in question, it will be necessary to distinguish the most grave forms of the use of force (those constituting armed attack) from other less grave forms. In determining the legal rule which applies to these latter forms, the Court can again draw on the formulations contained in the Declaration [concerning Friendly Relations]. . . . Alongside certain descriptions which may refer to aggression, this text includes other . . . less grave forms of the use of force. In particular, according to this resolution:

. . . Every State has the duty to refrain from organizing or encouraging the organization of irregular forces or armed bands . . . for incursion into the territory of another State.

Every State [also] has the duty to refrain from . . . assisting or participating in acts of civil strife or terrorist acts in another State or acquiescing in organized activities within its territory directed towards the commission of such acts, when the acts . . . involve a threat or use of force.

192. Moreover, in the part of this same resolution devoted to the principle of non-intervention in matters within the national jurisdiction of States, a very similar rule is found:

> Also, no State shall organize, assist, foment, finance, incite or tolerate subversive, terrorist or armed activities directed towards the violent overthrow of the regime of another State, or interfere in civil strife in another State.

In the context of the inter-American system, this approach can be traced back at least to 1928 (Convention on the Rights and Duties of States in the Event of Civil Strife, Art. 1 (1)); it was confirmed by resolution 78 adopted by the General Assembly of the Organization of American States on 21 April 1972. The operative part of this resolution reads as follows:

> *The [OAS] General Assembly Resolves:*
>
> 1. To reiterate solemnly the need for the member states of the Organization to observe strictly the principles of nonintervention and self-determination of peoples as a means of ensuring peaceful coexistence among them and to refrain from committing any direct or indirect act that might constitute a violation of those principles.
>
> 2. To reaffirm the obligation of those states to refrain from applying economic, political, or any other type of measures to coerce another state and obtain from it advantages of any kind.
>
> 3. Similarly, to reaffirm the obligation of these states to refrain from organizing, supporting, promoting, financing, instigating, or tolerating subversive, terrorist, or armed activities against another state and from intervening in a civil war in another state or in its internal struggles. . . .

◆ *Notes*

The ICJ ruled against the US in the above case in 1986. Nicaragua's claim for reparations was pending before the ICJ for the following five years. In 1991, the Nicaraguan government notified the Court that it had decided to "renounce all further right of action based on the case and did not wish to go on with the proceedings. . . ." As is typical in such cases, where a party has requested a discontinuance of the case, the US was given an opportunity to object to the "discontinuance." Two weeks later, the Legal Adviser to the US Department of State responded with a letter to the Court, "welcoming the discontinuance." The case was removed from the ICJ's list of active cases.

HOW IS ARTICLE 51 APPLIED?

"Armed" Attack Provision In 1945, the UN Charter expressed that self-defense could be justified only in the case of "armed attack." That year was also the dawn of the nuclear age when the US dropped atomic bombs on Hiroshima and Nagasaki, effectively ending World War II. The development of weapons technology mushroomed in the ensuing decades.

Other Sources There are divergent perspectives about whether the UN Charter is the *exclusive* source for defining the parameters of the Article 51 "self-defense" provision. The reason for this debate is that this article refers to self-defense only in the context of an "armed attack." Prior to World War II, an armed attack—such as Pearl Harbor—was not synonymous with annihilation of an entire country or region of the world. In 1945, however, only one nation had the monopoly on nuclear weapons. The sophistication of intercontinental weapon systems that would heavily influence international relations during the Cold War was unforeseeable.

The ensuing growth of the community of nuclear nations and the general development of weapons technology supported the view that the Charter-based definition of self-defense quickly became obsolete. Rather than States being limited to "armed attack," nations and commentators began to argue that the drafters could not have intended to prohibit self-defense until missiles were actually launched. Some analysts still claim that this UN Charter provision has only one clear meaning, however. Self-defense is characterized as being limited to cases where an "armed attack" is underway. Australian National University Professor D. W. Greig criticizes the circuitry of this narrow "plain meaning" argument as an unrealistic interpretation of the UN Charter. By using this term, the Charter did not become the *sole* source for defining the contours of self-defense. Customary State practice is thus a viable alternative for defining the contours of the justifications for self-defense. In Greig's aptly worded account:

> Because Article 51 refers solely to situations where *armed* attack has actually occurred, it has been argued that the Charter only reserves the right of self-defense to this limited extent. Supporters of this view have inevitably been led into tortuous distinctions between different situations to decide whether each situation qualifies as an "armed attack." Once a

missile is launched, it may be said that the attack has commenced; but does it also apply to the sailing of an offensive naval force? Does the training of guerrillas and other irregular forces for use against another state constitute an armed attack? . . .

However, there would appear to be no need to adopt such an unrealistic approach to Article 51, because it is possible to reconcile its wording with the reasonable interests of states. It has already been pointed out that [under] Article 51 [a State] retains the "inherent right of self-defence" independently of other provisions of the Charter in cases of an armed attack. In cases where there is no armed attack but where, under traditional [customary] rules of international law, there existed a wider right of action in self-defence . . . [it] still continues to exist, though made subject to the restrictions contained in the Charter [prohibiting the *aggressive* use of force].[17]

"Anticipatory" Self-Defense The Cuban Missile Crisis of 1962 presented another round in this debate. In 1959, communist-inspired revolutionaries seized power in Cuba. Their leader, Fidel Castro, pledged to spread that revolution to the other republics of Central America. The former Soviet Union was sending missiles to Castro.

In an incident unique in the history of the Organization of American States, Cuba was expelled in 1962. The OAS rationale was that the introduction of foreign armaments was "incompatible with the principles and objectives of the inter-American system." US President Kennedy advised the American people that the "Soviets have provided the Cuban Government with a number of anti-aircraft missiles." In October, he ordered a US naval "quarantine" of Cuba, thus avoiding the more aggressive (but appropriate) term *blockade*. Kennedy described the US action as "defensive" and taken in anticipation of an armed attack from Cuba. He also announced his willingness to go to war with the Soviet Union if it did not halt its missile shipments to Cuba.

The following materials describe US President Kennedy's position that, in this provocative scenario, the US could legitimately use force to counter Soviet missiles being stationed only ninety miles from US shores. The other two excerpts are the OAS position in support of Kennedy's statement of the need for force, followed by Kennedy's warning to Cuba and the Soviet Union about the clear US intention to take aggressive measures to blockade Cuba, thus preventing a Soviet missile buildup:

"The Soviet Threat to the Americas"

ADDRESS BY PRESIDENT JOHN F. KENNEDY

47 *US Department of State Bulletin* 715 (1962)

Neither the United States of America nor the world community of nations can tolerate deliberate deception and offensive threats on the part of any nation, large or small. We no longer live in a world where only the actual firing of weapons represents a sufficient challenge to a nation's security to constitute maximum peril. Nuclear weapons are so destructive and ballistic missiles are so swift that any substantially increased possibility of their use or any sudden change in their deployment may well be regarded as a definite threat to peace.

For many years both the Soviet Union and the United States, recognizing this fact, have deployed strategic nuclear weapons with great care, never upsetting the precarious status quo which insured that these weapons would not be used in the absence of some vital challenge. Our own strategic missiles have never been transferred to the territory of any other nation under a cloak of secrecy and deception; and our history, unlike that of the Soviets since the end of World War II, demonstrates that we have no desire to dominate or conquer any other nation or impose our system upon its people. Nevertheless, American citizens have become adjusted to living daily on the bull's eye of Soviet missiles located inside the USSR or in [its] submarines.

In that sense missiles in Cuba add to an already clear and present danger—although it should be noted the nations of Latin America have never previously been subjected to a potential nuclear threat. . . .

Acting, therefore, in the defense of our own security and of the entire Western Hemisphere, and under the authority entrusted to me by the Constitution as endorsed by the resolution of the Congress, I have directed that the following initial steps be taken immediately:

First: To halt this offensive buildup, a strict quarantine on all offensive military equipment under shipment to Cuba is being initiated. All ships of any kind bound for Cuba from whatever nation or port will, if found to contain cargoes of offensive weapons, be turned back. This quarantine will be extended, if needed, to other types of cargo and carriers. . . .

Second: I have directed the continued and increased close surveillance of Cuba and its military buildup. The Foreign Ministers of the OAS in their communiqué of October 3 rejected secrecy on such matters in this hemisphere. Should these offensive military preparations continue, increasing the threat to the hemisphere, further action will be justified. I have directed the Armed Forces to prepare for any eventualities; and I trust that, in the interest of both the Cuban people and the Soviet technicians at the sites, the hazards to all concerned of continuing this threat will be recognized.

Third: It shall be the policy of this nation to regard any nuclear missile launched from Cuba against any nation in the Western Hemisphere as an attack by the Soviet Union on the United States, requiring a full retaliatory response upon the Soviet Union. . . .

Fifth: We are calling tonight for an immediate meeting of the Organ of Consultation, under the Organization of American States, to consider this threat to hemisphere security and to invoke articles 6 and 8 of the Rio Treaty in support of all necessary action. . . .

Sixth: Under the Charter of the United Nations, we are asking tonight that an emergency meeting of the Security Council be convoked without delay to take action against this latest Soviet threat to world peace. Our resolution will call for the prompt dismantling and withdrawal of all offensive weapons in Cuba, under the supervision of U.N. observers, before the quarantine can be lifted.

Seventh and finally: I call upon Chairman Khrushchev to halt and eliminate this clandestine, reckless, and provocative threat to world peace and to stable relations between our two nations. . . .

This nation is prepared to present its case against the Soviet threat to peace, and our own proposals for a peaceful world, at any time and in any forum—in the OAS, in the United Nations, or in any other meeting that could be useful—without limiting our freedom of action.

"Resolution of Council of the Organization of American States Meeting as the Provisional Organ of Consultation"

October 23, 1962

47 *US Department of State Bulletin* 722 (1962)

Whereas,

The Inter-American Treaty of Reciprocal Assistance of 1947 (Rio Treaty) recognizes the obligation of the American Republics to "provide for effective reciprocal assistance to meet armed attacks against any American state and in order to deal with threats of aggression against any of them" . . .

The Council of the Organization of American States, Meeting as the Provisional Organ of Consultation, Resolves:

1. To call for the immediate dismantling and withdrawal from Cuba of all missiles and other weapons with any offensive capability;

2. To recommend that the member states, in accordance with Articles 6 and 8 of the Inter-American Treaty of Reciprocal Assistance, *take all measures, individually and collectively, including the use of armed force,* which they may deem necessary to ensure that the Government of Cuba cannot continue to receive from the Sino–Soviet powers military material and related supplies which may threaten the peace and security of the Continent and to prevent the missiles in Cuba with offensive capability from ever becoming an active threat to the peace and security of the Continent. . . .

"United States Proclamation: Interdiction of the Delivery of Offensive Weapons to Cuba"

47 *US Department of State Bulletin* 717 (1962)

[T]he United States is determined to prevent by whatever means may be necessary, including the use of arms, the Marxist–Leninist regime in Cuba from extending, by force or the threat of force, its aggressive or subversive activities to any part of this hemisphere, and to prevent in Cuba the creation or use of an externally supported military capability endangering the security of the United States; and

Whereas the Organ of Consultation of the American Republics meeting in Washington on October 23, 1962, recommended that the Member States, in accordance with Articles 6 and 8 of the Inter-American Treaty of Reciprocal Assistance, *take all measures, individually and collectively, including the use of armed force,* which they may deem necessary to ensure that the Government of Cuba cannot continue to receive from the Sino–Soviet powers military material and related supplies which may threaten the peace and security of the Continent and to prevent the missiles in Cuba with offensive capability from ever becoming an active threat to the peace and security of the Continent:

Now, Therefore, I, John F. Kennedy, President of the United States of America, acting under and by virtue of the authority conferred upon me by the Constitution and statutes of the United States, in accordance with the aforementioned resolutions of the United States Congress and of the Organ of Consultation of the American Republics, and to defend the security of the United States, do hereby proclaim that the forces under my command are ordered, beginning at 2:00 p.m. Greenwich time October 24, 1962, to interdict, subject to the instructions herein contained, the delivery of offensive weapons and associated matériel to Cuba.

For the purposes of this Proclamation, the following are declared to be prohibited matériel:

Surface-to-surface missiles; bomber aircraft; bombs, air-to-surface rockets and guided missiles; warheads for any of the above weapons; mechanical or electronic equipment to support or operate the above items; and any other classes of matériel hereafter designated by the Secretary of Defense for the purpose of effectuating this Proclamation.

To enforce this order, the Secretary of Defense shall take appropriate measures to prevent the delivery of prohibited matériel to Cuba, employing the land, sea and air forces of the United States in cooperation with any forces that may be made available by other American States. . . .

The US premised its Article 51 self-defense posture on the progressive development of International Law, which arguably now recognized "anticipatory" self-defense. A State could not stand by without taking decisive action when an arch-rival's missiles were being introduced into another nation only ninety miles from its shores. But the UN Security Council was not given an opportunity to take control of this crisis, as envisioned by Article 51. It provides that a State may take unilateral action "*until* Security Council has taken measures necessary to maintain international peace and security." Under the US view, however, the Charter made the Security Council the *primary* entity for monitoring the defensive use of force. It was not the *exclusive* one. Kennedy was fully aware that the Soviet Union would undoubtedly block any Security Council action by exercising its veto power. Kennedy's legal advisor, Leonard Meeker, later wrote, "The quarantine was based on a collective judgment and recommendation of the American Republics made under the Rio Treaty. It was considered not to contravene Article 2, paragraph 4, because it was a measure adopted by a regional organization in conformity with the provisions of the [UN] Charter. Finally, in relation to the Charter limitation on threat or use of force, it should be noted that the quarantine itself was a carefully limited measure proportionate to the threat and designed solely to prevent any further build-up of strategic missile bases in Cuba."[18]

The former Soviet Union and the People's Republic of China opposed the legality of the US-imposed "quarantine" of Cuba. They did not perceive it as a measure that fairly anticipated imminent danger. The Soviet Union introduced a resolution in the Security Council condemning the US "blockade" of Cuba. It characterized this US action as a hostile act of aggression—not defensive in nature—because the US did not first seek the Security Council's approval. While the Council did not act on the Soviet resolution to condemn the US action in Cuba, there was a general consensus that the UN Secretary-General should have been given the opportunity to negotiate a settlement. And in November 1962, an article in the Chinese Government's *Chinese People's Daily* newspaper summarized the Sino–Soviet perspective on why this was an illegal blockade under International Law:

> Disregarding the severe condemnation and strong protest of the world's people, United States President Kennedy ruthlessly declared that a military blockade of Cuba was being put into effect. . . .
>
> It is extremely clear that American imperialism frivolously hopes to use the military blockade to exterminate the revolutionary regime of Cuba, to wipe out the Cuban people's right of self-determination. It is a serious act of criminal intervention in the internal affairs of Cuba and infringement of the sovereignty and independence of Cuba. This naked aggression is also a thorough undermining of the Charter of the United Nations [Article 2.4] . . . and even [Article 15] of the "Charter of the Organization of American States". . . .
>
> This further proves that any rules or any rights confirmed by the Charter . . . can be torn to pieces by the United States in accordance with its own needs of aggression and war.[19]

Collective Self-Defense The next major development in the law of Charter Article 51 self-defense arose when the International Court of Justice considered Nicaragua's suit against the US. The US had worked with counterinsurgents for the purpose of undermining the mid-1980s Sandinista government of Nicaragua. This case presented an opportunity for the ICJ to address the applicability of *collective* self-defense arguments, which had not been determined during the Cuban Missile Crisis but were now ripe for decision. The issue was whether the US could assert *collective* self-defense as a legal justification for its political actions—including the work of US CIA operatives who arranged the mining of strategic harbors in Nicaragua.

While the US withdrew prematurely from participation in the proceedings, it made its position clear before doing so. The ICJ disagreed with the US position that its activities in Nicaragua constituted a proper case for an intervention that could be properly characterized as "collective self-defense." The US asserted that its intervention was justified as a form of self-defense against some *future* armed attack by Nicaragua on other OAS members. Citing both the UN Charter and the above OAS provisions providing for collective defense against an attack, the US claimed that it had the right to intervene *before* Nicaragua aided opposition forces in other Latin American States. Nicaragua was allegedly helping anti-government forces in countries such as El Salvador overthrow democratically elected governments in the region.

The ICJ was not receptive to the US claim of collective self-defense. The Court nevertheless examined whether there might be indications of a recognized practice to legitimize US intervention—directly or indirectly, with or without armed force—in support of anti-government forces in Nicaragua. The question posed by the US, then, was whether the "cause" of the opposition "Contras," which the US characterized as particularly worthy for political and moral reasons, could ripen into a right of intervention in the name of collective self-defense. US authorities supported intervention into the affairs of a foreign State based on factors including ideology, the level of its armaments, or the direction of its foreign policy—which the US would characterize as adverse not only to its own interests, but also to those of other countries in the region. The Court responded that this US policy was not supported by any existing rule of International Law. For such a general right to legally materialize, the US would have to prove a fundamental *modification* of the customary International Law principle of non-intervention. The ICJ disapproved the US basis for intervention in Nicaraguan affairs, reasoning that it was not being supported by the doctrine of self-defense. In the Court's words:

> [T]he United States has not claimed that its intervention, which it justified in this way on the *political* level, was also justified on the *legal* level, alleging the exercise of a new right of intervention regarded by the United States as existing in such circumstances. As mentioned above, the United States has, on the legal plane, justified

its intervention expressly and solely by reference to the 'classic' rules involved, namely, collective self-defence against an armed attack. Nicaragua, for its part, has often expressed its solidarity and sympathy with the opposition [anti-government forces] in various States, especially in El Salvador. . . .

The Court therefore finds that no such general right of [US] intervention, in support of an opposition within another State [Nicaragua], exists in contemporary international law. The Court concludes that acts constituting a breach of the customary principle of non-intervention will also, if they directly or indirectly involve the use of force, constitute a breach of the principle of non-use of force in international relations.[20]

The next major opportunity to analyze Article 51 occurred during the Persian Gulf War. Four days after Iraq invaded Kuwait, the UN Security Council issued Resolution 661. That statement identified the application of self-defense by ". . . *[a]ffirming* the inherent right of individual and collective self-defence, in accordance with Article 51 of the Charter. . . ."[21] The dozen resolutions during that war reflected a consensus about the existence of the inherent right of *collective* self-defense.

The novel question was whether either individual or collective self-defense could be undertaken at any time *without* the direct participation of the UN Security Council. Article 51 authorizes self-defense "until the Security Council has taken measures necessary to maintain international peace and security." Although time was allegedly of the essence, Article 51 does not condone a wholly *unilateral* exercise whether by the US or other States. Such action would be inconsistent with the Security Council's traditional concerns about State responses to aggression in the name of self-defense. The Council was motivated to quickly and incessantly issue resolutions so as to remain openly involved with the US-directed process of forcing Iraq to withdraw from Kuwait. It is at this point that one may integrate the Security Council's Chapter VII powers with self-defense.

Yet another unresolved situation occurred in 1998 when the US launched cruise missile attacks into Afghanistan and Sudan in retaliation for the August bombings of US embassies in Kenya and Tanzania. Some 250 were killed, including twelve American citizens, and more than 5,000 were wounded in the embassy bombings. While each bombing might arguably be considered an armed attack on the US, both occurred half a world away from US shores. Only a small fraction of those harmed were US citizens. Those responsible for the bombings were not State agents of either Afghanistan or Sudan. On the other hand, these countries took no action to prevent or find the perpetrators. But there was no resort to the UN Security Council—a decision that would likely have compromised the secrecy and timeliness of any forceful US reaction to the embassy bombings. To label the US response "acceptable" under International Law would require characterization of the missile attack as constituting a limited right of reprisal launched in the name of self-defense.

The "last word" on self-defense was uttered by the UN's judicial arm in 1996:

"Legality of the Threat or Use of Nuclear Weapons"

INTERNATIONAL COURT OF JUSTICE, 1996

General List No. 95

Advisory Opinion of 8 July 1996

Go to course Web page at http://home.att.net/~slomansonb/txtcsesite.html; click on Nuclear Weapons Case.

◆ *Notes & Questions*

1. What did the ICJ decide in the Nuclear Weapons Case?
2. What are the basic arguments for and against the use of nuclear weapons in self-defense?

HOW IS ARTICLE 39 APPLIED?

Charter Language This provision of the Charter provides that the "Security Council shall . . . decide what measures shall be taken in accordance with Articles 41 and 42, to maintain or restore the peace." The latter articles provide that the Council may initiate appropriate countermeasures. Those not involving force include the interruption of economic relations with the offending States. Countermeasures involving force include "action by air, sea, or land forces . . . includ[ing] demonstrations, blockade, and other operations by air, sea, or land forces of Members of the United Nations."

Sanctions *Sanctions* is a word used by journalists and other commentators, although typically avoided in international documents. "Sanctions" suggests the imposition of punishment—rather than mere deterrence. The UN Charter is most discreet in its Article 39 reference to "measures . . . to maintain or restore international peace and security."

The UN Charter envisions regional organizational measures undertaken as a means of regional dispute resolution. Like Security Council oversight, such action is not supposed to be unilaterally imposed in the absence of organizational endorsement. For example, the European Community's anti-investment measures against South Africa were imposed as a means of participating in the broader UN policy of encouraging member States to dismantle apartheid. The Organization of American States imposed economic sanctions on Haiti in 1991 after military leaders deposed the country's first democratically elected leader. The 1992 OAS sanctions barred oil deliveries to Haiti as a measure for securing Haiti's observation of the democratic principles contained in the OAS Charter. The OAS also considered sanctions against Peru in 1992 when its leader closed Congress and suspended the Peruvian Constitution.

In both instances, the US served as the "strongman" in terms of being the first among equals in regional military and economic power. However, the application of sanctions on an international level, rather than being unilaterally imposed, increased the likelihood of consensus appropriate for the *organizational* imposition of sanctions via a regional process. Regionally imposed sanctions encourage the elimination of threats to peace. Unilaterally imposed sanctions, on the other hand, encourage the escalation of threats to peace. When implementing countermeasures are imposed by a multilateral body, the sanctioning State is not as readily perceived as an aggressor, like a State that is merely taking advantage of the situation to achieve some less-than-altruistic objective.

One should not construe unilateral *State*-imposed sanctions that employed for the asserted purpose of furthering UN Charter principles as tantamount to compliance with Charter objectives. The UN, not its individual member States, has the official monopoly on the use of force. US President Carter applied a series of sanctions against Iran, during the 1979–1980 Hostage Crisis. Virtually every nation of the world condemned Iran's actions of seizing and then holding diplomatic hostages. This multilateral form of approval did not authorize President Carter's use of unilateral sanctions, however, in the absence of Security Council involvement.

US dealings with Cuba present a more blatant breach of UN Charter principles. In 1994, the UN General Assembly passed a resolution—for the third consecutive year—calling on the US to end its embargo against Cuba. Of the 184 UN member States, only Israel has supported the US-imposed Cuban economic sanctions. Cuba has always characterized US sanctions policy as a direct threat to its existence. A 1960 Cuban law characterized US economic countermeasures in the following terms: "the attitude assumed by the [US] government . . . constitutes an aggression, for political purposes, against the basic interests of the Cuban economy . . . [that] forces the Revolutionary government to adopt, without hesitation, all and whatever means it may deem appropriate or desirable for the due defense of the national sovereignty and protection of our economic development process."[22]

This type of economic affront can ripen into more serious forms of conflict. The US, for example, launched the infamous 1961 Bay of Pigs assault, which Cuba used to justify its introduction of Soviet missiles and then precipitated the Cuban Missile Crisis. Cuba has since had reason to harbor mistrust. The Castro government has feared the almost insatiable US desire to economically crush Cuba. The Cuban migrations to US shores of the 1980s and 1990s were caused, in part, by the resulting economic hardship of US sanctions policy. This is not a situation where the US has acted under Security Council principles to economically force compliance of some State to come to terms with UN-imposed sanctions. State sanctions against South African apartheid and the aggression of the Bosnian Serbs are different matters. The Cuba sanctions are a series of unilateral acts with the objective of the economic downfall of a particular government. One could draw a parallel with the Arab boycott of Israel. Both were designed to crush a particular government or State.[23]

The use of force displayed by the US during the Cuban Missile Crisis rebutted the UN Security Council's supposed monopoly. Although the US's supreme national interests were at stake, the Soviet Union would surely have disapproved any proposed Council action in support of the US concern about Soviet missiles only ninety miles from the US shoreline. Nevertheless, the US economic boycott of Cuba has been designed to topple the government of Cuba since 1959. The late 1998 White House proposal, which was essentially designed to authorize private individuals to legally send money to relatives, was a minor concession—especially in view of the 1996 Helms–Burton embargo legislation (discussed in Chapter 13). Princeton University Professor Richard Falk lamented that:

> In an era when economic relations with China are being actively promoted and relations with Vietnam are being gradually normalized, it would seem more anachronistic than ever for the United States to continue to regard its close neighbor Cuba as posing some sort of lethal threat to US interests and values. . . .
>
> In the end it will probably require pressure from US citizens to induce the White House to change US policy toward Cuba . . . [to expose] the extent to which economic warfare collides with international law and with the opportunities for peaceful and equitable international relations among sovereign states in the post–cold war world.[24]

Organizational Force The collective response during the 1991 Persian Gulf War expanded the concept of self-defense beyond merely repelling an aggressor. The objective was to defeat Iraq with sufficient force so as to eliminate its potential for further threats to international peace. Security Council Resolution 678 authorized "all necessary means" to force Iraq's withdrawal from Kuwait—in addition to restoring peace. The Council's Chapter VII powers indicate that the organization should authorize less forceful measures before escalating the use of force as happened in Kuwait. The Security Council normally authorizes forcible sanctions *only* after less severe ones have failed to work (as evinced by its patience with Iraq since the Persian Gulf War). But the Charter should also be a flexible document, one interpreted to ensure enforcement of its mandate to restore peace and *maintain* security. David Scheffer of the Carnegie Endowment for International Peace commented that "[t]he Iraq–Kuwait crisis served to remind us that the Charter is a flexible document that can be interpreted as such. Narrow, rigid interpretation of the Charter by U.N. enthusiasts may have the unintended result of creating unnecessary obstacles to the effective implementation of critical Charter provisions. For example, there was some discussion during the early months of the Iraq–Kuwait crisis that trade sanctions must be proven to have failed before the Security Council could authorize use of force under Article 42 of the Charter. However, the text of Article 42 offers more latitude. . . . The Security Council could make a determination at any time that trade sanctions "would be inadequate" [under Article 41] and move on to Article 42 and the use of force.[25]

Scheffer's argument favors a liberal Charter interpretation. It was borne out by the fact that Iraq was *militarily* defeated in the Persian Gulf War, yet it restationed a large military force near the Kuwait border in late 1994. Applying economic sanctions, for a long enough period to determine their deterrent effect would have had about the same effect as US economic sanctions against Iran during the 1979–1980 hostage crisis.

Problems have surfaced when one or more States seek the necessary consensus to impose or maintain UN sanctions against the targeted State. During the Cold War, the Council's ability to use sanctions as a basis for forcing State compliance with Charter principles was thwarted by the veto power. One permanent member's veto would block the ability of the Council to take decisive action. Since the end of the Cold War, the UN has been able to enter into geographical arenas (like Bosnia) that were once beyond its reach because of barriers imposed by the superpowers' respective spheres of influence. The US would not be likely to participate in a Bosnian conflict had it occurred while the Soviet Union was still functioning. Subsequently, however, the Security Council was able to impose an embargo on the former Yugoslavia—and NATO to insert military force—with the blessing or at least grudging acceptance of all UN Security Council members.

Maintaining UN sanctions policy may be another matter. Some States reportedly ignored the UN arms embargo by providing arms to Serbia and Montenegro and assisting parties on both sides of this conflict. The 1994 US decision to ignore the embargo adversely affected the Security Council's newfound activism—and alarmed US allies in Europe. The US was concerned about the embargo's impact on Muslim and Croatian forces, which did not enjoy the benefit of receiving illicit arms (as did the Bosnian Serbs). A unilateral national decision to ignore Security Council–imposed sanctions created somewhat of a diplomatic rift between the US and its NATO allies. The latter were concerned because the US Congress eliminated funding for the US enforcement of the UN's embargo on Yugoslavia. After the US officially withdrew its support of the UN-imposed sanctions, other Security Council members questioned the lasting value of such sanction orders.

One former UN Secretary-General advocated a more forceful method for applying Charter principles to future hostilities. In 1992, then UN Secretary-General Boutros Boutros-Ghali proposed that UN forces be made available for the rapid deployment of force under the Charter's Chapter VII powers. There had never been a standing army as envisioned by Article 43. Yet the time was ripe in the aftermath of the Cold War to establish some force capable of quickly responding to threats to peace. In his *Agenda for Peace,* which was prepared in response to a request from the heads of State of the Council members (*see* §3.3), Boutros-Ghali proposed that the Persian Gulf War had taught the community of nations an important lesson. A permanent body would need to be on call in order to serve as a deterrent to future threats to peace. He proposed "peace-enforcement units." Under this proposal, the "ready availability of armed forces could serve, in itself, as a means of deterring breaches of the peace since a potential aggressor [like Iraq] would know that the Council had at its disposal a[n immediate] means of response."

This proposal seeks the introduction of a UN rapid deployment force into any conflict deemed appropriate by the Security Council. Boutros-Ghali's perspective was that the Council should consider "the utilization of peace-enforcement units in clearly defined circumstances."[26] Adoption by the Council would bolster the UN's diplomatic role—but finally grant it the manpower to be a peacemaker, rather than continue to serve in its perennial role as mere peace*keeper.*

In 1994, President Clinton responded with new guidelines for US participation that would do two things. First, they would greatly limit future US involvement in UN operations incorporating the use of force (*see* §3.3, on UN Reform). The essential feature is that "the President will never relinquish command over US forces. However, the President will, on a case-by-case basis, consider placing appropriate US forces under the operational control of a competent UN commander for specific UN operations authorized by the Security Council."[27] Ample room is left within this new US executive policy for the provision of rapid deployment forces. It remains to be seen, however, whether this policy will survive congressional scrutiny.

◆ 10.3 PEACEKEEPING OPERATIONS

> "The new breed of intra-State conflicts have certain characteristics that present United Nations peace-keepers with challenges. . . .
>
> They are usually fought not only by regular armies but also by militias and armed civilians with little discipline and with ill-defined chains of commend. They are often guerilla wars without clear front lines. Civilians are the main victims and often the main targets. Humanitarian emergencies are commonplace and the combatant authorities . . . lack the capacity to cope with them. . . .
>
> Another feature of such conflicts is the collapse of State institutions, especially the police and judiciary, with resulting paralysis of governance, a breakdown of law and order, and general banditry and chaos."
>
> —UN Secretary-General, *Agenda for Peace* (1995), 8–9

Regional powers have established several significant non-UN peacekeeping operations. This section concentrates on UN peacekeeping and how it evolved without any express provision in the UN Charter.

NON-UN PEACEKEEPING OPERATIONS

The UN is not the only international organization for dispatching international peacekeeping forces. NATO, OAS, European Union, and other peacekeeping forces have attempted to control State uses of force.

NATO has authorized the use of air strikes since 1993, for example, under extensive international pressure to react to the Bosnian Serb attacks on civilian targets. NATO awaited UN authorization, before it carried out its "threat" by bombing some Serbian positions when the Serbs failed to retreat and then attacked UN-designated safe havens in Bosnia. NATO's 1994 air strikes were the first attacks on ground troops in NATO's existence.

NATO's earlier decision to conduct air strikes should be insulated from any responsibility in Serbia and Montenegro's 1994 suit against NATO, which was lodged in the International Court of Justice. Yugoslavia (now consisting of only Serbia and Montenegro) therein challenged NATO's February 1994 decision to use air strikes as an illegal use of international force in this civil war. This case is unlikely to proceed, however, because of jurisdictional problems. First, NATO States have not generally consented to the jurisdiction of the ICJ (choosing instead to do so via specific international treaties). Second, the current "Yugoslavia" no longer holds the former UN seat and must reapply for admission to the UN. The plaintiff State is no longer a UN member and not a party to the UN's Statute of the International Court of Justice (9.4 on ICJ jurisdiction).

Other less publicized operations and proposals have been conducted by several international organizations, including the following (chronologically listed).

- OAU (1998): African foreign ministers met in Ethiopia, rejecting Western nations' proposal to help train potential OAU peacekeeping force on the African continent.
- ECOMOG (1997): Economic Community of Western African States "Military Observer Group" was authorized by the UN Security Council to intervene to maintain order in Sierra Leone's civil war (between 7,000 and 20,000 peacekeepers by January 1999).
- High Readiness Brigade (1996): Seven nations signed an agreement in December 1996 to deploy a 4,000-person force to crisis spots under the direction of the Security Council: Austria, Canada, Denmark, Poland, Netherlands, Norway, and Sweden.
- OAS (1993): A sixteen-nation OAS civilian observer force was present in Haiti to assess the effect of the coup of its first democratically elected leader in 1991.
- WEU (1992): The Western European Union assisted NATO with enforcing a UN-imposed blockade. The warships of certain European States kept all vessels from passing in or out of the Adriatic Sea near the former Yugoslavia.
- WAC (1990): The sixteen-member West African Community sent a five-nation peacekeeping force into Liberia during its civil war to locate the leader of the rebel forces in Liberia.
- British Commonwealth (1979): One thousand troops from five nations of the British Commonwealth were sent into Southern Rhodesia. Their goal was to keep the peace achieved as a result of a ceasefire agreement between antigovernment guerrillas and the government of Southern Rhodesia. The presence of this force enabled Southern Rhodesia to transfer political power to the new Zimbabwe government in 1980.
- Arab League (1976): The six-nation Inter-Arab Deterrent Force was sent into Lebanon by the Arab League. On Lebanon's request, the League sent more than 30,000 troops there to monitor the peace "established" by an agreement between Muslim and Christian factions during Lebanon's civil war.
- OAS (1965): The Dominican Republic was on the verge of a civil war. The US sent more than 20,000 troops in a unilateral action that violated standing OAS regional security agreements. The OAS later replaced those troops with its own much smaller Inter-American Peace Force.

The Organization on Security and Cooperation in Europe is assuming an increased organizational role in maintaining peace in Europe. It has monitored election results, for example, and is a potential NATO "competitor" for broadening regional peacekeeping activity. However, it may be difficult to cultivate a smooth functioning relationship with the UN Security Council—a problem experienced throughout much of the "UN" peacekeeping process. As University of Pisa Professor Natalino Ronzitti writes:

> The usual pattern has been established by relations between the UN and regional organizations: regional organizations are entitled to take enforcement measures if so authorized by the UN Security Council [which] . . . can "utilize" regional organizations for enforcement action "under its authority." This concept is based on the supremacy of the Security Council, under the authority of which regional organizations can act.
>
> The way in which this concept has been implemented in practice is a moot point. During the Cold War, regional organizations often acted without any authorization from the Security Council (the best example is the Organization of American States). Even in the post–Cold War period, relations between regional organizations and the Security Council are still not easy (UNPROFOR and NATO in Bosnia

and Herzegovina is a case in point) and regional organizations sometimes act without real directions from the Security Council, as proven in the case of NATO in former Yugoslavia (Bosnia and Herzegovina), where the UN adopted an "enabling resolution" putting NATO under the nominal authority only of the UN.[28]

UN PEACEKEEPING

Introduction UN peacekeeping has been a focus of worldwide attention since its inception in 1947. That first operation involved no more than a handful of UN employees attempting to ascertain the degree to which the Balkans were a source of support for guerrillas fighting in the Greek civil war. The UN has actually conducted a number of "peacekeeping" operations—although the term was not employed officially until the 1956 Suez Canal Crisis. Since then, approximately one-half million UN troops have been deployed in many regions of the globe. As of the end of 1998, nearly 1,600 international civil servants thereby lost their lives.

The scope of these operations has dramatically increased over time, particularly during the period after the Cold War and just prior to the UN's end-of-millennium financial crisis. In 1992, the number of UN forces quadrupled from 11,000 to 44,000. By the end of 1993, there were 80,000 UN peacekeepers. And for the first time in UN history, US combat troops were assigned as UN peacekeepers, sent to Macedonia to aid in containing the Bosnian conflict so that it would not spill over into bordering States.

Exhibit 10.1 (pages 454–455) is a snapshot of UN peacekeeping operations to date.

Limitations From the outset, there were problems with the laudatory objective of the UN keeping the peace. No standing army ever materialized, as arguably contemplated by some participants in the drafting of Article 43 of the Charter. The Cold War blocked effective peacemaking. Contemporary UN peacekeeping problems include inadequate funding, insufficient national resolve to continue participation, and the severely limiting US guidelines promulgated by President Clinton in 1994 (§10.2).

An unwillingness to cede the requisite degree of State sovereignty to the UN is the basic limiting factor. The Charter was drafted with a view toward ensuring that the UN would not become a form of world government possessing the preeminence to override national sovereignty. Therefore, Article 2.7 of the Charter retained the primacy of State sovereign power: "Nothing contained in the present Charter shall authorize the United Nations to intervene in matters [that] are essentially within the domestic jurisdiction of any state. . . ." This constitutional limitation precluded the organization from operating in any theater, absent consent of the State, giving rise to the perennial UN role as "peacekeeper" rather than "peacemaker."

The UN learned this lesson the hard way in the unique expansion of its "Operation Restore Hope" in Somalia. In practice, a peacekeeping invitation had always been understood to mean that the UN troops would take on a somewhat passive role—not actively participating in local military conflicts and serving only as a buffer between hostile forces after an agreement at least temporarily ended hostilities. UN troops in Somalia seized arms and conducted raids to find a particular Somalian warlord. This organizational activity violated the practice that the organization would not use its presence to act in ways not authorized under its Charter-based peacekeeping role.

Another preliminary handicap limited the UN's peacekeeping potential. States did not stock the Article 43 "standing army." The UN Charter did not specify the intended composition of its peacekeeping forces. Under Article 43, members would "undertake to make available to the Security Council, on its call and in accordance with a special agreement or agreements, armed forces, [and] assistance . . . necessary for the purpose of maintaining international peace and security."

The framers of this article did not have the support, and apparently not the intent, to establish an international military force as of 1945. France had unsuccessfully attempted to gather support for an international police force during the League of Nations drafting conference. At the Dumbarton Oaks UN preparatory conference, the idea of a permanent international military force was again rejected. Instead, the participating governments favored subordination of national contingents to an international command. So that the Security Council (SC) would not be totally out of the picture, national staffing agreements were to be approved by the SC. Article 47 even provided for a Military Staff Committee that would supposedly assist the Council regarding its "military requirements for the maintenance of international peace and security, the employment and

EXHIBIT 10.1 UNITED NATIONS PEACEKEEPING OPERATIONS

Name	Year Began	Location	Function
MINURCA	1998	Central African Republic	Maintain and enhance security and stability
UNOMSIL	1998	Sierra Leone	Monitor military and security situation
UNTAES	1998	Croatia	Civilian Police Support Group
MONUA	1997	Angola	Consolidate peace and national reconciliation
MINUGUA	1997	Guatemala	Verify fulfilment of agreement on definitive ceasefire
MIPONUH	1997	Haiti	Civilian Police Mission
UNMOP	1996	Croatia	Monitor demilitarization
UNSMIH	1996	Haiti	Assist with professionalization of police
UNCRO	1996	Croatia	Replace UNPROFOR ◆ Confidence measures
ONUMOZ	1996	Mozambique	Help implement peace agreement
UNPREDEP	1995	Macedonia	Replace UNPROFOR and monitor any border area developments that undermine confidence and stability
UNMIBH	1995	Bosnia and Herzegovina	Monitor peace accords
UNMIH	1995	Haiti	Transition to democracy
UNMOT	1994	Tajikistan	Monitor ceasefire agreement
UNAMIR/UNOMUR	1993	Rwanda	Humanitarian assistance mission
UNMIH	1993	Haiti	Help Haiti's democratic government fulfill its responsibilities
UNOMIL	1993	Liberia	Humanitarian assistance
UNOMIG	1993	Georgia	Investigate reports of ceasefire violations
OUNMOZ	1992	Mozambique	Operation to maintain peace
UNOSOM	1992	Somalia	Humanitarian assistance ◆ Civil war
UNPROFOR	1992	former Yugoslavia	Civilian protection ◆ State breakup
UNAMIC/UNTAC	1991	Cambodia	Transitional authority subsequent to Vietnamese departure
UNUSAL	1991	El Salvador	Verify elections after US and Nicaraguan indirect involvement
MINURSO	1991	Western Sahara	Mission for Referendum on status

Additional details are available on the UN Web site, www.un.org; click on Peace and Security.

command of forces placed at its disposal, the regulation of armaments, and possible disarmament."

Article 43 was inserted into the UN Charter as an open-ended provision that was, in effect, an agreement to agree. The details would be worked out sometime after completion of the initial Charter-drafting process in 1945. Thus, Article 43 did not specify the size, makeup, and utilization of the international armed forces that were supposed to be placed at the Security Council's disposal. This particular lack of specificity allowed the national representatives to quickly conclude the drafting of the UN Charter. Unfortunately, it also

EXHIBIT 10.1 UNITED NATIONS PEACEKEEPING OPERATIONS (CONTINUED)

Name	Year Began	Location	Function
UNIKOM	1991	Iraq–Kuwait	Monitor post–Persian Gulf War Iraqi observance of UN resolution
UNIKOM	1991	Iraq–Kuwait	Observation mission to monitor demilitarized zone
UNAVEM I, II & III	1991	Angola	Verify withdrawal of Cuban troops and restore peace
UNTAG	1989	Namibia	Transition assistance group ◆ Implement independence from South Africa
UNUCA	1989	Central America	Observe Central American peace treaties
UNGOMAP	1988	Afghanistan ◆ Pakistan	Good office mission ◆ Control force
UNIIMOG	1988	Iran ◆ Iraq	Supervise postwar ceasefire
MFO & MFN	1982	Middle East	Enforce peace treaties between Egypt, Israel, and Lebanon
UNIFIL	1978	Lebanon	Interim force ◆ Restore sovereignty
UNDOF	1974	Israel-Syria	Disengagement observer force ◆ 1973 war between Israel and Syria
UNEF II	1973	Gaza	Supervise Egypt-Israeli ceasefire
UNTAG	1969	Namibia	Transition of Namibia to independence
UNIPOM	1965	India-Pakistan	Supervise border ceasefire
DOMREP	1965	Dominican Republic	Report on breaches of ceasefire
UNFICYP	1964	Cyprus	Buffer between Turkish and Greek Cypriot forces after Turkish invasion
ONUC	1964	Congo	Maintain independence from Belgium
UNYOM	1963	Yemen	Observe DMZ between Yemen and Saudi Arabia
UNSF	1962	West New Guinea	Security force ◆ Transfer to Indonesia
UNOGIL	1958	Lebanon	No illegal infiltration of personnel or arms supplies across borders
UNEF I	1956	Gaza	Buffer Egyptian–Israeli forces
UNMOGIP	1949	India ◆ Pakistan	Military observer group for ceasefire
UNTSO	1948	Palestine	Truce supervision ◆ Monitor ceasefires along Israeli borders
UNSCOB	1947	Balkans	Identify Greek guerrillas

vitiated the Security Council's power to effectively maintain peace, since it had no standing army available for potential police actions to deal with threats to international peace.[29]

The other early UN peacekeeping problem was the Cold War. For four decades, the UN peacekeeping operations would not be established within the US and Soviet spheres of direct influence (*see* Exhibit 10.1). Their respective interests in the Third World included the minimizing of one another's influence. William Durch, a prominent policy analyst at the Henry Stimson Center in Virginia, notes that "the UN offered a nominally impartial alternative that could meet this objective. . . . Peacekeeping missions more often served the West's interests in regional *stability*. Since Moscow's interest . . . was to foster regional *in*stability . . . lead[ing] to radical political change and greater Soviet regional influence, Soviet support for UN peacekeeping was intermittent at best throughout this period."[30]

Uniting for Peace Frustration with the Security Council's potential for inaction led the General Assembly to adopt the 1950 Uniting for Peace (UFP) Resolution. With the Security Council effectively precluded from controlling hostilities—due to the veto power of any one of the five permanent members—the UN General Assembly decided to fashion its own method for taking action independently of the Council. The Assembly's UFP Resolution was designed to remedy the potential failure of the Security Council to discharge its responsibilities on behalf of all the member States. The resolution's supporters devised a strategy, not contemplated by the terms of the Charter, that purported to authorize the General Assembly to initiate measures to restore peace, including the use of armed force. This novel resolution is set forth below:

"Uniting for Peace, Resolution 377 (V)"

UN GENERAL ASSEMBLY OFFICIAL RECORD
5th Session (1950), Supp. No. 20 (A/1775), p.10

. . . *Conscious* that failure of the Security Council to discharge its responsibilities on behalf of all the Member States . . . does not relieve Member States of their obligations or the United Nations of its responsibility under the Charter to maintain international peace and security,

Recognizing in particular that such failure does not deprive the General Assembly of its rights or relieve it of its responsibilities under the Charter in regard to the maintenance of international peace and security,

Recognizing that discharge by the General Assembly of its responsibilities in these respects calls for possibilities of observation which would ascertain the facts and expose aggressors; for the existence of armed forces which could be used collectively; and for the possibility of timely recommendation by the General Assembly to Members of the United Nations for collective action which, to be effective, should be prompt . . .

Resolves that if the Security Council, because of lack of unanimity of the permanent members, fails to exercise its primary responsibility for the maintenance of international peace and security in any case where there appears to be a threat to the peace, breach of the peace, or act of aggression, the General Assembly shall consider the matter immediately with a view to making appropriate recommendations to Members for collective measures, including in the case of a breach of the peace or act of aggression the use of armed force when necessary, to maintain or restore international peace and security. If not in session at the time, the General Assembly may meet in emergency special session within twenty-four hours of the request therefor. Such emergency special session shall be called if requested by the Security Council on the vote of any seven Members, or by a majority of the Members of the United Nations [General Assembly]. . . .

This resolution was important to the future of UN peacekeeping operations. The League of Nations had failed to prevent the outbreak of World War II. The promoters of this resolution did not want history to repeat itself. If the Security Council were unsuccessful in exercising its "primary" responsibility to maintain peace because of permanent member vetoes, then the General Assembly must assist in the achievement of the fundamental objectives of the organization. This resolution effectively amended the UN Charter's Security Council provisions by augmenting the organizational source for dispatching peacekeeping forces. The Uniting for Peace

Resolution was the basis for the next UN peacekeeping operation, which—unlike the US-driven Korean operation—was *actually* under UN control. This was the 1956 Suez Canal Crisis.

The Middle East has been the site of a number of UN peacekeeping operations. The events leading to the Suez Canal Crisis provided an initial post-war flashpoint. In 1956, the president of Egypt nationalized the Suez Canal, one of the major transshipping points of the world. Its closure would require time and great cost to circumnavigate continents to deliver goods and troops. Control of the canal could also affect the price of transporting Middle Eastern oil to the rest of the world.

The significant economic and military threats posed by Egypt's control of the Suez Canal concerned the entire international community. Great Britain, France, and Israel secretly decided that Israel would attack Egypt. Great Britain and France would rely on that attack as the basis for their own police action. After the Israeli attack, Great Britain and France then vetoed a Security Council resolution calling on Israel and Egypt to cease their hostilities. These vetoes by permanent members of the Council temporarily precluded the establishment of a UN peacekeeping force. Great Britain, France, and Israel presumed that they could protect their own interests in the canal without any UN interference.[31]

The United Nations Emergency Force (UNEF) was established in 1956. The General Assembly invoked the Uniting for Peace Resolution to enable it to act after the Security Council was stalemated by the British and French vetoes. A five-thousand-troop force was drawn from States that were *not* members of the Security Council. They were deployed to Egypt to serve as a buffer between Egypt and its British, French, and Israeli adversaries. In 1967, at the request of Egypt, the UN Secretary-General took the controversial step of withdrawing this force at the time of the Six Day War between Israel and its Arab neighbors. This suspended the UNEF operation until 1973, when it was revived to keep peace and order in the Sinai Desert and Gaza Strip. This time, the Security Council exercised its Charter powers to establish the next of many Council operations to follow in that theater.

Contemporary Limitations In 1991, Secretary-General Javier Perez de Cuellar analyzed the impact of the UN's financial crisis on peacekeeping. The national commitment to paying dues assessments to the UN had begun to falter (§3.3). The Secretary-General proposed a $1 billion Peace Endowment Fund to help defray costs of future peacekeeping operations. The UN was on the brink of insolvency. Some members, principally the US, were falling behind in their dues payments because of national concern about the soaring costs of membership in this organization. Only 67 of 159 countries had paid in full. By the end of 1992, the UN would learn that it had undertaken the most expensive operation in its history—in Cambodia—with a $2 billion price tag.

In 1992 (and again in 1995), UN Secretary-General Boutros Boutros-Ghali responded to a Security Council request for recommendations about the future of UN peacekeeping. In his report, he noted that demands were being placed on the UN for more peacekeeping operations than ever before. The end of the Cold War had thrust open new geographical peacekeeping possibilities that had been formerly suppressed by superpower politics. These demands surfaced when the UN's financial capacity was becoming quite diluted. He welcomed a broadening of the task of UN peacekeeping but was unable to present a suggestion that would provide any long-term answer to the perennial lack of national resolve.

The Secretary-General's most concrete peacekeeping suggestion was that the members' national budgets incorporate local infrastructure to execute tasks previously undertaken by UN peacekeeping forces. National expenditures might this way include the use of facilities and development of budgets with some form of UN component in mind. From his perspective, one must recognize that UN peacekeeping was headed for oblivion unless UN members decided that they wished to cooperate in unprecedented ways. Flashpoints were igniting costly conflicts in a global era of declining governmental resources.

One may, of course, draw upon the judicial precedent of a past generation for an explicit articulation of the *legal* obligation borne by members to pay for UN peacekeeping costs. A 1962 opinion of the International Court of Justice recorded the obligation of UN members to pay for extraordinary expenses incurred by the UN General Assembly for peacekeeping in the Congo and the Middle East. Article 17.2 of the Charter provides that the "expenses of the Organization shall be borne by the Members as apportioned by the General

Assembly." France then proposed that future "extraordinary" expenditures—specifically those associated with peacekeeping—would necessitate judicial review of whether they were calculated in conformity with the Charter. The Court effectively rejected this approach in the following passage:

> Turning to paragraph 2 of Article 17 . . . the term "expenses of the Organization" means *all* the expenses and not just certain types of expenses which might be referred to as "regular expenses." An examination of other parts of the Charter shows the variety of expenses which must inevitably be included within the "expenses of the Organization" just as much as the salaries of the staff or maintenance of the buildings. . . .
>
> For the reasons stated, financial obligations [that] . . . the Secretary-General incurred on behalf of the United Nations, constitute obligations of the Organization for which the General Assembly was entitled to make provision under the authority of Article 17.[32]

The most serious threat to UN peacekeeping came in February 1995 when the US Congress began to consider legislation that would ultimately:

- limit the president's authority to act in concert with the UN without prior consultation with Congress;
- reduce the US share of UN peacekeeping from 31 to 20 percent; and
- subject even that allocated US share to further deductions for costs incurred by the US when it is conducting unilateral "peacekeeping" missions.[33]

This legislation would significantly alter the US's long-standing commitment to the UN. Other States have already withheld their assessed shares of the UN peacekeeping budget, essentially following the US lead. The overall impact of such legislation, if passed, would jeopardize the ability of the UN to maintain any significant peacekeeping mission.

◆ 10.4 MULTILATERAL AGREEMENTS ON FORCE

Attempts to control the use of force by States are summarized in this section. The quest to limit the use of military force is not just a twentieth-century phenomenon. In 1789, English writer Jeremy Bentham published arms-control proposals that emphasized disarmament as the prerequisite to achieving peace. He hoped to pacify Europe through treaties that would limit the number of troops States could maintain. As an alternative, he envisioned an international court that would resolve any disputes regarding implementation. He did caution, however, with a relevance that has not faded with the passage of time, that "such a court was not to be armed with any coercive powers."[34]

In the nineteenth century, a number of European States considered the efficacy of drafting rules on the laws of war. They produced the Paris Declaration of 1856, a collection of principles on the methods for employing and conserving the use of force in armed conflicts. The major process, however, did not materialized until the end of the century.

HAGUE CONFERENCES

In 1899, Russia's Czar Nicholas invited a number of national representatives to The Hague, in the Netherlands, for the first of two turn-of-the-century international peace conferences. The second occurred in 1907. The objective was to limit the national use of armaments. Once the conference participants realized that there would be no international agreement *eliminating* war, the central theme became how to *conduct* war. For example, the representatives agreed to provide advance warning when any nation intended to use force to settle a dispute. The conference delegates also prepared numerous declarations in the form of draft treaties. A representative list is provided below:

1899 Hague Conference

- Convention for the Adaption to Maritime Warfare of the Principles of the Geneva Convention of 1864 on the Laws of War
- Declaration on Prohibiting Launching of Projectiles and Explosives from Balloons
- Declaration on Prohibiting the Use of Projectiles Diffusing Suffocating Gas
- Declaration on Prohibiting the Use of Expanding Bullets
- Hague Convention with Respect to the Laws and Customs of War on Land

1907 Hague Conference

- Convention for the Pacific Settlement of International Disputes
- Convention Respecting the Limitation of the Employment of Force for the Recovery of Contract Debts
- Convention Relative to the Opening of Hostilities
- Convention Respecting the Rights and Duties of Neutral Powers and Persons in War on Land
- Convention Respecting Bombardment by Naval Forces in Time of War

The Hague Conference representatives did not establish a system to *remedy* violations of the principles contained in the above agreements. There would be no international military force to act as a peacekeeper at the scene of hostilities. Instead, they announced an arbitration system to settle international disputes (Permanent Court of Arbitration; *see* §9.1 of this book). But no nation was *required* to resort to arbitration before using force. All of their draft treaties contained rights without effective remedies. Obligations were thus unenforceable.

Many of the Hague Conference principles nevertheless served as bases for later treaties and conferences. The Hague draft agreement on suffocating gas was reconsidered during the 1925 Geneva Protocols on the manufacturing of chemical weapons for future use. These post–World War I agreements prohibited the use of poisonous gases in warfare, although nations could continue to stockpile such weapons. In 1971, UN delegates considered both of these earlier documents when they resolved to prohibit the development, production, and stockpiling of biological and toxic weapons. The Hague Conference chemical weapons principles resurfaced in 1989. Discovery of a chemical weapons plant in Libya focused new attention on the need for international control of chemical weapons to avoid their use by terrorists. There was a renewed fear about the effects described in the preparatory work for the early twentieth-century chemical weapons conferences. The former Soviet Union and the US then pledged that they would reduce their arsenals of chemical weapons. Iraq was required to end its production of any such weapons as a consequence of the 1991 Persian Gulf War.

League of Nations The 1919 Treaty of Versailles established peace expectations after World War I, then referred to as "the war to end all wars." That treaty prohibited war until three months after an arbitral or judicial decision regarding the particular dispute (*see* League of Nations Covenant, Article 12).

Article 16 of the League's Covenant contained a significant innovation. It established the first collective security measure adopted by an international organization: War against one member of the League was tantamount to war against *all*. The League's representatives believed that they could deter hostile actions by agreeing to an interrelated mutual defense system. They opted for economic rather than military enforcement measures. Article 16 provided that "[s]hould any of the . . . Parties break or disregard its covenants under Article XII, it shall thereby *ipso facto* [by that act automatically] be deemed to have committed an act of war against all the other members of the League, which hereby undertake immediately to subject it [the offending nation] to the severance of all trade or financial relations, the prohibition of all intercourse between their nationals and the nationals of the covenant breaking State, and the prevention of all financial, commercial, or personal intercourse between nationals of the covenant breaking State and the nationals of any other State, whether a member of the League or not."

This Article was first tested in the mid-1930s during Italy's war against Abyssinia (now Ethiopia). The League did not intervene, even when Abyssinia sought its assistance to control Italy's aggression. The League instead responded by directing several nations to draft a report on Italy's hostile acts. Great Britain and France, with League approval, established an embargo against certain Italian exports. The products that were the object of this embargo, however, were insignificant. Great Britain and France did not want to risk war with their Italian trading partners. Japan then attacked Manchuria in 1939. The League's inability to respond decisively destroyed its credibility and exposed its inability to control the State use of force.[35]

Kellogg-Briand Pact The 1928 Treaty for the Renunciation of War, or Kellogg–Briand Pact, was advocated by France and the United States. It was not designed to be merely a regional peace process. The participants focused on Europe, however. It was the region most affected by World War I—not to mention the region most engaged in wars since creation of the modern State in 1648 (Peace of Westphalia, §1.3).

EXHIBIT 10.2 SELECTED MULTILATERAL ARMS CONTROL REGIMES

Date*	Title	Scope
1957	International Atomic Energy Agency	Intergovernmental organization to promote peaceful uses of nuclear energy
1959/1961	Antarctic Treaty	Prohibits establishment of military bases, maneuvers, and testing
1967	Outer Space Treaty	Prohibits orbit of weapons of mass destruction and military presence in space or on a celestial body
1967/1968	Treaty of Tlatelolco (Latin America)	Regional nuclear-free zone prohibiting acquisition, manufacture, or any use of nuclear weapons
1968/1970	Nuclear Non-Proliferation Treaty	Nuclear States may not transfer and others may not receive, manufacture, or develop nuclear weapons ◆ Effect limited; lacks ratification by key parties
1971/1972	Seabed Treaty	Prohibits nuclear weapons and other weapons of mass destruction on the seabed and ocean floor and in subsoil
1972/1975	Biological Weapons Convention	Prohibits the production and stockpiling of bacteriological and toxic weapons ◆ Seeks destruction or diversion of weapons to peaceful purposes ◆ National sovereignty withdrawal clause has rendered it ineffective
1977/1978	Enmod Convention	Prohibits military or other hostile use of environmental modification in, over, and above the Earth
1977	Mercenarism Convention (Africa)	Organization of African Unity prohibition on placing or training mercenaries in Africa ◆ Created crime of mercenarism whereby guilty person denied POW status
1981/1983	Inhumane Weapons Convention	Prohibits or restricts certain conventional weapons deemed too injurious: mines, booby traps, incendiary devices
1985/1986	Treaty of Rarotonga (South Pacific)	Declares nuclear-free zone ◆ Prohibits acquisition, testing of nuclear weapons, waste dumping
1986	Confidence and Security Building Measures and Disarmaments (CSCE; now OSCE) (Europe)	Facilitates abstention from threat or use of force, including advance notification of certain military activities such as major troop and battle tank movements

This pact *condemned* war. It contained the agreement that States "shall" use only peaceful means to settle their differences. Under Articles 1 and 2, the "Parties solemnly declare in the names of their respective peoples that they condemn recourse to war for the solution of international controversies, and renounce it as an instrument of national policy in their relations with one another. The . . . Parties agree that the settlement or solution of all disputes or conflicts of whatever nature or of whatever origin they may be . . . shall never be sought except by pacific means." It contained unassailable principles, but it also lacked any effective enforcement provisions to stop the outbreak of another world war.

Latin American Initiatives Other significant peace initiatives, like the 1928 Kellogg–Briand Pact, condemn war. The 1933 Montevideo Treaty provided that "settlement of disputes or controversies shall be effected only by the pacific means [that] shall have the sanction of international law." The 1948 Charter of the Organization of American States also prohibits the aggressive use of force. Its Article 21 provides that the "American

EXHIBIT 10.2 SELECTED MULTILATERAL ARMS CONTROL REGIMES (CONTINUED)

Date*	Title	Scope
1992	Conventional Armed Forces in Europe Treaty	Former Warsaw Pact nations to destroy 50,000 major weapons ◆ NATO nations to destroy few weapons ◆ All to reduce ground and air weapons ◆ Ceilings on certain combat equipment
1991	START I & II Treaties (Russia–US)	Would cut nuclear stockpiles by two-thirds ◆ Initially signed by US and USSR, now by US, Russia, and three former USSR republics
1991	Missile Technology Control Regime	UN Security Council permanent member–sponsored arms-export limitations and shared information regarding sales of all military weapons and control of missiles capable of delivering biological, chemical, nuclear weapons
1992/1997	Chemical Weapons Convention	UN General Assembly Resolution 47/39 prohibiting use, development, and stockpiling of chemical weapons ◆ Seeks destruction 10 years after entry into force
1992	Nuclear Power in Outer Space	UN General Assembly Resolution 47/68 would control use of nuclear power in outer space
1992	General and Complete Disarmament	UN General Assembly Resolution 46/36: 12 resolutions calling for complete disarmament, rather than mere controls ◆ Annex establishes UN Register of Conventional Arms to track importing or exporting of specified types of military systems
1996	UN Comprehensive Test Ban Treaty	Designed as universal and verifiable nuclear test ban, including States' duty not to explode nuclear weapons within their jurisdiction or control
1997	Land Mine Treaty	Prohibits use, stockpiling, production, and transfer of antipersonnel mines and requires their destruction

*Second date: year of entry into force; by minimum number of ratifications or by other special agreement

States bind themselves in their international relations not to have recourse to the use of force." This treaty does not contain a specific arms control regime, however.

Cold War The so-called Cold War between the former Soviet Union and the US began in the mid-twentieth century. It would dominate international affairs for the next forty years. During this period, States and international organizations concluded a number of agreements to prevent escalation of that conflict. The US and former Soviet Union agreed to a series of bilateral arms limitation agreements, beginning in 1972, to reign in their respective nuclear weapons arsenals.

Multilateral Agreements There have been many treaty-based regimes for controlling the use of force—on both regional and multilateral levels. Exhibit 10.2 provides a snapshot of selected instruments that were designed to control modern uses of *military* force.

One of the most serious problems with implementing multilateral agreements on the control of force surfaced in 1991. The Cold War had ended. North Korea had been admitted to the UN in 1991 as a "peace-loving state" under Article 4.1 of the UN Charter. It signed a Treaty of Reconciliation with South Korea. The US had announced a major withdrawal of its troops stationed in South Korea since the Korean War. North Korea had announced its agreement in principle with a US plan to purge the Korean peninsula of nuclear weapons. The US had already removed its nuclear weapons from South Korea.

Suddenly, it appeared that one remnant of the Cold War was about to resurface, another major threat to regional and global stability centered on the possession of nuclear weapons of mass destruction. North Korea announced that it would no longer permit inspections by the UN International Atomic Energy Agency as conducted under the 1968 Nuclear Non-Proliferation Treaty. All foreigners except accredited diplomats were asked to leave North Korea in 1993 as this disruptive scenario continued to unfold. North Korea then announced its withdrawal from the 1968 nuclear control treaty, which was later scaled back to a "suspension" after extensive UN-sponsored negotiations. Japan and South Korea pleaded with the US not to impose sanctions on North Korea. The world was once again perceived by many commentators as being near the brink of nuclear confrontation. In 1994, the US sent in scores of Patriot surface-to-air antimissile batteries to block North Korean Scud missiles in the event of the North's attack of the South. Later in 1994, North Korea finally agreed to permit inspectors to reenter the country to determine its nuclear weapons capability.

While the tension was ultimately diminished, the related compromise has arguably set a risky precedent. The US agreed to North Korea's demand that inspections of its suspected nuclear sites be postponed for several years. The US provision of $4 billion in aid would help North Korea pursue alternative energy resources. North Korea would freeze all nuclear programs for several years. This incident may have sent an unintended message to rogue States: Violating the 1968 treaty has its rewards. North Korea is effectively free to proceed as it wishes. The international community was "put off" for several years, and North Korea remains free again to disregard the nuclear control treaty when that time frame elapses.

One might thus consider the following question: Just how well can multilateral agreements effectively control the use of force as long as the international community tolerates such risks in the name of the preservation of sovereignty? Put another way, multilateral agreements on force have failed to vitiate the nationalist penchant for agreements "in principle" as opposed to the creation of effective enforcement machinery.

◆ 10.5 HUMANITARIAN INTERVENTION

Various modes of external intervention have been employed to assist people with insurmountable struggles in their homelands. Intervention may be military or non-military, unilateral or collective. The UN has authorized collective interventions with military forces that were designed to endorse the Charter's humanitarian objectives. Charter Article 2.7 eschews UN intervention "in matters essentially within the domestic jurisdiction of any State." However, this principle does "not prejudice the application of enforcement measures under Chapter VII." The UN Security Council relied on its Chapter VII powers, for example, to establish the *ad hoc* International Criminal Tribunals for the former Yugoslavia and Rwanda (§9.5). Because Article 39 authorizes the Council to "decide what measures shall be taken . . . to maintain or restore international peace and security," it authorized this form of non-military intervention to address the atrocities perpetrated within those arenas by forces within those countries.

Unilateral humanitarian intervention may conflict with the norms that encompass territorial sovereignty and the use of force. The extent to which a State may unilaterally intervene for the purpose of rescuing political figures or hostages is fraught with complex issues of legitimacy. This section thus focuses on situations that have been conveniently characterized as "humanitarian" interventions when certain States have had less than altruistic purposes in mind.

DEFINITIONAL CONTOURS

Multilateral intervention is often undertaken by a regional or global organization for the purpose of aiding people who are enduring shocking conditions. The underlying problem may be a civil war or degradation at the hands of a despotic political regime. The intervention may take the form of military or economic actions designed to bring about a change in the targeted State. Too often, intervention has been a euphemism for political domination. States have long recognized the practical utility of characterizing their actions as legal because they are undertaken for "humanitarian" purposes.[36]

The application of this form of force is typically justified on the basis that the inhabitants of another State are not receiving the protection they deserve under the International Law of Human Rights (Chapter 11). In other words, a particular government is arbitrarily and persistently abusing its inhabitants or a particular ethnic group. The US unilaterally intervened in Cuba in 1898, for example, to "put an end to barbarities, bloodshed, starvation, and horrible miseries."[37]

The permissible contours of humanitarian intervention have not been defined in a way that represents a meaningful State consensus. An essential reason is that the term "humanitarian intervention" has become part of the customary post–Cold War lexicon; however, neither word has been precisely defined. The US Department of State's Sean Murphy comments on this vacuum:

> The adjective "humanitarian" is very broad and in common parlance is used to describe a wide range of activities of governmental and nongovernmental actors that seek to improve the status and well-being of individuals. . . . The international community is not fully in agreement on the normative content of many human rights. . . .
>
> Assuming certain core human rights upon which there is more or less universal agreement, there is nevertheless an inherent subjectivity in assessing whether, for any given situation, those rights are threatened and must be protected. This subjectivity in turn raises important questions about who is competent to make the assessment. Is it important that the international community regard an intervention as "humanitarian," or is it sufficient that the state or group conducting the intervention consider it humanitarian? . . .
>
> The noun "intervention" is, likewise, quite broad and has been the subject of extensive debate in the United Nations and of scholarly treatises on international law. When a state, group of states, or international organization takes action against a state . . . [it] "intervenes" in the affairs of that state in the lay sense of the term, even if no military coercion is brought to bear. Indeed, all of international law and international relations consists of varying levels of states interacting and thereby "intervening" in each other's affairs.[38]

COLLECTIVE INTERVENTION

This form of intervention is readily more justifiable than unilateral intervention. A UN-based humanitarian mission, like the effort to rescue the failing State of Somalia in 1993, is the preferable form of humanitarian intervention. Chapter VII of the Charter gives the Security Council broad powers to intervene when there are threats to peace, although the Charter contains potentially conflicting norms. Members are expected to avoid the use of force because it threatens peace, while at the same time not acquiesce in ongoing human rights atrocities. The Charter's expressed expectation is that members pledge "to take joint *and separate* action" in cooperation with the UN for the achievement of its humanitarian purposes. They must therefore promote "universal respect for, and observance of, human rights and fundamental freedoms for all without distinction as to race, sex, language, or religion."[39] These provisions can, of course, be abused when a powerful State unilaterally acts in a way not condoned by the international community.

The UN Charter also authorizes *regional* arrangements in Chapter VIII. It does not specify the interplay between that chapter of the Charter and the Security Council's Chapter VII enforcement powers. A collective regional action undertaken in the name of humanitarian intervention would not be necessarily authorized by Security Council inaction or silence. Under Article 53, no enforcement actions are to be undertaken via regional arrangements without the authorization of the Security Council.[40]

On the other hand, there is room for the argument that customary State practice may augment or clarify the meaning of the term "humanitarian intervention," given the inherently imprecise nature of that term. As articulated by the International Court of Justice in the 1986 *Nicaragua* case: "There can be no doubt that the provision of *strictly* humanitarian aid to persons or forces in another country, whatever their political affiliation or objectives, cannot be regarded as unlawful intervention, or as in any other way contrary to international law."[41] This "right" might support another State's providing supplies in civil wars or other emergencies. It would not include the right of armed penetration or intervening in a way that violates the intervener's duty of neutrality.

This humanitarian intervention facet of customary (nontreaty) International Law had contemporary application in Rwanda in 1994 and Bosnia since 1991. More than one million people fled Rwanda during a civil war, wherein belligerent tribes armed with machetes indiscriminately killed or maimed members of a rival tribe. France sought to intervene. It was accused of employing this convenient basis for intervening in the affairs of its former colony as opposed to altruistically seeking an end to the massacres. France insisted that it was neutral and without such ulterior motives.

France and Belgium had previously sent "humanitarian aid" to Africa in the form of military troops to protect their respective citizens living in Zaire in 1991. That intervention provoked a number of protests, alleging that these countries had interfered in the internal affairs of a weaker sovereign nation once controlled by France during the colonial era. In Rwanda, the UN established a peacekeeping operation after the loss of hundreds of thousands of lives. This force consists of American, British, and Canadian troops. It has not been similarly accused of violating any norms associated with humanitarian intervention.

Post–Cold War cases for international humanitarian intervention arose in Bosnia and Kosovo. Claims of ethnic cleansing by Serbian military forces, mass rapes of Muslim women as a military tactic to drive them out, and other atrocities gave rise to the first International Criminal Court since Nuremberg (§9.5). Some food was sent, and NATO air strikes on Serb positions provided some small relief for the suffering of the civilian populace. In a January 1993 speech, the Pope claimed that the international community had a "duty to disarm the aggressor" if other means failed. This sentiment was premised in part on the appeals of non-Serbian leaders for *any* form of intervention that would balance the playing field in the Bosnian war—where the Serbs stood accused of genocidal acts and being in defiance of UN mandates regarding their conduct of the war in violation of human rights.

PRIVATE INTERVENTION

Given the difficulties of establishing criteria for legitimate humanitarian intervention, certain *non*-governmental actors have sought the right to *privately* intervene into appropriate conflicts. At France's insistence, the General Assembly supported this development in its three resolutions between 1988 and 1991 on "Humanitarian assistance to victims of natural disasters and similar emergency situations."[42] France sought to establish the right of private French groups to cross international borders unhindered by sovereign limitations that would otherwise prevent them from treating the victims of armed hostilities and other disasters.

These General Assembly resolutions paved the way for the 1991 Security Council Resolution 688. It demanded that Iraq provide immediate access to those in need of humanitarian assistance—especially its Kurdish population, which had been the subject of government poison gas attacks several years before. Resolution 688 did not, however, authorize *armed* intervention. Council members were reluctant to set any precedent, regardless of Iraq's extremely provocative conduct reminiscent of the Nazi Holocaust. International humanitarian organizations, such as the International Red Cross, were thus endowed with a new justification for humanitarian relief, so often blocked by competing notions of national sovereignty.

It is arguable that States have a duty under International Law to provide humanitarian assistance to their *own* populations or to accept external humanitarian assistance. If so, this duty would also give rise to the duty of all States to facilitate humanitarian assistance. In appropriate circumstances, other States could provide such help without the consent of the State whose populace is in need of such "intervention." Because the oft-stated basis for humanitarian intervention is to limit or eliminate human suffering, then accessibility to afflicted peoples by nongovernmental organizations would be a reasonable compromise. It would balance sovereign concerns with the developing human rights regime discussed in the next chapter of this book. As stated by University of Zurich Professor Dietrich Schindler:

> Access by private humanitarian organisations to victims without the consent of the government of the State concerned must be considered lawful in the following two cases. First, in a non-international armed conflict [civil war], an impartial humanitarian body, such as the International Committee of the Red Cross, may bring humane assistance to victims of the insurgent party without the consent of the legal government. . . . Second, if a State refuses a humanitarian organization [to have such] access to its territory in contradiction to its duties, such organizations can assert the same rights as a State. They may bring assistance to the victims in spite of the refusal of the government.[43]

RESCUE

Certain States employ clandestine forms of coercion in their international relations. One of these is the taking of hostages as a means of placing political pressure on another nation. The aggressor nation takes hostages or financially supports a group of individuals to force another nation to act pursuant to the captor's demands.

Hostage taking occurred with alarming frequency in the 1970s when it became a useful tool for accomplishing national political objectives. The UN responded to this phenomenon with the 1979 International Convention against the Taking of Hostages. The primary impetus for this convention was Iran's 1979 seizure of American diplomats and military personnel at the US embassy in Tehran. Article 1 of the Hostage Convention provides that any *person* who detains and threatens to kill another person in order to compel a State "to do or abstain from doing any act as an explicit or implicit condition for the release of the hostage commits the offense of taking hostages." Under International Law, a person acting on behalf of a State may not take a hostage to coerce another State to act in a certain way. When this occurs, the responsible State breaches this prohibition.

Some States have disregarded this principle, giving rise to a related issue in International Law. Danger invites rescue. When one nation's citizens are held hostage in another country, there is intense national pressure to free them. It is difficult to yield to that pressure because giving in to the captors' demands encourages further hostage taking. This dilemma has triggered the occasional but widely publicized use of an innovative form of countermeasure. Rescue missions have been carried out in other States to save hostages facing certain death.

Military rescue missions present both practical and legal problems. The nation launching the rescue mission clearly breaches the territorial sovereignty of the nation where the hostages are held. The rescuing nation claims, however, that necessity dictates this response. One reason for the necessity is that International Law cannot enforce the Hostage Convention's principles when a nation either takes or effectively condones hostage taking. Where no action appears to be on the horizon other than the usual diplomatic efforts to free the hostages, they have often been harmed or killed. It is therefore argued that the rescuing nation's right of self-defense supports the existence of a *limited* right to breach the sovereignty of the captor nation for this humanitarian purpose. States and international organizations have undertaken occasional rescue missions to extract their citizens or agents who are likely to die at the hands of some terrorist or government. While not a completely altruistic form of humanitarian intervention, there are similar concerns regarding the violations of sovereignty that may accompany such forms of self-help.

There is a viable legal basis for an organization's activities that extract its agents involved in Security Council enforcement actions. In 1992, a UN anti-mine team rescued a convoy that had braved two days of crossfire to deliver food to the besieged Bosnian town of Gorazde. While returning to the Bosnian capital of Sarajevo, this convoy was trapped by land mines. Neither warring faction would come to the aid of these UN workers to ensure their safe return. In this instance, no nation would loudly object to organizational action to retrieve such international civil servants from their dilemma.

The dominant problem is the unilateral use of force by a single nation. The US has been involved in a number of such rescue attempts. In 1980, a US military operation in Iran failed to retrieve US diplomats held captive for more than one year (§7.4). In 1992, a US Navy SEAL team conducted a secret rescue mission in Haiti. It extracted a handful of former Haitian officials aligned with the then-ousted but democratically elected President Aristide. Their lives were in danger, according to Pentagon officials. US Congressman Charles Rangel condemned this rescue, promising that Congress would conduct an inquiry into this matter. US President Bush did not comment on the raid, although a White House spokesman denied presidential knowledge of the rescue—a highly unlikely representation.

The classic hostage rescue mission occurred in 1976. A French passenger plane, containing mostly Israeli citizens, was hijacked in Athens by a Middle East terrorist organization and flown to Entebbe, Uganda. Some newspaper accounts of this event reported that a Middle Eastern nation clandestinely promoted this hijacking. The hijackers threatened to systematically kill the hostages unless other Middle Eastern citizens were freed from Israeli prisons. Uganda's President Idi Amin refused to help the hostages, arguably out of a desire to avoid harming his political position with any Arab nation that may have sponsored the hijacking. A group of Israeli commandos then flew into Uganda without permission and rescued the hostages. They killed a number of Ugandan soldiers at the airport where the hostages were being held. The Security Council's ensuing debate follows:

"Excerpts from United Nations Security Council Debate on the Entebbe Incident"

13 *UN Monthly Chronicle* (August–September 1976)

Author's Note: *The chairman of the Organization of African Unity initiated a complaint in the UN based on Israel's "act of aggression" against Uganda. Two draft resolutions condemning Israel's conduct were introduced in the Security Council, one by Great Britain and the United States—the other by Tanzania, Libya, and Benin. The draft resolutions condemned Israel's rescue mission as a violation of the principle prohibiting the use of force in international relations. The following summary from the UN debate suggests the delicate nature of this problem: How to simultaneously condemn both Israel's violation of Uganda's territory and the future taking of hostages.*

SECURITY COUNCIL DEBATE. In the debate, Kurt WALDHEIM, Secretary-General of the United Nations, said he had issued a statement on 8 July immediately after his return from Africa in which he had given a detailed account of the role he had played in efforts to secure the release of the hostages at Entebbe.

The case before the Council raised a number of complex issues because, in this instance, the response of one State to the results of an act of hijacking involved an action affecting another sovereign State. In reply to a specific question, he had said: "I have not got all the details, but it seems to be clear that Israeli aircraft have landed in Entebbe and this constitutes a serious violation of the sovereignty of a State Member of the United Nations." The Secretary-General said he felt it was his obligation to uphold the principle of the territorial integrity and sovereignty of every State.

However, that was not the only element involved in considering cases of the kind which the Council was discussing. That was particularly true when the world community was required to deal with unprecedented problems arising from acts of international terrorism, which Mr. Waldheim said he had consistently condemned and which raised many issues of a humanitarian, moral, legal and political character for which, at the present time, no commonly agreed rules or solutions existed. . . .

Percy HAYNES (Guyana) said the action taken by Israel against Uganda was nothing but naked and brutal aggression. Guyana strongly condemned Israel for its aggression against the black African country of Uganda.

It was being argued that the principle of sovereignty was subordinate to the principle of human freedom and that Israel had the right, whenever it chose, to violate the sovereignty of other States in order to secure the freedom of its own citizens. That was nothing but a modern-day version of gun-boat diplomacy.

Those who, like Israel, sought to give legitimacy to the violation of the sovereignty of other States were making many small States, whose faith in and commitment to international law were unshakable, hostage to the dictates of naked power. . . .

Kaj SUNDBERG (Sweden) said the drama was started by an abhorrent act of terrorism perpetrated by a group of extremist Palestinian Arabs and Europeans. There was no excuse for that criminal act.

The world must react vigorously against terrorist acts and take all possible protective measures. New efforts must be undertaken to achieve broad international agreement to combat terrorism, in the form of generally recognized standards of international conduct. The international community must work towards general recognition of the clear obligation resting on every State to do everything in its power, where necessary in collaboration with other States, to prevent acts of terrorism and, even more, to refrain from any action which might facilitate the perpetration of such acts.

Any State where hijackers landed with hostages must be prepared to shoulder the heavy responsibility of protecting all victims under circumstances which were bound to be difficult and delicate. . . .

Sweden, although unable to reconcile the Israeli action with the strict rules of the Charter, did not find it possible to join in a condemnation in such a case. . . .

Mr. SCRANTON (United States) said the United States reaffirmed the principle of territorial sovereignty in Africa. In addition to that principle, the United States was deeply concerned over the problem of air piracy and the callous and pernicious use of innocent people as hostages to promote political ends. The Council could not forget that the Israeli operation in Uganda would never have come about had the hijacking of the Air France flight from Athens not taken place.

Israel's action in rescuing the hostages necessarily involved a temporary breach of the territorial integrity of Uganda. Normally, such a breach would be impermissible under the Charter. However, there was a well established right to use limited force for the protection of one's own nationals from an imminent threat of injury or death in a situation where the State in whose territory they were located was either unwilling or unable to protect them. The right, flowing from the right of self-defence, was limited to such use of force as was necessary and appropriate to protect threatened nationals from injury.

The requirements of that right to protect nationals were clearly met in the Entebbe case. Israel had good reason to believe that at the time it acted Israeli nationals were in imminent danger of execution by the hijackers. In addition, there was substantial evidence that the Government of Uganda cooperated with and aided the hijackers. The ease and success of the Israeli effort to free the hostages suggested that the Ugandan authorities could have overpowered the hijackers and released the hostages if they had really had the desire to do so. . . .

Mikhail KHARLAMOV (USSR) said that the flight carried out, the material destruction wrought, the substantial number of Ugandans killed were all regarded by Israel as a measure which was just or at least justified. But there existed no laws in the world, no moral or international laws, which could justify such action.

However much the representative of Israel might have tried to refute the irrefutable, the armed action against Uganda was an act of direct, flagrant aggression and an outright violation of the Charter, especially of Article 2, paragraph 4, which stated: "All Members shall refrain in their international relations from the threat of use of force against the territorial integrity or political independence of any State, or in any other manner inconsistent with the purposes of the United Nations."

The Soviet Union consistently opposed acts of terrorism, and was prepared to do its part in order to end that phenomenon. But one could not replace one matter with another. The Council was considering not the matter of international terrorism but an attack on Uganda, the killing of Ugandans, the destruction of Entebbe Airport, and other material destruction inflicted by the Israeli action against that State. . . .

The Council must condemn in the most vigorous manner the Israeli aggression against the sovereignty and territorial integrity of Uganda and compel Israel to recompense Uganda for the material damage done in connection with the attack. In addition, the Council must extend a serious warning to Israel that such acts of aggression would not go unpunished in future. . . .

Isao ABE (Japan) said international terrorism, whatever form it might take, constituted an abhorrent crime against mankind and must be denounced in the strongest terms by the world community. The countries in the world must take effective measures to prevent and eliminate such a crime against humanity, and they were required to cooperate fully with each other in attaining that goal.

The Air France hijacking was terminated in an extraordinary circumstance—military action by a State within the territory of another State. Although the motives as well as the circumstances which led Israel to take such action were presented in detail, nevertheless there was an act of violation by Israel of the sovereignty of Uganda.

Japan reserved its opinion as to whether the Israeli military action had or had not met the conditions required for the exercise of the right of self-defence recognized under international law, as the Israeli representative contended.

The Security Council did not adopt either of the above draft resolutions condemning Israel's violation of Uganda's territorial sovereignty. Most nations were reluctant to officially condone Israel's acts, although their newspapers reported popular approval. One reason for this approval was that Israel did not initiate the crisis. Another was that Uganda's inaction acquiesced in terrorist hostage taking. Without some action by the Israeli government, the hostages faced certain death in Uganda at the hands of the hijackers. Whether State practice prohibits this limited use of reactionary force remains unclear. Rescue missions *may* be an acceptable way of responding to hostage crises. Although the US coauthored a resolution that would have condemned Israel for its rescue mission in Uganda, it later argued in favor of a limited right to rescue hostages from certain death when there was a diplomatic impasse. Three years later, the US would undertake its own hostage rescue mission in Iran. That mission did *not* generate an international reaction like the one that was thrust upon Israel.

◆ *Notes*

1. In 1984, the US Congress passed the Act for the Prevention and Punishment of Hostage Taking. *See* 18 *US Code* §1201 et seq. This legislation implemented the US commitment when it ratified the 1979 Hostage Convention.
2. In a 1998 conviction under this Act, the defendant claimed that neither the Act nor the treaty apply to domestic hostage taking. The courts decided, however, that the treaty requires ratifying countries to take "effective measures for the prevention, prosecution and punishment of all acts of taking hostages as manifestations of international terrorism. *US v. Wang Kun Lue,* 134 F. 3d 79 (2nd Cir. 1998).

SARAJEVO, Bosnia-Herzegovina, June 2, 1993—Serb mortar shells blasted a soccer game on a Muslim holy day yesterday, killing at least 15 people and wounding about 80 in one of the war's worst attacks on Sarajevo civilians.

An hour after two shells slammed into the crowd of spectators, the soccer ball remained on the parking lot where the game was played, surrounded by pools of blood."

—Associated Press

◆ 10.6 LAWS OF WAR

DEFINITIONAL INTRODUCTION

The "Laws of War" consist of customary State practices and treaties that govern the way in which belligerents conduct war. *National* laws prohibit war-related crimes, such as espionage or treason. It is *International* Law, however, that protects the innocent and defenseless against the excesses of State actors who believe that the end justifies the means. Democratic States tend to include certain of these expectations in their military field manuals.

Expediency during hostilities must sometimes yield to legal and moral concerns about humane treatment. The areas of concern include the following: summary executions of civilians and military personnel; ethnic cleansing and forcible displacement; mistreatment of detained prisoners of war; indiscriminate use of force against *nonmilitary* targets; attacks on medical and related relief personnel; looting and other destruction of civilian property with no military purpose; terrorizing and starving a civilian population; use of military or civilian human shields against a pending attack; and the use of particular types of warfare condemned under the international agreements mentioned in this section of the book.

The Laws of War are often categorized in three general theaters: on the ground, at sea, and in the air. Given the environmental terrorism perpetrated by Iraqi forces retreating from Kuwait during the Persian Gulf War, one must also include environmental Laws of War as a special category—because of the pervasive impact of this mode of conduct on all three territorial dimensions.

HISTORICAL SETTING

History is fraught with accounts of "man's inhumanity to man" in time of war. The Bible's Old Testament contains admonitions prohibiting the following: the slaughter of captured men; the transplanting of innocent women and children; the plunder of animals and other property; and the pillaging and wanton destruction of cities. In the Battle of Teutoburg Forest of 9 A.D., a Germanic tribal chieftain defeated several Roman legions. He declared at the point of victory that "those prisoners who were not hewn to pieces on the spot were only preserved to perish by a more cruel death in cold blood." During the medieval Crusades, combatant forces routinely slaughtered enemy prisoners. Women were raped, and inhabitants' goods were forfeited. These prizes of war were available as an incentive for soldiers facing periods of protracted siege.[44]

Sporadic efforts limited the cruelty of warfare. A few military leaders and heads of State required their soldiers to observe certain minimum standards of humane conduct in warfare. In 559 B.C. and 333 B.C., respectively, the King of Persia and Alexander the Great ordered their troops to spare the civilian population of conquered areas. They were also admonished not to intentionally desecrate religious sites. In 70 B.C., the Roman commander Titus arranged for the safe departure of women and children from Jerusalem when it was under his siege. In 410, the Visigoth leader Alaric—known for his cruelty to foreign soldiers—forbade his soldiers to violate the women of Rome when he captured the city. In the Middle Ages, certain Christian and Muslim leaders humanized the conduct of war, partially because of a more long-range strategy to avoid an overly desperate enemy otherwise facing some cruel form of extinction.

"Just wars" were a part of the new international legal system established by the seventeenth-century Peace of Westphalia that established the modern system of States (§1.3). The European perspective was that if the war was "just," then the enemy was by definition "unjust." Adversaries therefore were not entitled to humane treatment other than that within the discretion of the on-scene military commander.

The beginnings of more "civilized" modes for killing other humans began to emerge in the Middle Ages. In Latin America, for example, Spanish conquistadors—representing the crown and the Catholic Church—were required to read the *El Requerimiento* to the Indians, before hostilities could be legally commenced. Note the religious implications of the following declaration, which one could imagine as being read during contemporary Middle Eastern hostilities near Jerusalem. The South American Indian of the 1500s would be advised as follows in the presence of a notary public who would record the fact of the required prewar declaration:

"El Requerimiento: The Development of Regulations for Conquistadors"

CONTRABUCIONES PARA
EL ESTUDIO DE LA HISTORIA DE AMERICA
by Lewis Hanke, Buenos Aires, Argentina (1941)

On the part of the King [and Queen] . . . subduers of the barbarous nations, we their servants notify and make known to you . . . [that the Lord made known to] St. Peter, that he would be Lord and Superior of all men in the world, that all should obey him, and that he should head the whole human race, wherever men should live. . . .

And he commanded him to place his seat in Rome, as the spot most fitting to rule the world from; but also he permitted him to have his seat in any other part of the world and to judge and govern all Christians, Jews, Gentiles, and all other sects. This man was called Pope, as if to say, Admirable Great Father and Governor of men. . . .

One of these Pontiffs, who succeeded St. Peter as Lord of the world . . . made donation of these isles and Terra-firme [land territories] to the aforesaid King and Queen and to their successors. . . .

So their Highnesses are kings and lords of these islands and land. . . . Wherefore as best we can, we ask and require you that you consider what we have said to you, and that you take the time that shall be necessary to understand and deliberate upon it, and that you acknowledge the Church as the Ruler and Superior of the whole world . . . and that you consent and give place that these religious fathers should declare and preach to you the aforesaid.

If you do so, you will do well. . . . And besides this, their Highnesses will award you many privileges and exceptions and will grant you many benefits.

But if you do not do this, and wickedly and intentionally delay to do so, I certify to you that, with the help of God, we shall forcibly enter into your country and shall make war against you in all ways and manners that we can and we shall subject you and your wives and your children, and shall make slaves of them . . . and we shall take away your goods, and shall do all harm and damage that we can. . . . And that we have said this to you and made this Requisition, we request the notary here present to give us his testimony in writing, and we ask the rest who are present that they should be witnesses of this Requisition.

By the mid-nineteenth century, the various modes for conducting, declaring, and waging war were no more than pretenses for justifying aggressive tendencies. Both States and private organizations such as the Red Cross understood that increasingly sophisticated weapon systems were capable of inflicting alarming consequences. Military theorists, theologians, and moralists believed that certain State practices were too inhumane to be condoned by a civilized society. The desire for controlling such excesses began to materialize in national and treaty-based Laws of War. Although there were several predecessors, the 1864 Geneva Convention for the Amelioration of the Condition of the Wounded in Armies in the Field was the first such treaty to be drafted and widely ratified. The Laws of War would soon find their way into the national laws of many countries, as well as appear in major international treaties.

The year 1847 was an important turning point. Swiss General Dufour ordered his officers to protect wounded enemy soldiers who were prisoners of war. He was one of the original members of the "Committee of Five," which became the International Committee of the Red Cross in 1876.[45] The International Red Cross worked with the Swiss government on a project that would one day yield four treaties that are often referred to as the 1949 "Geneva Convention." Thus, it was actually a *nongovernmental* actor that ignited the international movement for regulating the treatment of civilians and prisoners in times of war.

No multilateral agreement has fully embraced the varied perspectives about the content of the Laws of War. In 1899, Russian Minister and Professor of International Law at Petersburg University Fredrick de Martens drafted the well-known clause. He therein provided that "Until a more comprehensive code of rules of war is prepared, . . . the people and belligerent parties are under the protection of principles of the law of nations stemming from the customs adopted by the civilized peoples, from the rights of humanity and public conscience." Although designed for a turn-of-the-century Hague Convention covering military combatants, it was later incorporated into the 1949 Geneva Conventions (common article 3).

Contrary to popular belief, the Laws of War are no longer applicable essentially to adult military combatants. In a 1998 UN report issued by the UN Secretary-General's special representative for children and armed conflict, Olara Otunnu reported that the twentieth-century impact of war on civilians had grown exponentially. In the First World War, civilians constituted 5 percent of all casualties. In the Second World War, this figure rose to 48 percent. By the last decade of the century, *90* percent of such casualties were civilians. He also shared the estimate that 300,000 military combatants are under age of eighteen, many children being used for mine clearance, spying, and suicide bombings. Thus, the need for international control applies to all sectors of society.

> During the last twenty-five years, fifty nations have produced and exported over 200,000,000 anti-personnel land mines. 26,000 people are thus killed and injured each year. 110,000,000 such mines remain buried and unexploded in sixty-eight countries.
>
> —From report at the Conference on an International Total Ban on Anti-Personnel Land Mines (Oslo, September 1997)

ESSENCE OF LAWS OF WAR

The content of this body of law evolved in terms of the environment wherein the particular military platform was operational—on land, in the air, or at sea.46 Given the range of modern weapons systems, even this simple categorization is not sufficiently encompassing—especially now that environmental warfare has become so devastating. This section surveys some illustrative problems, including the need for observance of the Laws of War by national contingents of international peacekeeping. Exhibit 10.3 (page 478) then illustrates some of the major treaties that contain the Laws of War.

Land Warfare is internationally regulated by widely promoted and somewhat obscure norms. Some of the commonly understood expectations arise in regard to the use of bacteriological and gaseous substances. Adolf Hitler considered the use of such weapons in World War II. His field marshals convinced him, however, that Germans would likely suffer more than the enemy. Germany did use Soviet prisoners and its own citizens to conduct experiments in anticipation of the war potential for possessing and using gas warfare.

Concentration camps have since been used by various captors for purposes regulated by the famous Geneva Conventions. One of the best—or worst—illustrations was the treatment of military prisoners and civilians by the infamous Nazi regime of World War II. The Nuremberg Military Tribunal's judgment describes the all-too-familiar scenario in which inhumane brutalization was relentlessly administered. The following passage succinctly describes a number of circumstances governed by the Laws of War. Each sentence, if not every phrase of this Tribunal's description, is the subject of a Geneva Convention provision. These international limitations were established after the war to prevent reoccurrences of the following violations:

> [T]he concentration camps were used to destroy all opposition groups. The persons arrested by the Gestapo . . . were conveyed to the camps in many cases without any care whatever being taken for them, and great numbers died on the way. Those who arrived at the camp were subjected to systematic cruelty. They were given hard physical labor, inadequate food, clothes and shelter, and were subject at all times to . . . the private whims of individual guards. . . .
>
> A certain number of concentration camps were equipped with gas chambers for the wholesale destruction of the inmates, and with furnaces for the burning of the bodies. Some of them were in fact used for the extermination of Jews. . . . Most of the non-Jewish inmates were used for labor although the conditions under which they worked made labor and death almost synonymous terms. Those inmates who became ill and were unable to work were either destroyed in the gas chambers or sent to special infirmaries, where they were given entirely inadequate medical treatment, worse food if possible than the working inmates, and left to die.[47]

This feature of the Laws of War received a great deal of attention in the last decade of the millennium because of two unrelated events. First, Iraq failed to cooperate with UN weapons inspectors, who are still seeking information about that nation's potential for producing weapons of mass destruction. The mere availability of such substances, let alone their use, would have a major impact on the balance of power in the Middle East. Second, the *ad hoc* tribunals for the former Yugoslavia (ICTY) and Rwanda were established in 1993 and 1994 (§9.5). While each is dealing with essentially internal conflicts, the Laws of War have played a prominent role in their jurisprudence.

In 1998, nations of the world gathered to draft the Rome Statute of the International Criminal Court. This is the latest word from the community of nations regarding the scope of war crimes:

Article 8 of the Rome Statute

(a) Grave breaches of the Geneva Conventions of 12 August 1949, namely, any of the following acts against persons or property protected under the provisions of the relevant Geneva Convention:
 (i) Wilful killing;
 (ii) Torture or inhuman treatment, including biological experiments;
 (iii) Wilfully causing great suffering, or serious injury to body or health;
 (iv) Extensive destruction and appropriation of property, not justified by military necessity and carried out unlawfully and wantonly;
 (v) Compelling a prisoner of war or other protected person to serve in the forces of a hostile Power;
 (vi) Wilfully depriving a prisoner of war or other protected person of the rights of fair and regular trial;
 (vii) Unlawful deportation or transfer or unlawful confinement;
 (viii) Taking of hostages.

(b) Other serious violations of the laws and customs applicable in international armed conflict, within the established framework of international law, namely, any of the following acts:
 (i) Intentionally directing attacks against the civilian population as such or against individual civilians not taking direct part in hostilities;
 (ii) Intentionally directing attacks against civilian objects, that is, objects which are not military objectives;
 (iii) Intentionally directing attacks against personnel, installations, material, units or vehicles involved in a humanitarian assistance or peacekeeping mission in accordance with the Charter of the United Nations, as long as they are entitled to the protection given to civilians or civilian objects under the international law of armed conflict;

(iv) Intentionally launching an attack in the knowledge that such attack will cause incidental loss of life or injury to civilians or damage to civilian objects or widespread, long-term and severe damage to the natural environment which would be clearly excessive in relation to the concrete and direct overall military advantage anticipated;

(v) Attacking or bombarding, by whatever means, towns, villages, dwellings or buildings which are undefended and which are not military objectives;

(vi) Killing or wounding a combatant who, having laid down his arms or having no longer means of defence, has surrendered at discretion;

(vii) Making improper use of a flag of truce, of the flag or of the military insignia and uniform of the enemy or of the United Nations, as well as of the distinctive emblems of the Geneva Conventions, resulting in death or serious personal injury;

(viii) The transfer, directly or indirectly, by the Occupying Power of parts of its own civilian population into the territory it occupies, or the deportation or transfer of all or parts of the population of the occupied territory within or outside this territory;

(ix) Intentionally directing attacks against buildings dedicated to religion, education, art, science or charitable purposes, historic monuments, hospitals and places where the sick and wounded are collected, provided they are not military objectives;

(x) Subjecting persons who are in the power of an adverse party to physical mutilation or to medical or scientific experiments of any kind which are neither justified by the medical, dental or hospital treatment of the person concerned nor carried out in his or her interest, and which cause death to or seriously endanger the health of such person or persons;

(xi) Killing or wounding treacherously individuals belonging to the hostile nation or army;

(xii) Declaring that no quarter will be given;

(xiii) Destroying or seizing the enemy's property unless such destruction or seizure be imperatively demanded by the necessities of war;

(xiv) Declaring abolished, suspended or inadmissible in a court of law the rights and actions of the nationals of the hostile party;

(xv) Compelling the nationals of the hostile party to take part in the operations of war directed against their own country, even if they were in the belligerent's service before the commencement of the war;

(xvi) Pillaging a town or place, even when taken by assault;

(xvii) Employing poison or poisoned weapons;

(xviii) Employing asphyxiating, poisonous or other gases, and all analogous liquids, materials or devices;

(xix) Employing bullets which expand or flatten easily in the human body, such as bullets with a hard envelope which does not entirely cover the core or is pierced with incisions;

(xx) Employing weapons, projectiles and material and methods of warfare which are of a nature to cause superfluous injury or unnecessary suffering or which are inherently indiscriminate in violation of the international law of armed conflict, provided that such weapons, projectiles and material and methods of warfare are the subject of a comprehensive prohibition and are included in an annex to this Statute, by an amendment in accordance with the relevant provisions set forth in articles 121 and 123;

(xxi) Committing outrages upon personal dignity, in particular humiliating and degrading treatment;

(xxii) Committing rape, sexual slavery, enforced prostitution, forced pregnancy, as defined in article 7, paragraph 2 (f), enforced sterilization, or any other form of sexual violence also constituting a grave breach of the Geneva Conventions;

(xxiii) Utilizing the presence of a civilian or other protected person to render certain points, areas or military forces immune from military operations;

(xxiv) Intentionally directing attacks against buildings, material, medical units and transport, and personnel using the distinctive emblems of the Geneva Conventions in conformity with international law;

(xxv) Intentionally using starvation of civilians as a method of warfare by depriving them of objects indispensable to their survival, including wilfully impeding relief supplies as provided for under the Geneva Conventions;

(xxvi) Conscripting or enlisting children under the age of fifteen years into the national armed forces or using them to participate actively in hostilities.[48]

At the *national* level, the US Congress passed the War Crimes Act of 1996. It amends US law by expressly incorporating the 1949 Geneva Conventions. It also provides criminal penalties for certain war crimes. US courts may now fine and imprison anyone who inside or *outside* the US violates the Geneva Conventions under specified circumstances. This broadens US jurisdiction over war crimes, although the legislation is limited to members of the US armed forces and US citizens. This legislation specifically provides as follows:

US Criminal Code

(a) Offense.—Whoever, whether inside or outside the United States, commits a war crime, in any of the circumstances described in subsection (b), shall be fined under this title or imprisoned for life or any term of years, or both, and if death results to the victim, shall also be subject to the penalty of death.

(b) Circumstances.—The circumstances referred to in subsection (a) are that the person committing such breach or the victim of such war crime is a member of the Armed Forces of the United States or a national of the United States. . . .

(c) Definition.—As used in this section the term 'war crime' means any conduct—

(1) defined as a grave breach in any of the international conventions signed at Geneva 12 August 1949, or any protocol to such convention to which the United States is a party;

(2) prohibited by Article[s] . . . of the Annex to the Hague Convention IV, Respecting the Laws and Customs of War on Land, signed 18 October 1907;

(3) which constitutes a violation of common Article 3 [*see* ICTY Article 3 above] of the international conventions signed at Geneva, 12 August 1949, or any protocol to such convention to which the United States is a party and which deals with non-international armed conflict; or

(4) of a person who, in relation to an armed conflict and contrary to the provisions of the Protocol on Prohibitions or Restrictions on the Use of Mines, Booby-Traps and Other Devices as amended at Geneva on 3 May 1996 (Protocol II as amended on 3 May 1996), when the United States is a party to such Protocol, willfully kills or causes serious injury to civilians.[49]

Had this legislation been in force before 1996, the most notorious breach would have taken place in the Vietnam village of My Lai in 1973. The superior orders defense, previously unsuccessful at the Nuremberg and Tokyo Trials of 1945, also failed in this more recent application. The resulting court-martial provides a realistic "in the field" perspective about the soldier who must—as a result of the Nuremberg precedent—choose between punishment for disobeying the order of a superior and, alternatively, like punishment for violating the Laws of War:

United States v. Calley

US COURT OF MILITARY APPEALS, 1973

22 *USCMA* 534, 48 *CMR* 19

Go to course Web page at http://home.att.net/~slomansonb/txtcsesite.html; click on Calley Court-Martial.

◆ *Notes & Questions*

1. US war crimes charges were brought against thirteen officers and enlisted men. Calley was the only one convicted. He was sentenced to twenty years in prison but was released pending appeal after three years due to the impact of pretrial publicity on this sensational case. In 1976, the Army decided not to return him to custody. He did not serve the remainder of his sentence. *See New York Times,* April 6, 1976, p. 1.
2. Regardless of what standard is applied, the combat soldier may have to choose between punishment for obeying a superior's order and that for disobeying the

order. Is it fair to expect the "simplest" soldier to break ranks with military discipline and disobey a superior's order in a combat environment?

What can a State do to limit the possibility of such dilemmas for its combat soldiers? The April 1992 US Department of Defense Report to Congress suggests one means of using national laws to ensure the observance of international limitations on State uses of force. This report was provided under the Persian Gulf Conflict Supplemental Authorization and Personnel Benefits Act of 1991. Section 501(b)(12) requires a report that must discuss the following matters:

> [T]he role of the law of armed conflict in the planning and execution of military operations by United States forces and the other coalition forces and the effects on operations of Iraqi compliance or noncompliance with the law of armed conflict, including a discussion of each of the following matters: (A) Taking of hostages. (B) Treatment of civilians in occupied territory. (C) Collateral damage and civilian casualties. (D) Treatment of prisoners of war. (E) Repatriation of prisoners of war. (F) Use of ruses and acts of perfidity. (G) War crimes. (H) Environmental terrorism. (I) Conduct of neutral nations. The Role of the Law of War Report to Congress requirements are reprinted in 31 *International Legal Materials* 612 (1992).

3. In 1985, a federal court in Ohio decided that it had the responsibility to honor Israel's request for the extradition of "Ivan the Terrible" Demjanjuk. Prior to his naturalization as a US citizen after World War II, he allegedly murdered tens of thousands of defenseless people while operating the gas chambers at the infamous Treblinka concentration camp in Poland in 1942. An Israeli court later found that there was insufficient evidence to establish that the defendant was in fact Ivan the Terrible. The US portion of this case is important for this reason: This decision is an expression of American case law addressing the Laws of War. A national *civilian* court, as well as a military tribunal, has the power to consider extradition for wartime crimes in appropriate circumstances. In other words, US law recognizes the power of both civilian and military tribunals to hear cases involving war crimes. *Matter of Demjanjuk,* 603 *Fed. Supp.* 1468 (No. Dist. Ohio, 1985), appeal dismissed 762 *Fed. Rptr.* 1012 (6th Cir. 1985). There were several appeals on a variety of grounds.
4. The UN's International Criminal Tribunal (Yugoslavia) addressed the increasingly frequent scenario in which paramilitary civilians are in charge of prisoners and mistreat them in ways prohibited by Geneva Convention standards. The Tribunal decided that the principle of superior responsibility is applicable in any situation in which a superior has effective control over the persons committing the underlying violations of international humanitarian law. The Trial Chamber embraced the view of the International Law Commission that the doctrine of superior responsibility extends to *civilian* superiors when they exercise a degree of control over subordinates similar to that of military commanders. The Trial Chamber concluded that a civilian superior should be held criminally responsible for failing to take measures "within his material possibility" to prevent illegal acts, and not merely those within his formal competence. *Prosecutor v. Delalic, Mucic, Delic, and Landzo,* IT-96-21-T (Nov. 16, 1998) (conviction of Muslim Bosnians for crimes committed in detention camp against Bosnian Serbs).

There are other serious breaches of the Laws of War. Victorious armies may not intentionally destroy cultural objects. These include certain buildings, works of art, libraries, and the like.[50] Under the early Lieber Code of 1856 and the ensuing 1907 Hague Regulations on the Laws of War, there would have been responsibility for arbitrarily destroying cultural property absent military necessity. One underlying reason is that property associated with a particular culture should be protected from arbitrary destruction in times of war. Hitler ordered the bombing of Paris, which would have destroyed the Cathedral of Notre Dame. His local military leader stabled German horses there, however, to avoid destruction of this special landmark in French history.

The 1949 Geneva Convention also prohibits the desecration of dead bodies. This provision was inspired by the Nazi policy of extracting gold teeth and fillings from the heads of corpses. After cremation, ashes were used as fertilizer. There were also attempts to use fat from deceased bodies to make soap.[51]

Civilians and prisoners of war cannot be forced to undergo physical or mental conditions designed to annihilate them. Civilians may not be deported from occupied territory. The Nazis deported millions of civilians from every occupied territory to meet the labor needs of the Third Reich. The Japanese undertook rather infamous measures against prisoners of war in World War II. The 1942 Bataan Death March drew the ire of the international tribunal that prosecuted Japanese defendants. After the American surrender in the Philippines, the US general was assured that his soldiers would be treated humanely. This seventy-five-mile march in intense heat was the last one for the sick and wounded. American and Filipino prisoners were shot if they fell behind. Others were taken from the ranks and beaten or killed. Approximately 8,000 died as a result of this forced march.[52] In 1994, a South Korean escaped from North Korea after forty-three years. He spent twenty-six of those years as a coal miner. This was an egregious violation of the State duty to repatriate prisoners of war after the war has ended.

Prisoners of war may not be tortured to compel them to divulge information. Nor can they be legally punished for giving false information during an interrogation. Article 17 of the 1949 Geneva (Third) Convention provides as follows: "No physical or mental torture, nor any other form of coercion may be inflicted on prisoners of war to secure from them information of any kind whatsoever. Prisoners of war who refuse to answer may not be threatened, insulted, or exposed to any unpleasant or disadvantageous treatment of any kind." During the Vietnam War, there were widespread reports that captured North Vietnamese soldiers and South Vietnamese Viet Cong were pushed from US helicopters for failing to answer questions during military interrogations. If true, this form of questioning clearly violated the Geneva Conventions.

War crimes against women are also prohibited. In 1994, Japan apologized to the surviving "Comfort Girls" (mostly Korean), who were forced to become sex slaves for occupying Japanese troops. During the Bosnian conflict, Serb forces mutated rape into a new form—a war crime committed with the intent to destroy a particular ethnic identity. As chronicled by US human rights attorney Kelley Askin in her four-year study on the treatment of women during periods of armed conflict:

> As a consequence of ethnic cleansing, by mid-1993, the policy of systematic rapes had reportedly resulted in thousands of pregnancies. Rape is such a formalized part of the Yugoslav conflict that soldiers may be castrated or killed for refusing to rape. There are reports on all sides that "women are held hostages until they become pregnant; and that once confirmed as pregnant, they are held by their captors until they are past the point of abortion." . . .
>
> The widespread prevalence of rape during war is, regrettably, nothing new. That it is committed opportunistically, sadistically, brutally, and viciously is not new. That rape is used as a weapon of war to terrify, humiliate, degrade, destroy, and subordinate is not new. But what is new, and extraordinarily horrifying, is that many of the rapes committed in the territory of the former Yugoslavia are also committed with the intent to impregnate, in an effort to destroy a particular ethnicity. In essence, some women are sexually assaulted with the specific intent to commit ethnic genocide either by impregnating females with a different ethnic gene or by destroying the community group through such ethnic cleansing practices.[53]

Sea There have been fewer reported incidents of violations of the naval Laws of War. This does not mean that they have not occurred or are less heinous in potential effect. During the Nazi war crimes trials at Nuremberg, two U-boat captains were accused of ordering totally unrestricted submarine warfare. One was found guilty of sinking all vessels within a neutral shipping zone. The other was charged (although there was insufficient evidence for conviction) with the crime of killing survivors of sunken ships. Naval captors may not deny quarters to or kill a defenseless enemy. He was not found guilty of this particular charge, partially because the tribunal found that this was also the US practice in the Pacific.[54]

The 1980–1988 Iran–Iraq war was the first opportunity since the 1945 UN Charter to more fully examine the relevant principles that States consider as being within the modern naval Laws of War. First, belligerents have a right to visit and search neutral-flagged merchant vessels. While this was done routinely during the Vietnamese conflict, it was basically just one State (the US) that exercised this "right." Visit and search occurred with much greater frequency during the 1991 Persian Gulf War, thus giving rise to the rather clear expectation that States at war may undertake this form of intrusion. It is a necessary incident to maintaining security from various forms of infiltration by belligerents and violations of neutrality by third parties (§2.4, on the recognition of belligerency).

Minelaying is permitted but not without limitation. The 1907 Hague Convention Relative to the Laying of Automatic Submarine Contact Mines precludes indiscriminate minelaying without proper monitoring by the responsible State. Notification is an essential requirement. The International Court of Justice commented on this expectation in both its 1949 *Corfu Channel* case and its 1986 *Nicaragua* decision. In the first case, Albania was at fault for not removing surface mines hit by British ships passing through an international strait. In the second case, the US was responsible for assisting indigenous forces to lay mines in key harbors to interrupt Nicaraguan shipping.[55] Another minelaying limitation is that States may not lay mines in the high seas if doing so endangers the shipping of nonbelligerent States. UN Security Council Resolution 540 of 1983 provides that States may not thereby threaten "the right of free navigation and commerce in international waters."

The right of passage by neutral ships through international straits cannot be suspended. The ICJ so ruled in the above 1949 *Corfu Channel* case. This norm was tested during the Persian Gulf War when Iran threatened to close the Straits of Hormuz, the only entry to the oil-exporting Persian Gulf. University of Pisa (Italy) Professors Andrea de Guttry and Natalino Ronzitti comment on the scope of this right of passage as follows:

> [N]eutral warships are granted the right of passage through international straits even if the littoral [coastal] State is at war. If such right is accorded to warships, so much the more will it be binding for merchant vessels flying a neutral flag. Not all scholars agree on this, but it seems to us that practice in the Gulf is perfectly in tune with what appears to be the dominant trend, a trend which probably now corresponds to precise customary rules.
>
> Faced with Iran's repeated threat to close the Strait, the USA, the United Kingdom, France and Italy . . . firmly emphasized that the right of passage through international straits can never be suspended, even when the littoral State is one of the belligerents.[56]

Air The comparatively recent appearance of the airplane for military warfare may account for the fact that there were no related charges made at either the Nuremberg or Tokyo trials. The only reference therein was a statement addressing the bombing of a city that kills innocent civilians (without mention of the 1945 US atomic bombings of Hiroshima and Nagasaki). In the words of the Nuremberg tribunal: "This is . . . an unavoidable corollary of battle action. The civilians are not individualized. The bomb falls, it is aimed at railroad yards, houses along the tracks are hit and many of their occupants killed. But that is entirely different, both in facts and in law, from an armed force marching up to these same railroad tracks, entering those houses abutting thereon, dragging out the men, women, and children and shooting them."[57]

Air warfare tactics are regulated by the 1977 Geneva Protocol and the 1980 Convention on Prohibition or Restrictions on the Use of Certain Conventional Weapons. Article 42 of the Geneva Protocol prohibits ground or air attacks on persons parachuting from aircraft in distress. Such individuals must also be given an opportunity to surrender before engaging them as enemy soldiers. *Airborne* troops are excepted from this protection. One reason for the Protocol was the North Vietnamese position that the 1949 Geneva Conventions did not apply to undeclared conflicts such as the Vietnam War.

Environmental Warfare This form of warfare is not limited to just one of the previous dimensions. A military commander can thus impact hostile forces on land, at sea, and in the air—simultaneously.

The 1976 Environmental Modification Convention prohibits military and other hostile uses of the environment to destroy the enemy. Ensuing protocols exhibited the international concerns regarding acts that affected lives far beyond the immediate military theater. The 1977 Protocol precludes any use that would cause "widespread, severe damage to the environment." Reprisals that use the environment are also prohibited.

These conventions proved ineffective when the most disastrous environmental act of war occurred. During its retreat from Kuwait during the 1991 Persian Gulf War, Iraq's military forces set fire to 700 oil wells. This wartime tactic sent flames and smoke into the upper atmosphere for a period of nine months until all wells could be capped. This event also generated the call for a new "Fifth" Geneva Convention dedicated solely to the protection of the environment in time of armed conflict.[58]

Laws Applicable to International Organizations? No treaties specifically address the responsibility of an international organization to observe the Laws of War. The UN is not a party to the Geneva Conventions governing the Laws of War. Those Conventions form the heart of the norms that address *State* practice. By analogy, however, national contingents operating in the service of the UN, NATO, or other organizations should be bound by the same requirements as if they were operating on behalf of their own States.

The International Committee of the Red Cross has requested that the UN promote the practice of having its State members provide renewed instructions to their national contingents prior to departure for UN service. In 1961, there were reports that UN emergency forces were violating the Laws of War during the UN operation in the Congo. Now that the UN peacekeeping operations have exercised the option of firing first in situations carefully prescribed in the Somalian conflict, this concern has taken on a new significance. Geneva Convention Articles 47, 48, 127, and 144 incorporate the State responsibility of instructing State military forces about the Laws of War. The Red Cross document, which is addressed to the UN member States within the organization, requests "that such contingents receive, before leaving their own countries, appropriate instruction so that they may acquire a sufficient knowledge of these Conventions."[59]

Members of the Canadian components of the UN peacekeeping mission in Somalia and the NATO action in Bosnia would be the modern test cases. In 1997, the Canadian Army's commanding officer said that forty-seven soldiers in Bosnia were accused of misconduct, including physically abusing mental hospital patients in 1993–1994. Ten other Canadians supposedly killed a Somalian during the UN operation there in an incident that was exposed after a cover-up. Because of a shift from the traditional national defense posture to international peacekeeping, Canada took steps to better train its soldiers in fulfilling these new duties.

Certain contemporary treaties contain the salient features of the Laws of War. Exhibit 10.3 (page 478) provides a succinct overview.

◆ 10.7 STATE TERRORISM AND ARMS SALES

THE "TERRORISM" PROBLEM

Another weapon in the State arsenal of force is international terrorism. What was once the high-water mark of such terrorism was the rash of commercial aircraft hijackings in the 1970s. On December 18, 1973, for example, Arab terrorists killed thirty-two people on a US *commercial* passenger jet in Rome's Leonardo Da Vinci Airport. Hostages were taken to Athens in support of a demand for the release of two Palestinian terrorists imprisoned in Greece. The aircraft was granted free passage to Kuwait, where local authorities indicated that they had no plans to try the hijackers.[60]

One key terrorist event of the 1980s drew immense international attention to terrorism: the 1985 hijacking of the *Achille Lauro* passenger cruiseliner by members of a faction within the Palestine Liberation Organization. The perpetrators succeeded in drawing attention to their cause by throwing a wheelchair-bound elderly Jewish man overboard to his watery grave. This incident was responsible in part for the 1987 US Anti-Terrorism Act. The legislative history for this congressional response includes the following findings:

> The Congress finds that—
> (1) Middle East terrorism accounted for 60 percent of total terrorism in 1985; (2) the Palestine Liberation Organization [PLO] . . . was directly responsible for the murder of an American citizen on the Achille Lauro cruise liner in 1985, and a member of the PLO's Executive Committee is under indictment in the United States for the murder of that American citizen; (3) the head of the PLO has been implicated in the murder of a United States Ambassador overseas; (4) the PLO and its constituent groups have taken credit for, and been implicated in, the murders of dozens of American citizens abroad. . . . *Therefore,* the Congress determines that the PLO and its affiliates are a terrorist organization and a threat to the interest of the United States, its allies, and to international law. . . .[61]

The 1990s spawned a new wave of what has been described as "terrorism" and "necessity," respectively, by victims and perpetrators. That is because one person's

EXHIBIT 10.3 SELECTED TREATIES ILLUSTRATING THE LAWS OF WAR

Date	Treaty	Scope
1907	Hague Second Conference on Laws and Customs of War (12 treaties, some updating 1899 Hague Conference draft)	Prohibits acts including uncontrolled unanchored contact mines, naval bombardment of undefended towns, capturing hospital ships ◆ Requires humane treatment of POWs who cannot be summarily killed or wounded
1925	Geneva Convention	Prohibits use of asphyxiating, poisonous, and bacteriological warfare
1945	London Charter (the Nuremberg Tribunal)	Prohibits conduct including: murder, ill treatment, deportation to slave labor, plunder of public or private property, destruction of cities in absence of military necessity
1946	UN General Assembly Resolution 95(1)	Prohibits the Crime of Genocide: includes annihilation of particular ethnic or national group
1949	Geneva Convention "I" on the wounded and sick in the field	Updated original 1864 Convention to adapt to modern warfare ◆ Requires respect and care for defenseless combatants
1949	Geneva Convention "II" on the wounded, sick, and shipwrecked at sea	Updated 1868 principles and 1907 Hague Convention laws in conduct of maritime warfare
1949	Geneva Convention "III" on prisoners of war	Most extensive of four 1949 Conventions ◆ Updates 1929 Geneva Convention ◆ Regulates conditions of captivity to safeguard human dignity
1949	Geneva Convention "IV" (Civilian protec--tion in time of war)	Second most extensive Geneva Convention ◆ Prohibits torture, mutilation, violence, outrages on personal dignity ◆ Designed to protect innocent civilians not involved in hostilities from being terrorized by enemy military forces
1972	Bacteriological Warfare Convention	Prohibits the production and stockpiling of bacteriological and toxic weapons ◆ Seeks destruction or diversion to peaceful purposes ◆ National sovereignty withdrawal clause has limited effectiveness
1976	Environmental Modification Convention	Prohibits military or other hostile use of environmental modifications in, over, and above the Earth
1977	Geneva Protocols to 1949 Conventions	Refinements: most significant one protects POWs in conflict described as noninternational or undeclared (North Vietnamese bases for nonapplication of Geneva POW Convention in Vietnam)
1981	Inhumane Weapons Convention	Prohibits and restricts certain conventional weapons deemed too injurious; e.g., land mines, boobytraps, incendiary devices, weapons escaping even X-ray detection in human body
1992	Chemical Weapons Convention	Priority is post–Cold War destruction of chemical and bacteriological weapons stock
1997	Land Mine Treaty	Prohibits the use, stockpiling, production, and transfer of antipersonnel mines and requires their destruction

"terrorist" is often another's "hero." This particular difference of opinion exists largely due to clandestine State-sponsored terrorism. A German court in Berlin issued a decision in 1997 that singled out Iran as an exporter of international terrorism. In the court's words: "[T]he evidence has revealed the decision-making procedures within the Iranian leadership, which in the final analysis has led to the liquidation of opposition politicians abroad. Decisions on such operations are in the hands of the secret, extra-constitutional 'Committee for Special Matters,' whose members include the President of Iran, . . . the foreign policy chief, . . . as well as the 'religious leader' [of Iran]."[62]

Even for those events considered to be the work of *individual* extremists, from where do they get the money to finance their operations? How do they manage to become so well armed when they must pass border checkpoints to gain access to the target population? Is there clandestine support for international terrorism by some State or States that privately support the effects caused by such force? These questions are the focus of this section, which does not address the "Bin Laden"–styled terrorism, which is not necessarily identified with a particular State.

Causes Traditional terrorism cannot be eradicated without recognizing and solving its cause: clandestine support from States that have something to gain from the resulting disruption. Many have blamed certain States for their alleged roles in promoting terrorism in the Middle East. Whether these accusations are true or not, the study of this form of force would be incomplete without recognizing two essential points: (1) the perpetrators do not consider their victims innocent; and (2) they believe that the end justifies the means.

The more democratic societies provide environments which may conveniently serve the needs of a terrorist operation, comparatively free of the constraints of less democratic societies. Travel, communications, and available weaponry are comparatively unrestricted. Private industry in some societies is also a potential contributor. One perspective is that corporate activity is guided by a profit motive in producing counter-terrorist devices to protect against terrorism. There is a vicious cycle, then, that feeds on the continued vitality of promoting the same products on "both sides of the fence."

The friction between societal human rights, and the need for antiterrorism legislation, also presents a problem in democratic societies. Under recent British law, for example, a suspected terrorist could be arrested and detained for seven days. But if there are no limits on the State's pursuit of terrorists, then the State may be in violation of human rights treaty obligations. In 1988, the European Court of Human Rights decided that Britain's power of extra-judicial arrest and detention in individual cases, *without a hearing,* violated the provision of the European Human Rights Convention that mandates a "prompt appearance" before a neutral judicial officer to determine the validity of the detention.[63]

Another distinction must be made between traditional modes of terrorism and contemporary "improvements." The 1988 bombing of Pan Am Flight 103 over Lockerbie, Scotland, is a useful illustration. Two Libyan nationals have been accused of blowing up that flight, killing hundreds of British and American citizens on the basis of their nationality—rather than targeting a *specific* individual. Libya and Iran allegedly planned this event. Iran supposedly participated, as its revenge for the midair destruction of an Iranian commercial airliner by a US warship in 1988. Iran thus commissioned the Popular Front for the Liberation of Palestine General Command to carry out the bombing.[64] Notwithstanding UN Security Council and International Court of Justice efforts to extract the two Libyans from Libya for trial, its leader has refused to comply. As discussed in §6.4, there are multilateral treaties prohibiting such conduct, and require all States to try and punish the perpetrators. The apparent perpetrators were allegedly aided by Libya's leader. Colonel Gadhafi shielded them from prosecution for this act by British and US authorities.

This terrorist event foreshadows the emergence of a terrorist's perspective. In the past, individuals including Prime Minister Gandhi of India, President Sadat of Egypt, and the prime ministers of Argentina and Italy, were killed by terrorist acts allegedly financed from external sources. These leaders were punished for legitimate political conduct while in office, through the clandestine support of other States. This brand of terrorism was then directed at *specific* individuals. But the Pan Am Flight 103 scenario suggests the emergence of international terrorism now directed at groups—rather than targeting a particular individual. The Muslim extremists who bombed New York's World Trade Center in 1993 had no particular person within their sights.

Such contemporary terrorism is being fueled by religious zealotry, as evinced in Bosnia. There, State-sponsored terrorism has been designed to accomplish the political goal of ethnic cleansing. The participation of groups with religious motivations is the principal reason for the deadliness of contemporary terrorism. According to a study done by Rand Corporation analyst Bruce Hoffman, secular terrorists understand that indiscriminate killing is antithetical to the goals of the well-trained and well-financed terrorists. Religious terrorists in the Middle East and South Asia, on the other hand, act in the name of religious values. Their logic is not so restrained because "[f]or the religious political terrorist violence is viewed as a sacramental act or divine duty. Terrorism thus assumes a transcendental dimension, and its perpetrators have none of the political, moral or practical constraints that affect other terrorists."[65]

This form of international terrorism has had its impact on international organizations, in addition to targeted States. Ironically, some of the great powers of the world view the UN as being controlled by the Third World. Yet, many religious terrorists view the UN as being antithetical to their struggles—in turn, necessitating the employment of terrorism. This is one reason why the UN itself was the target of terrorist threats, just after the 1993 World Trade Center bombing. The UN, in their view, is no longer capable of accomplishing "Third World" objectives. In a letter sent to the Secretary-General from the Islamic Jihad (Holy War), this terrorist organization described the conditions on which it relies, as the rationale for terrorism's utility:

"Conditions for Ending Hostage-Taking: A Letter from the Islamic Jihad"

LETTER TO THE UNITED NATIONS SECRETARY-GENERAL

Received and translated from Arabic on August 11, 1991

Reprinted in the *Washington Post,* August 13, 1991

. . . The role that the United Nations has played in our contemporary history . . . particularly the cause of the Muslim people of Palestine . . . the question of the occupied territories in Jordan, Syria and Lebanon and, subsequently, the [Persian] gulf crisis, gives us an extremely unfavorable impression of the situation of the United Nations, which has become a plaything in the hands of the superpowers.

Why has the United Nations been given an effective and important role . . . in solving the crisis that arose in the [Persian] gulf while it has been prevented from playing a role in helping to find a just solution to the question of the Muslim people in Palestine in spite of the fact that more than 50 years have passed since [the UN partition of Palestine creating Israel, whereby] the Israeli enemy usurped the land of Palestine?

Whenever an American, a Westerner or an Israeli is involved in [a] simple incident, there is an international hue and cry, all the United Nations organizations spring into action and governments throughout the world rise up in his defense under the slogan of protection of human rights, in contrast to their attitudes toward the massacres . . . [in various parts of the Muslim world including] the [US] shooting down of a civil aircraft over the gulf, which led to the death of its 300 passengers . . . and the other equally odious massacres that have been committed against our people engaged in the intifada in occupied Palestine. . . . [T]he conventions that have been adopted to protect human rights have been formulated in such a way as to protect the nationals of superpowers, which, in their customary statements, attach no value to persons who do not hold their citizenship. . . .

If the slogan of the need to combat international terrorism is an attempt to divert us from our course of holy struggle in the face of international arrogance, we will continue along the difficult path that we have chosen for ourselves without giving an inch. . . .

Consequently, the question of the detainees [hostages] was a reaction on the part of the Muslim freedom fighters to all those [above] practices and an endeavor to secure the release of our incarcerated fighters. This action will continue as long as they remain incarcerated.

The incalculable sorrow associated with such detentions was personified in the grief of the parents of the young Israeli soldier who was captured and held hostage by Hamas prior to his death in October 1994. The "terrorists," on the other hand, were seeking self-determination to secure their geographical version of the true State of Palestine. They are dissatisfied with the geographical version of Palestine accepted by PLO Chairman Yasir Arafat during the 1993 Washington Peace Accords with Israel, which brought some degree of autonomy to the Palestinians in Gaza and the city of Jericho. Absent the military power of the "occupying powers," terrorism is their only weapon. Funding and training necessarily involve the aid of one or more States that clandestinely support the objectives of the Islamic Jihad, Hamas, and other such "terrorist" organizations.

Solutions? There have been a number of UN attempts to cultivate solutions to international terrorism. The 1973 General Assembly Resolution on Measures to Prevent International Terrorism One was probably the first with significant potential. There was a lack of precision, however, in articulating a widely acceptable definition of "terrorism." This disconnect narrowed the Resolution's potential effectiveness. The General Assembly's underlying *Report of the Ad Hoc Committee on International Terrorism* (produced after seventeen meetings) did not arrive at any conclusions, except that this was a complex problem requiring further study. Only one of the delegations submitted a draft proposal dealing with State terrorism and the eradication of its underlying causes as a solution. This nonaligned delegation, led by Algeria, proposed that the following circumstances had to be changed for terrorism to be dissipated: eradication of colonial domination, elimination of racial discrimination, and strict implementation of the Declaration on Principles of International Law Concerning Friendly Relations and Co-operation Among States in Accordance with the Charter of the United Nations (*see* §10.2).[66]

The UN's 1979 Hostage Convention soon followed. It was spawned by events like the Iranian Hostage Crisis (*see* §7.4). The 1976 Entebbe incident was fresh on the minds of those who wanted to limit the problem of State rescue missions in response to international terrorism (*see* §10.5). Hostage taking had also violated various air hijacking conventions of the 1970s (*see* §6.4). Since their drafting, there had been a number of hostage-taking incidents in the Middle East, apparently supported by various States in the region. The reality, of course, is that significant steps will materialize only by steps taken at the *national* level within each State. There must be a willingness to directly address this problem through legislation to implement the principles of treaties like the 1979 Hostage Convention.

In 1985, the UN Security Council and General Assembly adopted similar terrorism declarations: the Resolution Condemning Hostage Taking (Council) and Measures to Prevent International Terrorism (Assembly).[67] The Security Council Resolution was adopted unanimously. The General Assembly Resolution was adopted without a vote. However, neither document mentioned specific instances of *State* terrorism. Both articulations were geared toward *individual* acts of terrorism rather than directly confronting the questions of *State* responsibility for conduct condemned in these unassailable resolutions. (Any State clandestinely pursuing international terrorism would not be likely to disagree in principle.)

UN attempts to control international terrorism have been dismal at best. The UN definition of aggression effectively works at cross purposes with controlling State-sponsored terrorism. As articulated by Chief Counsel to the US Senate Foreign Relations Committee Robert Friedlander in 1993:

> The Definition of Aggression, adopted by the General Assembly resolution of December 14, 1974, after a quarter-century of debate and disagreement, clearly indicates that forcible attacks against a victim state by "armed bands, groups, irregulars or mercenaries," sponsored by another state, are in direct violation of the U.N. Charter. However, there is an exception . . . for violent national liberation movements, legitimating a legal cloak which many terrorist organizations (such as the PLO) have since wrapped around themselves. Therefore, armed attacks—presumptively by terrorist groups—under the banner of self-determination become . . . not only permissible, but also legally justified. The implications for a global rule of law are distressingly self-evident.[68]

Some *regional* approaches to this global problem directly address State terrorism. Certain European pronouncements prohibit State-sponsored terrorism, although they are not treaties and do not yet have any legally binding force. But they do represent the most concrete consensus of a large bloc of States on applicable principles. The 1975 Helsinki Accords, or Final Act of the Conference on Security and Cooperation in Europe (now OSCE—*see* §3.5), *recommends* that members refrain from direct or indirect assistance to terrorist activities or employ subversive activities directed toward the violent overthrow of the regime of another State. Subsequent confidence-building measures add that no State member is to allow the use of its territory by terrorist groups.[69]

The other major denunciation of State terrorism was the 1978 Bonn Anti-Hijacking Declaration, promulgated under the auspices of the Group of Seven Economic Summit Industrial Powers (US, UK, France, Canada, Italy, West Germany, and Japan). It admonished State regimes about that group's reaction should any State harbor air hijackers or hostage takers. Members threatened to terminate air travel to any State that provided a safe haven for such individuals. Their first sanction was announced at the 1981 Ottawa Economic Summit and directed at Afghanistan for its harboring of international terrorists—long before the 1998 "bin Laden" affair whereby a Saudi citizen used Afghan bases to plan and execute terrorist bombings at US embassies in Kenya and Tanzania (*see* §7.2).

ARMS SALES

The unrestricted sale of weapons to States or private organizations is another dimension of State terrorism. This is a high-profit, high-demand international business.

The notion of limiting arms sales is not new. In 1789, English philosopher and writer Jeremy Bentham proposed an arms-control regime. This was his cure for curbing the widespread use of armaments. Otherwise, peace would not be attainable because Europe would fail to do the following: limit the number of troops, implement treaty controls on the quantity of armaments, and establish a court for settling international differences. One commentator aptly characterized the historical penchant for arms races: "The threat of war and the need to prepare for it are as old as civilization itself. . . . The reason is simple and stated in the [biblical] quotation from Joel: 'Let the weak say I am strong.' The status quo is not universally accepted and is challenged by a variety of groups with some frequency. War, the preparation for war, and strategies to change the status quo with the least cost to the challenger are an integral part of human history."[70]

The UN did not exactly beat swords into plowshares. The five permanent members of the UN Security Council account for 85 percent of the world's international trade in armaments. During Iraq's 1980–1988 war with Iran, the US exported huge amounts of weapons to Iraq. During the fourteen-year period prior to the Persian Gulf War arms embargo on Iraq, the five permanent members sold arms in the Middle East worth $163 billion. Then, in 1991, the five Council members agreed in principle on arms-export rules to limit the ability of States like Iraq to amass huge weapons arsenals. The 1991 "rules" contained no sanctions, however. Only peer pressure could limit their engagement in international arms sales on a smaller scale than in previous decades. By 1992, it appeared that these rules would not be considered in future negotiations. One source for this conclusion is the UN Conventional Arms Register established in 1992. Its purpose is to obtain disclosure of *all* international arms sales. Of course, not all are reported. Of those that have been disclosed, it is clear that arms sales are decreasing. But the decrease is not at the levels hoped for as a result of the 1991 "agreement" between the major arms exporters—the five permanent members of the UN Security Council.

Since the 1991 Security Council Permanent Five agreement, sales have both increased and decreased—depending on region. There was a reduction in the *world* aggregate military expenditure through the middle 1990s while procurement in two regions greatly *increased*. A Turkish economist, Dr. Saadet Deger, who is senior researcher for the Stockholm World Military Expenditure Project (1989–1992), traces the essential changes in such expenditures in the 1990s: "The central reason for the fall in world military expenditure in [the] aggregate is the halving of defence spending in one year by the Commonwealth of Independent States (CIS) countries [after the Cold War]. This aspect of 'shock therapy' in those countries has made the major contribution to international demilitarization. In the developing world [however], military spending rose in the Middle East and the Far East but fell in all other regions."[71] The 1996 report of the US Arms Control and Disarmament Agency reveals a significant increase in developing countries, starting in 1995. As stated by its director:

> Military spending took an upward turn in the developing countries as a group as well as in a number of regions, notably East Asia and South America, after

> dropping since 1986 except for the Gulf War years. Arms imports by the developing countries also turned up sharply in 1995, with increases appearing in the Middle East, East Asia, South America, and South and Central Asia.
>
> Although the long term implication of these trends may be cloudy, it is clear that the work of arms control and nonproliferation is far from over. That conviction is supported by the difficulties being encountered in many of the growing number of international peacekeeping efforts, the ominous threat of terroism, the military disorder in a number of regions, and the persistence of armed conflict around the globe.
>
> In fact, the work of arms control and nonproliferation is daily facing new challenges and taking new paths. It is imperative that the toilers in this vineyard maintain and even increase their dedication, their persistent efforts, and ultimately, their successes, despite setbacks and discouragements.[72]

The Middle East is not the only region adversely affected by the lucrative arms sales business. In 1994, Africa's Catholic bishops pleaded with Western nations to halt their arms sales on that continent. Weapons exports were kindling ethnic bloodshed in Rwanda, for example. They complained that the West was contributing to tribal warfare via the introduction of arms into African nations. What happened later that year in Rwanda is, unfortunately, proof positive of the significance of this warning.

The ultimate control of arms exports will depend, of course, on the degree to which the international community determines that there is a State obligation to regulate arms exports. If so, then there would be State responsibility for its breach. For example, Iraq's decade-long weapons buildup during its war with Iran was facilitated by Western arms sales for a variety of purposes: to defeat Iran, to spar with Cold War adversaries, to control *which* Middle East power would have superior weaponry, and to obtain the profits that another major weapons-exporting power would obtain in the event of any unilateral cutback. The 1998 India–Pakistani nuclear confrontation did not occur simply because a local scientist independently rediscovered nuclear fission.

In 1998, both the UN and the European Union conducted negotiations designed to curb the sale of arms. This was the first year that the US endorsed a UN firearms resolution. In 1997, the Organization of American States adopted similar regulations. The arms race is currently limited to the planet Earth. Will today's arms-exporting States comply with the international treaties (§6.4) that require that outer space remain a weapons-free environment?

◆ 10.8 UNITED STATES WAR POWERS RESOLUTION

This chapter on the use of force ends with *US* control of its own war potential. There is a growing trend toward democracy throughout the globe, evolving in the aftermath of the Cold War. However, the pressures of being the remaining superpower are also expanding. Other States, international organizations such as the UN and the European Union, non-governmental actors, and private entities often look to the US for various forms of support in this facet of their international relations. While many Americans do not want the US to act as the world's policeman, many others would like to see *more* American involvement in foreign conflicts. There may be no choice as new threats surface in the new millennium.

BALANCE OF POWER ENIGMA

Who controls the national war power? This separation-of-power dilemma hinges on the Constitutional allocation of power between the legislative and executive branches of government. Article I §8 of the US Constitution gives *Congress* the following powers: to declare war, to raise and support armies, to provide and maintain a navy, and to make rules governing their operations. Article II §2 makes the *President* the commander-in-chief of the army and navy, as well as the militia of the states (reserve units), when they are called on for active duty. The basic problem arises when Congress does *not* declare war but the President decides to use US military forces in foreign conflicts.

The *judicial* branch of the federal government plays a comparatively minor role in foreign affairs. It may interpret the Constitution or federal legislation when called upon to assess the use of power in ways that allegedly violate the Constitution. The courts usually dismiss cases involving such "political questions," however (*see* §9.8). The courts do not perceive themselves as capable of second-guessing the appropriateness of a decision to engage US troops in a foreign theater.

Prior to the 1973 "Watergate" incident, the US Supreme Court did exercise some degree of control over claimed executive excesses in the President's use of the national war power. For example, the US Supreme Court invalidated President Truman's seizure of US steel mills when he sought to thereby avert a strike during the Korean War.[73] Since the Korean conflict, US presidents have undertaken numerous foreign engagements that frustrated Congress. That body reacted to what its members perceived as relative powerlessness to control the presidential conduct of foreign military affairs. After the Watergate incident, which led to the first presidential resignation from office, Congress seized the opportunity to legislate a greater role for itself in military matters. Elliot Richardson, former US cabinet member and ambassador, stated that: "Congress became ever more frustrated as Presidents unilaterally committed this country to a series of controversial policies, including the Berlin airlift, the Bay of Pigs invasion, intervention in the Dominican Republic, and engagement in the Cuban Missile Crisis—seeking legislative approval after the fact, if at all. It was not until the Nixon Presidency was weakened by the dual political crises of Vietnam and Watergate that Congress was able to reassert itself. The stage was set, with a restless and increasingly active Congress seeking to assert its powers by confronting a President whose personal and political powers were waning."[74]

WAR POWERS RESOLUTION

Congress then passed the War Powers Resolution (WPR) in 1973. The stated purpose of this legislation is to "insure that the *collective* judgment of both the Congress and the President will apply to the *introduction* of United States Armed Forces into hostilities . . . and to the *continued use* of such forces in hostilities. . . ."[75] The WPR objective has been to limit the presidential exercise of the commander-in-chief's power to introduce military forces into foreign conflicts or potential conflicts *only* in the following circumstances: when Congress has already declared war, when Congress has specifically provided statutory authorization to do so, or in cases of national emergency created by an attack on the US.

This legislation requires the President "in every possible instance" to consult with Congress *prior* to introducing armed forces into hostilities—and after they are so engaged. This legislation requires the President, absent a declaration of war (the Vietnam impasse), to submit a written report to the House and the Senate within two days of sending forces abroad for combat purposes. The President must report on the need for such action, the constitutional or legislative authority for it, and the "estimated scope and duration of the hostilities or [other] involvement." Within sixty days of the report, the President must terminate the foreign involvement. Exceptions occur when Congress has declared war in the interim, has extended the involvement, or is unable to meet due to an armed attack on the US. And under *any* circumstances, the Congress may cause the President to withdraw US armed forces from a foreign involvement "if the Congress so directs by concurrent resolution."

This congressional augmentation of its role in foreign conflicts has by no means put to rest the question of its legitimacy. The WPR arguably invades the separation-of-powers doctrine if it unnecessarily restricts the commander-in-chief's ability to carry out his or her function of leading the nation's military in appropriate conflicts. Presidents always assert that they know best. Alternatively, the WPR gives Congress at least the apparent authority to exercise a significant role in foreign affairs. It would otherwise lie dormant, when Congress chooses not to go to war. In the final analysis, Congress could control the military purse strings by not continuing to finance US military operations abroad.

While there have been some two dozen general presidential reports to Congress, one could argue that the WPR is not working as Congress intended. Since its passage in 1973, the reporting requirement has not stopped US Presidents from introducing military forces into combat or near-combat situations—Haiti, Iraq, Panama, and Grenada, for example. Only President Ford thought it necessary to make the specific type of report that triggers the sixty-day reporting period and the ability of Congress to force termination of the action.

Imperfect WPR drafting yielded a number of circumventions by US Presidents to avoid making the type of report giving Congress the ability to terminate the particular action. As aptly characterized by New York University Professor Thomas Franck: "The War Powers Resolution was a good idea, but its drafting and execution were faulty. Instead of authorizing the President to use the armed forces in limited circumstances—such as armed attack on US forces, possessions or, perhaps, citizens—for as long as necessary, it authorized their use in unlimited circumstances for a fixed period. This stands the Constitution on its head."[76]

In August 1994, a unanimous vote of the Senate (100–0) determined that UN Security Council measures regarding Haiti would not relieve President Clinton of the obligation to comply with the WPR. This was reminiscent of the prior 177–37 House vote that "required" President Bush to obtain congressional approval for the deployment of troops for the Persian Gulf War. President Clinton nevertheless responded that "like my predecessors of both parties, I have not agreed that I was constitutionally mandated to get prior congressional authorization" [for US intervention in Haiti].

In May 1999, the Congress next "addressed" the WPR in the context of US forces previously committed to support and conduct NATO's military attack on Yugoslavia. Congress did not actually pursue application of the WPR, which could have squarely limited the President's authority to deploy troops without congressional authorization—a proposition of dubious constitutional validity because there is one commander-in-chief (not 535). The House of Representatives did not vote in favor of three articulated alternatives: declaring war, ending the bombing in Yugoslavia, or endorsing the air war. Members did vote, however, to require the President to seek congressional authority should he wish to commit US forces to a ground war. The Senate's parliamentarian ruled that a debate on Kosovo was required under the WPR. Senate leaders (and the White House), however, sidestepped this debate by raising—and then tabling—a resolution that would have authorized the President to use "all necessary force" to achieve NATO objectives in Kosovo. This scenario thus presented an eerie resemblance to the Vietnam conflict and the ensuing passage of the 1973 WPR.

The daunting question is whether the WPR makes sense in an International Law context. The UN supposedly has the monopoly to use force to deal with threats to peace. President Bush did not go to the Congress for approval when the US participated in the Persian Gulf War. There had been numerous UN Security Council resolutions that condemned Iraq's various threats to peace. Legislation introduced in 1995, if enacted into law, would significantly alter the existing war powers statute. It would limit US involvement in future UN peacekeeping operations and the ability of the US President to delegate control of US military forces to a foreign commander.

The activism of the UN Security Council—whether premised on the close of the Cold War or because of the widely condemned Iraqi takeover of Kuwait under Saddam Hussein—precipitated a new phase in the ongoing presidential–congressional rivalry about the source of authority for deploying military forces abroad. President Bush's somewhat radical position was that he did not have to act pursuant to the WPR. The UN Security Council had authorized US involvement in the Persian Gulf War (although Bush did request and obtain congressional approval to use armed forces for the purposes articulated by the Security Council).

◆ SUMMARY

1. In prior eras, war was not condemned. It was often waged as a "just" war, based on the alleged unjustness of another nation's conduct. At the beginning of the twentieth century, Russia promoted the Hague Conferences, which were designed to *control* the ways in which war would be conducted. While war was condemned in the 1928 Kellogg–Briand Peace Pact, this paradigm was ignored by many members of the international community. Now the most fundamental norm in International Law is the contemporary prohibition on the use of force as embodied in Article 2.4 of the UN Charter.
2. *Force* is a broad term that encompasses many variables. Some relevant factors in assessing its legality include whether the particular mode is aggressive or defensive; military, economic, or some other form of coercion; or used unilaterally by a State or multilaterally by an international organization whose function is to control threats to peace.
3. The various forms of force include coercive measures such as reprisals; low-intensity conflicts, such as when one State supports a rebel force within another State; economic countermeasures, such as freezing assets or boycotting goods from a certain country; embargoes to keep goods from entering the target nation; and "gunboat" diplomacy in which one State stations its forces near another's borders in a threatening show of military strength.
4. The key UN Charter provisions regarding the use of force are Articles 2.4 and 51. The first prohibits force or the threat of its use in International Relations. The latter article authorizes the use of force as a legitimate response to an "armed" attack. The "improvements" in weapons technology have

prompted reliance on "anticipatory" self-defense in State practice. Attempting to respond *after* an armed attack would be suicidal.

5. Chapter VII of the UN Charter legally vests the Security Council with the legal monopoly on the use of force. The standing army provision of Article 43 never materialized. The Council may authorize multilateral action via its resolutions, which other powerful States may then employ as bases for their use of force to alleviate the particular threat to peace.
6. Given the breadth of the Charter norms and the lack of definitional precision, the UN General Assembly promulgated two subsequent declarations. The 1970 Declaration prohibits "propaganda, terror, and finance" as means of coercing another State into acting in a particular way. The 1987 Declaration prohibits organizing or assisting in the execution of paramilitary, terrorist, or subversive acts. States must also avoid "economic, political, or any other type of measure to coerce another State" for the purpose of securing advantages of *any* kind. The 1998 Declaration generally prohibits coercive economic measures as a means of political and economic compulsion.
7. There is a contemporary problem with ascertaining the precise nature of the "right" of *collective* self-defense. In the 1986 *Nicaragua* case, the International Court of Justice denied US reliance on this principle as a basis for justifying its intervention in Nicaragua. This was a legal basis, however, for multilateral action in the UN-authorized Persian Gulf War against Iraq after its 1990 invasion of Kuwait.
8. UN operations have traditionally been undertaken as peace*keeping*, rather than peace*making*. State consent of the involved territories has been a condition precedent to UN involvement. UN efforts to incorporate an offensive or first-strike posture (e.g., Somalia) resulted in unforeseen problems and added dangers. There was a lack of clarity about the UN's role as a military force that traditionally maintains rather than seeks to alter the status quo.
9. The Security Council's impotence is the product of insufficient State resolve to endow the UN with the requisite degree of power to act independently of the wishes of its member States. The veto power of any one of the five permanent members is a contributing factor. The members' frustration materialized in the Uniting for Peace Resolution of 1950. The General Assembly therein proclaimed its right to act in lieu of the Security Council where the Council would not exercise its "primary" obligation to control threats to peace. This resolution served as the basis for certain peacekeeping operations.
10. There have been a number of multilateral attempts to control State uses of force via international treaties. Key regional and global initiatives are summarized in Exhibit 10.2.
11. Humanitarian intervention is often claimed as the legitimizing basis for State uses of force. The objective is to come to the aid of people in another nation when they are unable to fend for themselves in time of need. What constitutes the "need" is, of course, subject to disagreement. The UN Charter does not answer the question of the degree to which States may undertake collective humanitarian intervention without UN approval.
12. It is often said that danger invites rescue. There may be a limited basis for justifying unilateral rescue missions when a State's citizens face certain death at the hands of terrorists or a State that is unwilling to come to the aid of those in danger.
13. The Laws of War are designed to govern the treatment of various classes of individuals during military hostilities. The famous 1949 Geneva Conventions are the primary source of this control of the use of force. Defenseless civilians and prisoners of war are entitled to a minimum level of treatment so as to avoid the degradation that occurs in the absence of control.
14. Terrorism is a form of force that is theoretically subject to multilateral control via various treaties. Unfortunately, one person's terrorist is often another's hero. For the perpetrators, the end justifies the means. Methods include the sabotaging of commercial aircraft to indiscriminately kill civilian passengers. Such acts bring attention to the plights of the terrorist. But dealing with the effects, rather than the causes, will not eradicate this form of force.
15. The powerful States of the world are responsible for some of the contemporary problems with the many conflicts that have surfaced after the Cold War. The five permanent members of the Security Council—the US, Great Britain, France, Russia, and China—are responsible for approximately 85 percent of global arms sales. In 1991, they promulgated guidelines to limit such sales. These "rules" have not been followed, however.

◆ PROBLEMS

Problem 10.A (§10.2 after 1970, 1987 UN Declarations) Refer to the *Alvarez-Machain* case, contained in §5.3 of this book. Assume that the same incident occurred in Panama *prior* to General Noriega's extraction by US military forces during the US invasion of Panama in 1990 (discussed in §9.8). In this hypothetical scenario in Panama, a Panamanian doctor is extracted by US Drug Enforcement agents from Panama during a clandestine mission, resulting in Doctor X having to stand trial in the US on international drug-trafficking charges.

Noriega decides that he must take decisive action to strengthen his position because of the hypothetical US abduction of a Panamanian doctor from Panama. In a speech to the people of Panama, General Noriega declares as follows:

> The atrocity perpetrated this week by US authorities demonstrates the imperialistic attitude of the US toward Panama's political independence, territorial sovereignty, and its indisputable right to self-determination. I am thus forced to take measures to counter the continued unlawful operations of US forces in our beloved nation. Because humanitarian concerns do not guide the actions of the US, I must focus US attention upon our sovereign rights by using economic countermeasures. This morning, I ordered Panama's Minister of Banking and Commerce to seize all bank accounts and assets belonging to US citizens.

The US President responds to this expropriation by imposing an embargo on all goods from Panama. The US Customs Service refuses to allow any products from Panama to enter the US.

Do Panama's bank account seizures and the US embargo violate the principle of International Law that prohibits the State use of force? If so, *how?*

Problem 10.B (§10.2 after 1970, 1987 UN Declarations) In the 1970s, Ecuador and the US were embroiled in a fishing dispute over the breadth of Ecuador's territorial water zone. Ecuador claimed a territorial sea of 200 nautical miles. The US claimed that customary State practice permitted only a twelve-mile claim.

Ecuador seized fourteen US tuna fishing boats in its "territorial sea"—well beyond twelve miles from its coast—and would not return them unless the owners paid significant licensing fees. At the same time, the US encouraged its commercial fishing fleet to fish in Ecuador's two-hundred-mile zone. Congress passed legislation under which the owners of the captured tuna boats were reimbursed when their boats were seized or they had to pay Ecuador's license fees. The US responded to these boat seizures by suspending its sales of military supplies to Ecuador. Ecuador then claimed that the US had used illegal economic and political force by withholding these vital exports needed for its defense.

Assume that representatives of the US and Ecuador are debating this incident in the UN General Assembly. Two students (or groups) will present the positions of Ecuador and the US on the following question: Did either the US or Ecuador violate the UN Charter's prohibition against the use of force?

Problem 10.C (§10.2 after Cuban Missile Crisis Materials) Did the US properly invoke UN Charter Article 51's provision regarding the use of self-defense in the case of an "armed attack?"

Problem 10.D (§10.2 after Article 51 Materials) In April 1993, after US President Bush left office, he traveled to Kuwait. After returning, the US discovered that Saddam Hussein had planned the assassination of President Bush during this visit. The US responded in June 1993 by launching several missiles into Baghdad. The US claimed that an unsuccessful armed attack on a former head of State justified this responsive use of force as Article 51 self-defense.

The UN Security Council had authorized States to take "all necessary measures" to subdue Iraq's behavior related to the Persian Gulf War over its aggression in Kuwait. Not responding might suggest to Saddam Hussein that Iraq might continue to operate as a rogue State with no countermeasures to control his excesses.

Two students—one representing Iraq, and one representing the US—will debate whether a State's use of force in these circumstances is justifiable self-defense as opposed to a mere reprisal.

Problem 10.E (end of §10.4) In 1981 and 1982, fourteen petitions on behalf of approximately 5,000 inhabitants of the Marshall Islands were filed in the US Court of Claims (Washington, D.C.) to claim damages said to result from the US program to test nuclear weapons during the period from June 30, 1946, to August 18, 1958. The US program included detonation of 23 atomic and hydrogen bombs at Bikini Atoll and 43 nuclear bombs at Enewetak Atoll, and they required the removal of the inhabitants and their relocation. There was severe physical destruction at both atolls and radioactive contamination of parts of the Marshall Islands chain. Claimed damages ranged from $450 million to $600 million. This case and similar ones have been dismissed on a variety grounds including the statute of limitations, US sovereign immunity from suit, and lack of the court's power to hear this type of case because it poses a "political question." *See, e.g., Juda v. US,* 13 Claims Ct. 667 (1987), appeal dismissed by *People of Bikini v. US,* 859 *Fed. Rptr. 2d* 1482 (Fed. Cir. 1988). In 1994, US newspapers ran stories regarding the US disclosure of more than 200 previously undisclosed underground nuclear tests in the US since World War II.

Assume that some of these 200 nuclear tests occurred *in* 1994. Would the US thereby have violated any of the multilateral agreements mentioned in this chapter? Would it matter if the 1994 tests were conducted either inside or outside of the US?

Problem 10.F (end of §10.5) The border separating the hypothetical nations of North Alpha and South Bravo is lined with military installations on both sides. Both nations are members of the United Nations. Alpha and Bravo recently signed a bilateral treaty in which they agreed that neither State may use or encourage the use of coercive measures of an economic or political character. They further agreed that neither could force its objectives on the sovereign will of the other State or attempt to use force to obtain advantages of any kind.

Their international relations are now very poor. A small band of Alpha's military troops covertly crossed the border into Bravo and disappeared into Bravo's heartland. Bravo's leader learns about this clandestine military operation and decides that he must respond to this threat. He takes some prominent visiting Alpha citizens as hostages. He then announces that they will remain under house arrest in an unknown location in Bravo. The Alpha troops in Bravo are given an ultimatum by Bravo's leader in a widely broadcasted radio and television message: The Alpha soldiers must surrender to Bravo authorities or the Alpha civilian hostages will be executed, one each day, until Alpha's troops surrender.

Alpha's military forces in Bravo decide not to surrender. Instead, they plan a hostage-rescue mission. An Alpha military plane, loaded with specially trained Alpha soldiers, flies into Bravo to assist them. All of the Alpha soldiers in Bravo then join forces at a predetermined rendezvous point near the city where the Alpha citizens are being held. Bravo is not surprised. Bravo's military troops ambush and kill all of the Alpha soldiers. Bravo's leader then orders the mass execution of all Alpha hostages.

Did Alpha's rescue mission violate any international norms? Was there any justification?

Problem 10.G (end of §10.6) In 1972, the US conducted carpet bombing of Hanoi. During the negotiations to end the Vietnam War, President Nixon decided to bomb Hanoi in order to bring an end to the Vietnam War. The city contained many military targets. Being the seat of government for North Vietnam, the city was also home to a large number of civilians who were killed by the thousands. The following news report explains carpet bombing, its impact on the civilian populace, and the basis for a claim arising under the Geneva Conventions:

> Air raid sirens scream day and night. The earth trembles with the violence of an earthquake, and whole sections of the city crumble in a roar of flames and jagged steel. For the first time in the war the people seem afraid.
>
> This is Hanoi under attack by American B-52's, as described by Westerners who have been there. The big bombers, flying in wedges of three, lay down more than 65 tons of bombs at a time in a carpet pattern a mile and a half long and a half mile wide.
>
> For nearly two weeks now the city has been the focal point of a siege by American bombers that has extended across the densely populated heart of North Vietnam. Hundreds, if not thousands, of civilians are believed to have been killed. (*New York Times,* Dec. 31, 1972)

This incident focused attention on the 1949 Geneva Convention on the Protection of Civilian Persons in Time of War. A belligerent may not intentionally direct military force at civilian targets. While some civilian casualties cannot be avoided, a State cannot annihilate the civilian populace of the enemy to gain tactical or psychological advantages in time of war. North Vietnam's claimed violation of the Geneva Convention was never tested in an international tribunal. (Nor was its mistreatment of American POWs, particularly downed pilots captured in North Vietnam.)

The following account was written by a seven-year inmate of the infamous "Hanoi Hilton" (the subject of several American movies). This was a North Vietnamese prison complex where the interrogations brutalized mostly American pilots shot down over North Vietnam. One American inmate, Render Crayton, wrote that the Christmas bombings were responsible for bringing an end to the war (not unlike President Truman's 1945 decision to drop atomic bombs on the cities of Hiroshima and Nagasaki to end the war with Japan). In support of the US bombings, Crayton wrote as follows:

> Maybe North Vietnam was willing to *talk* about peace, but during the bombing pause that began in October 1972, Hanoi was resupplying its troops and rebuilding its air defense system. . . . The B-52 strikes during Christmas conveyed the required notice that it was time to talk seriously or else.
>
> From a cell in the Hanoi Hilton, I and many other Americans had close encounters during those 11 days of bombings. After seven years of sitting out an on-again, off-again war . . . it was clear to me that the B-52s carried a . . . message: this time we meant business. It was a long-awaited Christmas present. . . .
>
> The same fear that overcame the guards and the people in the streets undoubtedly was reflected in the willingness of their leaders to hustle back to the [negotiating] table [in Paris], this time ready for serious talks.
>
> [I]t was Congress . . . that helped drag out the Vietnam War. It was President Nixon, with the Christmas bombings, who put an end to it. (*San Diego Union-Tribune*, Jan. 7, 1993.)

Did the US carpet bombing violate any Laws of War? Was there any justification? Would the 1977 Protocol to the Geneva Convention play any role in your analysis?

◆ BIBLIOGRAPHY

§10.1 Defining "Force" and Its Role

I. Brownlie, *International Law and the Use of Force by States* (Oxford, Eng.: Oxford Univ. Press, 1963) (classic study).

W. Butler, *The Non-Use of Force in International Law* (Dordrecht, Neth.: Martinus Nijhoff, 1989).

E. Corr & S. Sloan (eds.), *Low-Intensity Conflict: Old Threats in a New World* (Boulder, CO: Westview Press, 1992).

W. Dixon, "Democracy and the Peaceful Settlement of International Conflict," 88 *American Political Science Review* 14 (1994).

T. Ehrlich & M. O'Connell, *International Law and the Use of Force* (Boston: Little, Brown & Co., 1993).

B. Jankovic, "International Conflicts," ch. 4 in *Public International Law* 347 (Dobbs Ferry, NY: Transnat'l Pub., 1984) (Yugoslavian perspective).

J. Lobel & M. Ratner, "Bypassing the Security Council: Ambiguous Authorizations to Use Force, Ceasefires, and the Iraqi Inspection Regime," 93 *Amer. J. Int'l Law* 124 (1999).

A. Rifat, *International Aggression—A Study of the Legal Concept: Its Development and Definition in International Law* (Stockholm: Almqvist & Wiksell Int'l, 1979).

§10.2 United Nations Charter Principles

S. Alexandrov, *Self-Defense Against the Use of Force in International Law* (The Hague, Neth.: Kluwer Law Int'l, 1996).

R. Amer, *The United Nations and Foreign Military Interventions: A Comparative Study of the Application of the Charter* (Uppsala, Sweden: Uppsala Univ., 1992).

Y. Dinstein, *War, Aggression and Self-Defence* (2nd ed. Cambridge, Eng.: Grotius, 1994).

L. Henkin, "Law and War after the Cold War," 15 *Maryland J. Int'l L. & Trade* 147 (1991).

T. Buergenthal & H. Maier, "International Organizations, Peace and Defense," §3-24 to §3-27 in *Public International Law in a Nutshell* 57 (2nd ed. St. Paul: West, 1990).

I. Johnstone, *Aftermath of the Gulf War: An Assessment of UN Action* (Boulder, CO: Lynne Reinner, (1994).

T. McCormack, *Self-Defense in International Law: The Israeli Raid on The Iraqi Reactor* (Jerusalem: Magnes Press, Hebrew University, 1996).

§10.3 Peacekeeping Operations

L. Davis, *Peacekeeping and Peacemaking After the Cold War* (Santa Monica, CA: Rand Inst., 1993).

P. Diehl, *International Peacekeeping* (Baltimore: Johns Hopkins Press, 1993).

R. Diekmann, *Basic Documents on United Nations and Related Peace-Keeping Forces* (2nd ed. Dordrecht, Neth.: Martinus Nijhoff, 1989).

G. Garvey, *United Nations Peacekeeping and Host State Consent,* 64 *Amer. J. Int'l Law* 642 (1984).

UN, *The Blue Helmets: A Review of United Nations Peace-Keeping* (2nd ed. New York: UN, 1990).

§10.4 Multilateral Agreements on Force

D. Bourantonis, *The United Nations and the Quest for Nuclear Disarmament* (Brookfield, VT: Dartmouth, 1993).

S. Croft (ed.), *The Conventional Armed Forces in Europe Treaty: The Cold War Endgame* (Brookfield, VT: Dartmouth, 1994).

D. Paul (ed.), *Disarmaments Mission Dimension: A UN Agency to Administer Multilateral Treaties* (Toronto: S. Stevens, 1990).

R. Powell, "Crisis Bargaining, Escalation and MAD," 81 *Amer. Pol. Sci. Rev.* 717 (1987).

D. Schindler & J. Toman (ed.), *The Law of Armed Conflict: A Collection of Conventions, Resolutions and Other Documents* (3rd rev. ed. Geneva: Henry Durant Inst., 1988).

§10.5 Humanitarian Intervention

P. Schraeder, *Intervention in the 1990s: US Foreign Policy in the Third World* (Boulder, CO: Lynne Reinner Pub., 1992).

F. Teson, *Humanitarian Intervention: An Inquiry into Law and Morality* (2nd ed. Irvington, NY: Transnat'l, 1997).

B. Weston, R. Falk, & A. D'Amato, *Unilateral Intervention,* in *International Law and World Order* 867 (2nd ed. St. Paul: West, 1990).

§10.6 Laws of War

L. Green, *Essays on the Modern Law of War* (2nd ed. Ardsley, NY: Transnat'l, 1999).

Helsinki Watch, *War Crimes in Bosnia-Hercegovina* (New York: Human Rights Watch, 1992).

L. Henkin et al., "The Law of War and the Control of Weapons," in *International Law* 1019 (3rd ed. St. Paul: West, 1993).

W. Krutzsch & R. Trapp, *A Commentary on the Chemical Weapons Convention* (Dordrecht, Neth.: Martinus Nijhoff, 1994).

T. McCormack & G. Simpson, *The Law of War Crimes: National and International Approaches* (The Hague, Neth.: Kluwer Law Int'l, 1997).

M. McDougal & F. Feliciano, *The International Law of War: Transnational Coercion and World Public Order* (Dordrecht, Neth.; Boston: Martinus Nijhoff, 1994).

M. Osiel, *Obeying Orders: Atrocity, Military Discipline & the Law of War* (New Brunswick, NJ: Transaction Publishers, 1998).

"Symposium: The International Humanitarian Law Applicable to Armed Conflict at Sea: Round Table of Experts," 14 *Syracuse Journal of International Law & Commerce* 571 (1988).

§10.7 State Terrorism/Arms Sales

M. Bassiouni (ed.), *Legal Responses to International Terrorism: US Procedural Aspects* (Dordrecht, Neth.: Martinus Nijhoff, 1988).

M. Crenshaw & J. Pimlott (eds.), *Encyclopedia of World Terrorism* (Armonk. NY: M.E. Sharpe, 1997) (three volumes).

D. Dahlitz & D. Dicke (eds.), *The International Law of Arms Control and Disarmament* (New York: UN, 1991) (symposium).

O. Elagab, *International Law Documents Relating to Terrorism* (London: Cavendish, 1995).

J. Lambert, *Terrorism and Hostages in International Law: A Commentary on the Hostages Convention 1979* (Cambridge, Eng.: Grotius, 1990).

§10.8 United States War Powers Resolution

T. Franck, "After the Fall: The New Procedural Framework for Congressional Control over the War Power," 71 *Amer. J. Int'l L.* 605 (1977).

L. Henkin, "Separation of Powers: Competition, Conflict, and Cooperation," ch. IV in *Foreign Affairs and the US Constitution* 83 (2nd ed. Oxford, Eng.: Clarendon Press, 1996).

E. Keynes, "The War Powers Resolution: A Bad Idea Whose Time Has Come and Gone," 23 *Univ. Toledo L. Rev.* 343 (1992).

◆ ENDNOTES

1. Aristotle, *Nichomachaean Ethics* 329 (New York: Penguin, 1976) (H. Tredennick revision, J. Thompson translation).
2. W. Reisman, "Private Armies in a Global War System: Prologue to Decision," in M. McDougal & W. Reisman, *International Law Essays* 142, 154–155 (Mineola, NY: Foundation Press, 1981).
3. "War as a Lawful Instrument of National Policy," 2 *Oppenheim's International Law* 177–178 (Essex, Eng.: Longman, 7th ed. 1952) (H. Lauterpacht edition).
4. *See* M. Mandelbaum, *The Fate of Nations: The Search for National Security in the Nineteenth and Twentieth Centuries* (New York: Cambridge Univ. Press, 1988).
5. "On Protracted War" (May 1938), reprinted in "Quotations from Chairman Mao Tse-Tung," in ch. 5 *On War and Peace* 59 (2nd ed. Peking: Foreign Language Press, 1966).
6. *See* G. Tunkin, "Law Functioning in the International System," ch. 2 in *Law and Force in the International System* 43, 80 (Moscow: Progress Publ., 1983) (1985 English translation).
7. D. Greig, "The Use of Force by States," ch. 16 in *International Law* 867 (2nd ed. London: Butterworths, 1976) (italics added).
8. Dept. of the Army and the Air Force, *Military Operations in Low Intensity Conflict,* Army Field Manual 100-20, Air Force Pamphlet 3-20, p. 1 (Dec. 1990).
9. *See, e.g.,* the representative comment of a critic that "American administrations have exaggerated the Soviet threat so as to keep in line their allies in the North and their clients in the South." "Introduction," G. Arnold, *Wars in the Third World Since 1945* xii (London: Casell, 1991).
10. *Commission on Integrated Long-Term Strategy, Discriminate Deterrence* 2–3 (Wash., DC: US Gov't Print. Off., 1988).
11. Gen. Ass. Res. 2625(XXXV), Part 1 Principles (1970).
12. *See* "The Development of the Doctrine of Reprisals in the Seventeenth and Eighteenth Centuries," ch. 1 in O. Elagab, *The Legality of Non-Forcible Counter-Measures in International Law* (Oxford, Eng.: Clarendon Press, 1988).
13. O. Schachter, "The Right of States to Use Armed Force," 82 *Mich. L. Rev.* 1620, 1633 (1984).
14. *Report of the Special Committee on the Definition of Aggression* 12 UN Gen. Ass. Off. Rec. (Supp. No. 16) 13 (1956). Further details are available in H. McCoubrey & N. White, "Aggression and Armed Attack," ch. 3 in *International Law and Armed Conflict* 39 (Brookfield, VT: Dartmouth Pub., 1992).

15. Gen. Ass. Res. 2625(XXXV 1970), reprinted in 9 *Int'l Legal Mat'ls* 1292 (1970).
16. Gen. Ass. Res. 42/22 (1987), reprinted in 27 *Int'l Legal Mat'ls* 1672 (1988).
17. D. Greig, *International Law* 892–893 (2nd ed. London: Butterworths, 1976) (italics added).
18. L. Meeker, "Defensive Quarantine and the Law," 57 *Amer. J. Int'l L.* 515, 523 (1963).
19. C. Li-hai, "American Imperialism Tramples on International Law," *Chinese People's Daily,* Nov. 14, 1962, at 4; reprinted in Vol. 2 J. Cohen & H. Chiu, *People's China and International Law: A Documentary Study 1461–1464* (Princeton: Princeton Univ. Press, 1974).
20. "Military and Paramilitary Activities in and Against Nicaragua, *(Nicaragua v. United States),*" 1986 *ICJ Rep.* 14, para. 208–209 (italics added) (hereinafter *Nicaragua case).*
21. The various Gulf War resolutions and numerous related documents are collected in W. Weller (ed.), *Iraq and Kuwait: The Hostilities and Their Aftermath* (Cambridge, Eng.: Grotius Pub., 1993).
22. Cuban law: No. 851, July 6, 1960.
23. **Bay of Pigs:** *See* P. Wyden, *Bay of Pigs: The Untold Story* (New York: Simon & Schuster, 1981) (detailing author's six-hour interview with Fidel Castro). **Cuban missile crisis:** *See* anticipatory self-defense analysis earlier in this section.
24. R. Falk, *Introduction* in M. Krinsky & D. Golove, *United States Economic Measures Against Cuba: Proceedings in the United Nations and International Law Issues* 1, 10–11 (Northhampton, MA: Aletheia Press, 1993).
25. D. Sheffer, "Commentary on Collective Security," ch. 8 in L. Damrosch & D. Scheffer (ed.), *Law and Force in the New International Order* 101, 103–104 (Boulder, CO: Westview Press, 1991) (hereinafter *Law and Force).*
26. B. Boutros-Ghali, *Agenda for Peace* 25–26 (New York: UN, 1992) and 1995 *Supplement* at 55–56.
27. Opening Statement of Dr. Edward Warner before the Senate Armed Services Subcommittee on Coalition Defense and Reinforcing Forces, in "US Department of Defense Statement on Peacekeeping," 33 *Int'l Legal Mat'ls* 814 (1994). *See also* D. Scheffer, "US Administration Policy on Reforming Multilateral Peace Operations," 33 *Int'l Legal Mat'ls* 795 (1994) and "US Department of State Statement on the Legal Authority for UN Peace Operations," 33 *Int'l Legal Mat'ls* 821 (1994).
28. N. Ronzitti, "OSCE Peace-Keeping," ch. 8 in M. Bothe et al. (eds.), *The OSCE in the Maintenance of Peace and Security: Conflict Prevention, Crisis Management and Peaceful Settlement of Disputes* 250-251 (The Hague, Neth.: Kluwer Law Int'l, 1997).
29. A succinct and authoritative account of the UN Charter drafting process, including Article 43, is available in B. Simma (ed.), *The Charter of the United Nations: A Commentary* 636–639 (New York: Oxford Univ. Press, 1995).
30. W. Durch (ed.), *The Evolution of UN Peacekeeping* 7 (New York: St. Martin's Press, 1993) (italics added).
31. A detailed account is provided in D. Neff, *Warriors at Suez* (New York: Simon & Schuster, 1981).
32. "Certain Expenses of the United Nations (Advisory Opinion)," 1962 *ICJ Rep.* 151, para. 161 and 177.
33. International Peacekeeping Policy Act of 1995, introduced in the Senate as S.420, 1st Sess., 104th Congress. For text, status, etc., *see* http://thomas.loc.gov/cgi-bin/query/z?c104:S.420.
34. This account is provided in J. McNeill, "Commentary on Dispute Resolution Mechanisms in Arms Control Agreements," ch. 26 in *Law and Force* 258, 259 (cited in note 25).
35. An account of this incident is provided in Spencer, "The Italian–Ethiopian Dispute and the League of Nations," 31 *Amer. J. Int'l L.* 614 (1937).
36. **Historical background:** J. Fonteyne, "The Customary International Law Doctrine of Humanitarian Intervention," 4 *Calif. West. Int'l L.J.* 203 (1974). **Varied definitions:** Bazyler, "Reexamining the Doctrine of Humanitarian Intervention in Light of the Atrocities in Kampuchea and Ethiopia," 23 *Stanford J. Int'l L.* 547 (1987).
37. *See* T. Franck & N. Rodley, "After Bangladesh: The Law of Humanitarian Intervention by Military Force," 67 *Amer. J. Int'l L.* 275, 285 (1973).
38. S. Murphy, *Humanitarian Intervention: The United Nations in an Evolving World Order* 8-10 (Phila., PA: Univ. Pennsylvania Press, 1996). This book was written while the author was on leave at the University of Virginia School of Law.
39. **Humanitarian purposes:** Article 55(c). **Action pledge:** Article 56.
40. *See* R. Lillich (ed.), *Humanitarian Intervention and the United Nations* (Charlottesville, Va.: Univ. Press of Va., 1973).
41. *Nicaragua* case, para. 242 (cited in note 20) (italics added).
42. **UN Gen. Ass. Resolutions:** 43/131, Dec. 8, 1988; 45/100, July 29, 1991; 46/182, Dec. 19, 1991.
43. D. Schindler, "Humanitarian Assistance, Humanitarian Interference and International Law," ch. 46 in R. Macdonald (ed.), *Essays in Honour of Wang Tieya* 689, 700 (Dordrecht, Neth.; Boston: Martinus Nijhoff, 1994).
44. These accounts are provided in "Historical Background," ch. 1 in H. Levie, *Terrorism in War—The Law of War Crimes* 9–10 (Dobbs Ferry, NY: Oceana, 1992) (hereinafter *Law of War Crimes).*
45. T. Kuhn, "Responsibility for Military Conduct and Respect for International Humanitarian Law," in *Dissemination* p. 1 (Aug. 1987) (magazine of the International Committee of the Red Cross).
46. The organization for any useful analysis of this field of law is conveniently structured by reference to Levie's *Law of War Crimes* (cited in note 44 above).
47. 1 *Trial of Military War Crimes* 234–235 (German defendants). This multivolume set contains an exhaustively complete record of the lengthy proceedings. An edited version of the case is set forth in the text of §9.5 (hereinafter referred to as the *Nuremberg Trial).* The same volumes also contain the record of the similar proceedings of the Tokyo defendants also tried by the Allies (hereinafter *Tokyo Trial*].

48. The full text of this Statute, including that part of Article 8 dealing with war crimes in cases of armed conflicts not of an international character, is available at www.un.org/icc/part2.htm.
49. 18 *US Code* §2441 et seq.
50. J. Toman, *The Protection of Cultural Property in the Event of Armed Conflict: Commentary on the Convention for the Protection of Cultural Property in the Event of Armed Conflict and Its Protocol* (Hants, Eng.: Dartmouth, 1996); and K. Jote, *International Legal Protection of Cultural Heritage* (Stockholm: Juristforlaget, 1994).
51. 1 *Nuremberg Trial,* 252 (cited in note 48).
52. 1 *Tokyo Trial,* 231 (cited in note 48).
53. K. Askin, *War Crimes Against Women: Prosecution in International War Crimes Tribunals* 273–274 (The Hague, Neth.: Martinus Nijhoff, 1997).
54. 1 *Nuremberg Trial,* 313 (cited in note 48).
55. **Corfu:** 1949 *ICJ Rep.* 4, p. 22. **Nicaragua:** 1986 *ICJ Rep.* 14, p.112.
56. A. Guttry & N. Ronzitti (eds.), *The Iran–Iraq War (1980–1988) and the Law of Naval Warfare* 7 (Cambridge, Eng.: Grotius, 1993).
57. 4 *Nuremberg Trial,* 466–467 (cited in note 48).
58. The London Conference of 1991 is discussed in G. Plant, *Environmental Protection and the Law of War: A "Fifth Geneva" Convention on the Protection of the Environment in Time of Armed Conflict* (London: Belhaven Press, 1992).
59. *Memorandum of the ICRC to the Governments of States Party to the Geneva Conventions and Members of the United Nations on the Application of the Geneva Conventions by the Armed Forces Placed at the Disposal of United Nations,* 10 November 1961, reprinted in *International Review of the Red Cross* (Geneva: 1961).
60. This widely reported event and others of that era are discussed in W. Slomanson, *ICJ Damages: Tort Remedy for Failure to Punish or Extradite International Terrorists,* 5 *Calif. West. Int'l L.J.* 121 (1973), reprinted in 14 *Comp. Juridical Rev.* 139 (1977).
61. Anti-Terrorism Act, Pub. Law No. 100–204, Title X, §1002, Dec. 22, 1987, 101 *Statutes at Large* 1406, Legislative Findings and Determinations, set forth in 22 *US Code* §5201.
62. Judgment of the Superior Court of Justice, Berlin, in *Sate v. Mykonos* (Apr. 10, 1997). As a result of this decision, security measures at German embassies and consulates, in various European and Middle Eastern cities were increased because this case directly linked the murder of three Kurdish politicians and the government of Iran.
63. *Case of Brogan and Others,* 145-B Euro. Ct. Hum. Rts. (series A) (1988). Analyzed in "Note: The United Kingdom's Obligation to Balance Human Rights and its Anti-Terrorism Legislation: The Case of Brogan and Others," 13 *Fordham Int'l L.J.* 328 (1990).
64. *See* Hearings of March 21, 1988, and April 25, 1989, Sub-Comm. on Aviation of the Comm. on Public Works and Transportation, US House of Representatives (Wash., DC: US Gov't Print. Off., 1989).
65. B. Hoffman, "The Contrasting Ethical Foundations of Terrorism in the 1980s," in *Terrorism and Political Violence* 360, 369 (July 1989).
66. **Report:** UN Gen. Ass. Off. Records: 28th Sess., Supp. No. 28 (A/9028). **Resolution:** UN Gen. Ass. Reso. 3034 (XXVII), UN Doc. A/RES/3068 (1973), reprinted in 13 *Int'l Legal Mat'ls* 218 (1973).
67. **Council:** Resolution 579, Dec. 9, 1985. **Assembly:** Resolution 40/61, Dec. 18, 1985. Both are reprinted in 25 *Int'l Legal Mat'ls* 239 and 243 (1986).
68. R. Friedlander, "Terrorism and the World Community," Epilogue to H. Han (ed.), *Terrorism and Political Violence: Limits and Possibilities of Legal Control* 447, 449–450 (New York: Oceana, 1993).
69. *See* 1983 Concluding Document of Madrid, 1986 Document of the Stockholm Conference, and the 1989 Concluding Document of Vienna, both reproduced in A. Bloed, *The Conference on Security and Cooperation in Europe: Analysis and Basic Documents, 1972–1993* (Dordrecht, Neth.: Martinus Nijhoff, 1993).
70. **1789 proposal:** This historical account of early attempts at arms control is available in J. McNeill, "Commentary on Dispute Resolution Mechanisms in Arms Control Agreements," ch. 26 in L. Damrosch & D. Scheffer (ed.), *Law and Force in the New International Order* 258 (Boulder, CO: Westview Press, 1991). **Quote:** G. Hammond, "Why Study Arms Races?" in *Plowshares into Swords: Arms Races in International Politics, 1840–1991* 3–4 (Columbia, SC: Univ. of So. Caro. Press, 1993).
71. S. Deger, "World Military Expenditure," ch. 9 in *SIPRI Yearbook 1993: World Disarmaments and Disarmament* 337 (Oxford, Eng.: Oxford Univ. Press, 1993). Earlier statistics are available in D. Galik (ed.), *World Military and Arms Transfers 1987* (Wash., DC: US Arms Control and Disarmament Agency, 1988).
72. J. Holum, *Foreward* to *World Military and Arms Transfers 1996* (Wash., DC: US Arms Control and Disarmament Agency, 1997).
73. *Youngstown Sheet & Tube v. Sawyer,* 343 US 579, 72 S.Ct. 863, 96 *L. Ed.* 1153 (1952).
74. E. Richardson, "Checks and Balances in Foreign Relations" in L. Henkin, M. Glennon, & W. Rogers (ed.), *Foreign Affairs and the US Constitution* 27 (Ardsley-on-Hudson, NY: Transnat'l, 1990) (hereinafter *Foreign Affairs and the Constitution).*
75. Pub. Law No. 93-148, 87 *Statutes at Large* 555, 50 *US Code* §1541 (italics added). The following quotes are taken from the remainder of this legislation contained in 50 *US Code* §§1541–1548.
76. T. Franck, *Rethinking War Powers: By Law or by "Thaumaturgic Invocation?"* in *Foreign Affairs and the Constitution* 56, 58–59 (cited in note 74 above).

CHAPTER ELEVEN

Human Rights

CHAPTER OUTLINE

INTRODUCTION

The first ten chapters of this book address the diverse mechanics of International Law. The remaining chapters contain cross-cutting themes, typically offered as separate courses in both undergraduate and law school curricula: human rights, the environment, and economic relations. This survey course in Public International Law would be incomplete without some exposure to the essentials of these pervasive topics.

This chapter addresses the first of these themes—human rights. After a preliminary exploration, these materials will summarize the "International Bill of

(i) JEAN KAMBANDA ADMITS THAT THERE WAS IN Rwanda in 1994 a widespread and systematic attack against the civilian population of Tutsi, the purpose of which was to exterminate them. Mass killings of hundreds of thousands of Tutsi occurred in Rwanda, including women and children, old and young who were pursued and killed at places where they had sought refuge, i.e. prefectures, commune offices, schools, churches and stadiums. . . .

(vii) Jean Kambanda acknowledges that, on or about 21 June 1994, in his capacity as Prime Minister, he gave clear support to Radio Television Libre des Mille Collines (RTLM), with the knowledge that it was a radio station whose broadcasts incited killing, the commission of serious bodily or mental harm to, and persecution of Tutsi and moderate Hutu. On this occasion, speaking on this radio station, Jean Kambanda, as Prime Minister, encouraged the RTLM to continue to incite the massacres of the Tutsi civilian population, specifically stating that this radio station was an indispensable weapon in the fight against the enemy. . . .

(ix) Jean Kambanda acknowledges that on 3 May 1994, he was personally asked to take steps to protect children who had survived the massacre at a hospital and he did not respond. On the same day, after the meeting, the children were killed. He acknowledges that he failed in his duty to ensure the safety of the children and the population of Rwanda.

—Judgment of 4 September 1998 by the International Criminal Tribunal–Rwanda, in *Prosecutor v. Kambanda,* ¶ 39.

Human Rights." To stimulate your appreciation of both successes and obstacles, the remaining sections highlight the prominent global and regional approaches to human rights—including the role of private non-governmental organizations in the evolution of this field of law.

The final section addresses the US record on ratification of human rights treaties and the emerging legislative and judicial policies regarding violations abroad.

◆ 11.1 HUMAN RIGHTS IN CONTEXT

What does the term *human rights* mean? Human rights are those rights possessed by an individual that cannot be withheld or withdrawn by the State. Scholars have typically referred to this significant feature of International Law as the "protection of individuals and groups against violations by governments of their internationally guaranteed rights. . . ."[1]

The English Magna Carta (1215), the French Declaration of the Rights of Man (1789), and the US Constitution's Bill of Rights (1791) are documents that have specifically listed the inherent, inalienable rights of the individual. These rights were expressed as being irrevocable by government action. Contemporary human rights norms originated in such documents. For example, the French Declaration and the US Constitution first expressed one of the most fundamental of all modern human rights: No person shall be deprived of life, liberty, or property without due process of law. The US Bill of Rights was added to the US Constitution in the form of Constitutional amendments guaranteeing freedom of religion, speech, press, and assembly, among others.

One must immediately acknowledge that human rights depend on the nature of the society that might lay claim to them. The level of economic development plays a role in the definition of basic rights. In democratic societies, individual rights routinely focus on *political* rights. In lesser developed societies, social and economic rights are the individual's primary concern. Food, shelter, health care, and a minimal education are the "human rights" of primary importance. Many individuals must therein struggle for their daily existence in obtaining essential food and shelter. The government is not in as good a position because of budgetary constraints to provide the full panoply of democratic rights enjoyed in more developed nations.

One could view World War II as the war that was fought to promote human rights. Certain States had deprived their inhabitants of life, liberty, and property by instituting sweeping social reforms to eliminate particular racial and ethnic groups. Germany's Nazi government deported a large portion of the German population (and occupied territories) to concentration camps in Poland and other occupied areas of Europe. Some nations entered the war, professing that the international community must fight to avoid the proliferation of such atrocities. During World War II, the Nazi political regime totally disregarded the inherent dignity of the individual. If anything positive can be drawn from that experience, it is that the Nazi form of fascism spawned an international consensus that the dignity of the individual is *not* solely a matter of State consent. After the war, these States formed an international organization of States (the United Nations) that would develop the various human rights initiatives discussed in this chapter. Post-war treaties, declarations, and commentaries stand as evidence of an international moral order that now limits the State's discretion in the treatment of its own citizens. States have been restrained, although only theoretically in the case of certain rogue regimes, in their historical discretion to exercise exclusive State power over human rights.

The development of human rights law is fraught with a number of ironies. Certain universal human rights are embraced publically by all States, even when some fail at merging word and deed. Many States that supported this facet of the UN's evolution have continued to *violate* human rights within their own territories while professing the importance of developing global and regional regimes to *protect* human rights. The UN Charter's human rights provisions were influenced by Hitler's "Final Solution." That State policy was designed to eradicate certain individuals and groups from all of Europe. This key event in the evolution of the "Holocaust" was probably the ultimate discrimination based on "race, sex, language, and religion"—a common phrase that appears in the UN Charter and ensuing human rights instruments. Yet in 1975, a UN resolution equated "Zionism" with racism. This General Assembly position was not repealed until 1991. And not until 1994 did the UN—through its Human Rights Commission, rather than the General Assembly—condemn anti-Semitism as a form of human rights abuse.

Unfortunately, the Nazi Holocaust was neither the first—nor the last—example of such widespread practice within a State. There was no international human rights program, for example, to limit the twentieth century's first major genocide: From 1915 to 1923, Turkey deported 1.75 million Armenians to arid deserts, where few survived. Nor did anyone stand in the way of Stalin's "Terror Famine" in the Ukraine during the winter of 1932–1933. Russia starved between 8 million and 10 million rural Ukranian farmers in pursuit of Stalin's State policy to splinter the Ukraine's populace, a plan based on centuries of class hatred. The Bosnian atrocities were premised on ethnic cleansing in the former Yugoslavia beginning in 1991 after the close of the Cold War.[2] This conflict generated a case in the International Court of Justice, wherein both sides claim that the other is responsible for genocide.[3] In 1994, the Hutu-controlled government sought to eliminate or drive the Tutsis out of Rwanda. The nature of these atrocities led the UN Security Council to establish the first *ad hoc* International Criminal Courts since Nuremberg (§9.5). Four years later, however, the UN would withdraw its first civilian operation dedicated exclusively to human rights—because it could not agree with the Rwandan government on how to monitor human rights abuses.

The mid-twentieth century was, practically speaking, the period for dating the development of the contemporary International Law of Human Rights. A brief history of the endeavors of States and their associations is provided below by a Canadian scholar. It provides a useful perspective for understanding how contemporary human rights developed, why certain States began to appreciate the importance of protecting individuals, and in what way the renewed fervor would form the basis of the contemporary UN human rights model. This passage further illustrates the early proposals that would have provided much greater definitional specificity—and offers reasons why these proposals were rejected (in the name of State sovereignty):

"The International Law of Human Rights in the Middle Twentieth Century"

JOHN HUMPHREY
UN DIRECTOR OF DIVISION OF HUMAN RIGHTS
FROM 1946 TO 1966

In *The Present State of International Law and Other Essays* 75 (1973)

I. TRADITIONAL DOCTRINE AND PRACTICE

[L]egal historians will surely be saying that one of the chief characteristics of mid-twentieth century international law was its sudden interest in and concern with human rights. The human rights were—and indeed still are—essentially a relationship between the State and individuals—usually its own citizens—residing in its territory, th[at] were, in *traditional theory* and practice, considered to fall *within domestic jurisdiction and hence beyond the reach of international law,* the norms of which governed the relations of States only [as opposed to relations between the State and its own citizens]. . . .

[I]n the nineteenth and early twentieth centuries an increasing number of treaties were entered into the purpose of which was to protect, if only indirectly, the rights of certain classes of people. The most important of these [treaties] were the treaties aimed at slavery and the slave trade. By 1885, it was possible to affirm, in the General Act of the Berlin Conference on Central Africa, that "trading in slaves is forbidden in conformity with the principles of international law." [This European "revelation" appeared after the success of the North in the American Civil War.] And in 1889, the Brussels Conference not only condemned slavery and the slave trade but agreed on measures for their suppression, including the granting of reciprocal rights of search, and the capture and trial of slave ships [on the high seas]. This work was continued by both the League of Nations and the United Nations. Steps were also taken in the nineteenth century for the relief of sick and wounded soldiers and prisoners of war. By the Geneva Convention of 22 August, 1864, twelve States undertook to respect the immunity of military hospitals and

Reprinted with permission of the International Law Association of London. Italics have been added in certain passages.

their staffs, to care for wounded and sick soldiers and to respect the emblem of the Red Cross. The Convention was revised in 1929 and has been widely ratified [by States as a binding obligation rather than being a mere statement of moral principles].

In 1906, the second Berne Conference opened two conventions for signature [so that States could later ratify them] which were forerunners of the many labor conventions which, after the First World War, would be adopted by the International Labor Organization: the International Convention respecting the Prohibition of Night Work for Women in Industrial Employment and the International Convention respecting the Prohibition of the Use of White (Yellow) Phosphorus in the Manufacture of Matches.

II. THE LEAGUE OF NATIONS

The peace settlement at the end of the First World War brought still more important developments. Attempts were made to enshrine human rights in the Covenant of the League of Nations. [US] President Wilson sponsored an article on religious freedom, but when the Japanese suggested that mention *also* be made of the equality of nations and the just treatment of their nationals (which frightened some countries the laws of which restricted Asiatic immigration) both suggestions were *withdrawn*. Wilson put into his second draft an article under which the League would have required all new States to bind themselves, as a condition precedent to their recognition, to accord all racial and national minorities "exactly the same treatment and security, both in law and in fact, that is accorded the racial and national majority of their [own] people." But the Peace Conference decided that the protection of minorities—though only in certain countries—would be dealt with *not in the Covenant* but by other treaty provisions and by declarations which certain States were required to make on their [subsequent] admission to the League. . . .

Human rights were expressly dealt with in Article 23 of the Covenant. Members of the League, it said, would "endeavour to secure and maintain" fair and humane labor conditions, undertake to secure just treatment for the native inhabitants of territories under their control, and entrust the League with the supervision of agreements relating to the [slave] traffic in women and children. [The US never joined the League.]

Although President Wilson's suggestion that the Covenant contain a provision protecting minorities was not pursued, the Allied and Associated Powers did require certain *newly created* States and [other] States, the territory of which had been increased by reason of the war, to grant the enjoyment of certain human rights to all inhabitants of their territories and to protect the rights of their racial, religious and linguistic minorities. These obligations were imposed by treaty and by the declarations which certain States were required to make on their admission to the League—the provisions relating to minorities being put under the guarantee of the League Council. . . .

The League of Nations also did important work on slavery. It created a special committee to *study* the question, was responsible for the drafting of the Slavery Convention of 1926, and, when Ethiopia applied for readmission to the League, it required from her an undertaking to make special efforts to abolish slavery and the slave trade, Ethiopia recognizing that this was not a purely internal matter but one on which the League had a right to intervene. . . .

To sum up, international law recognized, by the beginning of the Second World War, a whole series of rules and institutions . . . the effect of which was to protect the rights of individuals and groups, even though, in the dominant theory, *the individual was neither a subject of international law nor directly protected by it.* International law protected the rights of aliens through their States. . . .

III. THE IMPACT OF THE SECOND WORLD WAR AND THE UNITED NATIONS

The Second World War and the events leading up to it was the catalyst that produced the revolutionary developments in the international law of human rights that characterize the middle twentieth century. So potent was this catalyst that it produced not only an unprecedented growth in human rights law, but the very theory of international law had to be adapted to the new circumstances. *The individual now becomes a subject of international law.* . . . He is directly protected by this law and can even in some cases seek his own remedy. And States can no longer rely on the plea of domestic jurisdiction [over its own citizens to avoid human rights obligations under International Law]. It was not only a matter of new norms being added within the confines of an existing order, but the very nature of that order had changed. What had happened was revolutionary.

The Second World War was, as no other war has ever been, a war to vindicate human rights. This was recognized by the leaders of the Grand Alliance and perhaps best expressed by President Roosevelt when, in January 1941, before the United States entered the war, he defined four freedoms: freedom of speech, freedom of worship, freedom from want, freedom from fear—"everywhere in the world." He said that these were "the necessary conditions of peace. . . ." Yet, when the *Dumbarton Oaks Proposals* [creating the blueprint for the UN] were published in the fall of 1944 they contained only the [most] general reference to human rights. The United Nations would . . . "promote respect for human rights and fundamental freedoms"—something which considering its context and the generality of the language used *hardly met the expectations of a public opinion shocked by the atrocities of the war.*

The *relatively strong human rights provisions in the Charter* . . . were largely, and appropriately, the *result of determined lobbying by non-governmental organizations* at the San Francisco Conference. Some of the countries represented at San Francisco would have accepted even stronger human rights provisions than found their way into the Charter. There was even an attempt, which failed, to incorporate in the Charter an International Bill of Rights. But the Charter did provide for the creation of a Commission on Human Rights which, as [US] President Truman said in the speech by which he closed the Conference, would, it was generally understood, draft the bill [of rights. The UN Economic and Social Council later established the Commission that drafted the ensuing UN human rights instruments]. . . .

Implementation systems created by *treaty* have the *inherent weakness* that they are *unlikely to reach those countries where human rights are the least respected* and where, therefore, they are the most needed. There is no way by which the governments of such countries can be forced to ratify the treaties. Even those governments which are the most committed to respecting human rights are cautious about committing themselves in advance to limitations on their discretionary powers; and, in the experience of the United Nations in any event, treaty provisions for implementation have been extremely limited in their scope and operation. . . .

The principal characteristic of the twentieth century approach to human rights has been its unambiguous recognition of the fact that all human beings are entitled to the enjoyment not only of the traditional civil and political rights but also the economic, social and cultural rights without which, for most people, the traditional rights have little meaning. . . .

The United Nations, however, has always recognized that there is a *difference between* what can be expected from States in the implementation of economic and social rights and in the enforcement of *civil and political rights.* The former are looked upon as programme rights, [that is, mutually agreeable principles] the implementation of which is to be progressive. This is particularly true of economically underdeveloped countries with large populations to feed, which can hardly be expected to guarantee the immediate implementation of all economic and social rights. Even highly industrialized States will hesitate before guaranteeing the right, for example, to work—on any literal interpretation of the meaning of that right. . . .

[There is] the question of the increasing politicalization of human rights in the United Nations. Human Rights cannot, nor is it desirable that they should, be divorced from politics. To do so would be to divorce them from reality. And as a matter of fact there has always been a good deal of political controversy in the debates on human rights. . . . In recent years, however, the debates have become political to the exclusion of almost all constructive work, and one has the impression that governments are chiefly motivated by their [unrelated] conflicts with other countries. This, and *the absence of any effective public opinion capable of putting pressure on governments, has resulted in a slowing down,* in the United Nations at least, of effective work for the international promotion of respect for human rights.

This perspective from the UN's first Human Rights Director depicts the political reasons for disparate applications of the Charter and ensuing Charter-based "fundamental" human rights. The contemporary International Law of Human Rights—initiated by the UN—has not been adopted by all social and political systems. Thus, some States continue to assert that the parameters of human rights are a matter of internal law.[4] They perceive a conflict between two UN Charter objectives: first, State sovereignty, which precludes UN meddling in "matters [that] are essentially within the domestic jurisdiction of any state" (Art. 2.7); and second, "universal respect for . . . human rights and fundamental freedoms for all" (Art. 55c). What constitutes such rights is reserved exclusively for national implementation on a discretionary basis that must reflect local rather than internationally defined conditions. But, as stated by the Permanent Court of International Justice in 1923, long before the post–World War II "internationalization" of human rights: "The question whether a certain matter is or is not solely within the jurisdiction of a State is an essentially relative question; it depends on the development of international relations . . . [and] it may well happen that, in a matter [that] . . . is not, in principle, regulated by international law, the right of a State to use its discretion is nevertheless restricted by obligations [that] it may have undertaken towards other States. In such a case, jurisdiction [that], in principle, [allegedly] belongs solely to the State, is limited by the rules of international law."[5]

The study of human rights would be incomplete if the student merely viewed the UN's global regime as the only reasonable perspective. This chapter's analysis of human rights in distinct political regimes exposes the problem posed by contemporary Western thinking—that the UN's globally defined human rights regime is adaptable to *all* legal systems. However, some Western scholars disagree with that premise. They contend that the so-called global human rights regime *cannot* flourish in certain political systems such as the communist regimes of the People's Republic of China, North Korea, and Cuba. The human rights of the individual cannot prevail in a society where the rights of the State necessarily take priority over the rights of the individual in the event of a conflict. Internationally defined human rights are not common to all cultures and cannot be readily incorporated into all of the world's social and political systems. Canadian and US professors Rhoda Howard and Jack Donnelly make the point as follows:

> We argue, however, that international human rights standards are based upon a distinctive substantive conception of human dignity. They therefore require a particular type of "liberal" regime, which may be institutionalized in various forms, but only within a narrow range of variation. . . .
>
> Human rights are viewed as (morally) prior to and above society and the state, and under the control of individuals, who hold them and may exercise them against the state in extreme cases.
>
> In the areas and endeavors protected by human rights, the individual is the "king. . . ."
>
> Communitarian societies are antithetical to the implementation and maintenance of human rights, because they deny the autonomy of the individual, the irreducible moral equality of individuals, and the possibility of conflict between the community's interests and the legitimate interests of any individual. . . .
>
> Communist societies obviously must violate a wide range of civil and political rights during the revolutionary transition, and necessarily, not merely as a matter of unfortunate excesses in practice. Even after communism is achieved, the denial of civil and political rights remains necessary to preserve the achievements of the revolution. The permanent denial of civil and political rights is required by the commitment to build society according to a particular substantive vision, for the exercise of personal autonomy and civil and political rights is almost certain to undermine that vision.[6]

One must also acknowledge the impact of the general decline in economic commitments to UN processes discussed earlier in this book (§3.3). This diminished State commitment will have an adverse impact on the UN's ability to consummate its human rights objectives. The UN's annual human rights budget is approximately $11 million, or less than 1 percent of its regular (non-peacekeeping) budget. But the work of the UN Commission on Human Rights *tripled* during the ten years between the early 1980s and the early 1990s. The Human Rights Commission's increased caseload has not been offset by an increased economic commitment to the UN's role in monitoring State human rights observance.

◆ 11.2 UNITED NATIONS PROMOTIONAL ROLE

UN CHARTER PROVISIONS

Prior to the creation of the UN Charter, there were a variety of impediments to the fulfillment of human rights. Individuals had to rely on the internal law of their own States if they dared seek a remedy for abuses by State actors affiliated with the government. States were—and still are—quite reluctant to admit responsibility for human rights problems within their borders.

The concentration camps in Poland were the sites for implementing the Nazi government's "Final Solution." Hitler thus planned to destroy entire classes of people, including Europe's Jewish and Gypsy populations.

As discussed in §11.1, the lack of consensus about the definition and scope of the term *human rights* rendered external international legal control rather difficult to initiate.

During the early twentieth century, occasional bilateral treaty agreements would specify what two contracting nations would consider to be the fundamental rights of their citizens. League of Nations members occasionally expressed concern about this problem. No League effort prevented war crimes, genocide, and the other atrocities governed by the contemporary myriad of UN human rights treaties and declarations.

Because of the atrocities that occurred before and during World War II, the United Nations inaugurated a human rights program. Members incorporated a number of human rights provisions into this foundational document. The Preamble thus states that "WE THE PEOPLES OF THE UNITED NATIONS DETERMINED . . . to reaffirm faith in fundamental human rights, in the dignity and worth of the human person, in the equal rights of men and women . . . do hereby establish an international organization to be known as the United Nations." The third section of Article 1 provides that "[t]he purposes of the United Nations are . . . [t]o achieve international cooperation in solving international problems of an economic, social, cultural, or humanitarian character, and in promoting and encouraging respect for human rights for fundamental freedoms for all without distinction as to race, sex, language, or religion. . . ." Article 55 provides that "the United

Nations shall promote . . .(c) universal respect for, and observance of, human rights and fundamental freedoms for all without distinction as to race, sex, language, or religion." Article 56 adds that "All Members pledge themselves to take joint and separate action in co-operation with the Organization for the achievement of the purposes set forth in Article 55."

INTERNATIONAL BILL OF HUMAN RIGHTS

The UN Charter is the skeletal instrument that set the stage for the subsequent fleshing out of the global and regional human rights regimes presented in this chapter. The four cornerstones of the modern International Bill of Human Rights are as follows: (1) the 1948 Universal Declaration of Human Rights; (2) the 1966 International Covenant on Civil and Political Rights; (3) its optional protocols; and (4) the International Covenant on Economic, Social and Cultural Rights.

One might also add a number of ancillary conventions to the cache of contemporary human rights instruments. Many of them have been "declared" by the General Assembly and then opened for signature as treaties. Each addresses a specific agenda that builds upon the broad principles contained in the four principal UN documents. Exhibit 11.1 provides a snapshot of this expanded content of contemporary International Human Rights Law. The materials that follow in this section highlight the essentials of the four principal documents.

UN CHARTER LIMITATIONS

Contemporary instances of improper discrimination based on race, sex, and religion—prohibited by UN Charter, Article 55c, are all too familiar. For more than four decades, the white South African government refused to cease its State policy of discrimination against the black racial majority. Even today, women in many States are not given equal pay for equal work—contrary to the Charter's principles and the UN's Discrimination against Women Convention. States may also bear responsibility for violating human rights on the basis of linguistic discrimination. In the mid-1960s, for example, five French-speaking towns in Belgium lodged a claim against the Belgian government, asserting that it failed to provide education for their children in the French language. This failure allegedly violated the UN Charter and the European Human Rights Convention prohibitions against discrimination based on language.[7] In 1959 and 1960, an epidemic of anti-Semitism took the form of swastika-painting in Europe and Latin America. The UN's Sub-Commission on Prevention of Discrimination and Protection of Minorities condemned these manifestations of racial hatred as violations of the UN Charter.

The subcommittee's work ultimately resulted in the drafting of the 1981 Declaration on the Elimination of All Forms of Intolerance and of Discrimination Based on Religion or Belief.[8] The following circumstance may be a violation: In 1997, the Russian parliament enacted a controversial law that recognizes the Russian Orthodox Church as the nation's dominant church. The objective of this legislation is to curb religious cults, and it recognizes other religious groups. However, religious and secular groups throughout the world—as well as the US and the Vatican—oppose it. The most controversial clause requires religious groups to be in Russia for fifteen years before they can legally publish and distribute literature.

In 1970, the General Assembly announced the Declaration on the Occasion of the Twenty-Fifth Anniversary of the United Nations (Charter entering into force). State representatives therein lauded the UN's work, while recognizing that there remained much to be done. In the words of the Assembly, "serious violations of human rights are still being [routinely] committed against individuals and groups in several regions of the world."[9]

A preliminary question in this human rights assessment involves the legal nature of the UN Charter: Specifically, do the human rights provisions of the UN Charter impose legally binding obligations or are they merely a statement of goals? The answer is "no." The Charter, including its human rights provisions, contains a statement of aspirational standards for all member States. Article 56 does contain the oath that members "pledge themselves to take joint and separate action in cooperation with the Organization" to achieve the human rights goals specified in the Charter. If this language were designed to require *immediate* steps to implement the Article 56 pledge, however, joining the UN would have required instant compliance with the Charter's human rights provisions. States intended the Charter to be a broad statement of principle, requiring a *moral* commitment to provide the specified rights to all inhabitants.

When the Charter was being drafted, many States were in shambles as a result of World War II. It was read-

EXHIBIT 11.1 SELECTED HUMAN RIGHTS AGREEMENTS IN FORCE*

Year	Title and Objective
1948 ◆ 1951	Convention on the Prevention and Punishment of the Crime of Genocide [78 UN Treaty Series 277] ◆ Affirmed Nuremberg Principles (*see* case in §9.5) (US did not ratify until 1988)
1949 ◆ 1951	Convention for the Suppression of the Traffic in Persons and of the Exploitation of the Prostitution of Others [Gen. Ass. Reso. 260 A(III) of December 9, 1948] (US not party)
1951 ◆ 1954	Convention Relating to the Status of Refugees (*see* §4.2) (US not party to 1951 Convention regarding WWII refugees; ratified 1967 Protocol regarding refugees since WWII)
1952 ◆ 1954	Convention on the Political Rights of Women [Gen. Ass. Reso. 640(VII) of December 20, 1952]
1954 ◆ 1960	Convention Relating to the Status of Stateless Persons (US not party)
1957 ◆ 1958	Convention on the Nationality of Married Women [Gen. Ass. Reso. 1040(XI) of January 29, 1957] (US not party)
1960 ◆ 1962	Convention Against Discrimination in Education (General Conference of ECOSOC adopted December 14, 1960) ◆ Eliminates distinctions not expressed in Charter Articles 1.3 and 55c (US not party)
1962 ◆ 1964	Convention on Consent to Marriage, Minimum Age for Marriage and Registration of Marriages [Gen. Ass. Reso. 1763 A(XVII) of November 7, 1962] (US not party)
1965 ◆ 1969	International Convention on the Elimination of All Forms of Racial Discrimination [Gen. Ass. Reso. 2106 A(XX) of December 21, 1965]
1968 ◆ 1970	Convention on the Non-Applicability of Statutory Limitations to War Crimes and Crimes Against Humanity (*see* §10.6) (US not party)
1973 ◆ 1976	International Convention on the Suppression and the Punishment of the Crime of Apartheid [Gen. Ass. Reso. 3068(XXVIII) of November 30, 1973] (US not party)
1979 ◆ 1981	Convention on the Elimination of All Forms of Discrimination Against Women (Gen. Ass. Reso. 34/180 of December 18, 1979) (US not party)
1984 ◆ 1987	Convention Against Torture and Other Cruel, Inhuman or Degrading Treatment (Gen. Ass. Reso. 39/46 of December 10, 1984) (US did not ratify until 1994)
1989 ◆ 1990	Convention on the Rights of the Child (Gen. Ass. Reso. 44/25 of November 20, 1989) ◆ Protects children from discrimination (US has signed but not ratified)
1989 ◆ 1991	Convention Concerning Indigenous and Tribal Peoples in Independent Countries (General Conference of International Labour Organization adopted June 27, 1989) ◆ Maintain distinctions (US not party)

*Second date: year of treaty's entry into force

ily foreseeable that providing all such desired human rights would be prohibitively expensive. The precise date of compliance was expected to vary with the respective UN members' economic, social, and political ability to fully implement Charter expectations. Columbia University Professor Louis Henkin offers this explanation:

> [B]ecause, in general, the condition of human rights seemed to have little relation to the foreign policy interests of states, traditional policy-makers and diplomats tended to have little concern for the human rights movement, but neither did they see any need to court the public embarrassment of opposing it. In the United Nations General Assembly . . . governments could take part in the . . . [human rights] process without any commitment to adhere to the final product, trying nevertheless to shape emerging international norms so that their country's behaviour would not be found wanting . . . and it might even be possible to adhere to them [human rights norms] without undue burden if that later appeared desirable.[10]

The transformation from a moral imperative to a legal duty was to be accomplished by (a) ratifying *global* treaties such as those in Exhibit 11.1 above, (b) ratifying *regional* treaties containing human rights provisions acceptable to certain UN members in a localized context, and (c) enacting *national* legislation to actually implement the various UN Charter moral commitments (§11.5).

One could characterize the initial drafting process that produced the UN Charter's human rights provisions as saying one thing, but meaning another. No State would dare to openly object to the Charter's human rights provisions. However, no State was obliged to *act* on its "Article 56 pledge." Each State was implicitly authorized to defer the decision on the "how," "what," and "when" of implementation. The UN Charter was therefore devoid of any self-executing language (§8.2 on treaty formation). In the most prominent judicial opinion in US case law on this point, the 1952 California Supreme Court candidly analyzed the nonobligatory nature of UN Charter's human rights provisions:

> It is clear that the provisions . . . are not self-executing [binding by their own terms]. They state general purposes and objectives of the United Nations Organization and do not purport to impose legal obligations on the individual member nations or to create rights in private persons. . . . Although the member nations have obligated themselves to cooperate with the international organization in promoting respect for, and observance of, human rights, it is plain that it was contemplated that future legislative action by the several nations would be required to accomplish the declared objectives, and there is nothing to indicate that these provisions were intended to become [immediately binding] rules of law for the courts of this country upon the ratification [by the United States] of the charter.[11]

The States creating the UN had very practical reasons for characterizing the human rights provisions of the UN Charter as nonobligatory—in the *legal* rather than the *moral* sense. They did not want to accept an obligation that had not been precisely defined. Charter members might otherwise risk the embarrassment of a UN inquiry into matters that they could prefer to characterize as *national* rather than *international* in scope. There were too many "skeletons in the closet" in 1945. The internal laws of the US permitted racial segregation and prohibited interracial marriages in certain cases. The former Soviet Union had its *gulags*—the forced-labor camps where individuals who resisted State policy in peaceful ways were incarcerated.[12] Nor were the other powerful nations without their human rights problems.

THE INTERNATIONAL BILL OF HUMAN RIGHTS AT WORK

Universal Declaration The historical cornerstone in the UN program for building a global human rights culture is the Universal Declaration of Human Rights (UDHR). This 1948 UN General Assembly Resolution was adopted without dissent—although five members of the Soviet bloc, plus Saudi Arabia and South Africa, abstained from voting. This Declaration was the first *comprehensive* human rights document to be proclaimed on a global scale. Its specificity, while not intricate, readily transcended the Charter's breadth of purpose.

The UDHR promotes two general categories of rights. The first, "civil and political rights," includes the following: the right to life, liberty, and security of the person; the right to leave and enter one's own country; the prohibition of slavery and torture; freedom from discrimination, arbitrary arrest, and interferences with privacy; the right to vote; freedom of thought, peaceable assembly, religion, and marriage. The second category of rights consists of "economic, social, and cultural rights" such as the rights to own property, to work, to maintain an adequate standard of living and health, and the right to an education.

Like the UN Charter, the Declaration is also a statement of principles. It does not *require* a State to provide the listed rights to its populace immediately. The diversity of economic bases was one reason for this limitation. A poor country will not be able to give its citizens what a more developed country considers a minimum standard of living or education. UN member States were expected to pursue the laudatory purposes of the Universal Declaration at their own pace, according to their respective financial abilities to comply. Eleanor Roosevelt, Chair of the United States Commission on Human Rights and US Representative to the UN General Assembly, gingerly expressed the national sentiment regarding this post-war statement of "universal" principles. She carefully noted that "[i]n giving our approval to the declaration today, it is of primary importance that we keep clearly in mind the basic character of the document [Universal Declaration of Human Rights]. It is not and does not purport to be a statement of law or of legal obligation. It is a declaration of basic principles of human rights and freedoms, to be stamped with the approval of the General Assembly by formal vote of its members, and to serve as a common standard of achievement for all peoples of all nations."[13]

The UDHR was thus intended to be a statement of aspirations. Since its adoption in 1948, however, a number of commentators have characterized it as being something more. In 1971, the Vice President of the International Court of Justice perceived the Declaration's human rights provisions as having ripened into general practices that had become "accepted as law." In his separate opinion in the *Namibia* case, Judge Ammoun (Lebanon) expressed the view that:

> [the] Universal Declaration of Human Rights . . . stresses in its preamble that "it is essential, if man is not to be compelled to have recourse, as a last resort, to rebellion against tyranny and oppression, that human rights should be protected by the rule of law. . . . The Court could not remain an unmoved witness in face of the evolution of modern international law which is taking place in the United Nations through the implementation and the extension to the whole world of the principles of equality, liberty and peace in justice which are embodied in the Charter and the Universal Declaration of Human Rights. By referring . . . to the Charter of the United Nations and the Universal Declaration of Human Rights, the Court [in the main opinion of the *Namibia* case] has asserted the imperative character of the right of peoples to self-determination and also of the human rights whose violation by the South African authorities [the Court] has denounced. . . .
>
> The violation of human rights has not yet come to an end in any part of the world. . . . Violations of personal freedom and human dignity, the racial, social or religious discrimination which constitutes the most serious of violations of human rights . . . all still resist the currents of liberation on the five continents. That is certainly no reason why we should close our eyes to the conduct of the South African authorities. . . . Although the affirmations of the Declaration are not binding *qua* international convention [that is, not possessing legal capacity as an immediately binding treaty obligation] . . . they can bind states on the basis of custom . . . because they have acquired the force of custom through a general practice accepted as law. . . .
>
> The equality demanded by the Namibians and by other peoples of every colour . . . is something of vital interest here . . . because it naturally rules out racial discrimination and *apartheid*, which are the gravest of the facts with which South Africa, as also other States, stands charged. . . .
>
> It is not by mere chance that in Article 1 of the Universal Declaration of the Rights of Man there stands, so worded, this primordial principle or axiom: All human beings are born free and equal in dignity and rights. . . . The condemnation of *apartheid* has passed the stage of declarations and entered the phase of binding conventions.[14]

Some US commentators share Judge Ammoun's belief that certain human rights provisions of the UN Declaration are now binding under customary State practice. In 1987, a nationwide group of US judges, academicians, and government lawyers confirmed that

> [a]lmost all States are parties to the United Nations Charter, which contains human rights obligations. There has been no authoritative determination of the full content of those obligations, but it is increasingly accepted that states parties to the Charter are legally obligated to respect some of the rights recognized in the Universal Declaration. . . . It has been argued that the general pledge of the members in the Charter [to promote human rights] . . . has been made definite by the Universal Declaration, and that failure by any member to respect the rights recognized in the declaration is a violation of the Charter. Alternatively, it has been urged, the Charter, the Universal Declaration . . . and other practice of states have combined to create a customary international law of human rights requiring every state to respect the rights set forth in the Declaration.[15]

One persistent criticism of the 1948 UDHR has been its "Western" (sometimes referred to as "northern") derivation. It lacked input from lesser developed nations and those with more diverse political and social viewpoints. Norwegian author Ashborn Eide and Iceland's Gudmundur Alfredsson (of the UN Secretariat) characterized this criticism as being overstated. In their leading study of the UDHR, they depict its evolution as follows: "[P]articipants came from all over the world. Admittedly, there was only one participant from the African continent (Egypt). Indigenous peoples and minorities had no representation during the drafting and adoption stages. While this may be true, today the broad wording of the Declaration and its general principles together with subsequent standard-setting and implementation activities [see Exhibit 11.1] reduce the value of this statement to history."[16]

Ironically, the June 1993 Vienna World Conference on Human Rights appeared to take a step backward in terms of *globally* defining human rights entitlements. China and Indonesia were the front-runners in the final conference statement. It contends that Western-derived human rights standards should now be tempered by "regional peculiarities and various historical, cultural and religious backgrounds." This perspective, promulgated in the Vienna Declaration and Programme of Action,[17] arguably diminishes the efforts to eliminate barriers to the internationalization of human rights enforcement.

Furthermore, the UDHR is considered somewhat treacherous by some nations. The annual reports of Amnesty International (AI) furnish insight into the reason. AI is the most active of the private "watchdog" organizations that track claimed human rights abuses throughout the world. In its 1988 report, AI observed that many UN member nations consider the 1948 Declaration of Human Rights "subversive." It was the first UN document to assert that individuals have a right to direct protection by the international community. That clashes with the perceived national right to freedom from international interference with matters essentially within the local jurisdiction of every sovereign State. As reported by AI: "In at least half the countries of the world, people are locked away for speaking their minds, often after trials that are no more than a sham. In at least a third of the world's nations, men, women and even children are tortured. In scores of countries, governments pursue their goals by kidnaping and murdering their own citizens. More than 120 states have written into their laws the right to execute people convicted of certain crimes, and more than a third carry out such premeditated killings every year."[18]

International Covenant on Civil and Political Rights In 1966, the UN General Assembly added two core documents to the International Bill of Human Rights: the International Covenant on Civil and Political Rights (CPR)[19] and the International Covenant on Economic, Social and Cultural Rights (ESCR). Both were expressly cast as multilateral treaties opened for signature so that adopting States could ratify them and thus agree to their binding nature. By 1976, the minimum number of States had ratified both. They differ from the UN Charter and the Universal Declaration of Human Rights in that they are *not* mere declarations of principle.[20]

These two covenants (i.e., binding treaties when ratified) share a number of common substantive provisions. Both restate the human rights provisions contained in the Universal Declaration. The distinguishing feature of the Covenants is that they obligate States to establish conspicuous and effective machinery for filing charges of and dealing with alleged violations of human rights. Article 2 of the CPR Covenant requires parties "to adopt such legislative or other measures as may be necessary to give effect to the rights recognized in the present Covenant." States must also "ensure that any persons whose rights or freedoms as herein recognized are violated shall have an effective remedy . . . determined by competent judicial, administrative or legislative authorities, or by any other competent authority provided for by the legal system of the State. . . ."

Optional Protocols To monitor compliance with the CPR Covenant and other UN guidelines, a Human Rights Committee composed of eighteen State representatives examines the periodic compliance reports that the treaty parties must submit to the UN. That Committee cannot, however, conduct its own investigations to ensure the accuracy of the reports. A separate protocol to the CPR covenant permits *individuals* to submit their complaints directly to the Human Rights Committee. This was made possible under UN Resolution 1503 of 1970, which provides the individual right to petition the UN as a basic human right. This right of petition has not been particularly successful, partially because of difficulties with individual access, which is effectively controlled by the State.

The following example is an individual petition submitted to this Committee. It is also illustrates the human rights that are protected by the CPR Covenant. As you read this passage, note the subjectivity of the government's basis for the arrests in this case:

"Report of the Human Rights Committee"

24 *UN Monthly Chronicle* 66 (June 1979)

. . . The Committee also concluded, for the first time, consideration of a communication submitted to it by a Uruguayan national in accordance with the Optional Protocol to the International Covenant on Civil and Political Rights. Under the terms of the Protocol, individuals who claimed that any of their rights enumerated in the Covenant had been violated and who had exhausted all available remedies, might submit written communications to the Committee for consideration. The Committee, after examining the communication in question, took the view that it revealed a number of violations by Uruguay, the State Party concerned, of the Covenant provisions.

It held that the State Party was under an obligation to take immediate steps to ensure strict observance of the Covenant provisions and to provide effective remedies to the victims.

The communication was written by a Uruguayan national residing in Mexico, who submitted it on her own behalf, as well as on behalf of her husband, Luis Maria Bazzano Ambrosini, her stepfather, Jose Luis Massera, and her mother, Martha Valentini de Massera.

The author alleged, with regard to herself, that she was detained in Uruguay from 25 April to 3 May 1975 and subjected to psychological torture. She stated that she was released on 3 May 1975 without having been brought before a judge.

The author claimed that her husband, Luis Maria Bazzano Ambrosini, was detained on 3 April 1975 and immediately thereafter subjected to torture.

She also claimed that her stepfather, Jose Luis Massera, professor of mathematics and former Deputy to the National Assembly, had been arrested on 22 October 1975 and held incommunicado until his detention was made known in January 1976, and that her mother, Martha Valentini de Massera, had been arrested on 28 January 1976 without any formal charges and that in September 1976 she was accused of "assistance to subversive association," an offence which carried a penalty of two to eight years imprisonment. . . .

The Committee decided to base its views on the following facts which had not been contradicted by the State Party. Luis Maria Bazzano Ambrosini was arrested on 3 April 1975 on the charge of complicity in "assistance to subversive association." Although his arrest had taken place before the coming into force of the International Covenant on Civil and Political Rights and of the Optional Protocol thereto, on 23 March 1976, his detention without trial continued after that date. After being detained for one year, he was granted conditional release, but that judicial decision was not respected and the prisoner was taken to an unidentified place, where he was confined and held incommunicado until 7 February 1977. On that date he was tried on the charge of "subversive association" and remained imprisoned in conditions seriously detrimental to his health.

Jose Luis Massera, a professor of mathematics and former Deputy to the National Assembly, was arrested in October 1975 and has remained imprisoned since that date. He was denied the remedy of habeas corpus [whereby a neutral judge would assess the basis for his incarceration] and another application for remedy made to the Commission on Respect for Human Rights of the Council of State went unanswered. On 15 August 1976 he was tried on charges of "subversive association" and remained in prison.

Martha Valentini de Massera was arrested on 28 January 1976. In September 1976 she was charged with "assistance to subversive association." She was kept in detention and was initially held incommunicado. In November 1976 for the first time a visit was permitted, but thereafter she was again taken to an unknown place of detention. She was tried by a military court and sentenced to three-and-a-half years imprisonment.

The Committee, acting under article 5(4) of the Optional Protocol to the International Covenant on Civil and Political Rights, took the view that those facts, in so far as they had occurred after 23 March 1976, disclosed violations of the International Covenant on Civil and Political Rights [by Uruguay].

◆ *Notes*

Subsequent developments suggest that the shift to civilian control of Uruguay's government had a positive impact on its observance of international human rights norms. Ten years after the Commission's consideration of this claim of human rights abuses in Uruguay (June 1989), a court in Montevideo, Uruguay, ordered Uruguay's Defense Ministry to pay the equivalent of $47 million to an electrician tortured with his own equipment for eighteen months during 1976 and 1977. This was the first time that such a judgment was rendered in Uruguay—where such incidents were commonplace during the military dictatorship of the 1970s to the mid-1980s.

The Second Optional Protocol to the International Covenant on Civil and Political Rights is a separate treaty that, when ratified by a member State, precludes it from imposing the death penalty. There is a flourishing movement in the international community to treat this salient feature of State practice as a violation of International Law.[21] The International Criminal Tribunals (Yugoslavia and Rwanda) and the Rome Statute for a permanent tribunal all bar the death penalty. Their ultimate sanction is life imprisonment (§9.5). Under this Protocol, reservations are permitted only for "the most serious crimes of a military nature" committed during time of war.

During a 1994 debate in the UN's Third Committee, the Chair summarized the respective arguments by various national representatives for and against the death penalty as follows:

> [T]he Committee had clearly been divided into two camps: those favoring the *abolition* of capital punishment and those wishing to retain it. Arguments in favor of abolishing the death penalty had been the following: States could not impose the death penalty as a means of reducing crime because there was no evidence that it had a deterrent effect; the right to life was the most basic human right and, consequently, States did not have the right to take the life of any individual; the death penalty sometimes veiled a desire for vengeance or provided an easy way of eliminating political opponents; the death penalty, once applied, could not be reversed in the event of a judicial error; and capital punishment was excluded from the penalties used by international tribunals . . . and should consequently be less prevalent in national legislation.
>
> Arguments in support of *maintaining* the death penalty had been the following: certain legislative systems were based on religious laws; it was not possible to impose the ethical standards of a single culture on all countries; there was a need to discourage extremely serious crimes; and, in some countries, capital punishment was a constitutional or even a religious obligation.
>
> At the same time, all members agreed on certain fundamental points: the death penalty should be applied only in exceptional circumstances and subject to strict preconditions; and its scope of application should be extremely limited.[22]

International Covenant on Economic, Social, and Cultural Rights The CPR Covenant was one of two draft human rights treaties opened for signature by the UN in 1966. The other was the ESCR Covenant. It requires the State to provide adequate or improved living conditions for its inhabitants and to facilitate international cooperation to achieve this objective. Article 11 (and Article 28 of the Universal Declaration of Human Rights) provides as follows: "The States Parties to this Covenant recognize the right of everyone to an adequate standard of living for himself and his family including adequate food, clothing and housing, and to the continuous improvement of living conditions. The States Parties will take appropriate steps to ensure the realization of the right. . . ."

This second basket of rights was the subject of a separate 1966 UN draft treaty for good reason. It would be neither practical nor politically feasible to lump these non-political rights into a comprehensive treaty that could have lumped together the "universe" of rights set forth in the 1948 Universal Declaration of Human Rights—from which both the CPR Covenant and the ESC Covenant drew their inspiration. There is just too much diversity in the political, economic, social, and cultural fabric of the UN membership. This reality was especially evident to the treaty drafters because of the influx of new UN member States as a result of the decolonization movement of the 1960s. Developing nations consider the achievement of economic rights as a more immediate goal than the political rights contained in the other 1966 treaty. They must attend to basic food and shelter requirements as the most basic of human rights.[23] Then they can consider the extent to which issues such as minority rights regarding language or religion may become a governmental priority.

Economic, social, and cultural rights were thus identified as a distinct category of rights, based on their historical origin. As noted in a leading commentary about the evolution of the rights governed by the ESC treaty:

> Economic, social, and cultural rights are frequently termed 'second generation' rights, deriving from the growth of socialist ideals in the late nineteenth and early twentieth centuries and the rise of the labor movement in Europe. They contrast with the 'first generation' civil and political rights associated with the eighteenth-century [French] Declaration on the Rights of Man, and the 'third generation' rights of 'peoples' or 'groups,' such as the right to self-determination and the right to development. In fact the reason for making a distinction between first and second generation rights . . . [was] the ideological conflict between East and West pursued in the arena of human rights during the drafting of the covenants. The Soviet States, on the one hand, championed the cause of economic, social, and cultural rights, which they associated with the aims of socialist society. Western States, on the other hand, asserted the priority of civil and political rights as being the foundation of liberty and democracy in the 'free world.' The conflict was such that during the drafting of the International Bill of Rights the intended treaty was divided into two separate instruments which were later to become the ICCPR and the ICESCR.[24]

OTHER SOLUTIONS

Starting Over The UN's now-comprehensive human rights program has received much publicity. Commentators argue, however, that many State participants merely "pay lip service" to these programs while their inhabitants suffer. New York University Professor Theodore Meron espouses the representative view that rather than editing or beefing up existing treaties, a completely *new* instrument is needed. His perspective is that:

> [i]n recent years there has been a proliferation of human rights instruments, not all of them necessary and carefully thought out. It would nevertheless appear that the international community needs a short, simple, and modest instrument to state an irreducible and nonderogable core of human rights. . . .
>
> Some might argue that a solution could be found in better implementation of the existing law, rather than in the adoption of new instruments. But attainment of an effective system to implement the existing law, rather than in the adoption of new instruments. But attainment of an effective system to implement the existing law is not probable in the near future. Neither would it help to remedy the weakness inherent in the quantity and quality of the applicable norms.[25]

Individual Responsibility There is still another view. Insufficient emphasis has been placed on *individual* responsibility under International Law for serious human rights violations. Human rights instruments typically focus on the *State* as the primary actor in need of external controls. Of course, the State is the primary actor in International Law. It is vested with the power to control the lives of its inhabitants and to decide which international agreements it will ratify. Therefore, international human rights instruments obligate the State, as opposed to its citizens, not to act in ways that would deprive other individuals of their human rights. Some States are oblivious to their human rights obligations, as demonstrated by their failing to honor treaty commitments or their failure to follow customary State expectations.

Rather than "starting over," as suggested above by Professor Meron, Professor Lyal Sunga's study from the Graduate Institute of International Studies at Geneva proposes *supplementation* of the existing regime. There should be an increased emphasis on *individual* responsibility for human rights violations. His starting point would be to establish the legal liability of individuals for serious violations in the context of the Laws of War. The Nuremberg Judgment, followed by the 1949 Geneva Conventions, did this on an *ad hoc* basis.

Dr. Sunga argues that there should be a general rule of *individual* responsibility under International Law for serious human rights violations to supplement existing rules of *State* responsibility for such violations.[26] Just how this would be accomplished remains an open question.

UN High Commissioner The UN has a good track record in terms of being the primary entity to establish human rights standards on a global basis. According to the UN itself, however, more than half the people of the world suffer some form of violation of those rights. The lack of adequate enforcement resources has made it difficult for the UN to more fully implement its stated objectives.

In December 1993, the UN General Assembly thus added another cog in the wheel of human rights enforcement. The Assembly resolved to establish the post of "UN High Commissioner for the Promotion and Protection of All Human Rights," a proposal first made by Uruguay in 1951. The Commissioner is now appointed by the Secretary-General, subject to approval by the General Assembly. The first Commissioner was Jose Ayala Lasso, Ecuador's Education Ambassador to the UN (appointed in 1994).[27]

The Commissioner is the focal point for coordinating the UN's fragmented efforts to implement the rights enshrined in its numerous problem-specific treaties (*see* Exhibit 11.1). This UN official manages the UN's Center for Human Rights, which will move more swiftly than the overburdened Human Rights Commission—whose workload tripled between the early 1980s and the early 1990s.

The task of the first UN Commissioner began with a compromise. Western States agreed to modify language that would have given the Commissioner responsibility for "elimination and prevention" of human rights violations. The Commissioner's task is now worded so as to require only "an active role in removing the current obstacles" to the global enjoyment of human rights. This attenuated version of the Commissioner's role may ultimately relegate this office to bureaucratic obscurity.

Nevertheless, this officer does perform a valuable function, by questioning certain State practices through the medium of annual reports. The following is a classic instance:

Israeli Interrogation Cases

United Nations High Commissioner on Human Rights

Consideration of Reports Submitted by States Parties Under Article 19 of the Convention (Israel)

BY COMMITTEE AGAINST TORTURE

CAT/C/33/Add.2/Rev.1

(18 February 1997)

Go to Course Web page at http://home.att.net/~slomansonb/txtcsesite.html; click on Israeli Interrogation Cases.

◆ *Notes & Questions*

1. The UN Convention Against Torture and Other Cruel, Inhuman or Degrading Treatment or Punishment notes that "article 5 of the Universal Declaration of Human Rights and article 7 of the International Covenant on Civil and Political Rights, both of which provide that no one shall be subjected to torture or to cruel, inhuman or degrading treatment or punishment [and] . . . that the Declaration on the Protection of All Persons from Being Subjected to Torture and Other Cruel, Inhuman or Degrading Treatment or Punishment, adopted by the General Assembly on 9 December 1975" prohibit torture. Article 1 contains the agreement that:

> [T]he term "torture" means any act by which severe pain or suffering, whether physical or mental, is intentionally inflicted on a person for such purposes as obtaining from him or a third person information or a confession, punishing him for an act he or a third person has committed or is suspected of having committed, or intimidating or coercing him or a third person, or for any reason

based on discrimination of any kind, when such pain or suffering is inflicted by or at the instigation of or with the consent or acquiescence of a public official or other person acting in an official capacity. It does not include pain or suffering arising only from, inherent in or incidental to lawful sanctions.

2. Along with 101 other nations at the time of the Torture Committee's response to this report, Israel had ratified the Torture Convention. Is Israel violating the UN Torture Convention by continuing to employ the "shaking" interrogation technique, which had prevented ninety attacks in the two years prior to the Israeli Supreme Court decision? Would State security be of secondary importance to the Convention's general anti-torture prohibition?
3. In 1996, documents made public by the Pentagon revealed that the US Army's "School of the Americas" encouraged its Latin American police and military students to use torture against insurgents. Training manuals written in Spanish advocated tactics that violated express US domestic and foreign policy. This school opened in Panama in 1946 and was transferred to Fort Benning, Georgia, in 1984. The school's graduates include the leader of El Salvador's death squads and Panama's former dictator, Manuel Noriega. The manuals were destroyed in 1996, when their previously top secret contents became public ("Pentagon Details Army Manuals Urging Latin Military to Torture, Sept. 22, 1996, New York Times News Service).

Human Rights Police Force In 1992, Russia proposed a UN global "police force" for protecting human rights throughout the world. Russia's Foreign Minister to the UN, Andrei Kozyrev, made this proposal to the UN Human Rights Commission. The Russian Minister proposed an independent body of moral leaders who could study a particular situation and render advisory judgments about a State's conduct regarding its own citizens.

This proposal was a radical departure from prior Soviet doctrine. Human rights enforcement was uniformly characterized as an issue that fell exclusively within the internal affairs of the Soviet Union or its member States—as opposed to acknowledging the UN's role in human rights enforcement. Socialist States had routinely expressed the concern that UN programs intervened in the internal affairs of the targeted State. It was one thing to complain in a General Assembly context. It would be quite another to render such opinions regarding the conduct of a member of the international community toward its own citizens.

◆ 11.3 REGIONAL HUMAN RIGHTS APPROACHES

Several *regional* human rights programs coexist with the UN program. The degree to which they have been successful in comparison to the UN's global program depends on the political solidarity of the particular region. This section addresses human rights initiatives in Europe, Latin America, Africa, and Asia.

EUROPEAN PROGRAMS

Historical Evolution The Council of Europe is an international organization composed of thirty-nine European nations. The Council's essential goals are the maintenance of political and economic stability in Europe. Member States have characterized the preservation of individual rights as being an important method for achieving those goals. The constitution of the Council of Europe provides that each member must ensure "the enjoyment by all persons within its jurisdiction of human rights and fundamental freedoms." This provision was implemented by the creation of two human rights treaties: the European Human Rights Convention (EHR) and the European Social Charter. Upon ratification, the national participants bind themselves to grant the rights contained in various regional treaties to their inhabitants.[28] One of these is the 1992 Treaty of Maastricht, which deals with economic development. The pervasiveness of human rights as an element of development is evident in Article 130(u). It provides that "[c]ommunity policy in this area shall contribute to the general objective of developing and consolidating democracy and the rule of law, and to that of respecting human rights and fundamental freedoms."

The EHR treaty contains civil rights that are virtually identical to those set forth in the United Nations Covenant on Civil and Political Rights. The EHR treaty protects the rights to life, public and fair hearings, peaceful enjoyment of possessions, an education, freedom from torture or other degrading treatment, and the freedoms of thought, conscience, religion, expression, and peaceful assembly.

The European Social Charter provides for economic and social rights that are similar to those set forth in the United Nations Covenant on Economic, Social and Cultural Rights. The European Social Charter guarantees the rights to work, safe working conditions, employment protection for women and children, vocational training, and the right to engage in gainful occupations in the territories of other member states.

Enforcement The most effective tool for ensuring the enjoyment of these rights is the European Court of Human Rights. This is the judicial arm of the EHR treaty. The Court hears cases arising under the EHR treaty (*see* §9.6). The Court is seated with the Council of Europe in Strasbourg, France. It was this court's predecessor that directed Ireland to permit a pregnant minor to leave the country for the purpose of obtaining an abortion in Great Britain, although the Irish Constitution forbade abortions under the circumstances.[29]

A newly constituted court (as of 1998) replaced the two prior entities responsible for ensuring that the Contracting Parties comply with their obligations under the Convention: a court with the same name, and the European Commission on Human Rights. The reform was spawned by the growing difficulty experienced by the prior judicial body and the former administrative Commission's efforts to cope with an ever-increasing volume of cases. The reconstitution of the European Court of Human Rights into various chambers and the elimination of the European Commission on Human Rights avoided the time-consuming examination of cases by two separate bodies. Under Protocol No. 11 to the European Convention on Human Rights, the Court's jurisdiction is now compulsory; under the prior system, acceptance of both the right of individual petition to the Commission and the Court's jurisdiction was optional. Another feature of the system prior to 1998 was that the adjudicative role of the Committee of Ministers of the Council of Europe was eliminated. The Committee of Ministers will, however, retain its present responsibility for supervising the execution of the Court's judgments.[30]

The European Court of Human Rights has been a very useful force for preserving human rights in Europe. One reason is that, unlike other international venues, individuals may themselves be parties—rather than States only.[31] In a 1998 decision, the Court rendered a unanimous judgment against Bulgaria that had been brought by several individuals. They successfully claimed that, while a father had hit his plaintiff son on the day that injuries were also allegedly caused by the police, Bulgaria violated the European Convention on Human Rights. It failed to investigate "torture or degrading treatment or punishment" by public authorities, and thus failed to provide an effective remedy for police misconduct. The police also failed to adequately review the lawfulness of the son's two-year detention, during which the case should have come to trial.[32]

The court is also an effective advocate for addressing State excesses that threaten regional stability. The following case is a classic example:

Loizidou v. Turkey

EUROPEAN COURT OF HUMAN RIGHTS
No. 40/1993/435/514 (1996)
Judgment on the Merits
Go to course Web site at
http://home.att.net/
~slomansonb/txtcsesite.html;
click on Loizidou Case.

◆ *Notes & Questions*

1. What treaty-based human rights did plaintiff Loizidou rely on for her claim?
2. What obligations did Turkey breach?
3. What role did the Court play regarding the European Convention on Human Rights?

The existence of this comprehensive human rights machinery does not mean that the interests of the national participants always yield to the rights of the individual. For example, England's 1988 Prevention of

Terrorism Act extended pre-arraignment detention for those suspected of terrorism from two to seven days. In the major national case to be prosecuted under that act, four men from Northern Ireland were held for periods of from five to *seventeen* days. They were never charged with a crime. They were unable to seek redress in the English courts and thus filed a claim in the European Court of Human Rights. The Court in Strasbourg held that England's law permitting police to detain suspected terrorists for even seven days without a hearing violated the European Convention on Human Rights. The ECHR requires "prompt" access to a judicial officer after an arrest. The ECHR also provides for "an enforceable right to compensation." However, rather than complying with the court's ruling, the British government announced that it would withdraw from the applicable sections of the ECHR treaty.

On the other hand, this regional human rights process is the model for all regions of the world. The work of the ECHR and national willingness to abide by its judgments has greatly contributed to overcoming the historical national sovereignty barriers to effective enforcement of International Human Rights Law. As summed up by University of Connecticut Professors Mark Janis and Richard Kay:

> Nowadays, the European Court of Human Rights *regularly* finds nations in breach of their obligations under the international human rights law. . . . Remarkably, sovereign states have respected the adverse judgments of the Court . . . [and] have reformed or abandoned police procedures, penal institutions, child welfare practices, administrative agencies, court rules, labor relations, moral legislation, and many other important public matters. The willingness with which the decisions of the European Court have been accepted demonstrates the *emergence of a crucial new fact in the Western legal tradition:* an effective system of international law regulating some of the most sensitive areas of what previously had been thought to be fields within the exclusive domain of national sovereignty.[33]

OSCE Process Another European process is emerging as one of the regional guardians of human rights. Under the "Helsinki Final Act" of 1975, thirty-five nations (now fifty-two) convened the Conference on Security and Co-operation in Europe (CSCE—now OSCE). The initial driving force for this development was the former Soviet Union and other Warsaw Pact nations. They pursued the concept of a regional political and security arrangement for several decades. Canada and the US were invited to participate because of their prominent positions in NATO.[34] The organization now has several institutions dedicated to the preservation of human rights, including a High Commissioner on National Minorities and an OSCE Elections Commission whose task is to observe elections as an international observer.

The Final Act is not a treaty in the traditional sense. Its human rights work product more closely resembles the aspirational nature of the UN Charter and Universal Declaration of Human Rights—which is not surprising given the comparatively large number of members from all over Europe. They are not integrated in the many ways enjoyed by members of the Council of Europe. The Act is a declaration of "Principles Guiding Relations Between Participating States." It is a political statement of principles not intended to be immediately binding. It provides a regional standard of achievement. The State participants decided not to commit themselves to anything other than general principles, due to a lack of consensus on the question of how to achieve regional security.

The fundamental human rights provision of the Helsinki Final Act is Principle VII of its Declaration of Principles. It provides that in "the field of human rights and fundamental freedoms, the participating States will act in conformity with the purposes and principles of the Charter of the United Nations and the Universal Declaration of Human Rights. They will also fulfill their obligations as set forth in the international declarations and agreements in this field, including inter alia the [1966] International Covenants on Human Rights. . . ."

International disagreements about the individual's right to travel was one reason for the early inability of conference participants to achieve a concrete agreement on security and human rights. Certain nations, particularly the US, actively pursued implementation of the right of international travel. The US State Department issued annual reports for ten years *after* the initial 1975 CSCE conference, focusing on travel restrictions between East and West. The US therein denounced Eastern European travel restrictions, typified by the former "Berlin Wall," as being contrary to the human rights principles stated in the Helsinki Declaration.

The OSCE played a prominent role in monitoring the Russian assault on Chechnya, which began in 1994. In 1995, Russian President Boris Yeltsin agreed to allow a OSCE human rights mission to maintain a permanent presence in the region. Yeltsin assured the foreign ministers of Germany, France, and Spain, while on a mission from the European Union, that Russia was committed to a political settlement of the Chechnya crisis to be undertaken in conformity with OSCE human rights objectives. The recent work of the OSCE in Kosovo and other regions is covered in §3.5 (international organizations).

LATIN AMERICAN PROGRAMS

Human rights norms in Latin American are expressed in the Charter of the Organization of American States (OAS),[35] the American Declaration of the Rights and Duties of Man, and the American Convention on Human Rights. These norms are monitored by the Inter-American Commission on Human Rights.

The human rights provisions of the OAS Charter, like its UN counterpart, are aspirational statements of moral principles. They were designed to guide Latin American nations in their treatment of individuals, although neither charter imposes specific legal obligations. Article 5 provides that the "American States proclaim the fundamental rights of the individual without distinction as to race, nationality, creed or sex." This language is obviously drawn from Article 55c of the UN Charter (*see* §11.2 of this text). Article 16 provides that each "State has the right to develop its cultural, political and economic life freely and naturally. In this free development, the State shall respect the rights of the individual and the principles of universal morality."

State rights have priority over individual rights as expressed in the first sentence of Article 16. The State is thereby guaranteed the right to develop "freely and naturally." The delegates to the drafting conference ensured that each OAS member would retain its complete sovereignty upon affiliation with the OAS. The second sentence of the article says that States must also "respect the rights of the individual." This language ostensibly limits that sovereignty. The Charter is not specific, however, about the content of the rights to be respected. Nor does it express any obligation to treat the individual in a particular way.

Certain events have favorably affected the course of international human rights observance in Latin America. One was the OAS reaction to the harsh measures imposed by Cuba's revolutionary government beginning in 1959 when the Castro regime imprisoned anyone suspected of disloyalty. The OAS Inter-American Commission on Human Rights quickly conducted an international human rights investigation. Since Cuba did not allow the commission to inspect, the Commission conducted its hearings in Florida, where it interviewed Cuban refugees. The Commission found that there was a widespread suspension of the human rights implicit in the OAS Charter and the other Latin American human rights declarations discussed below. Cuba was ultimately expelled from the OAS. Yet many commentators—recognizing that similar problems occurred during the same period elsewhere in Latin America—espouse the conviction that superpower Cold War politics played a larger role in this expulsion than any claimed human rights abuses. Numerous military dictatorships in Latin America used similar tactics to control their people but were not the object of such human rights scrutiny.

Another regional development suggests the potential for greater adherence to the OAS Charter promise that the "State shall respect the rights of the individual." That development has been the shift away from military to democratic governments in all Latin American countries except Cuba. In the 1960s and the 1970s, the military dictators in this region were known for their *desaparecidos,* the "disappeared" individuals who were political or personal enemies of government officials. Many of these dictatorships exhibited little concern for human rights and subsequently became democracies in the next decade. The classic may have been that of Chile's former dictator, Augusto Pinochet (*see* Problem 7.A). This change has had a favorable impact on human rights in a number of Latin American nations. The evidence of improvement, however, is far from conclusive. Some commentators are reservedly positive. Others, however, soon realized that little actually changed in Latin America just because there was a shift from military to civilian rule. The collapse of military dictatorships during the 1980s did *not* minimize the degree of human rights violations for years to come. The following 1987 excerpt from the US-based Pacific News Service explains the apparent paradox:

The most telling clue to what sustains terror in democracies lies in Argentina where last April [1987], President Raul Alfonsin reached an accord with military officers. The accord followed protests in which some military [personnel] occupied bases to block the prosecution of fellow officers for human rights abuses committed during the 1970s.

The Argentine military functions almost like an American political party—with its own leaders, hierarchy, and civilian constituents who support it either out of blood ties or . . . the conviction that any drastic action to preserve law and order is justified. But it is a party with a difference—it has a monopoly on modern weapons and a fiercely loyal membership. Government officials have little weight with military officers, who have risen in rank because of their allegiance to generals, not to democracy.

Threatened with a coup, President Alfonsin agreed not to prosecute lower ranking officers—and to preserve democratic rule. He made a "convivencia," or "living together" [arrangement of convenience]. . . .

Nor is the convivencia unique to Argentina. Similar agreements exist in Guatemala, Peru, Columbia, Ecuador, Bolivia, El Salvador, and Uruguay, where civilian governments no longer [bother to] determine the level of human rights abuse.

In democratically ruled Guatemala, infamous secret police still "disappear" government critics—425 political assassinations were recorded by the local press in the first two months of 1987 alone, according to US Embassy sources. . . .

And death squads continue to haunt such democratically run countries as Brazil, El Salvador, and Ecuador.[36]

The OAS Charter was constituted in 1948. Also that year an international conference of Latin American States proclaimed the American Declaration of the Rights and Duties of Man. This declaration of principles contains various political and civil rights—basically the same rights contained in the UN's 1948 Universal Declaration of Human Rights (UDHR, §11.2). The *duties* include the specific duty of the *individual* to obey the law and a general duty to conduct oneself in a way that serves the immediate community and the nation.

Like the UN Charter and the UDHR, the rights contained in the (Latin) American Declaration were not intended to immediately bind the participating Latin American States. It would be better to obtain State participation in a process that at least paid lip service to modern human rights perspectives rather than risk an OAS with very few members. The signatories *did* agree to a general statement of principles, although States remain free to delay actual implementation of the American Declaration's human rights goals until ratification.

The most recent Latin American human rights document is the American Convention on Human Rights. In the mid-1970s, OAS members decide to expand the minimal human rights provisions contained in the 1948 OAS Charter (as amended in 1970) and the 1948 American Declaration of the Rights and Duties of Man. They were concerned because the latter document emphasized the duties of the individual rather than those of the State. The product of their work was the American Convention on Human Rights, which became effective in 1978. It contains many of the human rights mentioned in the UN Charter and Universal Declaration of Human Rights. The American Declaration was one response to the excesses of the military governments of the 1960s and 1970s. A number of Latin American countries had recently altered their form of governments, from military dictatorships to democracies.

Prior to 1978, the existing Inter-American Commission on Human Rights did not have a reliable legal foundation, which was traceable to any document drawn up by OAS member nations. The American Convention provided an express source for the Commission's power to hear and determine human rights violations. In theory, the American Declaration would also confirm the Commission's power to prevent several more decades of human rights violations in Latin America. State parties were not only supposed to respect human rights. They would now be required "to ensure" the free and full exercise of these rights.

Unlike the recent change in the European Court of Human Rights process, where the administrative European Commission was disbanded, the OAS still employs the Commission process. The Inter-American Commission on Human Rights encourages members to implement the human rights norms in the OAS Charter and the American Declaration of the Rights and Duties of Man. It conducts country studies and makes recommendations to member states. Latin American States are encouraged to use their national legislative processes to implement the recommendations of the Commission. However, cases must be first considered by the Commission—before they can be heard by the Court. The Commission will not normally consider a case unless the aggrieved person has sought his or her remedies in the courts of the State accused of the human rights violation. Another limitation is that individuals may present claims to the Commission but not the Court (also unlike the 1998 streamlined process in the European Court of Human Rights). After all remedies have been exhausted before the Latin American Human Rights Commission, a State party to a dispute may then lodge the matter—on behalf of the aggrieved individual—in the Inter-American Court on Human Rights.

Certain countries (including the US) have not ratified the American Convention on Human Rights. Their rationale is that they cannot determine the extent of their commitments under the "full and free exercise of human rights" provision of the Convention. Without specific obligations being set forth in that agreement, they are unwilling to commit themselves to a process that does not fully identify the outer parameters of the State's obligation to the individual.

Some OAS nations have been reluctant to ratify the 1978 American Convention for yet another reason. A unique human rights provision was inserted into the 1978 American Convention, stating that judicial remedies for certain rights cannot be suspended. The treaty right of *habeas corpus* means that prison officials can be forced to produce a prisoner for a prompt judicial examination of the legality of his or her incarceration. Under the Convention, that right *cannot* be suspended, *even in time of emergency.*[37]

Section 9.4 of this book addressed the extent to which the UN's International Court of Justice (ICJ) could advance International Law via its advisory opinions. This facet of the Court's judicial power may be initiated only by a UN organ when it is unlikely that the disputing States will agree to an adversarial resolution by the ICJ. In Latin America, by contrast, the ability of the Inter-American Court of Human Rights to enhance the development of human rights is broader. In addition to OAS organs, any member State—not just the State parties to the Inter-American Convention—may request an advisory opinion. Further, the Court's Article 64.1 advisory jurisdiction is not limited to interpreting just the Convention. It extends to all "other treaties concerning the protection of human rights in the American States."

The following case illustrates the Court's advisory jurisdiction at work:

◆

"Interpretation of the American Declaration of Rights and Duties of Man Within the Framework of Article 64 of the American Convention on Human Rights"

ADVISORY OPINION OC-10/89
INTER-AMERICAN COURT OF HUMAN RIGHTS, 1989
29 *International Legal Materials* 379

Go to course Web site at http://home.att.net/~slomansonb/Rxrcsesite.html; click on American Declaration Case.

◆ *Notes & Questions*

1. The Court decided that it was competent to render this advisory opinion. Having done so, what did the Court actually decide?
2. During 1994, the OAS promulgated two new human rights instruments: (1) the Inter-American Convention on Forced Disappearance of Persons, and (2) the Inter-American Convention on the Prevention, Punishment and Eradication of Violence Against Women. *See* 23 *Int'l Legal Mat'ls* 1529 and 1534 (1994). The OAS is taking important steps to eliminate the historical characterization of Latin America as a region of the world where States are only committed in principle to the international rule of law in human rights matters.

AFRICAN PROGRAMS

The Organization of African Unity (OAU) is Africa's political organization of States (§3.5). The 1963 OAU Charter reaffirms the human rights principles of the UN

Charter and the UN's Universal Declaration of Human Rights. It adds certain rights not contained in those documents, such as the rights to the "eradication of colonialism" and the well-being of the African people.

Like other regional human rights documents, the OAU Charter provisions are moral rights that exist on paper awaiting implementation. University of Calabar (Nigeria) Professor U. O. Umozurike characterizes this situation as follows:

> During the 1970s human rights appeared to enjoy low esteem in Africa. . . . The O.A.U. maintained an indifferent attitude to the suppression of human rights in a number of independent African states *by unduly emphasizing the principle of noninterference in the internal affairs of member states* at the expense of certain other principles, particularly the customary law principle of respect for human rights. . . . For instance, the massacres of thousands of Hutu [tribal people] in Burundi in 1972 and 1973 were neither discussed nor condemned by the O.A.U., which regarded them as matters of [Burundi's] internal affairs. The notorious regimes of Idi Amin of Uganda (1971–1979) [and other African leaders] escaped the criticism of the O.A.U. and most of its members.[38]

In his 1993 treatise on International Law, Professor Umozurike characterized the positive potential of the Banjul (African) Charter on Human and Peoples' Rights, which entered into force in 1986. It contains rights like those in the above UN's 1966 Covenants (*see* §11.2). A number of those rights can be derogated by law, however, without any significant limitations on the State parties. While the African Charter internationalizes human rights on the African Continent, "there are practically no effective measures for enforcement."[39]

Why do human rights in Africa not enjoy the degree of recognition found in Europe or the Americas? One reason is that the question just posed contains a degree of cultural relativism. The latter societies tend to perceive the human rights expressed by their instruments as having an undeniable universal character. A Danish scholar who has written extensively on comparative human rights issues commented as follows on the divergent paradigms on this planet:

> [W]hile the American approach reflects a strong ideological stance favorable to [the *natural* law] universality of human rights, the Europeans base their conclusions more on the degree to which the universality is reflected empirically in the various instruments [*positive* law—a distinction addressed in §1.3 of this textbook].
>
> The African approach can mainly be divided into two schools, the first of which constitutes the most radical opposition to [a] universalist approach. The main argument here is rooted in the different philosophical basis of Western Europe and Africa, with a particular emphasis on the lack of an individualistically perceived personality in traditional African culture, which would render most human rights inapplicable.[40]

The African perspective is generally one involving a distrust of *internationally* derived human rights measures. Some African scholars perceive these "global" rights as yet another attempt to impose Western cultural values on the African continent. University of Cape Town Professor T. W. Bennett summarized this position in his study of human rights in southern Africa (in 1991, just prior to South Africa's cessation of minority white political governance):

> The talk about human rights that currently permeates discussions about South African law has its origins in the [external] international and constitutional human rights movement. The universality claimed for this movement should not obscure its actual cultural provenance. Although the accession of many developing countries to United Nations' declarations and international [human rights] conventions gives a superficial impression of universalism, human rights are the product of bourgeois western values. In many parts of Africa this has given cause for suspicion about a renewed attempt to impose western cultural hegemony.
>
> [The author then refutes the argument that human rights are irrelevant to the situation in Africa, with counter-arguments including the following:] . . . Feminist studies, for instance, have revealed that women used to be assured of material protection and support within the framework of the extended family; after the introduction of capitalism, however, the system of labour migration caused the breakdown of this family structure to the detriment of women (amongst others). They have now been rendered vul-

nerable, and at the same time forced to undertake roles (for which they have no formal legal powers) that were previously prescribed for all men.[41]

Like Latin America's 1948 American Declaration on the Rights and Duties of Man, the 1986 Banjul (African) Charter on Human Rights focuses on *duties.* The individual has the duty to preserve family, society, the State, and even the OAU. For example, individuals must care for their parents and always conduct themselves in a way that "preserves social and national solidarity."

The fulfillment of these duties may be misused by a national leader. Idi Amin suppressed individual rights in Uganda, leading to thousands of citizens being killed or jailed without just cause in the 1970s. While no human rights document would mean anything to a leader like Amin, the 1986 African Charter conveniently emphasized *duties* rather than the minimal rights denied to Ugandans under Amin. As stated by Professor Umozurike, the "concept of duties stressed in the Charter is quite likely to be abused by a few regimes on the continent, if the recent past can be any guide to future developments. Such governments will emphasize the duties of individuals to their states but will play down their rights and legitimate expectations."[42]

The 1986 African Charter also established the African Commission on Human Rights. This Commission is an eleven-member body composed of representatives from the fifty-two member nations of the OAU. Seated in Bangul, Gambia, the Commission is supposed to promote national observance of human rights on the African Continent. Like the Inter-American Commission on Human Rights, the African commission may only study, report, and recommend. It has no enforcement powers. It conducts country studies and makes recommendations to member governments. The Commission has the power to publish its reports when it concludes that an OAU State has violated the human rights provisions of the African Charter.[43] This Commission's very existence, however, represents a significant aspirational improvement after centuries of slave trade, colonialism, and despotic regimes. But no regional mechanism has been able to halt egregious human rights violations exemplified by the Rwandan slaughter of 1994.

If one were to characterize the Commission's power of publication of negative reports as a voice for enforcing human rights in Africa, then that voice may be easily silenced. Individuals and States may report violations of the African Charter to the commission. The Commission then explores the basis for such claims, drafts confirming reports, and may publish them in all OAU countries. The allegedly offending nation's leader, however, may avoid that negative publicity by requesting a vote from the OAU Assembly (Africa's heads of State) to block publication. Since its creation, the Commission has not published one adverse report of mistreatment of individuals by an OAU member State.

That there are different human rights perspectives in a particular region of the world does not equate to the non-recognition of fundamental rights on the national and regional levels. For example, until 1994, Zimbabwe did not permit foreign citizens who married its women to reside with them in Zimbabwe—unless the husbands possessed a needed skill, had invested substantial capital in a government-approved project, or were retired with adequate income to sustain themselves without government assistance. While one might recognize the government policy behind the general exclusion, the Zimbabwe Supreme Court struck down this government policy. It infringed the wives' right to freedom of movement because they would have to live abroad to be with their husbands. This government policy also affected the enjoyment of one's home, as well as the right to leave and re-enter Zimbabwe without fear of expulsion.[44] On the regional level, a number of African nations have ratified the 1990 African Charter on the Rights and Welfare of the Child. Given the international community's general reluctance to ratify the global UN Convention on the Rights of the Child, this development also suggests the dangers of generalization about regional views on human rights.[45]

ASIAN PERSPECTIVES

A number of Chinese scholars view the existing International Law of Human Rights as a pretext for intervention in the internal affairs of socialist nations. They believe that the field of human rights is primarily a matter governed by the internal law of a State rather than one falling within the competence of International Law. Any pressure on China to apply Western standards to the government's treatment of its own citizens would interfere with Chinese sovereignty. The Chinese were quite offended, for example, when the 1989 government restraints of the student uprisings in Beijing were characterized by the Western press as a return to Maoist-era restrictions on internationally recognized human rights.

A representative Chinese scholar from the earlier Maoist era verbalized the perspective that human rights are intact in China. There is no need to embrace the approach expressed in the UN's International Bill of Human Rights. The elimination of private ownership of property, for example, is perceived as a guarantee of the genuine realization of human rights of the Chinese people. Chinese Professor Ch'ien Szu stated in 1960 that the "rights of landlords and bourgeoisie arbitrarily to oppress and enslave laboring people are eliminated; the privilege of imperialism and its agents to do mischief . . . is also eliminated. To the vast masses of people, this is a wonderfully good thing; this is genuine protection of the human rights of the people. The bourgeois . . . international law scholars, however, consider this to be a bad thing, since it encroaches upon the 'human rights' of the oppressors and exploiters."[46]

Contemporary human rights perspectives are not as State-centric as in previous eras. In the aftermath of the Cultural Revolution of 1966–1976, Professor Szu's perspective would no longer be representative of recent Chinese scholarship on human rights. Contemporary thought is that the way in which one country or group establishes a human rights model is not necessarily the sole criterion for judging the performance of other countries. Chinese citizens enjoy far greater human rights protection now than in the Maoist era.[47] Yet the PRC was rather irritated when Hong Kong incorporated the UN Covenant on Civil and Political Rights into its domestic law just prior to its takeover by China. The 1991 Bill of Rights Ordinance made the UN Covenant the essential source of human rights law in Hong Kong.[48]

Scholars in Asia's *democratic* States have a different criticism of what they characterize as arrogant Western human rights standards. Indian scholars believe that the Western-derived concepts of human rights—stated in the UN Charter and the various regional programs modeled after the Charter—benefit only developed States. Thus, the UN's international human rights program has little meaning for a State whose people do not all have the basic necessities of life. As articulated by Patna University (India) Dean Hingorini, traditional "human rights have no meaning for these States and their peoples. Their first priority is [obtaining] basic necessities of life. These are bread, clothing and shelter. These necessities of life could be termed as basic human rights for them."[49]

Dean Hingorini's perspective does not mean that Indian scholars *oppose* the human rights principles set forth in the various UN and regional charters. Rather, his perspective is that many of those politically oriented rights are irrelevant for the time being and of little practical value to the people of India today. Attaining such rights, as expressed in what might be considered an advanced UN model, cannot take precedence over India's need to first provide the more basic essentials to its populace. The more developed nations can afford to be the champions of political and economic human rights such as the rights to work and an education.

Indian scholars also perceive developed nations as proclaiming the importance of such rights for the convenient purpose of ensuring that their multinational corporations can exploit the Indian masses. East Indian Professor S.B.O. Gutto recalls that

> [h]istorical developments in the Third World countries in the last few decades have firmly fashioned the Third World as theaters for the violation of human rights. . . . Classical international law, under the umbrella of "law of nations" developed as a major super-structural tool for facilitating and justifying the actions of some states and their agents, in ensuring the dominant economic classes and institutions, and in dividing the world into spheres where . . . enslavement, dehumanization, super-exploitation of peoples labour and resources takes place. The unsatisfactory condition of human rights in the Third World today is therefore not solely a reflection of inherent social factors in the Third World but rather products of the historical relations in the world system corresponding to the international division of labor.[50]

The degree of national economic development may thus be correlated to the degree of affordable human rights enjoyed by a nation's populace. A high percentage of unemployment may be characterized under prevailing human rights norms as a State's failure to afford the right to work. An underdeveloped country like India is not economically equipped to create and implement such human rights, however, or to establish commissions to monitor human rights observance.

Such countries must first achieve a comparatively minimal degree of economic development. India's Professor T. O. Elias, formerly a judge of the International Court of Justice, published the following assessment of this correlation when he described the 1964 Seminars on Human Rights in Developing Countries conducted in Kabul, Afghanistan: "[T]he existence of adequate material means and a high standard of economic development were essential prerequisites of the full and effective enjoyment of economic, social and cultural rights, and contributed to the promotion of civil and political rights. . . . [T]he right to work was meaningless in countries where employment opportunities were grossly inadequate owing to overpopulation combined with economic underdevelopment."[51]

Under this view, a poor and undeveloped economy simply cannot afford the contemporary package of human rights espoused by the more developed nations. Any attempt to implement Western political and economic rights would detract less developed nations from other national priorities—one of which is the right to development.[52] They must necessarily delay realization of these "advanced" rights contained in the prevailing human rights instruments until the far more "basic" human rights to food and adequate living conditions are first realized.

One drawback with this "Third World" human rights perspective is that the State can continue to rely on economic grounds to indefinitely postpone implementation of the otherwise generally recognized regime set forth by the UN in the International Bill of Human Rights. A State could characterize the right to food, for example, as being too weighty to justify national attention to rights such as voting or being free from imprisonment without due process of law.

◆ 11.4 OTHER HUMAN RIGHTS ACTORS

The previous sections of this chapter addressed the global and regional efforts of international organizations to secure the human rights of the individual. Other human rights organizations and entities also act as advocates. The most common are the privately constituted non-governmental organizations (*see* §3.2 on NGOs in International Law). They have undertaken the rather daunting task of securing national observance of international human rights norms—when many State actors have paid only lip service to this objective. The State-centric system of International Law brands them as "*non*-governmental" institutions, notwithstanding their function of identifying grassroots human rights violations to governments and international organizations such as the UN.

There are limitations on what States are willing to actually accomplish. This is where NGOs routinely assist, but not without occasional blemishes on the State–NGO relationship. In mid-1993, for example, 167 State representatives convened the Second UN World Human Rights Conference in Vienna. Their work product was the "Vienna Declaration and Programme of Action."[53] Two key objectives were to advocate creation of an International Criminal Court and the Office of the UN High Commissioner for Human Rights (*see* §§9.5 and 11.2). The primary credit for these developments in the Law of Human Rights later accrued to other institutions—the UN Security Council, which established the first *ad hoc* court in 1993, and the UN General Assembly for creating the Office of the High Commissioner in 1994. The 1993 human rights conference in Vienna provided a spark, however, that helped kindle the fervor for such enforcement apparatus.

The 1993 World Human Rights Conference was the likely catalyst for the non-governmental organization movement. One thousand five hundred NGOs sent representatives. The UN ousted them, however, from the drafting of the Conference's resulting Vienna Declaration and Programme for Action. The more powerful NGOs such as Amnesty International bitterly protested. But China's threatened boycott succeeded in convincing the UN to bar NGOs from participation. China's perspective is that the UN does not need NGOs. The PRC's position reflects that of many Asian States. They perceive Western States as attempting to impose their religious and cultural values under UN authority when they denounce human rights abuses in politically targeted regions or countries. The NGOs responded by accusing the UN of bowing to such pressures and thereby retarding the achievable degree of accountability for human rights violations.

These private organizations have nevertheless played a very critical role in human rights monitoring. The International Red Cross is one of the most prominent. Its efforts included relentless pressure for internationalizing the Laws of War (*see* §10.6). The most significant work product was the 1949 Geneva Conventions and their Protocols, which deal with the treatment of civilians and prisoners during time of war and related hostilities (*see* Exhibit 10.3). The Red Cross is the NGO that routinely inspects various national detention centers that hold political prisoners so that inmates might receive medical and other basic necessities.

Amnesty International is probably the most prominent watchdog group. This NGO has offices and individual members throughout the world. AI produces annual reports on national compliance with the various human rights treaties and declarations on human rights. It is one of the many private monitors that publicize the human rights problems discussed in this chapter.

The major human rights NGOs enjoy consultative status in various international organizations including the Council of Europe, the OAS, and UNESCO. Their representatives may present reports to these organizations as a way to maintain public scrutiny of offending State practices.

Among the major human rights NGOs are Amnesty International (London), Canadian Human Rights Foundation (Montreal), Civil Liberties Organization (Nigeria), Committee for the Defense of Democratic Freedoms and Human Rights in Syria (Damascus), Human Rights Watch (New York), International Association of Democratic Lawyers (Brussels), International Commission of Jurists (Geneva), International Committee of the Red Cross (Geneva), International Federation for the Rights of Man (Paris), International Helsinki Federation for Human Rights (Vienna), International League for Human Rights (New York), Lawyers Committee for Human Rights (New York), and Punjab Human Rights Organization (Chandigarh).[54]

◆ 11.5 UNITED STATES HUMAN RIGHTS PERSPECTIVES

This section of the book focuses on several centerpieces of US human rights policy: first, the US Senate's dilemma with ratifying the relevant regional and global human rights treaties identified earlier in this chapter; second, US military and economic incentives for improving human rights via its foreign assistance policy; and third, US judicial perspectives on the availability of a remedy for human rights violations in other countries.

TREATY PARTICIPATION DILEMMA

The US is not a party to a number of international human rights instruments (*see* Exhibit 11.1 in §11.3). Ratification has typically taken decades. For example, the US Senate did not ratify the 1948 Genocide Convention until 1986.[55] It did not ratify the 1966 International Covenant on Civil and Political Rights until 1992. While a number of *bilateral* treaties with other countries contain human rights provisions, the US has not been willing to promptly ratify *multilateral* agreements. Why?

One reason is that—at the time of the 1945 UN Charter, the 1948 Universal Declaration of Human Rights (global), and the 1948 American Convention on Human Rights (regional)—racial discrimination was permitted or mandated in the US. Many southern Senators were not willing to embrace the post-war wave of UN human rights instruments. They feared that they could thereby subject the US to embarrassing international inquiries, based on noncompliance with certain human rights instruments. This form of discrimination was not limited to the South. In 1948, US Supreme Court Justice Black lamented that the majority of the judges (in the particular case before the Court) ignored the UN Charter's human rights provisions. The US Supreme Court's judges thus allowed a US state to legally discriminate against Japanese citizens residing in the US. Aliens were thereby prohibited from owning land under California law. In Justice Black's words:

> California should not be permitted to erect obstacles designed to prevent the immigration of people whom Congress has authorized to come into and remain in the country. . . . [I]ts law stands as an obstacle to the free accomplishment of our policy in the international field. One of these reasons is that we have recently pledged ourselves to cooperate with the United Nations to "promote . . . universal respect for, and observance of, human rights and fundamental freedoms for all without distinction as to race, sex, language, or religion." How can this nation be faithful to this international pledge if state laws which bar land ownership and occupancy by aliens on account of race are permitted to be enforced?[56]

Not until 1954 did the US Supreme Court decide in *Brown v. Board of Education* that "separate but equal facilities" were unconstitutional under US law. *De facto* racial discrimination did not end with *Brown,* however. Governmental agencies continued to struggle with the full implementation of *Brown* and its progeny.

At the same time, Ohio's Senator John Bricker sought an amendment of the US Constitution's treaty power that would have eliminated the president's executive agreement power (*see* §8.3). If successful, that measure would have required the president to obtain the advice and consent of the Senate for *all* treaties—not just the ones that the executive branch perceived as falling within the meaning of this constitutional phrase. The senator's underlying fear was the California *Sei Fujii* case (text set forth in §8.1). The trial court had just ruled against discriminatory land laws that barred alien ownership. This decision could be upheld by the US Supreme Court or some presidential executive agreement without input from Congress (neither of which occurred). Senator Bricker relentlessly expressed his concern that numerous state and federal laws might fall in the wake of presidential agreements that the Senate would not be able to bar or control.[57]

In the 1960s and 1970s, Presidents Kennedy and Carter submitted various human rights treaties to the US Senate for its advice and consent. Few were ratified. The Genocide Convention was ratified during the Reagan years, but not without significant concern about how it might later "haunt" the US. Like most multilateral instruments, it is broadly worded with rather general principled statements.

A new Constitutional concern supplanted the intergovernmental balance of power concerns expressed by Senator Bricker. Threats to the Constitutionally protected right to freedom of speech emerged as the contemporary argument for opposing US ratification of human rights treaties. Under US law, treaties cannot override the Constitution (*see* §9.7). A variety of international provisions might require the US to abandon its staunchly ingrained judicial posture—that the US Constitution cannot be overcome by a treaty. When the US Senate finally ratified the 1948 Genocide Convention forty years after the UN General Assembly's unanimous adoption, it did so on the basis of a US reservation providing that "nothing in the [Genocide] Convention requires or authorizes legislation or other action by the United States of America as interpreted by the United States."

Like a number of other human rights instruments, this Convention contains wording that essentially prohibits racial or religious hatred constituting an incitement to discrimination of any kind. In 1978, the American Civil Liberties Union successfully litigated the First Amendment right of Neo-Nazis to parade in Skokie, Illinois—complete with swastikas.[58] Assuming that the US had ratified the Genocide Convention before the time of that march, absent the above treaty reservation, the judicial approval and city-issued permit for this march would likely subject the US to international responsibility for government-approved activity that incited religious hatred.

The question of whether ratification of human rights treaties would yield unintended State responsibility is not limited to free speech concerns. Rationales include the following. First, many States of the world advocate abolition of the death penalty.[59] Many states of the US, however, punish certain crimes by imposing a death penalty. Second, US President Clinton discouraged the 1994 flogging of Michael Fay, an eighteen-year-old US citizen convicted of vandalism in Singapore. Yet the US has had a long history of public flogging. Until the 1960s, public flogging was authorized in several states for robbery and certain assaults. The most recently publicized event was the 1952 flogging of a young bricklayer in Delaware for beating an elderly woman. Third, the US invasion of Panama may have violated the 1977 Geneva Convention Protocol relating to the protection of civilian victims in armed conflict. The US Senate had previously declined ratification on grounds that the Protocol is "fundamentally unfair and irreconcilably flawed" because it "would undermine humanitarian law and endanger civilians in war."

FOREIGN ASSISTANCE ACT

Certain US statutes target conduct abroad that adversely impacts human rights. Title 22 of the United States Code, for example, contains the Foreign Assistance Act. Section 2304 provides:

> (a)(1) The United States shall, in accordance with its international obligations as set forth in the Charter of the United Nations and in keeping with the constitutional heritage and traditions of the United States, promote and encourage increased respect for human

> rights and fundamental freedoms throughout the world without distinction as to race, sex, language, or religion. Accordingly, a principal goal of the foreign policy of the United States shall be to promote the increased observance of internationally recognized human rights by all countries.
>
> (a)(2) Except under circumstances specified in this section, no security assistance may be provided to any country the government of which engages in a consistent pattern of gross violations of internationally recognized human rights.

This legislation prohibits providing police training to any offending foreign government unless the President certifies to Congress that extraordinary circumstances exist to warrant such assistance. The Act defines *gross violations* as "torture or cruel, inhuman, or degrading treatment or punishment, prolonged detention without charges and trial, causing the disappearance of persons by the abduction and clandestine detention of those persons, and [any] other flagrant denial of the right to life, liberty, or the security of person. . . ."

Section 2151(n) of the Foreign Assistance Act is also designed to protect abused children. No assistance may be provided to any government that fails to take appropriate measures, *within its means,* to protect children from exploitation, abuse, or forced conscription into military or paramilitary service. The "within its means" provision recognizes that certain governments may not have the economic competence to provide the degree of protection expected under US standards.

Under the Foreign Assistance Act, the US Secretary of State must transmit an annual report to the Speaker of the House of Representatives and the Senate Committee on Foreign Relations on practices of assisted nations involving "coercion in population control, including coerced abortion and involuntary sterilization. . . ." This provision places the relationship between the US and the People's Republic of China at odds because of the PRC's official policy of depriving State benefits to parents who have more than one child (generally enforced in urban areas).[60]

The Foreign Assistance Act formerly provided for an Assistant Secretary of State for Human Rights and Humanitarian Affairs. This position was statutorily repealed in 1994 under Vice President Gore's "restructuring" program to reduce the size of US government. The new title for the officer in charge of this monitoring function is the Assistant Secretary of State for the Bureau of Democracy, Human Rights, and Labor.[61] This arguably minor title change presents the issue of whether this "restructuring" effectively contracted this officer's human rights monitoring duties—because of the expanded job description.

1998 HUMAN RIGHTS EXECUTIVE ORDER

In December 1998, President Clinton issued the Executive Order on Implementation of Human Rights Treaties. Section 1 provides that it will be US "policy and practice . . . to fully respect and implement its obligations under the human rights treaties to which it is a party," specifically referring to the International Covenant on Civil and Political Rights; the Convention Against Torture and Other Cruel, Inhuman or Degrading Treatment or Punishment; and the Convention on the Elimination of All Forms of Racial Discrimination. Each executive department and agency of the US government was thereby directed to appoint a contact person who would be responsible for coordinating the implementation of human rights obligations within that department or agency. An Interagency Working Group on Human Rights was established to coordinate human rights implementation activities—including the preparation of responses to allegations of US human rights violations submitted to international organizations; the development of mechanisms to review legislation for conformity with human rights obligations; the monitoring of actions by state, municipal, and territorial governments for conformity with international human rights obligations; and the direction of an annual review of US reservations, declarations, and understandings to human rights treaties.[62]

In 1991, Congress had enacted a human rights statute—the Torture Victim Protection Act. This legislation evolved as a result of the major human rights case set forth below.

JUDICIAL PERSPECTIVES

Alien Tort Statute The following case was the springboard for a flourishing body of human rights law in the US judicial system:

Filartiga v. Pena-Irala

UNITED STATES COURT OF APPEALS, SECOND CIRCUIT

630 F.2d 876 (1980)

Author's Note: *Citations have been omitted and emphasis supplied in certain passages.*

COURT'S OPINION. IRVING R. KAUFMAN, Circuit Judge:

. . . Implementing the constitutional mandate for national control over foreign relations, the First Congress established original district court jurisdiction over "all causes where an alien sues for a tort only (committed) in violation of the law of nations." Judiciary Act of 1789, codified at 28 USC §1350. Construing this rarely invoked provision, we hold that deliberate torture perpetrated under color of official authority violates universally accepted norms of the international law of human rights, regardless of the nationality of the parties. Thus, whenever an alleged torturer is found and served with process by an alien within our borders, §1350 provides federal jurisdiction. Accordingly, we reverse the judgment of the district court dismissing the complaint for want of federal jurisdiction [to hear and decide this type of case].

I

The appellants, plaintiffs below, are citizens of the Republic of Paraguay. Dr. Joel Filartiga, a physician, describes himself as a longstanding opponent of the government of President Alfredo Stroessner, which has held power in Paraguay since 1954. His daughter, Dolly Filartiga, arrived in the United States in 1978 under a visitor's visa, and has since applied for permanent political asylum. The Filartigas brought this action in the Eastern District of New York against Americo Norberto Pena-Irala (Pena), also a citizen of Paraguay, for wrongfully causing the death of Dr. Filartiga's seventeen-year old son, Joelito. . . .

The appellants contend that on March 29, 1976, Joelito Filartiga was kidnapped and tortured to death by Pena, who was then Inspector General of Police in Asuncion, Paraguay. Later that day, the police brought Dolly Filartiga to Pena's home where she was confronted with the body of her brother, which evidenced marks of severe torture. As she fled, horrified, from the house, Pena followed after her shouting, "Here you have what you have been looking for so long and what you deserve. Now shut up." The Filartigas claim that Joelito was tortured and killed in retaliation for his father's political activities and beliefs.

Shortly thereafter, Dr. Filartiga commenced a criminal action in the Paraguayan courts against Pena and the police for the murder of his son. As a result, Dr. Filartiga's attorney was arrested and brought to police headquarters where, shackled to a wall, Pena threatened him with death. This attorney, it is alleged, has since been disbarred without just cause. . . .

In July of 1978, Pena sold his house in Paraguay and entered the United States under a visitor's visa. He was accompanied by Juana Bautista Fernandez Villalba, who had lived with him in Paraguay. The couple remained in the United States beyond the term of their visas, and were living in Brooklyn, New York, when Dolly Filartiga, who was then living in Washington, D. C., learned of their presence. Acting on information provided by Dolly the Immigration and Naturalization Service arrested Pena and his companion, both of whom were subsequently ordered deported on April 5, 1979 following a hearing. They had then resided in the United States for more than nine months.

Almost immediately, Dolly caused Pena to be served with a summons and civil complaint at the Brooklyn Navy Yard, where he was being held pending deportation. The complaint alleged that Pena had wrongfully caused Joelito's death by torture and sought compensatory and punitive damages of $10,000,000. The Filartigas also sought to enjoin Pena's deportation to ensure his availability for testimony at trial. The cause of action is stated as arising under "wrongful death statutes; the U.N. Charter; the Universal Declaration of Human Rights; the U.N. Declaration Against Torture; the American Declaration of the Rights and Duties of Man; and other pertinent declarations, documents and practices constituting the customary international law of human rights and the law of nations" . . . Jurisdiction is claimed . . . principally on this appeal, under the Alien Tort Statute, 28 USC §1350.

[Trial] Judge Nickerson stayed the order of deportation, and Pena immediately moved to dismiss the complaint on the grounds that subject matter jurisdiction was absent [in a case between citizens of Paraguay, regarding conduct occurring there] and for forum non conveniens [better forum elsewhere]. On the jurisdictional issue, there has been no suggestion that Pena claims diplomatic immunity from suit. The Filartigas submitted the affidavits of a number of distinguished international legal scholars, who stated unanimously that the law of nations prohibits absolutely the use of torture as alleged in the complaint. Pena, in support of his motion to dismiss on the ground of forum non conveniens, submitted the affidavit of his Paraguayan counsel, Jose Emilio Gorostiaga, who averred that Paraguayan law provides a full and adequate civil remedy for the wrong alleged. Dr. Filartiga has not commenced such an action, however, believing that further resort to the courts of his own country would be futile [where a criminal investigation had been pending against Pena for four years, Filartiga's lawyer was thus disbarred without cause, and Pena had left Paraguay to live in the US].

Judge Nickerson . . . dismissed the complaint on jurisdictional grounds. The district judge recognized the strength of appellants' argument that official torture violates an emerging norm of customary international law. Nonetheless, he felt constrained . . . to construe narrowly "the law of nations," as employed in §1350, as excluding . . . [the] law which governs a state's treatment of its own citizens i.e., precluding US jurisdiction over cases arising abroad.

The district court continued the stay of deportation for forty-eight hours while appellants applied for further stays. These applications were denied by a panel of this Court on May 22, 1979, and by the Supreme Court two days later. Shortly thereafter, Pena and his companion returned to Paraguay.

II

Appellants rest their principal argument in support of federal jurisdiction upon the Alien Tort Statute, 28 USC §1350, which provides: "The district courts shall have original jurisdiction of any civil action by an alien for a tort only, committed in violation of the law of nations or a treaty of the United States." Since appellants do not contend that their action arises directly under a treaty of the United States, a threshold question on the *jurisdictional issue is whether the conduct alleged violates the law of nations.* In light of the universal condemnation of torture in numerous international agreements, and the renunciation of torture as an instrument of official policy by virtually all of the nations of the world (in principle if not in practice), we find that an act of torture committed by a state official against one held in detention violates established norms of the international law of human rights, and hence the law of nations. . . .

The United Nations Charter (a treaty of the United States, *see* 59 Stat. 1033 [1945]) makes it clear that in this modern age a state's treatment of its own citizens is a matter of international concern. It provides: With a view to the creation of conditions of stability and well-being which are necessary for peaceful and friendly relations among nations . . . the United Nations shall promote . . . universal respect for, and observance of, human rights and fundamental freedoms for all without distinctions as to race, sex, language or religion. And further: All members pledge themselves to take joint and separate action in cooperation with the Organization for the achievement of the purposes set forth in Article 55. Id. Art. 56.

While this broad mandate has been held not to be wholly self-executing, . . . this observation alone does not end our inquiry. For although there is no universal agreement as to the precise extent of the "human rights and fundamental freedoms" guaranteed to all by the Charter, there is at present no dissent from the view that the guaranties include, at a bare minimum, the right to be free from torture. This prohibition has become part of customary international law, as evidenced and defined by the Universal Declaration of Human Rights, General Assembly Resolution 217 (III)(A) (Dec. 10, 1948) which states, in the plainest of terms, "no one shall be subjected to torture." The General Assembly has declared that the Charter precepts embodied in this Universal Declaration "constitute basic principles of international law." Gen. Ass. Reso. 2625 (XXV) (Oct. 24, 1970). [Here, the opinion notes that eighteen nations had—by 1978—incorporated the Universal Declaration into their own national constitutions.]

Particularly relevant is the Declaration on the Protection of All Persons from Being Subjected to Torture, General Assembly Resolution 3452 (1975). . . . The Declaration expressly prohibits any state from permitting the dastardly and totally inhuman act of torture. Torture, in turn, is defined as "any act by which severe pain and suffering, whether physical or mental, is intentionally inflicted by or at the instigation of a public official on a person for such purposes as . . . intimidating him or other persons." The Declaration goes on to provide that "(w)here it is proved that an act of torture or other cruel, inhuman or degrading treatment or punishment has been committed by or at the instigation of a public official, the victim shall be afforded redress and compensation, in accordance with national law." . . .

These U.N. declarations are significant because they specify with great precision the obligations of member nations under the Charter. Since their adoption, "(m)embers can no longer contend that they do not know what human rights they promised in the Charter to promote." Sohn, "A Short History of United Nations Documents on Human Rights," in The United Nations and Human Rights, 18th Report of the Commission (Commission to Study the Organization of Peace ed. 1968). . . .

Turning to the act of torture, we have little difficulty discerning its universal renunciation in the modern usage and practice of nations. The international consensus surrounding torture has found expression in numerous international treaties and accords. . . . *Although torture was once a routine concomitant of criminal interrogations in many nations,* during the modern and hopefully more enlightened era it has been universally renounced. According to one survey, torture is prohibited, expressly or implicitly, by the *constitutions* of over fifty-five nations, including both the United States and Paraguay. . . .

Having examined the sources from which customary international law is derived [including] the usage of nations, judicial opinions and the works of jurists we conclude that official torture is now prohibited by the law of nations. The prohibition is clear and unambiguous, and admits of *no distinction between treatment of aliens and citizens.* Accordingly, we must conclude that the dictum in *Dreyfus v. von Finck, supra,* 534 F.2d at 31, to the effect that "violations of *international* law do not occur when the aggrieved parties are nationals of the *acting* state," is clearly out of tune with the current usage and practice of international law. . . . We therefore turn to the question whether the other requirements for jurisdiction are met.

III

Appellee submits that even if the tort alleged is a violation of modern international law, federal jurisdiction may not be exercised consistent with the dictates of Article III of the Constitution [under US law]. The claim is without merit. . . .

It is not extraordinary for a court to adjudicate a tort claim arising outside of its territorial jurisdiction. A state or nation has a legitimate interest in the orderly resolution of disputes among those [who happen to later live] within its borders. . . .

[W]e proceed to consider whether the First Congress acted constitutionally in vesting jurisdiction over "foreign suits," alleging torts committed in violation of the law of nations. A case properly "aris(es) under the . . . laws of the United States" for Article III purposes if grounded upon statutes enacted by Congress or upon the common law of the United States. The law of nations forms an integral part of the common law, and a review of the history surrounding the adoption of the Constitution demonstrates that it became a part of the common law of the United States upon the adoption of the Constitution. Therefore, the enactment of the Alien Tort Statute was authorized by Article III.

During the eighteenth century, it was taken for granted on both sides of the Atlantic that the law of nations forms a part of the common law [of the courts of the US]. . . .

As ratified, the [US Constitution's] judiciary article contained no express reference to cases arising under the law of nations. Indeed, the only express reference to that body of law is contained in Article I, sec. 8, cl. 10, which grants to the Congress the *power to "define and punish . . . offenses against the law of nations."* Appellees seize upon this circumstance and advance the proposition that the law of nations forms a part of the laws of the United States *only to the extent that Congress has acted to define it.* This extravagant claim is amply refuted by the numerous decisions applying rules of international law uncodified in any act of Congress. . . .

The Filartigas urge that 28 USC §1350 be treated as an exercise of Congress's power to define offenses against the law of nations. While such a reading is possible, . . . we believe it is sufficient here to construe the Alien Tort Statute, not as granting new rights to aliens, but simply as opening the federal courts for adjudication of the rights already recognized by international law. The statute nonetheless does inform our analysis of Article III, for we recognize that questions of jurisdiction "must be considered part of an organic growth part of an evolutionary process," and that the history of the judiciary article gives meaning to its pithy phrases. The Framers' overarching concern that control over international affairs be vested in the new national government to safeguard the standing of the United States among the nations of the world therefore reinforces the result we reach today.

Although the Alien Tort Statute has rarely been the basis for [successfully asserting §1350] jurisdiction during its long history, in light of the foregoing discussion, there can be little doubt that [now] this action is properly brought in federal court. . . . Thus, the narrowing construction that the Alien Tort Statute has previously received reflects the fact that earlier cases did not involve such well-established, universally recognized norms of international law that are here at issue. . . .

In the twentieth century the international community has come to recognize the common danger posed by the flagrant disregard of basic human rights and particularly the right to be free of torture. Spurred first by the Great War, and then the Second, civilized nations have banded together to prescribe acceptable norms of international behavior. From the ashes of the Second World War arose the United Nations Organization, amid hopes that an era of peace and cooperation had at last begun. Though many of these aspirations have remained elusive goals, that circumstance cannot diminish the true progress that has been made. In the modern age, humanitarian and practical considerations have combined to lead the nations of the world to recognize that respect for fundamental human rights is in their individual and collective interest. Among the rights universally proclaimed by all nations, as we have noted, is the right to be free of physical torture. Indeed, for purposes of civil liability, the torturer has become like the pirate and slave trader before him *hostis humani generis,* an enemy of all mankind. Our holding today, giving effect to a jurisdictional provision enacted by our First Congress, is a small but important step in the fulfillment of the ageless dream to free all people from brutal violence.

◆ *Notes & Questions*

1. Several other issues were addressed by the various courts involved in the *Filartiga* litigation.

   First, Pena's US lawyer argued that the relevant human rights treaties were not "self-executing." As described in §8.1 of this book, a self-executing treaty either expressly or impliedly creates immediately binding obligations. The referenced multilateral human rights treaties are *not* "self-executing." Instead, they set aspirational standards of achievement—which all nations are at least morally obliged to achieve but only when ready to *ratify* the relevant human rights treaties. This treaty-based defense was correct, but it was not the end of the case. Customary State practice—and US national law—had already recognized the pervasive nature of the prohibition against torture.

   Second, defendant Pena claimed that the Act of State (AOS) doctrine barred US courts from hearing this case because Pena was a police official when the "alleged" torture occurred in Paraguay. As discussed in §9.8 of this book, the AOS doctrine would not apply. An action by a State official—in violation of the antitorture provision of the Constitution of the Republic of Paraguay, and not ratified by Paraguay—could hardly be characterized as an AOS.

   Third, Pena's *forum non conveniens* argument—essentially that Paraguay was a better forum for resolving this case—underscores the wisdom of the first US Congress in vesting jurisdiction over such claims in the federal district courts pursuant to the Alien Tort Statute (Judicial Code §1350). Put another way, if a US court were to dismiss this suit on the basis that Paraguay was a better forum, would it be discouraging the International Law of Human Rights? *Filartiga* sent a message abroad that US courts would apply international human rights doctrine even when foreign citizens torture other foreign citizens in foreign countries. The practical limitation is that the tortured plaintiff (or relative, in the case of wrongful death) must find a defendant in the US—who is not subject to some immunity while present—in order to serve the defendant with process in a *"Filartiga"* suit.
2. Four years after the appellate court's finding in *Filartiga* that the plaintiffs had stated a valid claim under US human rights law, which remanded the case back to the trial court for further proceedings, they were

awarded judgments totaling $10,385,364. The Pena defendants made no appearance in these subsequent proceedings. They had previously been deported from the US to Paraguay. The plaintiffs would then have to seek to enforce their judgments in Paraguay on the assumption that the defendants were not effectively judgment-proof because of insufficient funds to pay this sizable judgment. The final *Filartiga* judgment nevertheless makes the US position clear to perpetrators who commit such egregious conduct. The ultimate judicial opinion in *Filartiga* provides as follows: "The record in this case shows that torture and death are bound to recur unless deterred. This court concludes that an award of punitive damages of no less than $5,000,000 to each plaintiff is appropriate to reflect adherence to the world community's proscription of torture and to attempt to deter its practice." *Filartiga v. Pena,* 577 F.Supp. 860, 867 (E.D.N.Y. 1984).

3. Several scathing rebuttals by prominent writers in the field of International Law resist the *Filartiga* court's conclusion that the Alien Tort Statute (ATS) applies in this context. Chief among them is that by Tufts University Professor Alfred Rubin. In his view: (1) It is by no means clear that the "law of nations" was meant to apply to individuals, as opposed to States—especially in 1789, when the ATS was enacted; (2) the *Filartiga* plaintiffs alleged "wrongful death" as opposed to torture in their complaint—which raises doubts as to whether the "law of nations" can be breached in the case of a civil action for money damages based on "wrongful death;" (3) attempts to recover money damages from convicted Nazi war criminals or their heirs were rejected as not being based in law in decisions from both East and West German courts; (4) civil torts were not criminal "offenses" against the "law of nations" when the ATS was enacted in 1789; and (5) *Filartiga* is a vast expansion of rules of national jurisdiction that were rejected in the early days of the nation. *See* A. Rubin, "US Tort Suits by Aliens Based on International Law," 18 *Fletcher Forum* 65 (1994).
4. The accepted principles for international jurisdiction are set forth in §5.2 (Exhibit 5.1). None was expressly mentioned in Judge Kaufman's opinion. Which of these grounds would be a viable basis for jurisdiction on the facts of *Filartiga?* Did the US violate any obligation by deporting Pena back to Paraguay?

In another §1350 case, a federal appellate court in California was the first to decide that a political leader can be held liable for human rights violations committed by his subordinates during peacetime. After a fourteen-year rule in the Philippines, Ferdinand Marcos moved to Hawaii in 1986, where he was served with process in this case. The plaintiff Filipino victims and families received a huge damages award based on the disappearances, summary executions, and torture that occurred within Marcos' command authority while he was dictator. The court also approved of the class action device as a superior method for resolving such human rights claims when they are brought against a former leader who moves to the US after a despotic period of national rule.[63]

Torture Prevention Act In 1991, Congress enacted a refinement to the Alien Tort Statute (28 US Code §1350) that effectively codified the *Filartiga* decision. This legislation is called the Torture Victim Protection Act.[64] It prohibits torture and "extrajudicial killings." Congress defined the latter term to create liability for an "individual who, under actual or apparent authority, or color of law, of any foreign nation" tortures another human being or perpetrates "a deliberated killing not authorized by a previous judgment pronounced by a regularly constituted court affording all the judicial guarantees which are recognized as indispensable by civilized peoples." This term excludes "killing that, under international law, is lawfully carried out under the authority of a foreign nation." Congressional objectives for expanding jurisdiction over such conduct included the enhanced viability of the US as a forum for resolving the civil liability when foreign officials or State agents perform torture and then seek to defend their actions on the procedural grounds of sovereign immunity (*see* §2.6 of this book) or Act of State (*see* §9.8).

Torture is also prohibited by the 1966 International Covenant on Civil and Political Rights, to which the US is a party. Its terms provide that "[n]o one shall be subjected to torture or to cruel, inhuman or degrading punishment." However, the US 1991 Torture Prevention Act did *not* thereby adopt the 1984 *UN Convention* Against Torture. Principle 6 of the 1984 UN Convention on Torture provides that "[n]o circumstances *whatever* may be invoked as a justification for torture. . . ."

A widely publicized case arising out of the Bosnian conflict construed both the 1789 Alien Tort Statute (ATS) and the 1991 Torture Prevention Act (TPA). The self-styled leader of the Bosnian Serbs, Radovan Karadzic, was served with process in New York City in 1993. He was attending UN-brokered meetings of the various entities involved in the Bosnian conflict (prior to the 1995 Dayton Peace Accords). In its 1995 decision, the federal appellate court in New York distinguished between the types of claims that may be brought in US courts under these respective statutes. Under the ATS, personally planning and ordering a campaign of murder, rape, forced impregnation, and other forms of torture—which were designed to destroy religious and ethnic groups of Bosnian Muslims and Bosnian Croats—clearly violated both International Law (genocide) and the ATS (violation of the law of nations). Genocide generally violates the law of nations, as described earlier in this chapter. It also violates a specific US law—in this instance, the Genocide Convention Implementation Act of 1987, codified at 18 USC §1091. For the purpose of filing an ATS claim in a US court, it did not matter whether or not defendant Karadzic was acting under color of law. In other words, Karadzic's official or quasi-official status was irrelevant under the ATS. He was essentially accused of genocide, which violates "the law of nations."

The TPA, on the other hand, codifies the universally accepted norm prohibiting *official* torture. The TPA extends the ATS to cover summary executions, even when *not* perpetrated in the course of committing genocide or war crimes. This conduct may now be prosecuted under the TPA, but *only* when committed by state officials or under color of law. Karadzic was characterized as a state official because of his apparent authority over Serb forces in Bosnia. His alleged conduct was deemed a violation of the TPA. Thus, the plaintiffs could pursue their claim for civil damages—on the facts of this case—under both statutes.[65] On the other hand, if Karadzic had been a *private* citizen who acted in a way that violated International Law, he would be subject to liability under the ATS, but not the TPA.

◆ SUMMARY

1. Early "humanitarian interventions" were undertaken to enforce international human rights violations that were supposedly recognized by the community of nations. Some nations, however, abused this notion. They invaded other nations for political and military purposes. This fostered national distrust of human rights initiatives and retarded international attempts to secure those rights for oppressed individuals.
2. The UN inaugurated a human rights program that resulted in the International Bill of Human Rights. The essential rights are contained in various UN documents, especially the 1948 Universal Declaration of Human Rights (UDHR); the 1966 International Covenant on Civil and Political Rights; its protocols, which provide for the right of individual petition and abolition of the death penalty; and the 1966 International Covenant on Economic, Social and Cultural Rights.
3. All States profess their support for the human rights of their citizens. Many States disagree, however, about the precise content of this body of rights. Some deny that these rights are universal. Others "pay lip service" to the International Bill of Human Rights without actually observing them.
4. Human rights declarations such as the Universal Declaration of Human Rights are aspirational standards of achievement—as opposed to treaties necessitating immediately binding obligations. Treaties such as the 1966 International Covenants are binding—the reason why many States have either not ratified them or done so with significant reservations.
5. The 1948 UDHR was the first comprehensive human rights document to be drafted on a global scale. It is a General Assembly Resolution that was unanimously adopted by all UN members in 1948. It contains two general categories of rights. The first is civil and political rights. The second is economic, social, and cultural rights. Like the UN Charter, the Universal Declaration does not require a State to immediately provide these rights to its populace. Universal acceptance of this resolution arguably made it binding as a matter of *customary* international law, however.
6. In 1966, the UN General Assembly produced two key human rights instruments: the International Covenant on Civil and Political Rights, and the International Covenant on Economic, Social and Cultural Rights. They differ from earlier human rights instruments in that each is cast in the form of a multilateral treaty. Those countries that specifically accept their obligations by ratifying these Covenants must establish conspicuous and effective machinery to deal with alleged violations of human rights.

7. The UN's eighteen-nation Human Rights Committee examines periodic compliance reports submitted by the treaty parties. In 1993, the UN established the post of the UN High Commissioner on Human Rights for the purpose of monitoring and enhancing the various UN human rights programs.
8. There are various *regional* human rights programs. Most reiterate the same rights contained in the UN-based human rights documents. Europe has two basic human rights treaties: the European Human Rights Convention (EHR treaty) and the European Social Charter. The EHR treaty contains civil and political rights that are virtually identical to those set forth in the United Nation's Covenant on Civil and Political Rights. The European Social Charter contains the same economic and social rights set forth in the United Nation's Covenant on Economic, Social and Cultural Rights. Europe's enforcement machinery consists of specialized executive and judicial bodies. The executive body is Council of Ministers. The judicial body is the European Court of Human Rights.
9. Latin America's human rights norms are expressed in the 1948 Charter of the Organization of American States (OAS), the 1948 American Declaration of the Rights and Duties of Man, and the 1978 American Convention on Human Rights. These norms are monitored by the Inter-American Commission on Human Rights. In comparison to other regional instruments, the OAS Charter and the American Declaration are not as specific about the content of human rights in Latin America. The State's sovereignty to act is not as effectively limited as in European practice.
10. Africa's human rights program is premised on the 1986 African Charter on Human and Peoples' Rights. The African Charter contains many of the human rights principles mentioned in the UN Charter and the UN Universal Declaration of Human Rights. Like many other regional human rights documents, the African Charter contains "rights" in principle that have not been implemented by a binding multilateral treaty. Further, the African Charter establishes that individuals have a number of *duties* to society, the State, and the Organization of African Unity. The 1986 African Charter established the African Commission on Human Rights, which monitors human rights enforcement on the African Continent. Like its Latin American counterpart, the African Commission may only study, report, and recommend. It has no enforcement powers.
11. Some Asian scholars have traditionally characterized the International Law of Human Rights as an "imperialist" tool for intervening in the internal affairs of socialist nations. Their view is that the field of human rights is a matter governed *solely* by internal law. Human rights are considered intact in China. State ownership of most resources has been characterized as an effective guarantee of the genuine realization of human rights of the Chinese people. Contemporary, post–Cultural Revolution scholars claim that human rights in China are now more viable than in any prior generation.
12. Asian scholars in *democratic* nations criticize the UN's "global" human rights standards for a different reason. Indian scholars believe that the Western-derived conception of human rights has little meaning for people who lack the basic necessities of life. The human rights contained in the UN Charter and the "cloned" regional instruments address mostly political rights of little practical value for the people of India.
13. Advocacy of human rights is not limited to international organizations. Some States have expressly incorporated various human rights instruments directly into their constitutions or national laws. A number of non-governmental organizations—including the Red Cross and Amnesty International—also expose State violations of international human rights principles to public scrutiny.
14. The US Senate has historically shunned US ratification of global human rights instruments on the basis that such treaty commitments could subject the US to unintended obligations. One rationale is the lack of clarity in the precise content of the typically broadly worded human rights instrument. These documents typically contain morally unobjectionable but undefined principles with no specific content. Precise definitions are not a common characteristic of multilateral treaties, however. As discussed in Chapter 8, multilateral treaties depend on broad consensus for the incremental development of International Law.
15. US human rights policy nevertheless includes legislation that has been specifically designed to address

human rights violations abroad. The Foreign Assistance Act prohibits the provision of aid or technical assistance to States that perpetrate gross violations of legislatively defined human rights. The Alien Tort Statute implements the Constitutional provision authorizing Congress to "define and punish . . . offenses against the law of nations."The 1991 expansion of this Statue, the Torture Victim Protection Act, provides for a suit in the US for official conduct that does not amount to genocide or other war crimes.

◆ PROBLEMS

Problem 11.A (end of §11.2) The United Kingdom Human Rights Act of 1998 (legislation enacted November 9, 1998) gives further effect to rights and freedoms guaranteed under the European Convention on Human Rights (ECHR).[66] Sections 2 and 3 deal with the interpretation of Convention rights. All English courts and tribunals must take Convention rights into account in pending cases. Legislation must be interpreted in a way that is compatible with Convention rights. Legislation that is incompatible with Convention rights remains valid because UK courts must follow the will of the legislature. However, a court may make a declaration of incompatibility with human rights vested under the ECHR. Such a declaration does not affect the validity of the inconsistent legislative provision, and it is not binding on the parties. [Section 4(6)(a) and (b).] This declaration of incompatibility may serve as the basis for the Minister of the Crown to amend the legislation to remove the incompatibility with the treaty.

Section 19 of the Act introduces a "Statement of Compatibility" into England's parliamentary procedure. After the Second Reading of a Bill in either House of Parliament—Lords or Commons—the Minister of the Crown in charge has to either: (1) make this statement of compatibility with the ECHR, saying that, in his or her view, the provisions of the Bill are compatible with rights under the Convention; or (2) make a statement that he or she is *unable* to make this statement of compatibility, but the government nevertheless wishes the House to proceed with the Bill.

Assume that legislation is introduced that would extinguish a woman's right to an abortion under prior English caselaw. The ECHR contains a provision that recognizes the "right to life." (Article 2.1) This is the basis for the pending legislation, which would nullify the judicially created right to abortions in England (also enunciated in the *Roe v. Wade* decision by the United States Supreme Court, at 410 US 113).

Two students (or groups) will participate in a House of Commons debate regarding the compatibility of the pending legislation, which would abolish abortions in England pursuant to the right-to-life provision of the ECHR. Student 1 is the Minister of the Crown, who will present a Statement of Compatibility with the ECHR's right-to-life provision. Student 2 is a member of the House of Commons who demands that the Minister has no choice but to express that a Statement of Compatibility *cannot* be made.

Both students may rely on the resources in this chapter on human rights, including the various instruments within the International Bill of Human Rights—all of which contain a right-to-life provision—the Irish abortion case in Chapter 3 of this book *(Open Door and Dublin Well Woman v. Ireland)*; and the specialized treaties in Exhibit 11.1 regarding the rights of women and children. The key question is whether the anti-abortion legislation is compatible with the ECHR's right-to-life provision.

Problem 11.B (end of §11.3) Nicaragua's Sandinista government of the mid-1980s learned about a US Central Intelligence Agency plot that involved Nicaragua. Key harbors were mined, and US financial aid was provided clandestinely to a rebel group known as the "Contras." In a widely reported announcement, US President Reagan said, "I, too, am a Contra." (Additional details are available from the *Nicaragua* case set forth in the text of §10.2.)

Assume that you are the national leader in Nicaragua and have just learned about this foreign "presence" in your country. To defend your borders against this form of aggression, you declare martial law. Your military forces now control all of Nicaragua. Civil rights, including access to the courts, are suspended. Martial law has further limited opposition from the Roman Catholic Church, Nicaragua's human rights groups, and individuals who may incur criminal liability for the crime of "civil disobedience." Nicaragua previously ratified and has publicly embraced the UN's International Bill of Human Rights.

You now decide to dispatch a series of warnings to local groups that you suspect are supporters of the anti-government Contras. The basic Contra objective is to unseat your government. First, you warn the Catholic Bishop of Nicaragua that "the Church must stay out of political affairs and cannot be used as a vehicle for influencing governmental decision making on behalf of the people of Nicaragua." Amnesty International (AI) is part of a worldwide organization designed to monitor progress toward the accomplishment of UN human rights goals. AI has more offices in the US than in any other country. After opposition to martial law from AI's local office, you close the AI office in Nicaragua because it was publishing unapproved literature.

Martial law has also resulted in the arrest of Nicaraguan citizens charged with "civil disobedience." You believe that their detention is necessary because they are probably aiding the rebel Contra forces. On the basis of this national emergency, you have established "People's Tribunals" to accelerate the prosecution of subversion cases. These tribunals have the power to summarily imprison anyone in Nicaragua. They have exercised this power to jail Nicaraguan citizens who are Catholic, members of Amnesty International, and suspected of "civil disobedience." This term is not defined, so arresting authorities and the prosecuting tribunals will have the necessary discretion to deal with the rebellion and foreign intrusion on a case-by-case basis.

The national emergency has therefore temporarily suspended "due process of law," one of the fundamental features of various human rights treaties. The inhabitants of Nicaragua, in other words, are routinely charged with the broadly worded crime of "civil disobedience" when they are arrested. There is no independent judicial officer available to verify the propriety of incarcerations by the agents of the People's Tribunals. Each local tribunal has the complete discretion to orchestrate what Amnesty characterizes as the "disappearance" of many Nicaraguan citizens. No one jailed under your proclamation can question the legal basis for his or her incarceration. You will, of course, revive this right after this crisis passes and you can abolish martial law.

While in jail, prisoners are routinely tortured. Although this is not an official State policy, it is difficult to control. Your police force is your first line of defense in finding information about the US-supported Contras. Given this emergency, torture is an unpleasant necessity for extracting the vital information necessary to identify all citizens who seek the imminent overthrow of your government. You thus impose curfews on travel at night without a permit, and on travel between the rural and urban areas of Nicaragua. The Contra forces are located mostly in rural areas of your country.

You have undertaken all of the above steps to maintain public order in Nicaragua. It is clear that a major foreign power has effectively launched a military assault on your nation—including the bombing of your harbors, the financing of the Contras, and the potential use of the Church and other private organizations to disseminate information to incite the populace to rise against your government. Have you violated the UN's International Bill of Human Rights? If so, were you justified in doing so?

Problem 11.C (end of §11.5) In a December 1993 report, the World Health Organization (WHO) estimated that "over 80 million [living] female infants, adolescents, and women in over 30 countries . . . have been subject to female genital mutilation." In its 1997 Progress of Nations Report, the UNICEF Executive Director identified this figure as being 130 million living women. Further details are available from the UN Commission on the Status of Women, based on a report from the NGO called Equality Now. [*See* UN Doc. E/CN.4/Sub.2/1997/NGO/31 (7 Aug. 1997), and Esther Hicks, *Infibulation: Female Mutilation in Islamic Northeastern Africa* (New Brunswick, NJ: Transaction, 1993).]

This procedure is commonly referred to as "female circumcision." It is a tradition that dates from ancient Egypt. Now, in Somalia for example, it is estimated that *all* females undergo this process. Today's estimate for Egypt is 70 to 90 percent. Young women, mostly in Africa and the Middle East, are social outcasts if they do not endure this procedure, which has been associated with the retention of virginity and lack of physical sensation. In countries where this technique is practiced, most men will not marry women who have not undergone this procedure.

While it appears that no religion specifically endorses it, some Muslim scholars have endorsed female circumcision as "a noble practice [that] does honor to women" (*Washington Post,* Apr. 11, 1995, p. A14). While it is not officially endorsed as a State policy in any country, female circumcision is effectively condoned in a number of countries that have never taken any steps to curtail it, regardless of the known health risks. On the other hand, there are Muslims who advocate that Islam (The Koran) does *not* support this practice. The Egyptian

Organization for Human Rights specifically disputes this claim, noting that some Egyptian Christians also follow this practice—which predates Islam by 1,500 years.

In June 1997, an Egyptian court overruled a one-year-old government decree that had banned this practice. The judge noted that he was not ruling on the health aspects of the case, but rather on the legality of the ban that unduly restricted doctors. However, the court ruling left in place that portion of the ministerial decree that bars unlicenced midwives and barbers with no medical training from performing this procedure.

At approximately age ten, a young girl is held down by several women while a "practitioner" who does not necessarily have medical training uses a razor or paring knife to do this procedure in the home. It is extremely painful and performed without anesthesia. The WHO is concerned about the resulting hemorrhaging, tetanus, infection, infertility, and death that has occurred in an increasingly reported number of cases. In the West, women's rights groups seek the global abolition of female circumcision (the National Organization for Women, Global Campaign for Women's Human Rights, Population International, and Women's International Network).

This procedure is outlawed in France, Great Britain, and the US as of 1996. In 1993, US House of Representatives Resolution 3247 was the first congressional bill to deal with what Western newspapers have described as "the most widespread existing violation of human rights in the world." In 1994, the State Department first focused on this treatment of women in its annual human rights report (pursuant to a legislative enactment discussed in §11.5), referring to this practice as "ritual mutilation." An analysis of this phenomenon is available in Eugenie Gifford, "The Courage to Blaspheme," 4 *UCLA Women's L.J.* 329 (1994).

In 1994, a US immigration judge in Boston had to decide whether two US-born Nigerian girls—aged five and six—would be returned to their father in Nigeria or remain in the US with their mother after their parents divorced. The judge decided to overturn the mother's deportation order on humanitarian grounds. There are an estimated two million living women in Nigeria who have experienced the tradition of genital mutilation. The judge permitted the daughters to remain in the US with their mother. Had the girls returned home with their father, they would have been required to undergo this traditional procedure—just like their mother had when she was a child in Nigeria. In the judge's words: "This court attempts to respect traditional cultures, but this is cruel and serves no medical purpose." *INS v. Oluloro* (unreported case reviewed in *Maui News,* March 29, 1994). In a more recently reported case, the Board of Immigration Appeals (BIA) accepted the argument that a Togolese woman who fled her home country was being persecuted because she was threatened with forced genital mutilation. The BIA concluded that, despite her persecutor's benevolent intent, that petitioner Kasinga was a "refugee" because female genital mutilation can constitute "persecution" within the meaning of the Act [*In re Fauziya Kasinga,* Int. Dec. 3278, at 12 (BIA June 13, 1996) (en banc) (designated as precedent by the BIA); reprinted in 35 *Int'l Legal Mat'ls* 1145 (1996).]

As a result of the *Kasinga* case, the US Criminal Code prohibits this procedure from being performed on another person who is under eighteen years of age (18 US Code §116). Furthermore, the US Immigration and Nationality Act provides that "[i]n consultation with the Secretary of State, the Commissioner of Immigration and Naturalization shall identify those countries in which female genital mutilation is commonly practiced. . . ." The INS and Department of State thus make available to "all aliens who are issued immigrant or non-immigrant visas, prior to or at the time of entry into the United States . . . [i]nformation on the severe harm to physical and psychological health caused by female genital mutilation . . . *compiled and presented in a manner [that] is* limited to the practice itself and *respectful to the cultural values of the societies in which such practice takes place"* (8 US Code §1374; both statutes were enacted in 1996).

Assume that a wealthy African family vacations in the US each year when the heat is most intense in their home State—herein referred to as Country X. Mrs. X is a citizen of Country X. Her husband is a ranking government official in Country X. While it would be inappropriate for him to ever attend one of his wife's "procedures," he nevertheless agrees with the purpose of her work—as do most of the officials in the State X government, who are fully aware of this common practice.

Mrs. X is a devout religious woman who has herself undergone the "procedure"—and performed it on her own daughters, as well as hundreds of ten- to twelve-year-old girls in Country X. This practice has been passed on from generation to generation in her family for hundreds of years. She believes that it is her "God-given" duty to perpetuate her faith by performing this ritualistic procedure. She believes that this work is especially important in contemporary times when adolescent behavior in other regions of the world subject young women in Country X to many adverse influences that will certainly debase the family's cultural and religious beliefs.

During her annual vacation in New York City, she is served with process accusing her of torture in violation of International Law. The plaintiff is the mother of a Middle Eastern girl who underwent this procedure in Country X only after Mrs. X convinced the mother that this tradition cannot be changed and that "The Divine Order" requires that only faithful women be made available for marrying Country X males. "Otherwise," Mrs. X explained to the plaintiff mother, "the social, cultural, and religious traditions of Country X will be vitiated by Western influences." Although unusual, this particular child died of complications several very painful weeks after Mrs. X performed the "procedure."

The plaintiffs' lawyer decides not to sue on the basis of the gender-discrimination provisions in International Human Rights Law. Those instruments address *State* responsibility for discrimination rather than *individual* responsibility under International Law. Also, the plaintiff's lawyer decides not to name the father as a defendant in this matter because he will likely be entitled to immunity.

This case is filed in a New York court against Mrs. X. The deceased child's mother therein alleges torture resulting in her daughter's death. The plaintiff's lawyer also decides to bring this matter to the attention of the UN by filing a §1503 petition with the UN High Commissioner for Human Rights. In it, the plaintiff mother claims that her daughter's rights also have been violated by Country X because it has failed to provide sufficient information or any medical licensing regime for this procedure.

Four students will play the following roles in this hypothetical case: Students 1 and 2 as plaintiff's lawyer, and Students 3 and 4 as defense lawyer. The first of two sessions will occur in a New York trial court (Students 1 and 3), where the judge is deciding whether to dismiss this case. The second session will occur at the UN (Students 2 and 4) before the UN High Commissioner for Human Rights. In each instance, the defense lawyer for Mrs. X claims that neither decision maker can proceed with this case. The defense claims that US courts cannot exercise *Filartiga* "§1350 jurisdiction," given the facts of this case. Mrs. X's lawyer defends the "UN §1503 petition" on the ground that Country X is not thereby liable for torture under International Law. How should the US judge and the UN Commissioner rule?

◆ BIBLIOGRAPHY

§11.1 Human Rights in Context

T. Buergenthal, *International Human Rights in a Nutshell* (2nd ed. St. Paul: West, 1995).

G. Hoog & A. Steinmetz (eds.), *International Conventions on Protection of Humanity and Environment* (Berlin: Walter de Gruyter & Co., 1993) (full text of forty-eight treaties).

E. Lawson, *Encyclopedia of Human Rights* (2nd ed. New York: Taylor & Francis, 1996).

F. Newman & D. Weissbroadt, *International Human Rights: Law, Policy, and Process* (2nd ed. Cincinnati, OH: Anderson, 1996).

D. Robertson, *A Dictionary of Human Rights* (London: Europa, 1997).

§11.2 United Nations Promotional Role

P. Alston (ed.), *The United Nations and Human Rights: A Critical Appraisal* (Oxford, Eng.: Clarendon Press, 1992).

A. Eide & G. Alfredsson (eds.), *The Universal Declaration of Human Rights: A Commentary* (Oslo, Norway: Scandinavian Univ. Press, 1992).

A. Eide et al. (eds.), *Economic, Social and Cultural Rights: A Textbook* (Dordrecht, Neth.: Martinus Nijhoff, 1995).

L. Henkin (ed.), *The International Bill of Rights: The Covenant on Civil and Political Rights* (New York: Columbia Univ. Press, 1981).

UN, *The United Nations and Human Rights: 1945–1995* (New York: UN, 1995).

§11.3 Regional Human Rights Approaches

AFRICA

C. Heyns (ed.), *Human Rights Law in Africa* 1996 (The Hague, Neth.: Kluwer Law Int'l, 1996).

W. Nagan, "African Human Rights Process: A Contextual Policy-Oriented Approach," 21 *Southwestern L. Rev.* 157 (1992).

EUROPE

A. Rosas (ed.), *International Human Rights Norms in Domestic Law: Finnish and Polish Perspectives* (Helsinki: Finnish Lawyers' Pub., 1990).

J. Weiler, "Eurocracy and Distrust: Some Questions concerning the Role of the European Court of Justice in the Protection of Fundamental Human Rights within the Legal Order of the European Communities," 61 *Wash. Univ. L. Rev.* 1103 (1986).

INTER-AMERICAN

T. Burgenthal & D. Shelton, *Protecting Human Rights in the Americas: Cases and Materials* (4th rev. ed. Kehl, Germany: N.P. Engel, 1995).

O. Fitzgerald, *Understanding Charter Remedies* (Scarborough, Ontario: Craswell, 1994) (Canada).

A. Mower, *Regional Human Rights: A Comparative Study of the West European and Inter-American Systems* (New York: Greenwood Press, 1991).

MIDDLE EAST

"Human Rights and Peace in the Middle East: A Conference," 13 *Syracuse J. Int'l L. & Comm.* 391 (1987).

GLOBAL

B. Conforti & F. Francioni (eds.), *Enforcing International Human Rights in Domestic Courts* (The Hague, Neth.: Martinus Nijhoff, 1997).

"Symposium: Human Rights—Global Issues and Information Sources," 25 *Int'l J. Legal Inf.* 3–200 (1997).

UN, *A Compilation of International Instruments: Regional Instruments* (Vol. 1) (New York: Geneva Centre for Human Rights, 1994).

§11.4 Other Human Rights Actors

M. Bronson, *Amnesty International* (New York: Macmillan Children's Book Group, 1994).

R. Lillich, "When Do Individuals and Non-Governmental Organizations Have the Right to Petition the UN and What Happens?" in *International Human Rights: Problems of Law, Policy, and Practice* (2nd ed. Boston: Little, Brown & Co., 1991).

§11.5 United States Ratification and Legislation

H. Hannum & D. Fischer (eds.), *United States Ratification of the International Covenants on Human Rights* (Irvington-on-Hudson, NY: Transnational, 1993).

M. Gibney (ed.), *World Justice? US Courts and International Human Rights* (Boulder, CO: Westview Press, 1991).

K. Randall, *Federal Courts and the International Human Rights Paradigm* (Durham, NC: Duke Univ. Press, 1991).

B. Stark, "Economic Rights in the United States and International Human Rights Law: Toward an 'Entirely New Strategy,'" 44 *Hastings L.J.* 79 (1992).

B. Stevens & M. Ratner, *International Human Rights Litigation in US Courts* (Irvington-on-Hudson, NY: Transnational, 1996).

SPECIAL HUMAN RIGHTS ISSUES

Developing Countries

S. Chowdhury, E. Denters, & P. Waart, *The Right to Development in International Law* (Dordrecht, Neth.: Martinus Nijhoff, 1992).

Human Rights in Developing Countries 1986–1994 (Oslo, Norway: Norwegian Inst. Human Rts, 1994) (seven volumes).

Language & Religion

F. de Varennes, *Language, Minorities and Human Rights* (The Hague, Neth.: Matinus Nijhoff, 1996).

J. van der Vyver & J. Whitte, Jr. (eds.), *Religious Human Rights in Global Perspective: Legal Perspectives* (The Hague, Neth.: Martinus Nijhoff, 1996).

Minorities

S. Anaya, *Indigenous Peoples in International Law* (New York: Oxford Univ. Press, 1996).

S. Chandra (ed.), *International Protection of Minorities* (Delhi, India: Mittal, 1986).

Women & Children

P. Alston et al. (eds.), *Children, Rights and the Law* (rev. ed. Oxford, Eng.: Clarendon Press, 1993).

J. Berkey, "Circumcision Circumscribed: Female Excision and Cultural Accommodation in the Medieval Near East," 28 *Int'l J. Mid. East Studies* 19 (1996).

K. Engle, "International Human Rights and Feminism: When Discourses Meet," 13 *Mich. J. Int'l L.* 517 (1992).

M. Halberstam & E. Defels, *Women's Legal Rights: International Covenants an Alternative to ERA?* (Ardsley-on-Hudson, NY: Transnat'l Pub., 1987).

G. van Bueren, *International Law on the Rights of the Child* (Dordrecht, Neth.; Boston: Martinus Nijhoff, 1994).

Other

J. Acker et al. (eds.), *America's Experiment with Capital Punishment: Reflections on the Past, Present, and Future of the Ultimate Penal Sanction* (Durham, NC: Carolina Acad. Press, 1998).

S. Chowdhury, *The Rule of Law in a State of Emergency: The Paris Minimum Standards of Human Rights Norms in a State of Emergency* (New York: St. Martin's Press, 1989).

M. Jakobson, *Origins of the Gulag: The Soviet Prison-Camp System, 1917–1934* (Lexington, KY: Univ. Press of Kentucky, 1992).

◆ ENDNOTES

1. T. Buergenthal, "Historical Antecedents of International Human Rights Law," ch. 1 in *International Human Rights in a Nutshell* 1 (2nd ed. St. Paul: West, 1995).
2. Contemporary problems with ethnic cleansing are analyzed in A. Bell-Fialkoff, *Ethnic Cleansing* (New York: St. Martin's Press, 1996).
3. *Case Concerning Application of the Convention on the Prevention and Punishment of the Crime of Genocide (Bosnia and Herzegovina v. Yugoslavia)* (filed in 1993). The proceedings are available on the Court's Web site at www.icj-cij.org.
4. *See* J. Gardner (ed.), *Human Rights as General Norms and a State's Right to Opt Out: Reservations and Objections to Human Rights Conventions* (London: Brit. Inst. Comp. Law, 1997).
5. *Advisory Opinion on Nationality Decrees Issued in Tunis and Morocco, PCIJ*, ser. B, No. 4 (1923).
6. R. Howard & J. Donnelly, "Human Dignity, Human Rights, and Political Regimes," 80 *Amer. Pol. Sci. Rev.* 801 (1986).
7. *Belgian Linguistics Case (Merits),* European Court of Human Rights, 45 *Int'l Law Rep.* 114 (1968).
8. Gen. Ass. Reso. 36/55, reprinted in 21 *Int'l Legal Mat'ls* 205 (1982).

9. Gen. Ass. Reso. 2627(XXV) of Oct. 24, 1970, reprinted in E. Lawson, *Encyclopedia of Human Rights* 375, 376 (New York: Taylor & Francis, 1991).
10. L. Henkin, "Idealism and Ideology: The Law of Human Rights," ch. 12 in *How Nations Behave: Law and Foreign Policy* 231 (2nd ed. New York: Columbia Univ. Press, 1979).
11. *Sei Fujii v. State of California,* 38 Cal. 2d 718, at 722, 242 P.2d 617, at 620 (1952). This case is set forth in §8.1, illustrating the distinction between "self-executing" treaties and "standards of achievement."
12. **US segregation:** *Plessy v. Ferguson,* 163 US 537, 16 S.Ct. 1138, 41 *L. Ed.* 256 (1898). Plessy was not overruled until nearly ten years after the Charter was drafted, in 1954. **US interracial marriages:** The relevant state prohibitions were not ruled unconstitutional until 1967. *Loving v. Virginia,* 388 US 1, 87 S.Ct. 1817, 18 *L. Ed.* 2d 1010 (1967). **Soviet gulags:** A. Solzhenitsyn, *The Gulag Archipelago* (New York: Harper & Row, 1974).
13. M. Whiteman, 5 *Digest of International Law* 243 (Wash., DC: US Gov't Print. Off., 1965).
14. "Namibia (South-West Africa) Advisory Opinion," 1971 *ICJ Rep.* 16, 55 (Concurring Opinion of Judge Ammoun).
15. American Law Institute, 2 *Restatement of the Foreign Relations Law of the United States* §701, at 153 and 155 (3rd ed. Wash., DC: Amer. Law Inst., 1987).
16. A. Eide & G. Alfredsson (eds.), "Western Approach?" in *The Universal Declaration of Human Rights: A Commentary* 11 (Oslo, Norway: Scandinavian Univ. Press, 1992).
17. Reprinted in 32 *Int'l Legal Mat'ls* 1661 (1993).
18. "Rights Report Finds Continuing Abuses around the Globe," *Los Angeles Daily Journal,* October 5, 1988, p. 1.
19. *See* M. Nowak, *U.N. Covenant on Civil and Political Rights: CCPR Commentary* (Kehl, Germany: N.P. Engel, 1993) (leading English-language commentary on the CPR).
20. **ICCPR:** 999 *United Nations Treaty Series* 171 (1976). **ICESCR:** 993 *United Nations Treaty Series* 3 (1976).
21. W. Schabas, *The Abolition of the Death Penalty in International Law* (2nd ed. Cambridge, Eng: Cambridge Univ. Press, 1997) (hereinafter *Abolition of the Death Penalty).*
22. UN Doc. A/C.3/49/SR.43, §§74–76.
23. *See, e.g.,* A. Eide et al. (eds.), *Food as a Human Right* (Tokyo: UN University, 1984).
24. *See* M. Craven, *The International Covenant on Economic, Social, and Cultural Rights: A Perspective on Its Development* (Oxford, Eng.: Clarendon Press, 1995).
25. T. von Meron, "On the Inadequate Reach of Humanitarian and Human Rights Law and the Need for a New Instrument," 77 *Amer. J. Int'l L.* 589, 604–605 (1983).
26. *See* L. Sunga, *Individual Responsibility in International Law for Serious Human Rights Violations* (Dordrecht, Neth.: Martinus Nijhoff, 1992).
27. Gen. Ass. Reso. 48/141, of Dec. 20, 1993, reprinted in 33 *Int'l Legal Matl's* 303 (1994).
28. **Convention:** "European Convention for the Protection of Human Rights and Fundamental Freedoms," 213 *UN Treaty Series* 221 (1955). **Charter:** *See* D. Harris, *The European Social Charter* (Charlottesville, VA: Univ. Press of Va., 1984).
29. *See Case of Open Door and Dublin Well Woman v. Ireland* set forth in §3.4 of this book.
30. Further details are available on the Court's Web site at http://194.250.50.200/eng/PRESS/1st%20meeting%20of%20new%20ECHR.html.
31. *See* "European Convention for the Protection of Human Rights and Fundamental Freedoms: Report Regarding Its Differences from the UN Covenants," 9 *Int'l Legal Mat'ls* 1310 (1970).
32. *Assenov and Others v. Bulgaria,* 90/1997/874/1086 (Judgment of Oct. 28, 1998).
33. M. Janis and R. Kay, *European Human Rights Law,* vii (Hartford, CT: Univ. of Conn. Law School Foundation Press, 1990).
34. **Final Act:** Reprinted in "Declaration of Principles Guiding Relations between Participating States," 70 *Amer. J. Int'l L.* 417 (1976). **Conference documents:** A. Bloed (ed.), *The Conference on Security and Co-operation in Europe: Analysis and Basic Documents, 1972–1993* (Dordrecht, Neth.: Martinus Nijhoff, 1993); and A. Bloed (ed.), *The Conference on Security and Co-operation in Europe: Basic Documents, 1993–1995* (The Hague, Neth.: Martinus Nijhoff, 1997).
35. 119 *UN Treaty Series* 3 (1952) (as amended).
36. Robin Kirk, "Human Rights Challenge: Why Terror Still Persists in Latin American Democracies," *Los Angeles Daily Journal,* July 14, 1987, at 4.
37. *See generally,* Hartman, "Derogation from Human Rights Treaties in Public Emergencies," 22 *Harv. Int'l L.J.* 1 (1981).
38. U. Umozurike, "The African Charter on Human and Peoples' Rights," 77 *Amer. J. Int'l L.* 902–903 (1983) (italics added) (hereinafter "African Charter").
39. U. Umozurike, "Human Rights," ch. 12 in *Introduction to International Law* 153 (Ibadan, Nigeria: Spectrum Law Pub., 1993).
40. Lone Lindholt, "A Universal Concept of Human Rights?" Ch. 3 in *Questioning the Universality of Human Rights: The African Charter on Human and Peoples' Rights in Botswana, Malawi and Mozambique* 27 (Aldershot, Eng.: Dartmouth, 1997).
41. T. Bennett, *A Sourcebook of African Customary Law for Southern Africa* viii (Wetton, So. Africa: Juta & Co., 1991).
42. "African Charter," at 911 (cited in note 37 above).
43. *See* E. Ankumah, *The African Commission on Human and Peoples' Rights: Practice and Procedures* (The Hague, Neth.: Martinus Nijhoff, 1996).
44. *"Rattigan and Others v. Chief Immigration Officer, Zimbabwe and Others,"* 103 *Int'l L. Rep.* 224 (1994) (decided 1994).
45. **African Charter:** OAU Doc. CAB/LEG/TSG/Rev.1. **Global instruments:** *See* M. Saulle (ed.), *The Rights of the Child: International Instruments* (Irvington-on-Hudson, NY: Transnational, 1995).
46. C. Szu, "A Criticism of the Views of Bourgeois International Law on the Question of Population," reprinted in 1 J. Cohen and H. Chiu, *People's China and International Law* 607 (Princeton: Princeton Univ. Press, 1974).

47. H. Chiu, "Chinese Attitudes Toward International Law of Human Rights in the Post-Mao Era" in *Occasional Papers/Reprints Series in Contemporary Asian Studies,* Paper No. 5 (Baltimore: Univ. of Maryland, 1989).
48. R. Lillich, "Sources of Human Rights Law and the Hong Kong Bill of Rights" in H. Chiu (ed.), 10 *Chinese Yearbook Int'l L. & Affairs* 27 (Baltimore: Chinese Soc. Int'l Law, 1992).
49. R. Hingorini, *Modern International Law* 258 (New York: Oceana, 1984).
50. S. Gutto, "Violation of Human Rights in the Third World: Responsibility of States and TNCs," reprinted in F. Snyder and S. Sathirathai (ed.), *Third World Attitudes Toward International Law* 275 (Dordrecht, Neth.: Martinus Nijhoff, 1987).
51. T. Elias, *New Horizons in International Law* 167 (Alphen an den Rijn, Neth.: Sitjhoff & Noordhoff, 1979).
52. M. Bulajic, *Principles of International Development Law: Progressive Development of the Principles of International Law Relating to the New International Economic Order* (2nd rev. ed. Dordrecht, Neth.: Martinus Nijhoff, 1993).
53. Reprinted in 32 *Int'l Legal Mat'ls* 1661 (1993).
54. M. Posner & C. Whittome, "The Status of Human Rights NGOs," 25 *Colum. Hum. Rts. L. Rev.* 269 (1994).
55. Genocide Convention Implementation Act of 1987, codified at 18 *USC* §1091.
56. *Oyama v. California,* 332 US 633, 649–50, 68 S.Ct. 269, 277, 92 *L. Ed.* 249 (1948) (Justice Black, Concurring Opinion).
57. **Brown case:** 347 US 483, 74 S.Ct. 686, 98 *L. Ed.* 873 (1954). **Sei Fujii case:** 38 Cal.2d 718, 242 P.2d 617 (Cal. S.Ct., 1952). **Racial rationale:** *See* "The US Senate and Human Rights Treaties," §7.3 in *Nutshell* (cited in note 1 above).
58. *See Collin v. Smith,* 578 F.2d 1197 (7th Cir. 1978), *cert. den'd* 439 US 916.
59. **Treaties:** *International Covenant on Civil and Political Rights, Protocol* 2 (§11.2) and *Organization of American States Protocol on the American Convention on Human Rights to Abolish the Death Penalty,* 29 *Int'l Legal Mat'ls* 1447 (1990). **Scholarship:** *Abolition of the Death Penalty* (cited in note 21).
60. For a discussion of this US statute and related policy analysis, *see* S. Cohen, "Conditioning US Security Assistance on Human Rights Practices," 76 *Amer. J. Int'l L.* 246 (1982).
61. **Repealed position:** 22 *US Code* §2384(f). **New job description:** Provided by telephone call to US Department of State on January 18, 1995.
62. Executive Order of Dec. 10, 1998: www.pub.whitehouse.gov/uri-res/I2R?urn:pdi://oma.eop.gov.us/1998/12/11/4.text.1.
63. *Hilao v. Estate of Marcos,* 103 F.3d 789 (9th Cir., 1996). The estate paid $150 million to settle this case in February 1999.
64. Pub. L. 102-256, Mar. 12, 1992, 106 Stat. 73 (enacted as amendment to §1350 in 1991).
65. *Kadic v. Karadzic,* 70 Fed.3d 232 (2nd Cir., 1995), *rehearing den'd,* 74 Fed.3d 377 (2nd Cir., 1996), *cert. den'd,* 518 US 1005 (1997). The facts are also set forth in §2.1 of this book, after the excerpt "On Condition of Statehood," note 1.
66. Government's Internet version: www.hmso.gov.uk/acts/acts1998/19980042.htm.

CHAPTER TWELVE

International Environment

CHAPTER OUTLINE

ON THE NIGHT OF DECEMBER 2–3, 1984, THE MOST tragic industrial disaster in history occurred in the city of Bhopal . . . India. Located there was a chemical plant owned and operated by Union Carbide India Limited [50.9% owned by UC of New York]. . . . Methyl isocyanate (MIC), a highly toxic gas, is an ingredient in the production of both Sevin and Temik. On the night of the tragedy MIC leaked from the plant in substantial quantities for reasons not yet determined.

The prevailing winds . . . blew the deadly gas into the overpopulated hutments adjacent to the plant and into the most densely occupied parts of the city. The results were horrendous. Estimates of deaths directly attributable to the leak range as high as 2,100. No one is sure exactly how many perished. Over 200,000 people suffered injuries—some serious and permanent—some mild and temporary. Livestock were killed and crops damaged. Businesses were interrupted. [The official death count is now 10,000, with injuries to another 380,000 people.]

— *In re Union Carbide Corporation Gas Plant Disaster at Bhopal, India in December, 1984*, 634 F.Supp. 842, 844 (SDNY, 1986), *aff'd*, 809 F.2nd 195 (2nd Cir., 1987), *cert. den'd*, 484 US 871 (1987). *New York Times*, January 1997

INTRODUCTION

World wars, the Cold War, and the possibility of a nuclear holocaust have all subsided as perceived threats to the inhabitants of planet Earth. It is environmental problems that could cause the breakdown of international society as we now know it.

This chapter will identify the basic features of State responsibility for the environment, which knows no boundaries. It will focus on the UN environmental program, attempts to effect the shift from "soft law"—consisting of numerous draft principles like *transboundary environmental interference* when one State degrades another's environment—to "hard law," whereby nations would ratify the various instruments at the core of International Environmental Law. These materials also present arbitral and judicial perspectives about the competing considerations that militate in favor of establishing predicable outcomes on the one hand, while engaging sufficient flexibility to accommodate the respective interests of the "have" and "have not" members of the community of nations on the other.[1]

What *is* International Environmental Law? The contemporary international environmental regime is a confluence of themes and actors previously addressed in this course: customary law, State practice, international and non-governmental organizations, conference diplomacy, treaties, and the extraterritorial application of domestic law. For example, §6.3 dealt with the Law of the Sea. Article 235 of the UN Conference on the Law of the Sea Treaty, which entered into force in 1994, contains an important statement of the applicable environmental norms:

1. States are responsible for the fulfillment of their international obligations concerning the protection and preservation of the marine environment. They shall be liable in accordance with international law.
2. States shall ensure that recourse is available in accordance with their [national] legal systems for prompt and adequate compensation or other relief in respect of damage caused by pollution of the marine environment by natural or juridical [that is, corporate] persons within their jurisdiction.

In an attempt to use customary international law to protect the environment, commentators have spent the last two decades elaborating rules of State responsibility for transboundary pollution. States have begun to build on this liability regime by developing international principles for the prevention of harmful environmental activity. States also have been experimenting with different modes of regulation for special environmental problems, as well as searching for new methods of treaty enforcement. Meanwhile, numerous intergovernmental organizations now monitor pollution and regulate environmentally harmful behavior.[2] In the last decade of the prior millennium, a number of academic publications emerged as a core for both the teaching and research efforts to "catch up" with developments in International Environmental Law (IEL).[3]

The impact of the environmental disasters described in this chapter is not limited to the territorial borders of the State of occurrence. Environmental pollution knows no boundaries. States may no longer rely on territorial sovereignty to conveniently brush aside the applicability of international programs for avoiding and remedying the consequences of such incidents. Transboundary pollution is arguably the least logical of all modes of State conduct for invoking the familiar defense enshrined in Article 2.7 of the 1945 UN Charter—that certain matters fall exclusively within the national jurisdiction of the offending State and are not subject to international legal control.

◆ 12.1 THE ENVIRONMENT'S DOMINION

HISTORICAL DEVOLUTION

Ancient Greek and Roman smelters emitted enough lead to contaminate the entire northern hemisphere, rivaling gasoline as a cause of pollution in the modern era. Silver refining 2,500 years ago was the oldest large-scale hemispheric pollution ever reported prior to the Industrial Revolution of the nineteenth century.

Events in the mid-twentieth century were no improvement. There was a unique example: the radioactive fallout from the US bombing of Nagasaki and Hiroshima, Japan—which either killed or harmed an additional 100,000 people within several years *after* this dawn of the nuclear era. The resulting program of nuclear weapons development would spawn extensive atmospheric and underground testing. The ensuing Cold War wreaked havoc on more than just the political environment.[4]

A number of disasters in the last decade of the twentieth century dramatically illustrate the importance of solidifying a global environmental protection regime. In 1984, toxic chemical gas leaked from a plant at a US corporation's subsidiary in Bhopal, India.[5] In 1986, an explosion at the Chernobyl nuclear reactor in the Ukraine caused the first *officially* reported radiation deaths in a nuclear power plant accident. This incident released radioactive material into the atmosphere and was carried as far away as the US. Also in that year, a fire in Switzerland resulted in thirty tons of chemicals being washed into the Rhine River. This event was one of Europe's most serious environmental catastrophes. In 1991, near the close of the Persian Gulf War, retreating Iraqi forces set fire to 700 Kuwaiti oil wells. That single military campaign sent millions of tons of contaminants into the biosphere during the nine months it took to extinguish all of these fires. In 1993, a Norwegian tanker spilled 4,000 tons of sulfuric acid into the sea off the Mexican coast.

These are just examples of *sudden* disasters. Equally severe are the long-term *incremental* threats—ozone depletion, climate change, deforestation of entire regions, and many other potentially incalculable dangers to human survival. Many of these hazards have reportedly caused skin cancer, cataracts, suppression of the human immune system, and agricultural degradation. The circulation of industrial contaminants throughout the atmosphere may further lead to catastrophic rises in sea levels and even the so-called greenhouse effect, an unnatural warming of the biosphere that results in heat waves and the melting of polar icepacks.

Each year, the average greenhouse releases 23,000 pounds of carbon dioxide, compared to a car's release of 10,000 pounds. Everyday, vessels traversing the world's oceans and airways introduce pollutants and otherwise disturb the world's biodiversity. In 1993, for example, Russia's head environmental adviser revealed that the former Soviet Union clandestinely dumped vast amounts of highly radioactive waste at sea during the previous thirty years—twice the *combined* amount of all twelve other nuclear nations. This total included 2.5 million curies of radioactive waste and eighteen nuclear reactors dumped into the Arctic Sea and the Sea of Japan.

The pivotal crisis in the "incremental" category of environmental degradation may be overpopulation. In 1994, the Worldwide Watch Institute, a Washington, D.C., research academy, issued its grimmest annual report ever. According to Worldwide Watch, this planet is nearing its capacity to produce food. If the earth's growing population remains uncontrolled and soil and water resources continue to be degraded, then there will be no positive correlation between food production and human consumption. The Institute projected that the world's population (then 5.4 billion) would *increase* by 3.6 billion in the next forty years. But the world's per capita seafood catch fell 9 percent during the four-year period between 1989 and 1993. Grain production, which expanded by 3 percent between 1950 and 1984, dropped to a 1 percent annual growth rate between 1984 and 1994. Just as ideological conflict dominated the *last* four decades of the Cold War, the Earth's physical capacity to satisfy the growing demand for food may dominate the *next* four decades.[6]

The related problem of shelter is no less in crisis. The 1996 UN Conference on Human Settlements issued its Istanbul Declaration and the Habitat Agenda. It reports that, by the year 2001, more than 50 percent of the world's population will reside in cities. Housing will thus become an even greater problem for local and national governments. An estimated 1 billion people in developing nations will not have adequate shelter.

It was statistics such as these that motivated 180 nations to develop a twenty-year plan for slowing population growth at the 1994 UN Population Conference in Cairo. This conference focused on birth control, economic development, and providing women in certain societies and religious backgrounds with more power over their lives. The Vatican had rejected the final documents of the earlier world population conference debates held in 1974. At the 1994 conference, however, the Pope partially supported the results in principle—although he remained averse to the abortion alternative. The Cairo Program of Action calls on States to provide better education for women in traditionally male-dominated societies, wider access to modern birth-control methods, and the right to choose if and when to become pregnant. The consensus-oriented reservation is that these program objectives—while expressing the intended lack of conflict with national laws, religious beliefs, and cultural norms—does not necessarily match word and deed.[7]

◆ 12.2 UNITED NATIONS ENVIRONMENTAL PROGRAM

1972 STOCKHOLM CONFERENCE

This was the first UN Conference on the Human Environment.[8] The resulting proclamations recognized that preservation of the environment is essential to the continued enjoyment of life itself. The importance of preserving the environment was succinctly stated in the aspirational proclamation providing (in part) as follows:

1. . . . In the long and tortuous evolution of the human race on this planet a stage has been reached when, through the rapid acceleration of science and technology, man has acquired the power to transform his environment in countless ways and on an unprecedented scale. . . . [M]an's environment . . . [is] essential to his well-being and to the enjoyment of basic human rights—even the right to life itself.
2. The protection and improvement of the human environment is a major issue [that] affects the well-being of peoples and economic development throughout the world; it is the urgent desire of peoples of the whole world and the duty of all Governments.

The bulk of the Stockholm Conference work product consists of twenty-six principles that call on States and international organizations to "play a co-ordinated, efficient and dynamic role for the protection and improvement of the environment" (Principle 25). This UN conference thus established the Governing Council of the United Nations Environment Program. The functions of this Council include the implementation of environmental programs and "[t]o keep under review the world environmental situation in order to ensure that emerging environmental problems of wide international significance receive appropriate and adequate consideration by Governments. . . ."[9] The key provisions of the 1972 Stockholm Declaration on the United Nations Conference on the Human Environment are Principles 21 and 22, which set the stage for an evolving regime for establishing both standards and remedies:

> **Principle 21**
> States have, in accordance with the Charter of the United Nations and the principles of international law, . . . the responsibility to ensure that activities within their jurisdiction or control do not cause damage to the environment of other States or of areas beyond the limits of national jurisdiction.
>
> **Principle 22**
> States shall cooperate to develop further international law regarding liability and compensation for the victims of pollution and other environmental damage caused by activities within the jurisdiction or control of such States beyond their jurisdiction.

In 1972, States also began to focus on the emerging debate about whether environmental protection and economic development helped or hindered one another. There were few international agreements concerning the environment. Since then, however, virtually all States have enacted *national* legislation that provides for varying degrees of environmental protection. As of 1994, there were nearly 900 *international* instruments consisting of further UN declarations, regional, and multilateral treaties (Exhibit 12.1 sets forth the major environmental instruments).[10]

The new focus became *sustainable development.* This phrase represents a somewhat symbiotic relationship between economic development (the benefit) and environmental degradation (the cost). The improvement of underdeveloped economies is not supposed to be accompanied by unacceptable costs to the environment. As acknowledged in Proclamation 4 of the 1972 Stockholm Resolution, "In the developing countries most of the environmental problems are caused by under-development. . . . Therefore, the developing countries must direct their efforts to development, bearing in mind their priorities and the need to safeguard the environment." One might characterize this aspiration as an attempt to impose the rough equivalent of an environmental impact statement when a government undertakes any project with the potential for causing transboundary pollution—on land, in the sea, and in the air.

This is perhaps the major impasse in IEL today. It pits the generally industrialized North against the less developed South. Nations within the former group seek comparatively more regulation to control environmental degradation. Lesser developed nations seek economic prosperity with its attendant costs to the environment. This conflict is currently cast in terms of a "sustainable development" theme that is articulated in many yet-to-be-ratified international environmental instruments.

Several years prior to the 1992 Rio Conference (described below), a UN group of experts drafted principles that serve as a yardstick for measuring the acceptable scope of the "sustainable development" for developing countries. These nations must be vigilant about their responsibility not to use their territory in ways that harm other States. In 1987, this Experts Group on Environmental Law of the World Commission on Environment and Development promulgated its Principles for Environmental Protection and Sustainable Development.[11] Article 11 provides for liability when transboundary environmental harm results from *permissible* activities. An activity that creates a risk of substantial harm caused by "transboundary environmental interference" gives rise to State liability if "the overall technical and socio-economic cost . . . far exceeds the long run advantage." Article 21 provides that a State is responsible when it uses a natural resource or fails to prevent an environmental interference in a manner that causes an adverse environmental impact in another State.

The Article 21 alternative remedies against the offending State are that it must: (1) cease the wrongful act; (2) reestablish the circumstances, as they were prior to the wrongful act; or (3) provide compensation to the State harmed by the transborder environmental interference—or all three. Even assuming that liability is clear, which of these remedies is the most appropriate? Should the responsible State pay damages for the "environmental interference"? If so, *how much* would appropriately compensate the harmed State? Would it be fairer to require the offending State to *restore* the status quo as it existed prior to the environmental degradation? Developments in International Environmental Law have signaled a shift to the paradigm of "sustainable development." This new model attempts to balance the competing interests of protecting the environment, while encouraging underdeveloped nations to improve industrial growth. But attempting to strike this balance will surely make both liability and remedy assessments even more complex, given the ambiguities associated with the ill-defined term *sustainable development*.

The Council of Europe effectively responded in 1998 through its Convention on the Protection of the Environment Through Criminal Law. This Convention reflects the concern of the forty member States, expressed in the Preamble, that "the uncontrolled use of technology and the excessive exploitation of natural resources entail serious environmental hazards" and that ratifying parties should take "effective measures to ensure that the perpetrators of environmental hazards having serious consequences do not escape prosecution and punishment." The essential objective is to criminalize certain intentional or negligent forms of environmental offenses, which may be limited to acts of gross negligence. The intentional discharge of ionizing radiation into the air, soil, or water that causes death or serious injury—or creates a "significant risk" of death or serious injury—is thereby prohibited. States may not "unlawfully dispose, treat, store, transport, export, or import hazardous waste" that is likely to cause death or serious injury or "substantial damage to the quality of air, soil, water, animals, or plants." Aiding and abetting the intentional commission of an environmental offense is to be criminalized under domestic law.

To ensure the shift from "soft law" aspirations to "hard law" requirements, the Convention authorizes jurisdiction over an offense committed on a State's territory, on one of its ships or aircraft, or by one of its nationals—if the offense is punishable under criminal law where it was committed or when the site of the offense does not fall under any State's territorial jurisdiction. A State has jurisdiction in cases where an offender is present in its territory, but that State does not extradite the person to another State after a request for extradition. Natural or corporate offenders may be imprisoned, fined, and required to reinstate the previous condition of the environment. Each State must adopt measures that permit confiscation of property and proceeds.[12]

There are, of course, *defenses* to an alleged "transboundary environmental interference." The nature of the environment can obscure the diagnosis of how a degradation occurred. One must sometimes search for a causal link between the result and the actor supposedly responsible for the damage and the effect. An adverse result may occur long after the incident (if one is identifiable) that allegedly caused the degradation. *Existing* pollution may also be a factor. Carbon dioxide, or acid rain, was discharged into the atmosphere in the *Trail Smelter Arbitration* (§12.3) across the border from Canada to the US state of Washington. Assuming that the Washington fog became thicker and more dense over a period of time, it would be difficult for the state of Washington to conveniently trace the fog problem directly or exclusively to the Canadian smelter. Other contaminants in the US may have contributed to that fog, including industrialization in the region near the border. The pollution on the US side may have originated from a variety of sources, including US automobiles, forest depletion machinery operations, and other industrial activities—in addition to smelter operations on either side of the international border.

The 1991 joint research project of the Italian universities of Sienna and Parma analyzes the practical problems with international responsibility for environmental harm. The president of the European Council for Environmental Law therein cautions that environmental damage cases are comparable to a *legal steeplechase*. His analogy is as follows: "The procedure of compensation for environmental damage can be compared to a steeple-chase where different obstacles must be overcome before arriving to the final result. Some obstacles—and maybe the hardest ones to overcome—result from *facts* while others have a *legal* character. The first category characterizes all environmental compensation situations [that is, causation] while the second [the remedy] mainly consists in problems arising from the transnational nature of the damage."[13]

THE 1992 RIO CONFERENCE

On the twentieth anniversary of the Stockholm Conference, nations assembled once again to reassess the

EXHIBIT 12.1 MAJOR GLOBAL ENVIRONMENTAL INSTRUMENTS

Year	Event
1972	Stockholm Declaration of UN Conference on Human Environment ◆ First global statement of environmental principles (11 *Int'l Legal Mat'ls* [ILM] 1416).
1972	UN Gen. Ass. Reso. 2997 on Institutional and Financial Arrangement for International Environment Cooperation ◆ Established UN's environmental fund and Governing Council for policy guidance (13 ILM 234).
1973	UN Gen. Ass. Reso. 3129 on Cooperation in the Field of the Environment Concerning Natural Resources Shared by Two or More States ◆ Governing Council to report on measures taken (17 ILM 1097).
1974	Convention for the Prevention of Marine Pollution from Land-Based Sources ◆ Ecological protection (13 ILM 352).
1977	Environmental Modification Convention ◆ Prohibits military and other hostile uses of the environment (16 ILM 88).
1978	Protocol Relating to International Convention for the Prevention of Pollution from Ships ◆ Ecological protection (17 ILM 546).
1980	Gen. Ass. Reso. 35/48 on Historical Responsibility of States for Preservation of Nature for Present and Future Generations (UN Doc. A/35/48, GAOR, 35th Session, Supp. No. 48)
1983	World Charter for Nature ◆ Nature's essential processes not to be impaired; genetic viability not compromised; all areas of earth subject to conservation; ecosystems managed for optimum sustainable productivity; no degradation by warfare or other hostile activities (22 ILM 455).
1985	Vienna Convention for the Protection of the Ozone Layer ◆ Protects layer of atmospheric zone above planetary layer (26 ILM 1529; protocols in 28 ILM 1335).
1986	International Atomic Energy Agency Convention on Early Notification of a Nuclear Accident ◆ Designed to minimize consequences and protect life, property, and environment (25 ILM 1369).
1987	Experts Group on Environmental Law of World Commission on Environment and Development ◆ Legal principles for maintaining "sustainable development" of developing countries (UN Doc. WCED/86/23/Add. 1).
1988	Protocol to the 1979 Convention on Long-Range Transboundary Air Pollution Concerning the Control of Emissions of Nitrogen Oxides or Their Transboundary Fluxes ◆ States to control or reduce emissions to 1987 levels (28 ILM 212; 1979 treaty in 18 ILM 1442).
1989	Hague Declaration on the Environment ◆ Cooperation in controlling ozone-layer deterioration caused by emissions from industrialized States adversely affecting the right to live (28 ILM 1308).

interplay between the potentially conflicting objectives of maintaining the Earth's environment and sustaining development of the southern tier of nations. Nearly 180 States gathered in Rio de Janeiro, Brazil, for the second United Nations Conference on Environment and Development (UNCED). The fundamental principle resolved by this conference was that a State is liable for its conduct or omission that constitutes "transboundary environmental interference."

How to manage the connected but sometimes competing themes of environmental protection and economic development was a central issue. As provided in the relevant UN declaration, the Rio objectives were "to promote the further development of international environmental law, taking into account the [above 1992] Declaration of the UN Conference on the Human Environment, as well as the special needs and concerns of developing countries, and to examine . . . the feasibility of elaborating general rights and obligations of states, *as appropriate,* in the field of the environment. . . ."[14]

This widely heralded gathering of diverse States produced five major documents that set the international environmental agenda for the twenty-first century. The primary components are (1) Agenda 21, (2) Rio Decla-

EXHIBIT 12.1 MAJOR GLOBAL ENVIRONMENTAL INSTRUMENTS (CONTINUED)

Year	Event
1991	Protocol on Environmental Protection to the Antarctic Treaty ◆ Updates 1959 treaty (prohibiting nuclear testing and hazardous-waste disposal) to enhance protection of all ecosystems, prevent jeopardy of endangered species, and prohibit mineral resource activities except scientific (30 ILM 1461; 1959 treaty in 19 ILM 860).
1992	Rio Declaration on Environment and Development ◆ Second major conference of States; establishes current program for global partnership discouraging environmental degradation while encouraging sustainable development (31 ILM 874).
1992	Agenda 21 ◆ Most extensive statement of priorities including review and assessment of International Law, development of implementation and compliance measures, effective participation by all States in lawmaking process, study of range and effectiveness of dispute resolution procedures (800-page document, extensively analyzed in book cited in note 15).
1992	Framework Convention on Climate Change ◆ Measures to combat greenhouse effect of emissions of carbon dioxide and similar gases and to finance controls (31 ILM 849).
1992	Convention on Biological Diversity ◆ National monitoring and strategies for conserving biological diversity of all ecosystems (31 ILM 818).
1992	Non-Legally Binding Authoritative Statement of Principles for Global Consensus on the Management, Conservation and Sustainable Development for All Types of Forests ◆ Principles encourage sustainable development, reforestation, and reduction of pollutants, especially acid rain.
1993	UN Gen. Ass. Reso. on Institutional Arrangement to Follow Up the [1992] UN Conference on Environment and Development ◆ UN General Assembly follow-up resolution welcoming adoption of Agenda 21, stressing integration of environmental protection and sustainable development (32 ILM 238).
1997	UN Convention on International Watercourses ◆ Framework for development, conservation, management, and protection (36 ILM 700).
1997	IAEA Joint Convention on Safety of Spent Fuel Management and on the Safety of Radioactive Waste Management ◆ Obligation to establish a legislative and regulatory framework to govern spent fuel from both civilian reactors and military or defense programs (36 ILM 1431).
1997	Kyoto Protocol ◆ To strengthen 1992 Climate Change Convention by reducing greenhouse emissions to 1990 levels between 2008 and 2012 (37 ILM 22).
1998	UN Convention on Prior Informed Consent Procedure for Certain Hazardous Chemicals and Pesticides in International Trade ◆ Requires consent of importing nation (UN Doc. UNEP/FAO/PIC/CONF/2).

ration, (3) Biological Diversity Convention, (4) Climate Change Convention, and (5) the Forest Principles.[15]

(1) *Agenda 21* is the 800-page blueprint for managing the various sectors of the environment in the twenty-first century. Many of the action items are quite specific, yet they aspire to degrees of protection that are well beyond the existing capacity of many States. The most controversial of these was protection of the atmosphere, because financing is the critical issue. There was agreement that fresh funding sources were needed if the objective of sustainable development were to be something more than just lip service to an unattainable ideal. However, the developed States did not succumb to pressure to commit even a small fraction of their GNP to assisting developing States.

Agenda 21 has other drawbacks. It does not contain any *mandatory* rules and depends largely on follow-up processes to attain the laudable goals of its 800-page *Program of Action*. Stanley Johnson, author of several environmental books, laments in his description of Agenda 21 that it

> may suffer from its own sheer bulkiness . . . as well as from the fact that it does not lay down any manda-

> tory rules, nor on the whole does it require truly bankable commitments to be made by any of the [State] parties involved. Agenda 21 is in reality the softest of "soft law," exhortory in nature, a cafeteria where self-service is the order of the day.
>
> Much hope is placed in the "follow-up" process, i.e., how the implementation of Agenda 21 at [the] national and international level will be monitored, but this is an area where much confusion still has to be dissipated.
>
> UNCED [merely] agreed on new institutional arrangements, particularly an inter-governmental Commission on Sustainable Development reporting to the General Assembly through ECOSOC [the Economic and Social Council discussed in §3.3], whose primary responsibility would be to investigate the extent to which states were fulfilling their duties under Agenda 21.... With so many uncertainties, it is hard to enthuse ... over the creation of another new institution in the UN framework [referring to the UN Commission for Sustainable Development].[16]

(2) The *Rio Declaration* on Environment and Development consists of twenty-one principles. Principle 2 repeated *verbatim* the above-quoted Stockholm Principle 21 on the general duty not to permit any use that harms another State's interests. Principle 7 of the Rio Declaration expanded the above-quoted Stockholm Principle 22 statement of environmental expectations.

The 1992 articulation distinguished between the responsibilities of developed and other countries, specifically referring to the new goal of "sustainable development." Rio Principle 7 provides as follows: "States shall cooperate in a spirit of global partnership to conserve, protect and restore the health and integrity of the Earth's ecosystem. In view of the different contributions of global environmental degradation, States have common but differentiated responsibilities. The developed countries acknowledge the responsibility that they bear in the international pursuit of sustainable development in view of the pressures their societies place on the global environment and of the technologies and financial resources they command."

Principle 24 is certain to reappear in scholarly and judicial discussions of the relationship between novel environmental concerns and traditional international legal theory. It provides as follows: "Warfare is inherently destructive of sustainable development. States shall therefore respect international law providing protection for the environment in times of armed conflict and cooperate in its further development, as necessary." The drafters of this principle likely had in mind the virtually incomprehensible devastation wrought by Iraq's armed forces during their retreat from Kuwait earlier in the year of the conference (1992). They set fire to 700 Kuwati oil wells. It took nine months to bring these infernos fully under control. In the interim period, millions of tons of hazardous gases belched into the air over Kuwait. UN Security Council Resolution 687 affirmed that Iraq was "liable under International Law for any direct loss, [or] damage, including environmental damage and the depletion of natural resources ... as a result of Iraq's unlawful invasion and occupation of Kuwait." Yet it is unclear whether State *practice* (as opposed to nonbinding resolutions) would characterize this use of the environment as invoking criminal responsibility under customary International Law. One reason is that States may fear expansions of Resolution 687's principle, which could criminalize other less egregious forms of transborder pollution. Nevertheless, the UN Compensation Commission determined in 1996 that Iraq would have to pay the $610 million it cost to cap the burning oil wells.[17]

(3) The 1992 Rio Conference spawned another major dispute—involving the *Convention on Biological Diversity*.[18] This treaty was opened for signature at the Conference. The "Biodiversity Treaty" mandates national development, monitoring, and preservation of all forms of life. It also requires the maintenance of "variability" among living organisms from all sources and ecosystems—a form of endangered-species protection. The dispute occurred when President George Bush declared that the US would not endorse this treaty even in principle. He objected to the required transfer of technology and intellectual property rights held by US corporations, the sharing of access to profitable biotechnologies with developing countries, and a required financial commitment to advance the relative economic position of developing countries. The gist of the US objection was that the US did not want to donate its biotechnology nor provide financing for other countries to develop competitive capabilities.

The US then stood alone among the world's leading nations against implementation of the Biodiversity Treaty. Some 120 States had signed this treaty at or shortly after the Rio Convention. In 1993, however,

President William Clinton reversed the US position. He announced that the US would "sign" this treaty, meaning an agreement in principle, although the US would not then ratify it as a binding instrument. President Clinton announced that the US would subsequently work with the European Union to develop an interpretive agreement that would not debase the intellectual property rights of US and European companies that used genetic resources in their research and development programs.

Article 3 of the Biodiversity Treaty contains an important principle that will be of lasting value in dovetailing environmental protection and sustainable development: "States have, in accordance with the Charter of the United Nations and the principles of international law, the sovereign right to exploit their own resources pursuant to their own environmental policies, and the [concomitant] responsibility to ensure that activities within their jurisdiction or control do not cause damage to the environment of other States or areas beyond the limits of national jurisdiction." This is obviously another feature of the sustainable development doctrine that now permeates international environmental instruments.

(4) Environmental concerns with the atmosphere are expressed in various UN draft instruments, including the 1992 *Climate Change Convention*.[19] This was the only treaty opened for signature at the Rio Conference. It addresses greenhouse emissions, especially carbon dioxide. Parties submit periodic reports about their gaseous emissions that harm the atmosphere by depleting the ozone layer above the earth. Some 6 percent of the world's industrialized population now produce 30 percent of the gases responsible for this greenhouse effect. An environmental agency reviews national compliance with the treaty goal of limiting these environmentally adverse emissions to earlier levels—as opposed to unregulated increases. Article 9 of the Climate Convention also calls for continual assessment of scientific evidence, as it becomes available, for controlling climate change and incorporating the relevant technologies for achieving better national control. The initial agreement was to strive for a return to the emission levels of 1990—by the year 2000. As a result of the Kyoto Protocol, at the 1997 (Rio) follow-up conference, thirty-eight *industrialized* nations agreed to reduce greenhouse emissions to 1990 levels between 2008 and 2012. (It enters into force when fifty-five nations have ratified it.)

Finally, preventative measures are costly. The estimated cost would be $120 billion per year to control global warming. Not many States will have the economic capacity to provide the requisite funding. Future global warming conferences will have to focus on an acceptable framework for controlling nations like the US, with its highest rate of greenhouse gas emissions in the world—twenty tons per person in 1995.

The Climate Convention also provides for financial assistance to the lesser developed countries. Funding would become available through the Global Environmental Facility of the World Bank. This bank was the intergovernmental institution responsible for rebuilding post-war Europe through the establishment of national economic-development programs. The Global Environmental Facility would be the world's environmental banker. Given existing concerns with the objectivity of the World Bank, however, it is not clear that the more developed nations will ratify this device for financing sustainable development.[20]

(5) The key document—Non-Legally Binding Authoritative Statement of Principles for Global Consensus on the Management, Conservation and Sustainable Development for All Types of Forests, or *Forest Principles*—encourages *sustainable* development, as well as reforestation and the reduction of pollutants, especially acid rain.[21]

In conjunction with the International Monetary Fund, the World Bank is currently working to fund the cleanup and restoration of the Amazon forests in Brazil. These are the earth's "lungs" in the sense that 50 to 80 percent of the Western hemisphere's oxygen comes from these rain forests. Each year, approximately 25 million acres of forests are cleared from the world's rain forests. In 1994, the US Agency for International Development estimated that Guatemala and Colombia would ultimately lose 33 percent of their remaining forests; Ecuador and Nicaragua 50 percent. This form of environmental depletion affects all other nations throughout the hemisphere.

In 1997 and 1998, most nations of the world attended various follow-up Rio conferences. The delegates acknowledged the continuing problems: pollution of the atmosphere and oceans, growing water scarcity, declining fish stocks, and vanishing forests. They have deadlocked on most issues, however. One result was that lowering greenhouse gas emissions to previously agreed-upon 1990 levels was pushed back to somewhere between the years 2008 and 2012.

IEL INSTRUMENTS

The 1972 Conference on the Environment spawned an unprecedented political and diplomatic awakening. The UN, together with regional environmental organizations and world leaders, repositioned international environmental issues from the periphery to the center of national political and diplomatic agendas. Conferences of States, UN initiatives, and intergovernmental treaties permeated the public consciousness in the last portion of the twentieth century. As a result, environmental issues are finally sharing center stage with the other traditional concerns of International Law depicted in the first eleven chapters of this book.

This subsection provides a snapshot of some of the major international environmental instruments. The overview in Exhibit 12.1 will help you visualize the various campaigns designed to save the environment from further assaults—now undertaken with at least the acknowledgment of the body of principles involving environmental degradation.

◆ 12.3 ARBITRAL AND JUDICIAL PERSPECTIVES

The analysis of environmental issues by third-party decision makers often begins with the pivotal principle that the presence of an international border cannot vest total discretion in the border States to alter natural conditions on the basis of State sovereignty.

ARBITRATION

The 1941 *Trail Smelter Arbitration* may be the classic case for articulating the fundamental norm in contemporary International Environmental Law. This was the first to deal authoritatively with cross-border *air* pollution. A Canadian smelter seven miles from the US state of Washington emitted extraordinary amounts of sulfur dioxide fumes, harming the atmosphere and the agricultural industry in Washington for more than a decade. The US and Canada established a three-member arbitral tribunal that consisted of Canadian, US, and Belgian arbitrators (the third being a neutral arbitrator selected by the other two). The tribunal determined that Canada had incurred State responsibility for environmental damage, although the smelter was a non-governmental operation.

In one passage, the arbitrators effectively predicted the direction of future environmental analyses by referring to the competing interests of industrial development and agricultural degradation in the region surrounding British Columbia and Washington. Drawing from commonly accepted sources, the arbitral decision provides that "[i]t would not be to the advantage of the two countries concerned that industrial effort should be prevented by exaggerating the [environmental] interests of the agricultural community. Equally, it would not be to the advantage of the two countries that the agricultural community should be oppressed to advance the interest of industry."[22]

While the State parties ineffectively juggled the final resolution of this decision for the next forty years, *Trail Smelter* authoritatively restated an emerging principle, one subsequently cited in national and international litigation. A State must not knowingly permit the use of its territory to harm other States. It has the obligation to protect other States from the injurious acts of individuals and corporations within State borders. Sovereignty encompasses vital rights. However, it also includes the responsibility to respect the territory of other States.

INTERNATIONAL COURT OF JUSTICE AND THE ENVIRONMENT

Introduction Internationally imposed limitations appeared in the jurisprudence of the Permanent Court of International Justice in the 1920s and 1930s—wherein the Court restrained State activity in rivers and canals that were used for international navigation or irrigation.[23] Like perspectives surfaced in the jurisprudence of the current International Court of Justice (ICJ). Prior to deciding the major environmental cases set forth below in this section, the ICJ first pronounced the obligation of States not to allow the use of their territories to interfere with the rights of other States (in 1949). Albania was held liable for its failure to notify Great Britain about the presence of mines in Albanian waters within an international strait. In 1974, the Court ordered France to cease its nuclear atmospheric testing in the South Pacific because radioactive fallout would prejudice various health and agricultural interests of the citizens of Australia and New Zealand.[24]

In one of the two major environmental cases decided by the ICJ, its Vice-President Gregory Weermantry succinctly articulated the interplay of the evolving—and sometimes competing—rights to "development," "environmental protection," and "sustainable development" (*separate* opinion from the *Hungary v. Slovakia* case below):

The people of both Hungary and Slovakia are entitled to development for the furtherance of their happiness and welfare. They are likewise entitled to the preservation of their human right to the protection of their environment. . . . The present case [1997] thus focuses attention, as no other case has done in the jurisprudence of this Court, on the question of the harmonization of developmental and environmental concepts. . . .

Article 1 of the Declaration on the Right to Development, 1986, asserted that "The right to development is an inalienable human right." This Declaration had the overwhelming support of the international community. . . .

The protection of the environment is likewise a vital part of contemporary human rights doctrine, for it is a *sine qua non* [indispensable prerequisite] for numerous human rights such as the right to health and the right to life itself. It is scarcely necessary to elaborate on this, as damage to the environment can impair and undermine all the human rights spoken of in the Universal Declaration and other human rights instruments. . . .

While, therefore, all peoples have the right to initiate development projects and enjoy their benefits, there is likewise a duty to ensure that those projects do not significantly damage the environment. . . .

After the early formulations of the concept of development, it has been recognized that development cannot be pursued to such a point as to result in substantial damage to the environment within which it is to occur. Therefore development can only be prosecuted in harmony with the reasonable demands of environmental protection. Whether development is sustainable by reason of its impact on the environment will, of course, be a question to be answered in the context of the particular situation involved.

It is thus the correct formulation of the right to development that that right does not exist in the absolute sense, but is relative always to its tolerance by the environment. The right to development as thus refined is clearly part of modern international law. It is compendiously referred to as sustainable development.[25]

Recent ICJ developments have integrated the International Environmental Law principles discussed earlier in this chapter with factual contexts involving both sudden and long-term environmental degradations. In addition to the Court's *advisory* and *contentious* jurisdiction cases, it now has a special chamber of judges available to determine environmental cases on an expedited basis.[26]

Advisory Case Section 9.4 of this book dealt with the ICJ's advisory jurisdiction. The Court may thereby aid in the progressive development of International Law in those cases in which States would not be likely to consent to suit because of the sensitivity of the issue at hand.

Termination of the Cold War superpower nuclear threat did not diminish concerns about environmental disasters, which could still occur because of their potential use in more limited conflicts. Black marketeers, ethnic or religious zealots, and terrorists—like those who used poisonous gas in Tokyo's subways in March 1995—attest to the potential danger of *nuclear* environmental pollution. The UN's World Health Organization (WHO) thus requested an advisory opinion from the ICJ in 1993 regarding the legality of either using or threatening to use nuclear weapons. All States and international organizations with an interest in the resolution of this case submitted their written input to the Court by June 1995. One issue involved environmental degradation balanced against the national prerogative to use *any* means available to preserve the State. The relevant portions of the Court's 1997 decision follows:

"Legality of the Threat or Use of Nuclear Weapons"

INTERNATIONAL COURT OF JUSTICE

General List No. 95 (Advisory Opinion of 8 July 1996)

(To see the full case, check www.law.cornell.edu/icj/icj1/unan5afin.htm)

Author's Note: *The UN General Assembly requested an advisory opinion from the ICJ, based on information provided by the World Health Organization. The issue for the Court was the following: "Is the threat or use of nuclear weapons in* *any circumstance permitted under international law?" The Court did not authoritatively decide the question presented, regarding the legality of using nuclear weapons in self-defense* (see *§10.2 of this text).*

The Court did, however, enunciate some useful principles regarding International Environmental Law. The portion of the case, addressing nuclear weapons and the environment, is set forth immediately below. Italics have been added to certain words and phrases within this version of the Court's opinion.

COURT'S OPINION. THE COURT . . . gives the following Advisory Opinion: . . .

27. In both their written and oral statements, some States furthermore argued that any use of nuclear weapons would be unlawful by reference to existing norms relating to the safeguarding and protection of the environment, in view of their essential importance.

Specific references were made to various existing international treaties and instruments. These included Additional Protocol I of 1977 to the Geneva Conventions of 1949, Article 35, paragraph 3, of which prohibits the employment of "methods or means of warfare which are intended, or may be expected, to cause widespread, long-term and severe damage to the natural environment"; and the Convention of 18 May 1977 on the Prohibition of Military or Any Other Hostile Use of Environmental Modification Techniques, which prohibits the use of weapons which have "widespread, long-lasting or severe effects" on the environment (Art. 1). Also cited were Principle 21 of the Stockholm Declaration of 1972 and Principle 2 of the Rio Declaration of 1992 which express the common conviction of the States concerned that they have a duty "to ensure that activities within their jurisdiction or control do not cause damage to the environment of other States or of areas beyond the limits of national jurisdiction." These instruments and other provisions relating to the protection and safeguarding of the environment were said to apply at all times, in war as well as in peace, and it was contended that they would be violated by the use of nuclear weapons whose consequences would be widespread and would have transboundary effects.

28. Other States [countered, and thus] questioned the binding legal quality of these precepts of environmental law; or, in the context of the Convention on the Prohibition of Military or Any Other Hostile Use of Environmental Modification Techniques, denied that it was concerned at all with the use of *nuclear* weapons in hostilities. . . .

It was also argued by some States that the principal purpose of environmental treaties and norms was the protection of the environment in time of *peace*. It was said that those treaties made no mention of nuclear weapons. It was also pointed out that warfare in general, and nuclear warfare in particular, were not mentioned in their texts and that it would be destabilizing to the rule of law and to confidence in international negotiations if those treaties were now interpreted in such a way as to prohibit the use of nuclear weapons.

29. The Court recognizes that the environment is under daily threat and that the use of nuclear weapons could constitute a *catastrophe* for the environment. The Court also recognizes that the environment is not an abstraction but represents the living space, the quality of life and the very health of human beings, including generations unborn. The existence of the general obligation of States to ensure that activities within their jurisdiction and control respect the environment of other States or of areas beyond national control is now part of the corpus of international law relating to the environment.

30. . . . The Court does not consider that the treaties in question could have intended to deprive a State of the exercise of its right of self-defence under international law because of its obligations to protect the environment. Nonetheless, States must take environmental considerations into account when assessing what is necessary and proportionate in the pursuit of legitimate military objectives. Respect for the environment is one of the elements that go to assessing whether an action is in conformity with the principles of necessity and proportionality.

This approach is supported, indeed, by the terms of Principle 24 of the Rio Declaration, which provides that:

> "Warfare is inherently destructive of sustainable development. States shall therefore respect international law providing protection for the environment in times of armed conflict and cooperate in its further development, as necessary."

31. The Court notes furthermore that Articles 35, paragraph 3, and 55 of [Geneva Convention] Additional Protocol I provide additional protection for the environment. Taken together, these provisions embody a

general obligation to protect the natural environment against widespread, long-term and severe environmental damage; the prohibition of methods and means of warfare which are intended, or may be expected, to cause such damage; and the prohibition of attacks against the natural environment by way of reprisals.

These are powerful constraints for all the States having subscribed to these provisions.

32. General Assembly resolution 47/37 of 25 November 1992 on the Protection of the Environment in Times of Armed Conflict, is also of interest in this context. It affirms the general view according to which environmental considerations constitute one of the elements to be taken into account in the implementation of the principles of the law applicable in armed conflict: it states that "destruction of the environment, not justified by military necessity and carried out wantonly, is clearly contrary to existing international law." Addressing the reality that certain instruments are not yet binding on all States, the General Assembly in this resolution "[a]ppeals to all States that have not yet done so to consider becoming parties to the relevant international conventions." . . .

33. The Court thus finds that while the existing international law relating to the protection and safeguarding of the environment does not specifically prohibit the use of nuclear weapons, it indicates *important environmental factors that are properly to be taken into account in the context of the implementation of the principles and rules of the law applicable in armed conflict*. . . .

35. . . . The Court has noted the definitions of nuclear weapons contained in various treaties and accords. It also notes that nuclear weapons are explosive devices whose energy results from the fusion or fission of the atom. By its very nature, that process, in nuclear weapons as they exist today, releases not only immense quantities of heat and energy, but also powerful and prolonged radiation. According to the material before the Court, the first two causes of damage are vastly more powerful than the damage caused by other weapons, while the phenomenon of radiation is said to be peculiar to nuclear weapons. These characteristics render the nuclear weapon potentially catastrophic. *The destructive power of nuclear weapons cannot be contained in either space or time. They have the potential to destroy all civilization and the entire ecosystem of the planet.*

The radiation released by a nuclear explosion would affect health, agriculture, natural resources and demography over a very wide area. Further, the use of nuclear weapons would be a serious danger to future generations. Ionizing radiation has the potential to damage the future environment, food and marine ecosystem, and to cause genetic defects and illness in future generations. . . .

57. The pattern until now has been for weapons of mass destruction to be declared illegal by specific instruments. The most recent such instruments are the Convention of 10 April 1972 on the Prohibition of the Development, Production and Stockpiling of Bacteriological (Biological) and Toxic Weapons and on their destruction which prohibits the possession of bacteriological and toxic weapons and reinforces the prohibition of their use and the Convention of 13 January 1993 on the Prohibition of the Development, Production, Stockpiling and Use of Chemical Weapons and on Their Destruction which prohibits all use of chemical weapons and requires the destruction of existing stocks. Each of these instruments has been negotiated and adopted in its own context and for its own reasons. The Court does not find any specific prohibition of recourse to nuclear weapons in treaties expressly prohibiting the use of certain weapons of mass destruction.

58. In the last two decades, a great many negotiations have been conducted regarding nuclear weapons; they have not resulted in a treaty of general prohibition of the same kind as for bacteriological and chemical weapons. . . .

60. Those States that believe that recourse to nuclear weapons is illegal stress that the conventions that include various rules providing for the limitation or elimination of nuclear weapons in certain areas (such as the Antarctic Treaty of 1959 which prohibits the deployment of nuclear weapons in the Antarctic, or the Treaty of Tlatelolco of 1967 which creates a nuclear-weapon-free zone in Latin America), or the conventions that apply certain measures of control and limitation to the existence of nuclear weapons (such as the 1963 Partial Test-Ban Treaty or the Treaty on the Non-Proliferation of Nuclear Weapons) all set limits to the use of nuclear weapons. In their view, these treaties bear witness, in their own way, to the emergence of a rule of complete legal prohibition of all uses of nuclear weapons. . . .

76. Since the turn of the century, the appearance of new means of combat has[,] without calling into question the longstanding principles and rules of international law[,] rendered necessary some specific prohibi-

tions of the use of certain weapons, such as explosive projectiles . . . [c]hemical and bacteriological weapons . . . weapons producing "non-detectable fragments," of other types of "mines, booby traps and other devices," and of "incendiary weapons," was either prohibited or limited. . . .

78. . . . In conformity with the aforementioned principles, humanitarian law, at a very early stage, prohibited certain types of weapons either because of their indiscriminate effect on combatants and civilians or because of the unnecessary suffering caused to combatants, that is to say, a harm greater than that unavoidable to achieve legitimate military objectives. If an envisaged use of weapons would not meet the requirements of humanitarian law, a threat to engage in such use would also be contrary to that law. . . .

93. A similar view has been expressed with respect to the effects of the principle of neutrality. Like the principles and rules of humanitarian law, that principle has therefore been considered by some to rule out the use of a weapon the *effects* of which simply *cannot be contained within the territories of the contending States.*

94. The Court would observe that none of the States advocating the legality of the use of nuclear weapons under certain circumstances, including the "clean" use of smaller, low yield, tactical nuclear weapons, has indicated what, supposing such limited use were feasible, would be the precise circumstances justifying such use; nor whether such limited use would not tend to escalate into the all-out use of high yield nuclear weapons. This being so, the Court does *not* consider that it has a sufficient basis for a determination on the validity of this view. . . .

◆ *Notes & Questions*

1. Under International Environmental Law (IEL), what is a State's responsibility when contemplating whether to use nuclear weapons?
2. Must a State choose between preservation of the environment and self-defense?
3. Can one argue—because nuclear weapons are not mentioned in the various instruments of IEL—that such weapons may be used without regard to the environmental consequences? That environmental consequences could defeat a State's right to self-defense?

Contentious Cases The ICJ considered its first major environmental case in 1993. The small, formerly resource-rich State of Nauru alleged that Australia had incurred State responsibility for the environmental degradation of Nauru. It claimed that Australia (and others) mined the phosphate-rich soil of Nauru to satisfy the needs of Australia's agricultural industry for fertilizer. Nauru received a woefully inadequate share of the profits from its natural resources in addition to experiencing a depletion that also degraded its economic, social, and cultural environment—as previously determined by an independent Commission of Inquiry.[27]

The parties settled this case shortly after the ICJ announced its Environmental Chambers Constitution in 1993 (described below). One might presume that the Court's willingness to hear Nauru's contentious case, coupled with its establishment of a specialized environmental chamber, may have pressured Australia into pursuing a settlement—rather than facing the consequences of an adverse ICJ judgment. One possible consequence could have been a court-mandated requirement that Australia restore Nauru to the position it would have enjoyed but for the environmental degradation.

A book-length account of the work of the Commission of Inquiry (undertaken before Nauru's post-independence ICJ litigation) depicts the resulting environmental degradation of Nauru by the partnership of Australia, New Zealand, and Great Britain. A scientific report used by the Commission of Inquiry illustrates the relevant findings:

> Land shortage resulting from mining has given Nauru one of the most important social problems which the country now faces.
>
> In relation to fauna and flora, [scientists who prepared this report] . . . have described how centuries will be needed for the forest to reestablish itself naturally even in modified form, and how numerous plant species are scattered and stunted as compared with their growth in the unmined forest. . . . These scientists have stressed "the disastrous effects and almost total disruption of island ecosystems that resulted from inappropriate development projects

and land use." Natural forest microclimates have been transformed into new microclimates with increased sunlight and lower humidity, resulting in greatly altered patterns of vegetation. A number of indigenous plant species are endangered.

With the changes in vegetation, Nauruan diet too has suffered a drastic change.[28]

The most prominent environmental decision of the Court in a *contentious* case involving actual litigants involved a joint construction project on the Danube agreed to by Hungary and Czechoslovakia in 1977. (The above ICJ *Nuclear Weapons Case,* by contrast, was an *advisory* opinion sought by the World Health Organization.) After the breakdown of the former Soviet Union, there was a dispute regarding how to carry out their respective treaty obligations—especially after this project became quite unpopular with the people of Hungary. The following ICJ opinion did a great deal to solidify the basket of norms that had evolved in International Environmental Law, some during the twenty-year period spanning the 1977 treaty and the Court's decision:

Case Concerning the Gabcíkovo-Nagymaros Project (Hungary v. Slovakia)

INTERNATIONAL COURT OF JUSTICE

General List No. 92

(Judgment of 25 September 1997)

Go to course Web page at http://home.att.net/~slomansonb/txtcsesite.html; click on Gabcíkovo-Nagymaros Project.

◆ *Notes & Questions*

1. Hearings in the case were held between 3 March and 15 April 1997. The Court visited the Gabcíkovo-Nagymaros Project site (the first such visit in its history). The Court found that both Hungary and Slovakia had breached their obligations under the 1977 Budapest Treaty. It therefore called on both States to negotiate in good faith in order to ensure the achievement of the objectives of the treaty—which the Court declared as being still in force—while requiring the parties to take into account the factual situation that had developed since the 1989 collapse of the Soviet Union.
2. In September 1998, Slovakia filed a request for an *additional* judgment. Slovakia claimed that a fresh judgment was necessary because of Hungary's unwillingness to implement the 1997 Judgment of the Court by negotiating in good faith.
3. What was the "necessity" on which Hungary relied as its basis for not having to comply with its obligations under the Budapest Treaty (with Slovakia's predecessor Czechoslovakia)?
4. What principles of International Environmental Law did the Court enunciate in this case?
5. An excellent overview of this case in its historical and contemporary contexts is available in A. Schwabach, "Diverting the Danube: The Gabcíkovo-Nagymaros Dispute and International Freshwater Law," 14 *Berkeley J. Int'l L.* 290 (1996).

Environmental Chamber There is now a specialized Environmental Chamber *within* the ICJ. Section 9.4 of this book addressed the "Chambers" process whereby States may access the expertise of certain ICJ members to resolve their conflicts—rather than the usual decisions by the full bench of judges. Article 26.1 of the Statute of the ICJ provides for "chambers, composed of three or more judges . . . for dealing with particular categories of cases; for example labour cases and cases relating to transit and communications."

In 1993, the ICJ formed a "Chamber of the Court for Environmental Matters." That Chamber's constitution proclaims that the ICJ *was* willing until the 1990s to deal with environmental matters on an *ad hoc* basis. But due to increased concern with environmental conflicts between State parties, the judges of the Court implemented this novel environmental dispute-resolution procedure. The special "Constitution of a Chamber of the Court for Environmental Matters" provides as follows: "In view of the developments in the field of environmental law and protection which have taken place in the last few years [*see* Exhibit 12.1], and considering that it should be prepared to the fullest possible extent to deal with any environmental case falling within its jurisdiction, the Court has now deemed it appropriate to establish a seven-member Chamber for Environmental Matters. . . ."[29]

The Environmental Chamber has not yet decided any cases. Given the intense interest in major environmental disasters of the current generation, however, States will hopefully refer such matters to this specialized forum by treaty or other special agreement. The anticipated advantages include the development of a special body of expertise by a group of judges who are readily available for a quicker resolution than possible under the traditional full Court procedure. Judges can also be selected so as to seat those of particular nationalities rather than the full court—a preferred posture for some litigants.

US COURTS AND LEGISLATION

The US previously enacted environmental legislation originally intended to manage the environment *within* the US. In 1969, the US Congress enacted legislation designed to control degradation of the environment:

Title 42. The Public Health and Welfare
Chapter 55—National Environmental Policy

Subchapter I—Policies and Goals

§4332. Cooperation of agencies; reports; availability of information; recommendations; international and national coordination of efforts

Author's Note: *Italics have been added to certain words and phrases.*

[Legislation.] The Congress authorizes and directs that, to the fullest extent possible: . . . *all agencies of the Federal Government shall*—

(A) utilize a systematic, interdisciplinary approach which will insure the integrated use of the natural and social sciences and the environmental design arts in planning and in decisionmaking which may have an impact on man's environment;

(B) identify and develop methods and procedures, in consultation with the Council on Environmental Quality established by subchapter II of this chapter, which will insure that presently unquantified environmental amenities and values may be given appropriate consideration in decisionmaking along with economic and technical considerations;

(C) *include* in every recommendation or report on proposals for legislation and other major Federal actions significantly affecting the quality of the human environment, *a detailed statement* by the responsible official *on*—

(i) *the environmental impact of the proposed action,*
(ii) any adverse environmental effects which cannot be avoided should the proposal be implemented,
(iii) alternatives to the proposed action,
(iv) the relationship between local short-term uses of man's environment and the maintenance and enhancement of long-term productivity, and
(v) any irreversible and irretrievable commitments of resources which would be involved in the proposed action should it be implemented. . . .

(F) *recognize* the worldwide and long-range character of environmental problems and, where consistent with the foreign policy of the United States, lend appropriate support to initiatives, resolutions, and programs designed to maximize international cooperation in anticipating and preventing a decline in the quality of mankind's world environment. . . .

◆ Notes

1. In a 1993 case construing the US environmental legislation quoted above, the federal appellate court for the District of Columbia determined, despite the presumption against the extraterritorial application of national legislation, that US environmental standards could be applied to Antarctica. This area within the global commons (§6.2) is not subject to the sovereign control of any nation, although the US has a significant degree of legislative control. *Environmental*

Defense Fund, Inc. v. Massey, 986 F.2d 528 (D.C. Cir., 1993).

In 1996, Congress added a provision regarding space launches: "The licensing of a launch vehicle or launch site operator . . . under chapter 701 of title 49, United States Code . . . shall not be considered a major Federal action for purposes of . . . the National Environmental Policy Act of 1969 (42 USC 4332[C]) if—

"(1) the Department of the Army has issued a permit for the activity; and

"(2) the Army Corps of Engineers has found that the activity has no significant impact."

2. In 1990, Congress enacted the Oil Pollution Act (OPA) in response to the disastrous 1989 oil spill by the US tanker *Exxon Valdez*. The OPA is a comprehensive Act that contains measures to prevent oil spills and regulate liability and compensation for oil spills. There are lingering questions about its constitutionality under US law.[30] International conventions governing such oil spills have been in place for twenty-five years. These include some skeletal provisions in the 1982 UN Conference on the Law of the Sea, the 1969 International Convention on Civil Liability for Oil Pollution Damage, the 1971 International Oil Pollution Compensation Fund Convention, and the 1972 Convention on the Prevention of Marine Pollution by Dumping of Wastes and Other Matter.[31]

◆ SUMMARY

1. Environmental pollution is not an exclusively modern phenomenon. In the final decades of the twentieth century, however, sudden disasters and incremental degradations made it one of the most prominent of international concerns.
2. The term *International Environmental Law* is a blend of national and international attempts to legally control the effect of industrial development on the environment. The many draft treaties and declarations arguably consist of "soft law," in the sense that there are many principles but few binding obligations—due to the varying degrees of concern with the effects of development on the environment. It may be better, however, to have at least general principles with which few States disagree. The latter may facilitate a shift to "hard" law as State practice evolves. Numerous environmental instruments have thus been promulgated in the closing decades of the twentieth century. Two major conferences of States produced draft treaties, declarations, and principles designed to maintain the quality of the environment (1972 Stockholm and 1992 Rio Conferences).
3. There are twin objectives in contemporary environmental instruments: encouraging sustainable development while discouraging environmental degradation. Whether these will ultimately be compatible depends on the degree to which underdeveloped States will be able to close the gap with developed States—without significant adverse effects on regional and global ecosystems.
4. Both the 1972 and 1992 UN environmental conferences affirmed the expectation that States must cooperate in developing programs to jointly manage the environment. The latter conference added that developing countries in their pursuit of "sustainable development" must incorporate appropriate technologies and financial resources so that the *environmental* cost of development does not far exceed the economic benefit.
5. The 1992 UN Conference on the Environment and Development produced a series of draft treaties and declarations. The most prominent was Agenda 21—an extensive blueprint for environmental control and sustainable development in the twenty-first century. One potential drawback is the lack of mandatory obligations and Agenda 21's dependence on "follow-up processes."
6. There is legal liability for one State's "environmental interference" with another—now referred to as a "transboundary environmental interference." The emerging legal standards include the principle that States no longer have the *exclusive* discretion to manage and resolve environmental issues within their own borders, because degradations routinely have transboundary effects. The clearest norm is that a State may not use or allow the use of its territory in a way that harms another. Applications include a sudden disaster, like using a small nuclear device, that present environmental hazards in other countries.
7. The alternative remedies for such a degradation are that the offending State cease the wrongful act; reestablish the circumstances, as they were prior to the wrongful act; or provide compensation to the

State harmed by the transborder environmental interference.

8. Determining the legal cause of an "incremental" category of transboundary environmental interference may be rather complex. Assuming that liability is established, the alternative remedies are relatively clear. The offending State must halt its role in perpetuating the environmental degradation. It may have to restore the harmed State to the position it would have enjoyed but for the environmental interference. Money damages may also be an appropriate remedy, depending on the circumstances of the particular case and the theoretical ability to actually restore the harmed State to its prior position.
9. The 1992 Rio Declaration prompts States to develop environmental programs that will augment or implement international environmental efforts. The major US legislation, predating the conference, is the National Environmental Protection Act (NEPA). It requires federal agencies to prepare an Environmental Impact Statement (EIS) for proposed activities that may "significantly" affect the environment. International instruments tend to require assessments of even a "minor" impact on the environment.

◆ PROBLEM

Problem 12.A (end of Chapter)

Basic Facts: Greenpeace International is a non-governmental organization (NGO) headquartered in Amsterdam. Its objective is to protect the environment, often by monitoring threats to an increasingly fragile environment. It has thus operated a small fleet, including the former British-registered flagship *Rainbow Warrior,* which began to make international port calls in 1971. French nuclear testing has been a popular target for Greenpeace activity.

In 1973, New Zealand and Australia sued France in the International Court of Justice, seeking a judgment that would require France to cease its nuclear testing in the South Pacific. The plaintiff States feared that radioactive fallout would adversely affect the atmosphere throughout the South Pacific. Rather than participating in this litigation, France withdrew. The ICJ dismissed the case in 1974 on the basis of France's unilateral declaration that it would cease such testing—which, in fact, it later resumed.

The private multinational crews of Greenpeace vessels had recently begun to follow various oceangoing vessels suspected of excessive whaling and other fishing enterprises in violation of international norms, transporting and dumping of nuclear fuels and waste materials, and dumping other toxic substances into the ocean. Given the mid-1970s case filed by two State opponents of France's nuclear testing, Greenpeace believed that it was in a far better position to bring worldwide attention to France's resumption of nuclear testing.

The most famous "collision" between Greenpeace and the French government occurred in 1980 at a harbor's entrance to a port in France. A Japanese merchant vessel was carrying nuclear reactors to France; Greenpeace characterized the shipment as a major hazard due to the potential radiation hazard from transferring this material by sea. Put another way, this was a nuclear *Exxon Valdez* waiting to happen. As Greenpeace's *Rainbow Warrior* began to shadow the Japanese vessel, the Greenpeace vessel was rammed by a French police ship. After its seizure by French port authorities, the Greenpeace vessel was released and ordered never to return to French waters.

The primary newsworthiness of the *Rainbow Warrior* was its subsequent "shadowing" of French, Russian, and Spanish naval vessels in attempts to disrupt French nuclear testing in French Polynesia (not far from New Zealand). Greenpeace was the target of a plot by the Directeurat-Generale de Sécurité Extérieure (DGSE), a French governmental intelligence agency. A DGSE agent purporting to be a Greenpeace supporter worked undercover in the Auckland, New Zealand, office of Greenpeace International. She photographed Auckland's harbors as part of a plan to sink the Greenpeace ship after a decade of shadowing French military vessels. New Zealand, as part of its Nuclear Free Zone policy, had banned French nuclear vessels from its harbors. This agent's photographs were sent to Paris for intelligence-gathering purposes, which would soon bring worldwide attention to the ongoing Greenpeace–French connection.

While in Auckland Harbor in 1985, the *Rainbow Warrior* was bombed and sunk by a group of at least eight DGSE agents. Two bombs, exploding near midnight, resulted in the death of a Dutch citizen who was the ship's onboard photographer. The explosion injured several crew members of various nationalities (other than

New Zealand) and sank this British-flagged ship. Most of the French agents escaped. It appears that the nearby French submarine sank the boat in which they escaped from Auckland Harbor, after bringing them aboard for their probable return to France via French Polynesia.

New Zealand captured two of the French DGSE agents, tried them, and sentenced them to ten-year sentences for manslaughter and arson (to name a few of the charges). New Zealand's citizens were outraged. The *Rainbow Warrior* incident was the first operation by a foreign government involving a bombing, death, and sinking of a vessel in a New Zealand harbor. New Zealand thus lodged a diplomatic protest with France and demanded reparations based on France's alleged State responsibility for various violations of national and International Law. The UN Secretary-General then arbitrated an agreement between France and New Zealand whereby (1) France was to pay damages to New Zealand, but not damages on account of the death or damage to the vessel caused by the bomb blast; (2) New Zealand would transfer the two convicted agents to a prison in French Polynesia to serve out the remainder of their terms; and (3) France would not impose trade barriers against New Zealand's butter and meat exports, which it had threatened to do during the *Rainbow Warrior* negotiations. New Zealand thus agreed to release the two captured French army officers to French custody so that they would serve the remainder of their jail terms in a French Polynesian prison.[32]

Within four years, the two transferred prisoners "escaped" from the French island prison. They were repatriated to France but never taken into custody in France (for what would otherwise be their return to the prison in French Polynesia). France claimed that there was no basis for New Zealand to demand their continued incarceration, because they were acting on "superior orders." The other French agents were never arrested or tried. The French government conceded its role in the bombing of the *Rainbow Warrior* but claimed that its agents had exceeded their authority. France nevertheless threatened to use further force if any other Greenpeace vessel ever attempted to disrupt future French nuclear testing.

In 1991, another French agent involved in the *Rainbow Warrior* bombing was arrested in Switzerland. Greenpeace immediately pressured the New Zealand government to seek his extradition from Switzerland. New Zealand decided not to pursue the harbor-bombing incident any further. Switzerland allegedly bowed to French pressure to release the agent from custody, even providing a diplomatic escort to the French border.

Additional "Facts": In addition to the given facts, assume the following *hypothetical* facts:

The explosion and sinking of the *Rainbow Warrior* in Auckland Harbor contaminates the harbor due to the nature and large volume of the just-loaded chemicals that were to be used for testing purposes. New Zealand (NZ) authorities were unaware of the presence of these chemicals aboard the Greenpeace vessel when it entered the harbor. While testing aboard the vessel did nothing to pollute the air, the combination of existing pollutants in Auckland Harbor and the chemicals aboard the sunken *Rainbow Warrior* further contaminates the fish within the harbor. One month after the explosion and sinking, the fish in Auckland Harbor are no longer fit for human consumption.

France continues to conduct nuclear testing in French Polynesia. France actually conducted fifty such reported tests before and after the 1985 *Rainbow Warrior* incident. The people of New Zealand begin to experience a severe form of "cold" that makes the average healthy person sick for several months at a time. The common symptoms are flu, fever, and skin rash. This form of cold did not exist in New Zealand prior to the start of French and US nuclear testing in the South Pacific in the 1950s. Since the 1970s, a small percentage of the population has exhibited these symptoms. It has become a fact of life for most New Zealanders in the last five years.

NZ lodges a diplomatic claim with France in 1995, accusing France of "transboundary environmental interference" within the meaning of the various UN instruments—especially the various 1992 Rio declarations—which NZ characterizes as the essence of International Environmental Law. NZ and France agree to arbitrate this matter. Both are parties to the UN Law of the Sea Treaty, the only agreement *in force* containing relevant environmental provisions. NZ seeks remedies for the flu that its citizens now suffer and the contamination of Auckland Harbor.

The Forum: Two students (or groups) will represent France and NZ as the arbitrators chosen by the respective parties to today's "Flufish Arbitration." A third student will sit as the third and neutral arbitrator selected by the other arbitrators. This arbitral body will report on its resolution of whether France has incurred State responsibility under International Law for harm to NZ. In the event of a split decision, the dissenting arbitrator will report his or her decision for further class discussion.

Issues for Resolution:

1. What rule or rules should the arbitrators use to assess whether France is liable under International Environmental Law? (Another student may also report on what rules of International Law from prior chapters were breached by France on these facts.)
2. Is France responsible for a transboundary environmental interference in New Zealand? Elsewhere?
3. If France is found to be liable for New Zealand's claimed environmental degradation, what remedy would be appropriate?

◆ BIBLIOGRAPHY

Documents & Dictionaries

The Environment Encyclopedia & Directory (New York: Taylor & Francis, 1993).

H. Hohmann (ed.), *Basic Documents of International Environmental Law* (Dordrecht, Neth.: Graham & Trotman/Martinus Nijhoff, 1992).

Multilateral Treaties in the Field of the Environment (Cambridge, Eng.: Grotius Pub., 1991) (two volumes).

General

S. Chowdhury et al., *The Right to Development in International Law* (Dordrecht, Neth.: Martinus Nijhoff, 1992).

P. Dupuy, *Soft Law and the International Law of the Environment,* 12 *Mich. J. Int'l L.* 420 (1991).

M. Miller, *The Third World in Global Environmental Politics* (Boulder, CO: Lynne Reiner, 1995).

P. Muldoon & R. Lindgren, *The Environmental Bill of Rights* (Toronto: Edmond Montgomery, 1995).

M. Quinn, "International Environmental Law," in *Going International: International Trade for the Nonspecialist* 91 (Philadelphia: Amer. L. Inst., 1994).

E. Urbani & C. Rubin (eds.), *Transnational Environmental Law and Its Impact on Corporate Behavior* (Irvington-on-Hudson, NY: Transnat'l 1994) (Fletcher School symposium).

Special Problems

S. Johnson, *World Population—Turning the Tide: Three Decades of Progress* (Dordrecht, Neth.: Kluwer, 1994).

K. Kummer, *International Management of Hazardous Wastes: The Basel Convention and Related Legal Rules* (Oxford, Eng.: Clarendon Press, 1995).

B. Kwiatkowsa & A. Soons (eds.), *Transboundary Movements and Disposal of Hazardous Wastes in International Law: Basic Documents* (Dordrecht, Neth.; Boston: Graham & Trotman/ Martinus Nijhoff, 1992).

A. Libler, "Deliberate Wartime Environmental Damage: New Challenges for International Law," 23 *Calif. West. Int'l L.J.* 67 (1992).

G. Reijnen & W. de Graaf, *Pollution of Outer Space, in Particular the Geostationary Orbit: Scientific, Policy and Legal Aspects* (Dordrecht, Neth.: Martinus Nijhoff, 1989).

C. Stone, "Beyond Rio: 'Insuring' Against Global Warming," 86 *Amer. J. Int'l L.* 445 (1992).

Regional

H. Munoz, *Environmental Diplomacy in the Americas* (Boulder, CO: Lynne Reinner, 1992).

J. Salter, *European Environmental Law* (Dordrecht, Neth.: Graham & Trotman/Martinus Nijhoff, 1994).

G. Goldenman, *Environmental Liability and Privatization in Central and Eastern Europe* (Dordrecht, Neth.: Graham & Trotman/ Martinus Nijhoff, 1994).

"Note: The Long Arm of the Law? Extraterritorial Application of US Environmental Legislation to Human Activity in Outer Space," 6 *Georgetown Int'l Environmental L. Rev.* 455 (1994).

◆ ENDNOTES

1. *See* A. Hurrell & B. Kingsbury, "The International Politics of the Environment: An Introduction," ch.1 in *The International Politics of the Environment: Actors, Interests, and Institutions* (Oxford, Eng.: Oxford Univ. Press, 1992); and A. Boyle, "Economic Growth and Protection of the Environment: The Impact of International Law and Policy," ch. 8 in A. Boyle (ed.), *Environmental Regulation and Economic Growth* (Oxford, Eng.: Clarendon Press, 1994).
2. *See* "Developments in the Law—International Environmental Law," 104 *Harv. Law Rev.* 1487 (1991).
3. **Coursebooks:** D. Hunter et al., *International Environmental Law and Policy* 1–38 (New York: Foundation Press, 1998); L. Guruswamy et al., *International Environmental Law: A Problem-Oriented Coursebook* 323–359 (St. Paul, MN: West, 1994). **Treatises:** P. Birnie & A. Boyle, *International Law and the Environment* (rev. ed. Oxford, Eng.: Clarendon Press, 1994); A. D'Amato & K. Engel, *International Environmental Law Anthology* (Cincinnati, OH: Anderson, 1996); R. Lefeber, *Transboundary Environmental Interference and the Origin of State Liability* (The Hague, Neth.: Kluwer Law Int'l, 1996); V. Nanda, *International Environmental Law & Policy* (Irvington-on-Hudson, NY: Transnational, 1995). **Summary:** L. Guruswamy & B. Hendricks, *International Environmental Law in a Nutshell* (St. Paul, MN: West, 1997).

4. *See, generally,* Helsinki Symposium, *Nuclear Accidents: Liabilities and Guarantees* (Paris: Org. Econ. Coop. & Development, 1993).
5. J. Cassels, *The Uncertain Promise of Law: Lessons from Bhopal* (Toronto: Univ. Toronto Press, 1993).
6. **Population:** J. Cohen, *How Many People Can the Earth Support?* (New York: W.W. Norton, 1995). **Food:** L. Brown, *Worldwatch Paper 136—The Agricultural Link: How Environmental Deterioration Could Disrupt Economic Progress* (Danvers, MA: Worldwatch Inst., 1997).
7. **Conference:** *See, generally,* N. Taub, *International Conference on Population and Development* (Wash., DC: Amer. Soc. Int'l L., 1994). **Statistics:** "World Population Statistics 1985–2025" (appendix) in E. Osmanczyk, *The Encyclopedia of the United Nations and International Relations* 1085 (New York: Taylor & Francis, 1990).
8. *See Report on the UN Conference on the Human Environment,* UN Doc. A/CONF.48/14/Rev.1, reprinted in 11 *Int'l Legal Mat'ls* 1416 (1972).
9. Section I, 2(d), Resolution on the Institutional and Financial Arrangement for International Environment Cooperation, Gen. Ass. Reso. 2997, UN Doc. A/8370 (1973), reprinted in 13 *Int'l Legal Mat'ls* 234 (1974).
10. A comprehensive collection is available in L. Guruswamy et. al., *Supplement of Basic Documents to International Environmental Law and World Order* (St. Paul, MN: West, 1994).
11. UN Doc. WCED/86/23/Add. 1 (1986).
12. **Text:** www.coe.fr/eng/legaltxt/172e.htm.
13. A. Kiss, "Present Limits to the Enforcement of State Responsibility for Environmental Damage," ch. 1 in F. Francioni & T. Scovazzi, *International Responsibility for Environmental Harm* 3, 4–5 (Dordrecht, Neth.: Graham & Trotman/Martinus Nijhoff, 1991) (italics added).
14. UN Gen. Ass. Reso. 44/228 (1992) (italics added).
15. Rio Conference reprinted in 31 *Int'l Legal Mat'ls* 874 (1992).
16. S. Johnson, *Did We Really Save the Earth at Rio?* in *Introduction to The Earth Summit: The United Nations Conference on Environment and Development (UNCED)* 6 (Dordrecht, Neth.: Graham & Trotman/Martinus Nijhoff, 1993) (hereinafter *Earth Summit).*
17. Well Blowout Control Claim, UN Doc. S/Dec.40, 36 *Int'l Legal Mat'ls* 1343 (1997). A succinct analysis is available in R. Alford, "International Decisions," 92 *Amer. J. Int'l L.* 287 (1998).
18. Reprinted in 31 *Int'l Legal Mat'ls* 818 (1992).
19. **Treaty:** Framework Convention on Climate Change, reprinted in 31 *Int'l Legal Mat'ls* 849 (1992). **Background:** K. Vandevelde, "International Regulation of Fluorocarbons," 2 *Harv. Environmental L. Rev.* 474 (1977).
20. *See, generally,* B. Brown, *The United States and the Politicalization of the World Bank: Issues of International Law and Policy* (London: Kegan Paul Int'l, 1992).
21. For the principles and an analysis of their application, *see* "Authoritative Statement of Forest Principles," ch. 7 in *Earth Summit* 103–116 (cited in note 16).
22. *"Trail Smelter Arbitration (US v. Canada),"* 3 *UN Rep. Int'l Arb.* 1938 (1949).
23. *See, e.g.,* "Territorial Jurisdiction of the International Commission of the River Oder," 1929 *PCIJ,* ser. A, No. 23 (Versailles Treaty Commission jurisdiction over river running through former nations at war); and *"Diversion of Water from the Meuse Case (Netherlands v. Belgium),"* 1937 *PCIJ,* ser. A/B, No. 70 (Belgium's control of canal based on treaty).
24. **Mines case:** *"Corfu Channel Case (Great Britain v. Albania),"* 1949 *ICC Rep.* 4. **Nuclear case:** *"Nuclear Tests Cases (New Zealand v. France),"* 1974 *ICJ Rep.* 253.
25. Separate Opinion of Vice-President A. Weeramantry, "The Concept of Sustainable Development," in *Case Concerning the Gabcíkovo-Nagymaros Project (Hungary v. Slovakia),* available at www.law.cornell.edu/icj/icj6/ihsjudweeraman.htm.
26. The advisory, contentious, and chambers jurisdiction of the Court is discussed in §9.4 of this text.
27. **ICJ case:** *"Certain Phosphate Lands in Nauru (Nauru v. Australia),"* 1989 *ICJ Rep.* 12. **Settlement:** 1993 *ICJ Rep.* 322.
28. C. Weeramantry, "Social Impact of Phosphate Mining," ch. 3 in *Nauru: Environmental Damage under International Trusteeship* 28, 30–31 (Oxford, Eng.: Oxford Univ. Press, 1992).
29. International Court of Justice Communique No. 93/20 of 19 July 1993 (italics added).
30. *See, e.g.,* M. Harrington, "Necessary and Proper, but Still Unconstitutional: The Oil Pollution Act's Delegation of Admiralty Power to the States," 48 *Case W. Res. L. Rev.* 1 (1997).
31. **1982 Law of the Sea Convention:** Art. 235(3) (*see* §6.4 of this text for further citation). **1969 Civil Liability Convention:** 9 *Int'l Legal Mat'ls* 45 (1970). **1971 Compensation Fund Convention:** *1971 UN Jur. Yearbook* 103. 1972 **Marine Pollution Convention:** 11 *Int'l Legal Mat'ls* 129 (1972).
32. The UN Secretary-General's arbitral decision is available in 26 *Int'l Legal Mat'ls* 1346 (1987).

CHAPTER THIRTEEN

International Economic Relations

CHAPTER OUTLINE

ON HUMAN RIGHTS, OVERALL PROGRESS HAS BEEN hard to quantify. On the one hand, China's exposure to the outside world has brought increased openness, social mobility, choice of employment and access to information. On the other hand, as we have documented in our annual human rights report, China's official practices still fall far short of internationally accepted standards.

It is our hope that the trend towards greater economic and social integration of China will have a liberalizing effect on political and human rights practices. Given the nature of the Chinese government, that progress will be gradual, at best, and is by no means inevitable. . . .

It is important to remember, first of all, that MFN [Most Favored Nation trading status] is a powerful symbol of America's global commitment to open markets. . . .

Moreover, the revocation of normal trade relations would eliminate prospects for U.S.-China cooperation on a wide range of issues. . . .

Revoking MFN would not only damage our growing commercial relationship; it would also deny us the benefits of our entire strategic dialogue. And because China's politics are in flux, especially during the run-up to this fall's Party Congress, the withdrawal of MFN would almost surely strengthen the hand of those who have been seeking to fill the country's ideological void with a belligerent nationalism. It would postpone rather than hasten improved Chinese behavior in the areas where we have the greatest concern.

—US Secretary of State Madeleine K. Albright, Statement before the Senate Finance Committee, China MFN, Washington, D.C., June 10, 1997; http://secretary.state.gov/www/statements/970610.html.

INTRODUCTION

This final chapter deals with several components of a subject historically regarded as a distinct discipline: the *economic* relations of States. A primary objective is to identify the pervasive impact of international commercial policies on International Law.

The initial section of this chapter identifies some of the very practical problems that corporate management must contemplate when the enterprise is engaged in an international commercial venture. It also presents the tip of the economic iceberg that has sustained the historical and contemporary evolution of International Law. Some familiar themes will be revisited, but this time to further explore the economic underpinnings retained for this final chapter.

The materials focus on the tidal wave of contemporary international economic integration: the organizations, their objectives, major economic treaties, and the various forms for consolidating economic programs. Economic integration has been a positive development in international relations because of its potential for achieving lasting peace (as suggested by the MFN excerpt at the opening of this chapter). One section focuses on *global* economic business practices in the form of the World Trade Organization (WTO), while the next one addresses regional associations of States.

The waning New International Economic Order (NIEO) is included. This UN-driven process pits the majority of the nations against the more developed and economically more powerful nations in a contest that has not been particularly productive. Its purpose remains one of improving the economic position of *under*-developed States vis-à-vis the developed States.

The final section of this chapter highlights the problems and adverse impact of international bribery. Treaties began to surface in the late 1990s to augment the several national laws on this subject. A multilateral approach will hopefully overcome the imposition of cultural relativism into the smooth functioning of accepted business practices in many parts of the world.

◆ 13.1 ECONOMICS AND INTERNATIONAL LAW

HISTORICAL EVOLUTION

Trade was a pivotal theme for ancient and medieval nations. Some great powers like Persia and Rome could afford to be relatively indifferent to foreign trade. They maintained well-developed agricultural bases. For other nations, however, trade was a key method for raising revenue and exercising a degree of political power. From ancient Athens through the medieval city-States, the role of trade was to create wealth that, in turn, facilitated other advances. Trade provided access to broader social and cultural perspectives as merchants traveled in search of marketing opportunities. Civilization developed in part from the concentration of people on or near major trade routes and ports. Trade ultimately led to diplomatic and other exchanges among these congregations of people.

Early medieval agreements focused on economic matters. The treaty of A.D. 860 between Byzantium—the major trading empire of that era—and Russia formalized their diplomatic and commercial relations. Under Article 4 of that agreement, Russia removed its previous ban on Byzantine exports. Trade was the ideal vehicle for developing international relations and thus usher in an era of relative peace. That concession also launched Russia's development of international trade relations with other nations.[1]

Links between commerce and law were forged by exploration. Many territories of the world were "discovered" by explorers seeking new trading opportunities. The ancient Phoenicians traveled the Mediterranean Sea and the north Atlantic Ocean in search of new trading partners. Portuguese and Spanish explorers discovered the New World during their trade-development programs of the fifteenth and sixteenth centuries.

Modern international commercial law is rooted in the trade practices that developed during the resulting interaction of national legal systems. Many standard contractual expectations were expressed in the medieval "Lex Mercatoria" (Law Merchant). This body of law was created and applied by specialized commercial tribunals, typically located in major port cities. Private merchants could conveniently resolve their local and international business disputes by submitting their disagreements for resolution to a neutral third party. The Lex Mercatoria flourished in the twelfth-century Italian city-States and later spread to other commercial centers. The customary practices of these tribunals were ultimately incorporated into the commercial laws of many nations.[2]

An early twentieth-century English case suggests how judges continued to apply the Lex Mercatoria when resolving maritime disputes. A shipment of goods was en route from San Francisco to London. The contract did not include a clause about *when* payment was due—thus failing to express the buyer's and seller's intents. While the goods were en route, the seller's agent presented the bill of lading (document of title) to the buyer. The buyer refused payment. He wanted to inspect the goods on arrival in London. The seller sued the buyer for breach of contract before the goods arrived. Under the medieval maritime practice, a buyer was required to pay for goods when the seller's agent provided a bill of lading for cargoes still en route by sea—unless the parties expressly contracted for payment at *another* time. The London court effectively incorporated this vintage commercial practice into the contract that supplied the missing term.[3] Arbitrators and judges thus merged certain commercial practices into the decisional law of maritime nations. Those practices then became customary rules of international commercial practice. Some practices were then codified into national legislation and treaties.

The global business climate changed dramatically after World War II. The post-war Marshall Plan announced by the US in 1947 was the largest and most successful foreign assistance program ever devised. The US was unable to agree with the Soviet Union about the scope of German reparations for the latter's role in causing Europe's economic devastation. The Marshall Plan was the US substitute for the dismal failure of the post–World War I Versailles Treaty process—which had isolated Germany, rendering its economy stagnant. That earlier isolation contributed significantly to the conditions that enabled Hitler to lead Germany's resurgence as a military power in the 1930s.

After World War II, the US wanted Germany and Japan to rise from the ashes of defeat to become prosperous allies. Helping to rebuild their economies was an important factor in maintaining an enduring peace, which would later develop markets for US goods and its lifestyle. A prosperous *West* Germany would ultimately "showcase" the advantages of market capitalism during the Cold War. Improved economic conditions in Germany and Japan created new long-term markets for US exports. A similar concern drives the West's promotion of democracy through economic strategies in the former republics of the Soviet Union. Aid has thus been linked to reform, arms control, nonproliferation of nuclear weapons, and the development of new consumer markets.

What occurred in the US is a good example of the development of economic ties that can lead to lasting peace. US economic interaction with Germany and Japan strengthened the political and economic ties between these nations. The stage was set for a comparative frenzy of international business transactions, unlike the isolationist tendencies of earlier eras. The US government's post-war objectives impacted corporate life in the US, as well as other countries. Corporate managers had previously concerned themselves only with local or nationwide business ventures. The country's vast internal markets did not encourage medium and small entrepreneurs to engage in *foreign* commerce. By the 1970s, however, foreign competitors began to enter into US markets in unprecedented numbers. The rebuilding programs of an earlier generation had virtually created economic Frankensteins. As the US demand for foreign products increased, a trade imbalance developed. US export growth lagged behind that of imports. Jobs in the affected US industries were at risk for enterprises unwilling to accommodate the surge of foreign competition.

A price would have to be paid for the unexpected degree of success of the US plans to develop foreign consumer markets. In order to compete, many US companies had to develop an expertise in problems that they had not previously encountered in local or nationwide business contexts. Even those companies that did not engage in *international* business had to respond in their own markets to foreign competitors. There was a growing consumer demand for foreign-made goods, a major contributor to the commonly articulated problem of "the foreign trade deficit."

On the other hand, multinational enterprises in regions such as Europe had never been as isolated from international commercial transactions. There, natural proximity to foreign borders—coupled with some limitations in the local availability of natural resources—presented a business environment more intuitively driven toward foreign markets. The same aggregate space between the US borders—the Atlantic and Pacific Oceans—could be geographically occupied by virtually all of Europe with its ubiquitous international frontiers. One reason for the success of the European Union's economic integration is that many national economies contained a significant degree of international business activity.

In the US, however, contemporary managers contemplating international business opportunities had to become familiar with the intricacies of importing, exporting, and producing in or for foreign markets. Assume, for example, that the CEO of Widget Inc. (a large US manufacturer) is contemplating export sales of its generic product known as "widgets." Widget's product has been quite successful in the US. But there is no guarantee that foreign markets will similarly respond to the same product. A representative agenda for Widget Inc.'s contemplation would include the following:

- Should our company export widgets to another country or region of the world? By what percentage should we increase our current production in order to do this? Alternatively, should we merely *advertise* our product to foreign market wholesalers?
- Should we instead commit our capital to a joint venture with a foreign producer? We might combine our expertise in widget making with the reduced cost–benefit of producing widgets in the foreign market? *Which* foreign market?
- Would any export restrictions apply to our widgets, particularly if they contain high-technology components that could be copied or used for purposes contrary to US military interests? The technical components of our product may be subject to federal agency review. That decision may adversely impact our export plans after an inordinate amount of company resources have been committed to developing a foreign marketing plan.
- Will a foreign environmental regulation bar our product from the preferred market? If our widgets are defective or inoperable due to conflicting technologies, will our company be able make the necessary modifications to sell our product overseas?
- Would the laws of the country where we want to market our product preclude us from forming the type of enterprise that we prefer? Put up barriers to profitability? Require us to share our technology as a condition of marketing our product?
- What would be the tax consequences of our business transactions under US law? Under foreign tax law? Is there a tax treaty between the US and that country to insulate us from double taxation?
- What are the foreign investment risks if we establish a widget enterprise in another country? Will too much success lead to our corporate assets being nationalized?
- Will we be able to get insurance for our operations in a foreign country? Can we insure against losses such as nationalization? Or losses in the form of limitations or prohibitions on the repatriation of profits back to the US? Losses such as from the imposition of currency-exchange limitations that would preclude the free transfer of capital out of the country?
- Will the US intervene in the event of a dispute between Widget Inc. and the host country? Or, in the event of some other action that effectively wrestles control of our enterprise from Widget Inc.'s management?
- Does that country have national laws that preclude us from seeking US help as a condition of doing business? If so, might we lose the diplomatic protection normally afforded to aliens subject to governmental expropriation?

Coursebooks on Public International Law have traditionally avoided any detailed discussion of commercial transactions, given the complexity of the underlying business judgments that must be made on both day-to-day and cyclical bases. The rationale was that a course on Public International Law should deal with *State* behavior, and the work of international organizations of States with political and military objectives. Private International Law, by contrast, could be readily distinguished. That body of law deals primarily with the impact of differing national legal systems on individuals—like merchants engaged in cross-border commercial transactions (§1.5).

In the late 1970s and 1980s, however, the academic environment began to change. A law school casebook on International Economic Relations materialized in 1977. The first law school casebook on International Business Transactions appeared in 1986. Business and undergraduate schools in the United States were slow to respond to the internationalization of commercial life in the closing decades of the twentieth century. A number of teachers remained understandably reluctant to "cram" Private International Law themes into a course in Public International Law.

Now, however, international business and economics courses have become separate academic offerings in many universities. Terms like *Euro, NAFTA,* and *World Trade Organization* have become relatively commonplace in standard curricula. Students in this course will have the benefit of integrating and understanding the crucial role of international economics in the evolution of Public International Law—in their *first* course in this discipline.

INTERNATIONAL LAW LINKS

This portion of §13.1 annotates the connections between international economic relations and Public International Law—the general body of norms covered in the first twelve chapters of this book.

Private International Law (Chapter 1) "Private" International Law was distinguished from "Public" International Law in the first chapter, where the materials focused on the norms applied by States in their international relations—as opposed to rules applicable to private individuals, who trade between distant nations with different legal systems. It is becoming increasingly difficult, however, to justify this distinction.[4] Several differences in national legal culture follow that will identify some reasons for the "private" law integration with the materials in this course on "Public" International Law.

Different legal systems with divergent requirements for enforcing a contract may yield contrary results for the same transaction. Whether the contract is enforceable has often depended on which nation's tribunals are chosen by one of the parties. Also, traders in different countries may operate in quite diverse negotiating postures. Socialist countries, for example, have historically conducted their trade via national trade agencies rather than through private enterprise. Nonsocialist nations depend on a market economy for the conduct of trade, which is done by private enterprises for profit rather than for the direct benefit of all people of the State. The government agencies in socialist States are characteristically bureaucratic and desperately in need of predictability. This is one reason why such intersystem dealing is a much more cumbersome process than when negotiating transactions between traders in private market economies.[5]

To illustrate how differences might affect a common commercial setting, assume that X Corporation agrees to sell a load of widgets to Y Corporation. X is a corporation that does business in its home country of State X. Y corporation does business in its home country of State Y. X Corporation then sends its first shipment of widgets to Y corporation. That shipment contains defects. Their written contract does not include a seller's promise that the goods will arrive without defects. Under the national law of State Y, an importer cannot ask a Y court to *imply* a contractual term not expressed by the parties to a contract. The courts of State Y do not want to thereby rewrite business contracts for the parties—to supply terms that *might* have been included but were not necessarily intended by the parties to the shipping agreement. Under the national law of the exporting State X, the lack of contractual warranties does not preclude Y Corporation from seeking a judicial remedy in State X. Y Corporation could sue for breach of the contract in State X, based on an *implied* warranty (not mentioned in the contract) that the goods will arrive without substantial defects. In the absence of an international treaty that deals with this "private" international law problem, the result will depend on the country in which enforcement is sought.

Given this recurring type of problem generated by differences in national legal systems, the UN opened the 1980 Convention for the International Sale of Goods (CISG) for signature and ratification by interested nations.[6] Under Public International Law, two States that ratify the CISG treaty thereby chose a uniform rule that governs the contractual relationships of their

> 3.16 We cannot see how the drafters of the [Dutch] Import and Export Act, and the 1963 Export Decree, could have taken a different view on the matter: . . . good international relations are . . . the *raison d'être* of the international legal order. . . .
>
> 4.3 The applicant [Dutch exporter] contended that its interest in free international trade should in this case carry much weight, because if the delivery of submarines to Taiwan were canceled, the survival of 1000 or possibly all of the 2000 jobs in its enterprise would be greatly endangered. . . .
>
> 4.5 . . . [T]he respondent [Dutch Minister for Economic Affairs] further contended that granting the permission applied for [to export the submarines] would impair the interest of the international legal order in yet another respect: continued delivery of submarines implied support for Taiwan's rejection of proposals for peaceful reunification . . . and was therefore likely to thwart a settlement of the existing conflict between the PRC and Taiwan.
>
> —Netherlands Trade and Industry Appeals Tribunal (1984), *"Wilton Feyenoord BV v. Minister for Economic Affairs,"* 101 *Int'l Law Rep.* 419, 424–426

respective private traders. The CISG does not deprive the parties of some advantage that both might prefer under the law of one of the countries involved in their transaction. The CISG authorizes them to agree that the national law of either State X or State Y will apply to their contract. Freedom of contract is preserved. One of the best articulations for any nation to adopt the CISG was provided by US President Ronald Reagan in the following excerpt from his letter to the US Senate recommending that the US adopt this treaty:

> International trade law is subject to serious legal uncertainties. Questions often arise as to whether our law or foreign law governs the transaction, and our traders and their counsel find it difficult to evaluate and answer claims based on one or another of the many unfamiliar foreign legal systems [whose law might apply]. The Convention's uniform rules offer effective answers to these problems.
>
> Enhancing legal certainty for international sales contracts will serve the interests of all parties engaged in commerce by facilitating international trade.[7]

Until 1998, there was no authoritative judicial interpretation of the CISG. The following decision illustrates how the treaty is designed to facilitate international trade, especially when local commercial law would have resulted in dismissal of the case:

MCC-Marble Ceramic Center, Inc. v. Ceramica Nuova D'Agostino, S.P.A.

UNITED STATES COURT OF APPEALS, ELEVENTH CIRCUIT

144 F.3d 1384 (1998) (rehearing den'd)

Author's Note: *Plaintiff buyer MCC is a US corporation that sells tiles. Defendant seller D'Agostino is an Italian corporation that manufactures tiles. MCC's president, Juan Carlos Mozon, met representatives of D'Agostino at a trade fair in Bologna, Italy. He negotiated an agreement in 1990 to purchase ceramic tiles from D'Agostino based on samples he examined at the Bologna trade fair. Monzon, who spoke no Italian, communicated with Gianni Silingardi, then D'Agostino's commercial director, through a translator, Gianfranco Copelli, who was himself an agent of D'Agostino.*

The parties apparently arrived at an oral agreement on the crucial terms of price, quality, quantity, delivery, and payment. They then recorded these terms on one of D'Agostino's standard, pre-printed order forms. Monzon signed the contract on MCC's behalf. According to MCC, the parties also entered into a related but separate "requirements" contract in February 1991. D'Agostino thereby agreed to supply MCC with high-grade ceramic tile at specific discounts as long as MCC continued to purchase sufficient quantities of tile. MCC completed a number of additional order forms requesting tile deliveries pursuant to that agreement before their commercial dispute erupted. MCC brought suit against D'Agostino, claiming that the defendant manufacturer breached 1991 requirements discount contract by failing to fill orders that MCC placed in April, May, and August 1991.

Footnotes and citations to authority have been omitted. Bold type has been added to several phrases. The [FN] refers to the court's footnotes.

COURT'S OPINION. This case requires us to determine whether a court must consider parol [oral] evidence in a contract dispute governed by the United Nations Convention on Contracts for the International Sale of Goods ("CISG"). . . .

BACKGROUND . . .

In addition to other defenses, D'Agostino responded that it was under no obligation to fill MCC's orders because MCC had defaulted on payment for previous shipments. In support of its position, D'Agostino relied on the pre-printed terms of the contracts that MCC had executed. The executed forms were printed in Italian and contained terms and conditions on both the front and reverse. According to an English translation of the October 1990 contract, the front of the order form contained the following language directly beneath Monzon's signature:

> [T]he buyer hereby states that he is aware of the sales conditions stated on the reverse and that he

expressly approves of them with special reference to those numbered 1-2-3-4-5-6-7-8.

Clause 6(b), printed on the back of the form states:

[D]efault or delay in payment within the time agreed upon gives D'Agostino the right to . . . suspend or cancel the contract itself and to cancel possible other pending contracts and the buyer does not have the right to indemnification or damages. . . .

MCC . . . argued that the parties never intended the terms and conditions printed on the reverse of the order form to apply to their agreements. As evidence for this assertion, MCC submitted Monzon's affidavit, which claims that MCC had no subjective intent to be bound by those terms and that D'Agostino was aware of this intent. MCC also filed affidavits from Silingardi and Copelli, D'Agostino's representatives at the trade fair, which support Monzon's claim that the parties subjectively intended not to be bound by the terms on the reverse of the order form. The magistrate judge [in the Florida federal trial court] held that the affidavits, even if true, did not raise an issue [which a jury could resolve] . . . regarding the interpretation or applicability of the terms of the written contracts and the district court accepted his recommendation to award . . . judgment in D'Agostino's favor. MCC then filed this timely appeal.

DISCUSSION . . .

The parties to this case agree that the CISG governs their dispute because the United States, where MCC has its place of business, and Italy, where D'Agostino has its place of business, are both States Party to the Convention. Article 8 of the CISG governs the interpretation of international contracts for the sale of goods and forms the basis of MCC's appeal from the district court's grant of summary judgment in D'Agostino's favor. [FN7] MCC argues that the magistrate judge and the district court improperly ignored evidence that MCC submitted regarding the parties' subjective intent when they memorialized the terms of their agreement on D'Agostino's pre-printed form contract, and that the magistrate judge erred by applying the parol evidence rule in derogation of the CISG.

FN7. Article 8 provides:

(1) For the purposes of this Convention statements made by and other conduct of a party are to be interpreted according to his intent where the other party knew or could not have been unaware what that intent was [thus allowing oral evidence which might be contrary to the terms in a written contract]. . . .

I. Subjective Intent Under the CISG

Contrary to what is familiar practice in United States courts, the CISG appears to permit a substantial inquiry into the parties' subjective intent, even if the parties did not engage in any objectively ascertainable means of registering this intent. [FN8] **Article 8(1) of the CISG instructs courts to interpret the "statements . . . and other conduct of a party . . . according to his intent" as long as the other party "knew or could not have been unaware" of that intent.** The plain language of the Convention, therefore, requires an inquiry into a party's subjective intent as long as the other party to the contract was aware [or should have been aware] of that intent.

FN8. **In the United States,** the legislatures, courts, and the legal academy have voiced a preference for relying on objective manifestations of the parties' intentions. For example, Article Two of the Uniform Commercial Code, which most states have enacted in some form or another to govern contracts for the sale of goods, is replete with references to standards of commercial reasonableness. See e.g., U.C.C. §2-206 (referring to reasonable means of accepting an offer); . . . Justice Holmes expressed the philosophy behind this focus on the objective in forceful terms: **"The law has nothing to do with the actual state of the parties' minds. In contract, as elsewhere, it must go by externals, and [the law will] judge parties by their conduct."** Oliver W. Holmes, "The Common Law" 242 (Howe ed.1963) quoted in John O. Honnold, *Uniform Law for International Sales Under the 1980 United Nations Convention* §107 at 164 (2d ed.1991) (hereinafter Honnold, Uniform Law).

In this case, MCC has submitted three affidavits that discuss the purported subjective intent of the parties to the initial agreement concluded between MCC and D'Agostino in October 1990. All three affidavits discuss the preliminary negotiations and report that the parties arrived at an oral agreement for D'Agostino to supply quantities of a specific grade of ceramic tile to MCC at an agreed upon price. The affidavits state that the "oral agreement established the essential terms of quality, quantity, description of goods, delivery, price and payment." The affidavits also note that the parties memorialized the terms of their oral agreement on a standard D'Agostino order form, but all three affiants contend that the parties subjectively intended not to be bound by the terms on the reverse of that form despite a provision directly below the signature line that expressly and specifically incorporated those terms.

The terms on the reverse of the contract give D'Agostino the right to suspend or cancel all contracts in the event of a buyer's non-payment and require a buyer to make a written report of all defects within ten days. As the magistrate judge's report and recommendation makes clear, if these terms applied to the agreements between MCC and D'Agostino, summary judgment [on the law, which precludes the plaintiff's case from going to trial for the resolution of factual issues] would be appropriate because MCC failed to make any written complaints about the quality of tile it received and D'Agostino has established MCC's non-payment of a number of invoices amounting to $108,389.40 and 102,053,846.00 Italian lira.

Article 8(1) of the CISG requires a court to consider this evidence of the parties' subjective intent. Contrary to the magistrate judge's report, which the district court endorsed and adopted, article 8(1) does not focus on interpreting the parties' statements alone. Although we agree with the magistrate judge's conclusion that no "interpretation" of the contract's terms could support MCC's position, article 8(1) also requires a court to consider subjective intent while interpreting the conduct of the parties. The CISG's language, therefore, requires courts to consider evidence of a party's subjective intent when signing a contract if the other party to the contract was aware of that intent at the time. This is precisely the type of evidence that MCC has provided through the Silingardi, Copelli, and Monzon affidavits, which discuss not only Monzon's intent as MCC's representative but also discuss the intent of D'Agostino's representatives and their knowledge that Monzon did not intend to agree to the terms on the reverse of the form contract. [The defendant described them as disgruntled employees.] This acknowledgment that D'Agostino's representatives were aware of Monzon's subjective intent puts this case squarely within article 8(1) of the CISG, and therefore requires the court to consider MCC's evidence as it interprets the parties' conduct.

II. Parol Evidence and the CISG

Given our determination that the magistrate judge and the district court should have considered MCC's affidavits regarding the parties' subjective intentions, we must address a question of first impression in this circuit: [W]hether the parol evidence rule, which bars evidence of an earlier oral contract that contradicts or varies the terms of a subsequent or contemporaneous written contract, [FN12] plays any role in cases involving the CISG. . . .

FN12. The Uniform Commercial Code includes a version of the parol evidence rule applicable to contracts for the sale of goods in most states. . . . U.C.C. §2-202.

The CISG itself contains no express statement on the role of parol evidence. It is clear, however, that the drafters of the CISG were comfortable with the concept of permitting parties to rely on oral contracts because they eschewed any statutes of fraud provision and expressly provided for the enforcement of oral contracts. Compare CISG, art. 11 (a contract of sale need not be concluded or evidenced in writing) with U.C.C. §2-201 (precluding the enforcement of oral contracts for the sale of goods involving more than $500). Moreover, article 8(3) of the CISG expressly directs courts to give "due consideration . . . to all relevant circumstances of the case including the negotiations . . ." to determine the intent of the parties. Given article 8(1)'s directive to use the intent of the parties to interpret their statements and conduct, article 8(3) is a clear instruction to admit and consider parol evidence regarding the negotiations to the extent they reveal the parties' subjective intent.

Despite the CISG's broad scope, surprisingly few cases have applied the Convention in the United States, see *Delchi Carrier SpA v. Rotorex Corp.*, 71 F.3d

1024, 1027-28 (2d Cir.1995) (observing that "there is virtually no case law under the Convention"), and only two reported decisions touch upon the parol evidence rule, both in dicta. . . .

Our reading of article 8(3) as a rejection of the parol evidence rule [which prohibits proof of an oral agreement which varies a term in the parties' written contract] . . . is in accordance with the great weight of academic commentary on the issue. As one scholar has explained:

> [T]he language of Article 8(3) that "due consideration is to be given to all relevant circumstances of the case" seems adequate to override any domestic rule that would bar a tribunal from considering the relevance of other agreements. . . . Article 8(3) relieves tribunals from domestic rules that might bar them from "considering" any evidence between the parties that is relevant. This added flexibility for interpretation is consistent with a growing body of opinion that the "parol evidence rule" has been an embarrassment for the administration of modern transactions.

Honnold, Uniform Law §110 at 170-71. . . . [A]lthough jurisdictions in the United States have found the parol evidence rule helpful to promote good faith and uniformity in contract, as well as an appropriate answer to the question of how much consideration to give parol evidence, a wide number of other [foreign] States Party to the CISG have rejected the rule in their domestic jurisdictions. One of the primary factors motivating the negotiation and adoption of the CISG was to provide parties to international contracts for the sale of goods with some degree of certainty as to the principles of law that would govern potential disputes and remove the previous doubt regarding which party's legal system might otherwise apply. See *Letter of Transmittal from Ronald Reagan, President of the United States,* to the United States Senate, reprinted at 15 USC app. 70, 71 (1997) [quoted just prior to this case]. Courts applying the CISG cannot, therefore, [unwittingly] upset the parties' reliance on the Convention by substituting familiar principles of domestic law when the Convention requires a different result. We may only achieve the directives of good faith and uniformity in contracts under the CISG by interpreting and applying the plain language of article 8(3) as written and obeying its directive to consider this type of parol evidence.

This is not to say that parties to an international contract for the sale of goods cannot depend on written contracts or that parol evidence regarding subjective contractual intent need always prevent a party relying on a written agreement from securing summary judgment. To the contrary, most cases will not present a situation (as exists in this case) in which both parties to the contract acknowledge a subjective intent not to be bound by the terms of a pre-printed writing. In most cases, therefore, article 8(2) of the CISG will apply, and objective evidence will provide the basis for the court's decision. Consequently, a party to a contract governed by the CISG will not be able to avoid the terms of a contract . . . simply by submitting an affidavit which states that he or she did not have the subjective intent to be bound by the contract's terms. . . . Moreover, to the extent parties wish to avoid parol evidence problems they can do so by including a merger clause in their agreement that extinguishes any and all prior agreements and understandings not expressed in the writing.

Considering MCC's affidavits in this case, however, we conclude that the magistrate judge and the district court improperly granted summary judgment in favor of D'Agostino. Although the affidavits are, as D'Agostino observes, relatively conclusory and unsupported by facts that would objectively establish MCC's intent not to be bound by the conditions on the reverse of the form, article 8(1) requires a court to consider evidence of a party's subjective intent when the other party was aware of it, and the Silingardi and Copelli affidavits provide that evidence. This is not to say that the affidavits are conclusive proof of what the parties intended. A reasonable finder of fact, for example [at trial], could disregard testimony that purportedly sophisticated international merchants signed a contract without intending to be bound as simply too incredible to believe and hold MCC to the conditions printed on the reverse of the contract. [FN20] Nevertheless, the affidavits raise an issue of material fact regarding the parties' [arguable] intent to incorporate the provisions on the reverse of the form contract. . . .

FN20. D'Agostino attempts to explain and undermine the affidavit of its representatives during the transaction, by calling Silingardi a "disgruntled" former employee. Appellee's Br. at 11, 39. Silingardi's alleged feelings towards his former employer may indeed be relevant to undermine the credibility of his assertions, but that is a matter for the finder of fact, not for this court on summary judgment. . . .

CONCLUSION

MCC asks us to reverse the district court's grant of summary judgment in favor of D'Agostino [so that this case can go to trial]. The district court's decision rests on pre-printed contractual terms and conditions incorporated on the reverse of a standard order form that MCC's president signed on the company's behalf. Nevertheless, we conclude that the CISG, which governs international contracts for the sale of goods, precludes summary judgment in this case because MCC has raised an issue of material fact concerning the parties' subjective intent to be bound by the terms on the reverse of the pre-printed contract. **The CISG also precludes the application of the parol evidence rule, which would otherwise bar the consideration of evidence concerning a prior or contemporaneously negotiated oral agreement.** Accordingly, we REVERSE the district court's grant of summary judgment and REMAND this case for further proceedings consistent with this opinion.

◆ *Notes & Questions*

1. How would the result in *MCC* be different under US law—and why?
2. The *MCC* opinion says that "Courts applying the CISG cannot, therefore, upset the parties' reliance on the Convention by substituting familiar principles of domestic law when the Convention requires a different result." Is it likely that the parties even knew about the CISG when the plaintiff's representative signed the defendant's contract in Italy? Does this apparent presumption on the part of the court actually matter?
3. The plaintiff's representative traveled from Florida to the trade fair in Bologna but could not speak Italian. He negotiated a contract written in Italian. Plaintiff MCC basically appealed to secure the right to get this case to trial to introduce oral evidence, varying the terms of the written contract. Those terms, on the back of the written form contract, were expressly incorporated into the contract—immediately under the plaintiff representative's signature. The three affidavits were, as argued by the defendant, "relatively conclusory and unsupported by facts that would objectively establish MCC's intent not to be bound by the conditions on the reverse of the form." Without affidavits from the two representatives of the defendant and thus only an affidavit from the plaintiff's representative, would the appellate court have allowed this case to go to trial?

The Letter of Credit (LOC) is probably the most useful mechanism for enabling an international commercial transaction between merchants in distant countries, especially, when they have little or no prior business dealings. The LOC has a long history. It (or its functional equivalent) was used by bankers in ancient Egypt and Greece, Imperial Rome, and Renaissance Europe.[8]

The International Chamber of Commerce (ICC), located in Paris, now composes standardized commercial documents, contract terms, and rules of interpretation. One of the ICC's most prominent contributions is the Uniform Customs and Practices for Documentary Credits (UCP). The UCP contains a series of articles that standardize the use of the LOC in international banking. A letter of credit is not required merely because the contract is international in scope. Some governments require it for *all* transactions involving foreign trade.

The buyer (importer) makes credit arrangements with the buyer's local bank. The buyer obtains a letter of credit from the bank. The LOC guarantees that the seller (exporter) will be paid for the goods. The buyer's bank promises to pay. This promise is essentially substituted for that of the buyer. The buyer's bank is the "issuing bank," charging a fee to the buyer for issuing its LOC. The LOC is typically sent to the "confirming bank" in the seller's country. Assuming that everything is in order with the issuing bank's LOC, the confirming bank then advises the seller that payment has been guaranteed. There may be some condition that must be satisfied before the confirming bank forwards the payment, such as the buyer's right to inspect the goods. The seller is then willing to ship or release its goods to the buyer, because payment has been guaranteed by a local bank with which the seller is familiar.

An actual application and a letter of credit are reproduced in Exhibits 13.1 and 13.2 (pages 570 and 571). Exhibit 13.1 is the buyer's application for a LOC. Exhibit 13.2 is the issuing bank's LOC, which is forwarded to the confirming bank.

The LOC has an important but little known connection with Public International Law. It has been used to settle conflicts between States at war and to mitigate problems spawned by poor international relations. One classic example occurred during the 1961 Bay of Pigs invasion of Cuba by Cuban rebels who had previously migrated to the US. They were supported in this clandestine mission by US President Kennedy as part of a strategy to overthrow Fidel Castro. Shortly after landing, their presence was detected and they were captured. A US naval destroyer was shelled as it monitored these events. One reason this mission failed was that President Kennedy was reluctant to provide air support once the plot was discovered.

A New York law firm attempted to negotiate the release of the invading Cuban immigrants who had been sent to Cuba by the Central Intelligence Agency. The ensuing 1962 Cuban Missile Crisis did not derail the negotiations for their release. A secret bargain was struck. Cuba was to receive $53 million worth of food and medical supplies in return for their release. But Cuba had no way of knowing whether the US would renege on its part of the bargain once Cuba released these prisoners. Even if the US did comply, there was no guarantee about the quality of supplies that the US might ultimately ship to Cuba. It would be quite difficult to provide assurances via diplomatic representations—which the Cuban government was understandably unlikely to trust. The absence of formal diplomatic ties between Cuba and the US was but one of the problems with making this exchange.

The US negotiator successfully requested the Red Cross to apply for a LOC from a Canadian bank executed in favor of Cuba. Once the bank issued an irrevocable LOC, Cuba would collect $53 million from the Canadian bank should the US fail to provide the supplies or if they were inferior. Cuba could be assured that the bank would make the payment. To subsequently dishonor its LOC, even if prodded to do so by the US government, would ruin that bank's credibility in all future banking matters. LOCs are governed by the marketplace. Diplomacy is governed by politics. Thus, the US government's use of a LOC resolved this most sensitive of matters at a time when tensions were already peaked by the Cuban Missile Crisis (*see* §10.2).[9]

International Legal Personality (Chapter 2) The preliminary chapters on the actors in International Law introduced the concept of international personality—a State or international organization's legal capacity to participate in matters on an international level.

After World War II, States engaged in international commercial transactions with individuals and corporations in other States—and with each other—on an unprecedented scale. Previously, when State A was called upon to appear as a *defendant* in State B litigation, B's courts would automatically dismiss suits by individuals or corporations against State A—even if State A chose to appear as a *plaintiff* in B's courts. The increasingly routine appearance of States in the international marketplace, where their profit motive resembled that of any other trader, accordingly created the pressure to alter State sovereign immunity practice (*see* §2.6). National and international tribunals began to reconsider the historical practice of absolute immunity, resulting in today's *restrictive* approach to sovereign immunity.

Even business transactions *within* a State became subject to external control by *other* international actors who possessed the necessary international legal personality. The post–World War II evolution of international organizations of States, such as the UN and the European Union, amassed powers that were previously exercisable on the international level only by States. Organizational legal personality blossomed as it began to cultivate organizational objectives not unlike those of State members. Certain organizations, notably the European Economic Community (now European Union), possessed the legal capacity to require a State—once the *only* actor in Public International Law—to act in ways that it would not otherwise embrace.

This postwar expansion of organizational legal capacity is typically couched in a commercial context. A classic example is the "German Beer" case of 1987. The Commission of the European Communities sued the Federal Republic of Germany, claiming that it had breached obligations arising under European Commu-

EXHIBIT 13.1 APPLICATION FOR LETTER OF CREDIT

TO: **FIRST INTERSTATE BANK OF CALIFORNIA** LETTER OF CREDIT APPLICATION AND SECURITY AGREEMENT
Formerly United California Bank

Please issue your irrevocable Letter of Credit as follows: ☐ Airmail ☒ Cable L/C No. SAMPLE

IN FAVOR OF (name and address) PHILIPPINE LAUAN, LTD., C.P.O. BOX 1776, MAKATI, RIZAL, PHILIPPINES	
FOR ACCOUNT OF (person or firm requesting this credit) RED LAUAN PLYWOOD CO., 108 W. 6th ST., LOS ANGELES, CA	TENOR OF DRAFTS SIGHT
	AMOUNT US$25,000.00

(check only one)

DRAWINGS FOR 100 % OF INVOICE VALUE ☒ NOT TO EXCEED ☐ APPROXIMATELY

DRAFTS TO BE ACCOMPANIED BY THE FOLLOWING DOCUMENTS: (Which the negotiating bank is authorized to forward to you in one mailing.)

☒ COMMERCIAL INVOICE(S) (indicate number of copies) triplicate ☐ SPECIAL CUSTOMS INVOICE(S)

☐ INSURANCE POLICY(IES) COVERING THE FOLLOWING RISKS (such as marine and war risk, etc.)

INSURANCE EFFECTED BY OURSELVES (name of ins. co. and policy no.) I/We agree to furnish you, upon request, such policy.

☒ OTHER DOCUMENTS PACKING LIST IN TRIPLICATE

☒ FULL SET OF CLEAN ON BOARD OCEAN BILLS OF LADING, TO ORDER OF SHIPPER, BLANK ENDORSED

NOTIFY: PERSON OR FIRM TO BE NOTIFIED BY CARRIER UPON ARRIVAL OF SHIPMENT RED LAUAN PLYWOOD CO., 108 W. 6th ST., LOS ANGELES, CA

☐ AIRWAY BILL/AIR CONSIGNMENT NOTE CONSIGNED TO

☐ RAILROAD/TRUCK BILL OF LADING CONSIGNED TO

EVIDENCING SHIPMENT OF:
COMMODITY (omit details of price, quality, etc.) RED LAUAN PLYWOOD AS PER ACCOUNTEE'S PURCHASE ORDER NUMBER 1776

FROM (country or port of shipment)	DESTINATION (port of arrival)	SHIPPING TERMS (check one)
PHILIPPINE PORT	LOS ANGELES HARBOR, CA	☐ FAS ☒ FOB ☐ C&F ☐ CIF

SHIPMENT TO BE MADE NO LATER THAN	DATE THIS CREDIT TO EXPIRE	TRANSHIPMENT	PARTIAL SHIPMENTS (check one)
June 15, 1989	June 30, 1989	☒ ALLOWED ☐ NOT ALLOWED	☒ ALLOWED ☐ NOT ALLOWED

SPECIAL INSTRUCTIONS

We, and each of us, agree that the terms and conditions set forth on this and the reverse page hereof are hereby made a part of this application and are hereby accepted and agreed to by us.

March 31, 1989 — DATE

RED LAUAN PLYWOOD CO. — APPLICANT'S NAME

AUTHORIZED SIGNATURE — TITLE

FOR BANK USE ONLY	CUSTOMER'S CURRENT LIABILITY	
	OFFICE NO	SIGNATURE OF LOAN OFFICER AUTHORIZING CREDIT

IB-117 8-82

Source: First Interstate Bank (San Diego, California)

EXHIBIT 13.2 LETTER OF CREDIT

First Interstate Bank Ltd.

First Interstate Bank, Ltd.
401 'B' Street, Suite 303
San Diego, CA 92101
619 699-3026

TO: PHILIPPINE NATIONAL BANK
MAKATI, RIZAL, PHILIPPINES

FROM: FIRST INTERSTATE BANK, LTD.
SAN DIEGO, CALIFORNIA

PLEASE ADVISE BENEFICIARY THAT WE HAVE ISSUED OUR IRREVOCABLE DOCUMENTARY CREDIT AS FOLLOWS:

OUR NUMBER: SAMPLE 89-01
PLACE AND DATE OF ISSUE: SAN DIEGO, 31MAR89
DATE AND PLACE OF EXPIRY: 30JUN89, AT NEGOTIATING BANK

BENEFICIARY: PHILIPPINE LAUAN, LTD.
C.P.O. BOX 1776
MAKATI, RIZAL, PHILIPPINES

APPLICANT: RED LAUAN PLYWOOD CO.
108 WEST SIXTH STREET
LOS ANGELES, CALIFORNIA

AMOUNT: USD25,000.00 TWENTY FIVE THOUSAND AND 00/100 USD

THIS LETTER OF CREDIT IS AVAILABLE WITH: NEGOTIATING BANK
BY: NEGOTIATION, AGAINST PRESENTATION OF THE DOCUMENTS DETAILED HEREIN AND OF YOUR SIGHT DRAFT(S) AT SIGHT DRAWN ON FIRST INTERSTATE BANK, SAN DIEGO, CALIFORNIA

PARTIAL SHIPMENTS PERMITTED TRANSHIPMENT PERMITTED

SHIPMENT/DISPATCH TAKEN IN CHARGE
FROM/AT: PHILIPPINE PORT
NOT LATER THAN: 15JUN89
FOR TRANSPORTATION TO: LOS ANGELES HARBOR, CALIFORNIA

SIGNED COMMERCIAL INVOICE IN TRIPLICATE
PACKING LIST IN TRIPLICATE
FULL SET OF CLEAN ON BOARD OCEAN BILL OF LADING, TO ORDER OF SHIPPER, BLANK ENDORSED, NOTIFY: RED LAUAN PLYWOOD CO., 108 WEST SIXTH STREET, LOS ANGELES, CALIFORNIA

EVIDENCING SHIPMENT OF: RED LAUAN PLYWOOD AS PER ACCOUNTEE'S PURCHASE ORDER NUMBER 1776; FOB VESSEL PHILIPPINE PORT TO LOS ANGELES HARBOR, CALIFORNIA, NOT LATER THAN 15JUN89

WE UNDERSTAND THAT THE INSURANCE WILL BE EFFECTED BY RED LAUAN PLYWOOD CO.

DRAFTS DRAWN HEREUNDER MUST BE PRESENTED TO THE NEGOTIATING BANK WITHIN FIFTEEN DAYS AFTER DATE OF SHIPMENT, BUT WITHIN THE VALIDITY OF THIS LETTER OF CREDIT.

WE HEREBY ISSUE THIS DOCUMENTARY CREDIT IN YOUR FAVOR. IT IS SUBJECT TO THE UNIFORM CUSTOMS AND PRACTICE FOR DOCUMENTARY CREDITS (1983 REVISION, INTERNATIONAL CHAMBER OF COMMERCE, PARIS, FRANCE PUBLICATION NO.400) AND ENGAGES US IN ACCORDANCE WITH THE TERMS THEREOF. THE NUMBER AND DATE OF THE CREDIT AND THE NAME OF OUR BANK MUST BE QUOTED ON ALL DRAFTS REQUIRED. IF THE CREDIT IS AVAILABLE BY NEGOTIATION EACH PRESENTATION MUST BE QUOTED ON THE REVERSE OF THIS ADVICE BY THE BANK WHERE THE CREDIT IS AVAILABLE.

Source: First Interstate Bank (San Diego, California)

nity Law. The relevant treaty ceded the capacity to the Council of Europe to enact directives that limited a member State's ability to use restrictive business practices against other members of the European Community. The relevant German law, dating from the year 1516, prohibited additives in the manufacturing of beer. Germany's national beer law barred the importation of beer from *any* country whose beer contained *substitutes* for malted barley—the basic and unadulterated substance for making German beer. Other Community member States wanted to export a different kind of beer to the German market, one containing a substitute for malted barley. Germany defended its restrictive beer law, on the basis that consumers would be misled—thinking that imported non-German beer was the same as that produced in Germany for four centuries. The Court of Justice of the European Community ruled that Germany's vintage restrictions did not survive the 1985 European Council Directives barring nontariff barriers to imports from other countries within the European Community. Germany's legislative protection unlawfully impeded the free importation of member-State products throughout the Community.[10]

Sovereignty (Chapters 2, 6) The legal personality of international organizations also affects commerce in far more sensitive ways. After the breakup of the former Yugoslavia, one of the new republics took the same name as the neighboring Greek province of Macedonia. Greece imposed a trade ban on the new State of Macedonia. As discussed in the materials on statehood and recognition, Greece's objection was not limited to the resulting confusion of coexisting Macedonias with a common border. Greece questioned whether this fragment of the former Soviet Union would ultimately seek to expand its territorial boundaries to include the adjacent Macedonian portion of Greece (*see* Problem 2.5).

In April 1994, the European Union threatened legal action against Greece. This trade dispute involved significant sovereignty concerns for Greece. The EU nevertheless advised Greece of its intent to sue in the European Court of Justice—a somewhat awkward decision, because the president of the EU was a Greek citizen. The EU's concern was that Greece's trade blockade also affected the ability of fellow EU members to access the nearby Greek port of Salonika. This is the customary Greek port for the journey of goods to and from the new Republic of Macedonia. Salonika is the exchange point for 80 percent of Macedonian trade and all of its oil imports. EU member States Great Britain and Germany pressured the EU to take this action for political reasons. The continued trade blockage of Macedonia might trigger a new round of Balkan destabilization.

Jurisdiction (Chapters 5, 6) The limitations on "extraterritorial" jurisdiction are not limited to States. An international organization must also be cautious about overreaching. Such problems often arise in a commercial context.

A classic example was presented when an international cartel, including US wood pulp producers, conspired to fix prices in member States of the European Community during the 1980s. The organization's executive and judicial bodies fined them pursuant to European Community Law, because their price-fixing conspiracy violated the organization's antitrust laws. These legal actions, although taken against business entities as far away as the US, did *not* constitute an improper "extraterritorial" regulation of commercial transactions. The conduct of the foreign enterprises was characterized as having the requisite effect within the territory of the European Community.[11]

There is a "price," however, for applying local laws to foreign enterprises. A number of countries have legislatively reacted to what they construe as extraterritorial assertions of another State's law against their citizens. The primary international concern is with US applications of its law to foreign corporate activity involving the US—for example, when domestic law subjects foreign companies to conflicting demands. Specifically, other countries have enacted "blocking statutes." These statutes are countermeasures whereby State X "blocks" the potential application of US law to the corporate activities of State X individuals or corporations subjected to US legal processes. Blocking statutes typically make it a crime for its citizens to reveal information, such as with the famous Swiss bank secrecy laws.[12]

The Chinese State Secrecy Law generally forbids the disclosure of financial data by Chinese corporations. This statute is designed to protect Chinese State agencies from disclosing information requested by authorities in other countries. But it creates a problem for the Chinese entity that is subject to conflicting demands. When Chinese companies do business in the US, for example, they have generally been required to disclose financial information when demanded by a US judge. These companies are held to the more liberal disclosure standard in the US. In 1992, a federal judge in San Francisco imposed a fine of $10,000 per day for each day that a Chinese corporation refused to comply with an American company's right to obtain business information.

In other business litigation, the US Supreme Court similarly held that a French company could not rely on French blocking legislation. French law prohibited the defendant French company from giving evidence in foreign litigation. This case alleged that a French corporation was liable for a faulty aircraft involved in an accident that arose in the US. The corporation had injected itself into business activities and could not avoid its litigation responsibilities arising in the country where it was operating.[13]

Diplomacy (Chapter 7) Diplomacy often materializes in an economic format. In 1991, the European Community withheld a $1 billion food and aid package that was destined for what was then the Soviet Union. The Community also delayed execution of a one-half billion dollar technical assistance agreement with Moscow and announced its intent to file a human rights complaint with the Conference on the Security and Cooperation. Soviet president Mikhail Gorbachev had just imposed a military "crackdown" on pro-independence groups in the Baltic republics of the former Soviet Union. The European Community action effectively protested the Soviet response to the political violence in Latvia. France and Germany simultaneously announced that they would seek to temper the Soviet hardline attitude toward the independence movement in the Baltic States of Lithuania, Latvia, and Estonia.

The US also pursued trade-related diplomacy at the time. President George Bush negotiated with Gorbachev on the basis that the US Congress could grant the (former) Soviets special trading status. The objective was to normalize international economic relations between the two superpowers. Bush's announced "global partnership" was designed to prevent the US and the crumbling Soviet Union from rekindling the tensions that symbolized the Cold War. This was employing economic incentives to reduce the risk of political and military hostilities while exploring the possibility of new Eastern European markets for US exports.

Treaty Norms (Chapter 8) The treaty chapter presented the nearly half-century-old Arab economic boycott of Israel as the centerpiece for the political objective of bankrupting the State of Israel. The Arab League sought to drive Israel out of existence—effectively, a reaction to the UN's 1947 partition of Palestine to create the State of Israel.

The materials in the remaining sections of this chapter explore global and regional economic treaties that evolved out of the desire to advance the commercial interests of the participants. The last section delves into the new bribery framework for a treaty-based response to the scourge of corruption—which disrupts natural market forces.

Adjudication (Chapter 9) The adjudication chapter dealt with the resolution of disputes by specialized tribunals created for the finite purpose of winding down hostile relations. Dispute resolution, of course, typically arises in a commercial context. A classic example is the Iran–US Claims Tribunal, which still functions in a building near the International Court of Justice in the Netherlands. This commercial adjudication scenario effectively concluded an episode that involved numerous principles of International Law.[14]

At the conclusion of the 1979–1980 Iranian Hostage Crisis, Iran released the US hostages to Algeria. The US released a portion of Iran's assets, which were frozen by US President Jimmy Carter at the outset of the crisis. Since then, the Iran–US Claims Tribunal has steadily worked to resolve the private claims of US businesses. This third-party dispute-resolution mechanism (*see* §9.1) peacefully resolved one of the most sensitive disputes ever to arise under Public International Law.

Economic Force (Chapter 10) In this chapter on commerce, one may productively reconsider the materials on force to cultivate the commercial roots in the genealogy of Public International Law. During the Cold War, the UN Security Council invoked its UN Charter powers to impose international economic sanctions with varying degrees of success: on South Africa, to eliminate the State policy of apartheid; on parts of the former Yugoslavia, to reduce the flow of arms entering the Bosnian conflict; and on Iraq, to keep it from perpetrating additional affronts to Kuwait's sovereignty during and after the 1991 Persian Gulf War.

Modern States are increasingly using economics as their weapon of choice, as opposed to using or threatening military force. After the end of the Cold War, for example, the US became *the* global superpower. It continued to rely on unilateral sanctions policy in certain cases, however, rather than defer to either the UN Security Council or World Trade Organization (WTO). Despite being the leading voice in favor of the WTO, the US has threatened or used various legislative and executive policies without the approval of these international organizations. Under the authority of Title 50 of US Code §1701, for example, the president implemented the Iran and Libya Sanctions Act of 1996. This statute authorizes targeting certain countries to "deal with any unusual and extraordinary threat, which has its source in whole or substantial part outside the United States, to the national security, foreign policy, or *economy* of the United States, if the President declares a national emergency with respect to such threat" (italics added).

Probably the most prominent example is the "Helms–Burton" legislation. Rather than use economic tools to embrace Cuba, the US arguably perpetuated a form of Cold War in this 1996 law. This was the next step in the forty-year-old US economic embargo of Cuba, which does not have the blessing of the UN Security Council, the European Union, and many individual nations. It is a forceful example of the interplay between politics, economics, and International Law. This legislation has prompted diplomatic protests from many nations—including US NAFTA partners Canada and Mexico—and the European Union. You may now read the edited versions of the US law, the legislation enacted by Cuba, and references to the official objections to Helms–Burton on the course Web page:

United States 1996 Cuban Liberty and Democratic Solidarity Act

and the responsive

Republic of Cuba 1996 Reaffirmation of Cuban Dignity and Sovereignty Act

Go to course Web page at http://home.att.net/~slomansonb/txtcsesite.html; click on Cuban Liberty and Democratic Solidarity Act & Reaffirmation of Cuban Dignity and Sovereignty Act

The Helms–Burton legislation was initially vetoed by President William Clinton but later signed after Cuban military jets shot down two private US aircraft in 1996 (*see Alejandre v. Republic of Cuba,* cited in the text box on page 271). This was then the latest incident in the ongoing friction between the US and Cuba, initially spawned by Fidel Castro's 1959 coup d'etat (*see Sabbatino* case discussion under Act of State, §9.7, page 417). Its purpose was to tighten the economic embargo of Cuba by making it a crime to "traffic" in property—originally belonging to US nationals—that was confiscated by Cuba in 1959 after the US first imposed a quota on Cuban sugar products.

This legislation prohibits third-country companies from "trafficking" in such property, a term previously reserved for US drug laws. It creates civil liability and excludes visits to the US by officers, controlling shareholders, families of trafficking companies, and anyone else who violates its terms. As noted in the Web page excerpt (appearing just before the US legislation), Mexico, Canada, and the European Union were prominent US trade partners who characterized this Act as an illegal extraterritorial application of US law.

In 1997, the EU brought a claim before the World Trade Organization (WTO), regarding this US legislation. The EU dropped its claim against the US in 1998, however, for alternative reasons implying a "lose–lose" scenario for the then new WTO trade process (*see* §13.3). First, if the EU were to continue to prosecute this matter in the WTO, and even be successful, the case would effectively politicize the fledgling global trade organization. It was, after all, designed to *avoid* politics in international trade. There was no guarantee that the US would remain in the WTO—recalling that the US abandoned the International Court of Justice in the mid-1980s when its supreme national interests were at stake in Nicaragua (*see* §10.2). Second, if the US were to win this case, its "national security" defense to anti-competitive trade measures would have effectively made a mockery of the WTO. The organization was basically conceived to ensure free, non-discriminatory trade—which was expressly contrary to the heart of the Helms–Burton Act. During the eight-year Uruguay Round, the US was generally the first and loudest proponent to claim that a prospective defendant should not frustrate the dispute settlement provisions of the WTO.

President Clinton has waived key portions of Helms–Burton five times since passage of this Act (each has a six-month life span). He expressed the concern that there would be retaliation against US companies, especially because foreign business people operating in Cuba could be sued under this US law, regarding any transaction involving "trafficked" property. A 1998 bipartisan campaign was launched in the US Congress to ameliorate the potential impact of this Act and the forty-year embargo on the Cuban people (as opposed to the targeted government).

In an analysis of the arguments for and against the legality of Helms–Burton in the American Bar Association's *International Lawyer,* the Founding Executive Director of the Legal Center for Inter-American Free Trade and Commerce concludes:

> The moment for multilateral diplomacy with respect for Cuba and the Western Hemisphere could not be any more auspicious. [T]he European Union has adopted a new foreign policy strategy vis-à-vis Cuba. The purpose of the European plan is to address human rights abuses and, consistent with Title II of *Helms Burton,* to foster the transition to a democratically elected government in the Caribbean island. Harmonious with this plan, Pope John Paul II made an unprecedented visit to Cuba during the early part of 1998 as a favorable prelude to the Second Summit of the Americas. As the international legal system approaches the crossroads in its continued development, the door to multilateral diplomacy is open. The only question is whether the US President and the Congress will make the correct policy choice.[15]

Human Rights (Chapter 11) There is a significant link between human rights doctrine and international commerce. The US is the largest consumer nation in the world and one of its strongest economies. The US is therefore in a comparatively affluent position to employ international economic strategies to further global human rights objectives. Oppressive regimes do not facilitate lucrative markets for US goods and services.

There are numerous contemporary examples, but space for only several. In mid-1994, the US opposed Singapore as the initial host of the World Trade Organization's premier 1995 ministerial meeting. The US Trade Representative objected to a Singapore site, because of its 1994 "caning" (severe corporal punishment with a whiplike cane) of an eighteen-year-old US citizen. President Clinton was unable to dissuade Singapore from carrying out this punishment after the youth had spray-painted several cars. There were widely reported global concerns with this form of State action on the basis that it constituted torture or cruel and degrading punishment under International Human Rights Law. While US pressure did not prevent the caning, the US *was* able to sidetrack Singapore's bid for hosting this major event at the dawn of the new World Trade Organization's operations.[16]

Contemporary US presidential administrations have complained about human rights abuses in the People's Republic of China (PRC). They have reportedly threatened to revoke the PRC's "most favored nation" (MFN) trade status with the US. This institution (*see* §13.3) essentially means that one State gives trade concessions to another State on the same basis as its most favorable trading partner for that particular product.

There has been a relatively long and tortuous political history associated with the decisions of US presidents regarding China's "MFN" status since World War II. In 1951, in the early stages of the Cold War, US President Harry Truman denied MFN status to all communist countries. President Richard Nixon unsuccessfully attempted to extend MFN status to China in 1972 when he initiated US relations with the PRC. In 1980, President Jimmy Carter finally extended MFN status to that nation. In 1990, President George Bush decided that China would receive MFN status—but not the former Soviet Union because of obstacles it had erected to Jewish emigration to Israel. This appeared to set a double standard for US MFN policy. *Candidate* Clinton campaigned in 1991 that, if elected, he would revoke China's MFN status because of continuing concerns with China's human rights performance. In 1993, *President* Clinton scaled this pledge back to denying MFN status only to *State* entities. Full MFN status was revived that year and continued thereafter (*see* text box excerpt at the beginning of this chapter).

The threatened revocation of China's MFN status has been a continuing commercial wrinkle in Sino–US diplomatic relations. It has continued to resurface since the PRC's massacre of pro-democratic Chinese students in Tiananmen Square in 1989. In 1994, the US Trade Representative announced a new tactic in the pursuit of Chinese human rights improvement—a cutback of 25 to 35 percent on the US importation of Chinese textiles and clothing. Of course, the US is experiencing a major trade deficit with the PRC. But the expressed rationale for this particular round of human rights diplomacy was that China continues to display a poor human rights record after a decade of prodding by various human rights organizations.

Environmental Niche (Chapter 12) The environmental chapter embraced a variety of links between business and law. The 1992 Rio Conference and related UN environmental programs have strived to accomplish sustainable economic development for the underdeveloped countries of the world (*see* §12.2). But there is continuing concern about the environmental cost of such development. The flourishing industrial-chemical plants of the 1970s and 1980s in Ireland, for example, helped raise the economic standard of living in Ireland, one of the European Union's poorest members. But they also produced one of the most polluted atmospheres in the Northern Hemisphere.[17]

The insatiable desire of underdeveloped countries to obtain a more equitable share of global resources has at least one disadvantage (*see* §13.4). Many members of the community of nations are now free of *de jure* colonial rule under the UN-driven self-determination program (*see* §2.3). But they are now challenged by the sometimes mutually exclusive objectives of brisk economic development and the unfavorable drain of long-term environmental degradation. The citizens of Bhopal, India, certainly gained from the presence of a major US corporate operation in their territory making chemicals for agricultural use. Thousands of jobs were created. India's economy was favorably impacted by the presence of this multinational corporate enterprise. More money was spent locally in the form of the added spending power of corporate employees, steady jobs, and a decline in unemployment. There would be a significant environmental price to be paid in 1984, however, for hosting a foreign corporation's operations in Bhopal. Several thousand people were killed and hundreds of thousands became ill from a toxic gas leak in one of the worst environmental disasters in history (*see* text box at the outset of Chapter 12).

INTERNATIONAL BUSINESS NEGOTIATING CONTEXT

Assume that Widget Inc. decides to enter into a business arrangement with a foreign company to market and sell widgets. It is critically important to acknowledge differences in business customs, language, culture, and attitude. Merely speaking the language or having translators and lawyers present does not ensure that the parties will achieve their objectives. This is a significant component of the bargaining process between or among business negotiators from different countries. The following excerpt succinctly summarizes some of the significant highlights of this process:

International Business Transactions in a Nutshell (5th ed., 1996)

R. Folsom, M. Gordon, & J. Spanogle, Jr.

"Negotiating International Business Transactions," 26–36

TIMING

Understanding the . . . framework for a successful negotiation is sometimes difficult for . . . United States attorneys and business executives. . . . [I]t took the Vietnamese two years to agree about the shape of the negotiating table at the Paris Peace Talks. The Chinese people from many other countries negotiate with a recognition that what cannot be settled today perhaps can be settled tomorrow or next week. Japanese are reluctant to do business with someone in whom they do not have sufficient trust and with whom they do not sense reciprocal feelings of friendship. . . . It may take weeks spent together on a golf course before such trust is engendered. People in other countries do not prefer to negotiate during certain times of the years, e.g., Ramadan in Islamic nations. In some countries the "weekend" is on days other than Saturday and Sunday, those days being normal business days. Some hours which in the United States are considered the normal business day are not considered appropriate for doing business in other countries. In parts of Africa "noon" may be any time between 10 a.m. and 2 p.m. The hours between 2 p.m. and 5 p.m. are inappropriate for doing business in Saudi Arabia.

IMPORTANCE OF PROCEDURE

It may be, and often is, that the procedure employed in international business negotiations is the single most important cause of their success or failure. The careful lawyer or executive will make advance inquiry about whether contacts preliminary to the negotiation are advisable and about which locations may be preferable for conducting negotiations. Procedures calculated to facilitate the building of personal relationships increase prospects for a successful negotiation, especially in Asia. In tough moments during a negotiation, courtesy alone may keep a consensus momentum going. Enduring courtesy is the essential lubricant of international negotiations.

A negotiating opposite may not want to admit that an apparent unwillingness to agree to a suggested point is caused by bureaucratic foot dragging, lack of coordination, lack of technical understanding or simple confusion on its side. Procedures that are flexible enough to allow time to work out such problems may cultivate ego, avoid a loss of "face" and continue [meaningful] participation in the negotiations. For example, a negotiating opposite may be unwilling to let you know that failure to reach quick agreement is due to the fact that he or she, despite having a lofty sounding title or other credentials, does not have authority to make a final agreement or will not assume personal responsibility for the consequences of an agreement. The latter case occurs frequently in Japan. Some nations find it prudent to advertise publicly that only certain government agencies are authorized to carry out sales or purchases.

Procedures which cause surprise are intimidating and can engender hostility and distrust. Obvious examples include emotional displays used as smokescreens, changing the agreed agenda for negotiation, unannounced or late arrivals and departures of negotiating personnel, and retreating from agreements already made. The surprise introduction of a written document . . . the contents of which a negotiating opposite is asked to consider or even to read on the spur of the moment, often causes similar reactions. Taking [written] minutes of a negotiation and preparing written summaries of points of agreement often speeds the consensus building process, but the surprise transmission of such documents to a negotiating opposite can work a greater and opposite effect. Of course, these procedures may be useful if negotiating by contest rather than consensus. Because the intimidating nature of a written document increases with its thickness, a one page summary of the contents stands a better chance of being read. . . .

IMPORTANCE OF CULTURE

Cultural and language differences between negotiating opposites accentuate the importance attached to procedure in international negotiations. Self-praise is deprecated in virtually all cultures. A story is told of one multinational investor in Africa who inserted certain "whereas" clauses into a negotiated agreement to the effect that the local government was unable to perform a task and that the investor possessed world wide management and technical success at the same task. An African newspaper published those "whereas" clauses as evidence of "imperialist attitudes."

Although giving gifts of modest value is appreciated in virtually all cultures, it is an expected occurrence between negotiating opposites in some countries. Certain gifts, such as books depicting the natural beauty of the investor's home area, are generally appreciated while more specialized gifts may be preferred in a particular country. For example, Johnny Walker Black Label Scotch is appreciated in Japan, but Red Label is valued in Thailand and Burma.

There is an almost universal cultural importance attached to sharing a meal with a negotiating opposite. Meal time affords a good opportunity for an investor to show an interest in and sensitivity about the host's culture. In many cultures [however,] talking about business matters during a meal is considered impolite and is counter-productive.

There is considerable cultural diversity about the meaning in international negotiations of silence and delay. The common law rule [in English-speaking countries] that, under appropriate circumstances, "silence is acceptance" is not shared widely in many countries. In some countries silence may mean "no," while in other countries periods of silence are an acceptable and common occasion during which thoughts are arranged and rearranged. For example, an investor in Indonesia brought the final draft of a completely negotiated agreement to a counterpart for signature and, following some pleasant conversation, placed the agreement on the desk. In complete silence, the counterpart simply returned the document, unsigned, to the investor. The investor later learned that this day was not considered propitious in Indonesia for signing one's name. Delays of days or even of months may not be signs that a negotiation is in difficulty, nor represent an attempt at increasing the costs of negotiating. Such delays may simply be the minimum time period in which a necessary consensus or authority is being achieved within a negotiating team.

An excellent analysis of cultural variables affecting international negotiations, known as LESCANT, had been prepared by David A. Victor. See *International Business Communications* (1992). LESCANT involves identification of the following cultural variables: Language; environment and technology; social organization; contexting (a measurement of explicit and implicit communications); authority conception; non-verbal behavior; and temporal conception.

THE LANGUAGE OF NEGOTIATIONS

Differences in language skills between negotiating opposites raise some peril in every international business transaction. Each negotiating party prefers quite naturally to use the language whose nuances are best known. Words that have a clear and culturally acceptable meaning in one language may be unclear or culturally offensive in another tongue. The converse may be true as well.... Because some hand gestures and body movements are acceptable in one culture yet deeply offensive in another culture, they are rarely an appropriate communications aid in international negotiations. For example, raising an open hand in the direction of another party can mean in North Africa that you hope that person will lose all five senses.

The use of interpreters substantially slows the pace of negotiations and may spawn further difficulties because the interpreter is one more fallible person taking part in the negotiations. Interpreting is exhausting work and rarely exact. During an international commercial arbitration in Los Angeles, a witness testified in German alongside a skilled interpreter whose job it was to translate the testimony into English. While the arbitrators waited, it required the interpreter's efforts, the efforts of a United States lawyer fluent in German, and the efforts of a German lawyer fluent in English to produce an oral translation which all agreed was sufficiently accurate. Even assuming the availability of an accurate literal translation, a Japanese person saying "yes" in answer to a question may not be signifying agreement but may only mean, "Yes, I understand the question."

The peril of language difficulty can be equally acute in negotiations between a lawyer from the United States and a negotiating opposite who speaks the English language. Each party may be [too] embarrassed to raise a language question. For example, in the middle of a telephone conversation between a lawyer from the United States and a negotiator in England, a London operator interrupted to ask if the lawyer was "through." Not wishing to terminate the conversation, the American answered, "No, I am not through." The operator disconnected the circuit, apologized, and once again dialed to get the call "through." A few minutes later the London operator came on the line again, interrupting the parties' conversation, to ask again if the United States caller was "through." Desiring to continue the conversation without further interruption, the American lawyer this time said "Yes, thank you," and the operator left the line connected.

Certain foreign enterprises require their negotiators to speak English when negotiating with Americans. The problem is that their English seldom tracks American English, and embarrassing moments occur when US negotiators must delicately seek clarification of the opponent's words. Such clarifications must be undertaken with the utmost politeness and goodwill in order not to insult or intimidate the foreign party.

Even exceptionally able interpreters may have difficulty if a United States lawyer or executive uses American slang in communicating during an international negotiation. The American penchant for using "ball park" figures may not be shared or understood in countries where baseball is not a popular sport. Slow and distinct patterns of speech combined with simple declarative sentences will always facilitate international business negotiations.

LANGUAGE IN THE AGREEMENT

The person who controls the drafting of an international business agreement often drives the negotiations. United States lawyers will almost always seek to perform this leading role. The careful language normally used by American lawyers in commercial contracts may prove controversial. While legally trained persons in some countries share an affinity for written contracts that set out the full extent of every right and duty of each party, the practice in many other countries tends toward more generally worded agreements that leave it to the parties (e.g., in Japan) or to the courts (e.g., in Germany) to supply any necessary details. A detailed, exhaustively worded, draft contract which is introduced during negotiations with Japanese or Chinese persons may arouse distrust. To them, a contract relationship is perceived as something that is shaped mutually as understanding develops. A German negotiating opposite may not be willing to sign an exhaustively worded contract because German courts dislike such agreements. The German courts take the position that they know the law and do not need a contract to state what is known already.

This attitude may trap unwary parties. Chinese negotiators, for example, will resist bargaining on the details of a contract or joint venture, saying "All that is of course understood" or "a part of our law." They may even show resentment at attempts to detail business agreements. However, during performance at a later date, other representatives of a Chinese entity may . . . say: "That is not written expressly in the contract and is not our duty." If a detail is important to the transaction, spell it out in the agreement. Many US attorneys involved with Chinese business transactions have learned the hard way.

Permissible contract clauses in one country may be impermissible in another country and *vice versa.* For example, penalty clauses which are not legally enforceable in the United States are enforced routinely by French and, to a lesser extent, Italian courts. One-sided (adhesion) contracts may be fun for lawyers to draft, but they may serve only to raise suspicion by identifying the drafter as an adversary or to generate hostility and ill will. Draft adhesion contracts do not promote the consensus building style of international business negotiations. German courts will eviscerate an unfair adhesion contract without mercy.

One of the most frustrating features of international business agreements is the presence of texts in different languages, each of which is considered authoritative. Counsel to an American enterprise will always seek to make English the sole language of the agreement, and sometimes succeed since English has become the predominant language of international business. Especially when negotiations have been conducted exclusively in English, time, expense, clarity and mutual understanding favor such a result. Even parties who do not natively speak English may use it as the language of agreement for these reasons. Agreements between Japanese and Indonesian businesses, for example, are often in English. But cultural pride (especially with French speaking negotiators) or fear of unfair dealing (especially with Chinese negotiators) may leave multiple texts in different languages [as] the only acceptable solution once "agreement" is reached.

Another important linguistic feature of international transactions, particularly of concern to lawyers, is the existence of different language texts of relevant laws. In the European Union, for example, there are nine official, authoritative texts for every treaty, regulation, directive, parliamentary report, etc. The nuances of nine languages can significantly affect the legality of any business transaction subject to EU law. Those same nuances can undermine any carefully constructed "consensus" international negotiators have worked hard to create.

◆ 13.2 WORLD TRADE ORGANIZATION AND GATT

The World Trade Organization (WTO) became effective in 1995, emerging in the form of a 26,228-page document. This new global agreement embodies a six-part program designed to reduce barriers to international commerce, including the following restraints:

- *Tariffs.* Import taxes and other tariff barriers would be reduced on 85 percent of the world's trade with some tariff cuts taking effect immediately. These taxes are called *customs duties, charges, tolls, assessments,* or *levies.* The most common term is *tariff.*
- *Dumping.* The practice of temporarily selling imports at a price below the cost of selling in the target market would be controlled. It is a predatory tool for eliminating local competition. After market access is secured, the pricing structure increases significantly so that ultimate profits recoup previous losses after eradication of most or all competitors.

- *Agriculture.* Farm subsidies, which artificially reduce the cost of production, would be reduced by an average of 36 percent.
- *Textiles.* Import quotas on textiles from developing countries, which currently help the local market's competitors maintain a greater market share, would be phased out over a ten-year period.
- *Service sectors.* Markets in "service" sectors such as banking, shipping, and insurance will be subject to international trade controls for the first time. Only "goods" were regulated under the 1947–1994 version of the WTO.
- *Intellectual property.* This regime also extends protection against unauthorized copying of "intellectual" property such as books, films, music, and computer programs.

The WTO is the successor of the General Agreement on Tariffs and Trade (GATT) institution. A global trade arrangement first called GATT was implemented in 1947. This institution did not operate as an international organization as such. Nevertheless, it had been *the* global agreement in international trade for almost half a century. "GATT 1994," meaning GATT as amended due to interim negotiated changes, has continued to function, but only for those few nations that did not become charter members of or later accede to the WTO agreement.

The shift from GATT to WTO was a significant change. The GATT thus shifted from a *de facto* arrangement to a truly international organization intended to become the treaty-based centerpiece of International Trade Law.[18] The primary reason for this upgraded status was that the WTO has radically changed dispute settlement procedures in international commerce.

EVOLUTION OF GATT AND WTO

In the consummate economic world, managerial skill and economic efficiency would be the essential market forces driving international economics. Instead, governments have introduced a variety of impediments to the free flow of cross-border commerce. The tariff became the primary international trade barrier. When a government so taxes a foreign-made commodity, its tariff increases the cost of doing business in that particular market. The higher the tariff, the higher the cost—and the less likely the importation of foreign goods and international competition. One reason that governments impose tariffs is to raise revenue. But the intended or unintended economic effect is that tariffs help local manufacturers compete with cheaper imports from more efficient and established competitors in other countries. While the taxing nation's products are protected by such tariffs, that protection has a price. That nation can expect its trading partners to counter with their own tariffs. The cost of the import so taxed in the absence of free trade is that the protected product becomes more expensive for that nation's consumers. The wholesaler will pass this cost along to the customer as a cost of doing business.

The inverse relationship between the level of tariffs and degree of international trade is illustrated by the effect of the US tariff law of 1930. It imposed the highest tariffs ever levied on foreign-made products. The US Congress then believed that this trade restriction would *stimulate* local industry and agriculture, and that the US would not be harmed by this tariff legislation. Quite the opposite occurred, however. The other major industrial countries retaliated by placing higher tariffs on US exports. The foreign demand for American products fell immediately, resulting in a loss of jobs in the US. These events *contributed* to the Great Depression of the 1930s—and the global recession of that era.

As explained by University of South Carolina Business School Professor Christopher Korth:

> The economy will likely suffer if the government of a country accedes to [excessive] protective pressures, regardless of the specific nature of the argument and regardless of whether the interested group represents the private or governmental sector. *Protectionism* means that a higher price must be paid by the majority in order to benefit the few.
>
> The list of arguments on behalf of controls is long. The list of "reasonable" arguments from the viewpoint of the public good (as opposed to that of special interest groups) is very short. Even in these cases, however, both national and world efficiency, income, and living standards will decline.[19]

In 1934, US President Franklin Roosevelt and the Congress worked together to reverse this high-tariff scenario. There was a need to stimulate the domestic economy. Congress enacted the Reciprocal Trade Agreements Program to encourage international competition. It generally reduced tariff rates that, in turn, encouraged similar reductions by other countries. The legislative goal was to vitiate the adverse effect of the high tariffs that had strangled the flow of international commerce—both in and out of the US. Congress then authorized the president to negotiate mutual tariff reductions with individual nations. The US Trade Representative thus began to negotiate an exhaustive series of *bilateral* agreements to reduce tariffs. This program increased the volume of US exports, while stimulating worldwide trade benefits as other countries responded by reducing their tariffs. The US tariffs gradually declined to the lowest levels in the nation's history.

During World War II, certain nations explored the possibility of a *multilateral* trade institution. They advocated a single, global trade agreement that would replace the hundreds of independent bilateral agreements. The US pursued this objective by lobbying for creation of the International Trade Organization (ITO) to develop and maintain a global trade agreement. Representatives from several nations met to draft an ITO Charter. They simultaneously created a comparatively informal document called the General Agreement on Tariffs and Trade (GATT) at Geneva in 1947. The GATT was originally supposed to be a statement of principles related to—but distinct from—the anticipated ITO Charter.[20]

The ITO never materialized. The US Congress resurrected its isolationist trade posture after World War II and decided against US participation in the proposed ITO. The US had the most prosperous post-war economy. Many of today's major economic powers were in ruins or economically depressed after the war. Without US support, the ITO became impractical. After that, GATT continued to be a *de facto* arrangement that was useful, even if not legally enforceable when its obligations (discussed below) were breached by a participating State.

GATT became the device for coordinating policies on international commerce, accomplishing trade objectives, and overcoming the inertia of the US Congress. In 1948, twenty-two nations executed an interim Protocol of Provisional Application—the original GATT agreement referred to as "GATT 1947." A GATT General Secretariat and administrative staff were established by 1955 in Geneva. Their task was to implement the trade objectives of the participating countries—which could not be called "members," because the GATT did not achieve official status as an international organization of States. GATT did not possess its own power to act when a State decided to ignore its GATT "obligations" during the next forty years.

There was another barrier to GATT's success. Some market economies resisted membership out of the desire to protect their local industries from foreign competition. Mexico, for example, was opposed because it was not ready to open its economy to imports. Mexico's private industrialists equated GATT membership with a flood of cheap imports that would destroy certain domestic industries and remove the protective barriers designed to foster their growth. Mexico finally applied for GATT membership in 1985, however, to breathe life into its sagging export program. President Miguel de La Madrid convinced Mexico's private industrialists that the nation could not expand its export sales if it maintained barriers to imports from other nations. Mexico's participation in GATT removed many of those barriers.

In 1994, the status of the GATT arrangement changed. Most nations of the world either joined or sought accession to the various agreements produced by the eight-year "Uruguay Round" of GATT negotiations. This "GATT 1994" was the last of five such periodic rounds conducted since GATT's inception. During that session, the national representatives produced the "Final Act," referring to the World Trade Organization (WTO).[21] As of January 1995, sixty nations became charter members of the WTO. Some have signed but not yet ratified the WTO agreement. Twenty-one others immediately began to negotiate for admission. Some States, however, remained in just the GATT, rather than accept the *mandatory* dispute-settlement provisions of the 1995 WTO process.

A primary objective of the switch from GATT to WTO was to overcome the national distrust associated with submitting sensitive trade disputes to a third-party dispute-resolution body. The recent legal adviser to the WTO, Ernst-Ulrich Petersmann, authoritatively observes:

> Both the classical international law of coexistence and the post-War international law of economic cooperation, including the General Agreement on Tariffs and Trade (GATT), had focused on the rights of states and governments rather than on the rights of their citizens. . . . While *Alexis de Tocqueville* could describe the US Supreme Court as a model for the judicial control of protectionist abuses of government

powers [within a nation], the termination, in October 1985, of the US acceptance of the compulsory jurisdiction of the International Court of Justice . . . revealed a widespread distrust vis-à-vis judicial settlement of disputes with third countries [via a multilateral process].

How can such distrust of judicial control of foreign policy powers be overcome? How can . . . abuses of foreign policy powers be prevented? How can a liberal international trade order be protected more effectively? . . .

The 1994 WTO Agreement, adopted by 124 countries and the EC . . . [is] arguably the most important worldwide agreement since the UN Charter of 1945. . . .

As a global integration agreement, which regulates international movements of goods, services, persons, capital and related payments in an integrated manner, the WTO agreement reduces the current fragmentation of separate international agreements and organizations. . . . Fifty years after the Bretton Woods Conference, its entry into force on 1 January 1995 completed the legal structure of the Bretton Woods system based on the IMF, the World Bank Group and [now] the WTO. The WTO was designed to serve constitutional functions and rule-making functions . . . , in addition to its executive functions, surveillance functions and dispute settlement functions for the foreign economic policies of member states, more so than the IMF and the World Bank, whose statutes include few substantive rules for the conduct of government policies and for the [much needed] rule-oriented settlement of international disputes.[22]

The new comprehensive title, "WTO" as opposed to "GATT," was more than just a name change. First, now a *de jure* international organization is endowed with jurisdictional powers provided by its member States. Second, the WTO has a power that was withheld from the GATT process by its participating States. The WTO can force compliance when a member breaches the obligations of GATT—and now WTO (set forth below). Third, there is also room in the WTO for economies that have not been historically free-market economies. The former Soviet Union and the People's Republic of China had expressed interest in participating in the earlier GATT agreement.

The US opposed China's participation, however, due to its extensive piracy of patented and copyrighted US materials. These products include computer hardware and software, books, movies, and a host of other items protected by treaty. US estimates are that China's breach of international copyright and patent treaties has cost US companies more than $1 billion a year in lost revenues, because 94 percent of US-made products in China are pirated copies. Notwithstanding the US concern, China became a member of the WTO. Russia's relatively recent shift to a market economy—assuming that democracy and capitalism continue to flourish—renders it a likely candidate for ultimate inclusion.

One major difference between the WTO and GATT is that a GATT State could pick and choose from among which provisions of the various agreements were expedient. This selective incorporation produced a very complex web of varying obligations, doing little to promote GATT's universal appeal. This is one of the reasons why *regional* trade organization (*see* §13.3) virtually eclipsed the GATT in importance. The WTO agreement requires that participating States must agree to all of the *basic* provisions, with some temporary exceptions.

The WTO also differs from GATT because it expanded GATT's limited application to only commodities. WTO membership requires accession to the four fundamental parts of the 1994 Final Act: (1) trade in goods—which had been GATT's sole focus—and the new components regarding (2) services, (3) intellectual property rights, and (4) investment rules. The *goods* portion of international commerce continues to be the primary area of concern. It will be summarized below as the central portion of this section.

The primary *legal* difference between GATT and the WTO is the latter's *mandatory* dispute-resolution mechanism (Exhibit 13.3). The former GATT panels of experts often issued their determinations without the ability to force compliance with the basic obligations described below. A far more formal adjudicatory system currently provides enforceable remedies. The significance is succinctly explained by New York University Law School Professor Andreas Lowenfeld, a prominent international commercial arbitrator:

Until now dispute settlement in the GATT has generally reflected a certain ambivalence. Some states and many "old GATT hands" within the secretariat

EXHIBIT 13.3 WORLD TRADE ORGANIZATION DISPUTE RESOLUTION

Action	Nature	Actor(s)	Objective
Creation of rules and procedures	Administrative	DSB[a]	Administer procedure; establish panels and appeal process; monitor implementation
Request for consultation	Initiate resolution process	Plaintiff State (P)	Offending State has ten days to respond
Response	Initiates consultation	Defendant State (D)	Must respond within thirty days and settle within sixty days
Establish panel	Administrative	DSB	Either no D response or unsettled by P and D
Decision	Adjudicatory—first level	3 judges[b]	Complete work within six months; issue decision called "Report"
Appellate body	Adjudicatory—second level	3 judges[c]	Complete work within three months; three more months possible in complex cases
Adoption of report	Accept or reject	DSB	Panel or appellate report may be rejected by consensus of DSB
Compliance	Cease offending practice	Defendant State	Defendant must inform DSB of intent to comply and date by which it will comply
Arbitration agreement on *date* for compliance	Mutual agreement	P and D	Submit case to *binding* arbitration from which there can be no appeal
Arbitration	Final resort	Parties or WTO Director	Limited to time within which D must comply; no substantive issue considered

Source: Agreement Establishing WTO, reprinted in 33 *Int'l Legal Mat'ls* 13 (1994)

[a]DSB = Dispute Settlement Body formed by the WTO General Council.
[b]These will normally be members of GATT delegation in Geneva; panel member with same citizenship as a party may not serve on panel absent specific request—providing option for panelists knowledgeable on laws of countries of respective parties.
[c]Seven-person organ, three of whom serve during Appellate Body review of panel report.

and among the delegations in Geneva believed that GATT dispute settlement should aim at lowering tensions, defusing conflicts, and promoting compromise; others, notably American officials and writers, have looked to the dispute mechanism of GATT as an opportunity to build a system of rules and remedies. Over the forty years of GATT dispute settlement, there has been an ebb and flow between the diplomatic and the adjudicatory models. It seems clear that the adjudicatory model prevailed in the Uruguay Round.[23]

Under GATT, the losing party could essentially ignore or block a GATT "panel report." States could disregard the findings of the GATT panel when told to cease an offending practice. A powerful trading partner could even block the GATT Secretariat from organizing a panel that was supposed to decide a complaint.[24]

Another difference is that GATT formerly permitted States to make their own unilateral determination that there had been a violation of the GATT rules. The US, for example, had freely wielded its "§301" procedure of the 1974 Trade Act. The congressional statement of purpose was "to strengthen economic relations between the United States and foreign countries through open and nondiscriminatory world trade." But the US Trade Representative thereby made determinations that there had been an unfair trade practice emanating from another country. Such unilateral determinations often led to the opposite result. They preceded (or announced) threatened trade wars, which only exacerbated instability.

The WTO discourages unilateral fact-finding by an individual member of the organization. Article 23 of Annex 2 to the Agreement Establishing the World Trade Organization provides that should a member seek redress for a violation of GATT obligations it "shall have recourse to, and abide by, the rules and procedures of this Understanding. . . ." Members may not make their own determinations, and must instead seek "recourse to dispute settlement in accordance with the . . . [WTO] Understanding."[25]

Under this Understanding on Rules and Procedures Governing the Settlement of Disputes, there is still an adjudicatory "panel" process. But State members of the WTO can no longer ignore a panel decision for three reasons. First, there is an initial consultation process. The aggrieved party may institute a relatively informal consultation with the allegedly offending party. This informal process has a short fuse so that the aggrieved party may then secure the establishment of a formal panel if the matter remains unresolved for sixty days. Second, one State may not unilaterally block the establishment of a panel when another has lodged a complaint in the WTO's headquarters in Geneva. Third, the unlikely acceptance of an adverse panel decision without any form of review would place the WTO and the entire GATT process at risk.

States have been traditionally reluctant to yield sovereign powers to an external decision maker without any recourse. The panels can make mistakes. Thus, the losing party may *temporarily* block a panel decision—unlike the former panel "process," which could drag on for months with no resolution. The losing party must now seek immediate appellate review by the WTO's "Appellate Body" in Geneva. This standing organ consists of seven persons, three of whom review the lower panel decisions. The existence of an appellate process is an innovation that has been criticized on the basis that the availability of appellate review reduces the prestige of the "trial" panel. It offers a clear advantage, however. The losing party has the opportunity to rectify a perceived mistake—a common attribute of democratic systems of governance that *adds* to the integrity of the WTO process.[26]

The WTO's mandatory dispute-resolution mechanism described above was a major procedural hurdle to national acceptance, especially by the more powerful nations concerned about a devolution of sovereignty to a distant process in Geneva. This inertia has been overcome, however, now that most nations of the world have accepted the WTO and its mandatory settlement provisions. But what are the WTO's underlying *substantive* obligations?

WTO TRADE OBLIGATIONS

What exactly does participation in the WTO (and GATT) mean? What obligations does a State thereby undertake when it opts to join this international organization of States? The fundamental objective is to combat trade barriers. National representatives thereby attempt to reduce or eliminate the varied forms of trade barriers: tariffs, nontariff barriers, and discriminatory trade practices.

The essential obligations are set forth in Articles I, II, III, and VI. The relevant portion of each is provided immediately below, followed by a brief explanation. (Italics have been added in certain passages.)

> **Article I Most-Favored-Nation Treatment**
> (1) With respect to customs duties and charges of any kind imposed on or in connection with importation or exportation or imposed on the international transfer of payments for imports or exports, and with respect to the method of levying such duties and charges . . . any advantage, favor, privilege or immunity granted by any contracting country shall be accorded immediately and unconditionally to the like product originating in or destined for the territories of all other contracting parties.

Under International Law, States are generally free to discriminate in their economic dealings. That is an attribute of the sovereign power to engage in international relations with other States. University of London

Professor Georg Schwarzenberger explains that in "the absence of bilateral and multilateral treaty obligations to the contrary, international law does not ordain economic equality between States nor between their subjects. Economic sovereignty reigns supreme. It is for each subject of international law to decide for itself whether and, if so, in which form, it desires to grant equal treatment to other States and their subjects or give privileged treatment to some and discriminate against others."[27] A nation's tariffs may thus discriminate against the goods from one country and favor those of another. Groups of States may combine to charge discriminatory tariffs. If the States within the European Union want to *eliminate* tariffs on the exported commodities of *only* its own members, then they do not have to extend this favorable tariff treatment to other countries.

The Article I "Most Favored Nation" (MFN) clause has been a centerpiece of GATT (and now the WTO). Even prior to its creation, many bilateral trade treaties contained such a clause. Each nation thereby promised that the tariff rate on the imports of its trading partner would be the lowest rate imposed on *like* imports from any other nation. Then under the GATT, member nations agreed to grant MFN status to the imported products from other GATT members. Assume that South Africa imposes a 10 percent tariff on imported Italian shoes. Both of these countries are now members of the WTO. The MFN article requires South Africa to charge Italy the lowest shoe tariff that it levies on like shoes from any other country. South Africa may charge a *higher*, 12 percent tariff on shoes from State X if X is not a WTO member.

Article II Schedules of Concessions

(1.b) The products described in *Part I* of the Schedule relating to any contracting party, which are the products of territories of other contracting parties, shall, on their importation . . . be exempt from ordinary customs duties in excess of those set forth therein. . . .

(1.c) The products described in *Part II* of the Schedule relating to any contracting party which are the products of territories entitled under Article I to receive *preferential treatment* upon importation into the territory to which the Schedule relates shall, on their importation . . . be exempt from ordinary customs duties in excess of those set forth and provided for in Part II of that Schedule.

Each State's tariffs on imported products are listed in "concessions," referred to as "schedules." These schedules have been renegotiated during the various periodic GATT rounds since the original 1947 agreement. Members have thereby updated and published their latest tariff schedules, giving their tariff for each item on the list of items governed by the GATT.

There is a dual system of tariffs under the GATT. Article II(1.c) above authorizes a GATT member to place the imports of designated nations on its "*Part II* Schedule" of tariffs. This results in lower tariffs being imposed on imports from a developing nation. Each GATT member may publish *different* tariffs for the same category of import on its Parts I and II lists. The lower tariffs on a member's Part II Schedule of tariffs favor the products of certain developing countries. The more they can thus benefit by developing *their* markets through lower tariff schedules, the larger their markets will be for exports from developed nations.

Article III National Treatment on Internal Taxation and Regulation

(2) The products of the territory of any contracting party imported into the territory of any other contracting party shall not be subject, directly or *indirectly,* to internal taxes or other internal charges of any kind *in excess of* those applied, directly or indirectly, to like *domestic* products.

A tariff is supposed to be a *surmountable* barrier to the importation of a foreign product. It increases the cost of selling that product in a foreign market. A domestic business that is already operating in that market obviously does *not* have to pay any import tariff. It can compete without having to factor in a tariff on its products as a cost of doing business. If a US company wants to sell steel to Germany, for example, the latter's tariff on that steel is an added cost to the American company of doing business in Germany. German steel producers do not have to pay this same cost in their own German markets. If competition in the international steel market is very high, then price differences will normally be minimal. Thus, the German tariff—or a sudden increase—may present an *insurmountable* cost barrier, making it unprofitable for a US company to sell steel in the German steel market.

In addition to *direct* import tariffs, many States have imposed *indirect* barriers to trade called "nontariff" barriers (NTB) to competition from imports. NTBs protect local industries from foreign competition. They create an added cost that is effectively assessed on imports in addition to the import tax that has already been paid. Article III(2) prohibits such indirect barriers on imports. Why? If the importing company has already paid an express tax (tariff) on its product, then its cost of doing such business should be transparent in the tariff tax on that product—rather than being hidden in the form of some costly restriction imposed after the product has already been taxed through the importing nation's scheduled tariff rate.

Assume that a US steel company determines that, after accounting for the German tariff, it is still profitable to export steel to German markets. Representatives of the German steel industry then convince the German legislature to enact a law that requires new inspections for structural defects in steel. This new law applies *only* to foreign-made steel imported into Germany. The US steel company must now pay the added cost of this new inspection procedure. This law is a GATT-prohibited NTB, because it discriminates against foreign steel producers without imposing a like cost of doing business on domestic German steel producers.

There are various forms of NTB. The simplest is a quota on the quantity of foreign imports from a particular country. Another example is the so-called buy national law. It provides economic incentives to a country's consumers to buy domestically made rather than foreign-made products. There is also the dual-purpose protectionist NTB. The US Congress, for example, passed environmental protection legislation in 1986 that discriminated against foreign oil. Congress thereby created a new tax on oil to establish the "Superfund" for cleaning up US waste-disposal sites. The tax was set at 11.7 cents per barrel of *imported* oil—but only 8.2 cents per barrel for *domestic* oil. Many oil-exporting States complained that this was an indirect tariff on their oil sold in the US. A GATT dispute panel found that this tax violated the GATT, because it was an NTB to competition with foreign oil. The US accepted the findings of the GATT panel and changed the law to delete its discriminatory effect.[28]

NTBs can discriminate against foreign imports in even more subtle ways. A good example, although arising in a non-GATT context, was a French tax struck down in 1985 by the European Court of Justice. France had imposed a tax on automobiles based on their horsepower. This special French tax applied only to automobiles with a very high horsepower. It was five times the tax imposed on cars with the usual horsepower for cars in France. French automobile makers effectively could not be subject to this tax, because none made vehicles with this high rate of horsepower. Although the French tax law purportedly applied to *all* automobile makers, its actual impact was limited to *foreign* makers. France was required to repeal this tax. It was an unlawful NTB to international trade within the European Community that effectively imposed higher costs on foreign enterprises doing business in the French market.[29]

Article VI Dumping

(1) The contracting parties recognize that . . . dumping, by which products of one country are introduced into the commerce of another country at less than the normal value of the products, is to be condemned if it causes or threatens material injury to an established industry in the territory of a contracting party or materially retards the establishment of a domestic industry. . . .

A nation may not "dump" its products onto another nation's market at a price *below the fair market value* of that product in that market. Although a company could theoretically sell below cost without an anti-competitive effect, such conduct inherently "causes or threatens material injury to an established industry." Dumping is the type of business conduct that most likely "retards the *establishment* of a domestic industry" if none is already present when the import arrives in the target market. Cheaper imports are one of the intended benefits of participation in the GATT. This provision controls a predatory business plan designed to temporarily flood a foreign market with cheap imports that are sold initially at a price below their value (after considering shipping and insurance costs).

Article VI Countervailing Duties

(2) In order to offset or prevent dumping, a contracting party may levy on any dumped product an anti-dumping duty not greater in amount than the margin of dumping in respect to such product.

A State may *augment* its scheduled (published) tariff concession on a product when it suspects that imports are being dumped onto its domestic markets from another country. This is an antidumping or countervailing "duty"—meaning a special tax imposed on imports in addition to the usual tariff for that commodity. The purpose is to offset the anti-competitive effect of the dumped product.[30] The importing State raises the cost of exporting such offending products into the "dumped" market to a level that approximates their normal cost.

A major change from the former GATT to the "New GATT" (under the WTO process) is the introduction of the more specific "Agreements on Implementation of the General Agreement on Tariffs and Trade." This new feature embodies the results of the seven-year Uruguay Round of GATT negotiations. Article 3.5 of the Agreement on Implementation of Article VI provides as follows:

> It must be demonstrated that the dumped imports are, through the effects of dumping . . . causing injury within the meaning of this Agreement. The demonstration of a causal relationship between the dumped imports and the injury to the domestic industry shall [include] . . . any known factors other than the dumped imports which . . . are injuring the domestic industry, and the injuries caused by these other factors [such as contraction of demand, developments in technology, or domestic productivity].

Such implementing agreements flesh out the skeletal detail provided by prior versions of the GATT and clarify what factors should and should not affect the WTO's determination of whether dumping is actually occurring—and, if it is, whether it is in fact *causing* the alleged harm to the importing market's domestic industry.

Dumping accusations are regularly voiced when the importing nation learns that the exporting nation has somehow subsidized a product. With this government assistance, the product becomes marketable at a price that gives the exporting nation's company an improper financial advantage in the importing nations. Such advantages make a product competitive in a foreign market, because it may be sold comparatively cheaply. But subsidies are not known for being transparent. Thus, related litigation often turns on the issue of whether the government involvement constitutes a subsidy. If so, this situation could authorize the importing nation to levy a countervailing duty on the product, which is an adjustment for the foreign government's interference with unadulterated market forces.

In 1995, for example, an Australian federal court examined Pakistan's price-fixing policy. It indirectly assisted Pakistani cotton manufacturers, because they could buy raw materials at a price lower than fair-market value in the global market. Although the trial and appellate courts did not determine that Pakistani policy constituted an unfair "subsidy," they did make their assessment in terms of the GATT, because Australia was a party. Thus, the appellate court noted that this subsidy did not violate GATT. On the facts of this case, the Pakistani government's assistance did not constitute an illegal subsidy, because "there was no material injury to an Australian industry producing like goods."[31]

WTO PANEL AND APPELLATE BODIES AT WORK

Having studied the background and institutional framework for the WTO, read the following case in order to (1) obtain a snapshot of this new organization enmeshed in an actual trade dispute, and (2) see firsthand what may be the most important case of any to be decided in the early going of the relatively new WTO process:

European Communities: Regime for the Importation, Sale and Distribution of Bananas

European Communities [*Responding Party*]
and
Ecuador, Guatemala, Honduras, Mexico, and the United States [*Complaining Parties*]
Belize, Cameroon, Colombia, Costa Rica, Côte d'Ivoire, Dominica, Dominican Republic, Ghana, Grenada, Jamaica, Japan, Nicaragua, Saint Lucia, St. Vincent and the Grenadines, Senegal, Suriname, and Venezuela
[*Third Participants*]

WORLD TRADE ORGANIZATION
APPELLATE BODY REPORT
WT/DS27/AB/R
(Geneva) 9 September 1997

Go to course Web site at http://home.att.net/~slomansonb/txtcsesite.html; click on European Union Banana Imports Case

◆ *Notes*

1. In September 1997, the Dispute Settlement Body (DSB) adopted the above Appellate Body Report (and the Panel Reports as modified). In October 1997, the European Community informed the DSB, pursuant to Article 21.3 of the *Understanding on Rules and Procedures Governing the Settlement of Disputes* (DSU), that it would fully respect its international obligations with regard to this matter. The European Community stated that it intended to act expeditiously; however, in view of the complexity of the matter at issue, the organization would require time to examine all the options to meet its international obligations. The European Communities then requested consultations with the Complaining Parties in order to reach agreement on a "reasonable period of time" for the implementation of the recommendations and rulings of the DSB (September 1997). These consultations did not lead to an agreement.

   The Complaining Parties thus requested that the "reasonable period of time" issue be determined by binding arbitration pursuant to Article 21.3(c) of the DSU. Absent an agreement between the parties on the appointment of an arbitrator, the Complaining Parties requested (in December 1997) the Director-General of the WTO to appoint the arbitrator as provided for in the DSU. After consultation with the parties, the Director-General decided (in December 1997) to appoint Judge Said El-Naggar (of the Appellate Body in this case) to be the Arbitrator.
2. In the arbitrator's 1998 award, WT/DS27/15 (www.wto.org/wto/dispute/distab.htm), the European Community was given until January 1, 1999, to comply with the above 1997 decision. This additional time was reasonable, primarily because of the obvious complexity of this case.
3. Although this decision is rather complex, it does provide the reader with a sense of the policies and procedures now being implemented by the WTO. Arguably more important than content, this decision by a three-judge panel in Geneva does appear to resolve a highly sensitive matter in a mandatory fashion not plausible under the prior GATT procedure. In March 1999, however, the US imposed a 100 percent tariff on unrelated EU exports—roughly equal to the lost banana trade.
4. In the WTO's decision of April 12, 1999, Guatemala, Honduras, Mexico, and the United States successfully criticized the EU's new measures taken in response to earlier WTO decisions about the EU's preferential banana importation from Caribbean countries. A summary of the various decisions is available in E. Fabrizio & D. Levy, *International Law in Brief*, www.asil.org/ilib27.htm (April 19–30, 1999).

◆ 13.3 REGIONAL ECONOMIC ASSOCIATIONS

Chapter 3 analyzed various categories of international organizations of States. That material introduced the essential characteristics of these associations, while emphasizing military and political associations of States such as the European Union (*see* §3.4). This chapter focuses on *economic* associations of States.

REGIONAL ORGANIZATIONAL STRUCTURES

This section of Chapter 13 is a glimpse of the diverse array of *economic* international organizations. *Regional* economic organizations virtually eclipsed the importance of global devices such as the General Agreement on Tariffs and Trade—and certainly, prior to its 1995 appearance, the World Trade Organization with its attendant mandatory dispute-settlement procedure.

Regarding regional analysis, one should first ascertain the basic objectives of the particular economic network. There are basic categories in ascending order of degree of integration:

- *Preferential trade.* Trade preferences are granted in the form of freer access to the respective members' markets. This is the most basic form of trade association. The US negotiated this form of agreement with its Caribbean neighbors in the 1983 Caribbean Basin Initiative.
- *Free trade area.* Tariffs between the member States are initially reduced and ultimately eliminated. Each member may keep its original tariffs, as against countries outside of the free trade area. There is no organized policy among the members as to other countries. The North American Free Trade Agreement among Canada, Mexico, and the United States is an example.

- *Customs union.* The members liberalize trade among themselves, while erecting a common tariff barrier against all *non*-member States. The 1969 South African Customs Union is an example.
- *Common market.* Usually after a customs union has been established, the members remove restrictions on the internal movement of the means of production and distribution of all commodities. The European Union is the most successful of all common markets.
- *Economic union.* This is a true common market but with a unified fiscal and monetary policy within the union. The result is similar to the linkage among the fifty states of the US. The difference is that an economic union consists of *international* States, rather than states within one federated State. The European Union made a significant step toward becoming a fully integrated economic union through the implementation of the Single European Act commonly referred to as "1992." In 1999, the eleven members of the EU implemented a common currency for all citizens and agencies within those States.[32]

The contemporary regional trading blocs currently number more than thirty. They function in a variety of ways. Blocs range from those that act like super-States to those that are more like political arrangements merely cast in the form of economic blocs. Many commentators characterize trade blocs as sharing a common bond—each of them, however, being the product of protectionist fears. A Washington, D.C., legal practitioner offers the following assessment of the underpinnings of contemporary economic integration:

"The New World Order of Regional Trade Blocs"

JOSEPH BRAND, DISTRICT OF COLUMBIA BAR

8 *American University Journal of International Law & Policy* 155, 155–157 (1992)

. . . Our world today is dividing into trading blocs. Some have the superstructure of nation states. The European Communities (. . . the European Community), with a parliament and courts and the supremacy of Community laws over those of its members, begins to look more and more like a state; others are multinational agreements that may be more political negotiating arrangements than cohesive trading blocs. ASEAN (Association of Southeast Asian Nations) is a relevant candidate. These blocs, however strong or weak, are growing all around the world. Like the empires (from Rome to the Soviet Union) that preceded them, the regional trading blocs of the new economic world order may divide into a handful of protectionist superstates. If by the new political world order we mean increased American hegemony disguised as international cooperation, we may come to know the new economic world order as regional hegemony disguised as free trade. . . .

[A variety of reasons explain the formation of economic associations of States.] First, they are born of political fear. The European Community was proposed . . . just five years after the end of the Second World War. European unity was perceived as the antidote to European war. Fear of war gave birth to the union. Another kind of fear seems relevant to the extension of the US-Canada Free Trade Agreement into a wider hemispheric economic bloc. Critics of the North American Free Trade Agreement (Canada, Mexico, and the United States) believe fear of a successful EC 1992 and the economic eminence of Japan underlies the political imperative that moves these negotiations.

Second, blocs espouse trade liberalization internally, but achieve trade protection externally. For example, the Uruguay Round of trade liberalization is now held hostage to the Europeans' protective treatment of their farmers. . . .

This rather bleak perspective about the motivation for regional trade groupings is not necessarily the only one. Dalhousie University (Canada) Professor Gilbert Winham espouses a different perspective—not as negative, but certainly more buoyant—in his 1992 book on the evolution of trade agreements: "What is the role of international trade agreement[s] in the modern nation-state system? The answer is to *reduce* protectionist national regulation, but even more important [it is] to reduce the uncertainty and unpredictability of the international trade regime, and to promote stability. The greatest cause of uncertainty in the contemporary trading system comes from the self-serving actions of self-interested nation states. It can be said that one nation's sovereignty is another nation's uncertainty."[33]

This perspective explains why, for example, members of the Association of Southeast Asian Nations (ASEAN)—Brunei, Indonesia, Malaysia, Philippines, Singapore, Thailand, and potentially Vietnam—seek regional "economic" stability in the form of the ASEAN trade agreement. They may thereby seek protection by their economic integration with similarly situated powers who also seek freedom from external influences over their sovereign affairs. China and Japan, for example, have exhibited territorial designs over the affairs of these nations over a long period. The ASEAN States have expressed fears that history may repeat itself. From their perspective, there is no reason to believe that the contemporary epoch will necessarily differ. Domination by war or trade may be perceived as only a matter of degree.

Regardless of each particular motivation for pursuing international trade relations, economic integration is clearly going to be a prominent feature in international relations for the foreseeable future. To appreciate its current contours, Exhibit 13.4 (pages 592–593) lists the major economic associations of States and summits.

NAFTA STRUCTURE

Section 3.5 of this book addressed the European Union as the prime example of a successful international organization. This section briefly focuses on one other organization—the North American Free Trade Association (NAFTA)—to illustrate how an association of States accomplishes the economic objectives of its participating national members.

NAFTA is an economic association consisting of Canada, Mexico, and the United States. It is essentially a free trade area. Its members decided initially to reduce tariffs, with the objective of eliminating them after fifteen years. Unlike a customs union, each member State remains free to retain the tariffs of its choosing for non-member countries. Prior to NAFTA, Mexico had an *average* tariff (the combined rate on all tariff items) of about 10 percent. The US average tariff rate was then about 4 percent. The NAFTA agreement established a schedule to reduce tariffs between members and eliminate other barriers such as Mexico's special agricultural licensing system. Upon total elimination of tariffs and non-tariff barriers to importation, exporters will have free market access within this free trade area.

The projected benefits included a 6 percent "real" growth rate (factoring in the effect of inflation) and a doubling of US exports to Mexico. It was estimated that, in the first five years of NAFTA, the US would sell $17 billion *more* in goods and services just in Mexico than it would have without NAFTA. Mexico's exports were expected to amount to an additional $8 billion in the same period as a result of the NAFTA treaty. The US had its largest trade deficit in six years in 1998. The US believes, however, that there were non-NAFTA reasons for this deficit, including the 1998 Asian financial crisis.

NAFTA was not adopted without its critics. US presidential candidate Ross Perot predicted that the US–Mexican wage differential would unwittingly result in the mass exportation of US jobs to Mexico. US corporations would opt to relocate there because of Mexico's cheaper labor costs. He expressed another concern: US companies would be able to take undue advantage of the average Mexican worker, given Mexico's less stringent labor and occupational protection laws. Many opponents also criticized NAFTA, because it would result in greater environmental degradation. For example, the average US-licensed truck on US highways weighs 80,000 pounds when loaded. The Mexican equivalent is 170,000 pounds per truck. The added weight on US border-state highways and the less stringent pollution standards for vehicle licensing in Mexico would combine to bring further environmental damage to the US atmosphere and its highways. This difference is one reason why trucks cannot travel more than twenty miles beyond their national borders—although trucks transport 75 percent of the trade between Mexico and the United States. At that point, shipments must be unloaded and transferred to domestic carriers.

On the positive side, NAFTA spurred production to create more US jobs in certain industries. The NAFTA benefits included new restrictions in various trades that would make it more costly to import foreign (as opposed to North American–made) commodities. The US television industry has battled greatly increased foreign completion from Asia. Asian corporations previously took advantage of contemporary customs laws on both sides of the US–Mexico border—specifically, the 1985 twin-plant *maquiladora* program. Asian companies have been able to complete final assembly of their products in Tijuana—one of the largest television-assembly areas in the world. They shipped 10,000 units per month (in the non-recessionary period prior to 1995). In Tijuana alone, manufacturers including Sony, Hitachi, Matsushita, and Samsung employ thousands of Mexican workers in the maquiladoras. The final assembly of a completed television set in Tijuana allows these Japanese corporations to avoid the higher US tariff required when the same television is assembled in Japan and shipped directly to the US. Under the relevant "rules of origin," Mexico becomes the origin of the finished product for customs purposes. The US generally charges Mexico a lower tariff on imported goods than it does Japan. Under NAFTA, all televisions imported into the US will ultimately have to contain North American–made picture tubes to qualify for duty-free treatment. Some of these Asian producers may shift their production centers from the maquiladoras of Mexico to new production plants in the US, creating jobs and added governmental revenues.

The 3,755-page NAFTA agreement accords preferential treatment to 9,000 categories of goods exchanged among the three member nations.[34] This has certain benefits for the US. For example, the 1988 US–Canada Free Trade Agreement provided that an automobile was entitled to preferential tariff treatment if *50 percent* of its components were made in the US. It was considered to have its "origin" in North America and could be imported from Canada without the imposition of a US tariff. Under the NAFTA agreement, the same car will have to consist of *65 percent* US-made components to qualify for duty-free import into the US.

One may make several functional contrasts between NAFTA and other trade agreements. NAFTA contains protectionist measures. The above automobile example is one of them. There are preferential tariffs between the NAFTA members. Sometime early in the twenty-first century, no tariffs will be assessed on the imports of many industries. Each NAFTA member remains free to assess whatever tariff it wishes on products not imported from member nations. This is the type of regional protectionism that the global World Trade Organization will likely seek to change under the "most favored nation" tariff treatment (*see* §13.2). Another contrast is that the NAFTA does not yield sovereign powers to an international entity that will control the independent actions taken by member governments. The European Union, on the other hand, is an example of economic integration in which member States have ceded substantial sovereignty to the EU's organizational institutions (*see* Exhibit 3.5 in §3.4).

Whether NAFTA will achieve what its proponents claimed will depend on the continuing solidarity of its trading partners (a group that could expand if Chile and several other Latin American neighbors successfully advocate for admission to this trade group). One year after NAFTA went into effect, Mexico experienced major financial problems. The peso was devaluated, largely as a countermeasure to the intense borrowing of the prior Mexican presidential administration. Mexico began to experience a reversal of its ability to control inflation, coupled with a very troubled 1995 in terms of the stability of its stock market and other investment opportunities. In mid-1994, Mexico imposed a new 9 percent tariff on US milk exports to northern Mexico. That came at a time when NAFTA was supposed to reduce tariffs. US milk was temporarily banned from the shelves of Calimax, Tijuana's major supermarket chain store. If protectionist measures continue to emerge, the thrust that was necessary for NAFTA's implementation will likely dissipate, along with the national willingness to continue this experiment in regional economic integration.

On the other hand, the three national members became one another's biggest trading partners. In 1997, the total amount of goods they exchanged grew from $350 billion (1994) to $500 billion. In 1998, that figure rose to $525 billion. All three countries, however, experienced expansions and contractions during the first five years of NAFTA during a period when an authoritative attribution to just NAFTA would be difficult to make.

SUMMITS: ECONOMIC DIPLOMACY

There is another organizational structure for facilitating international economic integration. The major one is the *summit,* examples of which follow.

"G-8" National leaders have used economic summits as a basis for developing special-purpose economic associ-

EXHIBIT 13.4 SELECTED REGIONAL ECONOMIC ASSOCIATIONS OF STATES

Name[a]	Members and Objectives[b]
AEC	African Economic Community (1991) ◆ Economic organ of Organization of African Unity designed to promote solidarity and collective self-reliance of OAU nations[c]
ANCOM	Andean Common Market: Bolivia, Colombia, Ecuador, Peru, Venezuela ◆ Chile withdrew (1969) as moved toward integration ◆ Conflicting national interests have inhibited achieving common market
APEC	Asia–Pacific Economic Cooperation: Australia, Brunei, Canada, China, Hong Kong, Indonesia, Japan, Malaysia, Mexico, New Zealand, Papua New Guinea, Philippines, Singapore, South Korea, Taiwan, Thailand, US (1990) ◆ Chile has applied ◆ Pacific Rim trade cooperation[d]
ASEAN	Association of Southeast Asian Nations: Brunei, Indonesia, Malaysia, Philippines, Singapore, Thailand (1976) ◆ Vietnam potential member ◆ Promotes regional economic stability and protection from external influences (China, Japan); 1992—program to create common market responding to economic alliances in Europe, North America; 1998—Hanoi Plan of Action to address economic crisis[e]
CARICOM	Caribbean Community and Common Market: Anguilla, Barbados, Belize, Dominica, Grenada, St. Kitts-Nevis, St. Lucia, St. Vincent, Trinidad, Tobago (1974) ◆ Elimination of internal trade barriers and common external tariff[f]
ECOWAS (Lagos, Nigeria)	Economic Community of West African States: 16 West African nations (1975) ◆ Promotes cooperation and development; seeks creation of a customs union[g]
EFTA	European Free Trade Association: Austria, Denmark, Iceland, Norway, Portugal, Sweden, Switzerland (1959) ◆ Great Britain, initially refused membership in EU, led this rival scheme before withdrawing after becoming an EU member[h]
European Union (Brussels)	Austria, Belgium, Denmark, Finland, France, Germany, Greece, Ireland, Italy, Luxembourg, Netherlands, Portugal, Spain, Sweden, United Kingdom (1957) ◆ Only free trade zone with no tariff barriers (*see* §3.4)[i]
Group of Eight (G-8)	Canada, France, Germany, Great Britain, Italy, Japan, Russia, US (1974) ◆ Annual summits on economic policies of major industrial democracies (was "G-7" before Russia joined)[j]
Gulf Cooperation Council	Bahrain, Kuwait, Oman, Qatar, Saudi Arabia, United Arab Emirates (1981) ◆ Standardized subsidies; eliminating trade barriers; negotiating with European Union and other regional organizations to obtain favorable treatment[k]

ations. Solidarity of approaches to a variety of problems is promoted by emphasizing trade and financial issues. For nearly twenty-five years, the leaders of the world's major industrialized democracies have met at various locations for their annual "G-7" summit.

The Group of Seven consisted of the world's richest countries: Canada, France, Japan, Germany, Great Britain, Italy, and the United States. In mid-1994, the "G-7" became the "G-8" with the admission of Russia. At the Naples meeting of the association, President

EXHIBIT 13.4 SELECTED REGIONAL ECONOMIC ASSOCIATIONS OF STATES (CONTINUED)

Name[a]	Members and Objectives[b]
IECO (Islamabad, Pakistan)	Islamic Economic Cooperation Organization: Iran, Pakistan, Turkey (1964) ◆ Seven former Soviet republics joined in 1992 to promote trade among Islamic States
NAFTA	North American Free Trade Agreement: Canada, Mexico, US (1994) ◆ Free trade zone treaty promoting reduction and elimination of tariffs and other trade barriers
OECD (Paris)	Organization for Economic Cooperation and Development (1961): 24 mostly Western European industrialized States ◆ Promotes world trade on non-discriminatory basis for economic advancement of lesser-developed countries
OPEC (Vienna)	Organization of Petroleum Exporting Countries: Algeria, Ecuador, Gabon, Indonesia, Iran, Iraq, Kuwait, Libya, Nigeria, Qatar, Saudi Arabia, United Arab Emirates, Venezuela (1960) ◆ Control production and international pricing of oil[l]
SELA	Acronym for 25-nation Latin American Economic System (1975) ◆ Goal to establish system for pooling resources, creating agencies to sell resources on world market similar to OPEC
Summit of the Americas	Summit of Western Hemisphere's 34 heads of State (1994) ◆ Free Trade Area goal by 2005; 1998: Santiago Declaration and Plan of Action of second summit reaffirming 1994 Miami summit objectives[m]

[a]City: headquarters for those organizations that have a permanent seat

[b](Date): when the association was originally formed

[c]Treaty available in A. Yusef (ed.), 1 *African Yearbook of Int'l Law* 227 (Dordrecht, Neth.: Martinus Nijhoff, 1993).

[d]K. Okuizumi (ed.), *The US–Japan Economic Relationship,* in *East and Southeast Asia: A Policy Framework for Asia Pacific Economic Cooperation* (Wash., DC: CSI Studies, 1992).

[e]*See Framework Agreement on Enhancing ASEAN Economic Cooperation,* 31 *Int'l Legal Mat'ls* 506 (1992).

[f]*See* A. Payne, *The Politics of the Caribbean Community, 1961–1979: Regional Integration Among New States* (New York: St. Martin's Press, 1980).

[g]*See Economic Community of West African States: An Overview of the Economies of West African States* (Lagos, Nigeria: ECOWAS Secretariat, n.d.).

[h]*See* M. Sheridan, J. Cameron & J. Toulin, *EFTA Legal Systems: An Introductory Guide* (London: Butterworths, 1993).

[i]*See* R. Folsom, *European Community Law in a Nutshell* (St. Paul, MN: West, 1992).

[j]*See* A. Mep & H. Ulrich, *Partners for Prosperity: The Group of Seven and the European Community* (Upland, PA: Diane Pub., 1994).

[k]*See* G. Dietl, *Through Two Wars and Beyond: A Study of the Gulf Cooperation Council* (New York: Advent, 1991).

[l]*See OPEC Official Resolutions and Press Releases 1960–1990* (Vienna: OPEC Secretariat, 1990).

[m]**Miami Summit:** *See* R. Rosenberg & S. Stein (ed.), *Advancing the Miami Process: Civil Society and the Summit of the Americas* (Boulder, CO: North-South Center Press–Univ. Miami, 1994). **Santiago Summit:** 37 *Int'l Legal Mat'ls* 947 (1998).

Boris Yeltsin described this occasion as a "large step to[ward] full security of peace on Earth." During the Cold War, there could be no such association. The former Soviet Union was politically opposed to democracy and to the capitalist market system. Now the two superpowers have joined in a *loose* economic association that is designed to help extinguish the mistrust associated with their forty years as political adversaries.

The 1994 summit communiqué of this ostensibly economic grouping of States went much further than just economics. It contained joint positions on Bosnia, Haiti, the Middle East, and North Korea, as well as on nuclear proliferation. At the same time, the two most powerful members, Japan and the US, are involved in a major economic confrontation over the US trade deficit and US access to Japanese markets. Nevertheless, this annual summit procedure continued to provide the opportunity for the leaders to review their drive toward a coordinated economic policy.

Summit of the Americas In December 1994, the heads of the Western Hemisphere's thirty-four democracies met in Miami for the first Summit of the Americas. Their goal was to convert the hemisphere into a free-trade zone called the Free Trade Area of the Americas by the year 2005. Their first (and last) summit on this topic was in 1967. Although the General Agreement on Tariffs and Trade (GATT) has prodded freer trade since 1947, it was the 1993 North American Free Trade Agreement (NAFTA) that provided the impetus for this hemispheric economic summit.

The anticipated benefit for the US is that it would enjoy more trade within Latin America by 2010 than it would in its *combined* trade with Japan and the European Union. This economic goal also involves much more than what is expressed by its apparent economic emphasis. The Summit's final decree called for joint action to combat crime and poverty. The summit leaders further agreed in principle to promote environmental cooperation, democracy, and literacy.

The 1998 Santiago Summit of the Americas reconfirmed the Miami Summit programs. The documents signed at both summits are legally binding and signal strong political commitments by the democratic governments of the hemisphere. The Santiago Declaration builds on the first summit's aspirations: more education to improve the living conditions of its inhabitants; the commencement of negotiations for achieving the Free Trade Area of the Americas (by 2005); and renewing the struggle against corruption, money laundering, terrorism, and other impediments to trade and good relations.[35]

Some impediments may limit the potential for implementation by the target date of 2005. Due to the summit's rather progressive environmental and worker's rights objectives, it will be more difficult for certain States in the hemisphere to adopt or implement every item contained in both final decrees' statements of intent. Further, Latin American States do not support the US policy on Cuba (*see* §10.2)—the only State not invited to this summit of the hemisphere's "democracies."

APEC Summit In 1993, fifteen Pacific Rim nations met in Seattle, Washington. Members of this "rim" of nations all have borders on the Pacific Ocean. This Asia–Pacific Economic Cooperation (APEC) meeting was the largest of world leaders in the US since the 1945 UN Conference in San Francisco. It also brought a great deal of attention to APEC in the aftermath of President Clinton's success in negotiating NAFTA. This economic association of States contains just over 50 percent of the world's economic production capabilities and approximately 40 percent of the world's population. For the US, trade across the Pacific surpassed trade across the Atlantic by 1983. By 1992, Pacific trade amounted to $315 billion—one-third more than the US trade across the Atlantic.

APEC has thereby associated the world's three largest economies—China, Japan, and the US. The 1993 summit was the first opportunity for a US president to meet a Chinese leader since the 1989 Tiananmen Square massacre. That particular event widely impacted subsequent Sino–US trade and human rights discourses. Meeting under the auspices of APEC provided an opportunity to develop a personal dialogue that could ease tensions associated with the Beijing massacre (*see* §11.2).

The APEC nations established an inter-summit *Group of Eminent Persons* at the 1993 summit. Its task is to follow up on the declarations made at the 1993 summit. In September 1994, this group's report pronounced the objective to "commit the region to achieve trade in all goods, services, capital and investment by the year 2020 with implementation to begin by 2000." The 1994 follow-up summit in Indonesia generated the declaration that the *developed* members of APEC would remove such barriers by the year 2010.

This group rejected both the European Union and the NAFTA trade bloc approach to economic integration. Instead, it encourages "open regionalism." APEC is willing to accept new member States—*if* they internationalize their economies. Unlike the EU and NAFTA, APEC does not intend to sustain trade discrimination against outsiders. It encourages APEC members to extend trade liberalization to non-APEC members.

For the US, this economic association could be characterized as another example of the shift from the Cold War "East–West" focus to a "West–East" orientation in economic integration. The US attention to international economic matters is shifting away from the sagging economies of post–Cold War Europe and toward the comparatively vibrant markets on the Pacific Rim. The Asian financial crisis of 1998 did not appear to dampen the APEC resolve to continue the pursuit of a Pacific Rim economic association. One reason is that the arrival of the "Euro" in 1999 would allow nations of the Western Hemisphere to respond to the European Union's very successful European economic integration strategy.

APEC solidarity is limited by its being *the* most diverse regional economic organization of States. China has the least codified trade policies. Japan and South Korea have the most intricate non-tariff barriers to international trade. China and Taiwan are the two largest economies that were not members of the General Agreement on Tariffs and Trade. (China immediately sought access to the WTO, while Taiwan did not). The 1993 APEC summit was boycotted by the Prime Minister of Malaysia due to a concern that APEC will become a device for forcing Western-style democracy and market reforms on its smaller members.

◆ 13.4 NEW INTERNATIONAL ECONOMIC ORDER

HISTORICAL EVOLUTION

The Third World's "New International Economic Order" (NIEO) was announced at the UN in 1974. Its roots may be traced to the early years of the twentieth century. The major political and economic powers engaged in extensive overseas investment and took protective measures to ensure continued profitability. They did not conduct their business operations with a view toward improving conditions in the host countries. The decolonization movement of the 1960s did not extinguish smoldering claims that Western hegemony survived independence. A vast change affected the infrastructure of International Law (*see* Exhibit 2.1 in §2.2). A deluge of underdeveloped States suddenly appeared on the international level, now armed with access to a world forum where they could express their desire for equality.

An embryonic movement of these States, which would come to be known as the NIEO, erupted when these new UN General Assembly members united with other lesser developed States to articulate their perspective about the proper application of various UN Charter principles, including the following:

- "equal rights of . . . nations large and small" (Preamble)
- "international machinery for the promotion of the economic and social advancement of all peoples" (Preamble)
- "international cooperation in solving international problems of an economic . . . character" (Article 1.3)
- "the principle of the sovereign equality of all its Members" (Article 2.1)
- "promoting international cooperation in the economic . . . field" (Article 13b)
- "the United Nations shall promote: higher standards of living . . . and conditions of economic and social progress and development" (Article 55a)

A group of lesser developed States began to articulate their right to *economic* independence by challenging the international status quo—specifically, the international legal principles on foreign investment, nationalization, and required host State compensation for nationalization. They characterized International Law as a Eurocentric web of control spun by the more powerful members of the UN to entrap their former "colonial" partners.

A series of UN developments surfaced in the 1960s that forged an early statement of this "Third World" position during the concurrent decolonization movement. In 1962, the UN General Assembly proclaimed the Resolution on the Permanent Sovereignty over Natural Wealth and Resources. Developing States therein complained about their required abdication of sovereignty—the price tag for encouraging foreign investment. The follow-up Resolution (1973) expressed the essence of the NIEO movement, wherein the General Assembly expressed that it:

> 2. *Supports resolutely* the efforts of the developing countries and of the peoples of the territories under colonial and racial domination and foreign occupation in their struggle to regain effective control over their natural resources;
>
> 3. *Affirms* that the application of the principle of nationalization carried out by States, as an expression of their sovereignty in order to safeguard their natural resources, implies that each State is entitled to determine the amount of possible compensation and the mode of payment, and that any disputes which might rise should be settled in accordance with the national legislation of each State. . . .[36]

The next major development of the 1960s occurred when a group of "Third World" States known as "G-77" (Group of 77) advocated creation of a NIEO to address the objectives of equality expressed in the UN Charter (quoted above). They initiated a fresh debate on the question of whether the Western foundations of modern International Law could continue to be operative, given the inequitable distribution of global wealth. G-77 prompted creation of the United Nations Conference of Trade and Development (UNCTAD) in 1966—a form of collective bargaining—with the States that they characterized as economic rivals dominating their existence. An UNCTAD resolution purported to demolish the basic tenet that *International* Law rather than *national* law provided the yardstick for measuring the scope of compensation for nationalized property. UNCTAD then began to promulgate a series of codes that purported to govern the conduct of multinational corporations. These included a Restrictive Business Practices Code and a Transfer of Technology Code. These were essentially guidelines for an international antitrust law, designed to equitably distribute the proceeds of multinational corporate activity in developing nations.[37] Their efforts would later surface in the 1974–1982 negotiations during the UN Conference on the Law of the Sea, producing provisions designed to redistribute the natural wealth found in and under the high seas (*see* §6.3).

In 1966, the G-77 established the United Nations Industrial Development Organization (UNIDO). UNIDO's primary objective, contained in Article 1 of its Constitution, was the "promotion and acceleration of industrial development in the developing countries with a view to assist in the establishment of a New International Economic Order."[38]

The UN's establishment of UNIDO and UNCTAD was to be the precursor whereby developing nations would have a more prominent role on the economic–political horizon. The creation of these institutions reflected the growing thirst of the newly independent States for a greater role in global economic and political affairs. The G-77 nations firmly believed that the GATT operated primarily to preserve the economic hegemony of the relatively powerful and developed States. They were also dissatisfied with the operation of the post-war Breton Woods Agreement that established the International Monetary Fund. It was not designed to effectively further the economic interests of the developing nations.

Prior to this embryonic period for the NIEO, multinational corporations experienced a commanding expansion since World War II—roughly coinciding with the decolonization movement of the 1960s (*see* §2.3 on self-determination). Parent companies thus established foreign subsidiaries with the ability to rapidly shift capital in and out of the foreign theater of operations. The foreign subsidiary was incorporated under the national laws of the host State. But the corporate operation was not thereby subject to the effective control of the host State. The corporate parent in a developed State fostered this development, while the host State assisted because it sought the infusion of foreign investment.[39] The people of the host State became more and more dependent on the multinational corporation for economic survival—especially in nations where the cost of labor was cheap due to high unemployment. The multinational corporation's arrival created and supported a job base. This presence conferred economic benefits on the underdeveloped State. It improved the quality of life for its citizens where there was high unemployment.

The member States of G-77 nevertheless decided to change the state of International Law, particularly its special protection for aliens. Multinational corporations facing uncompensated nationalizations of their enterprises could resort to the "State responsibility for injury to aliens" feature of International Law (*see* §2.5). Developing States, in turn, perceived this reliance as perpetuating their economic independence long after the successful decolonization movement at the UN.

The G-77 promulgated the 1974 UN Charter of Economic Rights and Duties of States.[40] Its essential purpose was to further regulate the multinational corporations and change the legal status quo. The NIEO's Economic Charter, supported by a majority of the UN's member States, demanded that International Law be modified to accommodate their economic development in relation to the UN's economically dominant members. G-77's goal was to effectuate a redistribution of global wealth. One of the primary methods would be to recapture some of the wealth derived by multinational corporations, which were otherwise free to operate without constraints in the host State's sovereign territory.

The 1974 UN Economic Charter became the NIEO's centerpiece. In its capacity as a sovereign entity, the State could thereby set the standard of compensation for nationalizations of foreign enterprises or certain assets. Whether and how much to compensate a multinational enterprise was now to be characterized as a matter governed by the *host State* law—not the International Law created by the economically developed States long before many under-developed nations even existed. Under Article 2.2 of the NIEO's Economic Charter, each State has the following "right":

> To nationalize, expropriate or transfer ownership of foreign property, in which case appropriate compensation should be paid by the State adopting such measures, taking into account its relevant laws and regulations and all circumstances that the State considers pertinent. In any case where the question of compensation gives rise to a controversy, it shall be settled under the domestic law of the nationalizing State and by its tribunals, unless it is freely and mutually agreed by all States concerned that other peaceful means be sought [to resolve compensation issues] on the basis of the sovereign equality of States and in accordance with the principle of free choice of means.[41]

Article 2 is a variation on the "Calvo Doctrine." As a condition of doing business, the foreign enterprise must waive the protection of International Law that prohibits the discriminatory treatment of aliens. A Calvo clause, stated either in the contract or mandated by host State law, precludes a nationalized entity from seeking the diplomatic assistance of its home State. The enterprise is thereby treated as if it were a citizen of the nationalizing State—in which case, it must look to *national* law for a remedy. The nationalizing State's decision, *whether* and *how* to compensate, is thereby based on its national law rather than International Law (*see* §4.4 on confiscation of property).

The promoters of the NIEO hoped to alter the reliance of these past decisions, as well as to modify or create a legal principle that would deem all such compensation decisions as falling solely within the discretion of the host State. If, for example, a nationalizing State's court or other tribunal were to find that the multinational enterprise had taken unfair advantage of its position over a period of time, then the host State would not *necessarily* have to pay any compensation for its taking of property. Compensation would not *have to be* "prompt, adequate, and effective"—the common articulation of the Western-derived principle. Latin American States had already objected to "international" authority via the Calvo Clause. Now was the time to build on that model via the NIEO perception that host State law should govern such matters.[42]

The NIEO's obstacle would be the commonly applied standard, requiring prompt, adequate, and effective compensation for a governmental taking of foreign corporate assets. The source for this principle is ascertainable from customary State practice and international arbitrations. No multilateral treaty exists to express the consensus of States. The decisions of various international tribunals typically reasoned that a nationalizing State must compensate the owner of foreign assets under the "prompt, adequate, and effective" rule. (*See* §4.4—Iran–US Claims Tribunal). This meant the fair-market value of the seized property in freely transferable currency—the preferred yardstick of the Western capital exporters.

The posture of the International Court of Justice is that there is no clear rule on this point. The Court explains why in the following passage from a 1970 case involving Belgian stockholders, a Canadian corporation, and a Spanish nationalization: "Considering the important developments of the last half-century, the growth of foreign investments and the expansion of the international activities of corporations, in particular of holding companies, which are often multinational, and considering the way in which the economic interests of States have proliferated, it may at first sight appear surprising that the evolution of law has not gone further and that *no generally accepted rules* in the matter have crystallized on the international plane."[43]

Some Western commentators have relied on the 1928 *Chorzow Factory* case, decided by the Permanent Court of International Justice, for a clear statement of the compensation principle attacked by the NIEO. The Court therein stated that established international practice required compensation that would "wipe out all the consequences of the illegal act. . . . To this obligation, in virtue of the general principles of international law, must be added that of compensating loss sustained as the result of the seizure."[44] This reliance is misplaced because that case involved an *illegal* taking of alien property. In that instance, a treaty-based obligation precluded the sovereign State from exercising its customary power of nationalization.

NEW, NEW INTERNATIONAL ECONOMIC ORDER

During the 1980s, the multinational corporations in developed nations—particularly in the US—reacted to the G-77's UN-based articulation of the NIEO in a way that was not anticipated by its proponents. Corporate management diverted the flow of foreign investment from participating "Third World" nations to other developed nations. What was thought to be a clear legal standard—permitting nationalization but *requiring* compensation of foreign investment—had blurred. Corporate management decided to avoid the potential impact of the NIEO, stimulating a capital flight into other nations. The instability wrought by the NIEO backfired on the G-77, although it had grown to 120 nations during the 1970s and 1980s.[45]

As a result, the lesser developed countries began to negotiate bilateral investment treaties (BITs) with the capital-rich States in order to reattract foreign investment. These treaties are typified by clauses that protect the right of the multinational corporation to fair-market-value compensation in readily transferrable currency in the event of a nationalization.[46] This has been the wave of the 1990s. The Uruguay Round of the GATT process presented a similar device. Trade Related Investment Measures (TRIMs) have been employed to protect foreign investors and reverse the capital flight of the 1980s.

This bilateral treaty approach has not been accepted by all original members of the G-77. The BITs are virtually treasonous competitors with the UN process that pioneered the NIEO. One might argue that a *new* New International Economic Order surfaced, signaling a movement in the direction of the *old* international economic order that prevailed prior to the heyday of the G-77 movement. The new NIEO appears to be coming full circle, returning to the *old* order. Foreign investment could not be attracted without sufficient protection from uncompensated nationalizations.

One could characterize the 1974 UN Economic Charter that "established" the NIEO as showing evidence of excessive wear. Just as the global WTO–GATT process is scrambling to subdue the State penchant for regional economic integration, the NIEO is falling by the wayside. In both instances, sufficient attention may not have been paid to the reality that inherent developmental differences exist within the community of nations. Thus, attempts to develop bi-polarized paradigms may be doomed to failure or at least great frustration. The diverse nature of the State infrastructure, which drives the international legal system, need not be pressed into a dominant model for worldwide application. The key feature of a successful international legal system is the recognition by its decision makers that emphasizing differences may eclipse values common to all. Central European University (Budapest) Professor Helen Hartnell has aptly characterized this problem with the NIEO: "The failed Charter of Economic Rights and Duties of States, like the failed Soviet Union, was built by 'levelers.' Their failure is rooted in [not conceding] the inevitability of diversity. Today's scrambling toward political, economic and legal integration in the eastern and western hemispheres might be seen to stem from fear of the consequences of too much difference, or [alternatively] from a recognition that cooperation can erase destructive differences. In any case, integration always has its limits . . . the point at which differences begin to overshadow common values and interests."[47]

◆ 13.5 CORRUPT INTERNATIONAL TRANSACTIONS

> *Concerned* at the seriousness of problems posed by corruption, which may endanger the stability and security of societies, undermine the values of democracy and morality and jeopardize social, economic and political development, . . .
>
> *Convinced that,* since corruption is a phenomenon that currently crosses national borders and affects all societies and economies, international cooperation to prevent and control it is essential, . . .
>
> *Adopts* the International Code of Conduct for Public Officials annexed to the present resolution, and recommends it to member States as a tool to guide their efforts against corruption. . . .
>
> —UN General Assembly Resolution 51/59, On Action Against Corruption, reprinted in 36 *Int'l Legal Mat'ls* 1039 (1996)

The United States was virtually the only voice against corruption in international transactions when it enacted the 1977 Foreign Corrupt Practices Act (FCPA). That legislation placed US business enterprises at a distinct disadvantage—until other States and international organizations followed suit. While there have been regional treaties addressing this problem, the most prominent international instrument is the global Convention on Combating Bribery of Foreign Public Officials in International Business Transactions, which was opened for signature *twenty* years after the FCPA.

This section of the book will cover the US 1977 FCPA, briefly mention regional devices, and focus on the 1997 Bribery Convention.

INTRODUCTION

Corrupt business transactions are not limited to a few countries. This is a global phenomenon that encompasses every region of the world.[48] The Principle Deputy Assistant US Secretary of Commerce and an experienced Washington, D.C., law firm member succinctly describe the scope of this problem in contemporary terms:

> By all accounts, however, the corruption problem is most prevalent in the world's transitional economies. . . . While the problem is difficult to quantify (*i.e.,* there are no ways of collecting meaningful statistics on corrupt payments), anecdotal evidence indicates that the demand for illicit payments has significantly increased in recent years as these markets have opened their doors to foreign investment and procurement. From Russia to Eastern Europe to China, western businessmen are seeking to participate in these growth markets, thus creating significant opportunities for payments. The size, variety, and prevalence of these foreign payments . . . undoubtedly retards the formation of democratic institutions, economic development, and the rule of law in many societies.
>
> The problem is perhaps most acute in post-communist societies. After decades of communist dictatorship, with law serving as an instrument of, rather than a check on, arbitrary state power, the rule of law is fragile and largely undeveloped in these countries. . . . While reformist governments are rewriting new anti-corruption laws, business regulations, and ethical guidelines, these regulations contain significant gaps, and the development of institutions to implement and enforce these new laws is a long-term process.[49]

US Foreign Corrupt Practices Act (FCPA) In 1976, the US Securities and Exchange Commission published a report that more than 400 US companies—including 117 of the Fortune 500 companies—made "questionable" payments to foreign officials.[50] In 1977, US President Gerald Ford and the US Congress responded with an act that (1) was designed to restore public confidence in US business, (2) would have a significant impact on the ability of US business enterprises to do business abroad, and (3) lead to claims of cultural relativism, because the US was perceived as trying to legislate morality on an international scale.

While portions of the FCPA appear in various titles of the *United States Code,* the following representative provisions illustrate its basic content:

1977 Foreign Corrupt Practices Act and International Anti-Bribery and Fair Competition Act of 1998

UNITED STATES CONGRESS
(implementing the 1997 Bribery Convention analyzed below)

Go to course Web page at http://home.att.net/~slomansonb/txtcsesite.html; click on Foreign Corrupt Practices Act

Paying a foreign government official is thus illegal if the payment is intended to induce the recipient to misuse his or her position to direct business to the person who pays the bribe. Foreign officials include any officer or employee of a foreign government, department, agency, member of a royal family, or legislative body who is acting in an official capacity. Payment to an official to induce even a *private* company to award a contract is also prohibited. The Act excludes payments for routine governmental actions. Although referred to as "grease" payments, fees for obtaining a license or official document, processing governmental papers, or scheduling inspections do not violate the FCPA—as long as such payments are authorized under the written laws of the country where the payment is made.

There were some clarifying amendments in 1988, although US businesses nevertheless complained that—among other things—every country has a law that prohibits bribes *by* its own government officials; however, only the US forbids payments *to* foreign officials. Therefore, in emerging markets where corruption flourishes, US business enterprises shoulder the added burden of foreign competitors being free from such anti-bribery constraints (until the 1998 treaty discussed below).

The FCPA has been prosecuted more heavily than recognized by the general public. In 1995, for example, Lockheed Martin Corporation of Bethesda, Maryland, pled guilty to bribing an Egyptian official to ensure the purchase of three C-130 cargo planes. This resulted in a criminal fine of $21.8 million, a civil settlement of $3 million, and a prison sentence and criminal fine for one of two responsible corporate executives.[51]

In February 1999, the CIA received allegations that, between May 1994 and April 1998, bribes were used to influence the outcomes of 239 international contract competitions that totaled $108 billion. Seventy percent were allegedly offered or paid to ministry or executive branch officials.

Regional Attempts to Control Corruption The UN General Assembly resolution (*see* §13.5 text box excerpt) and the Secretary-General's report on which it was based[52] did little to control a problem that all nations acknowledged, but few were willing to act upon.

Regional organizations were willing to create draft treaties, however. These include the following:

- European Union Convention on the Fight Against Corruption Involving Officials of Member States of the European Union (1997);
- Interim Committee of the Board of Governors of the International Monetary Fund Code of Good Practices on Fiscal Transparency (1998 Declaration on Principles);
- Organization of American States Inter-American Convention Against Corruption (1996).[53]

While none of these instruments effectively eradicated this commercial nemesis, they did develop an environment conducive to the production of a draft convention for global consideration.

The 1997 OECD Bribery Convention The twenty-nine members of the Organization for Economic Co-operation and Development (OECD) drafted the most global of corruption treaty alternatives to date. These industrialized nations were joined in the drafting process by five non-members—Argentina, Brazil, Bulgaria, Chile, and the Slovak Republic.[54]

The preambular wording states the underlying premise regarding bribery in international business transactions: It undermines good governance and economic development, while distorting competitive conditions in the international marketplace. The twin purpose of this convention is to pressure member nations to criminalize bribery and to facilitate equivalent measures among the ratifying States.

The treaty essentially defines bribery and conspiracy to commit it as follows:

Article 1
The Offence of Bribery
of Foreign Public Officials

1. Each Party shall take such measures as may be necessary to establish that it is a criminal offence under its law for any person intentionally to offer, promise or give any undue pecuniary or other advantage, whether directly or through intermediaries, to a foreign public official, for that official or for a third party, in order that the official act or refrain from acting in relation to the performance of official duties, in order to obtain or retain business or other improper advantage in the conduct of international business.
2. Each Party shall take any measures necessary to establish that complicity in, including incitement, aiding and abetting, or authorization of an act of bribery of a foreign public official shall be a criminal offence. Attempt and conspiracy to bribe a foreign public official shall be criminal offences to the same extent as attempt and conspiracy to bribe a public official of that Party.
3. The offences set out in paragraphs 1 and 2 above are hereinafter referred to as "bribery of a foreign public official".
4. For the purpose of this Convention:
   a. "foreign public official" means any person holding a legislative, administrative or judicial office of a foreign country, whether appointed or elected; any person exercising a public function for a foreign country, including for a public agency or public enterprise; and any official or agent of a public international organization;

b. "foreign country" includes all levels and subdivisions of government, from national to local;
c. "act or refrain from acting in relation to the performance of official duties" includes any use of the public official's position, whether or not within the official's authorized competence.

There are clear requirements as to jurisdiction and sanctions. Article 3 of the Bribery Convention provides the sanction that each ratifying nation must take the necessary measures to provide that the bribe, the proceeds from bribery of a foreign public official, or its corresponding property value are subject to seizure and confiscation—or, alternatively, that monetary sanctions of comparable effect are applicable.

Regarding jurisdiction, Article 4 provides for both domestic and international jurisdiction, premised on the familiar jurisdictional principles of International Law (*see* §5.2 of this textbook). Thus, each ratifying State "shall take such measures as may be necessary" to establish its jurisdiction over the bribery of a foreign public official when the offence is committed in whole—or in part—within its territory. A State possessing the jurisdiction to prosecute its nationals for offenses committed *abroad* "shall take such measures as may be necessary" to establish its jurisdiction in cases of the bribery of a foreign public official. Further, should there be concurrent jurisdiction, "the Parties involved shall, at the request of one of them, consult with a view to determining the most appropriate jurisdiction for prosecution." Article 9 then requires member States to provide mutual assistance where needed. This would entail extradition to the most appropriate State under Article 10. To complete this comprehensive guide for ensuring prosecution, each ratifying nation "shall review whether its current basis for jurisdiction is effective" in the fight against the bribery of foreign public officials. If not, then that State must take remedial steps to create or modify its jurisdictional rules to comply with its treaty obligations to prosecute such cases.

What does it all mean? First, under Article 12 of the Bribery Convention, ratifying States will cooperate in carrying out a program of systematic follow-up to monitor and promote full implementation. This will most likely be done within the framework of the OECD Working Group on Bribery in International Business Transactions. Second, the US was one of the first nations to have created legislation to ratify and implement the 1997 Bribery Convention (*see* 1998 Act on Course Web Page). It has thus taken a leadership position, not unlike the lonely vigil it commenced with the 1977 Foreign Corrupt Practices Act. Assuming the requisite degree of acceptance by other ratifications, US enterprises will be freed from the double standard that has resulted since 1977 in the loss of successful bids because of graft associated with the competition for project work in foreign markets. The Convention went beyond the US 1977 FCPA by making it also illegal to receive a bribe. Third, not only will there be a uniform standard for defining and combating bribery in international business, but also the same rules will apply to both State officials and those of international organizations.

◆ SUMMARY

1. International economic relations have continuously influenced the creation and evolution of modern International Law. Early treaties, and the medieval "Lex Mercatoria," or merchant law that flourished in Mediterranean seaports, contained the norms for resolving disputes with distant buyers and sellers. National leaders and their diplomats soon recognized that a solid trade foundation with other areas of the world could lead to many benefits, including peace.
2. Recent applications of International Economic Law include the treaties that standardize the consequences of an international business transaction when it has different legal effects in the respective trading nations (and an anti-bribery regime, discussed below). States and traders typically use letters of credit to conclude international business transactions. Trade is now used as a political vehicle for improving the human rights and environmental performance of other nations.
3. The *global* trade organization established in 1994–1995 consists of "GATT 1994" and "WTO 1995." GATT is the General Agreement on Tariffs and Trade. WTO 1995, GATT's successor organization, is the World Trade Organization.
4. The GATT is basically a series of agreements that were periodically renegotiated and revised during multilateral trade negotiation "rounds" among the nations of the world. Its essential objective has been to combat trade barriers by limiting tariffs and discriminatory barriers to trade.

5. The original GATT was not an international organization in one sense because it could not command its "Participating States" to comply with its various negotiated trade rounds from 1947 to 1994. The WTO differs, largely because the State members *must* confer their dispute resolution authority to the WTO's panels in Geneva. The WTO now covers *additional* trade matters including services, intellectual property, and investment rules.
6. The essential WTO articles are I, II, III, and VI. Article I requires that "most favored nation treatment" be accorded to the traders of other member States. A nation must thereby charge the same tariffs on like goods imported from other members. That nation is free, however, to charge a higher tariff on imports from non-member nations.
7. Article II prohibits member nations from charging greater tariffs than those published in their tariff schedules, referred to as "concessions." They may charge *lower* tariffs in the case of certain lesser developed countries. These are called "preferential" tariffs. This is one of the major problems in the European Union–US banana litigation, which was resolved by the WTO Appellate Body and arbitrator in 1997 and 1998.
8. Article III prohibits non-tariff barriers (NTBs) to imports. NTBs are charges assessed on foreign commodities in addition to Article II import duties. NTBs discriminate against foreign goods because like goods made within the same market are not subject to these practices.
9. Article VI prohibits "dumping"—the exporter's sale of goods in a foreign market at prices below their fair-market value. When this occurs, importing nations may assess an additional "countervailing duty" on the dumped product to offset the effect of this anti-competitive practice.
10. States are also engaged in a frenzy of *regional* economic integration. They have undertaken preferential trade agreements, establishing free trade areas, customs unions, common markets, and economic unions to facilitate international commerce.
11. The essential premise of the New International Economic Order (NIEO) was proclaimed in the 1974 UN Economic Charter on the Rights and Duties of States. The host State would thereby have the sovereign right to determine *whether* and *how much* compensation is payable for the taking of foreign property. The NIEO was conceived for the purpose of increasing host State control over multinational enterprises.
12. The NIEO's announcement encouraged the large multinational corporations to withdraw their capital once the usual compensation standards were questioned by Third World nations. The Western capital-exporting nations believe the norm to be "prompt, adequate, and effective compensation in readily transferrable currency." They invested in other developed nations during the 1980s.
13. In the 1990s, a number of the G-77 countries began to negotiate bilateral investment treaties (BITs) to reattract foreign investment. These treaties are evidence of a withdrawal from the NIEO's 1974 Economic Charter.
14. Corrupt business transactions and bribery detract from natural business performance, in addition to negatively impacting social and other values. The US thus passed the 1977 Foreign Corrupt Practices Act, amended it in 1998, and so became the first nation to implement its obligation to do so under the 1997 OECD Bribery Convention. The treaty's intended impact is to make international business transactions more transparent and competitive.

◆ PROBLEMS

Problem 13.A (end of §13.3)

Hypothetical Problem: Brazil and the United States are parties to GATT 1994 and WTO 1995. In 1994, Brazil announced a major discovery. After years of research in its rain forests, Brazilian chemists developed a generic drug substitute for a popular but expensive drug made by a US company in the US. The brand name of the US drug is "A-1." The Brazilian generic substitute is called "B-2." Both drugs are the best nonprescription treatments for the "common cold."

Brazen Inc. is a Brazilian State-owned corporation. Brazil uses the profits to raise revenue for the social and economic advancement of its people. Brazen's corporate management realizes the extraordinary potential for B-2 to become a substitute for A-1. The latter drug has been used by most US consumers to treat their cold symptoms. Brazen begins its marketing plan by selling B-2 to associated US companies that wish to compete with the US maker of A-1. Several US importers are licensed to market B-2 to US consumers. The price charged is slightly less than what US consumers pay for a bottle of A-1. The US tariff rate is low enough to make the exportation and sales of B-2 sufficiently profitable to encourage Brazen's entry into the US market.

Brazen exports B-2 to the US for $2 per unit shipped. It costs Brazen the equivalent of $1 per unit shipped to produce B-2 in Brazil and then market it in the US. In 1995, some parts of the US market slowly begin to accept B-2 as the cheaper generic substitute for A-1. Brazen and its US associates then decide to lower the price charged to US consumers to 95 cents per unit. This price reduction yields immediate benefits for US customers. They now pay *substantially* less for B-2 than for A-1. More consumers can now afford this relatively inexpensive but very effective cold remedy. B-2's unusually low prices quickly generate a large US demand. A-1's sales plummet, because US consumers can obtain B-2 at a substantially lower cost than A-1. The maker of A-1 reduces its production capacity and begins to look for profits in some other line of pharmaceuticals.

In 1996, Brazil's Minister of Commerce authorizes an increase in B-2 prices via gradual steps. By the end of the year, the cost to US consumers increases beyond the initial cost of B-2. Brazen begins to profit again from the large volume of B-2 sales in the US. It had lost money during the 1995 marketing campaign. Brazen's 1995 "below cost" pricing strategy had resulted in US consumers relying almost exclusively on B-2. Brazen's cost remained constant at $1 per unit shipped. The retail price of B-2 has now settled at $2.50 per unit shipped and will remain the same for the foreseeable future. Charging more would likely lead other companies to pursue this particular market.

The maker of A-1 reconsiders its decision to completely withdraw from manufacturing A-1. It begins by having its lobbyist in Washington, D.C., convince the US Customs Service to issue a new series of special regulations that govern the importation of foreign cold remedies. These tests are not used on A-1. The expressed purpose of these new requirements is to ensure the quality control and consumability of imported drugs. The new customs procedures reduce the risk of unauthorized or unsafe pharmaceuticals entering the US. First, the new regulations require special customs inspections for imported cold remedies. Second, the new regulations impose strenuous quality testing of foreign cold remedies arriving at US ports of entry. All of these new procedures—the special inspections and quality testing—are uniformly applied to all pharmaceuticals, regardless of the source of origin. The new regulations result in the rejection of most of the Brazilian B-2 shipped to the US but very little of similar imported drugs.

Brazil lodges a complaint with the US Department of State, claiming discriminatory treatment that has targeted foreign-made cold remedies from Brazil. Brazen Inc. is unable to reap the benefits of the Brazilian discovery of B-2 for Brazil's economy. The US consumer is paying more for A-1 than the previous cost of B-2. Brazil therefore claims as follows: US consumers no longer have the ability to choose between B-2 and A-1; this predicament has resulted in the lack of any significant competition for the maker of A-1 in US markets; and there has been a lack of access to B-2, which can only hurt the US customer.

Questions

1. Did Brazil's state-owned company violate the GATT and WTO?
2. Did the US, through its new customs regulations, violate the GATT and WTO?

Problem 13.B (end of §13.5) You are the legal officer for Deftco, a US corporation doing business in Russia. You are transacting business in St. Petersburg when you meet Michael. He is the personal secretary for the Russian CEO of a state-owned company. This company is accepting bids for refurbishing the Hermitage—the government's world renowned art museum near the center of the city. Michael is the CEO's brother. Michael maintains copies of all documents involved in the bidding process.

Michael notices that your company has not yet paid the standard "Maintenance Fee"—a payment that does not (and will not) appear in any of the documents regarding this bidding process. Russian law does not prohibit this payment, nor is there any provision that authorizes such payments. You return to your hotel room, open your laptop computer, and research the Foreign Corrupt Practices Act and the OECD Bribery Convention.

You return to Michael's office to explain why you cannot pay this fee: It will subject you to prosecution. Your company is the strongest contender for successfully bidding on the Hermitage refurbishing job. Michael, a Russian lawyer, has studied law in the US, where he obtained a graduate law degree after completing law school in Russia. He has always been fascinated by what he describes as "the condescending and arrogant attitude of American lawyers, who think that they can impose their cultural values on the world."

Two students will assume your role and that of Michael. They will deliberate whether the Maintenance Fee is illegal.

◆ BIBLIOGRAPHY

§13.1 Economics and International Law

COURSEBOOKS AND SUMMARIES

R. Folsom et al., *International Business Transactions: A Problem-Oriented Coursebook* (2nd ed. St. Paul: West, 1991).

R. Folsom et al., *International Business Transactions in a Nutshell* (4th ed. St. Paul: West, 1992).

J. Jackson et al., *Legal Problems of International Economic Relations: Cases, Materials and Text* (3rd ed. St. Paul: West, 1995).

DOCUMENTS

P. Kunig, N. Lau, & W. Meng (eds.), *International Economic Law: Basic Documents* (2nd ed. Berlin: de Gruyter, 1993).

S. Zamora & R. Brand (eds.), *Basic Documents of International Economic Law* (Chicago: CCH, 1990) (two volumes).

TREATISES

S. Dell, *The United Nations and International Business* (Durham, NC: Duke Univ. Press, 1990).

T. Howell (ed.), *Conflict Among Nations: Trade Policies in the 1990s* (New York: Westview Press, 1992).

Y. Lambert, *The United Nations Industrial Development Organization: UNIDO and Problems of International Economic Cooperation* (Westport, CT: Praeger, 1993).

P. Stephan, D. Wallace, & J. Roin, *International Business and Economics: Law and Policy* (Charlottesville, VA: Michie, 1993).

H. van Houtte, *The Law of International Trade* (London: Street & Maxwell, 1995).

§13.2 World Trade Organization and GATT

DOCUMENTS

ABA Int'l Section, *Most-Favored-Nation Certification and Human Rights: A Case Study of China and the United States* (Chicago: ABA, 1996).

P. Raworth & L. Reif, *The Law of the WTO: Final Text of the GATT/Uruguay Round Agreements, Summary & Searchable Diskette* (New York: Oceana, 1995).

TREATISES AND ARTICLES

J. Jackson, *The World Trading System: Law and Policy of International Economic Relations* (6th rev. ed. Cambridge, MA: MIT Press, 1994).

T. Stewart (ed.), *The World Trade Organization: Multilateral Trade Framework for the 21st Century and US Implementing Legislation* (Chicago: A.B.A. Section Int'l Practice, 1996).

F. Swacker et al., *World Trade Without Barriers: The World Trade Organization (WTO) and Dispute Resolution* (Charlottesville, VA: Michie Butterworth, 1995).

"Symposium on the First Three Years of the WTO Dispute Settlement System," 32 *Int'l Lawyer* 609–958 (1998).

R. Weaver & D. Abellard, "The Functioning of the GATT System," in T. Stewart (ed.), *The GATT Uruguay Round: A Negotiating History (1986–1992)* (Boston: Kluwer, 1993).

§13.3 Regional Economic Associations

J. Adu, *OPEC Official Resolutions and Press Releases 1960–1990* (Vienna: OPEC Secretariat, 1990).

R. Bernal, "Regional Trade Agreements in the Western Hemisphere," 8 *Amer. Univ. J. Int'l L. & Policy* 683 (1993).

V. Nanda, R. Lake, & R. Folsom, *European Community Law after 1992: A Practical Guide for Lawyers Outside the Common Market* (Boston: Kluwer, 1993).

S. Sullivan, *From War to Wealth: 50 Years of Innovation* (Paris: OECD, 1997) (Organization of Economic Cooperation and Development).

A. Toth, *The Oxford Encyclopaedia of European Community Law* (Oxford, Eng.: Clarendon Press, 1990).

§13.4 New International Economic Order

P. Ghosh (ed.), *New International Economic Order: A Third World Perspective* (Westport, CT: Greenwood Press, 1984).

"Panel: The New International Economic Order," in *Proceedings of the 87th Annual Meeting of the American Society of International Law* 459 (1993).

Thessaloniki Institute of Public International Law and International Relations, *North-South Dialogue: The New International Economic Order* (Thessaloniki, Greece: Inst. Public Int'l Law, 1982).

§13.5 Corrupt International Transactions

S. Deming, "Foreign Corrupt Practices," 31 *Int'l Lawyer* 463 (1998).

M. Geroe, "Complying with US Antibribery Laws," 31 *Int'l Lawyer* 1037 (1997).

ABA Int'l Section Report, "Inter-American Convention Against Corruption," 31 *Int'l Lawyer* 1121 (1997).

N. Kofele-Kale, *International Law of Responsibility for Economic Crimes: Holding Heads of State and Other High Ranking Officials Individually Liable for Acts of Fraudulent Enrichment* (The Hague, Neth.: Kluwer Law Int'l, 1995).

◆ ENDNOTES

1. M. Braychevskiy, "On the Legal Content of the First Treaty of Russia with the Greeks," 1982 *Soviet Yearbk. Int'l L.* 296 (Moscow: Nauka Pub., 1983) (English translation).

2. *See* V. Nanda, U. Draetta, & R. Lake, *Breach and Adaptation of International Contracts: An Introduction to Lex Mercatoria* (Salem, NH: Butterworths, 1992).
3. *"E. Clemens Horst Co. v. Biddell Bros.,"* 1911–1913 *All England Law Reports* 93, at 101 (Loreburn, Judge) (London: Butterworths, 1962).
4. M. Janis, "Academic Workshop: Should We Continue to Distinguish between Public and Private International Law?" in *Proceedings of the 79th Annual Meeting of the American Society of International Law* 352 (Wash., DC: Amer. Soc. Int'l Law, 1985) (panel discussion).
5. Details on problems and conflict resolution mechanisms in different legal systems are available in P. North & J. Fawcett, *Private International Law* (12th ed. London: Butterworths, 1992).
6. **Convention:** www.cisg.law.pace.edu. **Analysis:** D. Magraw & R. Kathrein (eds.), *The Convention for the International Sale of Goods: A Handbook of Basic Materials* (2nd ed. Chicago: Amer. Bar Ass'n, 1990) (hereinafter *Handbook).*
7. Message from the President of the United States, *Handbook,* 75 (cited in note 6).
8. B. Wunnicke et al., *Standby and Commercial Letters of Credit* 4 (2nd ed. Rexdale, Ont., Canada: John Wiley & Sons, 1996).
9. **The invasion:** An account, including interviews with Fidel Castro, is available in P. Wyden, *Bay of Pigs: The Untold Story* (New York: Simon & Schuster, 1979). **The LOC:** McLaughlin, "How the Marketplace Can Help in International Crises," *Los Angeles Daily Journal,* Dec. 24, 1992, p. 6.
10. *Comm. of European Communities v. Fed. Rep. Germany,* Case No. 178/84 (1987).
11. *See Ahlstom Oy v. EC Comm.* case, in the text of §9.6.
12. The US Supreme Court at least recognized the dilemma faced by a foreign bank when it is subjected to the conflicting demands of US law, which require disclosure of bank statements, and foreign law that would make this a crime for the bank to do so anywhere. *See Société Internationale pour Participations Industrielles et Commerciales v. Rogers,* 357 US 197 (1958).
13. **Chinese case:** *Richmark Corp. v. Timber Falling Consultants,* 959 F.2d 1468 (1992), *cert. den'd* 113 S.Ct. 454. **French case:** *Société Nationale Industrielle Aerospatiale v. US Dist. Ct.,* 482 US 522 (1987). **Commentary:** W. Slomanson, "The US Supreme Court Position on the Hague Evidence Convention," 37 *Int'l & Comp. L.Q.* 391 (1988).
14. Regarding the contributions of this tribunal, *see* A. Mouri, *The International Law of Expropriation as Reflected in the Work of the Iran–US Claims Tribunal* (Dordrecht, Neth.: Martinus Nijhoff, 1994); and J. Westberg, *International Transactions and Claims Involving Government Parties: Case Law of the Iran/United States Claims Tribunal* (Wash., D.C.: Int'l Law Inst., 1991).
15. G. Giesze, "Helms–Burton in Light of the Common Law and Civil Law Legal Traditions: Is Legal Analysis Alone Sufficient to Settle Controversies Arising Under International Law on the Eve of the Summit of the Americas?" 32 *Int'l Lawyer* 51, 92 (1998).
16. For an insightful analysis of a 1989 Zimbabwe Supreme Court decision involving caning, *see* H. Hannum, *"Juvenile v. State,"* 84 *Amer. J. Int'l L.* 768 (1990).
17. A fascinating account of this phenomenon is available in R. Allen & T. Jones, *Guests of the Nation: People of Ireland Versus the Multinationals* (London: Earthscan Pub., 1990).
18. The most comprehensive treatise is R. Bhala & K. Kennedy, *World Trade Law: The GATT–WTO System, Regional Arrangements, and US Law* (Charlottesville, VA: Lexis Law Pub., 1998).
19. C. Korth, "Barriers to International Business," ch. 4 in *International Business: Environment and Management* 84 (2nd ed. Englewood Cliffs, NJ: Prentice-Hall, 1985).
20. **ITO:** U.N. ECOSOC Res. 13, UN Doc. E/22 (1946). **GATT:** 55 *UN Treaty Series* 194 (1950).
21. "Final Act," 33 *Int'l Legal Mat'ls* 1143 (1994). Explanatory introductions to the actual agreements are available in A. Porges, "General Agreement on Tariffs and Trade: Multilateral Trade Negotiations and Final Act," 33 *Int'l Legal Mat'ls* 1 (1994) (negotiations) and 33 *Int'l Legal Mat'ls* 1125 (1994) (Final Act).
22. **WTO quote:** E. Petersmann, *International Trade Law and the GATT/WTO Dispute Settlement System* 7 & 9 (London: Kluwer Law Int'l, 1996). **IMF:** J. Gold, *Interpretation: The IMF and International Law* (London: Kluwer Law Int'l, 1996).
23. A. Lowenfeld, "Remedies Along with Rights: Institutional Reform in the New GATT," 88 *Amer. J. Int'l L.* 477, 479 (1994) (hereinafter *New GATT).*
24. Blocking examples are available in *New GATT,* 478 notes 7 and 8 (cited in note 23 above).
25. **Statement of purpose:** 19 *US Code* §2102(1). **"301" procedure:** "Omnibus Trade and Competitiveness Act of 1988," 19 *US Code* §§2901–3111. *See* "Changing the Rules: The Rise of Administrative Trade Remedies," ch. 6 in I. Destler, *American Trade Politics* 139 (2nd ed. Wash., DC: Inst. Int'l Econ., 1992). **GATT/WTO limitation:** *Agreement Establishing the World Trade Organization, Part II, Annex 2, Final Act Embodying Results of the Uruguay Round of Multilateral Trade Negotiations,* GATT Doc. MTN/FA (Dec. 15, 1993), reprinted in 33 *Int'l Legal Mat'ls* 1, 13 (1994). *Note:* this agreement refers to a "Multilateral" Trade Organization. In a 1994 follow-up meeting, the State representatives substituted the word *World* in the organization's title.
26. **Rules:** Reprinted in 33 *Int'l Legal Mat'ls* 112 (1994). **Consultations:** Rule 4. **Panels:** Rule 6. **Appeals:** Rule 17. **Criticism of appellate process:** P. Pescatore, "The GATT Dispute Settlement Mechanism: Its Present Situation and Its Prospects," 10 *J. Int'l Arb.* 27 (1993).
27. G. Schwarzenberger, "Equality and Discrimination in International Economic Law," 25 *Yearbk. World Affairs* 163 (London: Sweet & Maxwell, 1971).
28. *See* discussion in 4 *Bureau Nat'l Affairs Int'l Trade Rep.* 786 (Wash., DC: BNA, 1987).
29. *Humblot v. Directeur* (Case No. 112/84), 46 *Common Mkt. L. Rep.* 338 (London: European Law Centre, 1986).

30. G. Marceau, *Anti-Dumping and Anti-Trust Issues in Free-Trade Areas* (Oxford, Eng.: Clarendon Press. 1994).
31. *"Rocklea Spinning Mills PTY, Ltd v. Anti-Dumping Authority and Another,"* 107 *Int'l Law Reports* 105 (Australia, Fed. Ct, Gen. Div., 1995).
32. **Caribbean initiative:** Caribbean Basin Recovery Act of 1983, as amended, 97 *Statutes at Large* 369 (1990). **Free trade area:** *See* NAFTA textual discussion in this section. **Customs union:** "1969 Agreement Establishing the South African Customs Union," 2 *Yearbk. Int'l Org.* 975 (1990–1991). **Common market:** *See* R. Keohane & S. Hoffman (ed.), *The New European Community: Decisionmaking and Institutional Change* (Boulder, CO: Westview Press, 1991). **Economic union:** Single European Act, reprinted in 25 *Int'l Legal Mat'ls* 503 (1986). The Treaty of Maastricht anticipated formation of a monetary union—the original objective of the "1992" program. *See* "Treaty on the European Union and Final Act," reprinted in 31 *Int'l Legal Mat'ls* 247 (1991). A valuable analysis is available in J. Brand, "The New World Order of Regional Trade Blocs," 8 *Amer. Univ. J. Int'l L. & Policy* 155 (1992).
33. G. Winham, "Lessons from History," ch. 1 in *The Evolution of International Trade Agreements* 3, 21 (Toronto: Univ. Toronto Press, 1992) (italics added).
34. **NAFTA Text:** www.sice.oas.org/trade/nafta/naftatce.stm.
35. *See* T. Peay, "Declaration and Introductory Note, Second Summit of the Americas: Santiago Declaration and Plan of Action," 37 *Int'l Legal Mat'ls* 947 (1998).
36. **Permanent Sovereignty resolution:** Gen. Ass. Reso. 1803 (XVII), reprinted in 2 *Int'l Legal Mat'ls* 223 (1963). **1973 resolution:** Gen. Ass. Reso. 3171(XXVIII), reprinted in 13 *Int'l Legal Mat'ls* 238 (1974).
37. **Business practices code:** "Report of the Intergovernmental Working Group on the Formulation of a Code of Conduct," 16 *Int'l Legal Mat'ls* 719 (1977). **Technology transfer code:** "Group of 77 Manila Declaration and Program of Action for Commodities, Trade Negotiations, Transfer of Resources and Technology, and Economic Cooperation," 15 *Int'l Legal Mat'ls* 426 (1976).
38. *See* Y. Lambert, *The United Nations Industrial Development Organization: UNIDO and Problems of International Economic Cooperation* 61 (Westport, CT: Praeger, 1993).
39. *See, generally,* M. Sornarajah, *The Internatinal Law on Foreign Investment* (Cambridge, Eng.: Cambridge Univ. Press, 1994).
40. UN Declaration on the Establishment of a New International Economic Order, Gen. Ass. Reso. 3201(S-VI), UN Doc. A/Res/3201(S-VI), reprinted in 13 *Int'l Legal Mat'ls* 715 (1974).
41. Gen. Ass. Reso. 3281, UN Doc. No. A/9631 (1975), reprinted in 14 *Int'l Legal Mat'ls* 251 (1975).
42. **Classic Western articulation:** 2 *Restatement of the Law of Foreign Relations of the United States* §712 (3rd ed. Wash., DC: 1987). **NIEO summary:** G. Sandrino, "The NAFTA Investment Chapter and Foreign Direct Investment in Mexico: A Third World Perspective," 27 *Vand. J. Transnat'l L.* 259 (1994). **Classic Calvo Clause analyses:** A. Freeman, "Recent Aspects of the Calvo Doctrine and the Challenge to International Law," 40 *Amer. J. Int'l L.* 121 (1940), and D. Shea, *The Calvo Clause: A Problem of Inter-American and International Law and Diplomacy* (Minneapolis: Univ. of Minn. Press, 1955).
43. *"Barcelona Light & Traction Company (Belgium v. Spain),"* 1970 *ICJ Rep.* 3, 46–47, para. 89 (italics added). An edited version of the full case is set forth in §4.3.
44. 1 *World Ct. Rep.* 646 (1928).
45. *See, e.g.,* M. Rewat, "Multilateral Approaches to Improving the Investment Climate of Developing Countries: The Cases of ICSID and MIEA," 33 *Harv. Int'l L.J.* 102 (1992).
46. An institutional analysis of BIT development is available in UN Centre on Transnational Corporations, *Bilateral Investment Treaties* (New York: UN, 1988). *See also* K. Vandevelde, *United States Investment Treaties: Policy and Practice* (Deventer, Neth.: Kluwer Law and Taxation, 1991).
47. H. Hartnell, "The New New International Economic Order: Private International Law," in *Proceedings of the 79th Annual Meeting of the American Society of International Law* 352 (Wash., DC: Amer. Soc. Int'l Law, 1985) (panel discussion).
48. Information is available by country in book form and on the Internet. **Book:** J. Bialos & G. Husisian, *The Foreign Corrupt Practices Act: Coping with Corruption in Transnational Economies* 9–11 (Dobbs Ferry, NY: Oceana, 1996) (hereinafter *Corruption in Transnational Economies*). **Internet:** Transparency International (NGO), www.transparency.de/organisation/chapters/all.html.
49. *Corruption in Transnational Economies,* 12–13 (cited in note 48).
50. S.E.C., *Report on Questionable and Illegal Corporate Payments and Practices,* 94th Cong., 2d Session 1 (1976).
51. *See* L. Low, "Led by the US, the World Wages War on Corruption," *National Law Journal* B9; and W. Schmidt & J. Frank, "FCPA Demands Due Diligence in Global Dealings," *National Law Journal* B16, (Mon., Mar. 3, 1997).
52. *Report of the Secretary-General on Action Against Corruption, submitted to the Commission on Crime Prevention and Criminal Justice,* UN Doc. E/CN.15/1996/5 (1996).
53. **EU:** 37 *Int'l Legal Mat'ls* 12 (1998). **IMF:** 37 *Int'l Legal Mat'ls* 942 (1998); OAS: 35 *Int'l Legal Mat'ls* 724 (1996).
54. "Convention on Combating Bribery of Foreign Public Officials in International Business Transactions" (Dec. 18, 1997), 37 *Int'l Legal Mat'ls* 1 (1998).

Glossary

Absolute Theory of Sovereign Immunity Historical theory precluding law suits against one nation in the courts of a second nation, even when the first was engaged in a commercial enterprise.

Accreditation General term describing the process of exchanging diplomats. Foreign diplomats thereby present their *credentials* to the appropriate representative of the host government.

Accretion A method for obtaining legal title to land through slow or imperceptible change. *Avulsion,* or a sudden change caused by natural events, does not affect the prior legal boundaries of the affected territory.

Act of State Doctrine Practice whereby the courts will not sit in judgment of another State that has allegedly violated International Law. Under the "Hickenlooper Amendment" to the US Foreign Assistance Act, courts are expected to hear such cases unless the president intervenes to request that the case be dismissed for political reasons.

Advisory Jurisdiction An alternative form of jurisdiction exercised by international tribunals, typically in response to an organization's request for guidance on some general question of International Law when there are no contentious parties before the court.

Anticipatory Self-Defense Rather than awaiting an "armed" attack (per the 1945 UN Charter requirement), a State takes what it characterizes as "defensive" action designed to avoid the aggressive conduct of another State.

Arbitration A third-party dispute-resolution mechanism whereby States appoint an experienced arbitrator or panel to decide their dispute.

Area Under the Law of the Sea Treaty, "the Area" is the ocean floor and its subsoil beyond the limits of national jurisdiction—that is, the deep seabed area *under* the oceans that does not otherwise fall within any other coastal zone. Its resources are the common heritage of all humankind.

Authority Under the Law of the Sea Treaty, an organization called the International Seabed Authority will control deep seabed mining in "the Area" (*see* **Area**).

Baseline The low-water line along the coast as marked on charts officially recognized by the coastal State. It marks the inner boundary of the various coastal sea zones.

Bay A well-marked indentation of internal water whose penetration constitutes more than a mere curvature of the coast. The indentation must be at least as large as a semicircle whose diameter is a line drawn across the mouth of that indentation. A *historic* bay may be larger, thus excluding any international waters, if State practice has honored the coastal State's territorial claim over the entire body of water.

Calvo Clause Foreign enterprises are treated as if they were citizens of the host State, thus depriving them of the special protection afforded aliens under International Law. Foreign nationals must thereby rely exclusively on local remedies for the resolution of disputes, usually over compensation for a nationalization, thereby waiving their right to diplomatic intervention on their behalf.

Cession The deeding of territory by one nation to another via international treaty. The grantee nation's right to title is thus derived from an agreement of the nations involved in the transfer.

Chambers Typically, a three-judge panel of the International Court of Justice, providing the option of proceeding without a decision by all fifteen members of the Court.

Charge d'Affaires Normally the second-ranking official in an embassy's delegation who takes charge of the mission and premises in the absence of the primary diplomat.

Collective Self-Defense A treaty provision whereby an armed attack on one member of the particular organization of States constitutes an attack on all, thus resulting in a *collective* response.

Comparative Law The comparative study of the *internal* law of States having varied legal systems. Rather than attempting standardization, it compares the variances in legal relationships in different legal systems.

Compulsory Jurisdiction The ability of an international tribunal to require a defendant State to litigate a dispute before the court.

Conciliation A commission of persons who clarify the facts in an attempt to facilitate a resolution, typically through a report that contains proposals for settlement.

Congressional-Executive Agreement Under US treaty practice, the president requests the consent of *both* houses in a joint resolution of Congress—rather than seeking the consent of just the Senate under the federal Constitution's Treaty Clause.

Conquest The forcible taking of another State's territory that is no longer an acceptable basis for acquiring title to land under contemporary International Law.

Constitutive Theory of Recognition Other States must recognize an entity's statehood before it is entitled to *de jure* status as an international legal person.

Consul Official agent of the sending State who is not "accredited" like a diplomat. Consular officers often conduct "diplomatic" negotiations in international trade matters.

Contiguous Zone Twenty-four-nautical-mile zone of water adjacent to coastal State wherein it may exercise certain limited authority, such as when deterring contraband or illegal entry.

Continental Shelf The coastal State's seabed and subsoil of the submarine areas extending beyond its territorial sea throughout the natural prolongation of its land territory. Its range varies from 200 nautical miles from the coastal baseline to 350 nautical miles, depending on the natural extension of the coastal State's underwater land mass.

Contractual Treaty Merely restates existing norms deemed to expressly apply between the contracting nations; does not create new norms of International Law.

Conventions Typically a multilateral lawmaking treaty, although sometimes used to describe bilateral contractual (as opposed to lawmaking) treaties. The former category of convention is a primary source for ascertaining the content of International Law (*see* **Treaty**).

Countermeasures Sanctions taken in response to another State's conduct; not necessarily undertaken as justifiable self-defense. Like other forms of force, the unilateral use of countermeasures is outside the scope of the UN Charter's objective of limiting the use of force to the UN Security Council.

Countervailing Duty An offsetting tax on an imported product suspected of being "dumped" on the market; designed to eliminate the anti-competitive conduct of dumping (*see* **Dumping**).

Custom; Customary International Law The component of International Law that is a blend of State practices and their related expectations. This category of International Law is based essentially on what States do and what they consider legally binding in their mutual relations. It is thus a general practice accepted as law.

Declarative Theory of Recognition Once the elements of statehood are achieved, formal recognition by other States merely acknowledges the previously existing *de facto* status of the territory as an international person.

Diplomatic Asylum Protection from arrest or extradition, typically given to a host State's political refugee by a foreign State's diplomat.

Diplomatic or Consular Immunity General treaty-based protection from host State laws and lawsuits. The "diplomatic bag" is thus immune from search and seizure, as are the premises of the mission and key diplomatic personnel.

Dualism Under this view of the legal relationship between national and International Law, each is a distinct legal system representing two separate legal orders—one binding the individual, and the other binding the State.

Dumping A foreign good sold at a price below fair-market value as part of a market strategy (1) to capture the market and (2) to eliminate competition in that market to achieve a dominant market position.

Economic and Social Council of the United Nations Promotes observance of human rights and the general welfare of the individual. ECOSOC thus conducts studies and issues reports on economic, social, cultural, educational, and health matters.

Effects Doctrine Application of territorial jurisdiction whereby a State may regulate conduct occurring abroad when that conduct has the requisite effect within the State.

Embassy Under the Vienna Convention on Diplomatic Relations, the function or position of the ambassador; used as a common reference to the building where diplomatic functions are carried out.

Environmental Degradation The contemporary concern of public and private environmental organizations that seek to protect the planet from pollution that does not respect any international boundary.

Environmental Impact Statement Under US law, a requirement that federal agencies prepare a report that considers the potential impact of proposed agency action on the local and global environments.

Euro New monetary unit used by eleven of the fifteen European Union member States as common currency.

European Community Law The European Union's body of rules and regulations that govern community legal relations on a regional basis. The sovereign members have given EU organs the power to require State compliance with Community Law.

Exclusive Economic Zone The economic zone that overlaps the Territorial Sea and Contiguous Zones, but extends coastal State authority as far out as 200 nautical miles from the baseline. Other States are therein subject to coastal State regulation of their economic activities, including fishing and deep seabed mining.

Executive Agreement Under US treaty practice, an international treaty concluded by the president *without* the advice and consent of the Senate. US practice thus distinguishes such agreements from the US Constitution's treaty provision that requires the Senate's consent to (certain) treaties.

Exhaustion of Local Remedies Requirement that an individual or corporate entity first seek redress in the courts of the State that allegedly violated International Law prior to resorting to international remedies.

Extradition The arrest and transfer of an individual from one State to another, typically based on a bilateral treaty containing a schedule of extraditable crimes.

Extraterritorial Jurisdiction (1) the State's legal ability to act or regulate conduct beyond its territorial borders; (2) alternatively, a State's illegal exercise of sovereign power beyond internationally recognized limits.

Force A broad term that encompasses an array of unacceptable State behavior prohibited by UN Charter principles—including military, economic, and political uses of force.

General Agreement on Tariffs and Trade (GATT) Originally the only global arrangement to cover import tariffs, and now one of several such agreements on services and other matters. It contains thousands of tariff "concessions" or negotiated tariff schedules within the context of the new World Trade Organization.

General Assembly of the United Nations A deliberative body, with many associated agencies, consisting of all UN member States. The General Assembly issues studies, reports, and resolutions that are designed to implement the UN's overall objectives.

General Principle of International Law A norm existing in the internal law of many nations that is commonly used in all major legal systems. When such a norm has the requisite degree of usage, it may thus be a source of the substantive content of International Law.

Good Offices A variation of the **mediation** technique (*see* below) in which a third party communicates statements of the disputing parties to each other. It is particularly helpful when the respective States do not have diplomatic ties.

Gunboat Diplomacy A prohibited form of force whereby one State instigates a hostile or threatening act, short of war or a violation of sovereignty, that is designed to intimidate another State.

High Seas That portion of the oceans not subject to the control of any State due to the applicable regime of **res communis** (*see* below).

Humanitarian Intervention A claimed basis for legitimizing territorial encroachment; often misused by States to unilaterally intervene in the affairs of another State. The expressed purposes include rescuing the populace at large, certain political figures, or hostages who possess the nationality of the intruding State.

Human Rights Those rights possessed by an individual that cannot be withheld by the State. Most are the subject of the UN-driven International Bill of Human Rights, which consists of a multitude of special-purpose treaties.

Injury to Aliens A form of State responsibility incurred when governmental action discriminates against a foreign citizen on the basis of nationality. A State is thus accountable for the acts of its agents who harm aliens in a way that treats them differently from the State's own citizens.

Innocent Passage Passage through territorial waters that does not disturb the peace, good order, or security of the coastal State (*see* **Strait Passage**).

Inquiry A commission of individuals who are not associated with the State parties to the dispute and who attempt to provide an objective assessment of the facts of the case.

Internal Waters Waters on the landward side of the baseline that marks the inner edge of the coastal State's territorial sea.

International Court of Justice The judicial arm of the United Nations headquartered in the Netherlands. Its fifteen judges rotate and resolve contentious disputes arising under International Law and issue advisory opinions when requested from certain UN organs and agencies.

International Criminal Court A formal judicial body, also referred to as a *war crimes tribunal,* established by treaty (e.g., Nuremberg) or by UN resolution (e.g., the former Yugoslavia). It tries individual defendants for their violations of International Law.

International Law The body of rules that international persons, such as States, recognize as binding in their mutual relations. Its major components are custom and treaties (*see* **Custom, Modern International Law, Opinio Juris,** and **Treaty**).

International Minimum Standard A State may treat both aliens and its own citizens alike, but such equal treatment may nevertheless fall below the minimum level of treatment required by International Law.

International Organization of States A governmental organization created by States to accomplish treaty-based objectives. Some organizations, including those of the European Union, have the juridical power to enforce State compliance with their decisions.

International Personality The legal capacity historically possessed only by States to act on the international level by bringing or defending claims between States. This legal personality, now possessed by certain organizations and individuals, yields reciprocal rights and duties that arise under International Law.

International Relations A broad scope of activities that involve inter-State relations; not limited to just legal expectations.

Jurisdiction The State's right under International Law to regulate conduct that is either within its borders or has an effect within its borders.

Jus Cogens Compulsory law or a peremptory norm from which no State may derogate. Such a norm does not depend on State sovereignty for its existence, thus constituting a derogation from unequivocal sovereignty.

Jus Sanguinis Individual nationality based on the blood or parentage rule applied by some countries.

Jus Soli Individual nationality based on the soil or place-of-birth rule applied by some countries.

Last in Time Rule US practice for resolving conflicts between federal statutes and treaties, because they are equal in rank under the US Constitution.

Lawmaking Treaty Creates new norms designed to modify existing State practice.

Laws of War Essentially, the Red Cross–generated Geneva Conventions that protect private citizens and foreign soldiers during time of war.

Letter of Credit A banking device that expedites completion of the transaction between a buyer and a seller in different countries. The financial transaction guarantees payment to the seller after the buyer applies for and receives the issuing bank's LOC.

Mediation Unlike a fact-finding "commission of inquiry" (*see* **Inquiry**), a mediator is expected to advance his or her own proposal for resolving the dispute.

Minitrial The parties confront each other in an abbreviated trial-like context with a view toward illustrating the weaknesses of the respective positions—before undertaking a comparatively costly arbitration or judicial proceeding.

Mission (1) Per treaty, the actual process of maintaining permanent diplomatic offices in another country; (2) popularly, the physical location of the embassy—the correct term being the *premises.*

Modern International Law Originated with the 1648 Peace of Westphalia. After a long period of war, European nations entered into a period of relative peace based on a broader notion of sovereignty. The "State" would effectively replace local sovereignty, which had been exercised by indigenous groups during the rather bellicose feudal period of the early Middle Ages.

Monism Under this view of the legal relationship between national law and International Law, each is part of a unified system that binds both the State and the individual.

Most Favored Nation (MFN) Treatment A nation promises to trade with a particular partner on the most favorable tariff terms available for like goods, thus taxing that MFN nation's imports at the lowest amount of any nation.

Municipal Law The historic description of the internal law of a nation, as opposed to the International Law applied by the community of nations.

Nation Although often used synonymously with "State," a nation may technically be limited to an entity that has not yet achieved statehood.

Nationality A legal bond based on individual or corporate attachment with the State that confers nationality. It is a genuine connection associated with the existence of reciprocal rights and duties between a State and its nationals.

Nationality Principle of Jurisdiction The State regulation of conduct based on the nationality of the *defendant,* regardless of the location of the conduct.

New International Economic Order A 1974 UN General Assembly resolution that established a revised Charter of Economic Rights and Duties of States. Its objective is to alter the traditional requirement of effective compensation for nationalizations. The internal law of the nationalizing State would thus govern rather than the traditional customary State practice that establishes a right of compensation for the taking of alien property.

Non-Governmental Organization (NGO) An association, not necessarily created by States, that may pursue objectives similar to those pursued by States and governmental international organizations.

Non-Tariff Barrier Special licensing or other restrictions that pose barriers to competition by exported goods—in addition to the import tax on that commodity (or service).

Occupation Exclusive occupation for an extended period of time as a basis for claiming valid ownership of territory. This mode of acquisition is referred to as an "original" claim to territory.

Open for Signature A step in the multilateral treaty process whereby States or international organizations may sign the draft of a treaty after it has been developed by a conference of States or declared by a General Assembly resolution.

Opinio Juris The short form of *opinio juris sive necessitatis.* It is not enough that States consistently engage in a particular practice. To qualify as a binding norm of customary International Law, States must also accept that practice as legally binding them to act or refrain from acting in a certain way. When this is established, the custom is referred to as being with the *opinio juris.*

Optional Clause A provision in the Statute of the International Court of Justice whereby States may give their advance consent to generally litigate their disputes before the Court as opposed to doing so on a treaty-by-treaty basis.

Pacta Sunt Servanda Good faith performance of treaty obligations; the expectation that treaty parties will do nothing to frustrate the purpose of a treaty.

Passive Personality Principle of Jurisdiction The State regulation of conduct based on the *victim's* nationality; normally requires the presence of some other jurisdictional basis for the State to exercise jurisdiction under International Law.

Persona Non Grata The host State declares a diplomat unwelcome. He or she must then leave the host State to return home.

Political Question Doctrine US judicial practice whereby a court will not resolve matters committed by the Constitution to the political branches of government.

Port A long entryway that consists of natural twists and turns and extends to the outermost permanent harbor facility forming an integral part of the harbor system.

Port Tranquility Doctrine While bilateral treaties normally cede primary jurisdiction over vessels to the State of the vessel's nationality, this common treaty exception authorizes the port State to exercise authority when activity aboard such vessels disturbs the port's tranquility.

Prescription Title derived from foreign occupation of a territory for some period of time without objection by the former sovereign occupant.

Private International Law The body of rules that governs the resolution of disputes when individuals or corporations have significant contacts with two or more States. The relevant treaties standardize the applicable law, which would otherwise yield different results—depending on which State's law is applied.

Protective Principle of Jurisdiction The State regulation of conduct when the State's interest is sufficiently strong that neither the conduct nor its demonstrable effect needs to occur within its territory.

Publicist International legal scholar whose writings are a subsidiary source for determining the rules of International Law.

Ratification The final step in the multilateral treaty process whereby an individual State or international organization expressly accepts all or a portion of the draft treaty.

Rebus Sic Stantibus A change in circumstances whereby a State or international organization seeks to avoid or renegotiate its treaty obligations because the objective of the treaty is rendered difficult or impossible.

Reciprocity A provision in the Statute of the International Court of Justice used by a State to limit its consent to the Court's **compulsory jurisdiction** (*see* above). This form of consent to suit imposes the condition that in future litigation that State may invoke a *plaintiff* State's narrower terms of general consent to an ICJ suit. Reciprocity thus enables the consenting State to avoid a suit on the same basis that would be available to the plaintiff State if the latter were a defendant in similar ICJ litigation.

Recognition One State's recognition of another State, government, or belligerency. It is a political act with legal consequences, such as the recognized entity's acquisition of international legal personality with its attendant rights and obligations.

Registration Sent to the UN Secretariat or other appropriate international institution for dissemination to interested parties. Registration ensures that international agreements are public documents, as opposed to secret treaties (such as those that led to World Wars I and II).

Renunciation One nation's relinquishment of title to territory without the formality of a **cession** treaty (*see* above). This mode of acquisition has often been orchestrated by victorious nations as a form of war reparation.

Reprisal A coercive measure that typically involves the State-authorized seizure of property or persons. It typically retaliates for a prior wrong to the State or its citizens, and is now an unacceptable means of seeking reparations.

Res Communis Territory that is not subject to legal ownership by any State, such as the oceans and outer space.

Reservation A unilateral variation submitted at the time of acceptance of the treaty. It excludes or modifies the legal effect of certain provisions as applied to the reserving State.

Restrictive Theory of Sovereign Immunity Under this modern theory, a foreign State *may* be subjected to a local suit when it is engaged in a commercial enterprise. If acting as a trader, the foreign State must defend itself in local suits that arise out of its commercial conduct.

Schools of Thought: Natural Law, Positivism, and Eclectics **Natural Law** reflects harmony with the essential nature of all peoples. The Naturalist school of thought thus espouses the belief that the rules of International Law are drawn from the moral law of nature rooted in human reason. These fundamental rules are thus discernible without regard to positive law. **Positive** International Law refers to custom and treaty-based norms in some cases and eras denying the existence of Natural Law. The **Eclectic** school covers a broad range of International Law theories that incorporate various components of either or both of the Natural and Positive Law schools.

Secession One territory secedes from its legal ties with another territory, such as when a State divides into two or more sovereign States. Unlike *succession,* there is no mere transfer of sovereignty. The seceding portion of the former territory exercises independent sovereignty as a new international legal person.

Secretariat of the United Nations Administers all United Nations programs and is headed by the

UN Secretary-General—the chief administrative officer of the UN.

Security Council of the United Nations The rotating fifteen-State body designed to manage threats to peace. It was formed as a smaller organ than the General Assembly of all members so that it could react more quickly to threats to peace.

Self-Determination The right of an indigenous population to choose self-governance or some related form of autonomy. The people within the affected territory acquire the right to govern themselves—free of another State's control.

Self-Executing Treaty Creates immediately binding obligations by the terms of the treaty, as opposed to stating a declaration of principled intent that constitutes a standard for future achievement.

Signature An interim step in the multilateral treaty process whereby representatives of the States or organizations generally agree on draft articles with a view toward ultimate ratification by the parties. A signature is a *provisional* acceptance, as opposed to *final* acceptance of the treaty's obligations through ratification.

Source of International Law Where a decision maker such as a judge or diplomat looks for evidence of the content of International Law: customary State practice, treaties, general principles of law found in civilized legal systems, judicial opinions, the teachings (writings) of highly qualified publicists, and possibly certain UN General Assembly resolutions or documents.

Sovereign Immunity The immunity from suit enjoyed by States (and certain international organizations) in the courts of other States. This status is an attribute of sovereignty, whereby one State does not allow its judicial processes to be exercised against another State.

Sovereignty The various attributes of statehood. A territory, coexisting with other such entities in an international system of independent States, is characterized as being a sovereign entity entitled to equality and territorial control.

State Historically, the only entity that possesses the capacity to act on the international level. It is a group of societies within a readily defined geographical area that are united to ensure their mutual welfare and security (*see* **Nation**). It consists of a permanent territory, a defined populace, and a government that is capable of engaging in international relations.

Statelessness The absence of nationality, whereby an individual is generally a refugee who lacks the international protection afforded by a legal connection with any particular State.

State Responsibility A body of evolving norms that contains the obligations incurred as a consequence of a State's international legal personality. Failure to observe a norm of State practice or a treaty obligation thus renders the State responsible under International Law for its wrongful act or omission.

Strait Passage Passage through territorial waters that is not subject to the restrictive rules of the coastal State due to the strategic nature of the particular strait. These waters are, for the purpose of strait passage, permitted free passage as if in high seas (*see* **Innocent Passage**).

Succession One or more States take the place of a former State. The new entity thus succeeds to the sovereign attributes of the predecessor State, which no longer exists due to this transfer of sovereignty.

Tariff A tax on imports.

Terra Nullius Territory capable of ownership, although not yet under sovereign control. The land is characterized as belonging to no one and thus is capable of ownership through some act of occupation.

Territoriality The State regulation of conduct based on acts or effects that are felt within its territory. Recognized extensions authorize the exercise of a State's jurisdiction over its aircraft and seagoing vessels regardless of location.

Territorial Sea Twelve-nautical-mile strip of water adjacent to the coast, wherein the coastal State exercises total sovereignty as if on land.

Treaty An international agreement concluded between States or international organizations, typically in written form. Oral agreements also qualify, although their use has receded in the twentieth century.

Trusteeship Council of the United Nations Consists of selected UN members responsible for the administration of territories until they are capable of self-government. The bulk of its work was completed with the decolonization movement of the 1960s.

United Nations The global association of States formed in 1945 to maintain international peace, as well as other social and economic objectives for the betterment of all individuals.

Universality Principle of Jurisdiction The State regulation of conduct in circumstances in which the actor's conduct is so heinous that it constitutes a crime against all nations. Each State may thus prosecute or extradite the individual criminal for trial, regardless of the location of the conduct.

War Powers Resolution US legislation, initially enacted in 1973 but never closely followed, that is designed to limit the president's ability to commit US combat troops to foreign conflicts for more than sixty days without congressional approval.

World Trade Organization The 1995 global trade entity based in Geneva, Switzerland. It will ultimately oversee all facets of **GATT** (*see* above) and the related 1994 Uruguay Round agreements that cover services and intellectual property.

Index

D

H

I

J

K

Q

R

V

W

Y

Z